Understanding
MEDICAL TERMINOLOGY

Tenth Edition

Understanding
MEDICAL TERMINOLOGY

Tenth Edition

Sr. Agnes Clare Frenay, FSM, RN, MS (deceased)

Sr. Rose Maureen Mahoney, FSM, RRA, MA
Healthcare Consultant, Franciscan Sisters of Mary, St. Louis, MO

WCB McGraw-Hill

Boston, Massachusetts   Burr Ridge, Illinois
Dubuque, Iowa   Madison, Wisconsin   New York, New York
San Francisco, California   St. Louis, Missouri

WCB/McGraw-Hill

A Division of The **McGraw·Hill** *Companies*

UNDERSTANDING MEDICAL TERMINOLOGY

Copyright 1998 by The McGraw-Hill Companies, Inc. All rights reserved. First edition published in 1958. Eighth edition published in 1989 by the Catholic Health Association of America. Ninth edition © 1993 by Wm. C. Brown Communications, Inc. Printed in the United States of America. Except as permitted under the United States Copyright Act of 1976, no part of this publication may be reproduced or distributed in any form or by any means, or stored in a data base or retrieval system, without the prior written permission of the publisher.

 This book is printed on recycled, acid-free paper containing 10% postconsumer waste.

1 2 3 4 5 6 7 8 9 0 QPD/QPD 9 0 9 8 7

Library of Congress Catalog Number: 96-086396

ISBN 0-697-21943-7

Publisher: *Michael D. Lange*
Sponsoring editor: *Kristine Noel Tibbetts*
Developmental editor: *Kelly A. Drapeau*
Marketing manager: *Keri L. Witman*
Project manager: *Margaret B. Horn*
Production supervisor: *Laura Fuller*
Photo research coordinator: *John C. Leland*
Art editor: *Renee A. Grevas*
Compositor: *Shepherd Incorporated*
Typeface: *10/12 Goudy*
Printer: *Quebecor, Inc.*

www.mhhe.com

C O N T E N T S

The tenth edition of *Understanding Medical Terminology* offers a structured approach to learning medical terms and an ongoing reference work for both professionals and adjunct personnel in all health care fields. Few specialized vocabularies in our culture are as important as medical terminology, given the life-and-death implications inherent in the enormously complex world of modern medicine and health care.

In addition to the traditional fields of medical practice and nursing, specialties and sub-specialties are constantly proliferating within the health care field. Health care is one of the fastest growing "umbrella areas" in higher education and includes programs in physical and occupational therapy, paramedical action and support specialties, health information management, and medical-technical assistance in a growing number of areas.

As programs have developed to meet this growing network of interests and needs, the need for a shared working vocabulary becomes a more urgent priority and is reflected in the number of people taking medical terminology courses.

The best comprehensive texts for courses in medical terminology, and for ongoing reference for those active in medicine, nursing, and allied health fields, differ primarily in quality and approach. *Understanding Medical Terminology* is set apart by its experience, rigorous research, breadth and depth of coverage, pedagogic approach, ease of use for both beginning and advanced student, and usefulness as a reference for the practicing health care professional. The two key words here are experience and research. The first edition of *Understanding Medical Terminology* was a pioneering text in this field in 1958. In the succeeding years, it has been expanded and revised continually to reflect the constantly changing and expanding vocabulary of the health care professions. This combination of experience over the past decades and constant research and revision has resulted in a text of unique quality and practicality.

CHAPTER ORGANIZATION—GENERAL

The text is divided into three parts. Part I (chapters 1–16) provides background and context. Clinical laboratory tests and values are listed where appropriate. Part II (chapters 17–20) concentrates on specialty areas. Part III contains answers to multiple-choice questions found in the chapter review guides, the references and bibliography, the credits, and the index.

CHAPTER ORGANIZATION—DETAILS

PART I

The first chapter, which covers background and context, introduces the student to the basic concepts that underlie medical terminology. It includes examples of base or root elements, prefixes, suffixes, compounding elements and combining-form elements, all of which are useful when analyzing terms. It is important to emphasize that not all medical terms can be broken down exactly or even consistently in this manner and that there are many exceptions to the general rules of word formation. The student is introduced to basic terms and systems of measurement used in the clinical laboratory. A medical terminology text is a guide to usage, and as such it must be combined with experience to achieve the ultimate goal of understanding.

Chapters 2 through 16 cover disorders of the major body systems. Within chapters 2–15, medical terms are divided into several pedagogical categories:

Origin of terms offers the student an orientation to key word elements that pertain to the body system or disorder.

Phonetic pronunciation of selected terms lists specific medical terms, divided into phonetic syllables with inflections indicated. For example, the phonetic pronunciation of the term *pyoderma* would be PIE-o-DER′mah. The syllables in capital letters receive more emphasis than those in small letters; and when capital letters are followed by an apostrophe (′), that syllable receives greater emphasis than syllables in capital letters alone.

Anatomic terms designate body system structure.

Diagnostic terms deal with specific clinical disorders.

General terms relate closely, although are not identical to, the body system or disorder. Where appropriate, general terms appear instead of anatomic terms (e.g., see chapter 3, "Psychiatric Disorders," p. 41), or in addition to the anatomic terms (e.g., see Chapter 12, "Obstetrical, Fetal, and Neonatal Conditions," p. 299).

Operative terms relate to methods of surgical intervention employed to relieve or cure the impact of the clinical disorder, trauma, or other conditions on the system.

Symptomatic terms describe the presence of subjective evidence or symptoms experienced by the patient that characterize system disorders or conditions. In this text, we also extend the meaning of *symptomatic terms* to include any evidence of disturbed physiology perceived by either the patient or physician.

Abbreviations are shortened forms of words or phrases used to represent the full form. Abbreviations are distributed throughout each chapter.

Verbalized terms can be found in boldface type in the oral reading practices at the end of each chapter. Pronunciation of medical terms may vary drastically, and some of the most widely accepted pronunciations have little validity linguistically. In addition to the sections on phonetic pronunciation of selected medical terms, this text offers oral reading practices, which are brief discussions of medical topics. The readings provide students with opportunities to pronounce terms within a particular scientific-medical context and to help them overcome inhibitions that limit the effective use of medical terminology.

Surgery-related terms are detailed in tabular listings (see specific chapter tables regarding conditions amenable to surgery). Each table lists anatomic sites involved, specific diagnoses, type of surgery performed, and a description of the operative procedures employed.

Clinical laboratory studies represent common clinical laboratory tests and values listed where appropriate throughout the core chapters (chapters 1–16).

Special-procedure terms relate to the type of method or mechanism employed for further investigation or utilized to cure or relieve impending disorders or conditions.

The final chapter in Part I (chapter 16, "Multisystem Disorders"), introduces the student to a threefold topical classification of infectious diseases, immunologic diseases, and diseases of connective tissue. Each of these topics has its own expository subcategories; the first of these always concerns the origin of terms. In outline form, the triad of disorder types, with subcategories, would read as follows:

Infectious Diseases
Origin of Terms
Phonetic Pronunciation of Selected Terms
General Terms
Infections Caused by Various Agents

Immunologic Diseases
  Origin of Terms
  Phonetic Pronunciation of Selected Terms
  General Terms
  Diagnostic Terms
Diseases of Connective Tissue
  Origin of Terms
  Phonetic Pronunciation of Selected Terms
  Anatomic Terms
  Diagnostic Terms
This chapter also contains abbreviations and an Oral Reading Practice passage.

PART II

Chapters 17 through 20 deal with medical terminology in several specialty areas, including on-cology, imaging technology, nuclear medicine, and physical therapy. This systematic approach, which begins with fundamental terms relating to the disorders of the major body systems and then moves to specialty area terms, acknowledges the widely accepted logic of moving from general medical practice to specialization.

PEDAGOGY

Special pedagogical aids and strategies have been incorporated into the text.
  Review guides at the end of each chapter offer the students the opportunity to review learned terms, as well as to practice newly acquired spelling skills.
  Illustrations organize terminology primarily with regard to anatomic structures and significant procedures. These elements assist the student with overall integration of material, and general comprehension of the subject matter.
  Phonetic assistance (discussed previously) enables the student to cope with the challenge of pronunciation.
  In addition, external learning aids are available.
  Transparencies for use in the classroom link anatomical illustrations with lectures and text material.
  Instructor's Manual with Test Item File provides the instructor with systematic testing materials.
  The Life Science Living Lexicon CD-ROM by William Marchuk contains a complete lexi-con of life science terminology. Conveniently assembled on an easy-to-use CD-ROM are com-ponents such as a glossary of common biological roots, prefixes, and suffixes (Word Parts); a cat-egorized glossary of common biological terms; and a section describing the classification system.

SYLLABUS STRUCTURE

Ideally, the course in medical terminology should be taught in forty-eight- to fifty-minute hours (three semester credits) to ensure adequate coverage of the subject. This schedule also gives the learner the opportunity to digest and assimilate the material. The more common practice, however, is to cover this material in thirty-two- to fifty-minute hours (two semester credits). This arrangement necessitates selective elimination of several key areas or chapters. Whatever the time constraints, it is recommended that chapters 1 through 16 be considered "core curriculum." The instructor can select material from the specialty chapters on the basis of student needs and amount of time available.

The thorough student will make a point of reading all the material and would be well ad-vised to keep the text at hand as a ready reference.

ACKNOWLEDGMENTS

A special note of appreciation is extended to the late Sr. Agnes Clare Frenay, FSM, RN, MS, who was a pioneer in the field of medical terminology. She single-handedly prepared the first six editions of this text in a monumental labor of love. The present author was blessed with Sr. Frenay's friendship and guidance during collaboration on the seventh edition. The eighth through tenth editions continue and complement the work of Sr. Agnes Clare. Although content has changed, I am indebted to her, for her contributions to the text structure and for her leadership in the field of health care education.

Recognition and gratitude are extended to those physicians, professors, and health care professionals who reviewed chapters or provided individual consultation: Vallee Willman, M.D., professor of surgery, St. Louis University School of Medicine, St. Louis; Munir Ahmad, M.D., associate professor of internal medicine, St. Louis University School of Medicine, and director of the Nuclear Medicine Department, St. Mary's Health Center, St. Louis; Roy Auer, M.D., staff radiologist, St. Mary's Health Center, St. Louis; Ronald Turgeon, M.D., director of the Clinical Laboratory and Pathology Department, St. Mary's Health Center, St. Louis. Special thanks go to Thomas E. Reh, M.D., director of radiology, St. Mary's Health Center, St. Louis, who reviewed terms and anatomic illustrations; and Sr. Mary Leo Rita Volk, FSM, for her assistance in the area of cytogenetic studies.

I wish to acknowledge the contributions of the reviewers of the tenth edition who critiqued the manuscript as it was being prepared and offered valuable suggestions. They include: Gloria M. Ahern, Central Oregon Community College; Ruth Anne Atnip, Casper College; Robert H. Blackwell, Utah Valley State College; Thomas W. Downs, Maple Woods Community College; Dorothy T. Fresolo, Brigham and Women's Hospital; Catherine C. McCandless, Cypress College; LaVerne Ramaeker, Indiana University Northwest; Sharon A. Tauke, Kirkwood Community College; M. Sue Treitz, Arapahoe Community College; Pam Ventgen, University of Alaska–Anchorage; Robin J. Wahto, University of Alaska–Anchorage; and Mary E. White, Sinclair Community College.

A very special debt of gratitude is owed to the Governing Board of the Franciscan Sisters of Mary for appointing the author to the mission of researching and developing the tenth edition of *Understanding Medical Terminology*.

Finally, I wish to acknowledge in a special way the contributions of Bernard C. Huger, attorney at law, for his legal expertise and advise; Rev. Robert J. Mahoney, Ph.D., for his encouragement and expertise in publication procedures and contracts; and my mother and lifelong best friend, Rose C. Mahoney, for her encouragement and support.

Sr. Rose Maureen Mahoney, FSM

PART

I

1

Orientation to Medical Terminology

OBJECTIVES AND VALUES

Medical terminology is the professional language of those who are directly or indirectly engaged in the art of healing. Its strangeness may seem bewildering at first to students, and its complexity may tax their powers of concentration. These difficulties gradually disappear as students assimilate a working knowledge of the elements of medical terms, which, in turn, enables them to analyze words etymologically and according to their meaning. Memorization may be somewhat annoying to the beginner, but memory work is only a stepping-stone to a keener understanding of the professional language. It is obvious that the intellect is constantly engaged in the study of medical terms in various types of mental processes: analysis, interpretation, and, to a moderate degree, transfer of knowledge by uniting word roots synthetically with prefixes, suffixes, combining-form elements, and compound words.

The primary goal of introducing students to medical terminology is to help them develop the ability to read and understand the language of medicine. Efforts are directed at promoting knowledge of the elements of medical terms, understanding standard abbreviations, being able to spell medical terms, and appreciating the logical method found in analyzing medical terms.

BASIC CONCEPTS

The majority of medical terms claim Greek and Latin ancestry. Some have been adopted from modern languages, especially German and French. The study of medical terminology can enrich one's understanding of history, language, and medicine. As time goes on, additional scientific advances will herald new terms and evoke usage of previously coined terms.

The pronunciation of medical terms follows no rigid rules; flexibility is one of its outstanding characteristics. Students will sometimes be faced with common usage of an unfamiliar pronunciation. This is a result of the different traditions of these languages. For instance, the German tradition of instruction uses a pronunciation of Latin words that would have been unfamiliar to ancient Romans or even their modern Italian counterparts. Nevertheless, the powerful influence of

German scholarship in medicine helped to entrench these linguistically bizarre pronunciations of Latin and Greek terms; their ancient meaning, grammatical usage, and modern application all contribute to the medical terminology of today.

Many medical terms are combinations of components from these ancient languages. As the student's vocabulary grows, he or she begins to notice patterns that employ some of these components. Over time, increased knowledge of the more common components will enable him or her to recognize more quickly or recall more easily the modern meaning of the term. Sometimes this process of recognition is called *word building,* which is a well-meaning but misleading term. Actually, students must take apart rather than build words to discover, remember, and use their meaning. Breaking words apart to arrive at their inner meaning helps students develop a knowledge of word form and usage that eventually will enable them to read modern medical terminology intelligently. Students should not expect to develop this analytic perception overnight—it comes only after extensive vocabulary study. One day students may use these building blocks to fashion new words for the medical vocabulary.

In this tenth edition, the text seeks to develop an analytic attitude in the student. Becoming aware of the structural design of words and developing the habit of analyzing terms leads to a better understanding of definitions throughout the book. To help students learn to speak the language of medicine, Oral Reading Practice passages, brief discussions of medical topics, have been included. As students study the various categories of disorders, they will note the recurrence of certain prefixes, suffixes, roots, combining-form elements, and compound words. A review of key terms is found in the Origin of Terms section at the beginning of each chapter. It is through learning terms and speaking them that students begin to understand their definitions.

Located at the end of each chapter is a revised and enlarged *review guide,* which reinforces concepts and terms learned and provides students with the opportunity to practice newly acquired spelling skills. The answers to the multiple-choice questions are found in part 3 (see p. 508).

The updated chapter references and bibliography also are found in part 3 (see pp. 509–544). Reference numbers are noted in parentheses throughout the text.

In analyzing terms, students need to understand the key concepts that will enable them to break terms into their component elements (e.g., identifying roots, prefixes, suffixes, combining-form elements, and compound words). The following list presents these key concepts:

1. Root or base word element—refers to the main body of the word. It may be accompanied by a prefix or suffix.
   Example: adenoma
          aden- (base or root) = gland
          -oma (suffix) = tumor
          adenoma = gland tumor
2. Prefix—refers to one or two syllables or word parts placed before a word to modify or alter its meaning.
   Example: hemigastrectomy
          hemi- (prefix) = half
          gastr- (base or root) = stomach
          -ectomy (suffix) = removal or excision of
          hemigastrectomy = removal of half the stomach
3. Suffix—one or two syllables or word parts attached to the end of a word to modify or alter its meaning.

Example: hysterectomy

     hyster- (base or root) = uterus

     -ectomy (suffix) = removal or excision of

     hysterectomy = removal of uterus

a. Suffix meaning *pertaining to*—selected suffixes meaning *pertaining to* include *-ac, -ic, -al, -eal, -ary,* and *-ous*

Example: hemic

     hem- (base or root) = blood

     -ic (suffix) = pertaining to

     hemic = pertaining to blood

b. Suffix meaning *one who*—selected suffixes meaning *one who* include *-er* and *-ist.*

    Example: pathologist

         path- (root or base) = disease or morbid condition

         o (combining-form element, vowel)

         -logy (suffix) = science or study of

         -ist (suffix) = one who

         pathologist = one who studies disease or morbid conditions

4. Combining-form element—results when a vowel, usually *a, i, e,* or *o,* is added to a word root or base. The vowels used most commonly as combining-form elements are *a, i,* or *o.* The vowel is usually deleted from a combining form when the next letter that follows is also a vowel.

    Example: proctitis

         procto- (combining form) = denoting relationship to the rectum

         -itis (suffix) = inflammation of

         proctitis = correct combination

         proctoitis = incorrect combination (o should be dropped)

         proctitis = inflammation of the rectum

5. Compound words—result when two or more root or base-word elements are used to form a word. Usually adjectives or nouns are added to a root word to form compound words. Compound words may include a combining form, a root or base-word element, and a suffix or word ending.

    Example: myocardiopathy

         myo- (combining-form element) = relationship to muscle

         cardio- (combining-form element) = relationship to heart

         -pathy (suffix) = disease or morbid condition

         myocardiopathy = disease of the heart muscle

Caution and flexibility are required in breaking down terms.

    Example: anemia

         -emia (suffix) = blood

         an- (prefix) = without, not

         anemia = without blood

In the strict sense, the term "anemia" might seem to mean no blood (absence or total lack of blood) rather than the attenuated quality of blood. This example shows that an exact correspondence does not usually exist between the meaning of a modern term and the ancient language roots from which the term derives.

When breaking down terms, it is more helpful to start the process by beginning with the suffix, then proceed to the root or root and prefix. This strategy provides a clue as to how the root is being used. There are numerous prefixes, suffixes, roots, and combining-form elements. In tables 1.1 and 1.2, some of the most commonly used and basic elements appear.

TABLE 1.1	Suffixes, Roots, and Prefixes

Diagnostic Suffixes

Suffix	Term	Analysis	Definition
-cele (G) hernia, tumor, protrusion	cystocele	*kystis:* bladder *kele:* hernia	Hernia of the bladder
	gastrocele	*gaster:* stomach; -;	Hernia of the stomach
	hydrocele	*hydor:* water, fluid *kele:* tumor	Collection of fluid in the tunica vaginalis of the testicle
	myelocele	*myelos:* marrow *kele:* protrusion	Protrusion of spinal cord through the vertebrae
-ectasis (G) dilatation, expansion	angiectasis	*angeion:* vessel *ektasis:* dilatation	Abnormal dilatation of a blood vessel
	bronchiectasis	*bronchos:* bronchus; -;	Abnormal dilatation of a bronchus or bronchi
-emia (G) blood	hyperglycemia hyperglycosemia	*hyper:* excessive *glykys:* sweet, sugar *haima:* blood	Abnormally high blood sugar
	polycythemia	*polys:* many, excessive *kytos:* cell; -;	Abnormal increase of red blood cells and hemoglobin in the blood
-iasis (G) condition, formation of, presence of	lithiasis	*lithos:* stone, calculi *iasis:* presence of	Presence of stones
	cholelithiasis	*chole:* bile, gall; -; -;	Presence of calculi in the gallbladder
	nephrolithiasis	*nephros:* kidney; -; -; -;	Stones present in the kidney
-itis (G) inflammation	carditis	*kardia:* heart *itis:* inflammation	Inflammation of the heart
	iritis	*iris:* rainbow, iris; -;	Inflammation of the iris
	poliomyelitis	*polios:* gray *myelos:* marrow; -;	Inflammation of the gray matter of the spinal cord
-malacia (G) softening	encephalomalacia	*enkephalos:* brain *malakia:* softening	Softening of the brain
	osteomalacia	*osteon:* bone; -;	Softening of the bones
	splenomalacia	*splen:* spleen; -;	Softening of the spleen
-megaly (G) enlargement, big	hepatomegaly	*megas:* big, enlargement *hepat:* liver	Enlargement of liver
	splenomegaly	*splen:* spleen; -;	Enlargement of spleen
-oma (G) neoplasm, tumor	adenoma	*aden:* gland *oma:* tumor	Glandular tumor
	carcinoma	*karkinos:* cancer	Malignant tumor of epithelial tissue
	sarcoma	*sark:* flesh; -;	Malignant tumor of connective tissue

NOTE: Throughout table 1.1 (G) means that the suffix, root, or prefix is a Greek derivative, (L) a Latin. A dash and semicolon in the analysis column represent the suffix, root, or prefix that has already been given. In the analysis, Greek and Latin words are used to show the derivation, but the student needs only to learn the English version.

TABLE 1.1   (continued)

Suffix	Term	Analysis	Definition
-pathy (G) disease	adenopathy	*aden*: gland *pathos*: disease	Any glandular disease
	myelopathy	*myelos*: marrow; -;	Any pathologic disorder of the spinal cord
	myopathy	*mys*: muscle; -;	Any disease of a muscle
-ptosis (G) falling, downward displacement	blepharoptosis	*blepharon*: eyelid *ptosis*: a falling	Drooping of the eyelid
	gastroptosis	*gaster*: stomach; -;	Downward displacement of the stomach
	nephroptosis	*nephros*: kidney; -;	Downward displacement of kidney
-rhexis (G) rupture	angiorrhexis[1]	*angeion*: vessel *rhexis*: rupture	Rupture of a vessel (blood or lymphatic)
	cardiorrhexis[1]	*kardia*: heart; -;	Rupture of the heart
	hysterorrhexis[1]	*hysteria*: uterus; -;	Rupture of the uterus

Operative Suffixes

Suffix	Term	Analysis	Definition
-centesis (G) puncture	paracentesis	*para*: beside *kentesis*: a puncture	Puncture of a cavity
	abdominal paracentesis	*abdomen*: belly; -;	Puncture of abdominal cavity for aspiration of peritoneal fluid
-desis (G) binding, fixation	arthrodesis	*arthron*: joint *desis*: fixation	Surgical fixation of a joint
	tenodesis	*tenon*: tendon; -;	Fixation of a tendon to a bone
-ectomy (G) excision, removal	myomectomy	*mys*: muscle *oma*: tumor *ektome*: excision	Excision of a tumor of the muscle
	oophorectomy	*oophor*: ovary; -;	Removal of an ovary
	tonsillectomy	*tonsilla*: tonsil; -;	Removal of tonsils
-lithotomy (G) incision for removal of stone(s)	cholelithotomy	*chole*: bile, gall; -;	Incision into gallbladder for removal of gallstones
	nephrolithotomy	*nephros*: kidney; -;	Incision into kidney for removal of stones
	sialolithotomy	*sialon*: saliva; -;	Incision into salivary gland for removal of stones
-pexy (G) fixation, suspension	hysteropexy	*hystera*: uterus *pexis*: fixation	Abdominal fixation or suspension of uterus
	mastopexy	*mastos*: breast; -;	Fixation of a pendulous breast
	orchiopexy	*orchis*: testis; -;	Fixation of an undescended testis

[1]The "rr rule": Use a double *r* (*rr*) with *rh* when preceded by a vowel.

TABLE 1.1 (continued)

Suffix	Term	Analysis	Definition
-plasty (G) surgical correction, plasty repair of	arthroplasty	*arthron:* joint *plassein:* to form	Reconstruction operation on joint
	hernioplasty	*hernos:* a young shoot; -;	Plastic repair of hernia
	proctoplasty	*proktos:* anus, rectum; -;	Surgical repair of rectum
-rhaphy (G) suture	perineorrhaphy[1]	*perinaion:* perineum *rhaphe:* suture	Suture of a lacerated perineum
	staphylorrhaphy[1]	*staphyle:* uvula; -;	Suture of a cleft palate
-scopy (G) inspection, examination	bronchoscopy	*bronchos:* windpipe *skopein:* to examine	Examination of the bronchi with an endoscope
	cystoscopy	*kystis:* bladder; -;	Inspection of the bladder with a cystoscope
-stomy (G) creation of an artificial opening	colostomy	*kolon:* colon *stoma:* opening	Creation of an opening into the colon through the abdominal wall
	cystostomy	*kystis:* bladder; -;	Creation of an opening into the urinary bladder through the abdomen
-tomy (G) incision into	antrotomy	*antron:* antrum *tome:* incision	Incision into an antrum to establish drainage
	neurotomy	*neuron:* nerve; -;	Dissection of a nerve
-tripsy (G) crushing, friction	cholelithotripsy	*chole:* bile, gall *lithos:* stone *tripsis:* crushing	Crushing of gallstones
	lithotripsy		Crushing of a stone
	phrenicotripsy	*phren:* diaphragm; -;	Crushing of the phrenic nerve

Symptomatic Suffixes

Suffix	Term	Analysis	Definition
-algia (G) pain	gastralgia	*gaster:* stomach *algos:* pain	Epigastric pain
	nephralgia	*nephros:* kidney; -;	Renal pain
	neuralgia	*neuron:* nerve; -;	Nerve pain
-genic (G) origin	bronchogenic	*bronchos:* windpipe *gennan:* to originate	Originating in the bronchi
	neurogenic	*neuron:* nerve; -;	Originating in the nerves
	osteogenic	*osteon:* bone; -;	Originating in the bones
	pathogenic	*pathos:* disease; -;	Disease producing
-lysis (G) dissolution, breaking down	hemolysis	*haima:* blood *lysis:* breaking down	Breaking down of red blood cells
	myolysis	*mys:* muscle; -;	Destruction of muscular tissue
	neurolysis	*neuron:* nerve; -;	Disintegration of nerve tissue

[1]The "rr rule": Use a double r (rr) with rh when preceded by a vowel.

TABLE 1.1   (continued)

Suffix	Term	Analysis	Definition
-oid (G) like	fibroid	*fibra:* fiber *eidos:* resembling	Tumor of fibrous tissue, resembling fibers
	lipoid	*lipos:* fat; -;	Fatlike
	lymphoid	*lympha:* lymph; -;	Resembling lymph
-osis (G) increase, excess, disease or condition	anisocytosis	*anisos:* unequal *kytos:* cell *osis:* condition	Inequality of size of cells
	lymphocytosis	*lympha:* lymph; -;	Excess of lymph cells
-penia (G) deficiency, decrease	leukopenia	*leukos:* white *penia:* decrease	Abnormal decrease of leukocytes in the blood
	neutropenia	*neuter:* neutral; -;	Abnormal decrease of neutrophils in the blood
-spasm (G) involuntary contractions	chirospasm	*cheir:* hand *spasmos:* spasm or contraction of muscles	Spasm or contraction of the hand (writer's cramp)
	dactylospasm	*dactylos:* digit (finger or toe)	Spasm or cramp in fingers or toes
-stasis (G) arrest, halt, standing still	hemostasis	*haima:* blood *stasis:* halt	Arrest or halting of bleeding

Roots

Root	Term	Analysis	Definition
aden- (G) gland	adenectomy	*aden:* gland *ektome:* excision	Excision of a gland
	adenoma	-; *oma:* tumor	Glandular tumor
	adenocarcinoma	-; *karkinos:* cancer	Malignant tumor of glandular epithelium
aer- (G) air	aerated	*aer:* air	Filled with air
	aerobic	-; *bios:* life	Pertaining to an organism that lives only in the presence of air
	aeroneurosis	-; *neuron:* nerve *osis:* condition, disease, process	Functional nervous disorder affecting airplane pilots
arthr- (G) joint	arhtralgia	*arthron:* joint *algos:* pain	Pain in the joints
	arthritis	-; *itis:* inflammation	Inflammation of joints
blephar- (G) eyelid	blepharoptosis	*blepharon:* eyelid *ptosis:* a falling	Drooping of the upper eyelid
	blepharoplasty	-; *plassein:* to form	Plastic operation on the eyelid

TABLE 1.1 (continued)

Root	Term	Analysis	Definition
card- (G) heart	cardiac	*kardia*: heart	Pertaining to the heart or esophageal orifice of the stomach
	electrocardiogram	*elektron*: amber; -; *gramma*: mark	Graphic record of the variations in electrical potential caused by electrical activity of the heart muscle
cephal- (G) head	cephalad	*kephale*: head *ad*: toward	Toward the head
	cephalic	-; *ic*: pertaining to	Pertaining to the head
cerv- (L) neck	cervical	*cervix*: neck *al*: pertaining to	Pertaining to the neck
	cervicectomy	-; *ektome*: excision	Excision of the neck of the uterus
	cervicovesical	-; *vesica*: bladder	Relating to the cervix uteri and bladder
cheil-, chil- (G) lip	cheilitis	*cheilos*: lip *itis*: inflammation	Inflammation of the lip
	cheiloplasty	-; *plassein*: to form	Plastic operation of the lip
	cheilosis	-; *osis*: disease condition	Morbid condition of the lips caused by vitamin B deficiency
chir-[2] (G) hand	chiromegaly	*cheir*: hand *megas*: enlarge	Enlargement of the hand
	chiroplasty	-; *plassein*: to form	Plastic surgery on the hand
	chiropody	-; *pous*: foot	Treatment of conditions of the hands and feet
chol- (G) bile, gall	cholangitis	*chole*: bile, gall *angeion*: vessel *itis*: inflammation	Inflammation of the bile duct
	cholecyst	-; *kystis*: bladder, sac	Gallbladder
	cholecystogram	-; -; *gamma*: mark	Radiograph of the gallbladder
chondr- (G) cartilage	chondrectomy	*chondros*: cartilage *ektome*: excision	Excision of a cartilage
	chondrofibroma	-; *fibra*: fiber *oma*: tumor	Mixed tumor composed of fibrous tissue and cartilage
	chondroma	-; -;	Cartilaginous tumor
cost- (L) rib	costochondral	*costa*: rib *chrondros*: cartilage *al*: pertaining to	Pertaining to a rib and its cartilage
	costosternal	-; *sternon*: sternum	Referring to ribs and sternum

[2]Chir may suggest *of* the hand as in *chiromegaly*, or *by* the hand, as in the broad sense of "*treatment*," as in *chiropody*.

TABLE 1.1   (continued)

Root	Term	Analysis	Definition
cyst- (G) bladder, sac	cyst	*kystis:* bladder, sac	Bladder; any sac containing a liquid
	cystoscope	-; *skopein:* to examine	Instrument for internal examination of the bladder
cyt- (G) cell	cytology	*kytos:* cell *logos:* study	Study of cell life
	erythrocyte	*erythros:* red; -;	Red blood cell
	lymphocyte	*lympha:* lymph; -;	Lymph cell (a nongranular leukocyte)
dactyl- (G) finger, toe, digit	dactylitis	*dactylos:* finger *itis:* inflammation	Inflammation of fingers or toes
	dactylogram	-; *gramma:* mark	Fingerprint
	dactylomegaly	-; *megas:* enlarge	Enlarged fingers or toes
derm- (G) skin	dermal	*derma:* skin *al:* relating to	Relating to skin
	dermatitis	-; *itis:* inflammation	Inflammation of the skin
encephal- (G) brain	encephalitis	*enkephalos:* brain *itis:* inflammation	Inflammation of the brain
	encephaloma	-; *oma:* tumor	Brain tumor
enter- (G) intestine	enteritis	*enteron:* intestine *itis:* inflammation	Inflammation of the intestines
	enterocele	-; *kele:* hernia	Hernia of the intestines
	enterocolitis	-; *kolon:* colon; -;	Inflammation of the intestines and colon
gastr- (G) stomach	gastrectasis	*gaster:* stomach *ectasis:* dilatation	Dilatation of the stomach
	gastroenteritis	-; *enteron:* intestine *itis:* inflammation	Inflammation of the stomach and intestines
hem-, hemat- (G) blood	hematemesis	*haima:* blood *emesis:* vomiting	Vomiting of blood
	hematoma	-; *oma:* tumor	Blood tumor
hepat- (G) liver	hepatitis	*hepat:* liver *itis:* inflammation	Inflammation of the liver
	hepatoylsis	-; *lysis:* destruction	Destruction of liver cells
hyster- (G) uterus	hysterectomy	*hystera:* uterus *ektome:* excision	Excision of the uterus
	hysteropexy	-; *pexis:* fixation	Fixation of a displaced uterus

| TABLE 1.1 | | (continued) | |

Root	Term	Analysis	Definition
ile- (L) ileum	ileum	*ileum:* ileum	Distal part of small intestine
	ileocecal valve	-; *caecum:* blind, blind gut *valva:* one leaf of a double door	Two lips or folds at opening between the ileum and cecum
ili- (L) ilium	ilium	*ilium:* flank	Wide upper part of the hip bone
	iliofemoral	-; *femoralis:* femur	Referring to ilium and femur
leuk- (G) white	leukocytosis	*leukos:* white -; *osis:* excess, condition *kytos:* cell	Excessive increase in number of white blood cells (leukocytes)
	leukopenia	-; *penia:* lack, decrease	Decrease in the number of leukocytes
lip- (G) fat	lipectomy	*lipos:* fat *ektome:* excision	Excision of fatty tissues
	lipemia	-; *haima:* blood	Fat in the blood
lith- (G) stone	lithiasis	*lithos:* stone *iasis:* presence of	Presence of stones
	lithocystotomy	-; *kystis:* bladder *tome:* incision	Incision into the bladder to remove stones
mening- (G) membrane	meningeal	*meninx:* membrane *al:* relating to	Related to the meninges
	meningioma	-; *oma:* tumor	Tumor of the meninges
	meningitis	-; *itis:* inflammation	Inflammation of the membranes of the spinal cord and brain
metr- (G) uterus	metritis	*metra:* uterus *itis:* inflammation	Inflammation of the uterus
	metrorrhexis[1]	-; *rhexis:* a rupture	Rupture of the uterus
my- (G) muscle	myitis or myositis	*mys:* muscle *itis:* inflammation	Inflammation of a muscle
	myocardium	-; *kardia:* heart	Heart muscle
myel- (G) marrow	myelitis	*myelos:* marrow *itis:* inflammation	Inflammation of the spinal cord or of the bone marrow
	myelosarcoma	-; *sark:* flesh -; *oma:* tumor	Malignant tumor of the bone marrow
nephr- (G) kidney	nephropexy	*nephros:* kidney *pexis:* fixation	Surgical fixation of a floating kidney
	nephrosclerosis	-; *sklerosis:* hardening	Hardening of the kidney
	nephrosis	-; *osis:* condition	Condition marked by degeneration of renal substance

[1]The "rr rule": Use a double *r* (*rr*) with *rh* when preceded by a vowel.

TABLE 1.1   (continued)

Root	Term	Analysis	Definition
ophthalm- (G) eye	ophthalmitis	*ophthalmos:* eye *itis:* inflammation	Inflammation of the eye
	ophthalmology	-; *logos:* study	Study of the eye and its diseases
pneum- (G) lung, air	pneumococcus	*pneumon:* lung *kokkos:* berry	Microorganism causing pneumonia and other diseases
	pneumothorax	*pneumon:* air *thorax:* chest	Introduction of air into the pleural cavity
proct- (G) rectum, anus	proctology	*proktos:* rectum *logos:* study or science	Medical specialty dealing with diseases of the rectum
	proctoscopy	-; *skopein:* examine	Instrumental examination of the rectum
psych- (G) mind, soul	psychiatry	*psyche:* mind *iatreia:* healing	Medical specialty dealing with treatment of mental disorders
	psychopathy	-; *pathos:* disease	Any mental disease
pyel- (G) pelvis	pyelitis	*pyelos:* pelvis *itis:* inflammation	Inflammation of the pelvis (of the kidney)
	pyelonephrosis	-; *nephros:* kidney -; *osis:* disease	Any disease of the kidney and its pelvis
pylor- (G) gatekeeper, pylorus	pylorus	*pyloros:* gatekeeper	Orifice between stomach and duodenum
	pylorostenosis	-; *stenosis:* narrowing or constriction	Constriction of pylorus
	pyloromyotomy	-; *mys:* muscle *tome:* a cutting	Incision of the pyloric sphincter to relieve pyloric stenosis
radi- (L) ray	radioactivity	*radius:* ray *activus:* acting	Ability to emit rays that can penetrate various substances
	radiosensitive	-; *sensitivus:* feeling	Capable of being destroyed by radioactive substances
	radiotherapy	-; *therapeia:* treatment	Use of radiation of any type in treating diseases
spondyl- (G) vertebra	spondylitis	*spondylos:* vertebra, spinal column *itis:* inflammation	Inflammation of vertebrae
	spondylolisthesis	-; *olisthesis:* a slipping	Forward dislocation of one vertebrae over another
	spondylosyndesis	-; *syndesis:* a binding together	Spinal fusion
trachel- (G) neck	tracheoplasty	*trachelos:* neck *plassein:* to form	Plastic operation of the cervix uteri

TABLE 1.1   (continued)

Root	Term	Analysis	Definition
tubercul- (L) tubercle	tubercle	*tuberculum*: a little swelling	Lesion of tuberculosis; also, a nodular bony prominence
	tuberculoma	-; *oma*: tumor	Tuberculous tumor
	tuberculosis	-; *osis*: process	Infectious condition marked by formation of tubercles in any tissue
viscer- (L) organ	visceral	*viscus*: organ *al*: pertaining to	Pertaining to the internal organs
	viscus	-;	Organ
	viscera	-;	Organs
	visceroptosis	-; *ptosis*: a dropping	Prolapse of the viscera (splanchnoptosis)

Prefixes

Prefix	Term	Analysis	Definition
a-, an- (G) without, not	anesthesia	*an*: without *aesthesis*: sensation	Loss of sensation
	asthenia	-; *sthenos*: strength	Debility; loss of strength
ab- (L) from, away from	abductor	*ab*: away from *ductor*: that which draws	That which draws away from a common center, as a muscle
	abruptio placentae	-; *ruptere*: break *placenta*: a flat cake	Tearing away from or premature detachment of a normally situated placenta
ad- (L) adherence, increase, near, to, toward	adductor	*ad*: toward *ductor*: that which draws	That which draws toward a common center
	adhesion	*ad*: to *haerere*: to stick	Abnormal joining of surfaces to each other
ante- (L) before, prior to, in front of	ante cibum	*ante*: before *cibus*: food	Before meals
	antenatal	-; *natus*: birth	Before birth
	antepartum	-; *partum*: labor	Before onset of labor
anti- (G) against	antipyretic	*anti-*: against *pyretos*: fever	Drug that reduces fever
	antitoxin	-; *toxikon*: poison	Protein that defends the body against a toxin
bi- (L) two, both, double	biceps	*bis*: two *caput*: head	Two-headed
	biceps brachii	-; *brachii*: arm	Muscle of the upper arm having two heads
	biconvex	-; *convexus*: rounded surface	Having two convex surfaces, as in a lens

TABLE 1.1   (continued)

Prefix	Term	Analysis	Definition
co-, con- (L) with, together	congenital defect	*con:* with *genitus:* born *defectus:* imperfection	Born with a defect; hereditary
	connective tissue	*con:* together *nectere:* to bind	Tissue that connects or binds together
contra- (L) against, opposite	contraception	*contra:* against *concipere:* to conceive	Prevention of conception
	contraindication	-; *indicare:* to point out	Condition antagonistic to a type of treatment
	contralateral	*contra:* opposite *latus:* side	Affecting the opposite side of the body
ec- (G) out	ectropion of eyelid, cervix uteria	*ek:* out *trepein:* to turn *cervix:* neck *uteri:* of womb	Eversion, as of the edge of the eyelid, or the turning out of the cervical canal of the
ecto- (G) outside	ectopic pregnancy	*ecto:* outside *topos:* place *prae:* before *natus:* birth	uterus Gestation outside the uterine cavity
em-, en- (G) in	empyema	*em:* in *pyon:* pus	Pus in a body cavity, e.g., in the pleural cavity
	encephalopathy	*en:* in *kephale:* head *pathos:* disease	Any disease of the brain
endo- (G) within	endocardial	*endon:* within *kardia:* heart *-ial:* pertaining to	Situated or occurring within the heart or pertaining to the endocardium
	endocrine gland	-; *krinein:* to secrete *glans:* gland	Ductless gland in which forms an internal secretion
epi- (G) upon, in addition to, at	epidermis	*epi:* upon *derma:* skin	Cuticle or outer layer of the skin
	epigastrium	-; *gaster:* stomach	Region over the pit of the stomach
ex- (L, G) away from, out, over	exacerbation	*ex:* over *acerbus:* harsh	Aggravation of symptoms
	exhale	*ex:* out *halare:* to breathe	To breathe out; to expel from the lungs by breathing
hemi- (G) half	hemigastrectomy	*hemi:* half -; *gaster:* stomach *ektome:* excision	Removal of half of the stomach
	hemiglossectomy	-; *glossa:* tongue -;	Removal of half of the tongue

TABLE 1.1 (continued)

Prefix	Term	Analysis	Definition
hyper- (G) above, beyond, excessive	hyperacidity hyperadrenalism	*hyper:* excessive *acidus:* sour -; *ad:* near *ren:* kidney *ismos:* state of	Excess acid (in the stomach) Excess adrenal secretion
hypo- (G) below, beneath, deficient	hypochondriac region hypoglycemia	*hypo:* beneath *chondros:* cartilage *regio:* area *hypo:* deficient *glykys:* sugar *haima:* blood	Part of abdomen beneath the ribs Low blood sugar
infra- (L) below, beneath	infracostal infrasternal	*infra:* below *costa:* ribs *infra:* beneath *sternon:* sternum	Below the ribs Beneath the sternum
inter- (L) between	interannular interarticular	*inter:* between *annulus:* ring -; *articulus:* joint	Situated between two rings or constrictions Situated between articular surfaces
intra- (L) within	intracordal intrapyretic	*intra:* within *cor:* heart -; *pyrexia:* fever	Within the heart During the stages of fever
iso- (G) alike, equal, same	isocellular isocytosis	*isos:* same *cellula:* cell -*ar:* pertaining to *isos:* equal *kytos:* cell *osis:* condition	Pertaining to same kinds of cells Equality of the size of cells
meso- (G) middle, intermediate	mesoderm mesotarsal	*meso:* middle *derma:* skin *meso:* middle *tarsalis:* tarsal	Middle layer of skin Midtarsal
pan- (G) all	panarthritis panhysterectomy	*pan:* all *arthron:* joint *itis:* inflammation of -; *hystera:* uterus *ektome:* removal	Inflammation of all joints Complete removal of uterus
par-, para- (G) beside, around, near, abnormal	paracentesis parasalpingitis	*para:* beside *kentesis:* a puncture -; *salpingx:* tube *itis:* inflammation of	Puncture of the abdominal cavity for aspiration of peritoneal fluid Inflammation of tissues around a fallopian or uterine tube

TABLE 1.1 (continued)

Prefix	Term	Analysis	Definition
peri- (G) around, about	pericardium pericarditis	*peri:* around *kardia:* heart -; -; *itis:* inflammation	Double membranous sac enclosing the heart Inflammation of the pericardium
post- (L) after, behind	postembryonic postprandial	*post:* after *embryon:* embryo -; *prandium:* breakfast	Occurring after the embryonic stage Occurring after a meal
pre- (L) before, in front of	precancerous precordium	*prae:* before *cancer:* crab -; *cor:* heart	Before the development of cancer Region over the heart
pro- (L, G) in front of, before, forward	procidentia prognosis	*procidentia:* a falling forward *pro:* before *gnosis:* a knowing	Complete prolapse, especially of the uterus Prediction of the probable outcome of a disease
retro- (L) backward, behind, back of	retroflexion retroperitoneal	*retro:* backward *flexio:* a bending *retro:* behind *peritonaion:* peritoneum	Bending or flexing backward; as of the uterus Located behind the peritoneum
semi- (L) half	semicircular canal semilunar valves	*semi:* half *circulus:* a ring *canal:* a channel -; *luna:* moon *valva:* one leaf of a double door	One of the three canals in the labyrinth of the ear Half-moon-shaped valves of the aorta and pulmonary arteries
sub- (L) under, beneath, below	subcostal subcutaneous	*sub:* beneath *costa:* rib -; *cutis:* skin	Beneath the ribs Beneath the skin
super-, supra- (L) above, beyond, excessive, superior	supraoccipital superextension	*supra:* above *occiput:* back part of the skull *al:* pertaining to *super:* excessive *extensio:* extension	Pertaining to area above the back part of the skull Excessive extension
sym-, syn- (G) with, along, together, beside	symphysis pubis syndactylism	*sym:* together *physis:* a growing *syn:* together *daktylos:* digit (finger or toe) *ismos:* condition	Fusion of pubic bones on mid-line anteriorly Fusion of two or more fingers or toes; webbing

TABLE 1.1 (continued)

Prefix	Term	Analysis	Definition
trans- (L) across, over	transection transfusion	*trans:* across *sectio:* cutting -; *fusio:* a pouring	Incision across the long axis; cross section Injection of the blood of one person into the blood vessels of another
tri- (G) three	tricuspid trigone	*tres, tria:* three *cuspis:* a point *trigonon:* a three-cornered figure	Having three cusps or points Triangular space, especially that of the lower part of the urinary bladder
uni- (L) one	uniarticular unicellular	*unus:* one *articulus:* joint -; *cellula:* cell	Pertaining to a single joint Made up of a single cell

COMBINING-FORM ELEMENTS

Combining-form elements result when a vowel, usually *a, e, i,* or *o,* is added to a word root or base. The vowels most commonly used as combining forms are *a, i,* or *o.* Table 1.2 lists examples of selected combining-form elements. (Note that the parentheses surrounding the vowel in these examples do not appear with the combining-form elements found in the Origin of Terms and Review Guide sections of the text.)

TABLE 1.2 Selected Combining-Form Elements and Definitions

angi(o)- (G) vessel	*anis(o)-* (G) unequal, uneven, dissimilar	*anthrop(o)-* (G) human being, man	*arthr(o)-* (G) joint(s)
blenn(o)- (G) mucus	*carcin(o)-* (G) cancer	*celi(o)-* (G) belly, abdomen	*cephal(o)-* (G) head
chlor(o)- (G) green	*chrom(o)-* (G) color	*colp(o)-* (G) vagina	*duoden(o)-* (L) duodenum
enter(o)- (G) intestine(s)	*fibr(o)-* (L) fiber(s)	*galact(o)-* (G) milk	*gam(o)-* (G) marriage, sexual union
gangli(o)- (G) ganglion	*gastr(o)-* (G) stomach	*geni(o)-* (G) chin	*ger(o)-* (G) old age, aged
glyc(o)- (G) sweet, sugar, glucose	*gon(o)-* (G) semen, seed	*gynec(o)-* (G) woman, female reproductive organ(s)	*gyr(o)-* (G) circle, gyrus
hal(o)- (G) salt	*hamart(o)-* (G) defect	*hemat(o)-* (G) blood	*heter(o)-* (G) different, other, abnormal

TABLE **1.2**	(continued)

hidr(o)- (G) sweat	hist(o)- (G) tissue, web	hol(o)- (G) entire, whole	hydr(o)- (G) water, fluid
kary(o)- (G) nucleus, kernel, nut	kerat(o)- (G) cornea, horn	kinesi(o)- (G) movement	mamm(o)- (L) breast
mast(o)- (G) breast	mening(o)- (G) membrane	micr(o)- (G) small	mon(o)- (G) one, single
neur(o)- (G) nerve(s)	olig(o)- (G) little, scanty	onc(o)- (G) tumor, swelling, mass	oophor(o)- (G) ovary, bearing eggs
oste(o)- (G) bone(s)	ov(o)- (L) egg(s)	pulmon(o)- (L) lung	py(o)- (G) pus
pyel(o)- (G) pelvis of the kidney	pyret(o)- (G) fever	rachi(o)- (G) spine	rect(o)- (L) rectum
ren(o)- (L) kidney	rhin(o)- (G) nose	sapr(o)- (G) rotten, decay	sarc(o)- (G) flesh
schiz(o)- (G) division, split	scot(o)- (G) darkness	strept(o)- (G) twisted	thel(o)- (G) nipple
thorac(o)- (G) thorax, chest	thromb(o)- (G) clot, thrombus	toxic(o)- tox(o)- (G) poison, toxin	urethr(o)- (G) urethra
uter(o)- (L) uterus	vas(o)- (G) vessel	vesic(o)- (L) bladder	xer(o)- (G) dry

PHONETIC PRONUNCIATION OF SELECTED MEDICAL TERM ELEMENTS

In table 1.3, which gives phonetic pronunciation for selected terms, the syllables in capital letters receive more emphasis than those in small letters.

TABLE **1.3**	Phonetic Pronunciation of Selected Medical Term Elements

angio-	AN-je-owe	fibro-	FI-bro	osteo-	OS-tee-owe
arthro-	AR-throw	hemo-	HE-moe	-pexy	PECK-see
bi-	BYE	hyper-	HI-per	-plasty	PLAS-tee
cardio-	CAR-de-owe	hypo-	HI-po	pleuro-	PLOOR-owe
-centesis	sen-TEE-sis	hystero-	HIS-ter-owe	pneumo-	NEW-moe
cephalo-	SEF-ah-low	intra-	IN-trah	pyo-	PIE-owe
cerebro-	SER-e-bro	-itis	I-tis	-rhexis	RECK-sis
colpo-	KOL-po	litho-	LITH-owe	salpingo-	sal-PING-go
dacryo-	DAK-re-owe	-malacia	mah-LAY-she-ah	thymo-	THY-moe
-ectasis	ECK-tah-sis	megalo-	MEG-ah-low	thyro-	THY-roe
ecto-	ECK-toe	micro-	MY-kro	tracheo-	TRA-key-owe
-ectomy	ECK-toe-me	nephro-	NEF-row	utero-	YOU-ter-owe
endo-	EN-doe	oligo-	OL-i-go	viscero-	VIS-er-owe
entero-	EN-ter-owe				

TERMS PERTAINING TO THE BODY AS A WHOLE

ANATOMIC DIVISIONS OF THE ABDOMEN (SEE FIG. 1.1.)

hypochondriac region (upper lateral regions beneath the ribs) 1
epigastric region (region of the pit of the stomach) 2
lumbar region (middle lateral regions) 4, 6
umbilical region (region of the navel) 5
inguinal region (lower lateral regions) 7, 9
hypogastric region (region below the umbilicus) 8

CLINICAL DIVISION OF THE ABDOMEN (SEE FIG. 1.2.)

upper right quadrant . . . . URQ
upper left quadrant . . . . ULQ
lower right quadrant . . . . LRQ
lower left quadrant . . . . LLQ

ANATOMIC DIVISION OF THE BACK

cervical region . . . . neck
thoracic region . . . . chest
lumbar region . . . . loin
sacral region . . . . sacrum

POSITION AND DIRECTION (SEE FIGS. 1.3 AND 1.4.)

afferent—conducting toward a structure.
anterior or ventral—front of the body (not synonymous in lower limb).
central—toward the center.
deep—away from the surface.

Figure 1.1 Anatomic division of abdomen into nine regions by two horizontal planes (subcostal and transtubercular or intertubercular) and two sagittal planes (left and right lateral) through the midinguinal points.

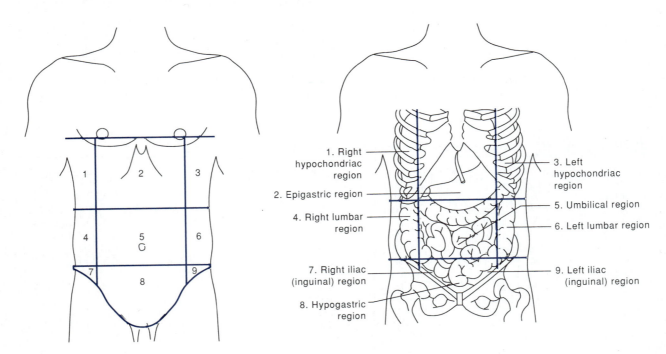

Figure 1.2 Clinical division of the abdomen into four quadrants by running a transverse plane across the midsagittal plane at the point of the navel.

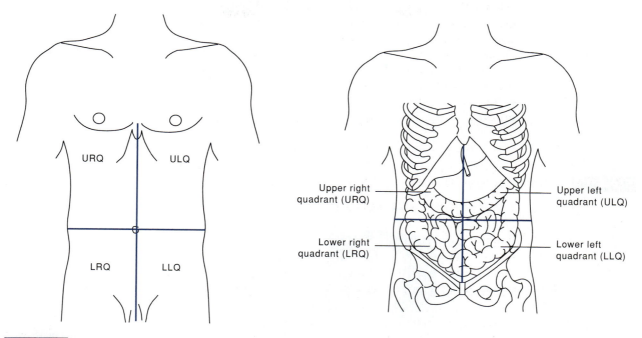

Figure 1.3 Posterior view of the body.

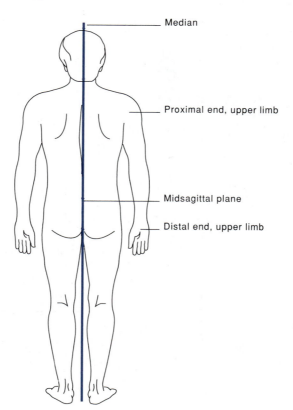

distal or peripheral—away from the beginning of a structure; away from the center.
efferent—conducting away from a structure.
inferior or caudal—away from the head; situated below another structure.*
intermediate—between median and lateral.
lateral—toward the side.*
medial—toward the median plane.*
median—in the middle of a structure.
posterior or dorsal—back of the body (not synonymous in lower limb). (See fig. 1.3 for posterior view of body.)
proximal—toward the beginning of a structure.
superficial—near the surface.
superior or cephalic—toward the head; situated above another structure.*

Figure 1.4   Directional planes of the body.

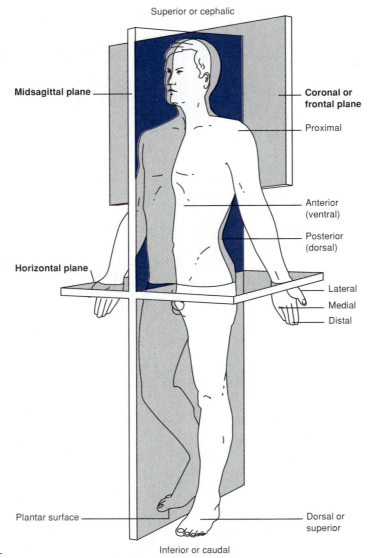

Superior or cephalic

Midsagittal plane
Coronal or frontal plane
Proximal
Anterior (ventral)
Posterior (dorsal)
Horizontal plane
Lateral
Medial
Distal
Plantar surface
Dorsal or superior
Inferior or caudal

*Refer to section on anatomic positions (p. 23).

PLANES OF THE BODY (SEE FIG. 1.4.)

frontal or coronal—vertical plane parallel to coronal suture of the skull; divides body or structure into anterior and posterior portions.
horizontal—plane parallel to the horizon.
longitudinal—plane parallel to the long axis of the structure.
median—lengthwise plane that divides the body or structure into right and left halves.
sagittal—any vertical plane parallel to the sagittal suture of the skull and the median plane.

ANATOMIC POSITION

Anatomists all over the world apply anatomic terms to the body as though it were in what is known as the "anatomic position." In this position, the body is erect, the eyes look straight to the front, the upper limbs hang at the sides with palms facing forward, and the lower limbs are parallel with the toes pointing forward. Whether the body lies face upward or downward, or in any other positions, the relationships of structure are always described as if the body were in the anatomic position.

BODY CAVITIES (SEE FIGS. 1.5 AND 1.6.)

A human's internal organs are termed *visceral organs*. These organs are located within specific cavities. Two main cavities are the dorsal cavity and the larger ventral cavity. The dorsal cavity can be further subdivided into the cranial cavity, which holds the brain, and the spinal cavity,

Figure 1.5 Major body cavities.

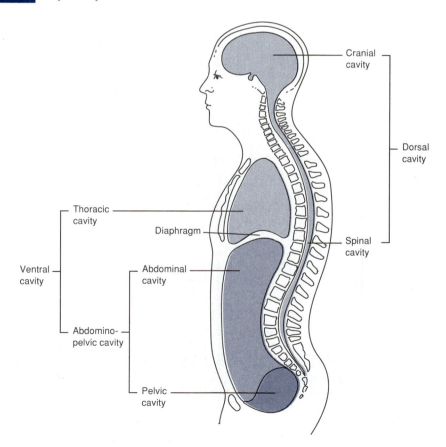

Figure 1.6 Minor body cavities.

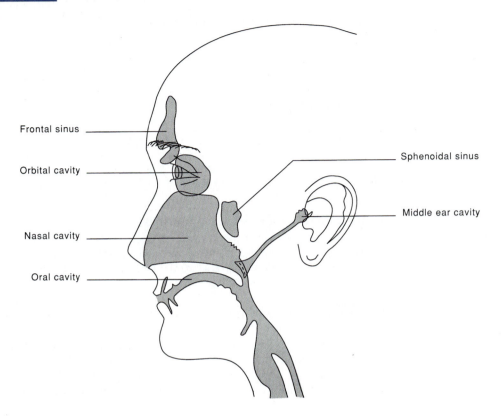

Frontal sinus

Orbital cavity

Nasal cavity

Oral cavity

Sphenoidal sinus

Middle ear cavity

which contains the spinal cord and is protected by sections of the vertebrae. The ventral cavity envelops the thoracic cavity and the abdominopelvic cavity. The thoracic cavity encloses the lungs, heart, esophagus, trachea, and thymus gland. The diaphragm separates the thoracic cavity from the lower abdominopelvic cavity. Two parts of the abdominopelvic cavity are the upper abdominal cavity and the lower pelvic cavity. The organs found in the abdominal cavity include the stomach, liver, spleen, gallbladder, and most of the large and small intestines.

The remaining portions of the large and small intestines are found in the pelvic cavity. The pelvic cavity also includes the rectum, urinary bladder, and internal reproductive organs.

Several smaller body cavities are located within the head. The oral cavity holds the teeth and tongue. The nasal cavity, which is divided into right and left sections by the nasal septum, is connected to several air-filled sinuses. The orbital cavities contain the eyes and related skeletal muscles and nerves. The middle ear cavities house the middle ear bones.

Not to be confused with the major body cavities are the possible spaces (but not actual spaces) for body cavities. For example, consider the pleural membranes that line the thoracic cavity and cover the lungs, and the pericardial membranes that surround the heart and cover its surface. The pleural cavity and the pericardial cavities are potential spaces between these membranes. Similarly, the peritoneal membranes line the abdominopelvic cavity and cover the organs inside. The peritoneal cavity is a potential space between these membranes.

GENERAL TERMS AND SYSTEMS OF MEASUREMENT USED IN THE CLINICAL LABORATORY

Clinical laboratory studies are located throughout the text. The system for reporting laboratory values used in most countries and in most scientific and medical journals is called the International System of Units (SIU). However, a majority of clinical laboratories in the United States still use conventional values, which is the traditional way of reporting normal test results. Where both types of values appear in this text, the SIU will appear in parentheses.*

GENERAL TERMS

assay—test or analysis of a substance to determine its biologic, chemical, or physical properties. (5)

bioassay—analysis of a living substance derived from a specific tissue or organ. (5)

biochemistry—chemistry that deals with components and processes of living organisms. **(5)**

conventional values—traditional way of reporting normal test results. (5)

factor—multiplication number for converting conventional units into international system (SI) units. (5)

hematology—medical science of the blood and blood-forming organs. (5)

immunohematology—hematologic specialty dealing with antigen-antibody or immune reactions and their effects on the blood.

International System of Units (SIU) (table 1.4)—modification of metric system using meter, kilogram, liter, mole, pascal, and second as basic units to ensure worldwide uniformity in presenting laboratory reports or other scientific data. (5)

metric system—a decimal system of measures and weights, using the meter, gram, and liter as basic units. (table 1.5)

reference range—reference intervals utilized for reporting laboratory values, formerly called normal range. It is recommended that reference ranges be utilized that are provided by your institution's clinical laboratory, since ranges may be method dependent. (5)

TABLE 1.4	Selected Reference Units

Units and subunits

Eq	=	equivalent	mEq/l, mEq/L	=	milliequivalent per liter
mEq	=	milliequivalent (measure of electrolytes)	μEq/l, μEq/L	=	microequivalent per liter
mμ	=	millimicron (same as nanogram)	μU	=	microunit
			IU	=	International unit
U	=	Units, units	mIU	=	milli-international unit

International System of Units

Basic units

A	=	ampere (electric current)	m	=	meter (length)
cd	=	candela (luminous intensity)	mol	=	mole (amount of substance)
Hz	=	hertz (frequency)	N	=	newton (force)
K	=	kelvin (thermodynamic temperature)	s	=	second (time)
Kg	=	kilogram (mass)	W	=	watt (power, radiant flux)

*(All clinical laboratory values cited in this text are from R. J. Elin, "Reference Intervals and Laboratory Values of Clinical Importance," in J. B. Wyngaarden and J. C. Bennett, eds., *Cecil Textbook of Medicine* [Philadelphia: W. B. Saunders Co. 1992]. Reprinted by permission.)

TABLE **1.4**	(continued)

Submits

mmol	=	millimole	mmol/L	=	millimole per liter
μmol	=	micromole	μmol/L	=	micromole per liter
nmol	=	nanomole	nmol/L	=	nanomole per liter
mol/kg	=	mole per kilogram	nmol/kg	=	nanomole per kilogram
Pa	=	pascal (unit of pressure: newton per square meter)	mOsm	=	milliosmole (measure of osmolarity)
molality	=	moles of solute in 1 kilogram of solvent	molarity	=	moles of solute in 1 liter of solution

Source: Adapted from personal communication with Ronald Turgeon, M.D.

sensitivity—frequency with which a laboratory test yields positive results in patients who have a particular disease; also, a state of reacting readily to stimuli or reagents. (5)

specificity—the frequency with which a laboratory test yields negative results in nondiseased persons. Test results apply to a single pathologic state, for example, indicating a disease produced by a distinct microorganism or condition. (5)

TABLE **1.5**	**Metric System Measurements**

Weights (in descending order)

kg	=	kilogram	=	1,000 grams	=	10^3g	
g, gm	=	gram	=	1,000 milligrams	=	10^3mg	
mg	=	milligram	=	1,000 micrograms	=	10^{-3}g	
μg	=	microgram	=	1,000 nanograms	=	10^{-6}g	
ng	=	nanogram	=	1,000 picograms	=	10^{-9}g	
pg	=	picogram	=	1,000 femtograms	=	10^{-12}g	
fg	=	femtogram	=	1,000 attograms	=	10^{-15}g	

Capacity (in descending order)

l, L	=	liter	=	1,000 milliliters	=	10 deciliters (dL, dl)	
l, L	=	liter	=	1,000 cubic centimeters	=	10 deciliters (dL, dl)	
dl, dL	=	deciliter	=	100 milliliters	=	0.10 liter (L,l)	
cl, cL	=	centiliter	=	10 milliliters	=	0.10 deciliter (dL, dl)	
ml, mL	=	milliliter	=	1,000 microliters	=	0.10 centiliter (cL, cl)	
μl, μL	=	microliter	=	1,000 nanoliters	=	0.001 milliliter (mL, ml)	
nl, nL	=	nanoliter	=	1,000 picoliters	=	0.001 microliter (μL, μl)	
pl, pL	=	picoliter	=	1,000 femtoliters	=	0.001 nanoliter (nL, nl)	
fl, fL	=	femtoliter	=	1,000 attoliters	=	0.001 picoliter (pL, pl)	

Length (in descending order)

m	=	meter	=	1,000 millimeters	=	100 centimeters (cm)	
dm	=	decimeter	=	100 millimeters	=	10 centimeters (cm)	
cm	=	centimeter	=	10 millimeters	=	0.01 meter (m)	
mm	=	millimeter	=	1,000 micrometers	=	0.001 meter (m)	
μm	=	micrometer	=	1,000 nanometers	=	0.001 millimeter (mm)	
nm	=	nanometer	=	1,000 picometers	=	0.001 micrometer (μm)	
pm	=	picometer	=	1,000 femtometers	=	0.001 nanometer (nm)	
fm	=	femtometer	=	1,000 attometers	=	0.001 picometer (pm)	

Source: Adapted from personal communication with Ronald Turgeon, M.D., and from Ronald J. Elgin, "Reference and Laboratory Values of Clinical Importance" in James B. Wyngaarden et al. (eds.), *Cecil's Textbook of Medicine*, 19th ed. Philadelphia: W. B. Saunders, 1992, 2370–2380.

REVIEW GUIDE

Instructions: Analyze the terms listed.

Example: ab—away from

Base or Root Words

arth-	derm-	ili-
blephar-	gastr-	lith-
chir-	hyster-	proct-
ile-	leuk-	myel-

Prefixes

an-	ec-	hypo-
bi-	em-	peri-
contra-	endo-	retro-

Suffixes

-algia	-oma	-oid
-cele	-pathy	-plasty
-ectasis	-lysis	-tripsy

Combining-Form Word Elements

angio-	glyco-	pyelo-
carcino-	neuro-	mono-
fibro-	schizo-	strepto-

Instructions: Break apart each term listed below, identify the medical term elements, and define the term.

Example: lipectomy   lip- = root = fat
                           -ectomy = suffix = excision

lithocystotomy

leukocytosis

hysteropexy

chiromegaly

gastroenterostomy

nephrosclerosis

trachelorrhaphy

electrocardiogram

Instructions: Supply the prefix, suffix, or combining-form element for each of the English words listed below.

Example: behind—post

pus	across	dilatation
all	between	enlargement
half	scanty	mucous

Instructions: Define the following terms.

Example: hematology—medical science of the blood and blood-forming organs

assay

conventional values

International System of Units

reference range

sensitivity

specificity

Instructions: Define the following abbreviations.

Example: m = meter

dm	fL	mol\kg
fm	mmol	nmol
nm	Pa	U
pm	mIU	mEq\L
pg	μU	μmol
Hz	kg	mμ

2

Disorders of the Skin

SKIN

ORIGIN OF TERMS

cutis (L)—skin
cryo- (G)—cold
cyan-, cyano- (G)—blue
derma-, dermat-, dermato-,
    dermo-, (G)—skin
erythema (G)—flush
hidro- (G)—sweat
kerato- (G)—horny, tissue, cornea
leuko-, leuco- (G)—white
macula (L)—spot, stain
melano- (G)—black, melanin
onych-, onycho- (G)—nail

papula- (L)—pimple
phyto- (G)—plant
pilo- (G)—hair
pruritus (L)—itching
pyo- (G)—pus
rhytido- (G)—wrinkle
sclero- (G)—hard
squama (L)—scale
stearo-, steato- (G)—fat
sudor (L)—sweat
tinea (L)—worm
vesico- (L)—blister, bladder

PHONETIC PRONUNCIATION OF SELECTED TERMS*

acne	ACK'nee
angioedema	an-gee-owe-e-DEE'mah
angioneurotic edema	an-gee-owe-new-ROT'ick e-DEE'mah
cellulitis	sell-you-LIE'tis
dermabrasion	DERM'a-BRAY-zhun
eczema	ECK'ze-mah
electrodesiccation	e-LECT-tro-DES-i-KAY'shun
keloid	KEY'loid
papule	PAP'ul
psoriasis	so-RYE'a-sis
pustule	PUS'tul
pyoderma	PIE-o-DER'mah
seborrheal	SEB-o-REAL'
stasis dermatitis	STAY'sis DER-mah-TIE'tis

*Syllables in capital letters receive more emphasis than those in small letters; capital letters followed by an accent (') receive greater emphasis than capital letters alone.

ANATOMIC TERMS (11, 23) (SEE FIGS. 2.1 AND 2.2.)

corium—true skin or deeper layer containing blood vessels, lymphatics, hair follicles, nerve endings, connective tissue fibers, and sweat and sebaceous glands.

derma, dermis—synonymous with corium.

epidermis—cuticle or outer layer of the skin.

epithelium—layers of cells covering the surface of the body, external as well as internal.

hair—develops from a group of epidermal cells at the base of a tubelike depression called a hair follicle. Hair grows from the base of a hair follicle when epidermal cells undergo cell division and older cells move outward and become keratinized. A group of smooth muscle cells, forming the **arrector pili muscle,** is attached to each hair follicle. This muscle is placed so that the hair within the follicle "stands on end" when the muscle contracts. Each hair follicle has one or more sebaceous glands associated with it.

integument—skin, composed of the corium and epidermis.

pigment—coloring substance. (See fig. 2.3.)

pilosebaceous—pertaining to hair and oil glands.

sebaceous glands—oil glands of the skin.

sebum—oily substance secreted by sebaceous glands.

subcutaneous tissue—layer of loose, connective tissue containing fat.

sudoriferous glands—sweat glands. There are many sweat glands present in all regions of the skin. Some of the sweat glands, termed **apocrine glands,** open into hair follicles in the anal region, groin, and armpits. Other sweat glands termed **eccrine glands,** open onto the surface of the skin.

Figure 2.1   Skin section.

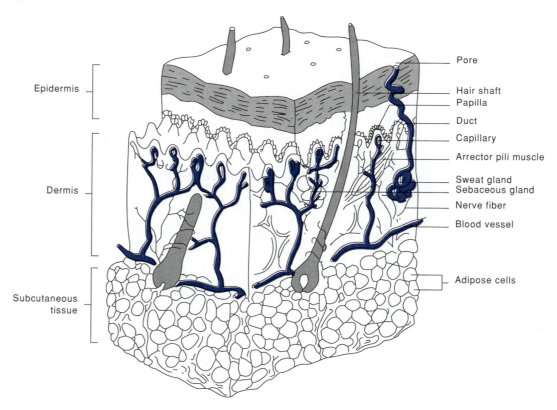

Epidermis

Dermis

Subcutaneous tissue

Pore

Hair shaft
Papilla

Duct

Capillary

Arrector pili muscle

Sweat gland
Sebaceous gland

Nerve fiber

Blood vessel

Adipose cells

Figure 2.2   Types of (a–d) simple epithelium and (e–g) glands.

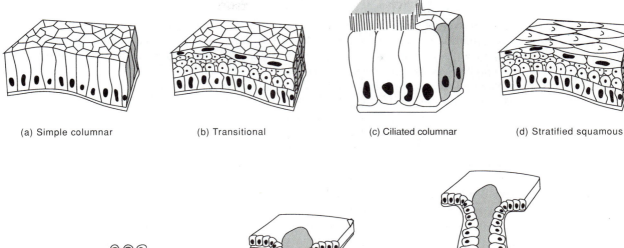

(a) Simple columnar   (b) Transitional   (c) Ciliated columnar   (d) Stratified squamous

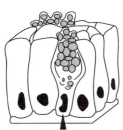

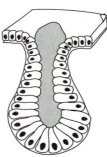

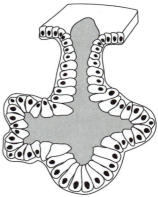

(e) Goblet cell located in simple columnar epithelium   (f) Simple alveolar gland   (g) Compound alveolar gland

Figure 2.3   Skin-coloring process. Skin coloring is caused by production of the pigment of melanin from (a) melanocytes in (b) the epidermis layer of the skin. Although people of all races have equal numbers of melanocytes, their genetic variations control the amount of melanin introduced into the cells. These cells are manufactured in the (c) germinative layer. Ultraviolet rays of the sun play a key role in melanin production. Melanin absorbs these rays, and as a result, the skin becomes tanned or sunburned. (d) Freckles result when only some melanocytes manufacture melanin.

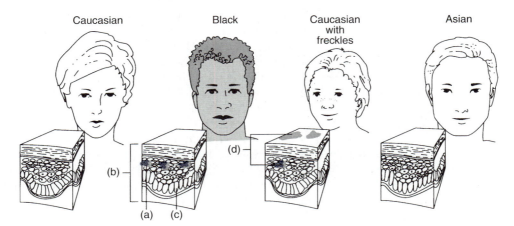

Caucasian   Black   Caucasian with freckles   Asian

DIAGNOSTIC TERMS

acne—any inflammatory condition of the sebaceous glands. The most common forms are:

acne conglobata—severe cystic process of acne with the appearance of multiple deep cysts, sinus tracts, and erythematous papules. (27)

acne pomade—seen mostly in the Black population. The pomade lesions are of the blackhead type and are usually found packed together around the hairline, scalp, and forehead. (27)

acne vulgaris—common form of acne involving the sebaceous follicles; marked by papules, pustules, and comedones. (11, 27)

albinism—congenital lack of normal skin pigment. (11, 22)

alopecia—loss of hair; baldness. (6, 23)

angioedema, angioneurotic edema, Quincke's edema—diffuse swelling of the loose tissues of the face, eyelids, lips, tongue, larynx, gastrointestinal tract, and other areas. (12)

atopic skin disorders—allergic skin conditions such as angioedema, urticaria, atopic drug reactions, and food allergy in atopic dermatitis. Atopy or allergy tends to be of the familial type. (12, 23)

burn—effect of exposure to heat, chemicals, electricity, or sunshine. (7, 10)

first-degree—redness or hyperemia involving superficial layers of skin.

second-degree—blisters or vesication involving deeper layers of skin.

third-degree—destruction involving any tissue below the skin.

callositas, keratosis—circumscribed thickening and hypertrophy of the horny cells of the epidermis. (12, 14)

carbuncle—circumscribed inflammation of the skin and deeper tissue causing necrosis and suppuration. (11)

cellulitis—inflammation of skin and subcutaneous tissue with or without formation of pus. (12)

decubitus ulcer, bedsore, pressure sore—ulcer that develops in an area where the skin covers a bony prominence and is damaged by continuous pressure, impoverished circulation, and nutrition. (12, 31)

dermatitis—inflammation of the skin. Some common forms are:

atopic dermatitis—chronic eczematous skin disorder usually associated with a personal or family history of asthma, allergic rhinitis, and atopic eczema. Pruritus is a common finding. Individuals exhibit dry, itchy skin, abnormal cutaneous vascular responses, and in some cases there is an elevation of serum IgE. Atopic persons present identifiable facies showing diffuse erythema, perioral pallor, and a redundant crease or fold below the lower eyelids (Dennie-Morgan fold). Although this disorder affects children, adolescents, and adults, its exact cause is unknown. (12, 23)

contact dermatitis, dermatitis venenata—inflammatory reaction to an irritant or a sensitizer; for example, poison ivy, ragweed, metal, chemical, rubber, and others. (23, 28)

exfoliative dermatitis—exfoliation or scaling off of dead skin, associated with crust formation, generalized redness, and edema. (12)

perioral dermatitis—facial dermatosis usually affecting females between the ages of 16 and 45. Its hallmarks are an erythematous, micropapular, fine scaling eruption affecting the nasolabial folds, the chin, and upper lip. (17, 23)

photodermatitis—various photosensitivity skin reactions that occur in response to exposure to ultraviolet light. Some of these reactions may be present as eczematous eruptions (termed *photoallergic dermatitis*) that may occur in response to topical and systemic substances in the presence of ultraviolet light. (23)

stasis dermatitis—brown, mottled hyperpigmentation. There may be evidence of scaling, thinning of the epidermis, pitting edema, varicosities, venous insufficiency, and ulceration. It is found most frequently on the skin over the medial malleolus. Stasis dermatitis may appear bilaterally. (23, 29)

dermatophytosis—superficial fungus infection (mycosis) that is readily transmitted from person to person; attacks the skin, nails, and hair; thrives in moisture and is caused by dermatophytes. (12, 16, 23)

> *Epidermophyton*—fungus that infects the skin.
> *Microsporum*—fungus that is found in the skin and hair.
> *Trichophyton*—fungus that attacks the skin, nails, and hair.

dermatophytosis of foot, epidermophytosis, tinea pedis, athlete's foot—parasitic or fungal infection, chiefly affecting the skin between the toes and associated with intense itching, sogginess, fissures, small blisters, and scaling of skin. (12, 16)

eczema—cutaneous inflammatory condition producing red papular and vesicular lesions, crusts, and scales. (12)

epidermolysis bullosa, acantholysis bullosa, Goldschneider's disease—hereditary condition characterized by dissolution of the layers of the skin and blister formation in response to slight irritation. (5, 12, 23)

erysipelas, St. Anthony's fire—a tender, erythematous area with sharp margin, with or without vesicle or bulla formation. The face and lower limbs are the most involved areas of the skin. (12)

gangrene—necrosis or putrefaction of tissue.

> *diabetic gangrene*—associated with diabetes mellitus. (20)
> *embolic gangrene*—caused by circulatory obstruction due to embolus. (29)
> *gas gangrene*—resulting from infection with bacillus *Clostridium perfringens*, an anerobic microorganism. (19, 20)

leukoderma—white patches of skin due to local absence of pigment. (12, 22)

lichen nitidus—asymptomatic chronic eruption of small sharply defined, flesh-colored papules localized in the penis, arms, and abdomen. Lichen planus resembles lichen nitidus and may coexist with it. (4)

lichen planus—inflammatory condition of skin and mucous membrane characterized by small, flat papules that appear shiny, dry, and violet. Linear, annular, and irregular patches are found on neck, wrists, and thighs. The Koebner phenomenon (see symptomatic terms) occurs in lichen planus, for example, linear streaks of papules at the sites of skin trauma may be seen. (3, 8, 12, 23)

lupus vulgaris—type of cutaneous tuberculosis, marked by reddish brown patches in which tiny nodules are embedded.

melanoderma—abnormal brown or black pigmentation of the skin.

onychia—inflammation of the nail bed.

paronychia—infected skin around the nail. (12)

pediculosis—infestation with lice. The three most common organisms are:

> *Phthirus pubis* (pubic louse or crab louse)
> *Pediculus humanus corporis* (body louse)
> *Pediculus humanus capitis* (head louse) (13, 18)

pemphigus—skin disease characterized by the appearance of crops of bullae (bubbles or blisters) of various sizes. (2, 12)

psoriasis—eruption appearing in circular patches of various sizes and showing a definite line of demarcation. Remissions and exacerbations are common. (23)

pyoderma—bacterial infection affecting:

> *skin*
>
> - *impetigo contagiosa*—infectious skin disease characterized by discrete vesicles that change to pustules and crusts; appear in crops, usually on the face, and are caused by *staphylococci* and *streptococci*. (12)
> - *pyoderma faciale*—cyanotic or reddish erythema associated with deep or superficial cystic lesions or abscesses.

pilosebaceous apparatus (hair and oil glands) causing:

- *furunculosis*—purulent infection of hair follicles usually by *Staphylococcus aureus*, which may result in necrosis of hair follicles and formation of furunculoid abscesses. (12)
- *staphylococcic folliculitis*—intradermal pustules surrounding hair follicles, usually due to *Staphylococcus aureus*. (12)

rhinophyma—red, large, nodular hypertrophic masses around the tip and wings of the nose; seen in men past 40 years of age. (12)

rosacea, simple rosacea—condition characterized by thickened skin, papules, and pustules occurring on a background of erythema and telangiectasia of facial skin. This process tends to affect mainly the middle third of the face from the forehead to the chin. Also, there may be hypertrophy of sebaceous glands present. Granulomatous changes can occur in the later stages of the disease. When this happens, this stage is referred to as *lupoid rosacea*. (24)

scabies—contagious skin condition caused by the mite *Sarcoptes scabiei*, which lays eggs in burrows under the skin, causing an intensely pruritic, vesicular eruption between the fingers, folds of axillae, buttocks, under the breasts, and in other areas. (12)

steatoma—sebaceous cyst.

tinea—any fungal skin disease, frequently caused by ringworms.

tinea barbae, tinea sycosis—ringworm of the beard.

tinea capitis, tinea tonsurans—ringworm of the scalp, forming bold circular patches.

tinea corporis, tinea circinata—ringworm of the body, usually noted by ring-shaped eruptions, scaling, vesiculation, and itching. It is transmitted by animal contact.

tinea pedis—athlete's foot. (16)

tinea unguium, onychomycosis—ringworm of the nails, especially toenails, causing thickening and scaling under the nail plate. (12, 23)

tumors of the skin—new growths of skin.

angiosarcoma—extremely aggressive malignant tumor arising from the vascular structures within the skin; lesions have a highly metastatic potential. (12)

basal cell carcinoma of the skin—present on sun-exposed skin as a small papule area, which in time forms a pearly, translucent surface. Lesions grow slowly. The large lesions may have a telangiectasia, which is a rolled, raised border with a depressed center. (12, 23, 30)

keloid—new growth of scar tissue.

keratoacanthoma—rapidly growing nodule arising from the epidermis and containing a horn-filled crater; usually a benign lesion. (14, 23, 29)

nevus, mole, birthmark—congenital pigmentation of a circumscribed area of the skin.

seborrheic keratosis, basal cell papilloma—benign superficial, epithelial tumor; few or many in number; light tan to black in color (depending on melanin content); characterized by horny overgrowth (hyperkeratosis); primarily occurring in middle-aged and elderly persons. (23)

squamous cell carcinoma—malignant tumor arising from epidermal or appendageal keratinocytes, or squamous mucosal epithelium. It often arises in skin areas that have been damaged or subjected to chronic irritation. Squamous cell carcinoma may evolve faster than basal cell carcinoma but not as rapidly as keratoacanthoma. (23, 30)

squamous cell carcinoma in situ—an intraepidermal neoplasm. Epidermal keratinocytes are arranged haphazardly with a windblown appearance. Characteristic of this tumor is the abnormal keratinization, which presents in the form of keratin pearls or individual dyskeratotic cells. Many cells are large and atypical, with large and hyperchromatic nuclei. (30)

ulcer—break in the skin or mucous membrane resulting from varicose veins or other causes. (12)

urticaria, hives, nettle rash—skin eruption of pale or reddish wheals, usually associated with intense itching. May occur as an acute self-limited episode caused by food allergy, drug reaction, emotional stress, or in chronic form as a characteristic feature of rheumatic and connective tissue disorders. (12, 23)

verruca vulgaris, warts—benign epithelial proliferations of the skin and mucosa caused by infection with papillomaviruses. These common warts appear as scaly, rough papules or nodules on any skin surface. (21, 23, 25)

OPERATIVE TERMS (SEE TABLE 2.1.)

cryosurgery of skin—freezing the skin with liquid nitrogen or solid carbon dioxide to destroy a lesion. (30)

curettage of skin—removal of superficial lesions with a skin curette. (30)

dermabrasion—surgical removal of nevi or scars using sandpaper or other abrasives. (12, 15)

> *dermabrasion and excision of*: (12, 15)
> - *furrowed brows*—application of dermabrader to frown furrows and removal of skin over the furrowed area.
> - *perioral wrinkles*—application of dermabrader to each vertical lip line for elimination of wrinkles around the mouth.

electrodesiccation—use of short, high-frequency electric sparks for drying cells and tissues. (9, 21)

electrosurgical excision of burn—excision of full-thickness burn using the electrosurgical unit at the level of the fascia. The procedure leaves a dry fascial bed for immediate grafting. (9)

face-lift operation—reconstructive plastic surgery of the face; the art of surgical sculpture applied to the human face to restore function, remove the marks of time, or correct defects. (See *rhytidectomy* definition listed in this section.) (31)

fulguration of skin—use of long, high-frequency electric sparks for destroying tissue.

incision and drainage—cutting through or into the infected skin lesion, and subsequent withdrawal of discharges from the lesion. (15)

laser therapy—technique that relies on devices that generate light amplification by stimulated emission radiation. Laser light lies in the infrared and visible light portions of the electromagnetic spectrum. Two lasers that have broad application in dermatology are the *argon* and *carbon dioxide laser*. The argon penetrates 1 to 2 millimeters in tissue depth and produces considerable scatter to the tissue. The carbon dioxide laser penetrates 0.1 to 0.2 millimeters in tissue depth and produces minimal scatter to the tissue.

> *Argon laser* is used for:
> - treatment of port wine hemangiomas
> - destruction of blood vessel lesions, hemangiomas, senile angiomas, pyogenic granulomas, telangiectasia, melanin-containing lesions, nevi, café-au-lait spots, and seborrheic keratoses.
>
> *Carbon dioxide laser* is used for:
> - removal of benign and malignant tumors
> - debridement of burns and decubitus ulcers
> - removal of viral verrucae, actinic keratosis, and leukoplakia. (1, 9, 12)

Linton flap procedure—operation for stasis dermatitis and ulceration refractory. All incompetent communicating veins are ligated and divided to relieve ambulatory venous hypertension in superficial veins. This prevents progression of dermatitis, ulceration, and pigmentation of overlying skin in the lower limb.

local excision of skin lesion—removal of skin lesion by cutting it out. A fusiform (elliptical) excision is indicated for removal of small- to moderate-sized benign or malignant neoplasms. Another technique is the disk excision, wherein the neoplasm is excised as a circle with adequate margins. (15)

plastic operation on skin—surgical correction of defect.

| TABLE **2.1** | Some Conditions of the Skin Amenable to Surgery |

Anatomic Site	Diagnosis	Type of Surgery	Operative Procedures
Skin	Seborrheic keratoses	Epidermal curettage	Lesions frozen with ethyl chloride and curetted
Skin	Basal cell carcinoma, small lesion	Curettage	Lesion and all extensions removed with skin curette
Skin	Basal cell carcinoma, small lesion	Electrodesiccation	Remaining cells destroyed by dehydration of tissues through the use of high-frequency electric current
Skin	Basal cell carcinoma, small lesion	Cryosurgery of skin lesion	Freezing with cryosurgical spray or by insertion of microthermocouple
Skin, Sebaceous glands, Hair follicles	Infected steatoma Furuncle or carbuncle of hair follicles	Incision and drainage of glands of skin; of hair follicles	Surgical opening of infected sebaceous glands or other infected areas to induce drainage
Nail bed Nail fold	Onychia, paronychia Infected ingrowing toenail	Incision and drainage of infected nail bed or nail fold	Surgical opening of infected areas to induce drainage
Subcutaneous areolar tissue	Cellulitis of forearm	Incision and drainage of subcutaneous areolar tissue	Surgical opening of infected area and insertion of drain
Skin, Subcutaneous tissue	Dermoid cyst of skin Lipoma of subcutaneous tissue	Local excision of dermoid cyst or lipoma	Removal of dermoid cyst or lipoma
Skin	Cicatrix of skin caused by burn (structures beneath the skin undamaged)	Excision of cicatricial skin lesion Use of split-thickness or full-thickness skin graft	Removal of excess scar tissue and replacement by covering area with either half or full thickness of skin removed by knife or dermatone
Skin, Subcutaneous tissue	Thermal burn injury	Electrosurgical excision of full-thickness burn	Burned skin and subcutaneous tissue removed by electro-surgery at level of fascia Immediate skin grafting of dry fascial bed

TABLE 2.1	(continued)		
Anatomic Site	*Diagnosis*	*Type of Surgery*	*Operative Procedures*
Skin of axilla	Cicatricial contracture of axilla	Z-plasty	Defect corrected by using sliding flaps of skin
Skin of neck, chin, or cheek	Contracture from scar of old burns or injuries	Reconstruction operation *First stage:* Preparation of pedicle or Gillies' tube flap *Second stage:* Excision of scar Coverage of denuded area with pedicle *Third stage:* Removal of pedicle	Skin and subcutaneous tissue from area raised and pedicle tubed Removal of deep scar; distal end of pedicle severed and sutured into defect with pedicle still attached Pedicle opened and returned to donor area

rhytidectomy—this technique usually consists of a major procedure involving extensive incisions hidden just in front of and behind the ear, in the temporal scalp, and behind the ear in the occipital hairline. Fat aspiration, such as **liposuction,** has been employed in the neck and face region, resulting in a more definitive chin and jaw line and correction of the double-chin appearance. This procedure may include surgical removal of subcutaneous fat pads and superfluous skin to eliminate wrinkles. For instance, fat may be removed from the cheeks and submental area, and the platysma muscle that forms the foundation for the neck may be altered to give support and provide a more youthful contour to the neck and submental angle. (31)

rhytidoplasty—surgical elimination of wrinkles achieved by removal of excess skin and by tightening remaining skin to restore youthful appearance. A dermal fat graft is inserted in the following forms of repair:

    cervicofacial rhytidoplasty—surgical correction of wrinkles of the neck and face.

    glabellar rhytidoplasty—operative procedure for removing the vertical furrows between the eyebrows. (15)

skin grafting—transfer of skin from a normal area to cover denuded areas. A dermatome may be used to obtain these skin transplants. A full-thickness skin graft (FTSG) consists of epidermis with full-thickness dermis. A split-thickness skin graft (STSG) consists of epidermis with a varying thickness of dermis. The cultured keratinocyte grafts are used for patients with burns, multiple wounds, and recalcitrant large wounds, and for patients who have a history of graft failure and limited graft donor sites, as well as for patients who are poor surgical risks. Two types of this graft are the keratinocyte autografts, which may be cultured from the patient's own skin and used only on that particular patient, or the keratinocyte allografts, which are cultured from human newborn foreskin and may be used on other patients. (15)

SYMPTOMATIC TERMS

anular (annular)—ring-shaped. (11, 23)

café-au-lait spots—light brown, flat spots, variable in shape and size, seen in neurofibromatosis (von Recklinghausen's disease). (23)

chloasma—patches of brown or yellowish pigmentation on skin that is otherwise normal. (23)

cicatrix of skin—scar left by a healed wound.

cicatrization—healing by scar formation.

comedo (pl. comedones), blackhead—excretory duct of skin plugged by discolored sebum.

confluent—lesions joined or run together.

depigmentation—partial or complete loss of pigment; occurs in albinism, atrophic skin, and scars. (22)

dermatographism, dermographia—skin writing. Urticarial wheals appear where skin was marked by pencil or blunt instrument. (11, 12)

discoid—shaped like a disk. (11)

discrete—lesions that are disconnected and separate from one another.

ecchymosis (pl. ecchymoses)—purple spot or bruise caused by seepage of blood into the skin. (11)

eczematoid, eczematous—eczemalike inflammatory lesion that tends to thicken and become scaly, vesicular, crusty, or weeping. (12, 23)

eruption—rash or skin lesion.

erythema—diffuse redness of skin. (3, 8, 23)

excoriation—linear break of skin or scratch mark resulting from surface trauma.

granulation—method of repair or healing following loss of tissue or pyogenic infection.

guttate—droplike. (11)

hyperpigmentation—presence of abnormal amount of pigment in the skin; seen in a number of systemic diseases, such as adrenal insufficiency, acromegaly, and others. In the familial progressive type of hyperpigmentation, patches of excessive pigmentation enlarge in size with increasing age. (11, 22, 23)

intertriginous—between two folds of skin. (12)

keratotic—pertaining to horny thickening. (11)

Koebner's phenomenon—present in some skin disorders that tend to evolve new lesions after traumatic injury in areas of apparently normal skin. For example, psoriasis may occur within surgical scars, after sunburn, or in a skin reaction to drugs. Lichen planus may exhibit this phenomenon. (23)

macule—discolored patch or spot on the skin. (11)

milia (sing. milium)—tiny white nodules appearing on the skin, frequently below the eyes.

moniliform—beaded.

multiform—several forms of a skin lesion.

Nikolsky's sign—friction or manual pressure, such as rubbing applied to healthy areas of skin near bullous lesions, causes the epidermis to wrinkle and separate. This sign is present in various forms of pemphigus and toxic epidermal necrolysis. (23)

papule—pimple. (11)

petechiae—pin-sized hemorrhagic spots in the skin. (11)

proliferation—process of rapid reproduction of similar cells.

pustule—small elevation of the skin containing pus or lymph. (11, 23)

seborrheal, seborrheic—pertaining to seborrhea, an oversecretion of sebaceous glands. (23)

ABBREVIATIONS

GENERAL

BP—blood pressure
CC—chief complaint
Dx—diagnosis

FH—family history
MH—marital history
PH—past history

PI—present illness
TPR—temperature, pulse, and respiration

MANUALS AND NOMENCLATURES
CPHA—*Commission on Professional Hospital Activities*
CPT—*Common Procedural Terminology*
DSM-IV—*Diagnostic and Statistical Manual of Mental Disorders*, 4th edition.
ICD-9-CM—*International Classification of Diseases, 9th Revision, Clinical Modification*, 4th edition.
SNDO—*Standard Nomenclature of Diseases and Operations*

PARAMEDICAL ORGANIZATIONS
AAMT—American Association for Medical Transcription
AAPA—American Academy of Physicians' Assistants
ADA—American Dietetic Association
AHIMA—American Health Information Management Association
APAP—Association of Physician Assistant Programs

ORAL READING PRACTICE

PEMPHIGUS

There are several forms of **dermatitis** in which a **bullous eruption** develops, but they are distinguished from true bullous diseases by a short duration and good prognosis.

The term **pemphigus,** derived from the Greek *pemphix,* meaning *blister,* points up the chief characteristic of **pemphigus vulgaris,** namely, the formation of blisters. These **blebs** arise suddenly on apparently normal or slightly **erythematous** skin and form oval shaped or round blisters containing clear **serum.** The blisters tend to be **flaccid** and break easily. The **epidermis** becomes detached, leaving increasingly larger areas of **denudation.** The **Nikolsky sign** is always positive. It is obtained by pressing on the skin with the fingertip. The epidermis then slides off, and a raw surface remains. The **denuded** areas are slow in healing and constitute a continuous threat of infection.

Pemphigus has been compared to a serious burn, but the trauma of a burn is a single occasion and the lesion is frequently localized. On the other hand, the injury inflicted on the skin by numerous crops of **bullae** followed by widespread denudation presents a still more serious problem than that of many burns. The blisters vary in size from a few **millimeters** to 10 **centimeters.** New lesions develop as old ones disappear. Since the crops arise rapidly, often overnight, and old lesions heal slowly, the areas of denudation are extensive. Eventually, crusts form over the raw surface. If **pyogenic bacteria** get beneath these crusts, foul-smelling pus collects and increases the patient's physical distress. There is no scarring; only a **hyperpigmented** lesion remains after healing. The formation of bullae in the **oral cavity** is particularly painful. Blebs about 5 millimeters in diameter are scattered over the **buccal mucosa.** They appear spontaneously, rupture, and leave new, painful ulcers. Blebs also may occur on other orificial mucous membranes.

The etiology of pemphigus is still unknown. Some authorities believe that it is metabolic in nature or caused by **bacterial** or **viral** infections; however, no theory has yielded convincing evidence.

The common type of pemphigus is a chronic, recurrent disease, afflicting only adults. Acute **exacerbations** may be followed by brief or prolonged periods of remission. As a rule, **pemphigus vulgaris** lasts from several months to years. Untreated, it is a fatal disease, but with judicious use of **cortisone,** the **prognosis** is favorable. (9, 16, 32, 38)

REVIEW GUIDE

Instructions: Break the following terms apart, identify the medical term elements, and define the term.

Example: dermatophytosis
    derma- = combining-form element = skin
    phyto- = combining-form element = plant
    -osis = suffix = condition, disease

cellulitis

cryosurgery

dermographia

epidermis

folliculitis

leukoderma

paronychia

perioral

pyoderma

rhytidectomy

steatoma

Instructions: Figure 2.1 in the text shows a skin section. For each line that extends from the figure below, provide the anatomic name of the site, as shown in the example.

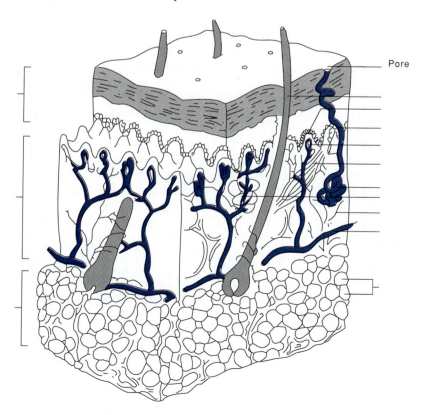

Pore

3

Psychiatric Disorders

ORIGIN OF TERMS

cata- (G)—against, along with, down, lower, under
dynamo- (G)—power
mania (G)—madness
phren- (G)—mind, diaphragm
psych-, psycho- (G)—mind
schizo- (G)—division, split
soma (G)—body
thymo- (G)—mind, thymus

PHONETIC PRONUNCIATION OF SELECTED TERMS

catalepsy	CAT'ah-LEP-see
catatonic	CAT-ah-TON'ick
cyclothymic	SIGH-clo-THY'mick
hebephrenic	HEB'e-fren-ick
psychogenic amnesia	SIGH-ko-GEN'ick am-NEE'ze-ah
schizoid	SKIZ'oid or SKIT'zoid
schizophrenia	SKIZ-o-FRE'nee-ah or SKIT-so-FRE'nee-ah

GENERAL TERMS

ego—in psychoanalytic theory, one of the three major divisions in the model of the psychic apparatus, the others being the id and superego. The ego represents the sum of certain mental mechanisms. The ego serves to mediate between the demands of primitive instinctual drives (the id), or internalized parental and social prohibitions (the superego), and of reality. The compromises between these forces achieved by the ego tend to resolve intrapsychic conflict and serve as an adaptive and executive function. As used in psychiatry, the term should not be confused with its common usage in the sense of "self-love" or "selfishness." (21)

psychiatry—the medical science that deals with the origin, diagnosis, prevention, and treatment of mental and emotional disorders.

forensic psychiatry—branch of medicine that deals with disorders of the mind and their relation to legal principles. The most common role of a forensic psychiatrist is to serve as an expert witness in court proceedings. (30)

geriatric psychiatry, geropsychiatry—branch of medicine that deals with the prevention, diagnosis, and treatment of physical and psychological disorders in the elderly. Geriatric psychiatry was declared an official subspecialty by the American Board of Psychiatry and Neurology (ABPN) in 1989. (29)

DIAGNOSTIC TERMS*

alcohol-use and alcohol-induced disorders:

alcohol abuse—a maladaptive pattern of alcohol use leading to clinically significant impairment or distress, as manifested by one (or more) of the following, occurring within a 12-month period: (1) recurrent alcohol use resulting in a failure to fulfill major role obligations at work, school, or home; (2) recurrent use of alcohol in situations in which it is physically hazardous, such as driving an automobile; (3) recurrent alcohol-related legal problems, such as arrest for alcohol-related disorderly conduct; (4) continued alcohol use despite having persistent or recurrent social or interpersonal problems caused by the effects of the alcohol, such as arguments with spouse about consequences of intoxication, or physical fights. (4)

> *Reference values alcohol abuse*
> - marked intoxication—0.3%–0.4% (SIU†: 65–87 mmol/L)
> - alcoholic stupor—4.0%–0.5% (SIU: 87–109 mmol/L)
> - alcoholic coma—greater than 0.5% (SIU: greater than 109 mmol/L)

alcohol intoxication—essential features are the presence of clinically significant maladaptive behavioral or psychological changes (e.g., inappropriate sexual or aggressive behavior, mood lability, impaired judgment, impaired social or occupational functioning) that develop during, or shortly after, alcohol ingestion. These changes are accompanied by evidence of slurred speech, incoordination, unsteady gait, nystagmus, impairment in attention or memory, stupor, or coma. (4)

alcohol withdrawal—essential feature of this disorder is the presence of a characteristic withdrawal syndrome that develops after the cessation of (or reduction in) heavy and prolonged alcohol use. The withdrawal syndrome includes two or more of the following symptoms (developing within several hours to a few days after cessation or reduction in alcohol): autonomic hyperactivity (e.g., sweating or pulse rate greater than 100); increased hand tremor and insomnia; nausea or vomiting; transient visual, tactile, or auditory hallucinations or illusions; psychomotor agitation; anxiety; and grand mal seizures. (4)

generalized anxiety disorder—the essential feature of this disorder is unrealistic or excessive anxiety and worry (apprehensive expectation), occurring more days than not for a period of at least 6 months, about a number of events or activities. The anxiety and worry are accompanied by at least 3 additional symptoms such as restlessness, being easily fatigued, difficulty concentrating, irritability, muscle tension, and disturbed sleep. The intensity, duration, or frequency of the anxiety and worry is far out of proportion to the actual likelihood or impact of the feared event. For example, the person worries about possible misfortunes to his or her child (who is in no danger) or worries about finances (for no good reason). Other specific anxiety disorders include:

anxiety disorder due to a general medical condition—characterized by prominent symptoms of anxiety that are judged to be due to the direct physiological effects of a general medical condition. The disturbance causes clinically significant distress or impairment in social, occupational, or other important areas of functioning.

---

*Substantial material in this section is taken verbatim from *Diagnostic and Statistical Manual of Mental Disorders*, 4th ed. (DSM-IV™) (Washington, D.C.: American Psychiatric Association, 1994). Reprinted with permission.
†SIU = International System of Units

substance-induced anxiety disorder—characterized by prominent symptoms of anxiety that are judged to be due to the physiological effects of a substance (e.g., a drug of abuse, a medication, or toxin exposure). The disturbance causes clinically significant distress or impairment in social, occupational, or other important areas of functioning. (7)

obsessive-compulsive disorder—essential features of this disorder are recurrent obsessions or compulsions that are severe enough to be time-consuming (i.e., they take more than 1 hour a day) or cause marked distress or significantly interfere with the person's normal routine, occupational or social functioning, or relationships with others.

- *obsessions*—persistent ideas, thoughts, impulses, or images that are experienced as intrusive and inappropriate and that cause marked anxiety or distress.
- *compulsions*—repetitive behaviors or mental acts, the goal of which is to prevent or reduce anxiety or distress, not to provide pleasure or gratification. Compulsions are either clearly excessive or are not connected in a realistic way with what they are designed to neutralize or prevent. (7)

panic disorder—essential features of this disorder are recurrent, unexpected panic attacks (discrete periods of intense fear or discomfort), followed by at least 1 month of persistent concern about having another panic attack, worry about possible implications or consequences of the panic attacks, or a significant behavioral change related to the attacks. An unexpected (spontaneous, uncued) panic attack is defined as one that is not associated with a situational trigger (i.e., it occurs "out of the blue"). At least two unexpected panic attacks are required for the diagnosis, but most individuals have considerably more. Persons with panic disorder frequently also have situationally predisposed panic attacks (i.e., those more likely to occur on, but not invariably associated with, exposure to a situational trigger). Situationally bound attacks (i.e., those that occur almost invariably and immediately on exposure to a situational trigger) can occur but are less common. (7)

post-traumatic stress disorder—development of characteristic symptoms following exposure to an extreme traumatic stressor involving direct personal experience of an event that involves actual or threatened death or serious injury, or other threat to one's physical integrity; or witnessing an event that involves death, injury, or a threat to the physical integrity of another person; or learning about unexpected or violent death, serious harm, or threat of death or injury experienced by family members or other close associates. Characteristic symptoms resulting from exposure to the extreme trauma include persistent reexperiencing of the traumatic event, persistent avoidance of stimuli associated with the trauma and numbing of general responsiveness, and persistent symptoms of increased arousal. The full symptom picture must be present for more than 1 month, and the disturbance must cause clinically significant distress or impairment in social, occupational, or other important areas of functioning. (7)

dissociative disorders—the dominant aspect is a disruption in the usually integrated functions of consciousness, memory, identity, or perception of the environment. The disturbance may be sudden or gradual, transient or chronic. Types of this disorder include:

dissociative amnesia—characterized by an inability to recall important personal information, usually of a traumatic or stressful nature, that is too extensive to be explained by ordinary forgetfulness.

dissociative fugue—characterized by sudden, unexpected travel away from home or one's customary place of work, accompanied by an inability to recall some or all of one's past and confusion about personal identity or the assumption of a new identity.

dissociative identity disorder (formerly *multiple personality disorder*)—characterized by the presence of two or more distinct identities or personality states (each with its own relatively enduring pattern of perceiving, relating to, and thinking about the environment and self). At least two of these identities or personality states recurrently take control of the person's behavior. Usually there is a primary identity that carries the individual's given name and is passive, dependent, guilty, and depressed. The alternate identities frequently have different names and characteristics that contrast with the primary identity (e.g., are hostile, controlling, self-destructive). Persons with this disorder experience frequent gaps in memory for personal history, both remote and recent. Transitions among identities are often triggered by psychosocial stress.

depersonalization disorder—characterized by a persistent or recurrent feeling of being detached from one's mental processes or body (e.g., as if one is an outside observer; feeling like one is in a dream). During the depersonalization experience, reality testing remains intact. The depersonalization causes clinically significant distress or impairment in social, occupational, or other important areas of functioning. Since depersonalization is a common associated feature of many other mental disorders, a separate diagnosis of depersonalization disorder is **not** made if the experience occurs exclusively during the course of another mental disorder (e.g., schizophrenia). (9)

eating disorders—characterized by gross disturbances in eating behavior. (2, 10) Some disorders in this category are:

anorexia nervosa—essential features of this disorder are refusal to maintain a minimally normal body weight for age and height; intense fear of gaining weight or becoming fat, even though underweight; a distorted body image; and amenorrhea (in postmenarcheal females). The weight loss is usually accomplished by a reduction in total food intake, often with extensive exercising. There may be frequent use of laxatives or diuretics and also self-induced vomiting. (The term *anorexia* is a misnomer because loss of appetite is rare.)

bulimia nervosa—essential features of this disorder are recurrent episodes of binge eating; a feeling of lack of control over eating behavior during the eating binges; use of laxatives or diuretics; strict dieting or fasting, or vigorous exercise in order to prevent weight gain; and persistent overconcern with body shape and weight. In order to qualify for the diagnosis, the person must have had, on average, a minimum of two binge-eating episodes a week for at least 3 months.

- *binge eating*—characterized by both of the following: (1) eating, in a discrete period of time (e.g., within any 2-hour period), an amount of food that is definitely larger than most people would eat during a similar period of time and under similar circumstances; (2) a sense of lack of control over eating during the episode (e.g., a feeling that one cannot stop eating or control how much one is eating).

pica—the essential feature is the persistent eating of nonnutritive substances for a period of at least 1 month. Infants and younger children with this disorder usually eat paint, plaster, string, hair, or cloth. Older children may eat animal droppings, sand, insects, leaves, or pebbles. Pica usually remits in early childhood but may persist into adolescence or on rare occasions continue through adulthood. This behavior must be developmentally inappropriate and not part of a culturally sanctioned practice.

mental retardation—significantly subaverage general intellectual functioning that is accompanied by significant limitations in adaptive functioning in at least two of the following skill areas: communication, self-care, home living, social-interpersonal skills, use of community resources, self-direction, functional academic skills, work, leisure, health, and safety. Significantly subaverage intellectual functioning is defined as an IQ (intelligence quotient) of 70 or below (approximately 2 standard deviations below the mean). The upper limit is intended as a guideline; it could be extended upward through an IQ of 75 or more, depending on the reliability of the intelligence test used. Onset is before 18 years and concurrent with deficits or impairments in adaptive functioning. *Adaptive functioning* refers to how effectively individuals cope with common life demands and how well they meet the standards of personal independence expected of persons in their particular age group, sociocultural background, and community setting. The degrees of severity reflecting level of intellectual impairment are:

mild mental retardation: IQ level 50–55 to approximately 70.

moderate mental retardation: IQ level 35–40 to 50–55.

severe mental retardation: IQ level 20–25 to 35–40.

profound mental retardation: IQ level below 20 or 25. (2)

mood disorders—disorders that have a disturbance in mood as the predominant feature. (6) Some subdivisions of mood disorders include:

mood episodes (8)

- *hypomanic episode*—essential feature is a distinct period that lasts at least 4 days during which the predominant mood is either elevated, expansive, or irritable. This period of abnormal mood must be accompanied by at least three additional symptoms from a list that includes inflated self-esteem or grandiosity (nondelusional), decreased need for sleep, more talkative than usual or pressure to keep talking, flight of ideas, distractibility, and/or other symptoms of the manic syndrome. If the mood is irritable rather than elevated or expansive, at least 4 of the above symptoms must be present. The disturbance is not severe enough to cause marked impairment in social or occupational functioning or to require hospitalization. Additional features of hypomanic episodes are similar to those of a manic episode except that delusions are never present and all other symptoms tend to be less severe than in manic episodes.

- *major depressive episode*—a period of at least 2 weeks (or less if hospitalization is required) during which there is either depressed mood or loss of interest or pleasure in nearly all activities. The person must also experience at least 4 additional associated symptoms such as appetite decline, change in weight, sleep disturbance, psychomotor agitation or retardation, decreased energy, feelings of worthlessness or guilt, difficulty in concentrating, recurrent thoughts of death, and suicidal ideation, plans, or attempts. To count toward a major depressive episode, a symptom must either be newly present or must have clearly worsened compared with the person's pre-episode status. (6)

- *manic episode*—distinct period (lasting at least 1 week) during which the predominant mood is either elevated, expansive, or irritable, and there are at least three additional associated symptoms that include inflated self-esteem or grandiosity (which may be delusional), decreased need for sleep, pressure of speech, flight of ideas, distractibility, increased involvement in goal-directed activity, psychomotor agitation, and excessive involvement in pleasurable activities that have a high potential for painful consequences that are not perceived by the patient. The disturbance during this period is sufficiently severe to cause marked impairment in occupational functioning or in usual social activities or relationships with others, or to require hospitalization to prevent harm to self or others.

- *mixed episode*—characterized by a period of time (nearly every day during at least a 1 week period) in which the criteria are met both for a manic episode and for a major depressive episode. The mood disturbance is sufficiently severe to cause marked impairment in occupational and social functioning or is characterized by the presence of psychotic features, or necessitate hospitalization to prevent harm to self or others. Symptoms frequently include agitation, insomnia, appetite dysregulation, psychotic features, and suicidal thinking.

depressive disorders (6)
- *major depressive disorder*—essential feature is a clinical course that is characterized by one or more major depressive episodes without a history of manic, mixed, or hypomanic episodes. Major depressive disorder may occur as a single or recurrent episode.
- *dysthymic disorder*—essential feature is a chronically depressed mood that occurs for most of the day more days than not for at least 2 years. Individuals with this disorder describe their mood as sad or "down in the dumps." (For children the period is 1 year and the mood may be irritable rather than depressed.) During the periods of depressed mood, at least two of the following additional symptoms are present: poor appetite or overeating, insomnia or hypersomnia, low energy or fatigue, low self-esteem, poor concentration or difficulty making decisions, and feelings of hopelessness.

bipolar disorders (6)
- *bipolar I disorder*—essential feature is a clinical course that is characterized by the occurrence of one or more manic episodes or mixed episodes.
- *bipolar II disorder*—essential feature of this disorder is a clinical course that is characterized by the occurrence of one or more major depressive episodes accompanied by at least one hypomanic episode.
- *cyclothymic disorder*—essential feature is a chronic, fluctuating mood disturbance for at least 2 years, involving numerous periods of hypomanic symptoms and numerous periods of depressive symptoms that do not meet criteria for a major depressive episode. (In children and adolescents, the duration must be at least 1 year.)

personality disorder—condition marked by maladaptive behavior pattern that is deeply ingrained in the personality. This disorder reflects an enduring pattern of inner experience and behavior that deviates markedly from the expectations of an individual's culture, is pervasive and inflexible, has an onset in adolescence or early adulthood, is stable over time and leads to distress or impairment. Personality traits are enduring patterns of perceiving, relating to, and thinking about the environment and oneself, and are exhibited in a wide range of important social and personal contexts. (11) Some examples of personality disorders are:

paranoid personality disorder—essential feature is a pattern of pervasive distrust and suspiciousness of others such that their motives are interpreted as malevolent. This pattern begins by early adulthood and is present in a variety of contexts; individuals with this disorder assume that other people will exploit, harm, or deceive them, even if no evidence exists to support this expectation.

schizoid personality disorder—essential features of this disorder are a pervasive pattern of detachment from social relationships and a restricted range of expression of emotions in interpersonal settings. Individuals with this disorder appear to lack a desire for intimacy, seem indifferent to opportunities to develop close relationships and do not seem to derive satisfaction from being part of a family or social group. The person is shy, seclusive, unsociable, eccentric, autistic, and almost always chooses solitary activities.

schizotypal personality disorder—essential features of this disorder are a pervasive pattern of social and interpersonal deficits marked by acute discomfort with, and reduced capacity for, close relationships as well as by cognitive or perceptual distortions and eccentricities of behavior. This pattern begins by early adulthood and is present in a variety of contexts, as indicated by five (or more) of the following: ideas of reference (excluding delusions of reference); unusual perceptual experiences, including bodily illusions; behavior or appearance that is odd, eccentric, or peculiar; suspiciousness or paranoid ideation; excessive social anxiety that tends to be associated with paranoid fears rather than negative judgments about self; odd thinking and speech; and lack of close friends other than first-degree relatives.

antisocial personality disorder—characterized by a pervasive pattern of disregard for, and violation of, the rights of others, as indicated by three or more of the following: failure to conform to social norms with respect to lawful behaviors as indicated by repeatedly performing acts that are grounds for arrest, deceitfulness (repeated lying, use of aliases, conning others for personal profit or pleasure), irritability and aggressiveness, reckless disregard for safety of self or others, consistent irresponsibility, and lack of remorse for the effects of their behavior on self or others. This disorder begins in early childhood or early adolescence and continues into adulthood. For this diagnosis to be made, the individual must be at least 18 years of age.

narcissistic personality disorder—essential features that begin by early adulthood are a pervasive pattern of grandiosity (in fantasy or behavior), hypersensitivity to the evaluation of others, and a lack of empathy. Persons with this disorder have a grandiose sense of self-importance. They tend to exaggerate their accomplishments and talents and expect to be noticed as "special," even without appropriate achievement.

histrionic personality disorder—essential feature is a pervasive pattern of excessive emotionality and attention-seeking behavior, beginning in early adulthood. Persons with this disorder constantly seek or demand reassurance, approval, or praise from others and are uncomfortable in situations in which they are not the center of attention. They tend to be dramatic and to draw attention to themselves. They consider relationships to be more intimate than they actually are, and interaction with others is often characterized by inappropriate sexually seductive or provocative behavior.

avoidant personality disorder—essential features are a pervasive pattern of social inhibition, fear of negative evaluation, and timidity, beginning by early childhood. These persons avoid social or occupational activities that involve significant interpersonal contact. These individuals are very hurt by criticism and are devastated by the slightest hint of disapproval.

dependent personality disorder—essential feature is an overall pattern of dependent and submissive behavior, beginning by early adulthood. Individuals find it difficult to make everyday decisions without an excessive amount of advice and reassurance from others. These individuals tend to agree with others even when they believe them to be wrong, for fear of being rejected.

obsessive-compulsive personality disorder—essential feature is a pervasive pattern of perfectionism and inflexibility, beginning in early adulthood. These persons tend to constantly strive for perfection, but adherence to their own strict and often unattainable standards frequently interferes with actual completion of tasks or projects. They are stingy with their emotions and material possessions and rarely give gifts or compliments. They tend to be overconscientious, scrupulous, and inflexible about matters of morality, ethics, or values (not accounted for by cultural or religious identification).

borderline personality disorder—essential feature is a pervasive pattern of instability of interpersonal relationships, self-image, and affects, and marked impulsivity that begins by early adulthood and is present in a variety of contexts. Individuals with this disorder make frantic efforts to avoid real or imagined abandonment. The perception of impending separation or rejection, or the loss of external structure, can lead to profound changes in self-image, affect, cognition, and behavior. They may display impulsivity by excessive gambling, spending money irresponsibly, binge eating, substance abuse, engaging in unsafe sex, or driving recklessly.

NOTE: The disorder formerly designated multiple personality disorder is now designated dissociative identity disorder. See page 43.

schizophrenia—severe mental disorder of psychotic depth marked by disturbances in behavior, mood, and ability to think. Altered concept formation may lead to a distortion of reality, delusions, and hallucinations, which tend to be self-protective. Emotional disharmony and bizarre regressive behavior are frequently present. The diagnosis of schizophrenia requires that continuous signs of the illness have been present for at least 6 months, which includes an active phase with psychotic symptoms. The development of the active phase of the illness is usually preceded by a prodromal phase in which there is a clear deterioration from the previous level of functioning. The American Psychiatric Association distinguishes several types, some of which are listed below:

catatonic type—marked disturbance in activity with either generalized inhibition (mutism, stupor, negativism, waxy appearance) or by excessive motor activity and excitement, as well as voluntary assumption of inappropriate bizarre postures. During catatonic stupor or excitement, the person needs careful supervision to avoid hurting himself/herself, or others.

disorganized type—features of this type are incoherence, marked loosening of associations or grossly disorganized behavior, and, in addition, flat or grossly inappropriate affect.

paranoid type—marked preoccupation with one or more systematized delusions or with frequent auditory hallucinations related to a single theme. Other features usually associated with this type include unfocused anxiety, anger, argumentativeness, and violence, as well as stilted, formal quality or extreme intensity in interpersonal interaction.

residual type—this category is used when there has been at least one episode of schizophrenia, but the clinical picture that occasioned the evaluation or admission to clinical care is without prominent psychotic symptoms, though signs of the illness persist. Emotional blunting, social withdrawal, eccentric behavior, illogical thinking, and mild loosening of associations are common.

undifferentiated type—marked by prominent psychotic symptoms (delusions, hallucinations, incoherence, or grossly disorganized behavior) that do not meet the criteria for paranoid, catatonic, or disorganized types. (5)

somatoform disorders—essential features are symptoms suggesting a physical disorder, with no evident organic findings or known physiologic mechanisms and no positive evidence, or with a strong presumption that the symptoms are linked to psychologic factors or conflicts. Examples of these disorders are:

body dysmorphic disorder (dysmorphophobia)—essential feature is preoccupation with some imagined defect in appearance in a normal-appearing person. Even if there is a slight physical anomaly present, the person's concern is markedly excessive. Most common complaints involve facial flaws, such as wrinkles, spots on the skin, excessive facial hair, shape of nose, mouth, or eyebrows, and swelling of the face.

conversion disorder—main feature is the presence of unexplained symptoms or deficits affecting voluntary motor or sensory function that suggest a neurological or other general medical condition. Psychological factors are judged to be associated with the symptom or deficit because the initiation or exacerbation of the symptom or deficit is preceded by conflicts or other stressors. The symptoms or deficit is not intentionally produced or feigned (e.g., as in malingering). The symptom or deficit causes clinically significant distress or impairment in social, occupational, or other areas of functioning or warrants medical evaluation. The symptom or deficit cannot, after appropriate investigation, be fully explained by a general medical condition, or by the direct effects of a substance, or as a culturally sanctioned behavior or experience.

hypochondriasis—preoccupation with the fear of having, or the idea that one has, a serious disease based on the person's misinterpretation of one or more bodily signs or symptoms.

This fear may be related to such bodily functions as heartbeat, sweating, peristalsis, or minor coughs. Social and work functioning may be impaired because the person is preoccupied with the disease. The preoccupation with these fears persists despite appropriate medical evaluation and reassurance.

somatization disorder—essential features of this disorder are recurrent and multiple somatic complaints, of several years' duration, for which medical attention has been sought, but that apparently are not due to any physical disorder. This disorder begins before the age of 30, extends over a period of years, and is characterized by a combination of pain, gastrointestinal, sexual, and pseudoneurological symptoms. Anxiety and depressed moods are frequent. Antisocial behavior and occupational, interpersonal, and marital difficulties are common.

pain disorder—characterized by pain in one or more anatomical sites that is the predominant focus of the clinical presentation, and that is of sufficient severity to warrant clinical attention. Psychological factors are judged to have an important role in the onset, severity, exacerbation, or maintenance of the pain. The pain causes clinically significant distress or impairment in social, occupational, or other important areas of functioning. The symptom or deficit is not intentionally produced or feigned. Pain disorder is not diagnosed if the pain is better accounted for by a mood, anxiety, or psychotic disorder, or if the pain presentation meets the criteria for dyspareunia. (12)

SYMPTOMATIC TERMS

aggression—forceful, self-assertive, attacking action, that is verbal, physical, or symbolic. (20)

agitation—chronic restlessness; important psychomotor reaction of emotional stress. (20)

ambivalence—opposing drives or emotions; for example, love and hatred for the same person. (23)

blocking—sudden interruption in the stream of thought. (23)

body image—conscious and unconscious picture a person has of his or her own body at any moment. The conscious and unconscious images may differ from each other.

catalepsy—diminished responsiveness usually characterized by trancelike states; an immobile position that is constantly maintained. (21)

catharsis—wholesome emotional release by talking about problems or repressed feelings.

confabulation—fabrication of stories in response to questions about situations or events that are not recalled.

defense mechanisms—refers to automatic intrapsychic processes that protects the individual against anxiety from awareness of internal or external stressors or danger. (21) Some examples of defense mechanisms are:

> *denial*—reality factors denied in an effort to resolve emotional conflict.
>
> *displacement*—tension-reducing mechanism in which an emotional response is transferred from its real source to a more acceptable substitute.
>
> *dissociation*—group of ideas, memories, and feelings that have escaped from normal consciousness and the control of the person.
>
> *identification*—unconscious imitation of another.
>
> *projection*—mental mechanism by which unacceptable desires are disowned and attributed to another.
>
> *regression*—anxiety-evading mechanism; readoption of immature patterns of thought, behavior, and emotional responses.
>
> *repression*—common mechanism that excludes unacceptable desires, impulses, and thoughts from conscious awareness.
>
> *sublimation*—channeling of undesirable impulses and drives away from their primitive objectives into activities of a higher order. This defense mechanism is nonpathogenic.

delirium—syndrome characterized by clouding of consciousness, incoherence of ideas, mental confusion, bewilderment, hallucinations, and illusions, over a short period of time. (3, 16, 20, 21, 24)

delirium tremens—occurs only in persons who are addicted to alcohol. Onset begins 24 to 48 hours after withdrawal from alcohol. Delusions, hallucinations, and agitated behavior usually occur. Autonomic hyperactivity such as tachycardia, sweating, and elevated blood pressure is present. If untreated, delirium tremens can be fatal. (20, 25)

delusions—false beliefs resulting from unconscious needs; maintained irrespective of contrary evidence.

> *delusions of grandeur*—exaggerated ideas about position and importance.
> *delusions of persecution*—false ideas that one is the target of persecution.
> *delusions of reference*—false belief that the behavior of others refers to oneself; that events, objects, or other persons in one's immediate environment have a particular and unusual significance, usually of a negative nature; derived from idea of reference, in which one falsely feels that one is being talked about by others. (21)

dementia—characterized by multiple cognitive deficits that include impairment in memory. Some types include dementia of the Alzheimer's type, vascular dementia; dementia due to drug abuse, a medication, or toxin exposure; and dementia due to Parkinson's disease. (3, 15, 16, 24)

empathy—objective insight into the feelings of another person, in contrast to sympathy, which is subjective and emotional.

hallucinations—false sensory perceptions without actual external stimulation. (20)

illusions—falsely interpreted sensory perceptions.

incoherence in speech—illogic flow of ideas that is difficult to comprehend by the listener.

libido—psychoanalytic term denoting the psychic drive that energizes living. Diminished libido refers to decreased sexual interest, drive, and performance. Increased libido is often associated with manic states. (21)

phobia—any morbid fear. (20)

sensory deprivation—experience of being cut off from usual external stimuli and the opportunity for perception. May occur in various ways, such as through loss of hearing or eyesight, by solitary confinement, by traveling in space. May lead to disorganized thinking, depression, panic, delusions, and hallucinations.

sleep apnea—sleep disruption or cessation of air flow at the nose or the mouth. The apneic period lasts approximately 10 seconds or more. Sleep apnea is considered pathological if the person has at least 5 apneic episodes an hour or 30 apneic episodes during the night. (20, 26)

somnambulism—sleepwalking, writing, or performing other acts automatically in a somnolent (sleepy) state without remembering the fact on awakening. (23)

SPECIAL PROCEDURES

TERMS RELATED TO PSYCHOMETRIC TESTS

intelligence tests—devices set up to determine a person's native intellectual ability including the level of functioning in various areas. The following tests have been widely accepted:

> *Stanford-Binet*—shows range of mental ability by age. It is assumed that mental growth stops at age 15.
> *Wechsler Adult Intelligence Scale*—verbal and performance test designed to measure the intellectual capacity of adults at different age levels.
> *Wechsler Intelligence Scale for Children*—test devised primarily to classify children according to their intellectual abilities. (20)

projective tests—methods employed to uncover a subject's unconscious attitudes, needs, and relationships to others. When taking a test, the subject projects the pattern of his or her own psychologic life and thus reveals the underlying dynamics of personality structure. Of value are the following:

Minnesota Multiphasic Personality Inventory—affords insight into various phases of the patient's personality.

Rorschach Personality Test—attempts to detect conscious or unconscious personality traits and conflicts through eliciting the person's associations to a set of ink blots.

Thematic Apperception Test—uses 20 pictures to stimulate projective expression of personality traits. (20)

TERMS RELATED TO PSYCHOPHARMACOLOGY

antianxiety agents—drugs that exhibit a central calming effect. They are used in the treatment of mild to moderate anxiety. (20)

antidepressants—psychic energizers that relieve despondency, tension, fatigue, and mental depression. (20)

antipsychotic agents—drugs used in treating psychoses and controlling excitation of the central nervous system. (20, 22)

ataractics—tranquilizing agents widely used in psychiatric disorders such as agitation, aggressive outbursts, psychomotor overactivity, and similar symptoms. They are the same as antianxiety agents.

drug toxicity—toxic effects of medication caused by incorrect dosage and related to age, impaired metabolism, faulty absorption or detoxification, renal dysfunction, and subsequent retention and cumulative effects of the drug. (22, 33)

hallucinogens—chemical agents producing hallucinations, disturbed thought processes, and depersonalization in normal persons. (20)

overdose—may result from overtreatment with medication by physician or intentional overuse of medicine by a suicidal patient or persons suffering with psychiatric or chemical dependency problems. (33)

pharmacokinetics—discipline dealing with the action of drugs on the body, including their absorption, distribution, metabolism, elimination, and pharmacologic response. (28)

pharmacology—discipline that studies the action of drugs on the body. (33)

psychedelics—drugs that apparently expand consciousness and enlarge vision. (20)

psychopharmacology—science dealing with drugs that affect the emotions. (28)

psychotogens—drugs producing psychotic behavior.

therapeutic drug monitoring (TDM)—measurement of serum drug levels to (1) ascertain if the drug regimen achieves the therapeutic serum concentrations with a narrow therapeutic ratio, for example, in administration of lithium and digoxin; (2) observe high-risk patients for drug interactions, e.g., with tricyclic antidepressants, lithium, and digoxin; (3) ascertain impaired renal clearance; e.g., with theophylline and digoxin; and (4) note potential toxic reactions; e.g., with theophylline and lithium. TDM is an important and essential tool for both the psychiatrist and the patient. It allows them to assess the target symptom over the course of the drug administration to determine whether the drug has been effective, as well as evaluating the drug's interaction with other drugs that the patient may be taking, and also noting type and severity of any adverse or toxic effects that may surface. (28, 83)

ELECTROCONVULSIVE THERAPY

electroconvulsive therapy (ECT)—electric current used to cause unconsciousness and/or initiate convulsions. ECT serves as a safe and effective treatment of persons with major depressive disorder, manic episodes and other serious mental disorders. The major alternatives to ECT are usually pharmacotherapy and psychotherapy. Electroconvulsive therapy is also referred to as electroshock therapy (EST). (28)

TERMS RELATED TO PSYCHOTHERAPY

psychotherapy—treatment of emotional and personality problems by psychologic means. (20, 27) The following terms refer to psychotherapeutic techniques:

abreaction—expressive form of psychotherapy that encourages a reliving of repressed emotional stress situations in a therapeutic setting. It releases painful emotions and increases insight.

activity therapy—program of activities prescribed for patients on the basis of psychologic understanding of their specific needs. Types of activity therapy include bibliotherapy, educational therapy, music therapy, occupational therapy, and recreational therapy.

behavior therapy—a therapeutic approach that attempts to bring about direct change by helping the person to unlearn maladaptive and destructive behavior and to enhance abilities for socially acceptable and productive behavior.

biofeedback—providing information to the subject based on the person's physiologic processes, such as brain-wave activity or blood pressure, often as an essential element of visceral learning.

cognitive therapy—treatment techniques are directed at correcting the cognitive distortions and specific, habitual errors in thinking (cognition). This therapy can assist the client to identify, to see the reality of, and to correct distortions and the dysfunctional conceptions underlying the cognitive distortions or habitual errors in thinking.

group psychotherapy—method of psychotherapy applied to a group. Group leaders help patients to understand the causes and gain insight into their emotional difficulties and conflicts, and translate their defensive reactions into acceptable behavior.

hypnosis—state of semiconscious suggestibility in which a person is able to respond to appropriate suggestions by experiencing alterations of perception, memory, or mood. Persons under hypnosis are in a trance state that may be heavy, light, or medium. Posthypnotic suggestion is important for successful completion of therapy.

milieu therapy—use of a modified and controlled environment in the treatment of mental disease.

play therapy—psychotherapeutic approach to children who tend to reveal their hidden resentments, feelings, and frustrations in play. An analytic therapist uses the interpretations of play as a guide to treatment.

psychoanalysis—type of insight therapy developed by Sigmund Freud. Psychoanalytic treatment seeks to influence behavior by bringing into awareness unconscious emotional conflicts in an effort to overcome them.

psychodrama—method of group therapy in which personality makeup, interpersonal relationships, conflicts, and emotional problems are explored by means of dramatic role playing.

supportive psychotherapy—therapeutic efforts directed toward a strengthening of the patient's ego to reduce anxiety. This particular technique can create a therapeutic relationship as a temporary bridge for the deficient patient. However, the real underlying problem may remain unsolved, and if this situation does occur, then these problems may become acute again at a crucial moment.

transference—patient's unconscious reaction to a psychiatrist that is a repetition of an early childhood relationship to a parent, sibling, or significant other. The psychiatrist uses the transfer situation to gain insight into the patient's disturbing emotional conflicts and to plan the psychotherapy accordingly.

ABBREVIATIONS

GENERAL

DT—delirium tremens
ECT—electroconvulsive therapy
EST—electric shock therapy
IQ —intelligence quotient

TESTS

CAT—Child Apperception Test
ITPA—Illinois Test of Psycholinguistic Ability
MMPI—Minnesota Multiphasic Personality Inventory
TAT—Thematic Apperception Test
WAIS—Wechsler Adult Intelligence Scale
WISC—Wechsler Intelligence Scale for Children
WPPSI—Wechsler Preschool and Primary Scale of Intelligence

ORGANIZATIONS

AA—Alcoholics Anonymous
AAMR—American Association on Mental Retardation
APA—American Psychiatric Association
MHA—Mental Health Association
NAMH—National Association of Mental Health
NARC—National Association for Retarded Children
NIMH—National Institute of Mental Health

ORAL READING PRACTICE

COCAINE-RELATED DISORDERS

Cocaine is an alkaloid that is derived from the shrub *Erythroxylon coca,* which is indigenous to South America. Cocaine is consumed in several different preparations, for example, **coca leaves, coca paste, cocaine hydrochloride,** and **cocaine alkaloid.** The cocaine available on the street differs greatly in potency due to varying levels of purity and speed of onset.

The most common method of using cocaine is by inhaling the finely chopped **cocaine hydrochloride powder** into the nose, a practice referred to as **snorting** or **tooting,** or it may be dissolved in water and injected intravenously. When mixed with **heroin,** it yields a drug combination known as a **"speedball."**

A commonly used form of cocaine in the United States is **"crack,"** a **cocaine alkaloid** that is extracted from its powdered hydrochloride salt by mixing it with sodium bicarbonate and allowing it to dry into small amounts called **"rocks."** Crack differs from other forms of cocaine because it is easily vaporized and inhaled, and its effect has a rapid onset. Before the advent of crack, cocaine was separated from its hydrochloride base by heating it with **ether, ammonia,** or some other volatile solvent. The resulting **"free base"** cocaine was then smoked. This was risky because the solvents could ignite and harm the person using it.

The misconception that cocaine is nonaddictive has resulted in its rapid proliferation. The intensity and frequency of cocaine administration is less in **cocaine abuse** as compared with **cocaine dependence.** When problems associated with use are accompanied by evidence of tolerance, withdrawal, or compulsive behavior related to obtaining and administering cocaine, a diagnosis of cocaine dependence rather than cocaine abuse should be considered.

The inability of a person to abstain from frequent compulsive use of cocaine may result in psychological dependence on the drug. **Psychological dependence,** or habituation, is manifested by an irresistible craving, compelling the person to use the drug as an escape from unpleasant situations and as a psychological crutch. Cocaine has extremely potent euphoric effects and persons exposed to it can develop **cocaine dependence** after using the drug for short periods of time. Because of its short life, there is a need for frequent cocaine dosing to maintain a **"high."** Regardless of the route of administration, tolerance occurs with repeated use.

Cocaine intoxication is the presence of clinically significant maladaptive behavioral or psychological changes that develop during, or shortly after, the use of cocaine. **Cocaine intoxication** often begins with a **"high" feeling** and includes one or more of the following: **euphoria** with enhanced vigor, **gregariousness, hyperactivity, restlessness, interpersonal sensitivity, talkativeness, anxiety, tension,** or **anger, stereotyped behaviors, impaired judgment,** or **impaired social** or **occupational functioning.**

Numerous studies have demonstrated an association between **cerebrovascular disease** and the use of cocaine. The most common cerebrovascular complication of the use of crack is **cerebral infarction.** Other cerebrovascular complications of crack include left **ataxic hemiparesis, headache, lethargy,** left or right **sensorimotor deficit, global aphasia,** and **dysarthria. Cerebral blood flow disorders** and **perfusion** in cocaine-dependent persons have been detected with **single photon emission computed tomography (SPECT) studies.**

Cocaine is the **substance of abuse** that is most commonly associated with **seizures.** The risk of a person having a cocaine-induced seizure appears highest in persons who have a history of **epilepsy,** who use high doses of cocaine, and who use crack. Cardiac rate and blood pressure increase in a dose-related manner. An increase in body temperature may occur following cocaine use, and large doses may induce **lethal pyrexia** or **hypertension. Cardiomyopathies** can develop with long-term use of cocaine. The most common cardiac effects of cocaine-induced abnormalities are **myocardial infarction** and the **arrhythmias.**

Women who abuse cocaine have reported **major derangements in menstrual cycle function** including **galactorrhea, amenorrhea,** and **infertility.** Cocaine abuse also may adversely affect **pregnancy. Neonates** who have become drug addicted in the womb because of a cocaine-using mother begin life physiologically damaged. These newborns have an increased risk of **congenital malformations** and **perinatal cardiovascular** and **cerebrovascular disease.** Findings observed in this class of infants include an increased rate of **seizures** after birth; the jitters, rapid **mood swings,** and heightened sensitivity to stimuli; increased prevalence of **fetal distress;** pronounced small head size compared with normal infants, suggesting **retardation in brain growth** with a high probability of **brain deficits** in the future; and a higher risk of **sudden infant death syndrome** or **crib death.**

Acute cocaine withdrawal symptoms ("a crash") are often seen after periods of repetitive high-dose use of cocaine. **Depressive symptoms with suicidal ideation or behavior** are usually the most serious problems that can occur during **"crashing."** Discontinuation of cocaine use (withdrawal) also may result in symptoms of **guilt, insomnia,** and **anorexia, psychomotor retardation,** or **agitation.** These symptoms cause significant impairment in social and occupational functioning. **Tricyclic antidepressants** such as **desipramine** may be of assistance in the long-term treatment of **cocaine dependency.** Individual and group psychotherapy and family and peer-group support programs are helpful in achieving long-range abstinence from drug use.

Cocaine use and its related disorders affect all racial, socioeconomic, age, and gender groups in the United States.

Cocaine-related disorders are commonly found in persons between ages 18 and 30 years; however, all age levels—neonates, teens, and even older adults—can be affected.

Cocaine-related disorders are almost equally distributed between males and females. (4, 12, 13, 19, 20, 25, 31, 32, 33)

REVIEW GUIDE

Instructions: Define the following abbreviations and terms.

Examples: CAT—Child Apperception test
phren- (G)—mind, diaphragm

AA	NAMH
AAMR	NARC
APA	NIMH
cata- (G)	psycho- (G)
DT	schizo- (G)
dynamo- (G)	soma (G)
ECT	TAT
EST	thymo- (G)
ITPA	WISC
MHA	WPPSI

Instructions: Define the following terms.

Example: psychiatry—the medical science that deals with the origin, diagnosis, prevention, and treatment of mental and emotional disorders.

alcohol withdrawal	dissociative identity disorder
anorexia nervosa	hallucinogens
antidepressants	hypnosis
catalepsy	mood disorders
cocaine intoxication	panic disorder
confabulation	psychotherapy
defense mechanisms	psychotogens
delusions	schizoid personality disorder
depersonalization disorder	

4

Neurologic Disorders and Anesthesia-Related Terms

NERVES

ORIGIN OF TERMS

axon (G)—axis
gangli-, ganglio- (G)—knot, ganglion
neur-, neuro- (G)—nerve(s)
nucleus (pl. *nuclei*) (L)—little kernel
plexus (L)—braid, network
radicle (L)—root, small branches
synapse (G)—clasp, connection

PHONETIC PRONUNCIATION OF SELECTED TERMS

ganglioneuroma	GANG-gle-owe-new-RO′mah
neurectomy	new-RECK′toe-me
neurilemoma	NEW-rye-lee-MO′mah
polyneuropathy	POL-e-new-ROP′ah-the
sciatic neuritis	sigh-AT′ick new-RYE′tis
sympathectomy	SIM-pah-THECK′toe-me
tic douloureux	tick doe-lou-RUE′
trigeminal neuralgia	tri-GEM′i-nal new-RAL′gee-ah
vagotomy	vay-GOT′owe-me

ANATOMIC TERMS (96, 101) (SEE FIGS. 4.1 AND 4.2.)

nerve—collection of many nerve fibers, bound together by connective tissue sheaths.
　　cranial nerves—12 pairs of nerves made up of either motor or sensory fibers or both.
　　spinal nerves—31 pairs of mixed nerves.
nerve cell, neuron—basic component of nerve tissue consisting of a cell body or neuron body and one or more processes. There are two types of processes: dendrites and axons.
　　structure of neurons:
　　　　• *axon, axone*—slender process of a neuron body arising from specialized protoplasm known as an axon hillock. It contains many neurofibrils but no Nissl bodies. The single axon carries the impulse outward from the cell body and transmits it to the

Figure 4.1   (*a*) Motor and (*b*) sensory neurons.

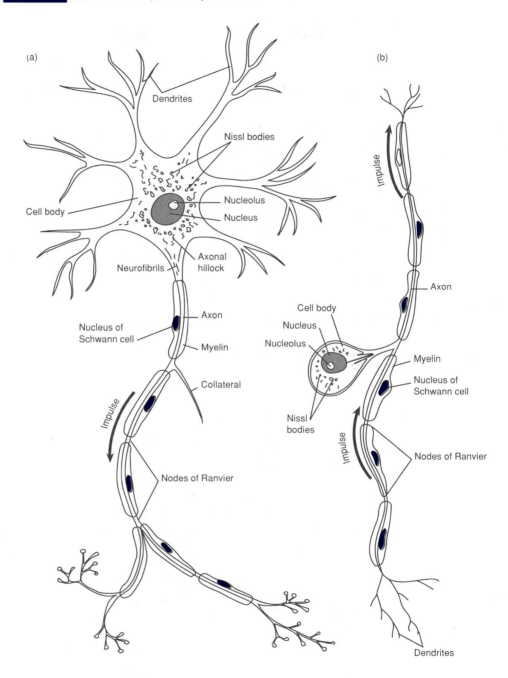

Figure 4.2 (a) Each spinal nerve has a posterior and an anterior branch. (b) The thoracic and lumbar spinal nerves also have a visceral branch.

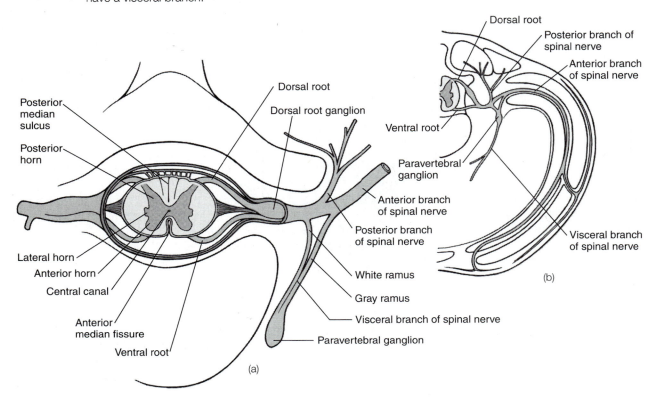

next cell. The axon and its sheath constitute a nerve fiber. The axon sheath is composed of myelin, and it is formed by glial cells, which wrap around the axon.

- *cell body*—neuron body composed of a nucleus embedded in cytoplasm, which contains neurofibrils, Nissl bodies, mitochondria, and various other organelles usually found in cells. The cell body maintains the nutrition of the whole neuron.
- *dendrite, dendron*—a protoplasmic extension from the cell body forming an irregular knobby process that is short and highly branched and that serves as the receptor surface of the neuron. These branches, combined with the membrane of the cell body, provide the main receptive surfaces of the neuron to which processes from other neurons communicate.
- *effector*—organ of response that reacts to the impulse, for example, a muscle or a gland.
- *ganglion* (pl. *ganglia*)—a collection of neural cell bodies lying outside the central nervous system.
- *myelin sheath*—protective covering of axons, composed of lipids and protein and interrupted by constrictions, called the nodes of Ranvier.
- *neurilemma, neurolemma, sheath of Schwann*—a thin, cellular membrane covering the axis cylinder of a nonmedullated (nonmyelinated) nerve fiber or enclosing the myelin sheath of a medullated (myelinated) nerve fiber of peripheral nerves. The neurilemma sheath is formed by a flattened neurilemma sheath cell with an oval nucleus and reticular cytoplasm.

- *neurofibrils*—delicate threads found in the cell bodies and processes of neurons.
- *Nissl bodies*—RNA (ribonucleic acid) granules present in the cell bodies of neurons.
- *receptor*—end organ that responds to various stimuli (pain, touch, and others) and converts them into nervous impulses.

classification of neurons according to function:

- *afferent neurons*—conduct impulses from receptor to central nervous system.
- *association, intercalated,* or *internuncial neurons*—located within the central nervous system; these transmit impulses between neurons.
- *efferent neurons*—conduct impulses away from the central nervous system to the effector organ.

nerve fiber—the axon with its sheaths.

plexus (pl. plexuses) of spinal nerves—a network of nerve fibers. For example:

brachial plexus—an intermingling of the fifth to the eighth cervical nerves and the first thoracic nerve, which supply the upper limb.

sacral plexus—an intermingling of the fourth and fifth lumbar and first four sacral nerves, which help to supply the lower limb.

roots of spinal nerves—attach the nerves to the spinal cord.

ventral (anterior) root—composed of efferent fibers, with no small ganglion.

dorsal (posterior) root—composed of afferent fibers, with a small ganglion.

synapse—the point of contact between the axon of one neuron and a dendrite or cell body of another neuron.

DIAGNOSTIC TERMS

Bell's palsy—functional disorder of the seventh cranial nerve may result in a unilateral paralysis of facial muscles and distortion of taste perception. Etiology is unknown. The onset of Bell's palsy is abrupt with maximal weakness being attained usually within 48 hours. Pain behind the ear may precede the paralysis for a day or two. Taste sensation may be lost unilaterally and the person may have an exceptionally acute sense of hearing but the hearing threshold is unusually low. (9, 37, 39)

causalgia—post-traumatic paroxysms of unbearable peripheral nerve pain of a burning quality, aggravated by heat, slight friction, anxiety, and emotion. It appears to be stimulated by efferent sympathetic nerve impulses. (16, 36)

Guillain-Barré syndrome, acute idiopathic polyneuropathy—widespread disorder of the peripheral motor nerves, characterized by progressive flaccid paralysis of an ascending type associated with sensory disturbances. When the chest muscles and diaphragm become affected, respiratory difficulties arise. Cranial nerve involvement, particularly that of the facial nerve, may develop in the course of the disease, or it may be the initial pathology followed by motor impairment of a descending type.

Plasmapheresis is the removal of plasma from withdrawn blood with retransfusion of the formed elements into the donor; most often, either fresh frozen plasma or albumin is used to replace the withdrawn plasma. Plasmapheresis has been shown to be an effective treatment in adults. Recently, results of a study indicated that plasmapheresis diminishes morbidity in child-hood Guillain-Barré syndrome by shortening the interval until recovery of independent ambulation is achieved. (9, 12, 36, 96)

herniated nucleus pulposus, herniated intervertebral disk—tear in posterior joint capsule and bulging of portions of intervertebral disk, resulting in nerve root irritation and compression followed by sciatic pain and paresthesia and occasionally by paresis or paralysis. (92, 99, 103)

neurilemmoma, neurilemoma (also neurolemoma, neurolemmoma)—often, growth occurs as a benign, encapsulated, solitary tumor, produced by the proliferation of Schwann cells. It may originate from a sympathetic, peripheral, or cranial nerve. (12)

neuroma—a tumor of tissue found in the nervous system. Neuroma is an obsolete term and a more specific designation is preferable. For example:

 acoustic neuroma, acoustic schwannoma—type of Schwann cell tumors of the vestibular portion of the eighth nerve originate in the internal auditory canal. Acoustic neuromas represent 2% of intracranial tumors and are the most common tumor of the cerebellopontine angle.

 ganglioneuroma—benign tumor consisting of nerve fibers and mature ganglion cells.

 pseudoneuroma—false neuroma. (17, 44, 46)

polyneuritis, polyneuropathy—widespread neural lesions caused by nutritional deficiencies, especially of vitamin B complex. The chief symptoms are pain and paresthesia. (12, 38)

radiculitis—any involvement of the spinal nerve roots due to infection, toxins, trauma, protrusion of intervertebral disk, or degenerative diseases. (38, 74)

sciatic neuritis, sciatica—a very painful involvement of the sciatic nerve. (9, 52)

OPERATIVE TERMS (SEE TABLE 4.1.)

ganglionectomy—excision of ganglion. (46)

neurectomy—excision of a nerve or lesion of a nerve. (22, 46)

neuroanastomosis—surgical communication between nerve fibers.

neuroplasty—plastic repair of a nerve. (16)

neurorrhaphy—suture of an injured nerve.

neurotomy—transection of a nerve.

procedures for trigeminal neuralgia relief: (99)

 avulsion of trigeminal nerve—surgical transection or division of the trigeminal nerve branches, for example, the infraorbital nerve.

 percutaneous trigeminal/gasserian rhizolysis—insertion of a needle through the cheek into the third division of the trigeminal nerve at the foramen ovale followed by advancement of the needle into the gasserian ganglion and the sensory root. The neural destruction is produced by injecting a neurolytic agent such as glycerol or by using a radiofrequency current to create a thermal lesion or by inflating a small balloon to compress the neural tissue.

 posterior trigeminal rhizotomy—partial division of the main sensory root of the trigeminal nerve adjacent to the pons.

 trigeminal microvascular decompression—using a microscope and a microsurgical technique, the area is exposed through a lateral posterior fossa approach, and following separating the vessels from the nerve, a material such as a synthetic sponge is inserted to maintain the separation and relieve the pain in tic douloureux.

 trigeminal nerve injection—one of the peripheral branches of the trigeminal nerve is injected with a neurolytic agent such as alcohol. This approach provides pain relief at the expense of sensation. If a peripheral branch is injected, numbness of the face in its distribution will result, but with time both sensation and pain return.

sympathectomy—excision of part of a sympathetic nerve. (36, 49)

 thoracic ganglionectomy—for causalgia or Raynaud's disease affecting the upper extremities.

 lumbar ganglionectomy—for causalgia, Raynaud's disease, and thromboangiitis obliterans affecting the lower extremities.

vagotomy—transection of a vagus nerve.

TABLE **4.1**	Some Conditions Amenable to Neurosurgery		
Anatomic Site	*Diagnosis*	*Type of Surgery*	*Operative Procedures*
Brain: Carotid arteries	Cerebrovascular insufficiency due to atherosclerotic plaque at bifurcation of common carotid artery	Carotid endarterectomy of extracranial lesion	Incision to expose plaque Peeling out lesion Arterectomy closed by suturing Dacron patch into it to widen artery
Brain: Internal carotid arteries Middle cerebral artery	Massive thrombotic occlusion of internal carotid artery with embolization of middle cerebral artery, causing cerebral ischemia	Microsurgical anastomosis of temporal artery to middle cerebral artery	Craniectomy or osteoplastic flap Use of operative microscope Creation of surgical union of temporal artery and patent segment of middle cerebral artery to support circulation
Brain: Subarachnoid space	Subarachnoid hemorrhage from ruptured aneurysm of internal carotid artery	Ligation of carotid artery Intracranial clipping or ligation of aneurysm	Tying carotid artery in neck Applying clip or ligature to aneurysmal sac
Brain: Subdural space	Subdural hematoma of the brain	Drainage of subdural space Craniotomy and excision of hematoma	Evacuation of clot through trephine opening in skull Surgical opening of skull and removal of subdural hematoma
Brain: Dura mater	Craniocerebral injury; open, depressed fracture with dural laceration	Decompression, suture of dura mater	Elevation of depressed fracture and repair of dural laceration
Brain: Meninges	Meningioma, benign	Craniotomy with excision of meningioma	Open skull, osteoplastic flap, remove tumor
Brain: Glial tissue	Primary malignant glioma	Craniotomy with resection of tumor	Open skull, osteoplastic flap, remove tumor
Brain: Choroid plexus Ventricles	Obstructive, noncommunicating hydrocephalus	Ventriculocisternostomy Torkildsen's operation	Shunting cerebrospinal fluid from third ventricle to cisterna magna by means of plastic catheter
	Nonobstructive, communicating hydrocephalus	Ventriculocaval shunt Insertion of Holter or Pudenz value	Shunting cerebrospinal fluid from lateral ventricle to superior vena cava via jugular vein by insertion of one-way valve
Brain: Trigeminal nerve	Trigeminal neuralgia (tic douloureux)	Retrogasserian neurotomy	Transection of sensory root of trigeminal nerve

TABLE 4.1	(continued)		
Anatomic Site	*Diagnosis*	*Type of Surgery*	*Operative Procedures*
Spinal cord: Ganglia	Intractable pain in extremity due to causalgia, Raynaud's disease, or Buerger's disease	Sympathectomy	Removal of sympathetic chain and ganglia
Spinal cord: Subarachnoid space	Intractable pain in malignant disease	Alcohol injection as nerve block	Injection of alcohol into subarachnoid space

SYMPTOMATIC TERMS

aural vertigo—episodic attacks of severe dizziness caused by lesion of the inner ear (labyrinthine lesion) or the vestibular portion of the eighth nerve. (29)

benign paroxysmal positional vertigo (BPPV)—occurs on lying down as well as sitting up. Also, there may be dizziness on turning the head from side to side or on flexing and extending the neck. Nystagmus for a brief period is associated with the dizziness. Fatigue also may be present. BPPV originates from the posterior semicircular canal of the inner ear on the side from which the symptoms may be provoked. Although this condition appears to occur after trauma, its cause is unknown. It usually resolves spontaneously, after a period of weeks or months. (29, 96)

labyrinthine vertigo, Ménière's syndrome—episodic sudden attacks of severe dizziness, accompanied by tinnitus and sensorineural hearing loss. Dizziness may last for a few minutes or several hours, but usually continuous vertigo that lasts for days is not due to Ménière's syndrome. Episodes are usually accompanied by nausea, vomiting, and profuse perspiration; however, mild attacks may cause nausea without vomiting. Nystagmus is present during the attack and may even persist for several days after the attack subsides. The hearing loss fluctuates, but if the condition remains untreated, the hearing loss slowly progresses to severe cochlear damage and total deafness. The cause of Ménière's syndrome is unknown. (96)

paroxysmal pain—sudden, recurrent, or periodic attack of pain, as in tic douloureux. (96)

tactile stimulation—evoking a response by touch. (38, 65)

trigeminal neuralgia, trifacial neuralgia, tic douloureux—paroxysms of lancinating pain of one or more areas innervated by the fifth cranial nerve. (9, 96)

trigger area—point from which the pain starts, as in trigeminal neuralgia. (65, 96)

BRAIN AND SPINAL CORD

ORIGIN OF TERMS

cerebro- (G)—brain
chordo- (G)—cord, string
cingulum (L)—girdle
encephalo- (G)—brain
gyrus (L)—convolution
hemi- (G)—one-half
lamina (L)—thin plate
medulla (L)—marrow
meninges (L)—membrane
meningo- (G)—membrane

myel-, myelo- (G)—marrow
neur-, neuro- (G)—nerve
-oma (G)—tumor
paresis (G)—relaxation
plexus (L)—braid, network
pons (L)—bridge
spina (L)—spine, thornlike projection or process
thalmo- (G)—chamber
ventricle (L)—small cavity

PHONETIC PRONUNCIATION OF SELECTED TERMS

anencephalus	AN-en-SEF'a-lus
carotid artery ligation	ka-ROT'id AR'ter-e lie-GAY'shun
cerebral ischemia	SER'e-bral is-KEY'me-ah
cerebrospinal rhinorrhea	SER-e-bro-SPY'nal RYE-no-RE'ah
Dawson's encephalitis	Daw-SONS en-SEF-a-LIE'tis
epilepsy	EP'i-LEP-see
glioblastoma	GLI-o-blast-TOE'mah
intracranial aneurysm	in-trah-KRA'nee-al AN'you-rizm
meningitis	MEN-in-JI'tis
myelitis	mile-LIE'tis

ANATOMIC TERMS (34, 96, 101) (SEE FIGS. 4.3 AND 4.4.)

brain, encephalon—major part of central nervous system. It is divided into the forebrain or prosencephalon, midbrain or mesencephalon, and hindbrain or rhombencephalon and comprises the following structural and functional components:

> *cerebellum*—second largest part of the brain, which serves as a reflex center for the coordination of muscular movements. It is divided into two hemispheres and a median portion, the vermis.
>
> *cerebrum*—largest part of the brain, which is divided into two hemispheres by a deep groove, the longitudinal fissure.
>
> *cerebral cortex*—surface of the cerebrum, composed of gray matter and arranged in folds known as convolutions or gyri.
>
> *cerebral localization*—definite regions of the cerebral cortex performing special functions:
> - motor areas influence voluntary muscular activity.
> - sensory areas are where sensations reach the conscious level.
>
> *corpus callosum*—bridgelike structure of white fibers that joins the two hemispheres.

brain stem—upward continuation of cervical cord that consists of numerous bundles of nerve fibers and nuclei. Its structural components include:

> *diencephalon, interbrain*—small but important part of the forebrain (prosencephalon) that bounds the third ventricle and connects the mesencephalon to the cerebral hemispheres. Each lateral half is divided by the hypothalamic sulcus into a dorsal part, comprising the epithalamus, dorsal thalamus, and metathalamus and a ventral part, comprising the ventral thalamus (subthalamus) and hypothalamus.
> - *epithalamus*—area including several nuclei and the pineal body or epiphysis.
> - *hypothalamus*—small mass below the thalamus containing nuclei and fibers; ventral part of the diencephalon that forms the floor and part of the lateral wall of the third ventricle. The hypothalamus is interconnected by nerve fibers to the cerebral cortex, thalamus, and other parts of the brain stem so that it can receive impulses from them and send impulses to them. The hypothalamus plays a major role in maintaining hemostasis by regulating a variety of visceral activities and by serving as a link between the nervous and endocrine systems.
> - *metathalamus*—part of the diencephalon inferior to the caudal end of the dorsal thalamus; area of the lateral and medial geniculate bodies.
> - *subthalamus, thalamus ventralis*—region of the ventral part of the diencephalon, placed between the dorsal thalamus, hypothalamus, and tegmentum of the mesencephalon; a mass of nuclei and fibers important in regulating muscular activities.
> - *thalamus*—mass of nuclei situated on either side of the third ventricle that functions as a sensory relay station.

Figure 4.3   Cerebrospinal fluid is secreted by choroid plexuses in the walls of the ventricles. The fluid circulates through the ventricles and central canal, enters the subarachnoid space, and is reabsorbed into the blood of the dural sinuses through arachnoid granulations.

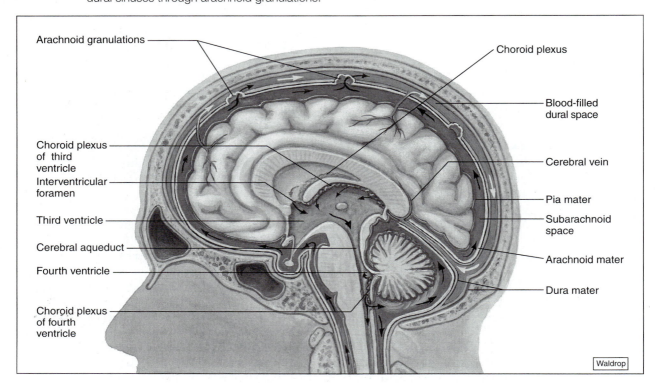

Arachnoid granulations

Choroid plexus

Blood-filled dural space

Choroid plexus of third ventricle

Interventricular foramen

Cerebral vein

Third ventricle

Pia mater

Cerebral aqueduct

Subarachnoid space

Fourth ventricle

Arachnoid mater

Choroid plexus of fourth ventricle

Dura mater

Waldrop

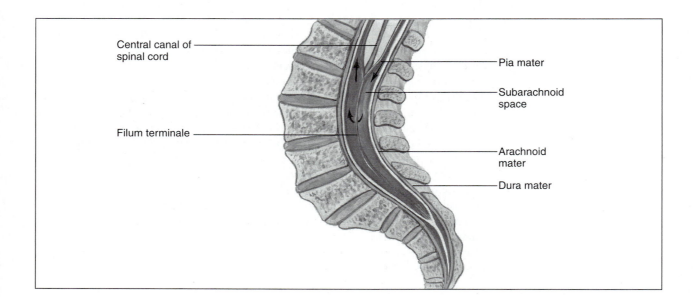

Central canal of spinal cord

Pia mater

Subarachnoid space

Filum terminale

Arachnoid mater

Dura mater

Figure 4.6 (a) Preganglionic fibers of the sympathetic division arise from thoracic and lumbar regions of the spinal cord. (b) Preganglionic fibers of the parasympathetic division arise from brain and sacral region of the spinal cord.

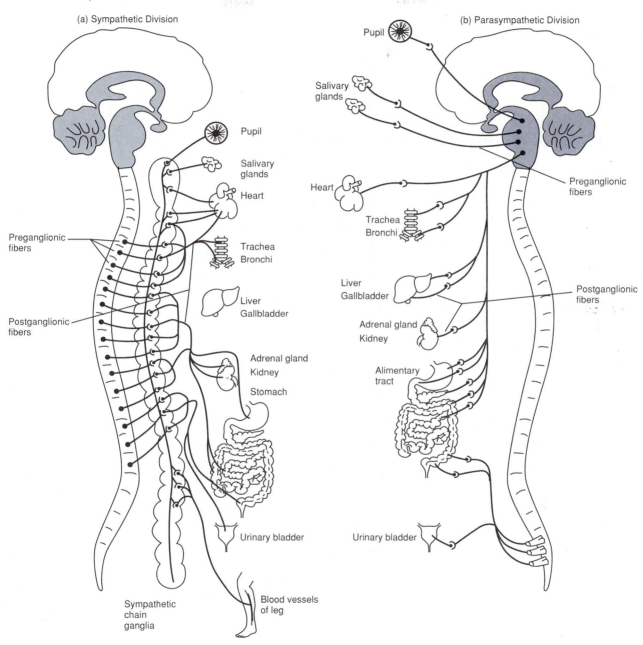

medulla oblongata, myelencephalon, marrow brain—extends from upper cervical cord to pons; contains vital centers regulating heart action, vasomotor activity, respiration, deglutition, and vomiting.

mesencephalon, midbrain—extends from pons below to forebrain above and is composed of nuclei and bundles of fibers.

pons—part of metencephalon (afterbrain) composed of bundles of fibers and nuclei that are located between the medulla and midbrain.

meninges—covering membranes of the brain and spinal cord.

dura mater—serves as outer protective coat and is composed of strong fibrous tissue.

arachnoid mater—middle layer consisting of thin meshwork. The subarachnoid space contains cerebrospinal fluid.

pia mater—fine, delicate, vascular membrane that covers the surface of the brain, spinal cord, roots of the spinal nerves, and blood vessels of the brain and cord.

nucleus (pl. nuclei)—group of nerve cells within the central nervous system.

ventricles and aqueduct:

lateral ventricles—fluid-filled spaces, one in each cerebral hemisphere.

third ventricle—fluid-filled space beneath the corpus callosum.

cerebral aqueduct—narrow canal that connects the third and fourth ventricles.

fourth ventricle—expansion of the central canal of the medulla oblongata.

The ventricles contain cerebrospinal fluid, which is formed by the capillaries of the choroid plexuses. The fluid seeps from the third ventricle into the cerebral aqueduct and fourth ventricle and from there into the central canal. It reaches the subarachnoid space through openings in the roof of the fourth ventricle and circulates around the cord and brain in this space, thus providing a water-cushion and shock absorber for the delicate nerve tissue.

spinal cord—portion of the central nervous system located in the vertebral canal and giving rise to 31 pairs of spinal nerves. The spinal cord extends from the foramen magnum to the second lumbar vertebra. Fissures and sulci extend along most of the external surface. The anterior median fissure and a posterior median sulcus and septum almost completely separate the cord into two equal halves, but these are joined by a commissural band containing a central canal.

The spinal cord is composed of white substance, which surrounds the inner gray matter of the cord. The white matter consists of myelinated fibers arranged in longitudinal bundles and grouped into three columns: anterior, lateral, and posterior funiculi. Afferent white fibers arise from the ascending nerve tracts, which carry impulses from the cord to the brain. Efferent white fibers represent descending nerve tracts, which bring messages from the brain to the cord. The gray matter is H-shaped in cross-section and consists mainly of cell bodies. The anterior horn contains motor cells from which the motor fibers of the peripheral neurons arise. Sensory relay neurons are located in the posterior horn.

The central nervous system comprises the brain and spinal cord, while nerves that connect the brain and spinal cord to other body parts form the peripheral nervous system. The peripheral nervous system can be further subdivided into the somatic system, which communicates with skin and skeletal muscles, and the autonomic system, which communicates with visceral organs. The autonomic nervous system includes two sections called the sympathetic and parasympathetic divisions. (See fig. 4.4.)

DIAGNOSTIC TERMS

Alzheimer's disease—degenerative disorder beginning in the fifth or sixth decade of life, pathologically characterized by neurofibrillar degeneration (with silver-staining plaques containing degenerating neuronal products grouped around an amyloid core being randomly pinpointed in the cortex and subcortex), cortical atrophy, and loss of nerve cells.

The disorder represents a complex picture. At least three different genetic loci that confer inherited susceptibility to this condition have been identified. The E4 allele of the Apolipo-protein E (apoE) gene is associated with Alzheimer's disease (AD in a significant proportion of cases with late onset, greater than 60 years). Mutations in the gene for β-amyloid precursor protein (BAPP) have been found in a small number of families (less than 3% of cases with disease onset before 65 years of age). A third locus (AD3) has been mapped by genetic linkage studies to chromosome 14q24.3, and may account for up to 70% of early-onset autosomal dominant AD. Early-onset AD is less common than late-onset AD; however, the AD3 locus is associated with the most aggressive form of this disorder (onset 30 to 60 years) making it likely that mutations at the AD3 locus initiates a biologically fundamental process leading to AD. AD is the most common cause of dementia. The most common signs are memory loss, language impairment, and deficits in spatial attention and visual perception. Apraxia is usually evident by the middle stages of the disease. Late in the disease course, persons may demonstrate involvement of primary motor, sensory, and visual pathways with evident weakness, spasticity, numbness, and visual field defects as well as urinary and fecal incontinence. Language impairment continues to progress from anomia to a transcortical sensory aphasia to Wernicke's aphasia and, in some individuals, to a global aphasia. Persons may develop depression, delusions, or hallucinations at any stage of the disease.

Tacrine is an acetylcholine esterase inhibitor that increases the availability of acetylcholine at the postsynaptic receptor. This drug has been approved for use by the U. S. Food and Drug Administration (FDA) for symptomatic treatment of patients with AD. At best, the drug appears to be of mild benefit and is associated with frequent elevation of liver enzymes, which requires stoppage of the medication. This medication has no effect on the course of the disease. No other medication is approved by the FDA for the treatment of AD. (19, 51, 53, 55, 59, 60, 66, 77, 82, 83, 85)

amyotrophic lateral sclerosis—degenerative disease of the lateral motor tracts of the spinal cord causing widespread muscle wasting, weakness, fasciculations, and usually a mild degree of spastic paralysis of lower extremities. (26, 56, 74)

anencephalia, anencephalus—absence of brain.

brain abscess—localized lesion of suppuration within the brain, generally secondary to ear infection, sinusitis, or other infections. (68, 76)

brain tumor, intracranial tumor—benign or malignant space-occupying brain lesion. (8, 33, 44, 98, 102)

> *congenital tumor*—slow-growing, highly invasive tumor; for example, a dermoid or teratoma.
>
> *medulloblastoma*—highly malignant cerebellar tumor that metastasizes freely to the subarachnoid space, cerebrum, and cord.
>
> *meningeal tumor*—neoplasm arising from the membranes covering the brain or cord. The meningioma may cause compression and distortion of the brain.
>
> *metastatic tumor*—most primary tumors may metastasize to the brain, especially breast and lung tumors.
>
> *pineal region tumors*—include germ cell neoplasms, tumors of the pineal body, such as pineocytoma and pineoblastoma, as well as uncommon occurrences of metastatic glial tumors and other meningeal growths.
>
> *pituitary tumor*—arises from the anterior pituitary (adenohypophysis) and may compress the normal portion of the pituitary, the hypothalamus, and optic chiasm.
>
> *primary brain tumors*—comprise a large number of intracranial tumors, especially the gliomas, which contain malignant glial cells. Some neoplasms of the glioma group are:
>
> > • *astrocytoma*—slow-growing tumor containing astrocytes that infiltrate widely into neighboring brain tissue and may undergo cystic degeneration.

- *ependymoma*—tumor that arises from the lining of the ventricular wall and is highly malignant and invasive.
- *glioblastoma multiforme*—the most malignant glioma, rapidly growing, causing edema and necrosis of brain tissue.
- *oligodendroglioma*—similar to astrocytoma in behavior, but different in histologic structure.

cerebral concussion—transient state of unconsciousness following head injury, caused by damage to the brain stem. (67, 74)

cerebral palsy—condition characterized by paralysis, incoordination, and other aberrations of motor or sensory functions caused by damage to the brain. This disorder is present from infancy or early childhood and it is due to a nonprogressive cerebral disorder. (27, 34)

cerebrovascular disease—any disorder in which one or more of the cerebral blood vessels have undergone pathologic changes.

cerebral aneurysm, intracranial aneurysm—dilatation of an artery of the brain, resulting in a thinning and weakening of the arterial wall. Rupture and hemorrhage may occur. The most common locations are the internal carotid and middle cerebral arteries. (9, 18, 36, 47, 76)

cerebral arteriovenous malformation—structural vascular defect that presents as congenital clusters of direct connections between the arterial and venous systems carrying high blood flow. The vessel walls contain elastin and smooth muscle. There is no normal capillary bed, and the malformation contains minimal intervening gliotic brain tissue. Arteriovenous malformations range in size from small simple shunts to massive hemispheric lesions, and generally are found in young patients who have recurrent subarachnoid hemorrhage and epilepsy. Cardiac failure and hydrocephalus is seen primarily in neonates and infants with malformation of the vein of Galen. (9, 36, 37, 71)

cerebral atherosclerosis—a primary degeneration of the intima by atheromatous plaques (lipid deposits) usually located in the basilar artery, in the middle and posterior cerebral arteries, and at the branching of the internal carotid arteries. The subsequent narrowing of the vessels may lead to inadequate oxygenation and nutrition of the brain by the reduced cerebral circulation. (47)

cerebral embolism—sudden occlusion of a cerebral blood vessel by a circulatory embolus composed of air bubble, blood clot, fat cells, or bacteria. (1, 47)

cerebral infarction—local necrosis of brain tissue resulting from loss of blood supply in vascular obstruction. (47)

cerebral ischemia—anemia of the brain resulting from diminished cerebral blood flow. Some important causes are circulatory obstruction of the intracranial or extracranial arteries by atheroma, thrombus, or embolus, severe hypotension, arteritis, or stenosis of an artery. Recurrent ischemic episodes are thought to signal impending stroke. (1, 13, 47) (See fig. 4.5.)

cerebral thrombosis—formation of a thrombus within an intracranial artery, leading to its occlusion and subsequent necrosis of the area supplied by the thrombosed vessel. (1, 47)

cerebrovascular accident, stroke—neurologic disorder caused by pathologic changes in the extracranial or intracranial blood vessels, primarily by atherosclerosis, thrombosis, embolic episodes, hemorrhage, or arterial hypertension. Cerebral infarction or necrosis of brain tissue may occur in the affected lesion. The completed stroke, usually recognized by a rather sudden loss of consciousness and other marked neurologic insult, is preceded by:

- *transient ischemic attacks (TIA)*—symptoms of minor brain damage evidenced by numbness, unilateral weakness, visual deficits, motor disability, and similar symptoms. They last from minutes to hours. A complete return to the preattack status may occur, or there may be residual damage.

Figure 4.5 Location of extracranial and intracranial vascular lesions in cerebrovascular disease.

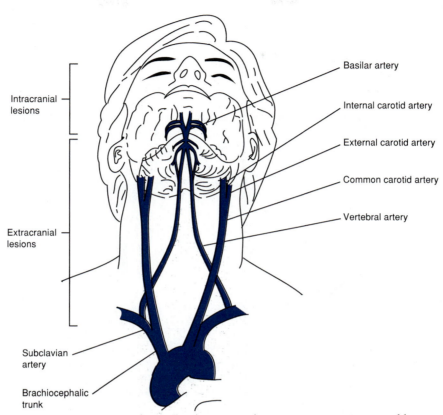

- *progressive stroke*—neurologic manifestations are persistent and become more serious, signaling impending stroke.

cerebrovascular insufficiency syndrome—clinical evidence of minor brain damage: numbness, motor weakness, slurred speech, and others; may develop from pathologic changes of the intracranial vessels, especially the anterior, middle, and posterior cerebral arteries. More frequently, it is caused by extracranial vascular obstruction leading to cerebral ischemia, as seen in the following:

- *internal carotid syndrome, internal carotid stenosis, internal carotid ischemia*—stenotic lesion usually resulting from atheromatous process near the bifurcation of the common carotid artery. It may cause contralateral hemiparesis or hemiplegia, speech difficulties, visual defects, and other changes. (1, 13, 36, 47) (See fig. 4.6.)
- *subclavian steal syndrome, proximal subclavian stenosis, skeletal muscle ischemia of arm*—syndrome caused by impaired blood flow to the basilar artery or brachiocephalic trunk near the origin of the vertebral artery. The decreased vascular pressure beyond the occluded segment initiates retrograde flow in the vertebral artery and siphons the blood away from the brain. This stealing of blood, which reduces the cerebral circulation, thus causing neurologic deficit, is demanded by the muscles for exercise of the affected arm. The low or absent blood pressure and pulse on the site of the subclavian occlusion, in contrast to those markedly

Figure 4.6 Occlusive lesion of the bifurcation of the common carotid artery extending into the internal carotid artery.

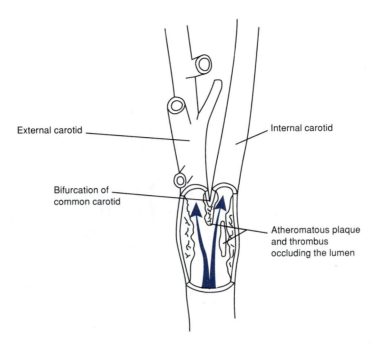

higher on the unaffected arm, are diagnostic evidence of this condition. (13, 36) (See fig. 4.7.)

- *vertebrobasilar syndrome, vertebral artery stenosis* or *basilar artery stenosis, vertebrobasilar ischemia*—syndrome manifests cerebellar involvement: vertigo, disequilibrium, ataxia, and cranial nerve damage, facial paralysis, motor and sensory disturbances. (13)

intracranial hematoma—local mass of extravasated blood formed as a result of intracranial hemorrhage. Chronic lesions may become encapsulated. Epidural and subdural hematomas, located above or below the dura mater, are usually caused by head injury. (67, 74)

intracranial hemorrhage—rupture of a vessel beneath the skull with seepage of blood into the brain coverings or substance. It may be caused by head injury, stroke, or ruptured aneurysm. Brain damage depends on the location and extent of the lesion involved. (13, 47)

subarachnoid hemorrhage—bleeding into the subarachnoid space, which in some cases is associated with excruciating headache, convulsions, and coma. It is due to head injury or ruptured intracranial aneurysm. (12, 46)

chorea—nervous disorder characterized by bizarre, abrupt, involuntary movements.

Huntington's chorea, adult chorea, Huntington's disease—disorder transmitted as an autosomal dominant disease usually occurring in midadult life (average age of onset about 35 to 40 years). The determining gene is located on the terminal segment of the short arm of chromosome 4. There is atrophy of the caudate nucleus, as well as other structures of the basal ganglia (putamen and globus pallidus). A combination of choreoathetotic movements and progressive mental decline occur. The involuntary movements include bizarre grimacing, respiratory irregularities, faulty articulation of speech, and irregular movements of the limbs, producing a gait with a peculiar dancing quality. The disorder progresses slowly and death usually occurs some 15 to 20 years after onset of symptoms. (19)

Figure 4.7 Subclavian steal syndrome. Proximal left subclavian artery stenosed by atheroma, resulting in impoverished blood supply to the arm. Cerebral circulation suffers due to a reversal of blood flow in the left vertebral artery.

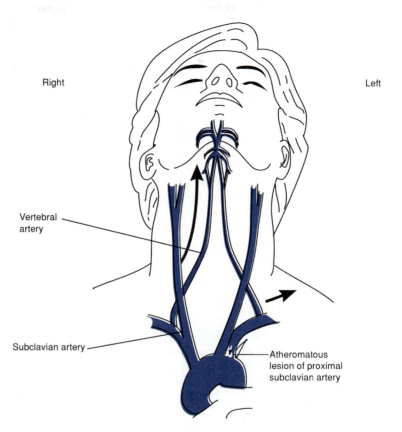

Right

Left

Vertebral artery

Subclavian artery

Atheromatous lesion of proximal subclavian artery

Sydenham's chorea, juvenile chorea—disorder of childhood and adolescence with insidious onset of jerky movements, usually occurring during rheumatic fever. (41)

encephalitis lethargica—inflammation of the brain marked by somnolence and ocular paralysis. It is caused by a filtrable virus.

encephalocele—protrusion of some brain substance through a fissure of the skull.

epilepsy—convulsive disorder consisting of recurrent seizures and impaired consciousness. (2, 30, 101)

Friedreich's ataxia—familial disease seen in young persons. Involvement of cerebellum, pyramidal tracts, and peripheral nerves results in sensory impairment, unsteady gait, contractures, and deformities, such as lordosis and high-arching feet with toe cocking up. Optic atrophy and myocardial disease may occur. Cardiac involvement may be present with such symptoms as progressive congestive heart failure and angina pectoris. Pathologically, the heart may be enlarged with fatty infiltration and fibrous replacement of myocardium, and often there is pathologic evidence of hypertrophic cardiomyopathy. (26)

head injury, craniocerebral trauma—injury to the head, usually associated with a fractured skull and directly or indirectly affecting at varying degrees one or more cerebral centers. The severity and extent of brain damage is usually but not exclusively indicated by state of consciousness, intracranial pressure, respiratory exchange, circulatory ability to supply the brain with oxygen and nutrients, and prevention or control of cerebral hemorrhage, edema, and infection. (67)

hydrocephalus—a pathologic condition characterized by a dilatation of the brain and an abnormal accumulation of intraventricular cerebrospinal fluid. It may be:

obstructive or noncommunicating hydrocephalus—due to an interference with the circulation of the cerebrospinal fluid through the ventricular system; indicates a block or obstruction within the ventricular system or located in its outlets to the subarachnoid space so that the ventricles and subarachnoid spaces are not in continuity.

nonobstructive or communicating hydrocephalus—due to an absorption of cerebrospinal fluid; indicates that the ventricular system is in communication with the subarachnoid spaces of the brain and spinal cord.

Other distinctions include the following:

adult hydrocephalus—presence of increased volume of cerebrospinal fluid, usually in the ventricular system.

infantile hydrocephalus—relatively common form that occurs before closure of fontanelles and is characterized by increasing cranial enlargement and prominent forehead. Occasionally the process is arrested.

post-traumatic hydrocephalus—type caused by head injury that may result in ventricular hemorrhage or subarachnoid bleeding and blockage of the aqueduct and fourth ventricle by blood clot.

Other types include:

ex vacuo hydrocephalus—denotes ventricular enlargement due to primary cortical atrophy.

external hydrocephalus—implies enlargement of subarachnoid spaces over the cortical surface.

internal hydrocephalus—denotes ventricular enlargement alone.

normal-pressure hydrocephalus—disorder depicted by normal cerebrospinal fluid pressure but enlarged ventricles. The distinction between normal-pressure hydrocephalus and high-pressure hydrocephalus seems to involve the severity of obstruction and ability of the brain to adapt rather than the cause of the ventricular enlargement. (7, 21, 34)

hypertensive encephalopathy—cerebral vasoconstriction and edema. Cerebral arteries are greatly constricted. The swollen, pale, and anemic brain is compressed against the skull and ventricles, causing increased intracranial pressure. (47)

meningitis—inflammation of the meninges resulting from infectious agents such as bacteria, fungi, and viruses. (79, 92)

acute septic meningitis, acute viral meningitis—syndrome involves signs and symptoms of meningeal irritation with mononuclear pleocytosis of the cerebrospinal fluid. Stiffness of the neck and back, occasionally along with muscular spasms, is the only neurologic sign in most cases. In about a third of the cases, Kernig's and Brudzinski's signs are present. This syndrome is caused mainly by viruses, especially the mumps virus, the enterovirus group, and herpesviruses.

meningocele—protrusion of the meninges through a cranial fissure.

microcephalus—abnormally small head, sometimes associated with idiocy. (91)

multiple sclerosis (MS)—autoimmune disease involving an integrated attack by T cells, B cells, and macrophages on the myelin sheath that surrounds nerve fibers. Potentially inflammatory cytokines such as τ-interferon and tumor-necrosis factor-α are found at the sites of damage. T cells and antibodies directed against myelin components can be isolated from inflamed regions in the central nervous system. Van Noort et al. describe the isolation of a protein that is a prominent target at the disease site in the myelin sheath. This autoantigen is a small heat-shock protein designed as αB-crystallin, which is induced in the diseased white matter. αB-crystallin was found in oligodendroglial cells as well as in astrocytes in plaques from patients with acute and chronic MS. αB-crystallin acts as immunodominant myelin antigen to human T cells when expressed at the increased levels found within and immediately around active MS lesions in the human brain. MS is a slowly progressive disease, striking persons ages 20 to 40. Areas of demyelination and scar tissue plaques are scattered throughout the nervous system, disrupting nerve transmission. Numbness, fatigability, clumsiness, difficulty in walking, and blurring vision may be followed by severe incoordination, spasticity, paralysis, incontinence, scanning speech, intention tremor, nystagmus, and blindness. (37, 42, 43, 85, 95)

myelitis—inflammation of the spinal cord.

neurofibromatosis-1 (NF-1) (formerly known as **von Recklinghausen's neurofibromatosis** or **peripheral neurofibromatosis**)—is present when two or more of the following criteria are present:

1. six or more café-au-lait macules over 5 mm in greatest diameter in prepubertal individuals and over 15 mm in greatest diameter in postpubertal individuals
2. two or more neurofibromas of any type or one plexiform neurofibroma
3. freckling in the axillary or inguinal regions
4. optic glioma
5. two or more Lisch nodules (iris hamartomas)
6. a distinctive osseous lesion such as sphenoid dysplasia or thinning of long bone cortex, with or without pseudoarthrosis
7. a first-degree relative (parent, sibling, or offspring) with NF-1 by the above criteria

The gene for NF-1 has been mapped to chromosome 17 by linkage analysis. (27)

neurofibromatosis-2 (NF-2)—criteria for NF-2 are met by persons who have bilateral eighth-nerve masses (seen with the appropriate imaging techniques) or a first-degree relative with NF-2 and either a unilateral eighth-nerve mass or two of the following: neurofibroma, meningioma, glioma, schwannoma, or a juvenile posterior subcapsular lenticular opacity. Results from linkage analyses have shown that the genetic abnormality of NF-2 is on the long arm of chromosome 22. Persons in the NF-1 group are not at risk for developing acoustic neuromas. The growth pattern of acoustic neuromas in persons with NF-2 is not predictable. Magnetic resonance imaging with gadolinium is able to detect tumors early and to follow growth patterns of individual tumors. At present, surgery is the definitive treatment for enlarging acoustic tumors. (27)

paralysis agitans, Parkinson's disease—slowly progressive neurologic disorder of middle life, primarily affecting the nuclei of the brain stem (substantia nigra, locus coeruleus), where there are varying degrees of nerve cell loss with reactive gliosis (most pronounced in the substantia nigra) along with distinctive eosinophilic intracytoplasmic inclusions (Lewy bodies). Depletion of striatal dopamine due to the nigra cell loss is the cause of bradykinesia (slowness and difficulty initiating movement) observed clinically. Other clinical findings include rigidity, tremors, masklike facies, and a monotonous voice. Characteristically, festination is present. The patient's body is stooped forward, the steps are short, and shuffling occurs with increasing pace once locomotion has started. The gait is propulsive or retropulsive. (2, 20, 65)

poliomyelitis—viral disease with lesions in the central nervous system and varying symptomatology. Forms include the following:

abortive poliomyelitis—minor illness characterized by fever, malaise, drowsiness, headache, nausea, vomiting, constipation, and sore throat. Recovery occurs within a few days.

nonparalytic poliomyelitis (aseptic meningitis)—in addition to the symptoms listed in abortive poliomyelitis, the person has stiffness and pain in back and neck. Illness lasts 2 to 10 days and recovery is rapid. In a small number of cases, the disease advances to paralysis. The polio virus is only one of many viruses that produce aseptic meningitis.

paralytic poliomyelitis:

- *bulbar poliomyelitis*—involves cranial nerve nuclei, particularly the respiratory center in the medulla. It is the most serious type of poliomyelitis, causing respiratory paralysis.
- *spinal paralytic poliomyelitis*—usually involves anterior horn cells of the spinal cord, resulting in characteristic stiffness of the neck and spine and tightness of the hamstring muscles, followed by paralysis of lower extremities. (70)

postpolio syndrome, postpoliomyelitis neuromuscular atrophy—a progressive muscle weakness beginning some 20 to 30 years after the initial occurrence of poliomyelitis. Symptoms vary from mild to moderate deterioration of function, with fatigue, muscle pain, fasciculations, and weakness that may stabilize or progress to muscle atrophy. The limbs are most often affected. The pathogenesis is considered to involve a dysfunction of surviving motor neurons, with slow disintegration of axon terminals, leading to late denervation of muscle. (70)

spina bifida—congenital defect resulting from absence of a vertebral arch of the spinal column. It may cause:

meningocele—protrusion of the meninges through the defect in the spinal column.

meningomyelocele—herniation of the cord and meninges through the defect of the vertebral column.

syringomyelocele—protrusion of cord and meninges through the defect in the spine. Cord tissue is a thin-walled sac filled with fluid from the central canal. (52)

spinal cord injury—trauma to cord produced by fracture or dislocation of spine may cause irreversible damage and disability.

compression of cervical cord—complete transverse compression of cervical cord may cause lifelong quadriplegia (paralysis of arms and legs) and loss of sphincter control or be fatal due to phrenic nerve injury and subsequent respiratory paralysis.

compression of thoracic or lumbar cord—pressure on this area may cause paraplegia (paralysis below the waist) and sphincter disturbances. Compression of spinal cord also may be caused by a cord tumor and a herniated intervertebral disk affecting the spinal nerve root of the lesion. (73)

spinal cord tumors—tumors involving the spinal cord are similar in cellular type to intracranial tumors. They usually arise from the parenchyma of the cord, nerve roots, meningeal coverings, intraspinal vascular network, sympathetic chain, or vertebral column. (44, 65, 75)

subacute sclerosing panencephalitis (SSPE), Dawson's encephalitis—uncommon form of inflammation of the brain occurring between 4 and 20 years of age. This is a slowly progressive demyelinating disorder of the central nervous system, and it is believed to be caused by a variant of the measles virus. Three stages are recognized:

1. behavioral disorders at the onset
2. mental deterioration, myoclonic jerkings, and convulsive seizures as the disease progresses
3. stupor, dementia, rigidity, blindness, and coma in the terminal phase (92)

tabes dorsalis, locomotor ataxia—syphilis of the central nervous system, resulting from involvement of the posterior columns and dorsal roots of the spinal cord. It is characterized by a loss of vibration sense and proprioception that results in a broad-based distinctive gait. In some cases, there may be associated impotence, bladder dysfunction, and optic atrophy. Argyll Robertson pupils may be present, as well as paresthesia, analgesia, or sharp recurrent pains in the leg muscles. (38, 74)

OPERATIVE TERMS (SEE TABLE 4.1.)

carotid aneurysmectomy—through a lateral neck incision at the base of the skull, the carotid artery is exposed and the aneurysm excised. In some cases, there is sufficient tortuosity and elongation of the carotid artery proximal and distal to the site of aneurysmal involvement to permit mobilization of the ends of the carotid artery and direct anastomosis, while other cases may require a vein graft to bridge the gap. (18)

carotid artery ligation—tying a carotid artery in its cervical portion (neck) or using a Selverstone or Crutchfield clamp to gradually occlude the blood flow in the extracranial portions of the common or internal carotid artery. (18)

carotid endarterectomy—removal of plaques on the intimal lining of a carotid artery in occlusive cerebrovascular disease. This removal may be carried out at the carotid bifurcation and followed by a reconstruction of an internal carotid artery with a Dacron graft. (1, 23, 32, 47)

cingulotomy, cingulumotomy—cingulum destruction by stereotaxic surgery with positioning of electrodes in target area. Operation is done under roentgenographic guidance for relief of severe disabling monopolar depression. (14, 88)

cordectomy—removal of a portion of the spinal cord to convert a spastic paraplegia to a flaccid paraplegia, which enhances rehabilitation. (22)

cordotomy, chordotomy—interruption of the lateral spinothalamic tract of the spinal cord, usually in the anterolateral quadrant, for relief of pain. Surgery may be performed by the open surgery approach or percutaneously by stereotaxic surgery. (22)

> *percutaneous cordotomy*—surgical interruption of pain fibers in the high cervical cord by means of percutaneous stereotaxic surgical techniques. This is done under biplane roentgenographic control.

> *selective cordotomy*—palliative surgery either by the open surgery approach or by stereotaxic surgery to obtain sensory loss in local pain region, for example, for pain surfacing in the arm, leg, or trunk.

craniectomy—removal of part of the skull; a method of approach to the brain.

craniotomy—opening of the skull. Burr or trephine openings into the skull are made to prepare a bone flap. This osteoplastic flap is separated from the skull during brain surgery and replaced when the skull is closed. Osteoplastic craniotomy is a common approach to the brain. (18, 88)

cryoneurosurgery—operative use of cold in destruction of neurosurgical lesions. (88)

decompression of: (75, 88)

> *brain*—removal of a piece of skull, usually in the subtemporal region, with opening of the dura mater to relieve intracranial pressure.

> *spinal cord*—removal of bone fragments, hematoma, or lesion to relieve pressure on cord.

drainage of meninges for abscess or hematoma—evacuation of subarachnoid or subdural space.

excision of brain lesion—complete removal if lesion does not encroach on vital centers.

laminectomy—excision of one or more laminae of vertebrae; method of approach to spinal cord. (75)

laser neurological surgery—procedure utilizing devices that convert disorganized forms of energy into highly organized electromagnetic radiation or light. Laser is an acronym for *l*ight *a*mplification by *s*timulated *e*mission of *r*adiation. The more common lasers employed in various neurosurgical procedures include the ND:YAG (neodymium: yttrium-aluminum-garnet) laser, the argon laser, and the carbon dioxide laser. Each type of laser should be carefully considered in light of its characteristic advantages and disadvantages. Lasers have been utilized in neurosurgery to perform commissural myelotomies, to make dorsal root entry lesions in the spinal cord for ablation of the descending tract of the trigeminal nerve, and for spinothalamic tractotomy. They also are useful in removing vascular malformations. The newer types of lasers, such as the frequency-doubled ND:YAG laser and the copper vapor lasers appear to interact with tissue in a manner similar to that of the argon lasers. (23)

microneurosurgery—use of the surgical binocular microscope that provides a powerful light source, up to 25 times magnification, and a clear stereoscopic view of the brain. Microneurosurgical techniques are employed for acoustic tumors, cerebral aneurysms, pituitary tumors, spinal cord tumors, and other neurosurgical procedures. (47, 102)

operations for parkinsonism—surgical procedures directed toward the destruction of areas of basal nuclei presumably affected by the disease. (2, 9, 50, 65, 88)

dopaminergic graft transplantation—procedure involving the grafting of human embryonic dopamine-rich mesencephalic tissue unilaterally into the putamen. Follow-up data indicate that this type of graft can survive in the parkinsonian brain and grow and exert functional effects up to at least 3 years postoperatively, despite an ongoing disease process. Optimal, long-term symptomatic relief may necessitate bilateral grafts.

pallidotomy—surgical interruption of nerve pathways coming from the globus pallidus to relieve intractable tremor and rigidity. Division of nerve fibers is usually achieved by use of electrocautery or chemical solution. Cryogenic agents, ultrasonic waves, and stereotaxic techniques are employed.

thalamotomy—partial destruction of thalamus for relief of tremors and rigidity. The stereotaxic instrument is applied to the skull. By means of roentgenographic visualization, the target area is located and lesions are created by electrolytic, chemical, ultrasonic, or cryogenic methods. Operations on the right hemisphere appear to be associated with a greater degree of relief of rigidity than operations on the left hemisphere.

stereotaxy—the use of a stereotaxic instrument fixed onto the skull with screws, as in a scaffold. From this, a probe containing either a chemical, electric, or cryogenic agent is introduced through a burr opening into the target area of the brain. Examples of this type of an approach are:

stereotaxic neurosurgery—operative procedure that uses three-dimensional measurement for precisely locating the neurosurgical target in acromegaly, cerebral aneurysm, diabetic retinopathy, manic depressive reactions, Parkinson's disease, psychogenic pain, and temporal lobe epilepsy. (2, 88)

gamma knife stereotactic radiosurgery—computerized way of blasting brain tumors, as well as a few other brain abnormalities, using an array of 201 separate beams of gamma rays. Instead of opening up the skull and cutting away the tumor, a specialized machine aims the gamma rays into the brain through a helmet that resembles a beauty salon hair dryer with 201 tiny holes in it. Separately, the gamma rays emitted by tiny pieces of cobalt 60 pass into the head and cause no harm to the skin, muscle, bone, and healthy brain tissue. However, when these rays converge, crisscrossing into a single point inside a tumor target, they act as a powerful glowing knife by blasting away tumor cells. Prior to performing the actual procedure, many magnetic resonance imaging brain scans are studied by the Gamma knife team to map a tumor's exact three-dimensional size, shape, and location. This technique is used to attack tumors that would be hard to reach with a scalpel. It only works on relatively small tumors, and it does little to retard the fast-growing tumors called *gliomas*. It is useful in buying time and improving the quality of life, but it will not take away the tumor; rather tumor control is the aim of this procedure. (2, 6, 88)

surgical shunts for hydrocephalus—detour channels, surgically created to relieve an accumulation of cerebrospinal fluid in the brain. (7, 21)

ventriculoatrial or *ventriculocaval shunt*—insertion of a Holter, Pudenz, or Hakim valve to channel the cerebrospinal fluid from the lateral ventricle to either an atrium or superior vena cava via the jugular vein. This operation is performed for communicating hydrocephalus.

ventriculocisternostomy, Torkildsen's operation—surgical procedure for obstructive hydrocephalus. A catheter is used to shunt the fluid from a ventricle to the cisterna magna. This operation is especially useful for obstructive hydrocephalus in aqueductal stenosis.

ventriculoperitoneal shunt—detour channel shunting the cerebrospinal fluid from the enlarged ventricular system into the peritoneal cavity.

trephination—cutting a circular opening or boring a hole into the skull; a method of approach to the brain.

SYMPTOMATIC TERMS

analgesia—loss of normal sense of pain.

aphasia—difficulty with the use or understanding of words due to lesions in association areas. Lesions in the brain's frontal region cause motor aphasia, and lesions affecting the brain's posterior region cause sensory aphasia. (61)

> *global (total) aphasia*—presence of a large lesion in the sylvian region, destroying a large part of the speech and language areas and leaving a severe aphasia. Infarction from occlusion of the left internal carotid or middle cerebral artery, a large hemorrhage, a large tumor, or penetrating trauma is usually responsible for this deficit. Persons with this type of aphasia appear initially mute or say a few stereotyped words (e.g., hi or yes), they do not read or write even the simplest words, and can understand only a few words of the speech of other persons.
>
> *motor aphasia, Broca's nonfluent aphasia, Broca's expressive aphasia*—verbal comprehension intact, but patient is unable to use the muscles that coordinate speech.
>
> *sensory aphasia, Wernicke's fluent aphasia, Wernicke's receptive aphasia*—inability to comprehend the spoken word, if the auditory word center is affected, and the written word, if the visual word center is involved. The patient will not understand the spoken or written word if there is an involvement of both centers.

ataxia—motor incoordination. (34)

aura—patient's awareness of pending epileptic seizure. (30)

cerebrospinal otorrhea—escape of cerebrospinal fluid from the ear following craniocerebral trauma. It is caused by a fistulous communication between the ventricular system or subarachnoid space and the ear. (67)

cerebrospinal rhinorrhea—escape of cerebrospinal fluid from the nose following craniocerebral trauma. It is caused by a fistulous passage leading from the ventricular system or subarachnoid space to the nose. (67)

coma—state of unconsciousness or deep stupor. (67)

convulsion—paroxysms of involuntary muscular contractions and relaxations.

diplegia—paralysis on both sides of the body. (27)

dysarthria—incoordination of speech muscles affecting articulation. (61)

dyskinesia—abnormal involuntary movement and body posture due to lesion or disease processes.

> *athetosis*—slow, wormlike, writhing movement, especially in hands and fingers.
> *ballism*—violent, flinging, shaking, or jerking movements of extremities.
> *chorea*—quick, explosive, purposeless movements.
> *choreoathetosis*—describes features of both chorea and athetosis.
> *dystonia*—abnormal posture from twisting movements, usually of limbs and trunk.
> (20, 34, 37, 41)

euphoria—sense of well-being associated with mild elation.

fasciculation—involuntary twitchings of groups of muscle fibers. (37)

festination—quick, shuffling steps; accelerated gait seen in Parkinson's disease. (34, 65)

hemiparesis—slight degree of paralysis of one side of the body. (34)

hemiplegia—paralysis affecting one side of the body. (27, 41)

hyperesthesia—increased sensibility to sensory stimuli. (11)

intention tremor—trembling when attempting voluntary movement; exhibiting rhythmic oscillation about the target of movement. (38, 65)

nystagmus—constant movements of the eyeballs, as seen in brain damage and disorders of the vestibular apparatus.

paraparesis—slight paralysis of lower limbs. (34)

paraplegia—paralysis of lower limbs and at varying degrees of lower trunk. (41) (Note: The word *paralysis* and the word ending *-plegia* are used to imply total loss of contractility; anything less than total is *paresis*.)

paresis—partial paralysis. (38, 41)

paresthesia—abnormal sensation; heightened sensory response to stimuli. (11)

scanning speech—hesitant, slow speech; pronouncing words in syllables.

syncope—fainting. (54)

tardive dyskinesia—persistent and often permanent movement disorder involving involuntary facial movements, choreoathetosis, and/or dystonia. It is often the most common complication for patients receiving long-term neuroleptic antipsychotic drugs. (62)

tic—involuntary, purposeless contractions of muscle groups, such as twitching of facial muscles, eye blinking, or shrugging of the shoulders. (91)

transient global amnesia (TGA)—of uncertain cause, with sudden loss of recent and remote memory. It is recognized by sudden inability to form new memory traces (anterograde amnesia) and retrograde memory loss for events of the preceding days, weeks, or even years. Other intellectual function remains intact. The amnesia terminates abruptly and the entire episode lasts less than 24 hours. There remains a permanent memory hiatus for the duration of the spell. (25)

SPECIAL PROCEDURES

SELECTED TERMS RELATED TO CEREBROSPINAL FLUID

cerebrospinal fluid (CSF)—produced in the capillaries of the choroid plexus, CSF circulates through the ventricles of the brain and enters the subarachnoid space. Its functions are to protect the brain and spinal cord from sudden pressure changes; to maintain a stable environment for both structures; and to remove waste products of brain and metabolism.

appearance of CSF:

turbidity of CSF—cloudy appearance caused by the presence of microorganisms, granules, or flaky material in spinal fluid.

xanthochromic—canary yellow. Xanthochromic CSF may occur in cerebral hematoma, subarachnoid hemorrhage, toxoplasmosis, abscesses, and tumors.

collection of CSF:

cisternal puncture—removal of CSF from the cisterna magna; for example, in the case of a blocked central canal of the spinal cord.

lumbar puncture—needle puncture of subarachnoid space of the lumbar cord used in determining CSF pressure and removing CSF for diagnostic evaluation or other purposes. (See fig. 4.8.)

ventricular puncture—removal of the ventricular fluids, rarely done on adults except for ventriculography, but a more common procedure for infants with open fontanels.

CSF examinations:

CSF cytology—cell count and differential count of CSF may aid in the detection of neurologic disease. Neutrophils in CSF signal an acute inflammatory process such as bacterial meningitis, and malignant cells shed in CSF may be derived from primary or metastatic brain tumors, lymphomas, or leukemias.

Figure 4.8 A lumbar puncture is performed by inserting a fine needle between the third and fourth lumbar vertebrae and withdrawing a sample of cerebrospinal fluid from the subarachnoid space.

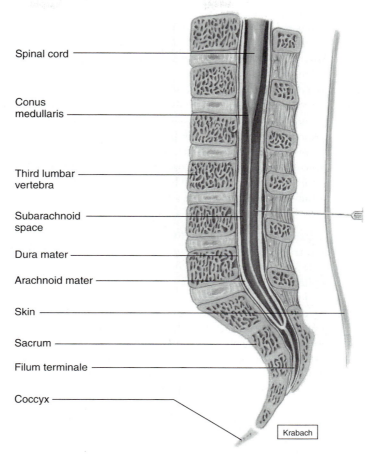

Spinal cord

Conus medullaris

Third lumbar vertebra

Subarachnoid space

Dura mater

Arachnoid mater

Skin

Sacrum

Filum terminale

Coccyx

Krabach

CSF glucose—elevated CSF glucose is of no diagnostic importance. Values less than 40 mg/dL may be present in tuberculous, bacterial, or fungal meningitis or malignant infiltration of meninges.

CSF glutamine—determination indirectly suggests the ammonia level in the central nervous system. Elevated ammonia concentrations have a toxic effect on nerve tissue. As a protective response, ammonia is converted to glutamine. Glutamine levels higher than 35 mg/dL indicate hepatic encephalopathy (hepatic coma).

CSF lactate dehydrogenase (LD)—test useful in distinguishing between aseptic and bacterial meningitis.

CSF lactic acid concentrations—if greater than 35 mg/dL, results suggest tuberculous or bacterial infection.

CSF total protein—reliable but nonspecific index of neurologic disease and a common abnormality in chemical analysis. Elevated immunoglobulin (IgG) levels are found in multiple sclerosis, neurosyphilis, and other central nervous system pathology.

microbiology of CSF—bacterial, fungal, tuberculous, protozoal, or viral infections may result from infiltration of CSF with microorganisms, hematogenous dissemination of microorganisms, or direct inoculation due to trauma or surgery. (31, 37, 91, 92)

TERMS RELATED TO NEUROLOGIC EXAMINATION

Babinski's reflex—extension of the great toe with or without plantar flexion of other toes when examiner strokes the sole. A positive Babinski's reflex suggests organic disease of the pyramidal tracts. (91)

blink reflex—is ascertained by stimulation over the supraorbital nerve, with surface recording over both ipsilateral and contralateral orbicularis oculi. This test is used in clinical medicine to assess trigeminal and facial nerve function, and can target disorders such as multiple sclerosis. (10, 91)

Brudzinski's sign—when head is passively flexed on chest, the patient draws up legs reflexively. This occurs in meningeal irritation and meningitis. (79, 91)

carotid compression test—evaluation of cerebral blood flow by compressing the carotid arteries digitally. This may lead to the detection of cerebrovascular insufficiency. An irritable carotid sinus reflex is evoked by unilateral compression. (36)

Kernig's sign—when the patient is supine with thigh flexed on the abdomen, he or she is unable to extend the leg. This sign is present in meningeal irritation and meningitis. (79)

Romberg's sign—inability of ataxic persons to stand steady with their eyes closed and feet together. (34, 38)

TERMS RELATED TO NEUROLOGIC STUDIES

electroencephalography—the tracing or recording of the electric current generated in the cerebral cortex by brain waves. Marked irregularities indicate pathologic conditions such as epilepsy, brain tumors, scars, and other disorders. The procedure is an aid to medical diagnosis and treatment. (10, 30)

electronystagmography—procedure that records changes in the corneoretinal potential due to eye movements that provide objective evidence of induced and spontaneous nystagmus.

evoked response, evoked potential—presents as the record of electrical activity produced by groups of neurons within the spinal cord, brain stem, thalamus, or cerebral hemispheres after stimulation of one or another sensory system effected by means of auditory, visual, or tactile input. Some tests employing this type of mechanism include:

brain stem auditory-evoked responses (BAERs)—type of auditory-evoked response effected by clicks transmitted to the client's ears by earphones. BAERs consist of 7 waves, which appear within the first 10 milliseconds after the click. The position of these waves in relation to the presence of structural lesions permits very good accuracy in targeting the level of the lesion within the brain stem auditory pathways, as well as providing the opportunity to correlate clinical findings with other neurological information.

pattern-reversal visual-evoked response (PRVER)—type of visual-evoked response used in clinical medicine in the diagnosis of subclinical optic neuritis or multiple sclerosis. The test is not specific. The difference between a demyelinating lesion, such as that seen in multiple sclerosis, and a compressive lesion, such as that involving the optic nerve, cannot be ascertained on the basis of this test.

somatosensory-evoked responses (SERs)—produced by repeated stimuli to the peripheral nerves, which can be recorded at many levels along the somatosensory pathways. A series of waves can be documented that show activity in peripheral nerve trunks, tracts in the spinal cord, gracile and cuneate nuclei, pontine and/or cerebellar structures, thalamus, thalamocortical radiations, and primary sensory fields of the cortex. (10)

facial thermography—photographic measurement of the skin temperatures of the face. In a controlled environment, the skin temperatures reflect variations in blood flow. The central portion of the supraorbital region is the only skin area of the face that receives its blood supply from the terminal branches of the internal carotid artery. In severe stenosis of the internal carotid artery, the decreased blood flow lowers the skin temperature in the medial supraorbital region. The cool area is detectable by a thermogram. (93)

ANESTHESIA-RELATED TERMS

ORIGIN OF TERMS

acus (L)—needle
-algia (G)—pain
anesthesia (G)—loss of sensation or feeling
cata- (G)—down, lower, under
cauda (L)—tail

dura (L)—hard
hypno- (G)—sleep
narco- (G)—stupor
-spasm (G)—involuntary contractions
vas-, vaso- (L)—vessel

GENERAL TERMS

analeptics—stimulants of the central nervous system, for example, Coramine and caffeine.

analgesia—loss of normal sense of pain. (63)

analgesics—drugs that relieve pain. (63)

anesthesia—inability to feel, lack of response to various stimuli. (84)

> *anesthesia state*—condition created by a broad range of drugs that effect anesthesia, for example, opioids, or inhaled anesthetics, and barbiturates. (84)
>
> *anesthesia depth*—occurs when the concentrations of agents are sufficient to produce a collage of effects needed for the comfort of the patient and conduct of surgical procedures. (84)
>
> *general anesthesia*—state of unconsciousness accompanied by varying degrees of muscular relaxation and freedom from physical pain. (100) (See table 4.2.)
>
> *local anesthesia*—absence of sensation and consequently of pain in a part of the body; consciousness retained. (57)

anesthesiologist—physician who specializes in anesthesiology.

anesthesiology—science and study of anesthesia. (57)

anesthetic—agent producing insensibility to pain. (57)

anesthetist—professional person, not necessarily a physician, who is qualified to administer anesthesia. (57)

antiemetic drugs—drugs that are therapeutically useful for control of nausea or vomiting, such as parasympatholytic agents (belladonna alkaloids), phenothiazines, and butyrophenones. (91)

arterial hypotension during anesthesia—lower arterial blood pressure during anesthesia may result from several causes. These include excessive premedication; potent therapeutic drugs administered prior to anesthesia; overdose of general anesthetics; circulatory effects of spinal and epidural anesthesia; raised airway pressure; compression of the vena cava; hypovolemia; hemorrhage; surgical manipulation; and change in the position of the patient. (94)

artificial ventilation—mechanism (respirator, ventilator, etc.) used to control rate and depth of breathing. Common indications for artificial ventilation are respiratory failure and deterioration of blood gas levels with progressive signs of tiring. (86)

dissociative anesthesia—selective blocking of pain conduction and perception, leaving those parts of the central nervous system that do not participate in pain transmission and perception free from the depressant effects of drugs. The profound analgesia induced by this type of anesthesia is associated with somnolence, in which the patient appears to be disconnected from the environment. (15, 72)

hypercarbia, hypercapnia—excess of carbon dioxide in the blood. (45)

hyperventilation—excessive respiration, causing an abnormal loss of carbon dioxide from the blood. (91)

hypotensive anesthesia—technique employed to diminish blood loss and oozing to create a dry surgical field and prevent risks of hypertension. It combines elements of pharmacologic blockage, monitoring of blood pressure and patient posture throughout the procedure, and use of the intermittent positive-pressure ventilator, when indicated. (94)

hypoxia—reduction of oxygen supply to the body tissues. (91)

| TABLE 4.2 | Classification of Selected General Anesthetics |

Anesthetic Agents	Systemic Effects

Volatile substances, administered by inhalation:
  Liquids producing vapors
    Chloroform
    Enflurane (Ethrane)
    Ether
    Ethyl chloride
    Halothane (Fluothane)
    Methoxyflurane (Penthrane)
    Trichloroethylene (Trilene)
    Vinyl ether (Vinethene)
  Gases
    Cyclopropane
    Ethylene
    Nitrous oxide
	Chemical substances and depressants of the central nervous system; surgically useful because they are complete anesthetics providing:
	  analgesia
	  suppression of reflex activity
	  muscular relaxation and loss of consciousness

Nonvolatile substances administered intravenously or rectally:
  Ultra-short-acting barbiturates:
    Methohexital (Brevital)
    Thiamylal (Surital)
    Thiopental (Pentothal)
  Derivatives of ethyl alcohol:
    Tribromoethanol (Avertin)
    Solution Avertin in amylene hydrate
	Basal narcotics, medullary depressants, and incomplete anesthetics; surgically useful as adjuncts to other anesthetics. They produce:
	  unconsciousness
	  inadequate control of reflex activity
	  unsatisfactory muscular relaxation
	  hypnosis and amnesia (following use of Avertin)

Nonvolatile substances administered intravenously or intramuscularly:
  Neuroleptics and nonbarbiturates:
    Ketamine (Ketalar)
    Droperidol (Inapsine)
  Neuroleptic and potent narcotic analgesic:
    Innovar (Droperidol and Fentanyl)
	Short-acting anesthetics, depressants of certain corticothalamic systems; useful as sole anesthetic and as adjunct to conventional anesthesia.
	They produce:
	  profound analgesia
	  amnesia
	  increased cardiovascular activity
	  unsatisfactory muscular relaxation

inhalation therapy—administration of inhalant gases such as oxygen or carbon dioxide to relieve oxygen insufficiency or to stimulate respiration. (91)

malignant hyperthermia syndrome—potentially fatal hypermetabolic syndrome that may be induced by any of the inhalation anesthetics, such as halothane, methoxyflurane, cyclopropane, and ethyl ether, or muscle relaxants, most notably succinylcholine. (See Oral Reading Practice for further information.) (40)

neuroleptanalgesics—potent analgesics and tranquilizers producing detached quiescence and somnolence, used for premedication and general anesthesia or as adjuncts to other anesthetic agents. (15)

neuromuscular blocking agents, skeletal muscle relaxants—drugs that serve as adjuncts to general anesthesia by producing muscular relaxation and thus reducing the need for deep levels of anesthesia.

    depolarizing agents—relaxants that block motor nerve impulses at the myoneural junction, such as succinylcholine chloride (Anectine) and decamethonium bromide (Syncurine). Depolarizing agents mimic the action of acetylcholine at the nerve-muscle junction, causing a discharge of the end-plate potential.

nondepolarizing agents—relaxants that inhibit transmission of motor nerve impulses at the myoneural junction, such as gallamine triethiodide (Flaxedil). Pancuronium bromide (Pavulon) is a competitive blocking neuromuscular agent that is longer acting and does not possess histamine or ganglionic blocking properties. (58, 69, 78, 90)

vasoconstrictors—drugs causing a constriction of the blood vessels. They are used in combination with local anesthetics to produce a vasoconstriction locally, thus preventing the anesthetic from being carried away from the site of injection. (91)

TERMS RELATED TO METHODS OF GENERAL ANESTHESIA

endotracheal anesthesia—introduction of a catheter into the trachea for the purpose of conducting the anesthetic mixture directly from the apparatus to the lungs. This may be achieved by oral or nasal intubation. The catheter is then attached to a closed or semiclosed inhaler. In present practice, this form of inhalation anesthesia is the method of choice for most major operations, since it permits a patent airway, aspiration of secretions, use of positive pressure, controlled breathing, adequate ventilation, and isolation of the respiratory tract from the gastrointestinal tract. (86)

hypercarbic anesthesia—excess carbon dioxide content of the blood and controlled hypertension causing improved oxygenation and decreased oxygen consumption during general anesthesia. The increased cerebral flow results from vasodilatation of hypercarbia and increased cerebral perfusion of induced hypertension. (45)

hypocarbic anesthesia—low carbon dioxide content and deliberate hypertension as an adjunct to general anesthesia. (45)

inhalation anesthesia—general anesthesia produced by the inhalation of vaporized liquids or gases. It is slower than intravenous anesthesia but is more readily controlled and may be safer. (48)

intravenous anesthesia—the intravenous administration of drugs to produce basal anesthesia. A stage of unconsciousness is produced, but analgesia and muscular relaxation may prove unsatisfactory. (15, 35, 72, 94)

rectal anesthesia—the rectal administration of drugs to produce basal anesthesia. The reflexes are partially abolished, and a hypnotic state ensues. Pentothal, Avertin, and ether have been used for this purpose. (28, 81)

SELECTED TERMS RELATED TO METHODS OF LOCAL ANESTHESIA

acupuncture analgesia—entails the insertion of stainless steel acupuncture needles at carefully selected points identified as being effective for producing the desired effect. This practice was developed in China and is widely accepted there as an anesthetic agent. The U.S. medical community views this practice as acupuncture analgesia rather than acupuncture anesthesia. (91)

axillary brachial block—with the patient's arm abducted at right angles and the elbow flexed, the axillary artery is palpated and outlined as high as possible. The anesthetist then places the forefinger of the left hand on the artery and inserts the needle, usually without the syringe attachment, at a right angle to the patient's skin. (97)

caudal or sacral anesthesia—method of epidural anesthesia in which the anesthetic solution is injected into the sacral canal. (24, 48, 97)

epidural block—spinal nerves blocked as they pass through the epidural space. (97)

infiltration anesthesia—injection of a dilute anesthetic agent under the skin to anesthetize the nerve endings and nerve fibers. (87)

intravenous regional anesthesia—method of producing analgesia in the extremities using lidocaine (or other drug) as a regional anesthetic to act at the main nerve trunks. (87, 97)

spinal anesthesia—anesthesia produced by the injection of a local anesthetic solution into the subarachnoid space of the lumbar region to block the roots of the spinal nerves. (24, 97)

supraclavicular brachial plexus block—point of injection is 1 centimeter above the midpoint of the clavicle. Insertion of the needle is downward and caudally, but not backward or medially. The supraclavicular approach to the brachial plexus results in a rapid onset of reliable blockade of the brachial plexus. This type of block offers excellent anesthesia for elbow, forearm, and hand surgery. (97)

topical or surface anesthesia—direct application of an anesthetic drug to a mucous membrane to produce insensibility to the nerve endings. Agents employed for topical anesthesia may include benzocaine, cocaine, dibucaine, cyclonine, lidocaine, and tetracaine. (87, 94)

ORAL READING PRACTICE

MALIGNANT HYPERTHERMIA SYNDROME

Malignant hyperthermia syndrome (MHS) is a potentially fatal hypermetabolic syndrome that may be induced by any of the **inhalation anesthetics,** such as **halothane, methoxyflurane, cyclopropane,** and **ethyl ether,** or **muscle relaxants,** most notably **succinylcholine.**

The etiology of **MHS** is believed to be an underlying pathophysiologic disorder of the muscle that may affect generalized body membrane dysfunction. Temperature increases rapidly to between 102.2°F and 107.6°F. Susceptibility to this disorder is transmitted by **autosomal-dominant inheritance** with variable frequency. Also, the syndrome may occur in **myotonic disorders, Duchenne dystrophy,** and in a **congenital myopathy** with **dysmorphic** features.

Continued progression of **MHS** depends on a combination of **myogenic, neurologic,** and **endocrinologic** derangements, including generalized membrane dysfunction. At the initiation and during the progression of **MHS,** hyperactivity of the **sympathetic nervous system** with release of **catecholamines** and **thyroid** hormone has been implicated in their effects on muscle cells. In some instances, following the intravenous injection of succinylcholine, muscle rigidity develops, especially **trismus-masseter spasm,** which involves jaw muscle rigidity in association with limb muscle flaccidity.

At the height of the malignant hyperthermia syndrome, the **serum creatine phosphokinase (CPK)** increases markedly along with the appearance of **myoglobinuria. Muscle biopsy** usually reveals depletion of **adenosine triphosphate (ATP),** as well as **CPK.** The clinical sequelae of **MHS** are usually initiated with a **hypermetabolic state** of muscle followed by a rapid rise in temperature. Most often, the first signal of **MHS** is **tachycardia.** This is followed by **tachypnea** as a result of **metabolic** and **respiratory acidosis.** The patient's skin is hot and **venous** blood in the operative field is dark because of the high oxygen consumption. Tachypnea is noted in the spontaneously breathing patient because of excess **carbon dioxide** production. It is essential to monitor closely the end-expired carbon dioxide and pulse oximetry in order to detect these symptoms.

Dantrolene is administered as soon as **MHS** is suspected and is continued until temperature begins to decline and other signs of **hypermetabolism** disappear. **Malignant hyperthermia** is a medical emergency. Anesthesia and the operative procedure should be concluded as quickly as possible and cooling mechanisms instituted. With the cooling mechanisms, it is important to avoid the **hypothermic** range. **Pulmonary hyperventilation** with **oxygen** is instituted simultaneously and **sodium bicarbonate** given intravenously to combat both **respiratory** and **metabolic acidosis.** It is important to monitor closely the **arterial blood gases** and **acid-base levels.** An osmotic diuretic is usually given to avoid **vasoconstrictive nephropathy** and **myoglobinemia-induced oliguria.** Late complications that may develop include **coma,** which may be irreversible, and a manifestation of **cerebral ischemia** and **hypoxia,** as well as **disseminated intravascular coagulopathy** and **vasoconstrictive nephropathy.**

Due to the tendency of this syndrome to run in families, it is essential that the anesthesiologist consider carefully the history of the patient or family members having anesthesia problems, as well as carefully monitoring the temperature of all patients under anesthesia. (40, 91)

ABBREVIATIONS

NEUROLOGIC
AD—Alzheimer's disease
BAPP—β-amyloid precursor protein
CNS—central nervous system
CP—cerebral palsy
CSF—cerebrospinal fluid
CVA—cerebrovascular accident
CVD—cerebrovascular disease
EEG—electroencephalogram
LP—lumbar puncture
MS—multiple sclerosis
PEG—pneumoencephalogram

ORGANIZATIONS
ABA—American Board of Anesthesiology
FDA—Food and Drug Administration

ANESTHESIA-RELATED
ACh—acetylcholine
Anes.—anesthesiology, anesthesia
C_{10}—decamethonium
C_3H_6—cyclopropane
C_2H_4—ethylene
$CHCl_3$—chloroform
C_2H_5Cl—ethyl chloride
C_2HCl_3—trichloroethylene (Trilene)
CO_2—carbon dioxide
HCl—hydrochloride
He—helium
N_2O—nitrous oxide
O_2—oxygen
Pent.—Pentothal

REVIEW GUIDE

Instructions: On the blank lines below, write the term that best fits each descriptive phrase or statement.

Example: Patient suffered from paralysis on both sides of his body. *diplegia*

Excision of a ganglion. _____

A benign tumor consisting of nerve fibers and mature ganglion cells. _____

Type of Schwann cell tumor of the vestibular portion of the eighth nerve, originating in the internal auditory canal. This is the most common tumor of the cerebellopontine angle. _____

Transection of a vagus nerve. _____

Surgical communication between fibers. _____

Incoordination of speech muscles affecting articulation. _____

Functional disorder of the seventh cranial nerve, which resulted in unilateral paralysis of facial muscles and distortion of taste perception. Etiology of this disorder is unknown. _____

Patient's awareness of a pending epileptic seizure. _____

Dilatation of an artery of the brain, resulting in a thinning and weakening of the arterial wall located at the middle cerebral artery. _____

Pathologic condition characterized by a dilatation of the brain and an abnormal accumulation of intraventricular cerebrospinal fluid. _____

Quick, shuffling steps and accelerated gait often seen in persons who have Parkinson's disease. _____

Degenerative disease of the lateral motor tracts of the spinal cord causing widespread muscle wasting, weakness, fasciculations, and a mild degree of spastic paralysis of the lower extremities. _____

A very painful involvement of the sciatic nerve. _____

Evoking a response by touch. _____

Paroxysms of lancinating pain of one or more areas innervated by the fifth cranial nerve. _____

Episodic attacks of severe dizziness caused by lesion of the inner ear (labyrinthine lesion) or the vestibular portion of the eighth nerve. _____

_____ is the partial division of the main sensory root of the trigeminal nerve adjacent to the pons.

Instructions: Define the following terms.

Example: analgesics—drugs that relieve pain.

antiemetic drug   hypercarbia

caudal anesthesia   hyperventilation

endotracheal anesthesia   hypoxia

epidural block   spinal anesthesia

Instructions: Figure 4.3 in the text shows how cerebrospinal fluid is secreted by choroid plexuses in the walls of the ventricles. For each line that extends from the figure below, provide the anatomic name of the site, as shown in the example.

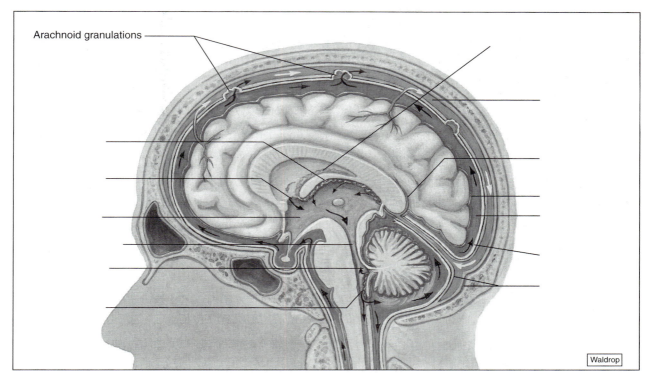

Arachnoid granulations

Waldrop

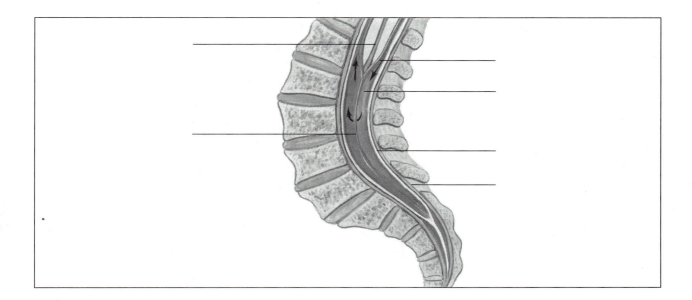

5

Musculoskeletal Disorders

BONES

ORIGIN OF TERMS

calcaneus (L)—heel bone
cancellus (L)—lattice
coxa (L)—hip bone
di- (G)—twice, double
dia- (G)—through, between
diploë (G)—fold
femur (L)—thigh
genu (L)—knee

ischio- (G)—hip
lacuna (L)—lake
medulla (L)—marrow
myel-, myelo- (G)—marrow
os (pl. *ossa*) (L)—bone
osteo- (G)—bone
pelvis (L)—basin
physis (G)—growth, generate

PHONETIC PRONUNCIATION OF SELECTED TERMS

callus	KALL′us
fibrosarcoma	FI′bro-sar-COE′mah
osteoblastoma	OS-tee-o-blas-TOE′mah
osteochondritis	OS-tee-o-kon-DRY′tis
osteoclasia	OS-tee-o-CLAY′ze-ah
osteolysis	OS-tee-o-LICE′sis
osteomalacia	OS-tee-o-mah-LAY′she-ah
osteomyelitis	OS-tee-o-mile-LIE′tis
osteotomy	OS-tee-OT′owe-me
plasmacytoma	PLAZ-mah-sight-TOE′mah
sequestrectomy	SEE-ques-TRECK′toe-me
trochanteric fracture	TRO-can-TER′ick FRACK′tur

ANATOMIC TERMS (74, 75) (SEE FIGS. 5.1 AND 5.2.)

bone, osseous tissue—hardest type of connective tissue, which provides a supporting framework for the body.

bone marrow, medulla—soft, central part of bone.

> *red marrow*—fills cancellous bone and manufactures red blood cells and hemoglobin.
> *yellow marrow*—fills the medullary cavity and contains fat cells.

cancellous bone—spongy bone composed of a loose latticework of bony trabeculae and bone marrow within the interspace.

compact bone, cortex of bone—solid bone rich in calcium.

diaphysis—shaft of long bone.

diploë—spongy bone between two tables of the skull.

endosteum—membrane lining the walls of the medullary cavity.

epiphysis (pl. epiphyses)—extremity of long bones and center of ossification for growing bone.

matrix of bone—collagenous fibers and a ground substance in which calcium is deposited.

medullary cavity—marrow-filled cavity within the shaft of long bones.

metaphysis—enlarged part of the shaft near the epiphysis of a long bone.

ossification—bone formation.

osteoblasts—bone-forming cells.

osteoclasts—bone-absorbing cells.

osteocytes—bone cells lying in lacunae with intercellular substance.

osteoid—resembling bone; young bone that has not undergone calcification, also the organic matrix of bone.

periosteum—outer covering of bone.

trabeculae—slender spicules or anastomosing bars of spongy bone.

trochanter—bony prominence of the upper extremity of the femur below the femoral neck.

> *major or greater trochanter*—large bony projection located externally and laterally between femoral neck and shaft.
>
> *minor or lesser trochanter*—conical bony prominence located medially and laterally at the junction of the femoral neck and shaft.

DIAGNOSTIC TERMS

bone neoplasms:

> *benign:*
>
> - *aneurysmal bone cyst*—solitary vascular lesion that usually arises from medullary or cancellous structures; affects the ends of the shaft and pushes outward, eroding soft and osseous tissue. Other possible sites of occurrence are the spine and scapula. (10, 16, 28)
> - *epidermoid cyst*—cyst filled with keratinaceous material and lined with squamous epithelium. Epidermoid cysts occur frequently in the skull and in the phalanges of the fingers. (10)
> - *ganglion cyst of bone*—intraosseous extensions of ganglia of local soft tissues that occur at the ends of long bones. The distal tibia is a common site for this cyst. (10, 30)
> - *giant cell tumor, benign*—osteolytic tumor containing numerous giant cells. It arises at the epiphysis and does not interfere with joint motion until late in its course. It may undergo malignant transformation or recur after removal. (11, 16, 28)
> - *hemangioma*—common benign vascular tumor of bone. These lesions are usually located in the vertebral body or skull. (10, 20)
> - *osteoblastoma*—benign lesion consisting of a collection of reparative bone reactions. It is found in the spine, where it may cause cord compression and paraplegia. (11, 28)
> - *osteochondromas*—cartilaginous nodules originating within the periosteum. The lesion consists of a bony mass generated by progressive endochondral ossification of a growing cartilaginous cap. Growth of the lesion usually parallels that of a person and ceases when skeletal maturity is reached. Osteochondromas may be found in any bone preformed in cartilage; however, they usually occur on the metaphysis of a long bone, near the epiphyseal plate. (10, 16, 28)
> - *osteoid osteoma*—small, benign, very painful tumor; found in almost any bone of the skeleton but occurs most frequently in the lower extremities. (10)

Figure 5.1 Skeleton, anterior view.

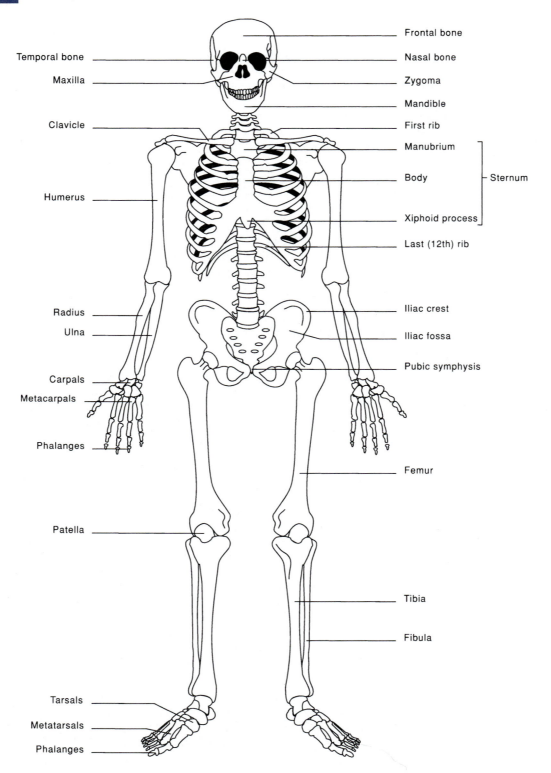

Frontal bone

Temporal bone

Nasal bone

Maxilla

Zygoma

Mandible

Clavicle

First rib

Manubrium

Body — Sternum

Humerus

Xiphoid process

Last (12th) rib

Radius

Iliac crest

Ulna

Iliac fossa

Pubic symphysis

Carpals

Metacarpals

Phalanges

Femur

Patella

Tibia

Fibula

Tarsals

Metatarsals

Phalanges

Figure 5.2   Skeleton, posterior view.

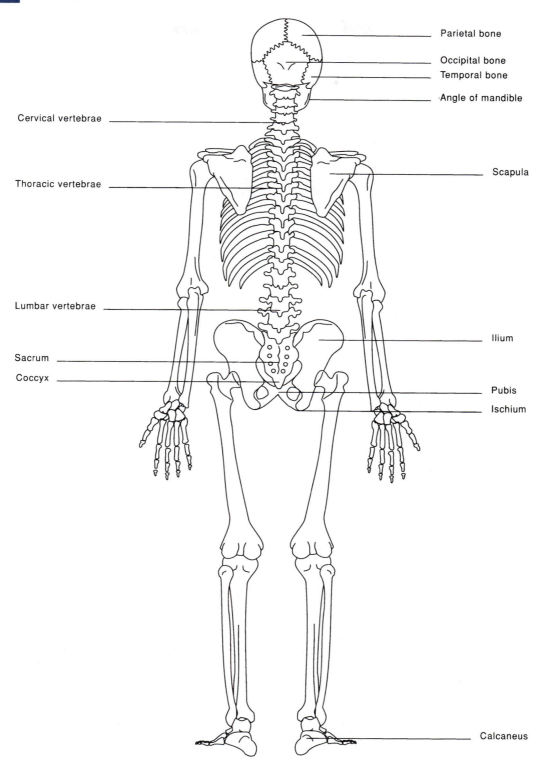

- Parietal bone
- Occipital bone
- Temporal bone
- Angle of mandible
- Cervical vertebrae
- Scapula
- Thoracic vertebrae
- Lumbar vertebrae
- Ilium
- Sacrum
- Coccyx
- Pubis
- Ischium
- Calcaneus

malignant:

- *Ewing's sarcoma*—malignant new growth originating in the shaft of long bones and spreading through the periosteum into soft tissues. Metastases occur early. The femur, tibia, humerus, fibula, and pelvic bones are frequently involved. (12, 16, 28, 34)
- *fibrosarcoma of the bone*—malignant tumor derived from bone marrow, metaphysis, or periosteum and found on the femur, humerus, and jawbone. (12, 16, 29)
- *myeloma, plasmacytoma*—malignant neoplasm derived from plasma cells and usually associated with abnormal protein metabolism. It may occur as:
  - *multiple myeloma*—malignant type of widespread bone destruction with gradual replacement of cancellous bone by neoplasm; usually seen in persons over 50 years old.
  - *osteogenic sarcoma*—highly malignant, vascular tumor usually involving the upper shaft of long bones, the pelvis, or knee. Metastases are common and life-threatening.
  - *solitary myeloma*—single lesions found in any location but most frequently in vertebral column. Back pain is severe. (12, 28, 34)

cervical rib—a supernumerary rib attached to cervical vertebra. (4)

coxa plana—flattening of the head of the femur. (See also **osteochondritis deformans juvenile, coxa plana, Legg-Calvé-Perthes' disease.**) (16)

coxa valga—widening of angle between shaft and neck of femur. (16, 47, 48)

coxa vara—diminishing of angle between shaft and neck of femur. (16, 47, 48)

epiphysitis, acute—inflammatory process of the epiphyseal region of a long bone, marked by tenderness and pain of the joint. (9)

fracture—broken bone. Long bone fractures are frequently associated with nerve injury. (See fig. 5.3.)

nonpenetrating or closed fracture—no external wound present.

penetrating or open fracture—an external wound communicating with the fracture.

Types of fractures include:

capillary—hairlike line of break.

comminuted—bone splintered into small fragments.

complicated—broken bone injuring adjacent structure; for example, fractured rib piercing the lung.

compound—an open wound leading down to the fracture.

depressed—bone broken inward, as in certain skull fractures.

fissured—fracture results in an incomplete longitudinal break.

greenstick—incomplete break that may be associated with bowing of shaft.

impacted—broken fragment wedged into another bony fragment.

oblique—occurs at an angle other than a right angle to the axis of the bone.

pathologic—spontaneous fracture caused by bone destruction in certain diseases: cancer, syphilis, osteomalacia, osteoporosis, and others.

simple—uncomplicated fracture with no open wound.

spiral—results from bone being twisted excessively.

transverse—break across the bone.

- *Colles' fracture*—transverse fracture of the radius above the wrist with displacement of the hand. (16, 43, 47, 54, 55, 56, 68)

fracture of hip—a break in the upper end of the femur. The two main types are:

femoral neck fracture—bone broken through the neck of the femur.

trochanteric fracture—bone broken below, around, or between the greater or lesser trochanters. (16, 55)

Figure 5.3 Types of traumatic fractures.

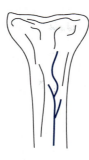

A *greenstick* fracture is incomplete, and the break occurs on the convex surface of the bend in the bone

A *fissured* fracture involves an incomplete longitudinal break

A *comminuted* fracture is complete and results in several bony fragments

A *transverse* fracture is complete, and the break occurs at a right angle to the axis of the bone

An *oblique* fracture occurs at an angle other than a right angle to the axis of the bone

A *spiral* fracture is caused by twisting a bone excessively

genu valgum—knock-knee. (9, 16)

genu varum—bowleg; deformity involving either tibia alone or femur, tibia, and fibula; seen in rickets and corrected by high doses of vitamin D. (9, 16)

osteitis deformans, Paget's disease of bone—slowly progressive disease occurring in advanced age; characterized by extensive bone destruction and followed almost immediately by abnormal bone repair of the weakened, deossified skeleton, which yields deformities and pathologic fractures. (13, 32, 59)

osteochondritis deformans juvenile, coxa plana, Legg-Calvé-Perthes' disease—self-limited disease in children aged 4 to 9; characterized by flattening of the femoral head and resulting in limping and restricted motion. (9, 16)

osteoclasia, osteolysis—resorption and destruction of osseous tissue. (16)

osteomalacia—softening of the bone caused by deficiency in calcium or phosphorus or both, which are needed for ossification of mature bones in adults. In children, the primary cause is lack of vitamin D and sunlight necessary for the normal absorption of the vitamin. (9, 42)

osteomyelitis—inflammation of the bone and bone marrow. Infective agents may be pyogenic bacteria, such as *Brucella, Salmonella, Staphylococcus aureus,* or other organisms. (16, 51, 78)

osteoporosis, porous bone—disorder of protein metabolism characterized by diffuse decrease of bone density and marked increase in porosity, which are most pronounced in the spine and pelvis. Recent research findings have linked a gene to the risk of osteoporosis. Two versions of the vitamin D receptor gene have been described. One is designated "B"—the one associated with weak bones; the other one is called "b"—the one for strong bones. Everyone inherits two copies of the gene, one from each parent. So it is possible to get a "bb" combination, or "BB" combination, or even a "Bb" combination in the genetic lottery. These findings indicate that vitamin D metabolism is extremely important in controlling the amount of bone that is found in the human skeleton. It is hoped that a test can be developed to identify persons at risk, even decades before the actual onset of the disease. (33, 41, 43, 45, 49)

renal (azotemic) osteodystrophy—bone disorder caused by defective mineralization, complicating chronic renal failure. (9)

rickets, rachitis—calcium and vitamin D deficiency of early childhood that leads to demineralization and deformities of bones. (9, 33)

sequestrum—dead bone separated from surrounding tissue. (5)

supernumerary bone—extra bone. (28)

vitamin D refractory rickets, familial hypophosphatemia—relatively common type of rickets in which abnormal phosphate loss and deficient mineralization are associated with renal tubule insufficiency. (33)

whiplash injury of neck—compression of cervical spine involving the bones, joints, and intervertebral disks. It results from a sudden throwing forward and then backward of the head, usually caused by a car accident when the collision is from the rear. (16)

OPERATIVE TERMS (SEE TABLE 5.1.)

amputation—partial or complete removal of limb necessitated by crushing injury, intractable pain, gangrene, vascular obstruction, or uncontrollable infection. (3, 35, 71, 72)

bone grafting, transplantation of bone—insertion of a bone graft.

> *autografting or autotransplantation of bone*—removal of bone from one site and implanting it at another site to promote bone union, to replace destroyed bone, or to immobilize joint in surgical fusion.

> *homografting or homotransplantation of bone*—surgical use of bone from bone bank obtained from amputations, ostectomies, or rib resections of nonmalignant, noninfectious cases. (69)

epiphyseal arrest—surgical procedure for retarding growth at the epiphysis by equalizing length of lower extremities. (3, 9)

epiphyseal stapling—temporary arrest of epiphyseal growth by stapling the epiphysis to control leg length discrepancy. (3)

epiphysiodesis—implanting bone grafts across the epiphyseal plate to secure immobilization of epiphysis. Operation is done for slipped femoral epiphysis following insertion of metal pins. (3)

exostectomy—removal of a benign bone tumor (exostosis), such as a bunion (hallux valgus). (52)

ostectomy—excision of a bone. (3)

osteoclasis—surgical refracture of a bone in case of malunion of broken parts. (4)

osteoplasty—reconstruction or repair of a bone.

osteotomy—surgical division or section of a bone. (9, 16, 52, 69)

replantation of an extremity—restorative surgery of an accidentally amputated limb to its functional capacity, including restoration of circulation by anastomoses of blood vessels, internal fixation of diaphyseal fracture of bone by intramedullary nail, with repair of nerves and tendons and debridement of devitalized tissue. Followed with closure by suturing undamaged soft tissue of dismembered limb to stump, and the application of split-thickness grafts for denuded skin areas. (15)

TABLE **5.1**	Some Orthopedic Conditions Amenable to Surgery		
Anatomic Site	*Diagnosis*	*Type of Surgery*	*Operative Procedures*
Carpal tunnel Transverse carpal ligament Median nerve	Carpal tunnel syndrome	Surgical division and partial excision of transverse carpal ligament Synovectomy of flexor synovialis	Complete section and partial removal of carpal ligament* Removal of thickened synovial membrane to decompress the median nerve
Spine	Scoliosis	Harrington's operation: instrumentation and fusion for correction of scoliosis	Implantation of metal rods and hooks directly on the spine, followed by fusion to provide distractive and compressive forces of spinal curve
Shoulder	Calcified deposits in rotator cuff	Curettement of rotator cuff	Split deltoid approach and scraping of cuff to remove deposits
Hip joint	Degenerative arthritis	Vitallium mold arthroplasty Austin Moore or Fred Thompson arthroplasty	Reconstruction of femoral head and placement of deep cup over femoral head Replacement of femoral head with hip prosthesis
Femur	Intertrochanteric fracture of femur	Internal fixation by insertion of hip nail (Jewett, Neufield, Holt, or Key type)	Nail driven over guide wire through femoral neck and into head of femur; side-plate fixed to shaft with screws
Femur	Transverse diaphyseal fracture of femur	Internal fixation by insertion of intramedullary nail (Kuntscher type or Lottes type)	Medullary nail driven over guide wire into medullary cavity occupying the entire canal
Femur	Fracture of femoral neck	Excision of femoral head and insertion of hip prosthesis (Fred Thompson or Austin Moore type) Internal fixation by insertion of Smith-Petersen nail	Removal of femoral head and most of neck with replacement by metal prosthesis Three-flanged nail driven over guide wire through femoral neck and head, then guide wire removed

*Many carpal tunnel repair techniques have been devised. Some of these are: endoscopic methods that include the two-portal procedures of Chow, Resnick, and Brown; the proximal uniportal techniques of Okutsu, Agee, and Menon; and the distal uniportal approach of Mizra. The limited open incision methods include the one-incision technique described by Naso and Bromley and the two-incision technique described by Biyani and Wilson. (41)

TABLE 5.1	(continued)		
Anatomic Site	*Diagnosis*	*Type of Surgery*	*Operative Procedures*
Knee	Chondromalacia of patella	Patellaplasty	Partial resection and plastic repair of patella
		Complete patellectomy	Removal of patella
Foot	Hallus valgus deformity	Keller operation	Resection of half of first phalanx of great toe and excision of bony prominence
Anterior cruciate ligament	Tear of anterior cruciate ligament; separation of anterior attachment	Reconstruction of torn anterior cruciate ligament	Repair of ligament by restoring the anterior attachment
Achilles tendon or Tendon calcaneus	Abnormal shortening of tendon calcaneus	Tenoplasty with lengthening of tendon calcaneus	Surgical repair of tendon

sequestrectomy—surgical removal of a piece of dead bone. (13)
surgical correction of fracture—this may be achieved by:
> *closed reduction*—manipulation and application of cast or application of splint or traction apparatus in selected cases when fracture ends are not in alignment. (54)
> *open reduction and internal fixation*—manipulation and
> - insertion of plate and screws
> - insertion of medullary nail for diaphyseal fractures (shaft of long bones); extraction of nail after bone union
> - insertion of a nail with a side plate, such as a Jewett nail, for trochanteric or femoral neck fractures
> - insertion of a hip prosthesis, Fred Thompson or Austin Moore type, in selected femoral neck fractures (54) (See fig. 5.4.)
>
> *simple immobilization*—application of cast or splint when fractured ends are in apposition. (48, 54, 68)

SYMPTOMATIC TERMS

callus—substance growing between ends of fractured bone that is converted into osseous tissue in the process of repair. (13)
crepitation—grating sound made by movement of fractured bones.
decalcification—removal of lime salts, especially from the bone. (73)
demineralization—deficiency or loss of bone minerals that occurs in osteoporosis, osteomalacia, cancer, or other disorders. (2, 49)
necrosis of bone—devitalization of osseous tissue; formation of dead bone. (17, 21, 73)
> *aseptic necrosis*—without infection.
> *avascular necrosis*—from deprivation of blood supply caused by fracture, loss of periosteum, exposure to radioactive substances, or other causes.
> *ischemic necrosis*—same as avascular necrosis of bone.

nidus—focal point from which a pathologic lesion develops. (73)
ostalgia, ostealgia, osteodynia—bone pain.
osteophyte—bony outgrowth (osseous excrescence). (2)
phantom limb pain—painful sensation felt by amputee, as if the limb were still intact. (71)
sequestration—process of bone necrosis resulting in dead bone. (73)

Figure 5.4 (a) Intertrochanteric fracture repaired by nail and side plate. (b) Insertion of femoral head prosthesis. (c) Medullary nailing of the femur.

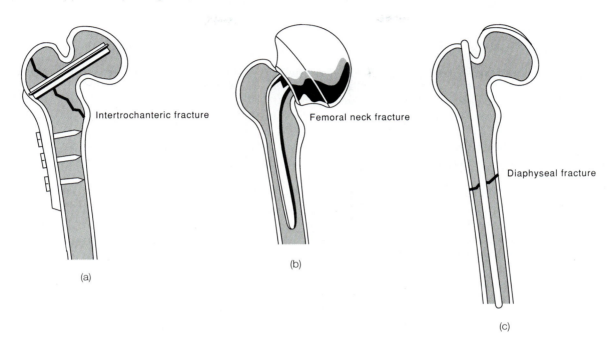

Intertrochanteric fracture

Femoral neck fracture

Diaphyseal fracture

(a)

(b)

(c)

JOINTS, BURSAE, CARTILAGES, AND LIGAMENTS

ORIGIN OF TERMS

arthr-, arthro- (G)—joint
bursa (L)—sac, saclike cavity
chondr-, chondro- (G)—cartilage, gristle
condyle (G)—rounded bone projection, knuckle
ligamentum (pl. *ligamenta*) (L)—that which ties, tissue that binds
scolio- (G)—twisted, crooked
spondyl-, spondylo- (G)—vertebra, spinal column
vertebro- (L)—vertebra, vertebral column

PHONETIC PRONUNCIATION OF SELECTED TERMS

ankylosis	ANG-ki-LOW′sis
arthrodesis	AR-throw-DE′sis
arthrotomy	ar-THROT′owe-me
bunionectomy	bun-yun-ECK′toe-me
chondritis	KON-DRY′tis
chondroblastoma	KON-dro-blas-TOE′mah
effusion, hemorrhagic	e-FUSE′shun, HEM-o-RAJ′ick
hemarthrosis	HEM-ar-THROW′sis
pseudogout	SUE′doe-gowt
pyogenic arthritis	PIE-o-GEN′ick ar-THRI′tis
rheumatoid arthritis	RUE′mah-toyd ar-THRI′tis
spondylolisthesis	SPON-dye-low-lis-THE′sis

ANATOMIC TERMS (1, 64, 76, 80) (SEE FIG. 5.5.)

acetabulum—cup-shaped socket on the external surface of the innominate bone in which the head of the femur lies.

articulation—joint

cartilaginous joint—bones united by fibrocartilage or hyaline cartilage.

fibrous joint—bones united by fibrous tissue.

synovial joint, diarthrodial joint—bones united by a joint capsule and ligaments. Cartilage covers the articular surface of the bones. The joint capsule is composed of a fibrous layer lined by synovial membrane.

bursa (pl. bursae)—connective tissue sac or saclike cavity filled with a viscid (glutinous or sticky) fluid and located at places in the tissues at which friction would otherwise develop.

intervertebral disc—fibrocartilage between the bodies of the vertebrae, composed of:

anulus fibrosus—outer fibrous ring encircling the nucleus pulposus.

nucleus pulposus—inner gelatinous mass.

ligaments—fibrous, connective tissue bands uniting articular ends of bones.

meniscus—fibrocartilage found in certain joints.

synovia—transparent alkaline viscid fluid resembling the white of an egg secreted by the synovial membrane, and contained in joint cavities, bursae, and tendon sheaths; also called **synovial fluid.**

synovial membrane—inner lining of a joint capsule, which secretes synovia.

volar—pertaining to the palm of the hand or sole of the foot.

DIAGNOSTIC TERMS

ankylosis—stiff joint. (16)

arthritis—inflammation of joints.

gouty arthritis—metabolic disorder, usually involving one joint (monarticular). Urate crystals are highly increased and found in various tissues. Pain is relieved by colchicine. (21, 82)

hypertrophic arthritis, osteoarthritis—degenerative condition of cartilage and enlargement of bone at the joint margins, occurring particularly in older persons. It often affects the terminal phalanges, knees, hips, and spine and results in contractures, deformities, and stiffness of affected joints. (6, 17, 18)

infectious arthritis, pyogenic arthritis, septic arthritis:

- *acute infectious arthritis*—acute inflammatory process affecting synovial and subchondral tissues and causing articular destruction. It is usually caused by pyogenic cocci such as gonococci, meningococci, pneumococci, staphylococci, and streptococci. (1, 21, 25, 51)
- *chronic infectious arthritis*—persistent infection of joint causing pain, swelling, restricted motion, and deformity. (79)

rheumatoid arthritis—produces constitutional symptoms in addition to painful, inflammatory, multiple joint involvement. (1, 17, 21, 25, 37, 73) Related terms include:

- *rheumatoid factor*—proteins belonging to a family of IgM antibodies that evolved in response to antigenic stimulation by an altered immunoglobulin. Consequently they are antiglobulins. Examples of associated tests to detect IgM rheumatoid factor are:
  - *bentonite flocculation test*—pooled human gamma globulin is used as antigen for coating particles.
  - *latex fixation test*—pooled human gamma globulin is absorbed to standard latex particles.
  - *Rheumanosticon*—a rapid slide test for the detection of the rheumatoid factor is performed on serum or whole blood. The rheumatoid factor reacts with the coating material, causing a visual agglutination of the inert latex particles.

Figure 5.5 Anatomy of the shoulder, elbow, hip, and knee joints.

Shoulder joint

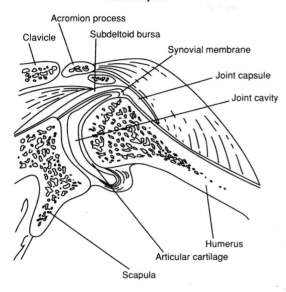

Acromion process
Clavicle
Subdeltoid bursa
Synovial membrane
Joint capsule
Joint cavity
Humerus
Articular cartilage
Scapula

Elbow joint

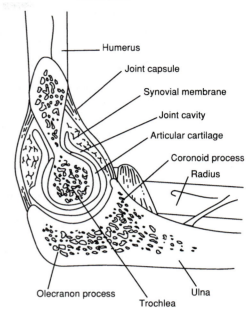

Humerus
Joint capsule
Synovial membrane
Joint cavity
Articular cartilage
Coronoid process
Radius
Olecranon process
Trochlea
Ulna

Hip joint

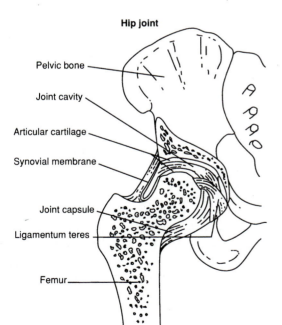

Pelvic bone
Joint cavity
Articular cartilage
Synovial membrane
Joint capsule
Ligamentum teres
Femur

Knee joint

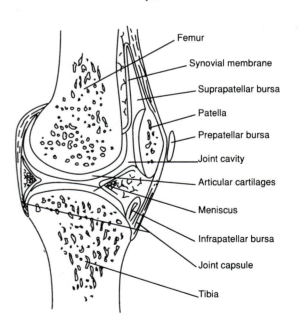

Femur
Synovial membrane
Suprapatellar bursa
Patella
Prepatellar bursa
Joint cavity
Articular cartilages
Meniscus
Infrapatellar bursa
Joint capsule
Tibia

juvenile rheumatoid arthritis—disorder of chronic synovitis beginning during the childhood years (under 16 years of age). Diagnosis depends on exclusion of other disease conditions known to be associated with chronic synovitis. Juvenile rheumatoid arthritis may persist in at least one joint for a minimum of 6 weeks. This process may be systemic, with the presence of spiking fevers, evanescent rash, and other extra-articular disease. Joint involvement in the disease process may range from a few joints to five or more joints. The term *Still's disease*, which was formerly used to describe this condition, is no longer used. (16, 17, 21)

Marie-Strümpell spondylitis, ankylosing spondylitis—painful inflammatory joint diease characterized by progressive erosion, stiffening, and hardening of bone adjacent to the sacroiliac joints. The condition is called **spondylodiscitis** when this erosive and hardening process extends into the intervertebral disc and adjacent bone. (67)

traumatic arthritis—a group of disorders resulting from single or repetitive trauma to joints: (16, 61)

- *acute synovitis, traumatic synovitis*—this may result from a single episode of articular trauma to the synovial membrane of a joint and may be associated with hemarthrosis and sprains. The articular cartilage is intact.
- *disruptive trauma of joint*—the major supporting structures have ruptured and the articular cartilage is damaged. Meniscal tears, intra-articular fractures, and severe sprains may be present.
- *post-traumatic osteoarthritis*—residual damage from disruptive trauma may lead to restricted mobility, deformity, and articular instability.
- *repetitive articular trauma*—chronic arthritis of the affected joints may develop due to occupational hazards or sports.
- *other types of trauma*—arthropathy may develop following decompression, radiation, frostbite, or the like.

arthropathy—any disease of the joints.

Baker's cyst, popliteal cyst—synovial fluid-filled, popliteal lesion found in muscles and other tissues, or near a joint in advanced osteoarthritis. Usually, Baker's cyst may be produced by either a herniation of the synovial membrane through the posterior part of the capsule of the knee or by the escape of fluid through the normal communication of a bursa with the knee, that is, either the semimembranous or the medial gastrocnemius bursa. Careful arthroscopic evaluation should be performed before excision of a popliteal cyst. (48)

bursitis—inflammation of a bursa. (10, 21, 47, 48)

calcium pyrophosphate dihydrate (CPPD) deposition disease—presence of CPPD crystal deposition in articular cartilage, synovium, and periarticular ligaments and tendons is most commonly seen in the elderly population. The cause is uncertain. The knee is affected most often, but other sites involved may include the wrist, shoulder, ankle, elbow, and hands. CPPD crystals were discovered in synovial fluids of patients who had acute goutlike attacks **(pseudogout).** CPPD crystals in the synovial fluids are detected by compensated polarized light microscopy. The radiologic appearance of calcified cartilage is called **chondrocalcinosis.** (21, 24)

chondritis—inflammation of a cartilage. (16)

destructive coxarthropathy—painful inflammatory disability of hip joint. Joint motion is moderately impaired.

dislocation—displacement of a bone from its natural position in a joint. (16)

hallux malleus—hammer toe. (3, 52)

hallux valgus (bunion)—lateral deflection of great toe to outer side of foot and subsequent development of bony prominence (bunion). In addition to the deflection of the great toe, this condition is frequently accompanied by deformities of the lesser toes. (52)

hallux varus—deflection of great toe to inner side of foot. (52)

hemarthrosis—bloody effusion in a joint cavity, likely to occur in hemophiliacs. (16, 21)

internal derangement of knee joint—refers to various joint lesions that interfere with motion (locking, snapping, buckling) due to atrophy of thigh muscles, tenderness or pain, and joint swelling. Some leading causes are tears of menisci, ligaments, and patellar or quadriceps tendons, loose bodies, fracture, or chondromalacia of patellae. (39, 61)

kyphosis—hunchback; abnormal posterior curvature of thoracic spine.

lordosis—hollow back; anterior convexity of lower spine.

neoplasms:
> *benign:* (10, 11, 16)
> - *chondroblastoma*—benign, vascular, cartilaginous tumor arising from the epiphysis of a long bone.
> - *hemartoma, benign mesenchymoma*—tumor containing multiple mesenchymal tissues, which have bizarre roentgenographic and histologic features and may be mistaken for malignant connective-tissue tumors. These tumors appear most often in bones, are hard to distinguish from other connective-tissue tumors, and tend to regress after puberty.
>
> *malignant:* (12, 13, 16, 32)
> - *chondrosarcoma*—malignant tumor derived from cartilage. These tumors usually affect the femur, pelvis, tibia, humerus, scapula, and ribs.
> - *chordoma*—originates from embryonic notochordal remnants. Ninety percent of tumors occur in the upper and lower ends of the vertebral column. Benign and malignant distinction is clinically and histologically difficult. Cellular differentiation, anaplasia, and mitotic activity do not relate to the usual indolent and progressive course, with presence for years without metastasis. When metastases do occur, it is usually late in the growth process.
> - *synovioma, synovial sarcoma*—highly malignant fibroblastic sarcoma, originating in periarticular structures and occurring in older children and young adults. The tumor presents as a slow-growing mass near a joint and spreads along tissue planes. The most common site of visceral metastases is the lung.

painful shoulder, cervicobrachial pain syndromes—articular or extra-articular disorders characterized by tenderness, moderate to agonizing pain, and limitation of motion in the shoulder girdle, neck, and arm. All or some of these symptoms are present in:
> *adhesive capsulitis, adhesive bursitis, frozen shoulder, periarthritis of the shoulder joint*—adhesions within the bursa, articular tendosynovitis, and calcareous deposits causing stiffness and atrophic changes. (16, 20, 21)
>
> *carpal tunnel syndrome*—painful condition resulting from a compression of the median nerve within the carpal tunnel, as evidenced by a flattening or circular constriction of the nerve. Tingling, aching, or burning pain in fingers, radiating to forearm and shoulder; may be constant or episodic and aggravated by strenuous, repetitive manual activity, especially in persons whose work requires repeated forceful finger and wrist flexion and extension. (16, 20, 36, 83)
>
> *cervical spondylosis, cervical disk disease*—degenerative disorder of cervical disk, characterized by progressive thinning of the joint cartilage; spinal cord and nerve root compression, resulting from extrusion of the nucleus pulposus; and subsequent pain radiating to the back of the neck and head, shoulder, and arm. (16)
>
> *epicondylalgia, epicondylitis, tennis elbow*—pain syndrome primarily affecting the lateral and median regions of the elbow and radiating to the upper arm and forearm. It is accentuated by repetitive grasping. (15)
>
> *hand-shoulder syndrome*—peculiar clinical entity in which pain radiates from shoulder to fingertips. The patient spontaneously immobilizes the affected extremity, which leads to atrophy and edema of the hand. Later overactivity of sympathetic nerves results in a

sweaty, cold, painful hand, followed by stiffness and fibrosis of joints. Syndrome may occur in myocardial ischemia, following myocardial infarction, and infrequently in bronchogenic carcinoma. (21)

supraclavicular nerve entrapment syndrome—compression of middle branch of supraclavicular nerve at its passage through the bone canal in the clavicle, causing pain and numbness. Neuralgia can be relieved by decompression of the nerve. (2)

supraspinatus syndrome—disorder caused by adhesions, calcium deposits, or tears in rotator cuff, resulting in a painful shoulder, limited motion, muscle atrophy, and spasm. (2)

Reiter's syndrome—triad of inflammatory states—urethritis (nongonococcal), conjunctivitis, and arthritis—probably due to chlamydial or mycoplasmal infection. (16, 25)

scoliosis—lateral spinal curvature. (19, 21, 57)

skeletal dysplasias—disturbances of bony growth, congenital or inherited; most severe if present in early infancy; less harmful if developing in adult life, causing progressive destruction of osseous tissue as a result of chondroid and osteoid abnormalities. Examples include:

dysplasias caused by impaired chondroid production—probably a metabolic defect of the maturation of chondroblasts (immature cartilage cells).

- *achondroplasia*—congenital, hereditary abnormality of chondroblastic cell growth at the epiphyses; subsequent development of a peculiar dwarfism.
- *enchondromatosis, dyschondroplasia, Ollier's disease*—a disorder affecting the growth plate in which hypertrophic cartilage is not resorbed and ossified in a normal manner. Masses of cartilage are present in the metaphyses in close association with the growth plate in very young children, but in the diaphyses in teenagers and adults. The usual sites of involvement are ends of long bones and the pelvis.
- *osteochondromatosis, hereditary multiple exostoses*—osteochondromas or bony outgrowths from the ends of long bones that may be associated with deformities of the knee, wrists, elbow, and long bones, or other defects. (10, 32)

dysplasias caused by impaired osteoid production—group of developmental abnormalities characterized by the presence of insufficient, excessive, or immature osteoid. Examples include:

- *fibrous dysplasia of bone, Albright's syndrome*—metabolic bone disease characterized by rapid resorption of bone and fibrous displacement of marrow, distortion of one or several bones, brownish pigmentation of skin, and precocious puberty in girls. (13, 34)
- *osteogenesis imperfecta, brittle bones*—inherited connective tissue disorder affecting the skeleton and occurring as:
  - *osteogenesis imperfecta congenita*—severe form that develops prenatally and may be fatal in infancy. (9)
  - *osteogenesis imperfecta tarda*—moderately severe form that develops in childhood. Clinical features include fragility of bones, fracture proneness at an early age, multiple pathologic fractures, deformities of long bones, excessive digital laxity, white or blue sclerae, deafness, a peculiar squeaky voice, and a crackling laugh. (9)
  - *osteopetrosis, marble bones, Albers-Schönberg disease*—rare congenital bone disorder thought to be caused by a persistence of primitive chondro-osteoid that interferes with its replacement by mature bone. Since osteoid formation is insufficient, the bones are fracture prone, marblelike, and chalklike. (34)
  - *spondyloepiphyseal dysplasia*—disorder in which growth abnormalities occur in various bones, including vertebrae, pelvis, carpal, and tarsal bones, and the epiphyses of tubular bones. (34)

spondylolisthesis—forward slipping of a lumbar vertebra on the adjacent vertebra below, usually associated with pelvic deformity. (21, 81)

spondylosis—ankylosis of vertebrae; also any degenerative lesion of the spine. (16)
sprain—injury to joint with tearing of tendons and ligaments. (16)
subluxation—incomplete dislocation.
talipes—clubfoot:
>   *equinus*—forefoot touches ground; walking on toes.
>   *planus*—arch broken; entire sole rests on ground.
>   *valgus*—foot everted; inner side of sole touches ground.
>   *varus*—foot inverted; outer side of sole rests on ground. (3, 16)

vertebral injuries—trauma to the spine resulting in compression fractures of the vertebrae, and fractures and dislocations or flexion fractures of the spine associated with minimal spinal cord damage. (81)

OPERATIVE TERMS (SEE TABLE 5.1.)

arthroclasia—surgical breaking of a stiff joint.
arthrodesis, artificial ankylosis—surgical fixation of a joint to immobilize it. (3, 14, 16, 21)
arthrolysis—freeing the joint from fibrous bands or excess cartilage to restore its mobility. (2)
arthroplasty—surgical repair of a joint. The hip, knee, elbow, and temporomandibular joints are best suited for reconstruction.

>   *arthroplasties of the hip joint:* (See fig. 5.6.)
>   - *Charnley low-friction arthroplasty*—total hip arthroplasty or total hip replacement for rheumatoid arthritis or any type of destructive hip disease. The prosthesis has two components: (1) an acetabular cup or socket of high-density polyethylene and (2) a femoral component of vitallium or stainless steel, consisting of a small femoral head for low friction that lodges in the socket and a prosthetic stem embedded in the intramedullary canal of the femur. Acrylic cement is used to seat the acetabular cup and prosthetic stem. The cement provides rigid fixation and stability. Modifications of Charnley total hip replacement are those of McKee and Watson-Farrar. (22)
>   - *Colonna capsular arthroplasty*—surgery for congenital dislocation of the hip. This procedure retains the gliding mechanisms between the displaced head of the femur and its capsule. The acetabulum is usually deepened and enlarged. (22)
>   - *Moore or Thompson prosthetic arthroplasty*—surgical repair of arthritic hip including amputation of head and neck of femur, acetabular remodeling and reconstruction, and seating of prosthesis in femoral shaft and acetabulum. (22)
>   - *vitallium-mold arthroplasty*—molding a joint, interposing a joint, and interposing a nonirritating substance between bony surfaces to improve joint function and lessen pain in rheumatoid arthritis and bony or fibrous ankylosis. Interposition of material between joint surfaces, such as autogenous fascia or inert metal (vitallium), also prevents recurrence of ankylosis. (22)

>   *arthroplasties of the knee:* (See fig. 5.7.)
>   - *compartmental total-knee arthroplasty*—reconstruction of the articulating surfaces limited to the affected compartment of the knee joint and correction of deformities in the presence of intact ligaments, providing joint stability. (64, 70)
>   - *geomedic (or geometric) total-knee arthroplasty*—removal of sufficient bone and insertion of femoral and tibial components of the geomedic prosthesis for total knee replacement. (70)
>   - *patellofemoral joint replacement*—conservative surgical procedure in which a minimum of diseased bone is removed, a knee implant for resurfacing the patellofemoral joint is inserted, and any interference with patellar ligaments is avoided to safeguard joint stability. (70)

Figure 5.6   (a) Acetabular component with socket for prosthetic head of femoral component. (b) Anterior/posterior view of hip after replacement arthroplasty.

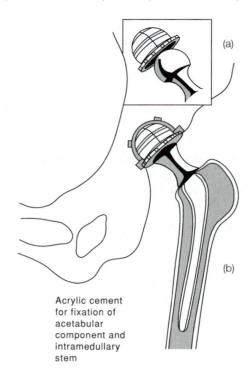

(a)

(b)

Acrylic cement
for fixation of
acetabular
component and
intramedullary
stem

Figure 5.7   Arthroplasties of the knee: total replacement. (a) lateral view; (b) anterior/posterior view.

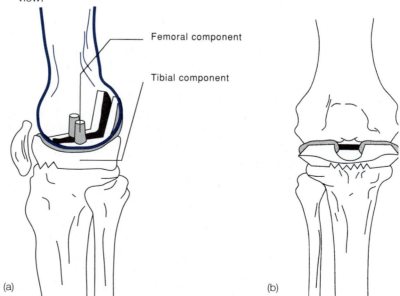

Femoral component

Tibial component

(a)

(b)

- *polycentric total-knee arthroplasty*—replacement of the involved articulating surfaces of the tibial plateaus and femoral condyles to relieve pain and restore joint motion and stability. (70)
- *Walldius arthroplasty*—salvage operation for severe pain and instability of the knee joint in rheumatoid arthritis using a vitallium hinge prosthesis (Walldius) with 10-centimeter (cm) stems. Insertion of the prosthesis is done by the anterior transverse approach with retention of the patella and usually without acrylic cement, since it fails to achieve joint stabilization. (70)

arthroplasties of the shoulder:

- *partial shoulder arthroplasty, hemireplacement of shoulder*—replacement of the articular surface of the humeral head by a Neer prosthesis in the presence of an intact rotator cuff and glenoid cavity. (60)
- *total shoulder arthroplasty, total glenohumeral joint replacement*—replacement of both the head of the humerus and the glenoid fossa in the presence of a massive tear or other defect in the rotator cuff. (60)

arthroplasty of temporomandibular joint—surgical breaking of a stiff joint to relieve disabling ankylosis caused by rheumatic, degenerative, infectious, or traumatic arthritis. The mandibular condyle is resected and remodeled. (44)

arthroscopy—endoscopic examination of the magnified joint, enhanced by fiberoptic light transmission; provides for joint irrigation to relieve pain from injury or arthritis. The procedure is primarily indicated in the detection of articular and meniscal lesions or other internal derangements of the knee. (38, 39, 40)

arthrotomy—surgical opening of a joint.

bunionectomy, surgical correction of valgus deformity—removal of bony prominence (bunion) from medial aspect of the first metatarsal head. (52)

chondrectomy—removal of a cartilage.

chondroplasty—plastic repair of a cartilage.

Harrington instrumentation and fusion—surgery for correcting scoliosis and spondylolisthesis. Metal rods and hooks are directly implanted on the spine. Articular fusion is achieved by inserting bone grafts from the ilium. (19, 63)

laminectomy: (62)

bilateral or total laminectomy—involves removal of both lamina and the spinous process.

unilateral laminectomy—involves removal of the lamina on one side of the spine.

laminotomy—refers to removal of only the inferior margin of the lamina. (62)

meniscal allotransplantation—replacement of meniscal structures with donor tissues harvested under aseptic surgical procedures. Meniscal allografts are utilized to provide a replacement of a normal structure and provide normal functions of a meniscus. All donor menisci should follow the criteria established by the American Association of Tissue Banks. (53)

synovectomy—partial or total removal of a synovial membrane lining of a joint capsule. (17)

SYMPTOMATIC TERMS

arthralgia, arthrodynia—joint pain.

capsular laceration—tear of a joint capsule. (2)

crepitus, articular—the grating of joints. (17)

detachment of cartilage—separation of cartilaginous material from a joint. Loose bodies limit motion. (2)

effusion, hemorrhagic—bleeding into synovial sac. (2, 73)

effusion, synovial—overproduction of joint fluid. (16)

Heberden's nodes—hard nodules at the distal phalangeal joints of the fingers in osteoarthritis. (6)

lipping—liplike bony growths at the joints in osteoarthritis; for example, the marginal lipping of the acetabular rim and head of the femur in degenerative hip disease. (6)

lumbago—dull ache in the lumbar region of the back. (21)

rheumatoid nodules—subcutaneous nodules located over bony prominences, such as the elbow or back of the heel. They exert pressure and are present in advanced rheumatoid arthritis. (1, 2)

spur—projection from a bone. (2)

tophus (pl. **tophi**)—deposit of urate crystals in subcutaneous tissue near a joint. (1, 2)

DIAPHRAGM, MUSCLES, AND TENDONS

ORIGIN OF TERMS

fascia (L)—band

leio- (G)—smooth

my-, myo- (G)—muscle

rhabdo- (G)—rod, striated

teno-, tenonto- (G)—tendon

tendo- (L)—tendon

PHONETIC PRONUNCIATION OF SELECTED TERMS

contracture	kon-TRACK′tur
diaphragmatic hernia	DI′ah-frag-MAT′ick HER′nee-ah
leiomyoma	LIE-o-my-OWE′mah
muscular dystrophy	MUS′koo-lar DIS′tro-fee
myoma	my-O′mah
myoplasty	MY′o-PLAS-tee
myosarcoma	MY-o-sar-COE′mah
polymyositis	POL-e-my-o-SIGH′tis
tenosynovitis	TEN-o-sin-o-VI′tis

ANATOMIC TERMS (77) (SEE FIGS. 5.8 AND 5.9.)

aponeurosis—flat sheet of fibrous tissue that usually serves as an attachment for a muscle.

diaphragm—the muscular, dome-shaped septum between the thoracic and abdominal cavities.

fascia—sheet of connective tissue that covers, supports, and separates muscles.

insertion of muscle—end attached to bone or cartilage that moves when the muscle contracts (or shortens).

muscle—contractile tissue composed of units that have the power to contract when stimulated by a nerve impulse.

origin of muscle—end attached to the bone or cartilage that does not move when the muscle contracts (or shortens).

tendons—bands of fibrous tissue that attach muscles to bones.

DIAGNOSTIC TERMS

carpoptosia—wristdrop.

claudication—limping, intermittent type caused by ischemia of leg muscles. (2)

contracture—permanent shortening of one or more muscles caused by paralysis, spasm, or scar formation.

   Dupuytren's contracture—shrinkage of palmar fascia, resulting in flexion deformity of one or more fingers. (27, 30)

   Volkmann's contracture—flexion deformity of the wrist and fingers that may be caused by circulatory interference from a tight cast. (26)

disuse atrophy—muscle wasting caused by immobilization. (30)

Figure 5.8 Skeletal muscles, anterior view.

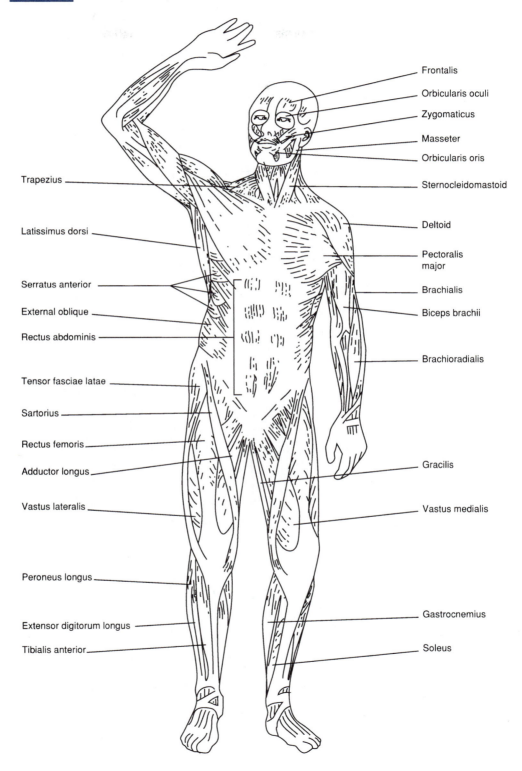

Frontalis

Orbicularis oculi

Zygomaticus

Masseter

Orbicularis oris

Sternocleidomastoid

Deltoid

Pectoralis major

Brachialis

Biceps brachii

Brachioradialis

Gracilis

Vastus medialis

Gastrocnemius

Soleus

Trapezius

Latissimus dorsi

Serratus anterior

External oblique

Rectus abdominis

Tensor fasciae latae

Sartorius

Rectus femoris

Adductor longus

Vastus lateralis

Peroneus longus

Extensor digitorum longus

Tibialis anterior

Figure 5.9 Skeletal muscles, posterior view.

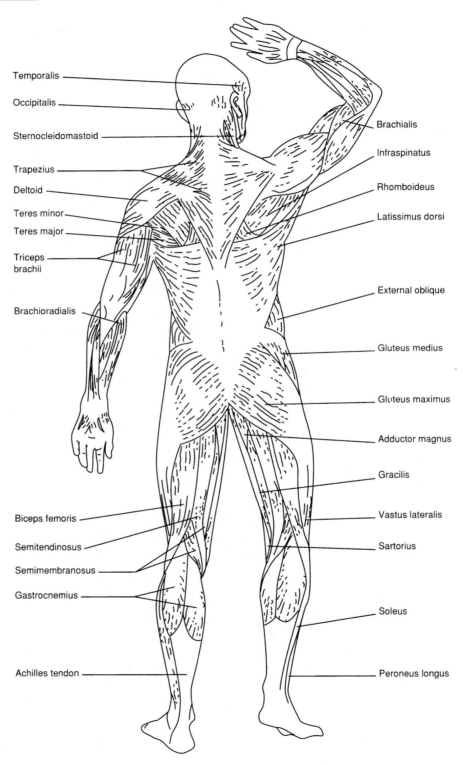

Temporalis

Occipitalis

Sternocleidomastoid

Trapezius

Deltoid

Teres minor

Teres major

Triceps brachii

Brachioradialis

Brachialis

Infraspinatus

Rhomboideus

Latissimus dorsi

External oblique

Gluteus medius

Gluteus maximus

Adductor magnus

Gracilis

Vastus lateralis

Sartorius

Biceps femoris

Semitendinosus

Semimembranosus

Gastrocnemius

Soleus

Achilles tendon

Peroneus longus

fascitis, fasciitis—inflammation of the fascia.

graphospasm—writer's cramp.

hiatus hernia, diaphragmatic hernia—protrusion of an abdominal organ, usually a portion of the stomach, through the esophageal opening of the diaphragm. (46)

muscular dystrophy—comprises a group of chronic diseases whose most prominent characteristic is progressive degeneration of skeletal musculature leading to weakness, atrophy, contracture, deformity, and progressive disability. Muscular dystrophy is most often inherited; however, in approximately 30% of patients with Duchenne's muscular dystrophy, the disease occurs as a result of spontaneous gene mutation (it occurs without any carrier state). There are two types of sex-linked muscular dystrophies: **Duchenne's muscular dystrophy (DMD)** and **Becker's muscular dystrophy (BMD).** Both the DMD and BMD gene has been identified on the X chromosome. These two types are similar in that the pattern of muscle weakness progresses, but Becker's muscular dystrophy begins later in life and progresses more slowly and is not as common as the Duchenne's type. The outcome of the two diseases is the same: a slow, progressive weakness, usually to wheelchair confinement and a premature death. Myocardial involvement is common in Duchenne's muscular dystrophy and is usually the cause of death; myocardial involvement is uncommon in Becker's type. (7, 19, 57)

myasthenia gravis—chronic neuromuscular disorder that has an autoimmune basis and is characterized by a 7 S gamma globulin antibody (AChR-ab) directed against the nicotinic acetylcholine recepter (AChR) of the neuromuscular junction. The disorder is manifested by weakness, usually affecting the ocular muscles, resulting in bilateral ptosis of eyelids and sleepy appearance. The myasthenic facies is apathetic and expressionless. There may be involvement of the muscles of speech, mastication, and swallowing. When the chest muscles are affected, dyspnea may develop. Infrequently, weakness of the legs interferes with walking. Symptoms fluctuate in severity, ranging from exacerbations to remissions. (58)

myositis—inflammatory process of muscles. (5)

neoplasms:

> *benign:*
> - *leiomyoma*—benign smooth-muscle tumor. (13)
> - *myoma*—benign muscular tumor. (13)
> - *rhabdomyoma*—striated-muscle tumor. (13)
>
> *malignant:*
> - *myosarcoma*—malignant muscular tumor. (13)
> - *rhabdomyosarcoma*—malignant tumor of striated muscle. (13)

paralysis—loss of sensation and voluntary movements, either temporary or permanent.

> *flaccid*—lower motor neuron involvement.
>
> *spastic*—upper motor neuron involvement. (16)

polymyositis—primary myopathy characterized by muscle weakness in pelvic and shoulder girdles, and distal lower and upper extremities, and muscle pain or tenderness. It may be associated with connective-tissue disease. (66)

tenosynovitis, tendosynovitis—inflammation of a tendon and its synovial sheath. (83)

torticollis, wryneck—contraction of a sternocleidomastoid muscle, drawing the head to one side and causing asymmetry of the face; may be congenital or acquired. (4)

OPERATIVE TERMS (SEE TABLE 5.1.)

myoplasty—surgical repair of a muscle—for example, by free muscle graft or pedicle graft. (2)

myorrhaphy—suture of a muscle.

myotasis—stretching of a muscle.

tenodesis—suture of end of tendon to skeletal attachment (tendon torn at point of insertion). (8)

tendoplasty—surgical repair of tendon. (4, 39)

tenosynovectomy—resection or removal of a tendon sheath.

SYMPTOMATIC TERMS

clonic spasm—rapid, repeated muscular contractions. (2)
cramp—prolonged, intense spasm of one muscle. (2)
hyperkinesia—purposeless, excessive involuntary movements. (73)
hypotonia—reduced muscle tension associated with muscular atrophy. (2)
rigidity, rigor—stiffness, muscular hardness. (2)
tonic spasm—excessive, prolonged muscular contractions. (2)
tremors—oscillating, rhythmic movements of muscle groups. (2)

ORAL READING PRACTICE

PAGET'S DISEASE OF BONE

Paget's disease of bone (**osteitis deformans**) is a peculiar bone disorder with an insidious onset, an **asymptomatic** early phase, a plateau of apparent stationary involvement, perhaps lasting years, followed by progressive disease and complications that may end in death. The **etiology** of **Paget's disease** is unknown. It is not a metabolic disturbance, since it primarily attacks bones under pressure of weight bearing, leaving those of the upper extremity relatively untouched. An exception is the skull, which shows **roentgenographic** evidence of **osteoporosis circumscripta,** so termed because **osteoporotic** changes are limited to circumscribed area. A lesion of **decalcification** forms, particularly in the outer **cranial** table. Gradually, dense areas resembling tufts of cotton appear in the **rarefied** lesion, and the **demarcation** between **diploë,** the two cranial tables, becomes indistinct. Another serious neurologic complication that may result from overgrowth of pagetic bone at the base of the skull (**platybasia**) is due to compression of the **brain stem.**

The incidence of Paget's disease of bone is highest in advancing years and greater in males than females. It is a rather common affliction, affecting 3% of persons over the age of 40. The pathologic characteristics comprise concurrent processes of **osteoclastic** and **osteoblastic activity,** resulting in **marked bone destruction** and **rapid bone repair, architectural abnormality of new bone,** and **increased vascularity** and **fibrosis.** Instead of normal resorption and replacement of bone, metabolic processes are disorganized and irregular. New bone may undergo **osteolysis** as soon as it is formed. **Osteoblasts** produce coarse, distorted **trabeculae** that **anastomose** in a peculiar fashion, exhibiting a **mosaic design.**

In **advanced Paget's disease,** the patient's **contour** portrays the influence of pathologic skeletal changes. The spine is **kyphotic,** stature shortened, position crouched, and abdomen **pendulous.** Pain develops with progressive bone involvement and varies from dull ache to intermittent or persistent **ostealgia.** Also, pain may be caused by involvement of the hip joint resembling **degenerative joint disease,** with varying degrees of **intrapelvic protrusion** of the **acetabulum, varus deformity** of the **femur,** and anterolateral bowing of the shaft. The **anterolateral bowing of the legs** results in a **waddling, slow gait.** The face appears small compared to the protruding skull, which characteristically shows **bitemporal enlargement.** Paget's disease produces one type of **spinal stenosis** that appears to respond to treatment with **calcitonin. Hearing loss deficits** can occur because of pagetic bone involvement of the **ossicles** of the inner ear or of the **cochlear** bone; they can also result from impingement of the **eighth cranial nerve** by pagetic bone narrowing the **auditory foramen.**

Fractures occur frequently, heal rapidly, and are the most common complication of **Paget's bone disease.** They may be caused by trivial incidents, such as tripping on stairs or turning in bed. The two most common sites of fracture are the **subtrochanteric area** and the **upper shaft area of the femur. Total hip arthroplasty** is usually the procedure of choice. **Heterotopic bone formation** may occur as a postoperative complication; however, the administration of **calcitonin** before and after surgery tends to decrease the **osteoclastic activity** and thereby hopefully reduce the risk of loosening secondary to inadequate support by **osteoporotic bone.**

The patient with Paget's disease, immobilized because of fracture or intercurrent disease, is likely to develop **hypercalciuria, renal calculi,** and **hypercalcemia.** Since bone repair is markedly decreased during immobilization, **osteoporosis** resulting from disuse becomes problematic. Bone destruction persists unabated, thus liberating an excessive amount of calcium, which is spilled into urine instead of being deposited in bone. This may lead to **nephrolithiasis** and serious **sequelae.** If the kidneys are unable to handle the high surplus of calcium, **hypercalcemia** is likely to develop. It is signaled by dryness of mouth and nose, nausea, and vomiting. Untreated, the **prognosis** may be death. Techniques of measuring disappearance rates of injected **radioisotopes** of **calcium** or **strontium** have shown that rates of bone turnover may be increased enormously in patients with active Paget's disease, occasionally more than 20 times normal. The magnitude of the increase varies with the extent and activity of the disease.

Malignant degeneration of diseased bone is a constant threat. Whenever **osteogenic sarcoma, chondrosarcoma,** malignant **fibrous histiocytoma, fibrosarcoma,** or **malignant osteoclastoma** develop, the patient has probably reached the terminal phase of life. **Palliative measures** must be instituted to bring relief of **ostealgia** and other distressing symptoms. (2, 13, 32, 50, 59, 73)

ABBREVIATIONS

GENERAL

AP—anteroposterior
ASS—anterior superior spine
C_1—first cervical vertebra
C_2—second cervical vertebra
EMG—electromyogram
FX—fracture
IM—intramuscular
IS—intercostal space
L_1—first lumbar vertebra
L_2—second lumbar vertebra

LIF—left iliac fossa
LLE—left lower extremity
LOM—limitation of motion
LUE—left upper extremity
RLE—right lower extremity
ROM—range of motion
RUE—right upper extremity
T_1—first thoracic vertebra
T_2—second thoracic vertebra

AMPUTATIONS AND PROSTHESES

AE—above the elbow
AK—above the knee
BE—below the elbow

BK—below the knee
PTB—patellar tendon bearing (prosthesis)
SACH—solid ankle cushion heel (foot prosthesis)

ORGANIZATIONS

MDAA—Muscular Dystrophy Association of America, Inc.
NSCCA—National Society for Crippled Children and Adults

REVIEW GUIDE

Instructions: On the blank lines shown below, **write the term** that best fits each descriptive phrase or statement.

Example: *cramp*—prolonged, intense spasm of one muscle.

_____ —surgical opening of a joint.

_____ —removal of a cartilage.

_____ —bleeding into synovial sac.

_____ —incomplete dislocation.

Another name for Albright's syndrome is _____ .

_____ —lateral spinal curvature.

_____ —hammer toe.

_____ —bunion.

_____ —bloody effusion in a joint cavity.

_____ —wristdrop.

_____ —suture of a muscle.

_____ —stretching of a muscle.

Torticollis is also called _____ .

Excision of a bone is termed _____ .

Extra bone is termed _____ .

_____ —knock-knee.

_____ —bowleg.

_____ —grating sound made by movement of fractured bones.

An incomplete break that may be associated with bowing of the shaft is called a _____ fracture.

A _____ fracture results from bone being twisted excessively.

_____ —benign tumor of smooth muscle.

_____ —malignant tumor of striated muscle.

_____ —benign tumor of striated muscle.

_____ —inflammation of the fascia.

Instructions: Figure 5.1 in the text is an anterior view of the skeleton. For each line that extends from the figure below, provide the name of the anatomic site, as shown in the example.

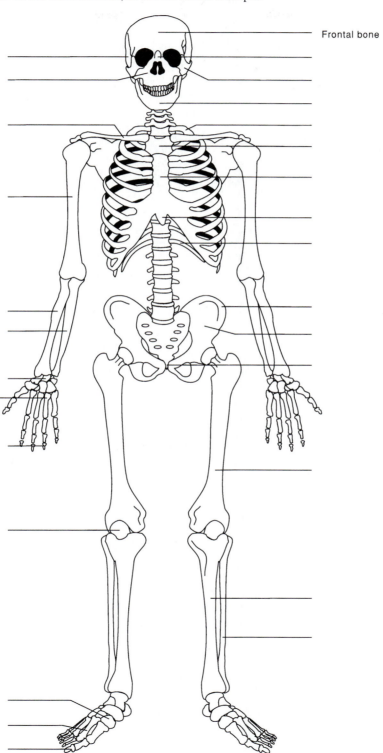

Frontal bone

Instructions: Figure 5.8 in the text is an anterior view of the skeletal muscles. For each line that extends from the figure below, provide the anatomic name of the site, as shown in the example.

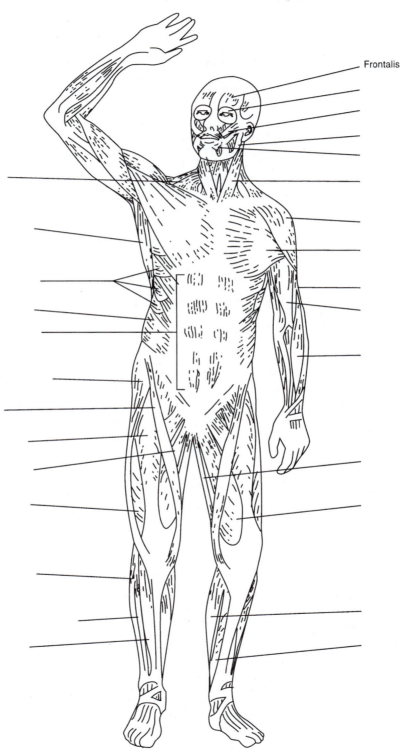

Frontalis

6

Cardiovascular Disorders

HEART AND CORONARY ARTERIES

ORIGIN OF TERMS

a-, an- (G)—without, not
angi-, angio- (G)—vessel
apico- (L)—top, summit
atrio- (L)—chamber, hall
brady- (G)—slow
card-, cardio- (G)—heart
cor- (L)—heart
dextro- (L)—right
-emia (G)—blood
endo- (G)—within

hem-, hemo- (G)—blood
my-, myo- (G)—muscle
-pathy (G)—disease
peri- (G)—around, about
septum (L)—dividing wall, partition
stetho- (G)—chest
tachy (G)—rapid, swift
topo- (G)—place
veno- (L)—vein
ventriculo- (L)—belly, ventricle

PHONETIC PRONUNCIATION OF SELECTED TERMS

angina pectoris	AN′ji-nah PECT′tor-is
atrial septal defect	A′tree-al SEP′tal DE′fect
bradycardia	BRAD-e-CAR′de-ah
cardiac edema	CAR′de-ack e-DEE′mah
ischemia	is-KEY′me-ah
systole	SIS′toe-lee
ventricular arrhythmia	ven-TRICK′you-lar a-RITH′me-a

ANATOMIC TERMS (47, 51, 91, 102, 106) (SEE FIG. 6.1.)

cavities of the heart—the four heart chambers.

> *atria* (sing. *atrium*)—two chambers that form the base of the heart and receive venous blood.

> *ventricles*—two chambers that lie anteriorly to the atria and propel blood into arteries.

Figure 6.1 Frontal section of the heart.

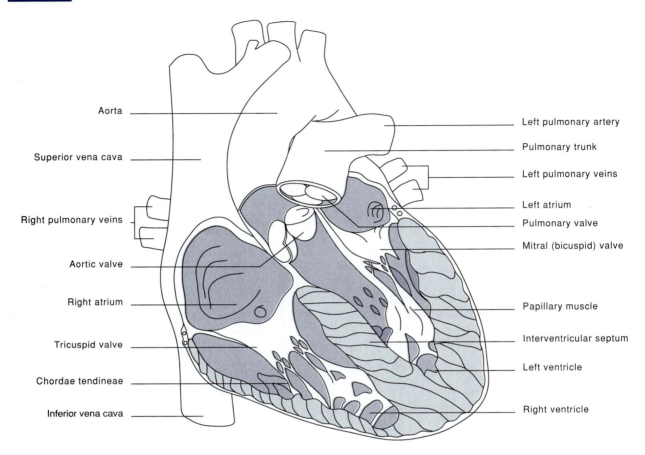

Aorta

Superior vena cava

Right pulmonary veins

Aortic valve

Right atrium

Tricuspid valve

Chordae tendineae

Inferior vena cava

Left pulmonary artery

Pulmonary trunk

Left pulmonary veins

Left atrium

Pulmonary valve

Mitral (bicuspid) valve

Papillary muscle

Interventricular septum

Left ventricle

Right ventricle

conduction system of the heart—neuromuscular tissue specialized for the conduction of electric impulses. (Components are arranged in order of function instead of alphabetic order. See fig. 6.2.)

sinoatrial node (S-A or SA node)—node situated in the wall of the right atrium. It is the pacemaker of the heart, since it transmits impulses to both atria, stimulating them to contract simultaneously.

atrioventricular node (A-V or AV node)—node found in the septum of the heart near the junction of the atria and ventricles. It relays impulses from the atria to the atrioventricular bundle.

atrioventricular bundle, bundle of His—a bundle of specialized neuromuscular tissue within the atrioventricular septum transmitting impulses from the AV node to the Purkinje fibers.

Purkinje fibers—cardiac muscle fibers of the conduction system that ramify beneath the endocardium and deliver impulses to the ventricular myocardium, initiating contraction of the ventricles.

heart and wall covering: (See fig. 6.3.)

endocardium—interior lining of the heart wall.

myocardium—the heart muscle.

myocardial sinusoids—endothelium-lined spaces lying between the myocardial muscle fibers and enabling the ventricular myocardium to absorb blood in a spongelike manner.

Figure 6.2 Cardiac conduction system. Impulses pass from the sinoatrial (S-A) node through both atria, stimulating them to contract. The atrioventricular (A-V) node is thereby activated and transmits impulses to the atrioventricular bundle and its right and left limbs, resulting in contraction of both ventricles.

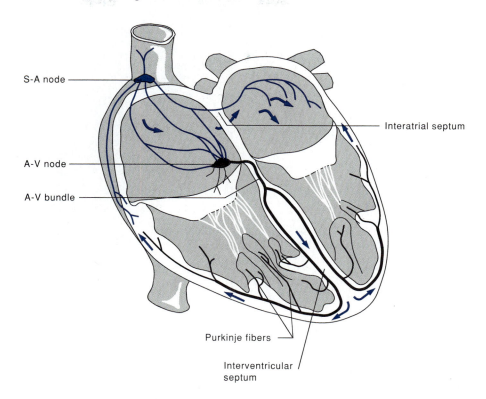

S-A node

A-V node

A-V bundle

Interatrial septum

Purkinje fibers

Interventricular septum

pericardium—covering of the heart composed of a fibrous tissue (pericardium fibrosum) and serous tissue (pericardium serosum). The former fits loosely around the heart. The latter consists of a visceral layer or epicardium that adheres closely to the myocardium and a parietal layer that lines the inner surface of the fibrous pericardium. The pericardial cavity is a narrow space between the parietal and visceral layers. It contains a minimal amount of serum that serves as a lubricant.

orifices and valves of the heart and great vessels:

atrioventricular orifices and valves—openings and cuspid valves between atria and ventricles. (See fig. 6.4.)

- *foramen ovale*—opening between the two atria in fetal life. It normally closes after birth.
- *mitral valve, bicuspid valve*—valve between left atrium and left ventricle. It contains two endothelial folds or cusps that come together when the ventricle contracts.
- *semilunar valves*—half-moon-shaped flaps within the aorta and pulmonary trunk that prevent the blood from flowing back into the ventricles.
- *tricuspid valve*—three endothelial folds or cusps that guard right atrioventricular orifice.

sinuses, arteries, and nerves:

aortic sinuses, sinuses of Valsalva—three dilated spaces at root of the aorta, related to the three cusps of the aortic valve.

Figure 6.3 The heart is enclosed by a layered pericardium.

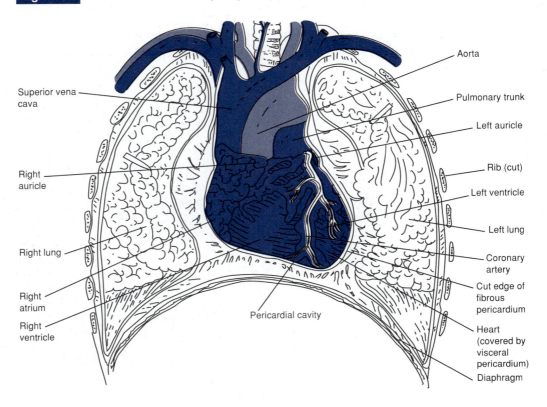

Aorta

Superior vena cava

Pulmonary trunk

Left auricle

Right auricle

Rib (cut)

Left ventricle

Left lung

Right lung

Coronary artery

Cut edge of fibrous pericardium

Right atrium

Pericardial cavity

Heart (covered by visceral pericardium)

Right ventricle

Diaphragm

Figure 6.4 The skeleton of the heart (superior view) consists of fibrous rings to which the heart valves are attached.

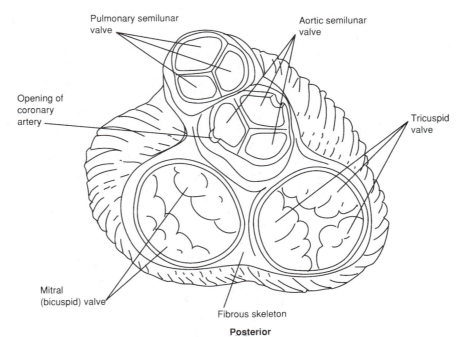

Pulmonary semilunar valve

Aortic semilunar valve

Opening of coronary artery

Tricuspid valve

Mitral (bicuspid) valve

Fibrous skeleton

Posterior

Figure 6.5 Blood vessels associated with the surface of the heart. (a) Anterior view; (b) posterior view.

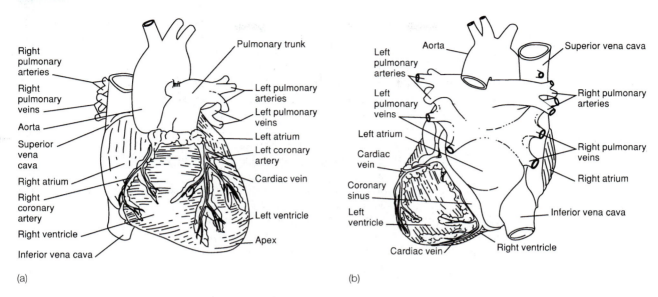

(a)

(b)

coronary arteries—branches of the ascending aorta arising from the right and left aortic sinuses. The blood vessels with their branches supply the heart muscle and form numerous anastomoses of small arteries and precapillaries. In the event of a sudden occlusion of a major coronary artery, these anastomotic channels may not be able to provide adequate collateral circulation. But if a major coronary artery is slowly occluded, these channels may enlarge and maintain a sufficient blood supply to the heart muscle. (See fig. 6.5.)

coronary sinus—short, broad vessel into which most of the veins of the heart empty. It in turn empties into the right atrium.

internal thoracic arteries, internal mammary arteries—blood vessels usually arising from the subclavian arteries and passing down on either side of the sternum. They are approximately the same caliber as the coronary arteries. They can be surgically relocated from the chest wall to a coronary artery distal to an obstructing lesion to revascularize the heart muscle.

parasympathetic fibers—preganglionic fibers that reach the heart via the vagus nerve. Ganglia in the heart have postganglionic fibers distributed to both the atria and the ventricles. Impulses slow the heart and depress contractions.

sympathetic fibers carried by the cervical and thoracic cardiac nerves to the heart muscle—fibers involved in control of the heart rate and the force of its contraction. Afferent fibers join the vagus nerve to aid in regulation of blood volume and heart rate.

DIAGNOSTIC TERMS

aneurysm—dilatation or bulging out of the wall of the heart, aorta, or any other artery. Thrombi may form in the sac, break off, and lead to embolism. The aneurysm may rupture. Ventricular aneurysms are usually complications of coronary atherosclerosis and myocardial infarction. (99, 109)

angina pectoris:

classic angina pectoris—syndrome characterized by short attacks of substernal precordial pain that radiates to the left shoulder and arm. It is more frequently associated with ST segment changes than conduction defects. Electrocardiographic (ECG) findings may show atrioventricular or intraventricular defects of conduction, nonspecific ST segment changes, previous myocardial scar, or other abnormalities. About 30% of the ECG studies are likely to be normal. This condition may be provoked by exertion and relieved by rest. (84, 89)

unstable angina pectoris—chest pain is more prolonged and severe than in classic angina and remains unrelieved by rest and nitroglycerin. ECG shows evidence of myocardial ischemia, but infarction or necrosis is absent in the early phase. A favorable prognosis depends on the evolution of the collateral circulation to compensate for the impoverished blood flow of the myocardium. Revascularization surgery has been reported to be about 80% successful. Untreated patients eventually develop myocardial infarction and die. (15, 82)

variant angina, Prinzmetal's angina—anginal chest pain at rest, prone to occur on awakening and tending to be cyclic. The spasm is the predominant factor and is usually but not always located in the proximal right coronary artery, as identified through coronary arteriography studies. Transient ST segment elevation or other ECG abnormalities may be associated with this syndrome. (98)

anomalies, congenital—gross structural defects of the heart or great intrathoracic vessels arising during fetal development, and in selected cases, associated with chromosomal abnormalities.

atrial septal defect—abnormality resulting in a shunting of oxygenated blood from the left into the right atrium. Atrial septal defects vary widely in size, position, and shape. Shunting is minimal when the defect is small. A persistent foramen ovale is one of the septal defects that may be encountered. (34, 104)

cor triatriatum—heart with three atrial chambers due to an obstructing membrane that partitions the left atrium, thus impeding the pulmonary venous circulation, causing pulmonary venous congestion, hypertension, and congestive heart failure. (34, 104)

cor triloculare—heart composed of three chambers, resulting from the absence of the interatrial or interventricular septum. (109)

coronary arteriovenous fistula—represented by a gross communication between a coronary artery and a cardiac chamber, the coronary sinus, or the pulmonary trunk. A fistula into the pulmonary trunk presents as one or more vessels opening into the pulmonary trunk and connecting with branches of each of the two main coronary arteries. The arteries feeding the fistula appear enlarged and tortuous. Saccular aneurysms may develop in segments of dilated vessels. (73)

pulmonary stenosis—a narrowing of the pulmonary valve or of the infundibulum associated with an intact ventricular septum. The stenotic defect causes pulmonary outflow tract obstruction. (The infundibulum is the cone-shaped area of the right ventricle from which the pulmonary artery begins.) This condition is usually congenital; however, acquired lesions of the pulmonary valve may lead to regurgitation. Pulmonary hypertension from such causes as mitral stenosis, chronic lung disease, or pulmonary emboli can cause pulmonary incompetence. (37, 73, 104)

patent ductus arteriosus—persistence of communication between pulmonary artery and aorta after birth. In normal infants, the closure of the ductus takes place during the first 6 weeks of life. (34, 65, 104)

tetralogy of Fallot—complex of congenital defects usually considered as having the following four parts, with the first two being the essential parts of the complex:
- *ventricular septal defect*—malformation of the septum of the ventricles.
- *pulmonic stenosis*—obstruction to pulmonary blood flow and involvement is associated with other defects. When the pulmonary stenosis is very severe, most of the pulmonary blood flow may be by way of collateral blood flow.
- *dextroposition of the aorta*—transposition of the aorta to the right.
- *hypertrophy of the right ventricle*—increased size of the ventricle, the body's way of compensating for the added load imposed by the defects. (73, 104)

ventricular septal defect (VSD)—abnormality allowing oxygenated blood to shunt from the left ventricle to the right ventricle. There are wide variations in size and position.

- *isolated*—absence of the ventricular septum, partial or total; occasionally multiple.
- *other*—defects associated with other anomalies. (65, 73)

artificial valve disease—disorders of artificial valves that are surgically implanted to correct diseases of the natural valves are designated as artificial valve diseases. These diseases include valvular stenosis, valvular regurgitation, thromboembolism, and infective endocarditis. Other diseases unique to artificial valves are mechanical breakdown, thrombotic obstruction, and hemolytic anemia. (43)

cardiac arrest—cessation of effective heart action, usually manifested by asystole or ventricular fibrillation. (65, 109)

cardiac arrhythmias, cardiac dysrhythmias—irregularities of heart action, including disturbances of rate, rhythm, and conduction, either related or unrelated to other cardiac disease, supraventricular (atrial) or ventricular. Primary arrhythmias result from electrophysiologic disturbance caused by a disease process, independent of a significant change in hemodynamic function. Secondary arrhythmia results from an electrical disturbance initiated by hemodynamic deterioration or metabolic abnormalities. Some major arrhythmias that seriously interfere with cardiac or circulatory efficiency are presented. (19, 51, 52, 70, 82)

atrial arrhythmias—disorders of rhythm having their origin in the SA node. They may be provoked by ischemia, drug toxicity, or atrial distention. If uncontrolled, atrial arrhythmias may become life threatening.

atrial fibrillation—extremely rapid, vermicular, ineffectual contractions of the atria resulting in irregularity of rhythm in the ventricles. The atrial rate is 350 beats per minute or more.

atrial flutter—rapid, regular cardiac action of 250 to 350 beats per minute, usually occurring in paroxysms, which are more prolonged than atrial tachycardia. The atrial impulse may produce a rapid ventricular rate or result in an atrioventricular block of varying degree (such as 2:1, 3:1, or 4:1 ratio).

paroxysmal atrial tachycardia (PAT)—rapid, regular contractions of the atria initiated by an irritable center within the atrium outside the sinoatrial node. Rate is about 160 to 200 beats per minute. Ventricular contractions are 1:1 ratio with atrial contractions. This arrhythmia (PAT) is practically indistinguishable from nodal paroxysmal tachycardia. The patient may experience a sudden forceful thump and subsequent attack of palpitation.

atrioventricular nodal arrhythmias—disorders arising in the atrioventricular node.

atrioventricular nodal rhythm—pacemaker function assumed by AV node in response to sustained failure of sinoatrial node to send impulses to the atrioventricular node.

premature atrioventricular nodal contractions (PNCs)—arrhythmia caused by irritation of the atrioventricular node, which produces an ectopic stimulus and subsequent premature nodal contractions (PNCs). Frequent recurrence of PNCs may signal progressive myocardial infarction.

ventricular arrhythmias—disorders of rhythm arising within the ventricles.

- *premature ventricular contractions (PVCs)*—the most common disturbance of rhythm, frequently an index of myocardial damage and anoxia. If more than six PVCs per minute occur, ventricular efficiency may be seriously impaired.
- *ventricular tachycardia*—disorder heralding a high degree of irritability, frequently associated with myocardial infarction. The irritable center within the ventricular wall produces a rapid ventricular rate that may change to ventricular fibrillation or ventricular standstill. The rate is 150 to 250 beats per minute or greater, and the rhythm slightly irregular. Sudden dizziness, precordial pain, dyspnea, and weakness are common complaints.

Figure 6.6 Ventricular fibrillation: life-threatening arrhythmia.

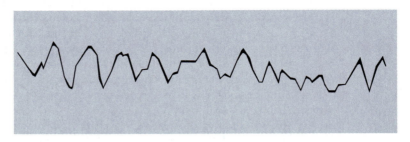

Figure 6.7 Terminal ventricular fibrillation and ventricular standstill—asystole.

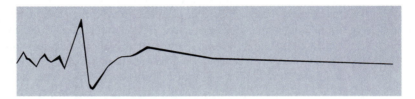

- *ventricular fibrillation*—extremely rapid, nonsynchronous contractions of ventricular muscle bundles; irregularities in rhythm and force result in no ejection of blood from fibrillating ventricles. It may terminate in ventricular standstill. (See figs. 6.6 and 6.7.)

conduction disturbances—abnormalities in the cardiac conduction system. Heart block refers to abnormalities of impulse that may be normal, physiological (e.g., vagal tone), or pathlogical. (51, 65, 70, 105)

- *atrioventricular block*—delay or obstruction of impulses arising above or within the atrioventricular node.

  first-degree heart block—prolongation of atrioventricular conduction time; delay of impulses on their ventricular pathway. Possible causes are increased vagal tone, myocardial ischemia, and drug toxicity.

  second-degree heart block (intermittent AV block)—present when some atrial impulses fail to conduct to the ventricles. Mobitz type I second-degree AV block (A-V Wenckebach block) is characterized by progressive PR interval prolongation prior to block of an atrial impulse. Mobitz type I can progress to complete heart block but this is uncommon. In Mobitz type II second-degree AV block, conduction fails suddenly and unexpectedly without preceding change in PR intervals; not all impulses are transmitted to the bundle of His by the atrioventricular node, resulting in various ratios (2:1, 3:1, 4:1, and others) of atrial contractions. Wrist pulse is 40 to 50 beats per minute.

  third-degree or complete block—no atrial impulses are transmitted to the bundle of His by the atrioventricular node. Wrist pulse is 30 to 40 beats per minute as a result of beats initiated within the conduction mechanism of the ventricle.

- *bundle branch block*—obstruction of the wave of excitation in either branch of the atrioventricular bundle.

- *hemiblock*—electrocardiographic patterns that precede or coexist with bundle branch blocks or are precursors of atrioventricular conduction abnormalities.

- *sick sinus syndrome, bradycardia-tachycardia syndrome*—sinoatrial dysfunction of the conduction system of the heart, characterized by abnormal impulse formation or transformation.
- *Stokes-Adams syndrome*—cardiac standstill that occurs with certain forms of heart block, causing syncope and possible fatal convulsions.
- *Wolff-Parkinson-White syndrome*—congenital disorder of atrioventricular conduction that may be associated with recurrent paroxysmal tachycardia, atrial flutter, or other ectopic rhythms.

cardiac tamponade, pericardial tamponade—compression of the heart by effusion or hemorrhage in the pericardium, which may seriously obstruct the venous inflow to the heart, raise the venous pressure, reduce the cardiac output, and cause hypotension, distention of the neck veins, and orthopnea. (2, 44, 84)

cardiomyopathies—miscellaneous group of heart muscle disorders of unknown etiology. These disorders may be classified as:

congestive dilatated cardiomyopathy—marked cardiac enlargement with systolic pump malfunction. Symptoms of congestive heart failure and arrhythmias may be present.

- *alcoholic cardiomyopathy*—persons who consume large quantities of alcohol over time may develop a clinical condition similar to idiopathic dilatated cardiomyopathy. Alcoholic cardiomyopathy is the major form of secondary dilatated cardiomyopathy in the Western world.
- *peripartum cardiomyopathy*—cardiac dilatation and congestive heart failure may develop in the last month of pregnancy or in the first few months after delivery. If the heart size returns to normal after the first episode of congestive heart failure, then subsequent pregnancies may be well tolerated; however, if it remains enlarged, future pregnancies often produce increasing myocardial damage, which may lead to refractory congestive heart failure and finally death.

hypertrophic cardiomyopathy—slight to moderate cardiac enlargement with left ventricular hypertrophy. The characteristic feature of this disorder is the asymmetric septal hypertrophy with or without obstruction to ventricular outflow and the presence of a systolic murmur. The most common symptom is dyspnea; however, other symptoms may occur, such as angina pectoris, fatigue, or syncope.

restrictive cardiomyopathy—slight cardiac enlargement with endomyocardial scarring and abnormal diastolic function. Interference with left ventricular filling and emptying cycle may be produced by the presence of infiltrative myocardial fibrosis, amyloid disease, and other disorders. (64, 65, 95, 110)

cardiopulmonary arrest—heart-lung arrest caused by sudden and unexpected cessation of respiration and functional circulation. (109)

Chagas' disease—acute or chronic myocarditis caused by *Trypanosoma cruzi*. Serious arrhythmias and congestive heart failure signal death. The disease is endemic in South and Central America and is fatal in 87% of those affected. (74)

congestive heart failure—the heart is unable to pump adequate amounts of blood to tissues and organs. This is generally caused by diseases of the heart, causing low cardiac output. It can result from other conditions (anemia, hyperthyroidism) in which the demand for blood is greater than normal, and the heart fails despite high cardiac output. In advanced disease, left-sided and right-sided congestive heart failure coexist. (9, 17, 93)

left-sided heart failure—failure of the left ventricle, precipitated by serious coronary, hypertensive, or valvular heart disease. Except in mitral stenosis, it produces variable degrees of left ventricular dilatation followed by pulmonary congestion and edema, salt and water retention, scanty urinary output, cerebral hypoxia, and coma.

right-sided heart failure—failure of the right ventricle characterized by venous congestion of the portal system, with ascites and enlargement of the liver and spleen.

latent heart failure—state in which heart failure is *not* present at rest, but is present during periods of increased stress or after an increase in blood volume.

compensated heart failure—condition in which heart failure was previously present, but in which cardiac output has returned to (or maintained at) a normal level by compensatory mechanisms or therapy.

atherosclerotic coronary heart disease (CHD)—the most common heart condition. Progressive thickening of the intima of the coronary arteries leads to occlusion, caused by narrowing of the lumen and intravascular clotting. (20, 65)

coronary risk factors—predispose to coronary heart disease (CHD) that may or may not be preventable. In addition to the major risk factors tabulated, obesity, a sedentary occupation or lack of physical activity, stress, and competitiveness may lead to heart disease. Oral contraceptives taken over years present a coronary risk, since they adversely affect the lipoprotein metabolism, even after the contraceptive has been discontinued. Epidemiological studies, such as the Framingham Heart Study, identified certain risk factors that demonstrate a positive link with the incidence of cardiovascular disease. (81, 88, 109) (See table 6.1.)

atherosclerotic occlusive disease—chronic disorder characterized by lipid deposits that form fibrous fatty plaques within the intima and inner media of the coronary arteries. These plaques are known as *atheromas*. (20, 99)

cor pulmonale—heart-lung disease characterized by right ventricular hypertrophy caused by pulmonary disorders that increase pulmonary vascular resistance and induce pulmonary hypertension; ventilatory insufficiency is not necessarily impaired. (12, 71)

acute form—caused by massive pulmonary embolism occurring within hours.

chronic form—caused by pulmonary fibrosis, obstructive emphysema, or obstructive vascular disease developing within months.

Ebstein's anomaly—tricuspid insufficiency caused by a spiral-like attachment of a valve leaflet of the tricuspid, resulting in atrial enlargement, defective ventricular filling, right-to-left shunting, other impairments, and variable clinical manifestations such as dyspnea, cyanosis, clubbing of fingers, precordial thrill, and systolic or diastolic murmurs. (34, 73, 104)

Eisenmenger's syndrome—right-to-left shunting of pulmonary circulation, usually recognized first in adolescence and thought to result from an unrepaired congenital defect in infancy. It is manifested by cyanosis, clubbing, chest pain, hemoptysis, syncope, and polycythemia. The clinical course is progressive, and death usually ensues before 50 years of age. (34)

endocarditis:

endocarditis, bacterial—acute or subacute infection of the lining of the heart and especially valve leaflets. It is caused by organisms that enter the bloodstream and initiate a bacteremia clinically recognized by fever, fatigue, heart murmurs, splenomegaly, embolic episodes, and areas of infarction. Acute bacterial endocarditis (ABE) evolves over days to weeks and the diagnosis is usually made in less than 2 weeks. ABE is most often caused by primary pathogens such as *Staphylococcus aureus*, which are capable of causing invasive infection at other sites of the body. Subacute bacterial endocarditis (SBE) evolves over several weeks or months. It is usually caused by low virulent organisms, such as *Streptococci viridans*. These types of organisms rarely infect other tissues. (23, 55) Other endocarditis distinctions include:

- *infective endocarditis*—caused by microbial infection of the endothelial lining of the heart. Its characteristic lesion is a vegetation that most often develops on a heart valve but may appear on the endocardium or on the lining of a large artery. The major trigger prompting the development of infective endocarditis is the attachment of microorganisms circulating in the bloodstream to an endocardial surface. (23, 55, 65)

- *Libman-Sacks endocarditis*—condition characterized by verrucose lesions found in the endocardium of patients with terminal disseminated lupus erythematosus. (8)

TABLE **6.1**	Coronary Risk Factors of Prime Importance According to Framingham Study	
Risk Factors	*Atherogenic Bases*	*Preventive Aspects*
Hyperlipidemia genetic defect

Diet induced | Familial predisposition to hyperlipidemia due to genetic defect
High dietary intake of cholesterol and saturated fatty acids | Intake low in cholesterol and saturated fat
Therapeutic diet rich in polyunsaturated fats and low cholesterol |
| Hypertension | Increased peripheral resistance due to vasoconstriction
If diastolic pressure is greater than 105 mm Hg, coronary risk is four times greater than in normotensive pressure | Reduction of blood pressure by appropriate hypotensive drugs
Lifestyle conducive to tranquility, and weight loss in obesity |
| Cigarette smoking | Constriction of coronary arteries by cigarette smokers who inhale nicotine while smoking one or two packs of cigarettes a day
Death rate from coronary heart disease is 70%–200% higher in smokers than in nonsmokers | Control of smoking habit over 10 to 20 years to reduce cardiovascular morbidity and mortality |
| Diabetes mellitus | Accelerated process of coronary, cerebral, renal, aortoiliac, and femoropopliteal atherosclerosis in diabetic persons
Wide distribution of microvascular changes in diabetes | Careful adherence to treatment regimen to maintain diabetic control |

Source: Adapted from (1) Charles E. Rackley and Robert C. Schlant, "Prevention of Coronary Artery Disease" in Robert C. Schlant and R. Wayne Alexander (eds.), *The Heart,* 8th ed. (New York: McGraw-Hill, Inc., 1994), pp. 1205–1222; (2) Russell Ross, "Factors Influencing Atherogenesis" in Robert C. Schlant and R. Wayne Alexander (eds.), *The Heart,* 8th ed. (New York: McGraw-Hill, Inc., 1994), pp. 989–1008; (3) Vallee L. Willman, M.D., Personal communication.

- *Löffler's endocarditis, fibroplastic endocarditis*—marked thickening of the ventricles affecting the underlying heart muscle and mural thrombi, thus diminishing the size of the ventricular cavities. (33, 95)
- *native valve endocarditis* (NVE)—infection engrafted upon a heart valve that was either previously normal or damaged by congenital or acquired disease. (23, 55)
- *noninfective endocarditis*—presence of sterile vegetations within the heart. (23, 55)
- *prosthetic value endocarditis* (PVE)—infection of an artificial valve. Early PVE occurs within the first 2 months after surgery and late PVE occurs after the first 2 months postsurgery. (23, 55, 65)

ischemic heart disease—the prominent feature is markedly reduced blood supply to the heart muscle, generally due to coronary atherosclerosis. The resultant myocardial ischemia may produce myocardial infarction, heart failure, or angina pectoris.

silent myocardial ischemia—temporary imbalance of myocardial oxygen supply and demand, which is usually not accompanied by angina or similar symptom. Silent myocardial ischemia may be detected by exercise testing and/or ambulatory electrocardiographic monitoring. The three main types of silent myocardial ischemia are:

- *Type I*—presents in asymptomatic patients, usually uncovered by a screening exercise test.
- *Type II*—occurs in patients asymptomatic following a myocardial infarction episode. Holter monitoring is a helpful procedure utilized to pinpoint this condition.

- *Type III*—includes those patients who have angina and who have sustained additional occurrences of silent myocardial ischemia. Ambulatory electrocardiographic monitoring studies indicate that 75% of all patients with angina have sustained some degree of silent myocardial ischemia. (26, 65, 89, 94)

mitral valve prolapse—slippage of one or more leaflets of the mitral valve into the atrium during ventricular systole, causing stress. The prolapse is associated with a systolic murmur and midsystolic click. The diagnosis is confirmed by auscultation, angiography, and echocardiography. (33)

myocardial disease, primary:

myocarditis—inflammation of the heart muscle that may result in myocardial fibrosis, followed by cardiac enlargement and congestive heart failure.

myocardosis—condition characterized by cardiac dilatation, congestive heart failure, and embolization. (74, 110)

myocardial disease, secondary—heart disease associated with noninfectious systemic diseases such as amyloidosis, carcinoidosis, collagen diseases, endocrinopathy, sarcoidosis, and systemic muscular and neurologic disorders. (45, 110)

myocardial infarction, acute—clinical syndrome manifested by persistent, usually intense cardiac pain, unrelated to exertion and often constrictive, followed by diaphoresis, pallor, hypotension, dyspnea, faintness, nausea, and vomiting. The underlying disease is usually coronary atherosclerosis that progressed to coronary thrombosis and occlusion and resulted in a sudden curtailment of blood supply to the heart muscle and myocardial ischemia.

inferior wall infarction, diaphragmatic infarction—occlusion of the right coronary artery.

lateral wall infarction—occlusion of the diagonal branch of the left anterior descending artery or left circumflex artery.

posterior wall infarction—infarction precipitated by occlusive lesions of the right coronary artery or circumflex coronary artery branch. (42, 65, 78, 86)

- *postmyocardial infarction (Dressler's) syndrome*—develops within the first week or weeks after myocardial infarction. It exhibits the clinical features of a benign form of pericarditis, with or without effusion. (65, 78, 86)

pericarditis—inflammation of the covering membranes of the heart. Its distinctive feature is pericardial friction rub, a transitory scratchy or leathery sound elicited on auscultation.

constrictive pericarditis, chronic—disorder characterized by a rigid, thickened pericardium that prevents adequate filling of the ventricles and may lead to congestive heart failure.

pyogenic (purulent) pericarditis—disease is usually secondary to cardiothoracic operations, immunosuppressive therapy, rupture of the esophagus into the pericardial sac, or rupture of a ring abscess in a person with infective endocarditis and with septicemia complicating aseptic pericarditis. It is not now commonly due to pneumonococcal pneumonia and pleuritis, which previously were the most common causes. (8, 45, 65, 96)

rheumatic heart disease—involvement of the heart in the course of rheumatic fever and attacking the myocardium, pericardium, and endocardium, with the valvular endocardium as the site of predilection. (83)

sudden cardiac death—unexpected death, either instantaneously or within 24 hours, excluding trauma, suicide, or terminal illness as possible causes. (16, 65)

valvular (valvar) heart disease, chronic—disorder referring to any permanent organic deformity in one or more of the valves. Some examples of this condition are: (33, 36, 65, 71, 82, 84, 85)

aortic regurgitation, aortic insufficiency—indicates regurgitation of small amounts of blood through the incompetent leaflets during diastole. As the valve deformity increases, larger amounts are regurgitated. The diastolic blood pressure is lowered, and the pulse wave assumes its characteristic contour. The left ventricle progressively enlarges. Left ventricular failure may suddenly occur, with acute pulmonary edema or recurrent paroxysmal nocturnal dyspnea and orthopnea. The murmur of aortic insufficiency may be absent during severe heart failure but may reappear following treatment.

aortic stenosis—reduction in the valve orifice, interfering with the emptying of the left ventricle. Characteristic signs include a systolic ejection murmur at the aortic area transmitted to the neck and apex and a systolic ejection click at the aortic area. In severe cases, there may be a palpable left ventricular heave, reversed splitting of the second heart sound, and a weak-to-absent aortic second sound. Eighty percent of patients with aortic stenosis are men.

mitral regurgitation, mitral insufficiency—mitral leaflets do not close normally during the ventricular systole, and blood is forced back into the atrium and through the aortic valve. This condition is characterized by a pansystolic murmur that is maximal at the apex and radiates to the axilla, a hyperdynamic left ventricular impulse, a brisk carotid upstroke, and a prominent third heart sound.

mitral stenosis—very common sequela of rheumatic fever, marked by the development of minute vegetations and thrombi that narrow the orifice of the valve leaflets. Calcifications form as the disease progresses. The characteristic sign is a localized, delayed diastolic murmur that is low in pitch and has a duration that varies with the severity of the stenosis and heart rate.

tricuspid regurgitation, tricuspid insufficiency—affects the right ventricle. This condition may occur in a variety of disorders other than disease of the tricuspid valve itself. The left ventricular overload resulting from left ventricular failure is usually due to coronary heart disease, hypertensive heart failure, cardiomyopathy, and mitral or aortic stenosis. The tricuspid insufficiency is characterized by a prominent regurgitant systolic wave in the right atrium and in the jugular venous pulse. Regurgitation of blood from the right ventricle to the right atrium may occur during systole, as noted by right ventricular angiography.

tricuspid stenosis—associated with mitral stenosis, this defect reduces the valve to a small, triangular opening that causes resistance in the flow of blood from the right atrium to the right ventricle and leads to congestion of the lungs and liver. Careful examination is required to differentiate the typical diastolic rumble along the lower left sternal border from the murmur of mitral stenosis. Women represent the majority of those affected, and mitral valve disease is usually present.

ventricular aneurysm, left—a sharply delineated area of scar that bulges paradoxically during systole. It rarely ruptures but may be associated with ventricular arrhythmias, and congestive heart failure. Aneurysms are recognized by persistent ST segment elevation (beyond 4 to 8 weeks), and a wide neck from the left ventricle can be demonstrated by echocardiography, scintigraphy, or contrast angiography. If medical treatment is not effective, ventricular aneurysmectomy can be performed. (65, 84)

TERMS RELATED TO CARDIAC AND CORONARY ARTERY CATHETERIZATION

cardiac catheterization, right side—a procedure of diagnostic value in detecting various cardiac defects and diseases. A radiopaque cardiac catheter is inserted into an accessible vein and passed into the heart and pulmonary artery. Various techniques may be employed. If the basilic or the cephalic vein is used as a starting point, the catheter passes through the innominate vein and superior vena cava into the right atrium, right ventricle, and pulmonary artery. If the saphenous vein is used, the catheter enters the heart through the inferior vena cava and traces its course through the cardiac chambers and pulmonary artery. Oxygen saturation of the blood in the chambers and the pressure recorded inside determine the defect within the heart, if present. Different indicator techniques aid in the detection and quantitation of shunts. Oxygen data or dye curves may be used for calculation of cardiac output. Although right cardiac catheterization is of great diagnostic value in certain heart lesions, it is incomplete if cineangiography does not accompany the hemodynamic data. (11, 31, 65, 109)

cardiac catheterization, left side—obtaining pressures and blood samples in the left side of the heart can be accomplished in several ways:

catheterization of the left atrium:

- *suprasternal or Radner method*—inserting a needle behind the suprasternal notch and directing it downward into the left atrium. The pulmonary artery, aorta, and left ventricle can be entered by the same method.
- *transseptal or Ross method*—inserting a long needle through a catheter up to the right atrium and then pushing the needle out the catheter and puncturing the atrial septum at the foramen ovale. Modifications of this method are:

    Brockenbrough technique—the cardiac catheter itself is slipped over the needle into the left atrium following transseptal puncture with the needle in the catheter.

    Shirey technique—the cardiac catheter is passed retrogradely through the brachial artery cutdown into the aorta, left ventricle, and left atrium.

    In the Radner method only the pressures may be recorded; in the Brockenbrough or Shirey technique, cineangiograms may be obtained by injection of opaque media through the catheter.

cardiac catheterization of left ventricle:

- *direct puncture of left ventricle*—use of a small-guage needle either through the apex (Brock technique) or through the subxiphoid approach (Lehman technique).
- *retrograde method*—femoral or arm approach using a percutaneous or cutdown technique, respectively.

catheterization of the coronary arteries: (11, 31)

Judkins' technique—technique uses percutaneous puncture of femoral artery and introduction of three differently shaped catheters in succession for catheterization of left and right coronary arteries and left ventricular cineangiography. Under fluoroscopic or television guidance, a catheter is introduced into the common femoral artery and advanced via the aortic arch to the coronary orifice. Catheter manipulation differs for selective left and right coronary artery catheterization. Following contrast injection, rapid direct serial radiography and cinephotofluorography provide coronary visualization, thereby revealing the presence and extent of occlusive arterial heart disease.

Sones' technique—technique uses approach through the brachial artery following a cutdown. A single catheter is inserted for the catheterization of both coronary arteries and left ventricular cineangiography. Selective catheterization of the coronary arteries is done according to an accepted technique to:

- assess the potential need for heart surgery in angina pectoris
- evaluate operative results such as the extent of revascularization following the Vineberg procedure
- assess the patency of aortocoronary saphenous vein grafts or internal mammary artery grafts following bypass surgery
- detect progression of coronary atherosclerotic heart disease leading to graft closure

directional coronary atherectomy (DCA)—a cardiac catheterization procedure performed with local anesthesia, in which fatty deposits known as plaque are cut, captured, and removed. An atherectomy catheter, equipped with a tiny balloon, a protected cutting surface, and a storage chamber, is inserted in the patient's artery via a small incision in the groin area. The catheter is then advanced to the blockage site and is precisely positioned next to the plaque. The balloon is inflated, causing the catheter's cutting surface to push against the plaque at high speed. The plaque is collected in a storage chamber on the catheter's tip. When the chamber is full, the catheter is removed, emptied, and reinserted until enough plaque has been removed to restore good blood flow to the artery. Whereas the traditional angioplasty uses a balloon to compress, stretch, or split the plaque in the artery's walls to restore blood flow,

Figure 6.8 How directional coronary atherectomy works.

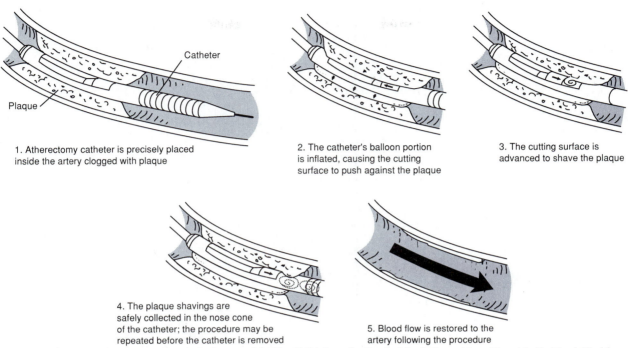

1. Atherectomy catheter is precisely placed inside the artery clogged with plaque

2. The catheter's balloon portion is inflated, causing the cutting surface to push against the plaque

3. The cutting surface is advanced to shave the plaque

4. The plaque shavings are safely collected in the nose cone of the catheter; the procedure may be repeated before the catheter is removed

5. Blood flow is restored to the artery following the procedure

Source: From Karen Price, "St. Mary's First in St. Louis to Offer New DCA Procedure" in *St. Mary's Center News*. Copyright St. Mary's Health Center, St. Louis, MO. Reprinted by permission.

DCA removes plaque. DCA is another alternative to treating certain types of blockages in the heart's circulation.* (57, 69, 80) (See fig. 6.8.)

endovascular stenting—balloon-expandable and self-expandable stents utilized to decrease the frequency of acute occlusion and restenosis that may occur following procedures such as percutaneous transluminal angioplasty (PTA). Types of stents include balloon-expandable Palmaz-Schatz stent and the Wiktor stent, and the Wallstent, a self-expanding stent. (24, 56, 58, 69, 100, 108)

percutaneous transluminal angioplasty (PTA)—nonoperative procedure used to dilate a stenosed artery by introducing a double-lumen balloon catheter (usually Grüntzig type) with the balloon deflated into the stenosed artery. After the catheter has crossed the stenotic lesion, the balloon is inflated to enlarge the arterial lumen and the deflated catheter is withdrawn. The procedure has been used to relieve angina pectoris caused by single high-grade coronary artery stenosis and ischemic atherosclerotic disease in the basilar, iliac, or femoral arteries. It is an effective method of treating renovascular hypertension due to renal artery stenosis. (11, 22, 80, 84, 109)

OPERATIVE TERMS (SEE TABLE 6.2.)

biopsy of pericardium—excision of a small piece of pericardial tissue for microscopic study. (67)

cardiac biopsy—excision of tissue from the heart for the purpose of diagnosing various disease states. This can be done at the time of the operation or by means of a biotome adapted to an intracardiac catheter. Under fluoroscopic control, the biotome is passed through a large peripheral vein into the right atrium and right ventricle for biopsy. Tissue studies aid in the evaluation of the patient's condition before cardiovascular surgery. Biopsy is the primary method of detecting rejection of the transplanted heart. (109)

*The description of directional coronary atherectomy is from Karen Price, "St. Mary's First in St. Louis to offer New DCA Procedure" in St. Mary's Center News. Copyright St. Mary's Health Center, St. Louis, MO. Reprinted by permission.

TABLE **6.2**	Some Cardiovascular Conditions Amenable to Surgery		
Anatomic Site	*Diagnosis*	*Type of Surgery*	*Operative Procedure*
Heart: Pulmonary artery Aorta	Patent ductus arteriosus	Complete division of ductus arteriosus	Obliteration of ductus by dividing ductus and suturing the cut ends
Heart: Pulmonary artery Aorta	Complete transposition of pulmonary artery and of aorta	Blalock-Hanlon operation	Right thoracotomy and exposure of interatrial groove Occlusion of vessels, application of Satinsky-type clamp, section of both atria Removal of segment and portion of septum
Heart: Atria Septum	Interatrial septal defect	Repair of interatrial septal defect Open method under direct vision	Interatrial septal defect closed by direct suture or patch Extracorporeal circulation
Heart: Ventricles Septum	Congenital heart disease Interventricular septal defect with pulmonary hypertension	Banding of pulmonary artery	Pulmonary artery constricted with umbilical tape in instances where direct closure is contraindicated
Heart: Ventricles Septum	Interventricular septal defect	Open cardiotomy and repair of interventricular septal defect under direct vision	Incision into right ventricle and exposure of defect Repair with suture or ventricular patch Extracorporeal circulation with or without hypothermia
Heart: Right atrium	Myxoma of right atrium with progressive right-sided heart failure	Atriotomy with excision of primary cardiac tumor Open heart surgery	Right atrium opened and myxoma removed Use of cardiopulmonary bypass with or without hypothermia
Heart: Atria Ventricles	Atherosclerotic heart disease Adams-Stokes syndrome, atrioventricular block	Insertion of transvenous endocardial pacemaker	Catheter electrode passed through incision in jugular vein and lodged in apex of right ventricle Subcutaneous tunnel and pocket constructed Catheter electrode fastened to pacemaker Pacemaker inserted into pocket

TABLE 6.2 (continued)

Anatomic Site	Diagnosis	Type of Surgery	Operative Procedure
Heart: Pericardium	Constrictive pericarditis Adherent pericardium	Pericardiectomy Pericardiolysis	Partial removal of the pericardium Breaking up of adhesions
Heart: Myocardium Coronary arteries	Obstructive coronary artery disease with myocardial ischemia and angina pectoris	Myocardial revascularization by aortocoronary bypass with autogenous grafts of saphenous vein Open heart surgery	Surgical creation of new ostium in ascending aorta and new openings into vessels of aortic arch for implanting proximal ends of vein grafts Anastomoses of distal ends of grafts with coronary arteries to bypass occlusive lesions Extracorporeal circulation with or without hypothermia
Heart: Mitral valve	Mitral valve incompetence	Mitral valve reconstruction	Anulus remodeling Leaflet resection Chordal shortening Chordal fenestration and resection
Heart: Ventricles Pulmonary artery	Tetralogy of Fallot —ventricular defect —pulmonic stenosis —dextroposition of aorta —hypertrophy of right ventricle	Shunting operations Blalock's method Potts-Smith's method Brock's operation Total correction of tetralogy of Fallot Open heart surgery	Joining right or left subclavian to pulmonary artery Anastomosis between pulmonary artery and aorta Removal of pulmonic obstruction Defects totally repaired using suture closure or patch for closure Infundibulum resected to correct pulmonary stenosis Cardiopulmonary bypass with or without hypothermia
Heart: Left ventricle	Ventricular aneurysm Left-sided heart failure	Ventricular aneurysmectomy Open heart surgery	Transverse sternotomy with bilateral thoracotomy; heart opened Removal of aneurysm, its sac, and related thrombus Reconstruction of left ventricle and closure of heart Extracorporeal circulation with or without hypothermia

TABLE 6.2 (continued)

Anatomic Site	Diagnosis	Type of Surgery	Operative Procedure
Tricuspid valve	Triscuspid incompetence	Tricuspid repair	Remodeling of anulus with prosthetic ring
Heart	Advanced occlusive coronary artery disease, diffuse myocardial damage, irreversible left ventricular failure	Median sternotomy Cardiac homotransplantation	Sternal split incision Simultaneous division of aorta, pulmonary artery, and atria followed by excision of donor and recipient hearts Implantation of donor heart by atrial and vascular anastomoses to recipient heart Extracorporeal circulation with or without hypothermia
Heart: Myocardium Coronary arteries	Progression of coronary atherosclerotic heart disease with graft closure and recurrence of disabling angina pectoris	Reoperative revascularization by internal mammary-coronary artery anastomoses	Median sternotomy Pericardium opened Circulatory support as needed Internal mammary artery grafts implanted in coronary branches to bypass occlusions Pump oxygenator primed with colloid electrolyte solution Moderate hemodilution with or without hypothermia
Heart: Aortic valve Mitral valve	Aortic stenosis and insufficiency Mitral stenosis and insufficiency due to rheumatic heart disease	Excision and replacement of aortic valve and mitral valve with Starr-Edwards aortic and mitral prostheses	Removal of calcified cups of aortic valve and seating of aortic prosthesis Total removal of calcified mitral valve and insertion of mitral valve prothesis Extracorporeal circulation, coronary artery perfusion, and hypothermia

TABLE 6.2   (continued)

Anatomic Site	Diagnosis	Type of Surgery	Operative Procedure
Heart: Myocardium Coronary arteries	Triple-vessel coronary artery disease Severe, unstable angina pectoris	Sequential or multiple grafts for triple-vessel disease One circular graft used less frequently	Standard cardiopulmonary bypass procedure Moderate hemodilution and hypothermia or cold cardioplegic solution infused into aortic root for myocardial arrest Sequential or multiple grafts reversed and implanted into anterior aortic arch Creation of 4 to 6 coronary artery anastomoses to bypass stenotic lesions and establish complete myocardial revascularization
Heart: Mitral valve	Mitral stenosis due to rheumatic carditis Combined mitral stenosis and mitral insufficiency	Mitral commissurotomy Mitral valvoplasty	Separation of commissure of stenotic valve Suture or plastic repair of valve; use of prosthesis
Artery	Occlusive femoropopliteal disease due to atherosclerotic lesions Pregangrenous state	Femoropopliteal reconstruction by the use of reversed autogenous vein graft	Removal of saphenous vein from knee to saphenofemoral junction Vein reversed and attached to patent vessel by end-to-end anastomosis bypassing the obstruction
Aorta	Dissecting aneurysm of thoracic aorta	Resection of aneurysm Replacement with plastic prosthesis	Aneurysm removed and defect bridged with prosthesis
Aorta	Aortic coarctation	Excision of coarctation Aortic anastomosis	Removal of constricted area and joining cut ends together with suture
Aorta	Atherosclerotic aortoiliac occlusion	Aortoiliac endarterectomy	Incision into left external iliac artery and removal of plaque Dissection of segmentally obstructed portion of intima of: —common iliac arteries near bifurcation of aorta; and —terminal aorta

TABLE 6.2	(continued)		
Anatomic Site	*Diagnosis*	*Type of Surgery*	*Operative Procedure*
Artery	Embolus in femoral artery	Embolectomy	Incision into femoral artery and removal of clot
Artery	Subclavian steal syndrome	Subclavian-subclavian crossover bypass graft	Extrathoracic approach Subclavian artery crossclamped Dacron graft anastomosed to vessel and tunneled subcutaneously in tissues of anterior neck Second anastomosis performed
Veins	Varicosity	Vein stripping	Ligation of saphenous vein; incision made and stripper introduced into vein; vein extirpated

cardiac massage, open—emergency thoracotomy and manual compression of the heart 40 to 60 times a minute, in an attempt to force blood from the ventricles into the aorta and pulmonary artery. (62, 109)

cardiac transplantation, heart transplantation—removal of a human cadaver heart for implantation into a recipient who is in irreversible cardiac failure. The procedure includes a median sternotomy, cannulation of vena cavae, cardiopulmonary bypass, surgical divisions of the ascending aorta, main pulmonary artery and atria, the excision of donor and recipient hearts, and implantation of donor heart by atrial and vascular anastomoses to recipient. (48, 109)

correction of congenital septal defects:

    atrial septal defect—closure of defect under direct vision using cardiopulmonary bypass with or without hypothermia.

    ventricular septal defect—repair of defect by direct suture or use of ventricular patch such as Dacron patch. Extracorporeal circulation (see p. 149) with or without hypothermia is employed. (34, 109)

correction of patent ductus arteriosus—complete division of patent ductus; the ductus is divided, and the pulmonic and aortic ends are closed separately by suture. (34, 73, 104, 109)

correction of transposition of the great vessels: (104)

    Blalock-Hanlon operation—surgical creation of an atrial septal defect as a palliative method, which provides increased intracardiac mixing of the oxygenated and unoxygenated blood.

    Mustard's operation—surgical revision of the atrial septum, transposing the venous return to match the transposed outflow tracts.

    Rashkind's operation, atrioseptostomy by balloon catheter—surgical creation of an atrial septal defect for palliation.

    Senning's operation, revised technique—reconstruction of a new atrial septum using the left atrial appendix to invert the atrial flow in transposition of the great arteries.

mitral commissurotomy—separation of the stenotic valve at points of fusion. (36)

percutaneous mitral valvuloplasty—a floating balloon catheter is advanced across the atrial septum, through the mitral and aortic valves. The guidewire is passed through the

Figure 6.9 Direct myocardial revascularization by triple aortocoronary artery bypass using autogenous vein grafts, anterior view.

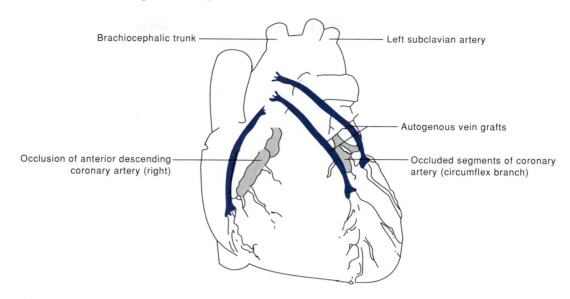

floating balloon catheter. The floating balloon is removed and the guidewire is left in place. Two 20-millimeter balloon catheters are advanced over the guidewire and placed across the stenotic mitral valve. After two or three inflations, the commissures split, thus widening the opening and relieving the stenosis. Percutaneous mitral valvuloplasty is an alternative approach to mitral commissurotomy. (6)

reconstruction of mitral valve—procedure to relieve mitral valve incompetence, including:

anulus remodeling—restoring the proper size and shape by prosthetic rings to establish normal valve orifice and function.

chordal fenestration and resection—improving leaflet motion by resecting fused chordae at triangular portion.

chordal shortening—shortening chordae by plastic repair of chordae or papillary muscle.

leaflet resection—resecting abnormal segments in the presence of abnormal leaflets or fibrotic lesions. (36)

myocardial revascularization—operative procedure that supplies the ischemic heart muscle with systemic arterial blood. Various techniques include:

aortocoronary artery bypass—revascularization of the heart muscle by attaching autogenous saphenous vein grafts (SVG) to the ascending aorta and the coronary arteries distal to the occlusions. Vascular obstructions are thus bypassed, and adequate blood flow to the heart is immediately restored. Since coronary atherosclerosis frequently involves several vessels, multiple grafts are often employed to safeguard permanent circulatory efficiency. (See fig. 6.9.)

internal mammary-coronary artery anastomoses—cardiac revascularization by joining internal mammary artery grafts (IMAG) to one or more coronary arteries to bypass occlusive lesions and relieve myocardial ischemia. Because IMA grafts have proved to be highly patent and stable, they are successfully used when recurrence of disabling angina caused by graft closure or progressive coronary atherosclerosis necessitates reoperative revascularization. Unstable angina may be effectively treated with venous autografts, internal mammary artery autografts, or both. (See fig. 6.10.)

Figure 6.10 Internal mammary artery bypass grafts for myocardial revascularization, anterior view.

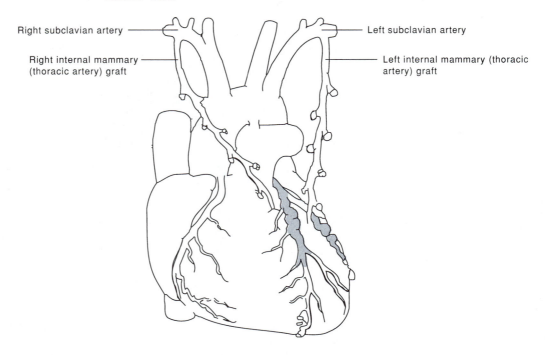

Right subclavian artery

Right internal mammary (thoracic artery) graft

Left subclavian artery

Left internal mammary (thoracic artery) graft

sequential vein graft for coronary artery bypass—procedure used for serious coronary disease with multiple vessel narrowing. Complete myocardial revascularization may be achieved by grafting distally to all or any of the following:
- *posterior descending right coronary artery;*
- *second marginal circumflex artery;*
- *first marginal circumflex coronary arteries;* or
- *diagonal branch and left anterior descending coronary arteries* (Cleveland's technique). (36, 50, 84)

pericardiectomy—incision and partial dissection of the pericardium to relieve the heart from constricting fibrous adhesions. (8, 67)

pulmonary banding—operation performed in infants with congenital defects and large left-to-right shunts at the ventricular level, which are not suitable for immediate complete correction. (34, 109)

tetralogy of Fallot: (34, 109)
 palliative operations:
- *Blalock-Taussig total repair*—anastomosis of the subclavian artery to the pulmonary artery to shunt some of the systemic circulation into the pulmonary circulation.
- *pulmonary valvotomy or infundibular resection*—correction of pulmonary stenosis by valvotomy or resection.
- *Waterston shunt initial repair*—anastomosis between the right pulmonary artery and ascending aorta for palliation of hypoxia in infants with tetralogy.
- *total correction by direct vision*—removal of pulmonary obstruction and closure of ventricular septal defect.

tricuspid repair—remodeling of anulus (annulus) with prosthetic ring. (109)

valve replacement surgery, cardiac—removal of incompetent or stenotic heart valve and replacement with a

> *bioprosthesis and homograft:* (36, 84, 109)
>> • *Carpentier-Edwards bioprosthesis*—porcine valve preserved in glutaraldehyde.
>> *pericardial valve*—designed to improve hemodynamics in small orifices. The septal bar projection is reduced in this model by mounting techniques that incorporate the bar into an asymmetric anulus. The mounting techniques avoid fixation sutures at the commissures. The design has a flexible stent to reduce stress at the commissures and at the base of the cusps.
>> *supra-anular porcine valve*—design characteristics aim at decreasing the transvalvular gradient and turbulence around the valve, as well as increasing longevity and decreasing calcification incidence.
>> • *Hancock bioprosthesis*—consists of the aortic valve of the pig secured to a flexible support with a stellite ring at the anulus to prevent distortion. The frame is covered with a fabric and a sewing ring allows the valve to be attached securely to the patient's tissues.
>> • *Hancock modified-orifice bioprosthesis*—valve has been modified by removing the right coronary cusp with its muscular shelf and replacing it with a noncoronary cusp (which has no muscle shelf) from another valve.
>> • *Ionescu-Shiley bioprosthesis*—valve is composed of three leaflets of bovine pericardium attached to a symmetrical titanium support covered with Dacron fabric.
>> • *unstented homograft valve*—"fresh" homograft for replacing the aortic valve.
>
> *mechanical prosthesis:* (36, 84, 109)
>> • *Björk-Shiley prosthesis*—tilting disc valve of pyrolite carbon that is retained by two struts. Other designs of the Björk-Shiley prostheses include:
>> *convex-concave disc of pyrolite carbon*—the inlet strut is formed from the same solid block of alloy as the valve housing and is no longer welded in place; however, the outlet strut is welded.
>> *monostrut valve with a single outlet strut*—the whole valve housing is constructed from one piece of metal alloy, eliminating all welds.
>> • *St. Jude Medical prosthesis*—bileaflet valve, made of pyrolytic carbon with no metal parts. The two leaflets open to give central flow, tilting nearly perpendicular to the anulus when the valve opens, eliminating the need for any supporting struts.
>> • *Medtronic-Hall prosthesis*—tilting disc prosthesis with pyrolytic carbon disc occluder in a titanium valve housing. The disc is retained by sliding along a central bar that allows the disc to move downstream, away from the orifice, during opening.
>> • *Sutter prosthesis*—caged ball prosthesis with a silicone rubber ball occluder and a titanium retaining cage on each side of the valve seat.
>> • *Starr-Edwards prosthesis*—caged ball prosthesis. Both models for aortic and mitral valve prostheses have a silicone rubber ball occluder with an uncovered stellite alloy cage.

valvotomy—incision into a valve.

> *mitral valvotomy*—splitting the two commissures (areas of fusion) of the mitral valve to widen its opening. (38)
> *pulmonary valvotomy*—incising the valve of the pulmonary artery to improve the pulmonary circulation. (109)

ventricular aneurysmectomy—excision of aneurysms, which are nonfunctional areas that weaken the pumping efficiency of the heart. Aneurysms may harbor clots, which can send embolisms to the brain or other vital organs. The procedure is sometimes combined with coronary revascularization using saphenous vein bypass grafts. (50, 84, 109)

SYMPTOMATIC TERMS

anasarca—massive, generalized edema with serous effusion, especially in the right pleural and peritoneal cavities. It occurs in right-sided heart failure and systemic congestion. (92)

Aschoff bodies—nodular lesions of the myocardium, pathognomonic (characteristic) of rheumatic disease. (83)

asystole—cardiac standstill; no contractions of the heart. (109)

bradycardia—slow heart action. (70)

cardiac edema—retention of water and sodium in congestive heart failure due to circulatory impairment. (92)

cardiac syncope—fainting associated with marked sudden decrease in cardiac output. (59)

cardiogenic shock—syndrome related to cardiovascular disease, primarily to myocardial infarction, ventricular failure, severe ventricular arrhythmias, cardiac tamponade, massive pulmonary embolism, and other disorders. The common denominator of shock, irrespective of its cause, is the reduced circulation to the vital organs. It is clinically characterized by mental torpor; reduction of blood pressure and pulse pressure; tachycardia; pallor; cold, clammy skin; and signs of congestive heart failure. (2, 21)

carotid sinus syncope, vasopressor type—fainting or clouded consciousness without change in heart rate. It is caused by hyperirritability of the carotid sinus or local disease. (49, 59)

ischemia—reduced blood supply to an organ, usually caused by arterial narrowing or occlusion in advanced atherosclerosis.

    cerebral ischemia—local anemia in the brain.

    myocardial ischemia—inadequate blood supply to the heart muscle. (75, 89, 94)

murmur—blowing sound heard on auscultation. (97)

palpitation—subjective awareness of skipping, pounding, or racing heartbeats. (97)

sinus rhythm—normal cardiac rhythm initiated at the sinoatrial node. (70)

systole—rhythmic contractions of the heart, particularly those of the ventricles that pump the blood through the body. (109)

tachycardia—rapid heart action. (109)

ARTERIES, CAPILLARIES, VEINS

ORIGIN OF TERMS

angi-, angio- (G)—vessel
arterio- (G)—artery
diastole (G)—expansion
hemangio- (G)—blood vessel

phleb-, phlebo- (G)—vein
pulsus (L)—stroke, beat
sclero- (G)—hard

systole (G)—contraction
thrombo- (G)—clot
veno- (L)—vein

PHONETIC PRONUNCIATION OF SELECTED TERMS

cardiogenic	CAR-de-owe-GEN'ick
hypovolemic	HI-po-vo-LE'mick
phlebitis	flee-BY'tis
septic	SEP'tick
vasoconstriction	VAS-owe-con-STRICK'shun
vasodepression	VAS-owe-de-PRESH'un

ANATOMIC TERMS (47, 51, 91, 102, 106) (SEE FIGS. 6.11–6.14.)

aorta—main artery of the trunk.

arteries—elastic vessels that carry blood away from the heart and distribute it to various parts of the body.

    arterioles—subdivisions of arterial vessels resulting in thinner tubes that progressively develop into fine branches. Arterioles have a relatively narrow lumen and thick muscular walls.

Figure 6.11   Wall of an artery.

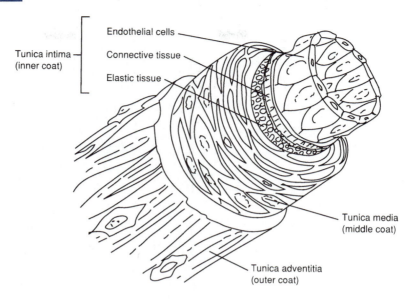

Tunica intima (inner coat)

Endothelial cells

Connective tissue

Elastic tissue

Tunica media (middle coat)

Tunica adventitia (outer coat)

Figure 6.12   Wall of a vein.

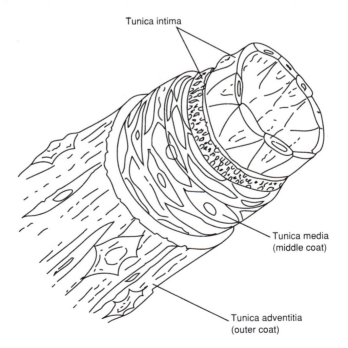

Tunica intima

Tunica media (middle coat)

Tunica adventitia (outer coat)

Figure 6.13 Major vessels of the arterial system (a. = artery).

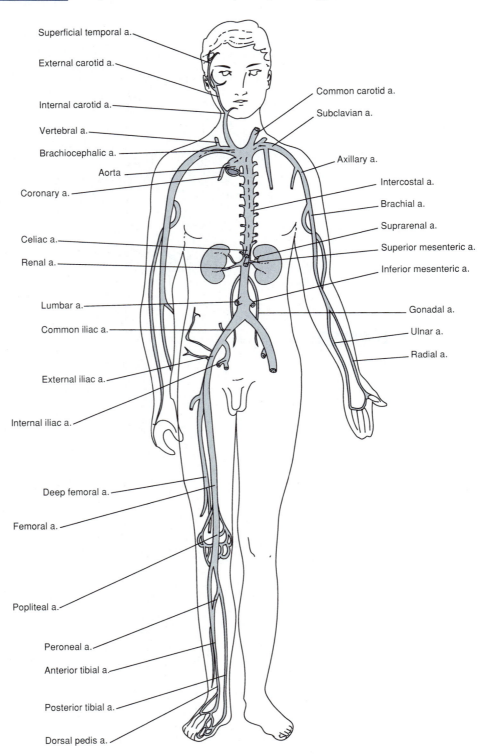

Superficial temporal a.

External carotid a.

Internal carotid a.

Vertebral a.

Brachiocephalic a.

Aorta

Coronary a.

Celiac a.

Renal a.

Lumbar a.

Common iliac a.

External iliac a.

Internal iliac a.

Deep femoral a.

Femoral a.

Popliteal a.

Peroneal a.

Anterior tibial a.

Posterior tibial a.

Dorsal pedis a.

Common carotid a.

Subclavian a.

Axillary a.

Intercostal a.

Brachial a.

Suprarenal a.

Superior mesenteric a.

Inferior mesenteric a.

Gonadal a.

Ulnar a.

Radial a.

Figure 6.14   Major vessels of the venous system (v. = vein).

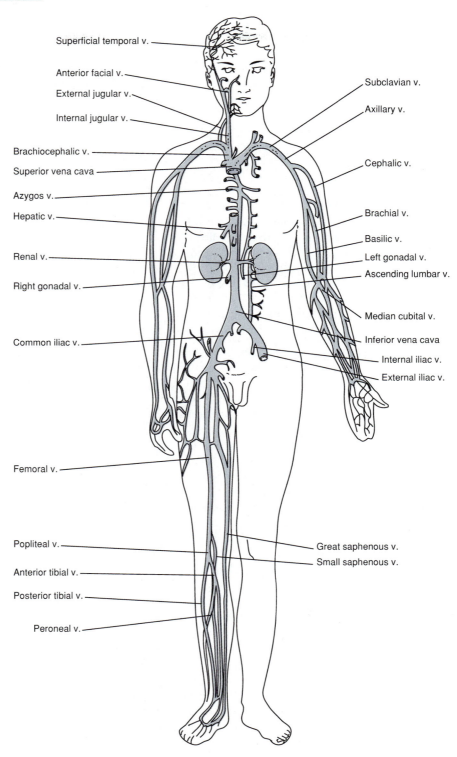

Superficial temporal v.

Anterior facial v.

External jugular v.

Internal jugular v.

Brachiocephalic v.

Superior vena cava

Azygos v.

Hepatic v.

Renal v.

Right gonadal v.

Common iliac v.

Femoral v.

Popliteal v.

Anterior tibial v.

Posterior tibial v.

Peroneal v.

Subclavian v.

Axillary v.

Cephalic v.

Brachial v.

Basilic v.

Left gonadal v.

Ascending lumbar v.

Median cubital v.

Inferior vena cava

Internal iliac v.

External iliac v.

Great saphenous v.

Small saphenous v.

coats or wall of arteries:
- *tunica adventitia*—outer coat.
- *tunica media*—middle coat.
- *tunica intima*—inner coat.

veins—vessels that return blood to the heart. Most veins contain valves that prevent backflow of blood and encourage the flow of blood toward the heart.

venules—smallest veins or tributaries that unite to form larger veins which commonly join together, forming venous plexuses.

venae comitantes—accompanying veins. The two veins that accompany medium-sized arteries, one on each side.

coats or wall of veins:
- *tunica adventitia*—outer coat.
- *tunica media*—middle coat.
- *tunica intima*—inner coat.

capillaries—microscopic vessels that connect arterioles to the venules. Capillaries are usually arranged in communicating networks called capillary beds. In some parts of the body, as in the fingers and toes, there are direct connections between arteries and veins, and there are no capillaries between them.

blood pressure: (77, 97)

systolic—force exerted by blood against the arterial walls at the end of the contraction of the left ventricle.

diastolic—force exerted by blood against the arterial walls at the end of the relaxation of the left ventricle.

DIAGNOSTIC TERMS

acute limb ischemia—sudden catastrophic interruption of blood flow to an extremity demanding reversal by surgery or clot lysis to save the limb. Vascular disorders such as acute arterial embolization and the deposition of atheromatous plaques associated with bleeding and a relatively rapid thrombus formation precipitate the occlusive event. The limb is waxy, pale, cold, painful, or insensitive to touch and exhibits rigidity or deep muscle tenderness. (109)

aneurysm of aorta—irreversible dilatation of a weakened part of the wall of the vessel. (35, 39, 109)

dissecting type—progressive splitting of middle coat that may involve the entire circumference of the aorta. When pulsating blood is driven between the media and intima, the tear may rapidly extend the whole length of the aorta, causing excruciating, ripping pain.

fusiform type—tubular swelling of the walls of the aorta involving the three coats and circumference.

sacculated type—saclike bulging of a weakened part of the aorta formed by the middle and outer coats.

aortic arch syndrome, pulseless disease, Takayasu's syndrome—group of disorders characterized by occlusion of vessels of the arch of the aorta associated with extremely weak or absent pulses, low blood pressure in upper extremities, and diminished circulation to the brain that may result in neurologic deficit. (60, 99)

aortic atresia—congenital narrowing or absence of the ascending portion of the aorta, usually involving the aortic valve as well. (109)

aortic stenosis—congenital or acquired narrowing of valvar opening into aorta. (34, 65, 84)

aortoiliac occlusive disease, Leriche's syndrome—gradual thrombosis of terminal aorta near the bifurcation and extending to the iliac arteries. Claudication and trophic changes may be present. (39)

arteriosclerosis—degenerative, vascular disorder characterized by a thickening and loss of elasticity of arterial walls. It affects small arteries and arterioles and seems to be secondary to hypertension. Arteriosclerosis and atherosclerosis are frequently used as synonyms.

atherosclerosis—disorder in which an intimal plaque or atheroma is produced by focal lipid deposits. In the beginning, the atheroma is soft and pasty. With time the plaque may undergo fibrosis and calcification, or it may ulcerate into the arterial lumen. Ulcerated plaques are prone to cause mural thrombosis and eventually arterial occlusion. It has been demonstrated that atherosclerosis is a biologial process similar to bone formation, possibly mediated by pericytelike cells. In the future, it may be possible to identify risk factors for atherosclerosis. (5, 7, 20, 88, 103, 107)

carotid occlusive disease—extracranial or intracranial vascular disorder usually caused by atheromatous lesions that obstruct carotid arteries; if progressive, may lead to reduced blood flow in the brain, transient ischemic attacks, cerebrovascular insufficiency, and stroke. (58, 99, 109)

coarctation of aorta—constriction of a segment of the aorta. (34, 65, 104, 109)

dilatation of aorta—abnormal enlargement of the aorta.

embolism—a "throwing in"; blocking of a blood vessel by a clot or other substance brought by the circulating blood. (3, 86, 90)

hypertension—pathologic elevation of the blood pressure; according to the World Health Organization (WHO), blood pressure that consistently exceeds 160/95 mm Hg. (32, 41, 66)

hypertensive cardiovascular disease—sustained high blood pressure associated with cardiovascular, renal, and retinal changes. (66)

Mönckeberg's medial calcific stenosis, medial calcinosis—vascular disorder in which ringlike calcifications occur in the media of muscular arteries. It is clinically of little importance, since the medial lesions fail to encroach on the arterial lumen. (5, 7, 20, 88, 103, 107)

peripheral arterial insufficiency of extremities—impaired circulation to the extremities, particularly to the lower limbs. It is characterized by claudication, coldness, pallor, trophic changes, ulceration, and gangrene in the involved extremity. (99)

peripheral vascular disease—any disorder directly affecting the arteries, veins, and lymphatics, except those of the heart. (99)

phlebitis—inflammation of the veins.

phlebosclerosis—hardening of the walls of the veins.

pulmonary hypertension—pathophysiological condition in which blood pressure in the pulmonary circulation is elevated above normal. This includes pressure in the pulmonary arterial system, as well as elevation of pressures in the pulmonary capillaries and veins. Pulmonary hypertension from any cause such as mitral stenosis, chronic lung disease, or pulmonary emboli can produce pulmonary incompetence. (28, 66)

pulmonary stenosis—occurs because of obstruction to systolic flow across the valve. It is usually congenital; acquired pulmonary stenosis is rare. (82)

Raynaud's disease—painful vascular disorder characterized by peripheral spasms of the digital arterioles of the fingers and toes, which may result in gangrene. Raynaud's disease should be differentiated from the numerous disorders that may be associated with Raynaud's phenomenon. Raynaud's disease appears between ages 15 and 45 and it tends to be progressive, and unlike Raynaud's phenomenon, which may be unilateral and involve only 1 or 2 fingers. (53, 99)

Raynaud's phenomenon—characterized by intermittent attacks of pallor or cyanosis, usually in the fingers (1 or 2 fingers usually affected), rarely in the toes. The patient's history and physical examination lead to the diagnosis of rheumatoid arthritis, systemic sclerosis, systemic lupus erythematosus, and mixed connective tissue disease. These disorders are commonly associated with Raynaud's phenomenon. (4, 53, 99)

rupture of an aneurysm—break in the weakened vascular wall of an aneurysm associated with hemorrhage. (53, 95)

small artery occlusive disease, arteriosclerosis obliterans—arterial obstruction of extremities, particularly affecting the lower limbs and causing ischemia. Obstructing lesions may occur in arteries less than 3 millimeters (mm) in diameter (e.g., radial, ulnar, tibial, or peroneal arteries). Those usually affected include persons with diabetes mellitus, vasculitis, or thromboangiitis obliterans (Buerger's disease). Hand, foot, or digital ischemia can result from these conditions, and amputation may be required. (58)

subclavian steal syndrome—a symptom complex of cerebrovascular insufficiency, usually due to segmental atheromatous occlusion of the subclavian artery proximal to the vertebral artery. Since the circulation through the vertebral artery is reversed, the subclavian is said "to steal" cerebral blood. A delay in the arrival time of the radial pulse on the affected side is diagnostic of reversed vertebral artery flow. A localized murmur and a difference in brachial blood pressure are common manifestations. The patient may experience dizziness, vertigo, light-headedness, tinnitus, blurred vision, headache, and ataxia. (63)

superior vena cava syndrome—obstruction of the superior vena cava, clinically recognized by numerous collateral veins distributed over the anterior chest, dilated neck veins, edema, and cyanosis of the upper body. Mayo Clinic studies indicate that superior vena cava syndrome is caused by malignancies in about 75% of cases. About 25% result from benign conditions, such as thrombosis of superior vena cava or clot formation around central venous catheters. (53, 99)

thoracic outlet syndromes—neurovascular compression syndromes affecting the structures of the thoracic outlet. Offending lesions are detected by angiography. Included are:

cervical rib and scalenus anticus syndrome—cutoff or torsion of subclavian artery may be present.
scalenus anticus and pectoralis minor syndrome—cutoff or torsion of subclavian artery and compression or thrombosis of axillary veins may be demonstrated by angiography.
scalenus anticus syndrome and tightness of costoclavicular space—a ridgelike compression of subclavian artery and venous compression or thrombosis may produce the syndrome. (53, 58, 109)

thromboangiitis obliterans, Buerger's disease—inflammatory, obstructive disease involving primarily the peripheral blood vessels of the lower extremities. (53, 99)

thrombophlebitis—inflammatory reaction of the walls of veins to infection, associated with intravascular clotting. (53, 99)

thrombosis—formation of blood clots in a blood vessel, leading to circulatory obstruction. (53)

varicose veins, varicosity—condition of having distended and tortuous veins, most commonly present in lower extremities. (40, 53, 99)

vascular injuries:

aortic lacerations—tears of the aorta occur most frequently at the aortic isthmus, the weakest part of the aorta, and less frequently in the ascending or descending aorta. Traumatic transection of the aorta may be followed by dissection of the entire vessel.
brachiocephalic lacerations—these injuries are frequently associated with aortic lacerations, and if multiple and severe, they are life threatening. (40)

OPERATIVE TERMS (SEE TABLE 6.2.)

anastomosis of blood vessels—end-to-end union of two different blood vessels or two segments of same blood vessels after excision of lesion. (34)

aneurysmectomy—removal of an aneurysm. (34)

aneurysm, resection of—excision of aneurysm and repair of arterial defect by insertion of homograft or prosthesis. (34, 39, 58)

aortic aneurysm resection, abdominal—clamping of aorta and iliac arteries, opening of the aneurysm, removal of thrombus, and reconstruction by means of a preclotted, knitted Dacron graft. (34, 39, 58)

aortofemoral bypass grafting—surgical procedure for aortoiliac occlusive (Leriche's) disease, consisting of appropriate vascular clamping and graft anastomoses, usually end to side, below, and above the obstructed segments to bypass circulatory occlusions. The formation of collateral vessels may maintain the circulation in graft failure. (39)

aortoiliac replacement grafting—excision of occluded segments of the aorta and iliac arteries followed by graft replacement. Graft failure is life threatening. (58, 109)

arterial homograft—arteries obtained at autopsies under aseptic technique and preserved by freezing or chemicals. They are used for replacing the excised segments of an artery. (109)

bypass graft, autogenous—implantation of an autograft, usually a segment of a saphenous vein to bypass a vascular obstruction, such as occlusive lesions of the coronary, femoropopliteal, or carotid-subclavian arteries. The occluded vascular segment is left in place. Circulatory efficiency is usually restored. (58, 109)

carotid endarterectomy—removal of the inner coat (intima) of the carotid artery for occlusive vascular disease. The integrity of the procedure may be evaluated intraoperatively by means of a sterile Doppler probe; real-time B-mode ultrasonography; or operative arteriogram. (99)

coarctation of the aorta repair:

subclavian flap angioplasty—suture ligation of the ductus arteriosus followed by the subclavian flap being sutured to the aortic incision.

resection of the coarctation and end-to-end anastomosis—dissection of the coarctation followed by aorta-to-aorta anastomosis.

resection with insertion of Dacron prosthesis—dissection of the coarctation followed by insertion of tubular woven Dacron prosthesis. Preclotting of the woven prosthesis is beneficial in preventing bleeding from the cloth interstices. This approach is used where the coarctation is too long for a primary anastomosis to be performed.

aortoplasty with Dacron patch—resection of the coarctation and application of a diamond-shaped Dacron patch sutured to the aorta. This procedure may be quite appropriate in the older adult who has undergone sclerotic changes of the aorta, where it would be hazardous to perform an end-to-end anastomosis.

insertion of Dacron prosthesis—approach avoids further resection of stenotic area resulting from previous resection and end-to-end anastomosis. (34, 104, 109)

embolectomy—emboli may be excised directly or removed by retrograde method via femoral arteries by balloon catheter. With balloon deflated, Fogarty catheter is inserted into a vein where embolus is located. When in proper position, the balloon is inflated. By withdrawing the catheter, the clot is pulled through the incision to the body surface. (40)

femoropopliteal arterial reconstruction—bypass surgery for restoring the circulation in femoral artery occlusion. The obstruction is bypassed using an autogenous saphenous vein, a bioprosthesis (umbilical vein), or an inert prosthesis (Dacron or expanded polytetrafluoroethylene [PTFE]). (37, 39, 40)

femorotibial bypass grafting—graft from femoral or posterior or anterior tibial or peroneal artery to bypass the obstructed arterial segment. (39)

phleborrhaphy—suture of vein.

phlebotomy—opening of a vein; for example, to reduce high red count in polycythemia vera by bloodletting.

profundaplasty, profundoplasty—reconstruction of the profunda femoris artery enabling relief of intermittent claudication; also may affect limb salvage. (109)

shunt for portal hypertension—method of diverting a large volume of blood from the hypertensive portal system into the normal systemic venous circulation. This operation prevents hemorrhages from esophageal varices, which result from portal hypertension. (109) (See chapter 9.)

subclavian steal syndrome operations: (39, 63)

axillo-axillary bypass graft—passing the graft subcutaneously in the anterior chest wall with end-to-side anastomosis of the graft to each axillary artery.

carotid-subclavian anastomosis—joining the carotid and subclavian arteries to improve cerebral blood flow.

carotid-subclavian bypass graft—implanting an autograft in carotid and subclavian arteries to bypass the occluded segment of the subclavian artery.

subclavian-subclavian bypass—inserting a knitted, preclotted Dacron graft and anastomosing one end of the graft with the right and the other end with the left subclavian artery, thus creating a crossover bypass of the occluded arterial segment.

thrombectomy—removal of a thrombus; for example, from an occluded portal vein. (40)

thromboendarterectomy (TEA)—initial arteriotomy followed by stripping of the diseased intima, removal of thrombus, and subsequent closure of vessel. Saphenous vein or Dacron patches may be used to prevent narrowing of the lumen following TEA. (99, 109)

vein stripping—surgical procedure to relieve varicosity. (40)

venesection—incision into a vein.

SYMPTOMATIC TERMS

acrocyanosis—bluish discoloration of fingertips and toes. (53)

angiospasm, vasospasm—involuntary contractions of the muscular coats of blood vessels; spasm of blood vessels. (109)

claudication:

lower-extremity claudication—limping caused by inadequate blood supply and associated with cramping pains in the calf muscles. It is usually relieved by rest and thus is intermittent.

upper-extremity claudication, brachial claudication—inadequate blood supply to an arm causing intermittent or persistent cramping pain. (53)

digital—referring to fingers and toes.

digital blanching—fingers and toes becoming pallid as a result of vasospasm of digital arterioles; seen in Raynaud's disease. (99, 109)

extravasation—escape of fluid (serum, lymph, blood) into the adjacent tissues. (109)

ischemia—local anemia of an organ or part resulting from circulatory obstruction or vasospasm. (75, 89, 109)

paroxysmal digital cyanosis—attacks of cyanosis caused by the interruption of blood flow in palmar and plantar arteries. (99)

pedal circulation—circulation in the foot.

pulse—rhythmical throbbing of regularly recurrent wave of distention in arteries that results from progress through an artery of blood injected into the arterial system at each contraction of the ventricles of the heart. This palpable rhythmic throbbing beat resulting from such pulse can be detected in a superficial artery, such as the radial artery.

bigeminal pulse—coupled beats.

Corrigan's or water-hammer pulse—strong, jerky beat followed by a sharp decline and collapse of beat.

dicrotic pulse—arterial beat with weak secondary wave that may be mistaken for two beats. (53, 77, 109)

pulse deficit—difference between apical heart rate and radial pulse rate, found in cardiac disease. (109)

shock—complex syndrome affecting the various body systems, resulting from the inability of cells to metabolize oxygen and needed substrates normally. Etiologic classifications include:

cardiogenic shock—phenomenon caused by decreased cardiac output, as in acute myocardial infarction, serious injury or cardiac surgery, ventricular arrhythmias, and ventricular failure.

hypovolemic shock—syndrome caused by markedly decreased blood volume.

septic shock—serious state resulting from infections, septicemia, or bacteremia.

Other distinctions of shock include:

early shock—initial arteriolar or venous constriction, accelerated contractibility of the heart, hyperventilation, and other effects.

late shock—life-threatening impairment of cellular metabolism causing advanced hypovolemia, intravascular clotting, and respiratory failure. (2, 21)

vasoconstriction—a narrowing of the vascular lumen, resulting in decreased blood supply. (109)

vasodepression—collapse caused by vasomotor depression. (109)

vasodilatation—widening of the vascular lumen, increasing the blood supply to a part. (109)

vasomotor—referring to nerves that control the muscular contractions of blood vessels. (109)

CLINICAL LABORATORY FINDINGS

TERMS PRIMARILY RELATED TO MYOCARDIAL ENZYMES AND ISOENZYMES

enzyme—catalytic protein that increases biochemical reactions in living cells; may possess marked specificity, and if present in the blood in large amount, usually indicates tissue damage. (101)

isoenzyme—distinct molecular fraction of a certain enzyme found in various tissues and separated by electrophoresis of serum. Diagnostic specificity is enhanced with the use of isoenzymes.

creatine kinase (CK) isoenzymes—isoenzymes of CK are dimers composed of muscle (M) or brain (B) subunits. Human myocardial CK constitutes approximately 14% as the MB isoenzyme (a species found only minimally in human tissues other than the heart). Usually, marked elevation of plasma MB-CK reflects irreversible myocardial damage.

lactate dehydrogenase isoenzymes (LD-1, LD-2)—both fractions prove to be useful indicators of myocardial infarction. LD-3 level is high in lung disease and LD-4 and LD-5 are moderately increased in liver disease. (42, 101)

serum enzymes of the heart muscle but also present in other organs include:

aspartate aminotransferase (AST), glutamate oxaloacetate transaminase (GOT)—enzyme widely distributed in body tissues but found in its highest concentration in the liver and heart muscle. AST/GOT were utilized in the past, but currently are no longer routinely used. This is due to the false-positive elevations that often occur, as well as the time course of elevation and fall of AST/GOT, which is intermediate between that of CK and LDH. Its incremental value for establishing the diagnosis of acute myocardial infarction is negligible.

creatine kinase (CK)—enzymes released into the blood following injury to the heart muscle or skeletal muscles. CK rises within 8 to 14 hours and usually returns to normal by 48 to 72 hours following infarction. (42)

lactate dehydrogenase (LD, LDH)—enzyme primarily found in the heart muscle, skeletal muscles, liver, and kidney. LDH rises later (24 to 48 hours) and may remain elevated as long as 7 to 14 days following infarction. (101)

serum enzyme tests in myocardial infarction (MI)—determinations based on the principle that high levels of enzyme activity reflect the evolution and extent of damage to the heart muscle. Since enzymes are also present in other organs, the tests are nonspecific.

serum aspartate aminotransferase (SAST) formerly *serum glutamate oxaloacetate transaminase (SGOT)*—diagnostic aid in myocardial infarction detection used in the past.

serum creatine kinase (SCK)—determination of serum CK activity, a very useful test due to the early CK rise after myocardial infarction and the absence of the enzyme from the liver and blood. (101)

Reference values: (25)
- *serum creatine kinase*
  - *Females:* 38–174 U/L (SIU: 38–174 U/L)
  - *Males:* 96–140 U/L (SIU: 96–140 U/L)
  - **Increase** in myocardial infarction and acute lung disease. Since CPK appears in skeletal muscle, muscular dystrophy of Duchenne may have to be ruled out. (101)

serum lactate dehydrogenase (SLD, SLDH) test—determination of LD activity in serum, a valuable test because of its late enzyme rise and its prolonged elevation in myocardial infarction. A disadvantage is its lack of specificity, resulting from the enzyme release into red blood cells, liver, lungs, and skeletal muscles. (101)

Reference values (method varies): (25)
- *Serum lactate dehydrogenase (SLDH):* 210–420 U/L (SIU: 210–420 U/L)
  - **Increase** in myocardial infarction, progressive muscular dystrophy, megaloplastic anemia, and cancer. (101)

SPECIAL PROCEDURES

actuarial method—statistical calculation, especially of life expectancy.

antistreptolysin-O titer—diagnostic aid for rheumatic fever. Also, it may be used as a standard assay in the measurement of pre- and postimmunization titers to tetanus toxoid. (54)

atherogenic index (pl. **indices**)—determination of serum lipoproteins by ultracentrifugal analysis used as a possible aid in the detection of factors causing atherosclerosis. (88)

cardiac index—cardiac output in relation to body size, useful in assessing the cardiovascular status, particularly after open-heart surgery. (109)

cardiac monitor—electronic device applied to a patient that reveals the electric activity of the heart by visual and auditory signals and thereby permits the immediate detection of dangerous arrhythmias. (109)

cardiac pressures—pressures created by the force of the contraction within the heart chambers on the circulating blood. (109)

cardioplegia (elective cadiac arrest)—the elminiation of the electrical and mechanical actions of the heart by crossclamping the aorta and perfusing the coronary arteries (antegrade cardioplegia) or the coronary venous system (retrograde cardioplegia) with blood (blood cardioplegia) or crystalloid solution (crystalloid cardioplegia) containing substances, usually potassium ions, that cause standstill of the heart. The injected solutions are frequently cooled to further reduce the nutrient requirements of the heart. Cardioplegia provides a motionless, dry operative field facilitating the sewing on of bypass grafts, valve procedures, and repair of congenital defects. (18, 109)

cardiopulmonary bypass—mechanism for diverting the blood around the heart and lungs for the purpose of providing inflow occlusion to the heart. This enables the surgeon to operate on a bloodless heart muscle under direct vision. (18, 109)

cardiopulmonary resuscitation—heart-lung revival achieved by establishing a patent airway and restoring respiratory and circulatory functions by drugs, electric myocardial stimulation, or closed or open chest cardiac compression. (109)

cardioversion—direct current (DC) countershock applied to the chest to convert abnormal rhythms to normal sinus rhythm. (61)

central venous pressure (CVP)—measurement of pressure within the superior vena cava reflecting the pressure of the right atrium and expressed in centimeters of water pressure. CVP provides some index of the adequacy of the pumping action of the heart and of the blood volume in the vessels.

CVP reference values: 5 to 8 centimeters of water pressure.
- *Increase of CVP*—indicates overload of right side of heart in congestive heart failure.
- *Decrease of CVP*—suggests reduced blood volume and need for fluid replacement. (40, 101, 109)

coronary artery perfusion—introduction of blood into the coronary arteries by catheters during procedures in which the root of the aorta is opened. (109)

counterpulsation—method of supporting the failing myocardium by removing arterial blood during the ejection of the ventricles and returning it to the circulation during diastole. (13)

countershock—use of an external electronic defibrillator to terminate the disorderly electric activity within the heart that provokes the arrhythmia. In ventricular fibrillation, a brief high-voltage shock abruptly stops the chaotic twitching of the ventricular muscle fibers. If effective, the natural cardiac pacemaker regains control and restores normal contractions. (109)

defibrillator—mechanical device for applying electric shock to the closed chest or to the open heart to terminate abnormal cardiac rhythms. (61)

diastolic augmentation procedure—circulatory assistive technique in which a balloon, placed in the aorta, is inflated during diastole and collapsed during systole (phase-shift). This reduces the pressure against which the heart pumps, yet increases diastolic pressure and thus favorably influences coronary flow. (109)

direct-current defibrillation—countershock by a capacitor discharge defibrillator (DC type) instead of the alternating current of the original type of defibrillator (AC type). (18)

Doppler blood flowmetry—modality that utilizes ultrasonic signals permitting transcutaneous auscultation of blood flow. Evaluation of the signal at various levels on the leg and thigh can assist in locating a lesion. (109)

exhaled-air ventilation—artificial respiration using the mouth-to-mouth, mouth-to-nose, or mouth-to-tracheal-stoma method to restore ventilatory lung function. (109)

external arteriovenous (AV) shunt—procedure used to facilitate access to the patient's circulation by cannulation of blood vessels for prolonged hemodialysis. One piece of Silestic tubing is inserted into an artery, the other into an adjacent vein. They are then brought on top of the skin and connected with each other by removable Teflon connector. (109)

external cardiac compression—the application of rhythmic pressure (60 times per minute) over the lower sternum to compress the heart and produce artificial circulation. (109)

extracorporeal circulation—blood circulating outside of the body, a form of cardiopulmonary bypass. It may be achieved by using a heart-lung machine. (109)

heart-lung machine—apparatus used to substitute for cardiopulmonary function. It permits a direct-vision approach to cardiac lesions requiring corrective surgery. Venous blood returning to the heart is not allowed to enter the right atrium but is sucked away by two tubes, one in each of the main veins. It is then pumped into an artificial lung. Then the oxygen-laden blood enters a reservoir, passes through filters, and is pumped to the patient's arterial system. Many different types of heart-lung machines are now in use. (109)

hemodilution—reduction of normal red cell mass of the blood and its subsequent oxygen content. It may be caused by injury, hemorrhage, or blood dyscrasias or may be therapeutically used, as in cardiovascular surgery to prime the pump oxygenator systems.

> *extreme hemodilution*—total washout achieved by removing most of the blood and replacing it with colloid electrolyte solution that maintains a normal circulating volume and a colloid osmotic pressure of plasma.
>
> *moderate hemodilution*—induced dilution of the normal blood that keeps the volume of the packed red cells (VPRC) greater than 20%. It may be used as a primer in cardiopulmonary bypass and in treating shock, polycythemia, and high-viscosity disorders. (109)

hemodynamics—a study of blood circulation and blood pressure. (109)

implantable cardioverter defibrillator (ICD)—therapeutic modality designed to detect and cardiovert ventricular tachycardia, as well as providing defibrillation. There is a pulse generator and lead electrodes for arrhythmia detection and for delivery of the cardioverting/defibrilating pulse. All ICD systems utilized endocardial or epicardial placed rate-sensing leads for arrhythmia detection. A variety of electrode configurations may be used for delivering electric shock energy to the myocardium. The ICD is now considered the treatment of choice for survivors of out-of-hospital ventricular fibrillation with drug-refractory arrhythmias not associated with a reversible predisposing cause (e.g., myocardial ischemia). Another class of patients in which ICD is being used with increasing frequency is those persons with spontaneous and induced sustained monomorphic ventricular tachycardia. (10)

intra-aortic balloon counterpulsation—method of circulatory assistance for left ventricular power failure and cardiogenic shock refractory to adrenergic stimulation. A balloon catheter is inserted in the femoral artery and advanced to the descending thoracic aorta. Circulatory assistance is provided by diastolic counterpulsation, which is monitored by electrocardiographic recordings. (13)

normothermia—environmental temperature that maintains body temperature and metabolic requirements at normal levels. (109)

> *systemic hypothermia*—artificial reduction of the body temperature in an effort to lower the metabolic requirements of the patient, who is then better able to tolerate the interruption of cardiac inflow. (18)

oscillation—movement to and fro. (109)

oscilloscope—instrument for displaying electric signals, such as those made by blood pressure, electrocardiogram, heart sounds, or other signals, on a cathode ray tube monitoring screen. (109)

oxymetry, oximetry—measuring the amount of oxygen in blood by one of a variety of techniques. (101)

pacemakers and related terms: (30, 46, 68, 101, 109, 111)

> *cardiac pacing, physiologic*—a normal response to myocardial stimulation initiated at the sinoatrial node, followed by atrial contractions, activation of the atrioventricular node, spread of the impulse through the bundle of His, and subsequent contractions of the ventricles. (89)

> *cardiac pacing, electronic*—substitution of normal cardiac pacing in Stokes-Adams syndrome, ventricular standstill, certain dysrhythmias such as tachyarrhythmias, and myocardial infarction.

> *basic pacemaker electronics*—includes four elements: energy source, electronic circuit, enclosure packet for the pulse generator, which protects the energy supply and circuit from contact with tissue and fluids, and pacemaker leads.

> *modes of pacemaker function:*
> - *single-chamber pacing*—utilization of pacemaker devise for single chamber, that is, for either atrial or ventricular pacing.
> - *dual-chamber pacing*—utilization of pacemaker devise for dual chambers, that is, for atrial and ventricular pacing.

> *pacemakers in use:*
> - *external cardiac pacemaker*—electronic device for stimulating the ventricles through the closed chest wall in cardiac standstill.
> - *implantable cardiac pacemaker for temporary or permanent use*—electronic device that achieves myocardial stimulation by epicardial or endocardial and unipolar or bipolar electrodes. Recent technical improvements include the reduced size of the pulse generator and a prolonged pacemaker life.
>   - *temporary cardiac pacing*—first system type to work well was introduced in 1959, and for several years after that, patients were paced transvenously with external generators on a long-term basis. Implantable permanent pacemakers were developed in 1960. Temporary pacing offers a bridge to permanent pacing. Temporary pacing is required most frequently in patients with severe infranodal block and less frequently with AV nodal block and sick sinus syndrome. Temporary pacing may also be indicated when symptomatic or hemodynamically significant bradycardia is due to drugs (e.g., an excess of digitalis). (23)

types of pacing:
- *demand pacing*—impulse is fired by pacemaker according to patient's need, usually triggered from a ventricular electrode. These are of two types: the R-wave-triggered pacemaker and the R-wave-inhibited pacemaker. A third type is the atrioventricular pacemaker, with an electrode through the atrium, or it may be atrioventricular pacing, stimulating first the atrium, then after an appropriate delay, the ventricle. All of these pacemakers have the capability of coordinating with the patient's own cardiac rhythm and supplying the required atrial stimulus when atrioventricular sequential pacing is employed. Nuclear pacemakers, usually powered by plutonium-238 have raised concern about the long-term effect of radiation on patients. For example, bone marrow is susceptible to induction of leukemia by radiation. Because of these potential hazards, nuclear pacemakers are not recommended for younger patients. One advantage is that these pacemakers should function for at least 10 years or even longer.
- *fixed rate pacing*—impulse is generated at a predetermined rate, irrespective of intrinsic cardiac rhythm.
- *synchronized pacing*—impulse is fired synchronously with the P wave of the patient. One electrode is placed in the atrium, the other in the ventricle. Since the atria are stimulated to pour their entire contents into both ventricles, cardiac function is almost normal and synchronous.

methods of pacing:
- *epicardial pacing*—asynchronous or synchronous pacing in response to impulses of electrodes firmly attached to the epicardium and to a pulse generator concealed in a subcutaneous pocket.
- *transthoracic pacing*—ventricular stimulation achieved by electrodes inserted through the chest wall into the ventricle. A battery-powered pacer serves as a power source. Since pacing can be quickly initiated, transthoracic pacing is an effective emergency measure for resuscitating patients in cardiac arrest.
- *transvenous pacing*—electrode catheter is introduced into the heart through the jugular or other suitable vein, and its tip lodged in the right ventricular apex; the battery case is located in a subcutaneous pouch below the clavicle. The rate is fixed, usually 75 impulses per minute. No thoracotomy is required. Transvenous pacing may be used temporarily for myocardial stimulation to control bradycardia and prevent ventricular standstill.

percutaneous angiographic embolization—deliberate therapeutic occlusion of a blood vessel by injecting an embolic pharmaceutical agent through an angiographic catheter to control acute or recurrent bleeding; to close an atriovenous fistula; to occlude an atriovenous malformation; or to devascularize bone, kidney, or other tumors. (109)

perfusion in intracardiac surgery—method of providing oxygenated blood to the body by a heart-lung machine while interrupting the circulation through the heart.

precordial shock—electric treatment of arrhythmias. The elective procedure for converting certain tachyarrhythmias to normal rhythm. It is known as cardioversion, and is the emergency procedure for controlling ventricular fibrillation. It is usually referred to as defibrillation. (109)

pulmonary artery balloon counterpulsation—counterpulsation applied to the pulmonary circuit to improve blood flow to the lungs and relieve ventricular failure. (13)

pulmonary wedge pressure (PWP)—measurement of filling pressure of the left heart using an open-ended catheter wedged into a small pulmonary artery. A Swan-Ganz catheter is one such device. The procedure aids in differentiating congestive heart failure, allergic drug response, and fat embolism. (109)

sphygmomanometer—instrument for measuring blood pressure.

stethoscope—instrument for listening to sounds within the body. (109)

Swan-Ganz pulmonary artery catheterization—insertion of balloon-tipped catheter by peripheral venipuncture to catheterize the pulmonary artery and achieve hemodynamic monitoring of critically ill patients. (46, 109)

synchronized direct-current (DC) countershock—electric shock producing cardioversion by the use of a synchronized capacitator. DC is the method of choice in converting chronic atrial flutter or fibrillation to normal sinus rhythm. (109)

transducer, medical use—transforms energy into electric signals for monitoring physiologic functions such as blood pressure. (109)

treadmill exercise tolerance—stress test for evaluating the ability of the coronary circulation to meet the metabolic demands of an increasing exercise load. The patient is subjected to graded exercise on the treadmill or bicycle ergometer until the electrocardiogram shows ischemic changes. (29, 109)

two-step exercise test, Master's test—exercise test of coronary reserve. Within 1 and 1/2 minutes the patient goes up and down two steps, 9 inches high, 15 to 25 times. A postexercise electrocardiogram is taken immediately. If it is negative, a 3-minute double two-step test is performed. As soon as the patient experiences pain, the exercise is discontinued. (29, 109)

Valsalva maneuver—effective treatment for paroxysmal atrial tachycardia and similar disorders. The patient is instructed to inhale deeply, hold his or her breath and then strain down forcefully while slowly counting for 10 seconds. The Valsalva maneuver is also used as a test for cardiac reserve. (32, 89)

TERMS RELATED TO SPECIAL RECORDINGS OF HEART ACTION

apexcardiogram (ACG)—recording low-frequency vibrations of the precordium when a transducer is placed against the chest wall. The graphic record of the movements reflects the apex beat of the heart. (77)

bipolar lead—lead with two electrodes, one negative and one positive. (109)

echocardiogram—transmission of pulsed-reflected ultrasound through the heart, with detection of the returning echoes detailing the position and movement of the cardiac acoustic interfaces. Echocardiography is a multidimensional and multiplanar imaging modality. Cardiac ultrasound consists of three main interrelated forms: M-mode echocardiography, two-dimensional echocardiography, and Doppler echocardiography. (27)

electrocardiogram computer analysis—a software program utilized in data processing to provide a computer analysis of the electrocardiograms. (15)

electrocardiogram (ECG)—graph obtained that reflects the electric waves of the cardiac cycle or spread of excitation throughout the heart that are recorded at the body surface. It is an invaluable diagnostic aid in the detection of arrhythmias and myocardial damage. (See fig. 6.15.)

> *P wave*—reflects the contraction of the atria.
>
> *PR interval*—period in which the impulse passes through the atria and AV node, normally 0.16 to 0.20 seconds.
>
> *QRS complex*—waves represent ventricular excitation or depolarization of the ventricular myocardium, normally 0.12 seconds.
>
> *Q wave*—downward deflection and beginning of the complex.
>
> *R wave*—large upward wave.
>
> *S wave*—second large downward deflection and end of the QRS complex.
>
> *ST segment*—interval between the completion of depolarization and recovery of ventricular muscle fibers. The segment may be depressed or elevated in myocardial injury.
>
> *T wave*—recovery phase following the contraction. Inversion of the T wave usually reflects injury or ischemia of the heart muscle. (14, 65, 109)

| **Figure 6.15** | Normal electrocardiographic cycle. |

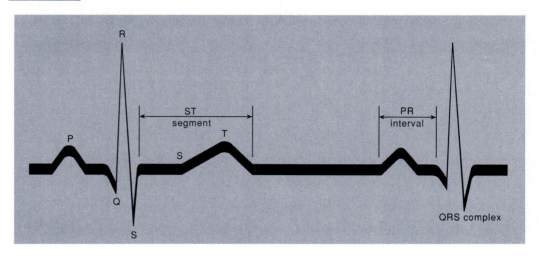

electrophysiological testing techniques: (1, 52, 65, 72)

ambulatory electrographic (Holter) monitoring—use of a portable ECG to permit continuous ECG recording of an ambulatory high-risk patient for early assessment and treatment of cardiac ischemia and ventricular arrhythmias or evaluation of response to activity or artificial pacemaker.

His bundle electrography (HBE)—combined atrial and ventricular ECG, showing the spread of the electric current throughout the heart muscle and separating conduction into two distinct subdivisions:

- *PH interval*—onset of P wave to His bundle activation or conduction time through both atria.
- *HR interval*—His bundle activation to onset of QRS complex, termed ventricular activation.

intracardiac electrography (IE)—adjunct to standard surface ECG using recordings by electrode catheters, percutaneously introduced into the heart via femoral or other suitable veins to assess arrhythmias and conduction disturbances.

impedance plethysmography—instrumental recording of variations in size of a part or organ caused by fluctuations in the size of the vascular bed. (40, 87)

phonocardiography—graphic recording of heart sounds, that includes not only the recording of auscultatory events of the precordium but also the recording of the carotid, venous, and apical precordial pulsations simultaneously with the electrocardiogram (ECG). This technique enhances the accuracy of the cardiac examination as it permits precise timing of cardiac auscultatory events as well as accurate and quantitative reproduction of physiologic events of the cardiac cycle. When phonocardiography is combined with echocardiography (phonoechocardiography), instantaneous valvular and ventricular wall motion can be correlated with sound and pressure events, further increasing this technique's diagnostic and instructional value. (80, 97)

phonoechocardiography—diagnostic method utilizing phonocardiography combined with M-mode echocardiography. The technique allows heart sounds to be timed precisely with valve motion. (80, 97)

pulse analysis—use of special transducer for recording of:

carotid pulse—initial abrupt rise corresponding to opening of aortic valve, subsequent brief tidal wave and decline with closing of aortic valve, and a gradual return to the baseline.

jugular venous pulse—accurate reflection of right atrial activity, recording waves of atrial systole, the filling of the right ventricle, and tricuspid function. (53, 76)

vectorcardiography—graphic recording of the direction and magnitude of the instantaneous electric forces of the heart from a cathode ray tube. A Polaroid photographic camera is frequently used. (13, 109)

ABBREVIATIONS

AMI—acute myocardial infarction
ASHD—arteriosclerotic heart disease
A-V, AV—atrioventricular, arteriovenous
BP—blood pressure
CCU—coronary care unit
CHD—coronary heart disease
CHF—congestive heart failure
CPR—cardiopulmonary resuscitation

CVP—central venous pressure
ECG or EKG—electrocardiogram, electrocardiographic, electrocardiography
HVD—hypertensive vascular disease
M—murmur
MI—myocardial infarction
mm Hg—millimeter of mercury
S-A or SA—sinoatrial (node)

ORAL READING PRACTICE

COARCTATION OF THE AORTA

Coarctation of the aorta, genetically identified as a **chromosomal abnormality,** is one of the most interesting congenital defects amenable to surgery. Coarctation occurs in approximately 7% of patients with **congenital heart disease** and is twice as common in men as in women, even though the lesion is frequently present in patients with **gonadal dysgenesis.** Clinical manifestations depend on the site and extent of obstruction and the presence of associated **cardiac anomalies. Aneurysmal dilatation** within the arterial supply of the **circle of Willis** produces a high risk of sudden rupture and death.

Coarctation consists of a constriction of a segment of the aorta and occurs in two types. The first type is a rare condition in which the aortic obstruction is located proximal to the **ductus arteriosus.** The lumen of the aorta is atretic or completely blocked, so that the impairment of the systemic circulation presents a serious problem. This defect is incompatible with life, and the child dies in infancy if corrective surgery cannot be performed.

The other type of coarctation is a common form that yields to surgical intervention. There may be either a narrowing or a complete **stenosis of the aortic lumen** distal to the left **subclavian artery** and to the insertion of the ductus. The latter is generally **ligamentous** and **obliterated.** The aorta near the constriction appears to be normal in size, but its major proximate branches are generally enlarged. The **intercostal arteries** distal to the obstruction also show an increase in size. The constriction of the aorta is usually limited to a short segment and permits a reasonable life expectancy, if not associated with other **cardiovascular** defects.

The outstanding diagnostic characteristic of aortic coarctation is high blood pressure in the arms and low blood pressure with a barely perceptible pulse in the legs. The differential diagnosis hinges on this disparity of the blood pressure in the extremities and the diminished or absent **femoral pulse.** Since the oxygenated blood reaches the systemic circulation, the patient's color remains normal. **Hypertension** may lead to **cerebrovascular accident.** In addition, infection presents a constant threat to the debilitated patient, since nutritional deficiency may accompany the impoverished systemic circulation.

When a short aortic segment is constricted, the clinical symptoms are absent or so minimal that they may escape notice, especially in childhood. In adolescence, symptoms of **fatigability,** decreased exercise tolerance, **epistaxis, syncope,** and coldness of the feet tend to develop and cause varying degrees of disability. In untreated cases, the life span rarely exceeds the fourth decade. Death may ensue from **rupture of the aorta, bacterial endocarditis,** or **congestive heart failure.**

The **electrocardiogram** can be utilized to reveal left **ventricular hypertrophy** of varying degree. **Doppler studies** can be employed to record and quantify the pressure gradient. **Magnetic resonance imaging** or **digital angiography** provide a visualization of the length and severity of the obstruction and associated **collateral arteries.** In the adult, **cardiac catheterization** is performed mainly to assess the status of the **coronary arteries.**

Adequacy of collateral circulation is vital for safe repair of the coarctation. Surgical treatment includes **resection, end-to-end anastomosis,** and **subclavian flap angioplasty.** It may be necessary to employ a **tubular graft, Dacron patch,** or **bypass conduit procedure** if the constricted segment is long.

The optimum age for surgical correction is between 4 and 6 years. In infants and children, this malformation accounts for approximately 8% of **congenital heart disease.** Although early repair is desirable, growth of a circular suture line at the site of an **end-to-end anastomosis** usually will not be adequate as the child grows, and it is likely that recurrent stenosis will develop, as well as the presence of **hypertension** during exercise.

In adults, prolonged degenerative changes in the aorta from **calcification** and **fibrosis** may make the insertion of a **prosthetic graft** necessary, because direct **anastomosis** cannot be achieved. Another approach is the insertion of a **bypass graft of Dacron** around the obstruction, without attempting to excise the coarctation. This approach relieves the obstruction without risking the hazards of excision.

The most dreaded complications are infection of the suture line, resulting in leakage, or dissolution of the anastomosis. **Postoperative paradoxical hypertension** is common between the second and tenth postoperative days and may be the causative factor of the **postcoarctation syndrome** in which **ileus, abdominal pain, mesenteric vasculitis,** and even **visceral infarction** can occur. It appears that treatment in the postoperative period with **propranolol** tends to prevent **paradoxical hypertension** following **repair of coarctation.** (34, 65, 104, 109)

REVIEW GUIDE

Instructions: Select the letter of the response that correctly completes each statement, as shown in the example.

Example: The suffix *-ectomy* in *thrombectomy* means
         a. repair <u>b.</u> removal c. closure d. fixation

1. Aneurysm means
   a. shunting of oxygenated blood from the left to right atrium.
   b. syndrome characterized by short attacks of precordial pain.
   c. node found in the atrioventricular bundle.
   d. dilatation or bulging out of the wall of the heart, aorta, or any other artery.
2. Variant angina may be called
   a. Purkinje's angina.
   b. Prinzmetal's angina.
   c. Valsalva's angina.
   d. none of the above.

3. Patent ductus means
   a. persistence of communication between pulmonary artery and aorta after birth.
   b. dextroposition of right ventricle after birth.
   c. shunting oxygenated blood to the right ventricle from the left ventricle.
   d. none of the above.
4. Coarctation of aorta is
   a. constriction of a segment of the aorta.
   b. dilatation of a segment of the aorta.
   c. both a and b are true.
   d. none of the above.
5. Mitral commissurotomy means
   a. separation of the stenotic valve at points of fusion.
   b. revision of chordae muscle.
   c. resection of mitral lesions.
   d. both a and b are true.
6. A strong, jerky beat followed by a sharp decline and collapse of a beat is called
   a. dicrotic pulse.
   b. bigeminal pulse.
   c. Corrigan's pulse.
   d. none of the above.
7. Cardiac standstill that occurs with certain forms of heart block, causing syncope and possible fatal convulsions is known as
   a. Eisenmenger's syndrome.
   b. Stokes-Adams syndrome.
   c. Wolff-Parkinson-White syndrome.
   d. Ebstein's anomaly.
8. The mitral valve is also called the
   a. foramen ovale.
   b. tricuspid valve.
   c. bicuspid valve.
   d. semilunar valve.
9. A short, broad vessel into which most of the veins of the heart empty is called the
   a. aortic sinus.
   b. coronary artery.
   c. coronary sinus.
   d. internal mammary artery.
10. The pacemaker of the heart is also called the
   a. atrioventricular node.
   b. conduction system of the heart.
   c. sinoatrial node.
   d. Purkinje fibers.
11. Which entry below is **not** among the four parts that make up the tetralogy of Fallot complex?
   a. ventricular septal defect
   b. pulmonic stenosis
   c. dextroposition of the aorta
   d. cor triloculare

12. The condition characterized by verrucose lesions found in the endocardium of patients with terminal disseminated lupus erythematosus is called
    a. ischemic heart disease.
    b. Löffler's endocarditis.
    c. Libman-Sacks endocarditis.
    d. Eisenmenger's syndrome.
13. Surgical revision of the atrial septum, transposing the venous return to match the transposed outflow tracts is called
    a. Blalock-Hanlon operation.
    b. Mustard's operation.
    c. Rashkind's operation.
    d. Senning's operation.
14. Suture of a vein is called
    a. venesection.
    b. profundaplasty.
    c. phlebotomy.
    d. phleborrhaphy.
15. Restoring the proper size and shape by using prosthetic rings to establish normal valve orifice and function is termed
    a. leaflet resection.
    b. chordal fenestration and resection.
    c. anulus remodeling.
    d. chordal shortening.

Instructions: Define the following terms.

Example: sclero- (G)—hard

angio-(G)	diastole (G)	thrombo- (G)
arterio- (G)	hemangio- (G)	topo- (G)
atrio- (L)	phlebo- (G)	veno- (L)
brady- (G)	tachy- (G)	ventriculo- (L)

Instructions: Figure 6.5 in the text shows the blood vessels associated with the surface of the heart: (a) anterior view; (b) posterior view. For each line that extends from the figure below, provide the anatomic name of the site, as shown in the examples.

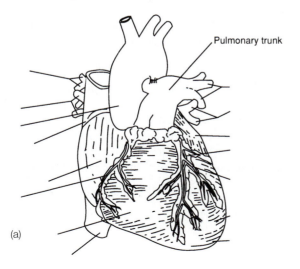

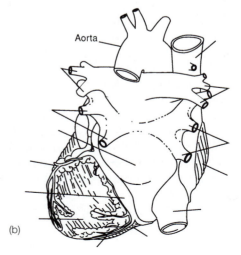

7

Disorders of the Blood and Blood-Forming Organs

BLOOD

ORIGIN OF TERMS

aniso- (G)—unequal, dissimilar

apheresis, pheresis (G)—removal

blasto- (G)—germ

cyt-, cyto- (G)—cell

-emia (G)—blood

erythro- (G)—red

hema-, hemato-, hemo- (G)—blood

leuko- (G)—white

megalo- (G)—large

myel-, myelo- (G)—marrow

-osis (G)—increase, disease, condition

-penia (G)—deficiency, decrease

-phage, -phagia (G)—to eat

-phoresis (G)—being carried, transmission

plasmo- (G)—plasma, cell substance

-poiesis (G)—to make, formation

poikilo- (G)—varied, irregular

polymorph (G)—many forms

reticulum (L)—network

sidero- (G)—iron

sphero- (G)—round, ball, sphere

PHONETIC PRONUNCIATION OF SELECTED TERMS

erythroblastosis fetalis	e-RITH-row-blas-TOE′sis fee-TAL′is
erythropoiesis	e-RITH-row-poy-E′sis
hereditary elliptocytosis	he-RED′i-ter-e e-LIP-toe-sigh-TOE′sis
megaloblastic anemia	MEG′a-low-BLAST-ick a-NEE′me-ah
polycythemia	POL-e-sigh-THE′me-ah

TERMS RELATED TO BLOOD ELEMENTS AND BLOOD GROUPINGS

blood—consists of a liquid portion called plasma and a solid portion that includes red blood cells (erythrocytes), white blood cells (leukocytes), and platelets. (52, 91)

blood group or blood type—inherited characteristic of human blood that remains unchanged throughout life. (60)

blood grouping systems—the classification of blood based on hemagglutinogens in red blood corpuscles. There are different types of blood factors (hemagglutinogens) requiring special methods of typing. These factors are (1) ABO system: A, B, AB, and O factors; (2) MN system: M, N, and MN factors; and (3) Rh-Hr system: Rh and Hr factors.

ABO system—the international system of Landsteiner, in which the four main blood groups are designated by the letters A, B, AB, and O. This system is universally used. The discovery of subgroups (A_1, A_2, A_3, A_4, and others for the ABO system) explains why the incompatibility of types of blood may occur within the same blood group. Rh studies are done routinely on all blood transfusions. In addition, subgroups may be checked to prevent reactions. Universal donor blood is only used for recipients of group A or B or AB in emergency when their respective type is not available.

MN system—classification based on the presence of MN factors in erythrocytes. This system is used in genetic blood group analysis and in medical-legal paternity studies when parental claims are disputed.

Rh-Hr system—a system of complex antigen structure. The Rh factor is an agglutinogen that occurs in the red blood corpuscles of 87% of White people. Originally only Rh-positive and Rh-negative agglutinogens were known; at present, subgroups of Rh factors are recognized. The Rh determinations are of clinical importance in blood transfusion and obstetrics. There is a reciprocal relationship between Hr and Rh factors. For more information on other blood group systems, such as Duffy, Kell, and Lewis, consult references 60 and 83. (60, 84, 85)

crossmatching—procedure done to determine the compatibility between the recipient's blood and donor's blood to prevent blood transfusion reaction. (See table 7.1.)

incompatible blood—blood that cannot be mixed without causing hemolysis or clumping of red blood cells.

universal blood donor—blood type O; blood has no agglutinogens, hence clumping does not occur. (52, 85, 91)

erythroblasts—immature red blood cells; possess a nucleus and are present in fetal blood. Within the red bone marrow, cells that are called hemocytoblasts give rise to erythroblasts, which in turn produce erythrocytes. (82) (See fig. 7.1.)

erythrocytes—red blood cells; mature cells have no nucleus. (88) (See fig. 7.1.)

erythropoiesis—entire process by which red blood cells are produced in the bone marrow. (29, 36) (See fig. 7.2.)

hematopoiesis, hemopoiesis—development of the various cellular elements of the blood—erythrocytes, leukocytes, platelets, and others. (82)

hemoglobin—chemical component of erythrocytes containing two substances: (1) globin, a protein, and (2) heme, an iron-containing portion responsible for the transport of oxygen to the cells. The heme is further decomposed into iron and a greenish pigment called biliverdin.

TABLE 7.1	Compatibility of Blood for Transfusion
Recipient's Blood	*Donor's Blood*
A	A or O
B	B or O
AB	AB, A, B, or O
O	O only

Source: Adapted from Robert J. Gresick, M.D., Personal Communication, and Ronald Turgeon, M.D., Personal Communication.

Figure 7.1 Origin and development of blood cells.

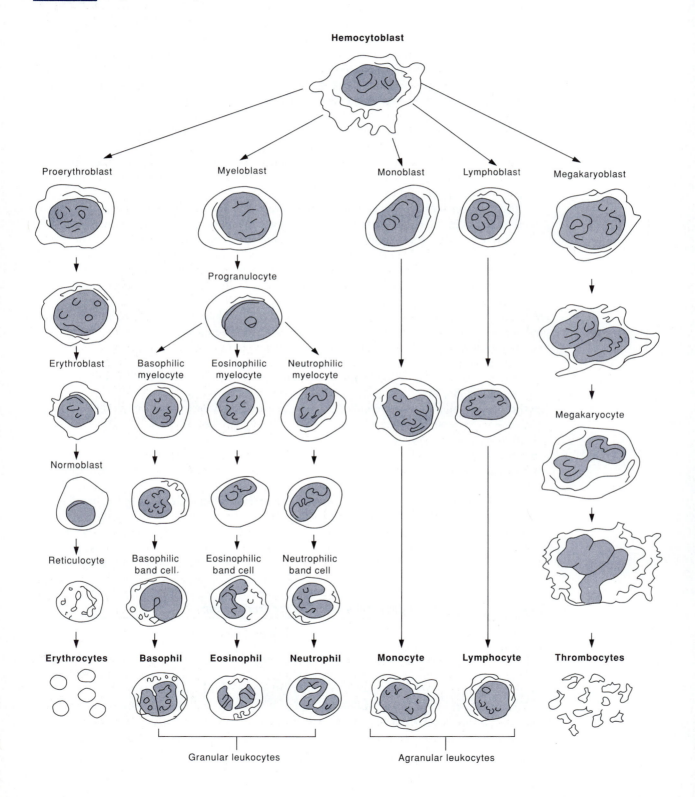

Figure 7.2 Life cycle of a red blood cell. (1) Essential nutrients are absorbed from the intestine; (2) nutrients are transported by blood to red bone marrow; (3) red blood cells are produced in red bone marrow by mitosis; (4) mature red blood cells are released into blood where they circulate for about 120 days: (5) damaged red blood cells are destroyed in the liver by macrophages: (6) hemoglobin from red blood cells is decomposed into heme and globin; (7) iron from heme is returned to red bone marrow and reused; (8) biliverdin is excreted in the bile.

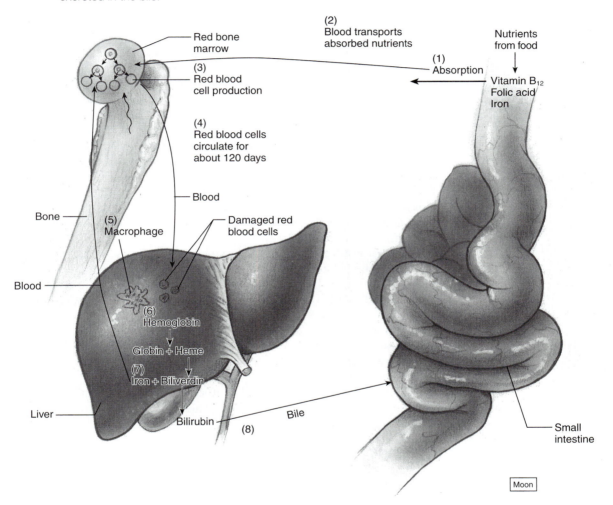

(See fig. 7.2.) The iron, together with a protein called transferrin, may be carried by the blood to the blood-cell-forming tissue in the red bone marrow where it can be reused in the synthesis of a new hemoglobin; or it may be stored in liver cells in the form of an iron-protein complex called ferritin. Over time, some of the biliverdin is converted to an orange pigment called bilirubin. Biliverdin and bilirubin are excreted in the bile as bile pigments. Physiologic jaundice of the newborn is considered to be the result of immature liver cells that are partially defective in excreting bilirubin into the bile. With this disorder, the newborn's skin and eyes become yellowish due to an accumulation of bilirubin in the tissues. (31)

leukocytes—white blood cells divided according to structure into those composed of granular cytoplasm, termed *granular leukocytes* or *granulocytes,* and those composed of cytoplasmic granules called *agranular leukocytes* or *agranulocytes.* (7, 49, 74, 75)

agranulocyte series includes:
- *lymphocytes*—leukocytes derived from lymphoid tissue. The cytoplasm contains few or no granules. Usually, the nucleus is large and round and is surrounded by a thin rim of cytoplasm. (26, 91)
- *monocytes*—cytoplasm contains few or no granules. Their nuclei vary in shape and may be round, kidney-shaped, oval, or lobed. Monocytes are the largest cells found in the blood, having diameters 2 to 3 times greater than those of red blood cells.

granulocyte series includes: (7, 13, 26, 44)
- *basophils*—irregular shaped cytoplasmic granules of cells that stain deep blue in basic stain. Basophils are similar to eosinophils in size and shape of their nuclei.
- *eosinophils*—cytoplasmic granules of cells that take an acid stain, staining a dark red. The nucleus is bilobed (has two lobes).
- *neutrophils, polymorphonuclear neutrophils*—cytoplasmic granules that stain pinkish with a neutral dye. Then nucleus of a neutrophil is lobed and consists of 2 to 5 parts connected by thin strands of chromatin. Neutrophils are called polymorphonuclear, which means their nuclei take many forms. Other neutrophilic designations include:
  - *neutrophilic band, staff cells*—immature nonfilamented cells in which the nucleus is T-, V-, or U-shaped and not divided into segments.
  - *neutrophilic lobocytes*—filamented mature cells with distinct segmentation.
  - *neutrophilic metamyelocytes, junge kernige*—immature cells in which the nucleus has become indented.
  - *neutrophilic myelocytes*—youngest neutrophils; nucleus round or ovoid. (See fig. 7.1.)

myelopoiesis—formation of blood cells and tissue elements from bone marrow. (52)

myeloproliferative—referring to an increased production of myelopoietic cells and tissue. (52)

normoblasts—nucleated red cells that precede normal erythrocytes in the developmental process. (52)

phagocytes—two classes of white cells:
  macrophages—absorb dead cells and tissues.
  microphages—ingest bacteria. (49) (See fig. 7.3.)

plasma—liquid portion of blood without cellular elements. (52)

plasma cells, plasmacytes—leukocytes, normally absent in blood film, occasionally seen in infection but rarely present in circulating blood. Their function is to synthesize immunoglobulins. (74)

platelets, thrombocytes—round or oval disks that control clot formation and clot retraction. (52, 60) (See fig. 7.1.)

polymorphonuclear—having nuclei of variable shape. (52, 91)

reticulocytes—immature red cells in intermediary stage of development between nucleate and anucleate forms. They contain a fine intracellular network and are normally present in the blood in small numbers. (52, 91)

serum—liquid portion of the blood after fibrinogen has been consumed in the process of clotting. (52, 91)

sideroblasts—nucleated erythrocytes containing stainable iron granules. (52, 91)

siderocytes—circulating red cells containing stainable iron granules. (52, 91)

transfusion—introduction of blood or blood component directly into the circulating bloodstream of recipients. (52, 60, 85)

types of transfusions:
- *autologous transfusions*—transfusions prepared from recipient's own blood. They are safe and of particular value to patients who have unusually rare blood types, react severely to homologous blood transfusions, or refuse donor blood on religious grounds. Two forms are used:

Figure 7.3 When bacteria invade the tissues, leukocytes migrate into the region and destroy bacteria by phagocytosis.

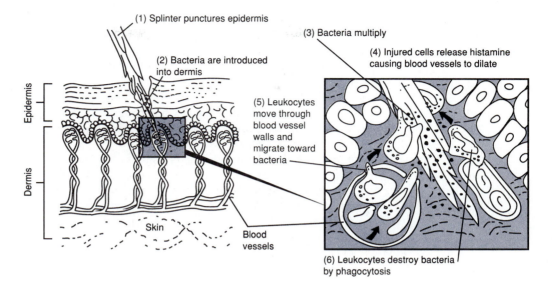

(1) Splinter punctures epidermis

(2) Bacteria are introduced into dermis

(3) Bacteria multiply

(4) Injured cells release histamine causing blood vessels to dilate

(5) Leukocytes move through blood vessel walls and migrate toward bacteria

Epidermis

Dermis

Skin

Blood vessels

(6) Leukocytes destroy bacteria by phagocytosis

- *intraoperative autologous transfusion*—blood salvaged in massive bleeding at surgery and reinfused in patient.
- *predeposit autologous transfusion*—recipient's blood withdrawn weeks before an anticipated need and stored in blood bank. Withdrawing blood from the body stimulates red cell production. When erythropoiesis is inadequate, iron supplements aid in maintaining the patient's iron storage. (85)
- *homologous transfusions*—donor's blood products obtained before an anticipated need of recipient and deposited in blood bank. Blood preparations are standardized by the National Institutes of Health (NIH) or *United States Pharmacopeia* (USP) or both. (91)

whole blood: (91)

- *banked whole blood, citrated whole blood, USP*—normal blood collected in acid citrate dextrose (ACD) solution, (USP) to prevent coagulation; primarily used for restoring or maintaining blood volume.
- *heparinized whole blood*—normal blood in heparin solution to prevent coagulation; formerly used for priming heart-lung machine to maintain extracorporeal circulation in open-heart surgery.

blood cells: (60, 85)

- *cytapheresis**—procedure in which one or more cellular elements of the blood (white cells, thrombocytes) are removed from the donor's blood and given to a recipient who has a marked deficiency of these components. The remainder of the blood is retransfused into the donor.
- *hemapheresis, pheresis*—any procedure in which leukocytes, thrombocytes, plasma, or other components are separated from the withdrawn donor blood and transfused into a patient who is deficient in these hemic elements. The donor is reinfused with the remaining part of the blood.

---

*Cyt- (G)—cell; *apheresis* (G)—removal. *Apheresis* is used to indicate that components are being separated out; *pheresis* is an abbreviated form also used in medical terminology, for example, *plateletpheresis*.

- *leukapheresis*—collection of granulocytes obtained by a blood cell separator or filtration leukapheresis device. The granulocytes are transfused into a patient, usually one with cancer, granulocytopenia, or sepsis, to stimulate bone marrow production of neutrophils. The leukocyte-poor blood is returned to the donor.
- *leukocyte transfusion, granulocyte transfusion*—white cell transfusion used in neutropenia and granulocytopenia, when neutrophils or other granulocytes are needed, and in immune deficiency, when cellular immune responses should be evoked.
- *packed red cells*—concentrated suspension of red cells (about 70%) in acid citrate dextrose (ACD) solution with most of the plasma removed. The procedure is indicated in anemia and hemorrhage when the oxygen-carrying capacity of the blood needs to be increased.
- *platelet concentrate*—platelet-rich plasma freshly drawn from a single donor or from pooled donors and widely used in thrombocytopenic disorders.
- *plateletpheresis, thrombocytapheresis*—platelet concentration obtained from withdrawn donor blood for transfusing a patient depleted of platelets (thrombocytes). The remaining platelet-poor blood is reinfused into the donor.
- *red blood cells, deglycerolized*—red blood cells are mixed with glycerol within 6 days of collection for freezing. Frozen red blood cells are stored at temperatures of 65° centigrade (C) to 80° C. Frozen red blood cells may be stored for at least 10 years. Prior to transfusion, red blood cells are deglycerolized as follows.
  - frozen cells are thawed at 37° C.
  - cells are first washed with a hypertonic saline solution followed by successively less concentrated saline containing glucose to remove the glycerol.
  - after thawing and deglycerolization, the red blood cells are resuspended in an isotonic electrolyte solution with glucose. The deglycerolized red blood cells must be used within 24 hours to avoid contamination.

blood proteins and plasma fractions: (85, 91)
- *antihemophilic human plasma, USP*—normal plasma, promptly processed to preserve antihemophilic globulin factor VIII, a component of fresh plasma. It is indicated in the treatment of hemophilia.
- *cryoprecipitate (Cryo)*—commercial product prepared by slowly thawing fresh frozen plasma to form cryoprecipitate rich in antihemophilic factor VIII. Cryo is the treatment of choice in hemophilia and other bleeding disorders.
- *fresh frozen plasma (FFP)*—plasma separated from whole blood and containing all clotting factors; useful as replacement therapy in depletion of coagulation factors.
- *gamma globulin (IgG)*—plasma fraction used for the amelioration of hepatitis and IgG deficiency.
- *plasma exchange (PE)*—the removal of several liters of plasma to rid the blood of unwanted substances, such as large immunoglobulins (IgM). The withdrawn plasma is replaced with normal plasma or suitable fluid, usually Ringer's lactate solution.
- *plasmapheresis*—plasma withdrawn from donor according to prescribed size and frequency of donation for the purpose of transfusing patient in need of plasma fraction therapy. The remaining cells are reinfused into the donor.
- *plasma protein fraction (PPF)*—effective therapeutic agent for hypovolemia. It contains serum albumin (5%) and a number of other plasma proteins.
- *serum albumin*—plasma fraction used in the treatment of shock and some protein deficiencies.

transfusion reaction—untoward response to intravenous infusion of a blood preparation. It may be caused by air embolism, allergy, bacterial contaminants, circulatory overload, and hemolysis due to incompatibility of cells. Reactions vary in degree from mild to life threatening; chills, fever, malaise, and headache are common warning signals.

- *post-transfusion disorders*—conditions transmissible through blood transfusions. These include *acquired immunodeficiency syndrome (AIDS), cytomegalovirus (CMV), viral hepatitis, hepatitis B virus, non-A, and non-B hepatitis virus.* (60, 85)

DIAGNOSTIC TERMS
Disorders primarily affecting the red cells
anemia—blood disorder characterized by a reduction in erythrocyte count, hemoglobin, and hematocrit, although not all three findings may be present. It is usually a manifestation or a complication of disease, not a diagnosis. (28, 85)

anemia of blood loss—disorder develops subsequent to an acute or chronic hemorrhage. (27, 28, 85) A condensed version of Wintrobe's etiologic classification of anemia follows:

deficiency factors in red cell production (erythropoiesis):

- *iron deficiency anemia*—depletion of body's iron storage, which may be followed by an inadequate production of hemoglobin and a reduction of the oxygen-carrying capacity of the blood. (27, 85)
- *megaloblastic anemias*—the common denominator is a disordered synthesis of DNA (deoxyribonucleic acid) due to deficiency of vitamin B_{12} or folic acid (B_c). Normally, dietary vitamin B_{12} interacts with a mucoid secretion of the gastric fundus, the intrinsic factor of Castle. In the absence of this factor, B_{12} cannot be absorbed by the ileum and nutritionally utilized by the body. Folic acid deficiency may be caused by malnutrition, malabsorption, increased requirement, or loss of folic acid and defective folate metabolism. (15, 62)
- *pernicious anemia (PA)*—prototype of a megaloblastic anemia, usually associated with marked vitamin B_{12} deficiency caused by failure of gastric mucosa to secrete an intrinsic factor. Pathologically, the most characteristic finding in pernicious anemia is gastric atrophy, which affects the acid and pepsin-secreting portion of the stomach; the antrum is spared. Anorexia, sore tongue, weakness, fatigue, a waxy pallor, and neurologic damage are common clinical manifestations. (15, 62)
- *sideroblastic anemias*—hereditary or acquired anemias exhibiting an excess of iron deposits within normoblasts, usually in association with hypochromia and microcytosis. The anemia may be present at birth but develops more frequently in young adults. The iron overload tends to initiate cardiac arrhythmias and liver fibrosis. Diabetes is frequently associated with sideroblastic anemia. (28, 85)

failure of bone marrow:

- *aplastic anemia*—marked reduction of red cells, white cells, and platelets or a selective reduction of red cells or platelets. Fat cells abound in the bone marrow. Clinical features are pallor, lassitude, bleeding, and purpura. The disease may be idiopathic or caused by toxic drugs or ionizing irradiation. (5, 78, 85, 93)
- *Fanconi's anemia, congenital pancytopenia*—idiopathic anemia that develops in early infancy, appears to be hereditary, and is associated with congenital abnormalities of the bones, heart, kidneys, eyes, and microcephaly. A common finding in Fanconi's anemia is patchy, brown pigmentation of the skin, resulting from the deposition of melanin. The dominant hematologic finding is pancytopenia; a reduction in all three formed elements of the blood—erythrocytes, leukocytes, and platelets. The bone marrow may be hypercellular or normocellular early in the disease course, but ultimately, progressive hypocellularity develops. An elevated level of fetal hemoglobin appears as a consistent feature. The exact cause of the disease is unknown, but is probably related to a recessive gene, or is the result of reciprocal

chromosomal translocation in one of the parents and a duplication deficiency in the affected offspring. (3, 5, 93)

- *myelodysplastic syndromes (MDS), refractory dysmelopoietic anemias*—heterogenous group of normocytic anemias often associated with neutropenia and thrombocytopenia, resulting from an acquired disorder of the hematopoietic pluripotent stem cell. The bone marrow varies in cellularity and usually displays disordered maturation of erythroid, myeloid, and megakaryocytic cells. Cytogenetic abnormalities include the deletion of the long arm chromosome 5, deletion of chromosome 7, or trisomy 8. Symptoms are usually related directly to the consequences of bone marrow failure, and include fatigue, pallor, infection, and bruising or bleeding. The FAB (French, American, British) Cooperative Group's classification of myelodysplastic syndromes include 5 categories: refractory anemia (RA), refractory anemia with ringed sideroblasts (RARS), refractory anemia with excess of blasts (RAEB), chronic myelomonocytic leukemia (CMML), and refractory anemia with excess of blasts in transformation (RAEB-T). (5, 78)
- *pure red cell aplasia (PRCA)*—disorder that involves a selective failure in the production of erythroid elements in the bone marrow. Severe reticulocytopenia is present. Normal cellular elements are present in the bone marrow with the exception of the virtual absence of any erythroid precursors. An increase in lymphocytes may be observed in the bone marrow. Pure red blood cell aplasia occurs as a congenital or acquired syndrome. (5, 78)

excessive destruction of erythrocytes:
- *hemolytic anemias*—congenital or acquired blood disorders characterized by a shortened red blood cell life span and an excessive destruction of mature red corpuscles. (28, 80, 85)
- *hemolytic disease of the newborn (HDN), erythroblastosis fetalis*—reduction of the life span of red cells, usually resulting from a hemolytic reaction of the Rh-positive infant to the sensitized Rh-negative mother. Uncontrolled high bilirubin levels may result in brain damage, evidenced by lethargy, characteristic spasms, and sharp cries. (34, 93) (See figs. 7.4 and 7.5.)
- *hereditary elliptocytosis (HE)*—inherited hemolytic disorder noted for the presence of a large proportion of elliptic-shaped erythrocytes in the circulating blood. In the majority of cases, individuals exhibit a structural abnormality of erythrocyte spectrin that leads to impaired assembly, while other afflicted persons may show a deficiency of erythrocyte membrane protein 4.1, which is important in stabilizing the interaction of spectrin and actin in the cytoskeleton. Degrees of hemolysis (mild to overt) may occur. Osmatic fragility test is usually normal but may be increased in patients with hemolysis. Red blood cell destruction occurs predominantly in the spleen, which is enlarged in persons with overt hemolysis. Hemolysis may be corrected by splenectomy. HE is transmitted as an autosomal dominant trait, with the exception of the Melanesian variant that appears to be autosomal recessive in inheritance. (65, 67, 80, 81)
- *hereditary spherocytosis (HS)*—mode of inheritance can be autosomal dominant or autosomal recessive. The most common mode of HS is autosomal dominant. Different biochemical defects can cause HS. The most common ones result from a molecular defect in ankyrin and depicts autosomal dominant inheritance. In the autosomal recessive form of HS, defects in alpha spectrin and protein band 4.2 have been reported. Affected persons have congenital hemolysis due to a defect in one of the proteins in the red cell membrane, leading to chronic hemolytic anemia characterized by the presence of spherical red cells, reticulocytosis, and increased

Figure 7.4 (a) If an Rh-negative woman is pregnant with an Rh-positive fetus, (b) some of the fetal red blood cells with Rh agglutinogens may enter the maternal blood at the time of birth. (c) As a result, the woman's cells may produce anti-Rh agglutinins.

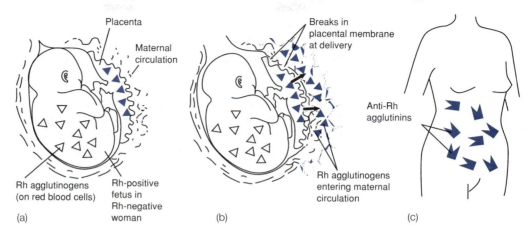

Figure 7.5 (a) If a woman who has developed anti-Rh agglutinins is pregnant with an Rh-positive fetus, (b) agglutinins may pass through the placental membrane and cause the fetal red blood cells to agglutinate.

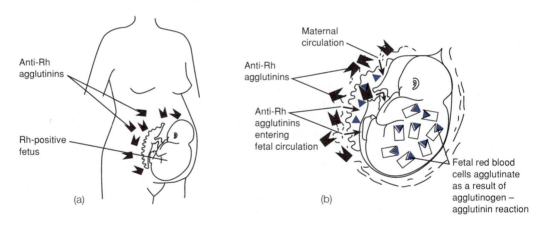

osmotic fragility. Clinical features may include anemia, splenomegaly, jaundice, a palpable liver, and a typical skeletal abnormality, the tower skull. Occasionally, chronic leg ulcers occur. (65, 67, 80, 81)

- *paroxysmal nocturnal hemoglobinuria (PNH)*—hemolytic disorder characterized by a defect of the red cell membrane that causes enzymatic and serologic abnormalities. The hemolysis ranges from mild to severe. Iron deficiency is present due to the loss of hemoglobin in urine at night. Episodes of fever, chills, and hemoglobinuria signal acute hemolysis. (52, 65, 81)

enzyme deficiency and increased red cell destruction:

- *glucose-6-phosphate dehydrogenase (G6PD) deficiency*—represents a group of hereditary abnormalities in which the activity of the enzyme G6PD is markedly diminished. Destruction of red blood cells occurs with this type of enzyme deficiency. G6PD is necessary for the normal metabolism of erythrocytes. The

G6PD is located on the X chromosome; therefore, the deficiency state is a sex-linked trait. Affected males (hemizygotes) inherit the abnormal gene from their mothers who are usually carriers (heterozygotes). Since there is inactivation of one of the two X chromosomes, the heterozygote has two populations of red blood cells: normal and deficient in G6PD. Most female carriers are asymptomatic, but those who have a high proportion of deficient cells resemble the male hemizygotes. Clinical problems appear to arise when the affected individual is subjected to some type of environmental stress. Hemolytic episodes most often are triggered by viral or bacterial infections. Also, drugs or toxins that pose an oxidant threat to the red blood cell cause hemolysis in deficient G6PD persons. Sulfa drugs, antimalarials, and nitrofurantoin are the most common offenders. Metabolic acidosis can precipitate an episode of hemolysis in the deficient G6PD person. There are approximately 300 electrophoretically separable variants of G6PD. (69, 80, 81)

- *pyruvate kinase (PK) deficiency*—the most common enzymatic deficiency, characterized by varying degrees of chronic hemolytic anemia and accelerated symptoms during stress or intercurrent infection. (65, 66, 68, 76)

increased destruction and decreased production of erythrocytes:
- *erythrocytosis*—designates an increase in the concentration of red corpuscles, whether measured as number of cells, hemoglobin, or packed cell volume.
  - *absolute erythrocytosis*—depicts a true increase in the total number (mass) of circulating red cells.
  - *relative (pseudo) erythrocytosis*—occurs when, through loss of blood plasma, the concentration of the red corpuscles is greater than normal; the total number in the circulating blood is not increased. (14)
- *sickle cell anemia (SCA)*—genetic abnormality of red blood cells due to the presence of the gene Hb S (homozygous genotype). Hemoglobin S produces progressive hemolysis and sickling of cells as the oxygen tension is lowered and deoxygenation increases. The resultant circulatory impairment may lead to vascular occlusions by plugs of sickled red cells, causing thrombosis, infarction, and leg ulcers. Sickle cell trait, the heterozygous state for Hb S gene, is present in approximately 8% of Black Americans and in about 30% of some African populations. Many other abnormal hemoglobins produce sickling without clinical symptoms. Hb S inherited from *one* parent may be asymptomatic. (32, 65, 77, 87)
- *thalassemia syndromes*—heterogenous group of hereditary anemias characterized by defects in the synthesis of one or more of the hemoglobin polypeptide chain subunits. The clinical symptoms produced with thalassemia arise from the combined consequences of inadequate hemoglobin accumulation and unbalanced accumulation of globin subunits. The former causes hypochromia and microcytosis and the latter promotes ineffective erythropoiesis and hemolytic anemia. Originally, the term *thalassemia* (loosely translated means the sea [Mediterranean] in the blood) was applied to the anemias encountered by peoples of the Greek and Italian coast areas. Today, the term refers to inherited defects in globin chain biosynthesis. Individual syndromes are named according to the globin chain whose synthesis is adversely affected. Some examples are:
  - *alpha (α)-thalassemia*—results from a decreased synthesis of alpha chain of hemoglobin so that insufficient amounts are available for combination with nonalpha globin and for the assembly of alpha globin genes. Each normal person inherits two alpha-chain genes from each parent. The homozygous form of α-thalassemia is incompatible with life, for example in the stillborn infant

> displaying severe hydrops fetalis, which is usually due to deletion of all four genes. The heterozygous form of α-thalassemia may be asymptomatic or only mild anemia may be present.

- *beta (β)-thalassemia*—caused by diminished synthesis of beta chains of hemoglobin. Many different mutations cause β-thalassemia and they are inherited in many genetic combinations responsible for a heterogeneous group of clinical syndromes. Two types are:
  - *beta (β)-thalassemia major, Cooley's anemia*—severe disorder due to inheritance of two β-thalassemia alleles, one on each copy of chromosome 11. Due to the diminished hemoglobin A synthesis, the circulating red cells are small, thin, and distorted. They contain very reduced amounts of hemoglobin. This type of homozygous genotype (both parents transmit the defect) usually causes severe anemia, enlargement of spleen and liver, jaundice, and mongoloid facies.
  - *beta (β)-thalassemia minor*—heterogenous genotype (one parent transmits thalassemia trait to offspring). β-thalassemia minor is due to the presence of a single β-thalassemia mutation and a normal β-globin gene on the other chromosome. Microcytosis with hypochromia and mild anemia occur. (32, 70, 87)

GENERAL TERMS

Disorders primarily resulting from a defective mechanism of coagulation

coagulation—hemostatic mechanism causing the formation of a blood clot. This process is triggered by a number of substances, most of which are synthesized by liver cells. It may involve (1) extrinsic clotting mechanism that is stimulated by the release of chemical substances from broken blood vessels or damaged tissues; and (2) intrinsic clotting mechanism that is stimulated by blood contact with foreign surfaces in the absence of tissue damage. The hemostatic mechanism by which blood coagulates is complex and involves many substances termed clotting factors. (15, 48, 50)

coagulation factors—various substances involved in the clotting of the blood that are designated by Roman numerals I to XIII, with the exception of the last two factors, which are without Roman numerals. According to Wintrobe, factor III, tissue factor, thromboplastin, and factor IV, calcium ions, are rarely used and factor VI does not exist. Effective hemostasis is dependent on the integrity of the following factors and cellular components of the blood and the walls of the blood vessels. A final step in the complex coagulation process involves the conversion of fibrinogen to fibrin. (15, 48, 50) The remaining coagulation factors according to International Nomenclature are listed in table 7.2.

DIAGNOSTIC TERMS

diffuse intravascular coagulation (DIC), consumption coagulopathy—pathologic clotting that differs from normal coagulation by being a diffuse instead of a local process; damaging the clotting site instead of giving it protection; consuming some coagulation factors (fibrinogen, factors V, VIII, XIII), thus predisposing to spontaneous bleeding; and forming fibrin-fibrinogen degradation products (FDP) due to intravascular fibrinogen breakdown, which occurs simultaneously with the pathologic clotting. Alternative names of FDP are *fibrin-fibrinogen split products (FSP)*, and *fibrin-fibrinogen related (FR) antigens*. Diagnostic essentials include platelet reduction, prolonged prothrombin time, marked fibrinolysis, and defective clot formation resulting in diffuse bleeding. Intravascular coagulation with massive hemorrhage may follow trauma, surgery, childbirth, gastrointestinal insult, and other causes. (23, 55)

Henoch-Schönlein syndrome, anaphylactoid purpura—acquired bleeding abnormality seen primarily in children and characterized by widespread vasculitis affecting many organs. Purpura is the dominant clinical feature. IgA is the antibody class most often seen in the immune complexes of persons afflicted with this syndrome. The syndrome may be accompanied by

TABLE 7.2	Coagulation Factors' Nomenclature

Factor's Roman Numeral	*Preferred Terminology*	*Alternative Terminology*
Factor I	fibrinogen	none
Factor II	prothrombin	none
Factor V	proaccelerin	labile factor, accelerator globulin (AcG), thrombogen
Factor VII	proconvertin	stable factor, serum prothrombin conversion accelerator (SPCA)
Factor VIII	antihemophilic factor (AHF)	antihemophilic globulin (AHG), antihemophilic factor A (AHF-A), platelet cofactor 1, thromboplastinogen
Factor IX	plasma thromboplastin component (PTC)	Christmas factor (CF), antihemophilic factor B (AHF-B), autoprothrombin II, platelet cofactor 2
Factor X	Stuart factor	Prower factor, autoprothrombin III, thrombokinase
Factor XI	plasma thromboplastin antecedent (PTA)	antihemophilic factor C (AHF-C)
Factor XII	Hageman factor (HF)	glass factor, contact factor
Factor XIII	fibrin-stabilizing factor (FSF)	Laki-Lorand factor (LLF) fibrinase, plasma, transglutaminase, fibrinoligase
_____*	Prekallikrein	Fletcher factor
_____*	HMW Kininogen	high-molecular-weight (HMW) kininogen, contact activation cofactor, Fitzgerald factor, Flaujeac factor, Reid factor, Washington factor, Williams factor

*Factors without Roman numerals.

Source: Thomas C. Bitchell, "Blood Coagulation," in C. Richard Lee, et al. (eds.), *Wintrobe's Clinical Hematology*, 9th ed., vol. 1. Philadelphia: Lea & Febiger, 1993, 567. Reprinted with permission.

intussusception (telescoping of intestines), abdominal pain, bleeding from digestive and urinary systems, kidney disease, and bone pain. (42, 54)

hemophilia-A, Factor VIII deficiency—hereditary disease in which a sex-linked trait is transmitted by females; the hemorrhagic disorder develops exclusively in males. In its classic form there is marked deficiency of the antihemophilic factor VIII, leading to spontaneous bleeding episodes. Common complications are hemarthroses and hematomas. (55, 92)

hemophilia-B, Factor IX deficiency, Christmas disease—familial disorder of blood coagulation attributed to a deficiency of the thromboplastin component, factor IX. The clinical picture of hemophilia B is the same as for hemophilia A. (52, 89)

hereditary hemorrhagic telangiectasia, Rendu-Osler-Weber syndrome—congenital defect in the vascular hemostatic mechanism, usually complicated by iron deficiency anemia. Localized dilatations of venules and capillaries are visible on the skin and mucous membranes. Epistaxis is common, and bleeding may occur from digestive, urinary, and respiratory tracts. The elderly tend to develop spiderlike skin lesions. (20, 79)

idiopathic thrombocytopenia purpura (cause unknown)—disorder resulting from a marked degree of platelet reduction. Symptoms vary from insignificant purpuric spots to serious bleeding from any body orifice or into any tissue. (19, 54, 81)

purpura—disorder characterized by pinpoint extravasations or petechiae and larger skin lesions, the ecchymoses. Bleeding may occur spontaneously, particularly from mucous membranes and internal organs. (20, 25)

von Willebrand's disease (vWD)—lifelong inherited bleeding disorder affecting both sexes. In its most common form (type I), the disorder is characterized by mild mucocutaneous hemorrhage, a prolonged bleeding time, deficiency of vWf (von Willebrand factor), and a proportionate reduction in levels of factor VIII. The vWf or one of its constituent subunits is required for normal platelet adhesion. The role of vWf in hemostasis is to act as a "carrier" for factor VIII and to promote adhesions of platelets to the subendothelium and to one another. When vWf is deficient or aberrant, both factor VIII deficiency and abnormalities in the early steps of primary hemostasis results. Both the factor VIII deficiency and the abnormal primary hemostasis display distinct laboratory abnormalities, and both defects contribute to the bleeding diathesis. The vWf gene is located on chromosome 12. Different types of vWD can be distinguished using vWf multimer analysis and other special tests. The disease is inherited in an autosomal manner. Types I, II-A, II-B, and II-C are autosomal dominant, while the most severe form, type III, is autosomal recessive. (17, 22, 54, 65, 92)

DIAGNOSTIC TERMS

Disorders primarily affecting the white blood cells

leukemia—neoplastic disease that primarily involves the bone marrow and lymphatic and reticuloendothelial systems. It is usually characterized by an overproduction of leukocytes. (67) The more common forms are:

acute leukemia, stem cell leukemia—an undifferentiated form of leukemia, since the cells are too young to be identified. Immature leukocytes usually abound in the peripheral blood and bone marrow. The onset is either abrupt or gradual, ushering in fever, pallor, prostration, bleeding, and joint and bone pains. Acute leukemia may occur in differentiated forms such as acute granulocytic, lymphoblastic, myeloblastic, monocytic, basophilic, or eosinophilic, and others, depending on the dominant cell. Anemia and thrombocytopenia may coexist. (50, 72, 83)

chronic lymphocytic leukemia (CLL)—great excess of lymphocytes, 50,000 to 250,000 white cells, enlargement of lymph nodes and spleen, anemia, and bleeding episodes. (44, 58, 65, 83)

chronic myelogenous leukemia (CML)—myeloproliferative disorder caused by a mutation in a pluripotential stem cell, which is characterized by extreme leukocytosis with an increase in immature and mature granulocytes and by splenomegaly. Most afflicted patients have a typical cytogenetic defect, the Philadelphia (Ph[1]) chromosome, a shortened G-22 chromosome resulting from the reciprocal translocation of genetic material between chromosomes 9 and 22. This abnormality is present in granulocytes, erythrocytes, and megakaryocytes. CML has chronic and acute phases. The mild chronic phase lasts approximately 3 and 1/2 years, and is characterized by a stable overproduction of leukocytes. Symptoms include anemia, fatigue, weakness, and splenomegaly. The acute phase (blast crisis) results in death in 90% of patients within several months. This is the aggressive form of CML. Transformation from the chronic phase to the acute phase may occur over several months or be sudden. Symptoms usually include fever, weight loss, severe anemia and thrombocytopenia, bone pain, purpura, and spleen enlargement. (12, 35, 50, 58, 65)

leukemoid reaction—blood disorder simulating leukemia because of its highly increased white count. Leukemoid reactions may occur in association with a variety of infections, malignant diseases, severe hemorrhage, or sudden hemolysis. (9)

leukemic reticuloendotheliosis, hairy cell leukemia—rare disorder in which an atypical cell with cytoplasmic projections (hair cells) characterizes the blood and replaces the bone marrow. Leukocytosis and marked splenomegaly are typical findings. (50, 52, 57, 58, 65, 83)

leukopenia, granulocytopenia, agranulocytosis—low white count, less than 5,000 leukocytes per cubic millimeter of blood caused by certain infections, nutritional deficiencies, hematopoietic disorders, chemical agents, and ionizing radiation. (9)

neutropenia—decreased concentration of neutrophils in the blood, predisposing to multiple severe infections. The normal median concentration is 3,650 neutrophils per cubic millimeter of blood. (10, 24)

polycythemia vera (PV)—an acquired myeloproliferative disorder resulting from clonal expansion of a transformed hematopoietic stem associated with prominent overproduction of erythrocytes and a lesser expansion of granulocytic and megakaryocytic elements. The bone marrow is hypercellular, with panhyperplasia of all hematopoietic elements. Iron stores are usually absent from the bone marrow, having been transferred to the increased circulating red blood cell mass. Iron deficiency may be due to chronic gastrointestinal blood loss. Thrombosis is the most common complication as well as the main cause of infection and death in polycythemia vera. Symptoms include headache, vertigo, tinnitus, blurred vision, and a variety of others related to expanded blood volume and increased blood viscosity. The skin has a reddish purple hue. Skin and mucous membrane hemorrhages are not uncommon. Epistaxis and bleeding of the gums may occur. Splenomegaly is present in most cases. The exact cause of PV is unknown. Onset of the disorder is gradual and progresses slowly. The disease occurs in midlife. It is less frequent among Blacks than Caucasians and is comparatively common in Jews. (13, 44, 46, 54, 58)

preleukemia—leukemia suspected but no definitive laboratory evidence to justify the diagnosis. The significant hematologic disorder is the presence of anemia—normochromic or normocytic, hypochromic or microcytic—associated with a low or normal reticulocyte count. Preleukemia occurs in all age groups, with some predilection for the elderly. The majority of children develop lymphoblastic leukemia; the majority of adults develop myeloblastic leukemia. (48, 91)

DIAGNOSTIC TERMS

Disorders primarily concerned with an unbalanced proliferation of cells

amyloidosis—presence of the extracellular deposition of the fibrous protein amyloid in one or more sites of the body. The current classification of amyloid syndromes is based on the biochemical composition of its constituent protein chains. The diagnosis of amyloidosis is based on the identification of amyloid in a tissue biopsy obtained from an involved organ or specifically involved site, such as tissues of the carpal tunnel, the endocardium, a peripheral nerve, or the skin. Two classifications of amyloidosis are:

primary systemic (or local) amyloidosis—a plasma cell dyscrasia and genetic metabolic disorder characterized by the deposition of immunoglobulin light chain-derived fibrils. Light chain-derived amyloidosis (AL) is seen in two clinical settings: in association with plasma cell dyscrasias, especially multiple myeloma, and as a primary nonhereditary form of systemic amyloidosis. There is cardiac and gastrointestinal involvement, arthropathy, peripheral neuropathy, and paresthesias.

secondary or reactive amyloidosis—condition caused by the deposition of amyloid protein A (AA). Recurring infections associated with AA deposition include tuberculosis, leprosy, chronic osteomyelitis, bronchiectasis, parenteral drug abuse, and hypogammaglobulinemia. Other chronic inflammatory conditions occasionally associated with AA include rheumatoid arthritis and inflammatory bowel disorders. (33, 46)

multiple myeloma, plasma cell myeloma—malignant neoplastic disease characterized by widespread bone destruction, intense bone pain, an excess of atypical plasma cells in the bone marrow, abnormal immunoglobulins, anemia, and recurrent pneumonia or other bacterial infections related to defective antibody synthesis. Renal damage may be associated with elevated calcium levels in blood and urine. (45, 66)

Waldenström's macroglobulinemia—plasma cell dyscrasia in which the production of gamma M globulin is greatly accelerated. The diagnosis of macroglobulinemia is established on the basis of the characteristic serum protein abnormality and the typical changes in blood and marrow. Plasmacytoid lymphocytes are the characteristic malignant cell seen in Waldenström's macroglobulinemia. Anemia and low hemoglobin levels are present in symptomatic disease. There may be involvement of the heart, nerves, muscles, and joints. The diagnosis of Waldenström's macroglobulinemia is confirmed by a demonstration of an IgM paraprotein by serum protein electrophoresis and immunoelectrophoresis. (1, 38, 47, 66)

PROCEDURAL TERMS

Allogeneic hematopoietic stem cell transplantation and bone marrow transplantations
allogeneic hematopoietic stem cell transplantation—procedure provides healthy stem cells from a compatible donor. These stem cells will differentiate into normal blood cells and replace impaired/diseased blood cells in a recipient patient. These stem cells are secured from the donor's peripheral blood. The donor receives injections of growth-colony-stimulating factor (GCSF) prior to harvesting to increase production of stem cells. Following collection of peripheral blood from the donor, the blood undergoes apheresis to separate out the stem cells. The remaining plasma and red blood cells are then reinfused into the donor. Prior to transplantation, the patient receiving the stem cells receives a 6-day period of chemotherapy to obliterate diseased blood cells. The stem cell transplant is carried out by infusion a few days after the chemotherapy regimen has been completed. Following the procedure, the patient is pancytopenic and is monitored for complications, such as rejection of the stem cell graft, protracted immunodeficiency, and recurrence of the disease itself. Those who benefit from this procedure include persons who have acute or chronic leukemia, neuroblastoma, myelodysplastic syndrome, multiple myeloma, Hodgkin's disease, and non-Hodgkin's lymphoma. (61)
bone marrow transplantation—bone marrow grafting in hematologic neoplasia, aplastic anemia, or leukemia. Bone marrow grafting has been applied in recent years to patients with genetic disorders of hematopoiesis.

allogenic marrow transplantation—bone marrow obtained from:
- *donor related to recipient, matched siblings*—histocompatibility usually present in members of the same family.
- *donor unrelated to recipient*—histoincompatibility frequently present. Infused marrow cells are prone to reject the patient's cells and patient is likely to develop:
  - *graft-versus-host disease (GVHD)*—major problem in the transplantation of tissues or organs, occurring when an immunoincompetent host receives histoincompatible lymphocytes. The chief targets of GVHD are the skin, gut, and liver.
  - *histoincompatibility*—tissue incompatibility between a donor and recipient.
  - *immunoincompetence*—deficient response to antigenic stimulus or congenital or acquired disease; also may be related to therapy and other causes.

autologous marrow transplantation—aspiration of the patient's own bone marrow before the initiation of aggressive radiotherapy with or without intensive chemotherapy and its infusion when bone marrow toxicity becomes life threatening.
isogeneic or syngeneic marrow transplantation—marrow grafting between identical twins. Since donor and host have the same tissue antigens, no immunologic barrier to transplantation should be present. (4, 5, 43, 60, 89)

SYMPTOMATIC TERMS

anisocytosis—variation in size of red cells, seen in pernicious anemia. (52)
blood dyscrasia—morbid blood condition. (52)
erythrocytosis—abnormal increase in the number of red blood cells. (52)
erythropenia—abnormal decrease in the number of red blood cells. (52)

fibrinolysis—dissolution of fibrin; blood clot becomes liquid. (17)

hemochromatosis—intracellular iron overload associated with organic damage. (39)

hemolysis—disruption of red cell membrane integrity producing release of hemoglobin. (52)

leukocytosis—abnormally high white cell count. (52)

leukopenia—abnormally low white cell count. (52)

macrocytosis—abnormally large erythrocytes in the blood. (52)

megaloblastosis—large, usually oval, embryonic red corpuscles found in bone marrow and blood. (52, 62)

microcytosis—abnormally small erythrocytes present in the blood.

neutropenia—excessively low neutrophil count. (10, 49, 63)

neutrophilia—increase in neutrophils including immature forms, seen in pyogenic infections. (49)

pancytopenia—reduction in all three formed elements of the blood: erythrocytes, leukocytes, and platelets. (93)

poikilocytosis—irregularly shaped red cells in the blood, seen in pernicious anemia. (52)

proliferation—increase in reproduction of similar forms of cells. (52)

reticulocytosis—increase in reticulocytes, as seen in active blood regeneration due to stimulation of red bone marrow or in congenital hemolytic anemia and some other anemias. (52, 81)

rouleaux formation, pseudoagglutination—false agglutination in which the erythrocytes appear as stacks of coins. It is seen in plasma cell dyscrasias such as multiple myeloma. (52)

spherocytosis—presence of spherocytes in the blood. A spherocyte appears as small globular, hemoglobinated erythrocyte without the central pallor, having a decreased mean corpuscular diameter and increased density. (52, 67)

thrombocytopenia—deficiency of thrombocytes or platelets in the circulating blood. (19, 52)

thrombocytosis—excess of thrombocytes or platelets in the circulating blood. (52)

LYMPHATIC CHANNELS AND LYMPH NODES

ORIGIN OF TERMS

aden-, adeno- (G)—gland

angi-, angio- (G)—vessel

cyt-, cyto- (G)—cell

hist-, histio-, histo- (G)—web, tissue

lymph-, lympho- (L)—lymph, water

-osis (G)—increase, disease, condition

-penia (G)—deficiency, decrease

PHONETIC PRONUNCIATION OF SELECTED TERMS

choriomeningitis	KO-re-owe-MEN-in-JI'tis
granuloma	GRAN-you-LOW'mah
histiocytosis X	HIS-tee-owe-sigh-TOE'sis X
lymphocytic	LIM-foe-SIT'ick
lymphocytosis	LIM-foe-SIGH-TOE'sis

ANATOMIC TERMS (8, 24, 49, 52, 71, 74) (SEE FIGS. 7.6–7.8.)

histiocytes, histocytes—tissue cells or macrophages that belong to the reticuloendothelial system and possess phagocytic properties.

lymph—clear or sometimes milky liquid found in lymphatics.

lymph nodes—encapsulated lymphoid tissue scattered along the lymphatics in chains or clusters.

lymphatic capillaries—appear as microscopic, closed-ended tubes that extend into the interstitial spaces of most tissues forming networks that parallel the networks of blood capillaries. Tissue fluid from the interstitial space is allowed to enter the lymphatic capillaries through its thin walls. When the fluid is inside the lymphatic capillaries, it is termed *lymph*.

Figure 7.6   Lymphatic vessels transport fluid from interstitial spaces to the bloodstream.

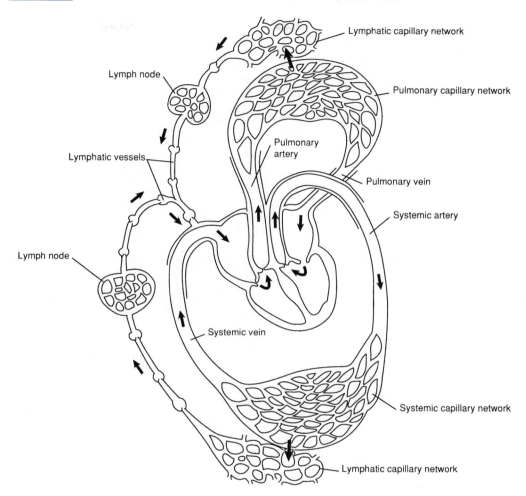

lymphatic duct, right—begins in the right thorax by the union of the right jugular, right subclavian, and right bronchomediastinal trunks. It empties into the right subclavian vein near the junction of the right jugular vein.

lymphatic trunks—drain lymph from large regions of the body, for example, the lumbar trunk drains lymph from the legs, lower abdominal wall, and pelvic organs; the intestinal trunk drains organs of the abdominal viscera; the intercostal and bronchomediastinal trunks receive lymph from areas of the thorax; the subclavian trunk drains the arm; and the jugular trunk drains portions of the neck and head. These lymphatic trunks then join one of two collecting ducts, either the thoracic duct or the right lymphatic duct.

lymphatics—thin-walled vessels widely distributed throughout the body and containing many valves. The lymphatic vessels have flaplike valves that help to prevent the backflow of lymph. The lymphatic vessels lead to specialized organs termed *lymph nodes*. After leaving the lymph nodes, these vessels come together to form larger lymphatic trunks.

reticuloendothelial system (mononuclear phagocyte system)—system includes highly phagocytic cells, such as macrophages or histiocytes, present in the loose connective tissue of

Figure 7.7   Major locations of lymph nodes.

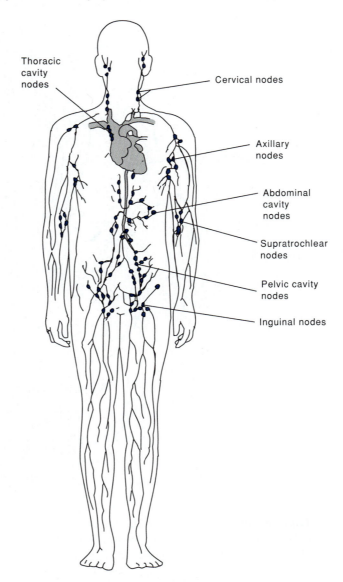

the body, the sinusoids of the lymph nodes, spleen, and liver, as well as in the bone marrow and lungs. It is thought that the function of these cells is:

under normal circumstances—removal of destroyed cells from the circulation and perhaps the storage of iron to be used in the regeneration of erythrocytes.

in pathologic disorders—removal of bacteria, dead tissue, and foreign bodies.

thoracic duct—originates in the abdomen, passes upward through the diaphragm beside the aorta, ascends in front of the vertebral column through the mediastinum, and empties into the left subclavian vein near the junction of the left jugular vein. The thoracic duct drains lymph from the intestinal, lumbar, and intercostal trunks, as well as from the left subclavian, left jugular, and left bronchomediastinal trunks.

Figure 7.8 Lymphatic vessels merge into larger lymphatic trunks, which in turn, drain into collecting ducts.

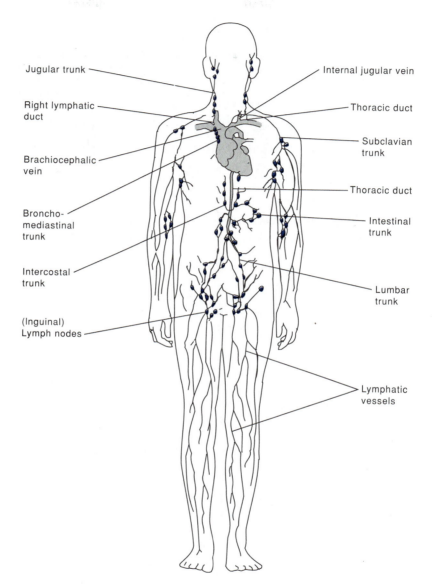

Jugular trunk

Right lymphatic duct

Brachiocephalic vein

Broncho-mediastinal trunk

Intercostal trunk

(Inguinal) Lymph nodes

Internal jugular vein

Thoracic duct

Subclavian trunk

Thoracic duct

Intestinal trunk

Lumbar trunk

Lymphatic vessels

DIAGNOSTIC TERMS

Burkitt's lymphoma—malignant tumor of lymphoid tissue that usually involves the facial bones and abdomen of young children. The etiologic agent is the Epstein-Barr virus. (47, 52)
Hodgkin's disease—life threatening, neoplastic disease producing widespread lymph node involvement, enlargement of the spleen and liver, serious blood disorders, pathologic changes in the bones and other organs, systemic manifestations such as recurrent bouts of fever, night sweats, malaise, and weight loss. Exacerbations and remissions are characteristic of the clinical course. (2, 37, 41, 48, 73) (See table 7.3.)

TABLE 7.3	Stage Grouping of Hodgkin's Disease
Stage I	Involvement of a single lymph node region (I) or single extralymphatic site (I_E)
Stage II	Involvement of two or more lymph node regions on the same side of the diaphragm (II) or localized involvement of a single associated extralymphatic organ or site and its regional lymph node(s) with or without involvement of other lymph node regions on the same side of the diaphragm (II_E)
Stage III	Involvement of lymph node regions on both sides of the diaphragm (III), which may also be accompanied by localized involvement of an associated extralymphatic organ or site (III_E), by involvement of the spleen (III_S) or both [$III_{(E+S)}$]
Stage IV	Disseminated (multifocal) involvement of one or more extralymphatic organs, with or without associated lymph node involvement, or isolated extralymphatic organ involvement with distant (nonregional) node involvement

Source: American Joint Committee on Cancer, *Manual for Staging of Cancer*, 4th ed. (Philadelphia: J. B. Lippincott Co., 1992), 253. Reprinted with permission.

Langerhans cell histiocytosis—currently preferred terminology for the group of histiocytic syndromes formerly known as *histiocytosis X, eosinophilic granuloma, Hand-Schuller-Christian disease,* and *Letterer-Siwe disease.* The basic histologic lesion of Langerhans cells histiocytosis is granulomatous, with collections of histiocytes and variable numbers of mature eosinophils and lymphocytes. Signs and symptoms vary due to which organs are infiltrated by histiocytes. Langerhans cells are classified as dendritic cells because of their capacity to form long cytoplasmic extensions through which they establish contact with other cells. Langerhans cell histiocytosis has a predilection for the skeleton. The most commonly affected sites are the skull, rib, mandible, femur, scapula, and vertebra. Histiocytoses involvement may range from solitary bone lesions to massive system involvement with multiorgan failure. Langerhans cell histiocytosis usually affects infants and young children, however young adults may also be afflicted. (8, 24, 71)

lymphadenitis—inflammation of the lymph glands. (90)

lymphadenopathy—any diseased condition of the lymph nodes, such as enlarged lymph nodes due to an unknown cause. (56)

lymphangioma—tumor composed of lymphatics. (90)

lymphangitis—inflammation of the lymphatics. (90)

lymphedema—congenital or acquired disorder of the lymphatics that prevents the removal of tissue fluids by the lymph channels and the absorption of protein and other substances by lymphatic capillaries, resulting in impairment of lymph flow and edema. (90)

malignant lymphomas, non-Hodgkin's lymphoma (NHL)—neoplasms that may arise in lymphoid tissue showing varying degrees of malignancy. They are distinguished by their histologic components and diffuse or nodular pattern. Malignant lymphocytes can be characterized as to their degree of cellular atypia (poorly differentiated or well differentiated). These factors—morphologic determinations (architectural pattern, cell size, and cellular atypia)—determine the histologic subtype of the lymphoma. The diagnosis of non-Hodgkin's lymphoma is made on morphologic criteria and the histologic subtype is classified to the Working Formulation. The Working Formulation tries to accommodate the terminology in the various systems used to classify non-Hodgkin's lymphomas. In the past, the Rappaport classification was the most used system in the United States. Tumor-specific DNA (deoxyribonucleic acid) sequences also occur at the sites of nonrandom chromosomal translocations and may be detected by molecular biologic techniques. The chromosomal translocation t (14;18) is present in 50% of patients with non-Hodgkin's lymphoma. Cloning of the t (14;18) break-points involving the *bcl-2* proto-oncogene on chromosome 18, and the immunoglobulin heavy chain region on chromosome 14 has made it possible to use polymerase chain reaction (PCR) amplification to identify cells containing this translocation. Since not all patients have a PCR-amplifiable translocation, it is unlikely that PCR analysis will replace morphologic assessment of the bone marrow. (6, 24, 48, 51, 53) (See table 7.4.)

TABLE 7.4	Stage Grouping of Non-Hodgkin's Lymphoma
Stage I	Involvement of a single lymph node (I) or localized involvement of a single extralymphatic organ or site (I_E)
Stage II	Involvement of two or more lymph node regions on the same side of the diaphragm (II), or localized involvement of a single associated extralymphatic organ or site and its regional nodes with or without regions on the same side of the diaphragm (II_E)
Stage III	Involvement of lymph node regions on both sides of the diaphragm (III) that may also be accompanied by localized involvement of an extralymphatic organ or site (III_E), by involvement of the spleen (III_S), or both [$III_{(E+S)}$]
Stage IV	Disseminated (multifocal) involvement of one or more extralymphatic organs with or without associated lymph node involvement, or isolated extralymphatic organ involvement with distant (nonregional) nodal involvement

Source: American Joint Committee on Cancer, *Manual for Staging of Cancer,* 4th ed. (Philadelphia: J. B. Lippincott Co., 1992), 258. Reprinted with permission.

> *polymerase chain reaction (PCR)*—technique that specifically amplifies DNA (deoxyribonucleic acid) and involves repeated cycles of denaturation of DNA, annealing of oligonucleotide primers, and extension of the primers using heat-stable bacterial DNA polymerase. (53)

mycosis fungoides, granuloma fungoides—chronic, progressive, lymphomatous tumor of the skin that tends to ulcerate and ultimately cause death. (52)

OPERATIVE TERMS (SEE TABLE 7.5.)

biopsy of lymph node—removal of small piece of lymphoid tissue for microscopic study. (90)
lymphadenectomy—excision of lymph nodes. (90)
lymphadenotomy—incision of lymph gland. Usually performed for drainage purposes.
multiple lymph node excision—removal of metastatic lymph nodes in a certain region, such as the axillary nodal cluster, the periaortic chain, or the pelvic and retroperitoneal nodes. (90)

SYMPTOMATIC TERMS

lymphocytopenia—deficient number of lymphocytes in the blood. (52)
lymphocytosis—abnormal increase in the number of lymphocytes in the blood. (52)
Pel-Ebstein pyrexia—cyclic fever in Hodgkin's disease and some other disorders, characterized by several days of pyrexia, followed by days or weeks of normal body temperature. The cycle repeats itself. (52)

SPLEEN

ORIGIN OF TERMS

aut-, auto- (G)—self
lien-, lieno- (L)—spleen
-oma (G)—tumor
splen-, spleno- (G)—spleen

PHONETIC PRONUNCIATION OF SELECTED TERMS

asplenia	a-SPLE'nee-a
hypersplenism	HI-per SPLEN'ism
splenectomy	sple-NECK'toe-me
splenic infarcts	SPLEN'ick IN'farks
splenitis	sple-NIE'tis
splenomegaly	SPLE-no-MEG'ah-lee
splenoptosis	SPLE-nop-TOE'sis
splenotomy	sple-NOT'owe-me

TABLE 7.5	Some Disorders of the Blood and Blood-Forming Organs Amenable to Surgery		
Cells or Anatomic Site	*Diagnosis*	*Type of Surgery*	*Operative Procedures*
White cells Bone marrow	Acute lymphoblastic leukemia	Marrow transplantation	Multiple marrow aspirations from iliac bones
		Allogenic grafting	Intravenous infusion of marrow from histocompatible donor
		Isogenic grafting	Intravenous infusion of marrow from identical twin
	Acute myelogenous leukemia Chronic myelogenous leukemia	Autologous grafting	Aspiration and storage of patient's own marrow Intravenous infusion of autologous marrow when blast crisis develops
Red cells	Hereditary sperocytosis	Splenectomy	Removal of spleen
Red cells Bone marrow	Aplastic anemia	Marrow transplantation Allogenic grafting	Multiple marrow aspirations from iliac bones Intravenous infusion of marrow from histocompatible donor
Platelets	Thrombocytopenia due to increased platelet destruction	Splenectomy	Removal of spleen
Blood cells Spleen	Congestive splenomegaly with cytopenia	Splenectomy	Removal of spleen
Spleen	Traumatic rupture of spleen	Splenectomy	Removal of spleen
Lymph nodes Spleen	Hodgkin's disease Lymphoma	Exploratory laparotomy and splenectomy	Surgical opening of abdomen with removal of spleen for the purpose of staging before initiating treatments
Lymph nodes	Embryonal cell carcinoma of testis Metastasis to lymph nodes	Radical retroperitoneal lymph node dissection (postorchiectomy)	Peritoneal cavity opened: peritoneum reflected off the aorta and vena cava Multiple pelvic and periaortic lymph nodes removed

ANATOMIC TERMS (8, 15, 41, 75, 85, 86, 90) (SEE FIG. 7.9.)

pulp—the tissues within the lobules of the spleen.

white pulp—distributed throughout the spleen in tiny islands. This tissue is composed of splenic nodules and contains large numbers of lymphocytes.

red pulp—contains many red blood cells, which, along with lymphocytes and macrophages, are responsible for its color. The red pulp fills the remaining spaces of the lobules and surrounds the venous sinuses.

Figure 7.9   (a) The spleen is located beneath the diaphragm in the upper left portion of the abdominal cavity; (b) it resembles a large lymph node.

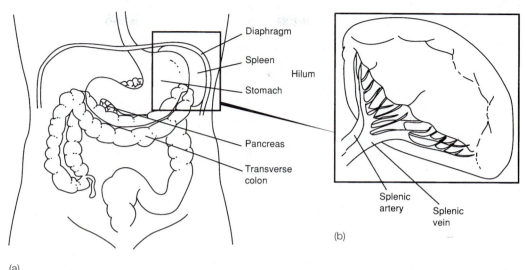

(a)

(b)

spleen—lymphoid organ located in the left hypochondriac region. The spleen is enclosed in connective tissue that extends inward from the surface and partially divides the organ into chambers or lobules. The venous sinuses (the spaces) within the lobules of the spleen are filled with blood instead of lymph. The spleen is active in the destruction of red blood cells and the manufacture of lymphocytes and phagocytes.

DIAGNOSTIC TERMS
accessory spleens—additional spleens. The occurrence of multiple accessory spleens is due to the failure of the lobules to fuse. (52)
asplenia—absence of the spleen. (86)
chronic congestive splenomegaly—condition characterized by long-standing congestion and enlargement of the spleen, usually caused by liver disease associated with portal or splenic artery hypertension. Leukopenia, anemia, and gastrointestinal bleeding are common manifestations. (25)
hypersplenism, hypersplenic syndrome—excessive splenic activity associated with highly increased blood cell destruction, leading to anemia, leukopenia, and thrombocytopenia. (11, 56, 80)
splenic infarcts—relatively common lesions usually caused by embolism, thrombosis, or infection. (11)
splenic sequestration crisis—the spleen rapidly enlarges, followed by a quick drop in blood volume and fatal hypovolemic shock. (9, 86)
splenitis, lienitis—inflammation of the spleen. (11, 90)
splenoptosis—downward displacement of the spleen. (52)
splenorrhexis—rupture of spleen due to injury or advanced disease.

OPERATIVE TERMS (SEE TABLE 7.5.)
splenectomy—removal of the spleen. (11, 71, 86)
splenopexy—fixation of a movable spleen. (56)
splenorrhaphy—suture of a ruptured spleen. (11, 90)
splenotomy—incision into the spleen.

SYMPTOMATIC TERMS

autosplenectomy—small, fibrotic spleen in adult with sickle cell anemia. Multiple splenic infarctions result in shrinkage of the organ. (48, 85)

splenomegaly, splenomegalia—enlargement of the spleen. (11, 56, 86)

ORAL READING PRACTICE

HODGKIN'S DISEASE

This peculiar and interesting disease is characterized by a painless enlargement of the lymph nodes that is initially confined to one lymph node group, frequently those located in the **cervical region.** From there, the lymph node involvement spreads to the axillary and inguinal regions and progressively assumes systemic proportions. If **mediastinal spread** with infiltration of the **lung parenchyma** and **pleura** occurs, the patient may experience substernal pain, cough, **dyspnea,** and **stridor.**

Retroperitoneal lymph node involvement may lead to the formation of a mass that presses on the stomach and produces a sense of fullness. This type of involvement tends to exert a deleterious effect, resulting in a dislodgement of the **kidneys,** compression of the **ureters** and **inferior vena cava,** and infiltrations into the neighboring structures, the spinal nerves and **vertebrae. Splenomegaly** and **hepatomegaly** are common signs and may be associated with progressive **anemia, obstructive jaundice,** and **ascites.**

Lesions of Hodgkin's disease are sometimes found in the reproductive system. **Osteolytic** and **osteoplastic** changes may occur in the **ribs, vertebrae, femur,** and **pelvis** and cause bone tenderness or intense pain. **Herpes zoster** is commonly seen during the course of **Hodgkin's disease** and can be a life-threatening illness. As the disease progresses, the patient will occasionally suffer from periodic fever episodes **(Pel-Ebstein pyrexia).** Near the terminal phase of the illness, the patient manifests a marked degree of **lassitude, debility, pallor,** and **cyanosis.**

The diagnostic feature of Hodgkin's disease is the **Reed-Sternberg cell,** a tumor cell containing irregularly shaped **cytoplasm,** a large nucleus, heavy clumps of **chromatin,** and distinctive **nucleoli** surrounded by a clear halo.

In 1902, Pusey reported the remarkable responsiveness of **Hodgkin's** and **non-Hodgkin's lymphomas** to **radiotherapy;** however, x-ray machines lacked technical efficiency, delivered inadequate depth dose, and caused painful skin burns. Radiation therapy continued to be a method of choice, but it was not until half a century later that Kaplan and the Stanford research team obtained dramatic results from the use of **megavoltage radiotherapy.**

Mantle field irradiation treats **cervical, supraclavicular, intraclavicular, axillary, hilar,** and **mediastinal nodes** down to the level of the **diaphragm. Inverted Y field irradiation** treats the **spleen** or **splenic pedicle, celiac, para-aortic, iliac, inguinal,** and **femoral nodes.** The **mantle** and the **inverted Y fields** compose the **total nodal irradiation (TNI)** or **total lymphoid irradiation (TLI).** When the pelvis is omitted from treatment, the terms are called **subtotal nodal irradiation (STNI)** or **subtotal lymphoid irradiation (STLI).**

Radiation pericarditis occurs in about 6% of the cases treated with 4,400 rad or less to the mantle field and is usually asymptomatic. Another common neurologic complication of radiotherapy is **Lhermitte's syndrome,** characterized by tingling, numbness, or electric sensations and is usually associated with bending of the head. This symptom gradually disappears over a period of several months.

Cyclic combination chemotherapy is the treatment of choice in advanced Hodgkin's disease. Several alternative programs are available. One alternative is the **MOPP** program of chemotherapy, which includes **nitrogen mustard (M); vincristine,** or Oncovin **(O); procarbazine (P);** and prednisone **(P).** It is known that the use of **antineoplastic** drugs requires much caution because of their potential toxicity. Another treatment alternative is the **ABVD** program, which is a combination of **Adriamycin (doxorubicin), bleomycin, vinblastine,** and **decarbazine.** This regime or variations of it has produced remission in some patients where the **MOPP** program has failed. A combination of **radiotherapy** and **chemotherapy** is reserved for advanced Hodgkin's disease that has not been controlled by a single treatment approach.

The most serious untoward effect of aggressive **megavoltage radiotherapy** and **chemotherapy** is **myelosuppression,** resulting in a reduction of all cellular elements of the blood **(pancytopenia). Granulocytopenia** with its lowered resistance to infection and **thrombocytopenia** with its hemorrhagic tendencies become life-threatening sequelae. The terminal phase of Hodgkin's disease is signaled by **lymphopenia,** a striking immunologic manifestation heralding a defective response to previously encountered antigens.

A **staging laparotomy** should include a careful abdominal inspection, **splenectomy,** and **sectioning of the spleen** in slices 1 centimeter apart. The procedure is only justifiable if done thoroughly. According to the Ann Arbor Conference, proper staging techniques include a complete history, signs and symptoms, detection of **extranodal involvement** and **adenopathy, biopsy** of **abnormal lymph nodes, bipedal lymphangiography,** and **chest roentgenography,** or **computed tomography. Bone marrow biopsy** is indicated in the presence of bone pain or **osseous lesions. Pathologic staging** of the extent of the disease is of practical significance as a guide to selecting the best therapeutic approach.

Early diagnosis, improved understanding of **Hodgkin's disease** and the **treatment modality** adapted to the stage of the disease now give rise to a more favorable prognosis than in the past. As a result of the addition of curative chemotherapy to the therapeutic regimen, the national mortality from Hodgkin's disease has fallen 58% during the past decade. Approximately 70% of all patients with Hodgkin's disease are curable. (2, 6, 28, 37, 41, 48, 52, 73)

ABBREVIATIONS

Ab—antibody
CBC-complete blood count
CF—complement fixation
DNA—deoxyribonucleic acid
ELISA—enzyme-linked immunosorbent assay
FDP—fibrin-fibrinogen degradation products
FR—fibrin-fibrinogen related
G6PD—glucose-6-phosphate dehydrogenase
Hb—hemoglobin
HB S—sickle cell hemoglobin

Hct, Ht—hematocrit
HLA—human leukocyte antigens
MCH—mean corpuscular hemoglobin
MCHC—mean corpuscular hemoglobin concentration
MCV—mean corpuscular volume
PCR—polymerse chain reaction
TIBC—total iron-binding capacity
VPRC—volume of packed red cells
vWf—von Willebrand's factor

RELATED TO HEMATOLOGIC DISORDERS

CML—chronic myelogenous leukemia
HE—hereditary elliptocytosis
HS—hereditary spherocytosis
MDS—myelodysplastic syndromes

PNH—paroxysmal nocturnal hemoglobinuria
PV—polycythemia vera
SCA—sickle cell anemia
vWD—von Willebrand's disease

RELATED ORGANIZATIONS

AABB—American Association of Blood Banks
ASCP—American Society of Clinical Pathologists

CLINICAL LABORATORY STUDIES

TERMS RELATED TO HEMATOLOGY

acid hemolysis test, Ham Test—test diagnostic for paroxysmal nocturnal hemoglobinuria (PNH), in which lysis of red cells occurs in acidified fresh serum. (81)

bleeding time—duration of bleeding from a standardized wound. It measures the integrity of the vessel wall and serves as a screening test for disorders of platelet function, both congenital and acquired, and for von Willebrand's disease (vWD). (18) (See table 7.6.)

capillary fragility tourniquet test—procedure measuring the resistance of the capillaries to pressure and stress. A blood pressure cuff is applied to the upper arm and kept inflated at 80 mm Hg pressure for five minutes. If a number of purpuric spots appear below the cuff area a few minutes after the cuff is released, the test is positive. (18)

coagulant—substance contributing to clot formation. (91)

coagulation time, clotting time—time taken for venous blood to clot. (17, 91)

coagulum, blood clot—lumpy mass formed in static blood in the laboratory and composed of platelets and red and white cells, irregularly scattered in fibrin network. (16)

clotlysis—dissolution of a clot. (91)

clot retraction—formation of a clot and the exuding of serum: a qualitative platelet function test. Normally, the retraction of blood begins within 30 to 60 minutes from the time it is drawn. A semiquantitative test method has been devised using platelet-rich plasma. Clot retraction depends on an adequate number of functionally normal platelets. The test is abnormal in thrombocytopenia and in Glanzmann's thrombasthenia. (16, 18)

FDP detection—direct latex test (Thrombo-Wellco test) and rapid slide test based on a latex reagent that is sensitized with anti-FDP antibodies. These are capable of detecting degradation products and fibrin in serum and urine. (40, 55, 91)

> *Reference values:* (Agglutination, Thrombo-Wellco test)
> - Fibrin degradation products
> - *Whole blood*—less than 10 µg/mL (SIU: less than 10 mg/L)
> - *Urine*—less than 0.25 µg/mL (SIU: less than 0.25 mg/L)
>   **Increased values** of serum FDP in thromboembolic disease, with peak level of 400 µg/ml and a drop to normal in about 24 hours; acute myocardial infarction with serum FDP rising 2 to 4 days after the attack. If, after the peak level subsides, a second rise of serum occurs, this signals extension of myocardial infarction or complications.

fibrin-fibrinogen degradation products (FDP)—protein fragments resulting from the digestive action of plasmin or related enzymes on fibrin or fibrinogen. (40, 91)

fibrinogen titer test—estimates the concentration of fibrinogen in plasma. (91)

fibrinogenolysis—proteolytic destruction of fibrinogen and other clotting factors in the circulating blood. (52)

fibrinolysis—destruction of fibrin in blood clots or the dissolution of fibrin due to enzymatic action. (62)

hematocrit (Hct, Ht) volume of packed red cells (VPRC)—measurement of the volume of packed red blood cells in the venous blood. (31)

hemoglobin (Hb) concentration—amount of hemoglobin recorded in grams per deciliter (g/dL) in the conventional system of units and in millimoles per liter (mmol/L) in the International System of Units (SIU). (59) (See table 7.6.)

hemogram, Schilling blood count—differential blood count in which neutrophils are divided into four groups: myelocytes, juvenile cells, staff cells, and segmented forms. (52)

mean corpuscular hemoglobin (MCH)—weight of hemoglobin in average red blood cells, conventionally expressed in picograms (pg); in the International System of Units (SIU), it is expressed in millimoles per liter (mmol/L). (59) (See table 7.6.)

| TABLE 7.6 | Selected Hematologic Findings in Disease | | | |

Test	Conventional Units (40)	SI Units (40)	Disease	Pathologic Response*
Bleeding time Duke Ivy	1–5 min. 2–7 min.	1–5 min. 2–7 min.	Thrombocytopenia von Willebrand's disease (18, 22)	Increase Increase
Clotting time Lee White	5–8 min.	5–8 min.	Hemophilia (22)	Increase
Clot retraction time	1–24 hr.	1–24 hr.	Thrombasthenia (Glanzmann's disease) (16, 18, 21)	Poor or absent
Hemoglobin Male Female	13.5–17.5 g/dL 12.0–16.0 g/dL	2.09–2.71 mmol/L 1.86–2.48 mmol/L	Polycythemia vera Anemias (28, 31)	Increase Decrease
Mean corpuscular hemoglobin (MCH)	26–34 pg/cell	0.40–0.53 fmol/cell	Hypochromic anemia (63)	Decrease
Mean corpuscular volume (MCV)	80–100 micra^3	80–100 fL	Macrocytic anemia Hypochromic microcytic anemia (28, 63)	Increase Decrease
Mean corpuscular hemoglobin concentration (MCHC)	31%–37% Hb/cell	4.81–5.74 mmol/Hb/L RBC	Hypochromic microcytic anemia (28, 63)	Decrease
Platelet count	150–400 × 10^3/μL (mm^3)	150–400 × 10^9/L	Idiopathic thrombocytopenic purpura (ITP) (19, 54, 81)	Decrease

mean corpuscular hemoglobin concentration (MCHC)—percentage of hemoglobin concentration in the average red blood cell. (54)

mean corpuscular volume (MCV)—mean volume of the average red blood cell. MCV may be measured in cubic micrometers (μm^3) or femtoliters (fl). (25, 59) (See table 7.6.)

osmotic fragility—measurement of the power of red cells to resist hemolysis in a hypotonic salt solution. This method of estimating the surface area/volume ratio of erythrocytes is used to establish the diagnosis of hereditary spherocytosis, as well as to screen for thalassemia. (64)

platelet aggregation test—test of the capability of platelets to aggregate in vitro to certain agonists. Aggregation may be measured spectrophotometrically and recorded by a platelet aggregometer. This test may be helpful in patients with prolonged bleeding times in the presence of normal platelet counts and in determining the cause of abnormal platelet function. This test is a useful aid in establishing the diagnosis of von Willebrand's disease, Bernard-Soulier syndrome, and Glanzmann's thrombasthenia. (16, 18)

prothrombin—coagulation factor II present in blood plasma. (10)

prothrombin time (PT)—time in seconds required for thromboplastin to coagulate plasma. PT is a screening test for abnormalities in the extrinsic pathways. It measures factors I, II, V, VII, and X. (18, 40)

Reference values:

Prothrombin time two-stage modified, whole blood (Na citrate)
- *PT*—18–22 seconds (SIU: 18–22 seconds)
- *PT* is prolonged in vitamin K deficiency, hypoprothrombinemia, liver disease, and obstructive jaundice. Also, PT is prolonged in heparin administration, in the presence of circulating anticoagulants, in disseminated intravascular coagulation (DIC), and in dysproteinemias.

serum hemic enzymes—enzymes of the formed elements of the blood; the abnormality is acquired or genetic. (52, 65, 91)

serum alanine aminotransferase (SALT)—acquired red cell defect of ALT is present in pyridoxine deficiency.

serum alkaline phosphatase (SALP)—acquired white cell defect of ALP occurs in granulocytic leukemia.

serum catalase—genetic red cell deficiency of catalase is found in acatalasia, in which the oral tissues become ulcerated and gangrenous.

serum phosphorylase, hepatophosphorylase—genetic white cell defect of this enzyme is present in brancher deficiency, type IV, one of the glycogen storage diseases. Measurement of the activity of phosphorylase of leukocytes confirms hepatophosphorylase deficiency.

serum glucose-6-phosphate dehydrogenase (G6PD)—deficiency of G6PD results in a mild or severe form of hemolytic anemia, which may be drug induced. If enzyme levels depress both erythrocytes and leukocytes, the disease is more serious. (65)

serum phosphatases—these enzymes are widely distributed throughout the body. The action of their isoenzymes has not been defined. (40, 52, 65)

serum acid phosphatase (SACP) measurement—concentration of ACP in the prostate, red cells, platelets, spleen, liver, and kidney, as reflected in the serum.

Reference values: (Method of King-Armstrong)
- *SACP*—0.13–0.63 U/L at 37° C (SIU: 2.2–10.5 U/L at 37° C)

  Increase in metastatic cancer of the prostate, particularly if the lesion has extended beyond the capsule of the prostate gland. SACP may also be elevated in Gaucher's disease, bone malignancy, and liver and kidney disease.

serum alkaline phosphatase (SALP) measurement—enzyme first noted for its high concentration in osteoblastic bone disease, since osteoblasts are rich in phosphatase. The present emphasis is on SALP levels in hepatobiliary disease.

Reference values: (Method of King-Armstrong)
- *SALP*—20–90 IU/L at 30° C (SIU: 20–90 U/L at 30° C)

  Increase is usually present in hepatic jaundice, posthepatic obstruction caused by gallstones or tumor, congenital atresia of intrahepatic bile ducts, biliary cirrhosis, metastases of prostatic carcinoma to bone, bone growth and repair, bone injury, Paget's disease of the bone, and other disorders.

serum iron level—iron concentration in serum. Iron is normally bound to transferrin. Iron deficiency depresses serum iron levels and boosts the total iron-binding capacity (TIBC). Serum iron and transferrin levels are depressed by such conditions as inflammation, cancer, and liver disease. (27, 40)

> *Reference values:*
> - *serum iron:*
>   *Males:* 50–160 µg/dL (SIU: 8.95–28.64 µmol/L)
>   *Females:* 40–150 µg/dL (SIU: 7.16–26.85 µmol/L)

total iron-binding capacity (TIBC)—valuable diagnostic test in anemia and related disorders to determine iron excess or iron deficit. The calculation of percentage saturation of iron provides additional information for differential diagnosis. (27, 40)

> *Reference values:*
> - *TIBC serum*—250–400 µg/dL (SIU: 44.75–71.60 µmol/L)
> - *Iron saturation*—20%–55% (SIU: Fraction of iron saturation—0.20–0.55)

transferrin, siderophilin—an iron-binding glycoprotein primarily synthesized by functional liver cells and referred to as transport iron due to its iron-transferring activity. Specific receptors on the plasma membranes of cells possess the capability to recognize transferrin, leading to the internalization of the protein and the release of iron into the cell cytoplasm. Transferrin saturated with iron is known as iron-binding capacity (IBC) or total iron-binding capacity (TIBC). (27)

plasma iron turnover (PIT)—represents the absolute amount of iron released from transferrin per unit of time, and is determined mostly by the rate of erythropoiesis.

> *fluorometric assay of free erythrocyte protoporphyrin (FEP)*—screening mechanism utilized to determine iron deficiency. This type of test can be utilized with large groups, such as school children. (27)

thromboplastin—coagulation factor III, thought to initiate clotting by converting prothrombin to thrombin in the presence of calcium ions. Tissue thromboplastin is chiefly found in the brain, thymus, placenta, testes, and lungs. (18, 40, 54)

> *complete thromboplastins*—substances causing clot formation as quickly with hemophilia as with normal blood.

> *partial thromboplastins*—substances causing clot formation less quickly with hemophilia than with normal blood.

> *partial thromboplastin time (PTT)*—valuable screening test for abnormalities of blood coagulation, measuring coagulation factors involved in the intrinsic pathways except for platelet factor III, factor VII, and factor XIII. The test is complementary to the prothrombin time and may point out other clotting factors' deficiencies or the presence of a circulating anticoagulant.

> *activated partial thromboplastin time (APTT)*—helpful screening test for the intrinsic coagulation system. Factor XII and cofactors are activated by particulate ingredients of a reagent such as celite. The other proteins are activated by phospholipid in the reagent.

> *Reference values:*
> - *PTT whole blood* (Na citrate) 60–85 seconds (SIU: 60–85 seconds)
> - *APTT whole blood* (Na citrate) 25–35 seconds (SIU: 25–35 seconds)
>   **Increase** in vitamin K deficiency, hepatic disease, and von Willebrand's disease in the presence of circulating anticoagulants, and other disorders.

thrombus—structure formed in circulating blood; chiefly composed of a head of agglutinated platelets and white cells and a tail of fibrin and entrapped red cells. (65)

thrombin time—period of time allowing plasma to clot upon addition of thrombin to the test solution. (18)

thrombin time test—screening test for marked reductions in fibrinogen concentration and the presence of fibrin in fibrinogen products. (18)

TERMS RELATED TO SEROLOGIC AND IMMUNOLOGIC TESTS

agglutination—clumping of erythrocytes when mixed with incompatible blood or antisera. (76)

agglutination test—serologic reaction in which the antibody combines with an antigen in agglutination. (76)

agglutinin—specific antibody in blood serum that causes agglutination. (65, 76)

> *autoagglutinin*—resembles cold agglutinin; reacts at temperature below 37° C with person's own cells and those of other groups.

> *cold agglutinin*—antibody causes clumping of human group O red cells. The cold agglutinins bind the antigen, thereby producing agglutination at temperatures below 37° C.

agglutinogen—substance that stimulates the production of agglutinins when introduced into the body. (76)

antibody—molecule belonging to a special group of proteins known as gamma globulins (IgG, IgM, others). (76)

antibody screen—combination of tests for detecting anti-red cell antibodies in serum, routinely used for transfusion crossmatching. An indirect Coombs' test is included in the antibody screen. (31, 76, 91)

antigen—substance that causes the formation of antibodies.

> *ABO antigens*—genetically determined, specific glycoproteins, primarily located on the surface of red blood cells but also in other body tissues.

> *human leukocyte antigens (HLA)*—antigens found on the surface of nucleated cells, including most body tissues and cellular components of the circulating blood, with exception of red cells. Peripheral blood leukocytes are suitable to access the HLA antigenic composite of a person. It is imperative that HLA typing is done for the detection of HLA antibodies before platelet or leukocyte transfusions or transplant procedures of bone marrow, kidney, heart, and other organs.

> *platelet antigens*—antigens specific for platelets and associated with ABO and HLA antigens. Matching for platelet transfusions is complex and problematic. (1, 51, 52, 81, 91)

blood factor for hemagglutinogen—serologic factor that occurs on the surface of red blood corpuscles. (1, 52, 91)

complement fixation (CF) test—antigen-antibody reaction requiring a complement for the union of antigen and antibody. (1, 48, 55, 76)

enzyme-linked immunosorbent assay (ELISA)—purified enzyme bound in a stable way to a specific antibody. With this procedure, there is no fading as with fluorescent tests and light microscopy. (1, 76, 91) (See chapter 16 for other immunologic tests.)

REVIEW GUIDE

Instructions: Break apart the following terms, identify each of the medical term elements, and define the term.

Example: lymphadenitis

lymph- = root = lymph   aden- = root = gland   -itis = suffix = inflammation

asplenia

erythroblastosis

hemapheresis

hematopoiesis

hemolysis

lienitis

macroglobulinemia

megaloblastosis

pancytopenia

poikilocytosis

splenorrhaphy

splenorrhexis

thrombocytopenia

Instructions: Define the following terms and abbreviations.

Examples: lien (L)—spleen   AB—antibody

aniso- (G)	-phagia (G)	sphero- (G)
-emia (G)	histio- (G)	lympho- (L)
leuko- (G)	poikilo- (G)	apheresis (G)
blasto- (G)	myel- (G)	sidero- (G)
polymorph (G)	-penia (G)	angio- (G)
adeno- (G)	auto- (G)	lieno- (G)
CML	PCR	VPRC
MCHC	DNA	vWf
PV	HLA	PNH
SCA	AABB	TIBC

Instructions: Figures 7.7 and 7.8 in the text show the lymphatic system. For each line that extends from the figures below, provide the anatomic name of the site, as shown in the example.

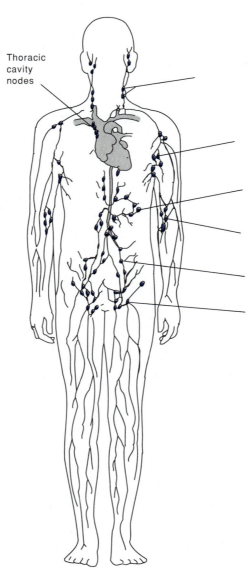

Thoracic
cavity
nodes

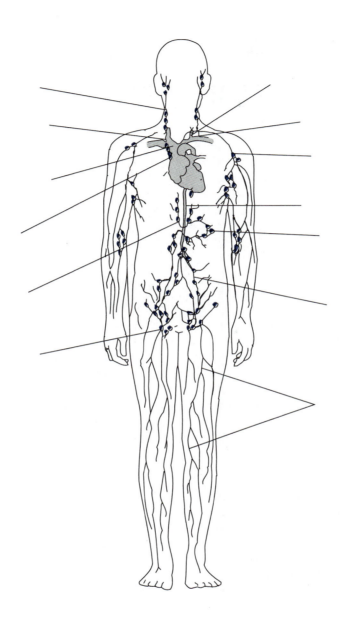

8

Respiratory Disorders

NOSE

ORIGIN OF TERMS

choana (G)—a funnel
concha (L)—a shell
meatus (L)—a passage
naso (L)—nose

osmo- (G)—sense of smell
pharyngo- (G)—pharynx
rhino- (G)—nose
septum (L)—partition

PHONETIC PRONUNCIATION OF SELECTED TERMS

atresia   a-TRE′ze-ah
coryza   ko-RYE′zah
nasal polyp   NA′zal POL′ip
nasopharyngeal cancer   NA-zo-fah-RIN′jee-al CAN′ser

ANATOMIC TERMS (24, 50) (SEE FIG. 8.1.)

choana (pl. choanae), posterior aperture—opening of the nasal cavity into the nasopharynx.
concha (pl. conchae), turbinate—one of the scroll-like bony projections on the lateral wall of the nasal cavity.
naris (pl. nares)—nostril.
nasal meatus (pl. meatuses)—space beneath each concha of the nose.
nasal septum—partition between the two halves of the nasal cavity.
nasopharynx—open chamber located behind the nasal fossa and below the base of the skull.

DIAGNOSTIC TERMS

atresia of choanae—malformation in which the opening of the nasal cavity into the nasopharynx is obstructed by a partition of mucous membrane and bone, or congenital absence of same. (50)
coryza—cold in head.
nasal polyp—benign lesion that may cause considerable obstruction of the nasal airway. (50)
nasal septal deformities—result from developmental anomalies or trauma at birth or later in life and produce nasal obstruction with sinusitis and/or chronic eustachian tubal obstruction with middle ear disease. Deviation of the nasal septum would be included in this category. (50)

Figure 8.1   (a) Major features of the upper respiratory tract. (b) Frontal section of the skull.

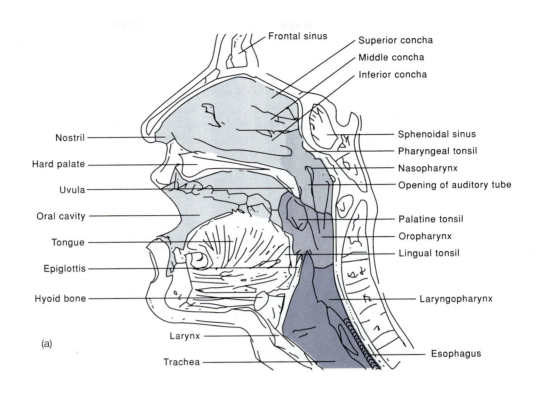

Frontal sinus
Superior concha
Middle concha
Inferior concha

Nostril
Hard palate
Uvula
Oral cavity
Tongue
Epiglottis
Hyoid bone

Sphenoidal sinus
Pharyngeal tonsil
Nasopharynx
Opening of auditory tube
Palatine tonsil
Oropharynx
Lingual tonsil

Laryngopharynx

Larynx
Trachea

Esophagus

(a)

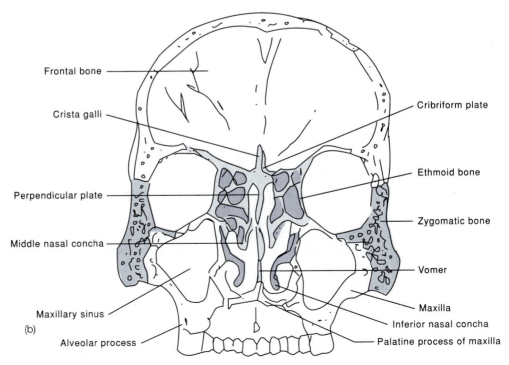

Frontal bone

Crista galli

Perpendicular plate

Middle nasal concha

Maxillary sinus

(b)

Alveolar process

Cribriform plate

Ethmoid bone

Zygomatic bone

Vomer

Maxilla
Inferior nasal concha
Palatine process of maxilla

nasal skin cancer—dermal lesion of the basal cell, squamous cell, epidermoid, or melanoma variety, differing in degree of malignancy and metastatic potential. (50)

nasopharyngeal cancer—usually an epidermoid carcinoma or lymphosarcoma of the nasopharynx, which may spread by direct extension to the meninges, compress cranial nerves, and cause cranial nerve paralyses, ptosis of the eyelid, and eventually loss of sight. Invasion of lymph nodes occurs frequently. (56)

nasopharyngitis—inflamed condition of the nasopharynx.

rhinitis—inflammation of the nasal mucosa.

> *allergic rhinitis*—hay fever.
>
> *atrophic rhinitis*—chronic infection with crust formation and nasal obstruction. (7, 46)
>
> *hypertrophic rhinitis*—form in which the mucous membrane thickens and swells, leading to nasal obstruction. (7, 46)

rhinolith—nasal concretion, or stone.

OPERATIVE TERMS (SEE TABLE 8.1.)

rhinoplasty—plastic reconstruction of the nose.

septectomy, submucous resection—excision of the nasal septum or part of it. (50)

septoplasty—corrective repair procedure whereby the deviated cartilage and bone are exposed and remodeled. Some septal deformities may be associated with external nasal deformities and there may be required additional external nasal reconstruction or rhinoplasty. (50)

transantral ligation of maxillary artery—application of vascular clips on the maxillary artery in uncontrolled recurrent epistaxis. (50)

turbinectomy—excision of a turbinate bone.

turbinotomy—surgical incision of a turbinate bone.

SYMPTOMATIC TERMS

anosmia—absence of sense of smell.

epistaxis—nosebleed. (46, 50)

rhinorrhea—thin, watery discharge from nose.

PARANASAL SINUSES

ORIGIN OF TERMS

antro- (L)—cavity, antrum

ethmo- (G)—sieve

maxilla (L)—jawbone

sinus (L)—hollow

PHONETIC PRONUNCIATION OF SELECTED TERMS

actinomycosis of sinus	ACK-tin-o-my-COE′sis of SIGN′us
antrotomy	an-TROT′owe-me
Caldwell-luc operation	CALD′well-LUCK′ OP-er-AY′shun
ethmoidectomy	ETH-moy-DECK′toe-me
pansinusitis	PAN-sign-new-SIGH′tis
sinusitis	SIGN-new-SIGH′tis

ANATOMIC TERMS (24, 50, 58) (SEE FIG. 8.1.)

ethmoidal cells—air cells in the ethmoidal labyrinth. The ethmoidal cells, collectively called a sinus, appear like a honeycomb.

ethmoidal sinus—collection of small cavities or air cells in the ethmoidal labyrinth between the eye socket (orbit) and nasal cavity.

frontal sinus—air space in the frontal bone above each orbit.

maxillary sinus, antrum of Highmore—large air sinus of the maxillary bone.

sphenoidal sinus—air space, variable in size, in the sphenoid bone. It is divided into right and left halves by a septum.

DIAGNOSTIC TERMS

actinomycosis of sinus—fungus infection in sinus. (58)
pansinusitis—inflammation of all the sinuses. (7)
sinusitis—inflammation of a sinus or sinuses. (58)

TABLE 8.1	Some Respiratory Conditions Amenable to Surgery		
Anatomic Site	*Diagnosis*	*Type of Surgery*	*Operative Procedures*
Nasal septum	Deflection of septum, congenital or posttraumatic	Septectomy or submucous resection	Removal of nasal septum, partial or complete
Nasal mucosa	Mucous polyp	Excision of lesion	Removal of polyp
Larynx	Papilloma or cyst of larynx	Laryngoscopy with excision of lesion	Endoscopic examination with removal of neoplasm
Larynx Epiglottis Vocal cords	Squamous carcinoma of larynx	Total laryngectomy	Removal of entire larynx
Trachea	Carcinoma of larynx	Tracheostomy (preliminary step to laryngectomy)	Fistulization of trachea
Bronchi	Endobronchial tuberculosis	Bronchoscopy with aspiration of bronchial secretions	Endoscopic examination of bronchi
Bronchopulmonary segment	Cystic disease of lung, tension air cyst	Segmental resection, lateral segment, middle lobe	Removal of segment, including tension air cyst of lung
Bronchopulmonary segment	Moderately advanced tuberculosis with cavitation	Segmental resection, upper lobe	Removal of two segments of upper lobe
Bronchus Bronchioli Lung	Bronchiectasis, postinfectional	Lobectomy, middle lobe	Removal of middle lobe of lung
Lobe of lung	Tuberculoma	Wedge resection, upper lobe	Excision of triangular-shaped tuberculoma
Lung	Far-advanced fibrocaseous tuberculosis	Lobectomy, upper lobe	Removal of upper lobe
Lung Visceral pleura	Carcinoma or far-advanced tuberculosis of lung	Pneumonectomy Pleurectomy	Removal of lung, including visceral pleura

OPERATIVE TERMS

antrotomy—opening of antral wall.
Caldwell-Luc operation—radical maxillary antrotomy. (50)
ethmoidectomy—excision of ethmoid cells. (50)
lavage of sinus—washing out a sinus for removal of purulent material. (50)

LARYNX

ORIGIN OF TERMS

chondro- (G)—cartilage, gristle
cornu (L)—hornlike projection
cricoid (G)—ringlike
glottis (G)—aperture of larynx
laryngo- (G)—larynx
larynx (G)—voice box
phono- (G)—voice
vox (L)—voice

PHONETIC PRONUNCIATION OF SELECTED TERMS

dilatation of larynx	dil-ah-TAY'shun of LAR'inks
epiglottitis	EP-i-glot-TIE'tis
laryngectomy	LAR-in-JECK'toe me
laryngitis	LAR-in-JI'tis
laryngoplasty	la-RING'owe-PLAS-tee
laryngotracheobronchitis	LAR-in-go-TRA-key-owe-brong-KI'tis

ANATOMIC TERMS (24, 50) (SEE FIG. 8.2.)

cricoid cartilage—ring-shaped cartilage of lowest part of larynx.
endolarynx—interior of larynx, divided into a supraglottic portion, the glottis, and a subglottic portion.
epiglottis—thin, leaf-shaped cartilage partially covered with mucous membrane. It closes the entrance of the larynx during swallowing.
glottis—two vocal folds with the rima glottidis between them.
larynx—tone-producing organ, the voice box, composed of muscle and cartilage. Its interior surface is lined with mucous membrane.
rima glottidis—narrowest portion of laryngeal cavity between the vocal folds.
vocal folds, vocal cords—mucosal folds, each containing a vocal ligament and muscle fibers.

DIAGNOSTIC TERMS

endolaryngeal carcinomas—malignant epithelial tumors of various laryngeal structures such as the glottis, subglottis, or supraglottis. Hoarseness is the presenting symptom in cancer of the vocal cord. (46, 50)
epiglottitis—inflammation of the epiglottis. (7)
hypoplasia of epiglottis—underdevelopment of epiglottis.
laryngitis—inflammation of larynx. (50)
laryngospasm, laryngismus, laryngeal stridor—adduction of laryngeal muscles and vocal cords resulting in obstruction of the airway, marked by sudden onset of inspiratory dyspnea. It is common in children.
laryngotracheobronchitis—inflammation of the mucous membrane of larynx, trachea, and bronchi. (7, 50)
perichondritis—inflammation of the perichondrium, a membrane of fibrous connective tissue that surrounds the cartilage.
stenosis of larynx—narrowing or stricture of the larynx. (46)

Figure 8.2 Cartilages of the larynx: (a) anterior view; (b) posterior view; (c) frontal section; and (d) sagittal section.

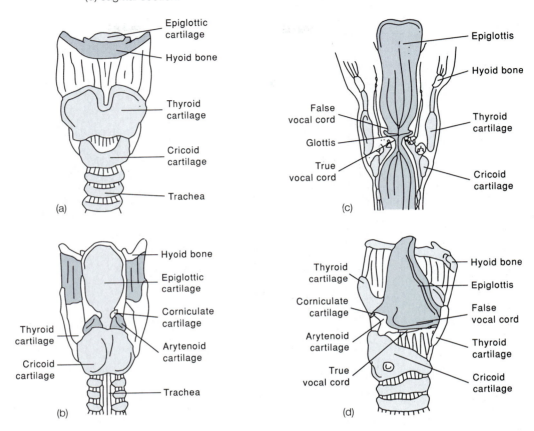

OPERATIVE TERMS (SEE TABLE 8.1.)

cordectomy—excision of vocal cord. (50)

dilatation of the larynx—instrumental stretching of the larynx.

hemilaryngectomy—removal of half of the larynx. (50)

laryngectomy—removal of the larynx for carcinoma. (50)

laryngofissure—surgical procedure to open the larynx by a median incision through the thyroid cartilage to remove cancerous growth from the larynx.

laryngoplasty—plastic repair of the larynx.

laryngoscopy—examination of interior larynx with a laryngoscope. (55)

laryngostomy—establishing a permanent opening through the neck into the larynx.

laser excision of laryngeal cancer—method of applying a suitable surgical laser to excise malignant vocal cord lesions, aided by an operating microscope attached to a laser micromanipulator. (46)

SYMPTOMATIC TERMS

aphonia—loss of voice due to local disease, hysteria, or injury to recurrent laryngeal nerve.

dysphonia—difficulty in speaking, hoarseness.

Figure 8.3 (a) The trachea transports air between the larynx and the bronchi; (b) the bronchial tree consists of the passageways that connect the trachea and the alveoli.

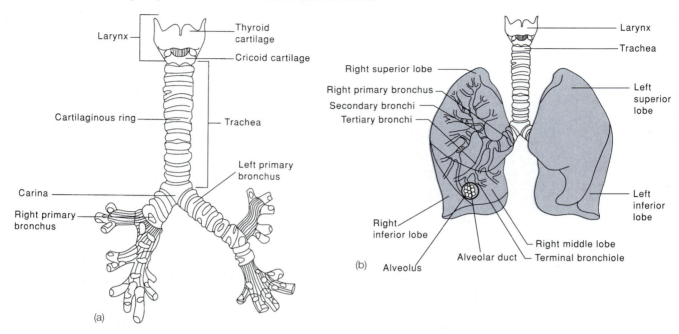

TRACHEA

ORIGIN OF TERMS

bi- (L)—two
furca (L)—fork

steno- (G)—narrow, contracted
trachea (G)—rough, tubelike

PHONETIC PRONUNCIATION OF SELECTED TERMS

tracheoesophageal fistula	TRA-key-owe-e-SOF'a-jee-al FIS'two-lah
tracheoplasty	TRA'key-owe-PLAS-tee
tracheoscopy	TRA-key-OS'ko-pe
tracheostomy	TRA-key-OS'toe-me
tracheotomy	TRA-key-OT'owe-me

ANATOMIC TERMS (24) (SEE FIG. 8.3.)

bifurcation—division into two branches.
carina—ridge between the trachea at the bifurcation.
trachea—tubelike structure composed of about 18 **C**-shaped cartilages, held together by elastic tissue and smooth muscle and extending from the larynx to the bronchi.

DIAGNOSTIC TERMS

calcification of tracheal rings—deposit of calcium in trachea.
stenosis of trachea—contraction or narrowing of lumen of trachea.
tracheobronchitis—inflammation of the bronchi and trachea. (7, 52)

tracheoesophageal fistula—communication of esophagus with trachea, a congenital or acquired anomaly.

tracheopleural fistula—communication of trachea with the pleura; may be caused by postoperative injury or pressure necrosis of inflated cuff of a tracheostomy tube.

OPERATIVE TERMS

tracheoplasty—plastic operation on trachea.

tracheoscopy—inspection of interior of trachea.

tracheostomy—formation of a more or less permanent opening into the trachea, usually for insertion of a tube. Tracheostomy (or laryngostomy) is imperative before total laryngectomy to establish an open airway. It may be necessary after thyroidectomy and brain or lung surgery to overcome a tracheal obstruction. Tracheostomy may be employed to control secretions in severely ill patients or to provide a route for ventilatory support in respiratory insufficiency. (23)

tracheotomy—incision into the trachea. (50)

BRONCHI

ORIGIN OF TERMS

bronchiolus (L)—air passage
bronchus (L)—bronchus, windpipe
-plasty (G)—surgical formation
-scope (G)—instrument to view or examine

PHONETIC PRONUNCIATION OF SELECTED TERMS

bronchi-	BRONG'ki
bronchiectasis	BRONG-key-ECK'tah-sis
bronchiolitis	BRONG-key-owe LIE'tis
broncho-	BRONG'KOE
bronchoscopy	brong-KOS'ko-pe
bronchotomy	brong-KOT'owe-me
emphysema	EM-fi-SEE'mah

ANATOMIC TERMS (24, 51) (SEE FIG. 8.3.)

bronchi (sing. **bronchus**), **main**—two primary divisions, one to each lung, pass inferolaterally from the termination of the trachea to the hila of the lungs.

> *right main bronchus*—shorter and more vertical than the left and therefore more prone to become lodged with foreign bodies when aspirated. Its upper and lower parts provide the air passages for the three lobes of the right lung.

> *left main bronchus*—gives rise to two lobar bronchi, which supply the lobes of the left lung.

bronchioles, bronchioli (sing. **bronchiole, bronchiolus**)—the smaller subdivisions of the bronchial tubes, which do not have cartilage in their walls. These small branches of the segmental bronchi enter the basic units of the lung—the lobules.

> *terminal bronchioles*—these tubes branch from a bronchiole. There are 50 to 80 terminal bronchioles within a lobule of the lung.

> *respiratory bronchioles*—two or more respiratory bronchioles branch from each terminal bronchiole. These are termed respiratory because a few air sacs bud from their sides, making these the first structures to engage in gas exchange.

> • *alveolar ducts*—2 to 10 long, branching alveolar ducts extending from each respiratory bronchiole.

> • *alveolar sacs*—thin-walled closely packed outpouchings of alveolar ducts.

- *alveoli*—thin-walled, microscopic air cells that open only on the side communicating with an alveolar sac. Air can diffuse freely from the alveolar ducts, through the sacs, and into the alveoli. The alveoli provide a large surface area of thin epithelial cells through which gas exchanges can occur. During these exchanges, oxygen diffuses through the alveolar walls and enters the blood in nearby capillaries, and carbon dioxide diffuses from the blood through these walls and enters the alveoli.

DIAGNOSTIC TERMS

aplasia of bronchus—undeveloped bronchus.

asthma—disorder characterized by increased responsiveness of the trachea and bronchi to various stimuli, resulting in narrowing of the airways. These changes are reversible either spontaneously or as a result of treatment. Symptoms vary in intensity and duration and include wheezing, coughing, and dyspnea. Asthma is an episodic type of disease, acute exacerbations being interspersed with symptom-free periods. Bronchial asthma occurs at all ages, but predominantly in early life. Allergic asthma is usually associated with a personal or family history of allergic diseases, such as rhinitis, urticaria, and eczema; positive wheal-and-flare skin reactions to intradermal injections of extracts of airborne antigens; increased levels of IgE in the serum and a positive response to provocation tests involving the inhalation of a specific antigen. The pathophysiologic hallmark of asthma is a narrowing of the airway diameter brought about by contraction of smooth muscle, vascular congestion, edema of the bronchial wall, and thick secretions. The result of these changes is an increase in airway resistance, decreased forced expiratory volumes and flow rates, hyperinflation of the lungs and thorax, increased work of breathing, and alterations in respiratory muscle function, ventilation, and pulmonary blood flow. The disorder of asthma is not only a disease of the airways but it affects most all aspects of pulmonary function.

    status asthmaticus—prolonged state of severe asthma. (25, 35)

bronchial carcinoid—slowly growing, highly vascular tumor, potentially malignant, usually found in mainstem bronchus as an obstructive endobronchial lesion. (55)

bronchiectasis—dilatation of a bronchus or bronchi, with secretion of large amounts of offensive pus. (4, 57)

bronchiectatic—pertaining to bronchiectasis. (4)

bronchiogenic carcinoma—lung cancer arises in the mainstem bronchus in 75% of patients with this malignant tumor. Metastasis occurs readily, since the great vascularity, rich network of pulmonary lymph nodes, and constant lung movements facilitate transport to neighboring and remote structures such as the brain, liver, and other organs. (6, 11)

bronchitis—inflammation of the bronchial mucous membrane. Several classifications of bronchitis are:

    chronic bronchitis—condition reflecting excessive tracheobronchial mucus production causing a chronic productive cough with expectoration for at least 3 months of the year for more than 2 consecutive years. Some types include:

- *simple chronic bronchitis*—condition characterized by mucoid sputum production.
- *chronic mucopurulent bronchitis*—characterized by ongoing or recurrent sputum with pus in the absence of localized suppurative disease, for example, bronchiectasis.
- *chronic obstructive bronchitis*—develops in a small percentage of persons suffering from simple chronic bronchitis and results in irreversible narrowing of airways. Chronic obstructive bronchitis is severe and disabling, and is manifested by increased resistance to airflow, hypoxia, and hypercapnia.
- *chronic asthmatic bronchitis*, *chronic infective asthma*—presence of chronic obstructive bronchitis with superimposed severe dyspnea and wheezing in association with inhaled irritants or an acute respiratory infection.

- *chronic obstructive lung disease*—condition in which there is chronic obstruction to airflow due to chronic bronchitis and/or emphysema.
- *emphysema*—distention of the air spaces distal to the terminal bronchiole with destruction of alveolar septa. Emphysema can be a severe disabling disorder. (25, 29, 35)

broncholithiasis—presence of one or more calcified stones within the tracheobronchial tree. The most common cause of stone formation results from erosion of a calcified lymph node into an adjacent bronchus. Eroding calcified lymph nodes are usually due to granulomatous infection, including histoplasmosis, tuberculosis, and coccidioidomycosis. Manifestations include cough, expectoration of calcified material, and hemoptysis. Pneumonia and atelectasis may develop secondary to the obstruction of the airway with the calcified material. (57)

bronchopleural fistula—open communication between a bronchus and the pleural cavity. This may be a complication of pulmonary resection.

OPERATIVE TERMS (SEE TABLE 8.1.)

bronchoplasty—plastic operation for closing fistula.

bronchoscopy—examination of the bronchi through a bronchoscope. (4)

bronchotomy—incision into a bronchus.

YAG laser therapy—application of the yttrium-aluminum-garnet (YAG) laser beam, which causes the tumor to vaporize on contact. This type of therapy has been used effectively in the treatment of malignant lesions of the trachea and bronchi.

LUNGS

ORIGIN OF TERMS

alveolus (L)—small saclike dilatation
apex (L)—tip
phthisis (G)—a wasting
pneumo- (G)—air, lung
pulmo-, pulmono- (L)—lung
segment (L)—a portion

PHONETIC PRONUNCIATION OF SELECTED TERMS

histoplasmosis	His-toe-plaz-MOS′sis
Legionnaires' disease	LEE-jah-NARS′ DIS′ease
lobectomy	lo-BECK′toe-me
pneumonectomy	NEW-mon-ECK′toe-me
pneumonitis	NEW-mo-NYE′tis
silicosis	SIL-i-CO′sis

ANATOMIC TERMS (24, 51) (SEE FIG. 8.4.)

alveoli (sing. **alveolus**)—air cells of the lungs in which the exchange of gases takes place.

apex of lung—most superior part of the lung above the clavicle.

base of lung—inferior part of the lung above the diaphragm.

bronchopulmonary segment—one of the subdivisions of a pulmonary lobe, supplied with a bronchial tube, blood, and lymph vessels. The right lung has 10 segments and the left lung has 9.

bronchopulmonary tree—the lung compared to a hollow tree upside down in the thorax. The tree trunk is the trachea, kept open and stiffened by C-shaped bars of cartilage. The main bronchi are two large branches that ramify into smaller and smaller ones until they become leaf stems or bronchioles. These in turn form tiny airways, the alveolar ducts, which lead to countless clusters of air cells surrounded by capillaries. There the exchange of gases takes place.

Figure 8.4   (a) Lobes of the lungs. (b) Bronchopulmonary segments of the lungs (anterior view).

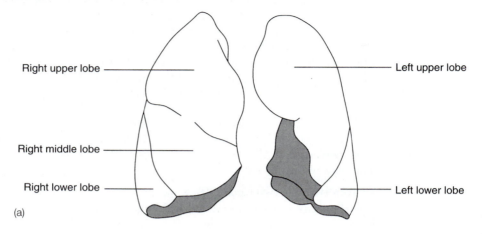

(a)

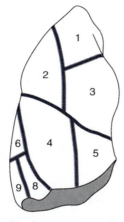
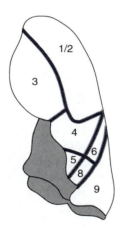

(b)

Right lung
1. Apical segment of upper lobe
2. Posterior segment of upper lobe
3. Anterior segment of upper lobe
4. Lateral segment of middle lobe
5. Medial segment of middle lobe
6. Apical segment of lower lobe
7. Medial basal segment of lower lobe†
8. Anterior basal segment of lower lobe
9. Lateral basal segment of lower lobe
10. Posterior basal segment of lower lobe†

Left lung
1. Apicoposterior segment of upper lobe
2. *Combined with (1) in left lung*
3. Anterior segment of upper lobe
4. Superior lingular segment of upper lobe
5. Inferior lingular segment of upper lobe
6. Apical segment of lower lobe
7. Medial basal segment of lower lobe†
8. Anterior basal segment of lower lobe
9. Lateral basal segment of lower lobe
10. Posterior basal segment of lower lobe†

†Not visible in anterior view.

hilus—triangular depression on the medial surface of the lung that contains the hilar lymph nodes and the entrance or exit of blood and lymph vessels, nerves, and bronchi. They form the root of the lung.

lobe—major division of the lung composed of bronchopulmonary segments.

parenchyma—the functional tissue of any organ; for example, the respiratory bronchioles, alveolar ducts, sacs, and alveoli, which participate in respiration.

DIAGNOSTIC TERMS

abscess of lung—localized area of suppuration in the lung with or without cavitation. It is accompanied by necrosis of tissue. (3)

acute respiratory failure—life-threatening condition characterized by excessively high carbon dioxide tension or abnormally low oxygen tension of the arterial blood. It may be caused by blockage of air passages by tenacious secretions from lung infection, by exposure to atmospheric smog or other irritant inhalants, or by brain damage to the respiratory center. (54)

adult respiratory distress syndrome (ARDS)—the essential feature is substantial intrapulmonary right-to-left shunt, a decreased functional residual capacity, and interstitial lung edema. Intubation and ventilation with positive end-expiratory pressure (PEEP) is used in the treatment of this syndrome. (30)

aplasia of lung—incomplete development of the lung.

asbestosis—occupational disease caused by protracted inhalation of asbestos particles. (34, 44)

atelectasis—functionless, airless lung or portion of a lung. (52)

blast injury—internal trauma of lungs, ears, and intestines resulting from high-pressure waves following an explosion. It may result in extreme bradycardia, severe cyanosis, dyspnea, hemorrhage, and deafness. (54)

byssinosis—chronic occupational lung disease caused by the inhalation of hemp, flax, or cotton. (38)

carcinoma of the lung: primary, secondary, or metastatic—malignant new growth and the most important of the neoplastic diseases of the lung. Common tumors are:

> *adenocarcinoma*—tumor forms acinar and glandular structures with or without mucin formation. Most adenocarcinomas develop in the peripheral area of the lung. Adenocarcinoma has been implicated in pulmonary fibrosis and may arise in areas of previous scars in the lung. Distant metastases occur early and frequently. Bone metastases may be blastic.

> *large cell carcinoma*—an anaplastic tumor arising in the lung periphery. The cells are large, bizarre, pleomorphic, multinucleated, and round or spindle shaped. The large cell carcinoma may invade locally or metastasize widely.

> *small cell carcinoma, oat cell carcinoma*—tumor arises most frequently in the proximal bronchi. The intramucosal site of origin of this carcinoma is difficult to identify, but the tumor is thought to arise from basal neuroendocrine or Kulchitsky cells (peptide hormone-secreting cells). In advanced stages, the bronchial lumina may be obstructed by extrinsic compression or endobronchial tumor. It is a very malignant tumor, notorious for its early, frequent, and life-threatening metastases.

> *squamous cell carcinoma, epidermoid carcinoma*—most common type of lung cancer that arises from the central bronchi in about 80% of patients. Squamous cell carcinoma tends to metastasize late. Lymph nodes, adrenal gland, and liver are frequent sites of metastases. (8, 9, 21, 27, 37)

chronic obstructive pulmonary disease (COPD)—refers to a class of diseases of uncertain etiology characterized by persistent slowing of airflow during forced expiration. This prolonged airway obstruction can cause disabling progressive respiratory disease, frequently with irreversible functional deterioration and fatal prognosis. (52)

histoplasmosis—fungus disease caused by *Histoplasma capsulatum;* sometimes associated with calcified pulmonary lesions. (59)

Legionellosis—refers to infections caused by bacteria of the genus *Legionella*. There are over 39 recognized species of *Legionella*. The most important of these infections is **Legionnaires' disease** caused by *Legionella pneumophila*. It was detected and described as a result of a dramatic outbreak of respiratory infections in persons attending an American Legion Convention in Philadelphia in 1976. Legionnaires' disease is acquired by inhaling aerosolized water containing *Legionella* organisms or possibly by pulmonary aspiration of contaminated water. A variety of contaminated aerosols' sources have been identified in the outbreak of Legionnaires' disease that are derived from air-conditioning systems, cooling towers, humidifiers, whirlpool baths, and showers. Symptoms may include weakness, malaise, anorexia, dry cough, purulent or nonpurulent sputum, pleuritic pain, nausea, headache, vomiting, and diarrhea. High fever, relative bradycardia, dyspnea, confusion, and signs of consolidation are usually present. Pulmonary infiltrates progress to form patchy, localized lesions leading to multilobar lesions and consolidation. Erythromycin is the drug of choice for the treatment of this disease.

    Pontiac fever—in July of 1968, 144 employees and visitors in a health department building in Pontiac, Michigan, developed a self-limited illness, consisting of fever, myalgias, headache, and malaise. The causative agent was assumed to be *L. pneumophila;* however, this was not proven. (5, 6, 10, 43)

pneumoconiosis—disease of the lungs due to injury by dust from any source. (19, 35, 40)

    coal worker's pneumoconiosis (CWP)—deposition of coal mine dust in the lung and parenchyma and the tissue's reaction to its presence. Simple CWP's chest radiographic abnormalities consist of small irregular opacities. With prolonged exposure, the radiographic picture is one of 1 to 5 millimeters in diameter of small rounded regular opacities. Complicated CWP is manifested by chest radiographs showing nodules ranging from 1 centimeter in diameter to the size of an entire lobe. Usually, these nodules are confined to the upper half of the lungs. (40)

pneumonia—inflammation of the lungs with exudation into lung tissue and consolidation. Predominant etiologic agents are pneumococci and mycoplasmas or pleuropneumonialike organisms (PPLO) and less frequently staphylococci, streptococci, meningococci, viruses, tubercle bacilli, and others. Classifications of pneumonia are:

    Community-acquired pneumonia affects 2 to 3 million adults annually in the United States. *Streptococcus pneumoniae*, a gram-positive bacterium, appears as the most common cause of community-acquired pneumonia in patients of all ages. Community-acquired pneumonia is usually not caused by enteric gram-negative bacilli in young adults; however, some of these organisms have been implicated in a small percentage of cases, most of which reflect debilitated or elderly patients with preexisting disease conditions.

    Hospital-acquired pneumonia is the second leading cause of nosocomial infections and accounts for 13% to 18% of all nosocomial infections. The causative agent is usually gram-negative organisms, which are responsible for 50% to 80% of nosocomial pneumonias. Among the gram-positive bacteria, *Staphylococcus aureus* is the most commonly occurring organism. *Legionella* species may cause nosocomial infection when the hospital water distribution is colonized with this organism.

Various types of pneumonia are:

    aspiration pneumonia—pulmonary inflammatory condition resulting from the abnormal entry of endogenous secretions to exogenous substances into the lower airways. Three conditions related to aspiration pneumonia are:

        • *chemical pneumonitis*—refers to fluids that are inherently toxic to the lower airways and can produce an inflammatory reaction that is independent of bacterial infection, for example, acid, gasoline, kerosine, mineral oil, and alcohol.

- *bacterial infection*—due to aspiration of bacteria that reside in the upper airways. Bacterial infection following aspiration may initially show pneumonitis, but if not medially treated early, pneumonitis may progress to suppurative complications that include lung abscess or emphysema.
- *airway obstruction*—due to aspirating fluids or particulate matter that are not inherently toxic to the lung but cause mechanical obstruction reflex airway closure. For example, vegetable matter can cause obstruction and inflammation. The *Heimlich maneuver*, which consists of firm, rapid pressure applied to the upper abdomen in an effort to force the diaphragm up and dislodge the offending particle, is the on-the-scene treatment of choice. Bacterial infection is a common complication to airway obstruction.

bronchopneumonia—inflammation of bronchioli and air vesicles with scattered areas of consolidation.

lobar pneumonia—acute inflammation of one or more lobes of the lung or lungs.

primary atypical pneumonia—infection caused by *Mycoplasma pneumoniae*. The type of this disease process may range from a mild illness to a fatal condition. (2, 8, 9, 16, 32, 59)

pneumonitis—inflammation of the lung; a virus form of pneumonia. (2)

pneumonocele, pneumocele—pulmonary hernia. (55)

pulmonary edema—excess of intra-alveolar and intrabronchial fluid in the lungs, inducing cough and dyspnea; common in left-sided heart failure. (25)

pulmonary embolism—lodgment of a clot or foreign substance in a pulmonary arterial vessel, cutting off the circulation. (42, 47)

pulmonary or vesicular emphysema—overdistention of alveoli and smaller bronchial tubes with air. (29)

pulmonary hypertension—condition due to increased pressure in the pulmonary artery resulting from obstruction by pulmonary embolism or thrombosis, tuberculosis, emphysema, or pulmonary fibrosis. (22, 42)

pulmonary infarction—necrosis of functional lung tissue (parenchyma) due to loss of blood supply usually caused by embolism. (42, 47)

pulmonary thrombosis—clot formation in any pulmonary blood vessel resulting in circulatory obstruction. (42)

pulmonary tuberculosis, phthisis—a specific inflammatory disease of the lungs caused by tubercle bacillus and characterized anatomically by a cellular infiltration that subsequently caseates, softens, and leads to ulceration of lung tissue; manifested clinically by wasting, exhaustion, fever, and cough. (12, 52, 60)

shock lung—pulmonary changes due to shock, closely resembling severe congestion and edema, both interstitial and intra-alveolar in nature. A shock lung is associated with marked hypoxia, diffuse intravascular coagulation, and formation of microthrombi. (54)

siderosis—chronic respiratory disorder caused by the inhalation of iron oxide, an industrial hazard of arc welding or steel grinding, leading to pulmonary irritation, chronic bronchitis, and emphysema. (40)

silicosis—occupational disease due to inhalation of silica dust usually over a period of 10 years or more. (39)

OPERATIVE TERMS (SEE TABLE 8.1.)

biopsies: (11, 49)

lung biopsy—small specimen of lung tissue used for pathologic, bacteriologic, and spectrographic studies to aid diagnosis.

lymph node biopsy—removal of tissue from scalene or supraclavicular lymph nodes for gross or microscopic examination to aid in the detection of cancer, tuberculosis, or other disease.

percutaneous needle biopsy—procedure used when tissue diagnosis is needed to plan radiation therapy and chemotherapy. The area to be biopsied is detected by television fluoroscopy. A biopsy needle is inserted through a small skin incision, and cells aspirated are used for cytologic and bacteriologic diagnosis. (1, 20, 31)

bronchofiberscopy—endoscopic examination of the tracheobronchial tree using a flexible bronchofiberscope to view the carina and right and left mainstem of bronchus. Under fluoroscopic control, transbronchial biopsies, brushings, or aspiration of secretions may be obtained for culture and cytologic examination. (11)

excisional surgery (extirpative, definitive)—partial or complete removal of the diseased lung. (11)

lobectomy—removal of a pulmonary lobe.

lung resection, pulmonary resection—partial excision of the lung, such as:
- *pneumonectomy*—removal of an entire lung.
- *segmental resection*—removal of a bronchopulmonary segment.
- *subsegmental resection*—removal of a portion of a bronchopulmonary segment.
- *wedge resection*—removal of a triangular portion of the lung, usually a small peripheral lesion, such as a tuberculoma.

extrapleural thoracoplasty—multiple rib resection without entering the pleural space. (11, 59)

lung transplantation—removal of patient's lung with subsequent replacement by implantation of a donor lung. Improved results from this type of surgical procedure have resulted from strict adherence to preoperative criteria in selecting one-lung transplant recipients; the availability of cyclosporine for immunosuppression combined with the avoidance of routine postoperative administration of prednisone in the first 2 or 3 weeks following transplantation; and a significant change in operative technique, which included the use of omentum (a long fold of membranes attached to the stomach and adjacent organs in the abdomen) to protect and revascularize the bronchial anastomosis. The omentum is wrapped around the ends of the bronchial tube where the new lung has been attached. When the omentum is placed in contact with damaged tissue, it is able to promote the growth of new blood vessels to facilitate the healing process. Patients suffering from various terminal pulmonary diseases and who are unresponsive to medical therapy may be candidates for single-lung transplantation. These disorders may include pulmonary fibrosis, chronic emphysema, cystic fibrosis, bronchiectasis, posttraumatic pulmonary insufficiency, and silicosis.

heart-lung transplantation—removal of patient's heart and lungs with subsequent replacement by implantation of a donor's heart and lungs. The use of cyclosporine for immunosuppression has been a pivotal improvement in the reduction in morbidity and in the improvement in survival. It has also provided a major element in the revival of heart-lung transplantation procedures. The combined replacement of heart and lungs offers several advantages, e.g., all the diseased tissue are replaced and removed, and since the coronary-bronchial vascular beds are undisturbed, blood is supplied immediately to the tracheal anastomosis. By using endomyocardial biopsy procedures, the clinician can evaluate the rejection factor of both the heart and lung grafts. Those who would benefit from a heart-lung transplantation include children with congenital heart disease complicated either by irreversible vascular disease from prolonged left to right shunting or by marked hypoplasia of pulmonary arteries that makes correction impossible. Patients with moderate to severe pulmonary hypertension could also benefit. (28, 34, 54)

pulmonary embolectomy—removal of lung embolus employing extracorporeal circulation in patients presenting with massive embolus and profound circulatory collapse. (47)

SYMPTOMATIC TERMS

anoxemia—deficient oxygen tension in arterial blood. (54)

anoxia—oxygen want in tissues and organs. (54)

apnea, apnoea—temporary absence of respiration; also seen in Cheyne-Stokes respiration. (54)
  sleep apnea—intermittent cessation of airflow at the nose and mouth during sleep. (44, 53)
bronchial or tubular breathing—harsh breathing with a prolonged high-pitched expiration that may have a tubular quality.
Cheyne-Stokes respiration—irregular breathing beginning with shallow breaths that increase in depth and rapidity, then gradually decrease and cease altogether. After 10 to 20 seconds of apnea, the same cycle is repeated. (44)
cyanosis—bluish color of skin due to deficient oxygenation. (52)
dyspnea, dyspnoea—difficult breathing. (44, 52)
expectoration—act of coughing up and spitting out material from the lungs, trachea, and mouth.
hemoptysis—expectoration of blood. (52)
hiccough, hiccup, singultus—spasmodic lowering of the diaphragm followed by spasmodic, periodic closure of the glottis. (44, 52)
hypercapnia, hypercarbia—excess of carbon dioxide in the circulating blood, with abnormally high carbon dioxide tension (PCO_2) causing overstimulation of respiratory center. (54)
hyperpnea—respirations with increased rate and depth. (44, 52)
hyperventilation syndrome—prolonged heavy breathing and long, sighing respirations causing marked apprehension, palpitation, dizziness, muscular weakness, paresthesia, and tetany. The attack may result from biochemical changes in neuromuscular and neurovascular function or from acute anxiety. (44, 54)
hypoxia—oxygen want due to decreased amount of oxygen in organs and tissues. (54)
orthopnea, orthopnoea—breathing possible only when person sits or stands. (54)
paroxysmal nocturnal dyspnea (PND)—attacks of difficult breathing, usually occurring in heart disease at night. (52)
rales—bubbling sounds heard in bronchi at inspiration or expiration. (42)
tachypnea—abnormally rapid breathing.

THORAX, PLEURA, AND MEDIASTINUM

ORIGIN OF TERMS
paries (L)—wall
phren (G)—diaphragm, mind
pleuro- (G)—pleura
pyo- (G)—pus
thorax (G)—breast plate, chest
viscero- (L)—organs, viscera

PHONETIC PRONUNCIATION OF SELECTED TERMS
hemothorax	HE-mo-THO′raks
pectus carinatum	PECK′tus CAR′i-nat-um
pleuritis	PLOOR-RYE′tis
pyothorax	PIE′owe-THO′raks

ANATOMIC TERMS (13, 16, 24, 49, 55) (SEE FIG. 8.5.)
mediastinum—the interpleural space containing the pericardium, heart, major vessels, esophagus, and thoracic duct.
pleura (pl. **pleurae**)—thin sac of serous membrane that is invaginated by the lung and lines the mediastinum and thoracic wall. Each lung has its own pleural sac.

Figure 8.5 Location of the lungs within the thoracic cavity.

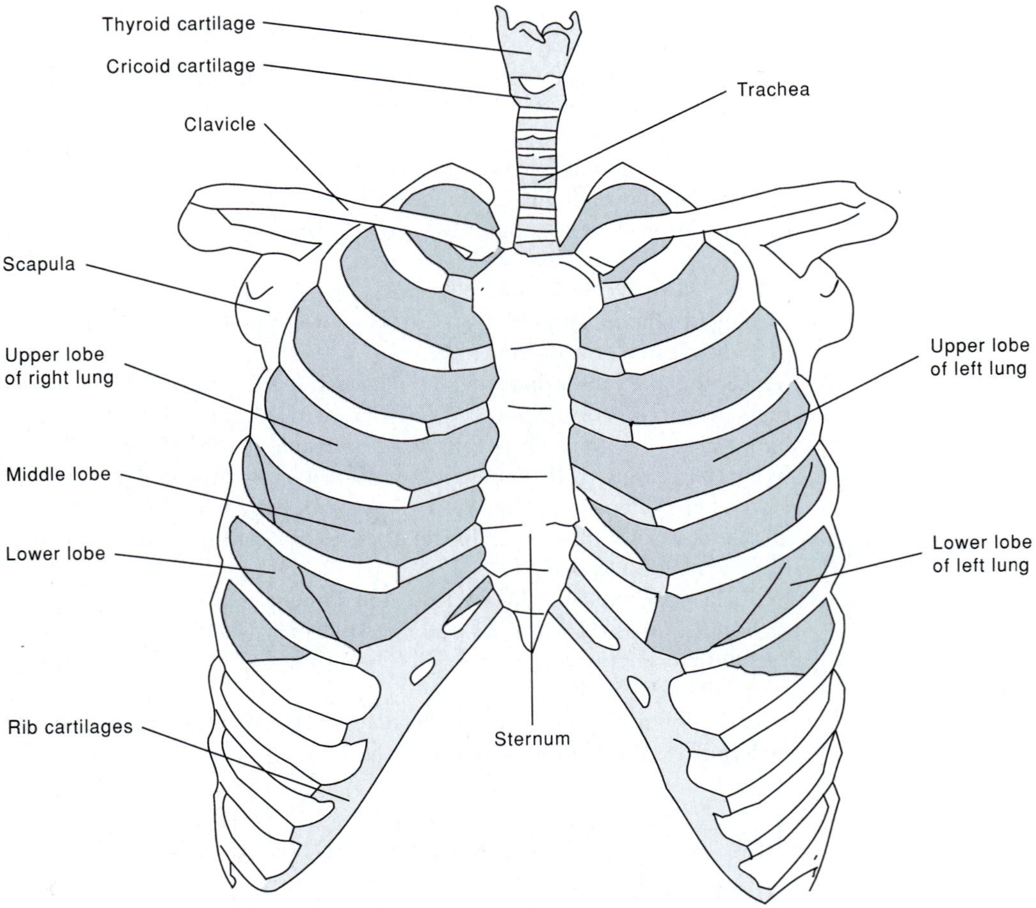

parietal pleura—the costal, mediastinal, and diaphragmatic parts of the pleura and the cupola, which covers the apex of the lung.

visceral pleura, pulmonary pleura—pleura that invests the lungs and lines the interlobar fissures.

pleural cavity—potential space between the parietal and visceral pleurae, lubricated by a thin film of serum.

thorax, chest—upper trunk composed of the thoracic vertebrae, sternum, ribs, costal cartilages, and muscles. The thoracic cage protects the vital organs of circulation and respiration as well as other mediastinal structures.

DIAGNOSTIC TERMS

abnormal chest:

barrel chest—barrel-like appearance of chest on inspiration in advanced emphysema.

flail chest, flapping chest cage—instability of thoracic cage due to fracture of ribs or sternum or both.

pectus carinatum—keeled chest. Presents as undue prominence of the chest. Condition also called chicken breast.

rachitic chest—chest condition affected with rickets. Chest contour resembles a pigeon breast. (15, 49)

empyema of pleura, pyothorax—pus in pleural cavity. (55)

hemothorax—blood in pleural cavity caused by trauma or ruptured blood vessel. (15, 49, 55)

hydropneumothorax—watery effusion and air in pleural cavity.

mediastinitis—acute or chronic inflammation of the mediastinum. (16, 55)

mesothelioma of the pleura—primary neoplasm arising from the surface lining of the pleura. Approximately 75% of the pleural mesotheliomas are malignant, and the remaining 25% present as localized tumors. (15, 38)

pleural effusion—excessive formation of serous fluid within the pleural cavity. (14, 33, 52)

pleurisy, pleuritis—inflammation of the pleura. (14, 52)

pyopneumothorax—pus and air in the pleural cavity. (14, 52)

spontaneous pneumothorax—entrance of air into the pleural cavity resulting in a collapse of a lung. (13, 15, 52)

tension or valvular pneumothorax—entrance of air into pleural cavity on inspiration; air exit blocked by valvelike tissue on expiration; enlargement of pleural cavity and collapse of lung as positive pressure increases, resulting in mediastinal shift and depression of diaphragm. (13, 15, 33)

tumors of mediastinum—may not cause patient distress until they become large. Such tumors are often discovered on routine chest x-ray films or fluoroscopy. Biopsy of the mass may prove the best technique to establish a definitive diagnosis. A computed tomography (CT) scan of the thorax is the most precise, noninvasive technique for detecting mediastinal tumors. Definitive treatment depends on the primary disease and extension of the tumor to other vital organs, such as heart, great vessels, esophagus, air passages, and surrounding nerves. Examples of these tumors are teratomas and neuroblastomas. Tumors locate in the posterior mediastinum and originate from the sympathetic ganglion (ganglioma, ganglioneuroblastoma, neuroblastoma, and neurofibroma), and the intercostal nerves (neurofibroma, neurilemoma, and neurosarcoma). Thyoma is the most common neoplasm of the anterosuperior mediastinum. (13, 36, 45)

OPERATIVE TERMS (SEE TABLE 8.1.)

artificial or therapeutic pneumothorax—introduction of a measured amount of air into the pleural cavity through a needle to give the diseased lung temporary rest. (49)

> *mediastinal node biopsy*—resection of a small piece of tissue from a regional lymph node for microscopy and culture. (20)
>
> *pleural biopsy*—aspiration of cells from parietal pleura with biopsy needle for bacteriologic and histologic studies. (20)

cervical mediastinotomy—small incision into the mediastinum in the neck region to obtain biopsy specimen from lymph node for diagnostic evaluation, and in staging of superiormediastinal lymph nodes before consideration of therapy in patients with lung cancer. (21)

mediastinoscopy—examination of the mediastinal organs by mediastinoscope under direct vision to aid in diagnosing disease and in assessing the resectability of bronchogenic carcinoma.

pleurectomy: (49)

> *partial*—removal of a portion of the pleura.
>
> *complete*—removal of the entire pleura; generally associated with pneumonectomy.

pulmonary decortication—removal of fibrinous exudate or pleural peel from the visceral surface of the imprisoned lung to restore its functional adequacy. (49)

thoracostomy, open—surgical excision of rib segment to create an opening in the chest wall for drainage of the empyemic space.

SYMPTOMATIC TERMS

pleural adhesions—fibrous bands that bind the visceral pleura to the parietal pleura. They may be loose, elastic, and avascular or firm, inelastic, and vascular. (33)

pleural effusion—abnormal accumulation of fluid within the pleural space. (13, 33, 55)

pleural exudate—pus or serum accumulating in the pleural cavity. Fibrinous exudate may lead to the formation of adhesions.

pleural peel—abnormal layer of fibrous tissue adherent to the visceral pleura and underlying diseased lung. The ever-thickening peel may inhibit respiratory function. (54)

pleuritic pain, pleurodynia—sharp, intense pain felt in intercostal muscles. (13, 55)

CLINICAL LABORATORY STUDIES

blood gas determinations—sensitive indicators of physiologic changes of lung function and tissue perfusion in acute illness. Measurements are obtained from hydrogen, carbon dioxide, and oxygen tensions (pressures) of arterial or venous blood. The P refers to partial pressure. (17, 54)

PCO_2—pressure or tension of carbon dioxide measured in millimeters of mercury.
Reference values:
- *arterial* PCO_2—35–50 mm Hg
- *venous* PCO_2—40–45 mm Hg
  Increase in PCO_2 (hypercarbia): Carbon dioxide retention in respiratory acidosis and metabolic alkalosis.
  Decrease in PCO_2 (hypocarbia): Excessive loss of carbon dioxide in hyperventilation due to respiratory alkalosis or metabolic acidosis.

pH—hydrogen ion concentration or acidity value of blood (urine).
Reference values:
- *arterial pH*—7.38 to 7.44
- *venous pH*—7.36 to 7.41
  Increase in acidosis.
  Decrease in alkalosis.

PO_2—pressure or tension of oxygen expressed in millimeters of mercury.
Reference values:
- *arterial* PO_2—95 to 100 mm Hg
  Patients with chronic lung disease normally have an arterial PO_2 of 70 mm Hg or less.
  Decreased values in arterial PO_2 in advanced lung or heart disease, venous PO_2 due to inadequate blood volume, exchange of gases, cardiac output, and tissue perfusion.

oximetry—determination of the oxygen saturation of arterial blood by means of bichromate photoelectric colormetry.

SPECIAL PROCEDURES

augmented ventilation—increased capillary circulation and gas exchange in respiration. The primary goal of assisted or augmented ventilation is to support ventilation until the patient can support ventilation for himself or herself. (28)

continuous positive airway pressure (CPAP)—measured in centimeters of H_2O pressure, this technique may be used when the respiratory drive is normal and the pulmonary disease is not overwhelming.

intermittent mandatory ventilation (IMV)—patient breathes without support, but mandatory respirations are supplied by the ventilator at intervals. This procedure permits a gradual weaning from mechanical ventilation to unaided breathing. (28)

peak inspiratory pressure (PIP)—peak positive pressure in centimeters of H_2O given at the top of the inspiration just before expiration.

positive end-expiratory pressure (PEEP)—maneuver used to increase the functional residual capacity of the lungs. It affects the airway during expiration, preventing intrathoracic pressures from returning to atmospheric pressure.

pressure-control ventilation (PCV)—ventilation is time triggered, time cycled, and pressure limited. The inspiratory airway pressure is specified by the operator, tidal volume and inspiratory flow rate are dependent variables and are not user specified. PCV requires that the patient passively accept ventilator breaths, and this may require heavy sedation for the patient to be maintained on this mode. This mode may be hazardous in the hemodynamically unstable patient.

pressure-support ventilation (PSV)—ventilation is patient initiated, flow cycled, and pressure limited. When PSV is used, the patient receives ventilator assist only when the ventilator detects an inspiratory effort. PSV is designed for use in the weaning process.

synchronized intermittent mandatory ventilation (SIMV)—similar to IMV except that mandated breaths are synchronized with the patient's own spontaneous breathing rate. Utilizing the SIMV techniques prevents delivery of a mandatory tidal volume from the ventilator on top of spontaneous inspiration.

thoracentesis, pleurocentesis—tapping of the pleural cavity to remove pleural effusion for diagnostic or therapeutic purposes. (31, 41, 48)

ORAL READING PRACTICE

DETECTING PLEURAL EFFUSION

The **pleural space** lies between the **lung** and **chest wall** and normally contains a very thin layer of fluid. The pleural space with its thin layer of liquid serves as a coupling system between the lung and chest wall. The **visceral pleura** is the serous membrane covering the **lung parenchyma.** The **parietal pleura** is the name of the serous membrane covering the **chest wall,** the **diaphragm,** and the **mediastinum.** When a person has an excess amount of fluid in the pleural space, that person has **pleural effusion.** Pleural fluid accumulates when pleural fluid formation exceeds pleural fluid absorption. The majority of causes have been classified as due to **congestive heart failure, malignancy, bacterial infection, pulmonary embolism, cirrhosis, pancreatitis, collagen vascular diseases,** and **tuberculosis.** The patient's history and physical examination usually can assist in narrowing the diagnosis of pleural effusion. Pleural effusions are detectable via **ultrasound, computed tomography (CT) scan,** and **magnetic resonance imaging (MRI),** but the **plain chest radiograph** remains the most commonly used procedure because of its availability, accuracy, and low cost.

Thoracentesis is one of the less-invasive procedures utilized to detect the cause of pleural effusion. Diagnostic thoracentesis may be performed when a clinically suspected pleural effusion has been confirmed on a chest radiography and remains undiagnosed. Helpful routine tests at the time of the diagnostic thoracentesis include **total protein, lactate dehydrogenase (LDH), cell count** and **differential,** and either pleural fluid **glucose** or **pH.** When an infectious cause for pleural effusion is considered, a **Gram-stained smear** of the pleural fluid should be done and the fluid cultured for **bacteria** as well as for **acid-fast bacilli (AFB). Fungal smears and cultures** can be obtained if clinically indicated. The combination of the pleural biopsy, histologic examination, and pleural tissue culture often are performed when there is suspicion of **tuberculous pleuritis.** A definitive diagnosis of tuberculous pleurisy can be established by demonstrating *Mycobacterium tuberculosis* in pleural fluid.

It is important to distinguish whether the pleural fluid is a **transudate** or **exudate.** A transudative type of effusion occurs as a result of unbalanced **hydrostatic** and **oncotic pressures** and usually signals **systemic disease** participation in contrast to direct pleural implication. The causes of transudative effusions are usually **congestive heart failure, cirrhosis, nephrotic syndrome,** and **hypoproteinemic states.** An exudative type of effusion is caused by inflammation or infiltration of the pleura or impairment of lymphatic drainage. This type of effusion contains excessive levels of **protein** and/or the enzyme **lactate dehydrogenase.** The differential diagnosis of an exudative effusion is more extensive; the most common causes are **infection, malignancy,** and **inflammatory disorders. Pleural biopsy** is only useful in the diagnosis of an exudative effusion, since exudative effusions occur due to direct pleural abnormalities. Pleural biopsy is not useful in the diagnosis of transudate effusion because this type of effusion signifies systemic disease.

Pleural fluid lymphocytosis is usually associated with **tuberculous pleurisy,** although **pleural carcinomatosis, lymphoma, sarcoidosis, rheumatoid pleuritis, fungal pleuritis (coccidiomycosis),** and **parasitic pleuritis** can cause a lymphocyte-predominant exudative effusion. The most common causes of **malignant pleurisy** are **lymphoma** and **carcinoma** of the **lung, breast, ovary,** or **stomach.** Chest x-ray during the diagnostic evaluation usually will demonstrate a moderate to large-sized effusion. The pleural fluid may appear as **serosanguinous** (straw-colored) or grossly bloody, suggestive of trauma or malignancy. Milky or very turbid pleural fluid can be due to the presence of numerous **leukocytes, chyle,** or **cholesterol.** An anchovy-colored fluid can result from rupture of an **amebic liver abscess** into the pleural cavity. A putrid or fecal odor of the pleural fluid may reflect infection of the pleural space with **anaerobic organisms.** The aspiration of frank pus is diagnostic of **empyema.**

Malignant pleurisy patients experience major symptoms of **dyspnea on exertion,** and **cough.** Other symptoms that may occur include **weight loss, chest pain, malaise,** and **anorexia.** Individuals exhibiting tuberculous infection may experience a **hypersensitivity reaction,** which results in the development of a **diffuse granulomatous pleuritis** or **tuberculous pleurisy.** The tuberculous pleurisy patient usually encounters symptoms such as **cough, pleuritic chest pain,** and **fever.** Diagnostic chest x-ray will demonstrate the presence of a small to moderate-sized unilateral effusion without parenchymal lung disease. The absence of a **parenchymal infiltrate** may be of assistance in differentiating **tuberculous pleurisy** from **bacterial pneumonia** with a **parapneumonic effusion.** The **tuberculin skin test** using **purified protein derivative (PPD)** is generally positive in the absence of **anergy.**

Percutaneous needle biopsy of the **parietal pleura** is performed under local anesthesia using a hook type of needle **(Cope** or **Abrams). Chronic nonspecific inflammation** is a frequent histologic finding of pleural biopsy. Other common entities presenting include **adenocarcinoma** and **caseating granulomatous inflammation** from tuberculous pleurisy. Percutaneous pleural biopsy is contraindicated when there is poor patient cooperation or when **uncontrolled coagulopathy** is present. Other contraindicated conditions associated with increased risk include chest wall infection, very small effusion, and unstable medical condition. Alternative techniques such as **thoracoscopy** and **thoracotomy** may be employed when pleural fluid studies fail to provide a diagnosis or are inconclusive. (1, 31, 33, 41, 48)

ABBREVIATIONS

GENERAL

ACD—anterior chest diameter
AFB—acid-fast bacillus
A&P—auscultation and percussion
AP—anterior-posterior, anteroposterior
  (projection of X-rays)
ARD—acute respiratory disease
ARDS—adult respiratory distress
  syndrome
ARF—acute respiratory failure
BS—breath sounds; bowel sounds
COPD—chronic obstructive pulmonary
  disease

IS, ICS—intercostal space
LSB—left sternal boarder
MCL—midcostal line
MSL—midsternal line
OT—old tuberculin
PA—posterior-anterior, posteroanterior
PCV—pressure-control ventilation
PEEP—positive end-expiratory pressure
PIP—peak inspiratory pressure
TB—tuberculosis
TLC—total lung capacity
URI—upper respiratory infection

ORGANIZATIONS
AART—American Association of Respiratory Therapy
ALA—American Lung Association
ATS—American Thoracic Society

REVIEW GUIDE

Instructions: Select the letter of the response that correctly completes each statement, as shown in the example.

Example: The partition between the halves of the nasal cavity is called the
     a. concha.   b. naris.   c. nasal meatus.   d. nasal septum.

1. A keeled chest may be called
   a. barrel chest.   b. pectus carinatum.
   c. flail chest.   d. rachitic chest.
2. Excessive formation of serous fluid within the pleural cavity is termed
   a. hydropneumothorax.   b. pleural effusion.
   c. empyema of pleura.   d. hemothorax.
3. Caldwell-Luc operation is associated with
   a. antrotomy.   b. bronchotomy.
   c. ethmoidectomy.   d. tracheotomy.
4. Opening of the nasal cavity into the nasopharynx is called
   a. concha.   b. carina.
   c. coryza.   d. choana.
5. Excision of nasal septum or part of it is called
   a. submucous resection.   b. turbinectomy.
   c. ethmoidectomy.   d. none of the above.
6. Disease of the lungs due to injury by dust from any source is termed
   a. histoplasmosis.   b. asbestosis.
   c. pneumoconiosis.   d. atelectasis.
7. Absence of sense of smell is called
   a. atresia of choanae.   b. asbestosis.
   c. aphonia.   d. anosmia.
8. The antrum of Highmore is also called
   a. frontal sinus.   b. ethmoidal sinus.
   c. sphenoidal sinus.   d. maxillary sinus.
9. Difficult breathing is termed
   a. dyspnea.   b. hyperpnea.
   c. hypoxia.   d. tachypnea.
10. Hay fever is termed
    a. allergic rhinitis.   b. atrophic rhinitis.
    c. hypertrophic rhinitis.   d. none of the above.

Instructions: Break apart each term listed below, identify the medical term elements, and define the term.

Example: rhinoplasty
              rhino- = combining-form element = nose
              -plasty = suffix = surgical correction; plasty repair

anoxemia

aphonia

bronchiectasis

bronchiogenic

broncholithiasis

dyspnea

ethmoidectomy

laryngospasm

laryngotracheobronchitis

lobectomy

mediastinoscopy

pleurodynia

pneumocele

pyopneumothorax

thrombosis

tracheostomy

Instructions: Figure 8.3 in the text shows the trachea and bronchial tree. For each line that extends from the figure below, provide the anatomic name of the site, as shown in the example.

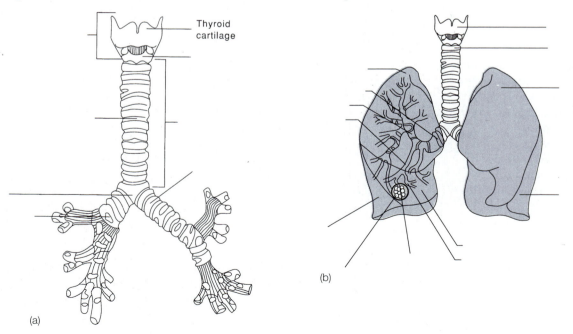

Thyroid
cartilage

(a)

(b)

9

Digestive Disorders

ORAL CAVITY AND SALIVARY GLANDS

ORIGIN OF TERMS

bucca (L)—cheek
cheilo- (G)—lip
dento- (L)—tooth
gingiva (L)—gum
glossa (G)—tongue
labium (L)—lip
lingua (L)—tongue
mandible (L)—lower jaw

odonto- (G)—tooth
os (pl. *ora*) (L)—mouth
parotid (G)—beside the ear
sialo- (G)—saliva
staphylo- (G)—bunch of grapes
stoma (G)—mouth
uvula (L)—little grape

PHONETIC PRONUNCIATION OF SELECTED TERMS

ankyloglossia	ANG-ki-low-GLOS'e-ah
cheiloplasty	KI'low-PLAS-tee
chilitis	ki-LIE'tis
giant cell epulis	JI'ant cell ep-YOU'lis
gingivitis	jin-ji-VI'tis
glossectomy	glos-SECK'toe-me
glossitis	glos-SIGH'tis
glossorrhaphy	glos-SOR'ah-fee
parotitis	PAR-o-TIE'tis
sialadenectomy	sigh-al-AD-e-NECK'toe-me
sialolithiasis	SIGH-ah-low-lith-THY'ah-sis
stomatitis	STO-mah-TIE'tis

GENERAL TERMS (30, 77)

deglutition—act of swallowing. When food enters the mouth, saliva, a fluid containing the digestive enzyme ptyalin, and mucus are secreted by the salivary glands. Saliva lubricates the food, helps to keep the mouth cavity moist and clean, and initiates chemical digestion. Once food passes over the epiglottis, the serial contraction of the superior, middle, and inferior constrictor muscles of the pharynx drives it forcibly into the esophagus below.

Figure 9.1 Sagittal section of the mouth and nasal cavity.

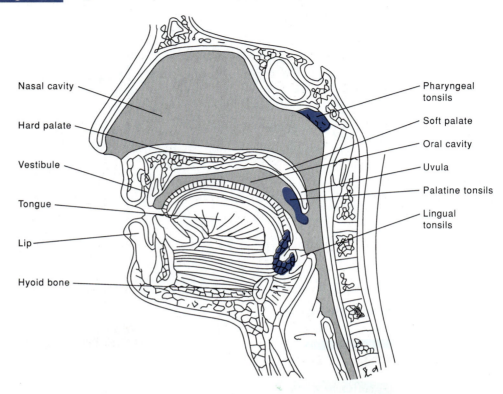

Nasal cavity

Hard palate

Vestibule

Tongue

Lip

Hyoid bone

Pharyngeal tonsils

Soft palate

Oral cavity

Uvula

Palatine tonsils

Lingual tonsils

digestion—process of converting food into chemical substances that can be absorbed and assimilated.

mastication—process of chewing food in preparation for swallowing and digestion.

regurgitation—backflow of gastric contents into mouth.

ANATOMIC TERMS (3, 30) (SEE FIGS. 9.1 AND 9.2.)

alimentary canal—the 9-meter-long tubular portion of the digestive tract. It extends from the mouth to the anus. It is also called *gastrointestinal (GI) tract.*

alveolus—bony tooth socket.

frenulum—median fold of mucous membrane that connects the inner surface of each lip in the midline to the corresponding gum.

frenulum linguae—mucous membrane between the floor of the mouth and the tongue in the midline, which is raised into a distinct vertical fold.

gums, gingivae—consists of dense fibrous tissue connected to the periosteum of the alveolar processes and surrounds the necks of the teeth.

lips, labia oris—two fleshy folds that surround the rima or orifice of the mouth. Externally the lips are covered by integument and internally by mucous membrane, between which are located the orbicularis oris muscle, the labial vessels, nerves, areolar tissue, fat, and many small labial glands.

oral cavity—the mouth. The oval-shaped cavity consists of two parts: (1) an outer, smaller part—the vestibule, and (2) an inner, larger part—the mouth cavity proper.

Figure 9.2 The mouth is adapted for ingesting food and preparing it for digestion.

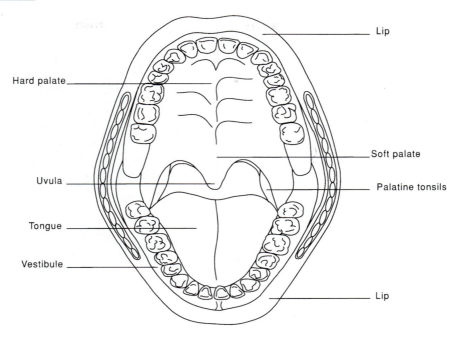

vestibule, vestibulum oris—slitlike space, bounded externally by the lips and cheeks and internally by the gums and teeth.

mouth cavity proper—bounded laterally and ventrally by the alveolar arches and their contained teeth. Dorsally, it communicates with the pharynx by a constricted aperture termed the isthmus faucium. It is roofed in by the hard and soft palates, with the majority of the floor being formed by the tongue.

palate:

hard palate, bony palate—anterior part of roof of mouth.

soft palate—posterior part of palate, partially separating the oral from the nasal part of the pharynx.

papillae of tongue—projections of the corium, thickly distributed over the anterior two-thirds of its dorsum, giving to this surface its characteristic roughness. The various types of papillae are the vallate papillae, fungiform papillae, filiform papillae, and papillae simplices.

tongue—located in the floor of the mouth, within the curve of the body of the mandible. The tongue assists in the mastication and deglutition of food. It serves as an important organ of speech and is the primary organ of the sense of taste.

tooth, teeth—three portions of the tooth are:

crown—projects from the gum.

root—embedded in the alveolus.

neck—constricted portion between the crown and the root.

The 20 teeth of the first set are termed the deciduous or milk teeth. The 32 teeth of the second set are termed the permanent teeth.

Figure 9.3   Salivary glands.

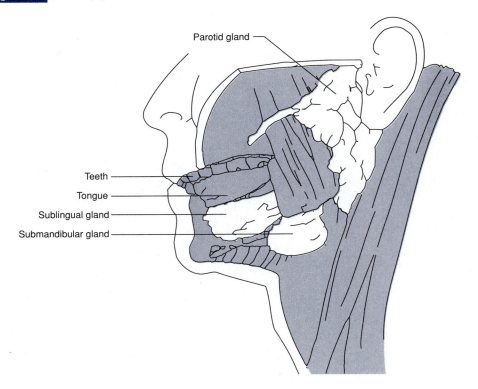

Parotid gland

Teeth

Tongue

Sublingual gland

Submandibular gland

uvula—small, cone-shaped, downward projection from the free lower edge of the soft palate in midline.

salivary glands: (See fig. 9.3.)

major salivary glands—three pairs of glands with ducts opening into the oral cavity. They secrete saliva, which moistens, dissolves, and transports food and produces a starch-splitting enzyme, amylase.

- *parotid glands*—the largest of the major salivary glands. One lies in front of and somewhat below each ear, between the skin of the cheek and masseter muscle.
  - *parotid duct (Stensen's duct)*—passes from the gland inward through the buccinator muscle, entering the mouth just opposite the upper second molar on either side of the jaw.
- *sublingual gland*—10 to 30 ducts situated on the floor of the mouth beneath the tongue; some of the ducts join to form a larger sublingual duct (duct of Bartholin), which opens into the submandibular duct.
- *submandibular glands*—located in the floor of the mouth, on the inside surface of the lower jaw.
  - *submandibular ducts (Wharton's ducts)*—situated mainly below the mandible. They open under the tongue near the frenulum.

minor salivary glands—numerous small glands in the tongue, cheeks, and lips.

DIAGNOSTIC TERMS

oral cavity:

ankyloglossia—tongue-tie. (58)

aphthous stomatitis—small ulceration of the mucous membrane of the mouth. (3, 9, 58)

benign mucous membrane pemphigoid—recurrent painful bullae that desquamate and leave a large, ulcerated area in the oral cavity. (77)

cavity of tooth, dental caries—localized progressive decay or loss of tooth structure. In addition to decay, other causes may be attrition, abrasion, erosion, or developmental defects. (28)

cheilitis, chilitis—inflammation of the lips.

cheilosis, chilosis—morbid condition of the lips caused by a vitamin deficiency.

cleft lip, harelip—congenital anomaly of upper lip consisting of a vertical fissure, often associated with cleft palate. (89)

cleft palate—congenital fissure of the roof of the mouth due to nonunion of bones. (89)

epulis, giant cell epulis—peripheral giant cell granulomatous lesion of the gingiva that develops in response to trauma or hemorrhage. (9)

gingivitis—inflammation of the gums. (28, 33)

glossitis—inflammation of the tongue. (33)

herpangina—coxsackie A viral infection, although coxsackie B and echoviruses also may be infecting agents. Ulcerating vesicles appear on the anterior of the tonsillar soft palate, uvula, and tonsils. (33)

periapical abscess—abscessed tooth, due to dental decay and leading to infection of the pulp. (28)

periodontal disease—dental disorders characterized by inflammation of the gums, destruction of alveolar bone, degeneration of periodontal ligament, and accumulation of microorganisms and plaque on tooth surfaces. Food, bacteria, or calcifications located between the gums and teeth areas (dental pockets) may cause the formation of pus (pyorrhea). (28)

pseudomembranous candidiasis (thrush)—curdlike, creamy patches in the mouth caused by overgrowth of *Candida albicans*. Pain, fever, and lymphadenopathy may be present. The fungal growth is prone to occur when antibiotics, corticosteroids, cytostatic therapy, or active illness upsets the balance of the normal flora. The buccal mucosa, palate, and tongue are favorite target sites for this fungal growth. (33, 58)

squamous cell carcinoma—most frequently occurring malignant neoplasm of the oral cavity. It usually presents as an infiltrative lesion with a fissurelike ulceration. Metastasis develops early and spreads to the contralateral side and mandible. (28, 33)

stomatitis—inflammation of the mucosa of the mouth and an oral manifestation of systemic disease, allergy, or toxic drug effect. Multiple lacerations and fissures of the corners of the mouth may be present. (3, 58)

torus palatinus—benign overgrowth of the hard palate. Bony, asymptomatic lesions may be present along the inner aspect of the mandible. (58)

Vincent's infection, acute necrotizing gingivitis, trench mouth—painful inflammatory condition of the gums, usually associated with fever, ulcerations, bleeding, and lymphadenopathy. (33)

salivary glands:

carcinoma of a salivary gland—malignant neoplasm arising from the glandular epithelium of a salivary gland. (28)

epidemic parotitis, mumps—painful, swollen viral disorder of the parotid gland. Exposure to this disease occurs 14 to 21 days prior to acute phase onset. Fever and malaise may be present, as well as swelling and tenderness of the sublingual and submandibular glands. (77)

parotitis—inflammation of the parotid gland. (28)

ptyalith, sialolith—stone in salivary gland. (58)

sialadenitis, sialoadenitis—inflammation of a salivary gland. (58)

sialolithiasis—calculi forming in the major ducts of the submandibular, sublingual, and parotid glands. (58)

OPERATIVE TERMS

oral cavity:

cheiloplasty—plastic repair of lip. (89)

cheilostomatoplasty—plastic repair of lip and mouth for cleft lip. (89)

clipping of frenulum (frenum) linguae—clipping of membranous fold below the tongue to relieve tongue tie. (58)

glossectomy, complete—removal of entire tongue, generally because of carcinoma. (9)

glossectomy, partial; hemiglossectomy—resection of the tongue. (9)

glossorrhaphy—suture of an injured tongue.

lip reconstruction—repair of lip that may be done following resection of malignant lesion of lip. (89)

oral cavity cancer resection—removal of cancerous tumor, usually followed by immediate reconstruction, either by direct primary closure of oral cavity defect, local tongue flap, or other procedure. (89)

palatoplasty—repair of cleft palate. (89)

periapical tissue biopsy—microscopic tissue study of the periapex (around the root of a tooth) to determine the benign or malignant character of the pathologic process. (9)

radical neck dissection—total removal of all metastatic lesions in the cervical region, together with the primary cancer. This includes lymph nodes, lymphatics, veins (such as the jugular), surrounding muscle, fascia, and fat, which constitute the repository for metastatic dissemination of the primary cancer. Neck dissection may be combined with glossectomy, laryngectomy, and thyroidectomy, as well as resection of the mandible, palate, and maxilla, depending on the extent of the malignant involvement. (9)

stomatoplasty—plastic repair of mouth.

salivary glands:

sialadenectomy—removal of a salivary gland. (9)

sialolithotomy—incision of salivary gland and removal of stone. (9)

subtotal parotidectomy—partial resection of parotid gland with removal of benign tumor. (9)

total parotidectomy—wide excision of malignant tumor and gland, sometimes including metastatic lesions. (9)

SYMPTOMATIC TERMS

glossodynia—a painful tongue due to a chronic inflammatory process of lingual papillae. (33)

halitosis—offensive odor of breath. (3, 28)

ptyalism, salivation—excessive secretion of saliva. (77)

PHARYNX AND ESOPHAGUS

ORIGIN OF TERMS

adeno- (G)—gland(s)

esophagus (G)—food-carrier, gullet

fauces (L)—throat

-phagia, -phagy (G)—to eat

pharynx (G)—throat

tonsilla (L)—almond, tonsil

varix (pl. *varices*) (L)—enlarged and tortuous vein, artery, or lymphatic vessel

PHONETIC PRONUNCIATION OF SELECTED TERMS

adenotonsillectomy	AD-e-no-TON-sil-LECK'toe-me
adenotonsillitis	AD-e-no-TON'sigh-LIE'tis
aphagia	a-FAY'jee-ah
esophageal varices	e-SOF-a-GEE'al VAR'i-sees
esophagoplasty	e-SOF-a-go-PLAS'tee
pharyngeal flap augmentation	fah-RIN'jee-al flap AWG-men-TAY'shun
pharyngitis	FAR-in-JI'tis

ANATOMIC TERMS (25, 30, 50, 58)

crypts—follicles or pits in tonsils.

esophagus—a 23- to 25-centimeter-long muscular canal extending from the pharynx to the stomach. (See fig. 9.4.)

> *abdominal esophagus*—portion of the esophagus that lies in the esophageal groove on the posterior surface of the left lobe of the liver.
>
> *cervical esophagus*—portion of esophagus in the neck.
>
> *thoracic esophagus*—portion of esophagus that passes through the thorax.

palatine tonsil, faucial tonsil—collection of lymphoid tissue lodged in the tonsillar fossa on either side of the oral part of the pharynx.

pharyngeal tonsil—collection of lymphoid tissue located in the posterior wall of the nasal part of the pharynx. During childhood, this tonsil may become hypertrophied into a considerable mass, at which time, it is termed *adenoid*.

pharynx—fibromuscular tube lined with mucous membrane and divided into oral, nasal, and laryngeal parts. It extends from the nose and mouth to the esophagus and serves as a common pathway for food and air. (See fig. 9.4.)

tonsillar fossa—forms part of the lateral oropharyngeal wall. It is bounded anteriorly by the palatoglossal fold (anterior tonsillar or faucial pillar). Posteriorly, the tonsillar fossa is bounded by the palatopharyngeal fold overlying the palatopharyngeal muscle.

DIAGNOSTIC TERMS

pharynx:

> *adenoids*—enlarged pharyngeal tonsils.
>
> *adenotonsillitis*—bacterial-viral disorder characterized by abnormal oropharyngeal or nasopharyngeal microflora caused by streptococci, adenoviruses, or other organisms. (58)
>
> *hypertrophy of tonsils*—enlarged palatine tonsils. (58)
>
> *peritonsillar abscess, quinsy*—localized collection of pus around the tonsil. (58)
>
> *pharyngitis*—inflammation of pharynx. (58)
>
> *tonsillitis*—inflammation of the tonsils. (58)

esophagus:

> *achalasia, dilatation of esophagus*—common disorder due to failure of the cardiac sphincter to relax. It is characterized by a dilated and hypertrophied esophagus, except for the distal segment, which may be atrophied. (25, 36, 41, 50)
>
> *Barrett's esophagus*—acquired disorder in which there is progressive columnar metaplasia of the distal esophagus due to long-standing gastroesophageal reflux and reflux esophagitis. Barrett's esophagus usually occurs in the older individual, but it may also occur in young patients with reflux esophagitis. (41, 50)
>
> *carcinoma of esophagus*—malignant neoplasm, commonly an epidermoid carcinoma, arising from the epidermis or squamous epithelium; metastatic spread to other organs is a frequent occurrence. Other than a very few rare esophageal malignancies, about 80% to 90% of

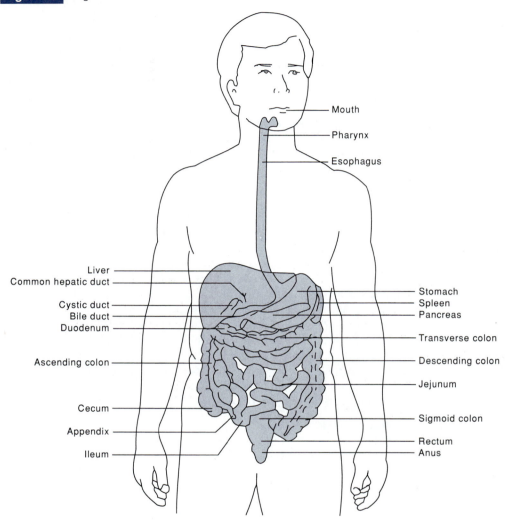

Figure 9.4 Digestive tract.

malignant tumors in the esophagus are squamous cell carcinomas, and the remaining 10% to 20% are adenocarcinomas arising in Barrett's mucosa. (5, 50)

diverticula (sing. *diverticulum*) *of esophagus*—outpouchings of esophageal wall. (1, 5, 50)

- *pulsion or true diverticula*—consist of a bulging of the mucosa through weakened parts of the esophageal wall.
- *traction or false diverticula*—result from pull exerted by diseased neighboring structures.

esophageal reflux ulceration—ulceration of the esophagus resulting from reflux of acid-peptic secretions into the esophagus due to incompetence of the gastroesophageal sphincter. Reflux esophagitis is the most common cause of superficial ulceration in the esophagus. Shallow ulcers and erosions may be caused by other types of esophagitis, including herpes esophagitis, drug-induced esophagitis, and esophageal involvement by Crohn's disease. (25, 36, 41, 50)

esophageal trauma—injury to the esophagus. (44, 50)
- *esophageal perforation*—hole in the esophageal wall, usually due to mechanical injury through ingestion of a foreign body, a gunshot wound, or other causes. (50)
- *esophageal stricture*—narrowing of the esophageal lumen, usually due to chemical injury, such as ingestion of lye or other caustic agents. (41)

esophageal varices—swollen, tortuous esophageal veins that may burst and result in massive hemorrhage. Condition is usually secondary to portal hypertension. (54, 56, 83)

esophagitis—inflammation of the esophagus. (25, 41, 50)

OPERATIVE TERMS

pharynx:

adenotonsillectomy—removal of adenoids and tonsils. (58)

esophagus:

bougienage for esophageal stricture—dilatation of the esophagus with bougies, flexible instruments resembling sounds, used to diagnose and treat strictures of tubular passages. A safe procedure is to insert the bougies by the retrograde method through a gastrostomy and pull them through the esophagus and the stricture and out through the gastrostomy. (50, 51)

esophageal diverticulectomy—excision of diverticulum and closure of the resulting defect. (50)

esophagojejunostomy—formation of a communication between the esophagus and jejunum. (48)

esophagoplasty—reconstruction or plastic repair of esophageal defect. (50)

esophagorrhaphy—suture of injured or ruptured esophagus.

fundic patch operation—surgical procedure for repair of ruptured esophagus or acid-peptic stricture and in the treatment of advanced achalasia. (50)

fundoplication—mobilization of the lower end of the esophagus and plication of the fundus of the stomach around it (fundic wrapping). The operative procedure relieves gastroesophageal reflux of large amounts of acid-peptic juice and restores gastroesophageal competence. (50) Some types include:
- *Belsy procedure*—fundoplication performed via a thoracotomy, during which the cardia of the stomach is wrapped partially around the lower esophagus.
- *Hill repair*—the plicated proximal curvature of the stomach is fixed to the preaortic fascia.
- *Nissen fundoplication*—the fundus of the stomach is wrapped totally around the intra-abdominal esophagus, thereby increasing the intra-abdominal length of the sphincter and accentuating the angle of His.
  - *laparoscopic Nissen fundoplication*—procedures identical to standard Nissen fundoplication (described above) except that the procedures are carried out by the laparoscopic route.
- *Toupet procedure*—a 270-degree posterior partial fundoplication is performed. (29)

Heller esophagomyotomy—incision into the circular muscle fibers of the distal esophagus to relieve achalasia. (50)

radical resection for esophageal cancer—excision of tumor-bearing portion of esophagus and regional lymph nodes, followed by restoration of continuity by anastomosis or interposition of loop of colon or jejunum. (58, 78)

resection for esophageal stricture—removal of extensive narrow segment, followed by colonic bypass. The right colon, with terminal ileum and ileocecal valve, is tunneled into the neck and anastomosed with the proximal esophagus. The operation is indicated when chronic stricture is unresponsive to bougienage. Sometimes a gastric tube is used as a means of reconstruction. (51)

SYMPTOMATIC TERMS

aphagia—inability to swallow, or abstention from eating. (24)
dysphagia—difficulty in swallowing, or painful to eat. (5, 46)

STOMACH

ORIGIN OF TERMS

duodeno- (L)—duodenum
fundus (L)—base
gastr-, gastro- (G)—stomach
jejuno- (L)—jejunum
myo- (G)—muscle

pyloro- (G)—gatekeeper, pylorus
ruga-, (pl. *rugae-*) (L)—fold, crease
sphincter (G)—binder, encircling band of
muscle fibers

PHONETIC PRONUNCIATION OF SELECTED TERMS

anorexia	AN-owe-RECK′see-ah
atrophic gastritis	a-TROF′ick gas-TRI′tis
bulimia	boo-LIM′e-ah
gastric sarcoma	GAS′trick sar-COE′mah
gastrojejunal anastomosis	GAS-tro-jay-JOO′nal a-NAS-toe-MO′sis

ANATOMIC TERMS (25, 30, 81)

antrum, gastric—distal nonacid secreting segment of the stomach or pyloric gland region that produces the hormone gastrin.
body of stomach—largest portion of the stomach, between the antrum and fundus. (See table 9.1 and fig. 9.4.)
cardia—small area of the stomach near the esophagogastric junction.
cardiac orifice—opening at the junction of the esophagus with the stomach.
cardiac sphincter, cardioesophageal sphincter—muscle fibers about the opening of the esophagus into the stomach.
curvatures of stomach:
    lesser—right and superior margin of the stomach.
    greater—left and inferior margin of the stomach.
fundus of stomach—enlarged portion to the left located above the level of the cardiac orifice.
gastroesophageal sphincter—the terminal few centimeters of the esophagus, which prevents reflux of gastric contents into the esophagus.
omenta (sing. **omentum**)—peritoneal sheets connecting the stomach with other viscera, such as the liver, spleen, and transverse colon.
pyloric part of stomach—distal segment of the stomach, including the antrum or pyloric gland area, and the pyloric canal.
pyloric sphincter—circular muscle around the pylorus.
pylorus—opening between stomach and duodenum.
rugae (sing. **ruga**)—irregular folds of the mucous membrane of the stomach in which gastric glands are embedded.

DIAGNOSTIC TERMS

gastric malignant neoplasms: (10, 81)
    carcinoma—usually adenocarcinoma, a malignant new growth of the glandular epithelium. These neoplasms develop mainly along the lesser curvature of the stomach.
    lymphoma—tumors arising from lymphoid tissue. These tumors may be found at any site in the stomach but favor the posterior wall, lesser curvature of the stomach, and antrum. Types of lymphoma include round cell lymphosarcoma, reticulum cell lymphosarcoma, non-Hodgkin's lymphoma, Hodgkin's lymphoma, and plasmacytoma.

TABLE 9.1	Gastric Types in Relation to Architectural Structures of Individuals		
Stomach Type	*Description of Stomach Type*	*Tonicity of Stomach*	*Graphic Representation*
Hypersthenic—individual stocky and short	Stomach high, wide above, narrow below; transverse position; pylorus to the right	Hypertonic—increased tone	
Sthenic—individual well built	Stomach tubular; as wide above as it is below; pylorus to the right, well above the umbilicus	Orthotonic—normal tone	
Hyposthenic—individual slender	Stomach long, narrow at the top; tendency to sag below greater curvature near umbilicus; pylorus swinging to the left	Hypotonic—decreased tone	
Asthenic—individual still more slender	Stomach sags far below umbilicus; is almost collapsed above, expanding into large sac below	Atonic—weak tone	

malignant smooth-muscle tumors of the stomach—nonepithelial malignant lesions involving the stomach. Some types of this tumor are leiomyosarcoma and epithelioid leiomyoma (leiomyoblastoma).

other mesenchymal tumors of the stomach—lesions that occur rarely and include such tumors as angiosarcoma, hemangiopericytoma, Kaposi's sarcoma, and liposarcoma.

linitis plastica (leather-bottle type of stomach)—occurs at the pylorus and spreads toward the cardia. The pyloric canal becomes constricted by overgrowth of fibrous tissue, resulting in dilatation of the stomach in its proximal part. When this occurs, the disorder is termed *chronic scirrhous carcinoma of the pylorus*. This type of cancer grows slowly and is confined to the wall of the stomach for a long period. Metastasis usually occurs late in the disease process. Finally, the stomach is transformed into a leathery rigid tube that cannot be distended, hence, its capacity is limited to a few ounces.

gastric polyps—lesions that project above the surface of the surrounding mucosa or submucosa. Most polyps are sessile (attached by a base); however, the larger polyps may be pedunculated (stalk or stemlike connecting part). When the major portion of the gastric mucosal surface reflects numerous polypoid lesions, the disorder is termed *diffuse polyposis*. Most of the polyps or benign tumors that occur in the stomach may be classified as follows:

epithelial polyps—include hyperplastic (regenerative) polyps and adenomatous polyps.

mesenchymal or mesothelial polyps—include leiomyomas, fibromas, neurogenic tumors, lipomas, and vascular tumors.

others—include aberrant pancreatic tissue polyps, inflammatory pseudotumors, hamartomas, and Peutz-Jeghers polyps. (81)

gastric ulcers—localized erosions of gastric mucosa that may result from digestive action of acid gastric secretion. Secondary involvement of muscle tissue may occur.

chronic gastric ulcer—chronic peptic ulceration, characteristically involving the non-acid-secreting antral area and seldom the acid-forming parietal cell region of the stomach. (81)

stress ulcer, stress erosive gastritis—presence of single or multiple ulcerative lesions of the fragile mucosa of the stomach in response to a stressful situation, such as trauma, major surgery, head injury, alcoholic excess, or increased steroid secretion. A gastric erosion represents a partial disruption of the epithelium, while an ulcer represents penetration through the muscularis mucosae. Superficial erosions rarely cause massive bleeding; however, deeper lesions may penetrate the large arteries that transverse the submucosa and massive bleeding may occur. (81)

gastritis—acute or chronic inflammation of the gastric mucosa. (46, 48, 81)

acute hemorrhagic gastritis—the most severe form of aspirin-induced gastritis and a frequent cause of upper gastrointestinal hemorrhage.

atrophic gastritis—chronic inflammatory process in which atrophic changes of the gastric mucosa are usually irreversible and progressive.

hyperplastic gastropathy—predominant feature is hyperplasia (number of normal cells increased) rather than hypertrophy (enlarged gastric folds in the body and fundus of the stomach and enlargement of the gastric mucosa) or inflammation. Some syndromes associated with hyperplastic gastropathy are:

- *Ménétrier's disease*—usually interpreted as a synonym for protein-losing gastropathy. Originally, Ménétrier's disease was concerned with the premalignant nature of the gastric lesion and not with its relation to protein loss.
- *mixed or combined type of hyperplastic gastropathy*—presents as a hyperplasia of mucous and specialized glandular cells and may be associated with hypersecretion of pepsin and acid without protein loss. Usually there are no clinical symptoms.
- *mucous cell or foveolate (pitted) type*—seen in Ménétrier's disease; characterized by hyperplasia of the mucous-secreting cells of the surface epithelium and foveolar pits. Hypochlorhydria and loss of albumin into gastric secretions, leading to hypoproteinemia and edema, may be associated with Ménétrier's disease.
- *Zollinger-Ellison syndrome*—excessive gastric secretion rapidly worsening, with refractory or recurrent peptic ulceration and hyperplasia of pancreatic islet cells; may be due to an ulcerogenic tumor in the pancreas.

gastrocele—hernia of the stomach, such as diaphragmatic gastric hernia.

gastrocolitis—inflammation of the stomach and colon.

gastroduodenitis—inflammation of the stomach and duodenum.

gastroenteritis—inflammation of the stomach and intestine.

gastroptosis—downward displacement of the stomach. (77)

hiatal hernia, hiatus hernia—protrusion of part of the stomach through the esophageal opening of the diaphragm. (44)

hypertrophic pyloric stenosis, congenital—condition seen in the newborn, characterized by an overgrowth of muscle fibers that markedly diminishes the lumen of the pyloric canal and gives rise to obstruction. (72)

Mallory-Weiss syndrome—longitudinal lacerations of the gastroesophageal mucosa causing upper-gastrointestinal bleeding. (46)

Peutz-Jeghers syndrome—mucocutaneous pigmentation and gastrointestinal polyposis. The polyps are usually large, pedunculated, and lobulated. The syndrome may involve the stomach, small intestine, and colon. (74)

OPERATIVE TERMS (SEE TABLE 9.2.)

anastomosis—surgical formation of a passage or opening between two hollow viscera or vessels; for example, gastrojejunostomy. (48, 65)

antrectomy, gastric—removal of the gastrin-producing pyloric gland area of the stomach. (81)

gastrectomy—removal of stomach. Total removal of the stomach with jejunal interposition has been advocated for the Zollinger-Ellison syndrome. (48, 80, 81)

> *hemigastrectomy, gastric resection*—subtotal or partial removal of the stomach. Gastric resection with removal of 50% to 75% of the stomach may be combined with one of the following procedures:
> - *gastroduodenal anastomosis, Billroth I*—joining the resected stomach to the duodenum.
> - *gastrojejunal anastomosis, Billroth II*—joining the remaining stomach to the jejunum by either the
>   - *Polya technique*—anterior anastomosis, large stoma, or
>   - *Hofmeister technique*—posterior anastomosis, small stoma.

gastroduodenostomy—creation of a communication between the stomach and duodenum. (48)

gastrojejunostomy—creation of a communication between the stomach and jejunum. (48)

gastrostomy—external fistulization of the stomach. This may be done for the purpose of maintaining nutrition. (48)

pyloromyotomy, Fredet-Ramstedt operation—incision of the hypertrophic pyloric muscle down to the mucosa. (72)

pyloroplasty—surgical reconstruction of the pyloric channel to relieve obstruction. Procedures of choice are usually those of Finney and Heinecke-Mikulicz. (81)

repair of hiatus hernia—several different methods are used, either by the transthoracic or transabdominal approach; for example, freeing the esophagus at the cardia and attaching the region of the esophagogastric junction to the defect in the diaphragm. (50)

vagotomy, gastric—the surgical interruption of vagal impulses to the pyloric gland area (antrum) and the gastric parietal cell region. (81)

vagotomy, selective gastric—vagal denervation restricted to the parietal cell mass of the stomach. (81)

vagotomy and antrectomy—surgical destruction of vagal impulses and excision of the gastric antrum for removing the major stimuli to acid production in gastric and duodenal ulcers. (81)

SYMPTOMATIC TERMS

achlorhydria—absence of hydrochloric acid in the gastric juice. (77)

anorexia—loss of appetite. (20)

bulimia—alternate cramming of food and induced vomiting. (20)

cyclic vomiting—periodic vomiting. (77)

dumping syndrome—symptoms occurring after meals following gastrectomy. The patient may experience such symptoms as palpitation, tachycardia, sweating, flushing, warmth, faintness, and sometimes diarrhea, and less frequently, postural hypotension. Abdominal discomfort and vomiting may also occur. The term *early dumping syndrome* refers to the vasomotor symptoms that are usually experienced within 30 minutes after eating and are thought to result from rapid emptying of hyperosmolar gastric contents into the proximal intestine. The *late dumping syndrome* refers to a symptom complex consisting of dizziness, light-headedness, palpitation, diaphoresis, confusion, and in some cases, syncope that occurs 90 minutes to 3 hours after eating. This syndrome appears to be caused by hypoglycemia due to insulin release stimulated by abrupt increases in blood glucose secondary to rapid emptying of sugar-containing meals into the proximal small intestine. (27, 77)

TABLE 9.2	Some Digestive Conditions Amenable to Surgery		
Anatomic Site	*Diagnosis*	*Type of Surgery*	*Operative Procedures*
Lip	Cleft lip	Cheiloplasty	Plastic repair of lip
Lip (lower)	Squamous call carcinoma of lower lip	Estlander's operation for carcinoma of the lower lip	V-excision of lesion-defect filled by flap from upper lip
Lip (upper)	Squamous cell or basal cell carcinoma of upper lip	Estlander's operation for carcinoma of the upper lip	V-excision and replacement of operative defect by triangular flap from lower lip
Tongue	Epidermoid carcinoma and/or metastatic cervical adenopathy	Partial glossectomy Radial neck dissection *or* Cautery excision with radon seed implantation in selected cases	Wide excision of malignant lesion, including removal of the jugular vein, muscles of the neck, and submaxillary and cervical lymph nodes
Parotid gland	Parotid tumor	Resection of parotid gland and tumor under direct vision	Y-shaped incision and dissection for flaps Partial removal of parotid gland with tumor, keeping facial nerve intact
Parotid gland Facial nerve	Parotid tumor widely infiltrating; facial nerve embedded in tumor	Total parotidectomy Elective excision of facial nerve	Removal of entire gland and tumor, including main trunk of facial nerve with plexus
Palate	Cleft palate	Staphylorrhaphy Palatoplasty	Suture of cleft palate Reconstruction of cleft palate
Floor of the mouth	Squamous cell carcinoma	Excision of lesion and/or Radiation therapy	Removal of neoplasm and/or irradiation
Tonsils, palatine	Hypertrophy of tonsils Chronic tonsillitis	Tonsillectomy	Removal of tonsils
Tonsils, pharyngeal	Adenoids	Adenoidectomy	Removal of adenoids
Esophagus	Esophageal lesion	Esophagoscopy with biopsy	Direct visualization of the esophagus with removal of bits of tissue
Esophagus	Esophageal diverticulum	Diverticulectomy	Extirpation of the diverticulum

TABLE **9.2**   (continued)

Anatomic Site	Diagnosis	Type of Surgery	Operative Procedures
Esophagus Stomach	Recurrent hiatus hernia	Repair of hiatus hernia, abdominal or thoracic approach	Direct vision reduction; sac sutured to undersurface of diaphragm; inclusion of gastric wall in fixation
Esophagus Stomach	Carcinoma of esophagus of the midthoracic portion	Radical resection of the carcinomatous segment of the esophagus Esophagogastric anastomosis or interposition of segment of bowel	Excision of malignant lesion and regional lymph nodes Anastomosis of remaining esophagus and stomach or use of bowel segment as substitute
Stomach Pyloric muscle	Congenital hypertrophic stenosis of pyloric sphincter	Pyloromyotomy Fredet-Ramstedt operation	Section of hypertrophic pyloric muscle down to mucosa
Stomach	Gastric carcinoma resectability unknown	Exploratory laparotomy	Opening abdomen to determine operability of lesion
Stomach Duodenum Jejunum	Carcinoma of the stomach	Subtotal gastrectomy Gastroduodenostomy Gastrojejunostomy	Partial removal of stomach including lymph glands Joining remaining portion of stomach and duodenum Joining remaining portion of stomach and jejunum

Stomach
Duodenum
Jejunum
	Chronic or recurrent gastric ulcer with obstruction or hemorrhage	Gastric resection
		Billroth I or
		Billroth II
		    Polya modification or
		    Hofmeister modification
			Partial removal of stomach and gastroduodenal anastomosis or gastrojejunal anastomosis using anterior approach or posterior approach

Stomach Duodenum	Duodenal ulcer	Selective vagotomy Mucosal antrectomy	Complete vagal denervation of the stomach Excision of entire gastrin-secreting antral mucosa
Duodenum	Progressive duodenal ulcer with obstruction *or* hemorrhage	Complete bilateral vagotomy Pyloroplasty	Section of vagus nerve fibers before they enter stomach Surgical repair of pyloric muscle
Duodenum Jejunum	Large duodenal perforation	Surgical reconstruction of perforated duodenum	Excision of duodenal ulcer Full-thickness jejunal pedicle graft for closure of large duodenal defect

TABLE 9.2 (continued)

Anatomic Site	Diagnosis	Type of Surgery	Operative Procedures
Jejunum Ileum	Morbid obesity Hyperlipidemia	Jejunoileal bypass	Division of jejunum a few inches distal to ligament of Treitz, and ileum a few inches proximal to ileocecal valve End-to-end anastomosis to restore continuity Closure of distal jejunum Implantation of proximal ileum into transverse colon or into left colon
Ileum Colon	Regional enteritis	Resection of involved ileum and colon Enteroanastomosis	Radical extirpation of bowel involved in regional enteritis Surgical joining of remaining parts
Colon Ileum	Chronic ulcerative colitis hemorrhage	Permanent ileostomy with total colectomy	Surgical creation of ileal stoma for fecal drainage and removal of colon
Cecum Colon	Intestinal obstruction Cancer of left colon	Cecostomy Gibson's technique Transverse colostomy	Creation of communication between cecum and body surface for fecal drainage Diversion of fecal content to the body surface
Appendix	Appendicitis	Appendectomy	Removal of appendix
Colon Rectum	Aganglionic megacolon (Hirschsprung's disease)	Modified Duhamel procedure or Modified Soave procedure	Side-to-side colorectal anastomosis Endorectal pull-through of ganglionated bowel to anus
Rectosigmoid	Rectal hemorrhage, cause unknown	Rectosigmoidoscopy	Endoscopic examination of the rectosigmoid
Rectosigmoid	Carcinoma of rectum and lower sigmoid	Abdominoperineal resection Miles' operation	Sectioning of bowel above the tumor; creation of permanent colostomy; removal of bowel above and below tumor; excision of anus
Rectum	Hemorrhoids, internal anal or external	Hemorrhoidectomy	Removal of hemorrhoids
Peritoneum	Hernia, inguinal, femoral, umbilical, ventral	Hernioplasty	Surgical repair of hernia

TABLE 9.2	(continued)		
Anatomic Site	*Diagnosis*	*Type of Surgery*	*Operative Procedures*
Liver	Hepatic necrosis	Exchange transfusion (fresh blood)	Construction of arteriovenous shunt
	Hepatic failure		Priming exchange transfusion circuit
	Hepatic coma		Exchange of equal volume of blood
Gallbladder	Cholecystitis Cholelithiasis	Cholecystectomy	Removal of gallbladder
Bile duct	Benign stricture bile duct	Repair of biliary stricture by ene-to-end anastomosis of bile duct	Excision of constricted part and surgical communication of the two ends of bile duct

dyspepsia—difficult digestion. (46)

eructation—belching.

hematemesis—vomiting blood. (56, 77)

hyperchlorhydria—excessive amount of hydrochloric acid in the gastric juice. (77)

hypergastrinemia—highly increased serum gastrin levels, found in Zollinger-Ellison syndrome and pernicious anemia. (77)

hypochlorhydria—deficient amount of hydrochloric acid in the stomach. (77)

intrinsic factor, Castle's intrinsic factor—factor normally present in gastric mucosa and gastric juice and required for absorption of vitamin B_{12}. It is absent in pernicious anemia. (45, 77)

polyphagia—excessive food intake.

pyrosis—heartburn. (20 46)

SMALL AND LARGE INTESTINES

ORIGIN OF TERMS

anus (L)—ring, circle
appendix (L)—appendage
cecum (L)—blind gut
celio- (G)—abdomen, belly
colon (G)—large intestine
duodeno- (L)—twelve, duodenum
enter-, entero- (G)—intestine

ileo- (L)—ileum
jejuno- (L)—jejunum
melano- (G)—black, melanin
procto- (G)—anus
recto- (L)—rectum
steato- (G)—fat
vermiform (L)—shape of worm

PHONETIC PRONUNCIATION OF SELECTED TERMS

appendectomy	ap-pen-DECK'toe-me
appendicitis	a-PEN-di-SIGH'tis
cecostomy	see-KOS'toe-me
colon resection	KO'lon re-SECK'shun
diverticulosis	DIE-ver-TICK-you-LOW'sis
duodenal ulcer	due-OD'en-al; DUE-owe-DEE'nal UHL'ser
enteritis	en-ter-I'tis
hemorrhoids	HEM'owe-royds
pruritus ani	pru-RYE'tus A'ni

ANATOMIC TERMS (30, 60, 61) (SEE FIG. 9.4.)

small intestine—proximal portion of intestine from pylorus to ileocecal junction.

duodenum—first part of small intestine; extends from pylorus to jejunum.

jejunum—second part of small intestine; extends from duodenum to ileum.

ileum—third part of small intestine; extends from jejunum to cecum.

mesentery—peritoneal fold that carries the blood supply and attaches the jejunum and ileum to the posterior abdominal wall.

large intestine—distal portion of intestine, including cecum, appendix, colon, rectum, and anal canal.

anus—outlet or orifice of anal canal.

appendix vermiformis—an intestinal diverticulum projecting 3 to 13 centimeters from the cecum and ending blindly.

cecum—blind pouch of large intestine at and below level of ileocecal junction.

colon—large intestine from cecum to rectum, including the ascending colon, transverse colon, descending colon, and sigmoid or pelvic colon.

- *flexures of colon:*
  - *right colic flexure, formerly hepatic flexure*—bend of colon near liver.
  - *left colic flexure, formerly splenic flexure*—bend of colon near spleen.
- *mesocolon*—mesentery attaching the colon to the posterior abdominal wall.

DIAGNOSTIC TERMS

appendicitis—inflammation of the appendix. (62, 85)

colitis:

granulomatous colitis—transmural involvement of colon presenting granulomas and fissures. (21, 61)

ischemic colitis—spontaneous reduction of the arterial blood flow of the large intestine associated with abrupt onset of abdominal pain, frequent bloody stools, and radiographic changes of colon. (40, 61)

mucous colitis—inflammatory condition marked by large amount of mucus in stool. (40, 61)

ulcerative colitis—inflammation and multiple erosions of the intestinal mucosa leading to hemorrhage and perforations, clinically noted for frequent evacuations of watery, purulent, and bloody stools. (21, 61)

congenital megacolon, Hirschsprung's disease—excessive enlargement of the colon associated with an absence of ganglion cells in the narrowed bowel wall distally. The aganglionic segment of the colon is the pathologic lesion. (40, 73)

diverticulitis—inflammation of a diverticulum or diverticula. Inflammation can occur in or around the diverticular sac. The inflammatory process may range from a small intramural or pericolic abscess to generalized peritonitis. Some attacks may reflect minor symptoms and resolve spontaneously. Most perforations of the diverticular sac are small and involve inflammation of the sac and the adjacent serosal surface. (1, 61)

diverticulosis—presence of diverticula in the intestinal tract. (1, 61)

duodenal ulcer—circumscribed erosion of duodenal wall that may involve its full thickness and that is usually located near the pylorus. (81)

dysentery—inflammation of the intestinal mucosa characterized by frequent small stools, chiefly of blood and mucus. It is due to specific bacillus or ameba (amoeba). (77)

enteritis—inflammation of the intestine. (21)

fissure, anal; fissure in ano—tear in anal mucosa that may become ulcerated, infected, spastic, scarred, and painful. (40, 59)

fistula:(40, 50, 59)

anal fistula, fistula in ano—abnormal communication between anal canal or lower rectum and skin near anus.

fecal fistula—abnormal passage from intestine to the body surface or another hollow viscus.

high-output gastrointestinal fistula—fistula that produces a minimum of 200 millimeters of gastrointestinal drainage in 24 hours, including salivary, gastric, pancreatic, and biliary secretions rich in enzymes and electrolytes. Consequently, there is a significant energy loss.

hemorrhoids, piles—dilated varicose veins of the anal canal and at the anal orifice. (40, 59)

ileitis—inflammation of the ileum.

intestinal malabsorption syndromes—disorders resulting from a faulty absorption of fat-soluble vitamins, proteins, carbohydrates, and minerals associated with copious excretion of fatty stools (steatorrhea). (26) Some associated disorders are:

adult celiac disease, gluten enteropathy, celiac sprue—genetic predisposition to gluten (protein of wheat, cereals) intolerance characterized by malnutrition, chronic diarrhea, edema, and muscle wasting, occurring within the third to sixth decades of life. (26)

childhood celiac disease, gluten enteropathy, celiac sprue—same as adult disease, except that it develops in infancy and causes retarded growth. (26)

Crohn's disease of small intestine—nutritional malabsorption due to damaged mucosa, fistulas, strictures, and decreased surface for absorption. (21, 60, 61)

short-bowel syndrome, short-gut syndrome—syndrome characterized by malabsorption of fat-soluble vitamins and depletion of fluid and electrolytes. (26)

Whipple's disease—rare disorder characterized by malabsorption of lipids (fat) with resultant steatorrhea, diarrhea, abdominal distress, fever, anemia, lymph node involvement, and bouts of arthralgia. (26, 46)

intestinal obstruction, ileus—obstruction of small intestine associated with variable symptoms: abdominal distention, colicky pain, nausea, vomiting, obstipation, or diarrhea. Interference with the blood flow to the obstructed intestine demands emergency surgery.

adynamic (paralytic) ileus—paralysis of intestinal muscles, absence of bowel sounds. It may be caused by electrolyte imbalance or operative handling of intestine.

dynamic (mechanical) ileus—intestinal occlusion from adhesions, strangulated hernia, volvulus, intussusception, emboli, or thrombi. (46, 60)

intussusception—telescoping of intestine; usually ileum slips into cecum, which leads to intestinal obstruction. (60)

Meckel's diverticulum—congenital pouch or sac that usually arises from the ileum and may cause strangulation, intussusception, or volvulus. (40, 46)

mesenteric ischemia and infarction—small intestine ischemia can be divided into:

nonocclusive type—mesenteric ischemia that does not involve an occlusion of a major vessel. The exact cause of nonocclusive disease has not been pinpointed, although contributing factors have been suggested, such as system arterial hypotension, cardiac arrhythmias, digitalis therapy, and dehydration.

occlusive type—results from arterial thrombus or embolus of the celiac or superior mesenteric arteries or from a mesenteric vein occlusion. (Venous occlusion is rare, but has been noted in women taking oral contraceptives.) Arterial embolus occurs most often in patients with chronic atrial fibrillation and valvular heart disease. Arterial thrombosis is associated with advanced atherosclerosis or low cardiac output. (60, 63)

multiple polyposis—polyps or tumors derived from mucous membrane; scattered throughout intestine and rectum; may undergo malignant degeneration. (61)

perforated viscus—ruptured internal organ due to advanced disease, malignancy, trauma, drugs, or a gunshot or stab wound. It may be complicated by hemorrhage, shock, and peritonitis.

proctitis—inflammation of rectum. (21)

prolapse of rectum—downward displacement of rectum, seen in infants and elderly people. (77)

rectal cancer—malignant tumor of the rectum or rectosigmoid. (6, 46)

rectocele—herniation of rectum into vagina.

volvulus—twisting of the bowel upon itself, leading to obstruction. Colicky abdominal pain is present. (61)

OPERATIVE TERMS (SEE TABLE 9.2.)

abdominal perineal resection—combined laparotomy and perineal operation for partial or complete removal of colon and rectum. (61)

appendectomy—removal of appendix. (61, 85)

cecectomy—excision of cecum.

cecostomy—external fistulization of the cecum to correct intestinal obstruction.

colectomy—either segmental colon resection or removal of entire colon. (61)

colon resection and end-to-end anastomosis—excision of involved colon with or without adjacent lymph glands; joining segments of colon. (61)

colostomy—formation of an abdominal anus by bringing a loop of the colon to the surface of the abdomen in an attempt to control fecal discharge. Another procedure is to bring the proximal segment of the colon to the skin, as in abdominoperineal resection. (61)

diverticulectomy—removal of diverticulum, including resection of involved bowel. (61)

endorectal ileoanal anastomosis—procedure aimed at preserving anorectal function with removal of all disease. Functioning is enhanced by incorporating an ileal reservoir proximal to the ileoanal anastomosis. Some types of pouches or reservoirs are: S type, J type, and H type. (88)

hemorrhoidectomy—removal of hemorrhoids. (59)

ileostomy—external fistulization of ileum for fecal evacuation, often done with total colectomy for ulcerative colitis. (61)

jejunoileal bypass—creation of a bypass of a considerable portion of the small intestine by joining the proximal jejunum to the terminal ileum and the distal end of the bypassed segment of the cecum. The procedure reduces the absorptive capacity of the small intestine and induces weight loss. Various techniques are used to control obesity and hyperlipidemia. (48)

operations for aganglionic megacolon (Hirschsprung's disease)—

    modified Duhamel procedure—side-to-side anastomosis of colon and rectum.

    modified Soave procedure—endorectal pull-through of ganglionated bowel to anus. (73)

proctocolectomy, total—removal of the entire rectum and resection of the colon, which may be done as emergency procedure for colonic perforation from ulcerative colitis. (38)

proctoplasty—plastic repair or reconstruction of rectum or anus.

reduction of intussusception—normal intestinal continuity restored either by barium enema or, if unsuccessful, by laparotomy. (38)

reduction of volvulus—manipulation of twisted bowel segment to ease or correct obstruction. Decompression of the twisted bowel segment by proctoscope, rectal tube, or flexible colonoscope usually results in a spontaneous untwisting of the involved segment. (38)

sphincterotomy, lateral internal—effective procedure for the control of an anal fissure using a small circular incision that is closed by suture and avoids fecal soilage. (38)

tube cecostomy—surgical decompression of the colon by tube drainage of the cecum. (33)

SYMPTOMATIC TERMS

borborygmus—rumbling or splashing sound of bowels. (77)

colic—spasm of any tubular hollow organ associated with pain.

diarrhea—frequency of bowel action, soft or liquid stools. (60)
fecalith—a fecal concretion. (40)
melena—black stool; also black vomit from blood. (40)
obstipation—extreme constipation, often due to obstruction.
pruritus ani—itching sensation around the anus. (59, 60, 61)
steatorrhea—increased fat content in feces as in malabsorption syndrome or in pancreatitis. (55)

LIVER, BILIARY SYSTEM, PANCREAS, AND PERITONEUM

ORIGIN OF TERMS

angi-, angio- (G)—vessel
celio- (G)—abdomen, belly
chol-, chole-, cholo- (G)—bile, gall
cholecyst (G)—gallbladder
choledocho- (G)—(common) bile duct
hepat-, hepato- (G)—liver
ictero- (G)—jaundice

jejuno- (L)—jejunum
lapro- (G)—abdominal wall, loin, flank
necro- (G)—death, dead
pancreato- (L)—pancreas
peritoneo- (L)—peritoneum
spleno- (G) spleen

PHONETIC PRONUNCIATION OF SELECTED TERMS

cholangitis	KO-lan-JI'tis
cholecystitis	KO-lee-SIS'tie-tis
empyema of gallbladder	EM-pie-E'mah of GAWL'blad-der
hemorrhagic	HEM-owe-RAJ'ick
herniorrhaphy	HER-nee-OR'a-fee
icterus	ICK'ter-us
jaundice	JAWN'dis
necrosis	nee-CROW'sis
pancreatic	PAN-kre-AT'ick
polycystic liver disease	POL-e-SIS'tick LIV'er dis-EASE'
sphincteroplasty	SFINGK'ter-owe-PLAS-tee
splenorenal shunt	SPLE-no-RE'nal shunt

ANATOMIC TERMS (4, 30, 32, 64, 66, 82)

bile duct—duct formed by union of common hepatic duct and cystic duct; carries bile into duodenum.
common hepatic duct—duct formed by union of right and left hepatic ducts, which receive bile from liver.
cystic duct—passageway for bile from gallbladder to bile duct.
gallbladder—pear-shaped, saclike organ that serves as a reservoir for bile.
inguinal canal—passage in the lower abdominal wall through which a testis descends into the scrotum.
pancreas—large endocrine and exocrine gland, its right extremity or head lying within the duodenal curve, its left extremity or tail ending near the spleen.
pancreatic duct—main passageway for pancreatic juice containing enzymes; runs from left to right and empties into duodenum.
pancreatic islets, islets of Langerhans—clusters of cells producing the hormone insulin.
pancreatic juice—clear secretion, 1,000 to 2,500 milliliters of fluid per day, composed of water, electrolytes, proteins, and enzymes.
peritoneum—sac of serous membrane composed of a parietal peritoneum that lines the abdominal wall and a visceral peritoneum that invests most viscera and holds them in position.

portal circulation—venous blood collected by the portal vein from the gastrointestinal canal, spleen, gallbladder, and pancreas, which enters the liver, passes through the sinusoids, and leaves the liver by the hepatic veins to pour into the inferior vena cava.

sphincter of bile duct (of Oddi)—circular muscle fibers around the end of the bile duct.

sphincter of hepatopancreatic ampulla—circular muscle fibers around end of ampulla (the union of the bile duct and main pancreatic duct).

DIAGNOSTIC TERMS

liver:

acute viral hepatitis—systematic inflammation of the liver caused by a specific viral agent. (See chapter 16 for the categories of viral agents.) (7, 13, 19)

acute yellow atrophy of liver—any severe form of hepatitis marked by shrinkage and necrosis of liver. (77)

Budd-Chiari syndrome—rare disease characterized by occlusion of hepatic veins, usually accompanied by ascites, hepatomegaly, and pain in abdomen. Caval venogram provides delineation of caval webs and occluded hepatic veins. Percutaneous liver biopsy may aid in revealing central lobular congestion. As the disease progresses, bleeding varices and hepatic coma develop. (19, 83)

chronic hepatitis—represents three related disorders: (1) chronic persistent hepatitis, (inflammatory process mostly confined to the portal areas; significant fibrosis and cirrhosis is absent); (2) chronic lobular hepatitis (predominant lesion is scattered single-cell necrosis in the lobule with minor portal inflammation present; does not progress to liver failure or cirrhosis); (3) chronic active hepatitis (continuing hepatic necrosis, active inflammation, and fibrosis present), which may lead to or be associated with liver failure, cirrhosis, and death. About 20% of chronic active hepatitis cases are caused by hepatitis B infection with or without superimposed hepatitis D infection. This syndrome also may follow posttransfusion or community-acquired hepatitis C or non-A, non-B hepatitis viruses (NANBHV). Drugs that cause chronic active hepatitis include amiodarone, dantrolene, isoniazid, methyldopa, nitrofurantoin, perhexilene maleate, phenytoin, propylthiouracil, and sulfonamides. Inborn errors metabolism such as Wilson's disease or alpha-1-antitrypsin deficiency also may cause chronic active hepatitis. (7, 14, 21)

cirrhosis of liver—organ diffusely nodular and firm. Stages of nodular development may include: (19, 54, 83)

- *biliary cirrhosis*—obstructive form is characterized by chronic jaundice and liver failure due to obstruction and inflammation of bile ducts.
- *macronodular cirrhosis*—features large nodules, measuring several centimeters in diameter.
- *micronodular cirrhosis*—features nodules measuring 1 millimeter in diameter or less.
- *presence of both macronodular and micronodular cirrhosis*—features the mixture of both small and large nodules. (72)

fatty liver—abnormal lipid increase in the liver, probably related to reduced oxidation of fatty acids or decreased synthesis and release of lipoproteins, causing inadequate lipid clearance from the liver. (19, 54)

hemochromatosis—excess of iron absorption and presence of iron-containing deposits (hemosiderin) in liver, pancreas, kidneys, adrenals, and heart. It may be associated with hepatic enlargement and insufficiency and esophageal bleeding from varices. (19)

hepatic calculi—stones originating in extrahepatic biliary tract or solely in the liver. They are also found in liver cysts. (77)

hepatic coma, cholemia—peculiar syndrome characterized by slow or rapid onset of bizarre behavior, disorientation, flapping tremors of extended arms, and hyperactive reflexes, and later lethargy and coma. It seems to be caused by intoxication with ammonia, a product of protein digestion that the diseased liver fails to convert into urea. (54)

hepatic encephalopathy—serious complication of advanced liver disease, probably caused by cerebral toxins, including ammonia, certain amines, and fatty acids. It is clinically manifested by personality changes and impaired intellectual ability, awareness, and neuromuscular functioning. (54, 84)

hepatic failure, fulminant—clinical syndrome caused by extensive necrosis of the liver, which may be induced by hepatotoxic drugs and may lead to progressive encephalopathy and a fatal prognosis. (68)

hepatic injury, drug-induced—liver injury may be:
- *cholestatic*—injury mimicking obstructive jaundice; for example, due to the use of chlorpromazine, erythromycin, steroids, and oral contraceptives. (19)
- *cytotoxic*—injury leading to severe hepatocellular jaundice and severe liver necrosis and failure; for example, due to the use of isoniazid, methyldopa, halothane, tetracycline. (67)

hepatic necrosis—destruction of functional liver tissue. (67)

hepatic trauma—liver injury resulting from blunt trauma or penetrating wounds. (67)

hepatoma—tumor of the liver. (8)

hepatorenal syndrome—combined liver and kidney failure; usually caused by serious injury to the liver associated with hemorrhage, shock, and acute renal insufficiency. (19)

liver abscess: (19, 82)
- *amebic abscess*—localized hepatic infection by *Entamoeba histolytica*; a common complication of intestinal amebiasis.
- *pyogenic abscess*—circumscribed area of suppuration. Infection brought to liver via portal vein, hepatic artery, or bile ducts.

malaria—infection caused by protozoa of the genus *Plasmodium*. The species commonly affecting humans are:
- *Plasmodium falciparum*—the most virulent type, which causes malignant tertian malaria.
- *Plasmodium malariae*—causes quartan malaria.
- *Plasmodium vivax* and *Plasmodium ovale*—causes benign tertian malaria. (87)

polycystic liver disease—cystic degeneration of the liver usually associated with congenital polycystic kidneys. (77)

portal hypertension—a portal venous pressure greater than 20 mm Hg, associated with splenomegaly, increased collateral circulation, varicosity, bleeding, and ascites. It may result from:
- *extrahepatic block*—block within the portal vein.
- *intrahepatic block*—block within the liver. (64)

primary carcinoma of the liver—hepatocellular tumor clinically manifested by an enlarged liver, ascites, jaundice, splenomegaly, edema, fever, and hepatic bruit. (8, 19, 82)

secondary carcinoma of the liver—metastatic malignant neoplasm, usually from lung, breast, or gastrointestinal cancer. (8, 19)

biliary system:

biliary stricture—contraction of a biliary duct that is prone to develop after gallbladder surgery. Strictures may present with bile leak or abscess formation in the immediate postoperative period. (19, 27)

carcinoma of the gallbladder—adenocarcinoma is the most common type, and remaining types originate either in squamous or mesothelial cells; early invasion of adjacent structures. Three kinds of adenocarcinoma that predominate are mucinous, papillary, and scirrhous. Scirrhous carcinomas are the most common and spread rapidly. Papillary carcinomas grow more slowly and result in polypoid-filling defects. Mucinous carcinomas occur least often. (19, 25)

cholangitis—inflammatory disease of bile ducts. (84)

cholecystitis—inflammatory disease of the gallbladder, frequently associated with the presence of gallstones. (19, 27, 84)

choledocholithiasis—gallstones in the biliary ducts. (17, 19, 84)

cholelithiasis, biliary calculi—the presence of gallstones in the gallbladder. (16, 17, 27, 84)

empyema of gallbladder—pus in the gallbladder. (27)

hydrops of gallbladder—distention of gallbladder with clear fluid. (27)

sclerosing cholangitis—disorder of unknown etiology resulting in a progressive fibrotic and inflammatory obliteration of the intrahepatic and extrahepatic biliary tree. In later stages of the disorder, secondary biliary cirrhosis associated with varices, ascites, and splenomegaly develops. The bile duct becomes irregularly thickened by the dense fibrosis, which may pervade the surrounding tissue as well. Death may result from chronic end-stage liver disease or variceal hemorrhage. (2, 19, 84)

pancreas:

pancreatitis—inflammation of the pancreas. All or part of the pancreas may be involved. (19)

- *acute pancreatitis*—inflammation of the pancreas. Its pathologic process is caused by irritation from enzyme activity, which results in pancreatic edema and vascular engorgement. The main tissue alterations in this disorder are acinar cell necrosis associated with an intense acute inflammatory reaction, and foci of necrotic fat cells. The physical and biochemical changes in the acinar cells affect synthesis, storage, and discharge of pancreatic digestive enzymes. In the initial disease process, pancreatic digestive enzymes are discharged from injured acinar cells into the blood and abdominal cavity. Clinical findings may include epigastric pain, nausea, vomiting, sweating, weakness, abdominal pain or distention, and fever. (19, 55, 71)

- *acute hemorrhagic pancreatitis, acute hemorrhagic pancreatic necrosis*—major medical emergency apparently caused by the destructive lytic action of pancreatic enzymes, clinically manifested by a sudden onset; acute abdomen; agonizing, constant pain; catastrophic peripheral vascular collapse; and shock. (19, 55)

- *chronic pancreatitis*—inflammatory disorder of the pancreas associated with permanent destruction of pancreatic tissue. When most of the pancreatic function declines, malabsorption and steatorrhea develop, as well as diabetes, which requires insulin treatment. Chronic abdominal pain and pancreatic calcifications also may be present. Many persons suffering from chronic pancreatitis may have bouts of recurrent acute pancreatic inflammation that may require hospitalization. This condition has been described as relapsing or recurrent chronic pancreatitis. (19, 55)

other types of pancreatitis include:

- *alcoholic pancreatitis*—caused by the ingestion of alcohol. It may result from an episode of binge drinking in the form of acute pancreatitis or from chronic alcohol ingestion, resulting in chronic pancreatitis. Individuals with chronic alcoholic pancreatitis appear at greater risk for the development of other diseases that affect their survival, such as extrapancreatic carcinoma, head and neck cancer, hepatic cirrhosis, and peptic ulceration. (19, 55)

- *gallstone pancreatitis*—presents as acute pancreatitis with gallstones, in which no other etiology is identified. It is caused by the migration of the gallstones through the ampulla of Vater. Acute gallstone pancreatitis is associated with an increased incidence of jaundice or hyperbilirubinemia. (55)

- *postoperative pancreatitis*—development of acute pancreatitis following operative procedures on the biliary tree, particularly those involving the sphincter of Oddi. Persons who have had prior episodes of acute pancreatitis are at greater risk to develop postoperative pancreatitis. Clinical findings that help to establish this diagnosis include an abnormal amount of postoperative abdominal pain, vomiting or large volumes of nasogastric aspirate with elevated plasma enzyme levels, or elevated urinary amylase excretion. (55)

pancreatic pseudocyst—fibrous capsule containing pancreatic juice with high levels of pancreatic enzymes, especially amylase. (55)

diabetes mellitus—the most significant pancreatic disease, in which pathogenic alterations of the islet cells cause a depletion of the insulin stores. (77) (See chapter 13.)

pancreatic tumors: (18, 19, 55)

- *carcinoma of pancreas*—highly malignant tumor, usually derived from glandular epithelium and involving the head of the pancreas. (19, 55)
- *islet cell tumors*—neoplasms originating from the islets of Langerhans. They tend to induce hyperinsulinism, which in turn produces hypoglycemia. Islet cell lesions may be benign, malignant, or metastasizing. (55)

peritoneum:

ascites—collection of fluid within the peritoneal cavity. (4, 19, 54)

hemoperitoneum—blood within the peritoneal cavity. (73)

hernia—rupture or protrusion of a part from its normal location; for example, an intestinal loop through a weakened area in the abdominal wall. Some locations where hernias occur include:

- *femoral*—organ passes through femoral ring.
- *inguinal*—organ protrudes through inguinal canal.
- *umbilical*—hernia occurs at the naval.
- *ventral*—hernia through the abdominal wall.

Some types of hernias are:

- *incarcerated*—hernia causes complete bowel obstruction.
- *incisional*—hernia complicates surgical intervention.
- *strangulated*—hernia cuts off circulation so that gangrene develops if emergency operation is not performed. (4, 50)

peritonitis—inflammation of peritoneum. (4, 11, 46)

OPERATIVE TERMS (SEE TABLE 9.2.)

liver:

biopsy of liver—removal of small piece of tissue for microscopic study. (34, 82)

hepatic lobectomy—removal of a lobe of the liver. (82)

hepatotomy—incision into liver substance.

liver transplantation—surgical procedure in which a healthy liver is implanted after the person's diseased liver has been removed. After the homograft has been implanted, suprahepatic and intrahepatic anastomoses are performed, followed by portal vein and biliary reconstruction. (12, 19, 82)

shunts for portal hypertension, portal decompression, portosystemic decompression—surgical method of diverting a considerable amount of blood of the hypertensive portal system into the normal systemic venous system to prevent or treat variceal hemorrhages. (57, 83)

- *mesocaval shunt*—surgical communication of the side of the superior mesenteric vein and the upper end of the inferior vena cava for thrombosis of the portal vein. (83)
- *portacaval shunt*—anastomosis of portal vein to vena cava for intrahepatic block. (83)
- *splenorenal shunt*—splenectomy followed by an anastomosis between the splenic artery and renal artery for extrahepatic block due to thrombosis of the portal vein. (83)

biliary system:

cholecystectomy—removal of the gallbladder. (16, 22)

- *laparoscopic laser cholecystectomy*—removal of gallbladder via laparoscopic approach. The laser fiber is advanced through a small, flexible endoscope and passed into the cystic and common ducts, until it contacts the stone and the laser is activated. Some fragments are pushed through the sphincter into the duodenum and, when necessary removed with small baskets or grasping instruments. (86)

cholecystojejunostomy—anastomosis between the gallbladder and jejunum to bypass the obstruction in the biliary ductal system. (84)

cholecystostomy—surgical creation of a more or less permanent opening into the gallbladder. This operation is indicated where removal of the gallbladder would be unduly hazardous. (16)

choledochoduodenostomy—surgical joining of the common bile duct to the duodenum. (17, 22)

choledocholithotomy—incision into bile duct for removal of gallstones. (27)

choledochoplasty—plastic repair or reconstruction of bile duct. (27)

Roux-en-Y procedures—jejunal loop or limb, surgically used to: bypass extensive trauma to the biliary ductal system by constructing a choledochojejunostomy, decompress a choleductal cyst or the biliary tract by performing a cholecystojejunostomy, and anastomose both ends of the completely transected pancreas following pancreatic injury, thus accomplishing a pancreaticojejunostomy. (55, 84)

sphincteroplasty (Oddi)—plastic repair of stenotic sphincter of Oddi. (84)

pancreas:

pancreatectomy—partial or total removal of pancreas; for example, for islet cell tumor. (55)

pancreatoduodenectomy—pancreatoduodenal resection indicated in major injury to the duodenum, pancreas, and adjacent viscera that precludes the salvage of these organs. (55)

pancreatojejunostomy—anastomosis of pancreas to jejunum; may be done for carcinoma of the ampulla of Vater. (55)

sphincteroplasty (Vater)—plastic repair of ampulla of Vater for alleviating ampullary obstruction by biliary stones and chronic pancreatitis. (55)

Whipple's operation, Whipple's pancreaticoduodenostomy— extensive resection for pancreatic cancer or serious injury, including the head, tail, and portions of the body of the pancreas, together with the duodenum, part of the bile duct, and stomach. The remaining pancreas is anastomosed to the bile duct, jejunum, and stomach. (55)

peritoneum:

exploratory laparotomy—surgical opening of the abdomen for diagnostic purposes. (84)

hernioplasty, herniorrhaphy—repair of hernia. (4, 11)

incision and drainage of abscess—opening and draining peritoneal, retroperitoneal, or subphrenic abscess. (4)

SYMPTOMATIC TERMS

arterial spiders, spider nevi—cutaneous vascular lesions occurring on face, neck, and shoulders in advanced hepatic disease, as well as in malnutrition and pregnancy. Each lesion consists of a central arteriole from which small vessels radiate. (67)

caput medusae—dilatation of the abdominal veins around the umbilicus, seen in severe portal hypertension with liver damage. (67)

cholestasis—impaired or obstructed bile flow.

fetor hepaticus—musty, sweet odor to the breath, characteristic of hepatic coma. (54, 67)

flapping tremor, liver flap—involuntary movements, elicited in the extended hand by supporting the patient's forearm. It consists of bursts of quick, irregular movements at the wrist similar to waving good-bye. The protruded tongue and dorsiflexed feet may likewise be affected. Flapping tremors occur in severe liver disease and signal impending hepatic coma. (54)

hepatic bruit—vascular bruit over liver, a blowing sound or murmur heard on auscultation, probably caused by pressure of enlarged liver on aorta. (77)

hyperammoniemia—excessive amount of ammonia in the blood, as in hepatic coma. (77)

icterus, jaundice—yellow discoloration of skin, sclera (white of eyes), membranes, and secretions due to excess bilirubin in the blood. (19)

palmar erythema, liver palms—bright or mottled redness of the palms and fingertips, seen in liver disease. Palmar erythema also occurs in malnutrition and rheumatoid arthritis. (67)

SPECIAL PROCEDURES

TERMS RELATED TO GASTROINTESTINAL ENDOSCOPIES

endoscopy with flexible fiberscope—visualization of a hollow organ using an endoscope with a tip for remote control and a biopsy channel for tissue sampling and histologic study of lesion. (21, 39)

> *colonoscopy, colonofiberoscopy*—method of examining the colon by using a colonic fiberscope with a four-way controlled tip to facilitate transversing the flexures of the sigmoid and transverse colon under fluoroscopic guidance. It may permit the removal of polyps up to the ascending colon. (21, 37, 38, 39)

> *duodenoscopy*—introduction of a flexible duodenoscope into the first part of the duodenum, for visualization and cannulation of papilla of Vater. Contrast material is injected into the orifice of the ampulla through a minute cannula to obtain a retrograde cholangiogram or pancreatogram. (39, 81)

> *esophagogastroduodenoscopy*—endoscopic examination of the entire esophagus, stomach, and duodenum, with all mucosal surfaces visualized and photographic recording of visualized abnormalities. Esophagogastroduodenoscopy is used in the evaluation of acid-peptic disorders, malignancy, and gastrointestinal bleeding. (81)

> *fiberoptic gastroscopy*—use of an end-viewing fiberscope as the usual method of choice for visualizing the esophagus, stomach, antrum, pylorus, duodenal bulb, and an anastomosis after surgery. In addition to the fiberoptic light source, the scope contains a channel for biopsies, for suction and air or water instillation, and for endoscopic photography. (81)

> *peritoneoscopy*—procedure for visualization of the peritoneal cavity using a peritoneoscope with a fiberoptic light source. It is possible to perform a percutaneous liver biopsy under direct vision, to photograph the lesions, to irrigate the peritoneal cavity, to aspirate ascitic fluid for cytoanalysis, and to finally arrive at a diagnosis of obscure abdominal disease by peritoneoscopy. (36)

> *proctosigmoidoscopy*—endoscopic procedure for visualization of benign and malignant lesions of the rectosigmoid. It permits excisional biopsy of small lesions, such as polyps, and segmental biopsy of large ones for diagnosis. (59)

endoscopic retrograde cholangiopancreatography (ERCP)—combined endoscopic and radiologic procedure that employs a specialized lateral viewing fiberoptic endoscope 1 centimeter in diameter to visualize the upper gastrointestinal tract and papilla of Vater. Under visual control, the pancreatic or biliary duct system is cannulated for the retrograde injection of radiopaque contrast media. An instrument channel of 1.6 centimeters provides passage of biopsy instruments, cannulating catheters, electrosurgical devices, and baskets or balloons for endoscopic manipulations. Another approach is use of the ultrasound-equipped endoscope for transmitting images within the abdominal cavity and for application of laser therapy in the treatment of intraluminal lesions of the biliary tree and pancreas. (34, 36)

TERMS RELATED TO MISCELLANEOUS PROCEDURES

balloon tamponade—emergency procedure to control bleeding from esophageal varices using a Boyce or Linton modification of the Sengstaken-Blakemore tube, which permits aspiration of secretions. (64, 83)

endoscopic sclerotherapy—procedure that involves the use of a rigid or flexible endoscope to directly inject the esophageal varices with a sclerosant. Usually, repeated injections are required to achieve variceal obliteration. Endoscopic sclerotherapy techniques may be used to stabilize the patient so that subsequent elective portosystemic shunt surgery can be employed. (83)

esophageal manometric studies—these studies measure intraesophageal pressure variations. Two other tests that may be performed in conjunction with esophageal manometric studies are:

> *acid perfusion test*—perfusion with water is begun for several minutes followed by perfusion, which is switched to 0.1 normal hydrochloric acid at a rate of 4 to 7 cubic centimeters per minute. The test serves as a method to differentiate pain of esophageal origin from true angina.

> *pH measurements*—measurements of esophageal pH using a long gastrointestinal electrode that provides direct and objective evidence of gastroesophageal reflux. (51)

exchange transfusion—exchange of equal volume of blood using a closed transfusion circuit for the purpose of lowering plasma bilirubin levels in cases at high risk for neurotoxicity. Fresh blood is used, and electrolytes are added as needed. (77)

hyperalimentation—long-term intravenous nutrition with an amino acid-glucose infusate using disposable tubing and infusion pump to maintain a constant infusion rate. A large intravenous catheter is inserted through a central vein, and its proper position is radiographically confirmed. Hyperalimentation should be reserved for patients with severe digestive abnormalities or seriously ill patients suffering from malnutrition, sepsis, and surgical or accidental trauma when use of gastrointestinal tract for feeding is not possible. (70)

pneumatic dilatation of lower esophageal sphincter (LES)— forceful dilatation of LES with a bag dilatator for reinstituting peristalsis and relaxing the sphincter in early achalasia. (51)

transhepatic embolization of varices—percutaneous insertion of a catheter through the liver and into the portal vein. The coronary vein is cannulated and a sclerosing agent is infused to obliterate the varices. The advantage of this technique is that a single application of variceal therapy is sufficient and repeated injections are not required to achieve variceal obliteration. (64)

CLINICAL LABORATORY FINDINGS

TERMS RELATED TO SERUM ENZYMES PRIMARILY CONCERNED WITH DIGESTION

> *amylase (AMS), diastase*—digestive enzyme acting on starches. It is found in the salivary glands, pancreatic juice, liver, and adipose tissue. (71)

> *amylase isoenzymes*—electrophoretic fractionation of salivary gland and pancreatic amylase, which falls into two general classes: (1) those arising from the pancreas (P isoamylases), and (2) those arising from nonpancreatic sources (S isoamylases). (79)

> *amylase (AMS) determination*—test of diagnostic value in pancreatic disorders. (71, 77)

> *Reference values* (Method of Somogyi): (15)

> - *serum amylase*—60–160 units/dl (SIU: 111–296 U/L)

>> **Increase** usually in acute pancreatitis, chronic recurrent pancreatitis, carcinoma of the head of the pancreas, salivary adenitis, and renal failure. (71, 77)

>> **Decrease** in chronic hepatic disease and in starvation. (77)

> *serum gamma glutamyl transferase (GGT)*—digestive enzyme probably involved in protein synthesis. It is found in kidney, lung, and prostate and in high concentration in the liver. GGT is an exquisitely sensitive indicator of hepatic disease and valuable in the detection

of alcoholic liver disease and in monitoring alcoholics who are involved in an abstention program. (52, 77)

> *Reference values* (varies with method): (15)
> - *Serum gamma glutamyl transferase (GGT)*
> - *Males:* 9–50 U/L (SIU: 9–50 U/L)
> - *Females:* 8–40 U/L (SIU: 8–40 U/L)
>> **Increase** in chronic hepatitis, obstructive hepatic disease, alcoholic cirrhosis of the liver, and hepatobiliary and pancreatic malignancies. (52, 77)

serum leucine aminopeptidase (SLAP) determination— measurement of LAP, a protein-splitting enzyme in the blood. (52, 77)

> *Reference values:* (15)
> - *Males:* 80–200 U/mL (SIU: 19.2–48.0 U/L)
> - *Females:* 75–185 U/mL (SIU: 18.0–44.4 U/L)
>> **Increase** in most types of liver disease but values are highest in biliary obstruction. Serum leucine aminopeptidase is sensitive in detecting obstructive infiltrative space-occupying lesions of the liver. (52, 77)

serum lipase (SLPS)—measurement of a lipase, a lipolytic (fat-splitting) enzyme in the blood. (52, 77)

> *Reference values* (method of Cherry-Crandall): (15)
> - *serum lipase*—0–1.5 U/mL (SIU: 10–150 U/L)
>> **Increase** in serum lipase activity in mumps, indicative of marked salivary gland and pancreatic involvement. (52, 77)

serum glycolytic enzymes—chiefly enzymes that catalyze the breakdown of glycogen to glucose in serum. Glycolytic enzymes are present in many tissues, and some are of diagnostic importance. (77)

> *serum aldolase (SALS)*—highly sensitive glycolytic enzyme.
>> *Reference values:* (15)
>> - *serum aldolase*—1.5–12.0 U/L (SIU: 1.5–12.0 U/L)
>>> **Increase** in muscle disease, hepatic necrosis, megaloblastic anemia, neoplastic disease, myocardial infarction, and pulmonary infarction. (77)

serum phosphohexoisomerase (SPHI)—increasing serum levels of this glycolytic enzyme reflect metastases, especially in patients with cancer of the prostate and breast. (77)

serum pyruvate kinase (SPK)—abnormally low glycolytic enzyme activity in red cells causes PK deficiency, a chronic hemolytic anemia. (77)

SELECTED TERMS RELATED TO GASTRIC ANALYSIS AND RELATED TESTS OF THE DIGESTIVE SYSTEM

augmented Histalog test—procedure in which the Histalog dose has been calculated according to body weight to induce maximal gastric acid secretion. If no acid is released, anacidity is present.

> *augmented histamine test*—an optional histamine dose is used to evoke a maximal gastric acid response, thus providing quantitative measurement of the secretory capacity of the stomach.

Note: To avoid the undesirable side effects of histamine, the augmented histamine test may be replaced by the pentagastrin test, which results in a similar magnitude of acid output with considerably fewer side effects. Pentagastrin is a synthetic pentapeptide derivative that contains four C-terminal amino acids of gastrin linked to substituted alanine. Pentagastrin retains a good portion of the biologic activity of gastrin and serves as a potent stimulus to the secretion of acid pepsin and the intrinsic factor of the stomach. Pentagastrin stimulates secretion of both bicarbonate and enzymes by the pancreas, as well as stimulating relaxation of the sphincter of Oddi and gallbladder contraction.

- *basal acid output (BAO)*—quantitative measurement of gastric acid secretion under basal conditions that is without histamine or Histalog stimulation.
- *maximal acid output (MAO)*—quantitative measurement of gastric acid secretion after stimulation with an augmented dose of histamine or Histalog.
- *gastric analysis (tube)*—aspiration of gastric contents for the purpose of determining the secretory ability and motility of the stomach. (23, 43, 45, 77, 79)

gastric exfoliative cytology—valuable method for detecting gastric malignancy by studying cells shed by the mucosa and obtained by aspiration, lavage, or abrasive brushes following the liquefaction of the mucosal coating. (77)

gastric juice—composite of water, hydrochloric acid, electrolytes, enzymes, blood group components, and the intrinsic factor of Castle. (77, 79)

gastrin—hormone formed by cells of the antral mucosa of the stomach and carried by the blood to the gastric fundus, stimulating the release of hydrochloric acid and evoking the secretion of pepsin, pancreatic enzymes, and the intrinsic factor of Castle. Gastrin is the most potent known stimulant of gastric acid secretion. (45, 79)

gastrin secretory test—use of a purified gastrin preparation in gastric secretory studies analogous to those of histamine and Histalog. (45, 79)

guaiac test—test for occult blood in feces (also in urine). (6)

Reference values: (15)

- *guaiac test:*
  Negative reaction—no blood, no greenish to blue color.
  Positive reaction—blood present, greenish to blue color.

Hemoccult test—test for occult blood in feces that can be done at home. Test depends on the presence of peroxidase activity of the heme in the sample. Usually two small fecal specimens are applied to prepared slides from three consecutive bowel movements. Bleeding from the upper gastrointestinal tract and oral doses of vitamin C diminish the sensitivity of the test. (6)

Reference values: (15)

- *Hemoccult test:*
  Negative reaction—no blood, no bluish color present.
  Positive reaction—blood present, bluish color present.
  Ulcerated carcinomas of the colon or stomach usually yield a positive reaction with use of the guaiac or Hemoccult tests.

histamine—powerful stimulant to gastric secretion used clinically in gastric function tests. (77)

Hollander insulin hypoglycemia test—use of insulin-induced hypoglycemia to evaluate the outcome of vagotomy. Positive results, a few months after surgery, may indicate the vagal nerve fibers are regenerating or that the vagotomy was incomplete. The Hollander test is no longer recommended because of the reported hypoglycemic seizures, strokes, and myocardial infarctions that are associated with it. The **sham feeding test** is employed for establishing the diagnosis of incomplete vagotomy. The contents of a meal are chewed but not swallowed. Acid output is determined during the test by aspirating gastric secretions through a nasogastric tube. If the acid output caused by the sham feeding is greater than 10% of the pentagastrin-stimulated peak acid output, this implies that the vagal innervation of the stomach is intact. (43)

intestinal absorption test, urinary D-xylose test—test that distinguishes between malabsorption due to small intestinal disease and that due to pancreatic exocrine insufficiency. Decreased urinary D-xylose values are seen in ascites. The urinary D-xylose test helps to differentiate whether steatorrhea is secondary to pancreatic disease or to small bowel disease.

An abnormal D-xylose test is found most frequently in disorders affecting the mucosal of the proximal small intestine, such as celiac sprue or tropical sprue. (26)

pepsin, protease—digestive enzyme present in gastric juice and capable of converting proteins into peptones and proteoses. (77)

secretin—hormone produced by the duodenal mucosa and acting as a potent stimulus to the release of pancreatic secretions. (43, 45)

secretin test (Dreiling and Hollander)—intravenous injection of secretin following the removal of the duodenal contents. The secretin stimulates pancreatic secretions, which enter the duodenum and are removed. The study of the duodenal aspirate, which includes volume of output, amylase activity, and content of bicarbonate, bile, and proteolytic enzymes, aids in the diagnostic evaluation of pancreatic and biliary disorders. (43)

stool examination—macroscopic and microscopic studies, chemical analysis, and examinations for parasites and protozoa; used as diagnostic aids, especially for detecting diseases of the digestive tract. (77)

sweat test, Gibson-Cooke technique—sweat electrolytes by pilocarpine iontophoresis into the skin to stimulate an increased secretion of the sweat glands. The laboratory diagnosis is based on the abnormally high content of sodium chloride (NaCl) in sweat. (42)

Reference values: (15)

- *sodium chloride concentration*—greater than 60 mEq per liter.
  Increased sodium and chloride concentration in sweat, exceeding 60 mEq/L in children and 70 mEq/L in adults is indicative of cystic fibrosis. (42)

SELECTED TERMS RELATED TO LIVER FUNCTION

aminotransferases (formerly called transferases)—enzymes that catalyze the transfer of biochemical substances. They are sensitive indicators of liver cell injury and other hepatocellular diseases such as hepatitis. (45)

They include:

serum alanine aminotransferase (SALT) or serum glutamate pyruvic transaminase (SGPT)
Reference values: (15)

- *SALT or SGPT (at 30° C)*—8–50 U/mL (SIU: 4–24 U/L)
  Increase in hepatitis, hepatic cirrhosis, metastatic cancer, obstructive jaundice, and other disorders. (52)

serum aspartate aminotransferase (SAST) or serum glutamate oxaloacetate transaminase (SGOT)
Reference values: (15)

- *SAST or SGOT (at 30° C)*—16–60 U/mL (SIU: 8–33 U/L)
  Increase in hepatitis, cirrhosis of liver, obstructive jaundice, myocardial infarction, and other disorders. (77)

serum gamma glutamyl transferase (SGGT) or serum gamma glutamyl transpeptidase (SGGTP)
Reference values: (15)

- *SGGT or SGGTP (at 37° C)*—5–40 IU/L (SIU: 5–40 U/L)
  Increase in hepatitis, obstructive jaundice, hepatic cirrhosis, alcoholic hepatitis, certain malignancies of liver and pancreas. (52)

liver function tests—of great importance not only in discovering the severity of hepatic disease, but also in determining the amount of liver damage caused by pathologic conditions of the gallbladder and pancreas. (52) (See table 9.3.)

TABLE 9.3	Useful Liver Function Tests	
Hepatic Function	*Tests*	*Comments*
Detoxification and excretion	Serum bilirubin	Increased in hepatocellular jaundice, hemolytic jaundice, obstructive jaundice, portal cirrhosis, and hepatic carcinoma
	Bilirubin in urine	Increased in hepatitis and liver disorders due to infectious or toxic agents, and obstructive biliary tract diseases
	Urobilinogen in urine	Increased in infectious and toxic hepatitis, biliary disease, malaria, cholangitis, hemolytic jaundice, and anemia, and acute liver cell damage
	Urobilinogen in feces	Increased in hemolytic jaundice, hemolytic anemia Decreased in biliary obstruction, obstructive jaundice, and severe liver disease
Prothrombin time (PT) activity	Prothrombin determination	Prolonged in alcoholic liver disease and cirrhosis, celiac sprue (owing to malabsorption of vitamin K), vitamin K deficiency, acute viral hepatitis, obstructive jaundice, and chronic hepatocellular disorders

Protein metabolism	Total serum proteins
	  Serum albumin
	  Serum globulin
	  Serum gamma globulin
	Serum immunoglobulins
		Increase of globulin in chronic active hepatitis and cirrhosis
		Decrease of total proteins and albumin in liver disease
		IgA increased in alcoholic hepatitis
		IgG increased in autoimmune chronic hepatitis
		IgM increased in biliary cirrhosis

	Blood ammonia levels	Increased in hepatocellular necrosis and portal hypertension
	Alpha$_1$ fetoprotein	Increased in hepatocellular carcinoma in adults and in some patients with hepatic necrosis
	Alpha$_1$ antitripsin	Deficiency in neonatal hepatitis, childhood cirrhosis, and in adults asymptomatic macronodular cirrhosis
Lipid metabolism	Serum cholesterol and serum cholesterol esters	Both increased in obstructive jaundice Both decreased in liver failure and hepatic necrosis

TABLE **9.3**	(continued)	
Hepatic Function	*Tests*	*Comments*
Enzyme activity	Serum alkaline phosphatase	Increased in obstructive jaundice, congenital intrahepatic biliary atresia, and hepatic carcinoma
	Serum alanine aminotransferase (SALT) or serum glutamic pyruvic transaminase (SGPT)	Highly elevated in acute hepatitis, toxic hepatitis, and hepatocellular damage
	Serum aspartate aminotransferase (SAST) or serum glutamic oxaloacetic transaminase (SGOT)	Increased in most hepatocellular disorders
	Serum gamma glutamyl transferase (SGGT)	Increased in alcoholism
Metals and electrolytes	Serum iron and iron-binding capacity	Increased in acute hepatitis and hemochromatosis Decreased in cirrhosis
	Serum copper and ceruloplasmin	Decreased in Wilson's disease (hepatolenticular degeneration)
	Urine copper	Increased in Wilson's disease

Adapted from personal communication with Ronald Turgeon, M.D.

ABBREVIATIONS

RELATED PRIMARILY TO TESTS

BA—barium
BAO—basal acid output
ERCP—endoscopic retrograde cholangiopancreatography

GI—gastrointestinal
MAO—maximal acid output
PP—postprandial (following a meal)

RELATED TO TIME SCHEDULE FOR MEDICATIONS

	Latin	**English**
ac	*ante cibos*	before meals
bid	*bis in die*	twice a day
hs	*hora somni*	at bedtime
pc	*post cibos*	after meals
po	*per os*	by mouth
prn	*pro re nata*	as necessary
qh	*quaque hora*	every hour
qid	*quarter in die*	four times a day
stat	*statim*	immediately
tid	*ter in die*	three times a day

ORAL READING PRACTICE

MALIGNANT NEOPLASMS OF THE ORAL CAVITY

Carcinomas of the mouth include malignant tumors of the lips, tongue, and floor of the **oral cavity. Neoplastic growth** may be preceded by gradual development of irregular, white, raised patches known as **leukoplakia.** This condition starts as a chronic, painless inflammation of the **oral mucosa.** It is usually considered a **premalignant lesion.** Although etiology is unknown, the relationship of tobacco and leukoplakia is a well established fact, since leukoplakia seen in heavy smokers tends to disappear after smoking has been discontinued. The white patches are caused by a **keratinization** of the **epithelium. Fissuring** or **ulceration** in a **leukoplakic area** may be a diagnostic sign that malignant changes are in progress.

Tumors of the upper lip are generally **basal cell carcinomas,** which tend to invade adjacent structures but rarely **metastasize.** Prompt treatment is imperative. **Carcinoma** of the lower lip may show a widespread involvement of the **epidermoid (squamous cell)** type. In its early phase, a fissure, flat ulcer, or chronic **leukoplakia** readily forms a **fungating mass,** malignant in character.

Carcinoma of the tongue begins as a fissure ulcer with raised borders. The areas of **induration** are prone to extend with time. Spontaneous bleeding occurs from ulcerating crevices and is distressing to the patient. With increasing **infiltration,** the movement of the tongue becomes restricted. **Metastatic adenopathy** may develop early or late and generally involves the **cervical** and **submaxillary lymph nodes.**

Any ulcer or new growth of the lips, tongue, or floor of the mouth that does not heal with treatment in three weeks should be **biopsied.** Suspicious lesions must receive prompt attention, since the progression to inoperability occurs before the patient feels the pain.

The treatment of choice in carcinoma of the mouth is surgical removal of the lesion with or without **irradiation,** or, if inoperable, **palliative radiotherapy** alone. For cancer of the lip, a **V-excision** of the **malignant lesion** may be done to provide relief from the discomfort and overcome disfigurement. Some surgeons treat metastatic cancer of the tongue with preoperative **supervoltage radiotherapy** to reduce the size of the tumor and subsequent **hemiglossectomy,** partial **mandibulectomy,** and **cervical lymph node dissection.**

Patients with advanced **squamous cell carcinoma** of the head and neck may have involvement of the **carotid artery.** There are a number of therapeutic options to be considered when this occurs, including supportive care alone, **radiation therapy, chemotherapy,** and **surgery.** If surgery is performed, the carotid artery should be saved whenever the tumor can be easily separated from the artery. Sometimes, the tumor can be peeled from the artery, but if the tumor has invaded the arterial wall, **carotid artery resection** is usually advocated. When carotid artery resection is performed, **interposition grafting** should be utilized to minimize the risk of **neurological morbidity.** Two other surgical approaches to be considered are **carotid artery ligation** and **carotid artery replacement.** Carotid artery replacement appears to be superior to carotid artery ligation in avoiding the neurological complications of carotid artery resection. Carotid artery resection can provide local control of the tumor but fails to achieve a high rate of disease-free survival.

Molecular techniques can now be utilized to identify specific **genetic mutations** in tumor samples providing a better understanding of the molecular events involved in malignant transformation. It has been found that over 5% of invasive head and neck squamous cell carcinomas have a **mutated p53 gene.** Because it is frequently mutated, the p53 gene is currently the most useful **genetic marker** available for head and neck squamous cell carcinomas. When a mutation is identified in the clonal cell population, the detection of that mutation in other cells serves as a strong evidence that they are derived from the same neoplasm. Precise linkage of metastatic and recurrent local lesions to a primary cancer containing the same mutation will provide a more accurate delineation of the incidence of metastasis and recurrence. In the future, a panel of probes representing the most common mutations found in head and neck squamous cell carcinomas may become available to screen at-risk patients. The potential ability to detect tumor cells exfoliated from a lesion by swabbing the oral mucosa with glove, tongue blade, or other device offers the future possibility of developing a screening test for the early detection of malignancy. (3, 8, 27, 32, 42, 71)

REVIEW GUIDE

Instructions: Break apart each term listed below, identify the medical term elements, and define the term.

Example: glossodynia
glosso- = combining form element = tongue
-dynia = suffix = painful

sialolithotomy	hematemesis
adenotonsillitis	choledocholithiasis
esophagorrhaphy	pancreaticoduodenostomy
hemigastrectomy	

Instructions: Select the letter of the response that correctly completes each statement, as shown in the example.

Example: Tongue-tie may be called
a. cheilosis. b. herpangina.
c. torus palatinus. <u>d.</u> ankyloglossia.

1. Meckel's diverticulum is associated with the
a. jejunum. b. ascending colon.
c. descending colon. d. ileum.
2. The Heinecke-Mikulicz procedure may be called
a. vagotomy. b. pyloroplasty.
c. pyloromyotomy. d. gastrojejunostomy.
3. The Fredet-Ramstedt operation may be called
a. vagotomy. b. pyloroplasty.
c. pyloromyotomy. d. gastrojejunostomy.
4. The sphincter of Oddi refers to
a. pancreatic duct. b. cystic duct.
c. bile duct. d. none of the above.
5. A collection of lymphoid tissue lodged in the tonsillar fossa on either side of the oral part of the pharynx is
a. pharyngeal tonsil. b. palatine tonsil.
c. both A and B. d. none of the above.
6. The alimentary canal extends from the
a. mouth to anus. b. ascending colon to anus.
c. mouth to duodenum. d. mouth to cecum.
7. Gingivitis is inflammation of the
a. gum. b. tongue.
c. lip. d. cheek.
8. Repair of cleft palate is called
a. palatoplasty. b. cheiloplasty.
c. glossorrhaphy. d. esophagorrhaphy.
9. The opening between stomach and duodenum is called
a. pylorus. b. cardiac orifice.
c. fundus of stomach. d. none of the above.
10. The parotid duct may be called
a. Wharton's duct. b. Stensen's duct.
c. Bernard's duct. d. none of the above.
11. Telescoping of intestine may be associated with
a. intussusception. b. steatorrhea.
c. borborygmus. d. none of the above.

12. Collection of fluid in the peritoneal cavity is
    a. hemoperitoneum.   b. ascites.
    c. melena.   d. cholemia.
13. Another term for belching is
    a. hypergastrinemia.   b. bulimia.
    c. eructation.   d. borborygmus.
14. Circular muscle around the pylorus is called
    a. cardiac sphincter.   b. gastroesophageal sphincter.
    c. pyloric sphincter.   d. none of the above.
15. Fundoplication performed via a thoracotomy, during which the cardia of the stomach is wrapped partially around the lower esophagus is termed
    a. Belsy procedure.   b. Hill repair.
    c. Nissen fundoplication.   d. Toupet procedure.

Instructions: Figure 9.4 in the text shows the digestive tract. For each line that extends from the figure below, provide the anatomic name of the site, as shown in the example.

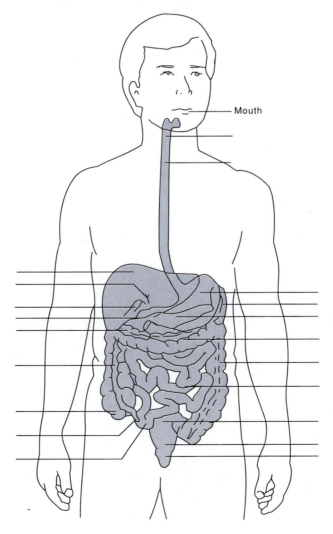

Mouth

10

Urogenital Disorders

KIDNEYS

ORIGIN OF TERMS

calyx (G)—cup

cortex (L)—rind, outer portion

glomerulus (pl. *glomeruli*) (L)—tuft, cluster

medulla (L)—marrow, inner portion

nephr-, nephro- (G)—kidney

ren (L)—kidney

PHONETIC PRONUNCIATION OF SELECTED TERMS

avulsion of kidney   a-VUL'shun of KID'nee

cortical adenoma   KOR'ti-kal AD-e-NO'mah

ecchymoses   ek-eye-MOE'seas

nephroblastoma   NEF-row-blas-TOE'mah

nephropexy   NEF'row-PECK-see

uremic frost   you-RE'mick frost

ANATOMIC TERMS (52, 64) (SEE FIGS. 10.1 AND 10.2.)

kidneys—paired, bean-shaped organs situated behind the peritoneum on both sides of the lumbar spine. Their function is to preserve the ionic balance of the blood and extract its waste products.

nephron—the functional unit of the kidney. Each nephron consists of a renal corpuscle and a renal tubule.

    renal corpuscle—composed of a tangled cluster of blood capillaries called a glomerulus, which is surrounded by a thin-walled, saclike structure called a glomerular capsule (Bowman's capsule).

- *glomerulus* (pl. *glomeruli*)—coiled capillary network that arises from an afferent arteriole (a branch of an interlobular renal artery). The capillary network ends in an efferent arteriole (which descends to form another capillary plexus in close relation to the straight and convoluted tubules). It filters urine from the blood.
- *glomerular capsule, Bowman's capsule*—double-layered envelope of epithelium that encloses a capillary tuft. It is the double-walled proximal portion of a renal tubule that encloses the glomerulus of a nephron. It filters water and solutes out of the blood into the tubule.

Figure 10.1 (a) Longitudinal section of a kidney; (b) a renal pyramid containing nephrons; (c) a single nephron.

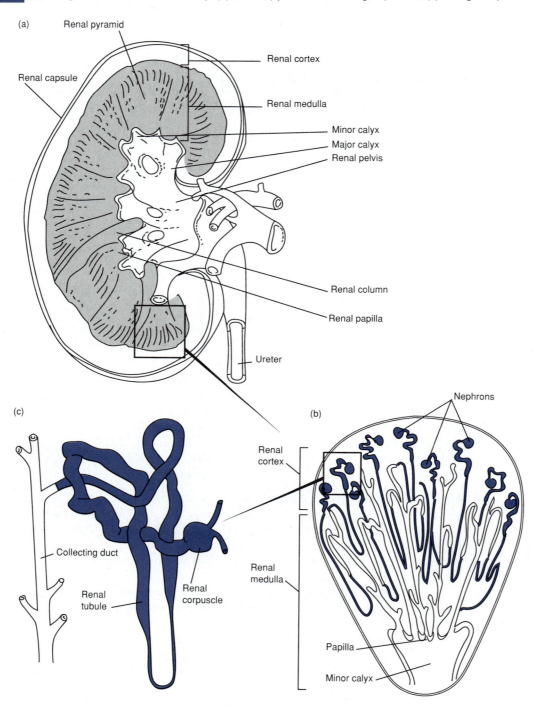

Figure 10.2   Structure of a nephron and the blood vessels associated with it.

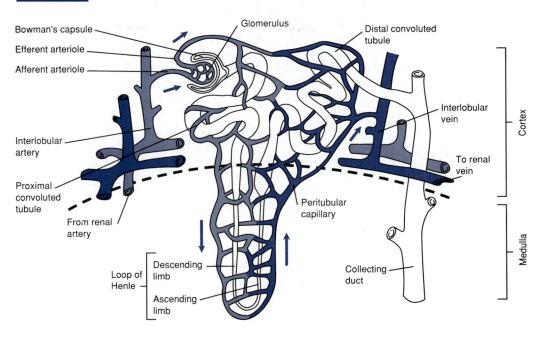

renal tubule—leads away from the glomerular capsule and becomes highly coiled. This coiled portion of the tubule is termed the proximal convoluted tubule. The proximal convoluted tubule dips toward the renal pelvis to become the descending limb of the loop of Henle. The tubule then curves back toward its renal corpuscle and forms the ascending limb of the loop of Henle. The ascending limb returns to the region of the renal corpuscle where it becomes coiled again and is called the distal convoluted tubule. Several distal convoluted tubules merge in the renal cortex to form a collecting duct.

- *collecting duct*—formed by several distal convoluted tubules that merge in the renal cortex. The collecting duct passes into the renal medulla, becoming larger as it is joined by other collecting ducts. The resulting tube, the papillary duct, empties into a minor calyx through an opening in a renal papilla.

renal cortex—outer portion of the kidney. It forms a shell around the medulla. Its tissue dips into the medulla between adjacent renal pyramids, forming renal columns. The granular appearance of the cortex is due to the random arrangement of very small tubules associated with the nephrons, the functional units of the kidney.

renal medulla—composed of conical masses of tissue called renal pyramids, whose bases are directed toward the convex surface of the kidney, and whose apexes form the renal papillae. The tissue of the medulla appears striated due to the presence of microscopic tubules leading from the cortex to the renal papillae.

renal pelvis—funnel-shaped enlargement of the ureter as it leaves the kidney. It contains:

calices (formerly calyces; sing. calyx)—cuplike indentations in the kidney pelvis. The collecting tubules open into the calices.

hilus—notch on the medial surface of the kidney through which the ureter and blood vessels enter or leave the kidney.

DIAGNOSTIC TERMS

acute tubular necrosis of kidney, acute reversible renal failure—a cellular necrosis affecting the renal tubules following shock, trauma, nephrotoxic damage, transfusion reaction, septicemia, and other causes. In acute renal failure, the glomerular filtration rate is abruptly reduced, causing a sudden retention of endogenous metabolites (urea, potassium, phosphate, sulfate, creatinine) that are normally cleared by the kidneys. (1, 3, 16, 38)

arteriolar nephrosclerosis—renal disorder characterized by an intimal thickening of the afferent glomerular arterioles, resulting in a narrowing of the arteriolar lumen and reduced blood supply to nephrons.

> *benign type*—neuropathy with benign hypertension.
> *malignant type*—neuropathy with malignant hypertension (diastolic often above 130 mm Hg) accompanied by papilledema, central nervous system manifestations, cardiac decompensation, and acute progressive deterioration of renal function. (7, 63)

glomerulonephritis—form of nephritis involving the renal glomeruli of both kidneys. There is evidence that the glomeruli may be injured by antigen-antibody complexes that develop from the immune responses to streptococcal infection. Hypertension, headache, malaise, puffiness around the eyes, oliguria, and blood, protein, and casts in the urine are common clinical findings. (5, 37, 66)

Goodpasture's syndrome, antiglomerular basement membrane nephritis—acute glomerulonephritis associated with severe diffuse lung disease, hemorrhagic and inflammatory, involving the basement membranes of the glomeruli and lungs. Recovery is rare. (66)

hereditary nephritis, Alport's syndrome—familial glomerulonephritis associated with defective hearing and sight. Two forms of the disease are:

> *classic Alport's syndrome*—is inherited as an X-linked disorder with hematuria, sensorineural deafness, and conical deformation of the anterior surface of the lens (lenticonus). The lenticonus rarely occurs without nephritis. The gene responsible for the X-linked disorder has been mapped to a particular site on the X chromosome (Xq21.1–q22.1).
> *nonclassic Alport's syndrome*—inherited as an autosomal trait that causes hematuria, but not deafness or lenticonus. (44)

injuries to the kidney—uncommon pathologic lesions usually caused by athletic, occupational, and traffic accidents. They include:

> *avulsion*—separation of kidney from blood supply.
> *contusions*—simple bruising of functional tissue of kidney.
> *ecchymoses*—black and blue spots of kidney substance due to escape of blood.
> *fissures*—slits in renal capsule or pelvis; may cause hematuria.
> *hematoma*—local mass of clotted blood, which may develop especially after injury to renal pelvis.
> *lacerations*—tears may involve renal pelvis and renal capsule and result in severe hematuria.
> *rupture*—extensive tear of the kidney may be the cause of massive bleeding and death. (15, 32)

interstitial nephritis—renal disease in which the interstitial connective tissue is involved. Its acute form appears to be a reaction to systemic infection or drug sensitivity; its chronic form exhibits a diffuse interstitial fibrosis and widespread atrophy of the renal tubules. (37, 38)

neoplasms of the kidney:

> *benign tumors:*
> - *cortical adenoma*—small nodule or papillomatous growth originating in the renal tubule and embedded in the renal cortex. (14)

- *lipomas*—common soft-tissue tumors that may appear with smooth muscle, abnormal blood vessels, or alone. Renal lipomas usually arise from the areas of the renal capsule or from perirenal adipose tissue. (14)
- *renomedullary interstitial cell tumor, medullary fibroma*—most common of the benign mesenchymal tumors of the kidney. These tumors develop from medullary interstitial cells and appear as small, unencapsulated, grayish-white round nodules.

malignant tumors:

- *embryoma, nephroblastoma, Wilms' tumor*—neoplasm common in children, infrequent in adults; may form huge abdominal mass that exerts pressure on functional renal tissue and metastasizes to the lungs, liver, bones, and brain. (15)
- *mesenchymal tumors*—large malignant soft-tissue tumors that arise from areas of the renal capsule and renal pelvis. (15)
- *renal cell carcinoma, hypernephroid carcinoma, Grawitz's tumor*—tumor clinically manifested by a palpable mass, hematuria, and pain in the costovertebral region. Widespread metastases are common. (15)

nephrolithiasis, renal calculi—stones in the kidney, generally in the pelvis and calices. They may be caused by renal tubular syndromes, enzyme disorders, hypercalcemia, increased uric acid, and other factors. (14, 43, 51)

nephropathy—any disease of the kidney, such as:

acute hyperuricemia—disorder resulting from a sudden high increase of serum uric acid level prone to occur in patients receiving massive antineoplastic therapy for lymphoma or leukemia. (51)

hypercalcemia—abnormal increase in serum calcium associated with hypercalciuria, renal calculi, and pyelonephritis. In its early phase, polyuria and tubular injury are present; in its late phase, there is progressive renal insufficiency. (63)

hypercalcemia crisis—serum calcium 15 to 20 milligrams per deciliter or more; may lead to renal failure. Normal laboratory range for serum calcium is 8.5 to 10.3 milligrams per deciliter. (63)

potassium depletion—inability of kidneys to concentrate urine due to the potassium deficiency. (63)

nephroptosis—a movable, floating kidney that is displaced downward. (63)

nephrotic syndrome—clinical state characterized by massive edema, excessive loss of protein in urine, and low albumin blood levels. It may develop during the course of glomerulonephritis, a collagen disease, toxic drug reaction, or specific allergy. (38, 45, 66)

obstructive uropathy—obstruction occurring anywhere along the urinary tract, from the renal pelvis to the external urethral meatus, causing changes in renal function, volume of urine, and amount of protein and sediment in urine. Obstructive lesions include renal, ureteral, vesical, and urethral calculi, strictures, and prostatic lesions, all of which may lead to renal failure. (63)

pyelonephritis, acute—infectious inflammatory disease that involves both the parenchyma and the pelvis of the kidney. Aerobic gram-negative bacteria are the dominant causative agents. (37)

pyelonephritis, chronic—generally no symptoms of urinary infection present. (37, 43)

renal abscesses:

abscess of kidney—usually a focal suppuration of the cortex.

perinephritic abscess—infection around the kidney. (4, 37)

renal anomalies:

agenesis—absence of one kidney.

dysplasia—multicystic kidney forming an irregular mass.

ectopy—displaced kidney, usually low in position. Condition may be bilateral or unilateral and is often associated with genital anomalies in 10% to 20% of the cases.

horseshoe—kidneys are fused at the midline; usually it is the inferior poles that are fused to form a horseshoe kidney. The isthmus joins the lower poles of each kidney; each renal mass lies lower than normal. The axes of these masses are vertical, in contrast to the axes of normal kidneys, which are oblique to the spine, because they lie along the edges of the psoas muscles. (33)

renal artery occlusion—acute blockage of renal artery due to embolus, thrombus, or other cause. The kidney is deprived of its blood supply when the occlusion is complete. Renal infarction and renal failure are rare complications. (63)

renal calcinosis, nephrocalcinosis—scattered foci of calcification within functional renal tissue. (14)

renal cystic diseases:

acquired cystic disease of kidney (ACDK)—uremic, multiple cystic disease acquired by patients with end-stage renal disease or dialysis. Long periods of dialysis increase the occurrence of ACDK. Cysts vary in size but are usually small in appearance. In contrast to polycystic disease, the outline of the kidney is maintained because of small cyst size. The cysts develop in the cortex, medulla, and in the area between the cortex and medulla. Complications may include gross hematuria, tumors (adenoma or adenocarcinoma), abscess, and calculus. (38, 43)

polycystic disease of the kidney—hereditary disorder that usually occurs bilaterally. Kidneys appear enlarged and are studded with various-sized cysts. Cysts scattered throughout the parenchyma tend to compress the adjacent parenchyma, destroy it by ischemia, and occlude normal tubules. Polycystic kidney disease also may involve other organs, such as the liver and pancreas. (14, 38, 43, 66)

simple cyst of the kidney—hereditary kidney disease presenting various cystic lesions of the medulla or cortex. They may be simple, multilocular, solitary cysts, and of the dermatoid type or similar to that of the polycystic kidney, with the only difference being in degree. They may replace and compress normal renal tissue and can be associated with cystic disease of the liver and pancreas. (14, 38)

sponge kidney—papillae and calices appear enlarged, with small cystic cavities within the pyramids. Usually, small calculi occupy the cysts. The condition is asymptomatic and is discovered when the patient has a urogram. (14, 34, 38, 63)

renal failure and related disorders:

azotemia—biochemical abnormality characterized by impaired renal function, an increase of blood urea nitrogen, and creatinine associated with retention of nitrogenous wastes in the blood. When clinical manifestations are present in addition to the biochemical abnormality, *uremia* is the proper term. (38)

renal failure, acute—clinical state marked by a sudden decrease in glomerular filtration rate and cessation of renal function subsequent to severe kidney damage due to toxins, disease, or trauma. Renal tubular necrosis is a dominant characteristic. The lumen of the renal tubules is occluded by debris, usually containing protein, epithelial cells, and hemoglobin. If the initial oliguric phase is followed by a diuretic phase, the patient recovers. Residual damage is common. (18, 27)

renal failure, chronic—clinical state resulting from irreversible, slowly progressive renal disorder, such as chronic glomerulonephritis or pyelonephritis, drug toxicity, systemic disease, or urinary tract obstruction. Marked glomerular damage, as evidenced by electrolyte imbalance and retention of nitrogenous wastes, signals a fatal prognosis. (10, 27)

uremia—syndrome resulting from greatly reduced excretory function in progressive bilateral kidney disease. The failure to remove metabolic waste end products from the urine, the subsequent retention of these products in the blood and tissue compartments, and their potential cumulative action as toxins are major components in the development of morbid conditions associated with the syndrome of uremia. Clinical symptoms vary widely, from lassitude and depression in the early phase to anuria, uremic frost, and peripheral neuropathy in the terminal phase. (10, 27, 63)

renal hypertension, renovascular hypertension—high blood pressure of the kidney resulting from marked thickening of arteriolar walls or stenosis of renal artery by atheromatous plaques and thrombi. It is not known why the ischemic kidney elevates the blood pressure. (41, 47, 48)

renal medullary necrosis, renal papillary necrosis—tissue death of renal papillae and medulla, usually a complication of pyelonephritis. (41, 47, 48)

renal tuberculosis—degeneration of kidney substance due to infection with tubercle bacilli. (55, 63)

renal vein thrombosis—occlusion of the renal vein by a thrombus, which may result in an elevation of the renal pressure, excessive proteinuria, and other manifestations of the nephrotic syndrome. A complete occlusion of the renal vein may be complicated by a hemorrhagic infarction of the kidney. (22, 30, 33)

OPERATIVE TERMS

nephrectomy—excision of kidney, primarily for advanced calculous pyonephrosis, hydronephrosis, or malignant tumor. (51)

nephrolithotomy—incision into kidney for removal of stones. (51)

> *percutaneous nephrolithotomy (PNL)*—needle puncture is directed by fluoroscopy, ultrasound, or both, and is usually placed from the posterior axillary line into a posterior inferior calix (puncture site may vary depending on location of stone). Once the puncture needle has entered the renal collecting system, fluoroscopy or ultrasound is essential for continued control and guidance of tract dilatation and intrarenal instrumentation to achieve stone disintegration and extraction. PNL is usually employed for removal of large calculi (e.g., staghorn stones), especially those resistant to extracorporeal shock wave lithotripsy (ESWL). (61)

nephrolysis—surgical destruction of renal adhesions.

nephropexy—surgical fixation of a displaced kidney.

nephrorrhaphy—suture of an injured kidney.

nephrostomy—surgical creation of a renal fistula for drainage, usually leading directly into the pelvis of the kidney. (61)

nephrotomy—incision into kidney.

nephroureterectomy—removal of kidney and ureter.

pyelolithotomy—incision into renal pelvis for removal of calculi. (51)

pyeloplasty—plastic repair of renal pelvis.

pyelotomy—incision into renal pelvis.

renal biopsy:

> *open renal biopsy*—through an incision made below the tip of and parallel to the twelfth rib, the muscle and fascia are divided and a wedge of tissue is excised from the kidney for histopathologic studies.
>
> *percutaneous renal biopsy*—removal of renal tissue by a pronged biopsy needle. The procedure is usually performed under fluoroscopic control. It aids in the diagnosis and prognosis of renal disease and also serves as a guide in designating the appropriate therapy. (38, 66)

renal transplantation, kidney transplantation—a form of replacement surgery in which a healthy donor kidney is implanted in a patient after his or her irreversibly diseased kidneys have been removed. The renal homograft may be obtained from a living donor or from a cadaver of a person who met with a fatal accident. Bilateral nephrectomies are imperative in the presence of renal infection or severe hematuria, since invariably the donor transplant will develop the disease of the collateral recipient's kidney if only one kidney has been removed. After the donated homograft is placed extraperitoneally, vascular anastomoses to the iliac vessels and hypogastric artery are performed, and an opening is surgically created between a ureter and the bladder (ureteroneocystostomy). (11, 38)

surgery for renovascular hypertension—operative procedure for the restoration of normal blood flow to the kidney, including: bypass grafting for unilateral or bilateral renal artery stenosis; excision of occluded lesion of renal artery followed by end-to-end anastomosis; and renal endarterectomy or surgical removal of intimal plaques from renal artery, with or without patch grafting. (41, 47, 48)

SYMPTOMATIC TERMS

anuria—total suppression of urine due to renal failure or blockage of urinary tract. (63)

renal pain—various degrees from dull ache to severe stabbing or throbbing pain in lumbar region. (43)

uremic frost—powdery deposit of urea on the skin due to the excretion of urea through perspiration. (59)

URETERS

ORIGIN OF TERMS

hydr-, hydro- (G)—water
junction (L)—joining
pyelo- (G)—pelvis, tub
pyo- (G)—pus
-stomy (G)—surgical creation of an artificial opening
uretero- (G)—ureter, duct

PHONETIC PRONUNCIATION OF SELECTED TERMS

calculus in ureter	CAL'cue-lus in u-RE'ter
ectopic ureteral orifice	ek-TOP'ick u-RE'ter-al OR'i-fis
pyoureter	PIE-owe-u-RE'ter
ureterolithotomy	u-RE-ter-owe-lith-OT'owe-me
ureteropelvioplasty	u-RE-ter-owe-PEL've-owe-PLAS-tee

ANATOMIC TERMS (52, 64) (SEE FIG. 10.1.)

ureter—muscular, distensible tube lined with mucous membrane. It carries urine from each kidney to the bladder.

ureteric orifice—opening of the ureter at the outer, upper angle of the trigone (base) of the urinary bladder.

ureteropelvic junction—meeting point between ureter and renal pelvis.

ureterovesical junction—meeting point between ureter and urinary bladder.

DIAGNOSTIC TERMS

calculus in ureter—ureteral stone causing obstruction. (43, 51)

congenital anomalies of the ureter: (19, 28)

> *duplication of ureters*—the most common ureteral abnormality. There are two kinds:
> - *complete duplication*—both ureters enter bladder on the same side.
> - *incomplete duplication*—ureters join supravesically.
>
> *ectopic ureteral orifice*—displaced opening, a developmental defect seen more frequently in women than men. It may result in incontinence.

incomplete ureter—embryonic development ceased before ureter reached kidney. Kidney may be absent or multicystic.

stricture of ureter—abnormal narrowing of the duct, usually occurring at the ureteropelvic junction or at ureterovesical orifice. It may be complicated by ureteral dilatation.

ureteral atresia—absence of ureter or ureter ending blindly after extending only part of the way to the flank.

ureterocele—cystic protrusion or ballooning sacculation of the lower end of the ureter into the bladder. It may be intravesical or ectopic. Usually, intravesical ureteroceles are involved with single ureters, and ectopic ureteroceles are involved with duplicated ureters.

hydroureter—ureter overdistended with urine due to obstruction.

injuries to ureter—uncommon pathologic states that may be due to external trauma (e.g., a penetrating bullet wound), or be associated with pelvic fractures, or occur inadvertently during surgery. (14, 32)

obstruction of ureter—blocking of ureter, usually resulting from pressure. It interferes with passage of urine. (19, 28)

occlusion of ureter—complete or partial closure of ureter.

pyoureter—an accumulation of pus in a ureter, generally secondary to infection of the bladder or kidney.

ureteritis—inflammation of the ureter.

OPERATIVE TERMS (SEE TABLE 10.1.)

ureteral resection—local excision of benign ureteral lesion. (69)

ureterectomy—partial or complete removal of ureter.

ureterocystostomy, ureteroneocystostomy—reimplantation of ureter into bladder. (69)

ureterolithotomy—incision into ureter for removal of calculi.

ureterolysis—freeing the ureter from adhesions to relieve secondary obstruction. (69)

ureteropelvioplasty—plastic operation at the ureteropelvic junction.

ureteropyelostomy—anastomosis of ureter and renal pelvis.

ureterostomy, cutaneous—transplantation of ureter to skin.

ureteroureterostomy—operation of joining portions of the same ureter. The urine is diverted by a linear ureterotomy. An oblique oval anastomosis is developed to ensure that healing occurs at different planes and that strictures do not occur. This procedure is performed in cases where the ureter has been severed, either deliberately or accidentally. (69)

ureterovesicoplasty—corrective surgery for persistent reflux by repair of the ureterovesical junction.

SYMPTOMATIC TERMS

ureteral colic—excruciating, stabbing pain usually caused by the passage of a stone or large clot into the ureter. (43)

ureteral spasm—contraction of ureter, frequently resulting from painful overdistention of ureter by a stone. (69)

BLADDER AND URETHRA

ORIGIN OF TERMS

bulb (L)—enlargement or rounded mass
cysto- (G)—bladder, sac
meatus (L)—passageway, opening

trigone (G)—triangular area
urethro- (G)—urethra
vesico- (L)—bladder

TABLE 10.1	Some Urologic Conditions Amenable to Surgery		
Anatomic Site	*Diagnosis*	*Type of Surgery*	*Operative Procedures*
Kidney	Nephroptosis	Nephropexy	Fixation or suspension of movable or displaced kidney
Kidneys	Chronic glomerulonephritis, preterminal Irreversible renal failure	Renal homotransplantation, including: bilateral nephrectomy, revascularization of homograft, ureterocystostomy	Removal of both kidneys Extraperitoneal donor homografting with vascular anastomoses to iliac and hypogastric vessels Creation of opening between ureter and bladder
Kidney	Posttraumatic fistula of kidney	Nephrorrhaphy	Suture of kidney
Ureter	Calculus in ureter associated with renal obstruction	Ureterolithotomy	Incision into ureter with removal of calculus
Renal pelvis	Calculus in renal pelvis, small	Pyelolithotomy	Removal of calculus from renal pelvis
Bladder	Diverticulum of bladder	Diverticulectomy of urinary bladder	Local excision of diverticulum
Bladder	Hemorrhage from urinary bladder	Cystoscopy with evacuation of blood clots	Endoscopic examination of the bladder with removal of blood clots

PHONETIC PRONUNCIATION OF SELECTED TERMS

cystectomy	sis-TECK′toe-me
cystolithotomy	SIS-toe-lith-OT′owe-me
cystostomy	sis-TOS′toe-me
panendoscopy	PAN-en-DOS′ko-pe
trabeculation, vesical	tra-BECK-u-LAY′shun, VES′i-kal
ureteroileostomy	u-RE-ter-owe-ILL-e-OS′toe-me
vesicoureteral reflux	VES-i-ko-u-RE′ter-al RE′fluks

ANATOMIC TERMS (52, 64) (SEE FIG. 10.3.)

bladder, urinary—a hollow, muscular, distensible organ. It serves as a temporary reservoir for urine. It is located within the pelvic cavity, behind the symphysis pubis, and beneath the parietal peritoneum. In a male, it lies against the rectum posteriorly, and in a female, it contacts the anterior walls of the uterus and vagina.

bulbourethral glands, Cowper's glands—these two glands are located posterolateral to the membranous urethra. The glands are above the bulb of the penis within the fibers of the sphincter urethra muscle. The ducts of these glands open into the ventral wall of the proximal part of the spongy urethra. These glands secrete a viscous fluid into the male urethra at times of sexual excitement.

detrusor urinae muscle—muscular network with bundles of muscle fibers running in various directions, intermingling, and decussating. Their contraction effects the expulsion of urine from the bladder.

neck of bladder—lowest angle of bladder.

TABLE 10.1	(continued)		
Anatomic Site	**Diagnosis**	**Type of Surgery**	**Operative Procedures**
Bladder	Early carcinoma of urinary bladder, no metastasis	Partial cystectomy with excision of tumor	Removal of bladder wall, including the carcinoma and surrounding cuff of normal bladder wall
Bladder	Papilloma encroaching on ureteral orifice	Suprapubic cystostomy with excision of tumor	Surgical opening of the bladder above the symphysis pubis and removal of tumor
		Ureterocystostomy	Anastomosis of ureter to bladder and reimplantation of ureter into bladder
Bladder	Rupture of bladder due to injury	Cystorrhaphy	Suture of bladder
Bladder Ureters	Neurogenic bladder with vesical calculi and recurrent pyelonephritis	Ureteroileostomy (Ileal conduit)	Transplantation of both ureters to isolated segment of ileum for conveying urine to external stoma
Bladder Ureters Urethra	Carcinoma of bladder	Cystectomy Colocystoplasty (neobladder or sigmoid bladder)	Excision of urinary bladder Creation of new bladder by isolating sigmoid segment and implanting ureters and urethra in segment

trigone—triangular internal surface of the posterior wall of the bladder. The vesical trigone is bounded by the openings of the ureters at its posterolateral angles and by the urethral aperature at its inferior (anterior) angle.

ureterovesical junction—meeting point between ureter and urinary bladder. The ureterovesical junction allows urine to enter the bladder but prevents urine from regurgitating into the ureter.

urethra—fibromuscular tube between the urinary bladder and external urethral orifice.

female urethra—passageway for urine that empties through the urethral orifice into the vestibule between the labia minora. The urethral orifice is positioned anterior to the vaginal orifice and is about 2.5 centimeters posterior to the clitoris.

male urethra—passageway for urine and seminal fluid. The male urethra is about 20 centimeters long and S-shaped because of the shape of the penis. It is composed of:
- *membranous portion*—passes through the pelvic and urogenital diaphragms.
- *prostatic portion*—passes through prostate.
- *spongy portion*—passes through the penis.

urethral glands of Littre—mucus-producing glands that are most dense on the dorsal surface of the spongy urethra.

vesical sphincter—thickened detrusor muscle fibers that surround the bladder neck.

vesicouterine—peritoneum extending between the bladder and the uterus.

Figure 10.3 Urinary bladder and urethra. (a) The urethra of a male transports both urine and seminal fluid. It consists of prostatic, membranous, and spongy portions. The prostatic portion is surrounded by the prostate. (b) The urethra of a female is considerably shorter and transports only urine.

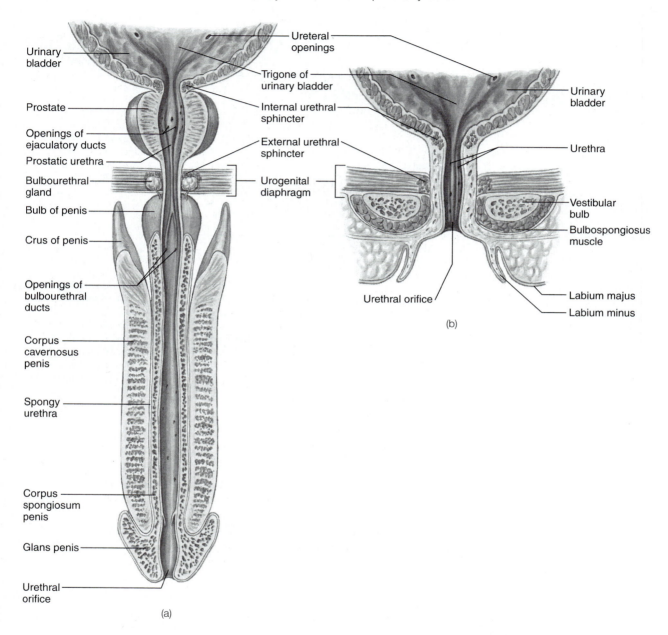

DIAGNOSTIC TERMS

atony of bladder—enormous distention of bladder associated with reduced expulsive force. It occurs in some diseases of the central nervous system. (63)

bladder neck obstruction—blockage of the lumen of the bladder outlet, resulting in overdistention of the urinary bladder, frequency, dysuria, persistent pyuria, retention with overflow and urinary backflow, dilatation of the ureters, renal pain, and stone formation. The obstruction may be due to:

> *contracture of vesical outlet, congenital or acquired*—form of urethral stricture. The bladder neck may be narrowed by hypertrophic muscle, fibrous tissue, or chronic inflammatory disease. (14, 53)
>
> *obstructive lesions of vesical outlet*—blood clots, calculi, diverticula, and tumors, especially prostatic enlargement. (14, 53)

calculus (pl. calculi) of bladder—bladder stone.

cystitis, acute or chronic—inflammation of bladder due to infection. (37, 43, 55)

exstrophy of bladder—congenital absence of the lower abdominal and anterior vesical walls with eversion of the bladder; absence of closure or formation of the anterior half of the bladder. It is often associated with epispadias. (14, 58)

hypospadias—congenital abnormality resulting in a defect in the ventral wall of the spongy urethra, so that it is open for a greater or lesser distance. The glandular and penile types of hypospadias occur due to failure of fusion of the urogenital fold. In the glandular type, the prepuce is usually deformed, and its frenulum may be absent. Scrotal hypospadias occurs from failure of the labioscrotal swellings to fuse. (14, 34)

injuries to:

> *urinary bladder*—direct trauma to the distended bladder may cause vesical compression or rupture. A bony spicule of a fractured bone may pierce the bladder, blood and urine will spill into the peritoneal cavity, and a hematoma may form. Accidental perforation of the bladder may occur during surgery.
>
> *urethra, bulb of spongy urethra*—injury to these sites may be more serious than to the bladder, including contusions, lacerations, and rupture associated with extravasation of urine and blood and formation of hematoma. Shearing injuries or straddle injuries may be complicated by urethral stricture. (14, 32)

interstitial cystitis, submucous fibrosis of bladder, Hunner's ulcer—bladder disorder predominantly seen in middle-aged women. Fibrosis of the vesical wall reduces the bladder capacity, which is clinically manifested by frequency, nocturia, distention of the bladder, and suprapubic tenderness or pain. (58)

megalocystis, megabladder—enormous dilatation of urinary bladder.

neoplasms: (43)

> *benign*—papilloma, polyp, and others.
>
> *malignant*—transitional cell carcinoma, epidermoid carcinoma, and others. The diagnosis is usually confirmed by cystoscopy.

neurogenic bladder—when sensory pathways are interrupted between sacral spinal neurons and cortical centers, there may be a loss of sensation of bladder fullness. If the sphincters are functioning, overflow incontinence occurs when bladder pressure exceeds pressure generated by sphincter contraction. Other conditions that may occur include:

> *dyssynergia*—outflow obstruction occurs when the detrusor contraction fails to inhibit sphincter contraction. This condition is seen in spinal cord and bilateral cortical lesions. This type of simultaneous contraction of the detrusor and sphincters gives rise to incomplete emptying and reflux. If untreated, hydroureter with renal damage may occur. (56)

flaccid atonic type—condition caused by lower motor neuron lesion due to trauma, ruptured intervertebral disk, meningomyelocele, or by peripheral neuropathy of diabetes or alcoholism, or the result of pelvic surgery, or other disorders and resulting in vesical dysfunction. The bladder has a large capacity, low intravesical pressure, and a mild degree of trabeculation (hypertrophy) of the bladder wall. Sphincter weakness may be caused by damage to pudendal nerves or sacral roots, or by trauma to the sphincter during childbirth or with perineal injuries.

spastic automatic type—condition caused by upper motor neuron lesion due to injury, multiple sclerosis, or other factors. Bladder capacity is reduced, the intravesical pressure is high, and there is marked hypertrophy of the bladder wall and spasticity of the urinary sphincter. (60)

prolapse of bladder—downward displacement of the bladder. (59)

stress incontinence—inability to retain urine under any tension and when sneezing, coughing, or laughing. (9, 57, 58)

stricture of urethra—narrowing of lumen of urethra due to infection or trauma, or prior instrumentation. (14, 34, 59)

stricture of vesicourethral orifice—narrowing of the opening between the bladder and urethra. (14)

syphilis of bladder and urethra—venereal infection due to *Treponema pallidum*. (63)

***Trichomonas* infection**—parasitic infection that may occur in the bladder and male urethra. (14, 63)

trigonitis—inflammation of the trigone, the triangular base of the bladder.

urethritis, acute or chronic—inflammation of urethra, which may be due to gonococcic infection. (59)

vesical fistulas—pathologic openings of bladder leading to adjacent organs.

vesicoenteric fistula—sinus tract between bladder and intestine.

vesicorectal fistula—fistulous connection between bladder and rectum.

vesicovaginal fistula—pathologic opening between bladder and vagina. (54, 58, 59)

vesicoureteral reflux (primary)—occurs from developmental ureterotrigonal weakness. Primary reflux is the most common type and is associated with some degree of congenital muscular deficiency in the trigone and terminal ureter. The severity of reflux is proportionate to the degree of this muscular deficiency. (54)

OPERATIVE TERMS (SEE TABLE 10.1.)

cold-punch transurethral resection of the vesical neck—endoscopic procedure for relief of bladder neck obstruction using a cold-punch resectoscope for transurethral resection of tumor tissue, calcareous deposit, or cicatrix. The Kaplan resectoscope permits fiberoptic illumination, magnification and sharp visualization of surgical area, free flow of irrigation fluid, and controlled movement of the knife.

cystectomy—excision of bladder.

partial—resection of bladder.

radical—removal of anterior pelvic organs. In men, this usually includes removal of the bladder with its surrounding fat, and peritoneal attachments, the prostate, and the seminal vesicles. In women, this procedure usually includes the bladder, and surrounding fat and peritoneal attachments, cervix, uterus, anterior vaginal vault, urethra, and ovaries. (12, 21)

cystolithotomy—incision into the bladder for removal of stones.

cystoplasty—surgical repair of the bladder.

cystorrhaphy—suture of a ruptured or lacerated bladder.

cystoscopy—endoscopic examination of the bladder. (49)

cystostomy—surgical creation of a cutaneous bladder fistula for urinary drainage.

meatotomy—incision of urinary meatus to increase its caliber.

suprapubic vesicourethral suspension, Marshall-Marchetti repair—elevation and immobilization of the bladder neck and urethra by suturing them to the pubis and rectus muscles for the establishment of urinary control. (58)

transurethral resection of the bladder neck—endoscopic resection of the bladder neck for removal of inelastic tissue using the transurethral approach. (43)

urethroscopy, panendoscopy—endoscopic examination of the male urethra or distal female urethra using a special panendoscope. (49, 51)

urinary diversion operations for incapacitated bladder:

ileal conduit, ureteroileostomy—transplantation of both ureters to an isolated segment of the ileum. The urine drains through an external ileal stoma into a bag glued to the skin. Candidates for an elective ileal conduit may be children with bladder exstrophy and incontinence, adults with neurogenic bladders caused by injury or neurologic disease, or victims of a vesical carcinoma. In malignancy and persistent bladder infection a cystectomy is done with an ileal conduit. (12)

sigmoid bladder, neobladder, colocystoplasty—replacement of bladder by creating a substitute bladder. A sigmoid segment is isolated, and the ureters and urethra are implanted in the segment. The cecum may also be used for urinary diversion. (13, 62)

SYMPTOMATIC TERMS

albuminuria, proteinuria—albumin or protein in urine.

dysuria—difficult or painful urination. (31, 43)

enuresis—incontinence or involuntary discharge of urine when asleep at night. (31, 58)

frequency of urination—voiding at close intervals, more often than every 2 hours. This is normal in infancy. (31, 41)

glycosuria—sugar in urine. (66)

hematuria—blood in urine. (66)

hesitancy—dysuria due to nervous inhibition or obstruction of the vesical outlet. (31, 43)

micturition—urination. (60)

nocturia—frequent voiding during the night; may be due to renal inability to concentrate urine. (31, 43)

obstruction in bladder or urethra—blockage causing backflow of urine and renal damage. (54)

oliguria—scanty urinary output due to acute tubular necrosis, fluid and electrolyte imbalance, organic kidney lesions, obstructive uropathy, and other causes. Oliguria is present when the daily urine volume is not sufficient to remove the endogenous solute loads that are the end products of metabolism. (1, 31)

orthostatic proteinuria, benign postural proteinuria—protein in urine when in upright position; no proteinuria during recumbency. (66)

overflow incontinence—involuntary urination caused by overdistention of bladder. (31, 60)

polyuria—excessive urinary output. (31)

pyuria—pus in the urine. (31)

residual urine—inability to empty bladder at micturition, resulting in urinary retention and vesical overdistention. (60)

spinal shock—sequela of transverse injury to cord. It may cause autonomous bladder paralysis and later automatic voiding. (60)

suprapubic discomfort—uncomfortable sensation that may be due to interstitial cystitis, ulceration of the vesical mucosa, or other disorders. It is usually present when the bladder fills and disappears when the bladder empties. (63)

tenesmus of vesical sphincter—painful spasm at the end of micturition. (63)

trabeculation, vesical—hypertrophy involving all muscle layers of the bladder. It may occur in benign prostatic hypertrophy. (54)

ureteral pain—usually acute, colicky pain radiating from renal pelvis to groin; may be due to a stone pressing against the ureteral wall. (31, 37)

urethral discharge—clear, thin, mucoid or purulent, scanty or profuse excretion from the urethra. (31, 43)

urgency—intense need to urinate. (31, 43)

urinary retention—inability to expel urine. This may be acute or chronic, complete or incomplete. It is frequently caused by obstruction of urinary outflow due to a stone, stricture, tumor, and similar blocks. (31)

SPECIAL PROCEDURES AND TESTS

TERMS RELATED TO NONSURGICAL PROCEDURES

fine-needle aspiration cytology—specimen is obtained via suction through a small-bore (21-, 22-, or 23-gauge) needle. Computed technology scanning, fluoroscopic studies, or ultrasonic techniques enhance the visualization and localization of lesions. The cytologic specimen is placed on slides and stained by either the Romanowsky method (usually the May-Grünwald-Giemsa stain) or the Papanicolaou (Pap) method. The procedure aids the physician in planning further therapy or diagnostic studies. (63)

percutaneous extraction of renal calculi, nephrolithotripsy—under fluoroscopic control or under direct vision with a nephroscope, a nephrostomy tract can be established, and subsequently dilatated to allow for stone manipulation and removal. When the lithotripsy probe comes in direct contact with the stone, electrical or sonic energy is transmitted through the probe to break up the stone. Small stones can be removed via the nephroscope and larger stones by means of a stone basket or forceps. Another disintegrative method applicable to kidney stone is:

> *extracorporeal shock wave lithotripsy (ESWL)*—pulverizes kidney stones by bombarding them with shock waves, which are produced outside the body, focused at the kidney stones, and transmitted by body tissues. Patients are immersed in water, since water serves as the medium through which the shock waves are transmitted by body tissues. Shock waves produce a selective disintegrative effect on kidney stones because of their high acoustical impedance compared to the brittle makeup of surrounding tissues. Periodic fluoroscopic monitoring of the treatment ensures that the stone is still in the shock wave's focal point. As the treatment progresses, video monitors may be employed to display the gradual pulverization of the kidney stone. (14, 51, 50, 61)

transcatheter embolization—therapeutic introduction of an inert embolic or sclerosing substance into a vessel to occlude it. Superselective engagement of branch vessels or use of an occlusive balloon catheter assists in preventing occurrence of inadvertent embolization of the distant organs. Occlusion of the vascular supply of the kidney makes possible early ligation of the renal vein. This ligation may prevent dissemination of tumor cells when the kidney and the tumor are subsequently mobilized. Transcatheter embolization with radioactive particles can create an interstitial infarct implant capable of delivering high doses of radiation to a tumor. This procedure can be used for reducing tumor size and thus making the inoperable tumor operable. (20, 29)

transluminal angioplasty—an intraluminal balloon catheter is used to dilate the stenotic area of the artery. After the lesion is located and evaluated by either angiography or digital subtraction angiography, the balloon catheter is advanced to the lesion by the Seldinger technique. A guide wire is advanced into the distal branches of the renal artery to ensure that the balloon remains in stable position. The balloon is then placed across the lesion and inflation is begun. To prevent thrombosis, the patient's blood should be heparinized.

Thereafter, aspirin may be given as an anticoagulant for a prolonged period of time. Transluminal angioplasty is quite effective in the treatment of lesions resulting from fibromuscular hyperplasia and arteriosclerotic lesions of the renal arteries causing hypertension. (20, 29)

TERMS RELATED TO DIALYSIS STUDIES

dialysis—the passage of solutes back and forth across a semipermeable membrane placed between two solutions. Each solute moves toward the fluid in which its concentration is lower. Dialysis is used in acute renal failure to remove urea from the body and terminate electrolyte imbalance. (2, 26, 63)

hemodialysis—employs the process of diffusion across a semipermeable membrane to remove unwanted substances from the blood while adding desirable components. Hemodialysis is a life-sustaining procedure in irreversible renal failure, since it removes excess water and the end products of protein metabolism and corrects acidosis as well as electrolyte imbalance.

> *continuous arteriovenous hemodialysis (CAVHD)*—technique that employs high-efficiency dialyzers with cardiac-generated blood flow (via a cannulated femoral artery) along with very slow dialysate flow rates. CAVHD is a useful therapy in the unstable, acute renal failure patient.

> *intermittent hemodialysis*—circulation established outside the body with the renal dialyzer 1 to 3 times a week, depending on the patient's residual kidney function. An arteriovenous fistula is surgically created, or an artery and vein are cannulated, permitting the repetitive use of hemodialysis. The blood of the patient who is connected to the renal dialyzer passes into a coil of semipermeable membrane immersed in a bath of rinsing fluid. This membrane substitutes for the glomerular membrane. The concentration of solutes in the blood differs from that in the bath to promote a solute transfer through the semipermeable membrane, which restores the electrolyte balance. After the solute exchange is completed, the blood reenters the patient's vein. (2, 17, 63)

peritoneal dialysis—perfusion of the peritoneum using commercially prepared electrolyte solutions, special catheters, and a closed system of infusion and drainage in the treatment of renal failure. The peritoneum functions basically as an inert semipermeable membrane, permitting the exchange of solutes in both directions. Two other types of peritoneal dialysis include continuous ambulatory peritoneal dialysis (CAPD) or continuous cyclic peritoneal dialysis (CCPD). (2, 17, 26, 63)

TERMS RELATED TO RENAL FUNCTION STUDIES

blood urea nitrogen (BUN)—renal function test that measures the concentration of urea in the blood. In health, the blood levels are low, since urea, an end product of protein metabolism, is freely excreted in the urine. In renal impairment and failure, urea nitrogen accumulates in the blood, and the patient may lapse into coma. (8, 63, 67)

> *Reference values:* (16)
> - *BUN*—8 to 18 mg of urea nitrogen per 100 mL of blood.
>   **Increase** in nephritis, urinary obstruction, and uremia. (63)
>   **Decrease** in amyloidosis, nephrosis, and pregnancy. (63)

concentration and dilution test—measures the functional capacity of the kidney to concentrate and dilute urine. Failure to concentrate urine indicates kidney damage. It may be partially caused by a faulty mechanism of the antidiuretic hormone (ADH) released from the pituitary gland. (8)

> *Reference values:* (16)
> *creatinine*, urine, 24 hr
> - *Males*—14–26 mg/kg/d (SIU: 124–230 μmol/kg/d)
> - *Females*—11–20 mg/kg/d (SIU: 97–177 μmol/kg/d)

endogenous creatinine clearance—renal function test that measures the removal of creatinine from plasma, as reflected by the glomerular filtration rate (GFR). (8, 63, 67)

Howard test; excretion of water, salt, and creatinine—renal function study to detect ischemia of the kidney caused by stenosis of the renal artery or its branch or by chronic pyelonephritis with arteriolar involvement. A low urine volume and a low-sodium and high-creatinine concentration are positive findings and indicate that the patient may benefit by renovascular surgery. (63)

phenolsulfonphthalein (PSP)—dye test for detection of kidney impairment. About 90% of the PSP is eliminated through the renal tubules and only 10% through glomerular infiltration. (63)

> *Reference values:* (16)
> - *PSP first hour*—40%–50%
> - *PSP second hour*—20%–25%

Note: A low urinary excretion of the dye of 40% or less in 2 hours is usually associated with nitrogen retention in the blood. Elimination of the dye is delayed in hypertrophy of the prostate gland complicated by hydronephrosis, malignant hypertension, and cystitis with urinary retention. (63)

plasma renin activity (PRA)—bioassay method of Gunnels measuring the enzyme activity of renin to screen patients for renovascular hypertension or malignant hypertension. (47)

renin—enzyme originating in the glomerulus. Renin levels rise with lowered perfusion pressure and lowered delivery of water and sodium to the glomerulus. High levels of renin formed by the diseased kidney may lead to renal hypertension and primary aldosteronism. (47)

urea clearance—test measures the glomerular function of the kidney to remove urea from the blood. It is calculated as plasma cleared of urea in one minute. Measurements of urea and creatinine concentrations in serum are often used to assess the glomerular filtration rate (GFR). (8)

TERMS RELATED TO BLADDER STUDIES

cystometrogram—graphic record of pressure reactions while the patient's bladder is being filled with water. Bladder capacity, residual urine, and sensory responses are checked. (56, 63)

cystometry—measurement of intravesical pressure during filling of the urinary bladder with fluid. (60, 63)

TERMS RELATED TO URINE FINDINGS

urinalysis—examination of physical and chemical properties of urine. Physical properties comprise quantity, color, specific gravity, odor, and other qualities. Chemical properties are concerned with quantitative or qualitative tests dealing with protein, glucose, bile pigments, ketone bodies, blood, calculi, and similar substances. In conditions of the urinary system, albumin and casts are frequently present, and the pH concentration is altered. (8, 38, 43, 63)

> *albumin, protein*—abnormal constituent of urine in renal and febrile diseases and toxemias of pregnancy. It is caused by increased permeability of the glomerular filter.
>
> *Bence Jones protein*—peculiar type of protein molecule that is excreted in the urine in the majority of cases of multiple myeloma (plasma cell myeloma), amyloidosis, and certain bone tumors.
>
> *calcium in urine (and feces)*—these tests are concerned with the calcium balance in the body. In health the calcium intake exceeds the calcium excretion in urine and feces.
>
> *casts*—cells abnormally formed in the renal tubules and shed in the urine as hyaline, granular, epithelial, blood, and pus casts.
>
> *hydrogen ion concentration (chemical symbol: pH)*—the reaction of the urine.
> - *pH concentration of 7*—normal neutrality.
> - *pH concentration less than 7*—acid in reaction.
> - *pH concentration greater than 7*—alkaline in reaction.
>   In acidosis, the urine is strongly acid; in chronic cystitis and in urinary retention, the urine is usually alkaline in reaction.

porphyrins (coproporphyrin, uroporphyrin, porphobilinogen)—pigments resembling bilirubin and apparently derived from the hemoglobin of the blood. Minute amounts of porphyrins are normally present in the urine. An increase is abnormal.

coproporphyrin urinary excretion—a valuable test in the detection of lead poisoning, acute porphyria, pellagra, and liver damage.

uroporphyrin urinary excretion—diagnostic aid in acute porphyria and acute intermittent porphyria.

Sulkowitch test—approximate estimate of amount of calcium in urine. Calcium excretion is increased in hypercalciuria, hyperthyroidism, and urinary calcium calculi. Calcium excretion is decreased in hypocalciuria and hypoparathyroidism. (63)

urinary calculi—stones found in the pelvis of the kidney, ureter, and bladder in the forms of:

crystine stones—white or pale yellow granules.

oxalate stones (calcium oxalate)—crystalline structure.

phosphate and carbonate stones—compact balls.

uric acid stones—smooth, round pebbles. (43)

TERMS RELATED TO PROPRIETARY URINE TESTS (24, 63)

Clinistix, Clinitest—reagent strip or tablet for testing glucose in urine.

Combistix—three separate reagent areas: pH, protein, and glucose in urine, providing information on acid-base balance, renal function, and carbohydrate metabolism.

Keto-Diastix—reagent strip for detecting glucose and ketones in urine.

Ketostix—reagent strip for checking ketones in urine, serum, and plasma.

MALE GENITAL ORGANS

ORIGIN OF TERMS

balano- (G)—glans
deferens (L)—carrying away
didymos (G)—testis, twin
gono- (G)—offspring, seed
oligo- (G)—little, scanty

orchido- (G)—testis (pl. testes)
scrotum (L)—bag
semen (L)—seed
spermato-, spermo- (G)—seed, male generative element
vaso- (L)—vessel, duct

PHONETIC PRONUNCIATION OF SELECTED TERMS

anorchism — an-OR′kizm
balanitis — BAL-a-NI′tis
epididymectomy — EP-i-DID-i-MECK′toe-me
hydrocele — HI′dro-seal
orchidectomy — OR-ki-DECK′toe-me
phimosis — fi-MOW′sis
prostatectomy — PROS-ta-TECK′toe-me
syphilis — SIF′i-lis

ANATOMIC TERMS (52, 65) (SEE FIG. 10.4.)

penis—highly vascular organ containing three erectile tissue components. The distal end is the glans penis, over which is folded the prepuce, or foreskin. The penis serves as the outlet for urine stored in the bladder (urination). During sexual intercourse its role is to deposit seminal fluid or semen in the vagina of the female (ejaculation).

prostate gland—organ composed of smooth muscle and fibrous and glandular tissue and divided into two lateral lobes and one medial lobe. An extension of the urinary bladder, the prostate is connected to the prostatic urethra and ejaculatory ducts. Its secretion, a type of milky alkaline fluid, is part of the seminal fluid.

Figure 10.4 Male reproductive organs: (a) sagittal view, (b) posterior view.

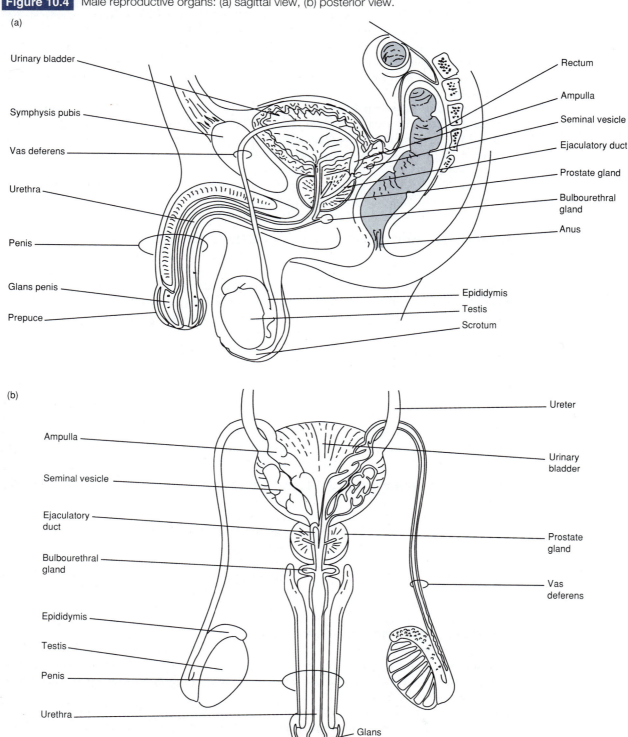

(a)

Urinary bladder

Symphysis pubis

Vas deferens

Urethra

Penis

Glans penis

Prepuce

Rectum

Ampulla

Seminal vesicle

Ejaculatory duct

Prostate gland

Bulbourethral gland

Anus

Epididymis

Testis

Scrotum

(b)

Ampulla

Seminal vesicle

Ejaculatory duct

Bulbourethral gland

Epididymis

Testis

Penis

Urethra

Ureter

Urinary bladder

Prostate gland

Vas deferens

Glans penis

scrotum—sac of loose, redundant skin containing testes and epididymides.

seminal vesicles—small, convoluted blind pouches about 5 centimeters long that secrete an alkaline constituent of the seminal fluid. They lie against the fundus of the bladder, diverging like the limbs of the figure V. Above the base of the prostate, each vesicle is constricted to form a short duct that joins the lateral side of the narrowed vas deferens at an acute angle. The common duct formed by this union is the ejaculatory duct.

testes (sing. **testis**)—paired male reproductive glands lying in the scrotum and divided into lobules by septa that are inward extensions of the outer covering. The lobules contain threadlike coils, the *seminiferous tubules*. The testes produce *spermatozoa*, a minute part of the seminal fluid, and androgen, the male hormone responsible for the secondary sex characteristics. Three ducts share in the transport of spermatozoa on each side:

> *epididymis* (pl. *epididymides*)—structure lying on top and at the side of the testis and composed of head, body, and tail. It stores spermatozoa before they are emitted. The greatly coiled duct of the epididymis, about 6 meters in length, merges into the vas deferens.
>
> *vas deferens, ductus deferens*—duct conveying spermatozoa from the epididymis to the ejaculatory duct.
>
> *ejaculatory duct*—duct formed by union of the vas deferens with the duct of the seminal vesicle. Its fluid is carried into the urethra.

tunica vaginalis testis—double-layered serous sheath partially covering the testis and epididymis. An abnormal collection of serum between the layers is known as *hydrocele*.

DIAGNOSTIC TERMS

actinomycosis—fungus disease that may affect the genital organs. (63)

adenocarcinoma of prostate—malignant tumor of glandular epithelium. It most commonly involves the prostate, less commonly the other genital organs. Metastases to bone occur frequently. Knowledge of the stage and grade of adenocarcinoma of the prostate may be helpful in treating this disease. Prostatic cancer is the most common cancer in men, with increasing incidence in older age groups. (See table 10.2.) (14, 39, 63)

anorchism—absence of testes. (35)

balanitis—inflammation of the glans penis.

chordee of penis—painful downward curvature of the penis as a result of a congenital anomaly (hypospadias) or urethral infection (gonorrhea). (34)

cryptorchism—improperly descended testis; descent arrested. (35)

ectopy of testis—testis outside the path of normal descent. (35)

epididymitis—inflammation of the epididymis. (14, 37)

hydrocele:

> *spermatic cord*—collection of fluid along the spermatic cord, usually within the inguinal canal. (35)
>
> *tunica vaginalis*—collection of fluid within the tunica of the testis. (35)

hypertrophy of prostate, benign—diffuse enlargement of the prostate, frequently seen in elderly men. The gland interferes with micturition and eventually results in hydronephrosis and dilatation of ureters. (39, 43)

orchitis—inflammation of the testes. (33)

paraphimosis—foreskin retracted behind the glans, with subsequent edema preventing restoration to normal position. (12)

phimosis—stenosis of the orifice of the prepuce or foreskin. It may be congenital or due to infection. The opening may be pinpoint or absent. (14, 31)

polyorchism, polyorchidism—more than two testes present.

prostatitis—inflammation of the prostate gland. (14, 33)

syphilis—venereal disease due to *Treponema pallidum*. Involvement of genital organs is common.

TABLE 10.2	TNM Classification for Carcinomas of the Prostate

Definition of TNM

Primary tumor (T)

TX Primary tumor cannot be assessed
TO No evidence of primary tumor
T1 Clinically inapparent tumor not palpable or visible by imaging
    T1a Tumor incidental histologic finding in 5% or less of tissue resected
    T1b Tumor incidental histologic finding in more than 5% of tissue resected
    T1c Tumor identified by needle biopsy (e.g., because of elevated PSA)
T2 Tumor confined within the prostate*
    T2a Tumor involves half of a lobe or less
    T2b Tumor involves more than half of a lobe, but not both lobes
    T2c Tumor involves both lobes
T3 Tumor extends through the prostatic capsule**
    T3a Unilateral extracapsular extension
    T3b Bilateral extracapsular extension
    T3c Tumor invades the seminal vesicle(s)
T4 Tumor is fixed or invades adjacent structures other than the seminal vesicles
    T4a Tumor invades any of: bladder neck, external sphincter, or rectum
    T4b Tumor invades levator muscles and/or is fixed to the pelvic wall

Regional lymph nodes (N)

NX Reginal lymph nodes cannot be assessed
NO No regional lymph node metastasis
N1 Metastasis in a single lymph node, 2 centimeters (cm) or less in greatest dimension
N2 Metastasis in a single lymph node, more than 2 cm but not more than 5 cm in greatest dimension;
    or multiple lymph node metastases, none more than 5 cm in greatest dimension
N3 Metastasis in a lymph node more than 5 cm in greatest dimension

Distant metastasis* (M)**

MX Presence of distant metastasis cannot be assessed
MO No distant metastasis
M1 Distant metastasis
    M1a Nonregional lymph node(s)
    MIb Bone(s)
    M1c other site(s)

Source: American Joint Committee on Cancer, *Manual for Staging of Cancer*, 4th ed. Philadelphia: J.B. Lippincott Co., 1992, p. 182. Reprinted with permission.

*Tumor found in one or both lobes by needle biopsy, but not palpable or visible by imaging, is classified as T1c.

**Invasion into the prostatic apex or into (but not beyond) the prostatic capsule is not classified as T3, but as T2.

***When more than one site of metastasis is present, the most advanced category (pM1c) is used.

testicular tumors—usually malignant neoplasms seen in young adults 18 to 35 years of age, less frequently in children, and rarely in other age groups. They include:
    choriocarcinoma—malignant tumor secreting chorionic gonadotropin. (14, 36, 42)
    embryonal carcinoma—aggressive, lethal, testicular neoplasm that is highly invasive and readily spreads to lymph nodes and internal organs. (36, 42)
    seminoma—common testicular germ cell tumor. (14, 36, 42)
    teratocarcinoma—malignant testicular tumor composed of various poorly differentiated tissues. (36, 42)
    teratoma, differentiated—benign cystic dermoid containing multiple tissues, including hair and teeth. (14, 42)

	TABLE 10.3	Some Conditions of the Male Reproductive Organs Amenable to Surgery		
Anatomic Site	*Diagnosis*	*Type of Surgery*	*Operative Procedures*
Prostate	Hypertrophy of prostate	Transurethral resection of prostate; cryosurgery of prostate	Partial removal of prostate using special endoscope and electrocautery or localized freezing of prostate
Prostate Seminal vesicles Vas deferens	Carcinoma of prostate	Retropubic prostatectomy Radical perineal prostatectomy	Radical extravesical removal of prostate Removal of prostate, seminal vesicles, and vas deferens through perineal incision
Testis	Undescended testis, unilateral	Orchiopexy Orchioplasty	Surgical fixation in the scrotum of undescended testis Plastic surgery of testis
Testes	Advanced carcinoma of the prostate gland with bone metastases	Orchiectomy, bilateral (castration for androgen control)	Removal of both testes

tuberculosis—systemic, contagious disease caused by tubercle bacilli. Involvement of genital organs is infrequent. (63)
varicocele—swelling and distention of veins of spermatic cord. (35)
vasovesiculitis—inflammation of the vas deferens and seminal vesicles.
(See chapter 16 for terms pertaining to infections caused by sexually transmitted diseases.)

OPERATIVE TERMS (SEE TABLE 10.3.)
circumcision—removal of an adequate amount of prepuce to permit exposure of the glans. (34)
epididymectomy—excision of the epididymis.
epididymovasostomy—anastomosis of the vas deferens to epididymis to produce fertility by circumventing the obstructive lesion in the vas deferens. (36)
excision of hydrocele—evacuation of serous fluid or removal of serous tumor from tunica vaginalis. (35)
orchiectomy, orchectomy, orchidectomy—removal of testis.
orchiopexy—suturing an undescended testis in the scrotum. (31)
orchioplasty—plastic repair of a testis.
prostatectomies: (6, 39, 40)
   transurethral cryogenic prostatectomy—use of special endoscope and freezing technique for destruction of prostatic tumor.
   transurethral laser prostatectomy—laser energy works by thermal destruction of tissue. Currently, there are two techniques of transurethral laser prostatectomy being evaluated. One technique causes coagulation and the other causes evaporation. The coagulation technique utilizes laser energy sufficient to coagulate but not evaporate adenoma tissue. Coagulated tissue eventually necroses and sloughs gradually over weeks to months. The evaporation technique uses a beam with high power density, which is achieved by decreasing divergence of the beam and increasing proximity of beam to tissue. This technique creates an immediate defect similar to that after transurethral prostatectomy.

There remains a rim of coagulated tissue around the evaporated tissue. Findings at this time indicate that there appears to be a lower incidence of urinary retention and a lower reoperation rate when the evaporation technique is employed. (39)

transurethral prostatectomy—removal of obstructing glandular tissue via the urethra using a transurethral resectoscope and electrocautery.

varicocelectomy—excision and ligation of the enlarged veins for varicocele.

vasectomy—removal of the vas deferens or a portion of it. Usually, this procedure is done to induce infertility. (36)

vasoligation—tying the vas deferens with ligature to produce sterility or to prevent epididymitis. (36)

vasovasostomy—anastomosis of the ends of the severed vas deferens. The procedure is done to restore fertility in vasectomized males.

vasovesiculectomy—excison of the vas deferens and seminal vesicles.

SYMPTOMATIC TERMS

azoospermia—semen without living spermatozoa, causing infertility in the male. (63)

oligospermia—scanty production and expulsion of spermatozoa. (31)

prostatism—urinary difficulty resulting from obstruction at the bladder neck by hypertrophy of prostate gland or other causes. (43)

SELECTED TERMS RELATED TO SEMINAL FLUID (23, 63)

semen—secretion containing spermatozoa, the male cells of reproduction.

semen culture—study of the seminal flora, useful in confirming a diagnosis of bacterial prostatitis.

seminal fluid—fluid chiefly secreted by the prostate and in minute amount by the testes.

sperm count—60 to 150 million/mL (SIU: 60 to 150×10^9/L) spermatozoa present in the seminal fluid of a healthy male.

sperm morphology—shape of cells indicating that more than 70% are normal mature spermatozoa.

sperm motility—sperm movement is greater than 60%.

volume of seminal fluid—1.50 to 5.0 mL of seminal fluid is produced by a healthy male.

ABBREVIATIONS

BPH—benign prostatic hypertrophy
BUN—blood, urea, nitrogen
Cysto.—cystoscopic/cystoscopy
ERPF—effective renal plasma flow
GFR—glomerular filtration rate
GU—genitourinary
KUB—kidney, ureter, bladder

pH—hydrogen ion concentration
PRA—plasma renin activity
PSA—prostatic specific antigen
RER—renal excretion rate
UA—urinalysis
UTI—urinary tract infection

ORAL READING PRACTICE

HYDRONEPHROSIS

Hydronephrosis is a by-product of mechanical obstruction of the urinary tract. When the interference with the outflow of urine is below the bladder, as in **urethral stricture** or **hypertrophy** of the **prostate gland, bilateral hydronephrosis** develops. When above the bladder, as in **unilateral ureteral stricture, calculus,** or **neoplasm,** the condition affects only one kidney. In addition, pressure from **tumors, adhesions,** or the **pregnant uterus** outside the urinary tract may interfere with the flow of urine and lead to **hydronephrosis. Congenital anomalies** of the **ureter** or **urethra** may also be responsible for this condition.

There are various degrees of **dilatation** of the **renal pelvis** and ureter. The pressure in the renal pelvis is normally close to zero. When this pressure increases because of obstruction or reflux, the pelvis and calices dilate. The degree of hydronephrosis that develops depends on the duration, degree, and site of the obstruction. The higher the obstruction, the greater the effect on the kidney.

In the initial phase of the disease, the pathologic changes are slight. As the condition progresses, the amount of fluid increases, the **papillae** assume a flattened appearance, the **renal cortex** becomes thinned, and the **pyramids** of the **medulla** undergo **atrophic changes.** The kidney resembles a hollow shell filled with fluid. In extreme cases, several liters of fluid may accumulate in the **renal pelvis,** leading to a complete loss of physiologic capacity. If the hydronephrosis is unilateral, the healthy kidney undergoes compensatory hypertrophic changes to adapt itself to the increased functional workload. In the presence of advanced bilateral hydronephrosis, the downhill clinical course is steady and terminates in **fatal uremia.**

The fluid in the kidney differs from normal urine in its reduced content of urea. Since it is locked up in the renal shell and unable to escape to its proper destination, it easily becomes a breeding place for invading bacterial organisms. Another **deleterious sequela** of fluid retention in the kidney is the formation of **renal calculi,** which adds insult to injury and completes the physiologic destruction of the organ.

In the early phase of hydronephrosis, symptoms may be absent or so mild that they escape notice. As the condition progresses, the kidney becomes palpable, tender, and painful, with unrelieved obstruction continued over weeks. The only symptom may be a dull pain. If intermittent obstruction occurs, attacks of pain develop periodically and are accompanied by **oliguria,** which is promptly reversed to **polyuria** when the obstruction is abolished. Should the damaged kidney become infected, **leukocytosis,** fever, and **pyuria** signal the onset of **pyonephrosis.**

Magnetic resonance imaging of the dilated collecting system in axial and/or coronal projections readily establishes the diagnosis of hydronephrosis. In the phase of acute obstruction, the corticomedullary demarcation is preserved. In contrast, the demarcation is absent in chronic hydronephrosis. The addition of dynamic gadopentetate dimeglumine in acute obstruction, shows cortical enhancement is similar to a normal kidney; however, medullary enhancement is higher. In chronic obstruction, cortical enhancement is lower than in the normal kidney and the tubular phase is prolonged.

The treatment of hydronephrosis consists in removing the cause of obstruction, such as the **ureteral stricture,** or compressing **prostatic** or **vesicular tumor.** If done early, the kidney may be saved. In advanced cases, the presence of irreparable damage demands the excision of the diseased organ, since it serves no useful function and is a constant threat of focal infection. (25, 46, 53, 60)

REVIEW GUIDE

Instructions: Break apart each term listed below, identify the medical term elements, and define the term.

Example: nephroptosis
nephro- = combining form element = kidney
-ptosis = suffix = downward displacement

anuria	nephrosclerosis	ureteroileostomy
balanitis	oligospermia	ureteropyelostomy
cystolithotomy	orchidectomy	uropathy
cystorrhaphy	pyelolithotomy	varicocelectomy
diverticulectomy	pyoureter	vasectomy
epididymovasostomy	ureterocele	vasovasostomy
glomerulonephritis	ureterocystostomy	vasovesiculectomy
nephroblastoma		

Instructions: Select the letter of the response that correctly completes each statement, as shown in the example.

Example: Improperly descended testis is termed
a. anorchism.   b. tenesmus.   c. cryptorchism.   d. trabeculation.

1. Blood in urine is termed
   a. glycosuria.
   c. nocturia.
   b. hematuria.
   d. oliguria.
2. The outer portion of the kidney is called
   a. renal medulla.
   c. renal cortex.
   b. renal pelvis.
   d. none of the above.
3. A pH concentration of less than 7 shows
   a. normal neutrality.
   c. acid in reaction.
   b. alkaline in reaction.
   d. none of the above.
4. Antiglomerular basement membrane nephritis may be called
   a. classic Alport's syndrome.
   c. Goodpasture's syndrome.
   b. nonclassic Alport's syndrome.
   d. none of the above.
5. Nephroblastoma may be called
   a. Grawitz's tumor.
   c. both a and b.
   b. Wilms' tumor.
   d. none of the above.
6. Lenticonus and sensorineural deafness occur in
   a. classic Alport's syndrome.
   c. nonclassic Alport's syndrome.
   b. Goodpasture's syndrome.
   d. none of the above.
7. The black and blue spots of the kidney's substance due to escape of blood is termed
   a. ecchymoses.
   c. avulsion.
   b. rupture.
   d. none of the above.
8. Renal cell carcinoma may be called
   a. Grawitz's tumor.
   c. Goodpasture's syndrome.
   b. Wilms' tumor.
   d. none of the above.
9. Surgical destruction of renal adhesions is called
   a. nephropexy.
   c. nephrostomy.
   b. nephrolysis.
   d. nephrotomy.
10. The glands located posterolateral to the membranous urethra are called
    a. glands of Littre.
    c. both a and b.
    b. Cowper's glands.
    d. none of the above.

11

Gynecologic and Breast Disorders

VULVA AND VAGINA

ORIGIN OF TERMS

aden-, adeno- (G)—gland(s)
-cele (G)—hernia, protrusion, tumor
colpo- (G)—vagina
fistula (L)—pipe, tube
hymen (G)—membrane
labia (L)—lips
-oma (G)—tumor
-rhaphy (G)—suture
vagina (L)—sheath
vulva (L)—covering

PHONETIC PRONUNCIATION OF SELECTED TERMS

atresia of vulva	a-TRE′ze-ah of VUL′vah
colpectomy	kol-PECK′toe-me
colpoperineoplasty	KOL-po-per-i-NEE′o-PLAS-tee
colpoperineorrhaphy	KOL-po-per-i-nee-OR′ah-fee
condyloma	KON-die-LOW′mah
leukoplakia of vulva	LU-KO-PLA′key-ah of VUL′vah
rectovaginal fistula	RECK-toe-VAJ′i-nal FIS′two-lah
vaginitis	VAJ-i-NI′tis
vesicovaginal fistula	VES-i-ko-VAJ′i-nal FIS′two-lah
vulvovaginitis	VUL-vo-VAJ-i-NI′tis

ANATOMIC TERMS (10, 36, 42, 67) (SEE FIG. 11.1.)

perineum—space between the vulva and anus.
Skene's glands—urethral glands in the female.
vagina—musculomembranous tube that connects the uterus with the vulva. It is the lower part of the birth canal.
vulva, pudendum—external female genital organ. Some of the vulvar structures of gynecologic importance include:
> *clitoris*—small body of erectile tissue that enlarges with vascular congestion.
> *hymen*—membranous fold that partially covers the vaginal opening in a virgin.
> *labia majora* (sing. *labium majus*)—two raised folds of adipose and erectile tissue covered on their outer surface with skin.

Figure 11.1 Organs of the female reproductive system.

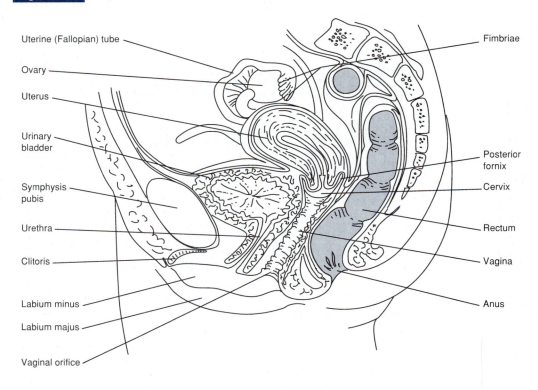

Uterine (Fallopian) tube

Ovary

Uterus

Urinary bladder

Symphysis pubis

Urethra

Clitoris

Labium minus

Labium majus

Vaginal orifice

Fimbriae

Posterior fornix

Cervix

Rectum

Vagina

Anus

labia minora (sing. *labium minus*)—two small folds covered with moist skin lying between labia majora.

vestibular glands (greater), *Bartholin's glands*—two small ovoid or round glands that secrete mucus. They lie deep under the posterior ends of the labia majora.

vestibule of vagina—space between the labia minora that contains the vaginal and urethral orifices and openings of greater vestibular glands.

DIAGNOSTIC TERMS

atresia of:

vagina—congenital absence of vagina.

vulva—congenital absence of vulva. (34)

Bartholin's adenitis—inflammation of Bartholin's glands, generally due to gonococci. (17, 23)

Bartholin's retention cysts—tumors retaining glandular secretions. They tend to undergo suppuration and form abscesses. (32, 45)

carcinoma of Bartholin's gland—carcinoma of Bartholin's gland accounts for about 1% of vulvar cancers. About 50% of the tumors are squamous cell carcinomas. Other tumor types arising in the Bartholin glands are adenomatous, adenoid cystic (an adenocarcinoma with specific histologic and clinical characteristics), adenosquamous, and transitional cell. (61)

carcinoma of vagina—usually:

clear-cell type—cancer characterized by glands and tubules lined by clear cells (hobnail cells) clustering in solid nests and containing glycogen. It occurs in adolescents and young women.

epidermoid type—cancer arising from epidermal cells. It occurs in women over 50 years of age. Cells are devoid of glycogen. Other forms of vaginal cancer are rare. (61)

carcinoma of vulva—usually a squamous cell cancer that begins with a small nodule, later undergoes ulceration, and may become invasive. Invasive cancers of the vulva progressively increase in size, encroach upon adjacent structures such as the vagina, urethra, and anus and can metastasize to the inguinal lymph nodes, which may become quite large and ulcerate through the overlying skin. It is the third most common cancer of the female organs. (45, 61)

condylomas—warty growths scattered over the vulva. (23)

fistula:

   rectovaginal—opening between rectum and vagina.

   vesicovaginal—opening between bladder and vagina. (34)

herpes simplex infection of the vulva—infection caused by herpes simplex virus, type 2. Painful vesicles, ulcerations, and pustular formations are present. Inguinal adenopathy, fever, and malaise also may be present. (54)

leukoplakia of vulva—whitish plaques on vulva that tend to form cracks and fissures. Condition results in leukoplakia vulvitis. (17)

vaginitis—inflammation of vagina.

   gonorrheal—gonococcal infection due to *Neisseria gonorrhoeae*.

   mycotic, monilial—due to fungus infection.

   senile—due to atrophic changes; occurs in elderly women.

   Trichomonas—due to infection with *Trichomonas vaginalis*. (23, 45)

vulvar dystrophies—disorders of epithelial growth and nutrition resulting in changes of the superficial cell layers of the vulva. In 1989, the International Society for the Study of Vulvar Disease (ISSVD) adopted a standard of reporting vulvar dysplastic lesions as vulvar intraepithelial neoplasia (VIN) I, II, and III depending on the degree of epithelial cellular maturation. The degree of loss of epithelial cellular maturation in a particular lesion defines the grade of VIN. Complete loss of cellular maturation in the full thickness of epithelium is defined as VIN III (which is synonymous with carcinoma in situ of the vulva). These lesions may be discrete or diffuse, single or multiple, flat or raised. They vary in color from the white appearance of hyperkeratotic tumors to a velvety red or black. Microscopic examination of these lesions reveals cellular disorganization and loss of stratification that involves the full thickness of the epithelium. (17, 61)

vulvar Paget's disease—form of vulvar cancer in situ, recurrent, noninvasive, spreading slowly, and presenting a discrete eruption that is initially velvety, soft, and red and later eczematoid and weepy with white plaques scattered about in the well-localized lesion. Pruritus and burning are distressing symptoms. The presence of Paget's cells in the lesion confirms the diagnosis. (61)

vulvovaginitis—inflammation of the vulva and vagina. (45, 54)

OPERATIVE TERMS (SEE TABLE 11.1.)

colpectomy—removal of vagina. (52)

colpocleisis—closure of vagina, one indication being prolapse of vagina following total hysterectomy. (52)

colpomicroscopy—use of the colpomicroscope, which affords higher magnification than a colposcope, in studying the superficial cervical epithelium for cytologic diagnosis.

colpoperineoplasty—surgical repair of vagina and perineum.

colpoperineorrhaphy—suture of vagina and perineum.

colporrhaphy—suture of vagina.

   anterior—repair of cystocele.

   posterior—repair of rectocele. (52)

colposcopy—examination of the vagina and cervix uteri, usually with a binocular microscope that allows the study of tissues under direct vision by magnifying the cells; makes possible colpophotography and the colposcopic selection of target biopsy sites. (29, 46, 62)

colpotomy—incision into the vagina to induce drainage.

TABLE 11.1	Some Gynecologic Conditions Amenable to Surgery		
Anatomic Site	*Diagnosis*	*Type of Surgery*	*Operative Procedures*
Hymen	Imperforate hymen	Hymenectomy	Excision of hymen
Clitoris	Hypertrophy of clitoris	Excision of hypertrophied clitoris	Removal of hypertrophied clitoris and creation of normal-looking genitalia
Bartholin's glands	Chronic Bartholinitis and Bartholin's gland cyst	Marsupialization of Bartholin's gland cyst	Partial excision of cyst wall Suture of cyst lining to the surrounding surface epithelium
Vulva	Carcinoma in situ	Excision of vulva with split-thickness graft	Removal of carcinoma in situ and abnormal vulva epithelium and replacement with normal epithelium via split-thickness graft
Vagina Bladder	Vesicovaginal fistula	Vesicovaginal fistula repair	Permanent closure of vesicovaginal fistula
Vagina Perineum	Rectocele	Posterior repair	Excess vaginal mucosa is excised; plication of perirectal and levator muscles over the anterior rectal wall, providing support to the perineal body, the posterior vaginal wall, and the pelvic floor
Vagina	Urinary stress incontinence	Marshall-Marchetti-Krantz operation	Surgical elevation and fixation of bladder neck and urethra by suture applications, using Cooper's ligament and conjoined tendon for suspension
Bladder Urethra	Cystocele Urinary stress incontinence	Anterior repair, Kelly plication	Construction of firm shelf of periurethral tissue to support bladder and urethra
Urethra Vagina	Urethrovaginal fistula Urinary stress incontinence	Urethrovaginal fistula repair	Excision of scarred, devascularized tissue surrounding fistula; approximation of healthy margins of tissue with multilayers by closing and bringing source of blood supply to base of urethra to cover fistula

TABLE **11.1**	(continued)		
Anatomic Site	*Diagnosis*	*Type of Surgery*	*Operative Procedures*
Vagina Cervix Uterus	Carcinoma of vagina, cervix, uterus	Radical Wertheim hysterectomy with bilateral pelvic lymph node dissection	Removal of uterus, tubes, parametrium, tissue surrounding the upper vagina, and pelvic lymphatics
Uterus	Irregular bleeding of undetermined origin	Dilatation and curettage	Instrumental expansion of the cervix and scraping of endometrial lining of the uterine cavity
Uterus	Prolapse of uterus	Manchester operation	Amputation of cervix uteri, tubes, and ovaries
Cervix uteri	Chronic cervicitis	Conization	Removal of mucous lining of cervical canal by high-frequency current
Uterine tubes	Hydrosalpinx	Salpingectomy	Removal of uterine tube
Uterine tubes	Fallopian tube obstruction	Fimbrioplasty	Opening of the obstructed uterine tube, salvaging functions of the fimbriae to allow entry and transport of sperm
Ovary	Polycystic ovary syndrome (Stein-Leventhal syndrome)	Wedge resection of the ovary	Removal of triangular wedge of ovary for stimulating ovarian activity in anovulation and infertility

episioplasty—plastic repair of the vulva.
excision of Bartholin's gland—removal of the gland. (34)
marsupialization of Bartholin's gland cyst—incision and drainage of the cyst and partial excision of the cyst wall, followed by suture of the cyst lining to the surrounding surface epithelium. Lubrication is preserved, since the gland is not removed. (34)
vulvectomy:
> *simple vulvectomy*—excision of vulvae, which may be done for vulvar carcinoma in situ.
> *radical vulvectomy*—total removal of the vulvae with regional lymphadenectomy.
>> • *regional lymphadenectomy*—involves excision of bilateral deep and superficial inguinal lymph nodes.

If the tumor extends anteriorly into the bladder, the involved organ must be removed by **anterior exenteration with urinary diversion.** If cancer involves the rectum, **abdominoperineal resection with sigmoid colostomy** is indicated. (61)

SYMPTOMATIC TERMS
leukorrhea—abnormal cervical or vaginal discharge of white or yellowish mucus. (11)
pruritus vulvae—severe itching of vulva. (11)
vaginismus—painful spasm of the vagina due to involuntary contraction of the vaginal musculature.

UTERUS AND SUPPORTING STRUCTURES

ORIGIN OF TERMS

cervix (L)—neck
cyst-, cysto- (G)—sac, cyst
fundus (L)—base
hyster-, hystero- (G)—womb, uterus
leio- (G)—smooth
meno- (G)—menses

metr-, metro- (G)—uterus
ostium (L)—small opening
-rhea (G)—flow
-rhage (G)—hemorrhage, excessive flow
trachelo- (G)—neck
uterus (L)—womb

PHONETIC PRONUNCIATION OF SELECTED TERMS

adenomyosis	AD-e-no-my-OWE′sis
culdocentesis	KUL-doe-sen-TEE′sis
endocervicitis	EN-doe-SER-vi-SIGH′tis
tracheloplasty	TRA′kel-owe-PLAS-tee
vulvectomy	vul-VEK′toe-me

ANATOMIC TERMS (10, 36, 42, 67) (SEE FIGS. 11.1 AND 11.2.)

cul-de-sac, rectouterine pouch, Douglas' pouch—pocket between the rectum and posterior uterus, formed by an extension of the peritoneum.

ligaments of uterus:

broad ligaments—double-layered peritoneal sheets that extend from the side of the uterus to the lateral pelvic wall.

round ligaments—two fibromuscular bands, one on each side arising anteriorly from the fundus, passing through the inguinal canal, and inserting into the labia majora.

uterus (nonpregnant)—pear-shaped, thick-walled, muscular organ, situated in the pelvis between the urinary bladder and the rectum. It is about 3 inches (7.5 centimeters) long and 2 inches (5 centimeters) wide in its upper segment. Anatomical distinctions of the uterus include:

body of uterus—main part extending from fundus to isthmus of the uterus.

cervix of uterus—lower part of uterus extending from isthmus to vagina.

cervical canal—passageway between uterine cavity and vagina.

external os, ostium of uterus—opening of cervix into vagina.

fundus of uterus—superior dome-shaped portion of uterus above the openings of the uterine tubes into the body cavity of the uterus.

isthmus of uterus—constriction of uterus between the body and the cervix.

uterine cavity—triangular space within the body.

uterine wall—thick and composed of three layers.

- *endometrium*—inner mucosal layer lining the uterine cavity.
- *myometrium*—thick, muscular layer, consisting of bundles of smooth muscle fibers arranged in longitudinal, circular, and spiral patterns, and interconnected with connective tissues.
- *perimetrium*—consists of an outer serosal layer that covers the body of the uterus and part of the cervix.

DIAGNOSTIC TERMS

diseases of the cervix uteri:

carcinoma of the cervix—malignant cervical lesion that may present as an ulceration or tumor associated with excessive and irregular uterine bleeding and a leukorrheic vaginal discharge.

- *adenocarcinoma*—highly malignant cancer assuming a glandular pattern.
- *squamous cell or epidermoid carcinoma*—most frequent form arising from squamous epithelium. (29, 45)

Figure 11.2 Female reproductive organs, anterior view, showing the relationship of ovaries, uterine tubes, uterus, cervix, and vagina.

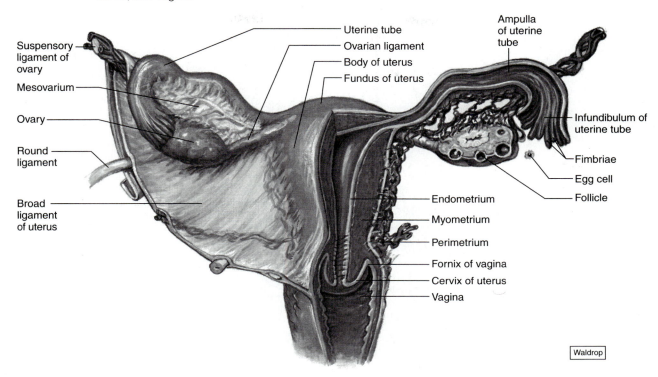

Terms adopted by the International Federation of Gynecology and Obstetrics:

invasive carcinoma—cancer of cervix (including the 4 stages presented in fig. 11.3).

microinvasive carcinoma—presence of preclinical cancer characterized by early stromal invasion. Diagnosis is based on microscopic examination from biopsy specimen.

preinvasive carcinoma—intraepithelial neoplasia where tumor cells are limited to the epithelium of origin, without invasion of the basement membrane. Also termed *carcinoma in situ*. (12, 29)

cervicitis—inflammation of the cervix uteri. (15, 35, 45)

acute—primary symptom is a purulent vaginal discharge. The discharge may be thick and creamy due to a gonorrheal infection; foamy and greenish-white due to a trichomonal infection; white and curdlike due to the presence of candidiasis; or a thin and graylike discharge in a *Gardnerella vaginalis* infection.

chronic—common condition caused by low-grade infection. It may be manifested by a purulent or mucopurulent exudate.

endocervicitis—inflammation of the mucous membrane of the cervix uteri.

erosion of cervix—red area produced by the replacement of squamous epithelium by columnar epithelium.

eversion of cervix, ectropion—rolling outward of a swollen mucous membrane resulting from chronic cervicitis. It may be associated with lacerations, cysts, and erosions.

polyps of cervix—soft, movable, pedunculated tabs that bleed readily.

diseases and malfunctions of the corpus uteri:

adenomyosis—endometrial invasion of the myometrium, which may be associated with dysmenorrhea and abnormal uterine bleeding. (50, 66)

Figure 11.3   Clinical stages of cervical cancer. **Stage 1:** Cancer is exclusively limited to the uterine cervix. **Stage 2:** Cancer has spread beyond the cervix but has not reached the pelvic wall. **Stage 3:** Cancer involves the lower third of the vagina or extends to the pelvic wall. **Stage 4:** Cancer has spread to the mucous membrane of the rectum and bladder or has extended beyond the true pelvis.

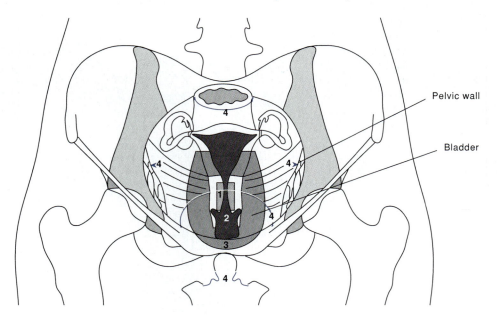

dysfunctional uterine bleeding—bleeding from the uterine endometrium unrelated to anatomic lesions of the uterus; functional bleeding not caused by any local disease. It may result from an irregular production of estrogen and/or progesterone by the ovary and may occur during puberty, the reproductive period of life, or during menopause. (26, 45)
endometriosis—aberrant endometrial tissue found in various pelvic and abdominal organs. (35, 45, 51)
endometritis—inflammation of the mucous membrane lining the corpus uteri. (45)
parametritis—cellulitis of the tissue adjacent to the uterus. (34)
perimetritis—pelvic peritonitis.

displacements of the uterus: (45) (See fig. 11.4.)
anteflexion—uterus, abnormally bent forward.
prolapse, procidentia, descensus uteri—downward displacement of the uterus, which may protrude from the vagina.
retrocession—dropping backward of the entire uterus; backward displacement of the uterus.
retroflexion—bending backward of the body of the uterus toward the cervix, resulting in a sharp angle at the point of bending.
retroversion—corpus uteri abnormally turned backward with cervix directed toward symphysis pubis.

neoplasms of the uterus:
benign tumors: (15, 28, 50)
  • *endometrial polyps*—small, projecting lesions that may be sessile and multiple, and may resemble cystic hyperplasia.

Figure 11.4   The uterus, variations in positions.

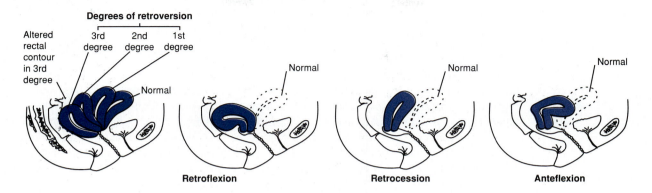

- *leiomyomas, myomas*—benign smooth-muscle tumors, erroneously referred to as fibroids, forming single or multiple, large or small, firm, encapsulated masses that may be:
  - *intraligamentous*—myoma protrudes into broad ligament.
  - *intramural*—myoma is embedded in myometrium.
  - *submucous*—sessile or pedunculated; myoma is located beneath the endometrium, may bleed profusely, and rarely undergoes sarcomatous transformation.

malignant tumors: (9, 12, 28)
  - *adenocarcinoma of the corpus uteri*—endometrial cancer, characteristically affecting the postmenopausal woman in two ways: (1) circumscribed lesion—small portion of endometrium is diseased, although myometrial invasion may be extensive; (2) diffuse type—the entire endometrium is involved; ulcerations and necrotic areas are present. Endometrial cancer may result from prolonged estrogen stimulation with inadequate progesterone or without progesterone and from other causes.
  - *leiomyosarcoma*—neoplasm usually arises from the uterine wall, recurs readily after removal, and metastasizes to the bone, brain, and lung.

OPERATIVE TERMS (SEE TABLE 11.1.)

cold conization cold knife biopsy of uterine cervix—cold knife removal of lining of cervical canal for locating the site of abnormal exfoliative cells in the absence of a visible lesion. The procedure is valuable in the detection of preinvasive lesions, cancer in situ, and occult cancer. (29)

culdocentesis—surgical puncture of the cul-de-sac used as diagnostic procedure whenever intraperitoneal bleeding is suspected, for example, in ectopic pregnancy. (23)

culdoscopy—endoscopic examination of the rectouterine pouch (cul-de-sac) and pelvic viscera to detect whether or not endometriosis, adnexal adhesions, tumors, or ectopic pregnancy are present or to determine the cause of pelvic pain, sterility, or other disorders. (29, 45)

dilatation and curettage (D&C)—instrumental expansion of the cervix and scraping of the uterine cavity to remove endocervical tissue and endometrial tissue for diagnosis, or to remove placental tissue to control bleeding, as in an incomplete abortion. D&C may be utilized to control bleeding due to submucous myoma, polyp, or other lesion. (32, 45)

electrocautery of endocervix—removing the mucous lining of the cervical canal by a high-frequency current to control chronic cervicitis. The procedure is also used to repair an incompetent cervix so that successful pregnancy may be achieved. (15)

hysterectomy—removal of the uterus. (9, 29, 32, 46, 52)

partial or subtotal excision—for example, supracervical removal.

panhysterectomy, total hysterectomy—removal of entire uterus, including the cervix.

vaginal hysterectomy—removal of the uterus by the vaginal approach.

Wertheim's operation—radical excision of entire uterus, tubes, and ovaries, and dissection of regional lymph nodes.

hysteroscopy, fiberoptic—endoscopic examination for intrauterine diagnosis or therapy by endometrial biopsy; identification of uterotubal junction, submucous myomas, polyps, and septa; detection and lysis of intrauterine adhesions, and female sterilization. (45, 46)

laparoscopy—through a small abdominal incision, endoscopic visualization of abdominal organs, especially the pelvic viscera (the uterus, tubes, and ovaries) is achieved. The procedure is of diagnostic value in primary and secondary amenorrhea, polycystic ovarian syndrome, unruptured ectopic pregnancy, pelvic inflammatory disease, and undiagnosed pain. (31, 45, 46)

myomectomy: (50)

abdominal approach—removal of intramural myoma or myomas from the uterus.

vaginal approach—removal of cervical myoma from uterine cervix.

suspension of uterus—correction of retrodisplacement of the uterus. (46)

Baldy-Webster procedure—creation of a surgical opening for the passage of the round ligaments, which are then sutured to the back of the uterus.

modified Gilliam procedure—surgical shortening of the round ligaments through the internal inguinal ring. This allows the stronger portion of the round ligament to bring the uterus forward.

trachelectomy, cervicectomy—removal of uterine cervix.

SYMPTOMATIC TERMS

amenorrhea—absence of menstruation for 3 months or more.

primary amenorrhea—no menstrual cycle initiated by age 18.

secondary amenorrhea—menstrual cycle ceased after initial menarche. (26, 32, 65, 68)

cryptomenorrhea—menses occur, but there is no external manifestation; due to obstructive lesion of lower genital canal. (26)

dysmenorrhea—painful menses. There are two types:

primary dysmenorrhea—menstrual distress is a functional disturbance, precipitated by emotional tension. It is prevalent in adolescence but may occur later in life.

secondary dysmenorrhea—menstrual pain has an organic basis; onset is usually after adolescence. (26, 45)

hypermenorrhea, menorrhagia—abnormal premenopausal bleeding due to irregular endometrial shedding, endometrial polyposis, uterine myoma or hypertrophy, or a bleeding disorder. (26, 45)

hypomenorrhea—diminished bleeding and number of days in menstrual period. (26)

metrorrhagia—irregular bleeding from uterus caused by hormone imbalance, not menses; sometimes induced by estrogen administration or hypothyroid state or caused by myoma, cervical or endometrial cancer, polyposis, or other disorders. (26)

oligomenorrhea—infrequent menstrual bleeding; interval of cycles is over 38 days but less than 3 months. (26)

polymenorrhea—recurrent uterine bleeding within 24 days related to an exceptionally short cycle or the interruption of the cycle by psychic or physical trauma.

premenstrual syndrome (PMS)—complex disorder recurring monthly before menstruation, characterized by fluid retention, weight gain, depression or agitation, mood swings, and fatigue. The symptoms increase progressively in some and suddenly in others. (26, 45) (See chapter 16 for toxic shock syndrome.)

OVARIES AND UTERINE TUBES

ORIGIN OF TERMS

albus (L)—white
ampulla (L)—little jug
fimbria (L)—fringe
folliculus (L)—little bag
infundibulum (L)—funnel

luteum (L)—yellow
oophor-, oophoro- (G)—ovary, bearing eggs
ovum, ova, ovi-, ovo- (L)—egg(s)
salpingo- (G)—tube, trumpet

PHONETIC PRONUNCIATION OF SELECTED TERMS

anovulation	AN-ov-u-LAY'shun
oophoropexy	o-OF-owe-row-PECK'see
pyosalpinx	PIE-owe-SAL'pinks
salpingolysis	SAL-ping-GOL'ice-sis
salpingostomy	SAL-ping-GOS'toe-me
tuboplasty	TU'bow-PLAS-tee

ANATOMIC TERMS (10, 36, 42, 67) (SEE FIGS. 11.2 AND 11.5.)

adnexae (sing. **adnexa**)—appendages or adjunct parts. Uterine adnexa or uterine appendages comprises the ovaries, uterine tubes, and ligaments of the uterus.
ova (sing. **ovum**)—female reproductive cells.
ovaries (sing. **ovary**)—two female reproductive glands producing ova after puberty.
> *ovarian follicle*—small excretory structure of the ovary. The primary ovarian follicle is immature, consisting of a single layer of follicular cells. The vesicular ovarian or graafian follicle develops, ruptures, and discharges the ovum. It also secretes the follicular hormone, estrogen.
> *corpus luteum*—small, yellow body formed in ruptured ovarian follicle. It secretes the corpus luteum hormone, progesterone.
> *corpus albicans*—white body that develops from the corpus luteum. It leaves a pitlike scar on ovary.

uterine tubes, fallopian tubes, oviducts—two muscular canals about 4 inches (10 centimeters) long that provide a passageway for the ovum to the uterus and a meeting place for the ovum and spermatozoon in fertilization. An ovum entering the tube through the abdominal opening of the fimbriated infundibulum passes through the:
> *ampulla*—wider, thinner-walled segment; longest part of the tube.
> *isthmic portion*—interstitial portion of the tube, narrower and thicker-walled than the ampulla.
> *uterine part*—tube within the myometrium.
> *uterine opening*—entrance into the uterine cavity.

DIAGNOSTIC TERMS

abscess, tubo-ovarian—localized suppuration of the uterine tube and ovary. (14, 54)
Brenner's tumor—peculiar, usually benign ovarian tumor containing epithelial cell nests within a matrix of fibrous tissue. It may undergo mucinous transformation or increased epithelial proliferation, as seen in malignancy. (14, 68)
cyst of ovary—fluid-containing tumor of the ovary.
> *graafian follicle cyst*—retention cyst appearing on the ovary as a fluid-filled bleb, resulting from the inability of the partially formed follicle to reabsorb.
> *corpus luteum cyst*—functional ovarian enlargement, resulting from the fluid increase by the corpus luteum following ovulation.

Figure 11.5 Path of egg and sperm cells through the female reproductive tract.

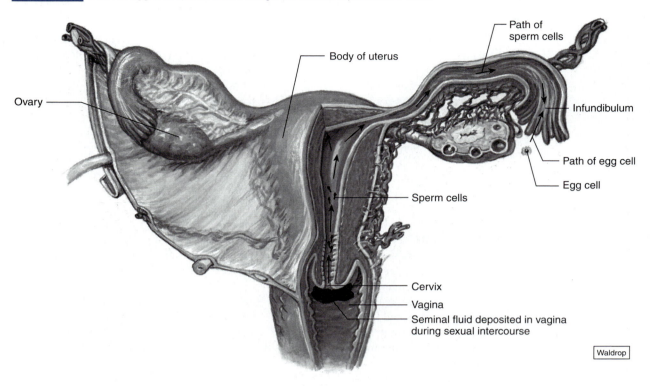

endometrial ovarian cyst—cyst formed by ectopic endometrial tissue and filled with decomposed blood due to bleeding into the cystic cavity. This cyst may be attached to other pelvic structures.

theca lutein cyst—cyst, prone to occur in both ovaries, is filled with straw-colored or serosanguineous fluid and may rupture. It develops in the presence of hydatidiform mole, choriocarcinoma, and excessive therapy with chorionic gonadotropin. (14, 68)

cystadenoma of ovary—silent tumor, nonproductive of hormone, constituting 70% of ovarian neoplasms.

mucinous cystadenoma—multilocular, large-sized cysts, lined with active mucin-secreting cells. Cysts may rupture, releasing mucinous cells that may transplant and grow on the omentum and the peritoneum. When this condition leads to a continuing collection of mucin in the peritoneum, it is termed *pseudomyxoma peritonei*.

serous cystadenoma—encapsulated multilocular glandular cyst filled with thin, yellowish fluid and growing in size, but not to great excess. (13, 14, 68)

dehiscence of abdominal wound—separation of the layers of a surgical wound. It may be partial (superficial) or it may be complete (disruption of all layers of the surgical wound). (16)

dysgerminoma—germ cell tumor occurring in small girls or in first decades of life, exhibiting variability in size and malignancy. The tumor may be associated with streak ovaries, rudimentary gonads seen in chromosome aberration. (14, 35)

hydrosalpinx—uterine tube distended by clear fluid.

infertility, female—temporary or permanent inability to conceive or become pregnant after a year of sexual exposure, dependent on multiple etiologic factors such as:
anovulation.
defects of the luteal phase.
condition of the cervix, or the status of uterine tubes.
chromosomal aberrations (e.g., Turner's syndrome or Klinefelter's syndrome).
immunologic responses.
male factors (e.g., high viscosity of semen, low sperm motility, and low volume of semen). (38, 48)
Associated terms include:
> *primary infertility*—pregnancy never achieved.
> *secondary infertility*—at least one previous conception has occurred, but currently, the couple is not able to achieve pregnancy.
> *sterility*—total inability to conceive. (38, 48)

Meigs' syndrome—solid, fibromatous, unilateral tumor of the ovary associated with hydrothorax and ascites. Other pelvic tumors may also form pleural and peritoneal effusions, which promptly disappear with surgical removal of the tumor. (14)

oophoritis, acute and chronic—inflammation of the ovary or ovaries. (23)

ovarian malignant epithelial neoplasms—tumors arising from the surface epithelium of the ovary, which is an extension of the primitive coelomic mesothelium. Common tumors include serous papillary cystadenocarcinoma, serous papillary peritoneal carcinoma, mucinous cystadenocarcinoma, endometrioid adenocarcinoma, and clear cell carcinoma. Less commonly occurring tumors include malignant mixed mesodermal tumors, small cell carcinoma, malignant Brenner and transitional cell carcinoma, and undifferentiated carcinoma. (2, 3, 5, 6, 17, 31, 41, 69)

pelvic inflammatory disease (PID)—broad term, including pelvic inflammations caused by gonococcal, streptococcal postabortal infections, as well as intestinal parasites; multiple infectious organisms may coexist. (23, 49, 54)

polycystic ovarian syndrome, Stein-Leventhal syndrome—symptom complex characterized by bilateral enlarged ovaries containing multiple follicular microcysts. Amenorrhea, infertility, obesity, hypertension, and hirsutism (hairiness) are common symptoms. (14)

pyosalpinx—pus in the uterine tube.

ruptured tubo-ovarian abscess—breaking open of the abscess and escape of purulent drainage into the peritoneal cavity. (14)

salpingitis, acute or chronic—inflammation of the uterine tube(s). (23, 35)

torsion of ovarian pedicle—twisting of the pedicle of an ovarian cyst resulting in circulatory disturbance and sharp persistent pain. (14)

OPERATIVE TERMS (SEE TABLE 11.1.)

adnexectomy—removal of uterine adnexa, the tubes, and ovaries. (32, 46)

oophorectomy, ovariectomy—partial removal of an ovary; complete removal of one ovary; castration—bilateral, complete removal of ovaries. (14)

oophoropexy—fixation of a displaced ovary.

oophoroplasty—plastic repair of an ovary.

ovarian wedge resection—removal of a triangular wedge of the ovary for the purpose of stimulating ovarian activity in anovulation and infertility. (14)

panhysterectomy and bilateral salpingo-oophorectomy—removal of complete uterus, both tubes and ovaries. (23)

salpingectomy—partial or complete removal of the uterine tubes.

salpingolysis—the breaking up of peritubal adhesions that damage the fimbriated end of the tube. This procedure is considered an effective means of correcting infertility.

salpingo-oophorectomy—removal of tubes and ovaries. (32)

salpingostomy—surgical creation of a new ostium in a tube whose fimbrial end is completely occluded, e.g., forming a hydrosalpinx.

tubal implantation—correction of the cornual block and implantation of the unobstructed tubes into the uterine cavity, to restore tubal patency following sterilization surgery, or tubes obstructed by the presence of chronic infection.

tubal ligation—tying or constricting the uterine tubes by means of ligatures to prevent pregnancy; sterilization surgery. (19)

tuboplasty, salpingoplasty—reconstructive tubal surgery for the correction of infertility. The constricted or occluded end of the uterine tube is excised, and the distal portion of the tube is reimplanted into the uterus. Also, the use of cone-shaped, spiral stents has been advocated as an effective method of maintaining tubal patency.

SYMPTOMATIC TERMS

anovulation—absence of ovulation due to cessation or suspension of menses. (45)

menarche—a human female's first menstrual cycle. This cycle begins after the ovaries and other organs of the female reproductive system have become mature and are responsive to certain hormones. (26, 45)

menopause—cessation of menses and reproductive period of life. (44)

menstruation—the hormone-controlled cyclic, physiologic discharge through the vagina consisting of blood and mucosal tissue from the nonpregnant uterus. This process occurs at approximately 4-week intervals (in the absence of pregnancy) during the reproductive period (from puberty through menopause) in the human female. (26, 45)

ovulation—expulsion of an ovum from the ruptured graafian follicle.

septic shock—sudden hypotension, renal dysfunction, peripheral blood pooling, and metabolic acidosis caused by gram-negative bacteremia due to septic abortion, puerperal sepsis, or pelvic infection. (7)

SPECIAL PROCEDURES

CYTOLOGIC STUDIES FOR GYNECOLOGIC CONDITIONS

cytopathologic studies—include cytogenetic, cytologic, and hormonal evaluation of gynecologic disorders. The specimen for study is usually obtained by microbiopsy. (55)

cytogenetic studies—deal with chromosomal structure of cells and aid to clarify issues of hermaphroditism, intersexuality, and antenatal sex determination. (12)

cytologic studies—detection of tumors of the cervix and endometrium in the preinvasive state when proper treatment can be instituted. Several methods have been devised to obtain smears for cytologic diagnosis. (12, 16, 54)

> *Papanicolaou's method (Pap smear)*—technique that employs an exfoliative cytological staining procedure for detection and diagnosis of various conditions, especially malignant and premalignant disorders of the female genital tract (e.g., cancer of the vagina, cervix, and endometrium), in which cells that have been desquamated from the genital epithelium are obtained by smears, fixed and stained, and examined under the microscope for evidence of pathologic changes.

hormonal studies—cytopathologic evaluation for detecting abnormal cytohormonal patterns, which may suggest the presence of functional ovarian neoplasms, endocrine or breast tumors, and endometrial or tubal lesions.

microbiopsy study—the cellular specimen obtained for tissue examination by the pathologist.

TERMS RELATED TO FERTILITY STUDIES

biopsy:

endometrial biopsy and histologic study—method of determining evidence of ovulation. If absent, the ovarian factor is thought to be the cause of sterility. The biopsy, however, does not indicate whether the ovary is primarily or secondarily involved. (28)

ovarian biopsies, bilateral—removal of ovarian tissue for the detection of the cause of infertility, evaluation, and resumption of ovarian function. Large ovarian biopsies with use of Palmer biopsy forceps may be done under laparoscopic control. (28)

hysterosalpingography—roentgenography of the uterus and uterine tubes following injection of opaque material. (26, 48)

laparoscopy—through a small abdominal incision, endoscopic visualization and examination of pelvic and reproductive organs is performed for diagnostic appraisal and/or therapeutic control. (8, 12, 31, 48, 69)

tubal insufflation (Rubin test)—tubal patency test in reproductive failure. Blocked tubes are a cause of sterility. (66)

OTHER TESTS

culture for *Neisseria gonorrhoeae*—use of Thayer-Martin (TM) medium in cultures for the detection of the gonococcus. (23, 66)

dark-field examination—most specific means of direct demonstration of *Treponema pallidum*, obtained from moist lesions of primary, secondary, or relapsing syphilis. (23, 66)

Schiller test—test helpful in the detection of superficial cancer, particularly that of the cervix. Normal epithelium is rich in glycogen and stained deeply by iodine solution. Cancerous epithelium has almost no glycogen and takes no stain. The test has its limitations. (12, 29, 66)

serologic tests for syphilis—tests that utilize either nontreponemal or treponemal antigens:

nontreponemal antigen tests:

- flocculation tests:
  - Venereal Disease Research Laboratories (VDRL) test
  - rapid plasma reagin (RPR) test
- complement fixation tests:
  - Wassermann test
  - Kolmer test

treponemal antibody tests:

- Fluorescent treponemal antibody absorption (FTA-ABS) test
- *T pallidum* immobilization (TPI) test
- *T pallidum* complement fixation (TPCF) test
- *T pallidum* hemagglutination (TPHA) test (20, 23, 39, 54)

tests for acquired immunodeficiency syndrome (AIDS)—specific tests for the human immunodeficiency virus (HIV) may include antigen and antibody detection and direct viral culture. AIDS may be detected by: enzyme immunoassay (EIA), immunofluorescent assay (IFA), enzyme-linked immunosorbent assay (ELISA), or radioimmunoprecipitation assay (RIPA). Positive specimens may be confirmed by the Western blot test. This test identifies antibodies to specific viral proteins. (20, 54, 66) (See chapter 16 for terms pertaining to infections caused by sexually transmitted diseases.)

ABBREVIATIONS

GENERAL TERMS

AIDS—acquired immunodeficiency syndrome
D&C—dilatation and curettage
GC—gonorrhea
Gyn—gynecology
IUD—intrauterine device

HIV—human immunodeficiency virus
LMP—last menstrual period
MH—marital history
PID—pelvic inflammatory disease
PMP—previous menstrual period

ORGANIZATIONS

ACOG—American College of
Obstetricians and Gynecologists
ACS—American College of Surgeons

FIGO—International Federation of
Gynecology and Obstetrics
ISSVD—International Society for the
Study of Vulvar Disease

BREASTS

ORIGIN OF TERMS

areola (L)—small area or space
-gram (G)—a writing, a mark
-graphy (G)—to write
lacto- (L)—milk
mamma- (L)—breast

mammo- (G)—breast
mast-, masto- (G)—breast
-pexy (G)—suspension, fixation
-plasty (G)—surgical correction or formation
thele- (G)—nipple

PHONETIC PRONUNCIATION OF SELECTED TERMS

amastia	a-MAS'tee-ah
athelia	a-THE'lee-ah
biopsy	BY'op-see
cystic mastitis	CYST'ick mas-TIE'tis
hyperplasia	HI-per-PLAY'ze-ah
lactiferous	lack-TIF'er-us
mammaplasty	MAM'a-PLAS-tee
mastectomy	mass-TECK'toe-me
mastitis	mas-TIE'tis
mastodynia	mast-o-DIN'i-ah
mastopexy	MASS'toe-peck-see
mastoplasty	MASS'toe-PLAS-tee
thelitis	the-LIE'tis

ANATOMIC TERMS (36, 47) (SEE FIG. 11.6.)

areola—area of pigmented skin surrounding the nipple. It becomes dark during pregnancy and remains so thereafter.

mammary gland—glandular tissue of the breast composed of 15 to 20 irregular shaped lobes, each of which includes tubular glands **(alveolar glands),** and a duct **(lactiferous duct)** that leads to the **nipple** and opens to the outside. The lobes are separated from each other by dense connective and adipose tissues. These tissues support the glands as well as attach them to the underlying pectoral muscles.

nipple, papilla mammae—at the tip of each breast at about the level of the fourth intercostal space, the nipple is located.

DIAGNOSTIC TERMS

abscess of breast, mammary abscess—localized collection of pus in mammary tissue.
amastia—absence of a breast. (27)

Figure 11.6 Structure of the breast: (a) sagittal section, (b) anterior view.

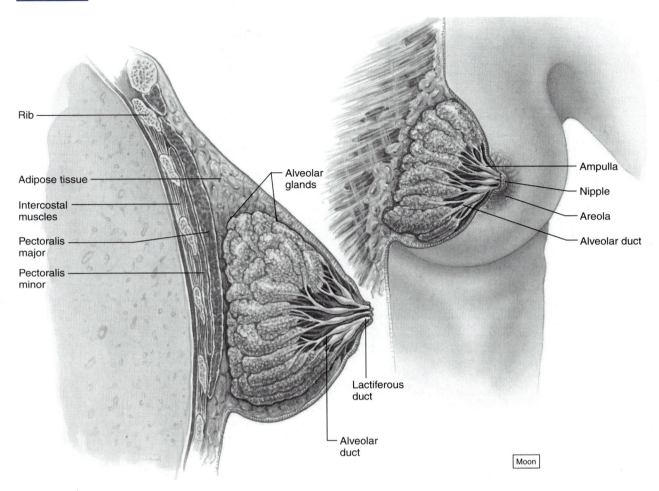

Rib

Adipose tissue

Intercostal muscles

Pectoralis major

Pectoralis minor

Alveolar glands

Lactiferous duct

Alveolar duct

Ampulla

Nipple

Areola

Alveolar duct

Moon

athelia—absence of a breast nipple.

breast calcifications—calcium deposits of the breast; viewed on mammograms as clustered calcifications of any morphology, multiple punctate calcifications of any configuration, and linear or ring-shaped calcifications. These calcifications should be carefully evaluated by periodic follow-up mammograms. Studies have indicated that these patients are at an increased risk for subsequent breast cancer. (64)

breast cancer—malignant mammary tumor, a painless or painful mass that may be associated with skin and muscle attachment, discharge, crusting, and retraction of nipple, changes in contour of affected breast; and metastasis to regional lymph nodes. (1, 4, 24, 27, 30, 43, 64, 66) (See the Oral Reading at the end of this section for additional information regarding breast cancer.)

chronic cystic mastitis—describes a family of lesions found in the breast. These include papillomatosis, blunt duct adenosis, periductal mastitis, fat necrosis, hyperplasia of duct epithelium, and fibroadenoma. Mastitis first appears in the late twenties age range, with increased evidence in the thirties and forties. Cyst may vary in size. (27)

fissure of nipple—a deep furrow in the nipple.

hyperplasia of breast, hypermastia—abnormally large breast, usually pendulous and sagging.

TABLE 11.2	Some Breast Conditions Amenable to Surgery		
Anatomic Site	**Diagnosis**	**Type of Surgery**	**Operative Procedures**
Breast	Abscess of breast caused by *Staphylococcus aureus* or other infectious agents	Mastotomy with drainage	Surgical opening and evaluation of abscess Insertion of drain
Breast	Carcinoma of breast	Radical mastectomy	Removal of breast, pectoral muscles, and lymph nodes
Breast	Overdevelopment of breast (pendulous breast)	Mastopexy	Fixation of pendulous breast
Breast	Unilateral hypomastia	Augmentation mammaplasty of underdeveloped breast	Implementation of Cronin silicone prosthesis in retromammary pocket
Breast	Cystic mastitis	Breast biopsy with frozen section	Excision of breast lesion for diagnostic evaluation Microscopic study of slides of biopsied lesion
Breast	Hypermastia right breast	Reduction mammaplasty of overdeveloped breast	Partial excision of mammary tissue, right breast

hypoplasia of breast, hypomastia—abnormally small breast.
   unilateral hypomastia—one breast underdeveloped, with the other normal or overdeveloped. This results in mammary asymmetry and disfigurement.
   bilateral hypomastia—both breasts are abnormally small.
occlusion of lactiferous ducts—blockage of lumen of milk-conveying ducts.
Paget's disease of nipple—cancer directly beneath the nipple, seen in elderly women. Areola, nipple, and surrounding skin may be weeping and eczematoid. (27)
thelitis—inflammation of the nipple. (47)
tuberculosis of breast—the breast is rarely infected by tubercle bacilli. The presenting lump may be mistaken for cancer or as sinuses discharging purulent material. Breast tuberculosis appears to be secondary to tuberculosis of the internal mammary lymph nodes.

OPERATIVE TERMS (SEE TABLE 11.2.)

biopsy of breast—excision of small piece of mammary tissue for diagnostic evaluation. (27, 47, 58)
frozen section—microscopic study of slides prepared with fresh tissue of a lesion. It is valuable for rapid diagnosis while the patient awaits surgery to determine the need for a conservative approach, if the tissue section shows a benign lesion, or a radical approach, if a malignant lesion is found. (27)
incisional biopsy—tissue of lesion obtained for pathologic verification. This procedure is indicated when the tumor mass is very large. Otherwise excisional biopsy is the method of choice.
mammaplasty, mammoplasty, mastoplasty—surgical reconstruction of a breast. (27, 43)
   augmentation mammaplasty—implantation of a retromammary prosthesis for an underdeveloped breast. (59)
   reduction mammaplasty—repair of an overdeveloped, pendulous breast by partial removal of the mammary gland and fixation of the breast to its normal position.

mastectomy, mammectomy—removal of a breast. (21, 27, 43, 58)

modified radical mastectomy—consists of an en bloc removal of the breast with the underlying pectoralis major fascia (but not muscle) and axillary lymph nodes. Modified radical mastectomy provides much better cosmetic and functional outcome compared to the standard radical mastectomy.

radical mastectomy—removal of an entire breast, including axillary dissection and surgical division of pectoralis major and minor muscles.

segmental mastectomy—quadrant excision, partial mastectomy, or lumpectomy may be another option available for consideration. An additional option may be to use radiation therapy with segmental mastectomy.

simple mastectomy—removal of a breast without dissection of axillary lymph nodes.

mastopexy—surgical fixation of a pendulous breast. (63)

mastotomy—incision and drainage of a breast abscess.

TRAMM flap procedure—breast reconstruction technique utilizing the transverse rectus abdominis musculocutaneous (TRAMM) flap technique. The procedure may be performed immediately following mastectomy or it may be delayed and performed as a separate secondary procedure. (21, 22, 63)

SYMPTOMATIC TERMS

mastalgia, mastodynia—breast pain occurring in premenstrual period, mastitis, breast cancer, and other disorders. (47)

peau d'orange—skin simulating orange peel; seen in inflammatory breast cancer. (43)

ORAL READING PRACTICE

BREAST CANCER

The exact cause of **breast cancer** remains unknown. What is known is that in terms of annual mortality, approximately **46,000 women** (and **300 men**) die of breast cancer. Breast cancer is a major health problem especially for women. Breast cancer represents a chronic type of illness with the potential threat for recurrence up to 40 years after removal of the primary tumor. Several factors impact the occurrence of breast cancer: age, family history, genetics and other risk factors.

Age: 15% of breast cancer cases occur before the age of 40. After age 40, the incidence of breast cancer steadily increases with two-thirds of the cases affecting postmenopausal women.

Family history: Daughters and sisters of a breast cancer patient have a two- to threefold probable risk of developing breast cancer than do women without this first-degree relationship. Women at higher risk for breast cancer should have very careful monitoring. Also, women with a history of prior treatment for breast cancer should be carefully monitored, since they have a 10% to 15% chance of developing a secondary primary breast cancer.

Genetics: Of breast cancer patients, 5% to 10% have inherited mutations leading to breast cancer. **Two genes** have been identified and may account for most of these mutations. BRCA1 was assigned by **genetic linkage** to the long arm of **chromosome 17.** It is associated with breast cancer and with ovarian carcinoma. **BRCA2** is assigned to the long arm of **chromosome 13.** It is associated with male and female breast cancer but not ovarian carcinoma. Ongoing research continues to study genetic linkages in breast cancer as well as work toward developing a diagnostic test for mutations within these genes.

Other risk factors: **Estrogens** have an impact on the development of breast cancer. A higher risk of breast cancer appears to correlate with early menarche, late menopause, and late or no pregnancy. However, premature loss of ovarian function, late menarche, early menopause, early or more numerous pregnancies correlate with a decreased risk. Other possible risk factors to carefully monitor include **breast calcifications, lesions** that cannot be palpated, **changes in breast architecture, ionizing radiation,** and **diet.**

Usually, breast cancer is detected by the patient, by routine physical examination, or by mammography. Breast cancer presents as a painless or painful mass that may be associated with skin and muscle attachment, discharge, crusting, and retraction of nipple, changes in contour of affected breast; and **metastasis** to **regional lymph nodes.** Breast cancer spreads directly to the **bloodstream** as well as to the draining **lymphatics. Leptomeningeal metastases** present with headache and focal sensory or motor changes suggestive of nerve root involvement. This diagnosis depends upon demonstration of breast cancer cells in the **cerebrospinal fluid.** Breast cancer is the most common source of metastases to the eye in women. When a metastatic focus is identified, routine studies to map the tumor extent include a complete blood count and the measurement of **serum levels of liver enzymes, bilirubin,** and **calcium. Hypercalcemia** may be present in patients with advanced breast cancer. **Estrogen** and **progesterone receptors proteins** are present in normal **mammary epithelium** and in a proportion of breast cancers. Assays for estrogen and progesterone receptors are helpful at the stage of initial diagnosis. **Endocrine therapy** (e.g., **Tamoxifen**) has proven to be beneficial for patients whose tumors have a positive estrogen or progesterone receptor. Receptor status may change as a result of **chemotherapy, endocrine therapy,** or **radiation therapy.** Should the patient develop metastases, knowing the receptor status at the time of initial diagnosis is helpful in deciding therapy options.

The **carcinoembryonic antigen titer** and the **CA 15-3 antigen titer** can be useful markers for following response to therapy. A chest radiograph is helpful to reveal **lung nodules, mediastinal** or **hilar node involvement,** or **pleural effusion.** Clinical or other physical findings may signal the need for further diagnostic studies, such as a **bone scan** and liver studies, including a **radionuclide scan of the liver,** a **liver sonogram,** or a **liver computed tomography (CT) scan.**

Persons who develop breast cancer during pregnancy tend to present with a more advanced stage of the disease than do nonpregnant women; however, when compared stage for stage, pregnant women have only a slightly less favorable prognosis than do nonpregnant women.

Most breast tumors derive from **mammary epithelium.** Of these, 80% are **infiltrating ductal carcinomas. Ductal carcinoma in situ** often evolves into an invasive type of cancer that requires surgery. **Inflammatory breast cancer** represents a virulent pathologic variant. Hallmarks of this cancer type is the red, swollen, warm breast with a **peau d'orange** appearance. Less common occurring neoplasms are **infiltrating lobular carcinoma, medullary carcinoma, comedocarcinoma,** and **tubular, papillary,** and **colloid carcinomas.**

Early detection of masses is essential. Helpful screening and detection mechanisms include self-examination and breast imaging techniques. **Ultrasonography** can distinguish cystic from solid lesions initially found on radiography. It may be used for patients who are less than 35 years of age and who have dense breast tissue on mammogram, or a negative mammogram in a person with persistent breast symptomatology, and/or a high-risk history.

Mammography is the current most reliable means of detecting breast cancer. A **mammogram** is not a replacement for **biopsy** when a suspicious mass presents. Mammograms may miss cancer in a very dense breast and mammograms do not always identify medullary types of cancer. Suspicious masses identified on mammogram may be pinpointed by placing needles or wires under radiologic guidance. The lesion can be excised and submitted for a definitive pathological diagnosis. **The current mammographic recommendations for asymptomatic women are:**

Mammography every 1 to 2 years for women aged 50 or older. Mammography annually for women at any age with a personal history of breast cancer. Mammography annually for women aged 40 and over who have a family history of breast cancer or who are otherwise at risk.

After the breast cancer has been diagnosed, the disease is staged to assist in planning the most beneficial course of treatment. The patient's decision regarding choosing a treatment plan is based on the consideration of several factors such as age, size of tumor, stage of disease, and the presence or absence of estrogen and progesterone receptors. Treatment options available are endocrine therapy, chemotherapy, and radiation therapy, as well as several surgical procedures. Surgical procedures might include: modified radical mastectomy, radical mastectomy, segmental mastectomy, or a simple mastectomy. (See the Breast Operative Terms section for definition of these surgical procedures. See chapter 17 for specific chemotherapy agents.) Following a surgical procedure, the goal of adjuvant systemic therapy (chemotherapy, endocrine therapy, or radiation therapy) is to control any micrometastases present and thus improve survival. (1, 4, 24, 27, 30, 43, 64, 66)

REVIEW GUIDE

Instructions: Select the letter of the response that correctly completes each statement, as shown in the example.

Example: Bartholin's glands are located deep to the
   a. levator ani.   b. clitoris.   c. bulbocavernosus muscles.   <u>d.</u> none of the above.

1. Infrequent menstrual bleeding is called
   a. hypomenorrhea.
   c. dysmenorrhea.
   b. cryptomenorrhea.
   d. oligomenorrhea.

2. The space between the vulva and anus is called
   a. the perineum.
   c. the vestibule.
   b. the pudendum.
   d. none of the above.

3. The cervical canal is
   a. the superior dome-shaped portion of the uterus.
   c. the lower part of the uterus extending from isthmus to vagina.
   b. the passageway between uterine cavity and vagina.
   d. none of the above.

4. An abnormally large breast that is usually pendulous and sagging is termed
   a. hypermastia.
   c. both a and b.
   b. hypomastia.
   d. none of the above.

5. Stein-Leventhal syndrome may be called
   a. ruptured tubo-ovarian abscess.
   c. polycystic ovarian syndrome.
   b. Meigs' syndrome.
   d. pyosalpinx.

6. Downward displacement of the uterus is called
   a. anteflexion.
   c. retrocession.
   b. procidentia.
   d. retroversion.

7. Skene's glands are
   a. urethral glands in the female.
   c. horny growths of the cervical canal.
   b. warty growths near the vagina.
   d. salivary glands in the female.

8. Myoma that is embedded in the myometrium is called
   a. intraligamentous.
   c. both a and b.
   b. intramural.
   d. none of the above.

9. Inflammation of the mucous membrane that lines the corpus uteri is called
   a. perimetritis.
   c. endometritis.
   b. parametritis.
   d. endocervicitis.

10. Condylomas are
   a. cancer arising from epidermal cells.
   c. warty growths scattered over the vulva.
   b. cancer arising from squamous cells.
   d. hobnail cells.

Instructions: Break apart each term listed below, identify the medical term elements, and define the term.

Example: hysterectomy
  hyster- = root = uterus
  -ectomy = suffix = removal or excision

amastia

colpoperineorrhaphy

culdocentesis

endocervicitis

dysmenorrhea

hysteroscopy

mammogram

mastopexy

mastotomy

metrorrhagia

oligomenorrhea

salpingolysis

salpingostomy

thelitis

vulvovaginitis

Instructions: Figure 11.1 in the text shows the organs of the female reproductive system. For each line that extends from the figure below, provide the anatomic name of the site, as shown in the example.

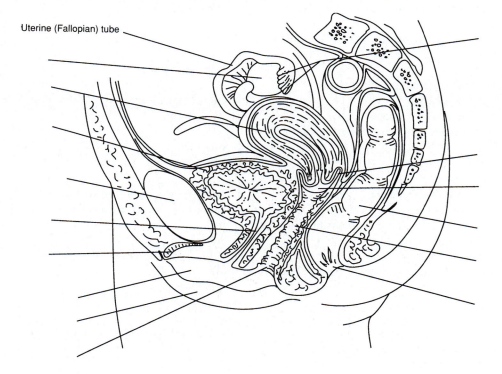

Uterine (Fallopian) tube

12

Obstetrical, Fetal, and Neonatal Conditions

THE OBSTETRICAL PERIOD

ORIGIN OF TERMS

contra- (L)—against, opposite
ec- (G)—out
ecto- (G)—outside
episio- (G) pubic region, vulva
galacto- (G)—milk
gravida (L)—pregnancy
multi- (L)—many
nulli- (L)—none

parous (L)—to bring forth, produce, birth
pelvis (L)—basin
placenta (L)—cake
pre- (L)—before, in front of
primi- (L)—first
puer- (L)—child, boy
toco- (G)—childbirth, labor

PHONETIC PRONUNCIATION OF SELECTED TERMS

choriocarcinoma   KO-re-owe-CAR-sin-NO'mah
eclampsia   e-KLAMP'see-ah
oligohydramnios   OL-i-go-hi-DRAM'nee-os
placenta abruptio   pla-SEN'tah a-BRUP'she-owe
puerperal hematoma   pu-ER'per-al HE-mah-TOE'mah

GENERAL TERMS

basal body temperature—body temperature taken under basal conditions before arising in the morning. Relatively lower levels are present in the preovulatory phase than in the postovulatory phase. (44, 54)

blighted ovum—impregnated ovum that has ceased to grow within the first trimester. (63)

contraception—voluntary prevention of pregnancy. (8)

gestation—intrauterine development of infant. (32)

    period of cleavage—during the first week, cells undergo mitosis, a blastocyst forms, and an inner cell mass appears; blastocyst becomes implanted in uterine wall.

    embryonic period—extends from the second week through the eighth week of development. The placenta is formed, the main internal organs develop, and major body structures appear during this time. In the early part of the embryonic period, the cells of the inner cell mass become organized into a flattened embryonic disk, which consists of two layers: outer (ectoderm) and inner (endoderm). Following this development, a third layer of cells (mesoderm) forms between the ectoderm and endoderm. These three layers of cells are termed *primary germ layers* and are responsible for forming all the body organs. (See fig. 12.1.) *fetal period*—ninth week to birth; approximately the second and third trimesters. Existing structures continue to grow; ossification centers appear in bones; reproductive organs develop; arms and legs reach final relative proportions; muscles become active; and head becomes positioned toward the cervix. (See fig. 12.2.)

gravida—pregnant woman. (3, 54)

high-risk gravida—there are multiple reasons for considering a pregnant woman a high-risk patient. She may be too young or too old or underweight or overweight, and may have diabetes, hypertension, urinary infection, rubella, hepatitis, Rh incompatibility, alcoholic or narcotic addiction, or be at risk for other health hazards. By identifying the problem during early gestation, appropriate treatment may be instituted to protect the mother and growing fetus. (61)

high-risk neonate—newborn in need of resuscitation due to abnormally brief or prolonged gestation, too low or too high birth weight, defective Apgar score, fetal diseases, congenital anomalies, chromosomal aberrations, and a host of maternal factors. (17)

immature infant—weight 500 to 1,000 grams and has completed at least 20 but less than 28 weeks of gestation. (54)

in vitro fertilization techniques: (13)

in vitro fertilization and embryo transfer (IVF-ET)—techniques involving removing eggs from the ovary, fertilizing them in the laboratory, and then placing them back into the patient's uterus. IVF-ET, which bypasses the mechanical transport functions of the female reproductive tract, was first instituted for patients with severe tubal disease. However, subsequently these techniques have been applied to a number of other infertility problems such as antisperm antibodies, endometriosis, oligospermia, and fertility of undetermined cause.

gamete intrafallopian tube transfer (GIFT)—superovulation is induced by a human chorionic gonadotropin (hCG) injection. Follicles are aspirated via laparoscopy. Prior to laparoscopy, the semen is collected and capacitated. In the laboratory, the eggs are identified and then mixed with sperm. The mixture of eggs and sperm is transferred to the uterine tubes, allowing fertilization and cleavage to occur. GIFT is applicable to women who have normal tubal function.

intracytoplasmic sperm injection (ICSI)—procedure that collects sperm from the male and then injects them into eggs retrieved from the female. The fertilized eggs are then transferred back into the female's uterus through the process of in vitro fertilization (IVF). This procedure, which places sperm directly into an egg, can offer help for some couples incapable of conceiving because of severe impairment in sperm production or function.

mature infant—a live-born infant who has completed 38 weeks of gestation and weighs 2,500 grams or more. (54)

multipara—woman who has given birth to two or more children. (3)

natural childbirth—childbirth in a normal physiologic manner without anesthetic or instruments. The woman participates actively and consciously in her delivery. (3, 53)

psychoprophylactic method as practiced by Lamaze, childbirth without pain—verbal analgesia based on antenatal training of the expectant mother and father. Words are used as therapeutic agents to create in the woman's mind a chain of conditioned reflexes applicable to childbirth (Pavlov's second system). The mother-to-be learns to give birth: to breathe, push, and relax effectively and to bring forth the child in a mentally alert state. The couple's united efforts make childbirth without pain a victory for both, since the husband plays an active part in the entire program.

Figure 12.1 Each of the primary germ layers is responsible for the formation of a particular set of organs.

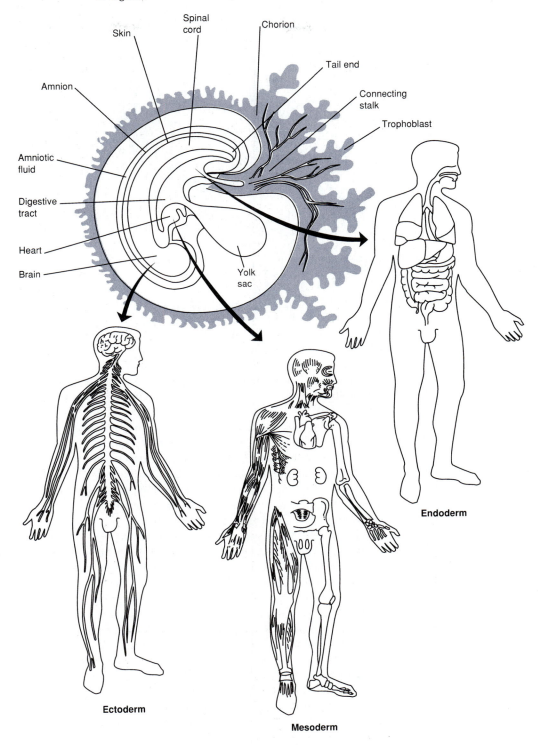

Skin

Spinal cord

Chorion

Tail end

Amnion

Connecting stalk

Trophoblast

Amniotic fluid

Digestive tract

Heart

Brain

Yolk sac

Endoderm

Ectoderm

Mesoderm

Figure 12.2 A full-term fetus usually becomes positioned with its head near the cervix.

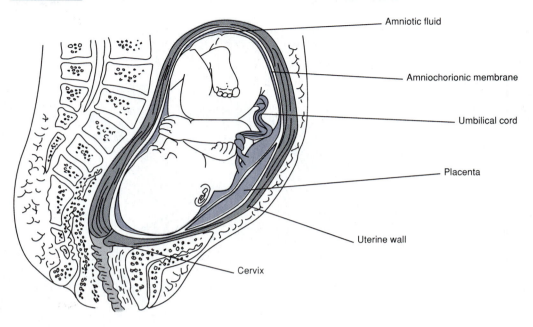

- Amniotic fluid
- Amniochorionic membrane
- Umbilical cord
- Placenta
- Uterine wall
- Cervix

Read's method, childbirth without fear—antenatal program for the mother-to-be, including education, psychological conditioning, abdominal breathing methods, exercises, and relaxation techniques preparatory to the three stages of labor. The natural childbirth preparation is focused on eliminating the fear-tension-pain syndrome.

natural family planning—method based on recognizing the fertile period of the menstrual cycle. (8, 32, 33)

calendar rhythm—a method of determining the approximate time of ovulation related to the length of a series of a woman's menstrual cycles. It is assumed that ovulation takes place within a range of 12 to 16 days before menstruation, that the maximal survival of the ovum is about 48 hours, and that the maximal survival of the sperm is about 72 hours. In obstetrics, rhythm refers to the alternating periods of sterility and fertility. Since fertility depends on the availability of the ovum, pregnancy may be avoided by practicing abstinence a few days before and after ovulation.

ovulation method, Billings method—study of the mucous pattern of fertility to predict the fertile period of the menstrual cycle. After menstruation, a discharge of sticky, cloudy mucus appears and lasts about 6 days. It is followed by a peak symptom of lubricative, clear, slippery mucus resembling egg white, which is present for 1 or 2 days. Typically, ovulation takes place within this phase. After the peak symptom, another kind of mucus forms, which is so thick, viscoid, and tenacious that the sperm cannot penetrate it. Conception may be avoided by practicing abstinence from the onset of the mucous discharge until 4 days after the appearance of the peak symptom.

temperature method—the recognition of body temperature changes during the normal menstrual cycle with a rise of temperature occurring following ovulation. The infertile period includes a preovulatory and postovulatory phase. Exact temperature recording during the postovulation phase may pinpoint the fertile period. If the body temperature is elevated for 3 consecutive days, fertilization of the ovum is no longer possible.

parturient—woman in labor. (3)

postmature infant—one that has completed 42 weeks or more of gestation. Also may be termed *postdate pregnancy*. (54)

premature infant—infant with birth weight of 1,000 but less than 2,500 grams and a gestation of at least 28 weeks but less than 38 weeks. (54)

primipara—woman who has had one pregnancy, delivered her first child resulting in the birth of a viable infant. (3)

teratogens—noxious agents (actinic, infectious, chemical, mechanical, or nutritional) capable of disrupting normal gestation, resulting in antenatal death or the birth of a misshapen, deformed neonate. (32, 61)

teratology—the study of disfiguring malformations caused by arrested embryonic growth and fetal development of organs or structures. (32, 61)

trimester of pregnancy—division of the pregnancy into a little less than 13 weeks or 3 calendar months each. (32, 61)

ANATOMIC TERMS (3, 31, 37, 54)

pelvis (pl. pelves)—bony basin is the reduced inferior portion of the abdomen. The pelvic cavity is directly continuous with the abdomen although angulated backward from it. The pelvis is adapted to childbearing in the female. Also, it is the region of transition from the trunk to the lower limbs, and the bony pelvis forms a pelvic girdle for the attachment of the limbs. The walls of the pelvis are bony and are composed of the sacrum, coccyx, and hip bones. The pelvis is closed inferiorly by the pelvic diaphragm, reinforced below by the perineal membrane. It contains the urinary bladder, the rectum, the internal genital organs, blood vessels and nerves, as well as the most dependent coils of the small intestine.

false pelvis—bounded posteriorly by lumbar vertebrae; supports pregnant uterus.
true pelvis—bounded posteriorly by sacrum; of practical significance in childbearing.
pelvic brim, pelvic inlet—upper opening into true pelvic cavity.
pelvic outlet—lower opening of the pelvis.
promontory of the sacrum—upper projecting part of the sacrum.

placenta—vascular structure that provides nutrition for the fetus. (See fig. 12.3.)

secundines, afterbirth—fetal membranes and placenta; their expulsion occurs in third stage of labor. (10)

DIAGNOSTIC TERMS

abortion—expulsion (natural spontaneous abortion or artifically induced abortion) of the products of conception, resulting in termination of the fetus. Abortions (medical or surgical) are less often performed after 20 weeks' gestation. Currently, medical beliefs indicate that viability begins at about 24 weeks. This means that the physical development of the fetus—as in development of the lung structure—is sufficient to sustain life outside the womb. The Supreme Court rulings of July 1989 require physicians to test for the viability of a fetus at 20 weeks, or two-thirds of the way through the second trimester of pregnancy. Viability has to do with *physical ability* to survive outside the womb.

habitual abortion—three or more consecutive, spontaneous abortions.
imminent, threatened abortion—vaginal bleeding, with or without pain, and cervical dilatation, usually ending in expulsion of fetus.
incomplete abortion—fetal expulsion with retention of total or partial placenta and subsequent bleeding.
induced abortion—voluntary expulsion of fetus, brought about by mechanical means or drugs.
inevitable abortion—rupture of membranes associated with cervical dilatation followed by fetal expulsion.
missed abortion—fetus dead, but retained in utero for days or weeks.

Figure 12.3   The placenta as it appears during the seventh week of development.

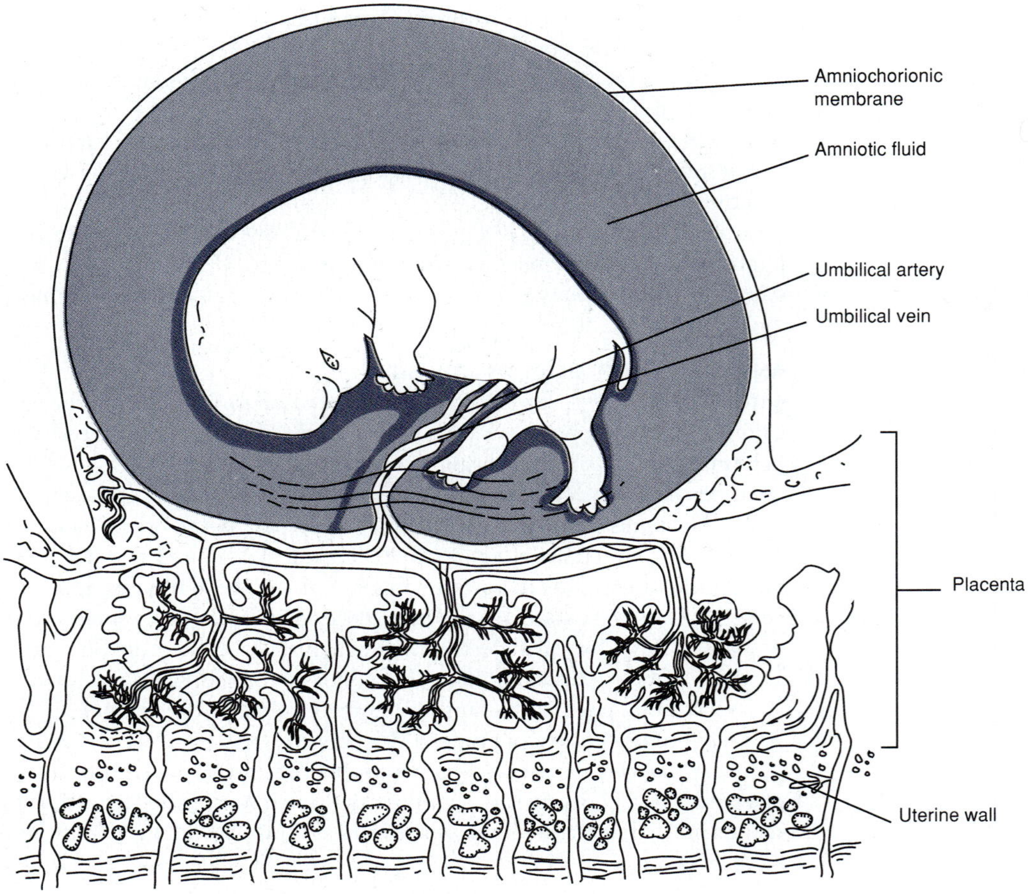

- Amniochorionic membrane
- Amniotic fluid
- Umbilical artery
- Umbilical vein
- Placenta
- Uterine wall

septic abortion—abortion with fever without any other known cause for temperature elevation, usually referred to as septic. Patients who have had interference, even if afebrile, may have a septic abortion. A foul-smelling vaginal discharge is a dominant feature. (12, 26, 40, 53)

(See *saline abortion* and *vacuum extraction,* pp. 312 and 313.)

atony of the uterus (See fig. 12.4.)—loss of uterine muscle tone, usually caused by prolonged labor, resulting in excessive uterine hemorrhage, unrelated to retained products or cervical lacerations, following the completion of the third stage of labor. (10, 61)

cervical incompetence—refers to obstetric condition characterized by painless dilatation of the cervix during the midtrimester of pregnancy, followed by rupture of the membranes and subsequent expulsion of the fetus. The cause of cervical incompetence has not been definitively determined, but several causative factors proposed include: prior trauma to the cervix, conization, cauterization, and traumatic delivery. (49)

ectopic pregnancy—fertilized ovum implanted outside of uterine cavity, for example, in a fallopian tube or ovary, or free in abdomen, attached to a viscus. (12, 53)

hyperemesis gravidarum—severe nausea and vomiting during the first months of pregnancy, which may cause dehydration and serious metabolic disturbances in mother and fetus. (12, 54)

Figure 12.4 Bimanual compression of the uterus and massage with the abdominal hand usually will effectively control hemorrhage due to uterine atony.

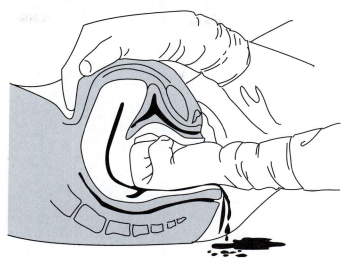

hypertensive disorders of pregnancy—blood pressure of 140/90 mm Hg and above, preceding pregnancy or developing during gestation or in early puerperium. Proteinuria, edema, convulsions, and coma may be present.

> *eclampsia*—major disorder of pregnancy and puerperium, manifested by high blood pressure, convulsions, renal dysfunction, headache, edema, and cases of severe coma.
> *preeclampsia*—usually a disorder of a first pregnancy but may also occur in multiparas who are severely hypertensive or diabetic; characterized by high blood pressure, sudden and excessive weight gain related to fluid retention and kidney dysfunction, proteinuria, or albuminuria. (40, 58)

inversion of the uterus (See fig. 12.5.)—sometimes during the postdelivery stage, the uterus begins to turn itself inside out. This usually starts in the area of the placental attachment of the fundus; the myometrium begins to prolapse downward through the remainder of the uterine cavity and can continue past the dilatated cervix into the vagina. (10)

involution of uterus—postpartum return of uterus to its former shape and size. (47)

oligohydramnios—deficient amount of amniotic fluid. (24)

phlegmasia alba dolens—phlebitis of femoral vein; may occur postpartum. (54)

placenta ablatio, placenta abruptio—premature detachment of the placenta, generally causing severe hemorrhage. (27, 52)

placenta accreta—placenta adheres directly to the myometrium without an intervening layer; placenta remains attached to the uterus after delivery. (10, 27)

placenta previa (See fig. 12.6.)—displaced placenta, implanted in lower segment of uterine wall.

> *marginal placenta previa insertion*—placenta comes up to the ostium uteri but does not cover it.
> *partial placenta previa*—placenta covers the ostium uteri incompletely.
> *complete or central placenta previa*—placenta entirely obstructs the ostium uteri. (27, 52)

polyhydramnios, hydramnios—excessive amount of amniotic fluid. (24, 38)

premature rupture of membranes—rupture of the chorioamniotic membranes prior to the onset of labor. (22)

puerperal hematoma—escape of blood into the mucosa or subcutaneous tissues of the external genitalia, forming painful vaginal or vulvar hematomas (blood tumors). They may also form in broad ligaments. (10, 47, 56)

Figure 12.5 (a) Incomplete inversion of the uterus. Diagnosis is determined by abdominal palpation of the fundal wall in the lower segment and cervix. (b) Progressive degrees of inversion.

(a)

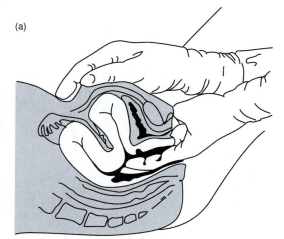

(b)

Figure 12.6 Placental types.

Normal | Marginal previa | Partial previa | Complete previa

puerperal infection, puerperal fever, childbed fever, puerperal septicemia, puerperal sepsis—infection of the genital tract occurring within the postpartum period. Fever is the dominant characteristic of puerperal infection; however, the puerpera may have fever from other causes, such as kidney, urinary tract, breast, or lung infections.

    puerperal febrile morbidity—temperature elevation of 100.4° F (38° C) or higher occurring after the first 24 hours postpartum on two or more occasions that are not within the same 24-hour period. (47, 56)

rupture of uterus, hysterorrhexis, metrorrhexis—laceration of uterus; a torn uterus. (52)

subinvolution—failure of the uterus to reduce to its normal size after delivery. (23)

trophoblast—layer of ectoderm that attaches the conceptus to the uterine wall, nourishes the embryo, and has invasive propensities and thus malignant potentials. (40, 48)

trophoblastic disease—disease originating in trophoblast.

    gestational trophoblastic neoplasms: (12, 38, 48)

- *chorioadenoma destruens*—malignant, nonmetastasizing, invasive tumor that may penetrate the muscular coat and even the serosa of the uterus and neighboring structures, rendering its removal difficult. Trophoblastic proliferation tends to be excessive.
- *choriocarcinoma*—highly malignant, invasive tumor derived from fetal trophoblast. Neoplastic cells infiltrate the myometrium and readily metastasize to the liver, lungs, brain, and pelvic organs. Choriocarcinoma may be a complication of a hydatidiform mole.
- *hydatidiform mole*—developmental abnormality of the placenta characterized by the conversion of chorionic villi into a mass of vesicles that resemble hanging grapes. Embryonic growth is usually terminated, but if it continues to full term, the neonate will probably be stillborn.

uteroplacental apoplexy, Couvelaire uterus—sudden, severe retroplacental bleeding into the myometrium. (27)

OPERATIVE TERMS (SEE TABLE 12.1.)

cesarean section—removal of the fetus through an incision into the uterus. (28)

episiotomy—incision of perineum to facilitate delivery and prevent perineal laceration. (3)

    median episiotomy—midline incision of perineum.

    mediolateral episiotomy—the incision is directed toward one side of the midline.

procedures for cervical incompetence: (49)

    McDonald cerclage procedure—multiple-bite suture of large-sized monofilament nylon is placed around the cervix and tied securely, resulting in reduction of the diameter of the cervical canal to a few millimeters.

    Shirodkar procedure—technique whereby mersaline tape encircles the cervix and is passed under the mucosa and anchored to the cervix anteriorly and posteriorly with silk ligatures.

    transabdominal cervicoisthmic cerclage procedure—technique utilizes mersaline band in an avascular space medial to the uterine vessels at the level of the cervicouterine junction.

SYMPTOMATIC TERMS

attitude, obstetric—intrauterine position of the fetus. (63)

ballottement—method of detecting pregnancy or testing for engagement of fetal head. The examiner sharply taps against the lower uterine segment with the forefinger in the vagina and tosses the fetus upward. (54)

Bandl's ring—groove seen on the abdomen between the pubis and umbilicus after hard labor.

Braxton-Hicks' sign—painless contractions of the uterus throughout gestation. They occur periodically and last until term. (54)

TABLE 12.1	Some Obstetrical Conditions Amenable to Surgery		
Anatomic Site	*Diagnosis*	*Type of Surgery*	*Operative Procedures*
Cervix uteri Endometrium	Early incomplete abortion	Dilatation and curettage	Instrumental expansion of cervix and scraping of endometrium to remove blood clots and tissue
Cervix uteri	Dystocia Cervical stenosis Carcinoma of cervix in pregnancy; viable fetus	Cesarean section	Removal of fetus through incision into uterus
Cervix uteri	Obstetric laceration of cervix	Trachelorrhaphy	Suture of torn cervix uteri
Uterine tube	Ruptured ectopic pregnancy with hemorrhage	Salpingectomy unilateral	Removal of one fallopian tube
Perineum	Second stage of labor, tense perineum	Episiotomy, mediolateral or midline	Incision into perineum
Perineum	Obstetric laceration of the perineum	Perineorrhaphy	Suture of torn perineum
Pelvis	Inlet contraction of pelvis	Cesarean section	Abdominal delivery of fetus
Pelvis	Prolonged labor, dystocia	Elective forceps delivery	Fetus delivered by horizontal traction
Uterus	Rupture of uterus, fatal hemorrhage, maternal death	Postmortem cesarean section	Delivery of fetus by incision through abdominal wall and uterus after death of mother
Uterus	Placenta previa, antepartum or intrapartum hemorrhage	Cesarean section	Incision into corpus uteri and delivery of fetus through abdomen

Chadwick's sign—violet discoloration of the vaginal mucosa, presumptive evidence of pregnancy. (54)

colostrum—yellowish fluid secreted by the mammary gland during pregnancy and for the first 2 or 3 days postdelivery. (63)

dilatation of cervix—gradual opening of the cervix to permit passage of fetus.

dystocia—difficult birth. (46)

effacement—obliteration of cervix; the process of thinning and shortening of the uterine cervix. (3)

engagement—descent of the fetal head through the pelvic inlet. (3)

engorgement—excessive venous and lymph stasis of lactating breasts, usually referred to as *caked breasts*. (3)

gestation—pregnancy.

Goodell's sign—cyanosis and softening of the uterine cervix due to increased vascularity of the cervical tissue, indicative of pregnancy. This change may occur as early as 4 weeks. (55)

Figure 12.7 Stages in the birth process: (a) Fetal position before labor; (b) dilatation of the cervix; (c) expulsion of the fetus; (d) expulsion of the placenta.

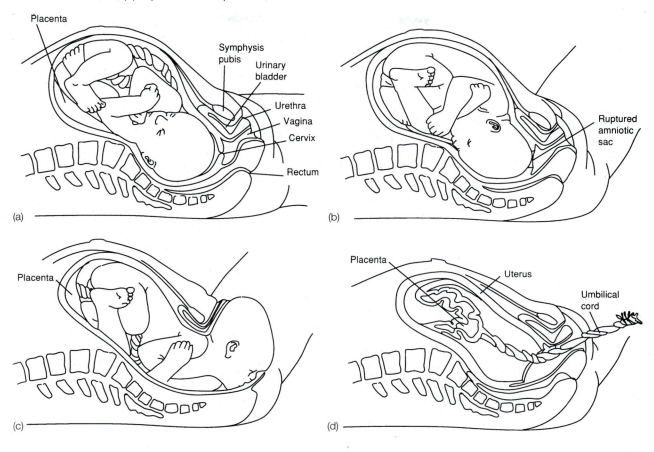

Hegar's sign—widening of the softened area of the isthmus, resulting in compressibility of the isthmus on bimanual examination. This occurs by 6 to 8 weeks. (55)

hemorrhage—excessive blood loss.

    antepartum—before birth.

    intrapartum—during delivery.

    postpartum—after delivery. (4, 10)

labor—normal uterine contractions that result in the delivery of the fetus. (3) (See fig. 12.7.)

    missed labor—a few contractions at full term, then cessation of labor and fetal retention, usually due to death of fetus in utero or extrauterine pregnancy.

    precipitate labor—hasty labor.

    premature labor—before full term.

    preterm labor—onset of labor prior to 37 completed weeks of gestation.

    protracted labor—unduly prolonged.

labor—three stages: (3, 5) (See fig. 12.7.)

    cervical dilatation, cervical stage—first stage begins with uterine contractions and terminates with complete cervical dilatation.

expulsion, pelvic stage—second stage, from complete dilatation of the cervix to the birth of the neonate.

placental separation and expulsion, placental stage—third stage, from delivery of neonate to expulsion of the placenta.

lie of the fetus—relation between the longitudinal axis of the fetus and the longitudinal axis of the mother.

transverse lie—the long axis of the body of the fetus crosses the long axis of the maternal body. In this situation, the shoulder usually presents first, but the arm, trunk, or any part of the trunk may be the first to appear. This condition also may be termed *torso, transverse,* or *trunk presentation.* (3, 5)

lochia—discharge from the birth canal following delivery.

pica—cravings of the pregnant woman for strange food or nonedibles. (61)

presentation or presenting part (See fig. 12.8.)—refers to the portion of the fetus that overrides the pelvic inlet. Cephalic presentation occurs in more than 95% of term labors. (3, 29) Presentation variations include:

breech presentation—presentation of the fetal buttock.
- *complete breech*—thighs flexed on abdomen and legs flexed on thighs.
- *footling*—the foot presents.
- *frank breech*—legs extended over ventral body surface.
- *knee*—the knee presents.

face presentation—presentation of the fetal head.
- *brow*—the forehead presents.
- *sinciput*—the large fontanel presents.
- *vertex*—the upper and back part of the head presents. This is the most common variety. (See transverse lie above.)

quickening—the pregnant woman's first perception of fetal life. In primigravidas, this occurs at 18–20 weeks, and at 14–16 weeks in the multigravidas. (54)

sterility—total inability to conceive. (64)

SELECTED PROCEDURES PERTAINING TO OBSTETRICAL CARE

anti-D antibody injection—preparation for passive immunization of Rh-negative mothers of D-positive babies, administered intramuscularly or intravenously within 72 hours after delivery. Its purpose is to prevent Rh isoimmunization and fetal hemolytic disease in future pregnancies. The individual sterile vaccine vials are prepared from plasma obtained from severely sensitized Rh-negative women who had stillborn hydropic fetuses or from gamma globulin from naturally or artificially sensitized donors. (5)

bimanual compression of uterus—massage of the posterior aspect of the uterus with abdominal hand massage and massage through the vagina of the anterior uterine aspect with the other fist, the knuckles of which contact the uterine wall. (10)

breech extraction—method of delivery when the presenting parts are the buttocks or feet. The fetus is pulled out. (61)

forceps application—instrumental delivery of child. (9, 28) The latest classification of the American College of Obstetricians and Gynecologists (1988) emphasized two factors: (1) the station of the fetal head in the pelvis was estimated in centimeters. Station referred to the level of the leading bony point of the head at or below the level of the maternal ischial spines. Engagement implied that the biparietal diameter (BPD) had passed through the pelvic inlet, and that the leading bony edge of the fetal head was usually at the level of the ischial spines (0 station); (2) the degree of rotation, which was classified as ≤ 45 degrees and greater than 45 degrees. The category of high forceps was elminiated. (See table 12.2.)

Figure 12.8 Selected variations in fetal presentations. Vertex presentation. (a) Right occiput anterior position; (b) left occiput anterior position. Vertex presentation. (c) Right occiput posterior position; (d) left occiput posterior position. Face presentation. (e) Right mentum posterior position; (f) left mentum anterior position. Breech presentation. (g) Left sacrum anterior position; (h) right sacrum posterior position.

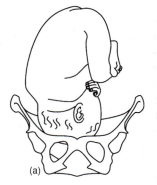
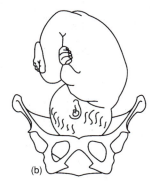

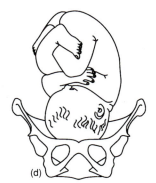

Vertex presentation. (a) Right occiput anterior position; (b) left occiput anterior position.

Vertex presentation. (c) Right occiput posterior position; (d) left occiput posterior position.

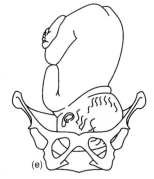

Face presentation. (e) Right mentum posterior position; (f) left mentum anterior position.

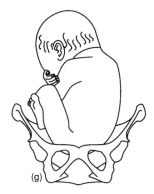
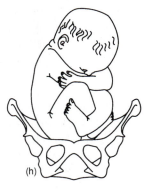

Breech presentation. (g) Left sacrum anterior position; (h) right sacrum posterior position.

TABLE 12.2	Criteria of Forceps Deliveries According to Station and Rotation
Type of Procedure	*Criteria*
Outlet forceps	1. Scalp is visible at the introitus without separating labia 2. Fetal skull has reached pelvic floor 3. Sagittal suture is anteroposterior diameter or right or left occiput anterior or posterior position 4. Fetal head is at or on perineum 5. Rotation does not exceed 45°
Low forceps	Leading point of fetal skull is at station ≥ +2 cm, and not on the pelvic floor a. Rotation ≤ 45° (left or right occiput anterior to occiput anterior, or left or right occiput posterior to occiput posterior) b. Rotation > 45°
Midforceps	Station above +2 cm but head engaged
High	Not included in classification

Source: American College of Obstetricians and Gynecologists, *Operative Vaginal Delivery*, Technical Bulletin No. 196 (Washington, D.C.: ACOG, 1994). Reprinted with permission.

Figure 12.9   Manual removal of the placenta. Fingers are alternately abducted, adducted, and advanced until the placenta is detached.

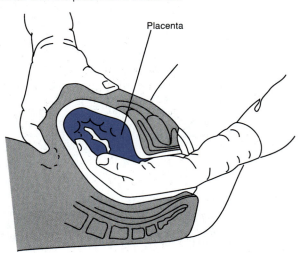

Placenta

manual delivery of placenta (See fig. 12.9.)—performed by using one hand to grasp the placenta, which is held in the vagina or the lower uterine segment by gentle traction on the umbilical cord. When the placenta has been delivered to the introitus, its weight is supported, allowing more gradual delivery to avoid torn and retained fetal membranes. A clamp placed across the membrane to provide even tension during this portion of the delivery may prove helpful. (10)

saline abortion—intra-amniotic injection of hypertonic salt solution after 14 weeks of gestation to induce abortion. (28)

vacuum extraction—instrumental delivery of infant with a vacuum extractor. Indicated in fetal distress, malpresentation, or prolapse of arm, as well as in cases of maternal inertia, prolonged labor, heart-lung disease, shock, and toxemia. (28)

version—the process of turning the fetus in the uterus. (28)

> *cephalic version*—the head is made the presenting part.
> *podalic version*—the breech is made the presenting part.

THE FETAL PERIOD

ORIGIN OF TERMS

amnion (G)—bowel, membrane enveloping the fetus

anti- (G)—against

chorion (G)—membrane around fetus
   (outermost extraembryonic membrane)

fetus (L)—offspring

terato- (G)—monster

toxico- (G)—poison

PHONETIC PRONUNCIATION OF SELECTED TERMS

fetal anomaly   FE′tal a-NOM′ah-lee

fetal anoxia   FE′tal a-NOK′see-ah

fetal hemolytic disease   FE′tal HE-mo-LIT′ick dis-EASE′

fetotoxicity   FE-to-tok-SIS′i-tee

intrauterine asphyxia   IN-tra-U′er-in as-FICK′see-ah

ANATOMIC TERMS (32) (SEE FIG. 12.10.)

amnion—the innermost fetal membrane, which forms the bag of waters and encloses the fetus.

amniotic fluid—fluid contained in the amniotic sac.

chorion—the cellular, outermost extraembryonic membrane composed of trophoblast lined with mesoderm. It develops villi about 2 weeks after fertilization and later gives rise to the placenta and persists until birth.

embryo—the product of conception, from about 2 weeks after fertilization to the end of the seventh or eighth week.

fetus—the unborn offspring in the postembryonic period, after the major structures have been outlined, usually from the seventh or eighth weeks after fertilization until birth.

DIAGNOSTIC TERMS

abortus (pl. abortuses)—fetus that weighs about 500 grams (17 ounces) when expelled from the uterus and thus is unable to survive. (63)

fetal alcohol syndrome (FAS)—alcohol produces a set of physical and mental abnormalities in the fetus, resulting from the pregnant woman ingesting alcohol (as little as 3 ounces per day or in binge drinking). The symptoms of this syndrome consist of abnormal facial features, small head size, impaired growth, organ malformations, mental retardation, and hyperactivity. (18)

fetal anomaly, preventable—malformed fetus caused by the mother taking teratogenic drugs during pregnancy; for example, anticarcinogens, such as methotrexate, ovarian or testicular steroids, such as androgen, estrogen, and progesterone, as well as thalidomide, cocaine, and alcohol. (42) (See table 12.3.)

fetal anoxia, intrauterine asphyxia—oxygen want of the fetus that may result from prolapse of the cord, placenta abruptio, compression of the umbilical vein, or other causes. Death is inevitable if fetus is not delivered promptly. (29)

fetal distress—life-threatening condition caused by fetal anoxia, hemolytic disease, or other disorders. (29)

Figure 12.10 (a–c) Changes occurring during the fifth week of development; (d–g) changes occurring during the sixth and seventh weeks of development.

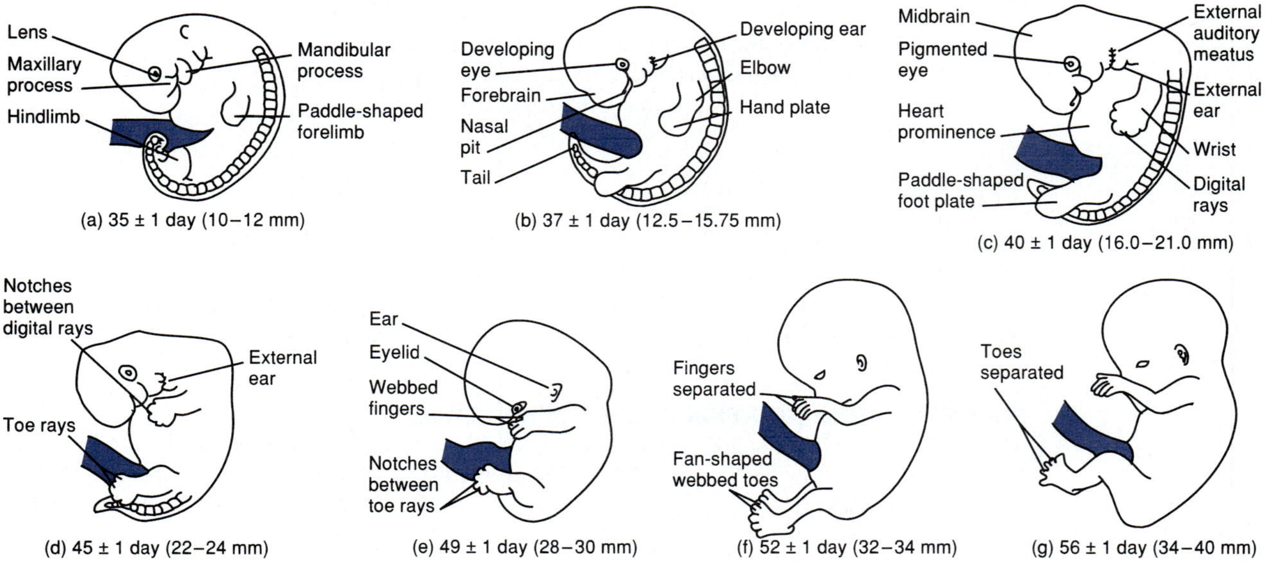

Lens

Maxillary process

Hindlimb

C

Mandibular process

Paddle-shaped forelimb

(a) 35 ± 1 day (10–12 mm)

Developing eye

Forebrain

Nasal pit

Tail

Developing ear

Elbow

Hand plate

(b) 37 ± 1 day (12.5–15.75 mm)

Midbrain

Pigmented eye

Heart prominence

Paddle-shaped foot plate

External auditory meatus

External ear

Wrist

Digital rays

(c) 40 ± 1 day (16.0–21.0 mm)

Notches between digital rays

Toe rays

External ear

(d) 45 ± 1 day (22–24 mm)

Ear

Eyelid

Webbed fingers

Notches between toe rays

(e) 49 ± 1 day (28–30 mm)

Fingers separated

Fan-shaped webbed toes

(f) 52 ± 1 day (32–34 mm)

Toes separated

(g) 56 ± 1 day (34–40 mm)

fetal hemolytic disease—blood disorder caused by antibody antigen reaction in ABO, Rh, or other blood group incompatibility. Maternal antibodies cross the placenta, agglutinate fetal blood cells, and destroy them. Fetal anemia develops. (27)

fetotoxicity—toxic effects of maternal medication on fetus and neonate. Hazards of fetotoxicity also include maternal immunization (Sabin) for poliomyelitis, smallpox vaccination, and compulsive nicotine smoking. (54) (See table 12.3.)

hypoxic-ischemic cerebral injury—condition results from a combination of hypoxemia and ischemia usually associated with impaired cerebrovascular autoregulation. The condition may be further exacerbated by diminished glucose supply to the brain, lactic acidosis, and other metabolic derangements. The extent of the hypoxic-ischemic cerebral injury is determined by the maturity of the brain at the time of insult and the severity and duration of the insult. Monitoring of fetal heart rate, fetal scalp blood gas sampling, and biophysical profile may aid in the diagnosis and timing of the antepartum insult. Infants who sustain hypoxic-ischemic cerebral injury early in gestation and before delivery may be asymptomatic in the neonatal period. Term newborns who sustain sufficient intrapartum insult may demonstrate clinical evidence of acute encephalopathy during the first days of life. (30)

intrauterine growth retardation (IUGR), intrauterine growth restriction (IUGR)—condition occurs in an infant whose birth weight occurs in the percentile ranking equal or less than the fifth percentile for gestational age and sex. The condition may result from:

maternal substrate factors (glucose, amino acids, and oxygen in the blood)—maternal nutrition before and during prgnancy is vital in terms of fetal growth. Lung disease, asthma, or alcohol consumption can affect fetal growth.

placental substrate transfer factors—vascular diseases, such as hypertension with constricted spiral arteries, affects the growth phases of the placenta, which may cease early, resulting in a smaller placenta that not only weighs less but also presents with a reduced surface area for exchange. The uterine blood flow can be restricted due to diseased blood vessels or vessels that are in spasm.

TABLE 12.3	Selected High-risk Agents Causing Fetotoxicity	
Drug Classification	*Name of Drug*	*Fetotoxic Complications*
Analgesics	Acetylsalicylic acid (aspirin, excessive use), other salicylates	Bleeding of neonate Convulsions Encephalopathy
Antianxiety drugs (ataractics, tranquilizers)	Diazepam (Valium) Meprobamate (Equanil)	Bleeding of neonate Retarded growth
Anticoagulants (coumarin)	Coumadin Dicumarol Warfarin	Bleeding of neonate Hypoprothrombinemia Fetal death
Hypnotics, sedatives	Barbiturates Phenobarbital Pentobarbital Thiopental	Withdrawal syndrome Retarded growth Bleeding of neonate Hyperbilirubinemia
Narcotics	Heroin Meperidine (Demerol) Methadone (Dolophine) Morphine	Withdrawal syndrome Convulsions Nerve damage Retarded growth Neonatal death
	Cocaine	Withdrawal syndrome Convulsions Nerve damage Retarded growth Congenital malformations
	Alcohol	Withdrawal syndrome Central nervous system dysfunction Mental retardation Attention deficit disorder Hyperactivity Growth retardation

fetal substrate utilization factors—diseases such as congenital cardiovascular abnormalities or trisomy 13 or 18 can interfere with fetal substrate utilization. Acclerated fetal metabolism may result from TORCH (toxoplasmosis, other [e.g. syphilis], rubella, cytomegalovirus, and herpes simplex).

In cases of suspected IUGR, weekly evaluation of the fetus should be instituted and may include:

ultrasonography—sonographic evaluation of head growth, biparietal diameter, and amniotic fluid volume, as well as fetal vessel Doppler velocimetry, which exhibits measurements of the sprectum of blood flow velocities, using pulsed or continuous-wave Doppler ultrasound to describe pattern of growth abnormality.

fetal heart monitoring—contraction stress test

placental insufficiency assessment—oxytocin challenge test.

chemical testing—estriol and hPL (human placental lactogen) levels. (11, 17, 27, 42, 61, 62)

meconium aspiration—occurs due to meconium staining of the amniotic fluid or fetus and occurs in utero in one-fifth of all deliveries and may be indicative of fetal distress. Meconium is usually not observed in the amniotic fluid before 34 weeks of gestation. Meconium in the amniotic fluid may stain the umbilical cord, placenta, and fetus. Despite aggressive obstetric and pediatric suctioning at birth, newborn meconium aspiration continues to occur in pregnancies complicated by meconium-stained fluid.

prolapse of cord—premature descent of the umbilical cord, a cause of fetal death. (9)

Figure 12.11 Fetal cells can be obtained by means of amniocentesis.

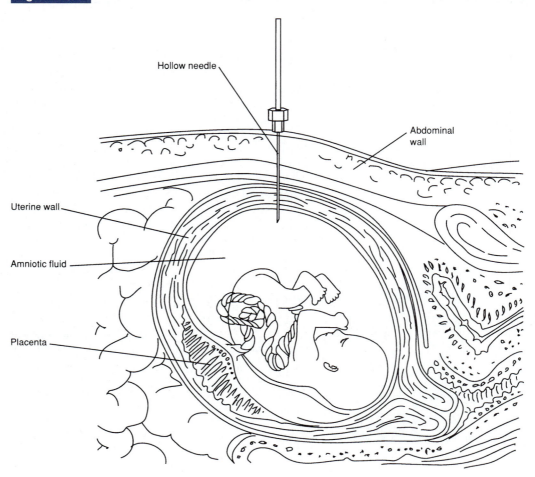

Hollow needle

Abdominal wall

Uterine wall

Amniotic fluid

Placenta

SELECTED PROCEDURES PERTAINING TO FETAL DEVELOPMENT

amniocentesis (See fig. 12.11.)—puncture of the amniotic cavity. This procedure may be performed to aspirate fluid for amniotic fluid analysis; inject radiopaque substance for amniography; administer intrauterine transfusions to the fetus with severe hemolytic disease; determine pressure changes of amniotic fluid, which permit the continuous monitoring of uterine contractibility; monitor the fetal heart rate; and detect possible genetic disorders antenatally. (6, 60, 62)

amnioinfusion—technique utilizing intrauterine catheters to infuse 1000 cc saline into women in labor with thick meconium. The infusion of normal saline solution dilutes the concentration of meconium in amniotic fluid and reduces fetal heart rate pattern abnormalities, both of which contribute to a decrease in meconium aspiration before birth. Infants born to women with meconium-stained fluid receiving amnioinfusion are less likely to have meconium below the vocal cords and less likely to have meconium aspiration syndrome than are infants born to women with meconium-stained fluid who did not receive amnioinfusion. (14, 68)

chorionic villus sampling (CVS)—under direct ultrasound guidance, the catheter is passed either transcervically, or transabdominally, or transvaginally, and placed within the villi of the chorion frondosum. The obtained fetal chorionic villi samplings are placed in a culture medium, and under a dissecting microscope, the villi are separated from maternal decidual tissue. The tissue obtained in CVS is fetal trophoblastic tissue that expresses nearly all the enzymes found in amniocytes and provides an excellent source of fetal deoxyribonucleic acid (DNA). The CVS can be performed at 9 to 12 weeks of gestation. Fetal disorders indicative of either cytogenetic, biochemical, or molecular nature can be ascertained by CVS. (60, 61)

fetal blood sampling—technique utilizing a 22-gauge spinal needle that is guided by ultrasound into one of the umbilical cord vessels, allowing access to fetal blood. Blood sampling has been helpful in the assessment of fetal infection (toxoplasmosis), coagulopathies (hemophilia A [factor VIII deficiency]), and white blood cell disorders such as chronic granulomatous disease), hemoglobinopathies (sickle cell disease and thalassemia major), resolution of mosaicism from amniocentesis sampling, and anemias. Fetal blood sampling provides a more direct and objective measurement of fetal anemias than studies of amniotic fluid, and therefore is a more accurate indicator when transfusions should be performed *in utero*. Fetal blood sampling also can be used to monitor the levels of drugs administered to the mother in order to treat the fetus, e.g., cardiac arrhythmias can be treated by administering drugs in this manner. (2, 60, 61)

fetal electrocardiography—method of detecting and recording electric impulses of the fetal heart. There are two distinct methods of detecting fetal electrocardiogram (FECG) signals:

direct recording—signal is obtained by direct attachment of the electrodes to the fetus.

indirect recording—signal is picked up from maternal electrodes.

The direct method gives a more accurate picture. The external maternal electrodes have been supplanted in favor of the more convenient Doppler ultrasonography for noninvasive monitoring. Doppler techniques can aid in obtaining functional information about the cardiovascular system in the fetus. Color Doppler techniques provide information about the flow of blood in the structures being visualized. A congenital malformation may lead to abnormalities of the velocity of flow on color Doppler, detecting clues for determining the correct diagnosis. Spectral Doppler velocimetry permits assessments of systolic fetal cardiac function, volume flows, diastolic function, and valvular insufficiency. (42, 61)

fetal heart rate monitoring—continuous record of fetal heart rate (FHR) patterns from a direct fetal electrocardiogram (FECG) electrode and uterine contractions using a transcervical catheter. Indications are clinical signs of fetal distress, FHR changes, suspected cephalopelvic disproportions, and high-risk pregnancies. Should the electronic fetal heart monitoring indicate fetal distress during oxytocin augmentation or induction of labor, the oxytocin infusion should cease until the fetal condition is evaluated and corrective measures instituted. (42, 57, 61)

fetal intrauterine transfusion—the injection of red cell concentrate prepared from Rh-negative whole blood (packed erythrocytes) into the peritoneal cavity of the fetus to combat fetal hemolytic anemia and prevent fetal death. (2, 6)

Other surveillance tests of fetal well-being: (42, 57, 61)

biophysical profile (BPP)—scoring method for antepartum fetal risk assessment based on a dynamic ultrasound survey of biophysical variables, which may include fetal breathing movements, gross body movements, fetal tone, reactive fetal heart rate, and qualitative amniotic fluid volume. In some health centers, the nonstress test may be included with this clinical study or performed only when one or more of the ultrasound-monitored variables are abnormal.

contraction stress test (CST)—measures the fetal response to a given stress. Uterine activity is evaluated for spontaneous contractions. This test attempts to mimic the stress of uterine contractions during labor. The **presence of late decelerations** is suggestive of fetal compromise. The **absence of late decelerations** correlates with fetal well-being.

Contractions are induced by means of intermittent nipple stimulation or dilute oxytocin infusion. When oxytocin is used, the test is referred to as the *oxytocin challenge test*. *nonstress test (NST)*—is an observational test in which the FHR response to fetal movement is noted. The test assesses the functional competence of the fetal central nervous system at the time of testing. The presence of normal movements accompanying fetal heart rate accelerations strongly suggest that the uteroplacental unit is functioning normally. The NST is usually the primary means of fetal surveillance for most conditions that place the fetus at high risk for placental insufficiency.

THE NEONATAL PERIOD

ORIGIN OF TERMS

blasto- (G)—germ, bud
chordo- (G)—cord
erythro- (G)—red
natus (L)—birth
neo- (G)—new, recent
neonate (L)—newborn
omphalo- (G)—navel
umbilicus (L)—navel

PHONETIC PRONUNCIATION OF SELECTED TERMS

asphyxia neonatorum	as-FICK'see-ah NEE-owe-nay-TOR'um
atelectasis neonatorum	AT-e-LECK'ta-sis NEE-owe-nay-TOR'um
erythroblastosis fetalis	e-RITH-ro-blas-TOE'sis FEE'tal-is
kernicterus	ker-NICK'ter-us
meconium	me-KO'nee-um
meningocele	me-NING'owe-seal
pylorospasm	pie-LOR'owe-spasm
vernix caseosa	VER'nicks KA-se-OWE'sa

ANATOMIC TERMS (31, 32)

fontanel, fontanelle—the junction point of cranial sutures that remain widely open in the newborn.
umbilical cord—cord connecting placenta with fetal umbilicus. At birth it is chiefly composed of one umbilical vein and two umbilical arteries surrounded by a gelatinous substance.

DIAGNOSTIC TERMS

asphyxia neonatorum—lack of oxygen in the blood of the newborn. (1, 55)
atelectasis neonatorum—failure of lungs to expand at birth.
caput succedaneum—tumorlike edema of presenting part of neonate's head. (25, 43)
cerebral hemorrhage—brain hemorrhage due to birth injury or coagulation defects, resulting in anoxia, cyanosis, and convulsions. (30)
congenital stridor—breathing disorders associated with a crowing noise from birth or first week of life caused by malformation, abnormal position, or malfunctioning of glottis, trachea, or vocal cords. (65)
cord hemorrhage—bleeding from umbilical cord. (9)
Down's syndrome, mongolism, trisomy G$_{21}$—chromosome aberration characterized by mental retardation and many physical features, such as slanting eyes; flat facial profile; thick, fissured tongue protruding from open mouth; pudgy, broad neck; hypotonia; and absence of the Moro reflex in the newborn. (33, 60)
drug addiction in neonate—withdrawal symptoms in the newborn appearing soon after birth. The infant is restless and has a shrill cry, tremors, twitching, and convulsions. Manifestations of withdrawal may closely parallel those of adult withdrawal, such as yawning, sneezing, anorexia, and diarrhea. (18, 64)

erythroblastosis fetalis (EBF)—hemolytic disease of the newborn. EBF presents as one of the most common and most severe diseases in the neonate. It results from ABO and Rh incompatibility and also by factors C, E, Kell, and others that belong to the IgG group and are able to cross the placenta. ABO incompatibility appears more frequently, but Rh incompatibility is more severe. Combined ABO and Rh incompatibility occurs rarely. Clinical findings that may be present in the newborn include jaundice, pallor, and hepatosplenomegaly. Synonyms for EBF are *icterus gravis neonatorum, hydrops fetalis,* and *congenital anemia of the newborn.*

> *anemic type*—damage to bone marrow, liver, and spleen; excessive hemolysis.
> *hydropic type*—extremely edematous, pleural, pericardial, and ascitic effusions are present. Stillborn or neonatal death may result. *Hydrops fetalis* refers to pathologically increased fluid accumulation in serous cavities or edema of soft tissue in a fetus. *Hydrops fetalis* secondary to red blood cell deficiency (usually due to isoimmunization-induced hemolysis) may be treated before birth by transfusing red blood cells into the fetus. Percutaneous umbilical cord puncture permits the blood to be transfused directly into the fetal vascular system.
> *icteric type*—marked jaundice; may be followed by kernicterus. Kernicterus may develop if the serum bilirubin is above 20 milligrams per deciliter (mg/dL). (4, 6)

hydrocephalus—abnormal fluid collection in the ventricles of the brain, resulting in an enlargement of the head. (30, 63)

hyperbilirubinemia, neonatal—abnormally high bilirubin content of the circulating blood, predisposing the newborn to kernicterus due to unconjugated bilirubin concentration within brain tissue. (1, 17, 41)

hypoxia of the newborn—reduction of oxygen supply to tissue below physiological levels despite adequate perfusion of the tissue by blood. After birth, the newborn's total bodily requirements of oxygen increase rapidly and if additional oxygen is not supplied immediately, permanent brain damage may result. It is important that the air passages be patent and not occluded by inhalation of amniotic fluid. It is essential that the inhaled oxygen reach the alveoli, so that adequate respiratory exchange can occur in the alveoli. (30, 50)

> *hypoxic-ischemic encephalopathy*—brain disorder usually resulting from an insult that is due to hypoxia-ischemia cerebral injury. Classifications of this disorder are:
> - *mild hypoxic-ischemic encephalopathy*—characterized by hyperalertness and jitteriness, and exaggerated tendon reflexes and Moro responses that do not last longer than 24 hours and are not associated with long-term sequelae.
> - *moderate hypoxic-ischemic encephalopathy*—characterized by lethargy and stupor, hypotonia, and suppressed tendon reflexes. Seizures may occur.
> - *severe hypoxic-ischemic encephalopathy*—characterized by coma, seizures, and brain stem and autonomic dysfunction. Seizures are often prolonged and may be resistent to anticonvulsants. Elevated intracranial pressure may occur. Infants with the severe form die or develop major neurologic disorders, such as microcephaly, spastic quadriplegia, and seizures. Clinical features worsen during the first 3 days of life and death usually occurs betwen 24 and 72 hours of life. (30)

idiopathic respiratory distress syndrome, hyaline membrane disease—serious breathing difficulty caused by hyaline material, a sticky exudate, filling the alveolar ducts and alveoli, thus obstructing the airway and preventing oxygenation. The condition, which occurs primarily in premature infants, may be fatal. (1, 17, 19, 34, 36, 65) (See Oral Reading Practice.)

imperforate anus, atresia of anus—rectum ending in a blind pouch. (63)

infections of the newborn: (17, 19, 20, 21)

> *congenital rubella syndrome*—neonate born with a rubella virus infection due to transplacental transmission, which is particularly serious when it occurs during the first trimester. The newborn may have cataracts, cardiovascular anomalies, microcephaly, mental retardation, deafness, and other defects.

epidemic diarrhea—loose, yellow-green stools, dehydration, and acidosis.

impetigo contagiosa—skin disease, with appearance of vesicles that change to pustules and later to crusts. Staphylococci frequently colonize impetiginous lesions, but most impetigo is due to group A streptococci.

ophthalmia neonatorum—purulent conjunctivitis.

thrush—fungus infection of oral mucous membrane that results in white patches or aphthae.

TORCH infections—acronym for toxoplasmosis, other (e.g., syphilis), rubella, cytomegalovirus, and herpes simplex. Effects of these viral infections may include abortion, fetal death, and growth retardation, as well as microcephaly, congenital heart disease, eye damage, deafness, or hepatosplenomegaly with jaundice or purpura.

kernicterus, nuclear jaundice, biliary encephalopathy—irreparable brain damage complicating severe erythroblastosis. Excess serum bilirubin, liberated by destroyed erythrocytes and not converted into an excretable form, stains the brain nuclei and results in mental retardation, cerebral palsy, or deafness. Kernicterus can be prevented by exchange transfusions. (41)

meningocele—meninges protruding through a defect in the spine or skull.

persistent pulmonary hypertension of the newborn—conditions such as perinatal asphyxia and meconium aspiration may result in persistent pulmonary hypertension. Hypoxia, acidosis, and hypercapnia acting through elevated plasma concentrations of vasoconstrictors such as thromoxane, prevent reduction of pulmonary vascular resistance and establishment of pulmonary blood flow that accompany normal delivery. Persistent pulmonary hypertension of the newborn may occur in association with sepsis, pulmonary hypoplasia, or congenital diaphragmatic hernia. Clinical symptoms include tachypnea, respiratory distress, and often rapidly progressive cyanosis. (1, 30, 50, 63)

phocomelia—congenital deformities such as absence or stunting of extremities, for example, infants born of mothers who took thalidomide during the first trimester of pregnancy developed these malformations. (63)

retinopathy of prematurity—disorder seen in premature infants who receive continuous oxygen therapy. The retina becomes edematous and detached. Partial or total blindness develops. (1, 20)

tongue-tie, ankyloglossia—short frenulum linguae that prevents the neonate from taking feeding. (63)

umbilical hernia—protrusion of part of the intra-abdominal contents at the umbilicus. At the time of birth, the umbilical ring usually has closed except for the small space occupied by the umbilical vein, and paired umbilical arteries. When the cord is ligated, the vessels undergo thrombosis, resulting in continued closure of the umbilical ring by scar tissue. If this scar formation does not occur normally or if the umbilical ring is enlarged, protrusion of the intra-abdominal contents will occur through this defect.

omphalocele—defect of the periumbilical abdominal wall in which the coelomic cavity is covered only by peritoneum and amnion. The omphalocele may house small and large bowel, liver, spleen, stomach, pancreas, and bladder. (63)

OPERATIVE TERMS

circumcision—removal of all or part of the prepuce or foreskin to permit exposure of the glans penis. (36)

clipping of frenulum linguae—minor operation to relieve tongue-tie.

herniorrhaphy—surgical repair or suture of hernia.

repair of imperforate anus—surgical creation of an opening.

SYMPTOMATIC TERMS

Apgar score—assessing a neonate's physical condition by evaluating heart rate, respiratory effort, reflex irritability, and skin color according to a scoring system. (27, 56)

congenital—born with a certain condition.

Moro reflex, startle reflex—reflex indicating an awareness of balance in the neonate. The reflex is stimulated by a sudden jarring of the crib or jerking of a blanket. The infant draws up the legs and throws the arms symmetrically forward. (30)

premature—before the proper time; in obstetrics before full term.

pylorospasm—spasm of circular muscle of lower end of stomach.

vernix caseosa—fatty substance that covers the newborn. (25)

SELECTED PROCEDURES PERTAINING TO THE NEONATE

exchange transfusion—replacing the blood of a neonate who has a severe antibody-antigen reaction caused by hemolytic disease with blood devoid of the offending antigen. (4)

extracorporeal membrane oxygenation (ECMO)—medical technique that takes over the heart-lung functions of the neonate to allow the diseased organs to heal. It is a modification of the heart-lung machine and procedure used in open heart surgery. Although ECMO was developed initially for adults, currently its most common usage is in the treatment of newborns with severe respiratory and cardiopulmonary disorders. (30)

phototherapy for the neonate—an effective method of lowering unconjugated bilirubin levels by exposing the newborn to fluorescent or other light, according to need. Infants with physiologic jaundice resulting from mildly elevated serum bilirubin benefit by the fluorescent lighting system of the nursery. This intense illumination of these newborns leads to the photoisomerization of bilirubin to water-soluble isomers that are quickly excreted in the bile without the prior need of conjugation. Other techniques include decreasing bilirubin production from heme by inhibitors of the enzyme, heme oxygenase. The synthetic protoporphyrins, when given to newborns with hyperbilirubinemia have markedly reduced the serum bilirubin. Also, infants with hyperbilirubinemia who may develop encephalopathy are exposed to intense fluorescent light therapy in special incubators to reduce their excessive bilirubin. (20, 41)

CLINICAL LABORATORY STUDIES

TERMS RELATED TO OBSTETRICAL, FETAL, AND NEONATAL TESTS AND PROCEDURES

ABO incompatibility—incompatibility in the A, B, AB, and O blood types. Usually the mother is type O and the baby type A or B. This incompatibility occurs in a considerable number of pregnancies, but erythroblastosis develops in a relatively small percentage of them. (4)

amniotic fluid—fluid contained in the amniotic sac.

amniotic fluid analyses—spectrophotometric tracings or other determinations on amniotic fluid in the antepartum management of Rh incompatibility, diabetes, and other conditions. Fetal involvement exists if there is an abnormal increase in the pigments that absorb light at wavelengths between 450 and 460 mμ. (1 mμ [millimicron] = 0.001 of a micron = 1 nm [nanometer]). Repeated amniotic fluid analyses are valuable guides for timing intrauterine transfusion or induction of labor. Numerous inborn errors of metabolism are identifiable by amniotic fluid analysis; for example, Gaucher's disease, galactosemia, and cystinosis, representing metabolic errors of lipid, carbohydrate, and amino acid metabolism. (63) Other associated tests include:

> *alpha$_1$-fetoprotein (AFP)*—major protein (glycoprotein) in fetal serum. It is synthesized by the embryonic liver. An elevated AFP in amniotic fluid is present in neural tube anomalies such as fetal anencephaly, myelocele, and spinal bifida. AFP also is increased in Turner's syndrome, tetralogy of Fallot, and other nonneural tube defects. (63)

bilirubin in amniotic fluid—spectrophotometric tracings detect bilirubin elevation in the Rh isoimmunization syndrome and predict the progress of fetal hemolysis and the risk of intrauterine death. When repeated amniocenteses signal a severely affected fetus, labor should be induced in 33 to 34 weeks to prevent perinatal death. (16, 34, 38, 60, 65)

creatinine levels of amniotic fluid—increasing levels provide information concerning fetal muscle development and renal concentration ability. They aid in the assessment of the fetal age. (60)

evaluation of the pulmonary maturity of the fetus—the development of the lungs is lined by the functional adequacy of the surfactant, a phospholipoprotein matrix that lines each alveolus and reduces the pulmonary surface tension during expiration. Since the fetal air passages communicate with the amniotic fluid, the surfactant is found in the amniotic fluid. Its presence in a sufficient amount signals lung maturity of the fetus; its absence or an insufficient amount signals lung immaturity. The following tests are done to detect the fetal pulmonary status:

- *amniotic fluid lung profile*—test to evaluate lung maturity. The lung profile detects lecithin, as well as two other phospholipids, namely phosphatidylglycerol (PG), and phosphatidylinositol (PI). PG appears after the 35th week of gestation and continues to increase until term. PI increases in the amniotic fluid after the 26th to 30th week of gestation and then slowly decreases. PI and PG act as surfactant-stabilizing substances, assisting to prevent alveolar collapse. The presence of PG in an amniotic fluid specimen, when the L/S ratio exceeds 2.0, is a strong indicator that respiratory distress syndrome (RDS) will not occur. PG is important in high-risk pregnancies such as those complicated by diabetes, isoimmunization, or by hydrops fetalis to document stable pulmonary stability.
- *foam stability index (FSI)*—test based on the surfactant being a foaming agent and ethanol inhibiting foam production. Ethanol (95% or 100%) is placed in a tube, 500 μl of amniotic fluid are added, and the tube is shaken for 30 seconds.
    - *Positive reaction:* presence of a complete ring of bubbles predictive of lung maturity of neonate; no respiratory distress syndrome will develop.
    - *Negative reaction:* no bubbles or an incomplete ring of bubbles predictive of lung immaturity of neonate with or without respiratory distress syndrome.
- *lecithin-to-sphingomyelin (L/S) ratio*—the ratio of these phospholipids reflects the extrusion of the surfactant into the amniotic fluid. An L/S ratio greater than 2.0 suggests adequate lung development in the third trimester. An L/S ratio less than 2.0 indicates lung immaturity, which is normal in early pregnancy but not before term. (1, 17, 19, 34, 36, 65)

fetal sex—determination of the sex of the fetus is possible at 15 to 18 weeks of gestation. Amniotic fluid studies commonly performed are: (1) the Barr test of nuclear sex; (2) Y chromosome staining in uncultured cells; and (3) tissue culture of human cells and karyotyping. (62, 63)

antiglobulin reaction, Coombs' test—test for antibodies.

direct Coombs' test—test for the antibody coating of erythrocytes (i.e., the ability of anti-IgG or anti-C3 antiserums to agglutinate the patient's red blood cells).

- *Negative reaction:* direct Coombs, no antibody coating on newborn's red cells.
- *Positive reaction:* direct Coombs, antibody coating on newborn's red cells, indicative of hemolytic disease. (26)

indirect Coombs' test—test determines presence of antibodies in serum. (36)

bilirubin—pigment in the bile derived from degenerated hemoglobin of destroyed blood cells. In newborns and particularly in premature and erythroblastic babies, the liver is unable to cope with the large amount of bilirubin liberated by destroyed erythrocytes. This results in an excess of bilirubin in the blood. (41)

bilirubin determinations (using cord blood of neonate):

Reference values: (15)

- *serum bilirubin, total*—0.2–1.0 mg/dL (SIU: 3.4–17.1 µmol/L)

    Increase in serum bilirubin is seen in physiologic jaundice, hyperbilirubinemia, and kernicterus. The less mature the neonate, the more marked is susceptibility to kernicterus. (41, 63)

blood group analysis of prospective parents—study of the parental blood groups in order to detect maternal and paternal grouping differences, predictive of mother-child incompatibilities. Routine procedures include ABO grouping, Rh typing, and screening for irregular antibodies. (33, 63)

blood group analyses for exclusion studies—tests used in medical-legal practice on the basis that parental blood groups are inherited by the child. Determinations are made to exclude allegation or denial of paternity. To clarify the issue, an example of the MN system of blood typing should be of interest. (33, 63)

Disputed Father = Type M; Mother = Type N

Child = Type N—Genotype NN

Conclusion = Since the child does not have the gene M, the person in question is not the father.

Blood group genetic marker—inherited characteristic determined by genes located on a pair of chromosomes. Markers are of value in paternity testing. Exclusion of paternity is based on the following: (1) the child cannot have a genetic marker that is missing in both parents; (2) the child inherits one of a pair of genetic markers from the mother and father; and (3) the child cannot possess a pair of identical markers (aa) if both parents do not have the marker (a). (2, 33)

fetal chromosome analysis—after 15 to 18 weeks of gestation, fetal cells can be grown in a satisfactory cell culture. Chromosomal abnormalities such as balanced translocation in either parent may be transmitted to the offspring. The incidence of Down's syndrome, trisomy 21, and spontaneous abortions increases with maternal age. The fetal chromosome analysis establishes an exact antenatal diagnosis of chromosome aberrations. (60)

genetic fingerprinting, DNA fingerprinting—molecular biologic technique displaying specific individual genetic makeup. DNA (deoxyribonucleic acid) carries an organism's genetic information. Each DNA molecule consists of four amino acids arranged in a code that is unique to each person. DNA has been used in prenatal diagnosis, paternity testing, zygosity of twins, carrier detection, premorbid diagnosis, such as in adult onset of polycystic kidney diseases, Huntington's chorea, and cancer detection. Forensic biology utilizes DNA fingerprinting in rape cases. (4)

glucuronyl transferase—enzyme absent from the liver of premature infants at birth and incompletely developed in full-term newborns. The absence of this enzyme seems to account for the liver's inability to handle the load imposed by the increased destruction of red cells in the first days of life. (63)

phenylalanine—essential amino acid present in protein foods. A blocking of its conversion into tyrosine causes phenylalanine blood levels to rise and phenylketone bodies to be excreted in the urine. As a result, brain development ceases. Mental retardation is preventable by early treatment with a low-phenylalanine diet. A serum phenylalanine test measures phenylalanine levels in blood serum. Plasma phenylalanine concentrations are maintained between 3 and 12 mg/dL. In classic phenylketonuria, plasma phenylalanine values are greater than 20 mg/dL.

Guthrie bacterial inhibition assay—simple screening test for the detection of phenylketonuria. Most children in Europe and North America are screened by determinations of blood phenylalanine concentration using this test. (35, 63)

placental hormones and related tests:

human choriogonadotropin (hCG), human chorionic gonadotropin (hCG)—glycopeptide secreted by the placenta during gestation. In 1 or 2 weeks after the implantation of the fertilized ovum, hCG is found in both blood and urine. Its rapidly rising levels reach a peak at 8 to 12 weeks of pregnancy, which is followed by a decline. After delivery, hCG becomes undetectable within 2 or 3 days. (63, 67)

Reference values: (RIA) (15)

- *serum chorionic gonadotropin*—less than 3 mIU/mL
- *urine chorionic gonadotropin*—less than 30 mIU/mL

immunologic pregnancy tests, immunoassays for pregnancy—sensitive tests for human chorionic gonadotropin (hCG) in serum and urine. Excess hCG is present in pregnancy. Techniques are simple, and results are read in 2 hours or less. The tests are designed for office use. Immunologic tests, however, also yield positive results in choriocarcinoma and hydatidiform moles. In menopause, elevated pituitary gonadotropin may produce a false-positive test. The following commercial immunologic pregnancy tests are in current use:

- *Gravindex 90*—slide test.
- *Neocept*—hemagglutination inhibition test.
- *Pregnosis*—slide test.
- *Sensi-Tex*—latex agglutination inhibition tube test. (7, 63)

human placental lactogen (hPL)—this hormone has been isolated in considerable amounts from human placentas at term. It maintains the pregnancy and initiates lactation. The hPL concentration of maternal serum is a sensitive indicator of placenta function and invaluable in monitoring high-risk pregnancies. The higher the blood pressure of hypertensive toxemia patients, the lower their placental lactogen. (63, 67)

Reference values: (serum hPL [RIA]) (15)

- *Males:* less than 0.5 μg/mL (μg same as mcg = microgram)
- *Nonpregnant females:* less than 0.5 μg/mL
- *Pregnant females:*
  - 5–27 weeks—less than 4.6 μg/mL
  - 28–31 weeks—2.4–6.1 μg/mL
  - 32–35 weeks—3.7–7.7 μg/mL
  - 36th week/at term—5.0–8.6 μg/mL
    Increase or normal urinary hPL and decrease of serum hPL after 8 weeks of menstrual cessation suggest the growth of hydatidiform mole. (7, 63, 67)

progestational hormones: (21, 67)

progesterone—steroid hormone formed by the corpus luteum and rapidly metabolized to pregnanediol; consequently, there is little progesterone in the blood. Plasma progesterone determinations aid in the detection of ovulatory and luteal deficiencies and hormonal imbalance in pregnancy.

pregnanediol—hormone produced in the liver by progesterone metabolism and excreted in urine.

Reference values: (method varies) (15)

- *Males:* 0.6–1.5 mg/d (SIU: 1.9–4.7 μmol/d)
- *Female cycle:*
  - *follicular*—less than 1.0 mg/d
    (SIU: less than 3.1 μmol/d)
  - *luteal*—2–7 mg/d
    (SIU: 6.2–22 μmol/d)
  - *postmenopausal*—0.2–1.0 mg/d
    (SIU: 0.6–3.1 μmol/d)

After delivery, pregnanediol excretion returns gradually to nonpregnant levels. (63)

Rh isoimmunization—sensitization that occurs when red cells containing Rh antigens not present in the cells of the recipient enter the circulation. This develops most commonly in

Rh-negative women carrying Rh-positive babies or receiving transfusion with Rh-positive blood. It usually occurs during the second Rh-positive pregnancy or subsequent pregnancies. (27, 51)

rubella, German measles, in early pregnancy—relatively mild disease with fever, rash, and lymph node involvement that causes serious deformities in the growing fetus when it occurs during the first trimester. Preventive measures are presented:

active immunization against rubella—live virus vaccine prepared in tissue cell culture derived from various sources and given as a single subcutaneous injection to nonpregnant, nonimmune women.

hemagglutination inhibition (HI) test for rubella—routine test to be performed within 10 days of exposure to rubella. An antibody titer of 1:10 or above usually indicates the patient is immune and will not develop rubella. An antibody titer below 1:10 suggests that the patient may develop rubella.

immune serum globulin (ISG)—prophylactic agent thought to prevent maternal and congenital rubella and rubella-induced congenital malformations. This passive immunization against rubella should be given to pregnant, nonimmune women within 7 or 8 days after exposure.

postpartum rubella immunization—procedure performed on nonimmune women during the puerperium to prevent rubella infection in future pregnancies. (19, 23, 63)

sickle cell disease screening tests—screening procedures for sickle cell hemoglobin (HbS) during the first months of life, preferably at the infant's first checkup. Tests primarily indicated include the tube solubility or microscopic test for HbS and the sickling test, a blood smear to detect sickled cells. Immunoglobulin levels are frequently increased. IgA levels are particularly elevated in all forms of sickle cell disease, while IgG levels appear elevated less often than IgA. IgM levels are elevated in sickle cell thalassemia. Sickle cell anemia can be diagnosed at birth by submitting cord blood samples to electrophoresis. Screening at birth is very important, especially if the mother has sickle cell trait. Chorionic villus biopsy performed in the first trimester has been used to obtain fetal DNA for diagnosis. (63)

steroid hormone—chemically interrelated organic compounds possessing a four-ring carbon structure. (7, 63, 67)

androgenic hormones—biologic substances that stimulate secondary sex characteristics in the male.

17-ketosteroids (17-KS) in urine—in men, a measurement of the adrenocortical steroids and adrenal and gonadal androgens; in women and children, primarily a measurement of adrenal gland secretion. The level of the 17-KS in urine aids in the detection of endocrine disorders.

Reference values: 17-KS excretion (significant daily variation in urine secretion) (14, 63)

- *Males*—6–18 mg/24 hr (SIU: 21–62 µmol/24 hr)
- *Females*—4–13 mg/24 hr (SIU: 14–45 µmol/24 hr)

Increase in adrenocortical tumor, especially if malignant; interstitial neoplasm of testes; adrenogenital syndrome; and occasionally Cushing's disease. (63)

Decrease in Addison's disease and myxedema. (63)

testosterone—steroid hormone and very potent androgen. (62)

Reference values: plasma testosterone (15)

- *Males*—275–875 ng/dL (SIU: 9.5–30 nmol/L)
- *Females*—23–75 ng/dL (SIU: 0.8–2.6 nmol/L)

Increase in adrenal hyperplasia or tumor, polycystic ovaries, and ovarian tumors. (63)

Decrease in estrogen therapy, hypogonadism, hypopituitarism, Klinefelter's syndrome, and orchidectomy. (63)

estrogenic hormones—internal secretions of the gonads, adrenal glands, and placenta that prepare the uterus and tubes for progesterone stimulation.

- *clomiphene*—antiestrogen used in diagnosis and therapy to detect anovulation and initiate a normal menstrual cycle, thus making pregnancy possible.
- *estriol* (E_3)—estrogenic hormone, synthesized in the placenta and highly elevated in pregnancy. Determinations of estriol are of clinical significance, since they reflect the status of the fetoplacental complex and may serve as treatment guides in a high-risk pregnancy. A marked decline in pregnancy estriol during the second or third trimester signals placental insufficiency and impending fetal death.
- *total estrogens*—these include estrone (E_1), estradiol (E_2), and estriol (E_3). They are measured to evaluate ovarian function. Estrogen excretion in urine is variable, with low levels at the menstrual period and peak levels at the midperiod of the cycle. (21, 63, 67)

Reference values: total estrogens (15)

- *serum*
  - *Males:* 40–115 pg/mL (SIU: 40–115 ng/L)
  - *Female cycle:*
    - 1–10 days 61–394 pg/mL (SIU: 61–394 ng/L)
    - 11–20 days 122–437 pg/mL (SIU: 122–437 ng/L)
    - 21–30 days 156–350 pg/mL (SIU: 156–350 ng/L)
    - *prepubertal and postmenopausal:* 40 pg/mL (SIU: 40 ng/L)
- *urine*
  - *Males:* 5–25 µg/24 hr (SIU: 15–90 nmol/24 hr)
  - *Females:* 5–100 µg/24 hr (SIU: 18–360 nmol/24 hr)
    Increase in pregnancy, ovarian tumors, testicular atrophy, and testicular tumors. (63)
    Decrease due to absence of ovulation, ovarian hormones, and corpus luteum function; amenorrhea, sterility; and other conditions. (63)

ORAL READING PRACTICE

RESPIRATORY DISTRESS SYNDROME (HYALINE MEMBRANE DISEASE)

Respiratory distress syndrome (RDS) is the result of a complex disturbance of early neonatal adaptation in which several factors interact, such as **gestational age (fetal maturity)** and environmental influences **(asphyxia hypothermia),** along with probable genetic factors entering into this interaction. Unfavorable combinations of these factors present defects in **lung stability** and **cardiopulmonary functions,** which are classified as a syndrome. The death rate is highest in the first 24 hours, and 90% of the deaths occur by the fourth day. The most characteristic finding is the **hyaline membrane lining** of the **alveoli,** which gives the disease its alternate name. The hyaline material is the result of damage to the **alveolar lining,** and consists of **fibrin** with additional transudates and secretions.

The main pathophysiological mechanism in RDS is a **surfactant deficiency** in the **alveoli.** The surfactant is a **lipoprotein** mainly composed of **dipalmitrol lecithin,** which begins to be secreted by the fetal lung about the 20th to 25th week of pregnancy. An important function of this surfactant is to form a film at the interface between the **alveolar lining** and oxygen in the **alveolus** per se. The result is an improvement in lung distensibility and lower alveolar surface tension. Without the surfactant, the alveoli collapse and greater **inspiratory pressure** is demanded on the next breath to expand the alveoli.

Since **lung compliance** is extremely low, the neonate's work of breathing is increased. The pulmonary defects present right-to-left **cardiopulmonary shunting,** which is the central reason for the **arterial oxygen unsaturation.** This resistance may result from lung collapse and congestion of the capillary bed due to **hypoxia** and **acidosis,** which cause **arteriolar vasoconstriction.** Should **asphyxia** be acute and of short term, the main defect presenting may be **pulmonary vasoconstriction;** rapid resolution may follow when the asphyxia is corrected. When asphyxia persists and is longer term, the result is a gradual deterioration, resulting in full-blown respiratory distress syndrome. Recovery in these cases is much slower, and treatment must be aggressive.

Another lipoprotein, **sphingomyelin,** also is present in the **amniotic fluid.** Sphingomyelin concentrations do not increase as much as the lecithin concentrations. The high increase is noted around the 32nd to the 34th week of gestation. The **L/S ratio** (ratio between lecithin and sphingomyelin concentrations) in the amniotic fluid provides an indication of the maturation of the fetal lung. An L/S ratio of 2.0 or more indicates that hyaline membrane disease is not likely to occur.

Recognition of respiratory distress syndrome is based on the respiratory effort, which may resemble **tachypnea** or may be slow; however, in all cases the neonate is laboring with **subcostal retractions** or retractions extending to the **sternum, intercostal spaces,** or **suprasternal spaces.** Grunting is often present with retractions and is indicative of serious disease; less grunting is usually a sign of improvement, unless it is associated with **apnea** or increasing **cyanosis** and deterioration, indications of failed respiratory effort.

Several pharmacologic agents or hormones may contribute to the acceleration of fetal pulmonary surfactant production. However, because of the potential maternal and fetal risk resulting from the usage of these drugs, it is essential that the drug of choice be individually justified and the risk-benefit ratio carefully evaluated prior to the administration of the drug. Natural synthetic and semisynthetic surfactants have been successfully administered into the lungs of premature infants for treatment of RDS. The surfactant preparations containing surfactant proteins provide highly surface-active material to the alveolus. Surfactant replacement therapy has become standard for prevention and treatment of RDS.

Monitoring of the neonate with respiratory distress syndrome includes serial **chest roentgenograms,** periodic **blood gas analysis, acid-base evaluations, fluid and electrolyte balance, L/S ratio,** as well as maintenance of good **ventilation** and **oxygenation,** temperature control, and close observation of vital signs. Approximately 70% to 90% of infants present with the disease in the moderately severe form. The remaining 10% to 30% of neonates are critically ill. Between 72 and 98 hours after birth, most infants will enter the recovery phase. The smaller the infant, the higher the mortality. The best site for care of RDS infants is in the neonatal intensive care unit where facilities and trained staff are available to monitor and provide treatment for those neonates on a continuous 24-hour basis. (1, 17, 19, 34, 36, 65)

ABBREVIATIONS

GENERAL

CDC—calculated day of confinement
CS—cesarean section
ECMO—extracorporeal membrane oxygenation
EDC—estimated date of confinement
FECG—fetal electrocardiogram
FHR—fetal heart rate
FHT—fetal heart tone
FTND—full term normal delivery
GIFT—gamete intrafallopian tube transfer
HDN—hemolytic disease of newborn

IUGR—intrauterine growth retardation; intrauterine growth restriction
IVF-ET—in vitro fertilization and embryo transfer
LBW—low birth weight
LMP—last menstrual period
NB—newborn
OB—obstetrics
RDS—respiratory distress syndrome
RH neg—rhesus factor negative
RH pos—rhesus factor positive

VERTEX PRESENTATIONS
LOA—left occipitoanterior
LOP—left occipitoposterior
LOT—left occipitotransverse
ROA—right occipitoanterior
ROP—right occipitoposterior
ROT—right occipitotransverse

FACE PRESENTATIONS
LMA—left mentoanterior
LMP—left mentoposterior
LMT—left mentotransverse
RMA—right mentoanterior
RMP—right mentoposterior
RMT—right mentotransverse

BREECH PRESENTATIONS
LSA—left sacroanterior
LSP—left sacroposterior
RSA—right sacroanterior
RSP—right sacroposterior

TRANSVERSE PRESENTATIONS
LScA—left scapuloanterior
LScP—left scapuloposterior
RScA—right scapuloanterior
RScP—right scapuloposterior

SIZE OF TERM INFANT
AGA—appropriate for gestational age
LGA—large for gestational age
SGA—small for gestational age

ORGANIZATIONS
AAMIH—American Association for Maternal and Infant Health
ACNM—American College of Nurse Midwifery
ACOG—American College of Obstetricians and Gynecologists
FACOG—Fellow of American College of Obstetricians and Gynecologists
FCMC—Family-Centered Maternity Care
ICM—International Confederation of Midwives
NAACOG—Nurses Association of the American College of Obstetricians and Gynecologists
USCB—United States Children's Bureau

REVIEW GUIDE

Instructions: Select the letter of response that correctly completes each statement, as shown in the example.

Example: Neonate refers to
    a. birth. b. new. <u>c.</u> newborn. d. navel.

1. Voluntary expulsion of fetus, brought about by mechanical means or drugs is termed
   a. threatened abortion.
   b. incomplete abortion.
   c. inevitable abortion.
   d. induced abortion.

2. Lack of oxygen in the blood of the newborn is called
   a. atelectasis neonatorum.
   b. caput succedaneum.
   c. asphyxia neonatorum.
   d. none of the above.

3. Down's syndrome may be called
   a. trisomy G_{13}.
   b. trisomy G_{21}.
   c. both a and b.
   d. none of the above.

4. The fatty substance that covers the newborn at birth is called
   a. meconium.
   b. vernix caseosa.
   c. phocomelia.
   d. none of the above.

5. The discharge from the birth canal following delivery is called
   a. pica.
   b. colostrum.
   c. dystocia.
   d. lochia.

6. Cyanosis and softening of the cervix due to increased vascularity of the cervical tissue, indicative of **pregnancy,** is called
   a. Chadwick's sign.   b. Goodell's sign.
   c. Hagar's sign.   d. none of the above.
7. Couvelaire uterus may be called
   a. hydatidiform mole.   b. subinvolution of uterus.
   c. involution of uterus.   d. uteroplacental apoplexy.
8. A fetus that is dead, but retained in utero for days or weeks is called
   a. an incomplete abortion.   b. a missed abortion.
   c. a septic abortion.   d. an induced abortion.
9. A deficient amount of amniotic fluid is called
   a. colostrum.   b. asphyxia.
   c. oligohydramninos.   d. eclampsia.
10. The upper opening into the true pelvic cavity is called
    a. pelvic inlet.   b. pelvic outlet.
    c. promontory of the sacrum. d. both b and c.
11. The painless contractions of the uterus throughout gestation is called
    a. ballottement.   b. Braxton-Hicks' sign.
    c. Chadwick's sign.   d. Goodell's sign.
12. The pregnant woman's first perception of fetal life is called
    a. ballottement.   b. Chadwick's sign.
    c. quickening.   d. none of the above.
13. Failure of lungs to expand at birth is called
    a. atelectasis neonatorum. b. caput succedaneum.
    c. asphyxia neonatorum.   d. none of the above.
14. The descent of the fetal head through the pelvic inlet is called
    a. colostrum.   b. effacement.
    c. engagement.   d. Hagar's sign.
15. Excessive venous and lymph stasis of lactating breast may be termed
    a. caked breasts.   b. engorgement.
    c. both a and b.   d. none of the above.

Instructions: Break apart each term listed below, identify the medical term elements, and define the term.

Example: chorioadenoma
          chorio- = combining-form element = chorion
          aden- = root = gland
          -oma = suffix = tumor

amniocentesis	fetotoxicity	metrorrhexis
ankyloglossia	hemorrhage	omphalocele
electrocardiography	hydrocephalus	pylorospasm
encephalopathy	hysteroscopy	retinopathy
erythroblastosis	meningocele	teratology

13

Endocrine, Metabolic, and Cytogenetic Disorders

ENDOCRINE GLANDS

ORIGIN OF TERMS

ad- (L)—near to, toward, in addition to
aden-, adeno- (G)—gland(s)
adreno- (L)—near kidney
crinin (G)—substance that generates
    glandular secretion
end-, endo- (G)—within
exo- (G)—outside
hormone (G)—to excite, to spur on

hyper- (G)—above, excessive
hypo- (G)—below, deficient
lacto- (L)—milk
pituita (L)—phlegm
thalamus (G)—inner chamber
thyro- (G)—shield, thyroid
toco- (G)—childbirth, labor
tropho- (G)—nourishment

PHONETIC PRONUNCIATION OF SELECTED TERMS

Addison's disease	ADD′i-sons dis-EASE′
adrenal crisis	ah-DRE′nal or a-DRE′nal CRY′sis
adrenalectomy	a-DRE-nal-ECK′toe-me
hyperparathyroidism	HI-per-PAR-ah-THI′royd-ism
hypoglycemia	HI-po-gly-SEE′me-ah
parathyroidectomy	PAR-ah-THI-roy-DECK′toe-me
thyroid adenoma	THI′royd AD-e-NO′mah
thyroiditis	THI-roy-DIE′tis
thyrotoxicosis	THI-row-TOKS-i-KO′sis

ANATOMIC TERMS (SEE FIG. 13.1.)

endocrine glands—ductless glands producing internal secretions that are absorbed directly into the bloodstream and influence various body functions. (47, 104)

hormone—substance secreted by a cell that has an effect on the functions of another cell. The physiological action of a specific hormone is restricted to its target cells. A particular hormone's target cells possess receptors that are distinctive to those cells and that other cells lack. (15, 86, 109)

pancreas—(See fig. 13.2.) lies transversely across the posterior abdominal wall extending from the duodenum to the spleen and is behind the stomach. The gland is divided into a neck, a

Figure 13.1 Locations of major endocrine glands.

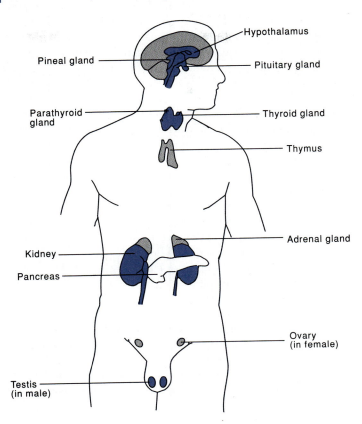

Figure 13.2 Hormone-secreting cells of the pancreas are arranged in clusters or islets surrounded by cells that secrete digestive enzymes.

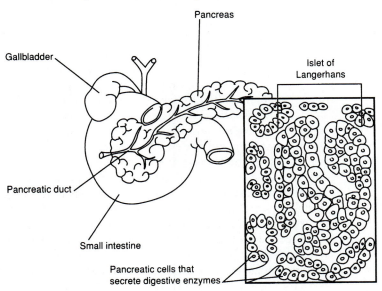

body, and a tail. Its pancreatic islets, the islets of Langerhans, are approximately 20% A cells, secreting glucagon; 75% B cells, secreting insulin; and 5% D cells, secreting somatostatin. A human pancreatic polypeptide has been added as a fourth type of cell. The types of pancreatic cells differ chemically, functionally, and microscopically. (47, 92, 104)

parathyroids—two to four small glands, usually a pair attached to each thyroid lobe. They secrete a hormone that regulates the metabolism of calcium and phosphorus. (76, 96, 104)

pineal gland—small, oval structure located deep between the cerebral hemispheres, where it is attached to the upper portion of the thalamus near the roof of the third ventricle. The pineal gland secretes a hormone called melatonin, which is synthesized from serotonin. (3)

pituitary gland, hypophysis—(See figs. 13.3 and 13.4.) small ovoid body situated in the hypophysial fossa of the sphenoid bone. It is composed of the adenohypophysis and neurohypophysis, each performing distinct functions. The adenohypophysis or anterior pituitary is known as the master endocrine gland because of its physiologic effect on the suprarenals, gonads, pancreas, and thyroid.

hypothalamus—small mass below the thalamus containing nuclei and fibers. It is an integrating center for the autonomic nervous system and through its relation to the hypophysis for the endocrine system. The axons in the posterior lobe of the pituitary gland are stimulated to release hormones by nerve impulses originating in the hypothalamus. The cells of the anterior lobe are stimulated by releasing hormones secreted by hypothalamic neurons.

pituitary anterior lobe hormones include:

- *adrenocorticotropic hormone* (ACTH)—affects the adrenal cortex and combats inflammatory processes. ACTH is essential to maintain life.
- *follicle-stimulating hormone* (FSH)—regulates development of egg-containing follicles in ovaries; stimulates follicle cells to secrete estrogen; in the male, stimulates production of sperm cells.
- *luteinizing hormone* (LH)—promotes secretion of sex hormones, and aids in release of egg cell in females.
- *growth hormone* (GH)—promotes normal long bone development, aids in movement of amino acids through membranes, and stimulates increase in size and rate of reproduction of body cells.
- *prolactin* (PRL)—stimulates the secretion of milk.
- *thyroid-stimulating hormone* (TSH)—controls secretion of hormones from the thyroid gland. (47, 52, 104, 107)

pituitary posterior lobe hormones include:

- *antidiuretic hormone* (ADH)—causes kidneys to reduce water excretion and, in high concentration, causes blood pressure to rise.
- *oxytocin* (OT)—causes contractions of muscles in uterine wall and causes contraction of muscles associated with milk-secreting glands. (47, 79, 101)

reproductive organs—organs that secrete important hormones, such as the ovaries, which produce estrogens and progesterone; the placenta, which produces estrogens, progesterone, and gonadotropin; and the testes, which produce testosterone. (See chapters 10 and 11 for anatomical descriptions of these reproductive organs.) (63, 104)

suprarenals, adrenals—two glands, one on top of each kidney. They are composed of an inner medullary substance and an outer cortex. The medulla produces the catecholamines— epinephrine (adrenaline), norepinephrine (noradrenaline), and dopamine. Catecholamines excess commonly results in hypertension. Deficient sympathetic neuronal norepinephrine release results in postural (orthostatic) hypotension (a sharp decrease in blood pressure when a person stands). The adrenal cortex forms the adrenocortical steroids, known as the corticosteroids or corticoids. They include the glucocorticoids and mineralocorticoids. The

Figure 13.3 Hormones released from the anterior lobe of the pituitary gland and their target organs.

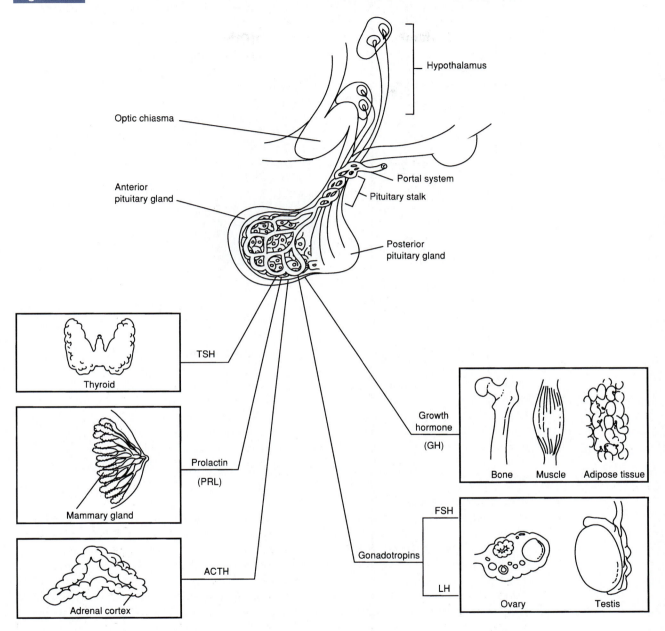

C-19 derivatives yield androgens, and the C-18 derivatives yield estrogens. Adrenocortical steroids help to regulate sodium, potassium, and chloride metabolism; water balance; and carbohydrate, protein, and fat metabolism. (47, 104, 107)

thymus gland—a bilobed organ that lies in the upper mediastinum, in front of the aorta, and behind the manubrium of the sternum, and between the lungs. It presents relatively large in young children but diminishes in size with age. The main function of the thymus is associated with the lymphatic system in maintaining body immunity through the maturation and

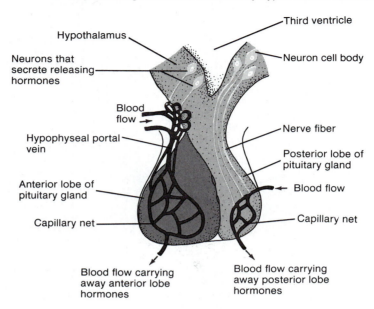

Figure 13.4 Axons in the posterior lobe of the pituitary gland are stimulated to release hormones by nerve impulses originating in the hypothalamus; cells of the anterior lobe are stimulated by releasing hormones secreted by hypothalamic neurons.

discharge of a specialized group of lymphocytes termed T lymphocytes. The thymus gland secretes a protein hormone called thymosin that stimulates the maturation of T lymphocytes after they leave the thymus and migrate to other lymphatic tissues. (47, 104)

thyroid gland—consists of two large lateral lobes and a central isthmus and is located just below the larynx on either side and in front of the trachea. This gland has a unique ability to remove iodine from the blood. It produces the hormones thyroxine (also called T_4, because its molecule includes 4 atoms of iodine) and triiodothyronine (also termed T_3, because its molecule includes 3 atoms of iodine). They help regulate the metabolism of carbohydrates, lipids, and proteins. (23, 47, 104)

DIAGNOSTIC TERMS

acromegaly—disease characterized by enlarged features, particularly of the face and hands. This is the result of oversecretion of the pituitary growth hormone in the adult after closure of epiphyses. When the growth hormone excess develops prior to epiphyseal closure in children, increased linear growth and giantism develops. Acromegaly usually occurs in middle age. (19, 28, 52)

Addison's disease—primary adrenal cortical insufficiency, a chronic syndrome due to progressive adrenocortical destruction. Hyperpigmentation is a dominant sign, but its absence does not exclude the diagnosis. (28, 62, 108)

adrenal crisis, Addisonian crisis—acute adrenocortical insufficiency and a life-threatening event resulting from a lack of glucocorticoids, hyperkalemia, and depletion of extracellular fluid during acute stress. Clinical manifestations are lassitude, headache, mental confusion, gastric upset, circulatory collapse, coma, and death. (28, 74, 108)

adrenal neoplasms:

adenomas and adenocarcinomas—benign or malignant glandular tumors arising from the adrenal cortex. Oversecretion of androgen by the tumor may cause virilization in women and children; excess estrogen production by tumor may result in feminization in men. (62)

neuroblastomas—tumors arising from the adrenal medulla. They are generally associated with metastases to bones.

pheochromocytomas—tumors usually arising from adrenal medulla and characterized by paroxysmal hypertension. (11, 28, 56, 107)

Conn's syndrome, primary aldosteronism—excessive secretion of aldosterone associated with pathology of adrenal cortex, resulting in potassium depletion, sodium retention, extreme exhaustion, paresthesias, cardiac enlargement, and increased carbon dioxide-combining power. (62, 83)

craniopharyngioma—arise in the remnants of Rathke's pouch, are more commonly suprasellar than intrasellar in location, and often show calcification, which enables the tumor to be diagnosed by imaging techniques. The tumor mass is usually filled with cholesterol-rich viscous fluid. Craniopharyngiomas may cause hypopituitarism by compressing or destroying adenohypophyseal tissue or the hypophyseotropic area of the hypothalamus. They can compress the pituitary stalk and can affect pituitary function by reducing the blood supply to the anterior lobe or by blocking flow of hypothalamic-regulating hormones to the adenohypophysis. (52)

Cushing's syndrome—symptom complex attributed to the hyperproduction of cortisone and hydrocortisone by the adrenal cortex. Typical manifestations of Cushing's syndrome may include obesity, hypertension, fatigability, weakness, amenorrhea, hirsutism, purplish abdominal striae, edema, glucosuria, osteoporosis, and a basophilic tumor of the pituitary. (23, 28, 64)

dwarfism, pituitary—congenital underdevelopment due to hyposecretion of the growth hormone. (52)

eunuchism—total gonadal underdevelopment.

eunuchoidism—partial gonadal underdevelopment. (63)

giantism—abnormal growth, particularly of long bones before the closure of the epiphyseal lines. It is caused by overproduction of the growth hormone of the anterior pituitary. (19, 28, 52)

goiter—an enlargement of the thyroid gland. Nontoxic goiter occurs periodically and is not associated with hyperthyroidism. These goiters may be either diffuse (e.g., the thyroid gland is quite enlarged) or nodular (e.g., containing small nodules). Graves' disease represents the toxic diffuse goiter. The toxic multinodular goiter represents the presence of hyperthyroidism due to an enlarged thyroid gland consisting of many rounded nodules. (23, 97)

hypercalcemic syndrome—abnormally high calcium levels of the blood seen in bone malignancies, endocrine and metabolic disorders such as multiple myeloma, acute adrenal insufficiency, hyperthyroidism, vitamin D intoxication, sarcoidosis, and milk-alkali syndrome. Prolonged bed rest may result in this hypercalcemic syndrome leading to the development of osteoporosis, Paget's disease, and similar disorders. (20, 29, 47, 76, 96)

hyperinsulinism due to islet cell tumor—condition marked by hypoglycemic episodes with a blood sugar below 30 or 40 mg/dL (milligram per deciliter), convulsions increasing in frequency and severity, and eventually coma. (16, 33, 55)

hyperparathyroidism, primary—overproduction and overactivity of the parathyroid hormone present in hypercalcemia, osteitis fibrosa, and tissue calcification. (28, 46, 70, 76, 96)

hyperthyroidism, thyrotoxicosis, exophthalmic goiter, Graves' disease—thyrotoxic state currently considered an immunologic disorder. The antigen, probably of thyroid origin, is still unknown. Excessive hormone secretion increases oxygen consumption, and this accounts for the high metabolic rate. Clinical characteristics are goiter, protrusion of the eyeballs, tachycardia, tremors, emotional instability, sweating, and weight loss. (23, 28, 57, 65)

hypoparathyroidism—abnormally decreased production of the parathyroid hormone causing hypocalcemia. It may be associated with reduced serum calcium and elevated serum phosphate levels. It usually occurs following thyroidectomy or surgery for hyperparathyroidism. (28, 29, 48, 76, 96)

hypothyroidism—condition resulting from insufficiency of thyroid hormones in the blood. (19, 21, 23, 51, 103)

multiple endocrine neoplasia (MEN)—endocrinopathies of tumors, genetically distinct and of autosomal dominant inheritance.

MEN Type 1, Wermer's syndrome—familial disorder in which the fully developed syndrome is characterized by the combined occurrence of primary hyperparathyroidism, pancreatic endocrine tumors, and neoplasms of the anterior pituitary gland. There is great variability in endocrine involvement and clinical manifestations. Localization of the MEN Type 1 gene has been assigned to the long arm of chromosome 11 (11q13), but the gene itself has not been identified. (9, 20, 28, 37, 51, 60, 91, 96, 99)

MEN Type 2A, Sipple's syndrome—an autosomal dominant genetic syndrome, usually comprising medullary thyroid carcinoma associated with bilateral pheochromocytomas of the adrenal medulla, and hyperparathyroidism. Localization of the MEN Type 2A gene has been mapped to the pericentrometric region of chromosome 10. (9, 28, 36, 42, 68, 78, 106)

MEN Type 2B, mucosal neuroma syndrome—autosomal dominant genetic syndrome that includes medullary thyroid carcinoma, pheochromocytoma, multiple mucosal neuromas, and a marfanoid habitus. There is absence of hyperparathyroidism. Localization of MEN Type 2B gene has been mapped to the pericentrometric region of chromosome 10 (same area as MEN Type 2A). (9, 28, 36, 42, 68, 78, 106)

myxedema—hypothyroidism causing lethargy, nonpitting edema, weakness, and slow speech. (23, 28)

pituitary apoplexy—acute headache occurring with known pituitary lesions and usually resulting from infarction or hemorrhage into the tumor. Growth and metastasis of the tumor may involve the overlying optic chiasm or the laterally lying cavernous sinus, producing either visual loss or ocular palsies. Surgical drainage should be instituted for removal of the hemorrhagic or infarcted material. (75, 81)

Sheehan's syndrome—pituitary apoplexy occurring during complicated parturition, particularly in the presence of massive blood loss, causes immediate or delayed hypopituitarism. Amenorrhea is followed by signs and symptoms of hypothyroidism. Hormone replacement is required. (107)

tetany—hypofunction of the parathyroids, resulting in intermittent, tonic spasms usually due to calcium deficiency, but also may occur with hypomagnesemia or severe respiratory alkalosis. (96)

thymoma—tumor of thymus that may be invasive and associated with myasthenia gravis or other syndromes. Tumor tends to recur after removal. (101)

thyroiditis—inflammation of the thyroid gland. (2, 23, 28)

acute thyroiditis—sudden onset of inflammatory process with local tenderness of thyroid.

Hashimoto's thyroiditis, struma lymphomatosa—lymphoid goiter or lymphocytic thyroiditis, thought to be an autoimmune, hereditary disease and not an infectious or inflammatory disorder as the name suggests. It occurs almost exclusively in women. A medium-sized, rubbery, firm goiter; low metabolism; and hypothyroidism are common clinical findings.

Riedel's thyroiditis, chronic fibrosing thyroiditis—rare chronic type characterized by fibrotic changes in the thyroid and surrounding structures, leading to induration of the tissues of the neck.

subacute thyroiditis—inflammation usually subsequent to viral infection in the respiratory tract indicative of an immunologic response to the virus.

thyroid neoplasms:

adenomas—benign glandular tumors. (21, 49, 64)

follicular carcinoma—malignant tumor more common in men than in women. It varies in appearance from well-differentiated types of tumors to nearly solid sheets of follicular epithelium with little evidence of follicle formation. (21)

lymphomas—malignant, nodular histiocytic tumor that usually arises in a gland affected by Hashimoto's thyroiditis. (21)

medullary carcinoma—malignant tumor originating from parafollicular or C cells and producing large amounts of calcitonin. These tumors are characterized by sheets of tumor cells separated by a hyaline-amyloid-containing stroma. Medullary carcinoma of the thyroid occurs in sporadic form (85%) and in familial form, which accounts for the remainder. Familial medullary carcinoma of the thyroid may be considered as part of a medullary thyroid carcinoma-pheochromocytoma syndrome, and it appears to be genetically determined as an autosomal dominant with a high degree of frequency. (20, 23, 28, 68)

papillary carcinoma—most common malignant type of thyroid tumor seen in younger patients. This type of thyroid carcinoma is more common in women than in men. (23, 28)

extrathyroidal tumor—extending through the thyroid capsule; involves surrounding tissue. (23)

intrathyroidal tumor—does not extend beyond the thyroid surface. Microscopically, these tumors consist of well-differentiated thyroid epithelium covering papillary fibrovascular stalks. (21, 23)

OPERATIVE TERMS (SEE TABLE 13.1.)

adrenalectomy—removal of adrenal gland or glands. (69, 94, 107)

cryohypophysectomy—one of several procedures that uses the stereotaxic transsphenoidal approach and achieves pituitary ablation (removal of hypophysis) by applying a cryoprobe.

hypophysectomy, total—removal of hypophysis. Total hypophysectomy is required to correct hypercortisolism in approximately 10% of patients. Postoperative radiation may be required for unresectable tumors and persistent hypercortisolism. (107)

microneurosurgery of pituitary gland—microdissection of tumor under magnification and with intense illumination using a binocular surgical microscope. Techniques are

Hardy's oronasal-transsphenoidal approach—entering the sphenoid sinus via nasal septum for removal of intrasellar tumor.

Rand's transfrontal-transsphenoidal approach—opening the sphenoid sinus through a frontal craniotomy for removal of tumor attached to optic chiasm. (52)

parathyroidectomy—removal of parathyroid tissue to control hyperparathyroidism. (70, 96)

thymectomy—removal of the thymus gland.

thyroid surgery: (21, 54)

lobectomy of thyroid—usually the removal of the isthmus and involved lobe for solitary thyroid nodule.

partial thyroidectomy—method of choice for removal of fibrous nodular thyroid.

subtotal thyroidectomy—removal of most of the thyroid to relieve hyperthyroidism.

SYMPTOMATIC TERMS

exophthalmos—abnormal protrusion of the eyeballs. (23, 28, 65)

hirsutism—excessive growth of hair. (28)

malignant exophthalmos—excessive protrusion of the eyeballs that fails to respond to treatment and leads to loss of sight.

orthostatic (postural) hypertension—high blood pressure associated with changes in posture. (18)

paroxysmal hypertension—sudden recurrence of high blood pressure after a remission. It may be caused by conditions of the adrenal gland. (101)

proptosis—forward displacement of the globes in the orbit; exophthalmos. (23, 28, 65)

virilism—masculinization in women. (28)

vitiligo—white patches on the skin of the hands and feet. They may be seen in hyperthyroidism. (74)

TABLE 13.1	Some Endocrine Conditions Amenable to Surgery		
Anatomic Site	*Diagnosis*	*Type of Surgery*	*Operative Procedures*
Adrenal gland	Adenoma of adrenal cortex (unilateral anterior to kidney)	Unilateral adrenalectomy with excision of adenoma	Abdominal approach with preliminary exploration of ovaries in the female followed by removal of anterior tumor
Adrenal gland	Cushing's syndrome secondary to adrenal neoplasm	Subtotal adrenalectomy Resection of tumor	Removal of one adrenal gland and tumor
Adrenal gland	Pheochromocytoma Paroxysmal hypertension	Adrenalectomy and tumor resection	Anterior transabdominal incision and removal of pheochromocytoma
Adrenal gland	Hyperadrenocorticism	Bilateral adrenalectomy followed by autotransplantation	Both adrenals removed and healthy portion of gland implanted to maintain adrenal function
Pancreas	Insulinoma: hyperinsulinism and marked hypoglycemia	Resection of pancreas and excision of insulinoma	Removal of part of pancreas containing insulinoma to restore glycemia
Parathyroid	Parathyroid adenoma Hyperparathyroidism Nephrolithiasis	Excision of parathyroid gland	Removal of parathyroid with adenoma to prevent recurrent renal calculi
Thyroid gland	Solitary thyroid nodule of unknown nature	Surgical exploration	Tissue from thyroid nodule removed Frozen section made
Thyroid gland	Papillary carcinoma with metastases to adjacent lymph nodes	Total thyroidectomy with neck dissection	Excision of entire thyroid gland with dissection of the upper portion of neck
Thyroid gland	Graves' thyrotoxicosis	Subtotal thyroidectomy	Removal of part of thyroid gland
Thymus gland	Myasthenia gravis, nonthymomatous	Transcervical thymectomy	Incision across the suprasternal notch, removal of thymus

METABOLIC DISORDERS

ORIGIN OF TERMS

a-, an- (G)—without, not
bio- (G)—life, living
melano- (G)—black

meli-, melito- (G)—honey, sweet, sugar
meta- (G)—after, beyond, over
xantho- (G)—yellow

PHONETIC PRONUNCIATION OF SELECTED TERMS

acidosis	AS-i-DOE′sis
alkalosis	AL′kah-LOW′sis
diabetes mellitus	DI-a-BE′tez mell-I′tus
galactosemia	gah-LAK-toe-SEE′me-ah
glycogenosis	GLI-ko-gen-OWE′sis
gouty arthritis	GOW′tee ar-THRI′tis
hyperchloremia	HI-per klo-RE′-me-ah
hypertriglyceridemia	HI-per-tri-GLIS-er-i-DEE′me-ah

GENERAL TERMS

basal metabolic rate (BMR)—measurement of the number of calories needed for the support of basic metabolic functions, such as respiration, circulation, and body temperature, in a resting person. The normal range is from −10% to +10%. (88, 101)

blood sugar level—concentration of glucose in the blood. (101)

glucagon—polypeptide hormone secreted by the alpha cells of the pancreatic islets. Glucose is mobilized from glycogen by a complex group of enzyme reactions. (5, 44)

glucose tolerance—the more sugar a healthy person takes, the more is utilized. The reverse is true in the diabetic person. (52, 72)

glycogenoses—glycogen storage diseases caused by an enzymatic defect in the buildup and breakdown of glycogen. (5, 38, 44)

insulin antibody, anti-insulin Ab—immunoglobin that may be present in diabetic persons receiving insulin and may account for allergic reactions and insulin resistance. (72, 101)

insulin resistance—a metabolic state in which a normal concentration of insulin produces a less than normal biological response. Insulin resistance is a characteristic feature of a patient with impaired glucose tolerance (IGT). Obesity is a well-known condition that also leads to the development of insulin resistance. For example, there may occur a tolerance to high daily dosage (200 units) due to obesity or to the development of antibodies that bind insulin. (72, 101)

insulin secretion radioimmunoassay—test determines insulin secretion response to glucose. Reference values are increased in insulinoma, acromegaly, and Cushing's syndrome. (101)

ketone bodies—acetone bodies, products of faulty metabolism in diabetic acidosis. Since sugar is not utilized normally in diabetes mellitus, excessive fat is mobilized and employed in energy production. Other clinical states characterized by faulty fat metabolism that result in ketoacidosis are starvation, prolonged diarrhea and vomiting, and von Gierke's disease. In ketoacidosis, ketone bodies accumulate in the blood (ketonemia) and are excreted in the urine (ketonuria). (101)

> *Reference values:* (26)
> *Ketoacidosis*
> - *serum ketone test (serum acetone test)*—greater than 2.0 mg/dL.
> - *urine ketone test (Acetest or Ketostix)*—purple color reaction with diabetic acid 5–10 mg/dL.

lipids—group of organic substances, mostly composed of carbon, hydrogen, and some oxygen; they may also contain nitrogen and phosphorus. Lipids are soluble in hydrocarbon and ether and insoluble in water. There are four types of principal circulating lipids: cholesterol esters, free cholesterol, phospholipids, and triglycerides. (12, 45, 101)

> *Reference values:* serum lipids (26)
> - *total lipids*—450–1000 mg/dL (SIU: 4.5–10 g/L)
> - *cholesterol*—150–265 mg/dL (SIU: 3.9–6.85 mmol/L)
> - *triglycerides*—10–190 mg/dL (SIU: 1.09–20.71 mmol/L)

- *phospholipids*—150–380 mg/dL (SIU: 1.50–3.80 g/L)
- *fatty acids (free)*—8–25 mg/dL (SIU: 0.30–0.90 mmol/L)
- *phospholipid phosphorus*—8.0–11.9 mg/dL (SIU: 2.85–3.55 mmol/L)

lipoproteins—lipids and proteins combined. Lipids alone cannot enter the circulation, but lipoproteins can be transported by the bloodstream.

alpha lipoproteins—tiny particles containing large amount of protein; do not predispose to atherosclerosis.

beta lipoproteins—tiny particles with high cholesterol content, predisposing to atherosclerosis.

prebeta lipoproteins—particles are relatively large and appear to be active in the transport of triglycerides.

chylomicrons—large particles present in serum during digestion of fat-containing foods. Chylomicrons undergo rapid metabolic transformations and are cleared from circulation within a few minutes and therefore are not detected in fasting plasma. (12, 14, 45, 94, 101)

Lipoproteins are classified according to specific differences into: HDL—high-density lipoproteins, LDL—low-density lipoproteins, and VLDL—very-low-density lipoproteins. (7, 13, 45)

lysosomes—cytoplasmic organelles that enclose environment and contain enzymes capable of hydrolyzing most macromolecules.

primary lysosomes—the original bodies derived from the Golgi apparatus, may fuse with their membrane-bound vesicles to form secondary lysosomes.

secondary lysosomes—contain material derived from outside the cell through endocytosis or from within the cell through autophagy. (4)

DIAGNOSTIC TERMS

acid-base imbalance—disturbance in acid-base balance of the blood concerned with carbon dioxide (carbonic acid) as the acid component and bicarbonate as the base component of the equation. As a result, abnormal changes develop in the carbon dioxide tension (PCO_2) and hydrogen ion concentration (pH). Lungs and kidneys play major roles in:

metabolic acidosis—primary alkali deficit characterized by a low pH and PCO_2. It occurs in Addison's disease, starvation, diarrhea, renal and liver diseases, and overtreatment with acids.

metabolic alkalosis—primary alkali excess marked by increased pH and PCO_2. It is caused by excessive loss of acid, gastric suction, potassium deficit, Cushing's syndrome, and overtreatment with alkaline salts.

respiratory acidosis—primary CO_2 excess, low pH, and high PCO_2 indicative of impaired gaseous exchange and hypoventilation resulting in carbon dioxide retention. Causes include depression of the respiratory center by cerebral disease or drugs, neuromuscular disorders, and cardiopulmonary arrest.

respiratory alkalosis—primary CO_2 deficit, high pH and low PCO_2 present in hyperventilation. It is seen in overstimulation of respiratory center, high altitudes, fever, hysteria, and anxiety. (49, 58, 73)

alkalosis—abnormal increase of alkalinity in the blood. (58, 73)

carcinoid syndrome, carcinoidosis—peculiar metabolic disorder characterized by flushing, diarrhea, dyspnea, and valvular heart disease. The symptoms are related to an overproduction of serotonin by the malignant carcinoid tumor of the gastrointestinal tract, usually the terminal ileum. Metastases to the liver and adjacent lymph nodes may occur. (105)

diabetes insipidus—metabolic disorder caused by hyposecretion of the antidiuretic hormone of the pituitary gland. Its clinical manifestations are polydipsia and polyuria. (28, 80)

diabetes mellitus—chronic metabolic disease complex, characterized by an insufficiency of insulin secretion and concomitant resistance to the metabolic action of insulin on tissues.

Diabetes mellitus's long-term complications involve the eyes, kidneys, nerves, and blood vessels with capillary basement membrane thickening, neuropathy involving both the somatic and autonomic nervous systems, neuromuscular dysfunction with muscle wasting, gangrene of the lower extremities, and decreased resistance to infection. According to the National Diabetes Data Group and standards from the World Health Organization, diabetes mellitus can be separated into two general disease syndromes:

> *Type I, insulin-dependent diabetes mellitus (IDDM)*—hyperglycemia caused by absent or insufficient secretion of insulin by B cells of pancreas in response to glucose. It is seen in the young and infrequently in adults, particularly nonobese or elderly individuals.

> *Type II, non-insulin-dependent diabetes mellitus (NIDDM)*—hyperglycemia related to varied amounts of pancreatic insulin; ketosis is limited to periods of stress or infection. Most persons afflicted with this type of diabetes are over 40 years of age. Two subgroups of persons with type II diabetes are characterized by the presence or absence of obesity. (27, 32, 55, 72)

secondary diabetic states—exist when some other readily identifiable primary disorder or pathophysiologic state causes or is associated with the diabetic state. Any disorder that limits insulin secretion or impairs insulin action can cause secondary diabetes. Some examples of these disorders are chronic pancreatitis, cystic fibrosis, hemochromatosis, Cushing's disease, pheochromocytoma, and others. (28, 72)

diabetic ketoacidosis (DKA)—due to insulin deficiency. Severe insulin deficiency leads to hyperglycemia and ketonemia, and from these states all of the other pathophysiologic sequelae may occur. Acidosis and ketonuria are primarily caused by the buildup of the ketoacids beta-hydroxybutyrate and acetoacetate. Hyperglycemia and hyperketonemia cause an osmotic diuresis that produces intravascular volume depletion and dehydration and urinary electrolyte loss. DKA is a serious complication in diabetic persons of all ages that may be precipitated in the young by infection, and in the elderly by acute stress, myocardial infarction, and infection. The onset is gradual, with symptoms of polydipsia and polyuria, fever, nausea, vomiting, and extreme fatigue. It is followed by increasing mental stupor and rapid deep respirations, with a fruity breath odor signaling ketoacetotic coma. This low blood pressure and rapid pulse reflect marked dehydration (5 to 10 liters) and salt depletion. (31, 32, 55)

Fabry's disease, α-galactosidase A deficiency—an X-linked inborn error of glycosphingolipid metabolism characterized by telangiectatic skin lesions, hypohidrosis, corneal and lenticular opacities, acroparesthesias, and vascular disease of the kidney. The disease results from the deficient activity of α-galactosidase A, a lysosomal enzyme encoded by a gene located on the long arm of the X chromosome. Fabry's disease is an X-linked recessive trait that is manifested in hemizygous males, with an estimated incidence of 1 in 40,000. Heterozygous females are usually asymptomatic or exhibit mild disease manifestations. Males are more severely affected with the disease, particularly males who are in blood group B or AB, as these blood group substances also accumulate because of the enzyme deficiency. (4, 39, 64)

galactosemia—inborn error of carbohydrate metabolism resulting in an incapacity for metabolizing galactose. Consequently, galactose blood levels increase abnormally, and galactose may be present in the urine. Other manifestations that may develop include gastrointestinal disorders, ascites, cirrhosis, proteinuria, and mental retardation. The key treatment is the institution of a galactose-free diet. Untreated patients with galactose deficiency may not survive, and those who do survive may be severely retarded mentally. (38, 44)

Gaucher's disease—hereditary metabolic defect resulting in faulty lipid storage. Abnormal reticuloendothelial (Gaucher) cells proliferate and cause progressive splenomegaly, pigmentation of the skin, anemia, and frequently bone involvement. (5, 10, 34, 64, 77)

glycogen storage diseases—caused by an enzymatic defect in the buildup and breakdown of glycogen. These disorders are a heterogeneous class of metabolic diseases affecting many different tissues. The main characteristic of these diseases is the excessive accumulation of glycogen, and usually there is organ dysfunction present also. (5, 44)

gout, gouty arthritis—disorder of purine metabolism and a recurrent form of arthritis manifested by an abnormal increase of uric acid in the blood, tophi, joint involvement, and in severe cases, uric acid nephrolithiasis or renal failure. (101, 110)

hyperglucagonemia—excess of glucagon in the circulating blood. It does not cause glucose intolerance in normal subjects or bring about deterioration of diabetic control. Glucagon in the insulin-deprived patient can worsen the condition. (32)

hyperlipoproteinemias—disturbances of lipid transport that result from accelerated synthesis of retarded degradation of lipoproteins that transport cholesterol and triglycerides through plasma. Hyperlipoproteinemias are classified as primary or secondary. Primary hyperlipoproteinemias can be divided into two categories: single-gene disorders that are transmitted by simple dominant or recessive mechanisms and multifactorial disorders with complex inheritance patterns in which multiple variant genes interact with environmental factors to cause varying degrees of hyperlipoproteinemia in members of a family. (12, 13, 45)

hypoglycemic states—low blood-sugar levels and neuroglycopenia (diminished glucose content of the brain) are essential characteristics of significant hypoglycemia. Nervousness, hunger, flushing or pallor, lethargy or somnolence, bizarre behavior, and syncopal attacks may be present in varying degrees. The most important cause of hypoglycemia is a pancreatic B-cell tumor, which may present as a solitary insulinoma and produce excessive amounts of insulin. Hypoglycemia may occur in the fasting state or postprandially.

fasting hypoglycemia—many are the causes of this type of hypoglycemia; however, in all the causes, there is an imbalance between the production of glucose by the liver and its utilization in peripheral tissues. Causes of underproduction of glucose during fasting can be grouped into 5 categories: (1) hormone deficiencies; (2) defects in glycogenolytic or gluconeogenic enzymes; (3) inadequate substrate delivery; (4) liver disease; and (5) drugs. Overutilization of glucose occurs when hyperinsulinism is present and when plasma insulin concentrations are low.

postprandial hypoglycemia—principal cause of postprandial hypoglycemia is alimentary hyperinsulinism. Other causes include hereditary fructose intolerance, galactosemia, leucine sensitivity, and idiopathic alimentary hypoglycemia.

- *Whipple's triad*—consists of (1) the symptoms of hypoglycemia; (2) a low fasting blood-sugar level of 40 milligrams per deciliter or less; and (3) a quick recovery after glucose administration. However, if insulinoma is the cause of hypoglycemia, the prognosis may be fatal. (16, 33, 55, 72, 90)

lactic acidosis—excess lactic acid in the blood due to inadequate removal causes circulatory, respiratory, renal, and hepatic failure; septic shock; and terminal cancer. Its clinical manifestations are hyperventilation and mental confusion, followed by coma and collapse. (32, 58)

lipid storage diseases—caused by functional deficiency of a certain enzyme. Some disorders representative of this classification include Gaucher's disease, Wolman's disease, granulomatous diseases with lipid storage such as histiocytosis, and other xanthomatoses. (7, 25, 39, 55)

lipodystrophies—represents a group of metabolic disorders characterized by abnormalities in adipose tissue, generalized or partial loss of body fat, abnormalities of carbohydrate and lipid metabolism, severe resistance to endogenous and exogenous insulin and immunologic dysfunction. (25)

lysosomal storage disease—includes most of the lipid storage disorders, the mucopolysaccharidoses, the mucolipidoses, glycoprotein storage diseases, and others. The enzyme deficiencies have an autosomal recessive basis, with the exception of Hunter mucopolysaccharidosis II, which is X-linked recessive, and Fabry disease, which is X-linked with frequent manifestations in females. (6)

Niemann-Pick disease—in disease type A and B, there is a deficiency of sphingomyelinase, an enzyme that hydrolyzes sphingomyelin to yield ceramide and phosphorylcholine. The most common disorder, type A, occurs shortly after birth with hepatosplenomegaly, failure to thrive, and neurologic impairment. The diagnosis is made by observing the presence of the distinctive Niemann-Pick cell in the bone marrow and can be confirmed by enzyme assay. Niemann-Pick type B disease presents with hepatosplenomegaly, sphingomyelinase deficiency, and, occasionally, pulmonary infiltrates, but there is no neurologic impairment. Niemann-Pick type C disease is not due to sphingomyelinase deficiency but is associated with a massive lysosomal accumulation of cholesterol due to an incompletely characterized defect in intracellular utilization of cholesterol. Type C disease is characterized by sphingomyelin lipidosis and progressive neurologic deterioration in childhood. (4, 39, 64)

obesity—excess of adipose tissue that presents a potential risk to good health. The metabolic factor causing obesity may be the steroid excess of glucocorticoids in Cushing's syndrome. Since obese persons usually have hypertriglyceridemia and hypercholesterolemia, they are more prone to develop atherosclerosis, hypertension, and diabetes mellitus than nonobese persons. (84)

phenylketonuria (PKU)—hereditary metabolic disorder causing mental retardation. Phenylketone bodies are found in serum and urine. The disease is caused by an inborn error of amino acid metabolism. (100, 101)

porphyria—inborn faulty porphyrin metabolism resulting in porphyrinuria. The disorders occur due to an excess accumulation and excretion of porphyrins and porphyrin precursors. The main clinical manifestations are cutaneous lesions, neurologic dysfunction, and hepatic disease.

> *congenital, erythropoietic type*—porphyria characterized by skin lesions due to photosensitivity from porphyrin in subcutaneous tissue.
>
> *hepatic intermittent acute type*—porphyria noted for liver damage, brownish pigmentation of the skin, and neurologic symptoms. (8, 22, 98)

xanthomatosis—widespread eruption of xanthomas on the skin and tendons. The xanthomas are yellow, lipid-containing plaques usually associated with hyperlipoproteinemia. (12, 74)

SYMPTOMATIC TERMS

exacerbation—aggravation of symptoms.

glycosuria—the presence of sugar in the urine. (50)

hypercholesterolemia—excessive cholesterol concentration in the circulating blood. (7, 45)

hyperglycemia—excessive sugar concentration in the blood. (51)

hyperkalemia—excessive potassium concentration in the blood. (58, 62, 77)

hypernatremia—excessive sodium concentration in the blood. (58)

hypertriglyceridemia—excessive triglyceride concentration in the blood. (7, 45)

hyperuricemia—excessive uric acid concentration in the blood. (101)

hyponatremia—abnormally low serum sodium level due to a disturbed ratio of water to sodium. (28, 32, 73)

insulinopenia—deficient insulin secretion by the pancreatic B cells present in diabetes mellitus. (55)

ketosis—excess ketone bodies in the body fluids and tissues due to incomplete combustion of fatty acids, which may result from a faulty or absent utilization of carbohydrates. Ketosis may produce severe acidosis. It develops in uncontrolled diabetes mellitus and starvation. (55)

Kussmaul breathing—classic manifestations in diabetic acidosis marked by unusually deep respirations associated with dyspnea. This type of breathing is caused by abnormally increased acid content of the blood, resulting in continuous overstimulation of the respiratory center. (31)

polydipsia—excessive thirst. (28)

polyphagia—overeating. (28)
polyuria—excessive urination. (21)
remission—symptoms decreased in severity.
steatorrhea—excess fecal fat due to malabsorption of lipids, an enzyme deficiency of the pancreas, or intestinal disease. (43)
tophi (sing. **tophus)**—sodium biurate deposits near a joint. Condition is peculiar to gout. (97, 110)

CYTOGENETIC DISORDERS

ORIGINS OF TERMS

acro- (G)—extremity, extreme
auto- (G)—self
centre (G)—center
chromo- (G)—color
cyto- (G)—cell
gamete (G)—mature germ cell, sperm, ovum
-gen (G)—to produce
karyo- (G)—nucleus

mono- (G)—single
mutant (G)—single
ovo- (L)—egg
soma, somato- (G)—body
spermato-, spermo- (G)—seed
syndrome (G)—concurrence, a set of symptoms that occur together

PHONETIC PRONUNCIATION OF SELECTED TERMS

D-trisomy	D-TRI′so-me
Klinefelter's syndrome	KLIN-fell-ters (syndrome)
hypomastia	HI-po-MAS′tee-ah
estrogen deficiency	ES′tro-gen de-FISH′en-see
hypoplasia of testes	HI-po-PLAY′ze-ah of TES′TEES
microphthalmia	my-krof-THAL′me-ah

GENERAL TERMS

acrocentric—centromere located at one end. (40)
autosomal aberration—abnormality of chromosomes.
    acquired—developed after birth, as in chronic myeloid leukemia.
    congenital—present at birth, as in Down's syndrome (mongolism). (39)
autosomal-dominant inheritance—one abnormal dominant gene of a pair is passed on to 50% of the offspring, although the affected parent has a normal mate. As a rule, autosomal-dominant inheritance delineates the following pattern:
    equal distribution of the abnormal trait among males and females.
    direct transmission of the trait over two generations or more.
    abnormal trait affecting close to 50% of the members of the pedigree. (41, 67)
autosomal-recessive inheritance—abnormality is produced by paired defective genes, since both parents contribute one recessive abnormal gene. Criteria for establishing recessive inheritance are (1) consanguinity increases the chance that the affected gene is passed on by the two related parents; (2) the same genetic disorder occurs in collateral family branches; and (3) the disease is present in 25% of the siblings. (41, 47, 67)
autosome, autosomal chromosome—non–sex chromosome. (40, 41, 83)
banding—banded or striped appearance of chromosomes when special staining is done to chromosomes at metaphase using the Giemsa method for karyotyping. (67, 83, 86, 93)
centromere—constriction in center of chromosome, dividing the chromosome into two lengths, or arms. (40, 86)
chromatid—one of the two halves of a chromosome.
chromatin—deoxyribonucleic acid (DNA) found in chromosomes and stainable by basic dyes. (40, 83)

Figure 13.5 Chromosomes from a normal human male cell, grown in tissue culture and arrested at metaphase (courtesy of Sister Leo Rita Volk, F.S.M.).

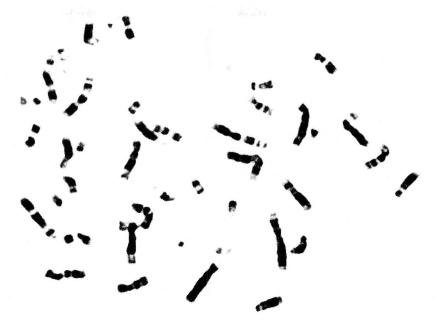

Sister Leo Rita Volk, F.S.M.

chromosomal aberration—abnormality of chromosomes.

acquired—developed after birth, as in chronic granulocytic leukemia, in which the Philadelphia (Ph[1]) chromosome is present.

congenital—present at birth, as in Down's syndrome (mongolism). (77)

chromosomal breakage, chromosomal fragmentation—anomaly frequently found in tumor cells.

chromosome—threadlike body of chromatin in cell nucleus. Chromosomes are bearers of hereditary substances, called *genes*. Normally, the number of chromosomes for each species remains constant. At present, chromosomes have become the prime target of genetic investigation. (40, 41, 67) (See figs. 13.5 and 13.6.)

chromosome analysis—karyotyping. (40, 67, 83, 87, 93)

chromosome defects: (37, 40, 67, 77, 86, 93)

aneuploid mosaics—modal numbers differing in two or more distinct cell populations.

aneuploidy—abnormal chromosome number.

heterosomal aneuploidy—all cells possessing uniform aneuploidy, including:

- *complex aneuploidy*—two or more individual chromosomes in the same person show defects in numbers.
- *monosomy*—one member of a chromosome pair is absent.
- *polysomy*—the same chromosome is present four times or more.
- *triploidy*—each chromosome occurs in triplicate.
- *trisomy*—one chromosome occurs in triplicate.

structural defects of chromosomes:

- *deletion*—partial loss of a chromosome that is prone to occur during cell division and may be a long-arm or short-arm deletion. Usually there are two breaks in a chromosome, and the segment between fractures is lost.
- *duplication*—condition in which a portion of a chromosome is represented more than once.

Figure 13.6 Human sex chromosomes, normal pattern and chromosomal aberrations (courtesy of Sister Leo Rita Volk, F.S.M.).

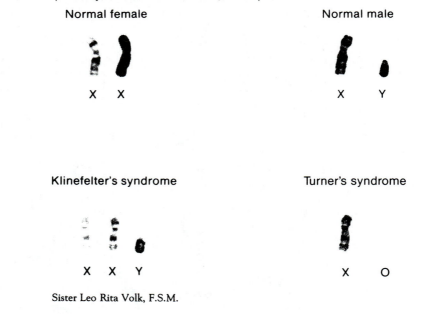

Normal female

X   X

Normal male

X   Y

Klinefelter's syndrome

X   X   Y

Turner's syndrome

X   O

Sister Leo Rita Volk, F.S.M.

- *isochromosome*—transverse division of the centromere during meiosis, which causes a chromosomal aberration.
- *translocation*—chromosome segment that shifts to a different position. It is balanced if there is a full complement of genetic material, even if the arrangement happens to be unusual. It is unbalanced if there is too much or not enough genetic material.

cytogenetics—branch of science concerned with the origin and development of cells in heredity, that is, the chromosomes. Examples of cytogenetic tests for chromosomal sex determination includes: (40, 67, 101)

biopsy of human skin—a microscopic examination of a small piece of epithelium to detect characteristic chromatin masses alongside the nuclear membrane in somatic cells. They are usually only found in females.

buccal or oral smear test, sex chromatin test, Barr test of nuclear sex—a stained smear of epithelial cells, scraped from the mucosa of the cheek, is studied under the microscope for chromatin bodies. Normally, males are chromatin negative and females chromatin positive.

leukocyte cell smear from peripheral blood—a cytologic test for chromosomal sex differentiation. A small number of circulating neutrophils forms a characteristic drumstick chromatin attachment distinguishable from the remaining nucleus. This drumstick formation on the cell nucleus has not been found in males.

tissue culture of human cells—new method of culturing permits growth without chromosomal disorganization. Tissue is cultured in vitro to obtain sufficient mitoses. The culture is treated with colchicine to arrest mitosis in metaphase and with hypotonic saline to attain spreading of the chromosomes. Preparations are then squashed, stained, and photographed under a microscope. The photomicrograph is enlarged, and the chromosomes cut out and paired to make a karyotype.

DNA, deoxyribonucleic acid—chromosomal material from which hereditary genetic characteristics may be transmitted. The major diagnostic impact of recombinant DNA technology has been in areas of carrier detection (e.g., in hemophilia, X-linked diseases, and cystic fibrosis), and in areas of premorbid diagnosis (e.g., Huntington's chorea). Studies indicate that about a fourth of the patients at risk for Huntington's chorea would consider suicide if found to carry the gene. In these cases, the genetic counselor could be advised which patients are most likely to have such suicidal ideation and tendencies and work closely with them to resolve the situation. Other areas include cancer detection, forensic pathology and archaeology, research, paternity testing, prenatal diagnosis, and zygosity of twins. (41, 51, 93, 101)

dominant—pertaining to a gene that exerts its effect even in the presence of a contrasting or opposite gene. (67, 77, 87)

euploidy—state pertaining to balanced sets of chromosomes in every number. (67, 93)

fragment—broken portion of a chromosome. In the acentric type, no centromere is present. (40, 67)

gamete—mature germ cell, sperm, or ovum. (40, 67, 84)

gene—basic unit of heredity found at a definite locus (place) on a particular chromosome. The exact location of a gene on a chromosome is its locus, and the array of loci constitutes the human gene map. There may be thousands of genes to one DNA molecule. Genes, like chromosomes, come in pairs and are either:

> *heterozygous*—each member of a gene pair carries a different instruction, or
> *homozygous*—both members of the gene pair carry the same instruction. (40, 51, 53, 67, 77, 87)

genome—a cell's or organism's entire genetic constitution. (6, 52, 87)

genotype—genetic constitution, irrespective of external appearance. (40, 67, 77, 87)

gonosome—sex chromosome Y or X. (40, 41, 67)

idiogram—diagram representing the karyotype (chromosome pattern) of the cells of an individual. (93)

karyotype—group of characteristics (form, number, size) used to identify an individual's chromosomal pattern, or that of a single cell. A karyotype of a normal person has 46 chromosomes, including 22 autosomal pairs and 2 sex chromosomes. (67, 83, 87, 93) (See fig. 13.7.)

marker chromosome—an abnormal chromosome recognized by its unusual structure. (83, 87)

meiosis—special cell division that occurs in maturation of sex cells and causes each daughter nucleus to receive half of the number of chromosomes of the species' somatic cells. (40, 83, 84)

metaphase—chromosomes lying on the equatorial plate. The equatorial plate is the same as the metaphase plate. (93)

mitosis—process of nuclear division; longitudinal splitting of chromosomes into halves and migration of the halves. (40, 67, 83)

mosaicism, chromosomal—population of normal chromosomes together with a population of one or more abnormal types, varying in proportion. Mental and physical retardation are common clinical characteristics. (40, 67, 85, 87)

mutation—change occurring in genes. (81, 85, 87, 93)

nondisjunction—chromatid pair failing to separate in cell division. (67, 87)

phenotype—person's appearance with visible characteristics that may be independent of genotype (hereditary type). It is the external expression of the genetic constitution of an organism. (40, 62)

Figure 13.7 Karyotype or idiogram of a normal human male, constructed from figure 13.5. Note banding of chromosomes (courtesy of Sister Leo Rita Volk, F.S.M.).

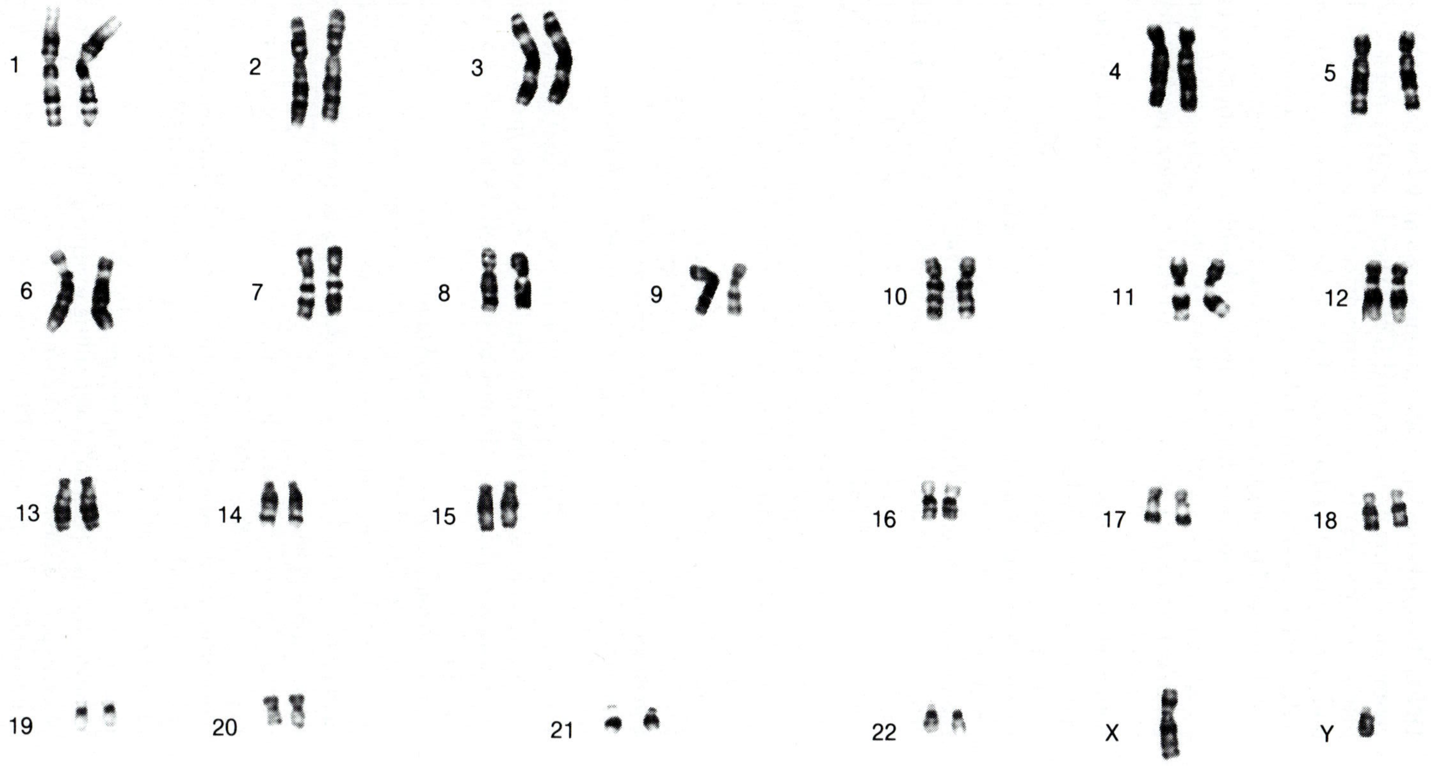

Sister Leo Rita Volk, F.S.M.

Philadelphia chromosome, Ph[1]—G group chromosome characterized by partial loss (deletion) of the long arm. It is present in typical chronic myelocytic leukemia (CML) and absent in atypical CML. (83)

recessive—pertaining to a gene that is ineffective in the presence of contrasting or opposite genes. (39, 65, 88)

sex chromosomes—those determining the sex of offspring; females have two X chromosomes (XX), and males have one X chromosome and one Y chromosome (XY). Normally, a person has 46 chromosomes; 44 (22 pairs) are autosomes and the other 2 are sex chromosomes. The normal female karyotype (i.e., the number and structure of chromosomes) is designated 46,XX. The normal male karyotype is designated 46,XY. (40, 41, 62, 85, 109)

> *X chromosome*—sex chromosome, normally found in the male and the female.
> *Y chromosome*—sex chromosome present in the male.

DIAGNOSTIC TERMS

ataxia telangiectasia (AT)—monogenic, autosomal recessive disorder characterized by progressive cerebellar ataxia, oculocutaneous telangiectasia, cellular and humoral immunodeficiency, chromosomal instability, cell cycle abnormalities, radiation sensitivity, and cancer predisposition. A gene, ATM, which is mutated in the autosomal recessive disorder ataxia telangiectasia (AT), was identified by positional cloning on chromosome 11q22–23. The disease is genetically heterogeneous, with four complementation groups designated as A, C, D, and E. ATM, which has a transcript of 12 kilobases, was found to be mutated in AT patients from all complementation groups, indicating that it is probably the sole gene responsible for this disorder. (17, 59, 71, 89, 102)

Down's syndrome—disorder with varying degrees of retardation and physical signs of mongolism, such as dwarfed stature, slanting eyes, open mouth, and protruding tongue. The genetic basis may be a numerical chromosome abnormality (aneuploy), such as trisomy 21 with 47 chromosomes, or a structural chromosome abnormality, such as translocation with 46 chromosomes. (85)

D-trisomy, trisomy 13–15—common chromosome abnormality with 47 chromosomes; clinically characterized by hemangiomas, polydactylia, and microphthalmia. Less evident are cardiovascular and neurologic anomalies, which are detectable by chromosomal analysis. (40)

Edwards' syndrome, trisomy 18 (E)—chromosome defect clinically manifested by a narrow long skull, prominent occiput, marked mental retardation, congenital cardiac disease, peculiar facies, and fingers with flexion deformities. Trisomy 18 (E) may be associated with cardiovascular involvement in such conditions as congenital polyvalvular dysplasia, ventricular septal defect, and patent ductus arteriosus. (35)

hermaphrodite—sex chromosome abnormality of variable phenotype and the presence of both ovarian and testicular tissue in gonads. (40)

Klinefelter's syndrome, seminiferous tubule dysgenesis—disorder in which chromosomal aberration results in sterility due to defective embryonic development of the seminiferous tubules. The common karyotype is either a 47,XXY chromosomal pattern (the classic form) or 46,XY/47,XXY mosaicism. Approximately 30 additional variants of the Klinefelter syndrome have been described. The symptom complex comprises various degrees of:

> *aspermia or oligospermia*—lack or scanty secretion of semen.
> *eunuchoidism*—sparsity of hair on face and body.
> *gynecomastia*—overdevelopment of the mammary glands in the male.
> *hypoplasia of testes, hypogonadism*—small, firm testes. Mental retardation and psychiatric disorders are common associated conditions. (28, 30, 85, 109)

Noonan's syndrome, Bonnevie-Ullrich syndrome, male Turner's syndrome—autosomal-recessive disorder characterized by cryptorchism, insufficient spermatogenesis, webbed neck, short stature, cardiovascular defects, and other anomalies. Males with Noonan's syndrome display primary testicular dysfunction with impairment of both sperm and androgen production, and elevated serum gonadotrophin levels. It is not a chromosomal abnormality. (28, 40)

Turner's syndrome, gonadal dysgenesis, ovarian dysgenesis—complex inherited disorder caused by chromosomal aberration. Constant clinical signs are rudimentary ovaries composed of a fibrotic streak in each broad ligament and infertility. The classic syndrome includes different degrees of:

estrogen deficiency—inadequate secretion of female hormones.

hypomastia—abnormally small breasts.

malformations—structural defects such as dwarfism, shieldlike chest, webbed neck, coarctation of the aorta, and others.

true primary amenorrhea—absence of menses. (28, 30, 40, 67, 85, 109)

SYMPTOMATIC TERMS

arachnodactylia—condition characterized by abnormal length and slenderness of the fingers and toes.

microphthalmia—condition of abnormal smallness in all dimensions of one or both eyes.

polydactylia—a developmental anomaly characterized by the presence of supernumerary digits on hands and feet.

xerostomia—dryness of mouth.

CLINICAL LABORATORY STUDIES

TERMS RELATED TO SOME ESSENTIAL BLOOD TESTS

blood gas determinations—sensitive indicators of physiologic changes of lung function and tissue perfusion in acute illness. Measurements are obtained from hydrogen, carbon dioxide, and oxygen tensions (pressures) of arterial or venous blood. The "P" refers to partial pressure. (101)

PCO_2—pressure of tension of carbon dioxide measured in millimeters of mercury. (101)
Reference values: (26)

- *arterial PCO_2*—35–50 mm Hg
- *venous PCO_2*—40–45 mm Hg

   Increase in PCO_2 (hypercarbia): Carbon dioxide retention in respiratory acidosis and metabolic alkalosis.

   Decrease in PCO_2 (hypocarbia): Excessive loss of carbon dioxide in hyperventilation due to respiratory alkalosis or metabolic acidosis. (101)

pH—hydrogen ion concentration or acidity value of blood (urine). (58, 101)
Reference values: (26)

- *arterial pH*—7.38 to 7.44
- *venous pH*—7.36 to 7.41

   Increase in acidosis. (58, 101)

   Decrease in alkalosis. (58, 101)

PO_2—pressure or tension of oxygen expressed in millimeters of mercury. (101)
Reference values: (26)

- *arterial PO_2*—95 to 100 mm Hg

   Patients with chronic lung disease normally have an arterial PO_2 of 70 mm Hg or less.

   Decreased values in arterial PO_2 in advanced lung or heart disease, venous PO_2 due to inadequate blood volume, exchange of gases, cardiac output, and tissue perfusion. (101)

TERMS RELATED TO ELECTROLYTES IN GENERAL (101)

anion—ion carrying a negative electric charge that travels toward the positive pole or anode.

anode—the positive pole or electrode toward which negatively charged ions (anions) or particles are attracted.

cathode—negative pole or electrode toward which positively charged ions (cations) or particles are attracted.

cation—ion carrying positive electric charge that travels toward the negative pole or cathode.

electrolyte—substance that conducts an electric current.

electrolyte balance—particular electrolyte performs its physiologic task, has the appropriate concentration in serum, body fluids, or tissues, and uses the proper channels of entry and exit, thus regulating its serum concentration.

electrolyte imbalance—particular electrolyte in the blood, body fluids, or tissues in too high or too low a concentration, which may adversely affect the body tissues and fluids.

ion—part of an electrolyte, an atom, or number of atoms carrying a positive or negative electric charge.

molality—concentration of a solution expressed in moles per kilogram of pure solvent.

molarity—concentration of a solution expressed in moles per liter of solution.

pascal (Pa)—derived unit of pressure in the International System of Units expressed in newtons per square meter.

valence—the number of charges on an electrolyte. The valence of the ion must be considered in the relationship of moles and equivalents. For example:

univalent, monovalent ions (Na^+, K^+, Cl^-, HCO_3^-)—molarity is equivalent.

divalent, bivalent ions (Ca^{++}, Mg^{++}, SO_4^{--})—these have two equivalents per mole.

trivalent ions (Fe_3^+, Po_4^{3-})—the relationship is three equivalents per mole.

TERMS RELATED TO SPECIFIC ELECTROLYTES

bicarbonate (HCO_3^-)—univalent anion that is part of the carbonate-bicarbonate buffering system for maintaining the pH (hydrogen ion concentration) and acid-base balance. (58, 101)

Reference values: (26)

- *serum bicarbonate*—18–23 mEq/L (SIU: 18–23 nmol/L)

    Increase in metabolic alkalosis resulting from protracted vomiting, gastric suction, hypokalemia, excessive aldosterone, renal artery stenosis, malignant hypertension, Cushing's syndrome, and other causes. (58, 101)

    Increase in respiratory acidosis caused by deficient elimination of carbon dioxide and subsequent rise of PCO_2 as occurs in severe lung emphysema, heart failure, or any other marked interferences with ventilatory function. (101)

    Decrease in metabolic acidosis resulting from prolonged diarrhea, starvation, diabetic ketosis, renal failure, and other causes. (58, 101)

    Decrease in respiratory alkalosis caused by hyperventilation. (58, 101)

calcium (Ca^{++})—divalent calcium cations play an important role in several major physiologic processes, including ion transfer, cell division and growth, bone mineralization and turnover, maintenance or hemostasis and blood coagulation, electric excitation of muscular contraction and cellular secretion, and electric activity of the heart. (48, 101)

Reference values: (26)

- *Serum calcium total*—8.4–10.2 mg/dL (SIU: 2.10–2.55 mmol/L)
- *urine calcium, 24 hr*—100–300 mg/d (SIU: 2.5–7.5 mmol/d)

    Increase in serum calcium in metastatic bone cancer, multiple myeloma, Paget's disease of bone, hyperparathyroidism, and other diseases. (48, 76)

    Decrease in serum calcium in rickets, hypoparathyroidism, osteomalacia, malabsorption syndrome, and severe pancreatitis with necrosis. (29, 48, 101)

chloride (Cl⁻)—important inorganic anion of extracellular fluid that maintains electrolyte and acid-base balance. Chloride retention or ingestion may initiate acidosis, chloride loss, and alkalosis. Sodium chloride aids in the control of osmolarity of body fluids. (101)

Reference values: (26)

- *serum chloride*—98–106 mEq/L (SIU: 98–106 mmol/L)

    Increase in serum chloride, or hyperchloremia, in dehydration, overuse of intravenous saline solution, selected cases of hyperventilation, renal disease, and other disorders. (101)

    Decrease in serum chloride, or hypochloremia, in chronic diarrhea, protracted vomiting, excessive sweating, renal failure, diabetic ketosis, and other conditions. (101)

magnesium (Mg⁺⁺)—divalent cation occurring in high intracellular concentration and serving as an activating ion to certain enzymes involved in carbohydrate, lipid, and protein metabolism. (1, 101)

Reference values: (26)

- *serum magnesium*—1.3–2.1 mEq/L (SIU: 0.65–1.05 mmol/L)

    Increase in magnesium levels may be present in renal failure. (1, 49, 101)

    Decrease in magnesium levels may occur in prolonged intravenous feeding, alcohol intoxication, hyperaldosteronism, hyperparathyroidism, malabsorption syndromes, diabetic coma, and other states. (1, 49, 96)

potassium (K⁺)—a univalent, essentially intracellular cation found in platelets and leukocytes. At present, determinations of potassium within human cells have not been achieved. Plasma or serum potassium measures the extracellular potassium concentration. When muscle weakness and paralysis develop, early potassium disturbance is suspected. It may progress to serious ventricular fibrillation and cardiac arrest, confirmed by electrocardiographic patterns (ECG or EKG). The EKG is of diagnostic importance in the detection of hyperkalemia and hypokalemia. (49, 58)

Reference values: (26)

- *serum potassium*—3.5–5.1 mEq/L (SIU: 3.5–5.1 mmol/L)
- *plasma potassium*—3.5–4.5 mEq/L (SIU: 3.4–4.5 mmol/L)

    Increase in renal failure, adrenal insufficiency, Addison's disease, and excessive potassium ingestion. (58, 101)

    Decrease in starvation, severe diarrhea, protracted vomiting, malabsorption syndromes, and metabolic alkalosis. (58, 101)

sodium (Na⁺)—univalent ion and major cation in extracellular fluid (ECF). Serum sodium concentration may serve as index of osmotic pressure of extracellular fluid (water) in healthy persons. (49)

Reference values: (26)

- *plasma sodium*—136–146 mEq/L (SIU: 136–146 mmol/L)

    Increase in dehydration, disease or trauma of central nervous system, and excess of aldosterone. (49)

    Decrease in low-salt intake; in sodium shift caused by burns or trauma; and with marked sodium loss via digestive tract or from fistula, obstruction, or other conditions such as hypertriglyceridemia due to uncontrolled diabetes. (32, 49, 101)

TERMS PRIMARILY RELATED TO ENDOCRINE FUNCTION STUDIES

adrenal hormones:

adrenal cortex—outer portion of adrenal gland. The cortex produces hormones, including three major groups: (1) steroids controlling the salt and water metabolism, such as aldosterone; (2) steroids regulating the glucose metabolism and promoting gluconeogenesis, such as hydrocortisone; and (3) steroids affecting androgenic activity, such as androsterone. (24)

adrenal medulla—inner portion of adrenal gland, which secretes epinephrine (adrenaline) and norepinephrine (noradrenaline). (62, 101)

aldosterone—potent salt-retaining hormone of adrenal cortex that affects electrolyte balance. (24, 62)

aldosterone in urine—quantitative measurement of aldosterone excreted in urine. (24, 62, 101)
Reference values: (26)
- *urinary aldosterone level*—3–20 µg/24 hr (SIU: 8.3–55 nmol/24 hr)

  Increase in primary and secondary aldosteronism, nephrosis with edema, congestive heart failure with edema, and hepatic cirrhosis with ascites, and in the second and third trimesters of normal pregnancy. (62, 101)

catecholamines in urine—determination of excretion of epinephrine, norepinephrine, total free catecholamines, and metanephrines. (90, 101)
Reference values: (26)
- *epinephrine*—10 µg/24 hr (SIU less than 55 nmol/24 hr)
- *norepinephrine*—less than 100 µg/24 hr (SIU: less than 590 nmol/24 hr)
- *total free catecholamines*—4 to 126 µg/24 hr (SIU: 24–745 nmol/24 hr)
- *total metanephrines*—0.1 to 1.6 mg/24 hr (SIU: 0.5–8.1 µmol/24 hr)

  Increase in pheochromocytoma, neuroblastoma. (62, 101)

corticosteroids—steroid hormones secreted by the adrenal cortex. (101)

corticotropin, adrenocorticotropic hormone (ACTH)—hormone of the hypothalamus under the negative feedback control of cortisol. ACTH and cortisol plasma levels are increased in the morning and low at night. (62, 69, 95, 101)
Reference values: (26)
- *plasma ACTH*—0800 hr: 25–100 pg/mL (SIU: 25–100 ng/L)
  —1800 hr: less than 50 pg/mL (SIU: less than 50 ng/L)
- *plasma cortisol*—0800 hr: 5–23 µg/dL (SIU: 138–635 nmol/L)
  —1600 hr: 3–15 µg/dL (SIU: 82–413 nmol/L)

17-hydrocorticosteroids—hormones regulating gluconeogenesis, the production of sugar from protein. (53, 95, 101)
Reference values: (26)
17-OH corticosteroids, 17-OH-CS, glucocorticoids:
- *Males*—3.9 mg/24 hr (SIU: 8.3–25 µmol/24 hr)
- *Females*—2–8 mg/24 hr (SIU: 5.5–22 µmol/24 hr)

  Increase usually in Cushing's syndrome, marked stress, acute pancreatitis, and eclampsia. (62, 101)

  Decrease in hypopituitarism and Addison's disease. (62, 101)

anterior pituitary hormones:

follitropin, follicle-stimulating hormone (FSH)—a glycopeptide hormone of the anterior pituitary that, together with the luteinizing hormone (LH), promotes the development and function of the sex organs. In the female, FSH stimulates the ripening of the ovarian follicle and thus prepares for ovulation; in the male, FSH stimulates the maturation of the sperm. (52, 101)
Reference values: (26)
serum FSH (radioimmunoassay [RIA])
- *Males*—4–24 mIU/mL
- *Females*—4–30 mIU/mL
  - *midcycle*—two times baseline
  - *postmenopause*—40–250 mIU/mL

Increase of FSH in primary gonadal failure, ovarian or testicular agenesis, castration, seminiferous tubule failure, Klinefelter's syndrome, and other disorders. (52, 82, 101)

Decrease of FSH in children before puberty; panhypopituitarism; anorexia nervosa; estrogen or androgen-secreting neoplasms of the adrenals, ovaries, or testes; and other conditions. (52, 82, 101)

lutropin, luteinizing hormone (LH)—potent hormone of the anterior pituitary. It exerts multiple effects on its target organ, the ovary; brings about follicular maturation, rupture of the follicle, and release of the mature ovum; develops the corpus luteum and progesterone; and stimulates estrogenic secretions. In the male it is primarily concerned with testosterone production and in conjunction with FSH promotes the maturation of sperms in the seminiferous tubules. (52, 101)

Reference values: (26)

serum LH (RIA)

- *Males*—7–24 mIU/mL
- *Females*—6–30 mIU/mL
  - *midcycle peak*—greater than three times baseline
  - *postmenopause*—greater than 30

Increase in primary gonadal dysfunction in men and in women with amenorrhea, if caused by ovarian failure. (52, 82)

prolactin (hPRL)—pituitary hormone that initiates and maintains lactation. During pregnancy prolactin concentration begins to increase in the second trimester and peak at term. (52, 79, 101)

For major thyroid tests, see chapter 19, Nuclear Medicine.

TERMS PRIMARILY RELATED TO METABOLIC STUDIES

calcitonin—calcium-reducing hormone derived from thyroid, parathyroids, and sometimes the thymus. It affects calcium metabolism and regulates plasma calcium levels and bone remodeling. Calcitonin secretion is excessive in medullary carcinoma of the thyroid. (20, 48, 101)

carbohydrate tolerance tests:

glucose tolerance tests—the intravenous or oral administration of a measured glucose load to discover disorders of the carbohydrate metabolism. (52, 101)

- *glucose tolerance test, oral*

CONVENTIONAL UNITS

Serum	Normal	Diabetic
Fasting:	70–105 mg/dL	>140 mg/dL
60 min:	120–170 mg/dL	≥200 mg/dL
90 min:	100–140 mg/dL	≥200 mg/dL
120 min:	70–120 mg/dL	≥140 mg/dL

INTERNATIONAL SYSTEM OF UNITS

Serum	Normal	Diabetic
Fasting:	3.9–5.8 mmol/L	>7.8 mmol/L
60 min:	6.7–9.4 mmol/L	≥11.0 mmol/L
90 min:	5.6–7.8 mmol/L	≥11.0 mmol/L
120 min:	3.9–6.7 mmol/L	≥7.8 mmol/L

postprandial blood sugar determination—screening procedure for the detection of diabetes mellitus. Blood to determine sugar content is drawn 2 hours after the patient started to eat a meal containing 50 to 100 grams of carbohydrates. (101)

Reference values: (26)

- *2 hr. postprandial glucose serum*—less than 120 mg/dL (SIU: less than 6.7 mmol/L)

carbon dioxide combining power—test for determining the acid-base balance in the blood. In health and with normal activity, the acid waste products of metabolism exceed the basic levels. (58, 99)

Reference values: (26)

carbon dioxide, total (TCO$_2$)

- *serum or plasma*—23–29 mEq/L (SIU: 23–29 mmol/L)

carbon dioxide content in serum:

Adults: **Increase** in alkalosis, hypercorticoadrenalism, and excessive alkali therapy. (58, 101)

Decrease in acidosis, diabetes, nephritis, and eclampsia. (58, 101)

Infants: **Increase** in respiratory conditions. (58, 101)

Decrease in severe diarrhea. (58, 101)

metabolite—any product of metabolism, for example, the mineral metabolites: sodium, potassium, and chloride, which are profoundly influenced by the activity of the adrenal cortex.

chloride salts—chiefly bound to sodium. In gastric juice, chlorides are present in the form of hydrochloride. (94, 101)

Reference values: (26)

- *plasma chloride*—98–106 mEq/L (SIU: 98–106 mmol/L)

Increase in many conditions resulting from decreased excretion or increased intake. (58, 101)

potassium salts: as *potassium chloride, phosphates,* and *bicarbonates*—found within tissue cells, especially in muscle cells and blood plasma. (58, 101)

Reference values: (26)

- *plasma potassium*—3.5–4.5 mEq/L (SIU: 3.5–4.5 mmol/L)

Increase in Addison's disease. (58, 101)

Decrease in Cushing's syndrome. (58, 101)

sodium salts: as *sodium chloride* and *sodium bicarbonate*—present in the blood plasma and extracellular fluids. (22, 24)

Reference values: (26)

- *plasma sodium*—136–146 mEq/L (SIU: 136–146 mmol/L)

Increase in Cushing's syndrome. (66, 69, 101)

Decrease in Addison's disease. (66, 69, 101)

osmolality—the number of moles of a solute per kilogram of pure solvent. (58, 101)

Reference values: (26)

- *serum osmolality*—275–295 mOsm/kg (SIU: 275–295 mOsm/kg)

ABBREVIATIONS

ACTH—adrenocorticotropic hormone
AD—autosomal dominant
ADH—antidiuretic hormone
AR—autosomal recessive
BMR—basal metabolic rate
CO_2—carbon dioxide
DKA—diabetic ketoacidosis
FBS—fasting blood sugar
FSH—follicle-stimulating hormone
GH—growth hormone

GTT—glucose tolerance test
HDL—high-density lipoprotein
K—potassium
LDL—low-density lipoprotein
LH—luteinizing hormone
NaCl—sodium chloride
NPH—neutral protamine Hagedorn (insulin)
VLDL—very low-density lipoprotein
XX—female sex chromosomes
XY—male sex chromosomes

ORAL READING PRACTICE

HYPOTHYROIDISM

Hypothyroidism is a functional disorder caused by insufficiency of circulating **thyroid** hormones. Any biological, chemical, or physical factors that reduce the hormone supply may result in thyroid failure.

Primary hypothyroidism is caused by an intrinsic defect in thyroid structure or biosynthetic mechanisms. In the **primary hypothyroid states,** the condition may be congenital, such as in **cretinism,** or acquired, such as in **juvenile myxedema** or **adult myxedema.** Surgical excision, **atrophy,** or disease of the thyroid gland stop or lower hormone production; a lack of **iodine** in food seriously hampers hormone synthesis. Dietary iodine deficiency results in inadequate thyroid hormone production, despite the presence of normal thyroid tissue. Iodine excess in addition to iodine deficiency can cause subclinical or overt hypothyroidism.

Secondary hypothyroidism is caused by insufficient thyrotropin stimulation of the thyroid due to pituitary failure. In the **secondary hypothyroid states,** the **pituitary gland** elaborates an inadequate amount of **thyroid-stimulating hormone (TSH),** which drastically reduces thyroid function. This deficit of **thyrotropin** occurs in **postpartum pituitary necrosis,** or **Sheehan's disease,** and **primary chronic hypopituitarism,** or **Simmond's syndrome.** A total absence of TSH is seen in **hypophysectomized** patients.

Tertiary hypothyroidism is caused by inadequate secretion of TSH from apparently normal **pituitary thyrotrophs** (any of the **basophils [beta cells]** of the **adenohypophysis** that secrete thyrotropin), and is probably the result of insufficient secretion of **hypothalamic thyrotropin-releasing hormone (TRH).**

The most helpful diagnostic test is the measurement of the **plasma TSH.** Results of this test usually are quite elevated in patients who have **primary hypothyroidism** and low in patients who have **pituitary** or **hypothalamic failure.** Measuring triiodothyronine (T_3) is not useful as a screening test, since T_3 is usually maintained within normal limits in hypothyroidism unless the gland is almost totally destroyed.

The judicious use of replacement therapy with **thyroxine** or **triiodothyronine** for thyroid failure and a thyrotropin preparation for pituitary failure is imperative to maintain relatively normal metabolic processes and overcome hypothyroidism. In patients with more general pituitary or hypothalamic failure, there also may be present **secondary adrenal insufficiency.** If this is the case, it is very important that adrenocortical therapy be instituted in conjunction with the thyroid therapy, since treatment of only the **hypothyroidism** may cause a fatal, acute adrenal crisis. (19, 24, 51, 78, 88, 101, 103)

REVIEW GUIDE

Instructions: Select the letter of the response that correctly completes each statement, as shown in the example.

Example: Hormone means to
    a. secrete. b. excite. c. swell. d. shield.

1. Graves' disease may be called
    a. hyperthyroidism.
    b. hyperparathyroidism.
    c. hypothyroidism.
    d. none of the above.
2. Seminiferous tubule dysgenesis may be called
    a. Noonan's syndrome.
    b. Edwards' syndrome.
    c. Klinefelter's syndrome.
    d. both a and b.

3. Masculinization in women is
   a. ovarian dysgenesis.
   b. hypogonadism.
   c. virilism.
   d. vitiligo.
4. A sudden recurrence after a remission is termed
   a. porphyria.
   b. paracusis.
   c. exacerbation.
   d. tophi.
5. The name Hashimoto is associated with disease of the
   a. pancreas.
   b. thyroid.
   c. pituitary gland.
   d. thymus.
6. α-galactosidase A deficiency may be called
   a. Edwards' syndrome.
   b. Fabry's disease.
   c. Gaucher's disease.
   d. Noonan's syndrome.
7. Plasma potassium is increased in
   a. Addison's disease.
   b. Cushing's syndrome.
   c. both a and b.
   d. none of the above.
8. Primary alkali deficit characterized by a low pH and PCO_2 is indicative of
   a. metabolic alkalosis.
   b. respiratory alkalosis.
   c. respiratory acidosis.
   d. metabolic acidosis.
9. When each chromosome occurs in triplicate, it is called
   a. triploidy.
   b. trisomy.
   c. translocation.
   d. none of the above.
10. The state pertaining to balanced sets of chromosomes in every number is called
   a. aneuploidy.
   b. polysomy.
   c. euploidy.
   d. triploidy.

Instructions: Break apart each term listed below, identify the medical term elements, and define the term.

Example: leukocyte   leuko- = combining form element = white
                              -cyte = suffix = cell

adrenalectomy

hyperparathyroidism

hypothalamus

lymphoma

microsurgery

parathyroidectomy

polydipsia

polyuria

thyroiditis

14

Disorders Pertaining to the Sense Organ of Vision

EYE

ORIGIN OF TERMS

cornea (L)—horny
crystal (G)—clear ice
cyclo- (G)—circle
cysto- (G)—sac
enucleate (L)—to remove
iris (G)—rainbow, halo
kerato- (G)—horny, cornea

nystagmus (G)—nod
oculo- (L)—eye
ophthalmo- (G)—eye
phaco-, phako- (G)—lens
pyo- (G)—pus
vitreous (L)—glassy
zonule (L)—tiny band

PHONETIC PRONUNCIATION OF SELECTED TERMS

aphakia	a-FAY'key-ah
aqueous	A'kwe-us
arcus senilis	AR'kus SE'nil-is
choroidal hemorrhage	ko-ROY'dal HEM'or-rage
corneal ulcer	KOR'nee-al UHL'ser
endophthalmitis	EN-dof-thal-MY'tis
glaucoma	glaw-KO'mah
iridodialysis	IR-i-doe-die-AL'ice-sis
keratitis	KER-a-TIE'tis
keratoconus	KER-a-toe-KO'nus
keratoplasty	KER-a-toe-PLAS'tee
retinoblastoma	RET-i-no-blas-TOE'MAH
thermokeratoplasty	THER-mo-KER'a-toe-PLAS-tee
trabeculectomy	trah-BECK'you-LECK'toe-me

ANATOMIC TERMS (63, 79) (SEE FIGS. 14.1 AND 14.2.)

bulb of the eye—the globe or eyeball. The eyeball is 2.4 centimeters long and is suspended in the anterior half of the orbital cavity in such a way that the six ocular muscles in the orbit can move the eye in all directions.

Figure 14.1 Transverse section of the eye.

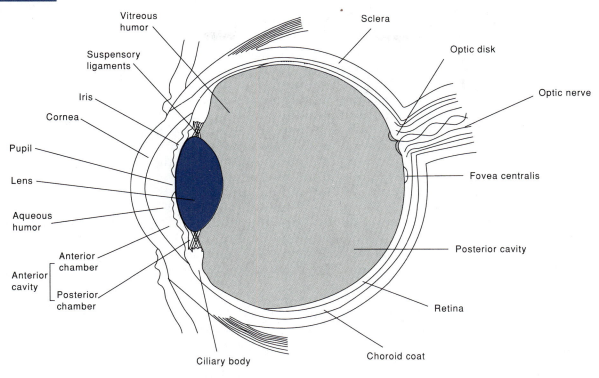

Figure 14.2 Anterior portion of the eye.

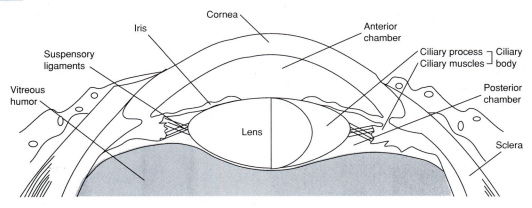

chambers of the eye:
> *anterior chamber*—lies behind the cornea and anterior to the iris.
> *posterior chamber*—narrow space situated behind the iris and in front of the lens, the suspensory ligament of the lens, and the ciliary processes.
> - *aqueous humor*—a clear, watery solution continuously secreted by the epithelium on the inner surface of the ciliary body into the *posterior chamber*. The fluid circulates from this chamber through the *pupil* (a circular opening in the center of the iris),

and into the *anterior chamber*. Aqueous humor fills the space between the cornea and the lens, helping to nourish these parts, as well as helping to maintain the shape of the front of the eye. Subsequently, the aqueous humor leaves the anterior chamber through veins and a special drainage canal (*canal of Schlemm*) located in its wall.

fundus oculi—inner posterior portion of the eye, which can be seen with an ophthalmoscope.

layers or **tunics (coats) of the eye:**

outer tunic (fibrous supporting layer):

- *cornea*—anterior transparent part of the outer fibrous tunic of the eye. The cornea serves as the window of the eye and helps focus entering light rays. The cornea is composed of connective tissue with a thin layer of epithelium on its surface. The transparency of the cornea is due to the fact that it contains few cells and no blood vessels. However, the cornea is well supplied with nerve fibers that enter its margin and radiate toward its center.

- *sclera*—white portion of the eye. The sclera is a firm fibrous cup that constitutes the posterior five-sixths of the outer layer of the eye. The sclera is continuous in front with the cornea at the corneoscleral junction, and behind, it is perforated by the optic nerve, forming a meshwork called the *lamina cribrosa sclerae*, which permits the fascicles of nerve and the central retinal artery and vein to pass through. Around the optic nerve entrance, other small apertures transmit the ciliary nerves and vessels.

middle tunic (vascular layer):

- *uvea, uveal tract*—middle or vascular tunic of the eyeball (uveal layer) that includes the *choroid coat*, the *ciliary body*, and the *iris*.

  - *choroid coat*—located in the posterior five-sixths of the globe of the eye, loosely joined to the sclera, and honeycombed with blood vessels that provide nutrition to the surrounding tissues. In addition, the choroid coat contains many pigment-producing *melanocytes* that give it a brownish black appearance. The melanin of these cells absorbs excess light and helps keep the inside of the eye dark.

  - *ciliary body*—thickened part of the vascular tunic of the eye. It extends forward from the choroid and forms an internal ring around the front of the eye. Within the ciliary body, there are two distinct groups of muscle fibers that constitute the *ciliary muscles*. The ciliary body has protrusions or folds on its internal surface called *ciliary processes*. These secrete *aqueous humor* (watery fluid) that fills the *anterior* and *posterior chambers* of the eye, which are spaces in front of and behind the iris. The *pars plana* is a thin, flat layer of ciliary vessels and muscle covered by ciliary epithelium.

  - *iris*—thin, contractile membrane having a central aperture called the *pupil*. The *sphincter pupillae muscle* surrounds the margin of the pupil and the *dilator pupillae muscle* is close to the posterior surface of the iris, converging from its circumference toward its center. The color of the eyes is determined largely by the amount and distribution of melanin in the irises and by the density of the tissue within the body of the iris. The iris extends forward from the periphery of the ciliary body and lies between the cornea and the lens. The iris divides the space separating these parts, which is called the *anterior cavity*, into the *anterior chamber* (between the cornea and the iris) and a *posterior chamber* (between the iris and the vitreous humor, and occupied by the lens).

    - *lens, crystalline lens*—transparent, biconvex body enclosed in a capsule and lying directly in back of the iris. It is a powerful refracting component of the visual system and focusing structure capable of changing its shape. The transparent lens is held in place by a series of fibrils, which constitutes the *suspensory ligaments (zonular fibers)*, which extend inward from the ciliary processes. The distal ends of these fibers are attached along the margin of a thin capsule that surrounds the lens. The *lens capsule* is a clear, membranelike structure composed mostly of intercellular material. The body of the lens contains no blood vessels, lies directly behind the iris, and is composed of specialized epithelial cells. .

inner tunic (layer of nerve elements):

- *retina*—the structure of the inner tunic that covers the choroid. The retina consists of a thin, outer pigmented layer in contact with the choroid and a thick, inner nervous layer, or visual portion. The visual layer of the retina terminates in a jagged margin near the ciliary body called the *ora serrata*. The pigmented layer extends anteriorly over the back of the ciliary body and iris. The retina perceives and transmits the sensory impulses of light to the optic nerve. Three regions delineated in the retina are:
  - *pars optica retinae*—occupies the posterior part of the bulb. It ends in a jagged line, the *ora serrata*. At the ora serrata, the nervous elements of the retina cease.
  - *pars ciliaris retinae*—extends forward over the ciliary body and has outer pigmented and inner nonpigmented epithelial cell layers.
  - *pars iridica retinae*—covers the posterior surface of the iris and ends at the pupillary margin.

anatomical areas associated with the retina include:

macula lutea—small avascular area in the central region of the retina around the fovea.

fovea centralis—a depression located in the center of the macula lutea, which provides the greatest visual acuity.

optic disk—situated medial to the fovea centralis. Here the nerve fibers leave the eye and become parts of the optic nerve. A central artery and vein pass through at the optic disk. These vessels are continuous with the capillary networks of the retina, and combined with the vessels in the underlying choroid coat, supply blood to the cells of the inner tunic. Because there are no receptor cells in the region of the optic disk, it is referred to as the *blind spot* of the eye.

posterior cavity—space bounded by the lens, ciliary body, and retina. It is the largest compartment of the eye. It is filled with a jellylike fluid called *vitreous humor*, which together with some collagenous fibers comprise the *vitreous body*. The vitreous body supports the internal parts of the eye and helps to maintain its shape.

orbit—bony cavity of the skull in which lies the *eyeball*.

trabeculae (sing. **trabecula**)—loosely arranged grayish white fibrous strands in the filtration angle of the anterior chamber through which the aqueous humor escapes.

DIAGNOSTIC TERMS

disorders of the cornea and sclera:

arcus senilis—degenerative change in the cornea that commonly occurs in persons past age 50; appears as a grayish-white ring about 2 millimeters wide. (83)

corneal dystrophy—idiopathic degeneration of the cornea that may seriously interfere with vision. This disorder affects the central cornea and is noninflammatory in origin. The aging process may encourage deterioration of the dystrophic cornea but is not a primary cause of the disorder. (74)

corneal injury—damage to cornea by foreign body; chemical, thermal, or radiation burn; laceration; or penetrating wound, frequently accompanied by intraocular damage, such as traumatic cataract and iris prolapse.

corneal ulcer—form of keratitis due to a pathogenic organism entering the corneal epithelium. The stroma may also break down.

dermoid—skinlike tumor or cyst generally located at the limbus and involving both cornea and sclera.

hypopyon—pus in the anterior chamber in back of the cornea; sometimes associated with corneal ulcer.

keratitis—inflammation of the cornea. (45)

- *actinic keratitis, ultraviolet keratitis*—ultraviolet burns caused by strong sunlight when skiing (snow blindness) or exposure to a welding arc, resulting in extreme eye pain and photophobia 24 hours later.
- *herpes simplex keratitis*—corneal ulcer caused by herpes simplex virus (HSV). Primary infection by herpes simplex type 1 often causes undiagnosed localized ocular lesions in children, which may be accompanied by regional lymphadenopathy, infection, and fever. Herpes simplex type 2 often produces infection in the cornea and retina. When a high rate of recurrence at one site initiates secondary herpes infection, the condition is referred to as *reactivation disease*. Reactivation disease presents as a severe inflammatory reaction and ulceration, but fever and lymphadenopathy are not present. (4, 64)
- *interstitial keratitis*—invasion of the deep layers of the cornea that may result in its perforation. Interstitial keratitis due to syphilis or tuberculosis may cause permanent opacification (loss of transparency) of the cornea. (45, 64)

keratoconus—conical bulging of the center of the cornea. (56)

scars of the cornea:

- *leukoma*—white, opaque cornea.
- *macula*—opaque spot seen on cornea.
- *nebula*—grayish opacity of cornea.

scleral injuries—cause of scleral damage may include penetrating or blunt trauma, thermal burns, irradiation, chemical burns, and scleral lacerations.

scleritis—inflammation of the sclera. (33, 35)

disorders of the uveal tract:

choroidal hemorrhage—local bleeding of choroid that may be associated with vascular disorder, trauma, choroiditis, diabetes, or other diseases. (53)

iridocyclitis—inflammation of the iris and ciliary body. (57)

iridodialysis—detachment of outer margin of the iris from ciliary body.

iritis—inflammation of the iris. (57)

sympathetic ophthalmia—inflammation of uveal tract, following a perforating wound of opposite eye, with incarceration or loss of uveal tissue. (46, 66)

synechia—two kinds:

- *anterior synechia*—adhesion of the iris to the cornea.
- *posterior synechia*—adhesion of the iris to the lens.

tumors of the uveal tract—intraocular tumors of the choroid, iris, or ciliary body.

- *choroidal cavernous hemangioma*—a hamartoma that may occur either as a solitary tumor or a component of the Sturge-Weber syndrome. The tumors are oval or round. It is soft, reddish-orange in appearance. (55)
- *malignant melanomas*—pigmented cancerous lesions, usually unilateral, which lead to loss of vision and occur in the fifth or sixth decade of life. (20, 55, 81)
- *nevi (sing. nevus), benign melanomas*—pigmented lesions that usually do not interfere with vision. (55)

uveitis—inflammation of the uveal tract caused by allergy, or organisms such as *Coccidioides immitis, Histoplasma capsulatum, Mycobacterium tuberculosis,* and *Toxoplasma gondii,* and by irritants and toxins, and connective tissue diseases. (57, 64, 66)

disorders of the vitreous:

vitreoretinal degeneration, Wagner's disease—hereditary disorder of vitreous and retina characterized by marked liquefaction of central vitreous, reduced vision, vitreous floaters, and vitreous traction on retina, resulting in retinal tears and breaks leading to retinal detachment. (73)

vitreous detachment—vitreous detached from retina in one or both eyes. It may lead to retinal tear. (67)

vitreous hemorrhage—rare but serious disorder, usually caused by rupture of a retinal vessel and followed by sudden loss of vision. (64)

vitreous infections—bacterial, fungal, or parasitic infections resulting in liquefaction, opacification, and shrinkage of vitreous. (64)

disorders of the lens and intraocular pressure:

aphakia—absence of the lens, congenital or acquired, due to surgical removal; binocular (in both eyes) or monocular (in one eye). (76)

cataract—an opacity in the lens, congenital or acquired. Lenticular opacity is usually linked with the process of aging. Insoluble proteins form in the lens and eventually lead to dehydration, lowered metabolism, and tissue necrosis. In the cataractous lens, sodium and calcium content tend to be increased, with potassium, protein, and ascorbic acid content decreased. Visual impairment is slowly progressive. (64)

ectopia lentis—displacement of the lens, seen primarily in Marfan's syndrome in its congenital form. It also may result from trauma. (76)

glaucoma—increased intraocular pressure; untreated, it leads to blindness. Some types of glaucoma are:

- *acute glaucoma*—severe obstruction of aqueous humor drainage, sharp rise of intraocular tension, and agonizing eye pain.
- *chronic glaucoma:*
  - *closed-angle glaucoma*—intermittent attacks of angle closure of anterior chamber; formation of adhesions in angle with gradual obliteration of angle, requiring peripheral iridectomy if unresponsive to medical therapy. (7, 48)
  - *open-angle glaucoma*—interference with aqueous outflow, creating an elevated intraocular pressure. The open type is bilateral and, if untreated, leads slowly to visual impairment and cupping of optic disk.
- *malignant glaucoma*—distinct type of angle closure with a forward movement of the lens and direct closure of the angle, occurring with or without glaucoma surgery. (20, 25)

disorders of the retina:

central serous chorioretinopathy—disorder in which occurs a serous detachment of the neurosensory retina caused by leakage from the retinal pigment epithelium. The cause of the disease is unknown. It appears that males with a type A personality are more prone to this disorder, which affects persons aged 20 to 55. (41)

Coats' disease—eye condition characterized by abnormalities of the retinal vasculature, retinal microaneurysms in areas of destruction of small vessels, retinal hemorrhage, and exudation. (23, 67)

diabetic retinopathy—condition characterized by pinpoint aneurysms, which may be caused by dilatation of the retinal capillaries in diabetes mellitus. Diabetic retinopathy is classified as nonproliferative diabetic retinopathy (NPDR) and proliferative diabetic retinopathy (PDR). NPDR is further delineated into stages of mild NPDR, moderate NPDR, severe NPDR, and very severe NPDR. PDR is characterized by new vessels arising from the surface of the retina or from retinal circulation elsewhere and grow along the partially detached posterior hyaloid. Fibroblasts and glial elements accompany the new vessels, and proliferation of this fibroglial tissue may become the predominant feature of retinopathy. Diabetic macular edema can occur with either NPDR or PDR. (3, 54, 67)

edema of the retina—condition due to active hyperemia, generally resulting from trauma. (82)

hypertensive retinopathy—retinal changes resulting from persistently high diastolic blood pressure. This condition may occur in essential hypertension, renal arteriolar sclerosis, glomerulonephritis, and toxemias of pregnancy. (67)

macular degenerations—group of degenerative disorders of the retina.

- *age-related macular degeneration*—rather common macular retinopathy, seen in the elderly. It is the leading cause of blindness in this age category; the exact cause of this disorder is unknown. There are two types:
  - *nonneovascular (nonexudative) age-related macular degeneration*—occurs with variable degrees of atrophy and degeneration of the outer retina, retinal pigment epithelium, Bruch's membrane, and choriocapillaris. Drusen are discrete, round, yellow-white deposits of variable size beneath the pigment and epithelium and are scattered throughout the macula and posterior pole. Drusens are visible with an ophthalmoscope and are the most common changes in the retinal pigment epithelium and Bruch's membrane. (14, 67)
  - *neovascular (exudative) age-related macular degeneration*—the impairment of Bruch's membrane as a barrier between the retinal pigment epithelium and the choriocapillaris; may cause occurrence of "wet" age-related macular degeneration. Serous fluid or blood from the choroid may seep through small defects in the collagenous membrane, causing a focal dome-shaped elevation of the pigment epithelium, or causing separation of the sensory retina. The sensory retina may be damaged by long-standing edema, detachment, or subretinal hemorrhage. A hemorrhagic detachment of the retina may, under fibrous metaplasia development, result in an elevated subretinal mass called a *disciform scar*. This fixed, but variably sized, fibrovascular mound represents the cicatricial stage of neovascular (exudative) age-related macular degeneration. If centrally located, it results in permanent loss of central vision. Also, degenerative breaks in Bruch's membrane can establish a pathway through which choroidal neovascularization can proliferate beneath the retinal pigment epithelium. (13, 64)

occlusion of central retinal artery—rare unilateral disorder due to thrombus, embolus, or atheromatous plaque suddenly causing total loss of sight in the affected eye. It may occur in advanced age or during oral contraceptive therapy. (22, 64)

occlusion of central retinal vein—thrombosis of the central retinal vein leading to sudden, painless loss of sight. (82)

retinal arteriolar sclerosis—form of sclerosis due to hypertension characterized by copper-wire arterioles in the retina. In the advanced stage of the sclerotic process, the arterioles resemble silver wire. (67)

retinal detachment—separation of the retina from the choroid. When the retina is torn, vitreous can pass through the tear and behind the sensory retina. The condition combined with vitreous traction and pull of gravity, results in progressive detachment. This disorder may result in blindness, if not relieved.

Note: The Greek word, *Rhegma,* means a break in continuity.

Two basic types of retinal detachment are termed *rhegmatogenous* and *nonrhegmatogenous.* Non-rhegmatogenous retinal detachment (without tear or hole) presents in tumors of the choroid and retinal vascular lesions, and in vitreous traction from proliferative retinopathy. The term *rhegmatogenous* retinal detachment designates those detachments due to a retinal hole or tear. Rhegmatogenous retinal detachment may be further delineated as to location:

- *equatorial*—near the equator or behind the equator.
- *macular*—at the fovea.
- *oral*—within the vitreous base or may occur between the posterior border of the vitreous base and the equator. (47, 67, 86)

retinal hemorrhage—moderate or massive bleeding from the retina. (82)

retinal necrosis, acute—syndrome consisting of peripheral necrotizing retinitis, arteritis, and vitreitis. It may be present in one or both eyes, and usually occurs in the third and fifth decade of life. Herpes simplex virus type 1, varicella-zoster virus, and cytomegalovirus have been implicated among the causative agents of this disorder. (10)

retinal tears—small holes or tears; unrepaired, they may enlarge and lead to retinal detachment and blindness. (47)

retinitis pigmentosa—hereditary degenerative disease principally affecting the rod and cone layer of the retina. Ophthalmologic examination reveals spider-shaped pigment spots on the retina. Night blindness is the dominant feature. (8, 67)

retinopathy of prematurity, retrolental fibroplasia—bilateral, retinal disease in premature infants; associated with high oxygen concentration in the infant's environment. (67)

retinoschisis—separation of the sensory retina into two layers appearing as a shallow elevation of the peripheral retina. Defect may not be progressive, but vision in the involved area is affected. (43)

von Hippel-Lindau disease, angiomatosis retinae cerebelli—retinal angioma usually associated with cerebellar angioma and polycystic kidneys. Angiomas are dark intraretinal tumors, consisting of capillaries and glial cells, with a dilated feeding artery and a draining vein. Clinical symptoms of angiomas are usually not present until serious damage occurs due to complications, such as hemorrhage, retinal detachment, or macular edema. von Hippel-Lindau disease is an autosomal dominant inherited disorder causing hemangioblastomas of the central nervous system, retinal hemangiomas, renal cell carcinomas, pheochromocytomas, pancreatic and liver cyst, and epididymal cystadenomas. The gene for von Hippel-Lindau disease is linked to DNA markers that map to the short arm of chromosome 3. Most of the lesions can be treated successfully when diagnosed in time. (29, 50)

disorders of the optic nerve:

optic atrophy—destruction of the fibers of the optic nerve; associated with loss of visual acuity. (65)

optic coloboma—congenital defect in the optic nerve resulting from imperfect closure of fetal cleft. Defects in the choroid and retina may coexist. Visual impairment is common. Typical colobomas may involve the iris, choroid, or any combination of these, and also may encompass the optic nerve. (28)

optic neuritis—inflammation of the optic nerve; may involve the sheaths of the nerve (optic perineuritis) or its main body. (6, 15, 85)

papilledema, choked disk—edema of the papilla or optic nerve head usually caused by increased intracranial pressure. (15, 64, 85)

papillitis—inflammation of the papilla or head of the optic nerve accompanied by optic disk swelling. (6, 15, 65)

retrobulbar neuritis—optic neuritis in which nerve involvement occurs behind the optic disk and cannot be seen ophthalmoscopically. Visual acuity is seriously affected or entirely lost. One of its most common causes is multiple sclerosis. (6, 15)

ocular infections:

endophthalmitis—intraocular infection due to various etiologic agents. Early treatment may salvage the eye. Two types of endophthalmitis are:

- *endogenous endophthalmitis, metastatic endophthalmitis*—infection of intraocular tissues due to spread of the infection to the eye via the bloodstream. There is a wide range of etiologic agents causing the disease. Signs and symptoms vary depending on the virulence of the organism. (51, 58)
- *exogenous endophthalmitis*—inflammation of the aqueous, vitreous, and internal tunics of the eye. Fungal or bacterial organisms are the most common causes of infection. The infecting organism enters the eye from the external environment. Exogenous endophthalmitis can be clinically classified into five distinct categories: (1) acute postoperative; (2) delayed-onset postoperative; (3) trauma-related; (4) associated with filtering blebs; and (5) intraocular extension of external ocular infections. (27)

panophthalmitis—extensive ocular infection, usually resulting from eye injury and leading to corneal ulceration and total destruction of the eyeball. (58)

ocular tumors:

melanomas of choroid or *iris*—malignant neoplasms derived from cells that form melanin, a black pigment. (55)

- *optic nerve tumors:* (44)
  - *gliomas*—are derived from astrocytes and oligidendroglial cells of the optic nerve and appear either as a solitary tumor or a component of von Recklinghausen's neurofibromatosis. (30)
  - *meningiomas*—usually orbital tumors arising in the sheath of the optic nerve. (30)
  - *retinoblastomas*—malignant tumors arising from the retina. They are hereditary, unilateral or bilateral, and readily metastasize to the optic nerve and brain. Other common tumors are hemangiomas and orbital lymphomas. (30)

OPERATIVE TERMS (SEE TABLE 14.1.)

cataract operations—various procedures for the removal of an opaque lens.

anterior chamber lens implantation—preparation of a 7.5 millimeter trephine opening followed by removal of cataract and insertion of anterior chamber lens through the trephine opening. Following an intraocular cataract extraction or as a secondary procedure, an anterior chamber type of lens is employed, while a posterior chamber type of lens is used after an extracapsular cataract extraction. (48)

posterior chamber lens implantation—after an injection of sodium hyaluronate (Healon), an anterior capsulotomy is performed. The nucleus may be removed with an irrigating vectis technique followed by removal of the cortex. Additional Healon may be injected and the posterior lens implant inserted. Healon may be removed by aspiration. (48)

aspiration and irrigation procedure—removal of a cataract by suction through a small limbal incision and simultaneous irrigation of the anterior chamber with normal saline solution through another limbal incision. The effective use of the operating microscope permits aspiration of virtually the entire opaque lens. Discission of the posterior capsule completes the procedure, which is used for patients under age 30.

cryoextraction of cataract—application of the tip of the cryoextractor to the anterior surface of the lens until the cataract firmly adheres to the instrument. When the freezing process has extended for 2 to 3 millimeters into the lens substance, the probe—with the lens frozen to it—is lifted out.

enzymatic zonulysis, zonulolysis—instillation of alpha-chymotrypsin, a fibrinolytic enzyme, into the anterior chamber to dissolve the ciliary zonules and thus facilitate the removal of

TABLE 14.1	Some Eye Conditions Amenable to Surgery		
Anatomic Site	*Diagnosis*	*Type of Surgery*	*Operative Procedures*
Eyeball	Penetrating wound of eyeball	Enucleation of eyeball	Removal of eyeball
Retina Uvea Iris Conjunctiva	Retinoblastoma Malignant melanoma Epidermoid carcinoma	Enucleation of eyeball	Removal of eyeball and as much as possible of optic nerve in retinoblastoma
Retina Choroid Sclera	Detachment of retina	Cryopexy	Application of freezing probe to sclera to promote formation of chorioretinal scar and thus fusion
Retina Choroid Sclera	Detachment of retina	Scleral buckling operation	Diathermy to sclera and choroid; release of subretinal fluid Inward buckling of treated area and insertion of silicone implant; firm contact of choroid with retina reestablished
Cornea	Corneal scar Keratoconus	Keratoplasty; lamellar transplant or penetrating transplant	Replacement of opaque cornea with transparent cornea using partial-thickness or full-thickness corneal graft
Cornea Iris Vitreous	Glaucoma: acute, primary	Keratocentesis Peripheral iridectomy Cyclodialysis	Paracentesis of cornea Surgical removal of part of iris Surgical communication between anterior chamber and suprachoroidal space
Sclera Vitreous	Aphakic glaucoma *or* Open-angle glaucoma	Pars plana filter including sclerotomy, vitrectomy	Sclera incised bilaterally Irrigation, fragmentation, and aspiration to remove formed vitreous Aqueous escaping through sclerotomy openings
Cornea Sclera Trabeculum	Glaucoma: open-angle or narrow-angle	Trabeculectomy	Positioning the operating microscope appropriately Raising a conjunctival flap to expose sclera Removing part of sclera together with trabecular meshwork

TABLE **14.1**	(continued)		
Anatomic Site	*Diagnosis*	*Type of Surgery*	*Operative Procedures*
Crystalline lens	Cataract: congenital; infantile; senile	Microsurgical phacoemulsification Kelman technique	Operating microscope in position Tiny limbal incision followed by excision of small capsular portion of prolapse lens into anterior chamber Insertion of phacoemulsifier into lens using ultrasound for its emulsification Aspiration of lens fragments and irrigation of eye
Crystalline lens Iris	Cataract: congenital; senile	Discission Peripheral iridectomy Intracapsular extraction of cataract	Needling of lens Approach to cataract by removal of part of iris Excision of cataract within capsule
Iris	Cyst of iris	Electrolysis	Insertion of an electrolysis needle in the center of cyst to induce shrinkage
Ocular muscle	Strabismus	Recession of ocular muscle	Correction of defect by drawing muscle backward
Canthus Eyelid Lacrimal sac	Basal cell carcinoma medial canthal region—eyelid	Surgical ablation of entire malignant lesion Reconstruction of canthal region and lid	Excision of tumor, lacrimal sac, canaliculus, medial half of lid Surgical creation of midline forehead flap covering the lid
Eyelid	Laceration of eyelid Hordeolum Blepharoptosis	Blepharorrhaphy Blepharotomy Repair of eyelid	Suture of eyelid Incision with drainage of meibomian gland Surgical correction of ptosis
Lacrimal sac	Abscess of lacrimal sac	Dacryocystotomy	Incision and drainage of tear duct
Lacrimal gland	Retention cyst of lacrimal gland	Dacryoadenectomy	Removal of tear gland
Lacrimonasal duct	Stenosis of lacrimonasal duct	Dacryocystorhinostomy	Fistulization of lacrimal sac into nasal cavity

the cataractous lens. The procedure is used in persons 20 to 50 years of age, who have tough zonules, making cataract extraction difficult. (32)

extracapsular cataract extraction—incision into anterior capsule to express the opaque nucleus of the lens and some of the cortical material. (48)

intracapsular cataract extraction—removal of entire lens in its capsule; a method of choice, especially for senescent (senile) cataracts. (32)

intraocular lens implantation—removal of cataract and insertion of plastic lens, such as:
- Binkhorst two-loop or four-loop lens
- Choyce anterior chamber lens
- Rayner perflex anterior chamber lens
- Shearing posterior chamber lens
- Sputnik or Fyodorow type II lens (48)

pars plana lensectomy—lens removal by:
- irrigation with balanced salt solution.
- ultrasonic fragmentation with Girard ultrasonic fragmentor.
- aspiration through minute pars plana incisions. The technique may be used for congenital and senescent (senile) cataracts, dislocated and traumatic cataracts, and other types.

phacoemulsification, Kelman technique—cataract removal by inserting a phacoemulsifier through a 2- to 3-millimeter incision and breaking up the sclerotic portion of the lens by ultrasonic vibration, followed by aspiration of the lens fragments and irrigation of the eye. (31)

phacoprosthesis—usually referred to as intraocular lens, a less-correct term, since the intraocular lens is either natural or artificial. (78)

corneal operations:

epikeratophakia—form of corneal refractive surgery that alters the anterior surface of the patient's cornea by the addition of a precarved lenticule of donor corneal tissue. The procedure has been used to facilitate the treatment of amblyopia, aphakia, and keratoconus. Another alternative technique that may be employed is epikeratophakia using commercially prepared tissue.

keratocentesis—puncture of the cornea.

keratoplasty, corneal graft, corneal transplant—surgical replacement of a section of an opaque cornea with a normal, transparent cornea to restore vision.
- *lamellar keratoplasty*—using partial-thickness corneal transplant. (31, 34)
- *penetrating keratoplasty*—using full-thickness corneal transplant. (11)

radial keratotomy—surgical procedure that aims at creating a given number of linear radial incisions at a prescribed depth through the corneal epithelium and stroma, while preserving an adequate clear central optical zone. (77)

thermokeratoplasty—procedure based on proper application of heat to shrink corneal collagen and thus prevent corneal scarring. A well-controlled temperature probe flattens the keratoconus and makes the cornea more spherical. This operation is not indicated when scarring has already developed or when the cornea is very thin.

enucleation—removal of the eyeball, indicated in penetrating injuries and malignant tumors of the eye, and as an emergency measure in threatened sympathetic ophthalmia. (59)

evisceration—removal of contents of eyeball but leaving the sclera and cornea.

exenteration—removal of the entire contents of the orbit, including the eyeball and lids. (80)

glaucoma operations—surgical procedures for highly increased intraocular pressure, irreducible by miotics or other medical treatment.

cyclocryosurgery—direct application of the cryoprobe to the conjunctiva over different locations in back of the limbus. The intense vascular response reduces ciliary body function and aqueous production. No incision is necessary.

cyclodialysis—filtering procedure allowing aqueous to drain into the suprachoroidal space to lower intraocular tension. (69)

iridencleisis—filtering technique permitting aqueous to escape into the space below the conjunctiva, where it is reabsorbed by the circulating blood and diffused into the tear film. (69)

goniotomy—incision across the anterior chamber for establishing normal aqueous outflow through regular channels in congenital and infantile glaucoma.

microsurgery in glaucoma—use of the operating microscope to facilitate direct surgery on Schlemm's canal and trabecular meshwork in treating glaucoma. (62)

Argon laser trabeculoplasty—procedure whereby laser energy is directed through a goniolens to burn the trabecular meshwork. This produces blanching or fine bubble formation, thereby causing a purse-string type of contraction in the trabecular meshwork, and the outflow mechanism opens to facilitate the emergence of aqueous humor. This procedure achieves a clinically significant decrease in intraocular pressure. (49, 62)

trabeculectomy—elevation of a conjunctival flap to expose the sclera at the limbus and excision of a scleral portion, including the trabecular meshwork. The appearance of a filtering bleb achieves ocular pressure control. Trabeculectomies have been successfully performed in adult phakic eyes with open-angle glaucoma. (49)

trabeculotomy—surgical fashioning of a scleral flap, meticulous dissection to locate Schlemm's canal, and insertion of a small probe into the canal and anterior chamber to relieve block to aqueous outflow, which is usually present in the trabecular meshwork.

laser gonioplasty—contracture of peripheral iris stroma by laser energy application is an alternative to laser iridectomy. Laser gonioplasty is less permanent than laser iridectomy and retreatment may be necessary. (7)

laser iridectomy—application of the argon laser to penetrate the iris, producing thermal destruction with removal of a portion of the iris. Application of the ND:YAG (neodymium: yttrium, aluminum, and garnet) laser in this procedure produces mechanical disruption and explosion of tissue in contrast to the thermal lesion produced by the argon laser. Other coherent light sources such as the krypton laser, the Q-switched ruby laser, and the organic dye laser can be employed to create successful iridectomies; however, the lack of widespread availability of these instruments has limited their clinical application. (7)

peripheral iridectomy—raising a small conjunctival flap at the limbus and entering the anterior chamber through a 4-millimeter incision to prevent pupillary block. This technique frees the filtration angle from the iris root and permits the aqueous to escape by the normal channel. (84)

thermal sclerostomy, Scheie's operation—filtering procedure for severe glaucoma. Anterior chamber is entered through limbal incision and posterior portion of incision is cauterized, resulting in tissue shrinkage. This is followed by a peripheral iridectomy, repositioning of conjunctival flap at the limbus, and wound closure. (13)

Some types of laser tissue interaction are:

- *photocoagulation*—use of light of appropriate intensity and wavelength at a given distance to cause coagulation of tissue. Thermal lasers are the principal lasers used in this procedure. They can be utilized to destroy intraocular neovascularization, as in diabetic retinopathy, and to shrink collagen, increasing tension in the trabecular meshwork or iris for treatment of retinal holes, as well as higher energy levels to evaporate tissue, thereby producing perforation, as in laser iridotomy. (24)

- *photodisruption*—application of high-powered laser pulse to achieve optical breakdown, plasma formation, and subsequent shock wave, which mechanically disrupts the tissue. These lasers are used principally for perforating cloudy posterior capsules following cataract extraction and for laser iridotomy. (24)

- *photoevaporation*—application of carbon dioxide lasers that can evaporate surface lesions, such as lid tumors, or be used for bloodless incisions in the skin or sclera. Although these lasers have been used to remove both malignant and benign lid tumors, possible scarring, lack of histological specimen, and inability to assess margins may defer the use of laser treatment to other methods.

repair of retinal holes or tears and retinal detachment—surgical reattachment of minor or major separations of the retina from the choroid. This can be accomplished by:

cryopexy of sclera—application of a supercooled probe to the sclera to produce a chorioretinal scar with minimal damage to the sclera.

retinopexy, pneumatic—procedure whereby small superior retinal breaks or rents are treated with cryotherapy, intravitreal gas injection, and patient positioning. This procedure is an alternative technique to scleral buckling for the treatment of selected cases of retinal detachment. (42)

scleral buckling operation—removal of strip of sclera near the retinal separation, drainage of subretinal fluid, placement of implant, and tightening of sutures around the implant to buckle the sclera. (42, 47)

vitrectomy, subtotal—removal of the vitreous for vitreous opacity in severe retinopathy with vitreous hemorrhage or for the control of fibrotic overgrowth in severe intraocular trauma. Also, vitrectomy is employed for creation of chorioretinal adhesions and for the closure of retinal breaks. (21)

SYMPTOMATIC TERMS

amaurosis fugax—fleeting blindness manifested by transient monocular blindness. It may result from transient embolization of retinal arterioles and suggest impending stroke. (17)

amblyopia—dimness of vision in one eye that is normal on ophthalmoscopic examination. (64, 70)

amblyopia ex anopsia—diminished visual acuity in one eye not caused by organic eye disease. It is known as the "lazy eye."

ametropia—optic defect or refractive error that does not permit parallel light rays to fall exactly on the retina. (18)

anisometropia—inequality in refractive power of right and left eye. (80)

Argyll-Robertson pupil—absence of light reflex without change in the contractile power of the pupil, a reliable sign of syphilis of the central nervous system. (9)

astigmatism—images are warped and distorted because of irregular corneal curvature that prevents clear focusing of light. (18)

binocular blindness—blindness in both eyes.

binocular vision—ability to focus both eyes on one object and fuse the two images produced into one. (18)

color blindness—reduced ability to distinguish between colors.

cystoid maculopathy, cystoid macular edema—vascular abnormality that may develop after cataract extraction and reduces the vision at variable degrees (20/40 to 20/200).

diplopia—double vision. (18, 64)

Elschnig's pearls—clusters of transparent vacuoles, remnants of lenticular epithelium seen in the eye after incomplete cataract removal.

emmetropia—normal vision; no refractive error. (18)

enophthalmos—recession of the eyeball into the orbit.

exophthalmos, exophthalmus—protrusion of the eyeball in hyperthyroidism and orbital space-taking lesions. (80)

hypermetropia, hyperopia—farsightedness; parallel rays of light from a distant object are focused behind the retina; a refractive error. (80)

hyphemia—blood in the anterior chamber in front of the iris. (80)

iridodonesis—a quivering of the iris when a person moves the eye is a common indication of lens dislocation and is caused by lack of lens support. This manifestation is characteristic of partially and completely dislocated lenses.

leukokoria, white pupil—white pupillary reflex referred to as amaurotic cat's eye, suggesting the presence of a sight-destroying condition such as a retinoblastoma, curable in its early phase.

malignant exophthalmos, progressive proptosis—increasing forward displacement of the eyeball in Graves' disease, causing severe ocular symptoms such as fullness of eyelids, lacrimation, epiphora, corneal ulcerations, chemosis, and edema of conjunctiva. (80)

monocular blindness—blindness in one eye.

myopia—nearsightedness; parallel rays from a distant object are focused in front of the retina; a refractive error. (80)

nyctalopia—night blindness.

nystagmus—constant involuntary movement of the eyeballs. It may be caused by a disease of the central nervous system. (80)

photophobia—marked intolerance to light. (64, 80)

presbyopia—gradual loss of accommodation, a common condition in persons past middle age. (80)

scotoma—blind spot in the vision. (80)

vitreous floaters—dark opacities within the vitreous that are perceived as moving spots by the retina. (18)

vitreous loss—leakage of vitreous into the anterior chamber that disrupts the normal contact of the vitreous with the retina, exerts traction on the retina, and predisposes to the formation of retinal holes and tears. (64)

ACCESSORY ORGANS OF VISION

ORIGINS OF TERMS

blepharo- (G)—eyelid
canaliculus (G)—small canal
cantho- (G)—angle
dacryo- (G)—tear
dacryoaden- (G)—tear gland
dacryocyst- (G)—tear sac
lacrima (L)—tear
palpebra (L)—eyelid

PHONETIC PRONUNCIATION OF SELECTED TERMS

blepharoptosis	BLEF-ar-OP′toe-sis
chemosis	key-MOW′sis
dacryoadenectomy	DACK-re-owe-ad-e-NECK′toe-me
dacryocystitis	DACK-re-owe-sis-TI′tis
dacryocystorhinostomy	DACK-re-owe-SIS-toe-ri-NOS′toe-me
exotropia	EKS-owe-TRO′pe-ah
strabismus	stra-BIZ′mus
symblepharon	sim-BLEF′ah-ron
tarsorrhaphy	tar-SOR′ah-fee

ANATOMIC TERMS (63, 79) (SEE FIGS. 14.3–14.5.)

canthus (pl. **canthi**)—lateral or medial angles at both ends of the palpebral fissures (slits between the eyelids).

cilia, eyelashes—rows of hairs at the free margin of the eyelids.

conjunctiva (pl. **conjunctivae**)—mucous membrane that lines the deep surface of the eyelid and is reflected over the front of the eyeball. It is divided into the:

Figure 14.3 Sagittal section of the eyelids and anterior portion of the eye.

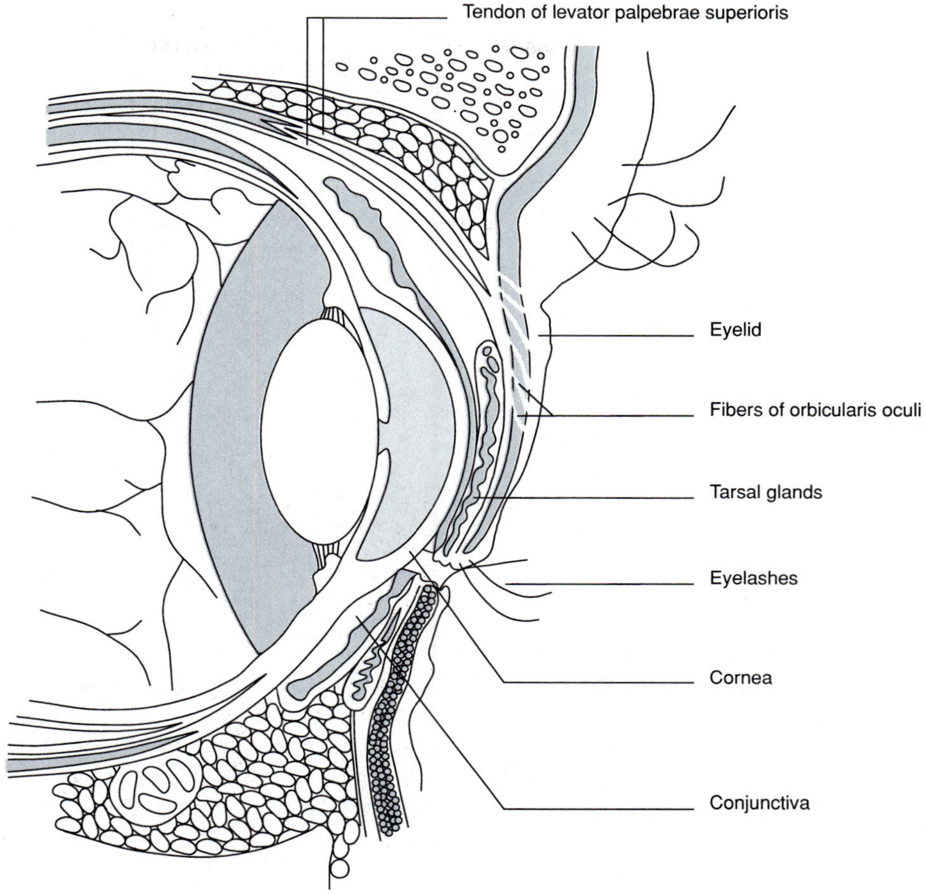

bulbar conjunctiva—colorless, transparent portion covering the anterior part of the globe.

palpebral conjunctiva—lining of the posterior or deep surface of the lids.

fornix (pl. fornices) conjunctivae—angle between the palpebral and bulbar conjunctivae.

lacrimal apparatus: (See fig. 14.4.)

lacrimal gland—tear gland; its orbital part lies in the lacrimal fossa of the upper, outer part of the orbit; its palpebral part lies in the upper eyelid.

lacrimal ducts—tear ducts extending from the gland to superior conjunctival fornix.

lacrimal canaliculi—one canaliculus (canal) for each eyelid to conduct tears from lacrimal punctum to lacrimal sac.

lacrimal puncta (sing. *punctum*)—minute openings, the beginning of the canaliculi.

lacrimal sac—tear sac situated in lacrimal groove or medial wall of orbit.

nasolacrimal duct—duct-draining lacrimal sac and opening into inferior nasal meatus.

muscles associated with the eye:

name of skeletal muscles and function:

- *orbicularis oculi*—closes eye
- *levator palpebrae superioris*—opens eye.

Figure 14.4 Lacrimal apparatus consists of a tear-secreting gland and a series of ducts.

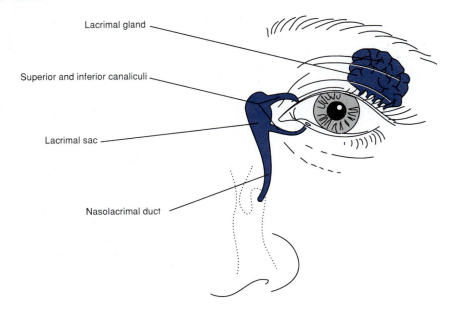

Lacrimal gland

Superior and inferior canaliculi

Lacrimal sac

Nasolacrimal duct

- *superior rectus*—rotates eye upward and toward midline.
- *inferior rectus*—rotates eye downward and toward midline.
- *medial rectus*—rotates eye toward midline.
- *lateral rectus*—rotates eye away from midline.
- *superior oblique*—rotates eye downward and away from midline.
- *inferior oblique*—rotates eye upward and away from midline.

name of smooth muscles and function:
- *ciliary muscles*—causes suspensory ligaments to relax.
- *iris, circular muscles*—causes size of pupil to decrease.
- *iris, radial muscles*—causes size of pupil to increase.

palpebral fissure—opening between the eyelids.
tarsal glands—secretory follicles in the tarsal plate.
tarsal plate—supporting connective tissue of the eyelid.

DIAGNOSTIC TERMS
disorders of the eyelid:

blepharitis—inflammation of the eyelid. (5, 64)

blepharoptosis—drooping of the upper eyelid, congenital or acquired.

chalazion (pl. *chalazia*)—true granuloma of the eye appearing as a painless swelling at the tarsus. (5)

distichiasis—on one or both of the eyelids, accessory row of lashes that are turned in against the eyeball.

ectropion—outward turning of the margin of the eyelid. (80)

entropion—inward turning of the margin of the eyelid. (80)

hordeolum (pl. *hordeola*) (5, 64, 80)
- *external hordeolum*—pyogenic infection of a sebaceous gland at the margin of the lid.

Figure 14.5 Extrinsic muscles of the eye.

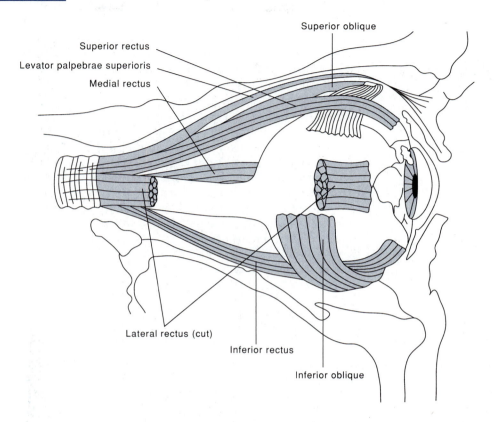

- *internal hordeolum*—purulent infection of a sebaceous gland embedded in the conjunctiva of the eyelid.

tumors of the lid—congenital or acquired; dermoids, fibromas, hemangiomas, and carcinomas.

disorders of the conjunctiva:

adenoviral conjunctivitis—caused by adenoviruses and marked by fever, malaise, pharyngitis, and glandular involvement. The palpebral conjunctiva looks red, and a copious watery discharge is present. (60)

allergic conjunctivitis—chronic hypersensitivity reaction of the conjunctiva, frequently associated with hay fever. (1, 64)

bacterial conjunctivitis—inflammation of the conjunctiva characterized by pain, edema, hyperemia, exudation, and infiltration. *Staphylococcus aureus*, *Streptococcus pneumoniae*, and Koch-Weeks and Morax-Axenfeld bacilli are common etiologic agents. (1, 64)

chlamydial keratoconjunctivitis—presents as:

- *inclusion conjunctivitis*—venereal infection transmitted to the eyes by contact with genital secretions from a chlamydial urethritis in men or chlamydial cervicitis in women. (2)
- *neonatal inclusion conjunctivitis*—chlamydial infection of newborns contracted by passage through birth canal of infected mothers. Blennorrhea (inclusion conjunctivitis) develops within the first 2 weeks of life. (2)

- *trachoma*—occurring endemically and a major cause of blindness, characterized by chronic inflammation of the follicular conjunctiva and followed by granulation, capillary infiltration of the cornea (pannus), and blindness. (2, 64)

keratoconjunctivitis sicca (KCS), dry eye syndrome, Sjögren's syndrome—ocular dryness caused by deficiency of one or more components of the tear film: mucin, aqueous, or liquid. Condition results in the appearance of dry spots on the conjunctival and corneal epithelium. (33, 39, 64)

ophthalmia neonatorum, gonococcal conjunctivitis of the newborn—the conjunctival sac of the infant is filled with pus containing gonococci. (36)

pterygium—membrane of conjunctival tissue that extends like a wing from the limbus toward the center of the cornea. (83)

disorders of the lacrimal apparatus:

acute dacryoadenitis—unilateral or bilateral inflammation of the lacrimal gland. It is frequently seen in children as a complication of measles and parotitis (mumps).

chronic dacryoadenitis—chronic, painless swelling of the lacrimal glands showing no signs of acute inflammation. (Acute or chronic inflammation of the lacrimal sac is usually due to nasolacrimal stenosis.) (61, 64, 72)

lacrimal gland abscess—localized accumulation of pus in the lacrimal gland.

disorders of ocular motility:

esotropia, convergent strabismus or *squint*—common type of eye disorder, usually referred to as crossed eyes. The eyes are directed toward the medial line.

exotropia, divergent strabismus or *squint*—known as walleyes. The eyes are turned laterally (outward).

hypertropia—one eye deviated upward.

hypotropia—one eye deviated downward.

vergences—disjunctive movements; the eyes move in opposite directions.

- *convergence*—eyes turning inward.
- *divergence*—eyes turning outward.

OPERATIVE TERMS (SEE TABLE 14.1.)

blepharectomy—excision of an eyelid.

blepharoplasty—plastic repair of an eyelid.

blepharorrhaphy—suture of a lacerated or injured eyelid.

dacryoadenectomy—removal of a lacrimal gland.

dacryocystectomy—removal of the lacrimal sac.

dacryocystorhinostomy—surgical creation of an opening into the nose for the tears.

Mohs' chemosurgery—micrographic technique utilized to excise tumors of the skin. The tumor is fixed in place and a layer is removed. That portion is examined microscopically; this procedure is repeated until all of the tumor is removed. This technique gives the highest cure rate for both primary and recurrent eyelid tumors. (40)

repair of strabismus:

application of adjustable suture—suture may be placed on the sclera at any point that will be accessible to the surgeon. The bow knot attached to the muscles may be adjusted as desired, that is, tightened or loosened to change the eye position as necessary. However, eye alignment may not be permanent and further surgery may be necessary. (27)

Faden procedure—technique whereby a new insertion site for the muscle is created far in the back of the eye by suturing the muscle to the sclera. This changes the functional insertion of a rectus muscle so that its vector force changes from a rotator to a retractor as the eye moves into the muscle's field of action. This procedure tends to weaken the muscle in its field of action. (38)

recession of ocular muscles—technique to weaken muscles. The muscle is detached from the eye, separated from its facial attachments, and allowed to retract. It is resewn to the eye a measured distance behind its original insertion site. (38)

resection of ocular muscles—technique used to strengthen muscles. The muscle is detached from the eye and stretched longer by a measured amount and then resown to the eye, usually at the original insertion site. Also, the muscle may be strengthened by tucking the tendon in graded amounts. (12)

tenotomy—procedure of cutting through a tendon. For example, the superior oblique muscle weakening may be accomplished by cutting through the tendon.

transposition procedures—techniques employed to move all or part of the extraocular muscles or tendons up or down or in any direction other than their natural line of action. The purpose of the procedure is to change the force generated by the muscle as well as the direction of that force. Transposition procedures are used to correct paresis and paralysis defects, torsional defects, and monocular concomitant hypertropia or hypotropia. (38)

tarsorrhaphy—surgical closure of an eyelid.

SYMPTOMATIC TERMS

blepharedema—puffy, swollen, edematous eyelids.

chemosis—conjunctival swelling near the cornea. (80)

epiphora—overflow of tears, often due to lacrimal duct obstruction. (80)

hyperemia—congestion.

lacrimation—secretion of tears.

limbal damage—injury at the corneoscleral junction that may be caused by the destruction of perilimbal blood supply, interfering with the nutrition of the cornea.

pannus—newly formed capillaries covering the cornea like a film. Pannus formation may be an inflammatory or a degenerative process. The connective tissue, which usually contains the blood vessels, invades beneath the corneal epithelium to separate it from Bowman's layer. When the pannus is associated with other ocular disease, fibrous vascular tissue may be involved. When the pannus is due to an inflammatory process, chronic inflammatory cells may invade. Scarring may be present in the late stages of both inflammatory or degenerative pannus. (83)

symblepharon—adhesion between the palpebral and bulbar conjunctiva. (80)

xerophthalmia—excessive dryness of the eye resulting from the destruction of mucin-producing goblet cells or lacrimal ducts and glands or from other causes.

SPECIAL PROCEDURES

TERMS RELATED TO BACTERIOLOGIC STUDIES

epithelial inclusion bodies—bodies found in conjunctival disease, such as inclusion blennorrhea of the newborn, some adult forms of diffuse, follicular conjunctivitis, and trachoma. Epithelial scrapings stained with Giemsa's or Wright's stain reveal the inclusion bodies.

epithelial scrapings from the cornea or conjunctiva—procedure used for identifying the etiologic organism of bacterial conjunctivitis or keratitis. A thin layer of epithelial cells is removed with a spatula or scalpel. The scrapings are transferred to slides and stained with Gram's method, or with Giemsa's or Wright's stain. These methods permit the identification of the predominant organism, as well as eosinophils and epithelial inclusion bodies. Since pathogenic organisms are freely present in epithelial cells before they appear in secretions, the study of scrapings offers a valuable aid to early diagnosis. Commonly seen etiologic organisms in conjunctival disease include *Diplococcus pneumoniae*, *Neisseria gonorrhoeae*, *Staphylococcus*, *Streptococcus*, and *Chlamydia*.

TERMS RELATED PRIMARILY TO FUNCTIONAL TESTING

accommodation—ability to see at various distances due to the contraction and relaxation of the ciliary muscle. The focusing power is measurable. (80)

contact lenses—small corneal lenses that fit directly on the eyeball under the eyelids, medically used to correct vision in keratoconus (cone-shaped cornea) and other eye conditions.

corneal sensitivity—the examiner touches the corneas with a cotton fiber to determine whether each cornea is normally sensitive.

dark adaptation—ability of retina to adjust to low levels of illumination. (80)

diopter—unit of measurement of refractive power or strength of lenses. (80)

electroretinography—the recording of retinal action currents. Procedure aids in the detection of degenerative disorders of the retina. (18)

"E" test, "E" game—series of tests for the detection of visual acuity in preschool children and illiterate persons. (18, 80)

fluorescein angiography—intravenous injection of fluorescein followed by ophthalmoscopy or funduscopy and rapid serial photography. Fluorescence of the vasculature aids in the detection of normal and abnormal states of the retinal and choroidal vessels, including microaneurysms, neovascularization, atriovenous shunts, vascular leakage, retinal hemorrhage, and subtle vascular conditions of the macula. (18)

gonioscopy—examination of the iris angle of the eye using an optical instrument. Obstruction of the filtration angle may occur in glaucoma. (18)

iris angiography—procedure shows the blood supply to the iris and the permeability of the blood vessels of the iris in normal subject. (19)

keratometry—measurement of the curves of the cornea with a keratometer. (80)

major amblyoscopy—test for evaluating the sensory status of the eyes; also used in orthoptic study before and after strabismus surgery.

ophthalmodynamometry—measurement of the pressure in the central retinal arteries for indirectly evaluating the blood flow in the carotid arteries. (18)

ophthalmoscopy—examination of the eye grounds (fundi) with an ophthalmoscope. (18, 19)

perimetry—instrumental measurement of field of vision. Computerized automated perimetry utilizes test lights projected into a hollow bowl but with a static threshold testing method that is more precise and comprehensive. Two basic perimetry methods are:

> *kinetic (moving) perimetry*—test object is moved from a peripheral area toward the center, and the patient indicates when the object is spotted.
>
> *static perimetry*—utilizes nonmoving test object presented at a particular location; the patient indicates at what point he or she fails to see the object. (18, 26)

probing of lacrimal drainage system—establishing drainage of obstructed system after unsuccessful irrigation. A metal probe is passed through the upper or lower punctum and canaliculus and into the lacrimal (tear) sac, nasolacrimal duct, and nose.

retinoscopy—light beam test for detecting refractive errors.

slit lamp biomicroscopy—use of a combination of slit lamp and biomicroscope for intense illumination and high magnification of the eyeball or lids. Layers of cornea and lens are clearly visualized, and pathologic processes such as opacities are detected with accuracy. (37)

tonometry—determination of intraocular pressure by a tonometer, such as that of Schiotz or the Goldmann applanation tonometer. (52)

visual acuity—determination of the minimum cognizable letter under standard conditions of illumination using the Snellen chart or one of its modifications. (19)

visual evoked potential (VEP), visual evoked response (VER)—response to 50 to 100 flash stimuli recorded from over the right and left occipital poles. Since each eye is stimulated separately, it is possible to recognize lesions of the optic nerve by the reduced amplitude and delayed conduction. Different responses of each hemisphere suggest retrochiasmatic pathology. VER is of particular use in evaluating the vision pathways in nonresponsive patients and infants and recognizing subclinical lesions in certain neurologic disorders such as multiple sclerosis. (18, 19)

ABBREVIATIONS

GENERAL

EM—emmetropia
EOM—extraocular muscles
ET—esotropia
IOP—intraocular pressure
OD—oculus dexter (right eye)
ODM—ophthalmodynamometry
Ophth., Oph.—Ophthalmology

OS—oculus sinister (left eye)
OU—oculus uterque (each eye)
PRRE—pupils, round, regular, and equal
VA—visual acuity
VE—visual efficiency
VEP—visual evoked potential
VER—visual evoked response

ORGANIZATIONS

AFB—American Foundation for the Blind
NINDB—National Institute of Neurological Diseases and Blindness
NSPB—National Society for the Prevention of Blindness

ORAL READING PRACTICE

GLAUCOMA

Glaucoma is a disease of the eye characterized by an elevated **intraocular pressure (IOP).** Normally, the internal pressure of the eye is about 18 to 22 mm Hg, a pressure higher than that of other organs. The maintenance of normal intraocular pressure depends primarily on the amount of **aqueous humor** present in the eye. The formation of aqueous humor and its elimination is a continuous process. If the production and absorption are in perfect balance, all is well, but if there is a disturbance of balance, the eye is seriously affected.

The **ciliary processes** form the **aqueous humor,** which passes through the pupil space to the **anterior chamber.** It leaves the anterior chamber through veins and a special drainage canal **(canal of Schlemm)** located in its wall. In most cases of glaucoma, the elevated intraocular pressure results from interference with the elimination of aqueous humor, although increased rate of production may be the source of imbalance.

Primary open-angle glaucoma presents spontaneously without the presence of related disorders and with no known origin other than **genetic** or **hereditary** predisposition. The disease is bilateral. The angle of the anterior chamber may be wide or narrow but it remains always open, whether the disease is in its initial stages or far advanced. The clinical picture is variable depending on the degree of elevation of intraocular pressure, which may vary from normal to significantly elevated pressures. Usually, there is a decreased facility of aqueous outflow, which tends to worsen over time with the progression of the disease.

Secondary open-angle glaucoma is characterized by partial or total blockage of the aqueous outflow to the tissues. This may result from the presence of **cells** and **particulate matter** carried into the **trabecular meshwork** along with aqueous humor or resulting from membrane or scar formation. Some types of **blunt trauma** to the anterior segment of the eye can produce blockage to aqueous outflow because of the simultaneous injury to the trabecular meshwork, the body of the **iris,** and the anterior aspect of the **ciliary body,** followed by scarring of the outflow channels.

Some types of secondary open-angle glaucoma may be of short duration, lasting until the obstructing blockage has passed through the angle structures, while some types may be of longer duration, lasting long after the causative agent has been removed.

Primary angle-closure glaucoma occurs in eyes with an anatomically narrow range. Abnormally small eyes **(nanophthalmus)** are more prone to angle closure. As the lens enlarges, the iris is held secure against the anterior lens surface, thus increasing the resistance to aqueous humor flow from the posterior chamber to the anterior chamber. In older adults, the anterior chamber loses depth and the lens enlarges with age, and thus this type of glaucoma is seen more often in that age category.

Secondary angle-closure glaucoma involves antecedent pathologic factors that cause closure of the angles. Some examples of these conditions are **iritis, iridocyclitis, intraocular neoplasms, dislocations of the lens, central vein occlusion,** and **trauma.**

Preventing loss of visual function is the goal of treatment in glaucoma disorders. The treatment regimen is geared to lower the pressure, either by increasing the facility of outflow or suppressing formation of **aqueous humor** or both. Treatment consists of judicious use of drugs such as **miotics,** which sometimes constrict the pupil so effectively that the aqueous humor can escape. If no alleviation can be achieved, operative intervention becomes imperative.

Argon laser trabeculoplasty (ALT) is usually considered before some of the more traditional surgical procedures are employed. ALT is an operative procedure by which laser energy is directed through a **goniolens** to burn the trabecular meshwork producing blanching or a fine bubble formation, thereby causing a purse-string type of contraction in the trabecular meshwork, with resultant opening of the outflow mechanism to facilitate the emergence of aqueous humor. A series of 100 burns may be made in a 360-degree angle within the trabecular meshwork. Another approach is to perform this procedure in a two-step phase by having only a 180-degree angle of the trabecular meshwork treated with 50 burns. Then after a 6-week period, if the intraocular pressure is not adequately controlled, the other 180-degree angle can be treated with 50 more burns. Whatever the choice of approach, this procedure achieves a clinically significant decrease in intraocular pressure.

Various other forms of surgical drainage may be indicated, depending on the kind of glaucoma and the presence or absence of **anterior synechiae.** Other procedures of choice may include **peripheral iridectomy, laser iridectomy, sclerectomy, cyclodialysis,** or **goniotomy.** Additional surgical procedures are combined **phacoemulsification, trabeculectomy,** and **capsulocleisis.** (17, 20, 62, 64, 68, 69, 71, 73)

REVIEW GUIDE

Instructions: Define the following terms.

Example: kerato-   (G)—horny

cornea (L)	canaliculus (L)	phaco- (G)
iris (G)	cantho- (G)	vitreous (L)
cyclo- (G)	ophthalmo- (G)	dacryo- (G)
palpebra (L)		

Instructions: Break apart each term listed below, identify the medical term elements, and define the term.

Example: endophthalmitis   endo- = prefix = within   ophthalm- = root = eye   -itis = suffix = inflammation

blepharoptosis

chorioretinopathy

conjunctivitis

dacryocystorhinostomy

electroretinography

hyperopia

iridocyclitis

keratitis

kerocentesis

lensectomy

melanomas

retinoblastoma

retinopathy

sclerostomy

trabeculoplasty

trabeculotomy

uveitis

vitrectomy

vitroretinal

Instructions: Figure 14 in the text shows a transverse section of the eye. For each line that extends from the figure below, provide the anatomic name of the site as shown in the example

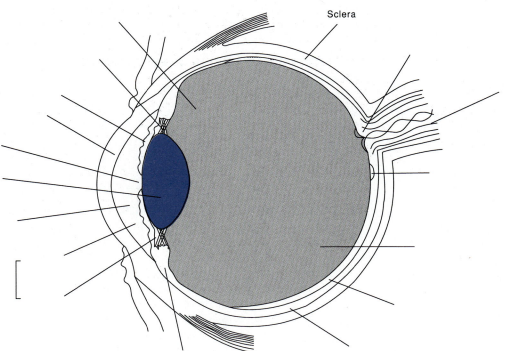

Sclera

15

Disorders Pertaining to the Sense Organ of Hearing

EAR

ORIGIN OF TERMS

acou- (G)—to hear, hearing
acoustic (G)—sound
auricle (L)—little ear
chemo-, chemi-, chemico- (G)—
    alchemy, chemical, chemistry
cholo-, chole- (G)—bile
cochlea (G)—snail, shell, spiral form
myringo- (L)—eardrum
-oma (G)—neoplasm, tumor

ossicle (L)—small bone
ot-, oto- (G)—ear
sacculus (pl. *sacculi*) (L)—sac, little bag
salpingo- (G)—tube, trumpet
stapes (L)—stirrup
stearo-, steato- (G)—fat
tympano- (G)—drum, tympanic
vestibule (L)—antechamber

PHONETIC PRONUNCIATION OF SELECTED TERMS

cholesteatoma	KO-lee-STE-a-TOE'mah
chemodectoma	KE-mow-deck-TOE'mah
glomus tympanicum	GLO'mus tim-PAN'ick-um
mastoiditis	MAS-toy-DI'tis
mastoidectomy	MAS'toy-DECK'toe-me
myringotomy	MIR-in-GOT'owe me
otosclerosis	O-toe-skle-ROW'sis
stapedectomy	STAY-pe-DECK'toe-me

ANATOMIC TERMS (3, 13, 23) (SEE FIGS. 15.1–15.3.)

external ear—division of ear consisting of the auricle and the external auditory canal or meatus.
    auricle, pinna—the external ear, made up chiefly of elastic fibrocartilage that is shaped to catch the sound waves.
    cerumen—ear wax, formed by the ceruminous glands of the skin lining the meatus.
    external auditory meatus—ear passage, composed of a cartilaginous and a bony part.
    helix—outer folded margin of the auricle.
middle ear—narrow cavity in the temporal bone, which lies just internal to the tympanic membrane and communicates with the pharynx by means of the auditory tube. It is the

Figure 15.1 Major parts of the ear.

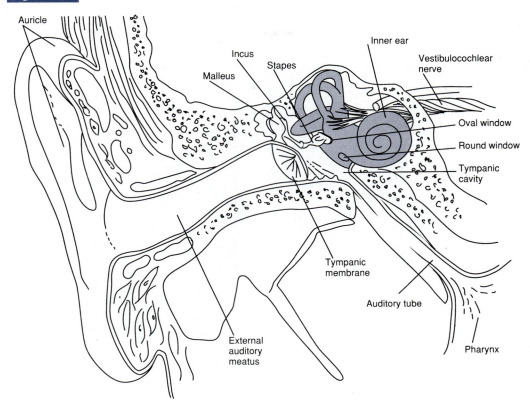

Figure 15.2 Middle ear, medial view. Two small muscles attached to the malleus and stapes, the stapedius and tensor tympani, serve as effectors in the tympanic reflex.

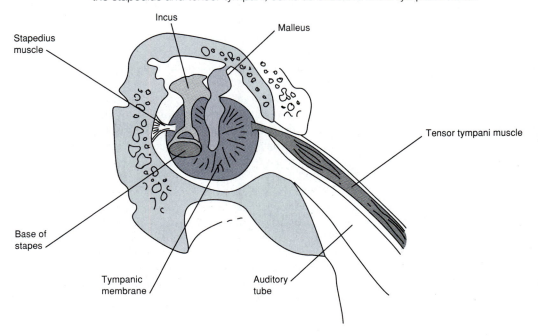

Figure 15.3 The osseous labyrinth of the inner ear is separated from the membranous labyrinth by perilymph. The membranous labyrinth contains endolymph.

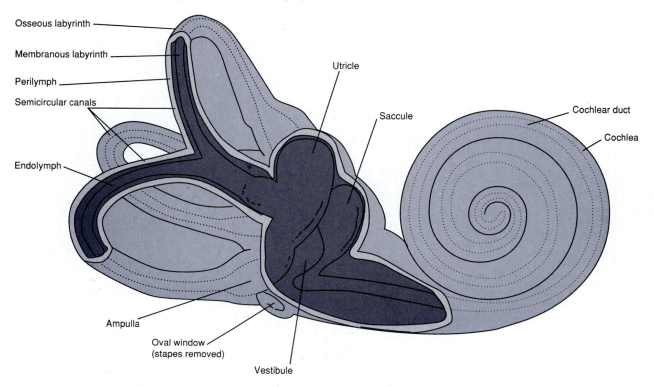

division of ear containing the ossicles. In this cavity, the energy of sound waves is converted into mechanical energy through a chain of ossicles.

tympanic cavity—the space directly internal to the tympanic membrane.

auditory tube—channel of communication between nasal portion of the pharynx and the tympanic cavity that allows for equalization of pressure on either side of the tympanic membrane.

epitympanic recess—space above the tympanic cavity.

orifices of the tympanic cavity:

- *aditus ad antrum*—opening to the mastoid antrum. This is a large, irregular aperture that connects the epitympanic recess with the mastoid antrum.
- *mastoid antrum*—the largest and most superior of the cavities in the mastoid bone. It communicates below and behind with the mastoid air cells. The antrum and the mastoid air cells are lined by mucous membrane continuous with that of the middle ear.
- *fenestra cochleae, fenestra rotunda*—round window facing the internal ear.
- *fenestra vestibuli, fenestra ovalis*—oval window in which the stapes lodges.

roof of the middle ear or *tympanic cavity*—formed by a thin plate of bone, the tegmen tympani, that separates the tympanic cavity from the dura mater on the floor of the middle cranial fossa. The tegmen tympani also roofs the mastoid antrum.

floor of the middle ear or *tympanic cavity*—a narrow fissure between the medial and lateral walls.

ossicles of the tympanic cavity—three tiny bones: malleus (hammer), incus (anvil), and stapes (stirrup). They transmit vibrations to the internal ear. (See fig. 15.3.)

Figure 15.4 (a) The cochlea consists of a coiled, bony canal with a membranous tube inside. (b) If the cochlea could be unwound, the membranous tube would be seen ending as a closed sac at the apex of the bony canal.

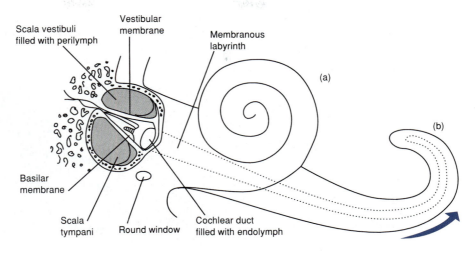

inner ear—division of ear composed of a number of fluid-filled spaces and the membranous labyrinth, which is a tube, that lies within the bony (osseous) labyrinth. The osseous labyrinth is a bony canal in the temporal bone. Between the osseous and membranous labyrinths is a fluid called *perilymph,* which is secreted by cells in the wall of the bony canal. The membranous labyrinth contains fluid termed *endolymph.* The perilymphatic space of the bony labyrinth contains the cochlea, which functions in hearing; three semicircular canals that function in providing a sense of equilibrium; and the vestibule, which is located between the cochlea and the semicircular canals, and contains membranous structures that serve both hearing and equilibrium.

 cochlea—the essential organ of hearing. It is a spiral tube whose shape represents the coiled shell of a snail. This spiral tube possesses a bony core, the modiolus, which contains the spiral ganglion and transmits the cochlear nerve, and a bony shelf, the spiral lamina, which winds around the core like threads of a screw. The shelf divides the bony labyrinth of the cochlea into upper and lower compartments:

  • *upper compartment, scala vestibuli*—leads from the open oval window to the apex of the spiral.
  • *lower compartment, scala tympani*—protrudes from the apex of the cochlea to a membrane-covered opening in the wall of the inner ear called the round window. (See fig. 15.4.)

These compartments constitute the bony labyrinth of the cochlea and are filled with perilymph. A portion of the membranous labyrinth within the cochlea is called the cochlear duct (scala media). The cochlear duct is filled with endolymph and lies between the two bony compartments. This duct terminates as a closed sac at the apex of the cochlea. The cochlear duct is separated from the scala vestibuli by a vestibular membrane (Reissner's membrane) and from the scala tympani by a basilar membrane. The basilar membrane extends from the bony shelf of the cochlea and forms the floor of the cochlear duct.

 organ of Corti—located on the upper surface of the basilar membrane; stretches from the apex to the base of the cochlea. The organ of Corti contains about 16,000 hearing receptor cells. The receptor cells, termed hair cells, are arranged in four parallel rows, and they possess numerous hairlike processes that extend into the endolymph of the cochlea.

Figure 15.5 Distribution of the vestibulocochlear nerve to the inner ear (n. = nerve).

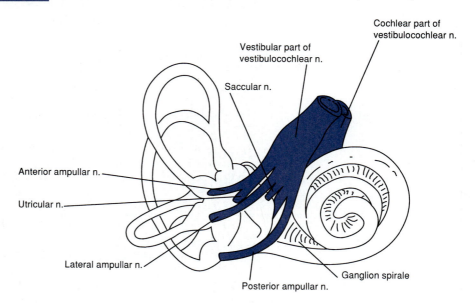

tectorial membrane—located above the hair cells; attached to the bony shelf of the cochlea and passes like a roof over the receptor cells, making contact with the tips of their hairs.
vestibular apparatus—the utricle and semicircular ducts, which aid in maintaining equilibrium.
vestibulocochlear nerve, eighth cranial nerve, formerly acoustic or *auditory nerve*—nerve comprising two distinct fiber sets. (See fig. 15.5.)
- *cochlear branch*—fibers distributed to the hair cells of the spiral organ. They are concerned with hearing.
- *vestibular branch*—fibers distributed to portions of the utricle, saccule, and semicircular ducts. They aid in maintaining body balance.

DIAGNOSTIC TERMS
conditions of the external ear:

atresia of external auditory meatus—absence of the normal opening of the ear or closure of the external auditory meatus. (20)
auricular hematoma—accumulation of blood and serous fluid in a plane between the perichondrium and cartilage. If left untreated, the perichondrium generates new cartilage that eventually results in a *cauliflower ear deformity*. Hematomas at the auricular site occur due to direct trauma to the ear, such as from a wrestling injury or as seen in victims of child abuse. (4, 26)
auricular keloid—result from trauma to the auricular dermis. Keloids are characterized histologically by broad bands of eosinophilic collagen. Keloids appear as irregular-shaped and rounded, and are firm nodules, usually located on the medial surface of the ear lobe. Keloids are often associated with ear lobe piercing. (4, 26)
congenital microtia—usually a deformed or misplaced, small aural tag associated with absence of meatus and tragus. (20)
external otitis—all the inflammatory processes that involve the skin of the external auditory canal are included in this term. For purposes of differentiation, these disorders

may be classified as infectious, eczematoid, or seborrheic and may be acute, recurrent, or chronic. (4) Some examples are:

- *abscess of auricle or of external auditory meatus*—localized collection of pus of auricle or meatus. (4)
- *acute diffuse external otitis, swimmer's ear*—a disease of the summer months when introduction of extraneous moisture from swimming or bathing increases the maceration of the canal skin and creates a condition favorable to bacterial growth. *Pseudomonas aeruginosa* is the most common bacteria found. Itching, hyperemia, and edema occur as the canal becomes inflamed and swollen. (4)
- *acute localized external otitis*—an infection of a hair follicle, beginning as a folliculitis but usually extending to form a furuncle. The infecting microorganism is usually *Staphylococcus*. (4)
  - *furuncle of the external auditory canal*—painful nodule of the skin formed by circumscribed inflammation of the skin and subcutaneous tissue: initially, may resemble a mild infection of the sebaceous glands and hair follicles. Staphylococci enter through the hair follicles. (4, 25)
- *dermatitis of external ear*—inflammation of skin of auricle and external auditory meatus. Types encountered include dry, moist, exfoliative, contact, eczematous, allergic, and seborrheic. (4)
  - *seborrheic external otitis*—condition associated with seborrheic dermatitis of other regions, particularly the scalp (dandruff). The lesions are typified by a greasy scaling that has a yellowish appearance due to the abnormal sebum production. The external cartilaginous canal, concha, and postauricular regions are most often involved. (4, 27)
  - *eczematoid external otitis*—the external canal, concha, tragus, antitragus, and lobule are involved with confluent weeping and crusted lesions. (4)
  - *otomycosis*—fungal infections of the external ear. Aspergillus and candida are the most common infections. Otomycosis is usually a chronic superficial infection. (4, 25)

frostbite of auricle—exposure to extreme cold resulting in hyperemia, blanching, and in severe cases, ulceration and gangrene. (4, 26)

traumatic avulsion of auricle—loss of pinna due to injury. (4)

tumors of external auditory canal:

- *benign tumors:*
  - *aural polyp*—benign tumor on a pedicle that may occlude the external auditory canal and thus interfere with sound conduction. (4, 25)
  - *cerumen gland adenoma*—benign tumor originating in ceruminous glands. (4, 27)
  - *osteoma*—occurs in the auditory canal as a single larger growth forming near the lateral end of the bony portion. The tumors may be pedunculated. (4)
- *malignant tumors:*
  - *carcinoma of the external ear canal*—malignant tumor, either basal cell or squamous cell type. Basal cell carcinoma occurs most often on the auricle, and squamous cell carcinoma constitutes 70% of the malignancies of the external canal. (4, 27)
  - *cylindroma*—a very malignant adenocystic carcinoma. The tumor is noted for its slow relentless growth, and neural invasion. (4, 27)
  - *embryonal rhabdomyosarcoma*—most common malignant tumor involving the external canal or middle ear in children. This tumor is associated with chronic ear drainage, ear pain, and hearing loss. (27)

conditions of the tympanic membrane:

myringitis, tympanitis—inflammation of the eardrum.

perforation of tympanic membrane—hole in eardrum; if small it will heal without treatment; if large, it may require tympanoplasty. (5)

rupture of tympanic membrane—condition usually due to trauma, such as direct injury to ear. (5)

tumors—rare disorders that may be endotheliomatous, fibromatous, or angiomatous or show other histologic patterns.

tympanosclerosis—involvement of the mucous membrane of the middle ear or drum by sclerosis of exudate, with fixation of the ossicles and drum, diffuse calcification, and thickening of the mucosal lining of the cavity. (25)

conditions of the middle ear:

cholesteatoma—globular pearly mass covered with a thin shell of epidermis and connective tissue. It usually forms following middle ear infection and is the body's way of arresting suppuration. Pseudocholesteatomas are common. (25)

glomus tumors, chemodectomas—common neoplasm of the head and neck. (27, 31, 34)

- *glomus tympanicum*—tumor originates in the middle ear and usually can be surgically removed. (27, 31)
- *glomus jugulare*—tumor containing chemoreceptor cells arises from the jugular bulb in the middle ear. It may cause episodes of dizziness, nystagmus, blackouts, and facial paralysis. Labyrinthine and cochlear invasion by the glomus leads to deafness. Complete surgical excision depends on the location and size of the tumor. (27, 31)
- *glomus vagale*—tumor arises along the course of the vagus nerve and is relatively uncommon. (21, 31)

mastoiditis—infection of the middle ear that has extended to the antrum and mastoid cells. Mastoiditis may be acute, subacute, chronic, and recurrent. (21, 25)

middle ear effusion—acute or chronic presence of fluid in the middle ear, generally without infection. (12, 33)

- *secretory otitis media, mucoid otitis media, glucotitis*— thick, cloudy, viscous exudate in middle ear; contains cells and mucous strands. Secretory otitis media is the main cause of hearing loss in children, and may follow acute otitis media. It may be secondary to such conditions as allergy, infection, barotrauma, and adenoid enlargement. (24, 33)
- *serous otitis media*—thin, clear amber fluid in middle ear. (33)
- *serous otitis media with hemotympanum*—serum and blood in middle ear space resulting from temporal bone fracture, tumor, or blood disorder. (33)

otitis media—inflammation of the middle ear. Common types encountered are:

- *acute suppurative otitis media*—marked by intense congestion of mucosa of middle ear, blockage of eustachian tube, serous exudate that becomes infected, and rupture of the eardrum. Bacterial invaders are *Staphylococcus aureus, Diplococcus pneumoniae, Streptococcus pyogenes, Haemophilus influenzae,* and others. (33)
- *chronic suppurative otitis media*—characterized by continuation of middle ear infection resulting in protracted suppuration. (5, 25, 33)

salpingitis of eustachian tube—inflammation of the auditory tube. It may be acute or chronic. (12)

conditions of the inner ear:

acoustic neuroma—benign tumor of the eighth cranial nerve affecting the vestibular branch more than the cochlear branch of the nerve and causing vertigo, tinnitus, and hearing impairment. (14, 21, 34) *labyrinthitis*—inflammation of the labyrinth, usually secondary to acute or chronic suppurative otitis media with or without cholesteatoma or to acute upper respiratory infection. (6, 31)

- *acute diffuse suppurative labyrinthitis*—characterized by complete deafness in the affected ear, associated with severe vertigo, nausea, vomiting, and ataxia. (6)

Ménière's disease, endolymphatic hydrops—neurologic disorder exhibiting a triad symptom complex in its classic form: explosive attacks of true vertigo, fluctuating hearing loss of the sensorineural type, and tinnitus. Dizziness, ataxia, and a feeling of fullness in the ear are usually present. Remissions may last years. (16, 21)

otosclerosis, otospongiosis—newly formed spongy bone replacing the hard bone of the labyrinth. It may result in conduction deafness with fixation of the stapes and stapedial footplate, followed later by nerve degeneration. (7, 19, 31)

tinnitus—auditory perception of internal origin (noise), usually localized as presenting from within and rarely heard by others. It affects both men and women and generally occurs between 40 and 80 years.

- *vibratory tinnitus*—real sounds, mechanical in origin, arising within or near the ear.
- *nonvibratory tinnitus*—neural excitation and conduction from anywhere within the auditory system to the auditory cortex, with a mechanical basis. Nonvibratory tinnitus appears to be more common than vibratory tinnitus. (19, 21)

hearing loss (two basic types):

conductive hearing loss—impairment of hearing resulting from obstruction of sound waves that do not reach the inner ear. The interference may be caused by impacted cerumen, exudate, blockage of external auditory canal or eustachian tube, otosclerosis, or other causes. Otitis media of some type is the most common cause of conductive hearing loss. (19, 21)

sensorineural hearing loss—inability of the cochlear division of the eighth cranial nerve to transmit electric impulses to the brain, or the hair cells of the organ of Corti to change sound to electric energy. Dysfunction may result from neural degeneration of the organ of Corti, alterations in endolymph, cochlear conductive disorder, or other causes.

Conductive or sensorineural hearing loss or both may be found in the following types.

- *congenital deafness*—loss of hearing from birth. (28)
- *hysterical deafness*—simulated hearing loss associated with neurotic behavior and emotional instability, thus psychogenic in nature.
- *Mondini's deafness*—genetic deafness caused by aplastic changes in the osseous and membranous labyrinth. (11)
- *noise deafness, industrial hearing loss, occupational hearing loss*—impairment or loss of hearing induced by constant noise, explosions, or blows to the head. It disappears in a quiet environment if neural damage is in its early phase. (2, 28)
- *sudden sensorineural hearing loss, spontaneous hearing loss*—usually an abrupt onset of sensorineural loss of hearing in one ear due to viral infection, vascular accident, trauma, shrinkage of organ of Corti, or other causes. Bilateral sudden hearing loss is uncommon. (11, 23)

OPERATIVE TERMS (SEE TABLE 15.1.)

microsurgery—the use of a high-power binocular dissecting microscope with built-in illumination for ear surgery.

external ear:

otoplasty—correction of deformed pinna. (15)

pedicle tube insertion—technique useful in repairing a large defect in the auricular area, such as results from trauma or from total excision of the auricle for extensive carcinomas. A skin incision is made over the defective area, the skin flap is raised, and a tube is inserted and closed with continuous or interrupted sutures. By sliding and undermining, the donor site can be closed beneath the tube, then defects at the end of the tube are closed. (4)

TABLE 15.1	Some Ear Conditions Amenable to Surgery		
Anatomic Site	**Diagnosis**	**Type of Surgery**	**Operative Procedures**
Ear	Carcinoma of ear	Amputation of ear Otoplasty	Removal of ear Plastic repair of ear
External auditory meatus	Foreign body in external auditory meatus Papilloma	Otoscopy with removal of foreign body Excision of papilloma	Endoscopic examination of external auditory meatus for removal of foreign body or lesion
Middle ear	Otitis media, acute serous	Paracentesis tympani Myringotomy	Puncture of eardrum and evacuation of fluid from middle ear Incision of eardrum and drainage of middle ear
Middle ear	Perforation of eardrum, chronic	Myringoplasty	Reconstruction of eardrum
Middle ear	Otitis media, chronic suppurative	Radical mastoidectomy or modified radical mastoidectomy	Endaural approach to temporal bone and thorough removal of diseased tissues
Middle ear Mastoid	Otitis media, acute Mastoiditis, acute	Mastoidectomy	Scooping out and obliterating infected air cells and removal of diseased mastoid process
Mastoid	Mastoiditis, chronic perforation of pars tensa	Tympanoplasty with or without mastoidectomy	Closure of perforation by skin graft or vein or fascia or perichondrium
Mastoid	Mastoiditis, chronic suppurative or recurrent	Repair of middle ear Tympanoplasty	Surgical creation of new cavity composed of healthy mastoid tissue, tympanum, and external auditory canal

repair of auricular deformity (microtia), excision of microtia—proper surgical revision of existing malformation as a foundation for prosthesis and prosthetic reconstruction of auricle. (4, 20)

sebaceous cyst and keloid excision—complete removal of entire sebaceous cyst and keloid from its site. (4)

middle ear:

insertion of plastic tubes—the process whereby plastic tubes may be introduced into the middle ear area; the tubes act temporarily or permanently as an artificial eustachian tube. (4)

mastoid antrotomy—surgical opening of mastoid antrum, usually done for children with middle ear infection.

mastoid obliteration—following the postauricular incision, the soft tissue over the mastoid cortex is exposed and elevated as an anteriorly based pedicle flap. The pedicle flap is fitted into the cavity reforming the shape of the canal. Bone paste and bone chips (if needed) are packed in behind the soft tissue flap. The incision is closed without drainage. (5)

TABLE 15.1   (continued)

Anatomic Site	Diagnosis	Type of Surgery	Operative Procedures
Middle ear	Otosclerosis, conductive deafness with fixation of stapes	Stapedectomy Stapedioplasty	Removal of stapes Insertion of delicate prosthesis to replace stapes
Middle ear Tympanum Mastoid	Tympanomastoiditis Cholesteatoma	Tympanomastoidectomy Tympanoplasty	Postauricular incision Removal of necrotic incus Malleus and stapes freed by dissection and typanosclerosis removed Complete enucleation of diseased mastoid Fascial graft placed on canal wall Tympanomeatal flap positioned and secured with Gelfoam and Silastic sponge
Internal ear	Ménière's disease unilateral	Labyrinthectomy Exenteration of air cells Avulsion of endolymphatic labyrinth	Endaural or postaural approach to inner ear Removal of air cells Destruction of membranous labyrinth
Vestibulocochlear nerve	Acoustic neuroma	Excision of neoplasm	Removal of neoplasm that involved some area of neural passageway of hearing

mastoidectomy, modified radical—procedures employed preserve the middle ear space while draining the attic and mastoid. It involves removal of the superior canal wall, removal of the posterior canal wall to the level of the facial nerve and creation of a canal skin flap, which is turned down to line the mastoid cavity and attic space. The severity of the disease condition may necessitate the removal of the incus and head of the malleolus. In some cases, staging is preferred, with the tympanic membrane grafted at the initial procedure and the ossicular repair performed at a second stage procedure. (5)

mastoidectomy, radical—removal of all diseased tissue in mastoid antrum and tympanic cavity and conversion of both into one dry cavity that communicates with the external ear. An operating microscope is used. Radical mastoidectomy is rarely indicated because it involves severe loss of function. Its application is usually employed for tumors of the middle ear or external meatus. (5)

myringotomy, tympanotomy—opening of the eardrum in an area that tends to heal readily, to avoid spontaneous rupture at a site that rarely closes.

myringoplasty—surgical repair of tympanic membrane by tissue grafts. (5)

ossiculectomy—surgical removal of an ossicle, or of the ossicles of the ear. (5)

ossiculoplasty—surgical repair of ossicles of the ear and the ossicular chain. (5)

paracentesis tympani—surgical puncture of the eardrum for evacuation of fluid from middle ear. (25, 33) *stapedectomy*—removal of stapes and reestablishment of the connection between incus and oval window by interposition of prosthesis and tissue or inert cover over the oval window. (7, 26)

tympanoplasty—repair of perforated tympanic membrane with erosion of malleus by closing tympanum with graft against incus or remnant of malleus. Several tympanoplastic procedures have been devised. (5, 26)

- *tympanoplasty with ossiculoplasty, without mastoidectomy*—repair of the middle ear conductive mechanism and tympanic membrane without involving the mastoid cavity.
- *tympanoplasty with ossiculoplasty, with mastoidectomy*—procedure that eradicates disease in both the mastoid and middle ear cavity with reconstruction of the tympanic membrane and ossicular chain.

tympanotomy, exploratory—exploration of middle ear through tympanomeatal approach. (5)

inner ear:

cochlear implant, cochlear prosthesis—electronic device assigned to initiate motion in the ossicular chain and cochlear fluid and depolarize peripheral neurons, thus producing auditory sensations. By generating electric stimulation of various segments of the cochlear branch of the eighth cranial nerve, the cochlear prosthesis promises to become a functional implantable hearing aid enhancing the speech rehabilitation of the totally deaf. (18, 28)

cochleosacculotomy—creation of a fistula between the perilymphatic and dilatated endolymphatic compartments by inserting a hook through the round window membrane and the osseous spiral lamina of the basal end of the cochlea. Penetration of the tip of the hook can be monitored by movement of the stapes footplate. The defect in the round window is obliterated with Gelfoam. (9)

decompression of endolymphatic sac—removal of bone around the sac for improvement of vascularization so that endolymph can escape to the cerebrospinal fluid system. (9)

labyrinthectomy—total destruction of labyrinth with or without removal of Scarpa's ganglion; for intractable vertigo. (9, 34)

labyrinthectomy transmeatal with cochleovestibular neurectomy—the transcanal labyrinthectomy can be extended, the internal auditory canal opened, and the cochlear and vestibular nerves sectioned. This procedure has the advantage of ruling out an acoustic neuroma and also may give better results in relieving tinnitus. (9, 34)

ligation of internal jugular vein—tying of the internal jugular vein to relieve objective venous tinnitus, formerly known as cephalic bruit. (34)

surgery of internal auditory canal—transvestibular approach to canal. The procedure is performed for relief of disabling vertigo and tinnitus by section of the vestibular nerve or excision of acoustic neuroma, and in cases of facial paralysis, by decompression of the facial nerve with facial nerve grafting. (9)

SYMPTOMATIC TERMS

anacusis—sound perception completely lost.

impacted cerumen—dried ear wax. (4)

nystagmus—involuntary rhythmic movements in one eye or both that may be horizontal, rotary, vertical, circulatory, oblique, or mixed type. They commonly occur in vestibular disease.

otalgia—pains in ear; severe earache. (21)

paracusis of Willis—ability of person with conductive hearing loss to hear better in the presence of noise.

presbycusis—impaired hearing that is part of the aging process. (17, 21)

vertigo—illusion of movement of a person in relation to the environment. The patient feels that he himself is spinning (subjective type) or the objects are whirling about him (objective type).

central vertigo—present in disorders of vestibular nuclei, cerebellum, or brain stem, characterized by slow onset, prolonged duration, and absence of hearing impairment or tinnitus.

peripheral vertigo—present in disorders of vestibular nerve and semicircular canals. It is episodic and explosive; marked by sudden, violent attack, lasting minutes to hours; and usually accompanied by tinnitus and impaired hearing. (8)

SPECIAL PROCEDURES

BASIC TERMS RELATED TO AUDIOLOGY

air conduction—aerotympanic route or aerial transmission of sound waves across the tympanic cavity (middle ear) and through the round window into the inner ear. (21, 29)

bone conduction—ossicular route or transmission of sound waves across the ossicles and through the oval window into the inner ear. The mechanical force of air and bone conduction is transformed in the inner ear into electric energy, which travels along the cochlear branch of the eighth cranial nerve to the brain, where it is perceived as speech. (21, 28, 29)

decibel—unit expressing intensity of sound. (21, 29)

discrimination—ability to distinguish accurately between similar-sounding words. (21)

frequency—the number of regularly recurrent sound vibrations emanating from a source and expressed in cycles per second. (21)

intensity of sound—pressure exerted by sound and measured in decibels. (21)

loudness—sound heard by person with normal hearing differing from that perceived by person with defective hearing while the intensity remains the same.

recruitment—abnormal condition of the inner ear characterized by an extremely rapid increase in loudness. (28)

sensitivity to sound—acuteness of hearing.

spondee words—in speech audiometry, bisyllabic words, such as nosebleed, headache, and eardrum. (28)

threshold—the lowest limit of initial sound perception; 50% of words heard correctly. (10, 28)

tone decay—the tone becomes inaudible.

tympanometry—measures the impedance of the middle ear. Tympanometry is a useful technique in the identification and diagnosis of middle ear effusions in children. (10, 28, 29)

TERMS RELATED TO FUNCTIONAL TESTS OF COCHLEAR APPARATUS

audiometry—measurement of hearing for the purpose of accurately evaluating the extent and nature of hearing impairment. (1, 18)

audiometric test—quantitative measurement of hearing loss. Results are plotted according to an established norm on an audiogram, which is a graphic representation of patient's threshold of hearing at different frequencies and intensities. (19, 29) (See fig. 15.6.)

Békésy audiometric test—test automatically presenting continuous pure tones and interrupted tones at different frequencies. The subject controls the intensity of the testing signal, and a needle plots the audiogram on a record form. (10, 28)

electrocochleography—new method of testing hearing, particularly in infants 1 to 6 months old. Electrodes are positioned on or near the cochlea, and a computer records low-voltage electric potentials obtained from the inner ear. (29)

pure tone audiometry—use of an electric instrument for quantitatively measuring pure tones both by air conduction and bone conduction at threshold levels. Test detects the type of hearing loss. (1, 10, 24)

Figure 15.6 Different frequencies create different wave patterns in the basilar membrane within the cochlea. High-frequency sound vibrates the basilar membrane at the base of the cochlea. Medium-frequency sound vibrates the middle area of the cochlea. Low-frequency sound vibrates the apex of the cochlea. Hearing depends on sound waves entering the inner ear.

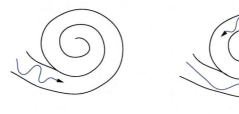

High   Medium   Low

short-increment sensitivity index—test presenting continuous pure tone to subject and superimposing short pips of 1 decibel increments on constant pure tone. Subjects with cochlear impairment experience no difficulty in perceiving the pips, whereas those with normal hearing do. (10, 24, 28)

speech audiometry—valuable aid in clinical audiology. The patient's functioning in the environment is estimated by a speech discrimination score. Speech discrimination is tested by giving phonetically balanced words at an intensity of 40 decibels (Db) above threshold and recording the percentage of correct responses. (10, 24, 28)

tone decay test—valuable special auditory test that demonstrates the phenomenon of a tone becoming inaudible. (24)

tuning fork tests—means for determining the type of hearing impairment in relation to sound conduction and sound perception. Two commonly used tests are the Rhine and Weber tests. A third test is the Schwabach test. This test allows the examiner to compare his or her own hearing, if normal, by bone conduction with the patient's bone conduction by alternately placing the vibrating tuning fork on the patient's mastoid and the examiner's mastoid process. (21, 24)

TERMS RELATED TO FUNCTIONAL TESTS OF THE VESTIBULAR APPARATUS

caloric test—procedure that conveys information of the functional capacity of each labyrinth and the presence of horizontal and rotary nystagmus. (24)

electronystagmogram—record of eye movements by electric tracing induced by caloric or positional stimulation. (1, 24)

Romberg test—procedure that tests body balance when eyes are closed and feet are together side by side.

ABBREVIATIONS

AC—air conduction
BC—bone conduction
ENT—ear, nose, and throat
ETF—eustachian tubal function

PTS—permanent threshold shift
SISI—short-increment sensitivity index
TDT—tone decay test
TTS—temporary threshold shift

ORAL READING PRACTICE

OTITIC MENINGITIS

Meningitis is one of the most serious sequelae of ear infections. Its incidence is higher in small children than in adults because of the intimate relation of the middle ear to the **middle cranial fossa** in early life. Symptoms may develop slowly, or there may be an abrupt onset of the disease with **prodromal** manifestations. A chill occasionally signals the beginning of the acute phase. With the cerebral invasion of pathogenic organisms, the cardinal symptoms make their appearance: a constantly high fever, a headache progressively becoming worse to the point of being excruciating, and **vertigo,** particularly in the presence of **labyrinthine** involvement. **Purulent labyrinthitis** can occur as the infection spreads from the **subarachnoid space** into the **cochlea** through the **cochlear aqueduct** or along the **vascular** and **nerve channels** of the **auditory canal.** As the disease progresses, prostration increases, **convulsions** occur, particularly in children, and the patient becomes very irritable, exhibiting marked personality changes. In infants, the large **fontanelle** is bulging, but there is no pulsation.

Bacterial meningitis is a common cause of unilateral or bilateral **sensorineural hearing impairment.** In children, the most common cause of **conductive hearing impairment** is **otitis media with effusion,** and a persistent effusion may cause a **conductive hearing loss. Chronic suppurative otitis media** causes **meningitis** by direct extension through bone and dura or through the inner ear via a **labyrinthine fistula** caused by a **cholesteatoma,** or through the bloodstream. **Bacteremia** is thought to be responsible for most **bacterial meningitis** (otitic and nonotitic). Acute or chronic **suppurative otitis media** may be followed by **intracranial complications** such as **thrombophlebitis** of the **lateral sinus, extradural** or **intradural abscess, facial paralysis,** and other disorders.

Kernig's sign is positive, as evidenced by pain and reflex contraction in the hamstring muscles when the examiner attempts to extend the leg after flexing the thigh upon the abdomen. Brudzinski's sign (which is flexion of the legs at the knee when flexion of the head is attempted), may also be present. These signs are elicited in only about 50% of adults with bacterial meningitis, and their absence does not rule out the possibility of meningitis. Muscular rigidity of back and neck and retraction of the head are characteristic manifestations. In addition, the patient suffers from **photophobia, hyperesthesia** at touch, and **opisthotonos.** If treatment remains ineffectual, progressive drowsiness and coma develop, the deep reflexes disappear, and the prognosis is poor. Spinal fluid findings confirm the diagnosis. The fluid appears cloudy and purulent, and the pressure is increased. The cell count is high in **lymphocytes** and **polymorphonuclear leukocytes.** The protein content of the spinal fluid markedly rises, whereas the sugar drops. An excessively high protein content is usually associated with **ventricular blockage** and signals a fatal outcome. Smear and culture findings generally indicate that the bacterial invaders causing the ear infection are the same as those of the otogenic complication in the brain.

Streptococcus pyogenes and *Diplococcus pneumoniae* are the common etiologic agents of **diffuse purulent meningitis,** whereas *Neisseria meningitidis,* a very pyogenic diplococcus, provokes **epidemic cerebrospinal meningitis.**

The treatment of meningitis consists of intravenous antibiotic therapy and adequate drainage of the suppurative focus in the ear. Monitoring the cerebral spinal fluid is important to ensure the adequacy of the **antibiotic therapy.** Progress may be monitored by periodic **lumbar puncture.** Once the disease has developed, vigorous treatment must be instituted to combat the infection, prevent ventricular blocking, and maintain electrolyte balance and nutrition. Surgical intervention is limited to the rapid eradication of the ear infection and any additional intracranial complications requiring surgery. (6, 19, 22, 25, 30)

REVIEW GUIDE

Instructions: Select the letter of the response that correctly completes each statement, as shown in the example.

Example: The suffix *-oma* in the term *chemodectoma* means
  a. infection. <u>b.</u> tumor. c. ear. d. none of these.

1. Pressure exerted by sound and measured in decibels is termed
   a. air conduction. b. discrimination.
   c. frequency. d. intensity of sound.
2. Which of the following is *not* part of the ossicles of the tympanic cavity?
   a. malleus b. cochlea
   c. incus d. stapes
3. Genetic deafness due to aplastic changes in osseous and membranous labyrinth is called
   a. congenital deafness. b. noise deafness.
   c. hysteric deafness. d. Mondini's deafness.
4. Thin, clear, amber fluid in the middle ear is indicative of
   a. serous otitis media. b. secretory otitis media.
   c. serous otitis media with hemotympanum. d. all of the above.
5. The helix is associated with
   a. external ear. b. inner ear.
   c. middle ear. d. none of the above.

Instructions: Break apart each term listed below, identify the medical term elements, and define the term.

Example: myringitis
      myring- = root = eardrum
      -itis = suffix = inflammation

cochleosacculotomy

cholesteatoma

otosclerosis

stapedectomy

tympanoplasty

vestibulocochlear

Instructions: Define the following terms.

Example: acoustic (G)—sound

auricle (L)	myringo- (L)	salpingo- (G)
cochlea (G)	ot-, oto- (G)	tympano- (G)

Instructions: Define the following abbreviations.

Example: AC = air conduction.

ENT	PTS	TDT
ETF	SISI	TTS

Instructions: Figure 15.1 in the text shows the major parts of the ear. For each line that extends from the figure below, provide the anatomic name of the site, as shown in the example.

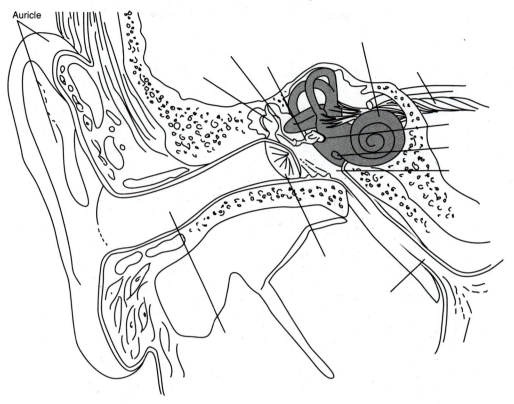

Auricle

16

Multisystem Disorders

INFECTIOUS DISEASES

ORIGIN OF TERMS

ameba- (G)—change
bacillus (L)—rod
coccus (G)—berry
gono- (G)—seed
helminth (G)—worm
lympho- (L)—lymph
myco- (G)—fungus
proto- (G)—first

pseudopod (G)—false foot
sapro- (G)—rotten
strepto- (G)—curved, twisted
tricho- (G)—hair
vecto (L)—carrier
virus (L)—poison
zoster (G)—girdle

PHONETIC PRONUNCIATION OF SELECTED TERMS

actinomycosis	ACK-tin-owe-my-COE′sis
erysipelas	ER-i-SIP′e-las
histoplasmosis	HIS-toe-plas-MOW′sis
infectious mononucleosis	in-FECK′shus MON-owe-NEW-kle-OWE′sis
rubella	rue-BEL′ah
rubeola	RUE-be-OWE′lah
trichinosis	TRICK-in-OWE′sis
variola	va-RI′owe-lah
viral hepatitis	VI′ral HEP-a-TIE′tis

GENERAL TERMS

acid-fast bacilli—organisms that resist acid-alcohol decolorization after they have been stained with a special dye (carbofuchsin). (91)

aerobes—organisms requiring oxygen for growth. (5)

agglutination—clumping of bacteria (or blood cells) after being mixed with antisera. (11)

allergen—substance capable of bringing about a hypersensitive state when introduced into the body.

allergy—state of hypersensitivity in which a person experiences certain symptoms when coming in contact with an allergen.

anaerobes—organisms capable of growing in the absence of atmospheric oxygen. (5)

antiseptic—substance that prevents bacterial growth.

antitoxin—immune serum that prevents the deleterious action of a toxin.

bacterium (pl. bacteria)—"little rod"; in general, any of the unicellular prokaryotic microorganisms that commonly multiply by cell division (fission) and whose cell is typically contained within a cell wall. Bacteria may be aerobic, anaerobic, phytic, parasitic, or pathogenic. (39)

blood culture—method of isolating the causative microorganisms in specific infectious diseases by placing blood withdrawn from a vein in a suitable culture media. (22, 91)

contagious—communicable.

culture medium—a milieu that promotes the growth of bacteria. (11, 91)

direct contact—spread of disease from person to person.

exudate—fluid or blood elements that have escaped into body cavities or tissues. (91)

fungus (pl. fungi)—a vegetable, unicellular organism that feeds on organic matter. (39)

gram-negative—pertaining to bacteria that do not retain Gram's stain (an iodine-crystal violet complex). (4)

gram-positive—pertaining to bacteria that retain Gram's stain after suitable decolorization. (4)

immunity—resistance to disease, either natural or acquired. (53)

inoculation—the process of introducing pathogenic organisms.

microorganism—plant or animal only recognized under microscopic vision. (91)

molds—plants belonging to a division of organisms known as fungi.

multisystem disorder—any disease with involvement of many systems; it need not have an immunologic basis. Examples are infections, connective tissue disorders, or metabolic diseases.

mycology—the study or science of fungi.

nosocomial infections—hospital-acquired infections; usually occur in patients who have defective host resistance or who receive cytotoxic drugs for malignancies or who have received organ transplants and are being treated with immunosuppressive therapy. Infective agents may be *Aspergillus*, *Candida*, *Nocardia*, *Pneumocystis carinii*, cytomegalovirus, and other pathogenic or opportunistic microorganisms. (39)

nosology—the science or study of disease classification.

nucleus—functional center of a cell.

opportunistic infection—pathogens that produce disease through some defect or group of defects in the ability of the host to defend against and destroy the potential invader. A number of normal flora, usually regarded as harmless in a specific location, may produce disease if introduced to another part of the body or if predisposing factors such as neoplasm, trauma, or immunosuppressive antibiotic therapy are present. *Candida* is an example of an opportunistic pathogen. Although part of the normal flora of the mouth, skin, vagina, and pharynx, when *Candida* is exposed to broad-spectrum antibiotic therapy or corticosteroid or other immunosuppressive chemotherapy, it may cause clinically significant local infection involving the mouth, skin, vagina, pharynx, or esophagus. In a patient who has an infected intravascular catheter or marked granulocytopenia, or in certain postopertive states, *Candida* may invade the bloodstream and produce disseminated systemic disease. (13, 91)

parasite—plant or animal that lives within or on another and derives nourishment from its host. Medical parasitology involves the study of parasites and their life cycle in humans, as well as pathogenic effect, prevention, and control. It deals with two major phyla: (See table 16.1.)

Metazoa—multicellular parasites; for example:

- *helminthic infection*—infestation by worms.
- *platyhelminthic infection*—infestation by flatworms (tapeworms or flukes).
- *polyhelminthism*—infestation by several species of worms.

TABLE 16.1	Laboratory Tests for Major Infectious Diseases

Major Viral Diseases

Diseases	Etiologic agents	Tests for diagnosis (91)
Acute respiratory disease Conjunctivitis Keratoconjunctivitis Pharyngitis	Adenovirus type 4, 7, and others type 3, and others type 3, 7, and 8 (68)	Virus isolation from throat and conjunctival swabs or washings Complement fixation Neutralization Hemaglutination inhibition
Common cold (Coryza)	Picornavirus Rhinovirus (10)	Virus isolation from nose and throat
Classic influenza	Orthomyxovirus influenza A, B, C (8)	Virus isolation from nasal swabs and throat washings Complement fixation Neutralization Hemagglutination inhibition

Laryngotracheitis
Bronchitis
Bronchiolitis
Pneumonitis
Croup
	Paramyxovirus
	Parainfluenza 1, 2, 3, 4 (26)
		Virus isolation from throat or
		    nasopharyngeal swab, wash,
		    or aspirate
		Hemagglutination inhibition
		Complement fixation
		Neutralization

Bronchitis
Bronchiolitis
Pneumonia
Coryza
	Respiratory syncytial virus (RSV) (26)	Virus isolation from nasopharyngeal
		    swab, aspirate, or wash
		Direct immunofluorescence with
		    RSV antiserum can be applied to
		    nasopharyngeal smears containing
		    exfoliated cells

Measles (rubeola)	Measles virus (26)	Virus isolation from blood and nasopharynx Hemagglutination inhibition Complement fixation Neutralization
German measles (rubella) Congenital rubella syndrome	Rubella virus (25, 26)	Virus isolation from cell culture ELISA* Hemagglutination inhibition Indirect immunofluoresence Virus isolation from throat, nasopharynx, urine, and blood
Mumps (epidemic parotitis)	Mumps virus (26)	Virus isolation from saliva, urine, and cerebrospinal fluid Complement fixation Hemagglutination inhibition Skin test antigen Hemadsorption

*ELISA indicates enzyme-linked immunosorbent assay; RIA indicates radioimmunoassay.

TABLE **16.1** (continued)

Major Viral Diseases

Diseases	Etiologic agents	Tests for diagnosis (91)
Herpangina Pleurodynia Aseptic meningitis Myocardiopathy Neonatal disease	Coxsackie A virus Coxsackie B virus (10)	Virus isolation from lesion, and from cerebrospinal fluid, rectal swabs, or throat swabs Neutralization Complement fixation

Poliomyelitis
  abortive
  nonparalytic
  paralytic
	Poliovirus types 1–3 (10)	Cytology of cerebrospinal fluid
		Virus isolation from throat and feces, rarely from cerebrospinal fluid
		Complement fixation
		Neutralization test

Acute hemorrhagic conjunctivitis (AHC) Meningitis Encephalitis	Enterovirus 70 (10) Enterovirus 71 (10)	Virus isolation in human cell culture Virus isolation from brain (postmortem)
Viral hepatitis A	Hepatitis A virus (HAV) (45, 48)	ELISA for IgM to HAV RIA for IgM to HAV Immune adherence hemagglutination Tissue from liver biopsy Liver function tests Serum alanine aminotransferase Serum aspartate transaminase
Viral hepatitis B Viral hepatitis Non-A, Non-B Post-transfusion hepatitis	Hepatitis B virus (HBV) (45, 48) Hepatitis C virus (HCV) (47, 48)	ELISA and RIA for HBsAg, HBsAb, HBcAB Serum alanine aminotransferase Serum aspartate transaminase Complement fixation Counterelectrophoresis Red cell agglutination (RCA) Serum alanine aminotransferase Serum aspartate transaminase RIA for antibodies to HCV
Herpes simplex Aphthous stomatitis Keratoconjunctivitis Meningoencephalitis	Herpesvirus Herpesvirus type 1 (25, 42, 62)	Virus isolation from herpetic lesions of skin, cornea, brain, throat, saliva, and feces
Genital herpes Neonatal herpes Varicella (chickenpox)	Herpesvirus type 2 (25, 43, 62) Varicella-zoster virus (VZV) (25, 42, 62)	Antibodies measured by neutralization, complement fixation, ELISA, RIA, or immunofluorescence tests Virus isolation from vesicular fluid of skin lesion Antibodies to varicella-zoster virus measured by complement fixation, neutralization, gel precipitation tests Indirect immunofluorescence to virus-induced membrane antigens tests

TABLE 16.1 **(continued)**

Major Viral Diseases

Diseases	Etiologic agents	Tests for diagnosis (91)
Cytomegalic inclusion disease	Cytomegalovirus (CMV) (25, 47, 62, 81)	Virus isolation from mouth, adenoids, urine, kidneys, liver, and peripheral leukocytes Detection of antibodies in human sera by ELISA, RIA, immunofluorescence, complement fixation, and neutralization tests DNA hybridization quantitative methods to identify virus in urine
Infectious mononucleois (glandular fever) Burkitt's lymphoma Nasopharyngeal carcinoma	Epstein-Barr virus (EPV) or EB herpesvirus (25, 42, 62)	Heterophil agglutination test Monospot test EBV-specific antibody test
Acquired immunodeficiency syndrome (AIDS)	Human immunodeficiency virus (HIV) (20, 33, 62)	Antibodies detected by ELISA, RIA, and immunofluorescence assay or by Western blot analysis and radio-immunoprecipitation (RIP) T4-T8 ratio

Major Rickettsial Diseases

Diseases	Etiologic agents	Tests for diagnosis (91)

Rickettsialpox	*Rickettsia akari* (25)	Serologic
		  Weil-Felix reaction
		  Complement fixation
		  Microimmunofluorescence
		  Microagglutination

Rocky Mountain spotted fever	*Rickettsia rickettsii* (12, 62)	Serologic (Same as for Rickettsialpox)
Endemic murine typhus Epidemic louse-borne typhus Brill-Zinsser disease Scrub typhus	*Rickettsia typhi* (12) *Rickettsia prowazekii* (12) *Rickettsia prowazekii* (12) *Rickettsia tsutsugamushi* (25)	Serologic (Same as for Rickettsialpox) Serologic (Same as for Rickettsialpox) Serologic (Same as for Rickettsialpox) Serologic (Same as for Rickettsialpox)

Q fever	*Coxiella burnetii* (12)	Serologic
		  Complement fixation
		  Microagglutination
		  Immunofluorescent antibody

Trench fever (quintan fever, shin bone fever, Volhynia fever, and His-Werner disease)	*Rochalimaea quintana* (25)
	Rochalimaea henselae
		Serologic
		  ELISA
		  Passive hemagglutination

Major Bacterial Diseases

Diseases	Etiologic agents	Tests for diagnosis (91)
Abscesses	*Staphylococcus aureus* (4, 29, 62)	Microscopic smears and cultures from infected lesions

TABLE **16.1**	(continued)

Major Bacterial Diseases

Diseases	Etiologic agents	Tests for diagnosis (91)
Bacterial endocarditis	*Streptococcus* (various kinds) (4, 62)	Microscopic Blood culture

Erysipelas
Puerperal fever
Sepsis
	Streptococcus pyogenes (4, 62, 87)	Microscopic
		    Smears and cultures obtained
		    from lesions

Pneumonia	*Streptococcus pneumoniae* (4, 47, 62, 88)	Microscopic
		    Capsule swelling (Quellung) reaction
		    Blood culture
		    Sputum smears

Gonococcal infections	*Neisseria gonorrhoeae* (gonococcus)
	    (34, 47, 62)
		Microscopic
		    Smears and cultures (Thayer-
		    Martin medium) from lesions

Enteric infections Genitourinary infections	*Enterobacteriaceae* *Escherichia (E. coli)* *Klebsiella-Enterobacter-Serratia* group *Proteus-Morganella-Providencia* group *Citrobacter* *Salmonella* *Shigellae* (38, 70)	Microscopic Smears and cultures

Meningitis	*Neisseria meningitidis*
	Haemophilus influenzae
	Streptococcus pneumonia (47, 62, 78)
		Microscopic
		    Culture of cerebrospinal fluid
		Quellung reaction with type-specific
		    serum helps with identification

Undulant fever (brucellosis)	*Brucella melitensis*
	Brucella abortus
	Brucella suis (4, 47)
		Serologic
		    Agglutination test for undulant
		    fever

Diphtheria	*Corynebacterium diphtheriae*
	    (Klebs-Löeffler bacillus) (4, 25, 32)
		Microscopic
		    Culture from throat or larynx
		Schick test (intradermal injection
		    of diluted diphtheria toxin)

Food poisoning (botulism)	*Clostridium botulinum* (4, 21)	Animal inoculation for toxin in suspected food

Whooping cough	*Bordetella pertussis* (4, 30, 62)	Microscopic
		    Culture on cough plate from
		    specimens from nasopharyngeal
		    swabs or cough droplets
		Direct fluorescent antibody (FA)
		    test is quite useful in detecting
		    B. pertussis after culture on solid
		    media

TABLE **16.1** (continued)

Major Bacterial Diseases

Diseases	Etiologic agents	Tests for diagnosis (91)

Legionnaires' disease	*Legionella pneumophilia* (4, 62, 94)	Serologic
		    Indirect fluorescent antibody (IFA)
		    Microagglutination (MA)
		    Direct fluorescent antibody
		    ELISA
		    Culture of organism

Leprosy (Hansen's disease)	*Mycobacterium leprae* (4)	Microscopic Smear and culture from cutaneous skin lesions, nodules, plaques, and ulcers Animal inoculation Lepromin test (skin reaction to extracts of M. *leprae*)

Tularemia	*Francisella tularensis* (4)	Serologic
		    Agglutination test
		    Animal inoculation
		    Skin test for tularemia

Tuberculosis, pulmonary and extrapulmonary	*Mycobacterium tuberculosis* (4, 35, 47)	Microscopic Smears and cultures from acid-fast bacilli from sputum, gastric and bronchial washings, drainage, and tuberculous lesions from organs Animal inoculation Tuberculin tests: Mantoux, Tine, and others Detection of antibodies by precipitation, complement fixation, passive hemagglutination, ELISA, and polymerase chain reaction (PCR) DNA amplification-based assays to identify mycobacterial DNA

Typhoid fever	*Salmonella typhi*
	Salmonella enteritidis
	    (bioserotype *paratyphi* A or B; only occasionally causes typhoid fever) (4)
		Microscopic
		    Culture from stool, urine, and blood
		Serologic
		    Widal's test

Parathyroid fever	*Salmonella paratyphi* A *Salmonella schottmuelleri* (*Salmonella paratyphi* B) *Salmonella hirschfeldii* (*Salmonella paratyphi* C) (4, 42)	Microscopic Culture from stool, and blood

Food infection
    Food products:
        egg
        cattle
        unpasteurized milk
        pig
	Salmonella enteritidis
	Salmonella dublin
	Salmonella choleraesuis (4, 42)
		Microscopic
		    Culture from stool, and blood

TABLE **16.1** **(continued)**

Major Mycotic Diseases

Diseases	Etiologic agents	Tests for diagnosis (91)

Actinomycosis	Actinomyces (*Actinomyces israelii*) (4, 23, 33)	Microscopic
		    Direct smears or cultures from
		      sinuses and sputum
		Animal inoculation
		Gel diffusion methods or
		    immunofluorescence can
		    differentiate A. *israelli* from other
		    Actinomycetes species

Blastomycosis	Blastomyces (*Blastomyces dermatitidis*) (4, 23, 33)	Microscopic
		    Direct smears and culture from
		      sputum, pus, exudates, urine,
		      and biopsies from lesions
		Animal inoculation
		Complement fixation
		Immunodiffusion test
		Sedimentation rate

Candidiasis	*Candida albicans* (and related species) (23, 33)	Microscopic
		    Direct smears and cultures from
		      skin, nail scrapings, and sputum,
		      and material from vagina
		Antigen detection by
		    immunodiffusion, precipitation,
		    counterimmunoelectrophoresis,
		    latex agglutination tests, and others

Coccidioidomycosis	*Coccidioides immitis* (22, 23, 33)	Microscopic
		    Direct smears or culture from
		      sputum, gastric content, pleural
		      fluid, and abscesses
		Animal inoculation
		Serologic
		Immunodiffusion, and latex
		    agglutination tests
		Skin test

Histoplasmosis	*Histoplasma capsulatum* (21, 33, 47)	Microscopic
		    Direct smears or cultures of bone
		      marrow and lymph nodes
		Animal inoculation
		Serologic
		Latex agglutination, immunodiffusion,
		    and complement fixation
		Skin tests: Tine and intradermal

Nocardiosis	*Nocardia asteroids*
	Nocardia brasiliensis (4)
		Microscopic
		    Cultures from sputum, pus, pleural
		      fluid, lung abscesses, sinus
		      drainage, spinal fluid, and biopsy
		      material

TABLE 16.1   (continued)

Major Spirochetal and Protozoal Diseases

Diseases	Etiologic agents	Tests for diagnosis (91)
Amebic dysentery	*Entamoeba histolytica* (22, 25, 46)	Microscopic 　Examination of fresh stools
Syphilis	*Treponema pallidum* (40, 47, 77)	Dark-field examination of scraping or 　fluid exudate from chancre Immunofluorescence microscopy for 　fluorescent spirochetes Nontreponemal antigen tests: 　Flocculation tests 　Venereal Disease Research 　　Laboratories (VDRL) 　Rapid plasma reagin (RPR) 　Complement fixation (CF) tests 　　(Wasserman, Kolmer) Treponemal antibody tests: 　Fluorescent treponemal 　　antibody absorption test 　*T. pallidum* immobilization test 　*T. pallidum* complement fixation test 　*T. pallidum* hemagglutination test
Leptospirosis	*Leptospira interrogans* serovars (serotypes) 　(40, 85)	Urine culture Blood culture Detection of genus-specific 　antibody using 　　counterimmunoelectrophoresis 　　and hemolytic assays Microscopic slide agglutination test
Lyme disease	*Borrelia burgdorferi* (transmitted by ixodid 　ticks, often by *Ixodes dammini*) 　(40, 85)	Specific immunoglobulin antibody 　titers Culture of *B. burgdorferi* (not often 　successful) Other elevated test values are reflected 　in serum glutamic-oxaloacetic 　transaminase (SGOT) and 　erythrocyte sedimentation rate
Giardiasis	*Giardia lamblia* (22, 24, 46)	Microscopic 　Identification of trophozoites 　and/or cysts in stool specimen Serologic 　Indirect immunofluorescence
Malaria	*Plasmodium vivax* *Plasmodium falciparum* *Plasmodium ovale* *Plasmodium malariae* (22, 46)	Microscopic 　Examination of blood smears
Pneumocystis pneumonia	*Pneumocystis carinii* (20, 21)	Puncture biopsy of lung

TABLE **16.1** (continued)

Major Spirochetal and Protozoal Diseases

Diseases	Etiologic agents	Tests for diagnosis (91)

Toxoplasmosis	*Toxoplasma gondii* (22, 46)	Microscopic
		    Smears and sections stained with
		    Giemsa's stain to detect organism
		Animal inoculation
		Serologic
		    Sabin-Feldman dye test
		    ELISA
		    Indirect fluorescent antibody test
		    Complement fixation test
		    Indirect hemagglutination test
		    Skin test

Major Helminthic Diseases

Diseases	Etiologic agents	Tests for diagnosis (91)
Ascariasis	Nematodes *Ascarius lumbricoides* (large intestinal roundworm) (22)	Stool specimen containing characteristic ova (eggs) Sputum occasionally containing larvae

Enterobiasis	*Enterobius vermicularis* (pinworm) (22)	Stool specimen containing adult
		    worms
		Microscopic
		    Pinworm ova smears

Filariasis in advanced stage: elephantiasis	*Brugia malayi, Brugia timori, Wuchereria bancrofti* (and other infective larvae) (22)	Day and night blood specimens for
		    identification of microfilariae
		    (motile larvae)
		Complement fixation test
		Skin test for microfilaria

Hookworm disease	*Ancylostoma duodenale*
	    (European hookworm)
	Necator americanus
	    (American hookworm) (22)
		Stool specimen containing
		    characteristic eggs, guaiac positive
		Microscopic
		    Fecal smears for eggs and larvae
		    detection

Onchocerciasis	*Onchocera volvulus* (filiarial roundworm)
	(22)
		Aspiration of nodules for detection
		    of eggs
		Excision of nodules for demonstrating
		    larvae and adult worms
		Microscopic
		    Skin shavings and conjunctival
		    snips
		Slit-lamp examination for ocular
		    onchocerciasis

Strongyloidiasis	*Strongyloides stercoralis* (threadworm)
	(22)
		Stool specimen containing larvae or
		    adult worms
		Duodenal aspiration if organism not
		    found in stool

TABLE 16.1 **(continued)**

Major Helminthic Diseases

Diseases	Etiologic agents	Tests for diagnosis (91)
Trichinelliasis Trichiniasis Trichinosis	*Trichinella spiralis* (Pork roundworm) (22)	Skin test Precipitation and complement fixation tests Muscle biopsy for encysted larvae
Trichuriasis Trichocephaliasis	*Trichuris trichiura* (whipworm) (22)	Stool specimen containing ova of whipworm Concentration by centrifugation if eggs not found in direct fecal smear
Echinococcosis Cystic hydatid disease Alveolar hydatid disease	Cestodes *Echinococcus granulosus* *Echinococcus multilocularis* (tapeworm) (22)	Microscopic Examination of cyst contents of hydatid tumor in liver or other organs Serologic Indirect hemagglutination test, complement fixation test, and immunoelectrophoresis
Fasciolopsiasis	Trematodes *Fasciolopsis buski* (large intestinal fluke) (10)	Stool specimen containing eggs and occasionally flukes Urine specimen containing eggs
Taenia infestation	*Diphyllobothrium latum* (fish tapeworm) *Taenia saginata* (beef tapeworm) *Taenia solium* (pork tapeworm) (51, 71)	Stool specimen containing eggs and parasites Stool specimen containing proglottids and eggs Stool specimen containing eggs and parasites
Schistosomiasis (Bilharziasis)	*Schistosoma haematobium* (vesical or urinary fluke) *Schistosoma japonicum* (intestinal fluke) *Schistosoma mansoni* (intestinal fluke) (22, 52)	Urine specimen containing eggs Cystoscopic biopsy Stool or urine specimen containing eggs Rectal biopsy Stool or urine specimen containing eggs Rectal biopsy

Protozoa—unicellular parasites; for example:
- *Leishmania donovani*—etiologic agent of visceral leishmaniasis or kala-azar, causing splenomegaly, bleeding, edema, and emaciation.
- *Trypanosoma*—protozoal parasites causing sleeping sickness in Africa and Chagas' disease in America. The latter, affecting primarily children, is characterized by intermittent parasitemia, fever, acute lymphadenitis, and eyelid edema. (22, 39)

pathogenic—disease producing.
putrefaction—decomposition of organic material.
pyogenic—pus forming.

saprophyte—an organism that grows on dead matter.

sensitivity (drug related)—ability of infective organism to respond to the bacteriostatic or bacteriocidal action of an antibiotic or other agent. (91)

susceptibility—ability to acquire an infection following exposure to pathogenic organisms. (91)

taxonomy—the classification of organisms of the plant or animal kingdom, including the following categories: phylum, class, order, family, genus, species, and variety. The scientific names of organisms are binomial, composed of a genus, which is capitalized, and a species, which is not.

    genus (pl. *genera*)—the division between family and species.

    species—the division between genus and variety. (91)

virus (pl. **viruses**)—infectious agent of protein-coated nucleic acid, either ribonucleic acid (RNA) or deoxyribonucleic acid (DNA), and submicroscopic size. Viruses replicate only in living cells, being parasites at the genetic level. (25)

yeast—unicellular organism that usually reproduces by budding.

INFECTIONS CAUSED BY VARIOUS AGENTS

TERMS PERTAINING TO INFECTIONS CAUSED BY VIRUSES

adenoviral infections—serotypes of DNA-bearing adenovirus, transmitted by person-to-person contact and capable of latency in lymphoid tissue. These viruses are nondeveloped viruses that contain double stranded DNA as their genetic material. There are over 40 of these serotypes. Adenoviruses may cause epidemic outbreaks of:

    febrile pharyngitis—inflammation of pharynx with exudate, enlarged cervical lymph nodes, and fever.

    keratoconjunctivitis, epidemic—serious eye infection with corneal infiltrates and follicular conjunctival lesions. Associated symptoms that may be present include headache and swelling of regional lymph nodes.

    pharyngoconjunctival fever—severe type of pharyngitis associated with acute follicular conjunctivitis, usually lasting 5 days.

    pneumonia, adenoviral—highly fatal bronchopneumonia in infants; accompanied by sore throat, cough, prostration, and high fever. (68)

arboviral infections—arthropod-borne viral infections that are usually transmitted to human beings by the bite of a blood-sucking (hemophagous) insect. The viruses multiply in susceptible arthropods without producing the disease. The arthropod vector acquires a lifelong infection by ingesting vertebrate blood from a viremic host and maintains a complex vertebrate-arthropod-vertebrate cycle. (49)

arbovirus encephalitides—various types of encephalitis, each having a specific host and viral vector according to its geographic distribution. Those prevalent in the Americas are:

    eastern equine encephalitis (EEE)—occurs in eastern and southern United States.

    St. Louis encephalitis (SLE)—occurs in nearly all the United States.

    Venezuelan equine encephalitis (VEE)—occurs in Central and South America and southern United States.

    western equine encephalitis (WEE)—occurs chiefly in Canada and western United States. The encephalitogenic arbovirus attacks the neural tissues of the central nervous system, especially those of the brain, the cerebral cortex, meninges, cerebellum, neurons, and supportive structures. (36, 49)

chickenpox, varicella—acute varicella-zoster virus infection, characterized by sudden onset, fever, and skin eruption. It is highly infectious. (42)

cytomegalovirus (CMV) infections—common viral infection occurring congenitally or in acquired forms in the newborn, child, or adult, with or without symptoms, as local or systemic disorders. Infected cells are oversized and contain intranuclear and cytoplasmic inclusion bodies. Diagnosis is made serologically or by obtaining a culture of white blood cells or urine.

acute acquired cytomegalovirus disease (CMV infectious mononucleosis)—clinical picture similar to that of infectious mononucleosis (Epstein-Barr virus). Symptoms include fever, malaise, muscle and joint pains, enlarged liver, and generalized lymphadenopathy. This disorder can occur spontaneously or after transfusions of fresh blood during surgery (postperfusion syndrome).

congenital cytomegalic inclusion disease—infection developing in utero, affects primarily premature infants. In the fatal form of the disease, viral foci infiltrate the neonate's lungs, kidneys, liver, spleen, pancreas, thymus, adenoids, parotid glands, and other organs.

cytomegalic inclusion disease in the immunosuppressed host—system disorder in immunocompromised persons whereby the cytomegalovirus can cause a severe opportunistic pneumonia. Persons who have acquired immune deficiency syndrome (AIDS) often are susceptible to severe infections with cytomegalovirus, including retinitis, enterocolitis, and pneumonitis. Other persons who may develop cytomegalovirus pneumonitis or hepatitis and occasionally generalized disease, include those with malignancies or immunologic defects or those receiving immunosuppressive therapy for organ transplantation. (42)

German measles, rubella—mildly contagious disease with catarrhal symptoms and a rash resembling measles. (26)

herpes simplex, herpes febrilis, fever blisters—acute infectious condition of the skin or oral or genital mucous membranes, marked by vesicular lesions that may become secondarily infected. After a primary infection, latency usually is established and may lead to recurrences. (42)

herpes zoster—recurrent varicella-zoster virus infection affecting primarily one or more dorsal root ganglia or extramedullary cranial nerve ganglia. It is characterized by a vesicular eruption in the affected ganglia. Contact with vesicular fluid can cause chickenpox in a nonimmune person. (42)

infectious mononucleosis—usually a benign infection caused by Epstein-Barr virus. It exhibits a characteristic lymphocytosis and irregular clinical pattern. Glandular swelling (lymph node enlargement), throat symptoms, fever, and splenomegaly are common manifestations. The disease occurs chiefly in adolescents and young adults. (42)

influenza—acute febrile disease caused by influenza virus A, B, or C. It is generally characterized by prostration, muscle ache, joint pains, and respiratory symptoms. It may occur in epidemic or even pandemic form. (8)

measles, rubeola—highly communicable disease; clinically manifested by Koplik's spots of the buccal mucosa (small, irregular, bright red spots on the buccal and lingual mucosa, with a very small, bluish-white speck in the center of each); a rash; and catarrhal symptoms. (26)

mumps, infectious parotitis—virus disease of the salivary glands, which tend to involve glandular tissues; inflammation of the lacrimal glands, thymus, thyroid, breast, ovaries, and testes. (26)

rabies, hydrophobia—acute encephalitis that causes paralysis, delirium, convulsions, and death. (6)

Reye's syndrome, fatty liver with encephalopathy—acute disorder found exclusively in children under 15 years of age. It is characterized by vomiting, signs of progressive central nervous system damage, signs of hepatic injury, and hypoglycemia. The exact cause of the disorder is unknown, although viral and toxic agents, especially salicylates (e.g., aspirin) have been implicated. However, this illness may also occur in the absence of exposure to salicylates. (41)

smallpox, variola—communicable disease characterized by a rash that changes from macules, papules, vesicles, and pustules to scabs. Vigorous control efforts by the World Health Organization appear to have eradicated this disease. (17)

viral hepatitis, acute—disease associated with jaundice and liver damage resulting from hepatic cell necrosis, followed by hepatomegaly, splenomegaly, and virema. Several forms, immunologically distinct but clinically similar, are recognized:

hepatitis A—incubation period of approximately 4 weeks. The infective agent is hepatitis A virus (HAV), transmitted by the fecal-oral route. Hepatitis A is enhanced by poor personal hygiene and overcrowded living conditions. Other outbreaks have been traced to contaminated food, water, milk, and shellfish.

hepatitis B—incubation period 50 to 80 days. The infective agent is hepatitis B virus (HBV). Transmission can occur via a percutaneous (through the skin) route, or a nonpercutaneous route, such as oral ingestion, sexual contact, and perinatal transmission. A circulating antigen, HBsAg, is present in the early phase of hepatitis B and in chronic carriers.

hepatitis D (delta agent)—the delta agent hepatitis D virus (HDV) is a defective RNA virus that coinfects and requires the presence and helper function of HBV for its infection of the host cell. Because the delta agent relies on HBV for its expression and replication, the duration of the delta infection is determined by the duration of (and cannot outlast) the HBV infection.

non-A and non-B hepatitis (NANBH)—clinically similar to hepatitis B. This entity represents the majority of transfusion-associated hepatitis cases in the United States. NANBH is a term to describe viral hepatitis not due to either HAV or HBV. Two identified forms of NANBH are:

- epidemic type transmitted enterically, the **hepatitis E** form, identified in India, Asia, Africa, and Central America. Hepatitis E resembles hepatitis A in its enteric mode of transmission. This type of disorder occurs after water supplies are contaminated (e.g., after monsoon flooding); however, some isolated cases have occurred. Although a few cases have been found in the United States, it is not known if the hepatitis E form occurs outside of the areas mentioned above.
- parenterally transmitted type caused by the **hepatitis C** form. **Hepatitis C** is a cloned genome of NANBH agent, designated the hepatitis C virus (HCV). HCV was the first virus discovered by molecular cloning without direct use of biologic or biophysical methods. Infection with HCV has been indentified as the major cause of posttransfusion non-A, non-B hepatitis. Chronic liver disease occurs in about 50% to 100% of patients with acute HCV infection, and cirrhosis develops in about 20% of these patients. HCV genotypes 1a and 1b are the most commonly found genotypes in patients with chronic HCV in the United States. Multiple HCV genotypes have been identified worldwide. HCV genotype 1b may be associated with more severe liver disease and may have a higher risk for the development of hepatocellular carcinoma. (18, 45, 48, 95)

viral hepatitis, chronic active—long-term infectious disorder of diverse etiologies, characterized by progressive destruction of liver cells and fibrotic changes followed by terminal cirrhosis. Liver biopsy is necessary to establish the diagnosis. (18, 45, 48)

TERMS PERTAINING TO INFECTIONS CAUSED BY CHLAMYDIAE

chlamydiae (sing. **chlamydia**)—large group of nonmotile intracellular parasites closely related to gram-negative bacteria that lack mechanisms for production of metabolic energy and cannot synthesize ATP (adenosine triphosphate). It is this defect that restricts them to an intracellular parasitic existence. Chlamydiae are divided into two species:

Chlamydia psittaci—species that produces diffuse intracytoplasmic inclusions that lack glycogen. It is inhibited by sulfonamides.

Chlamydia trachomatis—species that produces compact intracytoplasmic inclusions that contain glycogen. It is inhibited by sulfonamides. (4, 84)

psittacosis, ornithosis, parrot fever—infectious disease characterized by variable symptoms, mild to acute fever, headache, lung involvement, cough, delirium, prostration, and even death. Psittacosis is a disease of birds that may be transmitted to humans. In humans, the agent *Chlamydia psittaci* produces a wide range of clinical manifestations ranging from very mild infection to severe pneumonia and sepsis with a high mortality. Tetracycline is the drug of choice to inhibit growth or extension of the disease. (4)

trachoma and inclusion conjunctivitis (TRIC)—chronic infectious diseases of the conjunctiva that may be associated with infections of the urogenital tract. The etiologic agents, chlamydiae, are transmitted by human contact or flies. If left untreated, TRIC infections persist for years and produce corneal scarring and blindness. (84)

TERMS PERTAINING TO INFECTIONS CAUSED BY SEXUALLY TRANSMITTED DISEASES

acquired immunodeficiency syndrome (AIDS)—the causative agent is a retrovirus called human immunodeficiency virus (HIV). The virus is transmitted through intimate sexual contact, or through parenteral exposue to infected blood by transfusion, or needle sharing by intravenous drug users, and perinatal exposure. The HIV infection appears to ultimately result in the almost total collapse of the body's cell-mediated immune system, leaving the person susceptible to malignancies (Kaposi's sarcoma) and opportunistic infections (*Pneumocystis carinii* pneumonia), against which the body is unable to defend itself. (See pp. 423–24 for further AIDS information.) (7, 14, 20, 39, 50, 61, 63)

gonorrhea—sexually transmitted infection that usually begins in the urethra and attacks the genital mucosa membrane. The infection also may affect the conjunctiva and joints. The etiologic agent is *Neisseria gonorrhoeae* (gonococcus). The primary symptoms in males during acute infection include dysuria, urethritis, and a purulent discharge. Symptoms in females include endocervical infection, which extends to the urethra and vagina. Mucopurulent discharge is present and the infection may progress to the uterine tubes. A serious complication of gonorrhea in women is pelvic inflammatory disease (PID). (4, 34)

granuloma inguinale—a progressive granulomatous disease of the skin and mucosa. The causative agent is an intracellular gram-negative bacillus, *Calymmatobacterium granulomatis* (also called Donovan's bodies, when identified within the histiocytes of a typical lesion). It is transmitted mainly through sexual contact. The primary lesion of granuloma inguinale presents as a red granulated ulcer tissue, which readily bleeds on contact. The primary lesion involves the genital and/or perianal areas and may be single or multiple. (4)

herpes simplex genital infection—herpes simplex virus type 2 (HSV 2) is the causative agent of herpes simplex genital infection in both men and women. Infection is contracted from a person who is shedding viral particles at the time of intercourse. Vaginal or penile pain and/or urethral lesions occur in most cases. (25)

lymphogranuloma venereum (LGV)—*Chlamydia trachomatis* serotypes L-1, L-2, and L-3 can cause this sexually transmitted disease. The primary lesion of LGV may appear as a papule, small ulcer, or as a herpes-type lesion. The most frequent symptom is progressive lymphadenopathy. In its advanced course, the disease exhibits systemic manifestations such as fever, skin rashes, gastric upset, back pain, headache, and meningeal irritation. (4)

syphilis—*Treponema pallidum* is the causative agent of syphilis. Sexual contact accounts for almost all syphilitic infections. Syphilis is an infectious, relapsing disease characterized by a primary lesion or hard chancre. It is followed by a secondary skin eruption with typical reddish-brown, coppery spots; periods of latency; and later, lesions in the central nervous system and cardiovascular systems. A transient nephrotic syndrome also may occur in some cases. (40)

trichomoniasis—venereal infection caused by a flagellate protozoan, *Trichomonas vaginalis*. In the female, trichomoniasis usually is manifested by a persistent vaginitis. The characteristic finding on vaginal examination is the strawberry appearance of the vaginal mucosa and the portio vaginalis of the cervix due to the marked congestion and petechial hemorrhages. Patients may experience vulvovaginitis, urethritis, cystitis, cervicitis, and infections in the Skene's ducts and the Bartholin's gland. (76, 77)

urethritis, salpingitis, and pelvic inflammatory diseases—these diseases represent common sexually transmitted diseases, which may be caused by *Chlamydia trachomatis*. (4, 24, 77)

vulvovaginitis candidiasis—the causative agents of this vulvovaginal infection can be either *Candida albicans* or *Candida glabrata*. A frequent clinical finding is vulvar pruritus. Vaginal discharge is usually minimal and may resemble cottage cheese or have a watery consistency. Also present may be vaginal soreness, dyspareunia, dysuria, and erythema and swelling of the labia and vulva. (13, 76)

TERMS PERTAINING TO INFECTIONS CAUSED BY PATHOGENS OF THE FAMILY LEGIONELLACEAE

Legionellosis—the term used to describe infections caused by bacteria of the genus *Legionella*. The most prominent of these diseases is a pneumonia called *legionnaires' disease*. Either as part of legionnaires' disease or separate from it, the legionellae may cause infections elsewhere in the body, often in the form of abscesses. Twenty-nine *Legionella* species have been isolated: about half of these from patients with legionnaires' disease and half only from the environment. The species that most commonly cause the disease are *L. pneumophila*, *L. micdadei*, *L. bozemanii*, *L. dumoffi*, and *L. longbeachae*.

> *legionnaires' disease*—presents as a febrile systemic illness with pneumonia occurring in sporadic and epidemic outbreaks and in mild and fulminant form. The main etiologic agent is *Legionella pneumophila*. Legionnaires' disease is acquired by inhaling aerosolized water containing *Legionella* organisms. The contaminated aerosols are derived from humidifiers, shower heads, respiratory therapy equipment, industrial cooling water, and cooling towers. In mild cases, malaise, chills, fever, cough, sputum, diarrhea, and joint and muscle pain gradually subside. In the fulminant type, these symptoms rapidly increase in severity. A widespread pneumonia develops and is associated with shaking, chills, hypoxia, pleuritic pain, delirium, a deepening coma, and death. (15, 94)

TERMS PERTAINING TO INFECTIONS CAUSED BY MYCOPLASMAS

mycoplasmas—pathogenic bacteria without cell walls that may cause infections of the respiratory and urogenital tract.

> *Mycoplasma pneumoniae* causes pneumonia.
> *Ureaplasma urealyticum*, formerly called T-strain mycoplasma, has been associated with nongonococcal urethritis in men.
> *Mycoplasma hominis* has been associated with postpartum fever in women and has been found with other bacteria in fallopian tube infections. (69)

mycoplasmal pneumonia, primary atypical pneumonia—a pneumonitis that may range from asymptomatic to serious lung disease. It is clinically manifested by an insidious onset, headache, malaise, fever, severe cough, and sore throat. *Mycoplasma pneumoniae* is the causative agent. (69)

TERMS PERTAINING TO INFECTIONS CAUSED BY RICKETTSIAE

spotted fever group:

> *rickettsialpox*—benign, self-limited disease that develops from *Rickettsia akari* and is transmitted from the house mouse to human beings by mites. Its clinical manifestations are a papulovesicular skin eruption, chills, fever, headache, and aching muscles.
> *Rocky Mountain spotted fever*—acute febrile disease caused by *Rickettsia rickettsii* infection, and usually transmitted to human beings by infected ticks and clinically manifested by an abrupt onset with chills, high fever, delirium, excruciating headache, and atypical rash on extremities and trunk. Shock and kidney failure may occur in the severely ill person. (12)

typhus group:

endemic murine typhus—acute fever caused by *Rickettsia typhi* infection, transmitted to human beings by fleas and clinically manifested by a rash, muscle pain, and fever lasting about 2 weeks.

epidemic louse-borne typhus—acute febrile illness due to *Rickettsia prowazekii*, transmitted to human beings by body lice (*Pediculus humanus corporis*).

recrudescent typhus, Brill-Zinsser disease—recurrent epidemic typhus; develops years after recovery from epidemic typhus, has a similar rash, similar liver, kidney, and neural manifestations, and the same etiologic agent, *Rickettsia prowazekii*. (12, 25)

other rickettsial groups:

Q fever (Q for query)—severe febrile illness caused by *Coxiella burnetii* living in ticks. They infect dairy cattle, sheep, goats, or parturient cats. Human transmission results from inhalation of dust contaminated with rickettsiae from dried feces, urine, or milk or from aerosols in slaughterhouses. Headache, fever, chills, malaise, anorexia, and aching muscles are common symptoms. The disease occurs worldwide. (12, 25)

trench fever, quintan fever, shin bone fever, His-Werner disease, Volhynia fever—illness caused by *Rochalimaea quintana* and *Rochalimaea henselae*; found extracellularly in the gut of lice and transmitted to human beings by infected feces rubbed on broken skin or conjunctiva. A patient who has trench fever may be either afebrile or severely debilitated by the disease, which in its acute form, may cause headache, fever, malaise, bone pain, muscle soreness, and macular skin eruption. Relapses are common. (25)

TERMS RELATING TO INFECTIONS CAUSED BY COCCI (SEE FIG. 16.1.)

erysipelas—acute febrile, inflammatory disease marked by localized skin lesions that tend to migrate. The infection is caused by the *Streptococcus pyogenes*. (4)

furunculosis—condition resulting from boils, generally caused by *Staphylococcus aureus*. (4)

gonorrhea—sexually transmitted infection that usually begins in the urethra and attacks the genital mucous membrane. The infection also may affect the conjunctiva and joints. The etiologic agent is *Neisseria gonorrhoeae*. (4, 34)

meningitis—inflammation of meninges. The epidemic form is caused by *Neisseria meningitidis*. (4)

staphylococcal food intoxication—food poisoning caused by staphylococci and associated with more or less violent and abrupt onset of nausea, vomiting, and prostration. Severe diarrhea may occur. (4)

toxic shock syndrome (TSS)—severe multisystem illness with sudden onset of high fever, vomiting, diarrhea, and myalgia. An erythematous (sunburnlike) rash is noted during the acute phase of the illness. Hypotension with cardiac and renal failure occur in the most severe cases. TSS frequently occurs within 4 to 5 days of the onset of menses in young women who use tampons. *Staphylococcus aureus* has been found in the vagina and on tampons. Most *Staphylococcus aureus* strains isolated from individuals with toxic shock syndrome produce a toxin called toxic shock syndrome toxin 1 (TSST-1). This toxin is associated with fever, shock, and multisystem involvement. Prolonged use of certain brands of hyperabsorbent tampons linked with the capacity of these materials to bind magnesium have increased the growth of intravaginal *S. aureus* and TSST-1 production. Removal of the hyperabsorbent tampons from the market and public education concerning this disorder have decreased the number of TSS cases reported in the United States. (4)

TERMS PERTAINING TO INFECTIONS CAUSED BY BACILLI

bacillary dysentery, shigellosis—acute infection marked by diarrhea, tenesmus, fever, and in severe cases, mucus and blood in the stool. The condition tends to be serious in infants and debilitated elderly persons. The disease is caused by various species of *Shigella*. (80)

Figure 16.1   Selected microorganisms.

Bacilli are rod-shaped or club-shaped organisms.

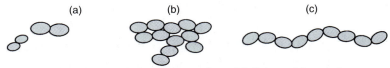

(a)   (b)   (c)

Cocci are spherical or oval organisms. (a) diplococci (in pairs);
(b) staphylococci (in cluster); (c) streptococci (in chains).

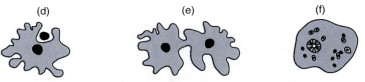

(d)   (e)   (f)

Amebae are unicellular animal organisms, capable of changing form by
throwing out footlike processes (pseudopodia), which help them
to move about and obtain nourishment. (d) Ameba; (e) ameba
dividing; (f) cyst of *Entamoeba histolytica*.

Salmonella or shigella are simple, non-spore-forming rods, often
joined end-to-end.

Treponema pallidum are coiled, virulent organisms containing 8 to 14 spirals.

diphtheria—acute infection, generally associated with fever and the formation of a grayish membrane in the throat, from which the Klebs-Löeffler bacillus (*Corynebacterium diphtheriae*) can be cultured. (4, 32)

food poisoning—disease characterized by an abrupt onset of gastrointestinal symptoms caused by food intoxication or infection.

botulism—afebrile condition, marked by weakness, constipation, headache, and forms of paralysis; may be fatal. The intoxication results from the botulinus bacillus (*Clostridium botulinum*) toxin. (4, 21)

Salmonella infection, salmonellosis—condition causing typhoid and paratyphoid fevers, bacteremia, and entercolitis. (81)

septic shock—manifested by inadequate tissue perfusion, following bacteremia, most often with gram-negative enteric bacilli. Frequent etiologic organisms include *Escherichia coli, Klebsiella-Enterobacter, Proteus, Pseudomonas,* and *Serratia.* The circulatory insufficiency is caused by diffuse cell and tissue injury and the pooling of blood in microcirculation. Hypotension, oliguria, tachycardia, and tachypnea occur in most cases. Respiratory failure is the primary cause of death in patients with septic shock. Septic shock also may be associated with gram-positive infections, and these usually result from *Staphylococcus, Pneumococcus,* and *Streptococcus.* (38, 39, 70)

undulant fever, brucellosis—general infection characterized by intermittent or continuous fever, headache, chills, and profuse perspiration. The etiologic agents are three species of *Brucella.* (31)

TERMS PERTAINING TO INFECTIONS CAUSED BY ACTINOMYCETES

actinomycetes—heterogenous group of filamentous bacteria related to the corynebacteria and mycobacteria. Actinomycetes superficially resemble fungi. They usually grow as gram-positive, branching organisms that fragment into bacterialike pieces. Most are free living in soil. Some are acid-fast. The anaerobic species are part of the mouth's normal flora. (23)

actinomycosis—chronic disease characterized by multiple abscesses that form draining sinuses. It is caused by *Actinomyces israelii* and related anaerobic filamentous bacteria. Lesions occur on the face, neck, lungs, and abdomen. Pelvic actinomycosis has occurred in women wearing intrauterine contraceptive devices (IUDs). (4, 23)

nocardiosis—infection chiefly caused by *Nocardia asteroides* and *Nocardia brasiliensis,* either localized in the lungs or disseminated through multiple systems: skin, subcutaneous tissue, brain, and other organs. Disorders caused by these organisms may be seen in patients immunosuppressed by leukemia, lymphoma, AIDS, and drugs. (4, 23)

TERMS PERTAINING TO INFECTIONS CAUSED BY FUNGI AND YEASTS

aspergillosis—infection with *Aspergillus* that attacks the lungs, skin, external ear, nasal sinuses, meninges, and bones. Severe infection is found in immunosuppressed patients. (23, 33)

blastomycosis—mycotic infection that follows inhalation of the conidia of *Blastomyces dermatitidis.* The infection may be limited to either subcutaneous tissue or disseminated throughout the lungs or multiple body systems. The most commonly affected organs are the lungs, skin, bones, and male genitourinary system. The disease is prevalent in the southeastern United States and in areas surrounding the Great Lakes; it also is found in Africa, Mexico, and in Central and South America. (23, 33)

candidiasis—represents a general term for diseases produced by *Candida* species. It may be an acute or subacute fungus infection that causes thrush, glossitis, vaginitis, onychia, and pneumonitis. Candidiasis occurs worldwide. (23, 33)

coccidioidomycosis—caused by *Coccidioides immitis,* a dimorphic fungus. It may occur as a primary, acute infection of the lungs, lymph nodes, or skin, which has a favorable prognosis or a generalized infection includes invasion of the meninges, which can be fatal. Patients with AIDS are at increased risk of coccidioidal dissemination. It is prevalent in the southwestern United States. (23, 33)

cryptococcosis—often presents as a noncontagious opportunistic mycosis characterized by acute or chronic pulmonary infection, or hematogenous dissemination, usually with meningitis. The mycotic infection forms multiple abscesses and lesions of skin, subcutaneous tissue, lungs, and meninges. The etiologic agent is *Cryptococcus neoformans.* The disease occurs worldwide. (33, 82)

histoplasmosis—mycotic disease caused by *Histoplasma capsulatum,* which produces benign pulmonary lesions. Histoplasmosis occurs worldwide and currently is considered the most common endemic respiratory mycosis in the United States. (23, 33)

mycosis (pl. **mycoses**)—any fungus disease.

TERMS PERTAINING TO INFECTIONS CAUSED BY SPIROCHETES

leptospirosis—acute infection by *Leptospira interrogans* or by one of the *Leptospira* serovars (serotypes). Transmission to human beings is by the ingestion of food that has been contaminated by the excretions of a reservoir animal (dog, rat, cattle, or swine). Clinical manifestations include sudden onset of fever, chills, abdominal and muscular pains, intense headache, a palpable liver, jaundice, conjunctival redness, purpura, erythema of skin, and, in severe cases, meningeal irritation. (93)

Lyme disease—an inflammatory arthropathy transmitted by small ixodid ticks, often *Ixodes dammini*, which carry the infectious spirochete organism called *Borrelia burgdorferi*. The first cluster of this disease was reported in Lyme, Connecticut, the town after which the disease is named. Lyme disease is widespread, and has been reported in 43 states, as well as throughout Europe and Asia. The symptoms include headache, stiff neck, fever, myalgia, arthralgia, lymphadenopathy, and an expanding red rash with a pale center that appears and then vanishes. The worst consequences of the disorder are the secondary symptoms that can develop after the initial infection, such as arthritis, meningitis, and occasional cardiac problems. Early treatment with penicillin or tetracycline usually results in prompt recovery and prevents complications from developing. (9)

rat-bite fever—there are two kinds, classified according to etiologic agent:

Streptobacillus moniliformis—organism causing rat-bite fever (Haverhill fever). High fever, chills, headache, vomiting, joint pain, and rash occur.

Spirillum minor—a gram-negative, spiral-shaped rod that causes one form of rat-bite fever (sodoku). The organism is inoculated into humans through the bite of a rat. The disease is characterized by a reddish brown rash spreading from the bite, accompanied by relapsing fever and local lymphadenopathy. (40)

relapsing fever—acute spirochetal infection by *Borrelia recurrentis*, transmitted to human beings by insect vectors (lice) or infected insects (ticks). Relapses of fever occur abruptly every week or two and gradually decrease in severity. The fever is accompanied by nausea and vomiting, joint and muscle pains, tachycardia, and psychic, neurologic, and hemorrhagic manifestations. Relapsing fever is endemic in the western United States and in many other countries. (9)

Weil's disease—severe leptospirosis with hepatic or renal involvement or both, hemorrhages, fever, and muscle pain. (93)

TERMS PERTAINING TO INFECTIONS CAUSED BY PROTOZOA

African trypanosomiasis, sleeping sickness—protozoal disease transmitted to human beings by the bite of infected tsetse flies. Its clinical manifestations are irregular fever, enlarged spleen and lymph glands, rapid pulse, and damage to the myocardium and central nervous system. (22, 62)

American trypanosomiasis, Chagas' disease—infection by *Trypanosoma cruzi* spread to the human host by blood-sucking insects. Usual clinical signs are unilateral eyelid and facial edema; intermittent fever; a chagoma (small painful, hard skin nodule); Romaña's sign (conjunctivitis); an enlarged liver; and myocardial and cerebral involvement. (22, 46)

amebic dysentery, amebiasis—parasitic infection marked by diarrhea, pain, and fever. It is caused by the protozoan *Entamoeba histolytica*. (22, 46) (See fig. 16.1.)

giardiasis—infectious disease caused by the intestinal parasite *Giardia lamblia* that produces a wide range of clinical symptoms, from gastrointestinal discomfort to acute or chronic diarrhea, which sometimes progresses to steatorrhea and malabsorption syndrome. Giardiasis is present in all climates. It is spread by two routes: waterborne infection (e.g., community water supplies) and direct person-to-person transmission. (22, 46)

leishmaniasis—infection by genus *Leishmania* and several species related to their geographic distribution. Transmission may result from bites by infected sandflies. Three forms are recognized:

cutaneous leishmaniasis—lesions may be ulcerating, moist, dry, or diffuse.

mucocutaneous leishmaniasis—manifests naso-oral lesions and erosions affecting the nasal septum. (46)

visceral leishmaniasis, kala-azar—fever is irregular and chronic; enlargement of liver and spleen is progressive and complicated by anemia, leukopenia, stomatitis, and dysentery.

malaria—disease caused by protozoa of the genus *Plasmodium*, which are parasitic in the red blood cells. It is manifested by fever, chills, splenomegaly, and anemia, and is transmitted to human beings by the bites of infected mosquitoes of the genus *Anopheles*. Some types of malaria include:

vivax malaria—caused by *Plasmodium vivax*.

ovale malaria—caused by *Plasmodium ovale*.

falciparum malaria—caused by *Plasmodium falciparum*. (22, 46)

pneumocystis pneumonia—lung infection caused by *Pneumocystis carinii*, which produces an interstitial plasma cell pneumonitis. Outbreaks may occur in nurseries, particularly among premature and marasmic infants. Adults receiving cytotoxic or corticosteroid therapy over a prolonged period are likely to develop this disease. This disease is the most common opportunistic infection in AIDS patients. (83)

toxoplasmosis—protozoal infection by *Toxoplasma gondii*. Types include:

congenital—the prenatal infection from the mother; if active after birth, it may be manifested in the neonate by fever, convulsions, enlarged liver and spleen, lymphocytosis, muscle and nerve involvement, microcephaly, and mental retardation.

acquired—infection is usually mild, with lymphadenopathy, malaise, fever, and rash present. If it is severe, encephalitis, pneumonia, retinochoroiditis, and myocarditis may develop, especially in the immunologically incompetent host.

Toxoplasmosis of the central nervous system is seen often in AIDS patients. (22, 46)

TERMS PERTAINING TO INFECTIONS CAUSED BY HELMINTHIC PARASITES

cestodes—tapeworms.

hydatid cyst disease—hydatid cyst of the liver or lung caused by larvae of *Echinococcus granulosus*. This small tapeworm is found sporadically in Alaska, Canada, California, and Utah. Human beings are usually infected hand-to-mouth by a host dog that harbors eggs in its fur. Ingested eggs deliver larvae that penetrate the intestinal wall and are carried by the circulating blood to the liver and sometimes to the lungs, where they form a hydatid cyst.

other intestinal and tissue cestode infections:

- *Diphyllobothrium latum*—the largest parasite that infects humans; may be up to 10 centimeters long and is found in many parts of the world. Infection is acquired by ingesting parasite cysts found in the tissues of smoked or uncooked freshwater fish.

- *Taenia saginata*—beef tapeworm infection that occurs in most countries with cattle husbandry. Humans are infected by eating undercooked beef containing viable cysticerci, which are larval forms of a tapeworm consisting of a single scolex enclosed in a bladderlike cyst.

- *Taenia solium*—pork tapeworm present in many countries. *T. solium* causes human infection in two forms. Persons who consume undercooked pork containing parasite cysts will develop intestinal *T. solium* tapeworms. Persons who consume parasite eggs in contaminated food may develop parasite cysts within the tissues of the body. This condition is called cysticercosis. Some types are:

  - *muscle cysticercosis*—larval invasion of muscles is followed by calcification of cysticerci after prolonged infestation, as confirmed by radiographic studies.

- *neurocysticercosis, cerebral cysticercosis*—invasion of the brain that results in epilepsy, mental decline, headache, cerebral edema, hydrocephalus, nerve palsies, and personality disorders.
- *ocular cysticercosis*—larval invasion of the eye resulting in a syndrome that presents as eye pain, scotomata, and decreasing vision due to iridocyclitis, clouding of the vitreous, and retina detachment. (22, 51)

nematodes—roundworms.

ascariasis—human infestation with the giant intestinal roundworm, *Ascaris lumbricoides*. Larvae of the roundworm may severely damage the lungs, causing an *Ascaris* pneumonitis prevalent in children. Adult ascarids may be expelled in vomitus or feces. Infection is common in Africa, Asia, and Latin America. (22, 71)

enterobiasis, pinworm infection—an intestinal infection of humans caused by *Enterobius vermicularis*. The gravid (pregnant) female migrates from the lower intestine to lay her eggs on the perianal skin, where they cause intense perianal itching (pruritus). The infection is acquired primarily by direct hand-to-mouth transmission from the perianal area. Spread within family and children's groups occurs readily. (71)

filariasis—filarial roundworm infection transmitted to human beings by the bite of certain mosquitoes that are the hosts of infective larvae. These larvae grow into adult worms near or in lymph nodes of the human host. The adults release numerous motile larvae, the microfilariae, which usually circulate in the blood during the night. In advanced filariasis, obstruction of the lymph flow leads to elephantiasis, lymphedema, lymphadenitis, lymphangitis, blindness, and dermatitis. (22, 71)

hookworm disease—infection by *Necator americanus*, the American hookworm of the southern states; it is 1 centimeter long. Its head curves backward and attaches to the intestinal mucosa. It is transmitted through direct contact of the skin with soil that has been contaminated with feces. During the invasion of the exposed skin by the larvae, an erythematous maculopapular skin rash, and edema with severe pruritus may occur. The most common site of lesions is around the feet, especially between the toes. This condition has been termed ground itch. Tarry, viscous stools associated with poor digestion, malnutrition, anemia, and moderate heart failure suggest heavy intestinal infection. (22, 71)

onchocerciasis—disease caused by *Onchocerca volvulus*. Humans are infected when the female blackfly *Simulium* deposits infective larvae while biting. Inflammation occurs in subcutaneous tissue, and pruritic papules and nodules form in response to the adult worm proteins. Microfilariae migrate through the subcutaneous tissue, ultimately concentrating in the eyes. There they cause lesions that lead to blindness. The disease is called river blindness because the blackflies develop in rivers and people who live along the rivers are affected. This disease is prominent in Africa and Central America. (22, 71)

strongyloidiasis—threadworm infection. *Strongyloides stercoralis* causes strongyloidiasis. The disease is characterized by a high degree of toxemia, urticaria, and prolonged mucous diarrhea, which is indicative of intestinal invasion. Strongyloidiasis occurs primarily in the tropics, especially in Southeast Asia. In the United States, Strongyloides is endemic in the southeastern states. (71)

trichiniasis, trichinosis—infection acquired by the ingesting the encysted larvae of *Trichinella spiralis* in poorly cooked pork. (71)

trichuriasis—whipworm infection producing serious toxic reactions in the host, such as marked emaciation, anemia, diarrhea, and bloody stools. (70)

trematodes—flukes.

fasciolopsiasis—infection with large intestinal fluke by eating uncooked infected water plants. The flukes may cause severe cramping pain, nausea, anorexia, diarrhea, and finally edema, ascites, cachexia, and death.

schistosomiasis, bilharziasis—chronic worm infection. Schistosomes are blood flukes that parasitize the venous channels of the human host. Infection is transmitted via freshwater snails. Humans may be infected by one of five species:

- *Schistosoma haematobium* (found in the Middle East and Asia).
- *Schistosoma mansoni* (widespread in Africa, the Arabian peninsula, and northeastern South America).
- *Schistosoma japonicum* (found in China, the Philippines, and Indonesia).
- *Schistosoma intercalatum* (found in Central Africa).
- *Schistosoma mekongi* (found in southeast Asia).

In the life cycle involving humans, the adult worms live in terminal venules of the bowel or bladder. Eggs may be eliminated in feces and urine or travel to the liver, provoking periportal fibrosis, and portal hypertension. Continuing embolization of eggs to the lungs may result in endarteritis, pulmonary hypertension, and cor pulmonale.

- *acute schistosomiasis*—2 to 6 weeks after exposure the infected person experiences abrupt onset of abdominal pain, weight loss, headache, malaise, chills, fever, myalgia, diarrhea, dry cough, hepatomegaly, and eosinophilia. Occurs most often with *Schistosoma japonicum* infection.
- *chronic schistosomiasis*—begins 6 months to 3 or 4 years after infection, and occurs as diarrhea, abdominal pain, bloody stools, hepatomegaly or hepatosplenomegaly, and bleeding esophageal varices (*Schistosoma mansoni* or *Schistosoma japonicum* infection); or terminal hematuria, urinary frequency, and urethral and bladder pain (*Schistosoma haematobium infection*). (22, 35, 69, 71)

TERMS PERTAINING TO SELECTIVE MULTISYSTEM DISEASES

cystic fibrosis—a hereditary genetic multisystem disease that follows an autosomal recessive pattern of transmission. It is characterized primarily by chronic obstructive pulmonary disease, pancreatic insufficiency, and increased sweat. The gene for cystic fibrosis is located on the long arm of chromosome 7. A genetic defect that causes cystic fibrosis apparently cripples the bacteria-fighting ability of cells lining the lungs, contributing to the tendency of people with the disease to get respiratory infections. The cystic fibrosis gene causes the lungs to lose the ability to regulate the flow of sodium and chloride in the airway. This leads to a buildup of thick mucus that can trap bacteria and cause infection. In addition to the presence of the mucus, the epithelial cells lining the airway lack a normal response against bacteria. Among the most serious manifestations of cystic fibrosis are chronic pulmonary infections with the bacterium *Pseudomonas aeruginosa*. The analysis of sweat for the presence of increased concentrations of chloride and sodium is an important part of the diagnosis of cystic fibrosis. Quantitative pilocarpine iontophoresis remains the standard criterion for diagnosing cystic fibrosis. In children, sodium and chloride concentrations exceeding 60 mEq per liter are considered diagnostic of cystic fibrosis; in adults, the level is 70 mEq per liter. The use of cDNA probes has produced fairly rapid and accurate assessment of the cystic fibrosis patient's genetic makup. The average life span of a cystic fibrosis patient is approximately 29 years. Research continues in gene therapy applications for cystic fibrosis. Cystic fibrosis may include a variety of clinical conditions:

abnormally raised levels of sweat electrolytes—causing salt depletion and cardiac collapse in hot weather.

chronic pulmonary disease—often leads to fatal complications. Most patients experience chronic progressive respiratory disease. The mucus and the infections cause inflammation in the lungs; over time, the lung tissue loses its elasticity, and its tiny air sacs become increasingly unable to extract oxygen from the air.

meconium ileus—causes intestinal obstruction in the newborn.

pancreatic insufficiency—enzyme deficiency leads to maldigestion of protein and fat, which produces bulky, foul-smelling stools. (3, 15, 18, 73, 90)

fever of unknown origin—persistent elevated body temperature, unexplained by serologic and bacteriologic studies or other diagnostic measures. (89)

Kawasaki disease, mucocutaneous lymph node syndrome—febrile multisystem disorder of undetermined cause. It is clinically manifested by prolonged fever, cracked lips, conjunctivitis, pharyngitis, strawberry tongue, red rash and edema of extremities with desquamation of hands and feet, lymphadenopathy, and in some cases angiitis of the coronary arteries. (37)

sarcoidosis—systematic granulomatous disease of undetermined etiology and pathogenesis. The sites affected most often include the mediastinal and peripheral lymph nodes, lungs, liver, spleen, skin, eyes, phalangeal bones, and parotid glands. (75)

IMMUNOLOGIC DISEASES

ORIGIN OF TERMS

auto- (G)—self
cyt- cyto- (G)—cell
histio-, histo- (G)—tissue, web

lysis (G)—dissolution, breaking down
phylaxis (G)—protection, guarding
-phoresis (G)—transmission, breaking down

PHONETIC PRONUNCIATION OF SELECTED TERMS

agammaglobulinemia — a-GAM-a-glob-you-li-NEE′me-ah
angioimmunoblastic — AN-gee-owe-IM-you-no-BLAS′tick
lymphadenopathy — LIM-fad-i-NOP′ah-the
hemolytic anemia — HE-mo-LIT′ick a-NEE′me-ah
macroglobulinemia — MACK-row-GLOB-you-lin-E′me-ah
myeloma — mile-LOW′mah

GENERAL TERMS AND TESTS

anaphylaxis—excessive hypersensitivity to foreign protein or other substance, clinically manifested by edema of the larynx, hypoxia, respiratory distress, hypotension, and vascular collapse. (65)

antibodies—specialized proteins or immunoglobulins formed in response to an antigen. (55, 72)

antibody labeling with fluorescein—histochemical technique for identifying antigen and antibody within tissues.

> *direct immunofluorescent staining*—sensitive serologic test in which the specific antibody is labeled with fluorescein and the fluorescing antigen-antibody complex is viewed in the tissues.

> *indirect immunofluorescent method*—procedure in which fluorescein-labeled antihuman globulin is employed in the detection of unlabeled antibody in human tissues. Since plasma cells show marked fluorescence, they are thought to be antibody-producing cells. Examples: immunofluorescent skin test in systemic lupus erythematosus and rheumatoid factor by indirect immunofluorescence. (1, 91)

antigens—substances that will cause the body to form antibodies. (44, 49, 55, 59)

antinuclear antibodies (ANA), antinuclear factor (ANF)—serum antibodies to cellular components, including:

> *autoantibodies*—antibodies formed by the patient against his or her own nuclear components, such as red-cell antigens of the blood. Autoantibodies are elicited by a person's own antigens.

> *non-organ-specific antibodies*—antibodies found in connective tissue diseases. The most characteristic finding in almost all patients with active lupus erythematosus is antinuclear antibodies directed against deoxyribonucleoprotein (DNP).

> *organ-specific antibodies*—antinuclear antibodies present in pernicious anemia, ulcerative colitis, and others. (21, 66, 72)

antinuclear antibody (ANA) determination—test performed by indirect fluorescent microscopy as a two-stage antigen-antibody reaction. Negative results show antinuclear antibody titer between 1:20 or less, and positive results indicate antinuclear antibody titer between 1:320 or over, which is strongly suggestive of systemic lupus erythematosus (SLE). (1, 66, 91)

autoimmunization—production of antibodies or other immunologic responses to antigens in a person without any artificial intervention. (72, 91)

cytopathic effect (of viruses)—biologic changes produced by the multiplication of viruses in cell culture. (19)

cytotoxicity—destruction of cells of autoantibodies, as seen in acquired hemolytic anemia, and other diseases. (54)

fluorescein—fluorescent dye used for diagnostic purposes.

histocompatibility—tissue compatibility between a recipient and donor based on immunologic identity or similarity of tissues; necessary for successful transplantation. (58)

hypersensitivity—exaggerated sensitivity to an infective, chemical, or other agent, such as an extreme allergic reaction to a foreign protein. Some types include:

> *immediate type hypersensitivity*—occurring within 1 to 30 minutes, such as anaphylactic shock. (92)
>
> *cell-mediated, delayed type hypersensitivity*—developing gradually within 48 to 72 hours or longer, such as a tuberculin reaction. This type of inflammatory reaction is induced by T-cell-mononuclear clear-cell accumulation of regulatory and effector T-cells and macrophages, and not by antibody alone. (19, 28, 53, 56, 57, 60)
>
> *subacute delayed type, Arthus reaction*—developing within 4 to 10 hours and characterized by a marked infiltration of small vessels, with polymorphonuclear leukocytes, local edema, and bleeding without thrombus formation. (45, 59)

immune response—formation of antibodies due to a specific stimulus. (86)

immunohematology—branch of hematology dealing with antigen-antibody reactions and their effects on the blood. (91)

immunoelectrophoresis—procedure employed to separate and identify multiple protein components. In the test, use is made of physiochemical and immunologic specificity. (1, 59, 91)

immunogen—one of a group of substances capable of stimulating an immune response or initiating a certain degree of active immunity under favorable conditions. Its effect may be detrimental or beneficial. (39)

immunogenicity—the ability of an immunogen to evoke an immune response, or the ability of an antigen to stimulate antibody formation. Immunogenicity is the same as antigenicity. (1)

immunoglobulins (Igs)—antibodies capable of reacting specifically with the antigen that caused their formation. They are similar in structure but diverse antigenically. Molecules of immunoglobulins are composed of:

> *heavy chains (H chains)*—large polypeptide chains. The major classes of antibody (isotypes) are defined by the heavy chain, the genes for which map to human chromosome 14q32. Each of the five classes of immunoglobulins are antigenetically distinct:
>
> - γ in IgG—immunoglobulin G
> - α in IgA—immunoglobulin A
> - μ in IgM—immunoglobulin M
> - δ in IgD—immunoglobulin D
> - ε in IgE—immunoglobulin E
>
> Molecular weights are 50,000 to 70,000 daltons.
>
> *light (L) chains*—small polypeptide chains, either of the kappa (κ) or lambda (λ) type, and are encoded on chromosomes 2 and 22 respectively. Molecular weight is 25,000 daltons. (1, 40, 55, 72)

immunoglobulin concentration—the amount of serum protein components determined by immunoelectrophoresis for establishing the presence or absence of elevated or depressed immunoglobulin levels. Thus, an exaggerated susceptibility to infection or antibody deficiency may be detected. (11, 91)

immunology—the medical science concerned primarily with immunity or resistance to disease in the human being. In its practical aspects it deals with methods of diagnosing or preventing disease or influencing its course by serotherapy and vaccination. (1)

immunopathology—the study diseases resulting from antigen-antibody reactions or alterations produced by immunologic responses. (1, 91)

immunosuppressive therapy—treatment instituted to suppress all immune responses and thus prevent the rejection of a graft. (1)

lymphocytes—white blood cells originating in lymphoid tissue and capable of responding to immunologic stimulation. This includes any of the mononuclear, nonphagocytic leukocytes found in the blood, lymph, and lymphoid tissues. Lymphocytes are divided into two classes: B lymphocytes, which are responsible for humoral immunity, and T lymphocytes, which are responsible for cellular immunity.

> *B lymphocytes*—account for about 20% of lymphocytes in the circulating blood. They live for a short time. When stimulated by antigen, a process that requires the assistance of helper T cells and macrophages, B cells are capable of proliferating, differentiating, and maturing into plasma cells.
>
> *T lymphocytes*—account for about 65% to 80% of lymphocytes in the circulating blood. They are long-lived. T cells have few immunoglobulin molecules and are thymus-dependent lymphocytes. T cells are primarily responsible for cell-mediated immunity. T cells develop from lymphoid stem cells that migrate from the bone marrow to the thymus and differentiate due to the action of the thymic hormones (thymopoietin and thymosin). Cytotoxic T lmyphocytes (CTLs) are differentiated T cells that can recognize and bring destruction to target cells carrying specific antigens that are recognized by their antigen receptors. These cells are also called killer cells or killer T cells. (53, 79, 91)

rejection phenomenon—reaction to a graft based on the formation of antibodies directed against the donated tissue or organ. (92)

transplantation immunity—immune responses to transplanting organs, depending on the histocompatibility of the type of graft.

> *allograft, homograft*—tissue or organ from one individual is transferred to another individual of the same species.
>
> *autograft*—tissue or organ is transplanted from one part of the body to another in the same person.
>
> *isograft*—tissue or organ is transplanted from one identical twin to another. Histocompatibility exists in its most complete form.
>
> *xenograft, heterograft*—tissue or organ from donor from one species is implanted in recipient from another species. Grafts between species are subject to intense medical research. (26, 91)

DIAGNOSTIC TERMS

acquired immune deficiency syndrome (AIDS)—an ultimately fatal disease first described in the United States in 1981. The disease is thought to have originated in central Africa. However, AIDS is a global disorder and most every country has reported cases. In 1984, the human immunodeficiency virus (HIV) was established as the etiologic agent of AIDS. Sexual contact is the major mode of HIV transmission. HIV has been transmitted by whole blood plasma, cellular components, and clotting factors, but not from other products produced in the United States from blood. HIV is transmitted by parenteral (injection) exposure to contaminated injection equipment, including needles. Infected mothers can transmit the virus to their infants perinatally (as early as the first and second trimesters of pregnancy). The virus can be transmitted from mother to infant via breast feeding. Despite the fact that the majority of cases have occurred among homosexual or bisexual men, the rate of new cases of AIDS now is rising among intravenous drug users. This trend has led to an increase in the number of people who have acquired AIDS through heterosexual contact, since intravenous drug users can infect their sexual partners. The number of pediatric cases of AIDS also is inceasing. The majority of infants are born of mothers who were either intravenous drug users themselves or the sexual partners of intravenous drug users. Approximately 11% of infants with AIDS were recipients of contaminated blood transfusions. HIV infection presents an occupational risk for health care workers. Workers may be exposed to the virus through penetrating injuries or through mucosal splash incidents involving large amounts of blood, for example, major surgical procedures.

The human immunodeficiency virus attacks T lymphocytes and severely damages the immune system. The HIV infection appears to ultimately result in the almost total collapse of the body's cell-mediated immune system, leaving the patient susceptible to malignancies (e.g., Kaposi's sarcoma) and opportunistic infections (e.g., *Pneumocystis carinii* pneumonia) against which the body is unable to defend itself. The presence of antibodies to AIDS retrovirus is helpful for screening blood donors but is not diagnostic of AIDS. Antibodies may be detected by enzyme-linked immunosorbent assay (ELISA). Other alternative tests include immunofluorescence assay, radioimmunoprecipitation assay, and the Western blot analysis. A positive test in a serum sample should be confirmed by a repeat alternative test method before notifying the serum donor. (7, 14, 20, 39, 50, 61, 63)

AIDS-related complex (ARC)—presence of such conditions as generalized lymphadenopathy, unexplained fever, weight loss, hematologic abnormalities (thrombocytopenia, anemia, and neutropenia), and neurologic abnormalities in a person with HIV infection but without the clinical picture of full-blown AIDS. (1, 20, 39)

angioimmunoblastic lymphadenopathy (AIL)—newly recognized systemic disorder with widespread involvement of peripheral and deep lymph nodes by movable and soft lesions that are 2 or 3 centimeters in diameter. The syndrome is marked clinically by an acute onset of chills, fever, diaphoresis, polyarthralgia, anorexia, edema, ascites, and vasculitis; it occurs primarily in the elderly. About 60% of affected patients die as a result of severe infection and immunologic incompetence. (27)

autoimmune diseases—characterized by production of either antibodies that react with host tissue or immune effector T cells that are autoreactive. Autoantibodies may arise in some cases by a normal T-cell and B-cell response activated by foreign substances that contain antigens, especially polysaccharides that cross-react with similar polysaccharides in body tissues. Laboratory tests for the detection of autoantibodies in serum and other biological fluids may be performed by using immunohistochemical techniques, such as immunofluorescence and enzyme-labeled techniques, or by serologic techniques, such as complement fixation, hemagglutination, latex particle aggregation, immunodiffusion, radioimmunoassay (RIA), and enzyme-linked immunosorbent assay (ELISA). Disorders associated with the autoimmune event tend to be distributed under organ-specific diseases or non-organ-specific diseases. The organ-specific diseases are characterized by antibodies directed to a single organ and the presence of inflammatory lesions within that single organ (e.g., Hashimoto's thyroiditis) or the autoantibodies are directed against multiple organs and the inflammatory lesions are widely dispersed (e.g., in systemic lupus erythematosus). Organs usually affected in organ-specific disease include thyroid, stomach, pancreas, and adrenal gland. In non-organ-specific diseases, circulating immune complexes deposit systemically, thereby giving rise to an extensive inflammatory process. Organs usually affected in non-organ-specific diseases include the kidneys, nervous tissue, skin, joints, and muscles. (87)

autoimmune hemolytic anemia—clinical syndrome of uncompensated hemolytic anemia caused by aberrant immune response initiated by a host and directed against the host's normal red cell antigens.

secondary autoimmune hemolytic anemia—hemolytic anemia characterized by the presence of autoantibodies and a coexisting disease that constitutes the basic ailment; for example, anemia caused by chronic infection or neoplasm. (1, 81)

heavy-chain diseases—disorders demonstrating a typical heavy-chain immunoglobulin fragment in urine, serum, or both.

alpha (α) heavy-chain disease—lymphocyte dyscrasia usually associated with malignant lymphoma of the intestine resulting in nutritional malabsorption. The diagnosis is based on the detection of an abnormal protein in the urine and serum that reacts with antiserums to alpha chains.

gamma (γ) heavy-chain disease—disorder primarily seen in the elderly, clinically manifested by weight loss, weakness, enlarged liver, recurrent infections, involvement of lymph glands, lymphocytosis, anemia, and platelet deficiency. (1, 81)

immunologic deficiency states—disorders reflecting defective cellular immunity, decreased antibody production, or both, resulting in increased susceptibility to infection.

Bruton's agammaglobulinemia—severe familial X-linked deficiency of all classes of immunoglobulins and absence of plasma cells. (1)

DiGeorge's syndrome—occurs because of failure of embryogenesis of the third and fourth pharyngeal pouches, resulting in aplasia of the parathyroid and thymus glands. The syndrome is an example of pure T-cell functional deficiency with intact B-cell function. (1, 2)

severe combined immunodeficiency (SCID)—syndrome caused by marked lymphopenia of both T cells and B cells, causing severe functional impairment of both humoral and cell-mediated immunity. This immunologic defect is related to deficiency of adenosine deaminase (ADA), an enzyme active in purine metabolism. This disorder is usually congenital, but may be inherited either as an X-linked or autosomal recessive defect, or may present sporadically. Severe fungal, bacterial, and viral infections may also occur. (1)

Wiskott-Aldrich syndrome—severe immunodeficiency disease of a familial type, characterized by eczema, low platelet count, and frequent infections and associated with abnormal immunoglobulins, lymphopenia, delayed hypersensitivity, and impaired immune response. (1, 2)

plasma cell and lymphocyte dyscrasias—disorders manifesting uncontrolled proliferation of cells usually active in antibody synthesis and homogenous immunoglobulin synthesis. Typical protein abnormalities in serum and urine confirm the diagnosis.

macroglobulinemia, Waldenström's macroglobulinemia—dyscrasia, including several clinical disorders, in which the common denominator is the presence of monoclonal macroglobulin formed by cells involved in immunoglobulin M (IgM) synthesis. Clinical features are anemia, bleeding, lymph gland involvement, and enlarged spleen and liver.

multiple myeloma—severe plasma cell dyscrasia associated with decreased antibody synthesis and low immunoglobulin levels resulting in recurrent infections. There is considerable infiltration of the bone marrow by neoplastic plasma cells, which proliferate in advanced disease, causing osteoporosis, typical punched-out skeletal lesions, and pathologic fractures, especially of the ribs and vertebrae. Renal disease and anemia are usually present. Multiple myeloma runs a progressive course, extending over one or more decades. (64)

DISEASES OF CONNECTIVE TISSUE

ORIGIN OF TERMS
arachno- (G)—spider
colla (G)—glue
dactylo- (G)—digit (finger/toes)
erythema (G)—redness
lupus (L)—wolf, meaning destructive

myo- (G)—muscle
peri- (G)—around
poly- (G)—many
sclero- (G)—hard

PHONETIC PRONUNCIATION OF SELECTED TERMS
arachnodactyly
dermatomyositis
polyarteritis
scleroderma

a-RACK-no-DACK′ti-le
DER-mah-toe-MY-owe-SI′tis
POL-i-AR-ter-I′tis
SKLE-row-DER′mah

ANATOMIC TERMS (42, 91)
collagen—a substance present between the fibers of connective tissue throughout the body.
connective tissue—a variety of tissues composed of widely spaced cells between which intercellular material is deposited. This intercellular substance offers the distinguishing mark of the specific connective tissue; for example, mineral salts are located in the interspaces of bone and are responsible for its hardness, whereas for blood the intercellular substance is liquid. Other variations of connective tissue are areolar, adipose, fibrous, cartilage, and lymphoid tissues.

DIAGNOSTIC TERMS
CREST syndrome—presence and coexistence of calcinosis, Raynaud's phenomenon, esophageal hypomotility, sclerodactyly, and telangiectasia. Initially, this disorder was considered a benign form of progressive systemic sclerosis. Pulmonary hypertension may occur during any phase of the syndrome's course. (67, 74)
dermatomyositis and polymyositis—inflammatory skeletal muscle disorder of unknown origin that may be accompanied by inflammation at other sites, such as the joints, lungs, and heart. **Dermatomyositis** is the term used for the disorder when those features are accompanied by inflammatory manifestations in the skin. The two most common rashes that occur are a lilac colored discoloration of the eyelids, usually accompanied by periorbital edema and Gottron's papules (dark red, raised, and scaly lesions). Inflamed joints, muscle weakness, and pulmonary dysfunction due to interstitial lung disease also may be present. **Polymyositis** is the term applied when the condition spares the skin. (74)
Marfan's syndrome, arachnodactyly—hereditary disorder of a connective tissue element resulting in skeletal, ocular, and cardiovascular abnormalities. Clinical features are spidery fingers; disproportionately long limbs; funnel chest; lax, redundant ligaments; and ectopia lentis (displaced lens) with impaired vision. Hemodynamic stress on the media of the aorta may lead to dissecting aortic aneurysm. Other disorders may be present. (44)
mixed connective tissue disease (MCTD)—clinical syndrome with overlapping features of systemic lupus erythematosus (SLE), scleroderma, polymyositis, and rheumatoid arthritis. Also present are high titers of antibodies directed against the ribonuclease-sensitive nuclear ribonucleoprotein (RNP) component of extractable nuclear antigen (ENA). (29)
polyarteritis, periarteritis nodosa—systemic disease characterized by nodules along the course of the muscular arteries. (29, 37)
scleroderma, progressive systemic sclerosis—chronic disease causing a leathery induration of the skin, progressive atrophy, and pigmentation. Systemic involvement of the mucous membranes and the musculoskeletal, vascular, and digestive systems may lead to death. Raynaud's phenomenon occurs in about 90% of these patients. (29, 67, 74)
Sjögren's syndrome—lymphadenopathy with hypergammaglobulinemia complicated by benign or malignant lymphoma. This chronic autoimmune disease is marked by dryness of the

mouth, caused by diminished secretion of saliva, resulting in difficult swallowing, eating, and speaking; dryness of the eyes, with smarting, burning, and itching; and numerous systemic involvements of the pancreas, pleura, pericardium, kidneys, and other organs. (16, 29) **systemic lupus erythematosus (SLE)**—collagenous inflammatory multisystem disorder that affects the synovial and serous membranes and vascular system. Clinical manifestations of this disorder include fever, anorexia, malaise, weight loss, joint symptoms, conjunctivitis, and rash over areas exposed to sunlight. Normocytic, normochromic anemia as well as leukopenia and lymphopenia also may be present. SLE is recognized by a typical butterfly lesion on the bridge of the nose and on the cheeks. (24, 43)

ABBREVIATIONS

TESTS

CF—complement fixation

CIE—counterimmunoelectrophoresis

ELISA—enzyme-linked immunosorbent assay

FTA-ABS—fluorescent treponemal antibody absorption

HI—hemagglutination inhibition

MHA-TP—microhemagglutination for *Treponema pallidum*

NT—neutralization test

RCA—red cell agglutination

RIA—radioimmunoassay

TPI—*Treponema pallidum* immobilization

VDRL—Venereal Disease Research Laboratories

ORAL READING PRACTICE

HERPES ZOSTER

Herpes zoster, or shingles, is an infectious disease caused by the zoster virus. It is characterized by vesicular lesions that follow the course of a **peripheral nerve** in a bandlike fashion. Before the eruption, the patient may experience pain for several days without other symptoms. Once the **erythema** and **vesicles** appear in a typical **zoniform** distribution, the diagnosis is readily made. In the beginning, the eruption exhibits slightly **edematous,** fairly well-defined **erythematous,** oval, or round areas on which vesicles form in groups. Generally sensory changes along the path of the affected **neutral zones** are associated with the eruption.

Pain precedes, accompanies, and follows the appearance of the skin lesion. It varies in duration and intensity from slight, brief **hyperesthesia** to **paroxysmal** attacks or persistent, excruciating **neuralgia.** Similar to other nerve root involvements, the pain is especially agonizing at night and is intensified by motion. In rare cases it has led to drug addiction and even suicide. **Paresthesia** of the skin may be brought on by touching the affected area or it may develop spontaneously. In addition, the patient may develop tender enlarged lymph nodes, rheumatic pains, and general malaise. Although the characteristic feature of the disease is the skin eruption, herpes zoster is essentially an inflammation of one or more posterior root ganglia. The rash is confined to the **dermal segment,** supplied by the sensory nerve arising from the involved **posterior (sensory) root ganglion.** The **neurotropic virus** destroys the ganglion cells and fibers. These changes result in a degeneration of the corresponding peripheral nerve.

Evidence now available suggests that herpes zoster virus is identical to the varicella virus that produces chickenpox; the varicella virus enters the body and may be incorporated within the **genome** of many cells, but it does not express itself until later in life as herpes zoster. The factors leading to the activation of herpes are unknown, but are thought to involve immune mechanisms, since the virus becomes active during immunosuppression. Also, the current evidence points to immunologic activity declining during the aging process, which may contribute to the onset of herpes zoster.

One of the most painful forms of herpes is **herpes zoster ophthalmicus,** caused by a viral infection of the **trigeminal nerve.** This may lead to **corneal ulceration, keratitis, iritis, conjunctivitis,** and **edema** of the **eyelids. Herpes zoster oticus** results from an inflammation of the **vestibulocochlear nerve** and is associated with deafness, **vertigo, tinnitus,** and severe pain. (25, 42, 62)

REVIEW GUIDE

Instructions: For each condition listed below, provide the corresponding etiologic agent(s).

Example: toxoplasmosis *toxoplasma gondii*

acquired immunodeficiency syndrome

blastomycosis

candidiasis

chickenpox

diphtheria

gas gangrene

genital herpes

Hansen's disease

histoplasmosis

Legionnaires' disease

meningococcal meningitis

rickettsialpox

rubeola

syphilis

trichuriasis

Instructions: Define the following terms and abbreviations.

Example: ameba (G)—change

gono- (G)

lympho- (L

myco-(G)

bacillus (L)

colla (G)

virus (L)

cyto- (G)

vector (L)

sapro- (G)

strepto- (G)

tricho- (G)

coccus (G)

sclero- (G)

pseudopod (G)

-lysis (G)

zoster (G)

P A R T

II

C H A P T E R

17

Selected Terms Pertaining to Oncology

ORIGIN OF TERMS

astro- (G)—star
carcino- (G)—cancer
histio-, histo- (G)—web, tissue
kerato- (G)—horny tissue, cornea
-oma (G)—tumor

onco- (G)—tumor, swelling, mass
papilla, (pl. *papillae*) (L)—small nipple-shaped
    projection
-plasia (G)—mold, formation
sarco- (G)—flesh

GENERAL TERMS

adjuvant—assisting. Chemotherapy given as an aid to surgery or to radiation in an attempt to reduce or eliminate the cancer cell burden. (1, 20, 32)

antineoplastic drugs—standard agents serve as the basic regimen in the treatment of neoplastic disease. This type of anticancer treatment involves drug metabolism, method of drug administration, drug stability, drug interactions, and drug incompatibilities and side effects. Common side effects may include pain, nausea, cerebral edema, hypercalcemia, and others. (11)

benign—mild, not malignant.

cancer—malignant disease characterized by uncontrolled cell growth.

carcinolysis—destruction of cancer cells.

carcinoma—malignant neoplasm that arises from epithelial tissue.

carcinoma in situ (CIS)—true malignant tumor of squamous or glandular epithelium in which no invasion of underlying or adjacent structures has occurred. Lesions may remain in situ (position) for an indefinite period before they become invasive. (25)

clone—population of cells derived from a single cell. This term is commonly used when a number of cells have the same abnormal chromosome complement. Gross colony morphology differs significantly from tumor type to tumor type, similar to differences in bacterial colony formation. (60)

deoxyribonucleic acid (DNA)—genetic substance within the nucleus of a cell responsible for controlling cell division and synthesis. (34, 60)

encapsulated—encased in a capsule, usually seen with benign neoplasms.

fractionation—radiation is administered to the patient in small repeated doses rather than using large doses.

implantation—spontaneous passage of tumor cells to a new site with subsequent growth.

lymphocyte—mononuclear leukocyte whose nucleus contains dense chromatin and a pale-blue-staining cytoplasm. Two major subclassifications of lymphocytes are:

T lymphocytes (T cells)—acted on by the thymus and concerned with the functional status of cell-mediated immune systems.

B lymphocytes (B cells)—become antibody-producing cells and are concerned with the functional status of the humoral immune system.

The combined activities of T cells and B cells provide immunity against infectious agents and oncogenic agents. For example, the cancer modalities (radiotherapy, surgery, chemotherapy) may affect the immune system, causing either a transitory or prolonged suppression. (60)

malignant—virulent; pertaining to the invasive, metastatic properties of a new growth. (33)

medullary—marrowlike; term used in oncology in reference to soft tumors, such as carcinomas of the breast or thyroid.

modality—refers to type of treatment regimen; for example, chemotherapy, radiation, or surgery, or a combination of these approaches. (11)

neoplasm (See table 17.1.)—an actively growing tissue composed of cells that have undergone an abnormal type of irreversible differentiation. The new growth is useless and progressive. Most neoplasms can be divided into three categories:

benign tumors—not invasive or metastatic.

invasive tumors—capable of invading or infiltrating and destroying surrounding tissue.

metastatic tumors—capable of developing secondary centers of neoplastic growth at some distance from the primary tumor. Other related terms:

- *behavior of neoplasm*—biologic interpretation indicating the potentialities of a new growth; for example, ability to spread, histologic appearance, rate of cellular proliferation (rapid cell division), and other aspects.
- *functioning neoplasm*—refers to tumor of endocrine derivation that synthesizes and releases hormones into the bloodstream and may cause some endocrine dysfunction. In a broader sense, any well-differentiated neoplasm capable of forming the product of a normal parent cell may be considered a functional tumor.
- *neoplastic growth patterns:*
  - *anaplasia, dedifferentiation*—loss of differentiation of cells and their orientation to each other, to their axial framework, and to blood vessels.
  - *differentiation*—specialization of a tissue or organ to perform a particular function. It is accompanied by characteristic morphologic alterations stimulating parent tissue.
  - *dysplasia*—loss in the regularity and normal arrangement of cells.
  - *fungating*—cauliflower-shaped pattern of growth. Cells grow rapidly, one on top of another, projecting from a tissue surface.
  - *hyperplasia*—abnormal increase in number of cells; cellular proliferation in excess of normal, not progressive (as in neoplasia), but reaching an equilibrium.
  - *metaplasia*—refers to a reversible process in which one type of differentiated cell is substituted for another. (33, 41, 60)

oncogene—viral gene carrying the potential to cause cancer; a transforming gene, since it has the potential to transform the host cell to a neoplastic phenotype. Cellular genes with potential for destabilizing growth regulation are termed proto-oncogenes. When proto-oncogenes become activated, they are termed oncogenes. Various alterations in these genes such as mutations, amplification, and chromosomal translocations may serve as mechanisms to activate the proto-oncogenes. The majority of oncogenes can be assigned to gene families based on the relatedness of nucleic acid or amino acid sequences or of enzyme activities of the oncogene product. Examples of some oncogenes implicated in the development of neoplasias are:

ras oncogene—identified in about 15% of the carcinomas affecting the lung, colon, and breast, as well as in several types of leukemias and sarcomas.

myc oncogene—implicated in Burkitt's lymphoma, neuroblastomas, retinoblastomas, and small-cell lung carcinomas. Human tumors may contain more than one oncogene. In the case of Burkitt's lymphoma, Lane and associates found a second oncogene, which they designated as *B-lym*. Ongoing research efforts continue to study the molecular aspects of cellular oncogene involvement with cell proliferation and differentiation, which represent key genetic elements associated with oncogenesis. (34, 36, 41, 42, 53, 57, 60)

oncogenesis—causation of tumors. (57, 60)

papillary—nipplelike or wartlike projection of cells.

papilloma—benign growth that resembles in its histologic structure the parent epithelium from which it is derived. Some skin papillomas are wartlike growths derived from squamous epithelium. Papillomas arising from the larynx, tongue, urinary bladder, or ureter are usually composed of transitional epithelium and tend to undergo malignant changes. Papillomatosis refers to the presence of multiple papillomata. (60)

radiocurability—refers to the tumor-normal tissue relationships; the interaction is such that curative doses of radiation can be regularly applied without excessive damage to the normal tissues. (44)

radioresponsiveness—clinical appearance of a tumor in regression following the initial dose of radiation. (44)

radiosensitivity—refers to innate sensitivity of cells to radiation. (44)

remission—refers to periods when no signs of disease are present. Periods may be described as partial, complete, or stable. Other related terms are:

disease-free interval (DFI)—refers to period of no active disease.

no evidence of disease (NED)—refers to periods when no signs of disease are present. (44)

scirrhous—hard; the term in oncology designates a hard tumor. (60)

sessile polyp—mass of tissue attached by a broad base. A polyp is a nonspecific term signifying tissue growth of a mucous membrane, which may be an inflammatory lesion or a true tumor. A pedunculated polyp is a mass of tissue attached to an organ by a freely movable, narrow stalk or pedicle. (60)

stem cell—describes a histologically primitive cell with the capacity to give rise to a large number of descendants through a process of self-renewal. (5, 60)

verrucous—wartlike; refers to projection usually occurring in the mouth and cheek areas. (60)

CANCER GRADING AND STAGING TERMS

grading—cancer grading refers to the degree of histologic and morphologic differentiation of the tumor, as determined by microscopic sections. (53, 60)

staging—cancer staging refers to the extent of the tumor's geographic spread at the time of the initial diagnosis. The joint efforts of the International Union against Cancer and the American Joint Committee for Cancer Staging and End Reporting developed a staging nomenclature entitled the *TNM system (T,* tumor; *N,* regional lymph node involvement; *M,* metastatic spread).

TNM System:

- *TO*—no evidence of primary tumor.
- *TIS*—tumor in situ.
- *T1, T2, T3, T4*—indicates size progression and involvement of tumor.
- *TX*—tissue cannot be assessed.
- *NO*—regional lymph node abnormality not demonstrated.
- *N1, N2, N3, N4*—indicated degree of node abnormality.
- *NX*—regional lymph node cannot be assessed.
- *MO*—no evidence of lymph node metastasizing.
- *M1, M2, M3, M4*—indicated degree and extent of metastases.

TABLE 17.1	Classification of Common Neoplasms

Benign Neoplasms	Malignant Neoplasms	Site of Predilection
Histologic derivation: Epithelial tissue (covering epithelium)		
Squamous papilloma—benign neoplasm composed of squamous epithelial cells, flat and pavementlike in appearance (60)	Carcinomas Eidermoid carcinoma Squamous cell carcinoma—a malignant neoplasm of squamous epithelial cells	Skin, buccal mucosa, tongue, salivary gland, lip, esophagus, larynx, lung, bladder, anus and vulva
	Oat cell carcinoma—very malignant undifferentiated, small cell tumor	Lung, esophagus, and other sites of low incidence
	Basal cell carcinoma—malignant neoplasm, frequently forming a rodent ulcer and destructive by invasion, rarely by metastasis (25, 29, 38)	Skin, especially face, canthus of eye, tip of nose, chin, lip, and others
Histologic derivation: Epithelial tissue (glandular epithelium)		
Adenoma—benign neoplasm arising from glands (38)	Adenocarcinoma—malignant neoplasm composed of glandular epithelium and characterized by many variations of anaplasia and metastases (19, 38, 39, 40)	Breast, bronchi, digestive tract, pancreas, endocrine glands, prostate
Cystadenoma—cystic neoplasm arising from glandular epithelium	Cystadenocarcinoma—cystic, malignant new growth of glandular epithelium	Ovary, salivary gland, breast, thyroid
• serous type—uni- or multilocular serous cyst composed of epithelial and connective tissue	• serous type—(rare) frequently bilateral loculations, and characteristic cyst contains transudate	Ovary
• pseudomucinous type—cystic neoplasm in which lining epithelium produces mucus (57)	• pseudomucinous type—malignant changes, cells undergoing stratification; implants on peritioneal surface; neoplasm characteristic—fluid of cyst viscid (60, 62)	Ovary
Histologic derivation: Embryonal tissue		
	Choriocarcinoma—a highly malignant tumor of chorionic epithelium; early metastasis common (6, 15, 17)	Uterus, testes, and mediastinum
Testicular adenoma—glandular tumor derived from germinal epithelium; extremely rare (60)	Embryonal carcinoma of testis— malignant new growth of germinal epithelium (6, 15, 17)	Testes
	Seminoma—testicular neoplasm of distinctive seminoma cells and lymphocytic stroma (15, 17)	Testes, epididymis, pelvic and para-aortic lymph nodes, and others
Teratoma, mature—mixed tumor composed of any type of embryonic and adult tissue (e.g., teeth, hair, bone, cartilage, and others) (17, 60)	Malignant teratoma, immature—mixed tumor malignant in one or the other tissue elements (15, 17)	Testes, ovaries, and retroperitoneal and sacrococcygeal regions

TABLE 17.1 (continued)

Benign Neoplasms	Malignant Neoplasms	Site of Predilection
	Histologic derivation: Connective tissue	
	Sarcomas	
Chondroma—benign neoplasm composed of cartilaginous elements (60)	Chondrosarcoma—malignant neoplasm of cartilaginous elements usually arising from end of long bones (28)	Femur, humerus, endolarynx, maxillary sinus, nasal fossa, and others
Lipoma—benign neoplasm composed of adipose tissue (fat) (61)	Liposarcoma—sarcoma composed of adipose tissue (43, 61)	Neck, shoulder back, gluteal region, thigh, and others
Fibroma—benign mass or firm nodule of fibroblasts or fibrocytes (61)	Fibrosarcoma—variable degrees of anaplasia and growth rate of tumor in subcutaneous or deeper structures (60, 61)	Extremities, head, neck, breast, and others
Leiomyoma—benign neoplasm of smooth muscle tissue (61)	Leiomyosarcoma—malignant neoplasm of smooth muscle tissue (38, 61)	Vulva, uterus, endometrium, esophagus, stomach, bladder, small intestine, and others
Rhabdomyoma—benign tumor arising in skeletal muscle (61)	Rhabdomyosarcoma—malignant poorly differentiated, bizarre mass in striated muscle (43, 61)	Any skeletal muscles, especially of the lower extremity
Osteoid osteoma—benign tumor derived from osteoblastic tissue (28)	Osteosarcoma—malignant tumor of osteoblastic or osseous tissue (5, 28)	Long bones, especially femur, humerus, fibula, pelvis, and others
	Histologic derivation: Nerve tissue or other tissue found in nervous system	
	Glioma group—primary intracranial tumors composed of glial tissues. Various types of cells are present:	Brain
	• Astrocytoma—neoplasm of glial tissue containing star-shaped cell or astrocytes	Cerebral hemisphere and brain stem
	• Ependymoma—neoplasm of the lining of the ventricles	Ventricles of the brain
	• Glioblastoma multiforme—highly invasive and destructive tumor; most malignant form of the gliomas	Cerebrum, cerebellum, brain stem, and spinal cord
	• Oligodendroglioma—slow growing neoplasm with areas of calcification (2, 24, 32, 60)	White matter of the frontal lobe
	Medulloblastoma—malignant tumor composed of medullary or neuroepithelial tissue (2, 24, 32)	Cerebellum
Meningioma—benign tumor arising from the meninges; common tumor (2, 24)		Meninges, cerebral hemisphere, and optic chiasm
	Neuroblastoma—highly malignant, lethal tumor of neuroblasts occurring in children (24, 32, 43)	Adrenal gland, sympathetic nerve chains, jaw, lip, nose, abdominal viscera, and others
Ganglioneuroma—benign tumor composed of ganglionic and nerve cells (45)	Ganglioneuroblastoma—malignant ganglioneuroma composed of ganglionic cells and neuroblasts (45)	Mediastinum and retroperitoneum
Neurilemoma—benign encapsulated tumor usually arising from peripheral nerve (45)		Peripheral or sympathetic nerves and eighth cranial nerve
Neurofibroma—tumor of peripheral nerve sheaths (45)	Neurofibrosarcoma—malignant neoplasm of peripheral nerve sheaths (61)	Peripheral nerves, hand, mediastinum, ureter, and others

TABLE **17.1**	(continued)	
Benign Neoplasms	*Malignant Neoplasms*	*Site of Predilection*
Histologic derivation: Nerve tissue and myelin-forming Schwann cells		
	Schwannomas—slow-growing malignant neoplasm originating from Schwann cells of the myelin sheath (24, 61)	Acoustic nerve fibers, spinal cord, and other cranial nerves
Histologic derivation: Nerve tissue, pigment-forming tissue		
Nervus—pigmented mole of developmental origin (4)	Malignant melanoma—malignant pigmented tumor (4, 59)	Skin, eye, and extremities
Histologic derivation: Reticuloendothelial tissue		
	Ewing's sarcoma—malignant tumor of reticuloendothelial tissue; early and wide metastases to other bones (28, 43, 61)	Femur, tibia, humerus, mandible, pelvic bones, and others
	Multiple myeloma, Plasma cell myeloma—malignant tumors derived from plasma cells of bone marrow (28, 35, 54, 60)	Flat bones, ribs, vertebrae, pelvis, skull, and others
Histologic derivation: Hematopoietic or hematologic tissue		
	Leukemias—stem cell, undifferentiated or differentiated forms (13, 27, 49, 55, 60)	Blood
Histologic derivation: Lymph-forming or lymphoid tissue		
	Lymphomas—stem cell or histiocytic, poorly or well-differentiated forms (60)	Lymph nodes, spleen, liver, and other viscera
	Hodgkin's lymphoma—lymphocytic predominance or depletion, mixed cellularity, or nodular sclerosis (12, 16, 36)	Lymph nodes, spleen, liver, bones, and other viscera
Histologic derivation: Vascular tissue		
Angioma Hemangioma—tumor of blood vessels (26)	Angiosarcoma Hemangiosarcoma—malignant blood vessel tumor (43, 61)	Blood vessels, subcutaneous tissue, muscles, and liver
Lymphangioma—tumor of the lymphatic vessels (61)	Lymphangiosarcoma—sarcoma of he lymphatic vessels (61)	Lymphatic vessels, neck, and others

Another staging approach is the classification system for staging malignant tumors in the female pelvis designed by the Cancer Committee of the International Federation of Gynecology and Obstetrics (FIGO). Other staging modalities include computed tomography (CT) and magnetic resonance imaging (MRI). Both of these radiologic modalities are noninvasive procedures. The staging laparotomy, which allows surgical exploration of the abdominal cavity to determine the exact spread of the disease is another avenue for staging tumors. (1, 18, 25, 31, 53)

SPECIAL STUDIES RELATED TO CANCER

bacille Calmette-Guérin (BCG) vaccine—immunotherapeutic agent used to destroy tumors or to prevent new or recurrent tumorigenesis (tumor formation). The immunopotentiating effect of BCG is increased by simultaneous use of antineoplastic agents at regular intervals. (4)

cancer detection diagnostic techniques: (37, 50, 51, 60)

cytogenetic studies:
- *fluorescence in situ hybridization*
- *DNA probes*

DNA analysis
- *southern blot technique*
- *restriction fragment length polymorphism analysis*
- *polymerase chain reaction*
- *RNase protection*
- *denaturing gradient gel electrophoresis*

RNA analysis
- *northern blot technique*
- *PCR enhancements*

protein analysis
- *western blot technique*
- *immunohistochemistry*

clinical cytogenetics—study of relationships between chromosomal aberrations and pathologic disorders. Cytogenetics focuses attention on chromosome defects related to malignancies. Primary tumors show more numeric than structural abnormalities, as seen by the Giemsa's banding method. Metastatic tumor cells are likely to reveal nearly triploid or tetraploid modes. Marker chromosome are very restricted in number in primary tumors but abound in metastatic tumors. Chromosome 1 is most frequently involved in marker formation, and chromosomes 2, 3, 5, 7, and 8 are next in frequency. Chromosome 22 is absent in about 75% of meningiomas. Leukemia and retinoblastoma occur with trisomy 21 or 13. In more than 90% of the cases of chronic myelogenous leukemia (CML), a Philadelphia (Ph[1]) chromosome is present in leukemic cells. Most CML patients have chromsomal translocations. Burkitt's lymphomas are characterized by reciprocal translocations, which in the majority of these cases involve chromosome 8 and either chromosome 2 or 22. Cytogenetic techniques and their related clinical techniques have established evidence that certain chromosomal disorders often precede and therefore predispose to specific types of neoplasms. The findings of recurrent chromosomal defects in numerous human cancers continue to support the theory that chromosomal rearrangements play a crucial role in carcinogenesis. (60)

exfoliative cytology—procedure in which cells are scraped from the diseased area, stained, and subsequently viewed under a microscope to detect the presence of cancer. The Papanicolaou (Pap) smear is a sample of this type of cytology. Cells are scraped from the cervix or vagina, and the procedure mentioned above is followed. Gastric exfoliative cytology is used to detect gastric malignancy by studying cells shed by the mucosa and obtained by aspiration, lavage, or abrasive brushes following the liquefaction of the mucosal coating. (60)

hormonal assays: (60, 62)

estradiol receptor assay (ERA)—test predicting the effectiveness of hormone therapy or hormone deprivation (endocrine ablation therapy) in particular breast cancers.

progesterone receptor assay—test used with estradiol receptor assay to select breast cancer patients who will benefit by hormone therapy.

monoclonal antibodies—homogeneous immunoglobulins directed at a single epitope or antigenic determinant. The most common method for producing monoclonal antibodies involves the use of hybridoma technology initiated in 1975 by Köhler and Milstein. Many tumor-associated antigens have been identified by monoclonal antibodies. Monoclonal antibodies have been developed against breast, colon, prostate, cervical, ovarian, lung, and pancreatic carcinomas. They have become important tools in the study of cell differentiation, tumor progression, and tumor immunology. (48, 60)

tumor-associated antigen (TAA)—antigens absent in normal tissues but found in leukemia, lymphoma, myeloma, melanoma, meningioma, neuroblastoma, hepatoma, osteogenic sarcoma, and tumors of urogenital organs. Monoclonal antibodies are ideal reagents for detection of TAA by immunohistochemical staining on biopsy tissue slides and immunocytologic evaluation of cell suspensions. CA-125 tumor-associated antigen is a glycoprotein recognized by a monoclonal antibody (OC-125) raised against a human epithelial ovarian cancer cell line. The function of CA-125 is unknown but it has been found to be distributed on various tissues, both normal and pathologic. In clinical practice, it is primarily used to monitor treatment response and to detect early recurrence in patients with ovarian cancer who have elevated preoperative levels. Other malignancies that have been reported to be associated with elevated CA-125 levels include carcinomas of endometrium, fallopian tube, lung, breast, stomach, liver, gallbladder, pancreas, kidney, and colon. (3, 48, 60)

tumor immunity—the presence of tumor antibodies toward the specific tumor, as detected by immunofluorescence, complement fixation tests, cytotoxicity tests, and immunohistochemistry analysis. (48, 60)

tumor marker—ideally, a specific and sensitive index of a microscopic tumor or metastatic lesion. Radioimmunoassay aids in the detection of tumor markers, since they are highly sensitive and measure antigens and hormones in nanograms. Other assays employed may include the enzyme-linked immunoassays (EIA) in which detection is by enzymatic activity rather than by radioactivity. Variations of EIA may include the enzyme-linked immunosorbent assay (ELISA) or the sandwich-type ELISA. Unfortunately, the specificity of tumor markers is very deficient or entirely lacking. Some examples of tumor markers are:

prostate-specific antigen (PSA)—a marker for human prostate epithelial cells used in the diagnosis of prostatic malignancy.

prostatic acid phosphatase (PAP)—biologic marker used in the diagnosis of metastatic prostatic cancer. Most metastatic adenocarcinoma of the prostate is positive for both markers; however, occasional metastatic deposits may be positive for one or the other. Current clinical practice encourages staining all cases of metastatic carcinoma of suspected prostatic origins for both markers.

ectopic polypeptides—immunoreactive adrenocorticotropic hormone (ACTH) in tissue extracts of pulmonary cancer; pancreatic polypeptide found in carcinoid tumors and medullary cancer of the thyroid and others.

placental proteins—human chorionic gonadotropin (hCG) and human placental lactogen (hPL); both hormones are normally present in fetal and maternal serum but undetectable 48 hours after delivery. Their continued presence in increasing amounts suggests the growth of a trophoblastic neoplasm in the male or nonpregnant female.

oncofetal antigens—immunologic substances that may serve as tumor markers.

- *alpha$_1$*, α_1, fetoprotein, fetal α_1, globulin (AFP)—alpha$_1$, globulin, synthesized by the embryo in the liver cell, normally present in serum and cord blood of the fetus and absent in the normal infant. If α_1 fetoprotein is found in a child or adult, a hepatoma or embryonal teratoblastoma is suspected.

carcinoembryonic antigen (CEA)—release of CEA into the underlying tissues of the gastrointestinal tract and its absorption into the blood and lymph channels account for the highly increased CEA concentrations in several entodermal and nonentodermal carcinomas and other disorders. (26, 30, 41, 52, 56, 60)

ORAL READING PRACTICE

CANCER MODALITIES

The combination of **radiation** and **chemotherapy** or **radiation** and surgery is used to increase the **therapeutic index** (relationship between desired and undesired effects of therapy). This purpose may be achieved by taking advantage of the different mechanisms of action of **systematic chemotherapy** and **regional irradiation.** Another approach toward increasing the therapeutic index is using drugs that specifically affect tumor response to radiation; a third approach is using a combination of drugs and **roentgen rays** with either independent action or additivity. The combined effect of drugs and radiation or of two drugs may be classified as:

independent—the agent's mechanisms of action are independent, and resulting damage is independent.

additivity—agents focus on the same loci; because of additive sublethal damage, the resulting damage may be greater than the lethal damage of each agent impacting alone.

synergism—two agents achieve a result that is more effective than pure additivity.

antagonism—cell-killing event is less than independent action.

The application of **ionizing radiation therapy** is aimed at killing malignant cells. By focusing enough radiation damage on the cell, it is hoped that the cell will lose its reproductive integrity. The critical target of this radiation is the **DNA (deoxyribonucleic acid),** the genetic substance within the nucleus of a cell responsible for controlling cell division and synthesis. Another mechanism, the **laser (light amplification by stimulated emission of radiation)** beam has had some effect on certain malignant tumors, such as **melanomas,** achieving some progressive regression. **Linear accelerators** refer to high-energy and advanced **radiotherapy** devices that accelerate charged particles in a straight line and provide various x-ray and electron therapies.

The **radioresponsiveness** of tumors may be predictable by histologic grading before therapy. The following tumors have proved to be **radiosensitive** and in selected cases **radiocurable** with a dose tolerable by normal tissue: **seminomas, lymphosarcomas, Hodgkin's disease, Wilms' tumors, neuroblastomas, medulloblastomas, retinoblastomas, Ewing's sarcomas,** and others. The biologic radiation effect of these mechanisms depends on interfacing several factors: length of radiation time, total dose, and number of treatments used in the delivery of the total dose. These variables are further delineated by consideration of tumor type, size, location, metastases, and the physical condition of the patient. Other related terms are:

boost technique—giving maximal tolerated dose to the target volume, then using a very localized radiation to raise the dose to the tumor bed.

shrinking field technique—giving the largest potential tumor bed a moderate dose of radiation, then reducing the volume to the tumor and its immediate confines.

brachytherapy (brachy = short)—radiation device is placed close or within short range of the target volume. Examples of brachytherapy include **interstitial** and **intracavitary radiation** used in the treatment of gynecologic and oral tumors.

teletherapy (tele = far)—radiation device is far removed from the target volume. Examples of teletherapy include the majority of orthovoltage or supervoltage machines.

The ranges of radiation utilized in clinical practice are:

superficial—radiation or roentgen rays from 10 to 125 keV (kiloelectron volts).

orthovoltage—radiation represents electromagnetic radiation between 125 and 400 keV.

supervoltage or megavoltage—for those energies greater than 400 keV.

Radiation and surgery modalities may be presented as a combined approach in therapeutic planning. For example, surgery is often limited by the required preservation of vital normal tissues adjacent to the tumor. Radiation can complement this situation, either preoperatively or postoperatively. As with any technique, the value and choice of method, dose of radiation, and the time between radiation and surgery should be viewed in light of goals planned for the patient. (20, 21, 23, 25, 31, 44, 53)

Surgery is the oldest treatment for cancer and plays a key role in the cancer diagnosis. A variety of techniques is available to obtain tissue for histologic diagnosis. Some of these techniques are:

excisional biopsy—refers to an excision of the entire suspected tumor tissue with little or no margin of surrounding tissue. When it is not necessary to cut directly into the tumor, this procedure is the choice of most surgeons.

incisional biopsy—refers to removal of a small wedge of tissue from a larger tumor mass. This type of procedure is often required for diagnosis of large masses that may require major surgical approaches even for local excision.

needle biopsy—refers to obtaining a core of tissue through a specially designed needle introduced into the suspect tissue. By suction, cells and tissue fragments are obtained through the needle and presented for cytologic analysis. When the tissue obtained is not sufficient for diagnosis, another type of biopsy procedure may be preferred, in which a larger amount of tissue may be obtained.

Surgery can also play a role in the staging of the tumor. For example, **staging laparotomies** allow the surgeon to explore the abdominal cavity to determine the exact spread of the disease. This information is of great assistance to the oncologist in planning treatment. Placement of **radio-opaque** clips during biopsy and staging procedure is important to delineate areas of known tumor mass and to guide later radiation application to these areas. Other surgical procedures may include:

cryosurgery—malignant tissue is destroyed by freezing techniques.

electrocauterization—malignant neoplasm is burned by an electric current.

The exact role of surgery varies with the type and involvement of the tumor. When feasible, the initial type of surgery may be that of biopsy. This may be followed by more radical surgery, such as radical mastectomy and lymph node dissection. Another approach may use other therapeutic modalities in the reduction of the tumor mass, such as chemotherapy, radiation, both of these modalities separately, or both combined. Then a second, less-extensive surgery to remove the reduced mass may follow. The interfacing of modalities in cancer treatment may provide the patient with optimal treatment while avoiding extensive radical procedures whenever possible. (25, 47, 53, 60)

Chemotherapy drugs provide multiple biochemical avenues to destroy tumor cells. They may be used independently, in combination, or as an aid to another modality **(adjuvant).** Tumors may be divided into **benign** and **malignant neoplasms.** Typical **benign tumors** are generally **encapsulated** by **connective tissue, not invasive,** and slow growing. They never

metastasize. Benign tumors may cause serious dysfunctions if they encroach on vital organs, obstruct the circulation or air passages, and compress nerves. Microscopically, the pattern of a benign neoplasm is orderly and well organized. In contrast, the microscopic pattern of the malignant tumor exhibits disorder. Typical **malignant tumors** have no capsule, **are invasive,** grow progressively, **metastasize,** and endanger physical well-being and even life. Most localized malignancies are controlled by surgery and radiation therapy, but it is the chemotherapy of cancer that is targeted at the treatment of metastases.

The term **adjuvant chemotherapy** usually is applied to the administration of drugs following the primary tumor's removal by an alternative method, when the residual tumor is small and clinically undetectable, and the cells are more actively dividing. The term **primary chemotherapy** refers to the use of chemotherapy as initial treatment for patients who have localized cancer for which there is an alternative, but less than completely effective treatment. The term **induction chemotherapy** refers to drug therapy administered as the primary treatment for patients who have advanced cancer and for which no alternative treatment exists. Selective terms pertaining to chemotherapy agents follow:

alkylating agents—highly reactive compounds with the ability to substitute alkyl groups $(R-H_2-Ch_2{}^+)$ for hydrogen atoms of certain organic compounds. The alkylation for DNA is the critical cytotoxic action. Alkylation produces breaks in the DNA molecule and cross-linking of its twin strands, thus interfering with replication and transcription. Even though alkylating agents as a class exert cytotoxic effects on cells throughout the cell cycle, there is a distinct difference in their pharmacokinetic features (chemical reactivity and membrane transport qualities), and these agents do not share cross-resistance in either experimental or clinical chemotherapy. Examples of this group include:

- *nitrogen mustard derivatives*—mechlorethamine, cyclophosphamide, cholorambucil, and melphalan.
- *ethylenimine derivatives*—such as thio-TEPA.
- *alkyl sulfonates*—such as busulfan.
- *triazene derivatives*—such as decarbazine.
- *nitrosureas*—such as carmustine (BCNU), lomustine (CCNU), and methyl-CCNU.

Streptomyces antibiotics—produce antibiotic and tumoricidal effects by directly binding to DNA, thus causing a major inhibitory effect on DNA and RNA synthesis. Examples include:

- *doxorubicin* (Adriamycin)
- *actinomycin D, dactinomycin* (Cosmegen)
- *bleomycin* (Blenoxane)
- *mithramycin* (Mithracin)
- *mitomycin* C (Mutamycin)

plants—may serve as useful antineoplastic agents, such as vincristine (Oncovin) and vinblastine (Velban). These alkaloids are extracted from the periwinkle plant.

western yew tree—an anticancer agent, Taxol is derived from the bark of the western yew tree (*Taxus brevifolia*).

antimetabolites—structural analogues (analog) of normal metabolites required for cell function and replication. Antimetabolites may interact with enzymes and cause damage to the cells. Examples of this group include:

- methotrexate
- 5-fluorouracil
- 6-mercaptopurine
- 6-thioguanine

hormonal therapy—tends to turn off tumor growth and interrupt hormone synthesis. Biologic antagonism is the primary reason for the application of most hormonal therapies, with the exception of estrogen use in postmenopausal breast cancer. Examples include:

- androgens (testosterone propionate, fluoxymesterone [Halotestin], and testosterone enanthate [Delatestryl]).
- antiandrogens (flutamide [Eulexin]).
- antiestrogens (tamoxifen [Nolvadex] used in the treatment of breast cancer).
- estrogens (ethingyl estradiol, estradiol, diethylstilbestrol).
- progestogens (hydroxyprogesterone, medroxyprogesterone).
- adrenal steroid hormones of the glucocorticoid class (prednisone, methylprednisolone, and dexamethasone).

Special uses of chemotherapy may include:

- instillation of drugs into the spinal fluid, directly using a lumbar puncture needle, or into an implanted Ommaya reservoir to treat central nervous system leukemia, lymphoma, and carcinoma.
- instillation of drugs into the pleural or pericardial space to control effusions.
- hepatic artery infusion to treat hepatic metastases.
- carotid artery infusion to treat head and neck cancers.
- use of chemotherapy through the intraperitoneal administration of drugs to treat ovarian cancers.

Special combinations of chemotherapy agents include:

- AC—doxorubicin (Adriamycin), cyclophosphamide
- BACON—blenomycin, doxorubicin (Adriamycin), lomustine (CCNU), vincristine (Oncovin), mechlorethamine (nitrogen mustard)
- CAF—cyclophosphamide, doxorubicin (Adriamycin, 5-fluorouracil [5-FU])
- CMF—cyclophosphamide, methotrexate, 5-fluorouracil (5-FU)
- MAP—melphalan, doxorubicin (Adriamycin), prednisone
- MCBP—melphalan, cyclophosphamide, carmustine (BCNU), prednisone
- MCP—melphalan, cyclophosphamide, prednisone
- MOB—mitomycin, vincristine (Oncovin), bleomycin
- VBAP—vincristine, carmustine (BCNU), doxorubicin (Adriamycin), prednisone
- VCAP—vincristine, cyclophosphamide, doxorubicin (Adriamycin), prednisone

A new form of cancer therapy (in addition to bone marrow transplantation) is evolving that includes the use of recombinant cytokines, growth factors, and monoclonal antibodies for the treatment of cancer. The term **biologic therapy** has been applied to describe this group of agents that either are normal mammalian mediators or achieve antitumor effects through endogenous host defense mechanisms. Biologic therapy approaches are still under study and development, but this modality does show promise for the future. The pivotal success of cancer therapy is dependent on the combination of two or more modalities and requires the coordinated expertise of the oncologist to ensure that the patient receives maximal benefit from the therapy regimen. (6, 7, 8, 9, 10, 11, 14, 22, 25, 33, 34, 46, 53, 57, 58, 60)

REVIEW GUIDE

Instructions: Define the following terms.

Example: -oma (G)—tumor

---

astro- (G)   onco-(G)

carcino- (G   papilla (L)

histo- (G)   -plasia (G)

Instructions: Define the following terms.

Example: benign—mild, not malignant

---

adjuvant chemotherapy

astrocytoma

bacille Calmette-Guérin (BCG)
   vaccine

brachytherapy

cystadenocarcinoma

DNA

dysplasia

encapsulated

fractionation

ganglioneuroblastoma

induction chemotherapy

invasive tumors

leiomyoma

medullary

oligodendroglioma

papillary

primary chemotherapy

prostate-specific antigen (PSA)

radioresponsiveness

radiosensitivity

ras oncogene

rhabdomyosarcoma

sessile polyp

stem cell

tamoxifen

teletherapy

therapeutic index

TNM system

tumor immunity

tumor marker

18

Selected Terms Pertaining to Imaging Technology

ORIGIN OF TERMS

echo- (G)—return of sound
endo- (G)—within
-genic (G)—origin
-gram (G)—a writing, a mark
lamina (pl. *laminae*) (L)—layer
radio- (L)—ray

-scopy (G)—to examine, inspection
sonus (L)—sound
tomo- (G)—section, cutting
ultra- (L)—beyond
xero- (G)—dry, dryness

RADIOLOGY

GENERAL TERMS

absorption of x-rays—one of the two main processes by which x-rays passing through an object are reduced in their intensity. The other main process is called scattering. (25)

artifact—an error in the reconstructed image that has no counterpart in reality. Artifacts represent unwanted false features in the image produced by the imaging process. (62)

attenuation of x-rays—the term covering both absorption and scattering of x-rays as they pass through an object. (25)

back projection—refers to both a process and a method of reconstructing an image. (62)

collimator—device that shapes the x-ray beam. (25)

computed tomography (CT)—the reconstruction by computer of a tomographic plane (slice) of a part of the human body. It is developed from multiple x-ray absorption measurements collected by detectors after the passage of the x-ray beam through the patient's body. The planes that can be visualized include axial, coronal, sagittal, and oblique sections. The computer is used to make the necessary calculations and synthesize the images. (62)

conventional tomography—body section radiography that delineates a thin layer of tissue of an organ; thus, the structures lying anteriorly and posteriorly are more or less blurred out. (62)

data acquisition system (DAS)—the components of a computed tomography (CT) machine used to produce and collect the x-ray attenuation information: x-ray tube, detectors, and detector preamplifiers. (62)

density—presence of an accumulation of black metallic silver crystals on the x-ray film. This accumulation of silver is directly related to the number of remnant photons that struck the film during exposure. Radiographic density refers to the amount of blackness seen on the film. Tissue density refers to the concentration of various molecules (mass) composing a particular body part or tissue. As the density of a body part or tissue increases, its absorption to x-rays increases. Tissue density is a causative factor in producing scatter. (62) (See *scattering of x-rays,* p. 447.)

digital computer—computer that uses numbers representing digits in a decimal or other system. (62)

digital radiography—the radiographic imaging in digital format, including various procedures applicable to angiography and radiography in general. Electronic digital records are used instead of film techniques. (62)

digital scan converters—computers that can accept image information in one scan mode, store it electronically, process it and transmit it to display units in a second scan pattern (as in a series of horizontal television-raster lines). Digital scan converters and auxiliary computers are the central elements of modern scanners. (62)

discrete—well-defined and clear-cut in appearance. (62)

display monitor—the television screen used to display the CT image. A monitor is distinct from a TV set in that it normally does not include the tuner that allows the selection of a particular channel. Monitors are used in closed-circuit applications. (62)

electron beam computed tomography (EBCT)—employs a stationary source-detector pair coupled to a unique technology whereby x-rays are produced as a rotating electron beam is swept across a series of 1 to 4 semicircular tungsten targets situated beneath the patient. For detection of coronary artery calcium on EBCT, a consecutive single-slice, 100-ms scans are performed. When performed in a "high-resolution" volume scanning mode, 20 to 40 sequential scans of the heart with electrocardiographic triggering during late diastole can be completed in about 20 to 40 seconds. There is no need for intravenous administration of contrast medium because calcific deposits in arterial walls demonstrate relatively high EBCT densities (measured as Hounsfield units), approximately 2- to 10-fold higher than the surrounding soft tissue. (66)

emission computed tomography (emission CT)—technique for obtaining cross-sectional images of the head or body based on the detection of the geometric distribution of the emissions or activity of radionuclides. The emissions may be single photons or coincidental photons arising from position decay. (62)

filter—technique for shaping the x-ray beam's intensity. Placing an aluminum plate between the x-ray tube and the patient is an example of this technique. Usually, different filters are used for head and body scanning. (62)

fluorescence—the property of becoming luminous through the influence of x-rays or other agents. (2)

gantry—the moveable frame on a CT machine that holds the x-ray tube, collimators, and detectors. (26)

gated computed tomography—process for synchronizing scanning or data collection with some physiologic process; technique employed for imaging the heart in different phases of the cardiac cycle by accumulating data for discrete portions of the cardiac cycle. The cardiac cycle is gated on the basis of the electrocardiogram. (62)

helical (spiral) computed tomography (CT)—technique involves continuous movement of the patient with concurrent scanning by a constantly rotating gantry and detector system that takes 1 second for a 360-degree rotation; thereby a helix of raw projecting data is obtained. An advantage of helical CT entails the acquisition of volumetric data during a single breath hold through the anatomic region of interest. Retrospective data reconstructions can be performed at any point; narrow reconstruction intervals facilitate multiplanar and three-dimensional

(3-D) imaging. Rapid acquisition of helical scan data set in a single breath hold eliminates discontinuities in the reconstructions due to variations in the patients' respiratory excursions. Due to the speed of the helical data acquisitions, other motion artifacts, such as bowel peristalsis, are suppressed. Helical CT is most beneficial when an entire organ or region is scanned in a single breath hold. Scan durations of 20 to 30 seconds are not unusual. (83, 91)

image intensifier—an electronic vacuum-tube device for increasing the intensity of a two-dimensional light image from a fluoroscopic screen. (62)

invasive technique—injection of contrast medium for enhancement of radiographic images. Invasive techniques also may imply the placement of needles, catheters, and such into the body. (62)

laminograph, planigraph, tomograph—body section radiographs imaging a thin layer of body tissue of varying depths without interference with the intervening structures. (62)

law of tangents—the radiographic image is determined primarily by the portions of the x-ray beam that pass tangentially or nearly tangentially along the borders between objects of different densities and thickness. (62)

linear accelerators—high-energy and advanced radiotherapy devices that accelerate charged particles in a straight line and provide various x-ray and electron therapies. Their primary usefulness is in the field of radiation oncology. (62)

linear amplifier—electric device producing an output signal proportioned to the input signal. The amplifier may be a transistor or electric tube. (62)

noninvasive technique—no injection of contrast material needed for radiographic procedures. Noninvasive technique also may imply no placement of needles or catheters into the body. (62)

pixel—short term for picture element cell. The pixel is a representation of the volume element on the display. (62)

positions of the body—the manner in which the patient is placed in reference to the surrounding space. Terms to describe body positions may include:

> *dorsal recumbent*—supine.
> *lateral recumbent*—lying on side.
> *ventral recumbent*—prone.

Terms used to describe part location or position may include:

> *anterior, ventral*—designates forward part of body or organ.
> *distal*—designates away from source.
> *lateral*—designates parts away from the median plane of the body or away from the middle of a part to the right or left.
> *proximal*—designates nearness to the source. (62)

profile—the plot of detector readings versus position made during a linear transverse of the scanning gantry (or its equivalent in a continuous rotation multielement detector system). Another word for profile is projection. (62) (The term projection can also be used in a different sense; see *back projection* (p. 444).

radiograph, radiogram, roentgenograph, roentgenogram—picture of an internal structure made on photographic film by means of x-rays. (62)

radiography, roentgenography—the making of x-ray photographs of internal structures. (62)

radiologist—physician who uses roentgen rays, ultrasound, and magnetic resonance imaging for diagnostic, therapeutic, and research purposes. (62)

radiology—the study or science concerned with the use of various forms of radiant energy and radioactive substances, as well as with the diagnosis and treatment of disorders by means of radiology, ultrasonography, and magnetic resonance imaging. (62)

reconstruction—an estimate of the density distribution or variation in x-ray attenuation, finite dimensional approximation of the x-ray attenuation distribution in a transverse section of the patient. (62)

resolution—in diagnostic radiology, the perception of two adjacent objects or points as being separate. (62)

roentgen ray, x-ray—form of radiant energy capable of penetrating solid and opaque objects and named after Wilhelm Conrad Roentgen (1845–1923), a German physicist who discovered x-rays in 1895. (62)

scan—the mechanical motion required to produce a CT image. During a typical scan, the x-ray tube rotates 360 degrees around the patient. Scan enhancement is achieved by increasing the clarity of a radiologic image with the injection of a contrast medium. (26, 68)

scattering of x-rays—one of the two ways in which the x-ray beam intensity is diminished in passing through an object. The x-rays are scattered in a direction different from the original beam direction and do not add to the production of the radiologic image. (25)

slice—the cross-sectional portion of the body that is scanned for the production of the CT image. (62)

slit-beam radiography—any imaging technique that uses a slitlike detector, in contrast to the large area used in conventional radiography. (62)

subtraction angiography—procedure that images arteries without their overlying or surrounding structures. (54, 56, 62)

thermography—an imaging technique based on the detection of the naturally occurring body emission of infrared radiation. (2)

SELECTED RADIOLOGIC STUDIES

TERMS RELATED TO MUSCULOSKELETAL RADIOGRAPHY

air arthrogram, pneumoarthrogram—air injection used as the contrast medium in a joint for radiologic evaluation. (63)

arthrography—contrast study of joints as an aid in establishing the diagnosis and selection of treatment modality for joint diseases and injuries. The most common joints evaluated by this technique include the knee, hip, and shoulder. (62)

hip arthrography—includes:
- evaluation of congenital hip dysplasias of infants and children to determine the type of corrective surgery needed while the bones are still partially cartilaginous.
- examination of complications of Legg-Calvé-Perthes disease, such as avascular necrosis and a detached hip fragment that may be covered by intact cartilage.
- detection of cartilaginous and synovial abnormalities of certain joint diseases in children and adults. Arthrograms are especially useful in prepuberty due to partial ossification of the skeleton.
- visualization of total hip arthroplasty immediately after surgery to determine the success or failure of the operation, or year later when pain indicates infection or a loosening of the prosthesis.

knee arthrography—includes:
- *meniscal injuries*—common knee injuries that may disrupt the meniscal cartilage and split the meniscus into fragments. Evaluation of meniscal abnormalities may be achieved by single- or double-contrast arthrography.
- *extrameniscal injuries*—abnormalities that include tears of ligaments, defects of articular cartilage, such as loose bodies, synovial disorders, and popliteal cysts (Baker's cyst). Double-contrast arthrography of the knee aids in the diagnosis of these injuries.

shoulder arthrography—includes evaluation of several bursal cavities and articulations present in the shoulder, as well as the glenohumeral joint. The data from these studies provide valuable information on various disorders, such as adhesive capsulitis, tears of the rotator cuff, subluxation of the joint, recurrent joint dislocations, bicipital tendon abnormalities, and articular diseases.

Other types of arthrography include:

ankle arthrography—to assess injury or disease of the ankle joint area, such as severe sprains with rupture of the ankle ligament. (62)

temporomandibular joint (TMJ) arthrography—the anatomic and physiologic complexity of TMJ requires careful arthrographic techniques to detect the possible cause of clicking, grinding, and locking of jaw; detachments; and perforations. There are several modalities for imaging TMJ. These include plain films, arthrography, CT arthrography, and magnetic resonance imaging (MRI). Arthrography and CT arthrography are adequate in assessing TMJ, but are invasive and deliver a significant radiation dose. MRI is becoming the modality of choice, as it provides direct visualization of the meniscus, is noninvasive, has excellent soft-tissue contrast, and does not use ionizing radiation. (36, 86)

computed tomography (CT) of mandible and maxilla—CT scanning of the mandible and maxilla is useful in preoperative planning of endosseous dental implants. For example, CT may show that the surface contour of the bone where the implant is needed is not capable of holding the implant. CT's oblique images offer the opportunity to recognize any developmental defects, foreign bodies, or osseous lesions that are present, and thus these entities can be avoided at the time of implantation of the dental fixtures.

Note: Other applications of CT in musculoskeletal diagnosis include: assessment of solid or cystic tumors, malignant, benign, or recurrent musculoskeletal masses; trauma; and metabolic bone diseases. (35, 44, 62)

conventional radiographs of skeleton—plain radiographs of bones that image fractures, metabolic or neoplastic bone disease, and other orthopedic deformities, as well as evaluate bone graft complications including pseudoarthrosis. Conventional radiographs are the primary method of following both the normal appearance of limb lengthening procedures and assessing complications. (48, 62)

scanography—method of x-ray examination for accurate measurement of the length of structures of the body, usually of the long bones, such as to determine a discrepancy in leg length. (48, 62)

TERMS RELATED TO NEURORADIOGRAPHY

cerebral angiography—conventional procedure or method of demonstrating the cervical and cerebral blood vessels by taking a series of radiographs during the injection of contrast medium. Extracranial atheromatous occlusions of the carotid, vertebral, and subclavian arteries producing cerebrovascular insufficiency can be readily detected and may be surgically correctable. A radiographic visualization of the intracranial vasculature may be of diagnostic value in locating space-occupying lesions, brain tumors, cerebral aneurysms, embolisms, and thrombosis. Various techniques have been devised. (54)

aortic arch catheterization, thoracic aortography—this procedure includes a percutaneous puncture with insertion of a catheter, with retrograde advancement into the aortic arch (usually by the transfemoral route) and an arterial injection of a contrast medium for each of the serial angiograms. In occlusive disease or tortuosity of the iliacs, a brachial or axillary artery may be used. The procedure demonstrates the site and extent of vascular occlusions and of collateral blood vessels and permits the determination of the regional circulation time. (54)

computed intracranial tomography—radiologic method using an automatic computerized tomographic scanner for establishing a diagnosis. The patient's head is placed in the center of the scanning ring, and the x-ray beam is directed to scan the brain from a number of different angles. Contiguous slices show differential tissue absorption, which is calculated by a computer and presented in a series of images of the cerebral structures. Computed tomography of the brain tends to detect primary or metastatic brain lesions, brain abscesses, subdural hematomas, and extent and location of cerebral infarction, and can exclude hemorrhage as the cause of focal stroke, and depict surrounding edema. However, CT cannot detect most cerebral infarctions for at least 48 hours. Also, when infarction occurs in the brain stem, CT is a less reliable scanning technique due to bone and motion artifacts and the small size of many infarcts. Magnetic resonance imaging (MRI) reveals more findings than CT scanning in patients with stroke. (56)

computed tomography of the pineal and pituitary regions—CT scanning of these areas tends to identify pinealomas, including solid and cystic teratomas, pineal blastomas, cystomas and gliomas, cystic changes within the pituitary gland, or a craniopharyngioma, an avascular mass in the suprasellar area with calcification and cystic components. In the case of hemorrhage due to a pituitary macroadenoma, CT scanning reveals a high-density area within the adenoma during the acute phase and a decreased density, with or without marginal enhancement as the hematoma is resorbed. (55)

discography—diagnostic aid in the detection of a herniated lumbar or cervical disk followed by radiographs of the spine. Discography may be performed prior to lower lumbar spinal fusion as a mechanism to evaluate the integrity of the disk immediately above the level of planned fusion. Discography may be performed in conjunction with chemonucleolysis and disk aspiration. (58, 62)

dynamic computed tomography—rapid scanning technique that delineates vascular perfusion and enhancement patterns of normal vessels, as well as abnormal lesions indicative of neoplasia, vascular occlusions, or other disorders. (62)

myelography—studies content of spinal canal following the injection of a radiopaque substance into the subarachnoid space by lumbar or cisternal puncture. The procedure permits the fluoroscopic observation of the contrast medium in the spinal canal as it rises and falls when the patient's position is changed. (58)

spinal cord computed tomography—CT procedure demonstrating the spinal cord, nerve roots and sheaths, nerves, ganglia, and intervertebral disks. (58)

ventriculography—the introduction of air or other contrast material into the ventricular system following the removal of cerebrospinal fluid. This procedure allows the radiographic examination of the brain. (57)

TERMS RELATED TO CARDIOVASCULAR IMAGING

angiocardiography:

peripheral angiocardiography—injection of contrast medium into the basilic or cephalic veins of the arm for examining the chambers of the heart and pulmonary circulation.

selective angiography—injection of contrast material through a catheter placed into the chamber or vessel of interest.

selective retrograde aortography and left ventriculography—retrograde aortic catheterization for passing a radiopaque catheter across the aortic valve into the left ventricle. The correct position of the catheter is ascertained either by fluoroscopic or television guidance or a radiogram. This method discloses ventricular septal defects, aneurysms, mitral and aortic regurgitation, and other pathology.

selective right ventricular angiography—visualization of the anatomic structures involved in tetralogy of Fallot, transposition of the great vessels, patent ductus arteriosus, and similar conditions. The catheter is placed into the right ventricle via either a brachial or femoral vein approach.

sequential angiocardiography—serial films taken at accurately recorded intervals. They reveal the time and sequence of filling of the great vessels and chambers of the heart, as well as their position, size, and configuration.

aortography—injection of opaque solution for x-ray examination of the aorta.

abdominal aortogram—injection of opaque solution into the abdominal aorta. The catheter may be introduced through either the femoral or axillary or brachial arteries or through a needle puncture of the aorta in the lumbar region.

thoracic aortogram—injection of opaque solution into the ascending aorta via retrograde introduction of catheter, either through femoral or axillary arteries or by a cutdown of the brachial artery. (62)

cardiac computed tomography—sectional imaging of the heart using a computerized machine to demonstrate the size and shape of cardiac chambers, intracavitary masses, septal defect, aneurysm, and graft patency or occlusion after coronary bypass. (62, 81)

digital subtraction angiography (DSA)—vascular imaging with a digital subtraction apparatus following intra-arterial, or infrequently, intravenous injection of a contrast medium. The purpose of substraction is to remove or subtract the image of the bony structures from the radiograph. DSA uses an electronic and computer method of performing the "subtraction" films. DSA has been successfully used to demonstrate vascular abnormalities of the aorta and carotid and renal arteries. This technique also has been helpful in studying the vessels of the base of the brain and in the study of the posterior fossa anatomy, in which there are dense overlying bony structures. (12, 54, 56)

digital video subtraction angiography—the video imaging system applied to digital subtraction angiography. It may be used to detect renovascular abnormalities and extracranial carotid artery disease, as well as congenital heart disease in children. (7, 62)

specific angiocardiography techniques: (2, 12, 62)

angiocardiography with large films—technique using regular x-ray films with rapid film changers of 2 to 12 films per second. Rapid filming of heart and vessels may be either single plane or biplane.

angiocardiography injection technique—injection of contrast media via a catheter or needle, using a suitable pressure injector.

- *standard injection of opaque substance*—injection with automatic high-pressure injector regardless of the time in the cardiac cycle.
- *time injection of contrast material*—technique in which beginning of the injection may be triggered by electronic timing devices at any point in the cardiac cycle, using the electrocardiogram as a reference. It can be limited to the duration of either systole or diastole, depending on the lesion of the opacified chamber of interest, such as a systolic injection into the atrium and a diastolic injection into the ventricle.

arteriography—radiographic examination of arteries following the injection of a contrast medium.

cardiac cine-computed tomography—fast computed tomogram that provides comprehensive cardiac imaging technique utilized for the evaluation of cardiac anatomy and function. This technique allows multiple sequential images to be obtained within a single cardiac cycle thereby providing a true real-time image. These images are laced together in a closed-loop cinematic format, called a cine-CT display. Cine-CT may be employed in the evaluation of hypertrophic congestive cardiomyopathies by quantitating ventricular volumes and myocardial mass. Cine-CT may be used also to monitor the effects of interventions on the right and left ventricles. Cine-CT performed at peak effort during supine bicycle exercise has detected an abnormal response in patients with suspected arterial stenosis.

cineangiocardiography—technique of recording the radiographic image of the heart and great vessels on motion picture film. This complex procedure combines cardiac catheterization and selective angiocardiography. Under fluoroscopic guidance, the cardiac catheter is maneuvered through the heart chambers and pulmonary artery. An image amplifier visualizes the cardiovascular structures. The frame speed of the motion picture camera ranges from a few frames up to 200 frames. Both cineangiographic and large film techniques require a power injector with or without timing devices.

digital fluorography—digital capabilities added to the conventional fluoroscopic procedure to provide clear, sharp images with the injection of a low-dose contrast medium.

electron beam computed tomography (EBCT)—technique employed for noninvasive identification and quantification of discrete coronary artery calcification. EBCT may be an effective means to assess and triage patients at risk for premature coronary artery disease or those with nondiagnostic chest pain syndromes. EBCT provides a noninvasive means to obtain quantitative information on cardiac anatomy, function, and flow and is a clinical alternative to conventional cardiac imaging. (66) (See the definition of electron beam computed tomography [EBCT] in the General Terms section.)

TERMS RELATED TO CHEST RADIOGRAPHY

bronchography—radiographic examination of the bronchial tree following the intrabronchial injection of an opaque solution. (35)

chest roentgenography—series of x-ray projections designed to evaluate chest, heart, lungs, and thoracic cage. These projections provide information about the size and configuration of the heart and great vessels and demonstrate pathophysiologic findings regarding pulmonary disease, blunt trauma to the chest, some congenital cardiac defects, and acquired heart disease. (35)

computed tomography (CT) of the bronchial tree—computerized device permits CT scanning of the bronchi to visualize diseases and tumors. (35, 62)

computed tomography (CT) of the lungs—CT imaging of thin slices of lung tissue for diagnostic evaluation. (23, 35)

computed tomography (CT) of the mediastinum—mediastinal CT techniques have the capability to identify different tissues by their attenuation characteristics, which can be very important in diagnosing mediastinal masses. The ability of CT to differentiate patients with a single chest mass from those with multiple masses is most helpful to the physician. In addition, the bolus intravenous injection of contrast material with dynamic CT scanning enhances intrathoracic structures, which in turn facilitates the differentiation of mediastinal from cardiac masses, and the depicting of mediastinal vascular abnormalities from mediastinal lymph nodes. (23, 35)

conventional tomography of the lungs and mediastinum—body section radiographs that delineate a thin layer of lung tissue; thus the structures lying anteriorly and posteriorly are more or less burned out. Tomographs demonstrate the presence of lung lesions. The widespread use of computed tomography (CT) has made conventional tomography less used in the localization of mediastinal masses. (62)

dynamic computed tomography of the lungs—rapid sequence (dynamic) CT following the injection of opaque medium into a peripheral vein for contrast enhancement to differentiate vascular and nonvascular lung lesions. (23, 62)

helical (spiral) computed tomography (CT)—technique involves continuous movement of the patient with concurrent scanning by a constantly rotating gantry and detector system. Helical CT serves as a primary screening tool in patients with thoracic metastases or lung cancer and as a problem-solving modality, for example with arteriovenous malformations. The airways can be displayed in detail on axial, coronal, or minimum intensity projection images, which is useful in planning interventional or surgical procedures. (83)

TERMS RELATED TO ABDOMINAL AND GASTROINTESTINAL RADIOGRAPHY

barium enema examination—fluoroscopic and radiographic examination of the colon after administrating a barium sulfate mixture rectally.

> *double-contrast enema*—examination of the colon using a small amount of barium to coat the mucosa of the colon and air to distend the colon. This procedure may demonstrate intestinal polyps and colonic carcinoma. (29, 62, 79)

barium upper gastrointestinal examination—radiologic study of the integrity of esophagus, duodenum, and upper small intestine. Study also may indicate some changes in the pancreatic or biliary system, alerting the radiologist to possible obstructive or disease processes in those areas. (19, 29, 43)

cholangiography—induction of radiopaque material into bile ducts for x-ray examination of the biliary system. (3, 90)

> *endoscopic retrograde cholangiopancreatography (ERCP)*—provides direct visualization of the biliary tree and pancreatic duct following the injection of these ducts with contrast material, through a catheter placed into the ducts via an endoscope in the duodenum. This study is of value in detecting common duct stones, inflammatory abnormalities, and neoplastic ductal abnormalities. (90)

> *percutaneous transhepatic cholangiography*—the injection of contrast material under fluoroscopic vision through a narrow-gauge needle positioned in the parenchyma of the liver. Like the ERCP procedure, this procedure is of value in detecting common duct stones, inflammatory problems, and neoplastic ductal abnormalities. (90)

cholecystokinin cholecystography (CCK-CCG)—procedure valuable in the diagnosis of chronic acalculous cholecystitis or biliary dyskinesia. The gallbladder is opacified, and serial radiographs are obtained after intravenous administration of cholecystokinin. (90)

oral cholecystography—oral cholecystographic contrast agents such as Telepaque (fat soluble) or Bilopaque (water soluble) are absorbed from the proximal small intestine, flow through the portal venous system, are conjugated within the liver and are excreted into the bile. Peak opacification of the gallbladder usually occurs about 14 to 21 hours after ingestion, except for water-soluble agents, whose peak opacification occurs approximately 10 hours after ingestion. The radiographs should be taken during this peak opacification period. (90)

esophagography, double contrast study—technique permits a detailed assessment of the esophageal mucosa for superficial ulceration or other changes of mild or moderate esophagitis that cannot be detected with conventional barium studies. The best technique for evaluating patients with suspected reflux esophagitis is a biphasic examination with upright double contrast and prone single contrast views of the esophagus. (19, 43, 45, 80)

computed tomography of the pancreas—CT procedure that demonstrates presence of pancreatitis and pancreatic cysts and tumors. CT's ability to provide detailed anatomic definition of the pancreas and surrounding structures has made it the single best imaging modality for the evaluation of suspected fluid collection. CT is also an excellent modality for detecting the secondary complications of fluid collections, such as infection and hemorrhage, or the involvement of adjacent structures (gastrointestinal tract, spleen or liver, blood vessels, urinary tract or kidney). Another important function of CT is to guide fine-needle aspiration of the fluid collection. CT can indicate secondary infection of pancreatic pseudocysts if it depicts gas bubbles or increased attenuation of the fluid contents. However, some fluid collections do not manifest any changes of infection, and a definitive diagnosis is possible only if cultures of the fluid yield organisms. (22)

helical (spiral) computed tomography (CT) of the pancreas and biliary tract—technique involves continuous movement of the patient with concurrent scanning by a constantly rotating gantry and detector system that takes 1 second for a 360-degree rotation. Helical CT provides the ability to relocate scan sections for visualization, detection, and staging of pancreatic neoplasms. Helical scanning of the bile duct has proved of value in detection of common bile stones, determination of the extent of cholangiocarcinoma, and preoperative assessment of patients undergoing laparoscopic cholecystectomy. (91)

TERMS RELATED TO UROGENITAL RADIOGRAPHY

plain radiography of abdomen (KUB—kidney, ureter, and bladder)—radiograph made without injection of air or radiopaque solution to serve as contrast medium. The procedure is a preliminary step when urologic diagnosis is anticipated. (34, 41, 62)

urography—radiography concerned with detection of urologic disorders. Some special procedures are:

cineradiography of urinary tract—urographic motion picture record of successive images appearing on fluoroscopic screen to demonstrate transient or persistent vesicoureteral reflux after having gradually filled the bladder with radiopaque medium.

computed renal tomography—use of a digital, x-ray-based, cross-sectional imaging modality that has the capability to detect subtle differences in the x-ray attenuation properties of various tissues and in its generation of cross-sectional images. CT provides detailed evaluation of renal anatomy and pathology. It has been useful in differentiating between normal renal tissue, renal tumors, and cysts and to provide cancer staging. CT is the procedure of choice for resolving most clinical problems relating to the adrenal gland. CT provides very good morphologic information but does not provide functional data. Radionuclide imaging of the adrenal gland is usually employed when functional information is required. (13, 15, 34, 41)

cystourethrography—cystography combined with urethrography to visualize abnormalities of the bladder and urethra following blunt pelvic trauma. A voiding cystourethrography is a procedure that demonstrates dilatation and elongation of the posterior urethra. Findings that may be seen include a linear radiolucent band representing the valve, the verumontanum is often enlarged, and the bladder neck commonly hypertrophies and, therefore, appears narrow in relationship to the dilatated posterior urethra. A voiding cystourethrography is useful in the assessment of anomalies of the posterior urethral valve. (31, 34, 41)

excretory urography—urograms demonstrating renal excretory function. They are obtained by intravenous injection of a contrast medium, which results in filling of renal calices and pelves with radiopaque solution. Excretory urograms visualize tumors, cysts, hydronephrosis, pyelonephritis, calculi, and other obstructive lesions of the urinary tract; vesicoureteral reflux; and renal ischemia. (13, 14, 41)

pedal lymphangiography—delineation of the lymphatic system after the injection of radiopaque material into both feet to visualize the lymphatic structures of the lower extremities, the groin, pelvis, periaortic region, and thoracic duct. (11, 34, 41)

retrograde cystography—vesical filling with opaque solution to detect bladder perforation due to injury, to study the neurogenic bladder, and to evaluate for vesicoureteral reflux, and bladder diverticula. (34, 41)

retrograde pyelography—roentgenograms are obtained following direct instillation of contrast material into the pelvis or ureters via catheters. The first roentgenograms are obtained after 3 to 5 milliliters of the contrast medium have been introduced through the ureteral catheter into the renal pelvis or ureters. The second roentgenograms are obtained after the catheters are withdrawn. The main advantage of this procedure is that a dense contrast substance can be injected directly under controlled pressure resulting in good visualization. This procedure usually is employed when excretory urography has been inconclusive. (41)

TERMS RELATED TO OBSTETRIC RADIOGRAPHY

amniography—radiography of the pregnant uterus after injection of a radiopaque substance into the amniotic fluid.

computed tomography (CT) pelvimetry—measurement of various obstetric diameters of the bony pelvis utilizing CT scanning techniques. Also, this procedure may be done employing magnetic resonance imaging techniques. Although the value of pelvimetry continues to be debated in obstetrical care circles, the main advantages of CT pelvimetry are that the results are more accurate than plain film pelvimetry. (62)

plain radiograph of abdomen and pelvis—abdominal x-ray films may identify the fetal skeleton after 16 weeks of gestation. (62)

TERMS RELATED TO BREAST RADIOGRAPHY

ductography—radiography procedure performed after injecting the mammary ducts with radiopaque contrast material. This technique is used to identify the discharging ductal system. It may provide a diagnosis (e.g., mass or suspicion of carcinoma) and it is helpful in localizing the origin of discharge prior to biopsy. (2, 51, 62)

mammography—soft-tissue mammary radiography based on varying degrees of absorption of the x-ray beam by fatty, fibroglandular, and cancerous tissue in the breast, in decreasing order of translucency. Two or three radiographic views of the breast (mammograms) outline benign lesions (nodules or cysts), or malignant lesions, which may be spiculated, ragged, and irregular in shape or poorly circumscribed, and can be associated with thickening and retracting of skin, nipple deformity, axillary lymph node involvement, microcalcifications, and venous congestion. Since the presence of fat serves to identify lesions, no radiopaque substance is injected into the lactiferous ducts. Mammography also may be used in screening studies of asymptomatic women and in postmastectomy follow-up examinations. (2, 51, 62)

TERMS RELATED TO OPHTHALMIC RADIOGRAPHY

angiography of ophthalmic artery—radiographic visualization of the ophthalmic artery for the detection of primary and metastatic tumors of the orbit, extraorbital neoplasms, vascular malformations, and occlusions and aneurysms of the ophthalmic artery. (62)

computed tomography (CT) in ophthalmology—use of CT scanning provides images of tissue planes at a given thickness. In ophthalmology, scans are made of the orbit, including the lateral and third ventricles, to detect orbital disease or tumors as well as intracranial lesions such as optic glioma, metastasis, or brain injury. Computed tomography used in ocular motility disorders can demonstrate the anatomy of extraocular muscles, and any intracranial neurologic cause. Extraocular muscle enlargement in Graves' disease and associated compressive neuropathy also may be visualized by CT scanning. (62)

distention dacryocystography—forceful injection of contrast medium into a canaliculus during x-ray exposure to outline the nasolacrimal duct system in its distended state. Direct x-ray magnification aids in the detection of obstructive lesion. (62)

optical coherence tomography (OCT)—a new medical diagnostic imaging technology that can perform micron resolution cross-sectional or tomographic imaging in biological tissues. This particular technology is similar to ultrasound B-mode imaging or radar except that light is used instead of acoustic or radio waves. Optical techniques have higher spatial resolution than ultrasound and do not require direct contact with the eye. OCT permits simultaneous viewing of the position on the ocular structure that is being scanned, as well as its transverse cross section. OCT can be used in real time to diagnose characteristic morphologies in the anterior eye, or the fundus, or it can be used to create a diagnostic record similar to fundus photography. (53)

orbital arteriography—serial angiograms of the orbital arteries, primarily via the ophthalmic branch of the internal carotid artery and secondarily via branches of the external carotid artery. The technique is used to detect arterial malformation or arteriovenous fistula of orbital vessels. (62)

TERMS RELATED TO OTOLOGIC RADIOGRAPHY

diagnostic angiography—method of evaluating glomus tumors preoperatively, assessing arterial supply and degree of vascularity, encasement of major arteries, degree of arteriovenous shunting, presence of major venous sinus occlusion by the tumor, multicompartmentalization or multifocality of tumor, confirmation of the expected diagnosis, and the exclusion of other vascular skull-base processes mimicking glomus tumors. (17)

otologic computed tomography—multiple serial section views of the ear that are of diagnostic value in middle and inner ear disorders, such as pure cochlear otosclerosis, Ménière's disease, and others. It is also helpful in detecting the site of facial nerve injury by cholesteatoma or glomus jugulare, intracranial extension of glomus tumor, translucent area of temporal bone, malformations of the middle and inner ear, and ossicular chain injury. Computer tomography's ability to visualize fine bony anatomy is important in evaluating the region of the temporal bone. (8, 17, 33)

> *high resolution computerized tomography (HRCT)*—thin-section HRCT renders exquisite bony detail. It is the preferred initial imaging modality when a lesion is clinically localized in the middle ear or mastoid and is the method of choice in cases of temporal bone trauma. (8)

venography—radiographic study of the venous system following the injection of a water-soluble radiopaque contrast agent. A cerebral or jugular venogram is performed to evaluate skull base tumors or conditions that cause *pulsatile tinnitus*. Procedure may be performed via puncture of a femoral vein, with navigation of the catheter through the vena cava to the internal jugular vein. The catheter can be placed at any location in the venous system and a venogram can be obtained. Small catheters are used for intracranial applications to limit the risk of venous sinus perforation. (12, 17)

TERMS RELATED TO RADIATION INJURY

over-irradiation—excessive radiation exposure. It may cause a syndrome characterized by nausea, vomiting, diarrhea, anorexia, and malaise within hours after overexposure, followed by blood dyscrasia within weeks or months. (62)

radiation anemia—usually aplastic anemia; no red cells are formed due to suppression of bone marrow activity. It occurs following excessive whole body radiation. (61, 62)

radiation sickness—untoward effects of radiation exposure, usually manifested by nausea, vomiting, and diarrhea, resulting from the breakdown of body tissue. (62)

radiodermatitis—inflammation of skin resulting from exposure to radiation. (62)

radioepithelitis—disintegration of epithelial tissue due to radiation, notably to that of the mucous membrane. (62)

radionecrosis—disintegration or death of tissue caused by radiation. (62)

radionephritis—acute condition caused by overexposure of the kidney to radiation. It is manifested by hypertension, edema, casts, and protein in the urine. (62)

radioneuritis—nerve involvement resulting from overexposure to radiation. (62)

DIAGNOSTIC ULTRASOUND

GENERAL TERMS

diagnostic ultrasonography—the recording of ultrasonic waves as they pass through deep structures of different reflectivity or echogenicity to locate pathologic lesions.

> *gray-scale ultrasound*—an ultrasound image containing various shades of gray rather than only black and white. A gray-scale image contains more complete information, since echoes of the intermediate strength are recorded.

real-time imaging—method of representation that displays images almost as fast as they are produced, permitting them to be viewed without delay.

real-time ultrasound instrument—provides diagnostic data for application in abdominal ultrasound, echocardiography, and peripheral vascular studies. (2, 89)

echography—reflections (echoes) of ultrasound waves directed at the tissues producing a record (image) of different acoustic densities resulting in differentiation between solid and cystic structures. (2, 87) Related terms are:

anechoic, sonolucent—echo-free, nonproductive of echoes.

echogenic—echo-producing; productive of echoes.

echogenicity—ability to produce echoes.

echogram—graphic record of reflected ultrasound imaging.

echographic elements:

- *attenuation sign*—decrease in reflective sound or echoes in solid tissue to differentiate solid from cystic fluid-filled lesions.
- *reflection*—the return of an echo from a surface, the strength of return being related to impedance.
- *strength of echo*—power of sound beam, capable of delineating differences in tissue reflectivity with minute precision.
- *ultrasonic tissue differentiation*—echogenicity of tissue is variable, since stiffness or bulk influence the sonographic beam.
  - *collagen*—supporting tissue of various organs is thought to be echogenic. When a tumor replaces normal collagen, the echogenicity is decreased in the organ.
  - *fat*—this tissue is of considerable echogenicity.
  - *fluid*—cell-free fluid is sonolucent. Tumors are echogenic; cysts are echo-free.

general measurements:

density—mass per unit of volume. (2)

frequency—number of cycles per second. (89)

hertz (Hz)—unit of frequency equivalent to one cycle per second. (89)

- *megahertz (MHz)*—1,000,000 Hertz or one million cycles per second. (89)

sonic—pertaining to audible range; sound is heard by human ear. (89)

- *infrasonic, subsonic*—below the audible range; sound is too low in frequency to be heard. (2)
- *ultrasonic, ultrasound*—above the audible range. This refers to sound beams of frequencies over 20,000 per second, which are inaudible to human hearing. (2)

sound wave—mechanical disturbance propagating through a liquid, solid, or gas medium. Sound waves are produced by vibrating sources that are in contact with the medium. (89)

- *longitudinal wave*—occurs as a sound wave travels through air, water, or soft tissue; the particles in the medium vibrate parallel to the direction of propagation of the sound wave. (89)
- *sound wave frequency*—the number of oscillations per second made by the vibrating source. (89)

velocity—product of frequency times the wavelength. (62, 87)

wave—distance traveled per unit of time. (2)

- *wave amplitude*—the maximum change in pressure caused by the wave and related to the intensity of the ultrasonic radiation; as the intensity increases, the amplitude also increases. (89)
- *wavelength*—distance between one given point and the next similar point of a wave measured in the direction of propagation. (89)

Figure 18.1 Three methods of ultrasound imaging. (B-mode and M-mode are schematic.)

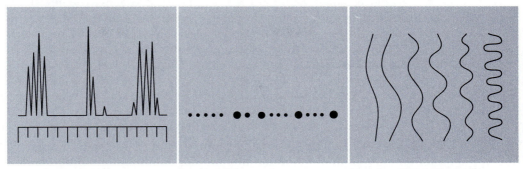

A-mode: amplitude, spikes   B-mode: brightness, dots   M-mode or T-mode: time motion

ultrasonic imaging methods:
> *modes*—methods of display or imaging. (87) (See fig. 18.1.)
>> • *A-mode*—amplitude modulation that portrays echoes as vertical spikes and reflects the height of the spike in proportion to the strength of the echoes. The transducer remains stationary. In the A-mode, a single beam of sound waves and its reflection create a simple linear display on an oscilloscope.
>> • *B-mode*—brightness modulation that depicts echoes on a linear trace as dots differing in size and intensity relative to the strength of the echoes and producing a two-dimensional cross-sectional display. Two methods are used:
>>> • *B-mode in time motion (TM)*—transducer remains in a fixed position while used to reflect echoes of a moving structure. Difference in strength of echoes may be portrayed by various shades of gray.
>>> • *B-mode, B scan, ultrasonography*—transducer is guided across the body region under study producing a transsectional, two-dimensional image of the structures. This method, known as real-time scanning, is dynamic.
>>> • *M-mode*—motion modulation that displays the changing pattern in echoes, with the transducer in a fixed position and the trace moving sideways. (2, 89)

Doppler ultrasound—continuous ultrasonographic technique concerned with the change in the frequency of sound waves, which are reflected from a pulsating target or circulating blood in a vessel and are transmitted as audible sounds. (89)

SELECTED ULTRASONIC STUDIES

TERMS RELATED TO DIAGNOSTIC ULTRASOUND OF THE BRAIN AND THYROID

carotid artery duplex sonography—this technique utilizes a combination of two modalities: high-resolution, real-time, two dimensional cross-sectional imaging, combined with pulsed Doppler ultrasound. Duplex sonography permits scanning of the extracranial portions of the carotid arteries, which are the most common sites of atherosclerotic lesions and has been very helpful as a noninvasive diagnostic tool in the evaluation of patients with suspected cerebrovascular arteriosclerosis and ascertaining the severity of carotid bifurcation disease. One advantage of color is speed in localization of the vessels. (2)

echoencephalography—studies of intracranial structures and vessels using ultrasonic pulse echo techniques. As soon as the density of the brain tissue is altered, a pulse beam of high-frequency sound, emitted by the transmitter, will echo back and be recorded on an oscillographic screen. This procedure detects pressure-producing and space-occupying brain lesions, cerebrovascular disease, seizure disorder, and hydrocephalus. (2)

ophthalmic echography—scanning technique utilizing:

> *A-mode echography*—depicts size of extraocular muscles, allowing the examiner to determine the presence of orbital congestion, since such congestion engorges and enlarges the extraocular muscles.
>
> *B-scan ultrasonography*—reflects the engorgement of the ethmoidal, superior, and vertical ophthalmic veins. Ophthalmic echography can be employed to confirm the diagnosis of a dural carotid-cavernous sinus fistula. B-scan ultrasonography using a water bath technique can distinguish the anterior sclera, but it is difficult to determine the precise borders between sclera and overlying episcleral tissue, and between sclera and underlying ciliary body and choroidal tissue with this particular technique. (49)
>
> *high-frequency ultrasound biomicroscopy*—method of producing high-resolution subsurface images of the eye at microscopic resolution. This procedure permits examination and assessment of anterior scleral disease. For example, localized anterior staphyloma can be differentiated from other causes of a black spot on the scleral surface. Episcleral thickening can be differentiated from involvement of the sclera itself. Scleral thinning can be assessed and quantified. Changes in the choroid, retina, and underlying vitreous can be detected as well. (49)

transcranial Doppler (TCD) sonography—ultrasonographic technique for recording blood flow velocities in cerebral arteries. Also, this technique is utilized to assess the time course and severity of vasospasm following subarachnoid hemorrhage, and to detect stenosis and occlusions of intracranial arteries, and to study intracranial hemodynamics in carotid artery disease. (2)

ultrasonography (Doppler) in supraorbital region—blood flow measurements by the transmission of a sound wave of ultrasonic frequency.

> *normal blood flow*—the direction of the blood flow is from the ophthalmic artery into the supraorbital artery and over some ramifications into the external carotid artery.
>
> *retrograde blood flow*—reversal of the blood flow occurs in occlusion of the internal carotid artery and is detectable by ultrasonography. (2)

ultrasonography of the thyroid gland—diagnostic ultrasound; a simple noninvasive method for ascertaining the size of the thyroid gland and nodules and differentiating solid from cystic lesions. B-mode ultrasonography offers information about hypofunctioning thyroid nodules and aids in establishing patterns for cystadenoma, multinodular goiter, and thyroiditis. It is a safe procedure in the assessment of pediatric and pregnant patients with thyroid lesions. (2)

TERMS RELATED TO CARDIOVASCULAR ULTRASONOGRAPHY

continuous-wave Doppler technique—method involving continuous transmission of ultrasound waves coupled with continuous ultrasound reception. The principal advantage of continuous-wave Doppler is its ability to measure high blood cell velocities. The main disadvantage of this method is its lack of depth discrimination. Usually this method is not incorporated into color flow systems. (2)

pulsed Doppler technique—noninvasive, nontraumatic method of comprehensive and quantitative assessment of blood flow to a structure or organ. (2)

Doppler ultrasonic flowmetry—ultrasound techniques for obtaining phasic, continuous, and instantaneous measurements of velocity (speed) of blood flow in various cardiovascular disorders, especially in aortic valvar disease and venous thrombosis. Doppler flow analysis has been found to be an excellent screening test for assessing the technical adequacy of the in situ saphenous vein bypass graft. (2)

Doppler color flow mapping—method whereby the characteristics of blood flow (direction, velocity, and size) are displayed on the two-dimensional echographic image by means of color encoding of the Doppler-generated flow signal. The usual method to visualize Doppler color flow data is in real-time at the time of the examination. However, images also may be recorded on video tape for review and analysis after examination. The brighter the hue, the faster the velocity; the duller the hue, the slower the velocity. Doppler color flow mapping is noninvasive, relatively inexpensive, with little patient risk in comparison to other imaging methods and makes flow information readily available for patient care. (59, 60, 62)

echoaortography—ultrasonic study of the aorta. (2)

gray-scale imaging—echographic method for detecting abdominal aortic aneurysm and measuring the vascular lumen distinct from the thrombus, which transmits denser internal echoes than the lumen.

echography of aortic root—screening technique for assessing bicuspid aortic valve, a congenital defect that predisposes to serious aortic disorders.

echocardiography—graphic recording of ultrasound waves reflected from the heart for the purpose of determining the development and severity of mitral stenosis, delineating such conditions as pericardial effusion as small as 15 milliliters (mL) and congenital and acquired heart disease. Echocardiography permits recognition of cardiomyopathy and classification into dilatated, hypertrophic, and restrictive-obliterative types. Intraoperative echocardiography includes assessment of left ventricular size and function; monitoring of left ventricular performance; imaging of coronary arteries; and assessment of coronary flow velocity, myocardial perfusion, and adequacy of mitral valve operations. Echocardiography may be utilized also to depict the structure and function of the transplanted heart and can be of assistance in detecting post-transplantation complications such as pericardial effusion and endocarditis. (2, 10, 30, 47, 60, 70)

Doppler echocardiography—utilizes ultrasound to record blood flow within the cardiovascular system. This technique focuses primarily on cardiac function in contrast to emphasis primarily on structure. Doppler echocardiography provides excellent noninvasive hemodynamic information. It may be used as a screening mechanism for suspected valvular disease, such as evaluating valvular incompetence. It may be employed to guide endomyocardial biopsy. Doppler echocardiography is the technique of choice for assessing the pressure gradient in valvular stenosis, as well as evaluating intracardiac shunt lesions. Color flow Doppler echocardiography is a quite effective technique for detecting early complications of endocarditis, paraprosthetic leaks, and valve dehiscence. It is also useful in detecting aortic disease and can depict the site of intimal tears in patients with aortic dissection. Color flow Doppler echocardiography is quite sensitive for regurgitation.

M-mode echocardiography—technique involves a single transducer emitting 1,000 to 2,000 pulses per second along a single line, providing an "icepick" view of the heart. The direction of the beam may be adjusted so that the heart can be scanned from the ventricles to the aorta and left atrium. M-mode echocardiography provides excellent temporal resolution.

two-dimensional real-time echocardiography—valuable noninvasive technique that uses a multiple transducer for imaging positions and permits appreciation of spatial relationships of cardiac anatomy. The introduction of digital recording and display to two-dimensional echocardiography has greatly enhanced this procedure. This addition gives the reviewer the ability to edit much of the respiratory artifact and to choose that cardiac cycle for evaluation in which no or little respiratory artifact is present. Since the digital acquisition can be done on line, the speed with which the study can be performed and evaluated is greatly enhanced. The digital format of the images allows the corresponding views at rest and during exercise to be viewed side by side for direct comparison. This type of two-dimensional real-time echocardiography is used for evaluating patients with coronary artery disease and exercise testing, as well as judging ventricular function with regard to wall thickening and wall functioning. Three-dimensional echocardiography is possible but difficult and not widely used at present.

stress echocardiography—procedure that evaluates regional wall motion abnormalities induced by either exercise on a bicycle or treadmill, or pharmacologic stress.

transesophageal echocardiography (TEE)—provides high-resolution real-time images of the heart. Most often, it can be performed without interfering with the surgical field, and has been helpful in detection of regional wall motion abnormalities. The availability of two-dimensional, transesophageal echocardiographic monitoring techniques were developed that allowed intraoperative wall motion analysis by real-time imaging of the beating heart in the anesthetized patient. Intraoperatively or during transcatheter closure, TEE is useful for confirming closing of septal defects, repair of valve defects, adequacy of conduits, outflow tract repair, or arterial switch. The superior spatial resolution and lack of acoustic shadowing associated with TEE are particularly valuable when investigating patients with disease involving the ascending aorta or small intracardiac abnormalities. This applies to acute aortic dissection, vegetations on cardiac valves, paraprosthetic leaks, and a variety of congenital heart diseases. TEE is also useful in the assessment of systemic and pulmonary venous return, sinus venous defects, fenestrated atrial septal defects, atrioventricular canal defects, subaortic stenosis, and pulmonary atresia.

TERMS RELATED TO ABDOMINAL AND GASTROINTESTINAL ULTRASONOGRAPHY

abdominal echography—the use of noninvasive diagnostic ultrasound for studying the liver, gallbladder, pancreas, spleen, kidney, aorta, and retroperitoneal space. It aids in the detection of intra-abdominal abscesses, cysts, or tumors. (2)

biliary echography—ultrasound imaging of the gallbladder and biliary ducts, which may be anechoic or display variable echoes, depending on the type of biliary pathology, such as dilatated bile ducts and gallbladder obstructed by cancer of the ampulla, hydrops of the gallbladder due to obstruction of the cystic duct, or gallstones seen by acoustic shadows. (2)

Doppler ultrasonography—permits detection of the presence and direction of blood flow based on changes in the frequency of back-scattered ultrasound waves produced by the movement of blood. Doppler ultrasonography can be utilized to evaluate the patency of surgically created portosystemic shunts. Doppler analysis enhanced by color flow imaging may detect vein patency by depicting flow around thrombus and flow in the distal portal veins. (2)

duodenum and stomach endosonography—technique permits introduction and advancement of the endosonographic scope to the first or second portion of the duodenum. After the scope is in the stomach, it is advanced through the pylorus. The proximal portion of the duodenum is then evaluated. The greater and lesser curves as well as the posterior and anterior walls of the stomach are assessed. (5, 6)

endosonography of the esophagus—initial investigation of the esophagus for esophageal and periesophageal disease. It is performed with the standard endoscope, then following local administration of pharyngeal anesthesia and sedation of the patient, the echoendoscope is inserted into the pharynx and passed down into the esophagus. Endoscopic ultrasound (EUS) is the most reliable imaging technique for the staging of esophageal carcinoma because of its ability to assess the depth of tumor infiltration and lymph node metastases. (4, 82)

gallbladder sonography—real-time ultrasound evaluation of the gallbladder aids in detecting gallstones and other forms of pathology. The gallstones can be diagnosed by identifying the curvilinear echo within the gallbladder and the acoustic shadow deep to the echo. The structures around the gallbladder can be surveyed with this technique as well. The right kidney should be surveyed to determine that there is no abscess, calculus, or tumor that could mimic gallbladder pain. (1)

hepatic sonography—ultrasonic investigation revealing either a normal liver or evidence of hepatic cirrhosis, ascites, liver abscess, fluid-filled cysts, hepatoma, cancer, and metastasis.

> *intraoperative ultrasonography*—utilizing the application of the ultrasound transducer to the exposed liver at surgery, results in an increased sensitivity of detecting occult hepatic metastasis.
>
> *ultrasound-guided liver biopsy*—technique of using echo-guided fine needle for liver biopsy. (85)

pancreatic endoscopic ultrasonography—endoscope is introduced into the periampullary region of the second part of the duodenum, where images of the head of the pancreas, portal vein, and papilla are observed. The endoscope is then repositioned in the duodenal bulb for images of the head and neck of the pancreas, portal vein, and distal common bile duct. The endoscope then is withdrawn into the stomach for imaging of the body and tail of the pancreas, and pancreatic duct, left kidney, spleen, and splenic vein. (22, 87)

sonographic colon examination—ultrasound imaging employed in finding and differentiating neoplastic masses, cysts, and abscesses.

> *endosonography*—by utilizing the attachment of an ultrasound transducer to the tip of an endoscope, there results ultrasonographic imaging from inside the colon's lumen. This technique permits a more accurate determination of the depth of tumor metastasis through the colon wall. (2)

ultrasound guidance of abdominal biopsy—ultrasound is one of the imaging modalities used for guiding percutaneous biopsy of the abdomen. The other methods are computed tomography and fluoroscopy. (42)

TERMS RELATED TO MUSCULOSKELETAL ULTRASONOGRAPHY

sonography of hip joint—ultrasound (US) real-time examination from lateral projections permits visualization of the unossified cartilaginous portion of the acetabulum and cartilaginous femoral head to determine the presence or absence of a dislocation. US is a sensitive modality for detecting suspected joint effusion. US has proved useful in the diagnosis and follow-up of transient synovitis of the hip. US depicts distention of the anterior recess by joint fluid that lifts up the capsule from the femoral neck for more than 3 centimeters (cms). Transient synovitis of the hip is the most common cause of painful hip in children. (2, 9, 35, 65)

ultrasonography of tendons and soft tissues—sonograms assist in the study and evaluation of tendon pathology. Different types of lesions may be identified such as tendinitis, peritendinous lesions, and ruptures. US is of assistance in the evaluation of clinically suspected infection by showing fluid collection around a joint prosthesis or fracture. Soft tissue abnormalities detected by US include thickening of subcutaneous tissue, fluid collections, abscess, and sinus tract formation. Because of the high resolution capability of US, discrimination between cellulitis and a deep fluid collection from abscess or joint effusion can be made. (9)

TERMS RELATED TO UROGENITAL ULTRASONOGRAPHY

renal sonogram, nephrosonogram—record of ultrasonic waves passing through the renal tissue for the purpose of determining the size and location of the kidney. Sonograms may detect congenital anomalies, such as horseshoe kidney, agenesis, and renal ectopy; aid in differentiating between hydronephrosis, unilateral multicystic kidney, and polycystic kidney; and demonstrate cysts or tumors. (2, 24, 34)

ultrasonic scanning of renal transplant—serial volume measurements of kidney transplant by ultrasound to detect changes in size, such as increase in renal size with or without scattered echoes from collecting tubules in acute rejection transplant, or a decrease in size, usually present in chronic rejection of transplant. (34)

Doppler ultrasonography—Doppler color flow imaging is a very helpful procedure in confirming the diagnosis of renal vein thrombosis.

duplex ultrasonography—this technique brings together two modalities; high-resolution, real-time, two-dimensional cross-section imaging combined with pulsed Doppler ultrasound. This procedure has been utilized for scanning of renal occlusive disease. (2)

urologic ultrasonography—the diagnostic use of sound beam echoes in the detection of renal tumors, or cysts, perirenal abscess, retroperitoneal mass, or hemorrhage, polycystic kidneys, testicular torsion, and prostatic disorders. Sonographic endorectal probes have the capability to image the prostate in a very detailed manner. Prostatic sonography provides information about the prostate gland and seminal vesicles, and the relationship of the prostate to the urinary bladder. (24, 34)

> *transrectal ultrasonography*—transrectal sonographic scanning technique that is useful in the early detection of prostatic cancer. Ultrasound has the capability of differentiating certain processes, such as calculi, cysts, ejaculatory duct dilatation, and others that can mimic carcinoma on digital rectal examination. However, prostatic ultrasound does not identify all cancers, and, therefore, it would be wise to consider ultrasound as a screening mechanism utilized in conjunction with the digital rectal examination, and the prostate-specific antigen (PSA), in a program of combined assault to detect the presence of prostatic cancer. (2, 62)

> *testicular ultrasonography*—testicular sonogram can be of help in establishing the presence of testicular parenchymal abnormalities, as well as to determine whether a palpable lesion is inside or outside of the testicle. If located inside, malignancy potential is greater. When a testicular neoplasm is suspected, blood for tumor marker determinations should be performed. A transscrotal biopsy of the testis or a transscrotal orchiectomy should not be performed if cancer is the likely potential diagnosis, as these procedures may predispose to the development of local recurrences and metastases to the inguinal lymphatics. This is usually not the case if a high inguinal orchiectomy is performed. Scrotal sonography is the most commonly used technique for evaluating the scrotal contents, depicting the testis as a homogeneous, moderately echogenic content; the mediastinum testis is depicted with a more increased echogenic texture, and the echo-consistency of the epididymis is similar to that of the testis. Doppler sonography (either pulsed or color) is an effective procedure to evaluate the blood supply to the testis. Duplex sonography (Doppler used in conjunction with sonographic imaging) allows direct visualization of the source of any detected vascular signal. (2, 62)

TERMS RELATED TO OBSTETRICS AND GYNECOLOGY ULTRASONOGRAPHY

ultrasound monitoring of fetus—high-resolution, dynamic ultrasound systems provide assessment of fetal well-being by documenting fetal activity. This type of sonographic biophysical data assesses variations of fetal heart rate, fetal breathing activities, coarse and fine motor activity, fetal tone, and amniotic fluid volume. Sonography's capability for high-resolution examination has allowed the identification and characterization of many fetal abnormalities. (40, 71)

> *amniotic fluid ultrasonography*—sonography estimation of amniotic fluid volume is an important element in fetal evaluation. The evaluation is usually carried out during the second or third trimester. Both oligohydramnios and polyhydramnios may be determined by amniotic fluid ultrasonography. Polyhydramnios has long been identified with serious congenital malformations. The most common disorders known to cause oligohydramnios are fetal renal disease, intrauterine growth retardation, preterm rupture of the membranes, and postmaturity. When antenatal sonography visualizes an aberrant sheet or band of tissue attached to the fetus with characteristic deformities and restriction of motion, a diagnosis of amniotic band syndrome can be established. Sonography has proved to be a major modality for identifying these fetal abnormalities. (45)

fetal echocardiography—ultrasound examination of human cardiac development and function in utero. By the early second trimester, the fetal heart is seen as a distinct, contracting fluid-filled structure. By the mid-second trimester, the cardiac chambers and valves can be depicted and studied. Cardiac structures are usually imaged by cross-sectional echocardiography and augmented by a combination of range-gated pulsed Doppler ultrasonography and M-mode echocardiography. The joining of Doppler ultrasonographic techniques with two-dimensional echocardiogram, and the representation in color of abnormalities in flow, volume, and direction serve to aid the physician in establishing a definitive diagnosis. Pulsed Doppler ultrasound examination combined with findings from fetal echocardiographic examination often detect such defects as hypoplastic heart syndromes or Ebstein's malformation of the tricuspid valve. (30, 45, 60, 70)

fetal musculoskeletal ultrasonography—real-time sonography provides the best current format for imaging fetal bones. The ossified portions of the fetal skeleton in the womb possess the highest level of contrast and are seen by sonography earlier and more consistently than any other fetal organ. This is not true of abortuses in which radiographs depict bony morphology more advantageously than would a sonogram. Direct visualization of neural tube defects can be ascertained by using a high-resolution real-time scanner for obtaining longitudinal and transverse sections of the fetal spine. (72)

ultrasonography of neonatal brain—noninvasive imaging modality providing detailed visualization of the ventricles, and intracranial structures of the neonate and promoting the assessment of hydrocephalus, cystic lesions, and cerebral hemorrhage. The skull defect in encephalocele also is delineated by ultrasound. (22, 40, 45, 73, 76) High-frequency transvaginal probes have been employed in the second and third trimesters to develop a systematic examination of the fetal brain. The procedure was developed from the standard neonatal neurosonographic examination. The transvaginal sonographic images are produced by scanning the fetal brain through the anterior fontanel using high-frequency transducers. The high-quality scans produced by this technique seem to indicate that transvaginal scanning is a major addition to evaluating and defining central nervous system abnormalities detected in utero. Transvaginal color Doppler sonography enables visualization of intracranial circulation earlier than it was possible by transabdominal sonography. (40, 45, 71)

fetal urologic ultrasonography—urologic sonographic scans can depict urethral obstruction of which the main signs include dilatation of the fetal urinary bladder, and proximal urethra with thickening of the urinary bladder wall. (2, 45)

gynecologic ultrasonography—the diagnostic use of ultrasound in detecting ovarian masses, pelvic inflammations, abnormalities of uterus, and tubo-ovarian abscesses. The ability to assess the flow to and within pelvic masses extends the capability of diagnostic sonography from an anatomical to a pathophysiological basis (39, 74)

color Doppler sonography—ultrasonographic technique that can be obtained with either transabdominal or transvaginal transducer/probes. Color Doppler sonography has a primary role in the detection of ovarian torsion. Color Doppler sonography can be used as an adjunct in differentiating morphologically similar pelvic masses. It is important to be aware that the areas of overlap in benign vs. malignant lesions tend to involve masses that contain vasodilated vessels or those that are actively hemorrhaging. (21, 39, 74)

obstetric ultrasonography—sonographic techniques for detecting fetal abnormalities, such as fetal hydrops and anencephaly, and maternal disorders: hydramnios, ectopic pregnancy, hydatidiform mole, fibroids, or cysts associated with pregnancy. Ultrasound is used in normal placental localization and the detection of placenta previa and twin placentas. (60, 73)

Other ultrasonic procedures may include:

antepartum fetal blood sampling—blood from the umbilical vein of an undelivered fetus obtained with the use of high-resolution dynamic ultrasound to direct a needle through the tissues of the maternal abdomen and uterus to the umbilical vein site, either where it enters the placenta or where it exits from the fetal abdomen. This procedure permits the determination of the fetal karyotype, assessment of biochemical and endocrine status of the fetus at risk for various inherited metabolic disorders, determination of hemoglobin structure in fetuses at risk for inherited hemoglobinopathies, the determination of erythrocyte and platelet membrane antigen status in the fetuses at risk for alloimmune disorders. In the affected fetus, the procedure permits determination of the presence and severity of disease, and the determination of the blood gas, acid-base, and biochemical status in the fetus at risk for antepartum asphyxial disease. Some complications may occur such as fetal hemorrhage either into the amniotic fluid, into the cord substance (cord hematoma), or into the maternal circulation (transplacental hemorrhage). Fetal death occurs at a frequency of approximately 1 per 500 procedures. Maternal complications are rare but include the risk of infection, placental abruptio, and hemorrhage. (45)

echosonography in early pregnancy—detection of intrauterine gestation. In the first trimester, ultrasonic data relate to pregnancy location, size of fetus/sac, and viability. During the second trimester, ultrasound data reflect fetal size and fetal growth. Fetal age is estimated by crown-rump length or gestational sac mean diameter. In the third trimester, data focus on size for growth considerations, fetal anatomy, and biophysical behavior. (45, 59, 60, 61)

obstetric echocardiography—cardiac evaluation of maternity patient with pericardial effusion, mitral valve disease, or cardiomyopathy by using ultrasound to assess the cardiac status and estimate the volume overload of the heart.

ultrasonic cephalometry—A-mode and B-mode ultrasonic techniques combined for determining the biparietal diameter (BPD) as a means of estimating the size, weight, and probable gestational age of the fetus. (61, 69)

MAGNETIC RESONANCE IMAGING

GENERAL TERMS

magnetic resonance imaging (MRI)—use of magnetic resonance to create images of objects such as the body. The image brightness depends jointly on spin density and relaxation times, with their relative importance depending on the particular imaging technique and choice of interpulse times. Image brightness is also affected by any motion such as blood flow and respiration. (1, 38)

magnetic resonance angiography (MRA)—technique represents a wide range of magnetic resonance sequences devised to provide angiographic contrast. MRA depicts and portrays blood vessels and blood flow by magnetic resonance imaging. Breathhold MRA has shown good visualization of the proximal coronary arteries. (16)

phosphorus-31 MR spectroscopy—noninvasive MR technique utilized for the investigation of high-energy phosphate metabolism of the heart. (16)

ultrafast magnetic resonance—refers to a group of techniques developed for acquiring images in a very rapid fashion. Ultrafast MR imaging of the heart allows imaging of individuals with irregular heart rhythm, making ultrafast MR imaging a major tool in clinical and research imaging of the cardiovascular system. (50)

SELECTED MAGNETIC RESONANCE TECHNICAL TERMS

magnetic field gradient—a magnetic field that changes in strength in a certain given direction. Such fields are used in nuclear magnetic resonance imaging with selective excitation to select a region for imaging and also to encode the location of nuclear magnetic signals received from the object being imaged. (38)

magnetic resonance (MR)—resonance phenomenon resulting in the absorption and/or emission of electromagnetic energy by nuclei or electron in a static magnetic field, after excitation by suitable RF magnetic energy. Continuous developments in pulse sequences, coil design, and gradient performance have extended the high-resolution capabilities of whole-body MRI systems. MR image resolution can be improved by increasing either gradient duration or gradient amplitude. Other associated terms include:

free induction decay (FID)—if transverse magnetization of the spins is produced, such as by a 90° pulse, a transient MR signal will result that will decay toward zero with a characteristic time constant T2* (T-two-star); this decaying signal is the FID. (38)

gradient—the amount and direction of the rate of change in space of some quantity, such as magnetic field strength. Also commonly used to refer to magnetic field gradient. (38, 86)

gradient echo—spin echo produced by reversing the direction of a magnetic field gradient or by applying balanced pulses so as to cancel out the position-dependent phase shifts that have accumulated because of the gradient. In the latter case, the gradient echo is usually adjusted to be coincident with the RF spin echo. Gradient-echo sequences are typically used in musculoskeletal imaging as a rapid method of acquiring images in which substances with long T1 relaxation, such as fluid, appear bright. (38)

gradient refocused echo (GRE)—type of MR pulse sequence that is characterized by reduced flip angle radio-frequency (RF) pulses and applied gradients that refocus the echo. Gradient refocused echo also is termed fast scan imaging. This type of MR pulse sequence is very sensitive to the magnetic susceptibility effects of paramagnetic substances. (38)

radiofrequency (RF)—wave frequency intermediate between auditory and infrared. The main effect of RF magnetic fields on the body is power deposition in the form of heating (mainly at the surface), and this is a major safety limits issue and concern. RF pulse is a burst of RF energy delivered to an object by a RF transmitter. (38, 88)

spin-echo—reappearance of a nuclear magnetic resonance signal after free induction decay has apparently died away, as the result of the effective reversal of the dephasing of the spins (refocusing) by techniques such as RF pulse sequences or pairs of magnetic field gradient pulses (gradient echo), applied in times shorter than or on the order of T2. Unlike RF spin echoes, gradient echoes will not refocus phase differences because of chemical shifts or in homogeneities of the magnetic field. (38)

spin-echo imaging—represents any of the many MR imaging techniques in which spin echo is used rather than FID. (38)

TI—inversion time. In inversion recovery, the time between the middle of the inverting (180°) RF pulse and the middle of the subsequent exciting (90°) pulse to detect amount of longitudinal magnetization. (38)

TR—repetition time. The period of time between the beginning of a pulse sequence and the beginning of the succeeding (essentially identical) pulse sequence. (38)

T1 (T-one)—spin-lattice, or longitudinal relaxation time; the characteristic time constant for spins to tend to align themselves with the external magnetic field. Starting from zero magnetization in the z direction, the z magnetization will grow to 63% of its final maximal value in a time T1. (38, 88)

T2 (T-two)—spin-spin, or transverse relaxation time; the characteristic time constant for loss of phase coherence among spins oriented at an angle to the static magnetic field, due to interactions between spins, with resulting loss of transverse magnetization and nuclear magnetic signal. Starting from a nonzero value of the magnetization in the xy plane, the xy magnetization will decay so that it loses 63% of its initial value in a time T2. (38, 88) *T2* (T-two star)*—the observed time constant of the FID due to loss of phase coherence among spins oriented at an angle to the static magnetic field, commonly due to a combination of magnetic field inhomogeneities. (38)

SELECTED MAGNETIC RESONANCE IMAGING (MRI) STUDIES

BRAIN, SKULL BASE, AND SPINAL CORD MRI

Magnetic resonance imaging (MRI) is capable of differentiating between **gray** and **white matter** with the brain substance, and providing excellent contrast between blood vessels and surrounding structures. Detection of disorders has been greatly enhanced with the addition of the **Federal Drug Administration's (FDA)** approval of the intravenous contrast agent, **gadolinium DTPA (Gd DTPA)** for MRI. High-dose (greater than 0.1 mmol/kg) intravenous gadolinium chelate administration provides superior lesion enhancement and detection of additional lesions, as well as lesion **necrosis** in metastatic brain disease. MR's ability to precisely identify the number and location of **brain metastases** is key for therapeutic decision making.

Primary hemangioblastomas of the **posterior fossa** are easily depicted by MRI. The separate cystic and solid components may be easily differentiated. **Hemangioblastomas** are a primary characteristic of **von Hippel-Lindau disease.** Individuals with this **familial neurocutaneous disorder** may exhibit multiple site tumors. Any type of change or insult to the structure of the brain associated with alteration in water content or myelin can be depicted in abnormal signal intensity on MR imaging. MRI is a sensitive instrument to be utilized in the detection of a wide variety of **non-neoplastic processes** that affect the brain. Within a short period, usually a few hours, following **vascular occlusion,** MRI is capable of detecting and localizing a **cerebral infarction.** MRI's ability to image flowing blood, has proven to be quite effective in detecting and localizing **arteriovenous malformations.** Also, MRI has detected **intracranial hemorrhage,** including hemorrhagic contusions and shearing injuries.

MR imaging of the **skull base** offers several benefits such as lack of artifact from bone, multiple plane imaging and fewer artifacts from dental fillings. Anatomic landmarks identified in the orbit by MR imaging are **globe, rectus muscles, optic nerve,** and **blood vessels.** MRI can demonstrate the posterior extent of the optic nerve through the **optic canal** and into the **chiasm,** thus MRI is a very helpful modality in evaluating **optic pathway gliomas.** The combination of multiple plane imaging and the high contrast of intraorbital structures makes the orbit and its contents an excellent area for evaluation by this modality. MRI appears to be playing a major complimentary role to CT scanning in most orbital disease entities. The inability of MRI to detect calcification may limit the specificity of MR in diagnosing **optic nerve sheath meningiomas,** and also, to a lesser extent, the **lacrimal tumors.**

The soft-tissue contrast and the direct multiplanar capability of MRI, supported by the elimination of artifacts from dense bone dental fillings or metal and the recently achieved spatial resolution comparable to that of CT, has made MRI the widespread accepted modality for the study of **pituitary** disease. The normal pituitary gland occupies a variable volume of the inferior portion of the **sella turcica.** The **pituitary stalk (infundibulum)** can be seen on MR imaging as it lies in the midline within the **suprasellar cistern.** Intravenous (IV) contrast enhancement is recommended for improved delineation of a **pituitary macroadenoma** from surrounding structures and, in particular, for improved definition of **cavernous sinus invasion.** An **intrasellar meningioma** can simulate a **pituitary macroadenoma.** The **extrasellar** extent of **macroadenomas** is readily depicted on MR contrast enhanced images, as are relationships to important **parasellar** structures, such as the **optic nerve, optic chiasm, cavernous sinuses,** and **carotid arteries.**

MR imaging is gradually becoming the procedure of choice used in the evaluation of the spinal axis. MRI has been helpful in the assessment of **intramedullary disease** (congenital, neoplastic, or demyelinating in origin). The ability to image the spinal cord in its entirety with MRI facilitates the diagnosis of intramedullary neoplasms. This is also important in patients with **vertebral metastatic disease,** since multiple lesions are usually present in these patients. MR imaging is site specific in defining **demyelinating plaques** associated with **multiple sclerosis.** MR imaging is effective in detecting **syringomyelia.** Another disorder, **agenesis** of the **corpus callosum,** causes characteristic brain abnormalities that are easily identifiable on MR scans. Some other anomalies that may be associated with this disorder are **Chiari II malformations, Dandy-Walker malformation, holoprosencephaly, neuronal migration abnormalities, encephaloceles,** and **interhemispheric cysts.** Although a plain radiographic film should be obtained to define bony anatomy, MRI with its multiplanar imaging capabilities depicts excellent morphologic detail of abnormal neural and soft-tissue anatomy, and is now the best means for the evaluation of **spinal dysraphism. Spina bifida occulta** is the most benign form of spinal dysraphism. In more severe forms of spinal dysraphism, **myelomeningoceles** protrude outside the skin with dilatation of the underlying subarachnoid space. (27, 46, 67)

MUSCULOSKELETAL, THORACIC, AND MEDIASTINAL MRI

MRI is utilized in evaluating derangements of the knee, abnormalities in the **temporomandibular joint (TMJ),** and **avascular necrosis,** as well as for depicting the extent of soft-tissue masses. MRI is quite sensitive in depicting marrow disease because the bone marrow is imaged directly. MR imaging demonstrates the severe marrow disorder of **Gaucher's disease** more effectively than other conventional methods. MRI can provide information on the extent of vascular invasion of **osteosarcoma** that is often difficult to assess on computed tomography (CT).

MRI's capability of using multiple planes of view provides for precise definition of the anatomic structures of the wrists and hand. The nerves, blood vessels, and tendons can be depicted through the **carpal tunnel** better than other imaging techniques. MRI's transaxial and coronal planes are used most in the evaluation of the hips. MR imaging provides a method of evaluating the **acetabular** and **epiphyseal cartilage** of the hip affected by **Legg-Calvé-Perthes disease,** permitting assessment of congruity of the acetabular and femoral articular surfaces and intracapsular soft-tissue irregularities. The coronal view is well suited for determining pathologic involvement along the vertically oriented muscle planes and femoral head, while the transaxial plane is more suited for the evaluation of long-bone marrow involvement. In the shoulder area, MRI's coronal and transaxial views are usually utilized for viewing the muscles and tendons of the **rotator cuff.** The major indication for MRI examination of the **lumbar spine** is for evaluation of possible **disc herniations.** The **nucleus pulposus** of the disc is easily identified in normal and degenerative conditions. When bone is examined, it is actually the **marrow** that forms the image, due to low levels of osseous water and high levels of fat. MR imaging depicts **aneurysmal bone cyst** as a well-defined expansive mass with cystic appearing characteristics of different signal intensities due to various stages of hemorrhage within the lesion.

MRI is an excellent modality for depicting the normal anatomy of the thorax and MRI is being employed more and more in the evaluation of **intrathoracic abnormalities. Cardiac** and **respiratory gating** techniques may be of assistance to help reduce **motion artifacts.** Fast imaging techniques are also used to decrease motion artifacts. The views reflected by the sagittal plane most often are applied to the mediastinal portion of the thorax, unless **apical** or **diaphragmatic** disease is suspected, although the sagittal plane also may be used to demonstrate pathologic processes in the anterior, middle, and posterior compartments of the **mediastinum.** Substernal and pretracheal lesions may best be delineated with this view. The oblique projections are particularly effective for cardiac imaging. The **thoracic wall** is easily visualized; however, there may be some loss of detail surrounding the lower thorax due to greater respiratory motion and cardiac activity. MR imaging reflects the ribs as a bright marrow signal surrounded by black cortical bone. MR imaging data for determining the anatomic association between **mediastinal masses** and great vessels are not always present with other types of modalities. Although computed tomography is the modality used for detection of **pulmonary nodules,** MRI's ability to visualize flowing blood is preferred to determine whether **hilar** or **parenchymal masses** are solid or vascular.

The skeletal and muscular components of the pelvis are well detected on T1-weighted images where the high-signal fat depicts the various muscle groups. MR imaging of the **iliopsoas** and other muscle groups appears to be superior to other modalities. The **knee, ligaments, menisci,** and regional **bone marrow** can be imaged quite effectively with MRI. A sagittal view provides visibility of the anterior and posterior **cruciate ligaments, menisci, popliteal vessels,** and surrounding tissue. Coronal views display collateral ligaments, and lateral aspects of the menisci, while transaxial views display **tendons, patellae, collateral ligaments,** and **diaphyseal** bone marrow spaces. **Cystic lesions** around the knee are common, for example, **Baker's cyst.** Other **cystic lesions** include **meniscal** and **ganglion cysts.** On MRI, cysts have low signal intensity on T1-weighted scans and bright signal intensity on T2-weighted scans.

MRI provides excellent soft tissue contrast features and delineates clearly the anatomy of the ankle joint. Utilization of coronal images reflects the relationship of the **tibia** and **fibula** to the adjoining **tarsal bones.** Sagittal images display the course of tendons best, as well as displaying the articular surfaces of the **tibia, fibula,** and **talus.** Axial images may be used to detect soft-tissue masses. The sagittal and axial images display the **Achilles tendon.** MRI of **Paget's disease of the bone (osteitis deformans)** shows both the changes of abnormal **bone remodeling** as well as the attendant changes in the **vertebral body marrow space.** In the active phase of the disease, the **hematopoietic bone marrow** is replaced by **fibrous connective tissue** with large numerous vascular channels. Cystlike lesions representing fat-filled marrow cavities may be present. (20, 23, 46, 63, 84, 88)

CARDIOVASCULAR MRI

MR imaging utilizing electrocardiographic gating techniques in conjunction with obtaining multisection single-echo images in the transverse plane best depict the entire **aorta** from the **aortic root** to the **aortic bifurcation;** it is also very effective in demonstrating **aortic dissection.** Aortic dissections are identified as definite when the characteristic **intimal flap** is visualized on the MR image. Additional views in the sagittal or coronal planes provide helpful assistance in determining branch vessel involvement, especially in the **aortic arch.** MRI can identify the most hazardous complication of dissection, namely, leakage of blood from the aorta resulting in **pleural effusion, pericardial effusion,** and **periaortic fluid collection.** MR imaging of congenital abnormalities of the aorta provides structural image detail that is useful in the evaluation of these aortic disorders, including **double aortic arch, vascular rings, supravalvular aortic stenosis,** and **coarctation.**

The **brachiocephalic vessels** appear to angle in a slightly oblique direction through the various coronal planes. MR imaging of the vena cava is an excellent technique to evaluate the presence of a **superior vena cava syndrome,** particularly in terms of differentiating extrinsic compression from the presence of a superior vena cava clot or tumor. Segments of the superior and inferior vena cava can be well defined, as well as their entry into the right atrium. The **descending aorta** and the **azygos vein** can be visualized easily. The main, left, and right **pulmonary arteries** may be followed throughout their mediastinal course. MRI appears to be the best imaging technique for defining the invasion or impingement of the **pulmonary arteries** by a tumor mass. The **pulmonary veins** intermittently can be visualized inserting into the left atrium.

MR imaging detects **thoracic aortic aneurysms** displaying concentric enlargement of the ascending or descending aortic aneurysms. Transverse MR images visualize the size of the residual lumen as well as the outer diameter of the aneurysm. Because of this, MR imaging can provide an accurate measure of the diameter of the aneurysm even in the presence of wall thickening or **mural thrombus.** MRI has been found effective in depicting **intracardiac thrombi** and **tumors.**

The development of **cine MRI** permits rapid dynamic imaging that allows evaluation of **ventricular performance,** as well as estimating the severity of **valvular regurgitation.** Cine MR imaging may prove to be the most effective technique for the noninvasive assessment of the severity of **valvular heart disease,** as well as a technique to monitor valvular and ventricular function. Cine MRI can be used to define the regional contractile abnormality caused by **ischemic heart disease.** Cine MRI may be used to determine **patency** of **coronary artery bypass grafts.** Cine MRI is able to demonstrate the abnormal flow pattern associated with **stenotic** and **regurgitant lesions.** The greater temporal and spatial resolution of cine MRI is one of its distinct advantages over radionuclide imaging in the evaluation of cardioventricular anatomy and function. **Radionuclide imaging** does not have the capability of demonstrating intracardiac flow patterns caused by shunt and regurgitant flow.

MRI techniques such as **ultrafast MR imaging** are dynamic techniques that acquire images at 300 to 500 milliseconds. An even faster MR imaging technique, **echoplanar** or **instant imaging,** in which single-snapshot images are acquired in 40 ms or less, is a technique that should be useful for imaging **cardiac** and **ventricular function** and for assessing **myocardial perfusion** when used in conjunction with paramagnetic contrast agents. (16, 18, 27, 32 50, 52, 78, 84, 88)

ADRENAL GLANDS AND KIDNEY MRI

MRI is utilized to assess patients with **adrenal cortical hyperfunction. Adrenal adenomas** larger than 2 centimeters in diameter can be detected by MRI. **Adrenal cortical carcinomas** that are usually larger than 10 centimeters in diameter and produce **Cushing's syndrome** can be depicted easily by MRI.

Computed tomography (CT) appears to be better than MRI in assessing **primary hyperaldosteronism,** because **aldosteronomas** and lesions of **nodular hyperplasia** tend to be very small and are poorly resolved on MR images. Both CT and MRI show high sensitivity for detection of **adrenal pheochromocytoma.** MRI possesses good sensitivity for detecting extra-adrenal and recurrent malignant pheochromocytomas. Views in the coronal plane offer an effective technique for scanning the **sympathetic chain,** thus increasing further the modality's ability to detect extra-adrenal lesions. The high soft-tissue contrast of MR imaging provides easy discrimination between the **adrenal gland** and adjacent organs. One disadvantage of MRI is that it is unable to detect adrenal calcification.

The kidneys are well delineated with MRI. MRI demonstrates morphological changes. Coronal views clearly define the **renal veins** and **inferior vena cava,** and enable **extrarenal metastases** to the **retroperitoneum, mediastinum,** and **liver** to be more effectively demonstrated. A major disadvantage of renal MRI is the poor demonstration of **calcification** and **calculi.** MR imaging of known **renal cell carcinoma** has advantages over computed tomography because of its better detection of tumor thrombus in major vessels and distinction of collateral vessels in the **renal hilus** from **renal hilar lymph nodes.** However, the staging process with MR imaging also has several limitations, such as its inability to allow reliable determination of tumors in **lymph nodes,** and MRI cannot currently be used to identify tumor spread through the **renal capsule.** (24, 31, 34)

PELVIC MRI

Over the past several years, MRI has shown to be a great diagnostic aid in depicting abnormalities of both sexes. MRI demonstrates anatomical features of the **prostate** and **seminal vesicles.** MRI detects prostatic parenchymal abnormalities. The high soft-tissue contrast of MRI is quite helpful in assessing the spread of **prostatic cancer** into adjacent structures, especially the **seminal vesicles.**

MRI of the **testes,** through its multiplanar imaging, provides superior tissue characterization along with its capability to detect **hemorrhage.** MRI demonstrates quite clearly the anatomical features of the **testis, scrotum,** and **inguinal region.** Both T1-weighted and T2-weighted sequences are required for a good evaluation of the **testis, epididymis,** and **spermatic cord.** The two **corpora cavernosa** and the **corpus spongiosum,** which combined make up the **penis,** are easily identified by MRI.

In the female pelvis, developmental abnormalities of the **reproductive tract** are very well suited to study by MRI, which clearly depicts the zonal anatomy of the **corpus uteri, cervix,** and **vagina.** T2-weighted images are utilized to best acquire optimal images of the internal organ anatomy and also for most disease processes. The use of MRI in the diagnosis of **placenta previa** is quite accurate. While abdominal ultrasound remains the most frequent diagnostic tool used for assessing placenta previa, vaginal probe ultrasound or MRI may be more helpful in cases of partial or posterior placenta previa. **MRI pelvimetry** enables fast, safe depiction of the birth canal.

Adenomyosis, a cause of uterine enlargement, can be diagnosed with MRI. MRI is useful in clarifying whether a mass is uterine or ovarian in origin. It can accurately measure the volume of an **uterine myoma,** and is also a valuable tool in distinguishing **leiomyomas** from other pelvic tumors when sonography has given indeterminate results. Studies have indicated that MRI can contribute to making a diagnosis of **leiomyoma** from an indeterminate solid pelvic mass and may save the patient from diagnostic surgery in selected cases.

Ovarian hemorrhagic cysts are well circumscribed and delineated by MRI. MRI appears to be more accurate than ultrasound for tissue characterization in differentiating simple fluid from that of more complex fluids. (28, 37, 64, 75, 77)

ABBREVIATIONS

GENERAL

A-mode—amplitude modulation
AP—anterior-posterior (projection of x-rays)
B-mode—brightness modulation
CAT—computed axial tomography
CT—computed tomography
DSA—digital subtraction angiography
M-mode—motion modulation

MRA—magnetic resonance angiography
MRI—magnetic resonance imaging
OCG—oral cholecystography
OCT—optical coherence tomography
RAD—radiology, radiation absorbed dose
US—ultrasound
USG—ultrasonography

RELATED TO SYMBOLS AND MEASUREMENTS

Bev—one billion electron volts
E—energy in ergs
erg—one unit of work
ev—one electron volt
f—frequency
Hz—hertz

Kev, keV—1,000 electron volts
Mev, MeV—one millon electron volts, megavolt, megavoltage
MHz—megaHertz, one million hertz
Q—volumetric flow rate
V—velocity

RELATED TO SCIENTIFIC ORGANIZATIONS
ABR—American Board of Radiology
ACR—American College of Radiology
ARRT—American Registry of Radiologic Technologists
ASRT—American Society of Radiologic Technologists

REVIEW GUIDE

Instructions: Define the following terms.

Example: density—mass per unit of volume.

absorption of x-rays	mammography
barium enema examination	noninvasive technique
computed tomography	optical coherence tomography
discography	oral cholecystography
dynamic computed tomography	radiofrequency
gray-scale ultrasound	radionecrosis
magnetic resonance angiography	testicular ultrasonography

Instructions: Define the following abbreviations.

Example: AP—anterior-posterior

Bev	CAT
DSA	RAD
ASRT	A-mode
M-mode	USG
OCT	MRA
erg	ev
Hz	ACR
ABR	ARRT
f	Mev

19

Selected Terms Pertaining to Nuclear Medicine

ORIGIN OF TERMS

atom (G)—indivisible

fission (L)—cleft, split

iso- (G)—equal

kine-, kinesio (G)—movement

GENERAL TERMS

activated water—water containing radioactive elements. (34)

activation analysis—method for identifying and measuring the chemical elements in a sample to be analyzed. The sample is first made radioactive by bombardment with neutrons, charged particles, or other nuclear radiation. The newly radioactive atoms in the sample give off characteristic nuclear radiations that can identify the atoms and indicate their quantity. (31)

alpha particle—positively charged helium nucleus characterized by poorly penetrating but strongly ionizing radiation. (31)

atom—smallest unit of any element, which consists of a central nucleus and outer orbital electrons. The nucleus is composed of protons and neutrons (except that of the hydrogen atom, which has no neutrons).

   electrons—negatively charged particles revolving around the nucleus.

   neutrons—electrically neutral particles present in the nucleus of an atom.

   protons—positively charged particles present in the nucleus of an atom; a mass approximately 1847 times that of the electron. The atomic number of an atom is equal to the number of protons in its nucleus.

   • *nuclear numbers:*
      • *atomic number (Z)*—number of protons in the nucleus of an atom.
      • *neutron number (N)*—number of neutrons in the nucleus of an atom.
      • *mass number (A)*—sum of neutrons and protons in the nucleus of an atom.
      Thus $A = Z + N$. (31)

atomic weight—relative weight of an atom compared to that of one carbon atom, which is 12. (31)

background radiation—the radiation of the natural environment, consisting of radiation from cosmic rays and from the naturally radioactive elements of the earth, including that from within the human body. The term also may mean radiation extraneous to an experiment. (34)

becquerel (Bq)—adopted by the International System of Units as the official unit of radioactivity. One Bq is defined as one nuclear transformation per second. One disintegration or decay per second (dps) equals one Bq. (34)

beta particle—nuclear particle either positively or negatively charged. When positively charged, the positron is useful for the gamma radiation produced when it interacts with a negatively charged beta particle. When negatively charged, the beta particle is essentially an electron, more penetrating and less ionizing than an alpha particle. The effect of beta particles is moderately destructive and usually limited to the first few millimeters of tissue. (31)

body burden—the amount of radioactive material present in the body of human beings or animals. (34)

bone seeker—a radionuclide that tends to lodge in the bones when it is introduced into the body; for example, strontium 90, which behaves chemically like calcium. (1, 34)

by-product material—any radioactive material (except source or fissionable material) obtained in the process of producing or using source or fissionable material. Includes fission products and many other radioisotopes produced in nuclear reactors. (34)

counter—device for making radiation measurements or counting ionizing events. (1)

curie—the unit for measuring the activity of all radioactive substances, or the quantity of radioactive material that undergoes 3.7×10^{10} disintegrations per second (dps). The International System of Units has adopted the becquerel (Bq) as the official unit of radioactivity. (See *becquerel*.) (34)

cyclotron—a particle accelerator in which charged particles receive repeated synchronized accelerations of "kicks" by electric fields as the particles spiral outward from their source. The particles are kept in the spiral by a powerful magnet. Cyclotrons are a valuable source of radionuclides for medical diagnosis and research. (34)

decontamination procedure—the removal of harmful radioactive material from persons, equipment, instruments, rooms, and so on. Some articles may be decontaminated by thorough washing with detergents or other chemicals. (34, 46, 54)

dosimeter—an instrument for measuring the dose of radiation.

emission computed tomography—consists of numerous techniques that produce a three-dimensional representation of the distribution of radionuclides within the patient. This technique eliminates the superimposed artifacts found in conventional two-dimensional gamma camera imaging, thus facilitating the monitoring of body physiologic changes and detecting abnormal pathologic lesions. In radionuclide emission computed tomography, photons are emitted from the patient. Two technologies associated with this concept are:

> *positron emission tomography (PET)*—a form of transaxial computed tomography utilized in the study of physiologic processes. With this process, it is possible to "label" compounds that have positron-emitting isotopes with proton emitters and subsequently "image" their distribution in the living body over time. PET may be used to localize tumors and to assess tumor viability before, during, and after therapy, both in primary and metastatic sites. Now available are whole-body PET scans that permit a survey of the entire body for metastatic tumors.

> *single photon emission computed tomography (SPECT)*—a form of transaxial computed tomography in which a set of planar views (projections) is obtained. These projections are stored in the computer memory and subsequently reconstructed into transaxial slices by algorithms. The projections are obtained by 1, 2, or 3 conventional gamma camera detectors with parallel-hole collimation. (6, 10, 12, 18, 28, 36, 41, 55)

film badge—photographic, dental-size x-ray film worn on the person for detecting radiation exposure. (34)

gamma ray—short wavelength electromagnetic radiation of nuclear origin. Gamma rays, which are similar to x-rays, are more penetrating than alpha and beta particles and are useful in diagnostic nuclear medicine. (6, 29, 31)

gamma stereotactic surgery—a therapy procedure for patients that utilizes several cobalt 60 beams focused by collimators on a finite target within the brain. Several diagnostic tests are performed to precisely identify the target area prior to the actual therapy procedure. (1, 34)

Geiger-Müller counter—a sensitive radiation detector composed of a tube filled with gas and a scaler. It is used to detect nuclear radiation. (31)

half-life, biologic—the time required for a biologic system, such as a human being or an animal, to eliminate, by natural processes, half the amount of a substance that has entered it. (31)

half-life, radioactive—time required for a radioactive substance to lose 50% of its activity by decay. For example, *Radiophosphorus* (^{32}P) has a half-life of 14 days. This means that a quantity of ^{32}P having a radioactivity of 250.0 mCi (millicuries) on a certain day will have an activity of 125.0 mCi (millicuries) 14 days later and 62.5 mCi (millicuries) 28 days later. (34)

ion—an atomic particle, charged atom, or chemically bound group of atoms. (31)

ionization—the process of producing ions.

isotopes—atoms having the same number of protons (atomic number) but differing by their atomic weight. (34)

labeled compound—a compound composed in part of a radionuclide. For example:

sodium radioiodide . . . . $Na^{131}I$
radiocobalt B_{12} . . . . $^{60}CoB_{12}$
chromic radiophosphate . . . . $Cr^{32}PO_4$ (34)

mass number—the sum of the neutrons and protons in a nucleus. The mass number of uranium 235 is 235. It is the nearest whole number to the atom's actual atomic weight. (31)

maximum permissible concentration—that amount of radioactive material in air, water, and foodstuffs that competent authorities have established as the maximum that would not create undue risk to human health. (34)

maximum permissible dose—that dose of ionizing radiation that competent authorities have established as the maximum that can be absorbed without undue risk to human health. (34)

median lethal dose (MLD, LD$_{50}$)—radiation that kills, in a given period, 50% of a large group of animals or other organisms. (34)

microcurie (μCi)—unit for measuring the energy of a radionuclide in a tracer dose. One microcurie is one millionth of a curie. (34)

millicurie (mCi)—unit for measuring the energy of a radionuclide in a therapeutic dose. One millicurie equals a thousand microcuries. (34)

nuclear fission—the splitting of a heavy nucleus into two or more nuclei, resulting in nuclear conversion and the release of powerful energy. (34)

nuclear medicine—a medical specialty involving the administration of radiopharmaceuticals to patients for the diagnosis and treatment of disease. (1, 34)

nuclides—atoms of an element distinguishable by their weight. The term denotes all nuclear species of chemical elements, both stable and unstable. It is used synonymously with isotope. (31)

photon—a discrete quantity of electromagnetic energy. Photons have momentum but no mass or electric charge. (34)

positron—a positively charged nuclear electron. (34)

radiation—the propagation of energy through matter or space in the form of waves. In atomic physics, the term has been extended to include fast-moving particles (alpha and beta rays, free neutrons, etc). (34)

radiation hazards:

external—exposure to ionizing radiation from radioactive sources outside the body.
internal—those caused by exposure to ionizing radiation from radioactive substances deposited inside the body. (34)

radiation exposure, acute type—a brief, intense radiation exposure, in contrast to prolonged or chronic exposure. (34)

radiation overexposure—excessive contamination by ionizing radiation that has deleterious effects on a person's health. In massive overexposure, symptoms of radiation injury develop in hours, days, or weeks; in chronic overexposure to small amounts of radiation, symptoms appear within months or years. (1, 34, 35)

radiation protection guide—the total amounts of ionizing radiation dose over certain periods that may safely be permitted to exposed industrial groups. These standards, established by the National Council on Radiation Protection and Measurements, are equivalent to what was formerly called the "maximum permissible exposure." (31, 34, 35)

radiation protection procedures—techniques used to safeguard patients and personnel from external and internal exposure. For example:

area monitoring—procedure for determining the amount of radioactive contamination present in a certain locality and at a given time.

personnel monitoring—individuals are monitored (namely, their breath, excreta, clothing, and so on) to detect health hazards and provide environmental safety. Monitoring records must be kept on all persons exposed to nuclear radiation in their employment.

Principles of safety in radiation protection procedures are concerned with:

time—the shorter the period of exposure, the lower the radiation dose.

distance—the further away from the radioactive substance, the less radiation received.

shielding—the denser the material between the person and the radioactive material, the lower the radiation hazard. Protection from the internal exposure is achieved by avoiding ingestion, inhalation, and direct contact with radioactive materials. (13, 31, 34)

radioactive contamination—the spread of radioactivity to places where it can have adverse effects on persons, experiments, and equipment. (29, 32)

radioactive decay, nuclear transformation—diminished nuclear properties (activity) of a radioactive substance in the course of time. (31, 34)

radioactive tracer—radionuclide used in minute amounts for diagnostic testing or evaluation, known as *tracer dose*. An element or compound that has been made radioactive can be easily followed (traced) in biologic and industrial processes. Radiation emitted by radionuclide pinpoints its location. In the treatment regiment, it is referred to as *therapeutic dose*. (1, 31, 34)

radioactive waste—equipment and materials (from nuclear operations) that are radioactive and have no further use. Wastes are generally referred to as *high level* (having radioactivity concentrations of hundreds to thousands of curies per gallon or cubic foot), *low level* (approximately one microcurie per gallon or cubic foot), and *intermediate* (between these extremes). (31)

radioactivity—the spontaneous decay or disintegration of an unstable atomic nucleus, accompanied by the emission of radiation. (31)

radioassay—quantitative analysis of substances using radionuclide tracer techniques to detect minute quantities not easily measured by other means. (31)

radioautograph, autoradiograph—a film record (radiograph) of an object or tissue made by recording the radiation emitted by the radioactive material within it, for example, after the introduction of radioactive material such as one of the technetium 99m phosphate complexes to detect metastases to osseous tissue. (31)

radiobiology—branch of biology dealing with the effects of radiation on biologic systems. (31)

radioimmunoassay (RIA)—technique of measuring minute amounts of substances by employing antigens and/or antibodies labeled with radioactive tracers. This technique has been applied to other biologically active substances, including nonimmune systems. Commonly used radioassay procedures measure serum levels of cardiac glycosides such as digoxin, cortisol, folic acid, triiodothyronine (T_3), thyroxine (T_4), and vitamin B_{12}. Radioimmunoassays offer reliable data and excel in specificity and sensitivity. (31, 51, 53)

radioisotopes—chemical elements that have been made radioactive by bombardment with neutrons in an atomic pile or cyclotron. Some occur in nature. By giving off radiation, they provide a valuable means for diagnosis and treatment. Radioisotopes differ from their nonradioactive partners by their atomic weight. For example, potassium, the stable isotope, has an atomic weight of 39; radiopotassium, the unstable isotope, has an atomic weight of 42. (31)

radiolabeled monoclonal antibodies—radiolabeling for imaging purposes uses a radionuclide whose gamma energy is suitable for gamma camera detection. It is essential that the immunoreactivity (how well the antibody binds to the target antigen before and after labeling) of the antibody be preserved following radiolabeling. The largest experience in radiolabeling antibodies exists with the use of radioactive iodine. Tumor staging with monoclonal antibodies is clinically useful in several conditions, such as colon carcinoma, ovarian cancer, melanoma, lung cancer, and choriocarcinoma. (38, 53)

radionuclides, radioactive nuclides—comprehensive terms including isobars, isomers, isotones, and isotopes, which exist for a measurable length of time and differ by atomic weight, atomic number, and energy state. The term *radioisotope* is obsolete and has been replaced by *radionuclide*.

> *isobars*—atoms have the same mass number (A) but have different atomic numbers (Z) and neutron numbers (N).
> *isomers*—atoms have the same atomic numbers (Z) and the same mass numbers (A) but differ in nuclear energy state.
> *isotones*—atoms have the same number of neutrons in the nucleus (N) but differ in atomic numbers (Z) and number of mass particles (A).
> *isotopes*—atoms have the same atomic numbers (Z) and, therefore, the same number of nuclear protons, but they have different numbers of mass particles (A), and therefore a different number of nuclear neutrons (N).
> A daughter radionuclide is a decay product produced by a radionuclide. The element from which the daughter was produced is called the parent. Radionuclidic purity refers to the amount of total radioactive species in a sample that represents the desired radionuclide. (31, 34)

radionuclidic imaging devices—Several instruments are in common use. Some examples are:

> *Anger camera, scintillation camera, gamma camera*—an instrument for presenting images of the distribution of radioactivity in any organ or part of the body. Its greatest assets are speed and sensitivity, which are of particular significance in dynamic function studies.
> *Anger multiplane tomographic scanner*—nuclear instrument that provides six complete synchronized images or readouts of variable depth or plane on a single scan (film).
> *rectilinear scanner*—the conventional scanner and a moving detector of radioactivity in selected areas of the body that is useful for static studies. (29, 34)

radiopharmaceuticals—radioactive pharmaceutical agents or drugs used for diagnostic or therapeutic procedures. The reason for using pharmaceutical agents that are radioactive is to follow their absorption, distribution, metabolism, and excretion through the use of appropriate detection devices, or to use these agents to target an organ or tissue for destruction. (38)

reactor—a device in which a fission chain reaction can be initiated, maintained, and controlled. Its essential component is a core with fissionable fuel. It usually has a moderator, a reflector, shielding, and control mechanisms. (34)

relative biologic effectiveness (RBE)—the relative effectiveness of a given kind of ionizing radiation in producing a biologic response as compared with x-rays. (13, 34)

scaler—an electronic instrument for counting radiation-induced pulses from Geiger counters and other radiation detectors. (32)

scan—image of the deposit of a radionuclide.

> *photoscan*—the pattern of radioactivity presented on x-ray film by a photorecorder.
> *scintillation scan*—image made by a scintillation counter to determine the size of a tumor, goiter, or other involvement and to locate aberrant, metastatic lesions. (1, 34)

scanning (nuclear medicine)—method of mapping out the deposition of a radionuclide in an organ using a rectilinear or other scanning device. (1)

scintillation counter—a highly sensitive detector for measuring ionizing radiation capable of counting scintillations (light flashes) induced by radiation in certain materials. (34)

scintiphotography, gammaphotography—the use of the Anger scintillation camera for obtaining photographs of the distribution of gamma-emitting radionuclides in living subjects. Scintiphotography may be employed for:

dynamic studies portraying rapidly changing images, as in the visualization of blood flow, vascular filling, or ventilation of radioactive xenon; static studies requiring highly technical performance of individual images (views); and, comparability of tracer concentration in related organs; for example, the intensity of radioactivity concentration in the spleen and marrow compared with that in the liver to demonstrate portal-systemic shunting of venous blood flow after surgery. (34, 47)

teletherapy with ^{60}CO—treatment of tumors within the body using an external source of cobalt 60 that is heavily shielded. The therapy beams may be rotated and shaped to permit a high dose to the tumor while sparing adjacent normal structures. (34)

whole body counter—device used to identify and measure the radiation in the body (body burden) of human beings and animals; uses heavy shielding to keep out background radiation and ultrasensitive scintillation detectors and electronic equipment. (34)

zipper effect—overlapping of two or more images. (1)

SELECTED RADIONUCLIDE IMAGING STUDIES

BLOOD FLOW, BONE AND BRAIN IMAGING STUDIES

blood flow imaging, perfusion studies—noninvasive, dynamic, nuclear uptake measurements to detect occlusive or stenotic vascular lesions or malformations of the brain, heart, lungs, kidneys, and other organs. (1, 47)

bone imaging—scintillation imaging following the intravenous injection of a bone-seeking radionuclide, such as one of the technetium 99m phosphate complexes, to detect metastases to osseous tissue and help to determine the extent of pathologic bone lesions or healing processes. Bone scintillation imaging has been used in the early detection of stress fractures and other fractures not demonstrated by usual radiographs. This particular type of imaging has detected minimal osseous trauma areas where radiographs of the same areas reflected normal findings in some child abuse cases. This technique serves as a diagnostic tool in the early detection of osteomyelitis, Legg-Calvé-Perthes disease, and other hip abnormalities. (9, 25, 40)

bone marrow imaging—delineation of areas of active bone marrow to detect abnormal expansion of bone marrow and areas of bone marrow destruction. (1, 25, 30, 41)

brain imaging—radionuclide uptake studies, dynamic or static, to detect intracerebral space-occupying lesions, malformations, trauma, or cerebrovascular disease. Diagnostic tracers frequently used are technetium 99m bound to diethylenetriamine pentaacetic acid and referred to as ^{99m}Tc DTPA, as well as ^{99m}Tc pertechnetate, ^{99m}Tc glucoheptonate, and others. Iofetamine HCL I-123 (SPECTamine) is the first lipid-soluble radiopharmaceutical for functional brain imaging approved by the FDA. Unlike earlier brain-imaging agents, SPECTamine easily crosses the intact blood-brain barrier because of its unique lipid solubility. Extraction efficiency is high, washout is slow, and blood-brain ratios are high. The initial distribution of SPECTamine is maintained for at least one hour despite slow washout. Transverse, coronal, and sagittal views may be obtained during brain imaging. Regional changes in brain physiology indicating impaired brain function are revealed, and this procedure is useful in documenting the site and extent of cerebrovascular accident (CVA).

cerebral circulation imaging—dynamic brain imaging to visualize cerebral blood flow to compare values in different regions and to analyze cerebrovascular disease or other vascular abnormalities. Images are taken in a sequential manner at 1- to 3-second intervals.

radionuclide cisternography—intrathecal injection of a tracer for diagnostic evaluation. Scans of cisterns are useful in delineating obstructive, nonobstructive, or ex vacuo types of hydrocephalus. This is the only diagnostic test used for establishing the diagnosis of normal pressure hydrocephalus. This test is also used to determine patency and drainage of neurosurgical shunts and to visualize the point of leakage associated with this type of shunt. (1, 5, 20)

HEART AND CIRCULATION IMAGING STUDIES

arteriovenous shunts—[99m]Tc human albumin microspheres (^{99m}Tc HAM) particle perfusion studies demonstrate collateral circulation when the surgically created shunts occlude. (1)

infarct-avid myocardial imaging—increased uptake of a radiopharmaceutical within an area of myocardial injury that permits its visualization as a "hot spot." Technetium 99m stannous pyrophosphate, ^{99m}Tc-labeled PYP, is commonly used as an imaging agent. The hot spot may be indicative of a subendocardial infarction, if increased uptake is 2 plus, and acute transmural infarction, if it is 3 or 4 plus. (12, 29, 38, 55)

myocardial perfusion studies—evaluation of blood flow through the heart muscle. The determination of regional blood flow depends on the tracers being uniformly mixed in the blood, extracted, and retained in the perfusion bed of the myocardium long enough to obtain static images. Blood flow and extraction are greatly reduced in ischemic and injured myocardial areas. This area is reflected as a "cold spot" or defect. Thallium 201 (^{201}Tl) scintigraphy is a sensitive technique for the detection of perfusion defects of the heart muscle in myocardial infarction. The larger the perfusion abnormality, the poorer the prognosis. Those patients with large perfusion defects may benefit from intracoronary streptokinase infusion or insertion of an intraaortic balloon pump to avert further hemodynamic deterioration. The use of myocardial perfusion scintigraphy early in the setting of myocardial infarction (MI) has been made more practical with the introduction of ^{99m}Tc-sestamibi, because it has very little washout once it enters the myocardium. ^{99m}Tc-sestamibi can be given when the patient presents and imaging delayed until the patient is stabilized. These images reflect the myocardium at jeopardy when the patient is first evaluated and obviate the delay in thrombolysis, which would be required if thallium 201 were used. Comparison with images acquired a few days later can demonstrate the amount of myocardium salvaged by thrombolysis or other interventional procedures. (1, 12, 38, 52, 55)

blood pool studies of the heart: (1, 37)

- *multigated (MUGA) blood pool studies*—these studies deal with ventricular wall motion and the ejection fraction and require that a tracer remain within the blood vessels during imaging. Technetium 99m–labeled red blood cells, ^{99m}Tc RBC, in vitro or in vivo, fulfill this condition. This study determines systolic, diastolic, and stroke volumes, cardiac output, ejection fraction, and regional and global wall motion abnormalities. (1, 19)

other radionuclide cardiovascular studies:

- *exercise thallium 201 (^{201}Tl) scintigraphy*—thallium 201 imaging in patients with exercise electrocardiograms is used for localizing and estimating the extent of significant coronary artery disease and evaluating the patient before and after myocardial revascularization. Serial studies are done to evaluate the patency or occlusion of postoperative grafts. This type of study is usually repeated 1 year after the graft procedure. (1, 2)

venous thrombosis radionuclide studies—nuclear medicine procedures available for the detection of deep-vein thrombosis include the following:

- *antifibrin scintigraphy*—antifibrin imaging is a new and innovative approach to the diagnosis of acute deep vein thrombosis. Antifibrin monoclonal antibodies labeled with Indium 111 or technetium 99m can be used. Initial clinical studies indicate accuracy with this approach and has the potential for overcoming many of the deficiencies of other methods for detecting deep vein thrombosis. Antifibrin imaging also has displayed excellent potential for use in patients with suspected acute, recurrent deep-vein thrombosis. (1, 22)

- *radionuclide venography*—bilateral injection of either ^{99m}Tc-human albumin microspheres (HAM) or ^{99m}Tc microaggregated albumin (MAA) into the dorsal veins of the foot. Application of tourniquets at the ankles assist to facilitate filling of the deep venous system. (20)
- *radiolabeled platelets technique*—employs indium 111 labeled autologous platelets to detect forming blood clots. This technique serves as a method for diagnosing focal atherosclerotic and thrombotic lesions, and for imaging vascular grafts. (22)

ADRENAL AND UROGENITAL IMAGING STUDIES

metaiodobenzylguanidine (MIBG) scintigraphy—MIBG acts as a tracer of catecholamine uptake and storage capacity by the sympathoadrenal system. The primary sites of normal uptake are the adrenal medulla, and in the sympathetic neuronal innervation of the heart, spleen, and salivary glands. The sensitivity of scintigraphy with either Iodine 123-MIBG or Iodine 131-MIBG for extra-adrenal tumors is 85% to 90%. For example, extramedullary pheochromocytomas occur in about 13% of patients. In adults, about 90% of malignant pheochromocytomas occur within the adrenal gland. In children, extra-adrenal tumors account for about 30% of pheochromocytomas and approximately 40% of these are malignant. Most primary neuroblastomas arise in the adrenal gland, although they can arise anywhere along the extra-adrenal sympathetic chain. Approximately 90% of neuroblastomas concentrate MIBG. MIBG scintigraphy is not a useful diagnostic technique to detect carcinoid tumors, but once carcinoid has been diagnosed, a total-body MIBG scintigraphy is useful to document disease extent, and this is helpful in choosing a therapeutic regiment. (1, 24, 27)

kidney imaging, renal imaging—radionuclide visualization of the kidney to study its structural and functional status and detect congenital abnormalities, perfusion defects, renovascular disease, obstructive lesions, kidney trauma, or other renal disorders. Radiopharmaceuticals for urologic diagnosis are various technetium 99m compounds, which label the renal cortex, define renal blood flow, or determine the rate of glomerular filtration. Abscesses and occult neoplasms may be detected by nuclear scans using gallium 67 citrate (^{67}Ga citrate). (26, 49)

kidney scintiphotography—use of a scintillation camera to visualize renal position and structure and evaluate renal function and blood flow distribution. Iodohippurate sodium ^{131}I (radioactive iodine) and technetium 99m cortical agent are diagnostic aids in evaluating renal blood flow in transplants, acute tubular necrosis, and uremia. (26, 49)

nuclear cystograms—accurate method of imaging bladder reflux. (2, 4, 49)

scrotal and testicular imaging—^{99m}Tc pertechnetate is an important tool in the evaluation of scrotal swelling and chronic testicular pain. Perfusion and tissue uptake are decreased in acute testicular torsion. In acute epididymoorchitis, perfusion and tissue uptake are increased. (4, 26, 49)

whole-body bone imaging—use of technetium 99m phosphate for skeletal scanning to demonstrate the extent of metastatic bone involvement of urologic malignancies. (2, 4, 49)

HEPATOBILIARY IMAGING STUDIES (8, 23, 41, 48)

hepatobiliary imaging—nuclear method of evaluating the liver or both liver and gallbladder.

xenon 133 (^{133}Xe)—retention in hepatic fatty infiltration due to alcohol abuse confirmed by scintigrams.

technetium 99m (^{99m}Tc) sulfur colloid—scintigram showing abnormal hepatic uptake in chronic alcoholics. Radionuclide demonstrates functioning of reticuloendothelial cells in liver, bone marrow, and spleen.

technetium 99m (^{99m}Tc) diethyl-IDA imaging—useful in noninvasive evaluation of hepatobiliary disorders. Nuclear cholescintigraphy provides accurate information about the biliary and hepatocellular function and the patency of the cystic duct and common bile duct. This is a reliable and often used test to demonstrate acute cholecystitis before surgery. This test may be used to evaluate postoperative status following cholecystectomy.

technetium 99m (^{99m}Tc) labeled red cell liver imaging—used to diagnose cavernous hemangiomas of the liver.

technetium 99m macroaggregated albumin (^{99m}Tc MAA) hepatic arterial perfusion imaging— used to evaluate intra-arterially administered chemotherapy of liver neoplasms.

PULMONARY IMAGING STUDIES

pulmonary imaging by: (32, 33, 36, 46, 47)

technetium 99m labeled macroaggregated albumin (^{99m}Tc-MAA)— injected intravenously and carried into the pulmonary circulation for perfusion studies. The particles lodge in the capillaries of the lung, except in areas of embolic obstruction or other blockage (about 70% of emboli are multiple).

xenon 133 (^{133}Xe)—for ventilatory studies inhaled to differentiate between emphysematous involvement or pulmonary emboli. Perfusion defects on lung scintigrams without any ventilation abnormality in the region are highly suggestive of pulmonary emboli. The diagnosis of pulmonary emboli is based on evaluation of blood flow to the lungs. Clearance of the perfusion defects after 4 to 5 days of anticoagulation therapy is presumptive evidence of recovery from embolic disease. No change in serial lung scans suggests presence of obstructive lung disease, such as emphysema, carcinoma, or other disorders.

gallium 67 (^{67}Ga)—used for staging of lung neoplasms (tumors less than 1.5 centimeters in diameter are not detectable), infections, and inflammatory conditions. Abnormal uptake of the ^{67}Ga in the mediastinum increases the prospect that mediastinal disease is present. The ^{67}Ga scans have been effectively used in patients with acquired immunodeficiency syndrome (AIDS) and the AIDS-related complex to identify *Pneumocystis carinii* pneumonia.

TERMS RELATED TO RADIONUCLIDES IN DIAGNOSTIC TESTS

SELECTED BLOOD TESTS

blood volume determination—sum total of red cell volume and plasma volume using chromium 51 (^{51}Cr) labeled red cells or technetium 99m (^{99m}Tc) labeled red cells used for measuring the blood volume. These findings are helpful in the diagnosis of polycythemia vera and in the management of fluid balance after surgery and severe burns. (51)

ferrokinetic tests include:

incorporation of iron (^{59}Fe) into red blood cells—in normal subjects this is 60% to 80% of the dose administered in 7 to 10 days. (51)

plasma iron clearance—iron (^{59}Fe) disappearance in half the time in plasma, which is normally 60 to 120 minutes. (51)

plasma iron pool (in milligrams)—determination by multiplying serum iron in milligrams by plasma volume per milliliter. Results may indicate iron deficiency anemias, polycythemias, and other disorders. (51)

red blood cell sequestration, RBC sequestration—measurement of rate of accumulation of chromium 51 (^{51}Cr) tagged red cells in spleen, liver, and pericardium by scintillation counting. The test aids in the diagnosis of hypersplenism due to any cause. (51)

red blood cells survival—determination of rate of disappearance of labeled erythrocytes from the circulating blood. Chromium 51 (^{51}Cr) is usually the tagging agent. The normal rate of RBC disappearance from circulation is 28 to 32 days. A decreased rate of cell survival is present in hemolytic anemias. (51)

SELECTED GASTROINTESTINAL TESTS

fat absorption test, lipid absorption test—measurement of fat digestion and absorption with radioiodine-labeled triolein and oleic acid, useful in distinguishing malabsorption syndromes. (50, 51)

gastrointestinal (GI) blood loss determination—localization of gastrointestinal bleeding by using technetium 99m labeled red blood cells (^{99m}Tc-labeled RBCs) or sulfur colloid for evaluation of GI bleeding. Serial images of the abdomen are done; if normal, the abdomen is clear; if bleeding is present, the activity can be localized. (50, 51)

GI protein loss determination—measurement of albumin leakage into the gastrointestinal tract using intravenous injection of albumin labeled with iodine 125 (^{125}I). (1, 50, 51)

vitamin B$_{12}$ absorption test, method of Schilling—determination of vitamin B$_{12}$ absorption as an aid in diagnosis of pernicious anemia and malabsorption of B$_{12}$ due to other causes. Using cobalt 57, 58, or 60 as a tracer, the amount of B$_{12}$ absorbed is indirectly measured by determining the percentage of the test dose that is excreted in the urine in 24 hours. Since the pathophysiology of pernicious anemia is the inability to absorb vitamin B$_{12}$, the urinary excretion in these patients is low (less than 10%). If a potent intrinsic factor is administered with the test dose B$_{12}$, it will permit absorption of B$_{12}$ in the presence of malabsorption caused by diseases other than pernicious anemia. (1, 41, 50, 51)

SELECTED RENAL TESTS

renal clearance test—functional renal imaging based on the fact that different radionuclear tracers measure the physiologic ability of specific areas of the kidney, such as effective renal plasma flow (ERPF) through glomeruli and proximal tubules, and glomerular filtration rate (GFR). (51)

renography—a graphic demonstration of both kidneys following the intravenous injection of a radioactive tracer and the placement of a sensitive detector over the kidneys. In the presence of unilateral disease, the curve of the moving nuclear bolus reflects reduced or increased tracer uptake by the affected kidney. (1, 49)

SELECTED THYROID TESTS (1, 6, 10, 21, 44, 51)

FTI, free thryoxine index, free T$_4$ index, FTE, free thyroxine estimate—an indirect measure of thyroxine-binding protein. FTI is increased in hyperthyroidism and decreased in hypothyroidism.

RAIU, radioactive iodine uptake determination—this test measures the ability of the thyroid gland to trap and organify the nuclide following the oral ingestion of a radioiodine tracer dose. A scintillation detector is used to determine the percentage of the thyroidal uptake of the radioiodine, usually at 6 and 24 hours after administration of the tracer dose. There tends to be an increase of radioactive iodine uptake in pregnancy and hyperthyroid and euthyroid states and a decrease in hypothyroidism.

TBG, thyroxine-binding globulin serum level—measurement of circulating levels of TBG. It is not to be confused with thyroxine-binding index (TBI). An increase of TBG may occur with hypothyroidism, estrogen therapy, oral contraceptives, and pregnancy; a decrease of TBG may occur with nephrotic syndromes, genetic hepatic disease, and other disorders.

TBI, thyroxine-binding index—a test of thyroxine-binding globulin levels in the patient's serum. A major problem is that the use of the contraceptive pill has become so prevalent that it interferes with the clinical interpretation of the test by elevating the level of the thyroxine-binding globulin (TBG) to elevations usually seen in pregnancy.

TRH, thyrotropin-releasing hormone—hormone produced by the hypothalamus, extrahypothalamic cerebral regions, and extracentral nervous system regions. TRH testing is an invaluable diagnostic procedure that is gradually replacing thyroidal stimulation and suppression studies.

TSH-RIA—this radioimmunoassay of the thyroid-stimulating hormone (TSH) is a highly sensitive test for detecting primary hypothyroidism. TSH may be increased in a goiter deficient in iodine, such as in myxedema.

TSH, thyroid stimulation hormone test—measurement of the thyroid response to the administration of the thyroid-stimulating hormone (TSH). The test aids in the differential diagnosis of thyroidal hypothyroidism, in which a diseased thyroid fails to respond to TSH. In pituitary hypothyroidism, the thyroid gland may begin to function after a TSH injection, since the gland may be simply dormant rather than diseased.

T_3 or T_3 RIA serum level—measurement of triiodothyronine (T_3) in human serum by radioimmunoassay. An elevated T_3 serum level in the presence of normal T_4 (thyroxine) concentration may indicate T_3 toxicosis or toxic nodular goiter.

T_3 or T_4 suppression test—measurement of the thyroidal uptake of radioiodine and a scan following the oral administration of triiodothyronine (T_3) or thyroxine (T_4). In euthyroid patients, there is usually a 50% suppression of the thyroidal uptake. In thyrotoxicosis, it does not drop below the normal range. The test is useful in distinguishing neurotic persons with borderline uptake from true hyperthyroidism. T_3 or T_4 suppression tests and TSH stimulation tests are gradually being replaced by TRH testing, since the procedure is safer for the patient.

Tg, thyroglobulin RIA—measurement of the protein thyroglobulin (Tg) in human serum by means of a radioimmunoassay. Serum Tg levels are elevated in Graves' disease, toxic adenomas, toxic multinodular goiter, and nontoxic diffuse or multinodular goiter.

Note: The therapeutic role of radionuclides may be seen in their employment in the treatment of polycythemia vera and in selected cases of leukemia and lymphoma. However, the application of radionuclides in therapy is more restricted than in diagnostic applications. For example, in the treatment of carcinomas, radionuclides serve as palliative agents with the potential for prolonging life, and they have a low capacity for inhibiting or destroying malignancies other than in certain thyroid or ovarian cancers. In nuclear medicine, radionuclides are primarily used for tracer studies, and their significance in diagnostic evaluation has been firmly established. (See table 19.1.)

ORAL READING PRACTICE

RADIONUCLIDE IMAGING OF THE THYROID GLAND

The **thyroid gland** lies in the anterior part of the neck, immediately in front of the trachea and below the **thyroid cartilage.** The two lobes of the thyroid are united by an **isthmus** in the form of a shield. The affinity of the thyroid for **iodine** is an interesting and unique characteristic of this **endocrine gland.** It is the basis of many thyroid function studies and the medical treatment of many thyroid diseases.

Associated with the development of **nuclear reactors** as part of the atomic weapons program, **radionuclides** (a species of atom whose nucleus disintegrates spontaneously, emitting radiation in forms of alpha or beta rays) became abundantly available as by-products, and many of these have been developed for use in the practice of nuclear medicine.

Nuclides are varieties of a chemical element that differ in their atomic weights but possess the same chemical properties. Some elements are available as both stable and **radioactive nuclides;** for example, iodine 127 (^{127}I), the stable element with an atomic weight of 127, and iodine 131 (^{131}I), one of the radionuclides, with an atomic weight of 131. The latter is a widely used radionuclide of iodine and is generally the one implied by the term "radioiodine."

The ^{131}I does not differ chemically from iodine, but differs physically in that it emits **beta particles** (radioactive particles emitted from the atomic nucleus; high-energy positively or negatively charged electrons) and **gamma rays** (high-energy, short-wavelength electromagnetic radiation emanating from the nucleus of some nuclides). Since the beta particles penetrate only 2 millimeters of tissue, they are almost all absorbed within the gland. On the other hand, about 90% of the gamma rays escape and can be accurately measured outside the body with a

TABLE 19.1	Some Radionuclides in Diagnosis		
Radionuclide	*Labeled Tracer*	*Diagnostic Procedures*	*Clinical Use*
Gallium 67 (^{67}Ga)		Identification of viral myocarditis and new onset of cardiomyopathy Localization of infection	Viral myocarditis Cardiomyopathy AIDS-related respiratory disease
Indium 111 (^{111}In)	Leukocytes (WBCs)	Abscess localization	Chronic abscess and other infections
Indium 111 (^{111}In)	Antimyosin	Identification of myocarditis and cardiac allograft rejection	Heart failure Myocarditis Cardiac allograft rejection
Iodine 123 (^{123}I)	Iofetamine (Spectamine)	Brain imaging	Brain function Cerebrovascular accident Dementia Epilepsy
Iodine 131 or 123 (^{131}I, ^{123}I)	Sodium iodide	Thyroid scan and RAIU uptake determination	Thyroid carcinoma Thyroid adenoma Thyroid nodule
Iodine 131 (^{131}I)	Hippuran	Measurement of effective renal plasma flow-ERPF	Renal clearance
Iodine 125 (^{125}I)	Human serum albumin	Blood volume determination, cardiac output, and circulation time	Vascular and cardiac disease
Iodine 125 (^{125}I)		TBI (Thyroxine-binding index) FTI (Free thyroxine index) T$_3$ (Triiodothyronine uptake test)	T$_3$ toxicosis
	Fibrinogen	Clot formation study ^{125}I fibrinogen uptake	Detection of thrombi in formative stage
Technetium 99m (^{99m}Tc)	Ceretec (HMPAO)	Cerebral perfusion studies	Detection of occlusive or stenotic vascular lesions malformations of the brain
Technetium 99m (^{99m}Tc)	Diethylenetriamine pentaacetic acid (DTPA) or DTPA chelate	Brain scan Perfusion studies Nuclear cisternography Renography or imaging Perfusion studies	Brain lesion Vascular disorder Hydrocephalus Renal disorder unilateral or bilateral obstructive renovascular hypertension Transplanted kidney
	Pertechnetate	Meckel's diverticulum (ectopic gastric mucosa)	Common cause of gastrointestinal bleeding in children

TABLE 19.1 (continued)

Radionuclide	Labeled Tracer	Diagnostic Procedures	Clinical Use
Technetium 99m (^{99m}Tc)	Red blood cells	Nuclear cardiology Angiocardiographic studies—blood pool imaging	1. Congenital cardiac defects Myocardial infarction Ventricular aneurysm Ischemic heart disease 2. Localization of gastrointestinal bleeding 3. Most sensitive test for diagnosis of liver hemangiomas
Technetium 99m (^{99m}Tc)	Sestambi (Cardiolite)	Myocardial perfusion studies	Myocardial perfusion studies; same as Thallium 201, but has better image quality; it shows no redistribution
Technetium 99m (^{99m}Tc)	Teboroxime	Myocardial perfusion studies	Myocardial agent with rapid washout Stress-rest study can be completed in 1 hour instead of 3 or 4 hours required with thallium study
Technetium 99m (^{99m}Tc)	Macroaggregated albumin (MAA) Erythrocytes Sulfur colloid	Lung perfusion studies Erythrocyte venography Imaging for functioning of reticuloendothelial cells in spleen, liver, and bone marrow	Pulmonary embolism Pulmonary venous hypertension Deep vein thrombosis Thrombophlebitis Evaluation of functional status of reticuloendothelial cells—chronic alcoholism
Technetium 99m (^{99m}Tc)	Stannous pyrophosphate	Bone imaging to detect osteogenic alterations Cardiac imaging Infarct-avid imaging Blood pool imaging	Metastatic bone lesions Osteomyelitis Acute myocardial infarction
Thallium 201 (^{201}Tl) and Technetium 99m (^{99m}Tc)		Parathyroid scan	Parathyroid adenoma
Thallium 201 (^{201}Tl)	Thallous chloride	^{201}Tl scintigraphy	Perfusion defects Myocardial ischemia Myocardial infarction

TABLE 19.1 (continued)			
Radionuclide	*Labeled Tracer*	*Diagnostic Procedures*	*Clinical Use*
Thallium 201 (^{201}Tl)	Thallous chloride	Exercise ^{201}Tl Myocardial scintigraphy	Evaluation of coronary artery disease Results of myocardial revascularization Postoperative graft occlusion
Chromium 51 (^{51}Cr)	Human red cells Human serum albumin	Blood volume determination Red cell survival Fecal analysis for blood loss and protein loss	Hemolytic disease Intestinal protein loss in hypoproteinemia
Iron 52 or 59 (^{52}Fe, ^{59}Fe)	Ferrous citrate	Plasma iron clearance Plasma iron turnover rate Plasma iron pool	Aplastic anemia Hemolytic anemia Iron deficiency anemia
Cobalt 57 or 60 (^{57}Co, ^{60}Co)	Cyanocobalamine (vitamin B$_{12}$)	Determination of intestinal absorption of vitamin B$_{12}$	Pernicious anemia Sprue

Source: Munir Ahmad, M.D. Personal communication.

radiation detector such as a **scintillation counter.** The ^{131}I has a **half-life** of 8 days. This means that every 8 days its radioactivity is reduced to half the intensity present eight days previously. The half-life is of clinical importance, since the nuclide must exert its effect long enough to ensure adequate results but not long enough to cause excessive radiation damage.

When a radioiodine uptake study is ordered, the patient receives a calibrated tracer dose of the radioiodide in a capsule form or in a solution. The tracer dose ranges from 5 to 25 **microcuries** (μCi), whereas therapeutic doses are measured in **millicuries** (1 mCi = 1000 μCi). After oral administration, radioiodine is rapidly absorbed from the **gastrointestinal (GI) tract** and selectively picked up by thyroid tissue. Within 4 to 6 hours, the gland has become the depot for about one-fourth of the nuclide ingested. In 24 hours, thyroid function can be estimated by the amount of radioiodine retained. The thyroidal uptake by the normal gland in 24 hours is 15% to 40% of the tracer dose. In **hyperthyroidism** it is 50% to 100%.

Radiopharmaceuticals employed for **thyroid imaging** to detect the presence and locations of metastases from thyroid cancer may include:

papillary and follicular carcinomas with ^{131}I-iodide or ^{123}I-iodide.

medullary carcinomas with ^{201}Tl-thallous chloride or Iodine 131-metaiodobenzylguanidine (^{131}I-MIBG) or ^{99}Tc-pentavalent dimercaptosuccinate (^{99m}Tc-DSMA). The major role of ^{111}In-Octreotide in thyroid imaging is to detect residual or metastatic medullary carcinoma.

undifferentiated carcinomas with ^{201}Tl-thallous chloride.

Also, **thallium 201 (^{201}Tl) and technetium 99m (^{99m}Tc) Sestamibi** have been used for thyroid carcinoma imaging because they do not require thyroid hormone withdrawal before imaging.

The major indications for thyroid radionuclide therapy include the treatment of hyperthyroidism and the elimination of metastases from **thyroid carcinoma.** Forms of hyperthyroidism that may be treated in this manner include **Graves' disease (diffuse toxic goiter), Plummer's disease (toxic multinodular goiter),** and **toxic adenoma.**

The following caution signals are important to note with the use of radioiodine: (1) Radio-iodine is excreted in human breast milk, and nursing should be stopped following diagnostic or therapeutic studies with radioiodine. (2) Pregnancy is another distinct caution flag for studies with radioiodine. The fetal thyroid concentrates radioiodine after the 12th week of gestation. Radioiodine crosses the placenta, and significant exposure of the fetal thyroid can occur and may result in **cretinism** following therapeutic doses to the mother. Large quantities of iodide administered to pregnant women have resulted in **goiter** in the newborn. The fetus can absorb **thyroid hormones** injected into the **amniotic fluid** and this has been used successfully in treatment of **hypothyroidism** and **goiter in utero.**

Autoimmune thyrotoxicosis, or **Graves' disease,** is the most common cause of **thyrotoxicosis** in the pregnant woman and accounts for approximately 90% of cases; the other 10% of cases usually are caused by **gestational trophoblastic neoplasia** and **hyperemesis gravidarum.**

Postpartum thyroiditis (PPT) may be associated with **thyroid autoimmunity** and **transient thyroid dysfunction** (either **hypothyroidism** or **hyperthyroidism**). Indeed, thyroid dysfunction is a well-known complication of the **puerperium.** A surveillance of the mother with thyroid disease (or with a history of thyroid disease) should be continued postdelivery. Usually, women of childbearing age are advised to avoid pregnancy for at least 1 year following iodide therapy, in case there would be a need to have iodide retreatment. (1, 3, 6, 11, 13, 15, 16, 44)

ABBREVIATIONS

SYMBOLS OF RADIONUCLIDES IN NUCLEAR MEDICINE

^{111}Ag—radiosilver
^{72}As, ^{74}As—radioarsenic
^{198}Au—radiogold
^{57}Co, ^{60}Co—radiocobalt
^{51}Cr—radiochromium
^{137}Cs—radiocesium
^{61}Cu, ^{64}Cu—radiocopper
^{18}F—radiofluorine
^{52}Fe, ^{59}Fe—radioiron
^{67}Ga—radiogallium
^{197}Hg, ^{203}Hg—radiomercury
^{125}I, ^{131}I—radioiodine

^{192}Ir—radioiridium
^{42}K—radiopotassium
^{81}Kr—radiokrypton
^{52}Mn—radiomagnesium
^{24}Na—radiosodium
^{32}P—radiophosphorus
^{86}Rb—radiorubidium
^{35}S—radiosulfur
^{85}Sr, ^{87}Sr—radiostrontium
^{99m}Tc—radiotechnetium
^{201}Tl—radiothallium
^{90}Y—radioyttrium

TESTS AND MISCELLANEOUS SYMBOLS

A—mass number
FTI—free thyroxine index
FUT—fibrinogen uptake test
GM—Geiger-Müller (counter)
MAA—macroaggregated albumin
MHP—mercuryhydroxypropane
MLD—maximum lethal dose
MPC—maximum permissible concentration
MPL—maximum permissible level or limit
N—neuron

RAIU—radioactive iodine uptake
RBE—relative biologic effectiveness
RIA—radioimmunoassay
TBG—thyroxine-binding globulin
TBI—thyroxine-binding index
TRH—thyrotropin-releasing hormone
TSH—thyrotropin, thyroid-stimulating hormone
Z—atomic number

MULTIPLE OF CURIE UNITS

1 Ci (curie) = 1 curie
1 mCi (millicurie) = 10^{-3} curie
1 μCi (microcurie) = 10^{-6} curie
1 nCi (nanocurie) = 10^{-9} curie
1 pCi (picocurie) = 10^{-12} curie

OTHER UNITS OF MEASUREMENT

1 becquerel (Bq)—2.7×10^{-11} curie
1 megabecquerel (MBq)—2.7×10^{-5} curie or 270 millicuries
1 gray (Gy)—100 rads
centigray (cGy)—1 rad
Bev, BeV—1 billion electron volts
E—energy in ergs
erg—1 unit of work
ev—1 electron volt
Kev, keV—1000 electron volts
Mev, MeV—1 million electron volts
r—roentgen
RAD, rad—radiation absorbed dose, 100 ergs/gm tissue
rem—absorbed dose equivalent used in radiation protection
sievert (Sv)—100 rems

SCIENTIFIC ORGANIZATIONS

ABNM—American Board of Nuclear Medicine
ACNM—American College of Nuclear Medicine
ACNP—American College of Nuclear Physicians
NRC—Nuclear Regulatory Commission
SNM—Society of Nuclear Medicine

REVIEW GUIDE

Instructions: On the blank lines below, write the term(s) that best describe the definition(s) given.

Example: activated water—water containing radioactive elements.

_____ positively charged helium nucleus characterized by poorly penetrating but strongly ionizing radiation.

_____ device for making radiation measurements or counting ionizing events.

_____ removal of harmful radioactive material from persons, equipment, instruments, rooms, and so on.

_____ a positively charged nuclear electron.

_____ the amount of radioactive material present in the bodies of human beings or animals.

_____ negatively charged particles revolving around the nucleus.

_____ electrically neutral particles present in the nucleus of an atom.

_____ positively charged particles present in the nucleus of an atom.

_____ branch of biology dealing with the effects of radiation on biologic systems.

_____ these studies deal with ventricular wall motion and the ejection fraction and require that a tracer remain within the blood vessels during imaging. This study determines systolic, diastolic, and stroke volumes, cardiac output, ejection fraction, and regional and global wall motion abnormalities.

_____ overlapping of two or more images.

_____ determination of rate of disappearance of labeled erythrocytes from the circulating blood.

_____ measurement of albumin leakage into the gastrointestinal tract using intravenous injection of albumin labeled with iodine 125 (^{125}I).

_____ determination of vitamin B_{12} absorption as an aid in diagnosis of pernicious anemia and malabsorption of B_{12} due to other causes.

_____ dynamic brain imaging to visualize cerebral blood flow to compare values in different regions and to analyze cerebrovascular disease or other vascular abnormalities.

_____ hormone produced by hypothalamus, extrahypothalamic cerebral regions, and extracentral nervous system regions.

_____ number of protons in the nucleus of an atom.

_____ sum of neutrons and protons in the nucleus of an atom.

_____ measurement of the thyroidal uptake of radioiodine and a scan following the oral administration of triiodothyronine (T_3) or thyroxine (T_4).

Instructions: Define the following abbreviations.

Example: Z—atomic number

A	FTI
Bev	Gy
ABNM	NRC
GM	RIA
1 μCi	^{61}Cu
MPL	^{67}Gal
1 pCi	^{52}Fe
^{131}I	^{198}Au
MPC	RAIU

20

Selected Terms Pertaining to Physical Therapy

ORIGIN OF TERMS

actino- (G)—ray
arthr-, arthro- (G)—joint
crymo-, cryo- (G)—*cold*
dia- (G)—through, between, apart, complete
dys- (G)—difficult, painful
esthesio- (G)—perception, sensation
-gnosis (G)—knowledge
hydr-, hydro- (G)—water
kine-, kinesio- (G)—movement
my-, myo- (G)—muscle
ortho- (G)—correct, straight

phon-, phono- (G)—voice, sound
phot-, photo- (G)—light
physio- (G)—physical, nature
praxio- (G)—action
pre- (L)—before, in front of
rachio- (G)—spine
radio- (L)—ray
retro- (L)—backward
schisto- (G)—split, cleft
therm-, thermo- (G)—heat

GENERAL TERMS

kinesiology—study of motion of the human body. (50)
modality—the application of any therapeutic agent, usually limited to physical agents. (25)
pathokinesiology—the study of kinesiology as related to abnormal human motion. (50)
physiatrist—physician who specializes in physical medicine and rehabilitation.
physical agents—active forces such as water, radiant energy, massage, exercise, electricity, and ultrasound energy. (25)
physical medicine—that branch of medical science that uses physical agents in the diagnosis and management of disease.
physical therapist—professional person qualified to provide physical therapy in such areas as direct patient care, consultation, supervision, teaching, administration, research, and community service. Problem identification, employment of the latest technological interventions through the physical therapist's personal contact and interaction with the patient continues to concretize the goal of the physical therapist, namely to enhance human movement and function and to assess, prevent, and treat movement dysfunction and physical disability. (25)
physical therapist assistant—skilled technical worker who administers physical therapy treatments under the supervision of a physical therapist. (25)

physical therapy—profession that uses knowledge and skills pertaining to physical medicine in caring for persons disabled by disease or injury. The primary focus is with the utilization of physical agents for the functional restoration of patients affected with skeletal, neuromuscular, cardiovascular, and pulmonary disorders. Steps to achieve and maintain this focus include an assessment of the patient's current level of function, and the degree of the patient's dysfunction coupled with the establishment of long-term and short-term goals supported by an appropriate treatment plan. Therapeutic measures specific to the patient's condition are applied, as well as periodic evaluation of the patient, treatment plan, and physical therapy modalities. (25)

rehabilitation—treatment process designed to help physically or mentally handicapped persons make maximal use of residual capacities and to enable them to obtain optimal satisfaction and usefulness in terms of themselves, their families, and their community. (42)

>   *FAS-TRAK*—a series of 67 task items that chart a patient's rehabilitation status and progress. Therapists rate most items on predefined scales of one through seven. Total dependence representing one (1), to total independence representing seven (7). (42)

torque—tendency of a force to cause a part of a structure to rotate about an axis. For example, the amount of force elicited by moving a limb over a specified angle. (50)

treatment plan—specific therapeutic action measures are developed according to the patient's needs and condition. Short-term and long-term goals are established based on these measures and the patient's potential to accomplish said goals. Periodic evaluation of the physical therapy modalities utilized in the patient's treatment plan presents opportunities to assess the patient's progress and response to these therapeutic measures. This approach ensures that the patient is gaining optimal benefit from the treatment plan. (25)

ORTHOTICS AND PROSTHETICS (50)

orthotics—usually refers to a device applied to patients for supportive assistance or for corrective purposes. Such devices include braces, splints, and so on. In contrast to prosthetics, an orthotic is utilized to supplement, not replace, human anatomy.

prosthetics—involves the study and technology of design, fabrication, and application of an artificial replacement for a body part, for example, to replace a limb.

TERMS RELATED TO PHYSICAL THERAPY PROCEDURES

biobehavioral treatment procedures—techniques that apply principles and practices from behavioral, physiological, and psychological life sciences in patient treatment. These procedures include:

>   *biofeedback*—using instrumentation to furnish information to an individual, usually in an auditory or visual mode, on one or more physiological variables or processes, such as heart rate, blood pressure, or skin temperature. Biofeedback may serve as a valuable potential adjunct to augment function; such a procedure often assists the person in gaining some voluntary control over the physiologic processes being sampled. (39)

>   *electromyographic biofeedback*—employs the use of instrumentation to transduce muscle potentials into auditory or visual cues for the purpose of increasing or decreasing voluntary activity. (16)

>   *myofeedback*—a type of biofeedback in which the physiologic process is muscular activity. (4)

>   *relaxation training*—technique employed to reduce emotional stress thus lessening or preventing the stress-related effects as well as the subsequent physiological effects produced by the presence of increased emotional stress in one's life. Examples of such techniques would be a progressive muscle relaxation (PMR) procedure, diaphragmatic breathing, guided imagery, or a combination of these techniques. (4)

cryotherapy, crymotherapy—the use of cold, especially cold packs, immersion in water, or ice massage. (12, 35)

electrical stimulation (ES)—represents a whole array of frequencies, pulse duration, intensities utilized by the physical therapist in establishing individual treatment regimens. Electrical stimulation may be employed to relieve muscle spasm, in exercise (covering such disorders as disuse atrophy, weakness, and paralysis), in relief of pain (occurring secondary to these conditions), and as an aid contributing to the healing process (for example, with open wounds or nonunited fractures). (31, 38) Related terms include:

electric current—stream of electrons flowing along a conductor.

alternating current (A/C)—bidirectional, intermittent, asymmetric current obtained from the secondary winding of an induction coil; also known as faradic, biphasic, and bipolar current.

direct current (D/C)—unidirectional current with distinct polarity; also called constant, galvanic, monophasic, and monopolar currents. Electrical current that flows in one direction for 1 second or longer is defined as a direct current. A direct current that flows unidirectionally for a few milliseconds or less is termed a pulsatile current. Some examples of current flow are: (31, 38)

- *alternating current continuous modulation*—refers to constant variation in rate of electron flow at any given intensity.
- *direct current continuous modulation*—rate of flow that is uniform at any given intensity.
- *interrupted modulation*—periods of current flow alternating with cessation of current flow.
- *surging modulation*—periods of current flow and cessation of flow, with a gradual increase and decrease in intensity. In surging modulation, the shift from energy flow to no flow is gradual, whereas in interrupted modulation it is abrupt.

The use of electric stimulation to test the reaction of muscles and motor nerves includes: (16, 32)

chronaxie—the minimal time required for a current twice the strength of the rheobase to elicit a muscle contraction.

electromyography (EMG)—the amplification and recording, both visually and audibly, of minute electric potentials generated by muscle contractions. Electromyograms are valuable in the study of neuromuscular disorders.

nerve conduction velocity—electric testing to determine the speed of nerve conduction and residual latency.

reaction of degeneration—the reaction of a muscle to galvanic but not faradic current.

rheobase—the minimal intensity of current required to elicit muscle contraction.

strength duration curve—the graphic representation of current strength and duration required to elicit a minimal muscle contraction.

electric stimulation therapy—use of electric current in the treatment of disease. Associated terms are:

high-voltage pulsed galvanic stimulation (HVPGS)—use of high voltage (greater than 100 volts) interrupted current, providing a series of pulses of fixed duration in the microsecond range. High-voltage pulsed galvanic stimulation has assisted with burn debridement, pain modulation, and the reduction of edema. (33)

iontophoresis—the introduction of medicinal ions into the tissues by means of direct current. (34, 52)

neuromuscular electrical stimulation (NMES)—use of high-frequency, low-amplitude neuromuscular electrical stimulation that serves as an adjunct to range-of-motion, strengthening, facilitation, and spasticity management programs. (38)

transcutaneous electric nerve stimulation (TENS)—the use of low-voltage or low-amperage current to produce sensory modulation for control of pain. TENS has been helpful in controlling the pain discomfort in labor and delivery. It has also been found helpful in the control of pain in those suffering from temporomandibular joint (TMJ) dysfunction. The combination of ultrasound with electrical stimulation is an another available treatment modality. The electrical stimulation causes the muscle to contract, whereas ultrasound is an effective muscle relaxant. (38, 41, 55)

hydrotherapy—the use of water in its various forms: liquid, solid, and vapor. Associated terms include:

Archimedes' principle—a body fully or partially immersed in a liquid experiences an upward thrust equal to the weight of the liquid it displaces.

burn hydrotherapy—use of water at approximately 37° C to 40° C (98° F to 100° F) for cleansing of patient, removal of clothing, and burned tissue. The addition of a suitable disinfectant and salt to the solution are helpful in preventing loss of fluids and electrolytes. Hubbard or whirlpool tanks also may be employed.

contrast bath—alternate use of hot and cold water.

hydrostatic weighing technique—reliable laboratory method for estimating body composition. This type of underwater weighing mechanism has been used to estimate body fat and lean tissue as part of an adult fitness program. Also, these techniques have been used to estimate percentage of body fat for research studies. In regard to persons who have body-composition analysis via underwater weighing techniques, it is very important that the therapist make sure they understand the results and their implications for weight reduction, nutrition, and exercise.

underwater exercise—immersion of the patient in water, a tank or a pool, to permit free active motion, relaxation, and full abduction of the extremities; sometimes it is used for gait training.

whirlpool—a treatment that offers temperature control in combination with mechanical effects of water in motion. (23, 51, 52)

thermotherapy—treatment of disease using various forms of heat. (22) Associated terms include:

conduction—heat transferred from a warmer object to a cooler one when both objects are in contact. (22, 52)

convection—heat exchange between a surface and a fluid moving adjacent to the surface. (22, 52)

diathermy—the therapeutic use of high-frequency currents to generate heat within parts of the body. (9, 52)

- *microthermy*—therapeutic use of 12.5-centimeter wavelengths to generate heat to delineated small regions of the body. Both diathermy and microthermy are utilized in physical therapy to generate heat in the tissues deeper than the superficial layers. (9, 52)
- *shortwave diathermy*—heat is generated by means of high-frequency oscillations obtained with high voltages and channeled through treatment drums, pads, or coils by means of insulated cables. (9, 52)

fluidotherapy—utilizes a dry heat agent that transfers energy by forced convection. The solid particles become suspended as air is forced through them. This type of therapy impacts mechanical as well as thermal stimulus to cutaneous receptors and has been found to be beneficial in the treatment of chronic musculoskeletal pain. (13, 52)

hot packs—a moist heat provided from a canvas case usually filled with a bentonite substance. Between applications, the hot packs are kept immersed in water at a temperature between 72° C to 79° C. Towels may be wrapped around the hot packs prior to placement at a particular body site. (13, 52)

paraffin baths—refers to mixture of paraffin, paraffin oil, or petroleum jelly used in a bath. Paraffin baths have been effective in relieving pain in rheumatoid arthritis and osteoarthritis, especially in areas of the joints distal to the elbow and knee. (13, 36, 52) *paraffin packs*—use of hot paraffin for therapeutic purposes. Paraffin packs are used most often for heat application to the lower extremities. (13, 36, 52)

therapeutic ultrasound—employment of high-intensity, high-frequency sound waves (considerably above the range of hearing) for therapeutic purposes. Therapeutic ultrasound is used in functional restoration and healing of soft-tissue conditions, as well as for tissue destruction in surgery and hyperthermia for tumor irradiation. Ultrasound may be used as a deep heating agent to increase the temperature of particular structures, especially in the treatment of musculoskeletal disorders. (47, 52)

phonophoresis—the introduction of medicinal ions such as hydrocortisone into the tissues by means of ultrasound. (47, 52)

massage—manipulation of the soft tissues of the body, most effectively performed with the hands, and administered to produce effects on the nervous and muscular systems and the local and general circulation of the blood and lymph. (3, 48)

acupressure—application of pressure to acupuncture sites to relieve pain. (3, 40)

cryokinetics—ice massage. (3)

effleurage—superficial or deep stroking movements. (3, 40, 49)

friction—deep circular or rolling movements. (3, 48, 49)

percussion—repeated taps or blows differing in force. (3, 48, 49)

petrissage—kneading or compression or compression movements. (3, 48, 49)

shiatsu—finger pressure type of Japanese physical therapy that involves the application of manual pressure over the body's acupuncture points. (3, 40)

Swedish—combination of effleurage or stroking, petrissage or kneading, and friction. The techniques are performed over the belly or over a portion of the muscle. (3, 40)

tapotement—percussion movements, including cupping, hacking, clapping, tapping, and beating. (3, 48)

thermassage—massage with heat.

vibratory massage—frequently performed with a mechanical device, especially to increase bronchial drainage. (3, 41)

radiation therapy—the therapeutic use of radiant energy. (54)

Various types may include:

electromagnetic—rays that travel at the speed of light and that may exhibit both magnetic and electrical properties. (54)

infrared—an invisible form of radiant energy, ranging from 760 to 1500 micrometers in the electromagnetic spectrum and producing heat on absorption. (54)

ionizing—radiation that directly or indirectly induces ionization of radiation-absorbing material used for diagnostic or therapeutic applications. (54)

ultraviolet—an invisible form of radiant energy, ranging from about 180 to 400 micrometers and producing chemical actions on absorption. (57)

Related terms are:

cold quartz—type of ultraviolet lamp used for local irradiation. (57)

cosine angle law—the intensity is greatest when the surface to be treated is at right angle to the lamp. (54)

electromagnetic spectrum (EMS)—graphic representation of the various waves of radiant energy in ascending order of length.

erythema—a latent inflammatory reaction caused by a chemical action that takes place in the skin. (54)

heliotherapy—exposure of the body to sunlight or solar radiation.

inverse square law—the intensity of radiation from any source varies inversely with the square of the distance from the source. (54)

minimal erythema dose—irradiation insufficient to cause reddening of the skin. (51, 57)

mottling—irradiation sufficient to produce abnormally white patches on the skin as well as red blotches.

reactive hyperemia—increased presence of blood in an area after restoration of blood flow following a decreased supply.

suberythema dose—irradiation insufficient to cause slight reddening of the skin. (51, 57)

third-degree erythema dose—irradiation sufficient to cause edema and blister formation. (51, 57)

therapeutic exercise: (21, 40, 50)

terms related to muscle action:

- *agonist, prime mover*—muscle that is considered the principal one used in a specific movement.
- *antagonist*—muscle that acts on a joint in the opposite direction.
- *concentric*—muscle contraction in which the external length of the muscle is decreased; the muscle tension overcomes the load.
- *eccentric*—muscle contraction in which the muscle lengthens as the load overcomes the tension developed by the muscle.
- *fixators*—muscles that act from the unconscious level to fix the attachments of the action of the agonists, antagonists, and synergists.
- *isometric or static*—muscle contraction in which the muscle is not allowed to shorten or lengthen.
  - *multiple-angle isometrics (MAI)*—involves the performance of isometric contractions by the quadriceps and hamstrings, reciprocally, at various positions within the client's available range of joint motion. This exercise combines proprioceptive and joint motion development influences with the muscle-strengthening effect of knee exercise, and it provides a proprioceptive stimulus that may assist progressive ambulation activities, especially in the subacute phase or repair stage of tissue inflammation.
- *isotonic or dynamic*—muscle contraction in which invisible shortening or lengthening of the muscle occurs.
- *synergist*—muscle that contracts together with another muscle and has an action identical or nearly identical to the agonist.

terms related to exercise: (21)

- *active exercise*—exercise in which movements are carried out by means of voluntary muscular effort by the person undergoing the exercise.
- *active assistive exercise*—exercise done voluntarily by a person with assistance from another person.
- *active resistive exercise*—exercise voluntarily by a person with resistance applied by another person.
- *corrective exercise*—exercise to recover normal function of an impaired or injured body part.
- *isokinetic exercise*—refers to control of speed of muscular performance achieved by an external mechanism that holds the speed of body movements to constant rates regardless of the degree of forces generated by the participating muscles. The isokinetic device allows suitable mechanical methods of receiving full muscular force of a body segment throughout a range of motion, but without permitting acceleration to occur.
- *isometric exercise, static exercise*—exercise in which there is active, voluntary contraction of muscles without producing motion of the joints to which they are attached.
- *neuromuscular facilitation exercise*—exercise used to enhance contraction or relaxation of muscles.
- *passive exercise*—exercise in which a person's body part is moved by another person or external force, without contraction of the person's muscles.

TERMS RELATED TO EVALUATION AND ASSESSMENT

ADL testing—test that serves to outline as accurately as possible how a patient functions in everyday life; how many activities of daily living (ADL) can be performed in the home and/or in connection with work. Functional assessment is a method for describing an individual's abilities and limitations. Associated terms include:

Barthel index—weighted index for assessing dependence in basic ADLs for chronic disabled patients. Health professionals judge the number of points to be awarded to a patient based on the amount of help that a person needs to perform an activity. This index rates independence in feeding, transferring from wheelchair to bed, getting on and off the toilet, controlling bladder and bowels, dressing, walking, and ascending or descending stairs. Overall the scores range from 0 to 100; 0 indicates complete dependence, and 100 indicates complete independence in activity performance.

Functional independence measure (FIM)—an ordinal scale with 18 items, 7-level scale with scores running from 18 to 126; areas of evaluation include self-care, sphincter control, transfers, locomotion, communication, and social cognition.

Katz ADL index—rating assessment in the range of 0 to 3 (0 = complete independence; 1 = use of a device; 2 = human help, and 3 = complete dependence). The six Katz ADLs rated include: bathing; dressing; going to the toilet; transfers; continence; and feeding.

Kenny self-care index—standardized protocol for recording the health professional's judgment of the patient's basic physical functions. The basic functions rated include bed activities; transfers; locomotion; dressing; personal hygiene; and feeding.

PULSES profile—a multidimensional evaluation mechanism employed by the health professional to judge physical and functional status of the client. PULSES is defined as: P—physical condition/health status; U—upper limb functions; L—lower limb functions; S—sensory components (sight and communications); E—excretory functions; and S—support factors, such as significant others and psychological, emotional, social, or financial assistance. (18, 28, 44)

balance behavioral evaluation—functional assessment of a patient's balance behavior deficits. Two associated tests are:

Fugl-Meyer sensorimotor assessment (FMSA)—a functional status assessment that indicates the amount of assistance needed during various balance tasks and the tolerated duration of each task. Performance is graded on a three-point ordinal scale: 0 = unable to perform; 1 = performs partially; 2 = performs faultlessly. (10, 26)

sensory organization balance test (SOT)—a timed balance test that assesses somatosensory, visual, and vestibular function for maintenance of upright posture. Vision, proprioception, and vestibular functions are the primary sensory systems that alert or trigger a balance response. The SOT is one vehicle to systematic evaluation of ability to switch reliance among somatosensory, visual and vestibular information for control of balance. Since the SOT does not quantify the ability to resist static loads during stance, control body-tilt angle, or compensate for unexpected balance perturbations, the SOT should be interfaced with other assessment tools such as the FMSA, tilt test, postural stress test, and others, so that the determinants of abnormal balance function can be fully identified. (10)

developmental evaluation—(see sensory testing p. 498.)

Other assessments are: (5, 6, 30)

Alberta Infant Motor Scale—an observational scale for assessing gross motor milestones in infants from birth through the stage of independent walking.

Bayle Scales of Infant Development, revised 1993—contain norm-referenced motor and mental scales for children from birth to 42 months of age.

developmental sequence testing—observing a child under 5 years of age and recording milestones in area of gross and fine motor reflexes, language, social, emotional, self-care, and cognitive development.

movement assessment of infants—tests that evaluate muscle tone, primitive reflexes, automatic reactions, and volitional movements in the first year of life. An assessment of risk for motor dysfunction at 4 months (age corrected for prematurity) can be tabulated.

Peabody developmental motor scale—refers to an instrument designed to assess gross and fine motor skills in children from birth to 42 months of age. Balance, locomotion, receipt, and propulsion of objects are measured by the gross motor scale, whereas the fine motor scale assesses grasping, hand use, eye-hand coordination, and finger dexterity. All items are arranged according to a normal developmental sequence.

gait analysis—methods used to detect deviations in gait resulting from pain, weakness, incoordination, or deformities. Examples of gait deviation include:

festination gait, Parkinsonian gait—refers to condition in which patients have a tendency to break into a run or trot. The pattern is slow to begin and may have a propulsive or retropulsive component. The length of steps is decreased and knee movements are diminished, producing a shuffling gait. In more severe cases, the patient may only cease this gait pattern when he or she encounters an object or wall.

hemiplegic gait—patient's leg is extended at the knee and circumducted at the hip, with toe brushing the floor. The arm is flexed at the elbow and the wrist and arm-swinging movements are decreased. Hemispheric stroke is the most common cause of hemiplegic gait.

scissor gait, spastic gait—patient walks slowly with knee extended. There are adduction movements of the hips along with pelvic tilting movements. Weight-bearing occurs on the lateral surface of the foot. The thighs scrape each other during adduction, which produces a scissorlike movement. Cerebral palsy and multiple sclerosis cause this type of gait.

senile gait—refers to difficulties with balance that occur with aging. The older adult man develops forward flexion of the upper portion of the body, as well as flexion of the arms and knees. There is decreased arm swinging and shorter step lengths. The older adult woman develops a waddling gait and shorter step lengths. Other individuals often express fear of falling and a sense of imbalance, which frequently makes them housebound.

sensory ataxia gait—refers to loss of joint position sense in which patients are unaware of the position of the lower extremities and usually stand with legs spread widely apart. The legs are lifted higher than necessary and are flung forward and outward in abrupt motions. Steps vary in length, and feet make a slapping sound as they make contact with the floor's surface.

steppage gait, equine gait—refers to condition caused by spasticity or contractures of the gastrocnemius and soleus muscles that prevent the heel from touching the ground. The gait is called equine since it is similar to the gait of the prancing horse. (11, 17, 45, 46)

manual muscle testing—an important tool used to determine the extent and degree of muscle weakness resulting from disuse, injury, or disease. The qualitative ranking of muscle strength by manual muscle testing can be utilized to ascertain change, especially in those muscles that are unable to move through the complete arc of motion against an externally applied resistance. There are quite a number of various types of testing mechanisms. Some examples include:

cable tensiometer—measures isometric tension.

hand-held dynamometer—device designed to test maximal voluntary isometric contraction. This mechanism has been employed in tests of normal children, children with Duchenne's muscular dystrophy, and individuals suffering from peripheral neuromuscular disorders.

other mechanisms—include isokinetic dynamometers, which can be used with recording devices, such as the Cybex II, which is designed to evaluate isometric or concentric contractions. Isokinetic training on Cybex II dynamometer is a practical strategy to increase adaptability in movement responses. (14, 39)

measurement of joint motion:

goniometry—testing the range of motion with the aid of a goniometer, a protractorlike instrument with one mobile and one stable arm, used manually in the clinical measurement of joint motion.

Figure 20.1 (a) Motor areas that control voluntary muscles; (b) sensory areas involved with cutaneous and other senses.

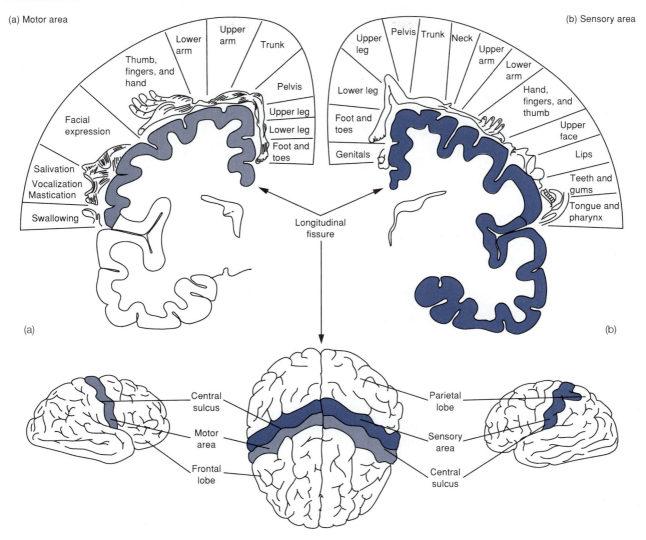

(a) Motor area

(b) Sensory area

electrogoniometry—testing the range of motion with the aid of an electrogoniometer. An electrogoniometer usually consists of a goniometer with a linear potentiometer substituted for the protractor at the axis of the goniometer. The potentiometer changes the electric resistance in direct proportion to the change in joint angle that moves the arm of the goniometer. (14) (See fig. 20.1.)

motor control testing—testing for perceptual motor skills: a response or family of responses in which receptor, effector, and feedback processes show a high degree of spatial and temporal organization. (5) (See fig. 20.1.)

posture evaluation—evaluating the position in which various parts of the body are held while sitting, walking, and lying. (5)

reflex testing—method by which the patient's involuntary response to a stimulus is tested to determine the status of the nervous system. (5)

sensory testing—using various tools and techniques to test the patient's responses to sensory stimuli. (2, 5) (See fig. 20.1.)

> *Sensory Integration and Praxis tests (SIPT)*—sensorimotor assessment for children between the ages of 4 and 9 years having mild to moderate learning impairment but who do not show symptoms of organic disease, mental retardation, or primary sensory deficit. This test is composed of 17 indices that look at balance, proprioceptive and tactile sensation, control of specific movements that are used to target sensory processing disorders in one of three areas: vestibular proprioception, tactile discrimination, or sensory modulation. (4)

SYMPTOMATIC TERMS

analgesia—loss of normal sense of pain. (41)

aphasia—difficulty with the use of understanding of words due to lesions in association areas. Lesions in the brain's frontal region cause motor aphasia, and lesions affecting the brain's posterior region cause sensory aphasia. (See Oral Reading Practice for the types of aphasia.) (See fig. 20.3.) (24, 37)

arthralgia, arthrodynia—joint pain. (16)

astereognosis—inability to recognize shape and form of objects by feeling or touch. (2)

ataxia—motor incoordination. (17)

ballismus—violent flinging movements. When affecting only one side of the body, it is called hemiballismus. (21)

bradykinesia—slowness in initiating and performing movement. (1, 11, 21)

clonic spasm—rapid, repeated muscular contractions.

contracture—permanent shortening of one or more muscles caused by paralysis, spasm, or scar formation. (45)

diplopia—double vision.

hemiplegia—loss of strength in the arm, leg, and sometimes the face on one side of the body. (21)

hyperkinesia—purposeless, excessive involuntary movements. (21)

hypotonia—reduced muscle tension associated with muscular atrophy. (21)

incoherence in speech—illogical flow of ideas that is difficult for the listener to comprehend.

Kernig's sign—when the patient is supine and the thigh is flexed on the abdomen, he or she is unable to extend the leg.

pallesthesia—ability to perceive or recognize vibratory stimuli.

paraplegia—paralysis of lower limbs and at varying degrees of the lower trunk.

Note: The word *paralysis* and the word ending *-plegia* are used to imply total loss of contractility; anything less than total loss is *paresis*. (21)

paresis—partial paralysis. (21)

paresthesia—abnormal sensation; heightened sensory response to stimuli. (2, 17)

phantom limb pain—painful sensation felt by amputee that the limb is still intact. (41)

quadriplegia—paralysis of all four limbs. The lesion resulting in a quadriplegic state occurs in the cervical segment rather than in the thoracic or lumbar segments of the spinal cord. (21)

Romberg's sign—person stands erect with feet together and head straight, first with eyes open and then with eyes closed to ascertain whether or not balance can be maintained. If when eyes are closed, the patient sways or begins to fall, Romberg's sign is said to be positive. (17)

tonic spasm—excessive, prolonged, muscular contraction. (20)

tremors—oscillating, rhythmic movements of muscle groups. (11)

vasoconstriction—narrowing of the vascular lumen, resulting in decreased blood supply.

vasodilatation—widening of the vascular lumen, increasing the blood supply to a part. (36)

vasomotor—referring to nerves that control the muscular contractions of blood vessels. (36)

vertigo—illusion of movement of a person in relation to the environment. The person feels that he or she is spinning (subjective type) or that objects are whirling about (objective type).

central vertigo—present in disorders of vestibular nuclei, cerebellum, or brain stem, characterized by slow onset, prolonged duration, and absence of hearing impairment or tinnitus.

peripheral vertigo—present in disorders of vestibular nerve and semicircular canals. It is episodic and explosive, marked by sudden, violent attacks, lasting minutes to hours, and usually accompanied by tinnitus and impaired hearing.

Other vertigo disorders encountered are:

pathologic vertigo—occurs with the presence of lesion disorders of the visual, somatosensory, or vestibular system.

physiologic vertigo—occurs when the brain is faced with a mismatch among the three stabilizing sensory systems (vestibular system, visual system, and somatosensory system), or when the vestibular is subjected to unfamiliar head movements to which it has never adapted, such as seasickness.

Vestibular dysfunction also may be a causative factor in such dissimilar disorders as spastic cerebral palsy, developmental delays, learning disabilities and Down's syndrome. (8)

ORAL READING PRACTICE

HEMIPLEGIA

Hemiplegia is one of the most common muscular disorders resulting from lesions occurring in the **brain** or upper segments of the **spinal cord** that affects the human population. Individuals afflicted with hemiplegia demonstrate a severe loss of strength in the arm, leg, and occasionally the face, and associated loss of voluntary movement with alteration of muscle tone and sensation throughout one side of the body. Hemiplegia is one of the most indicative manifestations of a neurological lesion, and one of the prime manifestations of serious neurological illness. **Vascular disease** of the **cerebrum** and **brain stem** rank as the primary causes of hemiplegia. Secondary causes include **brain contusion, epidural,** and **subdural hemorrhage,** followed by less frequently occurring causes such as **brain abscess, brain tumor,** and **encephalitis.** Hemiplegia may present as part of a more diffuse neurological syndrome, for example, in **adrenomyeloleukodystrophy,** or in other **demyelinating diseases** closely associated with **multiple sclerosis,** such as **Balo's concentric sclerosis.** Hemiplegia also may occur with seizures and coma in the acute demyelinating disorders, and complications of **meningitis, syphilis,** or **tuberculosis.**

Motor neurons, with cell bodies located in the **cortex** and **axons** extending into the cord, are known as **upper motor neurons,** in contrast to those in the **anterior horn** of the cord, called **lower motor neurons,** which extend toward the muscles. A similar division exists for the **cranial nerves** in the regions where their nerve nuclei perform a function corresponding to that of the spinal cord. When paralysis occurs suddenly and rapidly, it is referred to as a **stroke** or a **cerebrovascular accident (CVA).** The involvement affects the **corticospinal** and **corticobulbar** fibers. (See fig. 20.2.) Damage to the corticospinal and corticobulbar tracts in the upper portion of the brain stem will cause paralysis of the face, arm, and leg on the opposite side.

Lesions of the lower part of the brain stem, such as in the **medulla,** affect the **tongue** and occasionally the **pharynx** and **larynx** on one side and arm and leg on the other side. This condition is referred to as **crossed paralysis.** It is a well-known fact that hemiplegia occurs on the side opposite to the brain injury or insult. The reason for this is that about 90% of upper motor neurons cross over to the contralateral side at the level of the **medulla oblongata.** Those affected with left hemiplegia (right **hemisphere CVA**) usually have impairment in visual, spatial, and perceptual operations involving the discrimination and appreciation of form, distance, position, and movement. Right-sided hemiplegia appears to involve integration of sensory modalities that impinge on the development of body scheme and body awareness.

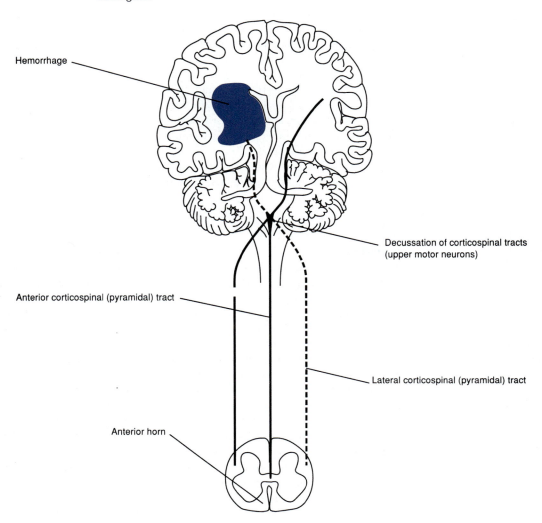

Figure 20.2 Cerebral hemorrhage in the left internal capsule resulting in right-sided hemiplegia because of crossing (decussation) of corticospinal (pyramidal) tracts in the medulla oblongata.

Hemorrhage

Decussation of corticospinal tracts (upper motor neurons)

Anterior corticospinal (pyramidal) tract

Lateral corticospinal (pyramidal) tract

Anterior horn

Approximately one-third of strokes are the result of **cerebral thrombosis.** A cerebral thrombosis tends to devitalize an upper motor neuron, resulting in its degeneration all the way from the thrombotic lesion to the cord. The lower motor neuron remains uninvolved. Following the initial period of shock, the muscles respond to **reflex arcs** mediated by the cord. Since these reflexes tend to be exaggerated, the muscles of the hemiplegic patient become spastic. This **spasticity** may interfere seriously with the exercise of voluntary muscle power that the patient has regained.

Drugs and therapies have tried to overcome the unfortunate handicap and, in extreme cases, surgical intervention has been imperative. It consists of a **transection** of the motor nerve to the extremity, resulting in **flaccid musculature,** which is preferred to the incapacitating spasticity.

Lower motor neuron paralysis results from the physiologic block or destruction of the anterior horn cells or their axons in anterior roots and nerves. Hemiplegia that occurs suddenly is usually caused by involvement of the **internal capsule** resulting from a rupture of a small branch of the **middle cerebral artery (MCA).** An occlusion of the main trunk affects a large portion of the **cerebral hemisphere** and causes contralateral hemiplegia. The arterial distribution of the brain provided by the **MCA** is the site of most strokes. It is occluded most frequently by **emboli** rather than by **thrombi.** Small infarcts may produce transient and permanent paralysis. **Vascular occlusion** may also involve the **cervical** segment of the **internal carotid artery.**

THE HEMIPLEGIC PATIENT

The hemiplegic patient may face several significant obstacles. Some of these include:

autotopagnosia—loss of awareness, rejection, or denial of bodily disease or dysfunction. The patient tends to look away from the hemiplegic side, rejecting the implication that there is anything wrong with it.

heteronymous hemianopia—visual disturbance in which the left visual field is obliterated. Because the patient tends to deny this condition, the patient may become overconfident and more accident prone, especially when alone, since the patient often moves impulsively and quickly resulting in disturbed judgments in speed and time.

balance and weight shift—early in the patient's treatment program, problems of balance and weight should be addressed, otherwise these problems may tend to become habit forming and difficult to overcome. When first learning to sit or stand, the patient has a tendency to fall toward the affected side, with no control or stability. If the patient is not helped to overcome balance and weight shift problems, he or she will not acquire the skills to move correctly.

confusion—results in inability to follow and/or remember given directions. The physical therapist may need to reinforce verbal commands with demonstration and actually involve the patient in the specific demonstration to assist the patient in overcoming the deficit. Simple repetition of movement without the subject knowing whether or not the movement is correct will not result in learning. One of the key effective reinforcers is the patient's own knowledge of the extent of improvement in the performance of a particular task or movement.

flaccidity—affects lower extremity when knee is kept extended on standing, thus making standing and walking harder for the patient. Flaccidity in the upper extremity may be demonstrated by a limp arm, which tends to get in the patient's way.

spasticity—may be a great aid to helping the patient stand or walk. It may prove a problem only when it is sufficiently marked to interfere with function, which might result in the presence of secondary soft-tissue contractures. Severe spasticity may be helped by drugs or by various surgical procedures. Other methods to reduce spasticity may include application of heat or cold, deep rhythmical massage over the muscle insertion areas, and rotation of trunk and limbs. Limb rotations have proven effective in providing a more normal control of muscle tone to the patient.

hemiplegic gait—patient's leg is extended at the knee and circumducted at the hip, with the toe brushing the floor. The arm is flexed at the elbow and wrist, and arm-swinging movement is decreased. Hemispheric stroke is the most common cause of hemiplegic gait. **Neuromuscular electrical stimulation (NMES)** has been utilized to improve the gait pattern of hemiplegics by increasing the **torque output** of the ankle **dorsiflexors** and reciprocally decreasing spastic reflexes in the **plantar flexors.** NMES may be applied to **gluteal muscles** and/or to the **quadriceps muscles** in an effort to enhance the stance phase of the gait. NMES also can be used to facilitate the swing phase of gait in the hemiplegic person by giving stimulation to the sole, dorsum of the foot, or lower posterior thigh. This last application of NMES tends to induce the **flexion reflex.**

speech and language disorders—inability to conceive thoughts, formulate meaningful sentences, or execute purposeful acts represent deficits that can be extremely painful and frustrating for the hemiplegic patient. When the physical therapist approaches a patient with left hemiplegia, it is important to make sure that the significant objects are in the right visual field, but it is vital to include the left side of the body and the left portion of the environment

Figure 20.3 Broca's area and Wernicke's area of the brain.

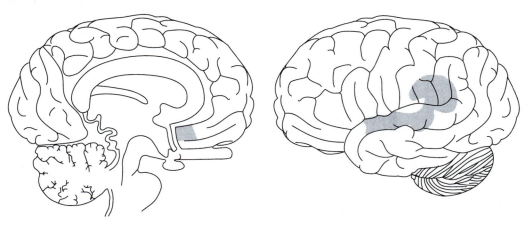

Broca's area   Wernicke's area

to help minimize denial. Because the major deficits in patients with right-sided hemiplegia is in communication, it is important for the physical therapist to understand that although it is difficult for such patients to follow directions, utilization of visual instructions (pictures or positive feedback demonstrated by approval gestures, smiling, hand-clapping, or shaking hands) is a more appropriate communication technique than words in the treatment and rehabilitation settings. Some speech and language disorders frequently encountered are: **aphasia**—difficulty with the understanding of words due to lesions in association areas. Lesions in the brain's frontal region cause motor aphasia, and lesions affecting the brain's posterior region cause sensory aphasia. (See fig. 20.3.) Some types of aphasia are:

- *motor aphasia, Broca's nonfluent aphasia, Broca's expressive aphasia*—the verbal comprehension is intact, but the patient is unable to use muscles to coordinate speech. The cerebral lesion is anterior and nearly always associated with hemiplegia or hemiparesis. Spontaneous speech is nonfluent and indistinct, and the vocabulary is limited. Comprehension and reading may be intact.
- *sensory aphasia, Wernicke's fluent aphasia, Wernicke's receptive aphasia*—inability to comprehend the spoken word, if the auditory word center is affected, and the written word, if the visual word center is involved. The patient will not understand the spoken or written word if both centers are involved. In Wernicke's aphasia, the lesion is posterior; spontaneous speech is fluent, but comprehension is defective. There may be logorrheic outpouring of words associated with bizarre, euphoric, or paranoid behavior.
- *mixed aphasia*—condition in which both expressive and receptive aspects are present.
- *nominal aphasia*—inability to name objects but recognition of the object's name when told.

dysarthria—inability to speak properly or formulate words due to muscle weakness involved with speech production. Dysarthric patients are able to read, write, and understand what they hear, even though they are unable to utter a single intelligible word.

Other associated problems may include physical and emotional conditions that negatively affect the patient's progress. Examples of such conditions are poor lung expansion from **hypotonus** and relative immobility, **bladder** and **bowel dysfunction, depression, helplessness,** and

loneliness. The assessment of the hemiplegic patient by the physical therapist should include key information related to the patient's ability to function with his or her deficits. Criteria employed for such an assessment should include:

intellectual and cognitive abilities and deficits.
visual and perceptual abilities and deficits.
motion, motor, sensory, and coordination abilities and deficits.
current functional activity level.

The assessment findings can be interwoven into planning long-term and short-term goals for the patient and correlated with the overall treatment plan. The therapeutic quality of care assessment is an ongoing process, and periodically it is important to assess and evaluate the patient's progress toward achievement of indicated goals, so that corresponding adjustments can be initiated in the patient's overall treatment program to meet the patient's current status and needs.

In contemplating various therapeutic approaches applicable to the hemiplegic patient, it is well to remember that the hemiplegic patient cannot sustain long periods of activity because of increased energy demands for motor involvement and the emotional and psychic stress placed on the patient in dealing with a major deficit. There may be occasions when the hemiplegic patient perceives the activity or desired task to be accomplished as beyond his or her control. In such circumstances, especially with the older adult, the patient may show cognitive, motivational, and emotional deficits of helplessness. This type of situation presents a challenge to the physical therapist to prevent or lessen this helplessness. Some approaches to assisting the hemiplegic patient might include providing a series of successful experiences, closely monitoring the patient's expectations of improvement, especially when such expectations cannot be achieved by the patient realistically, and whenever possible allowing the patient to make positive choices.

To ensure that rehabilitation of the hemiplegic patient continues after the physical therapist's treatment session, it is vitally important that other nursing staff and family members and friends be involved in the rehabilitation process. Gradually, the family must be prepared for the termination of the physical therapist's activities and the need to continue the rehabilitation process in the home. (7, 15, 17, 20, 21, 27, 37, 43, 44, 45)

ABBREVIATIONS

GENERAL

ADL—activities of daily living
AE—above elbow
AK—above knee
AKO—ankle-knee orthoses
BE—below elbow
BK—below knee
CMR—comprehensive medical rehabilitation
CPR—cardiac pulmonary resuscitation
DOE—dyspnea on exertion

DTR—deep tendon reflexes
LOM—limitation of motion
MAI—multiple-angle isometrics
PROM—passive range of motion
RD—reaction of degeneration
ROM—range of motion
SOB—shortness of breath
TENS—transcutaneous electric nerve stimulation

ORGANIZATIONS

AART—American Association of Rehabilitation Therapy
ACPMR—American Congress of Physical Medicine and Rehabilitation
ACRM—American Congress of Rehabilitation Medicine
APTA—American Physical Therapy Association
NARF—National Association of Rehabilitation Facilities.

REVIEW GUIDE

Instructions: Define the following terms.

Example: actino- (G)—ray

arthr- (G)	cryo- (G)	hydro- (G)
kinesio- (G)	myo- (G)	phono- (G)
photo- (G)	rachio- (G)	thermo- (G)
schisto- (G)	radio- (G)	pre- (L)
physio- (G)	ortho- (G)	actino- (G)
esthesio- (G)	-gnosis (G)	praxio- (G)
dia- (G)	dys- (G)	retro- (L)

Instructions: On the lines below, write the term that best describes the given definition.

Example: Loss of strength in the arm, leg, and sometimes the face on one side of the body is called <u>hemiplegia</u>.

Abnormal sensations or heightened sensory response to stimuli is termed _____ .

Violent flinging movements are termed _____ .

Exposure of body to sunlight or solar radiation is called _____ .

Study of motion of the human body is called _____ .

Slowness in initiating and performing movement is called _____ .

The use of cold, especially cold packs, immersion in water, or ice massage is called _____ .

Two other terms for motor aphasia are _____ and _____ .

Irradiation sufficient to produce abnormally white patches on the skin as well as red blotches is called

_____ .

The use of water in its various forms—liquid, solid, and vapor—is called _____ .

An invisible form of radiant energy, ranging from about 180 to 400 micrometers and producing chemical actions on

absorption is called _____ .

Ice massage is termed _____ .

The introduction of medicinal ions such as hydrocortisone into the tissues by means of ultrasound is called

_____ .

The reaction of a muscle to galvanic but not faradic current is called _____ .

The use of low-voltage or low-amperage current to produce sensory modulation for control of pain is called

_____ .

Heat transferred from a warmer object to a cooler one when both objects are in contact is called

_____ .

Heat exchange between a surface and a fluid moving adjacent to the surface is called _____ .

Two other terms for sensory aphasia are _____ and _____ .

Instructions: Define the following abbreviations.

Example: AE—above elbow

ADL	DTR	AART
BK	PROM	ACRM
CPR	ROM	APTA
DOE	SOB	TENS

III

Answers to Multiple Choice Questions in Chapter Review Guides

References and Bibliography

Credits

Index

Answers to Multiple-Choice Questions in Chapter Review Guides

Chapter 6	Chapter 8	Chapter 9	Chapter 10
pp. 155–157	p. 213	pp. 249–250	p. 276
1. D	1. B	1. D	1. B
2. B	2. B	2. B	2. C
3. A	3. A	3. C	3. C
4. A	4. D	4. C	4. C
5. A	5. A	5. B	5. B
6. C	6. C	6. A	6. A
7. B	7. D	7. A	7. A
8. C	8. D	8. A	8. A
9. C	9. A	9. A	9. B
10. C	10. A	10. B	10. B
11. D		11. A	
12. C		12. B	
13. B		13. C	
14. D		14. C	
15. C		15. A	

Chapter 11	Chapter 12	Chapter 13	Chapter 15
p. 297	pp. 328–329	pp. 356–357	p. 396
1. D	1. D	1. A	1. D
2. A	2. C	2. C	2. B
3. B	3. B	3. C	3. D
4. A	4. B	4. C	4. A
5. C	5. D	5. B	5. A
6. B	6. B	6. B	
7. A	7. D	7. A	
8. B	8. B	8. A	
9. C	9. C	9. A	
10. C	10. A	10. C	
	11. B		
	12. C		
	13. A		
	14. C		
	15. C		

Chapter 1

1. *Dorland's Illustrated Medical Dictionary,* 28th ed. Philadelphia: W.B. Saunders Co., 1994.
2. Elgin, Ronald J. Reference intervals and laboratory values of clinical importance. In Wyngaarden, James B., et al., eds., *Cecil's Textbook of Medicine,* 19th ed. Philadelphia: W.B. Saunders Co., 1992, pp. 2370–2380.
3. Nicoll, Diana. Appendix: Therapeutic drug monitoring and laboratory reference ranges. In Tierney, Lawrence M., Jr., et al., eds., *Current Medical Diagnosis & Treatment,* 35th ed. Stamford, CT: Appleton & Lange, 1996, pp. 1439–1446.
4. *Steadman's Medical Dictionary,* 26th ed. Baltimore: Williams & Wilkins, 1995.
5. Turgeon, Ronald M.D. Personal communications.

Chapter 2

1. Anderson, R. Fox, et al. Lasers in dermatology. In Fitzpatrick, Thomas B., et al., eds. *Dermatology in General Medicine,* 4th ed. New York: McGraw-Hill, Inc., 1993, pp. 1755–1766.
2. Anhalt, Grant J. Bullous diseases. In Rakel, Robert E., ed., *Conn's Current Therapy—1995.* Philadelphia: W.B. Saunders Co., 1995, pp. 766–772.
3. Arndt, Kenneth A. Lichen planus. In Fitzpatrick, Thomas B., et al., eds., *Dermatology in General Medicine,* 4th ed. New York: McGraw-Hill, Inc., 1993, pp. 1134–1143.
4. ———. Lichen nitidus. Ibid., pp. 1144–1148.
5. Bauer, Eugene A., and Briggaman, Robert A. Hereditary epidermolysis bullosa. In Fitzpatrick, Thomas B., et al., eds., *Dermatology in General Medicine,* 4th ed. New York: McGraw-Hill, Inc., 1993, pp. 654–670.
6. Bertolino, Arthur P., and Freedberg, Irwin M. Hair. In Fitzpatrick, Thomas B., et al., eds., *Dermatology in General Medicine,* 4th ed. New York: McGraw-Hill, Inc., 1993, pp. 671–695.
7. Burke, John F., and Bondoc, Conrado. Burns: The management and evaluation of the thermally injured patient. In Fitzpatrick, Thomas B., et al., eds., *Dermatology in General Medicine,* 4th ed. New York: McGraw-Hill, Inc., 1993, pp. 1592–1598.
8. Daniels, Troy E. Diseases of the mouth and salivary glands. In Wyngaarden, James B., et al., eds., *Cecil's Textbook of Medicine,* 19th ed. Philadelphia: W.B. Saunders Co., 1992, pp. 635–639.
9. Davis, Ira C., and Leshin, Barry. Cancer of the skin. In Rakel, Robert E., ed., *Conn's Current Therapy—1995.* Philadelphia: W.B. Saunders Co., 1995, pp. 709–711.
10. Demling, Robert H., and Way, Lawrence W. Burns and other thermal injuries. In Way, Lawrence W., ed., *Current Surgical Diagnosis & Treatment,* 10th ed. Norwalk, CT: Appleton & Lange, 1994, pp. 241–256.
11. Fitzpatrick, Thomas B., and Bernhard, Jeffrey D. The structure of skin lesions and fundamentals of diagnosis. In Fitzpatrick, Thomas B., et al., eds., *Dermatology in General Medicine,* 4th ed. New York: McGraw-Hill, Inc., 1993, pp. 27–55.
12. Goldstein, Sanford, M., and Odom, Richard B. Skin and appendages. In Tierney, Lawrence M., Jr., et al., eds., *Current Medical Diagnosis & Treatment,* 35th ed. Stamford, CT: Appleton & Lange, 1996, pp. 89–155.
13. Hashimato, Ken, and Sharata, Harry H. Parasitic infections of the skin. In Rakel, Robert E., ed., *Conn's Current Therapy—1995.* Philadelphia: W.B. Saunders Co., 1995, pp. 745–749
14. Hayes, Christine M., and Whitaker, Duane. Premalignant lesions. In Rakel, Robert E., ed., *Conn's Current Therapy—1995.* Philadelphia: W.B. Saunders Co., 1995, pp. 733–736.
15. Hruza, George J., and Feuikes, Jessica L. Dermatologic surgery: Selected aspects. In Fitzpatrick, Thomas B., et al., eds., *Dermatology in General Medicine,* 4th ed. New York: McGraw-Hill, Inc., 1993, pp. 2917–2937.
16. Karam, John H. Diabetes mellitus and hypoglycemia. In Tierney, Lawrence M., Jr., et al., eds., *Current Medical Diagnosis & Treatment,* 34th ed. Norwalk, CT: Appleton & Lange, 1995, pp. 1004–1040.
17. Kerr, Rebecca E. I., and Thomson, John. Perioral dermatitis. In Fitzpatrick, Thomas B., et al., eds., *Dermatology in General Medicine,* 4th ed. New York: McGraw-Hill, Inc., 1993, pp. 735–740.
18. Krinsky, William L. Arthropods and leeches. In Wyngaarden, James B., et al., eds. *Cecil's Textbook of Medicine,* 19th ed. Philadelphia: W.B. Saunders Co., 1992, pp. 2201–2027.
19. Levinson, Warren E., and Jawetz, Ernest. Pathogenesis. In *Medical Microbiology & Immunology,* 3d ed. Norwalk, CT: Appleton & Lange, 1994, pp. 23–33.
20. ———. Gram-positive rods. Ibid., pp. 80–87.
21. Lowy, Douglas R., and Androphy, Elliot J. Warts. In Fitzpatrick, Thomas B., et al., eds., *Dermatology in General Medicine,* 4th ed. New York: McGraw-Hill, Inc., 1993, pp. 2611–2621.
22. Mosher, David B., et al. Disorders of pigmentation. In Fitzpatrick, Thomas B., et al., eds., *Dermatology in General Medicine,* 4th ed. New York: McGraw-Hill, Inc., 1993, pp. 903–995.
23. Parker, Frank. Skin diseases. In Wyngaarden, James B., et al., eds. *Cecil's Textbook of Medicine,* 19th ed. Philadelphia: W.B. Saunders Co., 1992, pp. 2280–2330.
24. Plewig, Gerd. Rosacea. In Fitzpatrick, Thomas B., et al., eds., *Dermatology in General Medicine,* 4th ed. New York: McGraw-Hill, Inc., 1993, pp. 727–735.
25. Purvis, Robert S., and Lewis, Luke. Viral diseases of the skin. In Rakel, Robert E., ed., *Conn's Current Therapy—1995.* Philadelphia: W.B. Saunders Co., 1995, pp. 740–745.
26. Stanley, John R. Pemphigus. In Fitzpatrick, Thomas B., et al., eds., *Dermatology in General Medicine,* 4th ed. New York: McGraw-Hill, Inc., 1993, pp. 606–614.
27. Straus, John S. Sebaceous glands. In Fitzpatrick, Thomas B., et al., eds., *Dermatology in General Medicine,* 4th ed. New York: McGraw-Hill, Inc., 1993, pp. 709–726.
28. Taylor, James S. Occupational dermatoses. In Rakel, Robert E., ed., *Conn's Current Therapy—1995.* Philadelphia: W.B. Saunders Co., 1995, pp. 781–784.
29. Tierney, Lawrence M., Jr. Blood vessels and lymphatics. In Tierney, Lawrence M., Jr., et al., eds., *Current Medical Diagnosis & Treatment,* 35th ed. Stamford, CT: Appleton & Lange, 1996, pp. 403–433.
30. Tong, A. K. F., and Fitzpatrick, T. B. Neoplasms of the skin. In Holland, James F., et al., eds., *Cancer Medicine,* 3d ed., vol. 2. Philadelphia: Lea & Febiger, 1993, pp. 1775–1792.
31. Vasconez, Luis O., and Vasconez, Henry C. Plastic and reconstructive surgery. In Way, Lawrence W., *Current Surgical Diagnosis and Treatment,* 10th ed. Norwalk, CT: Appleton & Lange, 1994, pp. 1130–1164.

Chapter 3

1. Al-Mefty, Ossama, and Origitano, T. C. Meningiomas. In Rengachary, Setti S., and Wilkins, Robert H., eds., *Principles of Neurosurgery.* London: Wolfe Publishing, 1994, pp. 28.1–29.14.
2. American Psychiatric Association. Disorders usually first diagnosed in infancy, childhood, or adolescence. In *Diagnostic and Statistical Manual of Mental Disorders,* 4th ed. (DSM-IV). Washington, D.C.: American Psychiatric Association, 1994, pp. 37–121.
3. ———. Delirium, dementia, and other amnestic and cognitive disorders. Ibid., pp. 123–163.
4. ———. Substance-Related disorders. Ibid., pp. 175–272.
5. ———. Schizophrenia and other psychotic disorders. Ibid., pp. 273–315.
6. ———. Mood disorders. Ibid., pp. 317–391.
7. ———. Anxiety disorders. Ibid., pp. 393–444.
8. ———. Somatoform disorders. Ibid., pp. 445–469.
9. ———. Dissociative disorders. Ibid., pp. 477–491.
10. ———. Eating disorders. Ibid., pp. 539–550.
11. ———. Personality disorders. Ibid., pp. 629–673.
12. Bauer, Richard L., and Watson, William A. Clinical toxicology. In Stein, Jay H., ed.-in-ch., *Internal Medicine,* 4th ed. St. Louis: Mosby, 1994, pp. 2789–2799.
13. Bauer, Richard L., et al. Substance abuse. In Stein, Jay H., ed.-in-ch., *Internal Medicine,* 4th ed. St. Louis: Mosby, 1994, pp. 2799–2804.
14. Beal, M. Flint. Parkinson's disease and other extrapyramidal disorders. In Isselbacher, Kurt J., et al., eds., *Harrison's Principles of Internal Medicine,* 13th ed. New York: McGraw-Hill, Inc., 1994, pp. 2275–2280.
15. Beal, M. Flint, et al. Alzheimer's disease and other dementias. In Isselbacher, Kurt J., et al., eds., *Harrison's Principles of Internal Medicine,* 13th ed. New York: McGraw-Hill, Inc., 1994, pp. 2269–2275.
16. Brown, Martin M., and Hachinski, Vladimir C. Acute confusional states, amnesia, and dementia. In Isselbacher, Kurt J., et al., eds., *Harrison's Principles of Internal Medicine,* 13th ed. New York: McGraw-Hill, Inc., 1994, pp. 137–146.
17. Brown, Robert H. Motor neuron disease and the progressive ataxias. In Isselbacher, Kurt J., et al., eds., *Harrison's Principles of Internal Medicine,* 13th ed. New York: McGraw-Hill, Inc., 1994, pp. 2280–2286.
18. Caviness, Verne S., Jr. Neurocutaneous syndromes and other developmental disorders of the central nervous system. In Isselbacher, Kurt J., et al., eds., *Harrison's Principles of Internal Medicine,* 13th ed. New York: McGraw-Hill, Inc., 1994, pp. 2339–2344.
19. Chiriboga, Claudia A. Fetal effects: Neurologic complications of drug and alcohol abuse. *Neurologic Clinics* 11:707–723, August 1993.
20. Eisendrath, Stuart J. Psychiatric disorders. In Tierney, Lawrence M., Jr., et al., eds., *Current Medical Diagnosis & Treatment,* 35th ed. Stamford, CT: Appleton & Lange, 1996, pp. 915–971.
21. Kaplan, Harold I., et al. Theories of personality and psychopathology. In Kaplan, Harold I., et al., eds., *Kaplan and Sadock's Synopsis of Psychiatry,* 7th ed. Baltimore: Williams & Wilkins, 1994, pp. 237–266.
22. ———. Clinical examination of the psychiatric patient. Ibid., pp. 267–299.
23. ———. Typical signs and symptoms of psychiatric illness. Ibid., pp. 300–308.
24. ———. Delirium, dementia, and amnestic and other cognitive disorders and mental disorders due to a general medical condition. Ibid., pp. 336–373.
25. ———. Substance-related disorders. Ibid., pp. 383–456.
26. ———. Normal sleep and sleep disorders. Ibid., pp. 699–716.
27. ———. Psychotherapies. Ibid., pp. 824–864.
28. ———. Biological therapies. Ibid., pp. 865–1015.
29. ———. Geriatric psychiatry. Ibid., pp. 1155–1170.
30. ———. Forensic psychiatry. Ibid., pp. 1171–1188.
31. Kokkinos, James, and Levine, Steven R. Recreational drug abuse. In Feldmann, Edward, ed., *Intracerebral Hemorrhage.* New York: Futura Publishing Co., Inc., 1994, pp. 65–82.
32. Mendelson, Jack H., and Mello, Nancy K. Cocaine and other commonly abused drugs. In Isselbacher, Kurt, J., et al., eds., *Harrison's Principles of Internal Medicine,* 13th ed. New York: McGraw-Hill, Inc., 1994, pp. 156–162.
33. Turgeon, Ronald, M.D., Personal communications.

Chapter 4

1. Adams, Harold P., Jr., and Biller, José. Ischemic cerebrovascular disease. In Bradley, Walter G., et al., eds., *Neurology in Clinical Practice,* 2d ed., vol. 2. Boston: Butterworth-Heinemann, 1996, pp. 993–1031.
2. Adams, John E., and Barbaro, Nicholas M. Movement & psychopathologic disorders responsive to surgery. In Way, Lawrence W., ed., *Current Surgical Diagnosis & Treatment,* 10th ed. Norwalk, CT: Appleton & Lange, 1994, pp. 847–851.
3. Adams, Raymond D., and Victor, Maurice. Neurology of the aging. In *Principles of Neurology,* 5th ed. New York: McGraw-Hill, Inc., 1993, pp. 527–536.
4. ———. Disturbances of cerebrospinal fluid circulation, including hydrocephalus and meningeal reactions. Ibid., pp. 539–553.
5. ———. Degenerative diseases of the nervous system. Ibid., pp. 957–1009.
6. Adler, Eric. No need for the knife: Gamma surgery attacks tumors without cutting. *The Kansas City Star,* 11 September, 1995, pp. E1–E2.
7. Albright, A. Leland. Hydrocephalus in children. In Rengachary, Setti S., and Wilkins, Robert H., eds., *Principles of Neurosurgery.* London: Wolfe Publishing, 1994, pp. 6.1–6.23.
8. Al-Mefty, Ossama, and Origitano, T. C. Meningiomas. In Rengachary, Setti S., and Wilkins, Robert H., eds., *Principles of Neurosurgery.* London: Wolfe Publishing, 1994, pp. 28.1–29.14.
9. Aminoff, Michael J. Nervous system. In Tierney, Lawrence M., Jr., et al., eds., *Current Medical Diagnosis & Treatment,* 35th ed. Stamford, CT: Appleton & Lange, 1996, pp. 858–914.
10. Aminoff, Michael J. Electrophysiologic studies of the central and peripheral nervous systems. In Isselbacher, Kurt J., et al., eds., *Harrison's Principles of Internal Medicine,* 13th ed. New York: McGraw-Hill, Inc., 1994, pp. 2217–2223.
11. Asbury, Arthur K. Numbness, tingling, and sensory loss. In Isselbacher, Kurt J., et al., eds., *Harrison's Principles of Internal Medicine,* 13th ed. New York: McGraw-Hill, Inc., 1994, pp. 133–137.
12. ———. Diseases of the peripheral nervous system. Ibid., pp. 2368–2378.
13. Award, Issam A. Cerebrovascular occlusive disease. In Rengachary, Setti S., and Wilkins, Robert H., eds., *Principles of Neurosurgery.* London: Wolfe Publishing, 1994, pp. 10.1–10.20.
14. Baer, Lee. Cingulotomy in a case of concomitant obsessive-compulsive disorder and Tourette's syndrome. *Archives of General Psychiatry* 51: 73–74, January 1994.
15. Bailey, Peter L., and Stanley, Theodore H. Intravenous opioid anesthetics. In Miller, Ronald D., ed., *Anesthesia,* 4th

ed., vol. 1. New York: Churchill Livingstone, 1994, pp. 291–387.

16. Barbaro, Nicholas M., and Edwards, Michael S. Traumatic peripheral nerve lesions. In Way, Lawrence W., ed., *Current Surgical Diagnosis & Treatment*, 10th ed. Norwalk, CT: Appleton & Lange, 1994, pp. 827–828.

17. Barbaro, Nicholas M., and Wilson, Charles B. Tumors of the peripheral nerves. In Way, Lawrence W., ed., *Current Surgical Diagnosis & Treatment*, 10th ed. Norwalk, CT: Appleton & Lange, 1994, p. 837.

18. Batjer, H. Hunt. Intracranial aneurysm. In Rengachary, Setti S., and Wilkins, Robert H., eds., *Principles of Neurosurgery*. London: Wolfe Publishing, 1994, pp. 11.1–11.26.

19. Beal, M. Flint, et al. Alzheimer's disease and other dementias. In Isselbacher, Kurt J., et al., eds., *Harrison's Principles of Internal Medicine*, 13th ed. New York: McGraw-Hill, Inc., 1994, pp. 2269–2275.

20. Beal, M. Flint, et al. Parkinson's disease and other extrapyramidal disorders. In Isselbacher, Kurt J., et al., eds., *Harrison's Principles of Internal Medicine*, 13th ed. New York: McGraw-Hill, Inc., 1994, pp. 2275–2280.

21. Black, Peter McL., and Matsumae, Mitsunori. Hydrocephalus in adults. In Rengachary, Setti S., and Wilkins, Robert H., eds., *Principles of Neurosurgery*. London: Wolfe Publishing, 1994, pp. 7.1–7.7.

22. Blumenkof, Bennett. Chronic pain. In Rengachary, Setti S., and Wilkins, Robert H., eds., *Principles of Neurosurgery*. London: Wolfe Publishing, 1994, pp. 48.1–48.9.

23. Boggan, J. E., and Powers, S. K. Use of lasers in neurological surgery. In Youmans, Julian R., ed., *Neurological Surgery*, 3d ed., vol. 2. Philadelphia: W.B. Saunders Co., 1990, pp. 1236–1276.

24. Brown, David L. Spinal, epidural, and caudal anesthesia. In Miller, Ronald D., ed., *Anesthesia*, 4th ed., vol. 2. New York: Churchill Livingstone, 1994, pp. 1505–1533.

25. Brown, Martin M., and Hachinski, Vladimir C. Acute confusional states, amnesia, and dementia. In Isselbacher, Kurt J., et al., eds., *Harrison's Principles of Internal Medicine*, 13th ed. New York: McGraw-Hill, Inc., 1994, pp. 137–146.

26. Brown, Robert H. Motor neuron disease and the progressive ataxias. In Isselbacher, Kurt J., et al., eds., *Harrison's Principles of Internal Medicine*, 13th ed. New York: McGraw-Hill, Inc., 1994, pp. 2280–2286.

27. Caviness, Verne S., Jr. Neurocutaneous syndromes and other developmental disorders of the central nervous system. In Isselbacher, Kurt J., et al., eds., *Harrison's Principles of Internal Medicine*, 13th ed. New York: McGraw-Hill, Inc., 1994, pp. 2339–2344.

28. Coté, Charles J. Pediatric anesthesia. In Miller, Ronald D., ed., *Anesthesia*, 4th ed., vol. 2. New York: Churchill Livingstone, 1994, pp. 2097–2124.

29. Daroff, Robert B. Dizziness and vertigo. In Isselbacher, Kurt J., et al., eds., *Harrison's Principles of Internal Medicine*, 13th ed. New York: McGraw-Hill, Inc., 1994, pp. 96–99.

30. Dichter, Marc C. The epilepsies and convulsive disorders. In Isselbacher, Kurt J., et al., eds., *Harrison's Principles of Internal Medicine*, 13th ed. New York: McGraw-Hill, Inc., 1994, pp. 2223–2233.

31. Easton, J. Donald. Spinal fluid examination. In Stein, Jay H., ed.-in-ch., *Internal Medicine*, 4th ed. St. Louis: Mosby, 1994, pp. 963–964.

32. Easton, J. D., and Wilterdink, J. L. Carotid endarterectomy: Trials and tribulations. *Annals of Neurology* 35:5–17, January 1994.

33. Edwards, Michael S. Brain tumors. In Way, Lawrence W., ed., *Current Surgical Diagnosis & Treatment*, 10th ed. Norwalk, CT: Appleton & Lange, 1994, pp. 829–835.

34. Gilman, Sid. Ataxia and disorders of balance and gait. In Isselbacher, Kurt J., et al., eds., *Harrison's Principles of Internal Medicine*, 13th ed. New York: McGraw-Hill, Inc., 1994, pp. 125–130.

35. Glass, Peter S. A., et al. Intravenous drug delivery systems. In Miller, Ronald D., ed., *Anesthesia*, 4th ed., vol. 1. New York: Churchill Livingstone, 1994, pp. 389–416.

36. Green, Richard M., and Ouriel, Kenneth. Peripheral arterial disease. In Schwartz, Seymour I., ed.-in-ch., *Principles of Surgery*, 6th ed., vol. 1. New York: McGraw-Hill, Inc., 1993, pp. 925–987.

37. Greenberg, David A., et al. Motor deficits. In *Clinical Neurology*, 2d ed. Norwalk, CT: Appleton & Lange, 1993, pp. 146–180.

38. ———. Disorders of somatic sensation. Ibid., pp. 181–207.

39. Griggs, Robert C. Muscle spasms, cramps and episodic weakness. In Isselbacher, Kurt J., et al., eds., *Harrison's Principles of Internal Medicine*, 13th ed. New York: McGraw-Hill, Inc., 1994, pp. 130–133.

40. Gronert, Gerald A., and Antognini, Joseph F. Malignant hyperthermia. In Miller, Ronald D., ed., *Anesthesia*,

4th ed., vol. 1. New York: Churchill Livingstone, 1994, pp. 1075–1093.

41. Growdon, John, and Fink, J. Stephen. Paralysis and movement disorders. In Isselbacher, Kurt J., et al., eds., *Harrison's Principles of Internal Medicine*, 13th ed. New York: McGraw-Hill, Inc., 1994, pp. 115–125.

42. Gutrecht, José A., et al. Anatomic radiologic basis of Lhermitte's sign in multiple sclerosis. *Archives of Neurology* 50:849–851, August 1993.

43. Hauser, Stephen L. Multiple sclerosis and other demyelinating diseases. In Isselbacher, Kurt J., et al., eds., *Harrison's Principles of Internal Medicine*, 13th ed. New York: McGraw-Hill, Inc., 1994, pp. 2287–2295.

44. Hochberg, Fred, and Pruitt, Amy. Neoplastic diseases of the central nervous system. In Isselbacher, Kurt J., et al., eds., *Harrison's Principles of Internal Medicine*, 13th ed. New York: McGraw-Hill, Inc., 1994, pp. 2256–2269.

45. Hornbein, Thomas I. Acid-base balance. In Miller, Ronald D., ed., *Anesthesia*, 4th ed., vol. 2. New York: Churchill Livingstone, 1994, pp. 1383–1401.

46. Kilgore, Eugene S., et al. Hand surgery. In Way, Lawrence W., ed., *Current Surgical Diagnosis & Treatment*, 10th ed. Norwalk, CT: Appleton & Lange, 1994, pp. 1165–1189.

47. Kistler, J. Philip, et al. Cerebrovascular diseases. In Isselbacher, Kurt J., et al., eds., *Harrison's Principles of Internal Medicine*, 13th ed. New York: McGraw-Hill, Inc., 1994, pp. 2233–2256.

48. Koblin, Donald D. Inhaled anesthetics: Mechanisms of action. In Miller, Ronald D., ed., *Anesthesia*, 4th ed., vol. 1. New York: Churchill Livingstone, 1994, pp. 67–99.

49. Krupski, William C., and Effeney, David J. Arteries. In Way, Lawrence W., ed., *Current Surgical Diagnosis & Treatment*, 10th ed. Norwalk, CT: Appleton & Lange, 1994, pp. 739–771.

50. Lindvall, Olle, et al. Evidence for long-term survival and function of dopaminergic grafts in progressive Parkinson's disease. *Annuals of Neurology* 35:172–180, February 1994.

51. Maestre, Gladys, et al. Apoliprotein E and Alzheimer's disease: Ethnic variation in genotypic risks. *Annals of Neurology* 37:254–259, February 1995.

52. Mankin, Henry J., and Borges, Lawrence F. Back and neck pain. In Isselbacher, Kurt J., et al., eds., *Harrison's Principles of Internal Medicine*, 13th ed. New York: McGraw-Hill, Inc., 1994, pp. 72–81.

53. Markesbery, William R. The diagnosis of Alzheimer's disease. *Archives of Pathology & Laboratory Medicine* 117:129–131, February 1993.

54. Martin, Joseph B., and Ruskin, Jeremy. Faintness, syncope, and seizures. In Isselbacher, Kurt J., et al., eds., *Harrison's Principles of Internal Medicine*, 13th ed. New York: McGraw-Hill, Inc., 1994, pp. 90–96.

55. Mayeux, Richard, and Schofield, Peter W. Alzheimer's disease. In Hazzard, William R., et al., eds., *Principles of Geriatric Medicine and Gerontology*, 3d ed. New York: McGraw-Hill, Inc., 1994, pp. 1035–1050.

56. McDonald, Evelyn R., et al. Survival in amyotrophic lateral sclerosis. *Archives of Neurology* 51:17–23, January 1994.

57. Miller, Edward D., Jr., and Miller, Ronald D. Scope of modern anesthetic practice. In Miller, Ronald D., ed., *Anesthesia*, 4th ed., vol. 1. New York: Churchill Livingstone, 1994, pp. 3–8.

58. Miller, Ronald D. Use of neuromuscular blocking drugs in intensive care unit patients. *Anesthesia & Analgesia* 81:1–2, July 1995.

59. Mirra, Susanne S., et al. Making the diagnosis of Alzheimer's disease. *Archives of Pathology & Laboratory Medicine* 2:132–144, February 1993.

60. Missouri Hospital Association. Medical briefs. Healthstat 1:5, September/October 1993.

61. Mohr, J. P. Disorders of speech and language. In Isselbacher, Kurt J., et al., eds., *Harrison's Principles of Internal Medicine*, 13th ed. New York: McGraw-Hill, Inc., 1994, pp. 156–162.

62. Morgenstern, Hal, and Glazer, William M. Identifying risk factors for tardive dyskinesia among long-term outpatients maintained with neuroleptic medications. *Archives of General Psychiatry* 50:723–733, September 1993.

63. Murphy, Terence M. Chronic pain. In Miller, Ronald D., ed., *Anesthesia*, 4th ed., vol. 2. New York: Churchill Livingstone, 1994, pp. 2345–2373.

64. Nockels, Russ P., and Pitts, Lawrence H. Spinal cord injury. In Way, Lawrence W., ed., *Current Surgical Diagnosis & Treatment*, 10th ed. Norwalk, CT: Appleton & Lange, 1994, pp. 823–827.

65. Ojemann, G. A., and Ward, A. A., Jr. Abnormal movement disorders. In Youmans, Julian R., ed., *Neurological Surgery*, 3d ed., vol. 6. Philadelphia: W.B. Saunders Co., 1990, pp. 4227–4262.

66. Petersen, Ronald C., et al. Apolipoprotein E status as a predictor of the development of Alzheimer's disease in memory-impaired individuals. *Journal of the American Medical Association* 273:1274–1278, 26 April 1995.

67. Pitts, Lawrence H., and Nockels, Russ P. Craniocerebral trauma. In Way, Lawrence W., ed., *Current Surgical Diagnosis & Treatment*, 10th ed. Norwalk, CT: Appleton & Lange, 1994, pp. 817–823.

68. Pitts, Lawrence H., and Ross, Donald A. Intracranial aneurysms. In Way, Lawrence W., ed., *Current Surgical Diagnosis & Treatment*, 10th ed. Norwalk, CT: Appleton & Lange, 1994, pp. 842–845.

69. Prielipp, Richard C., et al. Comparison of the infusion requirements and recovery profiles of Vecuronium and Cisatracurium 51W89 in intensive care unit patients. *Anesthesia & Analgesia* 81:3–12, July 1995.

70. Ray, C. George. Enteroviruses and reoviruses. In Isselbacher, Kurt J., et al., eds., *Harrison's Principles of Internal Medicine*, 13th ed. New York: McGraw-Hill, Inc., 1994, pp. 821–825.

71. Regli, Luca, and de Tribolet, Nicolas. Arteriovenous malformations and angiomas of the brain. In Fisher, Marc, and Bogousslavsky, Julien, eds., *Current Review of Cerebrovascular Disease*, 2d ed. Philadelphia: Current Medicine, 1996, pp. 133–146.

72. Reves, J. Gerald, et al. Nonbarbiturate intravenous anesthetics. In Miller, Ronald D., ed., *Anesthesia*, 4th ed., vol. 1. New York: Churchill Livingstone, 1994, pp. 247–289.

73. Ropper, Alan H. Trauma of the head and spine. In Isselbacher, Kurt J., et al., eds., *Harrison's Principles of Internal Medicine*, 13th ed. New York: McGraw-Hill, Inc., 1994, pp. 2320–2328.

74. Ropper, Alan H., and Martin, Joseph B. Diseases of the spinal cord. In Isselbacher, Kurt J., et al., eds., *Harrison's Principles of Internal Medicine*, 13th ed. New York: McGraw-Hill, Inc., 1994, pp. 2352–2359.

75. Rosegay, Harold. Tumors of the spinal cord. In Way, Lawrence W., ed., *Current Surgical Diagnosis & Treatment*, 10th ed. Norwalk, CT: Appleton & Lange, 1994, pp. 835–836.

76. Rosenblum, Mark L. Surgical infections of the central nervous system. In Way, Lawrence W., ed., *Current Surgical Diagnosis & Treatment*, 10th ed. Norwalk, CT: Appleton & Lange, 1994, pp. 857–859.

77. Roth, Stuart. New findings may lead to Alzheimer's test. *The Kansas City Star*, 8 November 1993, p. A-3.

78. Savarese, John J., et al. Pharmacology of muscle relaxants and their antagonists. In Miller, Ronald D., ed., *Anesthesia*, 4th ed., vol. 1. New York: Churchill Livingstone, 1994, pp. 417–487.

79. Scheld, W. Michael. Bacterial meningitis and brain abscess. In Isselbacher, Kurt J., et al., eds., *Harrison's Principles of Internal Medicine*, 13th ed. New York: McGraw-Hill, Inc., 1994, pp. 2296–2309.

80. Selkoe, Dennis J. Missense on the membrane. *Nature* 375:734, 29 June 1995.

81. Shapiro, Harvey M., and Drummond, John C. Neurosurgical anesthesia. In Miller, Ronald D., ed., *Anesthesia*, 4th ed., vol. 2. New York: Churchill Livingstone, 1994, pp. 1897–1946.

82. Sherrington, R., et al. Cloning of a gene bearing missense mutations in early-onset familial Alzheimer's disease. *Nature* 375:754–760, 29 June 1995.

83. Small, Gary W., et al. Apolipoprotein E type 4 allele and cerebral glucose metabolism in relatives at risk for familial Alzheimer disease. *Journal of the American Medical Association* 273:942–947, 2/29 March 1995.

84. Stanski, Donald. Monitoring depth of anesthesia. In Miller, Ronald D., ed., *Anesthesia*, 4th ed., vol. 1. New York: Churchill Livingstone, 1994, pp. 1127–1159.

85. Steinman, Lawrence. Presenting an odd autoantigen. *Nature* 375:739–740, 29 June 1995.

86. Stone, David J., and Gal, Thomas J. Airway management. In Miller, Ronald D., ed., *Anesthesia*, 4th ed., vol. 2. New York: Churchill Livingstone, 1994, pp. 1403–1435.

87. Strichartz, Gary R., and Berde, Charles B. Local anesthetics. In Miller, Ronald D., ed., *Anesthesia*, 4th ed., vol. 1. New York: Churchill Livingstone, 1994, pp. 489–521.

88. Tasker, Ronald R., and Bernstein, Mark. Stereotactic surgery. In Rengachary, Setti S., and Wilkins, Robert H., eds., *Principles of Neurosurgery*. London: Wolfe Publishing, 1994, pp. 49.1–49.32.

89. Tobert, Daren G., and Gay, Peter C. New directions for pulse oximetry in sleep disorders. *Mayo Clinic Proceedings* 70:591–592, June 1995.

90. Tobias, Joseph D., et al. Pancuronium infusion for neuromuscular block in children in the pediatric intensive care unit. *Anesthesia & Analgesia* 81:13–16, July 1995.

91. Turgeon, Ronald, M.D., Personal communications.

92. Tyler, Kenneth L. Viral and prion diseases of the nervous system. In Isselbacher, Kurt J., et al., eds., *Harrison's Principles of Internal Medicine*, 13th ed. New York: McGraw-Hill, Inc., 1994, pp. 2309–2320.

93. Uemastu, S. Thermography. In Youmans, Julian R., ed., *Neurological Surgery*, 3d ed., vol. 1. Philadelphia: W.B. Saunders Co., 1990, pp. 500–508.

94. Van Aken, Hugo, and Miller Edward D., Jr. Deliberate hypotension. In Miller, Ronald D., ed., *Anesthesia*, 4th ed., vol. 2. New York: Churchill Livingstone, 1994, pp. 1481–1503.

95. Van Noort, Johannes, M., et al. The small heat-shock protein αB-crystallin as candidate autoantigen in multiple sclerosis. *Nature* 375:798–801, 29 June 1995.

96. Victor, Maurice, and Martin, Joseph B. Disorders of the cranial nerves. In Isselbacher, Kurt J., et al., eds., *Harrison's Principles of Internal Medicine*, 13th ed. New York: McGraw-Hill, Inc., 1994, pp. 2347–2352.

97. Wedel, Denise J. Nerve blocks. In Miller, Ronald D., ed., *Anesthesia*, 4th ed., vol. 2. New York: Churchill Livingstone, 1994, pp. 1535–1564.

98. Weinstein, Philip R., and Hoff, Julian T. Intervertebral disk disease. In Way, Lawrence W., ed., *Current Surgical Diagnosis & Treatment*, 10th ed. Norwalk, CT:. Appleton & Lange, 1994, pp. 851–856.

99. Wilkins, Robert H. Trigeminal neuralgia. In Rengachary, Setti S., and Wilkins, Robert H., eds., *Principles of Neurosurgery*. London: Wolfe Publishing, 1994, pp. 47.1–47.6.

100. Willenkin, Robert L., and Polk, Susan L. Management of general anesthesia. In Miller, Ronald D., ed., *Anesthesia*, 4th ed., vol. 1. New York: Churchill Livingstone, 1994, pp. 1045–1056.

101. Williams, Peter L., et al. Neurology. In *Gray's Anatomy*, 37th ed. Edinburgh: Churchill Livingstone, 1989, pp. 860–1243.

102. Wilson, Charles B. Pituitary tumors. In Way, Lawrence W., *Current Surgical Diagnosis & Treatment*, 10th ed. Norwalk, CT: Appleton & Lange, 1994, pp. 838–839.

103. Wood, George W., II. Lower back pain and disorders of intervertebral disc. In Crenshaw, A. H., ed., *Campbell's Operative Orthopaedics*, 8th ed., vol. 5. St. Louis: Mosby Year Book, 1992, pp. 3715–3790.

Chapter 5

1. Akeson, Wayne H., et al. Articular cartilage: Physiology and metabolism. In Resnick, Donald, ed., *Diagnosis of Bone and Joint Disorders*, 3d ed., vol. 2. Philadelphia: W.B. Saunders Co., 1995, pp. 769–790.

2. Anderson, David, M.D., Personal communication.

3. Beaty, James H. Congenital anomalies of the lower extremity. In Crenshaw, A. H., ed., *Campbell's Operative Orthopaedics*, 8th ed., vol. 3. St. Louis: Mosby Year Book, 1992, pp. 2061–2158.

4. ———. Congenital anomalies of trunk and upper extremity. Ibid., vol. 3, pp. 2199–2212.

5. ———. Paralytic disorders. Ibid., vol. 4, pp. 2383–2463.

6. Brandt, Kenneth D. Osteoarthritis. In Isselbacher, Kurt J., ed., et al., *Harrison's Principles of Internal Medicine*, 13th ed. New York: McGraw-Hill, Inc., 1994, pp. 1692–1698.

7. Brown, Robert H., Jr. Muscle disease. In Stein, Jay H., ed.-in-ch., *Internal Medicine*, 4th ed. St. Louis: Mosby, 1994, pp. 1108–1115.

8. Calandruccio, James H., and Jobe, Mark T. Paralytic hand. In Crenshaw, A. H., ed., *Campbell's Operative Orthopaedics*, 8th ed., vol. 5. St. Louis: Mosby Year Book, 1992, pp. 3233–3289.

9. Canale, S. Terry. Osteochondrosis or epiphysitis and other miscellaneous affections. In Crenshaw, A. H., ed., *Campbell's Operative Orthopaedics*, 8th ed., vol. 3. St. Louis: Mosby Year Book, 1992, pp. 1959–2003.

10. Carnesale, Peter G. Benign tumors of bone. In Crenshaw, A. H., ed., *Campbell's Operative Orthopaedics*, 8th ed., vol. 1. St. Louis: Mosby Year Book, 1992, pp. 235–252.

11. ———. Sometimes malignant tumors of bone. Ibid., vol. 1, pp. 253–262.

12. ———. Malignant tumors of the bone. Ibid., vol. 1, pp. 263–289.

13. ———. Soft tissue tumors and noneoplastic conditions simulating bone tumors. Ibid., vol. 1, pp. 291–314.

14. ———. Arthrodesis of ankle, knee and hip. Ibid., vol. 1, pp. 317–352.

15. Crenshaw, Andrew H., Jr. Shoulder and elbow injuries. In Crenshaw, A. H., ed., *Campbell's Operative Orthopaedics*, 8th ed., vol. 3. St. Louis: Mosby Year Book, 1992, pp. 1733–1766.

16. Day, Lorraine J., et al. Orthopedics. In Way, Lawrence W., ed., *Current Surgical Diagnosis & Treatment*, 10th ed. Norwalk, CT: Appleton & Lange, pp. 1011–1129.

17. Dulkowsky, Joseph P. Miscellaneous nontraumatic disorders. In Crenshaw, A. H., ed., *Campbell's Operative Orthopaedics*, 8th ed., vol. 3. St. Louis: Mosby Year Book, 1992, pp. 2005–2057.

18. Eckardt, Jeffrey, et al. An aggressive surgical approach to the management of chronic osteomyelitis. *Clinical Orthopaedics and Related Research* 1:229–239, January 1994.

19. Edmonson, Allen S. Scoliosis. In Crenshaw, A. H., ed., *Campbell's Operative Orthopaedics*, 8th ed., vol. 5. St. Louis: Mosby Year Book, 1992, pp. 3605–3654.

20. Gilliland, Bruce C. Relapsing polychondritis and miscellaneous arthritides. In Isselbacher, Kurt J., ed., et al., *Harrison's Principles of Internal Medicine*, 13th ed. New York: McGraw-Hill, Inc., 1994, pp. 1703–1710.

21. Hellmann, David B. Arthritis & musculoskeletal disorders. In Tierney, Lawrence M., Jr., et al. *Current Medical Diagnosis & Treatment*, 35th ed. Stamford, CT: Appleton & Lange, 1996, pp. 719–767.

22. Harkness, James W. Arthroplasty of hip. In Crenshaw, A. H., ed., *Campbell's Operative Orthopaedics*, 8th ed., vol. 1. St. Louis: Mosby Year Book, 1992, pp. 441–626.

23. Health Update. Program offers new hope for children with short limbs. In *St. Louis Post Dispatch Sunday Supplement*, p. 5, November 1993.

24. Hoffman, Gary S., and Reginato, Antonio J. Arthritis due to deposition of calcium crystals. In Isselbacher, Kurt J., et al., eds. *Harrison's Principles of Internal Medicine*, 13th ed. New York: McGraw-Hill, Inc., 1994, pp. 1698–1701.

25. Jobe, Mark T. Cerebral-palsied hand. In Crenshaw, A. H., ed., *Campbell's Operative Orthopaedics*, 8th ed., vol. 5. St. Louis: Mosby Year Book, 1992, pp. 3281–3299.

26. ———. Volkmann's contracture and compartment syndromes. Ibid., vol. 5, pp. 3341–3351.

27. ———. Dupytren's contracture. Ibid., vol. 5, pp. 3427–3434.

28. ———. Tumors and tumorous conditions of hand. Ibid., vol. 5, pp. 3447–3478.

29. Jobe, Mark T., and Wright, Phillip E., II. Congenital anomalies of hand. In Crenshaw, A. H., ed., *Campbell's Operative Orthopaedics*, 8th ed., vol. 5. St. Louis: Mosby Year Book, 1992, pp. 3353–3425.

30. Kilgore, Eugene S., et al. Hand surgery. In Way, Lawrence. W., ed., *Current Surgical Diagnosis & Treatment*, 10th ed. Norwalk, CT: Appleton & Lange, 1994, pp. 1165–1189.

31. Kraay, Matthew J., and Goldberg, Victor M. Cementless total knee arthroplasty. In Scott, W. Norman, ed., *The Knee*, vol. 2. St. Louis: Mosby, 1994, pp. 1105–1116.

32. Krane, Stephen M. Paget's disease of bone. Isselbacher, Kurt J., et al., eds., *Harrison's Principles of Internal Medicine*, 13th ed. New York: McGraw-Hill, Inc. 1994, pp. 2190–2193.

33. Krane, Stephen M., and Holick, Michael F. Metabolic bone diseases. In Isselbacher, Kurt J., et al., eds., *Harrison's Principles of Internal Medicine*, 13th ed. New York: McGraw-Hill, Inc., 1994, pp. 2172–2183.

34. Krane, Stephen M., and Schiller, Alan L. Hyperostosis, neoplasms, and other disorders of bone and cartilage. In Isselbacher, Kurt J., et al., eds., *Harrison's Principles of Internal Medicine*, 13th ed. New York: McGraw-Hill, Inc. 1994, pp. 2193–2201.

35. Krupski, William C., et al. Amputation. In Way, Lawrence W., ed., *Current Surgical Diagnosis & Treatment*, 10th ed. Norwalk, CT: Appleton & Lange, 1994, pp. 772–782.

36. Kulick, Roy G. Carpal tunnel syndrome. *Orthopedics Clinics of North America* 27:345–354, April 1996.

37. Lipsky, Peter E. Rheumatoid arthritis. In Isselbacher, Kurt J., et al., eds., *Harrison's Principles of Internal Medicine*, 13th ed. New York: McGraw-Hill, Inc., 1994, pp. 1648–1655.

38. Miller, Robert H., III. General principles of arthroscopy. In Crenshaw, A. H., ed., *Campbell's Operative Orthopaedics*, 8th ed., vol. 3. St. Louis: Mosby Year Book, 1992, pp. 1769–1786.

39. ———. Arthroscopy of lower extremity. Ibid., vol. 3, pp. 1787–1864.

40. ———. Arthroscopy of upper extremity. Ibid., vol. 3, pp. 1865–1891.

41. Mirza, M. Ather, and King, Eugene T. New techniques of carpal tunnel release. *Orthopedic Clinics of North America* 27:355–371, April 1996.

42. Morrison, Nigel A., et al. Prediction of bone density from Vitamin D receptor alleles. *Nature* 367:284–287, January 1994.

43. Mundy, Gregory R. Boning up on genes. *Nature* 367:216–217, 20 January 1994.

44. Murphy, William A., Jr., and Kaplan, Phoebe A. Temporomandibular joint. In Resnick, Donald, ed., *Diagnosis of Bone and Joint Disorders*, 3d ed., vol. 3. Philadelphia: W.B. Saunders Co., 1995, pp. 1699–1754.

45. Newsday. Scientists link gene, risk of osteoporosis. In *The Kansas City Star*, p. 4, 20 January 1994.

46. Pellegrini, Carlos A., and Way, Lawrence W. Esophagus and diaphragm. In Way, Lawrence W., ed., *Current Surgical Diagnosis & Treatment*, 10th ed. Norwalk, CT: Appleton & Lange, 1994, pp. 411–440.

47. Phillips, Barry B. Traumatic disorders. In Crenshaw, A. H., ed., *Campbell's Operative Orthopaedics*, 8th ed., vol. 3. St. Louis: Mosby Year Book, 1992, pp. 1895–1938.

48. ———. Nontraumatic disorders. Ibid., vol. 3, pp. 1939–1955.

49. Resnick, Donald, and Niwayama, Gen. Osteoporosis. In Resnick, Donald, ed., *Diagnosis of Bone and Joint Disorders*, 3d ed., vol. 4. Philadelphia: W.B. Saunders Co., 1995, pp. 1783–1853.

50. ———. Paget's Disease. Ibid., pp. 1923–1968.

51. ———. Osteomyelitis, septic arthritis, and soft tissue infection. Ibid., pp. 2448–2558.

52. Richardson, E. Greer. Disorders of the hallux. In Crenshaw, A. H., ed., *Campbell's Operative Orthopaedics*, 8th ed., vol. 4. St. Louis: Mosby Year Book, 1992, pp. 2616–2692.

53. Rodkey, William G., and Steadman, J. Richard. Meniscal allograft replacement. In Scott, W. Norman, ed., *The Knee*, vol. 1. St. Louis: Mosby, 1994, pp. 573–581.

54. Russell, Thomas A. General principles of fracture treatment. In Crenshaw, A. H., ed., *Campbell's Operative Orthopaedics*, 8th ed., vol. 2. St. Louis: Mosby Year Book, 1992, pp. 725–784.

55. ———. Fractures of the hip and pelvis. Ibid., vol. 2, pp. 895–987.

56. ———. Fractures of shoulder girdle, arm, and forearm. Ibid., vol. 2, pp. 989–1051.

57. Sage, Fred P. Inheritable progressive neuromuscular diseases. In Crenshaw, A. H., ed., *Campbell's Operative Orthopaedics*, 8th ed., vol. 4. St. Louis: Mosby Year Book, 1992, pp. 2465–2498.

58. Seybold, Marjorie E. Diseases of the neuromuscular junction. In Stein, Jay H., ed.-in-ch., *Internal Medicine*, 4th ed. St. Louis: Mosby, 1994, pp. 1104–1108.

59. Singer, Frederick R. Paget's disease of the bone. In Stein, Jay H., ed.-in-ch., *Internal Medicine*, 4th ed. St. Louis: Mosby, 1994, pp. 1529–1532.

60. Sisk, T. David. Arthroplasty of shoulder and elbow. In Crenshaw, A. H., ed., *Campbell's Operative Orthopaedics*, 8th ed., vol. 1. St. Louis: Mosby Year Book, 1992, pp. 627–673.

61. ———. Knee injuries. Ibid., vol. 3, pp. 1487–1732.

62. Slone, Richard M., et al. Principles and imaging of spinal instrumentation. *Radiologic Clinics of North America* 33:189–211, March 1995.

63. ———. Fixation techniques and instrumentation used in the thoracic, lumbar, and lumbosacral spine. Ibid., pp. 233–265.

64. Sprague, Norman F., III. Arthroscopic meniscal resection. In Scott, W. Norman. ed., *The Knee*, vol. 1. St. Louis: Mosby Year Book, 1994, pp. 527–557.

65. SSM Rehabilitation Institute. Product line management at SSM Rehabilitation Institute leads to major patient benefits. *Insights*, Winter 1993, pp. 1, 3, 5, and 7.

66. Tandan, Rup. Dermatomyositis and polymyositis. In Isselbacher, Kurt J., et al., eds., *Harrison's Principles of Internal Medicine*, 13th ed. New York: McGraw-Hill Inc., 1994, pp. 2379–2383.

67. Taurog, Joel D., and Lipsky, Peter E. Ankylosing spondylitis, reactive arthritis, and undifferentiated spondyloarthropathy. In Isselbacher, Kurt J., et al., eds., *Harrison's Principles of Internal Medicine*, 13th ed. New York: McGraw-Hill, Inc., 1994, pp. 1664–1669.

68. Taylor, J. Charles. Fractures of lower extremity fractures. In Crenshaw, A. H., ed., *Campbell's Operative Orthopaedics*, 8th ed., vol. 2. St. Louis: Mosby Year Book, 1992, pp. 785–894.

69. ———. Delayed union and nonunion of fractures. Ibid., vol. 2, pp. 1287–1345.

70. Tooms, Robert E. Arthroplasty of ankle and knee. In Crenshaw, A. H., ed., *Campbell's Operative Orthopaedics*, 8th ed., vol. 1. St. Louis: Mosby Year Book, 1992, pp. 389–439.

71. ———. General principles of amputations. Ibid., vol. 2, pp. 677–687.

72. ———. Amputation of lower extremity. Ibid., vol. 2, pp. 689–893.

73. Turgeon, Ronald, M.D., Personal communications.

74. Van De Graaff, Kent M. Skeletal system: Introduction and the axial skeleton. In *Human Anatomy*, 4th ed. Dubuque, IA: Wm. C. Brown Publishers, 1995, pp. 129–167.

75. ———. Skeletal system: Appendicular skeleton. Ibid., pp. 169–189.

76. ———. Articulations. Ibid., pp. 191–222.

77. ———. Muscular system. Ibid., pp. 223–282.

78. Warner, William C. Jr. Osteomyelitis. In Crenshaw, A. H., ed., *Campbell's Operative Orthopaedics*, 8th ed., vol. 1. St. Louis: Mosby Year Book, 1992, pp. 131–150.

79. ———. Infectious arthritis. Ibid., vol. 1, pp. 151–175.

80. Wilson, Stephen A., et al. Anatomy. In Scott, W. Norman, ed., *The Knee*, vol. 1. St. Louis: Mosby Year Book, 1994, pp. 15–71.

81. Wood, George W., II. Other disorders of the spine. In Crenshaw, A. H., ed., *Campbell's Operative Orthopaedics*, 8th ed., vol. 5. St. Louis: Mosby Year Book, 1992, pp. 3825–3870.

82. Wright, Philip E., II. Arthritic hand. In Crenshaw, A. H., ed., *Campbell's Operative Orthopaedics*, 8th ed., vol. 5. St. Louis: Mosby Year Book, 1992, pp. 3301–3339.

83. ———. Carpal tunnel and ulnar tunnel syndromes and stenosing tenosynovitis. Ibid., vol. 5, pp. 3435–3445.

Chapter 6

1. Akhtar, Masood. Technique of electrophysiological testing. In Schlant, Robert C., and Alexander, R. Wayne, eds., *The Heart*, 8th ed. New York: McGraw-Hill, Inc., 1994, pp. 881–892.

2. Alpert, Joseph, S., and Becker, Richard C. Pathophysiology, diagnosis, and management of cardiogenic shock. In Schlant, Robert C., and Alexander, R. Wayne, eds., *The Heart*, 8th ed. New York: McGraw-Hill, Inc., 1994, pp. 907–925.

3. Alpert, Joseph S., and Dalen, James E. Pulmonary embolism. In Schlant, Robert C., and Alexander, R. Wayne, eds., *The Heart*, 8th ed. New York: McGraw-Hill, Inc., 1994, pp. 1875–1887.

4. Bacharach, J. Michael, and Olin, Jeffrey W. Raynaud's phenomenon. *Heart Disease and Stroke* 3:255–259, September/October 1994.

5. Bierman, Edwin L. Atherosclerosis and other forms of arteriosclerosis. In Isselbacher, Kurt J., et al., eds., *Harrison's Principles of Internal Medicine*, 13th ed. New York: McGraw-Hill, Inc., 1994, pp. 1106–1116.

6. Block, Peter C. Percutaneous balloon valvotomy. In Schlant, Robert C., and Alexander, R. Wayne, eds., *The Heart*, 8th ed. New York: McGraw-Hill, Inc., 1994, pp. 1567–1582.

7. Boström, K., et al. Bone morphogenetic protein expression in human atherosclerotic lesions. *Journal of Clinical Investigation* 91:1800–1809, April 1993.

8. Braunwald, Eugene. Pericardial disease. In Isselbacher, Kurt J., et al., eds., *Harrison's Principles of Internal Medicine*, 13th ed. New York: McGraw-Hill, Inc., 1994, pp. 1094–1101.

9. ———. Heart failure. Ibid., pp. 998–1009.

10. Brooks, Ross, and Ruskin, Jeremy N. The implantable cardioverter-defibrillator. In Schlant, Robert C., and Alexander, R. Wayne, eds., *The Heart*, 8th ed. New York: McGraw-Hill, Inc., 1994, pp. 847–857.

11. Buller, Christopher, et al. Cardiac catheterization and percutaneous coronary angioplasty. In Sabiston, David C., Jr., ed., *Textbook of Surgery*, 14th ed. Philadelphia: W.B. Saunders Co., 1991, pp. 1826–1843.

12. Butler, John, and Braunwald, Eugene. Cor pulmonale. In Isselbacher, Kurt J., et al., eds., *Harrison's Principles of Internal Medicine*, 13th ed. New York: McGraw-Hill, Inc., 1994, pp. 1085–1088.

13. Carver, Joseph M., and Connolly, Mark W. The percutaneous intra-aortic balloon pump and ventricular assist devices. In Schlant, Robert C., and Alexander, R. Wayne, eds., *The Heart*, 8th ed. New York: McGraw-Hill, Inc., 1994, pp. 621–628.

14. Castellanos, Austin, et al. The resting electrocardiogram. In Schlant, Robert C., and Alexander, R. Wayne, eds., *The Heart*, 8th ed. New York: McGraw-Hill, Inc., 1994, pp. 321–356.

15. Chandra, Nisha Chibbler, and Weisfeldt, Myron L. Cardiopulmonary resuscitation and subsequent management of the patient. In Schlant, Robert C., and Alexander, R. Wayne, eds., *The Heart*, 8th ed. New York: McGraw-Hill, Inc., 1994, pp. 959–969.

16. Cobb, Leonard A. The mechanisms, predictors, and prevention of sudden cardiac death. In Schlant, Robert C., and Alexander, R. Wayne, eds., *The Heart*, 8th ed. New York: McGraw-Hill, Inc., 1994, pp. 947–957.

17. Cohn, Jay N., and Sonnenblick, Edmund H. Diagnosis and therapy of heart failure. In Schlant, Robert C., and Alexander, R. Wayne, eds., *The Heart*, 8th ed. New York: McGraw-Hill, Inc., 1994, pp. 557–571.

18. Connolly, Mark W., and Guyton, Robert A. Cardiopulmonary bypass and intraoperative protection. In Schlant, Robert C., and Alexander, R. Wayne, eds., *The Heart*, 8th ed. New York: McGraw-Hill, Inc., 1994, pp. 2443–2450.

19. Cox, James L. Surgical treatment of cardiac arrhythmias. In Schlant, Robert C., and Alexander, R. Wayne, eds., *The Heart*, 8th ed. New York: McGraw-Hill, Inc., 1994, pp. 863–871.

20. Davies, Michael J. The pathology of coronary atherosclerosis. In Schlant, Robert C., and Alexander, R. Wayne, eds., *The Heart*, 8th ed. New York: McGraw-Hill Inc., 1994, pp. 423–440.

21. Domanski, Michael J., and Topol, Eric J. Cardiogenic shock: Current understandings and future research directions. *American Journal of Cardiology* 74:724–726. 1 October 1994.

22. Douglas, John S., Jr., and King, Spencer B., III. Techniques of percutaneous transluminal angioplasty and atherectomy of the coronary arteries. In Schlant, Robert C., and Alexander, R. Wayne, eds., *The Heart*, 8th ed. New York: McGraw-Hill, Inc., 1994, pp. 1345–1358.

23. Durack, David T. Infective and noninfective endocarditis. In Schlant, Robert C., and Alexander, R. Wayne, eds., *The Heart*, 8th ed. New York: McGraw-Hill, Inc., 1994, pp. 1681–1709.

24. Eeckhout, Ric, et al. Comparison of the Wallstent, Palmaz-Schatz stent and Wiktor stent late after intracoronary stenting. *American Journal of Cardiology* 74:609–612, 15 September 1994.

25. Elgin, R. J. Reference intervals and laboratory values of clinical importance. In Wyngaarden, James B., et al., eds., *Cecil Textbook of Medicine*, 19th ed. Philadelphia: W.B. Saunders Co., 1992, pp. 2370–2380.

26. Factor, Stephen M., and Bache, Robert J. Pathophysiology of myocardial ischemia. In Schlant, Robert C., and Alexander, R. Wayne, eds., *The Heart*, 8th ed. New York: McGraw-Hill, Inc., 1994, pp. 1033–1053.

27. Felner, Joel M., and Martin, Randolph P. The echocardiogram. In Schlant, Robert C., and Alexander, R. Wayne, eds., *The Heart*, 8th ed. New York: McGraw-Hill, Inc., 1994, pp. 375–422.

28. Fishman, Alfred P. Pulmonary hypertension. In Schlant, Robert C., and Alexander, R. Wayne, eds., *The Heart*, 8th ed. New York: McGraw-Hill, Inc., 1994, pp. 1857–1874.

29. Fletcher, Gerald F., and Schlant, Robert C. The exercise test. In Schlant, Robert C., and Alexander, R. Wayne, eds., *The Heart*, 8th ed. New York: McGraw-Hill, Inc., 1994, pp. 423–440.

30. Fletcher, Ross D., et al. Temporary cardiac pacing. In Schlant, Robert C., and Alexander, R. Wayne, eds., *The Heart*, 8th ed. New York: McGraw-Hill, Inc., 1994, pp. 807–813.

31. Franch, Robert H., et al. Techniques of cardiac catheterization including coronary arteriography. In Schlant, Robert C., and Alexander, R. Wayne, eds., *The Heart*, 8th ed. New York: McGraw-Hill, Inc., 1994, pp. 2381–2418.

32. Froblich, Edward D. Pathophysiology of systemic arterial hypertension. In Schlant, Robert C., and Alexander, R. Wayne, eds., *The Heart*, 8th ed. New York: McGraw-Hill, Inc., 1994, pp. 1391–1401.

33. Gaasch, William H., et al. Mitral valve disease. In Schlant, Robert C., and Alexander, R. Wayne, eds., *The Heart*, 8th ed. New York: McGraw-Hill, Inc., 1994, pp. 1483–1518.

34. Galloway, Aubrey, et al. Congenital heart disease. In Schwartz, Seymour I., ed.-in-ch., *Principles of Surgery*, 6th ed., vol. 1. New York: McGraw-Hill, Inc., 1994, pp. 779–843.

35. ———. Diseases of great vessels. Ibid., pp. 903–924.

36. Galloway, Aubrey, et al. Acquired heart disease. In Schwartz, Seymour I.,

ed.-in-ch., *Principles of Surgery*, 6th ed., vol. 1. New York: McGraw-Hill, Inc., 1994, pp. 845–902.

37. Gilbert, Edward M., and Bristow, Michael R. Idiopathic dilated cardiomyopathy. In Schlant, Robert C., and Alexander, R. Wayne, eds., *The Heart*, 8th ed. New York: McGraw-Hill, Inc., 1994, pp. 1609–1619.

38. Gott, John Parker, and Guyton, Robert A. Techniques of valvular surgery. In Schlant, Robert C., and Alexander, R. Wayne, eds., *The Heart*, 8th ed. New York: McGraw-Hill, Inc., 1994, pp. 1547–1555.

39. Green, Richard, and Ouriel, Kenneth. Peripheral arterial disease. In Schwartz, Seymour I., ed.-in-ch., *Principles of Surgery*, 6th ed., vol. 1 New York: McGraw-Hill, Inc., 1994, pp. 925–987.

40. Greenfield, Lazar J. Venous and lymphatic disease. In Schwartz, Seymour I., ed.-in-ch., *Principles of Surgery*, 6th ed., vol. 1. New York: McGraw-Hill, Inc., 1994, pp. 989–1014.

41. Hall, W. Dallas, et al. Diagnostic evaluation of the patient with systemic arterial hypertension. In Schlant, Robert C., and Alexander, R. Wayne, eds., *The Heart*, 8th ed. New York: McGraw-Hill, Inc., 1994, pp. 1403–1425.

42. Hamm, Christian W. New serum markers for acute myocardial infarction. *New England Journal of Medicine* 331:607–608, 1 September 1994.

43. Hancock, E. William. Artificial valve disease. In Schlant, Robert C., and Alexander, R. Wayne, eds., *The Heart*, 8th ed. New York: McGraw-Hill, Inc., 1994, pp. 1539–1545.

44. Hancock, E. William. Cardiac tamponade. *Heart Disease and Stroke* 3:155–158, May/June 1994.

45. Healy, Bernadine P. The heart and connective tissue disease. In Schlant, Robert C., and Alexander, R. Wayne, eds., *The Heart*, 8th ed. New York: McGraw-Hill, Inc., 1994, pp. 1921–1935.

46. Herbert, Kathy A., and Glancy, David Luke. Indication for Swan-Ganz Catheterization. *Heart Disease and Stroke* 3:196–200, July/August 1994.

47. Hole, John W., Jr. Cardiovascular system. In *Human Anatomy and Physiology*, 6th ed. Dubuque, IA: Wm. C. Brown Publishers, 1994, pp. 650–713.

48. Hunt, Sharon A., et al. Cardiac transplantation. In Schlant, Robert C., and Alexander, R. Wayne, eds., *The Heart*, 8th ed. New York: McGraw-Hill, Inc., 1994, pp. 629–636.

49. Hurst, J. Willis, and Morris, Douglas C. The history: Symptoms and past events related to cardiovascular disease. In

Schlant, Robert C., and Alexander, R. Wayne, eds., *The Heart*, 8th ed. New York: McGraw-Hill, Inc., 1994, pp. 205–215.

50. Jones, Ellis L., Jr., and Hatcher, Charles R., Jr. Techniques for surgical treatment of atherosclerotic coronary artery disease and its complications. In Schlant, Robert C., and Alexander, R. Wayne, eds., *The Heart*, 8th ed. New York: McGraw-Hill, Inc., 1994, pp. 1381–1388.

51. Josephon, Mark E., et al. The bradyarrhythmias: Disorders of the sinus node function and AV conduction disturbances. In Isselbacher, Kurt J., et al., eds., *Harrison's Principles of Internal Medicine*, 13th ed. New York: McGraw-Hill, Inc., 1994, pp. 1011–1019.

52. ———. The tachyarrhythmias. Ibid., pp. 1019–1036.

53. Joyce, John W. The diagnosis and management of diseases of the peripheral arteries and veins. In Schlant, Robert C., and Alexander, R. Wayne, eds., *The Heart*, 8th ed. New York: McGraw-Hill, Inc., 1994, pp. 2181–2206.

54. Kaplan, Edward L. Acute rheumatic fever. In Schlant, Robert C., and Alexander, R. Wayne, eds., *The Heart*, 8th ed. New York: McGraw-Hill, Inc., 1994, pp. 1451–1456.

55. Kay, Donald. Infective endocarditis. In Isselbacher, Kurt J., et al., eds., *Harrison's Principles of Internal Medicine*, 13th ed. New York: McGraw-Hill, Inc., 1994, pp. 520–526.

56. Kiemeneij, Ferdinand, and Laarman, Gert Jan. Percutaneous transradial artery approach for coronary Palmaz-Schatz stent implantation. *American Heart Journal* 128:167–174, July 1994.

57. King, Spencer B., and Douglas, John S., Jr. Indications for percutaneous transluminal coronary angioplasty and atherectomy. In Schlant, Robert C., and Alexander, R. Wayne, eds., *The Heart*, 8th ed. New York: McGraw-Hill, Inc., 1994, pp. 1339–1344.

58. Krupski, William C., and Effeney, David J. Arteries. In Way, Lawrence W., ed., *Current Surgical Diagnosis & Treatment*, 10th ed. Norwalk, CT: Appleton & Lange, 1994, pp. 739–771.

59. Lewis, Richard P., et al. *Diagnosis and management of syncope*. In Schlant, Robert C., and Alexander, R. Wayne, eds., *The Heart*, 8th ed. New York: McGraw-Hill, Inc., 1994, pp. 927–945.

60. Lindsay, Joseph, Jr., et al. Diagnosis and treatment of diseases of aorta. In Schlant, Robert C., and Alexander, R. Wayne, eds., *The Heart*, 8th ed. New York: McGraw-Hill, Inc., 1994, pp. 2163–2180.

61. Lown, Bernard, and de Silva, Regis A. Cardioversion and defibrillation. In Schlant, Robert C., and Alexander, R. Wayne, eds., *The Heart*, 8th ed. New York: McGraw-Hill, Inc., 1994, pp. 843–846.

62. Lutz, Jerre F. The technique of myocardial biopsy. In Schlant, Robert C., and Alexander, R. Wayne, eds., *The Heart*, 8th ed. New York: McGraw-Hill, Inc., 1994, pp. 637–642.

63. Mannick, John A. Subclavian steal syndrome. In Sabiston, David C., Jr., ed., *Textbook of Surgery*, 14th ed. Philadelphia: W.B. Saunders Co., 1991, pp. 1584–1588.

64. Maron, Barry J., and Roberts, William C. Hypertensive cardiomyopathy. In Schlant, Robert C., and Alexander, R. Wayne, eds., *The Heart*, 8th ed. New York: McGraw-Hill, Inc., 1994, pp. 1621–1635.

65. Massie, Barry M. Heart. Tierney, Lawrence M., Jr., *Current Medical Diagnosis & Treatment*, 35th ed. Stamford, CT: Appleton & Lange, 1996, pp. 295–383.

66. ———. Systemic hypertension. Ibid., pp. 373–390.

67. Miller, Joseph I., Jr. Surgical management of pericardial disease. In Schlant, Robert C., and Alexander, R. Wayne, eds., *The Heart*, 8th ed. New York: McGraw-Hill, Inc., 1994, pp. 1675–1680.

68. Mond, Harry G. Permanent cardiac pacemakers: Techniques of implantation, testing, and surveillance. In Schlant, Robert C., and Alexander, R. Wayne, eds., *The Heart*, 8th ed. New York: McGraw-Hill, Inc., 1994, pp. 815–841.

69. Moscucci, Mauro, et al. Peripheral vascular complications of directional coronary atherectomy and stenting: Predictors, management, and outcome. *American Journal of Cardiology* 74:448–453, 1 September 1994.

70. Myerburg, Robert J., et al. Recognition, clinical assessment, and management of arrhythmias and conduction disturbances. In Schlant, Robert C., and Alexander, R. Wayne, eds., *The Heart*, 8th ed. New York: McGraw-Hill, Inc., 1994, pp. 705–758.

71. Newman, John H., and Ross, Joseph C. Chronic cor pulmonale. In Schlant, Robert C., and Alexander, R. Wayne, eds., *The Heart*, 8th ed. New York: McGraw-Hill, Inc., 1994, pp. 1895–2094.

72. Noble, R. Joe, and Zipes, Douglas P. Long-term continuous electrographic recording. In Schlant, Robert C., and Alexander, R. Wayne, eds., *The Heart*, 8th ed. New York: McGraw-Hill, Inc., 1994, pp. 873–880.

73. Nugent, Elizabeth W., et al. The pathology, pathophysiology, recognition, and treatment of congenital heart disease. In Schlant, Robert C., and Alexander, R. Wayne, eds., *The Heart*, 8th ed. New York: McGraw-Hill, Inc., 1994, pp. 1761–1828.

74. O'Connell, John B., and Renlund, Dale G. Myocarditis and specific myocardial diseases. In Schlant, Robert C., and Alexander, R. Wayne, eds., *The Heart*, 8th ed. New York: McGraw-Hill, Inc., 1994, pp. 1591–1607.

75. Orencia, Anthony J., et al. Sinus node dysfunction and ischemia stroke. *Heart Disease and Stroke* 3:91–94, March–April 1994.

76. O'Rourke, Robert A. Chest pain. In Schlant, Robert C., and Alexander, R. Wayne, eds., *The Heart*, 8th ed. New York: McGraw-Hill, Inc., 1994, pp. 459–467.

77. O'Rourke, Robert A., et al. General examination of the patient. In Schlant, Robert C., and Alexander, R. Wayne, eds., *The Heart*, 8th ed. New York: McGraw-Hill, Inc., 1994, pp. 217–251.

78. Pasternak, Richard C., and Brunwald, Eugene. Acute myocardial infarction. In Isselbacher, Kurt J., et al., eds., *Harrison's Principles of Internal Medicine*, 13th ed. New York: McGraw-Hill, Inc., 1994, pp. 1066–1077.

79. Pearlman, Alan S. Technique of Doppler and color flow Doppler in the evaluation of cardiac disorders and function. In Schlant, Robert C., and Alexander, R. Wayne, eds., *The Heart*, 8th ed. New York: McGraw-Hill, Inc., 1994, pp. 2229–2251.

80. Price, Karen. St. Mary's First in St. Louis to offer new DCA Procedure. *St. Mary's Center News*. St. Louis: St. Mary's Health Center, Fall 1990, p. 6.

81. Rackley, Charles E., and Schlant, Robert C. Prevention of coronary artery disease. In Schlant, Robert C., and Alexander, R. Wayne, eds., *The Heart*, 8th ed. New York: McGraw-Hill, Inc., 1994, pp. 1205–1222.

82. Rackley, Charles E., et al. Triscuspid and pulmonary valve disease. In Schlant, Robert C., and Alexander, R. Wayne, eds., *The Heart*, 8th ed. New York: McGraw-Hill, Inc., 1994, pp. 1519–1529.

83. Rackley, Charles E., et al. Multivalvular disease. In Schlant, Robert C., and Alexander, R. Wayne, eds., *The Heart*, 8th ed. New York: McGraw-Hill, Inc., 1994, pp. 1531–1538.

84. Rankin, J. Scott, et al. The heart: I. Acquired diseases. In Way, Lawrence W., ed., *Current Surgical Diagnosis & Treatment*, 10th ed. Norwalk, CT: Appleton & Lange, 1994, pp. 358–382.

85. Rapaport, Elliot, et al. Aortic valvular disease. In Schlant, Robert C., and Alexander, R. Wayne, eds., *The Heart*, 8th ed. New York: McGraw-Hill, Inc., 1994, pp. 1457–1481.

86. Roberts, Robert, et al. Pathophysiology, recognition, and treatment of acute myocardial infarction and its complications. In Schlant, Robert C., and Alexander, R. Wayne, eds., *The Heart*, 8th ed. New York: McGraw-Hill, Inc., 1994, pp. 1107–1184.

87. Rooke, Thom W. Impedance plethysmography. In Schlant, Robert C., and Alexander, R. Wayne, eds., *The Heart*, 8th ed. New York: McGraw-Hill, Inc., 1994, pp. 2223–2225.

88. Ross, Russell. Factors influencing atherogenesis. In Schlant, Robert C., and Alexander, R. Wayne, eds., *The Heart*, 8th ed. New York: McGraw-Hill Inc., 1994, pp. 989–1008.

89. Schlant, Robert C., and Alexander, R. Wayne. Diagnosis and management of chronic ischemic heart disease. In Schlant, Robert C., and Alexander, R. Wayne, eds., *The Heart*, 8th ed. New York: McGraw-Hill, Inc., 1994, pp. 1055–1082.

90. Schlant, Robert C., and Alpert, Joseph S. Special types of pulmonary embolism. In Schlant, Robert C., and Alexander, R. Wayne, eds., *The Heart*, 8th ed. New York: McGraw-Hill, Inc., 1994, pp. 1887–1893.

91. Schlant, Robert C., and Sonnenblick, Edmund H. Normal physiology of the cardiovascular system. In Schlant, Robert C., and Alexander, R. Wayne, eds., *The Heart*, 8th ed. New York: McGraw-Hill, Inc., 1994, pp. 113–151.

92. ———. Miscellaneous cardiovascular symptoms and signs. Ibid., pp. 481–483.

93. ———. Pathophysiology of heart failure. Ibid., pp. 515–555.

94. Selwyn, Andrew P., and Braunwald, Eugene. Ischemic heart disease. In Isselbacher, Kurt J., et al., eds., *Harrison's Principles of Internal Medicine*, 13th ed. New York: McGraw-Hill, Inc., 1994, pp. 1077–1085.

95. Shabetai, Ralph. Restrictive cardiomyopathy. In Schlant, Robert C., and Alexander, R. Wayne, eds., *The Heart*, 8th ed. New York: McGraw-Hill, Inc., 1994, pp. 1637–1646.

96. ———. Diseases of the pericardium. Ibid., pp. 1647–1674.

97. Shaver, James A., and Salerni, Rosemarie. Auscultation of the heart. In Schlant, Robert C., and Alexander, R. Wayne, eds., *The Heart*, 8th ed. New York: McGraw-Hill, Inc., 1994, pp. 253–314.

98. Théroux, Pierre, and Walters, David. Diagnosis and management of patients with unstable angina. In Schlant, Robert C., and Alexander, R. Wayne, eds., *The Heart*, 8th ed. New York: McGraw-Hill, Inc., 1994, pp. 1083–1106.

99. Tierney, Lawrence M., Jr. Blood vessels & lymphatics. In Tierney, Lawrence M., Jr., et al., eds., *Current Medical Diagnosis & Treatment*, 35th ed. Stamford, CT: Appleton & Lange, 1996, pp. 403–433.

100. Topol, Eric J. Caveats about elective coronary stenting. *New England Journal of Medicine* 331:539–541, 25 August 1994.

101. Turgeon, Ronald, M.D. Personal communications.

102. Van De Graaff, Kent M. Circulatory system. In *Human Anatomy*, 4th ed. Dubuque, Iowa: Wm. C. Brown Publishers, 1995, pp. 507–565.

103. Van Zanten, G. Henrita, et al. Increased platelet deposition on atherosclerotic coronary arteries. *Journal of Clinical Investigation* 93:615–632, February 1994.

104. Verrier, Edward D. The heart: II. Congenital diseases. In Way, Lawrence W., ed., *Current Surgical Diagnosis & Treatment*, 10th ed. Norwalk, CT: Appleton & Lange, 1994, pp. 383–410.

105. Waldo, Albert L., and Wit, Andrew L. Mechanisms of cardiac arrhythmias and conduction disturbances. In Schlant, Robert C., and Alexander, R. Wayne, eds., *The Heart*, 8th ed. New York: McGraw-Hill, Inc., 1994, pp. 659–704.

106. Walker, Bruce F., and Schlant, Robert C. Anatomy of the heart. In Schlant, Robert C., and Alexander, R. Wayne, eds., *The Heart*, 8th ed. New York: McGraw-Hill, Inc., 1994, pp. 59–111.

107. Watson, Karol E., et al. TGF-β1 and 25-hydroxycholesterol stimulate osteoblast-like vascular cells to calcify. *Journal of Clinical Investigation* 93:2106–2113, May 1994.

108. White, Christopher J., et al. Effective placement of the Wiktor stent after coronary angioplasty. *American Journal of Cardiology* 74:274–276.

109. Willman, Vallee L. Personal communication.

110. Wynne, Joshua, and Brunwald, Eugene. The cardiomyopathies and myocarditides. In Isselbacher, Kurt J., et al., eds., *Harrison's Principles of Internal Medicine*, 13th ed. New York: McGraw-Hill, Inc., 1994, pp. 1088–1094.

111. Zaim, Bulent, et al. Indications for use of permanent cardiac pacemakers. *Heart Disease and Stroke* 3:71–76, March/April 1994.

Chapter 7

1. Adelman, Daniel C., and Terr, Abba. Allergic & immunologic disorders. In Tierney, Lawrence M., Jr., et al., eds., *Current Medical Diagnosis & Treatment,* 35th ed. Stamford, CT: Appleton & Lange, 1996, pp. 894–718.
2. Aisenberg, Alan C. Hodgkin's disease. In Handin, Robert I., et al., eds., *Blood: Principles and Practice of Hematology.* Philadelphia: J.B. Lippincott Co., 1995, pp. 2105–2130.
3. Alter, Blanche. Inherited bone marrow failure syndromes. In Handin, Robert I., et al., eds., *Blood: Principles and Practice of Hematology.* Philadelphia: J.B. Lippincott Co., 1995, pp. 227–291.
4. Appelbaum, Frederick R. Bone marrow transplantation. In Stein, Jay H., ed.-in-ch., *Internal Medicine,* 4th ed. St. Louis: Mosby, 1994, pp. 754–757.
5. ———. Bone marrow failure. Ibid., pp. 873–881.
6. Armitage, James O. Non-Hodgkin's lymphomas. In Handin, Robert I., et al., eds., *Blood: Principles and Practice of Hematology.* Philadelphia: J.B. Lippincott Co., 1995, pp. 851–884.
7. Athens, John W. Granulocytes— Neutrophils. In Lee, G. Richard, et al., eds., *Wintrobe's Clinical Hematology,* 9th ed., vol. 1. Philadelphia: Lea & Febiger, 1993, pp. 223–266.
8. ———. The reticuloendothelial (mononuclear phagocyte) system and the spleen. Ibid., vol. 1, pp. 311–325.
9. ———. Variations of leukocytes in disease. Ibid., vol. 2, pp. 1564–1588.
10. ———. Neutropenia. Ibid., vol. 2, pp. 1589–1612.
11. ———. Disorders primarily involving the spleen. Ibid., vol. 2, pp. 1705–1722.
12. ———. Chronic myeloid leukemia. Ibid., vol. 2, pp. 1969–1998.
13. ———. Polycytemia vera. Ibid., vol. 2, pp. 1999–2017.
14. Athens, John W., and Lee, G. Richard. Polycythemia: Erythrocytosis. In Lee, G. Richard, et al., eds., *Wintrobe's Clinical Hematology,* 9th ed., vol. 1. Philadelphia: Lea & Febiger, 1993, pp. 1245–1261.
15. Babior, Bernard M., and Bunn, H. Franklin. Megaloblastic anemias. In Isselbacher, Kurt J., et al., eds., *Harrison's Principles of Internal Medicine,* 13th ed. New York: McGraw-Hill, Inc., 1994, pp. 1726–1732.
16. Bitchell, Thomas C. The physiology of primary hemostasis. In Lee, G. Richard, et al., eds., *Wintrobe's Clinical Hematology,* 9th ed., vol. 1. Philadelphia: Lea & Febiger, 1993, pp. 540–565.
17. ———. Blood coagulation. Ibid., vol. 1, pp. 566–615.
18. ———. The diagnostic approach to the bleeding disorders. Ibid., vol. 2, pp. 1304–1324.
19. ———. Thrombocytopenia caused by immunologic platelet destruction: Idiopathic thrombocytopenic purpura (TTP), drug-induced thrombocytopenia, and miscellaneous forms. Ibid., vol. 2, pp. 1329–1355.
20. ———. Bleeding disorders caused by vascular abnormalities. Ibid., vol. 2, pp. 1374–1389.
21. ———. Qualitative disorders of platelet function. Ibid., vol. 2, pp. 1397–1421.
22. ———. Hereditary coagulation disorders. Ibid., vol. 2, pp. 1422–1472.
23. ———. Acquired coagulation disorders. Ibid., vol. 2, pp. 1473–1514.
24. Boldt, David H. Abnormalities of phagocytes, eosinophils, and basophils. In Stein, Jay H., ed.-in-ch., *Internal Medicine,* 4th ed. St. Louis: Mosby, 1994, pp. 882–887.
25. Bolognia, Jean, and Braverman, Irwin M. Skin manifestations of internal disease. In Isselbacher, Kurt J., et al., eds., *Harrison's Principles of Internal Medicine,* 13th ed. New York: McGraw-Hill, Inc., 1994, pp. 290–307.
26. Braunwald, Eugene. Hypoxia, polycythemia, and cyanosis. In Isselbacher, Kurt J., et al., eds., *Harrison's Principles of Internal Medicine,* 13th ed. New York: McGraw-Hill, Inc., 1994, pp. 178–183.
27. Bridges, Kenneth R., and Bunn, H. Franklin. Anemias with disturbed iron metabolism. In Isselbacher, Kurt J., et al., eds., *Harrison's Principles of Internal Medicine,* 13th ed. New York: McGraw-Hill, Inc., 1994, pp. 1721–1726.
28. Bunn, H. Franklin. Anemia. In Isselbacher, Kurt J., et al., eds., *Harrison's Principles of Internal Medicine,* 13th ed. New York: McGraw-Hill, Inc., 1994, pp. 313–317.
29. ———. Pathophysiology of the anemias. Ibid., pp. 1717–1721.
31. ———. Anemia associated with chronic disorders. Ibid., pp. 1732–1734.
32. ———. Disorders of hemoglobin. Ibid., pp. 1734–1743.
33. Cohen, Alan S. Amyloidosis. In Isselbacher, Kurt J., et al., eds., *Harrison's Principles of Internal Medicine,* 13th ed. New York: McGraw-Hill, Inc., 1994, pp. 1625–1630.
34. Crombleholme, William R., and Evans, Arthur T. Obstetrics. In Tierney, Lawrence M., Jr., et al., eds., *Current Medical Diagnosis & Treatment,* 35th ed. Stamford, CT: Appleton & Lange, 1996, pp. 671–693.
35. Deisseroth, Albert B., et al. Chronic leukemias. In DeVita, Vincent T., et al., eds., *Cancer Principles & Practice of Oncology,* 4th ed., vol. 2. Philadelphia: J.B. Lippincott Co., 1993, pp. 1965–1979.
36. Desypris, Emmanuel N. Erythropoiesis. In Lee, G. Richard, et al., eds., *Wintrobe's Clinical Hematology,* 9th ed., vol. 1. Philadelphia: Lea & Febiger, 1993, pp. 124–157.
37. DeVita, Vincent T., Jr., et al. Hodgkin's disease. In DeVita, Vincent T., et al., eds., *Cancer Principles & Practice of Oncology,* 4th ed., vol. 2. Philadelphia: J.B. Lippincott Co., 1993, pp. 1819–1858.
38. Dimopoulos, Meletios A., and Alexanian, Raymond. Waldenstrom's macroglobulinemia. *Blood* 83:1452–1459, 15 March 1994.
39. Edwards, Corwin Q. Hemochromatosis and other iron storage disorders. In Lee, G. Richard, et al., eds., *Wintrobe's Clinical Hematology,* 9th ed., vol. 1. Philadelphia: Lea & Febiger, 1993, pp. 872–894.
40. Elin, Ronald J. Reference intervals and laboratory values of clinical importance. In Wyngaarden, James B., et al., eds., *Cecil's Textbook of Medicine,* 19th ed. Philadelphia: W.B. Saunders Co., 1992, pp. 2370–2380.
41. Eyre, Harmon J. Hodgkin's disease. In Lee, G. Richard, et al., eds., *Wintrobe's Clinical Hematology,* 9th ed., vol. 2. Philadelphia: Lea & Febiger, 1993, pp. 2054–2081.
42. Fauci, Anthony S. The vasculitis syndromes. In Isselbacher, Kurt J., et al., eds., *Harrison's Principles of Internal Medicine,* 13th ed. New York: McGraw-Hill, Inc., 1994, pp. 1670–1679.
43. Foerster, John. Bone marrow transplantation. In Lee, G. Richard, et al., eds., *Wintrobe's Clinical Hematology,* 9th ed., vol. 1. Philadelphia: Lea & Febiger, 1993, pp. 701–711.
44. ———. Chronic lymphocytic leukemia. Ibid., vol. 2, pp. 2034–2053.
45. ———. Multiple myeloma. Ibid., vol. 2, pp. 2219–2249.
46. ———. Amyloidosis. Ibid., vol. 2, pp. 2271–2283.
47. ———. Waldenström's macroglobulinemia. Ibid., vol. 2, pp. 2250–2259.
48. Freedman, Arnold S., and Nadler, Lee M. Malignant lymphomas. In Isselbacher, Kurt J., et al., eds., *Harrison's Principles of Internal Medicine,* 13th ed. New York: McGraw-Hill Inc., 1994, pp. 1774–1788.
49. Gallin, John I. Quantitative and qualitative disorders of phagocytes. In Isselbacher, Kurt J., et al., eds., *Harrison's Principles of Internal Medicine,* 13th ed. New York: McGraw-Hill, Inc., 1994, pp. 329–337.

50. Golde, David W., and Gulati, Subhash C. The myeloproliferative diseases. In Isselbacher, Kurt J., et al., eds., *Harrison's Principles of Internal Medicine*, 13th ed. New York: McGraw-Hill, Inc., 1994, pp. 1757–1764.

51. Greer, John P., et al. Non-Hodgkin's lymphomas. In Lee, G. Richard, et al., eds., *Wintrobe's Clinical Hematology*, 9th ed., vol. 2. Philadelphia: Lea & Febiger, 1993, pp. 2082–2142.

52. Gresick, Robert J., M.D. Personal communications.

53. Gribben, John G., and Nadler, Lee M. Detection of minimal residual disease in patients with lymphomas using the polymerase chain reaction. In DeVita, Vincent T., et al., eds., *Important Advances in Oncology 1994*. Philadelphia: J.B. Lippincott Co., 1994, pp. 117–129.

54. Handlin, Robert I. Disorders of the platelet and vessel wall. In Isselbacher, Kurt J., et al., eds., *Harrison's Principles of Internal Medicine*, 13th ed. New York: McGraw-Hill, Inc., 1994, pp. 1798–1803.

55. ———. Disorders of coagulation and thrombosis. Ibid., pp. 1804–1810.

56. Haynes, Barton F. Enlargement of lymph nodes and spleen. In Isselbacher, Kurt J., et al., eds., *Harrison's Principles of Internal Medicine*, 13th ed. New York: McGraw-Hill, Inc., 1994, pp. 323–329.

57. Hess, Charles E. Hairy cell leukemia, malignant histiocytosis, and related disorders. In Lee, G. Richard, et al., eds., *Wintrobe's Clinical Hematology*, 9th ed., vol. 2. Philadelphia: Lea & Febiger, 1993, pp. 2170–2201.

58. Hutton, John J. The leukemias and polycythemia vera. In Stein, Jay H., ed.-in-ch., *Internal Medicine*, 4th ed. St. Louis: Mosby, 1994, pp. 887–899.

59. Kjeldsberg, Carl R. Principles of hematologic examination. In Lee, G. Richard, et al., eds., *Wintrobe's Clinical Hematology*, 9th ed., vol. 1. Philadelphia: Lea & Febiger, 1993, pp. 7–37.

60. Klein, Harvey G. Blood groups and blood transfusion. In Isselbacher, Kurt J., et al, eds., *Harrison's Principles of Internal Medicine*, 13th ed. New York: McGraw-Hill, Inc., 1994, pp. 1788–1793.

61. Laing, June M. ICD-9-CM Coordination and Maintenance (C&M) Committee discusses possible coding changes. *Advance for Health Information Professionals* 6:20–23, 1 July 1996.

62. Lee, G. Richard. Megaloblastic and nonmegaloblastic macrocytic anemias. In Lee, G. Richard, et al., eds., *Wintrobe's Clinical Hematology*, 9th ed.,

63. ———. Microcytosis and the anemias associated with impaired hemoglobin synthesis. Ibid., vol. 1, pp. 791–807.

64. ———. The hemolytic disorders: General considerations. Ibid., vol. 1, pp. 944–964.

65. Linker, Charles A. Blood. In Tierney, Lawrence M., Jr., et al., eds., *Current Medical Diagnosis & Treatment*, 35th ed. Stamford, CT: Appleton & Lange, 1996, pp. 434–488.

66. Longo, Dan L. Plasma cell disorders. In Isselbacher, Kurt J., et al., eds., *Harrison's Principles of Internal Medicine*, 13th ed. New York: McGraw-Hill, Inc., 1994, pp. 1618–1625.

67. Lukens, John N. Hereditary spherocytosis and other hemolytic anemias associated with abnormalities of the red cell membrane and cytoskeleton. In Lee, G. Richard, et al., eds., *Wintrobe's Clinical Hematology*, 9th ed., vol. 1. Philadelphia: Lea & Febiger, 1993, pp. 965–989.

68. ———. Hereditary anemias associated with abnormalities of erythrocyte anaerobic glycolysis and nucleotide metabolism. Ibid., vol. 1, pp. 990–1005.

69. ———. Glucose-6-phosphate dehydrogenase deficiency and related deficiencies involving the pentose phosphate pathway and glutathione metabolism. Ibid., vol. 1, pp. 1006–1022.

70. ———. The thalassemias and related disorders: Quantitative disorders of hemoglobin synthesis. Ibid., vol. 1, pp. 1102–1145.

71. ———. Langerhans cell histiocytosis. Ibid., vol. 2, pp. 1640–1649.

72. ———. Acute lymphocytic leukemia. Ibid., vol. 2, pp. 1892–1917.

73. Miller, Thomas P., and Grogan, Thomas M. Hodgkin's disease and non-Hodgkin's lymphoma. In Stein, Jay H., ed.-in-ch., *Internal Medicine*, 4th ed. St. Louis: Mosby, 1994, pp. 899–911.

74. Paraskevas, Frixos, and Foerster, John. The lymphatic system. In Lee, G. Richard G, et al., eds., *Wintrobe's Clinical Hematology*, 9th ed., vol. 1. Philadelphia: Lea & Febiger, 1993, pp. 326–353.

75. ———. The lymphocytes. Ibid., vol. 1, pp. 354–430.

76. ———. Immunodiagnosis. Ibid., vol. 1, pp. 484–508.

77. Platt, Orah S. The sickle syndromes. In Handin, Robert I., et al., eds., *Blood: Principles and Practice of Hematology*. Philadelphia: J.B. Lippincott Co., 1995, pp. 1645–1700.

78. Rappeport, Joel M., and Bunn, H. Franklin. Bone marrow failure: Aplastic anemia and other primary bone marrow

disorders. In Isselbacher, Kurt J., et al., eds., *Harrison's Principles of Internal Medicine*, 13th ed. New York: McGraw-Hill, Inc., 1994, pp. 1754–1757.

79. Richter, James M., and Isselbacher, Kurt J. Gastrointestinal bleeding. In Isselbacher, Kurt J., et al., eds., *Harrison's Principles of Internal Medicine*, 13th ed. New York: McGraw-Hill, Inc., 1994, pp. 223–226.

80. Roodman, G. David. Hemolytic anemia. In Stein, Jay H., ed.-in-ch., *Internal Medicine*, 4th ed. St. Louis: Mosby, 1994, pp. 863–873.

81. Rosse, Wendell, and Bunn, H. Franklin. Hemolytic anemias. In Isselbacher, Kurt J., et al., eds., *Harrison's Principles of Internal Medicine*, 13th ed. New York: McGraw-Hill Inc., 1994, pp. 1743–1754.

82. Rothstein, Gerald. Origin and development of the blood and blood-forming tissues. In Lee, G. Richard, et al., eds., *Wintrobe's Clinical Hematology*, 9th ed., vol. 1. Philadelphia: Lea & Febiger, 1993, pp. 41–78.

83. Scheinberg, David A., and Golde, David W. The leukemias. In Isselbacher, Kurt J., et al., eds., *Harrison's Principles of Internal Medicine*, 13th ed. New York: McGraw-Hill, Inc., 1994, pp. 1764–1774.

84. Schroeder, Marlis L., and Rayner, Harry L. Red cell, platelet, and white cell antigens. In Lee, G. Richard, et al., eds., *Wintrobe's Clinical Hematology*, 9th ed., vol. 1. Philadelphia: Lea & Febiger, 1993, pp. 616–650.

85. ———. Transfusion of blood and blood components. Ibid., vol. 1, pp. 651–700.

86. Shurin, Susan Blakely. Disorders of the spleen. In Handin, Robert I., et al., eds., *Blood: Principles and Practice of Hematology*. Philadelphia: J.B. Lippincott Co., 1995, pp. 1359–1380.

87. Steinberg, Martin H. Hemoglobinopathies and thalassemias. In Stein, Jay H., ed.-in-ch., *Internal Medicine*, 4th ed. St. Louis: Mosby, 1994, pp. 852–863.

88. Telen, Marilyn J. The mature erythrocyte. In Lee, G. Richard, et al., eds., *Wintrobe's Clinical Hematology*, 9th ed., vol. 1. Philadelphia: Lea & Febiger, 1993, pp. 101–133.

89. Thomas, Donnall E. Bone marrow transplantation. In Isselbacher, Kurt J., et al., eds., *Harrison's Principles of Internal Medicine*, 13th ed. New York: McGraw-Hill, Inc., 1994, pp. 1793–1798.

90. Tierney, Lawrence M., Jr. Blood vessels and lymphatics. In Tierney, Lawrence M., Jr., et al., eds., *Current Medical Diagnosis & Treatment*, 35th ed. Stamford, CT: Appleton & Lange, 1996, pp. 403–433.

91. Turgeon, Ronald, M.D., Personal communications.

92. White, Gilbert C., II. Disorders of blood coagulation. In Stein, Jay H., ed.-in-ch., *Internal Medicine*, 4th ed. St. Louis: Mosby, 1994, pp. 804–822.

93. Williams, Darryl M. Pancytopenia, aplastic anemia, and pure red cell aplasia. In Lee, G. Richard, et al., eds., *Wintrobe's Clinical Hematology*, 9th ed., vol. 1. Philadelphia: Lea & Febiger, 1993, pp. 911–943.

94. Wolfe, Laurence C. Neonatal anemia. In Handin, Robert I., et al., eds., *Blood: Principles and Practice of Hematology*. Philadelphia: J.B. Lippincott Co., 1995, pp. 2105–2130.

Chapter 8

1. American Thoracic Society. Guidelines for thoracentesis and needle biopsy of the pleura. *American Review of Respiratory Diseases* 140:257–258, 1989.

2. Bartlett, John G. Aspiration pneumonia. In Baum, Gerald L., and Wolinsky, Emanuel, eds., *Textbook of Pulmonary Diseases*, 5th ed., vol. 1. Boston: Little, Brown and Co., 1994, pp. 593–606.

3. ———. Lung abscess. Ibid., vol. 1, pp. 607–620.

4. Baum, Gerald L., and Hershko, Elie P. Bronchiectasis. In Baum, Gerald L., and Wolinsky, Emanuel, eds., *Textbook of Pulmonary Diseases*, 5th ed., vol. 1. Boston: Little, Brown and Co., 1994, pp. 623–646.

5. Bernstein, Michael S., and Locksley, Richard M. Legionella infections. In Isselbacher, Kurt J., et al., eds., *Harrison's Principles of Internal Medicine*, 13th ed. New York: McGraw-Hill, Inc., 1994, pp. 654–658.

6. Blatt, Stephen P., et al. Legionnaires' disease in human immodeficiency virus—Infected patients: Eight cases and review. *Clinical Infectious Diseases* 18:227–232, February 1994.

7. Blinkhorn, Richard J. Upper respiratory tract infections. In Baum, Gerald L., and Wolinsky, Emanuel, eds., *Textbook of Pulmonary Diseases*, 5th ed., vol. 1. Boston: Little, Brown and Co., 1994, pp. 399–409.

8. ———. Community-acquired pneumonia. Ibid., vol. 1, pp. 411–456.

9. ———. Hospital-acquired pneumonia. Ibid., vol. 1, pp. 457–479.

10. Brooks, Geo. F., et al. Legionellae and unusual bacterial pathogens. In *Jawetz, Melnick & Adelberg's Medical Microbiology*, 19th ed. Norwalk, CT: Appleton & Lange, 1991, pp. 263–267.

11. Bruderman, Israel. Bronchogenic carcinoma. In Baum, Gerald L., and Wolinsky, Emanuel, eds., *Textbook of Pulmonary Diseases*, 5th ed., vol. 1. Boston: Little, Brown and Co., 1994, pp. 1345–1392.

12. Chambers, Henry F. Infectious diseases: Bacterial and chlamydial. In Tierney, Lawrence M., Jr., et al., eds., *Current Medical Diagnosis & Treatment*, 35th ed. Stamford, CT: Appleton & Lange, 1996, pp. 1192–1225.

13. Connors, Alfred E., and Altose, Murray D. Pleural anatomy, pleural fluid dynamics, and the diagnosis of pleural disease. In Baum, Gerald L., and Wolinsky, Emanuel, eds., *Textbook of Pulmonary Diseases*, 5th ed., vol. 2. Boston: Little, Brown and Co., 1994, pp. 1839–1851.

14. ———. Pleural inflammation and pleural effusion. Ibid., vol. 2, pp. 1853–1868.

15. ———. Hemothorax, chylothorax, pneumothorax, and other pleural disorders. Ibid., vol. 2, pp. 1869–1875.

16. Davis, R. Duane, Jr., and Sabiston, David C., Jr. The mediastinum. In Sabiston, David C., Jr., ed., *Textbook of Surgery*, 14th ed. Philadelphia: W.B. Saunders Co., 1991, pp. 1771–1796.

17. Elin, Ronald J. Reference intervals and laboratory values of clinical importance. In Wyngaarden, James B., et al., eds., *Cecil's Textbook of Medicine*, 19th ed. Philadelphia: W.B. Saunders Co., 1992, pp. 2370–2380.

18. Ettinger, Neil A., and Cooper, Joel D. Lung transplantation. In Baum, Gerald L., and Wolinsky, Emanuel, eds., *Textbook of Pulmonary Diseases*, 5th ed., vol. 2. Boston: Little, Brown and Co., 1994, pp. 1245–1261.

19. Fekety, Robert, and Lynch, Joseph P., III. Community-acquired pneumonia: What role for new antibiotics? *Journal of Respiratory Diseases* 15:132–147, February 1994.

20. Floreani, Anthony A., et al. Diagnostic procedures: The pleura. In Baum, Gerald L., and Wolinsky, Emanuel, eds., *Textbook of Pulmonary Diseases*, 5th ed., vol. 1. Boston: Little, Brown and Co., 1994, pp. 367–378.

21. Ginsberg, Robert J., et al. Non-small cell lung cancer. In DeVita, Vincent T., et al., eds., *Cancer Principles & Practice of Oncology*, 4th ed., vol. 1. Philadelphia: J.B. Lippincott Co., 1993, pp. 673–723.

22. Greenberg, Harly E., and Scharf, Steven M. Pulmonary hypertension: Pathophysiology and clinical disorders. In Baum, Gerald L., and Wolinsky, Emanuel, eds., *Textbook of Pulmonary Diseases*, 5th ed., vol. 1. Boston: Little, Brown and Co., 1994, pp. 1285–1304.

23. Grillo, Hermes C., and Nathisen, Douglas J. Tracheostomy and its complications. In Sabiston, David C., Jr., ed., *Textbook of Surgery*, 14th ed. Philadelphia: W.B. Saunders Co., 1991, pp. 1704–1709.

24. Hole, John W., Jr., Respiratory system. In *Human Anatomy and Physiology*, 6th ed. Dubuque IA: Wm. C. Brown Publishers, 1993, pp. 580–617.

25. Hudgel, David W. Bronchial asthma. In Baum, Gerald L., and. Wolinsky, Emanuel, eds., *Textbook of Pulmonary Diseases*, 5th ed., vol. 1. Boston: Little, Brown and Co., 1994, pp. 647–687.

26. Iannuzzi, Michael C., and Toews, Galen B. Neoplasms of the lung. In Stein, J. H., ed.-in-ch., *Internal Medicine*, 4th ed. St. Louis: Mosby, 1994, pp. 1733–1741.

27. Ihde, David C., et al. Small cell lung cancer. In DeVita, Vincent T., et al., eds., *Cancer Principles & Practice of Oncology*, 4th ed., vol. 1. Philadelphia: J.B. Lippincott Co., 1993, pp. 723–758.

28. Ingenito, Edward P., and Drazen, Jeffrey M. Mechanical ventilatory support. In Isselbacher, Kurt J., et al., eds., *Harrison's Principles of Internal Medicine*, 13th ed. New York: McGraw-Hill, Inc., 1994, pp. 1244–1248.

29. Ingram, Roland H., Jr. Chronic bronchitis, emphysema, and airways constriction. In Isselbacher, Kurt J., et al., eds., *Harrison's Principles of Internal Medicine*, 13th ed. New York: McGraw-Hill, Inc., 1994, pp. 1197–1206.

30. ———. Adult respiratory distress syndrome. Ibid., pp. 1240–1243.

31. Kennedy, Lisa, and Sahn, Steven A. Noninvasive evaluation of the patient with a pleural effusion. *Chest Surgery Clinics of North America* 4:451–466, August 1994.

32. Levison, Matthew E. Pneumonia, including necrotizing pulmonary infections (lung abscesses). In Isselbacher, Kurt J., et al., eds., *Harrison's Principles of Internal Medicine*, 13th ed. New York: McGraw-Hill, Inc., 1994, pp. 1184–1191.

33. Light, Richard W. Disorders of the pleura, mediastinum, and diaphragm. In Isselbacher, Kurt J., et al., eds., *Harrison's Principles of Internal Medicine*, 13th ed. New York: McGraw-Hill, Inc., 1994, pp. 1229–1234.

34. Low, Donald E., and Cooper, Joel D. Lung transplantation. In Sabiston, David C., Jr., ed., *Textbook of Surgery*, 14th ed. Philadelphia: W.B. Saunders Co., 1991, pp. 446–455.

35. McFadden, E. R., Jr. Asthma. In Isselbacher, Kurt J., et al., eds., *Harrison's Principles of Internal Medicine*, 13th ed. New York: McGraw-Hill, Inc., 1994, pp. 1167–1172.

36. Merrick, Scot H., and Fishman, Noel H. Tumors of the mediastinum, pleura, chest wall, and diaphragm. In Baum,

Gerald L., and Wolinsky, Emanuel, eds., *Textbook of Pulmonary Diseases*, 5th ed., vol. 2. Boston: Little, Brown and Co., 1994, pp. 1415–1441.

37. Minna, John D. Neoplasms of the lung. In Isselbacher, Kurt J., et al., eds., *Harrison's Principles of Internal Medicine*, 13th ed. New York: McGraw-Hill, Inc., 1994, pp. 1221–1229.

38. Morgan, Keith W. Occupational lung diseases: Occupational asthma, byssinosis, and industrial bronchitis. In Baum, Gerald L., and Wolinsky, Emanuel, eds., *Textbook of Pulmonary Diseases*, 5th ed., vol. 1. Boston: Little, Brown and Co., 1994, pp. 791–814.

39. ———. Occupational lung diseases: Asbestos, silica, silicates, and miscellaneous fibrous substances. Ibid., vol. 1, pp. 815–844.

40. ———. Occupational lung diseases: Coal workers', beryllium, and other pneumoconioses. Ibid., vol. 1, pp. 845–885.

41. Moser, Kenneth M. Diagnostic procedures in respiratory diseases. In Isselbacher, Kurt J., et al., eds., *Harrison's Principles of Internal Medicine*, 13th ed. New York: McGraw-Hill, Inc., 1994, pp. 1163–1167.

42. Moser, Kenneth M. Pulmonary embolism. In Baum, Gerald L., and Wolinsky, Emanuel, eds., *Textbook of Pulmonary Diseases*, 5th ed., vol. 2. Boston: Little, Brown and Co., 1994, pp. 1305–1325.

43. Phair, John. P. Bacterial pneumonia. In Shulman, Stanford T., et al., eds., *The Biologic & Clinical Basis of Infectious Diseases*, 4th ed. Philadelphia: W.B. Saunders Co., 1992, pp. 165–176.

44. Phillipson, Eliot A. Disorders of ventilation. In Isselbacher, Kurt J., et al., eds., *Harrison's Principles of Internal Medicine*, 13th ed. New York: McGraw-Hill, Inc., 1994, pp. 1234–1240.

45. Rosenberg, J. C. Neoplasms of the mediastinum. In DeVita, Vincent T., et al., eds., *Cancer Principles & Practice of Oncology*, 4th ed., vol. 1. Philadelphia: J.B. Lippincott Co., 1993, pp. 759–775.

46. Rowe, Lee D. Otolaryngology—Head and neck surgery. In Way, Lawrence W., ed., *Current Surgical Diagnosis & Treatment*, 10th ed. Norwalk, CT: Appleton & Lange, 1994, pp. 860–893.

47. Sabiston, David C., Jr. Pulmonary embolism. In Sabiston, David C., Jr., ed., *Textbook of Surgery*, 14th ed. Philadelphia: W.B. Saunders Co., 1991, pp. 1502–1512.

48. Schwartz, Mitchell L., and Sessler, Curtis N. When—and how—to perform percutaneous pleural biopsy. *Journal of Respiratory Diseases* 12:1155–1169, December 1991.

49. Scott, Stewart M. The pleura and emphysema. In Sabiston, David C., Jr., ed., *Textbook of Surgery*, 14th ed. Philadelphia: W.B. Saunders Co., 1991, pp. 446–455.

50. Snow, James B. Surgical disorders of the ears, nose, paranasal sinuses, pharynx, and larynx. In Sabiston, David C., Jr., ed., *Textbook of Surgery*, 14th ed. Philadelphia: W.B. Saunders Co., 1991, pp. 1187–1208.

51. Sobonya, Richard E. Normal anatomy and development of the lung. In Baum, Gerald L., and Wolinsky, Emanuel, eds., *Textbook of Pulmonary Diseases*, 5th ed., vol. 1. Boston: Little, Brown and Co., 1994, pp. 3–21.

52. Stauffer, John L. Lung. In Tierney, Lawrence M., Jr., et al., eds., *Current Medical Diagnosis & Treatment*, 35th ed. Stamford, CT: Appleton & Lange, 1996, pp. 215–294.

53. Strohl, Kingman P. Sleep apnea syndrome and sleep-disordered breathing. In Baum, Gerald L., and Wolinsky, Emanuel, eds., *Textbook of Pulmonary Diseases*, 5th ed., vol. 2. Boston: Little, Brown and Co., 1994, pp. 1097–1116.

54. Turgeon, Ronald, M.D., Personal communications.

55. Turley, Kevin. Thoracic wall, pleura, mediastinum, and lung. In Way, Lawrence W., ed., *Current Surgical Diagnosis & Treatment*, 10th ed. Norwalk, CT: Appleton & Lange, 1994, pp. 317–357.

56. Urist, Marshall M., et al. Head and neck tumors. In Way, Lawrence W., ed., *Current Surgical Diagnosis & Treatment*, 10th ed. Norwalk, CT: Appleton & Lange, 1994, pp. 257–273.

57. Weinberger, Steve E. Bronchiectasis and broncholithiasis. In Isselbacher, Kurt J., et al., eds., *Harrison's Principles of Internal Medicine*, 13th ed. New York: McGraw-Hill, Inc., 1994, pp. 1191–1194.

58. Willett, Laura Rees, et al. Current diagnosis and management of sinusitis. *Journal of General Internal Medicine* 9:38–45, January 1994.

59. Wolinsky, Emanuel. Mycotic, actinomycotic and nocardial pneumonia. In Baum, Gerald L., and Wolinsky, Emanuel, eds., *Textbook of Pulmonary Diseases*, 5th ed., vol. 1. Boston: Little, Brown and Co., 1994, pp. 503–520.

60. ———. Tuberculosis. Ibid., vol. 1, pp. 521–573.

Chapter 9

1. Balthazar, Emil J. Diverticular disease. In Gore, Richard M., et al., eds., *Textbook of Gastrointestinal Radiology*, vol. 1. Philadelphia: W.B. Saunders Co., 1994, pp. 1072–1097.

2. Bass, Nathan M. Sclerosing cholangitis and recurrent pyogenic cholangitis. In Sleisenger, Marvin H., and Fordtran, John S., eds., *Gastrointestinal Disease*, 5th ed., vol. 2. Philadelphia: W.B. Saunders Co., 1993, pp. 1868–1890.

3. Berger, Timothy and Silverman, Sol, Jr. Oral and cutaneous manifestations of gastrointestinal disease. In Sleisenger, Marvin H., and Fordtran, John S., eds., *Gastrointestinal Disease*, 5th ed., vol. 1. Philadelphia: W.B. Saunders Co., 1993, pp. 268–285.

4. Boey, John H. Peritoneal cavity. In Way, Lawrence W., ed., *Current Surgical Diagnosis & Treatment*, 10th ed. Norwalk, CT: Appleton & Lange, 1994, pp. 453–471.

5. Boyce, Worth H., Jr. Tumors of the esophagus. In Sleisenger, Marvin H., and Fordtran, John S., eds., *Gastrointestinal Disease*, 5th ed., vol. 1. Philadelphia: W.B. Saunders Co., 1993, pp. 401–418.

6. Bresalier, Robert S., and Kim, Young S. Malignant neoplasms of the large intestine. In Sleisenger, Marvin H., and Fordtran, John S., eds., *Gastrointestinal Disease*, 5th ed., vol. 2. Philadelphia: W.B. Saunders Co., 1993, pp. 1449–1493.

7. Brooks, Geo. F., et al. Hepatitis viruses. In *Jawetz, Melnick, & Adelberg's Medical Microbiology*, 19th ed. Norwalk, CT: Appleton & Lange, 1991, pp. 451–468.

8. Chopra, Sanjiv. Hepatic tumors. In J. H. Stein, ed.-in-ch., *Internal Medicine*, 4th ed. St. Louis: Mosby, 1994, pp. 638–643.

9. Coleman, John J., III, and Sultan, Mark R. Tumors of the head and neck. In Schwartz, Seymour I., ed.-in-ch., *Principles of Surgery*, 6th ed., vol. 1. New York: McGraw-Hill Inc., 1994, pp. 595–658.

10. Davis, Glenn R. Neoplasms of the stomach. In Sleisenger, Marvin H., and Fordtran, John S., eds., *Gastrointestinal Disease*, 5th ed., vol. 1. Philadelphia: W.B. Saunders Co., 1993, pp. 763–789.

11. Deveney, Karen E. Hernias and other lesions of the abdominal wall. In Way, Lawrence W., ed., *Current Surgical Diagnosis & Treatment*, 10th ed. Norwalk, CT: Appleton & Lange, 1994, pp. 712–724.

12. Dienstag, Jules L. Liver transplantation. In Isselbacher, Kurt J., et al., eds., *Harrison's Principles of Internal Medicine*, 13th ed. New York: McGraw-Hill, Inc., 1994, pp. 1501–1504.

13. Dienstag, Jules L., and Isselbacher, Kurt J. Acute hepatitis. In Isselbacher, Kurt J., et al., eds., *Harrison's Principles of Internal Medicine*, 13th ed. New York:

14. McGraw-Hill, Inc., 1994, pp. 1458–1478.

14. ———. Chronic hepatitis. Ibid., pp. 1478–1483.

15. Elgin, Ronald J. Reference intervals and laboratory values of clinical importance. In Wyngaarden, James B., et al., eds., *Cecil's Textbook of Medicine*, 19th ed. Philadelphia: W.B. Saunders Co., 1992, pp. 2370–2380.

16. Ellis, Harold. Cholecystostomy and cholecystectomy. In Schwartz, Seymour I., and Ellis, Harold, eds., *Maingot's Abdominal Operations*, 9th ed., vol. 1. Norwalk, CT: Appleton & Lange, 1989, pp. 1413–1430.

17. ———. Choledocholithiasis. Ibid., vol. 2, pp. 1431–1450.

18. Friedman, Arnold C. Pancreatic neoplasms. In Gore, Richard M., et al., eds., *Textbook of Gastrointestinal Radiology*, vol. 2. Philadelphia: W.B. Saunders Co., 1994, pp. 2161–2186.

19. Friedman, Lawrence S. Liver, biliary tract, and pancreas. In Tierney, Lawrence M., Jr., et al., eds., *Current Medical Diagnosis & Treatment*, 35th ed. Stamford, CT: Appleton & Lange, 1996, pp. 576–613.

20. Friedman, Lawrence S., and Isselbacher, Kurt J. Anorexia, nausea, vomiting, and indigestion. In Isselbacher, Kurt J., et al., eds., *Harrison's Principles of Internal Medicine*, 13th ed. New York: McGraw-Hill, Inc., 1994, pp. 208–213.

21. Glickman, Robert M. Inflammatory bowel disease: Ulcerative colitis and Crohn's disease. In Isselbacher, Kurt J., et al., eds., *Harrison's Principles of Internal Medicine*, 13th ed. New York: McGraw-Hill, Inc., 1994, pp. 1403–1417.

22. Gliedman, Marvin L., and Gold, Michael. Choledochoduodenostomy. In Schwartz, Seymour I., and Ellis, Harold, eds., *Maingot's Abdominal Operations*, 9th ed., vol. 2. Norwalk, CT: Appleton & Lange, 1989, pp. 1451–1462.

23. Goldschmiedt, Markus, and Feldman, Mark. Gastric secretion in health and disease. In Sleisenger, Marvin H., and Fordtran, John S., eds., *Gastrointestinal Disease*, 5th ed., vol. 1. Philadelphia: W.B. Saunders Co., 1993, pp. 524–544.

24. Goyal, Raj K. Dysphagia. In Isselbacher, Kurt J., et al., eds., *Harrison's Principles of Internal Medicine*, 13th ed. New York: McGraw-Hill, Inc., 1994, pp. 206–208.

25. ———. Diseases of the esophagus. Ibid., pp. 1355–1363.

26. Greenberger, Norton J., and Isselbacher, Kurt J. Disorders of absorption. In Isselbacher, Kurt J., et al., eds., *Harrison's Principles of Internal Medicine*, 13th ed. New York: McGraw-Hill Inc., 1994, pp. 1386–1403.

27. ———. Diseases of the gallbladder and bile ducts. Ibid., pp. 1504–1516.

28. Greenspan, John S. Oral manifestations of disease. In Isselbacher, Kurt J., et al., eds., *Harrison's Principles of Internal Medicine*, 13th ed. New York: McGraw-Hill Inc., 1994, pp. 199–205.

29. Hinder, Ronald A., et al. Laparoscopic Nissen fundoplication in an effective treatment of gastroesophageal reflux disease. *Annals of Surgery* 220:472–483, October 1994.

30. Hole, John W., Jr. Digestive system. In *Human Anatomy & Physiology*, 6th ed. Dubuque, IA: Wm. C. Brown Publishers, 1993, pp. 502–547.

31. Isselbacher, Kurt J. Bilirubin metabolism and hyperbilirubinemia. In Isselbacher, Kurt J., et al., eds., *Harrison's Principles of Internal Medicine*, 13th ed. New York: McGraw-Hill Inc., 1994, pp. 1453–1458.

32. Isselbacher, Kurt J., and LaMont, J. Thomas. Diseases of the peritoneum and mesentery. In Isselbacher, Kurt J., et al., eds., *Harrison's Principles of Internal Medicine*, 13th ed. New York: McGraw-Hill, Inc., 1994, pp. 1435–1436.

33. Jackler, Robert K., and Kaplan, Michael J. Ear, nose, and throat. In Tierney, Lawrence M., Jr., et al., eds., *Current Medical Diagnosis & Treatment*, 35th ed. Stamford, CT: Appleton & Lange, 1996, pp. 181–214.

34. Kaplan, Marshall M. Evaluation of hepatobiliary disease. In Stein, J. H. ed.-in-ch., *Internal Medicine*, 4th ed. St. Louis: Mosby, 1994, pp. 544–552.

35. ———. Primary biliary cirrhosis, Wilson's disease, hemochromatosis, and other metabolic and fibrotic liver diseases. Ibid., pp. 618–632.

36. Kimmey, Michael B., and Silverstein, Fred E. Gastrointestinal endoscopy. In Isselbacher, Kurt J., et al., eds., *Harrison's Principles of Internal Medicine*, 13th ed. New York: McGraw-Hill Inc., 1994, pp. 1350–1355.

37. Koch, Wayne M., et al. p53 gene mutations as markers of tumor spread in synchronous oral cancers. *Archives of Otolaryngology—Head & Neck Surgery* 120:943–947, September 1994.

38. Kodner, Ira J., et al. Colon, rectum, and anus. In Schwartz, Seymour I., ed.-in-ch., *Principles of Surgery*, 6th ed., vol. 2. New York: McGraw-Hill, Inc., 1994, pp. 1191–1306.

39. Kovacs, Thomas O. G. Endoscopic studies of the small intestine and colon. In Sleisenger, Marvin H., and Fordtran, John S., eds., *Gastrointestinal Disease*, 5th ed., vol. 1. Philadelphia: W.B. Saunders Co., 1993, pp. 433–443.

40. LaMont, J. Thomas, and Isselbacher, Kurt J. Diseases of the small and large intestine. In Isselbacher, Kurt J., et al., eds., *Harrison's Principles of Internal Medicine*, 13th ed. New York: McGraw-Hill Inc., 1994, pp. 1417–1424.

41. Levine, Marc S. Gastroesophageal reflux disease. In Gore, Richard M., et al., eds., *Textbook of Gastrointestinal Radiology*, vol. 1. Philadelphia: W.B. Saunders Co., 1994, pp. 360–361.

42. Lopez, James M., and Grand, Richard J. Hereditary and childhood disorders of the pancreas. In Sleisenger, Marvin H., and Fordtran, John S., eds., *Gastrointestinal Disease*, 5th ed., vol. 2. Philadelphia: W.B. Saunders Co., 1993, pp. 1601–1627.

43. Matthews, Jeffrey B., and Silen, William. Operations for peptic ulcer disease and early postoperative complications. In Sleisenger, Marvin H., and Fordtran, John S., eds., *Gastrointestinal Disease*, 5th ed., vol. 1. Philadelphia: W.B. Saunders Co., 1993, pp. 713–730.

44. McDonald, George B. Esophageal diseases caused by infection, systemic illness, medications, and trauma. In Sleisenger, Marvin H., and Fordtran, John S., eds., *Gastrointestinal Disease*, 5th ed., vol. 1. Philadelphia: W.B. Saunders Co., 1993, pp. 427–455.

45. McGuigan, James E. Peptic ulcer and gastritis. In Isselbacher, Kurt J., et al., eds., *Harrison's Principles of Internal Medicine*, 13th ed. New York: McGraw-Hill, Inc., 1994, pp. 1363–1382.

46. McQuaid, Kenneth R. Alimentary tract. In Tierney, Lawrence M., Jr., et al., eds., *Current Medical Diagnosis & Treatment*, 35th ed. Stamford, CT: Appleton & Lange, 1996, pp. 489–575.

47. Meleca, Robert J., and Marks, Steven C. Carotid artery resection for cancer of the head and neck. *Archives of Otolaryngology—Head & Neck Surgery* 120:974–978, September 1994.

48. Moody, Frank G., and Miller, Thomas A. Stomach. In Schwartz, Seymour I., ed.-in-ch., *Principles of Surgery*, 6th ed., vol. 1. New York: McGraw-Hill, Inc., 1994, pp. 1123–1152.

49. Ostrow, J. Donald. Jaundice and disorders of bilirubin metabolism. In J. H. Stein, ed.-in-ch., *Internal Medicine*, 4th ed. St. Louis: Mosby, 1994, pp. 556–570.

50. Pellegrini, Carlos A., and Way, Lawrence W. Esophagus and diaphragm. In Way, Lawrence W., ed., *Current Surgical Diagnosis & Treatment*, 10th ed. Norwalk, CT: Appleton & Lange, 1994, pp. 411–440.

51. Peters, Jeffrey H., and DeMeester, Tom R. Esophagus and diaphragmatic

hernia. In Schwartz, Seymour I., ed.-in-ch., *Principles of Surgery*, 6th ed., vol. 1. New York: McGraw-Hill, Inc., 1994, pp. 1032–1122.

52. Podolsky, Daniel K., and Isselbacher, Kurt J. Diagnostic tests in liver disease. In Isselbacher, Kurt J., et al., eds., *Harrison's Principles of Internal Medicine*, 13th ed. New York: McGraw-Hill, Inc., 1994, pp. 1444–1448.

53. ———. Derangements of hepatic metabolism. Ibid., pp. 1448–1453.

54. ———. Alcohol-related liver disease and cirrhosis. Ibid., pp. 1483–1495.

55. Reber, Howard A., and Way, Lawrence W. Pancreas. In Way, Lawrence W., ed., *Current Surgical Diagnosis & Treatment*, 10th ed. Norwalk, CT: Appleton & Lange, 1994, pp. 567–594.

56. Richter, James M., and Isselbacher, Kurt J. Gastrointestinal bleeding. In Isselbacher, Kurt J., et al., eds., *Harrison's Principles of Internal Medicine*, 13th ed. New York: McGraw-Hill Inc., 1994, pp. 223–226.

57. Rössle, Martin, et al. The transjugular intrahepatic portosystemic stent— Shunt procedure for variceal bleeding. *New England Journal of Medicine* 330:165–171, 20 January 1994.

58. Rowe, Lee D. Otolaryngology—Head and neck surgery. In Way, Lawrence W., ed., *Current Surgical Diagnosis & Treatment*, 10th ed. Norwalk, CT: Appleton & Lange, 1994, pp. 860–893.

59. Russell, Thomas R. Anorectum. In Way, Lawrence W., ed., *Current Surgical Diagnosis & Treatment*, 10th ed. Norwalk, CT: Appleton & Lange, 1994, pp. 693–711.

60. Schrock, Theodore R. Small intestine. In Way, Lawrence W., ed., *Current Surgical Diagnosis & Treatment*, 10th ed. Norwalk, CT: Appleton & Lange, 1994, pp. 615–643.

61. ———. Large intestine. Ibid., pp. 644–692.

62. Schrock, Theodore R. Acute appendicitis. In Sleisenger, Marvin H., and Fordtran, John S., eds., *Gastrointestinal Disease*, 5th ed., vol. 2. Philadelphia: W.B. Saunders Co., 1993, pp. 1339–1347.

63. Schuster, Marvin M. Irritable bowel syndrome. In Sleisenger, Marvin H., and Fordtran, John S., eds., *Gastrointestinal Disease*, 5th ed., vol. 1. Philadelphia: W.B. Saunders Co., 1993, pp. 917–933.

64. Schwartz, Seymour I. Liver. In Schwartz, Seymour I., ed.-in-ch., *Principles of Surgery*, 6th ed., vol. 2. New York: McGraw-Hill, Inc. 1994, pp. 1319–1366.

65. Schwartz, Seymour I. Intestinal resection and anastomosis. In Schwartz, Seymour I., and Ellis, Harold, eds., *Maingot's Abdominal Operations*, 9th ed., vol. 1. Norwalk, CT: Appleton & Lange, 1989, pp. 933–952.

66. Sherlock, Sheila, and Dooley, James. Anatomy and function. In *Diseases of the Liver and Biliary System*, 9th ed. Oxford: Blackwell Scientific Publications, 1993, pp. 1–16.

67. ———. Hepato-cellular failure. Ibid., pp. 72–85.

68. ———. Fulminant hepatic failure. Ibid., pp. 102–113.

69. ———. The portal venous system and portal hypertension. Ibid., pp. 132–178.

70. Shires, G. Tom, et al. Fluid, electrolyte, and nutritional management. In Schwartz, Seymour I., ed.-in-ch., *Principles of Surgery*, 6th ed., vol. 1. New York: McGraw-Hill Inc., 1994, pp. 61–93.

71. Soergel, Konrad H. Acute pancreatitis. In Sleisenger, Marvin H., and Fordtran, John S., eds., *Gastrointestinal Disease*, 5th ed., vol. 2. Philadelphia: W.B. Saunders Co., 1993, pp. 1628–1653.

72. Spitz, Lewis. Infantile pyloric stenosis and pyloric mucosal diaphragm. In Schwartz, Seymour I., and Ellis, Harold, eds., *Maingot's Abdominal Operations*, 9th ed., vol. 1. Norwalk, CT: Appleton & Lange, 1989, pp. 567–573.

73. ———. Hirschsprung's disease and anorectal anomalies. Ibid., pp. 977–1005.

74. Townsend, Courtney M., Jr., and Thompson, James C. Small intestine. In Schwartz, Seymour I., ed.-in-ch., *Principles of Surgery*, 6th ed., vol. 2. New York: McGraw-Hill Inc., 1994, pp. 1153–1189.

75. Trier, Jerry S. Celiac sprue. In Sleisenger, Marvin H., and Fordtran, John S., eds., *Gastrointestinal Disease*, 5th ed., vol. 2. Philadelphia: W.B. Saunders Co., 1993, pp. 1078–1096.

76. ———. Whipple's disease. Ibid., vol. 2, pp. 1118–1127.

77. Turgeon, Ronald, M.D. Personal communications.

78. Urist, Marshall M., et al. Head and neck tumors. In Way, Lawrence W., ed., *Current Surgical Diagnosis & Treatment*, 10th ed. Norwalk, CT: Appleton & Lange, 1994, pp. 257–273.

79. Walsh, John H., and Mayer, Emerson A. Gastrointestinal hormones. In Sleisenger, Marvin H., and Fordtran, John S., eds., *Gastrointestinal Disease*, 5th ed., vol. 1. Philadelphia: W.B. Saunders Co., 1993, pp. 18–43.

80. Wastell, Christopher. Partial and total gastrectomy. In Schwartz, Seymour I., and Ellis, Harold, eds., *Maingot's Abdominal Operations*, 9th ed., vol. 1. Norwalk, CT: Appleton & Lange, 1989, pp. 731–770.

81. Way, Lawrence W. Stomach and duodenum. In Way, Lawrence W., ed., *Current Surgical Diagnosis & Treatment*, 10th ed. Norwalk, CT: Appleton & Lange, 1994, pp. 472–504.

82. ———. Liver. Ibid., pp. 505–519.

83. ———. Portal hypertension. Ibid., pp. 520–536.

84. ———. Biliary tract. Ibid., pp. 537–566.

85. ———. Appendix. Ibid., pp. 610–614.

86. Wherry, David C., et al. An external audit of laparoscopic cholecystectomy performed in medical treatment facilities of the Department of Defense. *Annals of Surgery* 220:626–634, November 1994.

87. White, Nicholas J., and Breman, Joel G. Malaria and babesiosis. In Isselbacher, Kurt J., et al., eds., *Harrison's Principles of Internal Medicine*, 13th ed. New. York: McGraw-Hill, Inc., 1994, pp. 887–896.

88. Wong, Douglas W., et al. Ileoanal pull-through procedures. In Schwartz, Seymour I., and Ellis, Harold, eds., *Maingot's Abdominal Operations*, 9th ed., vol. 2. Norwalk, CT: Appleton & Lange, 1989, pp. 1077–1096.

89. Wood, Robert J., and Jurkiewicz, M. J. Plastic and reconstructive surgery. In Schwartz, Seymour I., ed.-in-ch., *Principles of Surgery*, 6th ed., vol. 2. New York: McGraw-Hill, Inc., 1994, pp. 2025–2074.

Chapter 10

1. Amend, William J. C., Jr., and Vincenti, Flavio G. Oliguria: Acute renal failure. In Tanagho, Emil A., and McAninch, Jack W., eds., *Smith's General Urology*, 14th ed. Norwalk, CT: Appleton & Lange, 1995, pp. 604–608.

2. ———. Chronic renal failure and dialysis. Ibid., pp. 609–611.

3. Anderson, Robert J., and Schrier, Robert W. Acute tubular necrosis. In Schrier, Robert W., and Gottschalk, Carl W., eds., *Diseases of the Kidney*, 5th ed., vol. 2. Boston: Little, Brown & Co., 1993, pp. 1287–1318.

4. Andriole, Vincent T. Renal and perirenal abscesses. In Schrier, Robert W., and Gottschalk, Carl W., eds., *Diseases of the Kidney*, 5th ed., vol. 2. Boston: Little, Brown & Co., 1993, pp. 959–971.

5. Atkins, Robert C., and Thomson, Napier M. Rapidly progressive glomerulonephritis. In Schrier, Robert W., and Gottschalk, Carl W., eds., *Diseases of the Kidney*, 5th ed., vol. 2. Boston: Little, Brown & Co., 1993, pp. 1689–1713.

6. Babayan, Richard K. Benign prostatic hyperplasia—Invasive therapies. In

Krane, Robert J., et al., eds., *Clinical Urology*. Philadelphia: J.B. Lippincott Co., 1994, pp. 892–905.

7. Badr, Kamal F., and Brenner, Barry M. Vascular injury to the kidney. In Isselbacher, Kurt J., et al., eds., *Harrison's Principles of Internal Medicine*, 13th ed. New York: McGraw-Hill, Inc., 1994, pp. 1319–1323.

8. Barchman, M. J., and Bernard, David B. Clinical and laboratory evaluation of altered renal function. In Krane, Robert J., et al., eds., *Clinical Urology*. Philadelphia: J.B. Lippincott Co., 1994, pp. 17–45.

9. Blaivas, Jerry G., et al. When sphincter failure is the cause of female stress incontinence. *Contemporary Urology* 5:33–34, 38–40, 43–44, 47, 51–54, March 1993.

10. Brenner, Barry M., and Lazarus, J. Michael. Chronic renal failure. In Isselbacher, Kurt J., et al., eds., *Harrison's Principles of Internal Medicine*, 13th ed. New York: McGraw-Hill, Inc., 1994, pp. 1274–1281.

11. Bretan, Peter N., Jr., and Burke, Edmund C. Renal transplantation. In Tanagho, Emil A., and McAninch, Jack W., eds., *Smith's General Urology*, 14th ed. Norwalk, CT: Appleton & Lange, 1995, pp. 612–625.

12. Carroll, Peter R. Urothelial carcinoma: Cancers of the bladder, ureter, and renal pelvis. In Tanagho, Emil A., and McAninch, Jack W., eds., *Smith's General Urology*, 14th ed. Norwalk, CT: Appleton & Lange, 1995, pp. 353–371.

13. Carroll, Peter R., and Barbour, Susan. Urinary diversion and bladder substitution. In Tanagho, Emil A., and McAninch, Jack W., eds., *Smith's General Urology*, 14th ed. Norwalk, CT: Appleton & Lange, 1995, pp. 448–461.

14. Donovan, James F., Jr., and Williams, Richard D. Urology. In Way, Lawrence W., ed., *Current Surgical Diagnosis & Treatment*, 10th ed. Norwalk, CT: Appleton & Lange, 1994, pp. 907–973.

15. Dreicer, Robert, and Williams, Richard D. Renal parenchymal neoplasms. In Tanagho, Emil A., and McAninch, Jack W., eds., *Smith's General Urology*, 14th ed. Norwalk, CT: Appleton & Lange, 1995, pp. 372–391.

16. Elgin, Ronald J. Reference intervals and laboratory values of clinical importance. In Wyngaarden, James B., et al., eds., *Cecil's Textbook of Medicine*, 19th ed. Philadelphia: W.B. Saunders Co., 1995, pp. 1411–1422.

17. Garnick, Marc B., and Brenner, Barry M. Tumors of the urinary tract. In Isselbacher, Kurt J., et al., eds., *Harrison's Principles of Internal Medicine*, 13th ed. New York: McGraw-Hill, Inc., 1994, pp. 1336–1339.

18. Glassock, Richard J., and Brenner, Barry M. The major glomerulopathies. In Isselbacher, Kurt J., et al., eds., *Harrison's Principles of Internal Medicine*, 13th ed. New York: McGraw-Hill, Inc., 1994, pp. 1295–1306.

19. ———. Glomerulopathies associated with multisystem diseases. Ibid., pp. 1306–1313.

20. Grünfeld, Jean-Pierre, et al. Acute interstitial nephritis. In Schrier, Robert W., and Gottschalk, Carl W., eds., *Diseases of the Kidney*, 5th ed., vol. 2. Boston: Little, Brown & Co., 1993, pp. 1331–1353.

21. Hautmann, Richard E. Bladder replacement surgery. In Krane, Robert J., et al., eds., *Clinical Urology*. Philadelphia: J.B. Lippincott Co., 1994, pp. 725–734.

22. Hill, Edward C. Gynecology. In Way, Lawrence W., ed., *Current Surgical Diagnosis & Treatment*, 10th ed. Norwalk, CT: Appleton & Lange, 1994, pp. 974–1010.

23. Honig, Stanton C., and Oates, Robert Davis. Infertility. In Krane, Robert J., et al., eds., *Clinical Urology*. Philadelphia: J.B. Lippincott Co., 1994, pp. 1102–1130.

24. Karam, John H. Diabetes mellitus and hypoglycemia. In Tierney, Lawrence M., et al., eds., *Current Medical Diagnosis & Treatment*, 35th ed. Stamford, CT: Appleton & Lange, 1996, pp. 1030–1068.

25. Kaude, Juri V., and Torres, Gladys M. Kidney. In Ros, Pablo R., and Bidgood, W. Dean, Jr., *Abdominal Magnetic Resonance Imaging*. St. Louis: Mosby, 1993, pp. 363–385.

26. Khanna, Ramesh, and Oreopoulos, Dimitrios G. Peritoneal dialysis. In Schrier, Robert W., and Gottschalk, Carl W., eds., *Diseases of the Kidney*, 5th ed., vol. 3. Boston: Little, Brown & Co., 1993, pp. 2969–3030.

27. Kjellsbrand, Carl M., and Solez, Kim. Treatment of acute renal failure. In Schrier, Robert W., and Gottschalk, Carl W., eds., *Diseases of the Kidney*, 5th ed., vol. 2. Boston: Little, Brown & Co., 1993, pp. 1371–1404.

28. Kogan, Berry A. Disorders of the ureter and ureteropelvic junction. In Tanagho, Emil A., and McAninch, Jack W., eds., *Smith's General Urology*, 14th ed. Norwalk, CT: Appleton & Lange, 1995, pp. 626–641.

29. Lange, Erich K. Vascular interventional radiology. In Tanagho, Emil A., and McAninch, Jack W., eds., *Smith's General Urology*, 14th ed. Norwalk, CT: Appleton & Lange, 1995, pp. 121–128.

30. Llach, Francisco, and Nikekhtar, Bijan. Acute renal thrombosis. In Schrier, Robert W., and Gottschalk, Carl W., eds., *Diseases of the Kidney*, 5th ed., vol. 2. Boston: Little, Brown & Co., 1993, pp. 1319–1330.

31. McAninch, Jack W. Symptoms of disorders of the genitourinary tract. In Tanagho, Emil A., and McAninch, Jack W., eds., *Smith's General Urology*, 14th ed. Norwalk, CT: Appleton & Lange, 1995, pp. 31–40.

32. ———. Injuries to genitourinary tract. Ibid., pp. 314–333.

33. ———. Disorders of the kidney. Ibid., pp. 570–591.

34. ———. Disorders of the penis and male urethra. Ibid., pp. 658–672.

35. ———. Disorders of the testes, scrotum, and spermatic cord. Ibid., pp. 681–690.

36. McClure, R. Dale. Male infertility. In Tanagho, Emil A., and McAninch, Jack W., eds., *Smith's General Urology*, 14th ed. Norwalk, CT: Appleton & Lange, 1995, pp. 739–771.

37. Meares, Edwin M., Jr. Nonspecific infections of the genitourinary tract. In Tanagho, Emil A., and McAninch, Jack W., eds., *Smith's General Urology*, 14th ed. Norwalk, CT: Appleton & Lange, 1995, pp. 201–244.

38. Morrison, Gail. Kidney. In Tierney, Lawrence M., et al., eds., *Current Medical Diagnosis & Treatment*, 35th ed. Stamford, CT: Appleton & Lange, 1996, pp. 795–821.

39. Narayan, Perinchery. Neoplasms of the prostate gland. In Tanagho, Emil A., and McAninch, Jack W., eds., *Smith's General Urology*, 14th ed. Norwalk, CT: Appleton & Lange, 1995, pp. 392–433.

40. Paulson, David F., and Frazier, Harold A., II. Radical prostatectomy. In Krane, Robert J., et al., eds., *Clinical Urology*. Philadelphia: J.B. Lippincott Co., 1994, pp. 1020–1047.

41. Pickering, Thomas G., et al. Renovascular hypertension. In Schrier, Robert W., and Gottschalk, Carl W., eds., *Diseases of the Kidney*, 5th ed., vol. 2. Boston: Little, Brown & Co., 1993, pp. 1451–1474.

42. Presti, Joseph C., Jr., and Herr, Harry W. Genital tumors. In Tanagho, Emil A., and McAninch, Jack W., eds., *Smith's General Urology*, 14th ed. Norwalk, CT: Appleton & Lange, 1995, pp. 434–447.

43. Presti, Joseph C., Jr., et al. Urology. In Tierney, Lawrence M., et al., eds., *Current Medical Diagnosis & Treatment*, 35th ed. Stamford, CT: Appleton & Lange, 1996, pp. 822–857.

44. Prockop, Darwin J., et al. Heritable disorders of connective tissue. In

Isselbacher, Kurt J., et al., eds., *Harrison's Principles of Internal Medicine*, 13th ed. New York: McGraw-Hill, Inc., 1994, pp. 2105–2117.

45. Schnaper, William, H., and Rabson, Alan M. Nephrotic syndrome, minimal change disease, focal glomerulosclerosis, and related disorders. In Schrier, Robert W., and Gottschalk, Carl W., eds., *Diseases of the Kidney*, 5th ed., vol. 2. Boston: Little, Brown & Co., 1993, pp. 1731–1784.

46. Seifter, Julian L., and Brenner, Barry M. Urinary tract obstruction. In Isselbacher, Kurt J., et al., eds., *Harrison's Principles of Internal Medicine*, 13th ed. New York: McGraw-Hill, Inc., 1994, pp. 1333–1336.

47. Sosa, R. Ernest, and Vaughan, E. Darracott, Jr. Renovascular and renal parenchymal hypertension. In Krane, Robert J., et al., eds., *Clinical Urology*. Philadelphia: J.B. Lippincott Co., 1994, pp. 303–313.

48. Sosa, R. Ernest, and Vaughan, E. Darracott, Jr. Renovascular hypertension. In Tanagho, Emil A., and McAninch, Jack W., eds., *Smith's General Urology*, 14th ed. Norwalk, CT: Appleton & Lange, 1995, pp. 728–738.

49. Stoller, Marshall L. Retrograde instrumentation of the urinary tract. In Tanagho, Emil A., and McAninch, Jack W., eds., *Smith's General Urology*, 14th ed. Norwalk, CT: Appleton & Lange, 1995, pp. 160–171.

50. ———. Extracorporeal shock wave lithotripsy. Ibid., pp. 305–313.

51. Stoller, Marshall L., and Bolton, Damien M. Urinary stone disease. In Tanagho, Emil A., and McAninch, Jack W., eds., *Smith's General Urology*, 14th ed. Norwalk, CT: Appleton & Lange, 1995, pp. 276–304.

52. Tanagho, Emil A. Anatomy of the genitourinary tract. In Tanagho, Emil A., and McAninch, Jack W., eds., *Smith's General Urology*, 14th ed. Norwalk, CT: Appleton & Lange, 1995, pp. 1–16.

53. ———. Urinary obstruction and stasis. Ibid., pp. 172–185.

54. ———. Vesicoureteral reflux. Ibid., pp. 186–200.

55. ———. Specific infections of the genitourinary tract. Ibid., pp. 245–261.

56. ———. Urodynamic studies. Ibid., pp. 514–535.

57. ———. Urinary incontinence. Ibid., pp. 536–551.

58. ———. Disorders of the bladder, prostate, and seminal vesicles. Ibid., pp. 642–657.

59. ———. Disorders of the female urethra. Ibid., pp. 673–680.

60. Tanagho, Emil A., and Lue, Tom F. Neuropathic bladder disorders. In Tanagho, Emil A., and McAninch, Jack W., eds., *Smith's General Urology*, 14th ed. Norwalk, CT: Appleton & Lange, 1995, pp. 496–513.

61. Thüroff, Joachim W. Percutaneous endourology and ureterorenoscopy. In Tanagho, Emil A., and McAninch, Jack W., eds., *Smith's General Urology*, 14th ed. Norwalk, CT: Appleton & Lange, 1995, pp. 129–147.

62. Truss, Michael C., and Jonas, Udo. Supravesical diversion. In Krane, Robert J., et al., eds., *Clinical Urology*. Philadelphia: J.B. Lippincott Co., 1994, pp. 705–724.

63. Turgeon, Ronald, M.D. Personal communications.

64. Van de Graaff, Kent M. Urinary system. In *Human Anatomy*, 4th ed. Dubuque, IA: Wm. C. Brown Publishers, 1995, pp. 637–659.

65. ———. Male reproductive system. Ibid., pp. 663–688.

66. Vincenti, Flavio G. and Amend, William J. C., Jr. Diagnosis of medical renal diseases. In Tanagho, Emil A., and McAninch, Jack W., eds., *Smith's General Urology*, 14th ed. Norwalk, CT: Appleton & Lange, 1995, pp. 592–603.

67. Williams, Richard D., and Kreder, Karl J., Jr. Urologic laboratory examination. In Tanagho, Emil A., and McAninch, Jack W., eds., *Smith's General Urology*, 14th ed. Norwalk, CT: Appleton & Lange, 1995, pp. 50–63.

68. Winfield, Howard N., and Donovan, James F. Ligating varicoceles through the laparoscope. *Contemporary Urology* 5:19–20, 22, 24, and 26. September 1993.

69. Zinman, Leonard, and Swierzewski, Mark J. Surgery of the ureter. In Krane, Robert J., et al., eds., *Clinical Urology*. Philadelphia: J.B. Lippincott Co., 1994, pp. 416–432.

Chapter 11

1. Albertsen, H. M., et al. A physical map and candidate genes in the BRACA1 region on Chromosome 17q12-21. *Nature Genetics* 7:472–479, August 1994.

2. Althek, Albert. General considerations. In Deligdisch, Liane, et al., eds., *Atlas of Ovarian Tumors*. New York: Igaku-Shoin, 1994, pp. 3–47.

3. ———. Management of nonepithelial germ cell and sex cord—stromal tumors of the ovary. Ibid., pp. 53–62.

4. Backer, J. W., M.D. Personal communications.

5. Baker, Vicki V. Premalignant and malignant disorders of the ovaries and

oviducts. In DeCherney, Alan H., and Pernoll, Martin L., eds., *Current Obstetrics & Gynecologic Diagnosis and Treatment*, 8th ed. Norwalk, CT: Appleton & Lange, 1994, pp. 954–966.

6. Bast, Robert C., and Berchuck, Andrew. Ovarian cancer. In Isselbacher, Kurt J., et al., eds., *Harrison's Principles of Internal Medicine*, 13th ed. New York: McGraw-Hill, Inc., 1994, pp. 1853–1858.

7. Bottoms, Sidney F., and Scott, James R. Transfusions and shock. In Scott, James R., et al., eds., *Danforth's Obstetrics and Gynecology*, 7th ed. Philadelphia: J.B. Lippincott Co., 1994, pp. 659–674.

8. Cohen, Carmel J. Management of malignant epithelial tumors of the ovary. In Deligdisch, Liane, et al., eds., *Atlas of Ovarian Tumors*. New York: Igaku-Shoin, 1994, pp. 49–52.

9. Creasman, William T. Malignant lesions of the uterine corpus. In Scott, James R., et al., eds., *Danforth's Obstetrics and Gynecology*, 7th ed. Philadelphia: J.B. Lippincott Co., 1994, pp. 1040–1054.

10. Cruikshank, Stephen H., and Davies, Jack. Anatomy of the female genital tract. In Scott, James R., et al., eds., *Danforth's Obstetrics and Gynecology*, 7th ed. Philadelphia: J.B. Lippincott Co., 1994, pp. 1–38.

11. Curry, Stephen L., and Barclay, David L. Benign disorders of the vulva and vagina. In DeCherney, Alan H., and Pernoll, Martin L., eds., *Current Obstetrics & Gynecologic Diagnosis & Treatment*, 8th ed. Norwalk, CT: Appleton & Lange, 1994, pp. 689–712.

12. DiSaia, Philip J. Malignant lesions of the uterine cervix. In Scott, James R., et al., eds., *Danforth's Obstetrics and Gynecology*, 7th ed. Philadelphia: J.B. Lippincott Co., 1994, pp. 995–1012.

13. ———. Tumors of the fallopian tube. Ibid., pp. 1055–1066.

14. ———. Ovarian disorders. Ibid., pp. 1067–1120.

15. DiSaia, Philip J., and Stafl, Adolf. Disorders of the uterine cervix. In Scott, James R., et al., eds., *Danforth's Obstetrics and Gynecology*, 7th ed. Philadelphia: J.B. Lippincott Co., 1994, pp. 987–995.

16. DiSaia, Philip J., and Walker, Joan L. Perioperative care. In Scott, James R., et al., eds., *Danforth's Obstetrics and Gynecology*, 7th ed. Philadelphia: J.B. Lippincott Co., 1994, pp. 875–885.

17. DiSaia, Philip J., and Woodruff, J. Donald. Disorders of the vulva and vagina. In Scott, James R., et al., eds., *Danforth's Obstetrics and Gynecology*, 7th ed. Philadelphia: J.B. Lippincott Co., 1994, pp. 959–986.

18. Dorr, Clyde H., II. Relaxation of pelvic supports. In DeCherney, Alan H., and Pernoll, Martin L., eds., *Current Obstetrics & Gynecologic Diagnosis and Treatment*, 8th ed. Norwalk, CT: Appleton & Lange, 1994, pp. 809–830.

19. Dunn, Leo J. Cesarean section and other obstetric operations. In Scott, James R., et al., eds., *Danforth's Obstetrics and Gynecology*, 7th ed. Philadelphia: J.B. Lippincott Co., 1994, pp. 639–658.

20. Elgin, Ronald J. Reference intervals and laboratory values of clinical importance. In Wyngaarden, James B., et al., eds., *Cecil's Textbook Medicine*, 19th ed. Philadelphia: W.B. Saunders Co., 1992, pp. 2370–2380.

21. Elkowitz, Andrew, et al. Various methods of breast reconstruction after mastectomy: An economic comparison. *Plastic and Reconstructive Surgery* 92:77–83, July 1993.

22. Elliott, L. Franklyn, et al. Immediate TRAM flap breast reconstruction: 1238 consecutive cases. *Plastic and Reconstructive Surgery* 92:217–227, August 1993.

23. Eschenbach, David A. Pelvic infections and sexually transmitted diseases. In Scott, James R., et al., eds., *Danforth's Obstetrics and Gynecology*, 7th ed. Philadelphia: J.B. Lippincott Co., 1994, pp. 933–957.

24. Fisher, Bernard, et al. Neoplasms of the breast. In Holland, James F., et al., eds., *Cancer Medicine*, 3d ed., vol. 2. Philadelphia: Lea & Febiger, 1993, pp. 1706–1774.

25. Fitzgerald, Paul A. Endocrinology. In Tierney, Lawrence M., Jr., et al., eds., *Current Medical Diagnosis & Treatment*, 35th ed. Stamford, CT: Appleton & Lange, 1996, pp. 972–1029.

26. Gerbie, Melvin D. Complications of menstruation: Abnormal uterine bleeding. In DeCherney, Alan H., Pernoll, Martin L., eds. *Current Obstetrics & Gynecologic Diagnosis & Treatment*, 8th ed. Norwalk, CT: Appleton & Lange, 1994, pp. 662–669.

27. Giuliano, Armando E. Breast. In Tierney, Lawrence M., Jr., et al., eds., *Current Medical Diagnosis & Treatment*, 35th ed. Stamford, CT: Appleton & Lange, 1996, pp. 614–637.

28. Goodman, Annekathryn. Premalignant and malignant disorders of the uterine corpus. In DeCherney, Alan H., and Pernoll, Martin L., eds., *Current Obstetrics & Gynecologic Diagnosis & Treatment*, 8th ed. Norwalk, CT: Appleton & Lange, 1994, pp. 937–953.

29. Goodman, Annekathryn, and Hill, Edward C. Premalignant and malignant disorders of the uterine cervix. In DeCherney, Alan H., and Pernoll, Martin L., eds., *Current Obstetrics & Gynecologic Diagnosis & Treatment*, 8th ed. Norwalk, CT: Appleton & Lange, 1994, pp. 921–936.

30. Harris, Jay R. Cancer of the breast. In DeVita, Vincent T., Jr., et al., eds., *Cancer: Principles & Practice of Oncology*, 4th ed., vol. 1. Philadelphia: J.B. Lippincott Co., 1993, pp. 1264–1332.

31. Hasson, Harrith M. Laparoscopic diagnosis and treatment of ovarian masses. In Sugarbaker, Paul H., ed., *Pelvic Surgery and Treatment for Cancer*. St. Louis: Mosby, 1994, pp. 181–203.

32. Herbst, Arthur L., and Hatch, Richard. Gynecology. In Schwartz, Seymour I., ed.-in-ch., *Principles of Surgery*, 5th ed., vol. 2. New York: McGraw-Hill Book Co., 1989, pp. 1781–1829.

33. Hightower, Randall D., et al. National survey of ovarian carcinoma IV: Patterns of care and related survival for older patients. *Cancer* 73:377–383, 15 January 1994.

34. Hill, Edward C. Gynecology. In Way, Lawrence W., ed., *Current Surgical Diagnosis & Treatment*, 10th ed. Norwalk, CT: Appleton & Lange, 1994, pp. 974–1010.

35. Hill, Edward C., and Pernoll, Martin L. Benign disorders of the uterine cervix. In DeCherney, Alan H., and Pernoll, Martin L., eds., *Current Obstetrics & Gynecologic Diagnosis & Treatment*, 8th ed. Norwalk, CT: Appleton & Lange, 1994, pp. 713–730.

36. Hole, John W., Jr. Reproductive systems. In *Human Anatomy and Physiology*, 6th ed. Dubuque, IA: Wm. C. Brown Publishers, 1993, pp. 804–851.

37. Hoskins, William J., et al. Gynecologic tumors. In DeVita, Vincent, Jr., et al., eds., *Cancer Principles & Practice of Oncology*, 4th ed., vol. 1. Philadelphia: J.B. Lippincott Co., 1993, pp. 1142–1225.

38. Hughes, Claude L., and Hammond, Charles B. Infertility. In Scott, James R., et al., eds., *Danforth's Obstetrics and Gynecology*, 7th ed. Philadelphia: J.B. Lippincott Co., 1994, pp. 807–820.

39. Jacobs, Richard A. Infectious diseases: Spirochetal. In Tierney, Lawrence M., Jr., et al., eds., *Current Medical Diagnosis & Treatment*, 35th ed. Stamford, CT: Appleton & Lange, 1996, pp. 1227–1245.

40. Jahshan, Antoine E., et al. Hot-knife conization of the cervix: Clinical and pathologic findings from a study introducing a new technique. *Obstetrics and Gynecology* 83:97–103, January 1994.

41. Kosary, Carol L. FIGO histology, histologic grade, age determining survival for cancers of the female gynecological system: An analysis of 1973–87 SEER cases of cancers of the endometrium, cervix, ovary, vulva, and vagina. *Seminars in Surgical Oncology* 10:31–46, January/February 1994.

42. Krantz, Kermit E. Anatomy of the female reproductive system. In DeCherney, Alan H., and Pernoll, Martin L., eds., *Current Obstetrics & Gynecologic Diagnosis & Treatment*, 8th ed. Norwalk, CT: Appleton & Lange, 1994, pp. 5–53.

43. Lewis, Brian J., and Conry, Robert M. Breast cancer. In Bennett, J. Claude, and Plum, Fred, eds., *Cecil's Textbook of Medicine*, 20th ed. Philadelphia: W.B. Saunders Co., 1996, pp. 1320–1325.

44. London, Steve N., and Hammond, Charles B. The climacteric. In Scott, James R., et al., eds., *Danforth's Obstetrics and Gynecology*, 7th ed. Philadelphia: J.B. Lippincott Co., 1994, pp. 853–874.

45. MacKay, H. Trent. Gynecology. In Tierney, Lawrence M., Jr., et al., eds., *Current Medical Diagnosis & Treatment*, 35th ed. Stamford, CT: Appleton & Lange, 1996, pp. 638–670.

46. Malinak, L. Russell, et al. Therapeutic gynecologic procedures. In DeCherney, Alan H., and Pernoll, Martin L., eds., *Current Obstetrics & Gynecologic Diagnosis & Treatment*, 8th ed. Norwalk, CT: Appleton & Lange, 1994, pp. 884–905.

47. Marchant, Douglas J. Nonmalignant diseases of the breast. In Wyngaarden, James B., et al., eds. *Cecil's Textbook of Medicine*, 19th ed. Philadelphia: W.B. Saunders Co., 1992, pp. 1378–1381.

48. Martin, Mary C. Infertility. In DeCherney, Alan H., and Pernoll, Martin L., eds., *Current Obstetrics & Gynecologic Diagnosis and Treatment*, 8th ed. Norwalk, CT: Appleton & Lange, 1994, pp. 996–1006.

49. McCormack, William M. Pelvic inflammatory disease. *New England Journal of Medicine* 330:115–119, 13 January 1994.

50. Merrill, James A., and Creasman, William T. Disorders of the uterine corpus. In Scott, James R., et al., eds., *Danforth's Obstetrics and Gynecology*, 7th ed. Philadelphia: J.B. Lippincott Co., 1994, pp. 1023–1039.

51. Muse, Kenneth N., Jr., and Fox, Michael D. Endometriosis. In DeCherney, Alan H., and Pernoll, Martin L., eds., *Current Obstetrics & Gynecologic Diagnosis & Treatment*, 8th ed. Norwalk, CT: Appleton & Lange, 1994, pp. 801–808.

52. Nichols, David H. Relaxation of pelvic supports. In Scott, James R., et al., eds., *Danforth's Obstetrics and Gynecology*,

7th ed. Philadelphia: J.B. Lippincott Co., 1994, pp. 887–903.

53. Querleu, Dennis, and LeBlanc, Eric. Laparoscopic infrarenal paraaortic lymph node dissection for restaging of carcinoma of the ovary or fallopian tube. *Cancer* 73:1467–1471, 1 March 1994.

54. Ramin, Susan M., et al. Sexually transmitted diseases and pelvic infections. In DeCherney, Alan H., and Pernoll, Martin L., eds., *Current Obstetrics & Gynecologic Diagnosis & Treatment,* 8th ed. Norwalk, CT: Appleton & Lange, 1994, pp. 754–784.

55. Rosenwaks, Zev, and Davis, Owen K. *In vito* fertilization and related techniques. In Scott, James R., et al., eds., *Danforth's Obstetrics and Gynecology,* 7th ed. Philadelphia: J.B. Lippincott Co., 1994, pp. 821–843.

56. Rubin, Stephen C., et al. Prevalence and significance of HER-2/*neu* expression in early epithelial ovarian cancer. *Cancer* 73:1456–1459, 1 March 1994.

57. Scott, James R. Ectopic pregnancy. In Scott, James R., et al., eds., *Danforth's Obstetrics and Gynecology,* 7th ed. Philadelphia: J.B. Lippincott Co., 1994, pp. 221–235.

58. Shapiro, Charles L., and Henderson, I. Craig. Diseases of the breast. In Rakel, Robert E., ed., *Conn's Current Therapy—1993.* Philadelphia: W.B. Saunders Co., 1993, pp. 1041–1047.

59. Shestak, Kenneth C., et al. Breast masses in the augmentation mammaplasty patient: The role of ultrasound. *Plastic & Reconstructive Surgery* 92:209–216.

60. Singleton, Timothy P., et al. Activation of *c-erb*B-2 and prognosis of ovarian carcinoma. *Cancer* 73:1460–1466, 1 March 1994.

61. Smith, Donna M., and Barclay, David L. Premalignant and malignant disorders of the vulva and vagina. In DeCherney, Alan H., and Pernoll, Martin L., eds., *Current Obstetrics & Gynecologic Diagnosis & Treatment,* 8th ed. Norwalk, CT: Appleton & Lange, 1994, pp. 906–920.

62. Staff, Adolf. Colposcopy. In Scott, James R., et al., eds., *Danforth's Obstetrics and Gynecology,* 7th ed. Philadelphia: J.B. Lippincott Co., 1994, pp. 1012–1022.

63. Stevenson, Thomas R., and Goldstein, Jeffrey A. TRAM flap breast reconstruction and contralateral reduction or mastopexy. *Plastic & Reconstructive Surgery* 92:228–233, August 1993.

64. Thomas, David B., et al. Mammographic calcifications and risk of subsequent breast cancer. *Journal of*

the *National Cancer Institute* 85:30–34, 3 February 1993.

65. Thorneycroft, Ian H. Amenorrhea. In DeCherney, Alan H., and Pernoll, Martin L., eds., *Current Obstetrics & Gynecologic Diagnosis & Treatment,* 8th ed. Norwalk, CT: Appleton & Lange, 1994, pp. 1007–1015.

66. Turgeon, Ronald, M.D. Personal communications.

67. Van de Graaff, Kent M. Female reproductive system. In *Human Anatomy,* 4th ed. Dubuque, IA: Wm. C. Brown Publishers, 1995, pp. 690–716.

68. Wheeler, James E., and Woodruff, J. Donald. Benign disorders of the ovaries and oviducts. In DeCherney, Alan H., and Pernoll, Martin L., eds., *Current Obstetrics & Gynecologic Diagnosis & Treatment,* 8th ed. Norwalk, CT: Appleton & Lange, 1994, pp. 744–753.

69. Young, Robert C., et al. Cancer of the ovary. In DeVita, Vincent T., Jr., et al., eds., *Cancer Principles and Practice of Oncology,* 4th ed., vol. 1. Philadelphia: J.B. Lippincott Co., 1993, pp. 1226–1263.

Chapter 12

1. Baker, Emily R., and Shephard, Barbara. Neonatal resuscitation and care of the newborn at risk. In DeCherney, Alan H., and Pernoll, Martin L., eds., *Current Obstetric & Gynecologic Diagnosis & Treatment,* 8th ed. Norwalk, CT: Appleton & Lange, 1994, pp. 594–612.

2. Berkowitz, Richard L., and Lynch, Lauren. Fetal blood sampling. In Creasy, Robert K., and Resnik, Robert, eds., *Maternal-Fetal Medicine: Principles and Practice,* 3d ed. Philadelphia: W.B. Saunders Co., 1994, pp. 359–381.

3. Biswas, Manoj K., and Craigo, Sabrina D. The course and conduct of normal labor and delivery. In DeCherney, Alan H., and Pernoll, Martin L., eds., *Current Obstetric & Gynecologic Diagnosis & Treatment,* 8th ed. Norwalk, CT: Appleton & Lange, 1994, pp. 202–227.

4. Blanchette, Victor, et al. Hematology. In Avery, Gordon B., et al., eds., *Neonatology: Pathophysiology and Management of the Newborn,* 4th ed. Philadelphia: J.B. Lippincott Co., 1994, pp. 952–999.

5. Bowes, Watson A., Jr. Clinical aspects of normal and abnormal labor. In Creasy, Robert K., and Resnik, Robert, eds., *Maternal-Fetal Medicine: Principles and Practice,* 3d ed. Philadelphia: W.B. Saunders Co., 1994, pp. 527–557.

6. Bowman, John M. Hemolytic disease (Erythroblastosis fetalis). In Creasy, Robert K., and Resnik, Robert, eds.,

Maternal-Fetal Medicine: Principles and Practice, 3d ed. Philadelphia: W.B. Saunders Co., 1994, pp. 711–743.

7. Branch, D. Ware, and Scott, James E. The immunology of pregnancy. In Creasy, Robert K., and Resnik, Robert, eds., *Maternal-Fetal Medicine: Principles and Practice,* 3d ed. Philadelphia: W.B. Saunders Co., 1994, pp. 115–127.

8. Burkman, Ronald T. Contraception and family planning. In DeCherney, Alan H., and Pernoll, Martin L., eds., *Current Obstetric & Gynecologic Diagnosis & Treatment,* 8th ed. Norwalk, CT: Appleton & Lange, 1994, pp. 670–688.

9. Collea, Joseph V. Malpresentation and cord prolapse. In DeCherney, Alan H., and Pernoll, Martin L., eds., *Current Obstetric & Gynecologic Diagnosis & Treatment,* 8th ed. Norwalk, CT: Appleton & Lange, 1994, pp. 410–427.

10. Craigo, Sabrina D., and Kapernick, Peter S. Postpartum hemorrhage and the abnormal puerperium. In DeCherney, Alan H., and Pernoll, Martin L., eds., *Current Obstetric & Gynecologic Diagnosis & Treatment,* 8th ed. Norwalk, CT: Appleton & Lange, 1994, pp. 574–593.

11. Creasy, Robert K., and Resnik, Robert. Intrauterine growth restriction. In Creasy, Robert K., and Resnik, Robert, eds., *Maternal-Fetal Medicine: Principles and Practice,* 3d ed. Philadelphia: W.B. Saunders Co., 1994, pp. 558–574.

12. Crombleholme, William R., and Evans, Arthur T. Obstetrics. In Tierney, Lawrence M., et al., eds., *Current Medical Diagnosis & Treatment,* 35th ed. Stamford, CT: Appleton & Lange, 1996, pp. 671–693.

13. DeCherney, Alan H., et al. *In vitro* fertilization and related techniques. In DeCherney, Alan H., and Pernoll, Martin L., eds., *Current Obstetric & Gynecologic Diagnosis & Treatment,* 8th ed. Norwalk, CT: Appleton & Lange, 1994, pp. 1026–1029.

14. Dye, Timothy, et al. Amnioinfusion and the intrauterine prevention of meconium aspiration. *American Journal of Obstetrics & Gynecology* 171:1601–1602, December 1994.

15. Fakhoury, George, et al. Lamellar body concentrations and the prediction of fetal pulmonary maturity. *American Journal of Obstetrics and Gynecology* 170:72–76, January 1994.

16. Elgin, Ronald J. Reference and laboratory values of clinical importance. In Wyngaarden, James B., et al., eds., *Cecil's Textbook of Medicine,* 19th ed. Philadelphia: W.B. Saunders Co., 1992, pp. 2370–2380.

17. Fanaroff, Avroy A., et al. Identification and management of high-risk problems in the neonate. In Creasy, Robert K., and Resnik, Robert, eds., *Maternal-Fetal Medicine: Principles and Practice*, 3d ed. Philadelphia: W.B. Saunders Co., 1994, pp. 1135–1172.

18. Feingold, Murray. Congenital malformations. In Avery, Gordon B., et al., eds., *Neonatology: Pathophysiology and Management of the Newborn*, 4th ed. Philadelphia: J.B. Lippincott Co., 1994, pp. 744–763.

19. Freij, Bishara, and Sever, John A. Chronic infections. In Avery, Gordon B., et al., eds., *Neonatology: Pathophysiology and Management of the Newborn*, 4th ed. Philadelphia: J.B. Lippincott Co., 1994, pp. 1029–1081.

20. Friendly, David S. Eye disorders. In Avery, Gordon B., et al., eds., *Neonatology: Pathophysiology and Management of the Newborn*, 4th ed. Philadelphia: J.B. Lippincott Co., 1994, pp. 1195–1210.

21. Ganong, William F. Physiology. of reproduction in women. In DeCherney, Alan H., and Pernoll, Martin L., eds., *Current Obstetric & Gynecologic Diagnosis & Treatment*, 8th ed. Norwalk, CT: Appleton & Lange, 1994, pp. 124–145.

22. Garite, Thomas J. Premature rupture of the membranes. In Creasy, Robert K., and Resnik, Robert, eds., *Maternal-Fetal Medicine: Principles and Practice*, 3d ed. Philadelphia: W.B. Saunders Co., 1994, pp. 625–638.

23. Gibbs, Ronald S., and Sweet, Richard L. Clinical disorders. In Creasy, Robert K., and Resnik, Robert, eds., *Maternal-Fetal Medicine: Principles and Practice*, 3d ed. Philadelphia: W.B. Saunders Co., 1994, pp. 639–703.

24. Gilbert, William M. Disorders of amniotic fluid. In Creasy, Robert K., and Resnik, Robert, eds., *Maternal-Fetal Medicine: Principles and Practice*, 3d ed. Philadelphia: W.B. Saunders Co., 1994, pp. 620–634.

25. Gill, William L. Essentials of normal newborn assessment and care. In DeCherney, Alan H., and Pernoll, Martin L., eds., *Current Obstetric & Gynecologic Diagnosis & Treatment*, 8th ed. Norwalk, CT: Appleton & Lange, 1994, pp. 228–239.

26. Glass, Robert H., and Golbus, Mitchell S. Recurrent abortion. In Creasy, Robert K., and Resnik, Robert, eds., *Maternal-Fetal Medicine: Principles and Practice*, 3d ed. Philadelphia: W.B. Saunders Co., 1994, pp. 445–452.

27. Green, James R. Placenta previa and abruptio placentae. In Creasy, Robert K., and Resnik, Robert, eds., *Maternal-Fetal Medicine: Principles and Practice*,

28. Hale, Ralph W. Operative delivery. In DeCherney, Alan H., and Pernoll, Martin L., eds., *Current Obstetric & Gynecologic Diagnosis & Treatment*, 8th ed. Norwalk, CT: Appleton & Lange, 1994, pp. 543–573.

29. Herrera, Eduardo A., and Pernoll, Martin L. Complications of labor and delivery. In DeCherney, Alan H., and Pernoll, Martin L., eds., *Current Obstetric & Gynecologic Diagnosis & Treatment*, 8th ed. Norwalk, CT: Appleton & Lange, 1994, pp. 506–519.

30. Hill, Alan, and Volpe, Joseph J. Neurologic disorders. In Avery, Gordon B., et al., eds., *Neonatology: Pathophysiology and Management of the Newborn*, 4th ed. Philadelphia: J.B. Lippincott Co., 1994, pp. 1117–1138.

31. Hole, John W., Jr. Reproductive systems. In *Human Anatomy & Physiology*, 6th ed. Dubuque, IA: Wm. C. Brown Publishers, 1993, pp. 804–851.

32. ———. Human growth and development. Ibid., pp. 852–881.

33. ———. Human genetics. Ibid., pp. 882–907.

34. Jobe, Alan H. Fetal lung development, tests for maturation, induction of maturation, and treatment. In Creasy, Robert K., and Resnik, Robert, eds., *Maternal-Fetal Medicine: Principles and Practice*, 3d ed. Philadelphia: W.B. Saunders Co., 1994, pp. 423–441.

35. Jones, Oliver W., and Cahill, Timothy C. Basic genetics and patterns of inheritance. In Creasy, Robert K., and Resnik, Robert, eds., *Maternal-Fetal Medicine: Principles and Practice*, 3d ed. Philadelphia: W.B. Saunders Co., 1994, pp. 3–60.

36. Kelly, Joan McGregor. General care. In Avery, Gordon B., et al., eds., *Neonatology: Pathophysiology and Management of the Newborn*, 4th ed. Philadelphia: J.B. Lippincott Co., 1994, pp. 301–311.

37. Krantz, Kermit E. Anatomy of the female reproductive system. In DeCherney, Alan H., and Pernoll, Martin L., eds., *Current Obstetric & Gynecologic Diagnosis & Treatment*, 8th ed. Norwalk, CT: Appleton & Lange, 1994, pp. 5–53.

38. Knuppel, Robert A. Maternal-Placental-Fetalunit: Fetal and early neonatal physiology. In DeCherney, Alan H., and Pernoll, Martin L., eds., *Current Obstetric & Gynecologic Diagnosis & Treatment*, 8th ed. Norwalk, CT: Appleton & Lange, 1994, pp. 155–182.

39. Lucas, Michael J. The role of vacuum extraction in modern obstetrics.

3d ed. Philadelphia: W.B. Saunders Co., 1994, pp. 602–619.

Clinical Obstetrics & Gynecology 37:794–905, December 1994.

40. Mabie, William C., and Sibai, Baha M. Hypertensive states of pregnancy. In DeCherney, Alan H., and Pernoll, Martin L., eds., *Current Obstetric & Gynecologic Diagnosis & Treatment*, 8th ed. Norwalk, CT: Appleton & Lange, 1994, pp. 380–397.

41. Maisels, M. Jeffrey. Jaundice. In Avery, Gordon B., et al., eds., *Neonatology: Pathophysiology and Management of the Newborn*, 4th ed. Philadelphia: J.B. Lippincott Co., 1994, pp. 630–725.

42. Manning, Frank A. Ultrasonography. In Avery, Gordon B., et al., eds., *Neonatology: Pathophysiology and Management of the Newborn*, 4th ed. Philadelphia: J.B. Lippincott Co., 1994, pp. 154–170.

43. Margileth, Andrew M. Dermatologic conditions. In Avery, Gordon B., et al., eds., *Neonatology: Pathophysiology and Management of the Newborn*, 4th ed. Philadelphia: J.B. Lippincott Co., 1994, pp. 1229–1268.

44. Martin, Mary C. Infertility. In DeCherney, Alan H., and Pernoll, Martin L., eds., *Current Obstetric & Gynecologic Diagnosis & Treatment*, 8th ed. Norwalk, CT: Appleton & Lange, 1994, pp. 996–1006.

45. McDonald, John S., and Yarnell, Ralph W. Obstetric analgesia and anesthesia. In DeCherney, Alan H., and Pernoll, Martin L., eds., *Current Obstetric & Gynecologic Diagnosis & Treatment*, 8th ed. Norwalk, CT: Appleton & Lange, 1994, pp. 520–542.

46. Naef, Robert W., III, and Morrison, John C. Guidelines for management of shoulder dystocia. *Journal of Perinatology* 14:435–441, November/December 1994.

47. Novy, Miles J. The normal puerperium. In DeCherney, Alan H., and Pernoll, Martin L., eds., *Current Obstetric & Gynecologic Diagnosis & Treatment*, 8th ed. Norwalk, CT: Appleton & Lange, 1994, pp. 240–174.

48. O'Quinn, April G., and Barnard, David E. Gestational trophoblastic diseases. In DeCherney, Alan H., and Pernoll, Martin L., eds., *Current Obstetric & Gynecologic Diagnosis & Treatment*, 8th ed. Norwalk, CT: Appleton & Lange, 1994, pp. 967–984.

49. Parisi, Valerie M. Cervical incompetence. In Creasy, Robert K., and Resnik, Robert, eds., *Maternal-Fetal Medicine: Principles and Practice*, 3d ed. Philadelphia: W.B. Saunders Co., 1994, pp. 453–466.

50. Parker, Julian T. Fetal heart rate. In Creasy, Robert K., and Resnik, Robert, eds., *Maternal-Fetal Medicine: Principles and Practice*, 3d ed. Philadelphia: W.B. Saunders Co., 1994, pp. 298–325.

51. Pernoll, Martin L. Late pregnancy complications. In DeCherney, Alan H., and Pernoll, Martin L., eds., *Current Obstetric & Gynecologic Diagnosis & Treatment*, 8th ed. Norwalk, CT: Appleton & Lange, 1994, pp. 331–343.

52. ———. Third-trimester hemorrhage. Ibid., pp. 398–409.

53. Pernoll, Martin L., and Garmel, Sara H. Early pregnancy risks. In DeCherney, Alan H., and Pernoll, Martin L., eds., *Current Obstetric & Gynecologic Diagnosis & Treatment*, 8th ed. Norwalk, CT: Appleton & Lange, 1994, pp. 306–330.

54. Pernoll, Martin L., and Taylor, Cathy Mih. Normal pregnancy and prenatal care. In DeCherney, Alan H., and Pernoll, Martin L., eds., *Current Obstetric & Gynecologic Diagnosis & Treatment*, 8th ed. Norwalk, CT: Appleton & Lange, 1994, pp. 183–201.

55. Phibbs, Roderic H. Delivery room management. In Avery, Gordon B., et al., eds., *Neonatology: Pathophysiology and Management of the Newborn*, 4th ed. Philadelphia: J.B. Lippincott Co., 1994, pp. 248–268.

56. Resnik, Robert. The puerperium. In Creasy, Robert K., and Resnik, Robert, eds., *Maternal-Fetal Medicine: Principles and Practice*, 3d ed. Philadelphia: W.B. Saunders Co., 1994, pp. 140–143.

57. ———. Post-term pregnancy. Ibid., pp. 521–526.

58. Roberts, James M. Pregnancy-related hypertension. In Creasy, Robert K., and Resnik, Robert, eds., *Maternal-Fetal Medicine: Principles and Practice*, 3d ed. Philadelphia: W.B. Saunders Co., 1994, pp. 804–843.

59. Scott, James R., and Branch, D. Ware. Immunologic disorders. In Creasy, Robert K., and Resnik, Robert, eds., *Maternal-Fetal Medicine: Principles and Practice*, 3d ed. Philadelphia: W.B. Saunders Co., 1994, pp. 467–481.

60. Simpson, Joe Leigh, and Elias, Sherman. Prenatal diagnosis of genetic disorders. In Creasy, Robert K., and Resnik, Robert, eds., *Maternal-Fetal Medicine: Principles and Practice*, 3d ed. Philadelphia: W.B. Saunders Co., 1994, pp. 61–88.

61. Sokol, Robert J., et al. Methods of pregnancy assessment for pregnancy at risk. In DeCherney, Alan H., and Pernoll, Martin L., eds., *Current Obstetric & Gynecologic Diagnosis & Treatment*, 8th ed. Norwalk, CT: Appleton & Lange, 1994, pp. 275–305.

62. Stenchever, Morton A., and Jones, Howard W., Jr. Genetic disorders and sex chromosome abnormalities. In DeCherney, Alan H., and Pernoll, Martin L., eds., *Current Obstetric & Gynecologic Diagnosis & Treatment*, 8th ed. Norwalk, CT: Appleton & Lange, 1994, pp. 93–123.

63. Turgeon, Ronald, M.D. Personal communications.

64. Varner, Michael W. Disproportionate fetal growth. In DeCherney, Alan H., and Pernoll, Martin L., eds., *Current Obstetric & Gynecologic Diagnosis & Treatment*, 8th ed. Norwalk, CT: Appleton & Lange, 1994, pp. 344–356.

65. Whitsett, Jeffrey A., et al. Acute respiratory disorders. In Avery, Gordon B., et al., eds., *Neonatology: Pathophysiology and Management of the Newborn*, 4th ed. Philadelphia: J.B. Lippincott Co., 1994, pp. 429–452.

66. Woods, James R., Jr., and Glantz, J. Christopher. Significance of amniotic fluid meconium. In Creasy, Robert K., and Resnik, Robert, eds., *Maternal-Fetal Medicine: Principles and Practice*, 3d ed. Philadelphia: W.B. Saunders Co., 1994, pp. 413–421.

67. Yen, S. S. C. Endocrinology of pregnancy. In Creasy, Robert. K., and Resnik, Robert, eds., *Maternal-Fetal Medicine: Principles and Practice*, 3d ed. Philadelphia: W.B. Saunders Co., 1994, pp. 382–412.

68. Yeomans, Edward R., and Gilstrap, Larry C., III. The role of forceps in modern obstetrics. *Clinical Obstetrics and Gynecology* 37:785–793, December 1994.

Chapter 13

1. Alfrey, Allen C. Disorders of magnesium metabolism. In Bennett, J. Claude, and Plum, Fred, eds., *Cecil's Textbook of Medicine*, 20th ed. Philadelphia: W.B. Saunders Co., 1996, pp. 1137–1138.

2. Amino, Nabuyuki, and Tada, Hisato. Autoimmune thyroid disease/thyroiditis. In DeGroot, Leslie J., et al., eds., *Endocrinology*, 3d ed., vol. 1. Philadelphia: W.B. Saunders Co., 1995, pp. 726–741.

3. Arndt, Josephine. The pineal gland: Basic physiology and clinical implications. In DeGroot, Leslie J., et al., eds., *Endocrinology*, 3d ed., vol. 1. Philadelphia: W.B. Saunders Co., 1995, pp. 432–444.

4. Beaudet, Arthur L. Lysosomal storage diseases. In Isselbacher, Kurt J., et al., eds., *Harrison's Principles of Internal Medicine*, 13th ed. New York: McGraw-Hill, Inc., 1994, pp. 2090–2099.

5. ———. The glycogen storage diseases. Ibid., pp. 2099–2105.

6. Beaudet, Arthur L., and Ballabio, Andrea. Molecular genetics and medicine. In Isselbacher, Kurt J., et al., eds., *Harrison's Principles of Internal Medicine*, 13th ed. New York: McGraw-Hill, Inc., 1994, pp. 349–365.

7. Bierman, Edwin L., and Glomset, John A. Disorders of lipid metabolism. In Wilson, Jean D., and Foster, Daniel W., eds., *Williams Textbook of Endocrinology*, 8th ed. Philadelphia: W.B. Saunders Co., 1992, pp. 1367–1395.

8. Bloomer, Joseph R., and Straka, James G. Disorders of porphyrin metabolism. In Stein, Jay H., ed.-in-ch., *Internal Medicine*, 4th ed. St. Louis: Mosby, 1994, pp. 1487–1493.

9. Boyd, Aubrey E., and Gagel, Robert F. Disorders affecting multiple endocrine systems. In Isselbacher, Kurt J., et al., eds., *Harrison's Principles of Internal Medicine*, 13th ed. New York: McGraw-Hill, Inc., 1994, pp. 2052–2058.

10. Brady, Roscoe O., et al. The role of neurogenetics in Gaucher disease. *Archives of Neurology* 50:1212–1224, November 1993.

11. Bravo, Emmanuel L. Evolving concepts in the pathophysiology, diagnosis, and treatment of pheochromocytoma. *Endocrine Reviews* 15:356–368, June 1994.

12. Brewer, Bryan H., Jr., et al. Disorders of lipoprotein metabolism. In DeGroot, Leslie J., et al., eds., *Endocrinology*, 3d ed., vol. 3. Philadelphia: W.B. Saunders Co., 1995, pp. 2731–2753.

13. Brown, Michael S., and Goldstein, Joseph L. The hyperlipoproteinemias and other disorders of lipid metabolism. In Isselbacher, Kurt J., et al., eds., *Harrison's Principles of Internal Medicine*, 13th ed. New York: McGraw-Hill, Inc., 1994, pp. 2058–2069.

14. Browner, Warren S. Lipid abnormalities. In Tierney, Lawrence M., Jr., et al., eds., *Current Medical Diagnosis & Treatment*, 35th ed. Stamford, CT: Appleton & Lange, 1996, pp. 1069–1080.

15. Chin, William W. Hormonal regulation of gene expression. In DeGroot, Leslie J., et al., eds., *Endocrinology*, 3d ed., vol. 1. Philadelphia: W.B. Saunders Co., 1995, pp. 6–16.

16. Comi, Richard J. Approach to acute hypoglycemia. *Endocrinology and Metabolism Clinics of North America* 22:247–262, June 1993.

17. Cooper, Max D., and Lawton, Alexander R., III. Primary immune deficiency diseases. In Isselbacher, Kurt J., et al., eds., *Harrison's Principles of Internal Medicine*, 13th ed. New York: McGraw-Hill, Inc., 1994, pp. 1559–1566.

18. Cryer, Philip E. Orthostatic (postural hypotension). In DeGroot, Leslie J., et al., eds., *Endocrinology*, 3d ed., vol. 3. Philadelphia: W.B. Saunders Co., 1995, pp. 2935–2942.

19. Daniels, Gilbert H., and Martin, Joseph B. Neuroendocrine regulation and

diseases of the anterior pituitary and hypothalamus. In Isselbacher, Kurt J., et al., eds., *Harrison's Principles of Internal Medicine*, 13th ed. New York: McGraw-Hill, Inc., 1994, pp. 1891–1918.

20. Deffos, Leonard J. Calcitonin and medullary thyroid carcinoma. In Bennett, Claude J., and Plum, Fred, eds., *Cecil's Textbook of Medicine*, 20th ed. Philadelphia: W.B. Saunders Co., 1996, pp. 1373–1375.

21. DeGroot, Leslie J. Thyroid neoplasia. In DeGroot, Leslie J., et al., eds., *Endocrinology*, 3d ed., vol. 1. Philadelphia: W.B. Saunders Co., 1995, pp. 834–854.

22. Desnick, Robert J. Porphyrias. In Isselbacher, Kurt J., et al., eds., *Harrison's Principles of Internal Medicine*, 13th ed. New York: McGraw-Hill, Inc., 1994, pp. 2073–2079.

23. Dillmann, Wolfgang H. The thyroid. In Bennett, Claude J., and Plum, Fred, eds., *Cecil's Textbook of Medicine*, 20th ed. Philadelphia: W.B. Saunders Co., 1996, pp. 1227–1245.

24. Ehrlich, Edward N., et al. Hormonal regulation of electrolyte and water metabolism. In DeGroot, Leslie J., et al., eds., *Endocrinology*, 3d ed., vol. 2. Philadelphia: W.B. Saunders Co., 1995, pp. 1685–1710.

25. Elders, Joycelyn, M. Lipodystrophies. In Stein, Jay H., ed.-in-ch., *Internal Medicine*, 4th ed. St. Louis: Mosby, 1994, pp. 1456–1462.

26. Elin, Ronald J. Reference intervals and laboratory values of clinical importance. In Wyngaarden, James B., et al., eds., *Cecil's Textbook of Medicine*, 19th ed. Philadelphia: W.B. Saunders Co., 1992, pp. 2370–2380.

27. Fajans, Stefan S. Diabetes mellitus: Definition, classification, tests. In DeGroot, Leslie J., et al., eds., *Endocrinology*, 3d ed., vol. 2. Philadelphia: W.B. Saunders Co., 1995, pp. 1411–1422.

28. Fitzgerald, Paul A. Endocrinology. In Tierney, Lawrence M., Jr., et al., eds., *Current Medical Diagnosis & Treatment*, 35th ed. Stamford, CT: Appleton & Lange, 1996, pp. 972–1029.

29. Fitzpatrick, Lorraine A., and Arnold, Andrew. Hypoparathyroidism. In DeGroot, Leslie J., et al., eds., *Endocrinology*, 3d ed., vol. 2. Philadelphia: W.B. Saunders Co., 1995, pp. 1123–1135.

30. Forest, M. G. Diagnosis and treatment of disorders of sexual development. In DeGroot, Leslie J., et al., eds., *Endocrinology*, 3d ed., vol. 2. Philadelphia: W.B. Saunders Co., 1995, pp. 1901–1937.

31. Foster, Daniel W. Diabetes mellitus. In Isselbacher, Kurt J., et al., eds., *Harrison's Principles of Internal Medicine*, 13th ed. New York: McGraw-Hill, Inc., 1994, pp. 1979–2000.

32. Foster, Daniel W., and McGarry, J. Dennis. Diabetes mellitus: Acute complications, ketoacidosis, hyperosmolar coma, lactic acidosis. In DeGroot, Leslie J., et al., eds., *Endocrinology*, 3d ed., vol. 2. Philadelphia: W.B. Saunders Co., 1995, pp. 1506–1521.

33. Foster, Daniel W., and Rubenstein, Arthur H. Hypoglycemia. In Isselbacher, Kurt J., et al., eds., *Harrison's Principles of Internal Medicine*, 13th ed. New York: McGraw-Hill, Inc., 1994, pp. 2000–2006.

34. Frenkel, Eugene P. Southwestern Internal Medicine Conference. Gaucher disease: A heterogeneous clinical complex for which effective enzyme replacement has come of age. *American Journal of the Medical Sciences* 305: 331–344, May 1993.

35. Friedman, William F., and Child, John S. Congenital heart disease in the adult. In Isselbacher, Kurt J., et al., eds., *Harrison's Principles of Internal Medicine*, 13th ed. New York: McGraw-Hill, Inc., 1994, pp. 1037–1046.

36. Gagel, Robert F. Multiple endocrine neoplasia type 2. In DeGroot, Leslie J., et al., eds., *Endocrinology*, 3d ed., vol. 3. Philadelphia: W.B. Saunders Co., 1995, pp. 2832–2845.

37. Gagel, Robert F. Multiple endocrine neoplasia type 1: Clinical features and screening. *Endocrinology and Metabolism Clinics of North America* 23:1–18, March 1994.

38. Garber, Alan J. Heritable disorders of carbohydrate metabolism. In Stein, Jay H., ed.-in-ch., *Internal Medicine*, 4th ed. St. Louis: Mosby, 1994, pp. 1430–1436.

39. ———. Lysosomal storage diseases. Ibid., pp. 1472–1483.

40. German, James. Cytogenetic aspects of human disease. In Isselbacher, Kurt J., et al., eds., *Harrison's Principles of Internal Medicine*, 13th ed. New York: McGraw-Hill, Inc., 1994, pp. 366–374.

41. Goldstein, Joseph L., and Brown, Michael S. Genetic aspects of disease. In Isselbacher, Kurt J., et al., eds., *Harrison's Principles of Internal Medicine*, 13th ed. New York: McGraw-Hill, Inc., 1994, pp. 340–349.

42. Goodfellow, Paul J. Mapping the inherited defects associated with multiple endocrine neoplasia type 2A, multiple endocrine neoplasia type 2B, and familial medullary thyroid carcinoma to chromosome 10 by linkage analysis. *Endocrinology and Metabolism Clinics of North America* 23:177–185, March 1994.

43. Greenberger, Norton J., and Isselbacher, Kurt J. Disorders of absorption. In Isselbacher, Kurt J., et al., eds., *Harrison's Principles of Internal Medicine*, 13th ed. New York: McGraw-Hill, Inc., 1994, pp. 1386–1403.

44. Greene, Harry L. The glycogen storage diseases. In Bennett, J. Claude, and Plum, Fred, eds., *Cecil's Textbook of Medicine*, 20th ed. Philadelphia: W.B. Saunders Co., 1996, pp. 1082–1083.

45. Grundy, Scott M. Disorders of lipids and lipoproteins. In Stein, Jay H., ed.-in-ch., *Internal Medicine*, 4th ed. St. Louis: Mosby, 1994, pp. 1436–1456.

46. Habener, Joel, et al. Hyperparathyroidism. In DeGroot, Leslie J., et al., eds., *Endocrinology*, 3d ed., vol. 2. Philadelphia: W.B. Saunders Co., 1995, pp. 1044–1060.

47. Hole, John W. Endocrine system. In *Human Anatomy & Physiology*, 6th ed. Dubuque, IA: Wm. C. Brown Publishers, 1993, pp. 460–497.

48. Holick, Michael F., et al. Calcium, phosphorus, and bone metabolism: Calcium-regulating hormones. In Isselbacher, Kurt J., et al., eds., *Harrison's Principles of Internal Medicine*, 13th ed. New York: McGraw-Hill, Inc., 1994, pp. 2137–2151.

49. Humphreys, Michael H. Fluid and electrolyte management. In Way, Lawrence W., ed., *Current Surgical Diagnosis and Treatment*, 10th ed. Norwalk, CT: Appleton & Lange, 1994, pp. 129–142.

50. Isselbacher, Kurt J. Galactosemia, galactokinase deficiency, and other rare disorders of carbohydrate metabolism. In Isselbacher, Kurt J., et al., eds., *Harrison's Principles of Internal Medicine*, 13th ed. New York: McGraw-Hill, Inc., 1994, pp. 2131–2132.

51. Jameson, J. Larry. Applications of molecular biology in endocrinology. In DeGroot, Leslie J., et al., eds., *Endocrinology*, 3d ed., vol. 1. Philadelphia: W.B. Saunders Co., 1995, pp. 119–150.

52. Jameson, J. Larry. Anterior pituitary. In Bennett, J. Claude, and Plum, Fred, eds., *Cecil's Textbook of Medicine*, 20th ed. Philadelphia: W.B. Saunders Co., 1996, pp. 1205–1221.

53. Jordan, Richard M., and Kohler, Peter O. Laboratory diagnosis in endocrinology. In Stein, Jay H., ed.-in-ch., *Internal Medicine*, 4th ed. St. Louis: Mosby, 1994, pp. 1238–1253.

54. Kaplan, Edwin L., et al. Surgery of the thyroid. In DeGroot, Leslie J., et al., eds., *Endocrinology*, 3d ed., vol. 1. Philadelphia: W.B. Saunders Co., 1995, pp. 900–916.

55. Karam, John H. Diabetes mellitus and hypoglycemia. In Tierney, Lawrence M., Jr., et al., eds., *Current Medical Diagnosis & Treatment*, 35th ed. Stamford, CT: Appleton & Lange, 1996, pp. 1030–1068.

56. Keiser, Harry R. Pheochromocytoma and related tumors. In DeGroot, Leslie J., et al., eds., *Endocrinology*, 3d ed., vol. 2. Philadelphia: W.B. Saunders Co., 1995, pp. 1853–1880.

57. Klee, George G. Biochemical thyroid function testing. *Mayo Clinic Proceedings* 69:469–470, May 1994.

58. Kokko, Juha P. Disorders of fluid volume, electrolyte, and acid-base balance. In Bennett, J. Claude, and Plum, Fred, eds., *Cecil's Textbook of Medicine*, 20th ed. Philadelphia: W.B. Saunders Co., 1996, pp. 525–551.

59. Lange, Ethan, et al. Localization of an ataxia-telangiectasia gene to an 500-kb interval on chromosome 11q23.1: Linkage analysis of 176 families by an international consortium. *American Journal of Human Genetics* 57:112–119, July 1995.

60. Larsson, Catharina, and Friedman, Eitan. Localization and identification of the multiple endocrine neoplasia type 1 disease gene. *Endocrinology and Metabolism Clinics of North America* 23:67–79, March 1994.

61. Lernmark, Åle. Insulin-dependent (type 1) diabetes: Etiology, pathogenesis, and natural history. In DeGroot, Leslie J., et al., eds., *Endocrinology*, 3d ed., vol. 2. Philadelphia: W.B. Saunders Co., 1995, pp. 1423–1435.

62. Loriaux, D. Lynn. Adrenal cortex. In Bennett, J. Claude, and Plum, Fred, eds., *Cecil's Textbook of Medicine*, 20th ed. Philadelphia: W.B. Saunders Co., 1996, pp. 1245–1252.

63. Matsumoto, Alvin M. The testis. In Bennett, J. Claude, and Plum, Fred, eds., *Cecil's Textbook of Medicine*, 20th ed. Philadelphia: W.B. Saunders Co., 1996, pp. 1325–1341.

64. McGovern, Margaret M., and Desnick, Robert J. Lysosomal storage diseases. In Bennett, J. Claude, and Plum, Fred, eds., *Cecil's Textbook of Medicine*, 20th ed. Philadelphia: W.B. Saunders Co., 1996, pp. 1095–1099.

65. McKenzie, J. Maxwell, and Zakarija, Margita. Hyperthyroidism. In DeGroot, Leslie J., et al., eds., *Endocrinology*, 3d ed., vol. 1. Philadelphia: W.B. Saunders Co., 1995, pp. 676–711.

66. Miller, Jeffrey W., and Crapo, Lawrence. The medical treatment of Cushing's syndrome. *Endocrine Reviews* 14:443–458, August 1993.

67. Moses, Robb E., and Magenis, R. Ellen. Principles of genetic disorders. In Stein, Jay H., ed.-in-ch., *Internal Medicine*, 4th ed. St. Louis: Mosby, 1994, pp. 1222–1238.

68. Nelkin, Barry D., et al. Molecular abnormalities in tumors associated with multiple endocrine neoplasia type 2. *Endocrinology and Metabolism Clinics of North America* 23:187–213, March 1994.

69. Nieman, L. K., and Cutler, G. B., Jr. Cushing's syndrome. In DeGroot, Leslie J., et al., eds., *Endocrinology*, 3d ed., vol. 2. Philadelphia: W.B. Saunders Co., 1995, pp. 1741–1769.

70. Norton, Jeffrey A., and Sugg, Sonia L. Surgical management of hyperparathyroidism. In DeGroot, Leslie J., et al., eds., *Endocrinology*, 3d ed., vol. 2. Philadelphia: W.B. Saunders Co., 1995, pp. 1106–1122.

71. Nowak, Rachel. Discovery of AT gene sparks biomedial research bonanza. *Science* 268:1700–1701, 23 June 1995.

72. Olefsky, Jerrold M. Diabetes mellitus (type II): Etiology and pathogenesis. In DeGroot, Leslie J., et al., eds., *Endocrinology*, 3d ed., vol. 2. Philadelphia: W.B. Saunders Co., 1995, pp. 1436–1463.

73. Papadakis, Maxine A. Fluid and electrolyte disorders. In Tierney, Lawrence M., Jr., et al., eds., *Current Medical Diagnosis & Treatment*, 35th ed. Stamford, CT: Appleton & Lange, 1996, pp. 768–794.

74. Parker, Frank. Skin diseases of general importance. In Bennett, J. Claude, and Plum, Fred, eds., *Cecil's Textbook of Medicine*, 20th ed. Philadelphia: W.B. Saunders Co., 1996, pp. 2197–2220.

75. Posner, Jerome B. Disorders of sensation—Headache and other head pain. In Bennett, J. Claude, and Plum, Fred, eds., *Cecil's Textbook of Medicine*, 20th ed. Philadelphia: W.B. Saunders Co., 1996, pp. 2031–2036.

76. Potts, John T., et al. Parathyroid hormone: Physiology, chemistry, biosynthesis, secretion, metabolism, and mode of action. In DeGroot, Leslie J., et al., eds., *Endocrinology*, 3d ed., vol. 2. Philadelphia: W.B. Saunders Co., 1995, pp. 920–967.

77. Pyeritz, Reed E. Medical genetics. In Tierney, Lawrence M., Jr., et al., eds., *Current Medical Diagnosis & Treatment*, 35th ed. Stamford, CT: Appleton & Lange, 1996, pp. 1417–1437.

78. Raue, Friedhelm, et al. Multiple endocrine neoplasia type 2: Clinical features and screening. *Endocrinology and Metabolism Clinics of North America* 23:137–156, March 1994.

79. Reichlin, Seymour. Endocrine-immune interaction. In DeGroot, Leslie J., et al., eds., *Endocrinology*, 3d ed., vol. 3. Philadelphia: W.B. Saunders Co., 1995, pp. 2964–2989.

80. Robinson, Alan G. Posterior pituitary. In Bennett, J. Claude, and Plum, Fred, eds., *Cecil's Textbook of Medicine*, 20th ed. Philadelphia: W.B. Saunders Co., 1996, pp. 1221–1226.

81. Rolih, Catherine A., and Ober, K. Patrick. Pituitary apoplexy. *Endocrinology and Metabolism Clinics of North America* 22:291–302, June 1993.

82. Rosenberg, Leon E. Inherited disorders of amino acid metabolism and storage. In Isselbacher, Kurt J., et al., eds., *Harrison's Principles of Internal Medicine*, 13th ed. New York: McGraw-Hill, Inc., 1994, pp. 2117–2125.

83. Rothwell, Norman V. Chromosomes and distribution of the genetic material. In *Understanding Genetics: A Molecular Approach*. New York: Wiley-Liss Publication, 1993, pp. 15–33.

84. ———. Chromosomes and gamete formation. Ibid., pp. 35–53.

85. ———. Sex and inheritance. Ibid., pp. 91–126.

86. ———. Changes in chromosome structure and number. Ibid., pp. 183–209.

87. ———. Glossary. Ibid., pp. 609–624.

88. Sarne, David H., and Refetoff, Samuel. Thyroid function tests. In DeGroot, Leslie J., et al., eds., *Endocrinology*, 3d ed., vol. 1. Philadelphia: W.B. Saunders Co., 1995, pp. 617–664.

89. Savitsky, Kinneret, et al. A single ataxia telangiectasia gene with a product similar to PI-3 kinase. *Science* 268: 1749–1753.

90. Service, E. John. Hypoglycemia, including hypoglycemia in neonates and children. In DeGroot, Leslie J., et al., eds., *Endocrinology*, 3d ed., vol. 2. Philadelphia: W.B. Saunders Co., 1995, pp. 1605–1623.

91. Skogseid, Britt, et al. Multiple endocrine neoplasia, type 1: Clinical features and screening. *Endocrinology and Metabolism Clinics of North America* 23:1–18, March, 1994.

92. Soergel, Konrad H. Pancreatitis. In Bennett, J. Claude, and Plum, Fred, eds., *Cecil's Textbook of Medicine*, 20th ed. Philadelphia: W.B. Saunders Co., 1996, pp. 729–736.

93. Speroff, Leon, et al. Molecular biology for clinicians. In *Clinical Gynecologic Endocrinology and Infertility*, 5th ed. Baltimore: Williams & Wilkins, 1994, pp. 3–29.

94. ———. Hormone biosynthesis, metabolism, and mechanisms of action. Ibid., pp. 31–92.

95. ———. Clinical assays. Ibid., pp. 967–989.

96. Spiegel, Allen M. The parathyroid glands, hypercalcemia, and hypocalcemia. In Bennett, J. Claude,

and Plum, Fred, eds., *Cecil's Textbook of Medicine*, 20th ed. Philadelphia: W.B. Saunders Co., 1996, pp. 1365–1373.

97. Studer, Hugo, and Gerber, Hans. Multinodular goiter. In DeGroot, Leslie J., et al., ed., *Endocrinology*, 3d, ed., vol. 3. Philadelphia: W.B. Saunders Co., 1995, pp. 769–782.

98. Tefferi, A., et al. Porphyrias: Clinical evaluation and interpretation of laboratory tests. *Mayo Clinic Proceedings* 69:289–290, March 1994.

99. Thakker, Rajesh V. The role of molecular genetics in screening for multiple endocrine neoplasia type 1. *Endocrinology and Metabolism Clinics of North America* 23:117–135, March 1994.

100. Thoene, Jess G. Disorders of amino acid metabolism. In Stein, Jay H., ed.-in-ch., Internal Medicine, 4th ed. St. Louis: Mosby, 1994, pp. 1462–1472.

101. Turgeon, Ronald, M.D. Personal communications.

102. Uhrhammer, Nancy, et al. Sublocation of an ataxia-telangiectasia gene distal to D11S384 by ancestral haplotyping in Costa Rican families. *American Journal of Human Genetics* 57:103–111, July 1995.

103. Utiger, Robert D. Hypothyroidism. In DeGroot, Leslie J., et al., eds., *Endocrinology*, 3d ed., vol. 1. Philadelphia: W.B. Saunders Co., 1995, pp. 752–768.

104. Van De Graaff, Kent M. Endocrine system. In *Human Anatomy*, 4th ed. Dubuque, IA: Wm. C. Brown Publishers, 1995, pp. 431–460.

105. Vinik, Aaron I., and Renar, Ivana Pavlic. Neuroendocrine tumors of carcinoid variety. In DeGroot, Leslie J., et al., ed., *Endocrinology*, 3d ed., vol. 3. Philadelphia: W.B. Saunders Co., 1995, pp. 2803–2814.

106. Wells, Samuel A., Jr., and Donis-Keller, Helen. Current perspectives on the diagnosis and management of patients with multiple endocrine neoplasia type 2 syndromes. *Endocrinology and Metabolism Clinics of North America* 23:215–228, March 1994.

107. Wells, Samuel A., Jr., and Soybel, David I. The pituitary and adrenal glands. In Sabiston, David C., Jr., ed., *Textbook of Surgery*, 14th ed. Philadelphia: W.B. Saunders Co., 1991, pp. 616–654.

108. Werbel, Sandra S., and Ober, K. Patrick. Acute adrenal insufficiency. *Endocrinology and Metabolism Clinics of North America* 22:303–328, June 1994.

109. Wilson, Jean D., and Griffin, James E. Disorders of sexual differentiation. In Isselbacher, Kurt J., et al., eds., *Harrison's Principles of Internal Medicine*, 13th ed. New York: McGraw-Hill, Inc., 1994, pp. 2039–2051.

110. Wortmann, Robert L. Gout and other disorders of purine metabolism. In Isselbacher, Kurt J., et al., eds., *Harrison's Principles of Internal Medicine*, 13th ed. New York: McGraw-Hill, Inc., 1994, pp. 2079–2088.

Chapter 14

1. Abelson, Mark B., et al. Allergic and toxic reactions. In Albert, Daniel M., and Jakobiec, Frederick A., eds., *Principles and Practice of Ophthalmology*, vol. 1. Philadelphia: W.B. Saunders Co., 1994, pp. 77–100.

2. Adamis, Anthony P., and Scheim, Oliver D. *Chlamydia* and *Acanthamoeba* infections of the eye. In Albert, Daniel M., and Jakobiec, Frederick A., eds., *Principles and Practice of Ophthalmology*, vol. 1. Philadelphia: W.B. Saunders Co., 1994, pp. 179–190.

3. Aiello, Lloyd M. Diagnosis, management, and treatment of nonproliferative diabetic retinopathy and macular edema. In Albert, Daniel M., and Jakobiec, Frederick A., eds., *Principles and Practice of Ophthalmology*, vol. 2. Philadelphia: W.B. Saunders Co., 1994, pp. 747–760.

4. Armesto, David, and Goosey, John D. Herpes simplex keratitis. In Margo, Curtis E., ed., *Diagnostic Problems in Clinical Ophthalmology*. Philadelphia: W.B. Saunders Co., 1994, pp. 189–198.

5. Bajart, Ann M. Lid inflammations. In Albert, Daniel M., and Jakobiec, Frederick A., eds., *Principles and Practice of Ophthalmology*, vol. 1. Philadelphia: W.B. Saunders Co., 1994, pp. 101–116.

6. Beck, Roy W. Optic neuritis. In Margo, Curtis E., ed., *Diagnostic Problems in Clinical Ophthalmology*. Philadelphia: W.B. Saunders Co., 1994, pp. 639–643.

7. Belcher, C. Davis, III, and Greff, Linda J. Laser therapy of angle-closure glaucoma. In Albert, Daniel M., and Jakobiec, Frederick A., eds., *Principles and Practice of Ophthalmology*, vol. 3. Philadelphia: W.B. Saunders Co., 1994, pp. 1597–1609.

8. Berson, Eliot L. Retinitis pigmentosa and allied diseases. In Albert, Daniel M., and Jakobiec, Frederick A., eds., *Principles and Practice of Ophthalmology*, vol. 2. Philadelphia: W.B. Saunders Co., 1994, pp. 1214–1237.

9. Bienfang, Don C. Neuroophthalmology of the pupil and accommodation. In Albert, Daniel M., and Jakobiec, Frederick A., eds., *Principles and Practice of Ophthalmology*, vol. 4. Philadelphia: W.B. Saunders Co., 1994, pp. 2470–2482.

10. Blumenkranz, Mark S., et al. Acute retinal necrosis. In Albert, Daniel M., and Jakobiec, Frederick A., eds., *Principles and Practice of Ophthalmology*, vol. 2. Philadelphia: W.B. Saunders Co., 1994, pp. 945–962.

11. Boruchoff, S. Arthur. Penetrating keratoplasty. In Albert, Daniel M., and Jakobiec, Frederick A., eds., *Principles and Practice of Ophthalmology*, vol. 1. Philadelphia: W.B. Saunders Co., 1994, pp. 325–337.

12. Bozkir, Naci, and Stern, George A. Chronic conjunctivitis. In Margo, Curtis E., ed., *Diagnostic Problems in Clinical Ophthalmology*. Philadelphia: W.B. Saunders Co., 1994, pp. 139–150.

13. Bressler, Neil M., et al. Age-related macular degeneration: Choroidal neovascularization. In Albert, Daniel M., and Jakobiec, Frederick A., eds., *Principles and Practice of Ophthalmology*, vol. 2. Philadelphia: W.B. Saunders Co., 1994, pp. 834–852.

14. Bressler, Susan B., et al. Age-related macular degeneration: Drusen and geographic atrophy. In Albert, Daniel M., and Jakobiec, Frederick A., eds., *Principles and Practice of Ophthalmology*, vol. 2. Philadelphia: W.B. Saunders Co., 1994, pp. 826–833.

15. Bryan, J. Shepard, and Hamed, Latif M. Optic disc swelling. In Margo, Curtis E., ed., *Diagnostic Problems in Clinical Ophthalmology*. Philadelphia: W.B. Saunders Co., 1994, pp. 644–656.

16. Bullross, Melanie, and Stern George A. Acute conjunctivitis. In Margo, Curtis E., ed., *Diagnostic Problems in Clinical Ophthalmology*. Philadelphia: W.B. Saunders Co., 1994, pp. 130–138.

17. Caplan, Louis R. Transient ischemia and brain and ocular infarction. In Albert, Daniel M., and Jakobiec, Frederick A., eds., *Principles and Practice of Ophthalmology*, vol. 4. Philadelphia: W.B. Saunders Co., 1994, pp. 2653–2669.

18. Chang, David F. Ophthalmologic examination. In Vaughn, Daniel G., et al., eds., *General Ophthalmology*, 14th ed. Norwalk, CT: Appleton & Lange, 1995, pp. 29–61.

19. Chylack, Leo T., et al. Prediction of postoperative visual function in cataract patients. In Albert, Daniel M., and Jakobiec, Frederick A., eds., *Principles and Practice of Ophthalmology*, vol. 1. Philadelphia: W.B. Saunders Co., 1994, pp. 669–682.

20. Cyrlin, Marshall N. Malignant glaucoma. In Albert, Daniel M., and

Jakobiec, Frederick A., eds., *Principles and Practice of Ophthalmology*, vol. 3. Philadelphia: W.B. Saunders Co., 1994, pp. 1520–1528.

21. D'Amico, Donald J. Vitreoretinal surgery: Principles and applications. In Albert, Daniel M., and Jakobiec, Frederick A., eds., *Principles and Practice of Ophthalmology*, vol. 2. Philadelphia: W.B. Saunders Co., 1994, pp. 1121–1142.

22. Destro, Maryanna, and Gragoudas, E. S. Arterial occlusions. In Albert, Daniel M., and Jakobiec, Frederick A., eds., *Principles and Practice of Ophthalmology*, vol. 2. Philadelphia: W.B. Saunders Co., 1994, pp. 727–735.

23. ———. Coats' disease and retinal telangiectasia. Ibid., vol. 2, pp. 801–809.

24. Dieckert, J. Paul. Posterior segment trauma. In Albert, Daniel M., and Jakobiec, Frederick A., eds., *Principles and Practice of Ophthalmology*, vol. 5. Philadelphia: W.B. Saunders Co., 1994, pp. 3403–3425.

25. Doyle, J. William, and Sherwood, Mark B. Malignant glaucoma. In Margo, Curtis E., ed., *Diagnostic Problems in Clinical Ophthalmology*. Philadelphia: W.B. Saunders Co., 1994, pp. 293–297.

26. Drake, Michael V. Glaucomatous visual field loss. In Albert, Daniel M., and Jakobiec, Frederick A., eds., *Principles and Practice of Ophthalmology*, vol. 3. Philadelphia: W.B. Saunders Co., 1994, pp. 1301–1310.

27. Driebe, William T., Jr. Exogenous endophthalmitis. In Margo, Curtis E., ed., *Diagnostic Problems in Clinical Ophthalmology*. Philadelphia: W.B. Saunders Co., 1994, pp. 394–401.

28. Eagle, Ralph C., Jr. Congenital, developmental, and degenerative disorders of the iris and ciliary body. In Albert, Daniel M., and Jakobiec, Frederick A., eds., *Principles and Practice of Ophthalmology*, vol. 1. Philadelphia: W.B. Saunders Co., 1994, pp. 367–389.

29. Ebert, Eleanore M., and Albert, Daniel M. The phakomatoses. In Albert, Daniel M., and Jakobiec, Frederick A., eds., *Principles and Practice of Ophthalmology*, vol. 5. Philadelphia: W.B. Saunders Co., 1994, pp. 3301–3328.

30. Feldon, Steven E. Tumors of the anterior visual pathways. In Albert, Daniel M., and Jakobiec, Frederick A., eds., *Principles and Practice of Ophthalmology*, vol. 4. Philadelphia: W.B. Saunders Co., 1994, pp. 2578–2592.

31. Floyd, Richard P. History of cataract surgery. In Albert, Daniel M., and Jakobiec, Frederick A., eds., *Principles and Practice of Ophthalmology*, vol. 1. Philadelphia: W.B. Saunders Co., 1994, pp. 606–613.

32. ———. The intracapsular cataract extraction. Ibid., pp. 613–621.

33. Foster, C. Stephen. Immunologic disorders of the conjunctiva, cornea, and sclera. In Albert, Daniel M., and Jakobiec, Frederick A., eds., *Principles and Practice of Ophthalmology*, vol. 1. Philadelphia: W.B. Saunders Co., 1994, pp. 191–217.

34. ———. Lamellar keratoplasty. Ibid., vol. 1, pp. 319–325.

35. Foster, J. David, and Rao, Narsing A. Scleritis. In Margo, Curtis E., ed., *Diagnostic Problems in Clinical Ophthalmology*. Philadelphia: W.B. Saunders Co., 1994, pp. 261–267.

36. Foulks, Gary N. Bacterial infections of the conjunctiva and cornea. In Albert, Daniel M., and Jakobiec, Frederick A., eds., *Principles and Practice of Ophthalmology*, vol. 1. Philadelphia: W.B. Saunders Co., 1994, pp. 162–172.

37. Friberg, Thomas R. Examination of the retina: Ophthalmoscopy and fundus biomicroscopy. In Albert, Daniel M., and Jakobiec, Frederick A., eds., *Principles and Practice of Ophthalmology*, vol. 2. Philadelphia: W.B. Saunders Co., 1994, pp. 686–697.

38. Fricker, Stephen J. Adult strabismus. In Albert, Daniel M., and Jakobiec, Frederick A., eds., *Principles and Practice of Ophthalmology*, vol. 4. Philadelphia: W.B. Saunders Co., 1994, pp. 2736–2754.

39. Gilbard, Jeffrey P. Dry eye disorders. In Albert, Daniel M., and Jakobiec, Frederick A., eds., *Principles and Practice of Ophthalmology*, vol. 1. Philadelphia: W.B. Saunders Co., 1994, pp. 257–276.

40. Goldstein, Sanford M., and Odom, Richard B. Skin and appendages. In Tierney, Lawrence M., et al., eds., *Current Medical Diagnosis & Treatment*, 35th ed. Stamford, CT: Appleton & Lange, 1996, pp. 89–155.

41. Guyer, David R., and Gragoudas, E. S. Central serous chorioretinopathy. In Albert, Daniel M., and Jakobiec, Frederick A., eds., *Principles and Practice of Ophthalmology*, vol. 2. Philadelphia: W.B. Saunders Co., 1994, pp. 818–825.

42. Haynie, Gary D., and D'Amico, Donald J. Scleral buckling surgery. In Albert, Daniel M., and Jakobiec, Frederick A., eds., *Principles and Practice of Ophthalmology*, vol. 2. Philadelphia: W.B. Saunders Co., 1994, pp. 1092–1110.

43. Hirose, Tatsuo. Retinoschisis. In Albert, Daniel M., and Jakobiec, Frederick A., eds., *Principles and Practice of Ophthalmology*, vol. 2. Philadelphia: W.B. Saunders Co., 1994, pp. 1071–1084.

44. Karcioglu, T. Tumors of the optic nerve. In Margo, Curtis E., ed., *Diagnostic Problems in Clinical Ophthalmology*. Philadelphia: W.B. Saunders Co., 1994, pp. 105–114.

45. Kelley, Curtin G. Interstitial keratitis. In Margo, Curtis E., ed., *Diagnostic Problems in Clinical Ophthalmology*. Philadelphia: W.B. Saunders Co., 1994, pp. 215–219.

46. King, W. T., et al. Sympathetic ophthalmia. In Albert, Daniel M., and Jakobiec, Frederick A., eds., *Principles and Practice of Ophthalmology*, vol. 1. Philadelphia: W.B. Saunders Co., 1994, pp. 496–503.

47. Kroll, Arnold J., and Patel, Samir C. Retinal breaks. In Albert, Daniel M., and Jakobiec, Frederick A., eds., *Principles and Practice of Ophthalmology*, vol. 1. Philadelphia: W.B. Saunders Co., 1994, pp. 1056–1063.

48. Lawrence, Mary Gilbert. Extracapsular cataract extraction. In Albert, Daniel M., and Jakobiec, Frederick A., eds., *Principles and Practice of Ophthalmology*, vol. 1. Philadelphia: W.B. Saunders Co., 1994, pp. 621–640.

49. Lee, Paul P., et al. Penetrating keratoplasty and glaucoma. In Albert, Daniel M., and Jakobiec, Frederick A., eds., *Principles and Practice of Ophthalmology*, vol. 3. Philadelphia: W.B. Saunders Co., 1994, pp. 1541–1551.

50. Levin, Marc R., and Gragoudas, Evangelos S. Retinal arterial macroaneurysms. In Albert, Daniel M., and Jakobiec, Frederick A., eds., *Principles and Practice of Ophthalmology*, vol. 2. Philadelphia: W.B. Saunders Co., 1994, pp. 795–801.

51. Mao, Lisa Kay, et al. Endophthalmitis caused by *Staphylococcus aureus*. *American Journal of Ophthalmology* 116:584–589.

52. McDermott, John A. Tonometry and tonography. In Albert, Daniel M., and Jakobiec, Frederick A., eds., *Principles and Practice of Ophthalmology*, vol. 3. Philadelphia: W.B. Saunders Co., 1994, pp. 1329–1335.

53. McMeel, J. Wallace. Uveal tract circulatory problems. In Albert, Daniel M., and Jakobiec, Frederick A., eds., *Principles and Practice of Ophthalmology*, vol. 1. Philadelphia: W.B. Saunders Co., 1994, pp. 389–396.

54. Miller, Joan W., and D'Amico, Donald J. Proliferative diabetic retinopathy. In Albert, Daniel M., and Jakobiec, Frederick A., eds., *Principles and Practice of Ophthalmology*, vol. 2. Philadelphia: W.B. Saunders Co., 1994, pp. 760–782.

55. Mukai, Shizuo, and Gragoudas, Evangelos S. Diagnosis of choroidal melanoma. In Albert, Daniel M., and

Jakobiec, Frederick A., eds., *Principles and Practice of Ophthalmology*, vol. 5. Philadelphia: W.B. Saunders Co., 1994, pp. 3209–3217.

56. Mulet, Miguel, and Kastl, Peter R. Keratoconus. In Margo, Curtis E., ed., *Diagnostic Problems in Clinical Ophthalmology*. Philadelphia: W.B. Saunders Co., 1994, pp. 255–260.

57. O'Brien, Joan M., et al. Anterior uveitis. In Albert, Daniel M., and Jakobiec, Frederick A., eds., *Principles and Practice of Ophthalmology*, vol. 1. Philadelphia: W.B. Saunders Co., 1994, pp. 407–423.

58. Okada, Annabelle A., and D'Amico, Donald J. Endogenous endophthalmitis. In Albert, Daniel M., and Jakobiec, Frederick A., eds., *Principles and Practice of Ophthalmology*, vol. 5. Philadelphia: W.B. Saunders Co., 1994, pp. 3120–3126.

59. Olsen, Karl R., and Curtin, Victor T. Enucleation and plaque treatment. In Albert, Daniel M., and Jakobiec, Frederick A., eds., *Principles and Practice of Ophthalmology*, vol. 5. Philadelphia: W.B. Saunders Co., 1994, pp. 3217–3233.

60. Pavan-Langston, Deborah. Viral diseases of the cornea and external eye. In Albert, Daniel M., and Jakobiec, Frederick A., eds., *Principles and Practice of Ophthalmology*, vol. 1. Philadelphia: W.B. Saunders Co., 1994, pp. 117–161.

61. Purdy, Eric P., and Bullock, John D. Acute dacryocystitis. In Margo, Curtis E., ed., *Diagnostic Problems in Clinical Ophthalmology*. Philadelphia: W.B. Saunders Co., 1994, pp. 119–127.

62. Richter, Claudia U. Laser therapy of open-angle glaucoma. In Albert, Daniel M., and Jakobiec, Frederick A., eds., *Principles and Practice of Ophthalmology*, vol. 3. Philadelphia: W.B. Saunders Co., 1994, pp. 1588–1595.

63. Riodan-Eva, Paul. Anatomy and embryology of the eye. In *General Ophthalmology*, 14th ed. Norwalk, CT: Appleton & Lange, 1995, pp. 1–28.

64. Riordan-Eva, Paul, and Vaughann, Daniel G. Eye. In Tierney, Lawrence M., et al., eds., *Current Medical Diagnosis & Treatment*, 35th ed. Stamford, CT: Appleton & Lange, 1996, pp. 156–180.

65. Sadun, Alfredo A. Optic atrophy and papilledema. In Albert, Daniel M., and Jakobiec, Frederick A., eds., *Principles and Practice of Ophthalmology*, vol. 4. Philadelphia: W.B. Saunders Co., 1994, pp. 2529–2538.

66. Sahel, José A., et al. Pathology of the uveal tract. In Albert, Daniel M., and Jakobiec, Frederick A., eds., *Principles and Practice of Ophthalmology*, vol. 4. Philadelphia: W.B. Saunders Co., 1994, pp. 2145–2179.

67. Sahel, José A., et al. Pathology of the retina and vitreous. In Albert, Daniel M., and Jakobiec, Frederick A., eds., *Principles and Practice of Ophthalmology*, vol. 4. Philadelphia: W.B. Saunders Co., 1994, pp. 2239–2280.

68. Samuelson, Thomas W. Low tension glaucoma. In Margo, Curtis E., ed., *Diagnostic Problems in Clinical Ophthalmology*. Philadelphia: W.B. Saunders Co., 1994, pp. 284–292.

69. Saornil, Maria A., and Allingham, R. Rand. Pathology of glaucoma. In Albert, Daniel M., and Jakobiec, Frederick A., eds., *Principles and Practice of Ophthalmology*, vol. 4. Philadelphia: W.B. Saunders Co., 1994, pp. 2280–2288.

70. Saunders, Richard A. Ambylopia. In Margo, Curtis E., ed., *Diagnostic Problems in Clinical Ophthalmology*. Philadelphia: W.B. Saunders Co., 1994, pp. 745–750.

71. Schott, Louis J., and Allen, Robert C. Angle-closure glaucoma. In Margo, Curtis E., ed., *Diagnostic Problems in Clinical Ophthalmology*. Philadelphia: W.B. Saunders Co., 1994, pp. 298–305.

72. Snebold, Neal G. Noninfectious orbital inflammations and vasculitis. In Albert, Daniel M., and Jakobiec, Frederick A., eds., *Principles and Practice of Ophthalmology*, vol. 3. Philadelphia: W.B. Saunders Co., 1994, pp. 1923–1942.

73. Sofinski, Sandra J., and Burke, Joseph F., Jr. Glaucoma associated with disorders of the retina, vitreous, and choroid. In Albert, Daniel M., and Jakobiec, Frederick A., eds., *Principles and Practice of Ophthalmology*, vol. 3. Philadelphia: W.B. Saunders Co., 1994, pp. 1551–1568.

74. Starck, Tomy, et al. Corneal dysgeneses, dystrophies, and degenerations. In Albert, Daniel M., and Jakobiec, Frederick A., eds., *Principles and Practice of Ophthalmology*, vol. 1. Philadelphia: W.B. Saunders Co., 1994, pp. 13–77.

75. Stern, George A. Ulcerative keratitis. In Margo, Curtis E., ed., *Diagnostic Problems in Clinical Ophthalmology*. Philadelphia: W.B. Saunders Co., 1994, pp. 199–209.

76. Streeten, Barbara W. Pathology of the lens. In Albert, Daniel M., and Jakobiec, Frederick A., eds., *Principles and Practice of Ophthalmology*, vol. 4. Philadelphia: W.B. Saunders Co., 1994, pp. 2180–2239.

77. Talmo, Jonathan H., and Steinert, Roger F. Keratorefractive surgery. In Albert, Daniel M., and Jakobiec, Frederick A., eds., *Principles and Practice of Ophthalmology*, vol. 1. Philadelphia: W.B. Saunders Co., 1994, pp. 342–362

78. Tortora, Christopher M., et al. Optics of intraocular lenses. In Albert, Daniel M., and Jakobiec, Frederick A., eds., *Principles and Practice of Ophthalmology*, vol. 5. Philadelphia: W.B. Saunders Co., 1994, pp. 3648–3663.

79. Tortora, Gerard J., and Grabowski, Sandra R. The special senses. In *Principles of Anatomy and Physiology*, 7th ed. New York: HarperCollins College Publishers, 1993, pp. 465–515.

80. Vaughn, Daniel G., et al. Glossary of terms relating to the eye. In *General Ophthalmology*, 14th ed. Norwalk, CT: Appleton & Lange, 1995, pp. 419–422.

81. Weber, Alfred L. Radiologic evaluation of the globe. In Albert, Daniel M., and Jakobiec, Frederick A., eds., *Principles and Practice of Ophthalmology*, vol. 5. Philadelphia: W.B. Saunders Co., 1994, pp. 3511–3520.

82. Weinberg, David V., and Seddon, Johanna M. Venous occlusive diseases of the retina. In Albert, Daniel M., and Jakobiec, Frederick A., eds., *Principles and Practice of Ophthalmology*, vol. 2. Philadelphia: W.B. Saunders Co., 1994, pp. 735–746.

83. Weiss, Jayne S. Conjunctival and corneal pathology. In Albert, Daniel M., and Jakobiec, Frederick A., eds., *Principles and Practice of Ophthalmology*, vol. 4. Philadelphia: W.B. Saunders Co., 1994, pp. 2126–2145.

84. Wilson, M. Roy. Peripheral iridectomy and chamber deepening. In Albert, Daniel M., and Jakobiec, Frederick A., eds., *Principles and Practice of Ophthalmology*, vol. 3. Philadelphia: W.B. Saunders Co., 1994, pp. 1618–1622.

85. Wray, Shirley H. Optic neuritis. In Albert, Daniel M., and Jakobiec, Frederick A., eds., *Principles and Practice of Ophthalmology*, vol. 4. Philadelphia: W.B. Saunders Co., 1994, pp. 2539–2568.

86. Young, Lucy H. Y., and D'Amico, Donald J. Retinal detachment. In Albert, Daniel M., and Jakobiec, Frederick A., eds., *Principles and Practice of Ophthalmology*, vol. 2. Philadelphia: W.B. Saunders Co., 1994, pp. 1084–1092.

Chapter 15

1. Adour, Kedar Karim. Facial paralysis. In Ballenger, John Jacob, and Snow, James B., Jr., eds., *Otorhinolaryngology: Head and Neck Surgery*, 15th ed. Baltimore: Williams & Wilkins, 1996, pp. 1153–1165.

2. Alberti, Peter W. Occupational hearing loss. In Ballenger, John Jacob, and Snow, James B., Jr., eds., *Otorhinolaryngology: Head and Neck Surgery*, 15th ed. Baltimore: Williams & Wilkins, 1996, pp. 1087–1101.

3. Austin, David F. Anatomy of the ear. In Ballenger, John Jacob, and Snow, James B., Jr., eds., *Otorhinolaryngology: Head and Neck Surgery*, 15th ed. Baltimore: Williams & Wilkins, 1996, pp. 838–857.

4. ———. Diseases of the external ear. Ibid., pp. 974–988.

5. ———. Chronic otitis media. Ibid., pp. 1010–1036.

6. ———. Complications of acute and chronic otitis media. Ibid., pp. 1037–1053.

7. ———. Otosclerosis. Ibid., pp. 1054–1063.

8. Daroff, Robert B. Dizziness and vertigo. In Isselbacher, Kurt J., et al., eds., *Harrison's Principles of Internal Medicine*, 13th ed. New York: McGraw-Hill, Inc., 1994, pp. 96–98.

9. Gacek, Richard R. Surgery of the vestibular system. In Harker, Lee A., ed., *Otolaryngology—Head and Neck Surgery*, 2d ed., vol. 4. St. Louis: Mosby Year Book, 1993, pp. 3199–3216.

10. Hall, James W., III, et al. Diagnostic audiology and hearing aids. In Ballenger, John Jacob, and Snow, James B., Jr., eds., *Otorhinolaryngology: Head and Neck Surgery*, 15th ed. Baltimore: Williams & Wilkins, 1996, pp. 953–973.

11. Harris, Jeffrey P., and Ruckenstein, Michael J. Sudden sensorineural hearing loss, perilymph fistula and autoimmune inner ear disease. In Ballenger, John Jacob, and Snow, James B., Jr., eds., *Otorhinolaryngology: Head and Neck Surgery*, 15th ed. Baltimore: Williams & Wilkins, 1996, pp. 1109–1118.

12. Healy, Gerald B. Otitis media and middle ear effusions. In Ballenger, John Jacob, and Snow, James B., Jr., eds., *Otorhinolaryngology: Head and Neck Surgery*, 15th ed. Baltimore: Williams & Wilkins, 1996, pp. 1003–1009.

13. Hole, John W., Jr. Somatic and special senses. In *Human Anatomy and Physiology*, 6th ed. Dubuque, IA: Wm. C. Brown Publishers, 1993, pp. 414–459.

14. Jackler, Robert K., and Kaplan, Michael J. Ear, nose, and throat. In Tierney, Lawrence M., Jr., et al., eds., *Current Medical Diagnosis & Treatment*, 35th ed. Stamford, CT: Appleton & Lange, 1996, pp. 181–214.

15. Kotler, Howard S., and Tardy, M. Eugene, Jr. Reconstruction of the outstanding ear (otoplasty). In Ballenger, John Jacob, and Snow, James B., Jr., eds., *Otorhinolaryngology: Head and Neck Surgery*, 15th ed. Baltimore: Williams & Wilkins, 1996, pp. 989–1002.

16. Mattox, Douglas E. Ménière's disease, vestibular neuronitis and paroxysmal positional vertigo and nystagmus. In Ballenger, John Jacob, and Snow, James B., Jr., eds., *Otorhinolaryngology: Head and Neck Surgery*, 15th ed. Baltimore: Williams & Wilkins, 1996, pp. 1119–1132.

17. Mills, John H. Presbycusis. In Ballenger, John Jacob, and Snow, James B., Jr., eds., *Otorhinolaryngology: Head and Neck Surgery*, 15th ed. Baltimore: Williams & Wilkins, 1996, pp. 1133–1141.

18. Miyamoto, Richard T., et al. Cochlear implants in aural rehabilitation of adults and children. In Ballenger, John Jacob, and Snow, James B., Jr., eds., *Otorhinolaryngology: Head and Neck Surgery*, 15th ed. Baltimore: Williams & Wilkins, 1996, pp. 1142–1152.

19. Parker, Stephen W. Otoneurology. In Stein, Jay H., ed.-in-ch., *Internal Medicine*, 4th ed. St. Louis: Mosby, 1994, pp. 1042–1046.

20. Parisier, Simon C., and Kimmelman, Charles P. Microtia, canal atresia, and middle-ear anomalies. In Ballenger, John Jacob, and Snow, James B., Jr., eds., *Otorhinolaryngology: Head and Neck Surgery*, 15th ed. Baltimore: Williams & Wilkins, 1996, pp. 1064–1074.

21. Rowe, Lee D. Otolaryngology—Head and neck surgery. In Way, Lawrence W., ed., *Current Surgical Diagnosis & Treatment*, 10th ed. Norwalk, CT: Appleton & Lange, 1994, pp. 860–893.

22. Scheld, W. Michael. Bacterial meningitis and brain abscess. In Isselbacher, Kurt J., et al., eds., *Harrison's Principles of Internal Medicine*, 13th ed. New York: McGraw-Hill, Inc., 1994, pp. 2296–2309.

23. Schuller, David E., and Schleuning, Alexander J., II. Anatomy and physiology. In DeWeese and Saunders' *Otolaryngology—Head and Neck Surgery*, 8th ed. St. Louis: Mosby, 1994, pp. 353–376.

24. ———. Special diagnostic procedures in testing for hearing. Ibid., pp. 377–397.

25. ———. Infection and inflammation of the ear. Ibid., pp. 403–433.

26. ———. Trauma to the external ear. Ibid., pp. 435–440.

27. ———. Tumors. Ibid., pp. 441–452.

28. Snow, James B., Jr., and Martin, Joseph B. Disturbances of smell, taste, and hearing. In Isselbacher, Kurt, J., et al., eds., *Harrison's Principles of Internal Medicine*, 13th ed. New York: McGraw-Hill, Inc., 1994, pp. 109–115.

29. Stelmachowicz, Patricia G., and Gorga, Michael P. Auditory function tests. In Harker, Lee A., ed., *Otolaryngology—Head and Neck Surgery*, 2d ed., vol. 4. St. Louis: Mosby, 1993, pp. 2698–2717.

30. Tunkel, Allan R., and Scheld, W. Michael. Acute meningitis. In Stein, Jay H., ed.-in-ch., *Internal Medicine*, 4th ed. St. Louis: Mosby, 1994, pp. 1886–1899.

31. Valvassori, Galdino E. Imaging of the temporal bone. In Ballenger, John Jacob, and Snow, James B., Jr., eds., *Otorhinolaryngology: Head and Neck Surgery*, 15th ed. Baltimore: Williams & Wilkins, 1996, pp. 798–826.

32. Wehrs, Roger E. Reconstruction of the tympanic membrane and ossicular chain. In Bailey, Bryon J., et al., eds., *Head and Neck Surgery—Otolaryngology*, vol. 2. Philadelphia: J.B. Lippincott Co., 1993, pp. 1666–1675.

33. Winther, Birgit, and Gwaltney, Jack M., Jr. Upper respiratory infections (colds, pharyngitis, sinusitis). In Stein, Jay H., ed.-in-ch., *Internal Medicine*, 4th ed. St. Louis: Mosby, 1994, pp. 1860–1868.

34. Zappia, John J., et al. Surgery of the skull base. In Ballenger, John Jacob, and Snow, James B., Jr., eds., *Otorhinolaryngology: Head and Neck Surgery*, 15th ed. Baltimore: Williams & Wilkins, 1996, pp. 1166–1186.

Chapter 16

1. Adelman, Daniel C., and Terr, Abba. Allergic and immunologic disorders. In Tierney, Lawrence M., Jr., et al., eds., *Current Medical Diagnosis & Treatment*, 35th ed. Stamford, CT: Appleton & Lange, 1996, pp. 694–718.

2. Bluestein, Harry G. Immunodeficiencies. In Stein, Jay H., ed.-in-ch., *Internal Medicine*, 4th ed. St. Louis: Mosby, 1994, pp. 2372–2377.

3. Bone, Roger C. Cystic fibrosis. In Bennett, J. Claude, and Plum, Fred, eds., *Cecil's Textbook of Medicine*, 20th ed. Philadelphia: W.B. Saunders Co., 1996, pp. 419–422.

4. Chambers, Henry F. Infectious diseases: Bacterial and chlamydial. In Tierney, Lawrence M., Jr., et al., eds., *Current Medical Diagnosis & Treatment*, 35th ed. Stamford, CT: Appleton & Lange, 1996, pp. 1192–1226.

5. Chow, Anthony W. Infections caused by bacteroides and other mixed nonsporulating anaerobes. In Stein, Jay H., ed.-in-ch., *Internal Medicine*, 4th ed. St. Louis: Mosby, 1994, pp. 2158–2169.

6. Chuck, Steven L. Rabies. In Stein, Jay H., ed.-in-ch., *Internal Medicine*, 4th ed. St. Louis: Mosby, 1994, pp. 2012–2017.

7. Cooper, Max D., and Lawton, Alexander R., III. Primary immune deficiency diseases. In Isselbacher,

Kurt J., et al., eds., *Harrison's Principles of Internal Medicine*, 13th ed. New York: McGraw-Hill, Inc., 1994, pp. 1559–1567.

8. Couch, Robert B. Orthomyxovirus infections (influenza). In Stein, Jay H., ed.-in-ch., *Internal Medicine*, 4th ed. St. Louis: Mosby, 1994, pp. 1993–2000.

9. Dennis, David T., et al. Infections caused by Borrellia (relapsing fever and Lyme disease). In Stein, Jay H., ed.-in-ch., *Internal Medicine*, 4th ed. St. Louis: Mosby, 1994, pp. 2187–2193.

10. Douglas, R. Gordon, Jr. Picornavirus infections (enterovirus and rhinovirus). In Stein, Jay H., ed.-in-ch., *Internal Medicine*, 4th ed. St. Louis: Mosby, 1994, pp. 1984–1992.

11. Drake, Thomas A. Use of laboratory tests in infectious diseases. In Stein, Jay H., ed.-in-ch., *Internal Medicine*, 4th ed. St. Louis: Mosby, 1994, pp. 1829–1841.

12. Durack, David T., and Walker, David H. Rickettsial infections. In Stein, Jay H., ed.-in-ch., *Internal Medicine*, 4th ed. St. Louis: Mosby, 1994, pp. 2062–2068.

13. Edwards, John E., Jr. Infections caused by *Candida, Actinomyces,* and *Nocardia* species. In Stein, Jay H., ed.-in-ch., *Internal Medicine*, 4th ed. St. Louis: Mosby, 1994, pp. 2227–2235.

14. Fauci, Anthony S., and Lane, H. Clifford. Human imunodeficiency virus (HIV) disease: AIDS and related disorders. In Isselbacher, Kurt J., et al., eds., *Harrison's Principles of Internal Medicine*, 13th ed. New York: McGraw-Hill, Inc., 1994, pp. 1506–1618.

15. Fick, Robert B., Jr. Cystic fibrosis and bronchiectasis. In Stein, Jay H., ed.-in-ch., *Internal Medicine*, 4th ed. St. Louis: Mosby, 1994, pp. 1725–1732.

16. Fox, Robert I. Sjögren's syndrome. In Stein, Jay H., ed.-in-ch., *Internal Medicine*, 4th ed. St. Louis: Mosby, 1994, pp. 2418–2422.

17. Friedman, Harvey M. Smallpox, vaccina, and other poxviruses. In Isselbacher, Kurt J., et al., eds., *Harrison's Principles of Internal Medicine*, 13th ed. New York: McGraw-Hill, Inc., 1994, pp. 797–799.

18. Friedman, Lawrence S. Liver, biliary tract, and pancreas. In Tierney, Lawrence M., Jr., et al., eds., *Current Medical Diagnosis & Treatment*, 35th ed. Stamford, CT: Appleton & Lange, 1996, pp. 576–613.

19. Geppert, Thomas D., and Lipsky, Peter E. Cellular immunity. In Stein, Jay H., ed.-in-ch., *Internal Medicine*, 4th ed. St. Louis: Mosby, 1994, pp. 2312–2320.

20. Gerberding, Julie Louise, and Sande, Merle A. Acquired immunodeficiency syndrome. In Stein, Jay H., ed.-in-ch., *Internal Medicine*, 4th ed. St. Louis: Mosby, 1994, pp. 1970–1979.

21. Gilbert, David N. Clostridial infections. In Stein, Jay H., ed.-in-ch., *Internal Medicine*, 4th ed. St. Louis: Mosby, 1994, pp. 2096–2112.

22. Goldsmith, Robert S. Infectious diseases: Protozoan and helminthic. In Tierney, Lawrence M., Jr., et al., eds., *Current Medical Diagnosis & Treatment*, 35th ed. Stamford, CT: Appleton & Lange, 1996, pp. 1246–1305.

23. Graybill, John R. Infections caused by fungi. In Stein, Jay H., ed.-in-ch., *Internal Medicine*, 4th ed. St. Louis: Mosby, 1994, pp. 2212–2227.

24. Hahn, Bevra Hannahs. Systemic lupus erythematosus. In Isselbacher, Kurt J., et al., eds., *Harrison's Principles of Internal Medicine*, 13th ed. New York: McGraw-Hill, Inc., 1994, pp. 1643–1648.

25. Hashmey, Rayhan, and Shandera, Wayne X. Infectious diseases: Viral and rickettsial. In Tierney, Lawrence M., Jr., et al., eds., *Current Medical Diagnosis & Treatment*, 35th ed. Stamford, CT: Appleton & Lange, 1996, pp. 1158–1191.

26. Hayden, Frederick G., and Hayden, Gregory F. Paramyxovirus (measles, parainfluenza, mumps, and respiratory syncytial virus), rubella virus, and coronavirus. In Stein, Jay H., ed.-in-ch., *Internal Medicine*, 4th ed. St. Louis: Mosby, 1994, pp. 2000–2012.

27. Haynes, Barton F. Enlargement of lymph nodes and spleen. In Isselbacher, Kurt J., et al., eds., *Harrison's Principles of Internal Medicine*, 13th ed. New York: McGraw-Hill, Inc., 1994, pp. 323–329.

28. Haynes, Barton F., and Fauci, Anthony S. Cellular and molecular basis of immunity. In Isselbacher, Kurt J., et al., eds., *Harrison's Principles of Internal Medicine*, 13th ed. New York: McGraw-Hill, Inc., 1994, pp. 1543–1559.

29. Hellmann, David B. Arthritis and musculoskeletal disorders. In Tierney, Lawrence M., Jr., et al., eds., *Current Medical Diagnosis & Treatment*, 35th ed. Stamford, CT: Appleton & Lange, 1996, pp. 719–767.

30. Hendley, J. Owen. *Bordetella pertussis* infection (whooping cough). In Stein, Jay H., ed.-in-ch., *Internal Medicine*, 4th ed. St. Louis: Mosby, 1994, pp. 2169–2172.

31. Henry, Nancy K., and Wilson, Walter R. Infections caused by *Brucella, Francisella tularensis, Pasteurella,* and *Yersina* species. In Stein, Jay H., ed.-in-ch., *Internal Medicine*, 4th ed. St. Louis: Mosby, 1994, pp. 2147–2158.

32. Ho, John L., and Johnson, Warren D. Gram-positive aerobic bacillary infections: *Corynebacterium* and *Listeria*. In Stein, Jay H., ed.-in-ch., *Internal Medicine*, 4th ed. St. Louis: Mosby, 1994, pp. 2092–2096.

33. Hollander, Harry. Infectious diseases: Mycotic. In Tierney, Lawrence M., Jr., et al., eds., *Current Medical Diagnosis & Treatment*, 35th ed. Stamford, CT: Appleton & Lange, 1996, pp. 1306–1316.

34. Hook, Edward W., III. *Neisseria gonorrhoeae* infections. In Stein, Jay H., ed.-in-ch., *Internal Medicine*, 4th ed. St. Louis: Mosby, 1994, pp. 2116–2122.

35. Hopewell, Philip C., and Small, Peter M. Tuberculosis and nontuberculous mycobacterial infections. In Stein, Jay H., ed.-in-ch., *Internal Medicine*, 4th ed. St. Louis: Mosby, 1994, pp. 2193–2212.

36. Hruska, Jerome F. Bunyavirus and togavirus infections (viral encephalitis, dengue, and yellow fever). In Stein, Jay H., ed.-in-ch., *Internal Medicine*, 4th ed. St. Louis: Mosby, 1994, pp. 2025–2031.

37. Hunder, Gene G., and Lie, J. T. The vasculitic syndromes. In Stein, Jay H., ed.-in-ch., *Internal Medicine*, 4th ed. St. Louis: Mosby, 1994, pp. 2430–2441.

38. Istorico-Saunders, Lisa J., and Cobbs, C. Glenn. Gram-negative bacteremia and the sepsis syndrome. In Stein, Jay H., ed.-in-ch., *Internal Medicine*, 4th ed. St. Louis: Mosby, 1994, pp. 1941–1952.

39. Jacobs, Richard A. General problems in infectious diseases. In Tierney, Lawrence M., Jr., et al., eds., *Current Medical Diagnosis & Treatment*, 35th ed. Stamford, CT: Appleton & Lange, 1996, pp. 1111–1134.

40. ———. Infectious diseases: Spirochetal. Ibid., pp. 1227–1245.

41. Kaplan, Marshall M. Primary biliary cirrhosis, Wilson's disease, hemochromatosis, and other metabolic and fibrotic liver diseases. In Stein, Jay H., ed.-in-ch., *Internal Medicine*, 4th ed. St. Louis: Mosby, 1994, pp. 618–632.

42. Katzenstein, David A., and Joran, M. Colin. Herpesvirus infections (herpes simplex virus, varicella-zoster virus, cytomegalovirus, Epstein-Barr virus). In Stein, Jay H., ed.-in-ch., *Internal Medicine*, 4th ed. St. Louis: Mosby, 1994, pp. 2035–2045.

43. Klippel, John H., and Decker, John L. Systemic lupus erythematosus. In Stein, Jay H., ed.-in-ch., *Internal Medicine*, 4th ed. St. Louis: Mosby, 1994, pp. 2422–2430.

44. Krane, Stephen M. Heritable and developmental disorders of connective tissue. In Stein, Jay H., ed.-in-ch., *Internal Medicine*, 4th ed. St. Louis: Mosby, 1994, pp. 2514–2520.

45. LaBrecque, Douglas R. Acute and chronic hepatitis. In Stein, Jay H., ed.-in-ch., *Internal Medicine*, 4th ed. St. Louis: Mosby, 1994, pp. 586–601.

46. Leech, James H. Infections caused by protozoa. In Stein, Jay H., ed.-in-ch., *Internal Medicine*, 4th ed. St. Louis: Mosby, 1994, pp. 2241–2270.

47. Levinson, Warren E., and Jawetz, Ernest. Laboratory diagnosis. In *Medical Microbiology & Immunology*, 3d ed. Norwalk, CT: Appleton & Lange, 1994, pp. 37–42.

48. ———. Hepatitis viruses. Ibid., pp. 203–208.

49. ———. Arboviruses. Ibid., pp. 208–213.

50. ———. Human immunodeficiency virus. Ibid., pp. 226–230.

51. ———. Cestodes. Ibid., pp. 266–271.

52. ———. Trematodes. Ibid., pp. 272–276.

53. ———. Immunity. Ibid., pp. 288–293.

54. ———. Cellular basis of the immune response. Ibid., pp. 294–304.

55. ———. Antibodies. Ibid., pp. 305–312.

56. ———. Humoral immunity. Ibid., pp. 312–314.

57. ———. Cell-mediated immunity. Ibid., pp. 314–316.

58. ———. Major histocompatibility complex & transplantation. Ibid., pp. 316–317.

59. ———. Antigen-antibody reactions in the laboratory. Ibid., pp. 323–329.

60. ———. Hypersensitivity (allergy). Ibid., pp. 329–333.

61. ———. Immunodeficiency. Ibid., pp. 338–341.

62. ———. Brief summaries of medically important organisms. Ibid., pp. 342–383.

63. Levy, Jay A. Human retrovirus infections. In Stein, Jay H., ed.-in-ch., *Internal Medicine*, 4th ed. St. Louis: Mosby, 1994, pp. 2045–2050.

64. Longo, Dan L. Plasma cell disorders. In Isselbacher, Kurt J., et al., eds., *Harrison's Principles of Internal Medicine*, 13th ed. New York: McGraw-Hill, Inc., 1994, pp. 1618–1625.

65. Marquardt, Diana L. Anaphylaxis. In Stein, Jay H., ed.-in-ch., *Internal Medicine*, 4th ed. St. Louis: Mosby, 1994, pp. 2398–2400.

66. Martin, Liam, and Fritzler, Marvin J. Autoantibodies. In Stein, Jay H., ed.-in-ch., *Internal Medicine*, 4th ed. St. Louis: Mosby, 1994, pp. 2349–2356.

67. Medsger, Thomas A., Jr. Systemic sclerosis (scleroderma). In Stein, Jay H., ed.-in-ch., *Internal Medicine*, 4th ed. St. Louis: Mosby, 1994, pp. 2443–2449.

68. Mills, John. Adenovirus. In Stein, Jay H., ed.-in-ch., *Internal Medicine*, 4th ed. St. Louis: Mosby, 1994, pp. 2050–2053.

69. ———. Mycoplasmal infections. Ibid., pp. 2058–2062.

70. Mumford, Robert S. Sepsis and septic shock. In Isselbacher, Kurt J., et al., eds., *Harrison's Principles of Internal Medicine*, 13th ed. New York: McGraw-Hill, Inc., 1994, pp. 511–515.

71. Olds, G. Richard. Infections caused by helminths. In Stein, Jay H., ed.-in-ch., *Internal Medicine*, 4th ed. St. Louis: Mosby, 1994, pp. 2274–2288.

72. Perlmutter, Roger M. Antibodies: Structure and genetics. In Stein, Jay H., ed.-in-ch., *Internal Medicine*, 4th ed. St. Louis: Mosby, 1994, pp. 2306–2312.

73. Pier, Gerald, et al. Role of mutant CFTR in hypersusceptibility of cystic fibrosis patients to lung infections. *Science* 271:64–63, 5 January 1996.

74. Provost, Thomas T., et al. Cutaneous manifestations of connective tissue diseases. In Stein, Jay H., ed.-in-ch., *Internal Medicine*, 4th ed. St. Louis: Mosby, 1994, pp. 2520–2525.

75. Pueringer, Robert J., and Hunninghake, Gary W. Sarcoidosis. In Stein, Jay H., ed.-in-ch., *Internal Medicine*, 4th ed. St. Louis: Mosby, 1994, pp. 1692–1697.

76. Rein, Michael F. Sexually transmitted diseases (urethritis, vaginitis, cervicitis, proctitis, genital lesions). In Stein, Jay H., ed.-in-ch., *Internal Medicine*, 4th ed. St. Louis: Mosby, 1994, pp. 1931–1941.

77. ———. Infections caused by Treponema species (syphilis, yaws, pinta, bejel). In Stein, Jay H., ed.-in-ch., *Internal Medicine*, 4th ed. St. Louis: Mosby, 1994, pp. 2177–2184.

78. Reinarz, James A. Neisseria meningitidis infections. In Stein, Jay H., ed.-in-ch., *Internal Medicine*, 4th ed. St. Louis: Mosby, 1994, pp. 2112–2116.

79. Rich, Robert R. Human immune response. In Stein, Jay H., ed.-in-ch., *Internal Medicine*, 4th ed. St. Louis: Mosby, 1994, pp. 2290–2299.

80. Riley, Lee W., et al. Infections caused by *Salmonella* and *Shigella* species. In Stein, Jay H., ed.-in-ch., *Internal Medicine*, 4th ed. St. Louis: Mosby, 1994, pp. 2140–2146.

81. Roodman, G. David. Hemolytic anemias. In Stein, Jay H., ed.-in-ch., *Internal Medicine*, 4th ed. St. Louis: Mosby, 1994, pp. 863–873.

82. Saag, Michael S. *Cryptococcus neformans* infections. In Stein, Jay H., ed.-in-ch., *Internal Medicine*, 4th ed. St. Louis: Mosby, 1994, pp. 2235–2240.

83. Safrin, Sharon. *Pneumocystis carinii* infection. In Stein, Jay H., ed.-in-ch., *Internal Medicine*, 4th ed. St. Louis: Mosby, 1994, pp. 2270–2274.

84. Schachter, Julius. Chlamydial infections. In Stein, Jay H., ed.-in-ch., *Internal Medicine*, 4th ed. St. Louis: Mosby, 1994, pp. 2053–2057.

85. Sheagren, John N. *Staphylococcus aureus* infections. In Stein, Jay H., ed.-in-ch., *Internal Medicine*, 4th ed. St. Louis: Mosby, 1994, pp. 2068–2074.

86. Steinberg, Alfred D. Tolerance and autoimmunity. In Stein, Jay H., ed.-in-ch., *Internal Medicine*, 4th ed. St. Louis: Mosby, 1994, pp. 2334–2337.

87. Stevens, Dennis L. *Streptococcus pyogenes* infections. In Stein, Jay H., ed.-in-ch., *Internal Medicine*, 4th ed. St. Louis: Mosby, 1994, pp. 2078–2087.

88. Strausbaugh, Larry J. Enterococcal and other non-group A streptococcal infections. In Stein, Jay H., ed.-in-ch., *Internal Medicine*, 4th ed. St. Louis: Mosby, 1994, pp. 2087–2092.

89. Tauber, Martin G. Fever of unknown origin. In Stein, Jay H., ed.-in-ch., *Internal Medicine*, 4th ed. St. Louis: Mosby, 1994, pp. 1841–1848.

90. *The Kansas City Star*. Gene causes problems in preventing infection. *The Kansas City Star*, 5 January 1996, p. A-5.

91. Turgeon, Ronald, M.D. Personal communications.

92. Wasserman, Stephen I. Immediate hypersensitivity. In Stein, Jay H., ed.-in-ch., *Internal Medicine*, 4th ed. St. Louis: Mosby, 1994, pp. 2328–2334.

93. Wenger, Jay D., and Kaufmann, Arnold F. Infections caused by Leptospires (Leptospirosis). In Stein, Jay H., ed.-in-ch., *Internal Medicine*, 4th ed. St. Louis: Mosby, 1994, pp. 2184–2186.

94. Winn, Washington C., Jr., and Grace, Christopher J. Infections caused by Legionellae. In Stein, Jay H., ed.-in-ch., *Internal Medicine*, 4th ed. St. Louis: Mosby, 1994, pp. 2172–2177.

95. Zein, Nizar N., and Persing, David H. Hepatitis C genotypes: Current trends and future implications. *Mayo Clinic Proceedings* 71:458–462, May 1996.

Chapter 17

1. Alexander, H. Richard, et al. Cancer of the stomach. In DeVita, Vincent T., Jr., et al., eds., *Cancer Principles & Practice of Oncology*, 4th ed., vol. 1. Philadelphia: J.B. Lippincott Co., 1993, pp. 818–848.

2. Aminoff, Michael J. Nervous system. In Tierney, Lawrence M., et al., eds., *Current Medical Diagnosis & Treatment*, 35th ed. Stamford, CT: Appleton & Lange, 1996, pp. 858–914.

3. Apel, Robyn L., and Fernandes, Bernard J. Malignant lymphoma presenting with an elevated serum CA-125 level. *Archives of Pathology and Laboratory Medicine* 119:373–376, April 1995.

4. Balch, Charles M., et al. Cutaneous melanomas. In DeVita, Vincent T., Jr., et al., eds., *Cancer Principles & Practice of Oncology*, 4th ed., vol. 2. Philadelphia: J.B. Lippincott Co., 1993, pp. 1612–1661.

5. Baserga, Renato. Principles of molecular cell. Biology of cancer: The cell cycle. In DeVita, Vincent T., Jr., et al., eds., *Cancer Principles & Practice of Oncology*, 4th ed., vol. 1. Philadelphia: J.B. Lippincott Co., 1993, pp. 60–66.

6. Bast, Robert C., Jr., and Berchuck, Andrew. Ovarian cancer. In Isselbacher, Kurt J., et al., eds., *Harrison's Principles of Medicine,* 13th ed. New York: McGraw-Hill, Inc., 1994, pp. 1853–1858.

7. Berger, Nathan A. Alkylating agents. In DeVita, Vincent T., Jr., et al., eds., *Cancer Principles & Practice of Oncology,* 4th ed., vol. 1. Philadelphia: J.B. Lippincott Co., 1993, pp. 400–409.

8. Chabner, Bruce A. Anticancer drugs. In DeVita, Vincent T., Jr., et al., eds., *Cancer Principles & Practice of Oncology,* 4th ed., vol. 1. Philadelphia: J.B. Lippincott Co., 1993, pp. 325–340.

9. Chabner, Bruce A., and Myers, Charles E. Antitumor antibiotics. In DeVita, Vincent T., Jr., et al., eds., *Cancer Principles & Practice of Oncology,* 4th ed., vol. 1. Philadelphia: J.B. Lippincott Co., 1993, pp. 375–384.

10. Chu, Edward, and Takimoto, Chris H. Antimetabolites. In DeVita, Vincent T., Jr., et al., eds., *Cancer Principles & Practice of Oncology,* 4th ed., vol. 1. Philadelphia: J.B. Lippincott Co., 1993, pp. 358–375.

11. DeVita, Vincent T., Jr. Principles of chemotherapy. In DeVita, Vincent T., Jr., et al., eds., *Cancer Principles & Practice of Oncology,* 4th ed., vol. 1. Philadelphia: J.B. Lippincott Co., 1993, pp. 276–292.

12. DeVita, Vincent T., Jr., et al. Hodgkin's disease. In DeVita, Vincent T., Jr., et al., eds., *Cancer Principles & Practice of Oncology,* 4th ed., vol. 2. Philadelphia: J.B. Lippincott Co., 1993, pp. 1819–1858.

13. Deisseroth, Albert B., et al. Chronic leukemias. In DeVita, Vincent T., Jr., et al., eds., *Cancer Principles & Practice of Oncology,* 4th ed., vol. 2. Philadelphia: J.B. Lippincott Co., 1993, pp. 1965–1983.

14. Donehower, Ross C., and Rowinsky, Eric K. Anticancer drugs derived from plants. In DeVita, Vincent T., Jr., et al., eds., *Cancer Principles & Practice of Oncology,* 4th ed., vol. 1. Philadelphia: J.B. Lippincott Co., 1993, pp. 409–417.

15. Einhorn, Lawrence H., et al. Cancer of the testis. In DeVita, Vincent T., Jr., et al., eds., *Cancer Principles and Practice of Oncology,* 4th ed., vol. 1. Philadelphia: J.B. Lippincott Co., 1993, pp. 1126–1151.

16. Freedman, Arnold S., and Nadler, Lee M. Malignant lymphomas. In Isselbacher, Kurt J., et al., eds., *Harrison's Principles of Medicine,* 13th ed. New York: McGraw-Hill, Inc., 1994, pp. 1774–1788.

17. Garnick, Marc B. Testicular cancer and other trophoblastic diseases. In Isselbacher, Kurt J., et al., eds., *Harrison's Principles of Medicine,* 13th ed. New York: McGraw-Hill, Inc., 1994, pp. 1858–1862.

18. Garnick, Marc B., and Brenner, Barry M. Tumors of the urinary tract. In Isselbacher, Kurt J., et al., eds., *Harrison's Principles of Medicine,* 13th ed. New York: McGraw-Hill, Inc., 1994, pp. 1336–1339.

19. Hanks, Gerald E., et al. Cancer of the prostate. In DeVita, Vincent T., Jr., et al., eds., *Cancer Principles & Practice of Oncology,* 4th ed., vol. 2. Philadelphia: J.B. Lippincott Co., 1993, pp. 1073–1113.

20. Harris, Jay R., et al. Cancer of the breast. In DeVita, Vincent T., Jr., et al., eds., *Cancer Principles & Practice of Oncology,* 4th ed., vol. 2. Philadelphia: J.B. Lippincott Co., 1993, pp. 1264–1332.

21. Hellman, Samuel. Principles of radiation therapy. In DeVita, Vincent T., Jr., et al., eds., *Cancer Principles and Practice of Oncology,* 4th ed., vol. 2. Philadelphia: J.B. Lippincott Co., 1993, pp. 248–275.

22. Henderson, Brian E., et al. Hormones. In DeVita, Vincent T., Jr., et al., eds., *Cancer Principles & Practice of Oncology,* 4th ed., vol. 2. Philadelphia: J.B. Lippincott Co., 1993, pp. 474–480.

23. Henderson, I. Craig. Breast cancer. In Isselbacher, Kurt J., et al., eds., *Harrison's Principles of Medicine,* 13th ed. New York: McGraw-Hill, Inc., 1994, pp. 1840–1850.

24. Hochberg, Fred, and Pruitt, Amy. Neoplastic diseases of the central nervous system. In Isselbacher, Kurt J., et al., eds., *Harrison's Principles of Medicine,* 13th ed. New York: McGraw-Hill, Inc., 1994, pp. 2256–2269.

25. Hoskins, William Jr., et al. Gynecologic tumors. In DeVita, Vincent T., Jr., et al., eds., *Cancer Principles and Practice of Oncology,* 4th ed., vol. 1. Philadelphia: J.B. Lippincott Co., 1993, pp. 1152–1225.

26. Keating, Michael J., et al. Acute leukemias. In DeVita, Vincent T., Jr., et al., eds., *Cancer Principles & Practice of Oncology,* 4th ed., vol. 2. Philadelphia: J.B. Lippincott Co., 1993, pp. 1938–1964.

27. Krane, Stephen M. Paget's disease of bone. In Isselbacher, Kurt J., et al., eds., *Harrison's Principles of Medicine,* 13th ed. New York: McGraw-Hill, Inc., 1994, pp. 2190–2193.

28. Krane, Stephen M., and Schiller, Alan L. Hyperostosis, neoplasms, and other disorders of bone and cartilage. In Isselbacher, Kurt J., et al., eds., *Harrison's Principles of Medicine,* 13th ed. New York: McGraw-Hill, Inc., 1994, pp. 2193–2201.

29. Lebovics, Robert S. Malignant tumors of the head and neck. In Isselbacher, Kurt J., et al., eds., *Harrison's Principles of Medicine,* 13th ed. New York: McGraw-Hill, Inc., 1994, pp. 1850–1853.

30. Lee, Cheryl T., and Osterling, Joseph E. Diagnostic markers of prostate cancer: Utility of prostate-specific antigen in diagnosis and staging. *Seminars in Surgical Oncology* 11:23–35, January 1995

31. Levin, Bernard, and Raijman, Issac. Malignant tumors of the colon and rectum. In Haubrich, William S., et al., eds., *Bockus Gastroenterology,* 5th ed., vol. 2. Philadelphia: W.B. Saunders, 1995, pp. 1774–1772.

32. Levin, Victor A., et al. Neoplasms of the central nervous system. In DeVita, Vincent T., Jr., et al., eds., *Cancer Principles & Practice of Oncology,* 4th ed., vol. 2. Philadelphia: J.B. Lippincott Co., 1993, pp. 1679–1737.

33. Liotta, Lance A., and Stetler-Stevenson, William G. Principles of molecular cell biology of cancer: Cancer metastasis. In DeVita, Vincent T., Jr., et al., eds., *Cancer Principles & Practice of Oncology,* 4th ed., vol. 1. Philadelphia: J.B. Lippincott Co., 1993, pp. 134–149.

34. Liu, Edison T. Oncogenes and suppressor genes: Genetic control of cancer. In Bennett, J. Claude, and Plum, Fred, eds., *Cecil's Textbook of Medicine,* 20th ed. Philadelphia: W.B. Saunders Co., 1996, pp. 1011–1012.

35. Longo, Dan L. Plasma cell disorders. In Isselbacher, Kurt J., et al., eds., *Harrison's Principles of Medicine,* 13th ed. New York: McGraw-Hill, Inc., 1994, pp. 1618–1625.

36. Longo, Dan L., et al. Lymphocytic lymphomas. In DeVita, Vincent T., Jr., et al., eds., *Cancer Principles & Practice of Oncology,* 4th ed., vol. 2. Philadelphia: J.B. Lippincott Co., 1993, pp. 1859–1927.

37. Mehne, Carol. Genetic genius. *MT Today* 3:6–7, 13 December 1993.

38. Mayer, Robert J. Neoplasms of the esophagus and stomach. In Isselbacher, Kurt J., et al., eds., *Harrison's Principles of Medicine,* 13th ed. New York: McGraw-Hill, Inc., 1994, pp. 1382–1386.

39. ———. Tumors of the large and small intestine. Ibid., pp. 1424–1431.

40. ———. Pancreatic cancer. Ibid., pp. 1532–1535.

41. Mendelsohn, John. Principles of neoplasia. In Isselbacher, Kurt J., et al., eds., *Harrison's Principles of Medicine,* 13th ed. New York: McGraw-Hill, Inc., 1994, pp. 1814–1826.

42. Perkins, Archibald S., and Vande Woude, George F. Principles of molecular cell biology of cancer:

Oncogeneses. In DeVita, Vincent T., Jr., et al., eds., *Cancer Principles & Practice of Oncology,* 4th ed., vol. 1. Philadelphia: J.B. Lippincott Co., 1993, pp. 35–59.

43. Pizzo, Phillip A., et al. Solid tumors of childhood. In DeVita, Vincent T., Jr., et al., eds., *Cancer Principles & Practice of Oncology,* 4th ed., vol. 1. Philadelphia: J.B. Lippincott Co., 1993, pp. 1738–1791.

44. Reh, Thomas E., M.D. Personal communications.

45. Rosenberg, J. C. Neoplasms of the mediastinum. In DeVita, Vincent T., Jr., et al., eds., *Cancer Principles & Practice of Oncology,* 4th ed., vol. 2. Philadelphia: J.B. Lippincott Co., 1993, pp. 759–775.

46. Rosenberg, Steven A. Gene therapy of cancer. In DeVita, Vincent T., Jr., et al., eds., *Cancer Principles & Practice of Oncology,* 4th ed., vol. 2. Philadelphia: J.B. Lippincott Co., 1993, pp. 2598–2613.

47. Rosenberg, Steven A. Principles of surgical oncology. In DeVita, Vincent T., Jr., et al., eds., *Cancer Principles & Practice of Oncology,* 4th ed., vol. 2. Philadelphia: J.B. Lippincott Co., 1993, pp. 238–247.

48. ———. Principles and applications of biologic therapy. Ibid., vol. 1, pp. 293–324.

49. Rowley, Janet D., and Mitelman, Felix. Principles of molecular cell biology of cancer: Chromosome abnormalities in human cancer and leukemia. In DeVita, Vincent T., Jr., et al., eds., *Cancer Principles & Practice of Oncology,* 4th ed., vol. 1. Philadelphia: J.B. Lippincott Co., 1993, pp. 67–91.

50. Rowley, Janet D., et al. The clinical applications of new DNA diagnostic technology on the management of cancer patients. *Journal of American Medical Association* 270:2331–2337, 17 November 1993.

51. Rowley, Janet D., et al. The impact of new DNA diagnostic technology on the management of cancer patients. *Archives of Pathology and Laboratory Medicine.* 117:1104–1109, November 1993.

52. Sagalowsky, Arthur I., and Wilson, Jean D. Hyperplasia and carcinoma of the prostate. In Isselbacher, Kurt J., et al., eds., *Harrison's Principles of Medicine,* 13th ed. New York: McGraw-Hill, Inc., 1994, pp. 1862–1865.

53. Salmon, Sydney E., and Bertino, Joseph R. Principles of cancer therapy. In Bennett, J. Claude, and Plum, Fred, eds., *Cecil's Textbook of Medicine,* 20th ed. Philadelphia: W.B. Saunders Co., 1996, pp. 1036–1049.

54. Salmon, Sydney E., and Cassady, J. Robert. Plasma cell neoplasm. In DeVita, Vincent T., Jr., et al., eds., *Cancer Principles & Practice of Oncology,* 4th ed., vol. 2. Philadelphia: J.B. Lippincott Co., 1993, pp. 1984–2025.

55. Scheinberg, David A., and Golde, David W. The leukemias. In Isselbacher, Kurt J., et al., eds., *Harrison's Principles of Medicine,* 13th ed. New York: McGraw-Hill, Inc., 1994, pp. 1764–1774.

56. Schwartz, Morton K. Cancer markers. In DeVita, Vincent T., Jr., et al., eds., *Cancer Principles & Practice of Oncology,* 4th ed., vol. 1. Philadelphia: J.B. Lippincott Co., 1993, pp. 531–542.

57. Simone, Joseph V. Oncology introduction. In Bennett, J. Claude, and Plum, Fred, eds., *Cecil's Textbook of Medicine,* 20th ed. Philadelphia: W.B. Saunders Co., 1996, pp. 1004–1008.

58. Slapak, Christopher A., and Kufe, Donald W. Principles of cancer therapy. In Isselbacher, Kurt J., et al., eds., *Harrison's Principles of Medicine,* 13th ed. New York: McGraw-Hill, Inc., 1994, pp. 1826–1840.

59. Sober, Arthur J., and Koh, Howard K. Melanoma and other pigmented skin lesions. In Isselbacher, Kurt J., et al., eds., *Harrison's Principles of Medicine,* 13th ed. New York: McGraw-Hill, Inc., 1994, pp. 1867–1871.

60. Turgeon, Ronald, M.D. Personal communications.

61. Yang, James C., et al. Sarcomas of soft tissues. In DeVita, Vincent T., Jr., et al., eds., *Cancer Principles & Practice of Oncology,* 4th ed., vol. 2. Philadelphia: J.B. Lippincott Co., 1993, pp. 1436–1488.

62. Young, Robert C., et al. Cancer of the ovary. In DeVita, Vincent T., Jr., et al., eds., *Cancer Principles & Practice of Oncology,* 4th ed., vol. 1. Philadelphia: J.B. Lippincott Co., 1993, pp. 1226–1263.

Chapter 18

1. Abuhamad, Alfred, and Copel, Joshua A. Doppler color imaging in obstetrics. In Sabbagha, Rudy E., ed., *Diagnostic Ultrasound Applied to Obstetrics and Gynecology,* 3d ed. Philadelphia: J.B. Lippincott Co., 1994, pp. 491–498.

2. Auer, Roy, M.D. Personal communications.

3. Baron, Richard L., and Campbell, William L. Nonneoplastic diseases of the bile ducts. In Freeny, Patrick C., and Stevenson, Giles W., eds., *Margulis and Burhenne's Alimentary Tract Radiology,* 5th ed., vol. 2. St. Louis: Mosby, 1994, pp. 1294–1324.

4. Botet, Jose F., and Lightdale, Charles J. Normal anatomy and techniques of examination of the esophagus: Endosonography. In Freeny, Patrick C., and Stevenson, Giles W., eds., *Margulis and Burhenne's Alimentary Tract Radiology,* 5th ed., vol. 1. St. Louis: Mosby, 1994, pp. 186–191.

5. ———. Endosonography: Normal anatomy and techniques of examination of the stomach and duodenum. Ibid., vol. 1, pp. 311–317.

6. ———. Normal anatomy and techniques of examination of the colon and rectum: Endosonography. Ibid., vol. 1, pp. 725–729.

7. Boxt, Lawrence M., et al. Angiocardiography in the diagnosis of congenital heart disease. *Radiologic Clinics of North America* 32:435–460, May 1994.

8. Chandrasekhar, Sujana S., et al. Imaging of the facial nerve. In Jackler, Robert K., and Brackmann, Derald E., eds., *Neurotology.* St. Louis: Mosby, 1994, pp. 341–359.

9. Chhem, Rethy K., et al. Ultrasonography of the musculoskeletal system. *Radiologic Clinics of North America* 32:275–289, March 1994.

10. Come, Patricia C., et al. Noninvasive methods of cardiac examination. In Isselbacher, Kurt J., et al., eds., *Harrison's Principles of Internal Medicine,* 13th ed. New York: McGraw-Hill, Inc., 1994, pp. 966–972.

11. Cooperberg, Peter L. Gallbladder sonography. In Freeny, Patrick C., and Stevenson, Giles W., eds., *Margulis and Burhenne's Alimentary Tract Radiology,* 5th ed., vol. 2. St. Louis: Mosby, 1994, pp. 1246–1250.

12. Crummy, Andrew B. Angiography. In Juhl, John. H., and Crummy, Andrew B., eds., *Paul and Juhl's Essentials of Radiologic Imaging,* 6th ed. Philadelphia: J.B. Lippincott Co., 1993, pp. 380–386.

13. Davidson, Alan J., and Hartman, David S. Renal sinus and periureteral abnormalities. In *Radiology of the Kidney and Urinary Tract,* 2d ed. Philadelphia: W.B. Saunders Co., 1994, pp. 533–569.

14. ———. The retroperitoneum. Ibid., pp. 671–714.

15. ———. The adrenal. Ibid., pp. 715–748.

16. de Roos, Albert, and van der Wall, Ernst E. Evaluation of ischemic heart disease by magnetic resonance imaging and spectroscopy. *Radiologic Clinics of North America* 32:581–592, May 1994.

17. Dowd, Christopher F., et al. Diagnostic and therapeutic angiography. In Jackler, Robert K., and Brackmann, Derald E., eds., *Neurotology.* St. Louis: Mosby, 1994, pp. 399–436.

18. Duerinckx, André J., and Higgins, Charles B. Valvular heart disease. *Radiologic Clinics of North America* 32:613–630, May 1994.

19. Ekberg, Olle. Normal anatomy and techniques of examination of the esophagus: Fluoroscopy, CT, MRI, and scintigraphy. In Freeny, Patrick C., and Stevenson, Giles W., eds., *Margulis and Burhenne's Alimentary Tract Radiology*, 5th ed., vol. 1. St. Louis: Mosby, 1994, pp. 168–185.

20. Fernandez-Madrid, Felix, et al. MR features of osteoarthritis of the knee. *Magnetic Resonance Imaging* 12: 703–709, 25 July 1994.

21. Fleischer, A. C., et al. Color Doppler sonography of benign pelvic masses: The spectrum of findings. In Kurjak, Asim, ed., *An Atlas of Transvaginal Color Doppler*. London: Parthenon Publishing Group, 1994, pp. 279–289.

22. Freeny, Patrick C., and Rohrmann, Charles A., Jr. Inflammatory disease of the pancreas. In Freeny, Patrick C., and Stevenson, Giles W., eds., *Margulis and Burhenne's Alimentary Tract Radiology*, 5th ed., vol. 2. St. Louis: Mosby, 1994, pp. 1052–1090.

23. Friedman, Paul J. Imaging in pulmonary disease. In Isselbacher, Kurt J., et al., eds., *Harrison's Principles of Internal Medicine*, 13th ed. New York: McGraw-Hill, Inc., 1994, pp. 1159–1163.

24. Ghiatas, Abraham A. Imaging of renal disorders. In Stein, Jay H., ed.-in-ch., *Internal Medicine*, 4th ed. St. Louis: Mosby, 1994, pp. 2589–2598.

25. Goaz, Paul D., et al. Radiation physics. In Goaz, Paul D., and White, Stuart C., eds., *Oral Radiology: Principles and Interpretation*, 3d ed. St. Louis: Mosby, 1994, pp. 1–23.

26. Gore, Richard M., and Fitzgerald, Steven W. Computed tomography of the abdomen and pelvis. In Gore, Richard M., et al., eds., *Textbook of Gastrointestinal Radiology*, vol. 2. Philadelphia: W.B. Saunders Co., 1994, pp. 1500–1505.

27. Goske, Marilyn J., et al. Pediatric spine: Normal anatomy and spinal dysraphism. In Modic, Michael T., et al., eds., *Magnetic Resonance Imaging of the Spine*, 2d ed. St. Louis: Mosby, 1994, pp. 352–387.

28. Graebe, Robert A. The role of imaging techniques in gynecology. In DeCherney, Alan H., and Pernoll, Martin L., eds., *Current Obstetric & Gynecologic Diagnosis & Treatment*, 8th ed. Norwalk, CT: Appleton & Lange, 1994, pp. 54–60.

29. Harris, K. M., et al. Normal anatomy and techniques and examination of the stomach and duodenum. In Freeny, Patrick C., and Stevenson, Giles W., eds., *Margulis and Burhenne's Alimentary Tract Radiology*, 5th ed., vol. 1. St. Louis: Mosby, 1994, pp. 282–317.

30. Hartnell, George G. Developments in echocardiography. *Radiologic Clinics of North America* 32:461–475, May 1994.

31. Hayes, Wendelin S. The urethra. In Davidson, Alan J., and Hartman, David S., eds., *Radiology of the Kidney and Urinary Tract*, 2d ed. Philadelphia: W.B. Saunders Co., 1994, pp. 649–667.

32. Higgins, Charles B. New cardiac imaging techniques. In Isselbacher, Kurt J., et al., eds., *Harrison's Principles of Internal Medicine*, 13th ed. New York: McGraw-Hill, Inc., 1994, pp. 972–979.

33. Hirsch, William L., Jr., and Curtin, Hugh D. Imaging of the lateral skull base. In Jackler, Robert K., and Brackmann, Derald E., eds., *Neurotology*. St. Louis: Mosby, 1994, pp. 303–340.

34. Hricak, Hedvig, and Tanagho, Emil A. Radiology of the urinary tract. In Tanagho, Emil A., and McAninch, Jack W., eds., *Smith's General Urology*, 13th ed. Norwalk, CT: Appleton & Lange, 1992, pp. 61–114.

35. Juhl, John H. Methods of examination, anatomy, and congenital malformations of the chest. In Juhl, John H., and Crummy, Andrew B., eds., *Paul and Juhl's Essentials of Radiologic Imaging*, 6th ed. Philadelphia: J.B. Lippincott Co., 1993, pp. 779–820.

36. ———. The teeth, jaws, and salivary glands. Ibid., pp. 1193–1216.

37. Kawada, Charles. Gynecologic history, examination, and diagnostic procedures. In DeCherney, Alan H., and Pernoll, Martin L., eds., *Current Obstetric & Gynecologic Diagnosis & Treatment*, 8th ed. Norwalk, CT: Appleton & Lange, 1994, pp. 613–632.

38. Kressel, Herbert Y. Magnetic resonance imaging. In Gore, Richard M., et al., eds., *Textbook of Gastrointestinal Radiology*, vol. 2. Philadelphia: W.B. Saunders Co., 1994, pp. 1518–1532.

39. Kurjak, Asim. Color Doppler velocimetry of the ovary: Vaginal approach. In Sabbagha, Rudy E., ed., *Diagnostic Ultrasound Applied to Obstetrics and Gynecology*, 3d ed. Philadelphia: J.B. Lippincott Co., 1994, pp. 683–689.

40. Kurjak, Asim, et al. Fetal intracranial circulation. In Kurjak, Asim, ed., *An Atlas of Transvaginal Color Doppler*. London: Parthenon Publishing Group, 1994, pp. 71–79.

41. Lee, Fred T., Jr., and Thornbury, John R. The urinary tract. In Juhl, John H., and Crummy, Andrew B., eds., *Paul and Juhl's Essentials of Radiologic Imaging*, 6th ed. Philadelphia: J.B. Lippincott Co., 1993, pp. 641–740.

42. Lee, Robert A., et al. Percutaneous biopsy of abdominal masses. In Freeny, Patrick C., and Stevenson, Giles W., eds., *Margulis and Burhenne's Alimentary Tract Radiology*, 5th ed., vol. 2. St. Louis: Mosby, 1994, pp. 1987–1997.

43. Levine, Marc S. Gastroesophageal reflux disease. In Gore, Richard M., et al., eds., *Textbook of Gastrointestinal Radiology*, vol. 1. Philadelphia: W.B. Saunders Co., 1994, pp. 360–402.

44. Magid, Donna. Computed tomographic imaging of the musculoskeletal system. *Radiologic Clinics of North America* 32:255–274, March 1994.

45. Manning, Frank A. Ultrasonography. In Avery, Gordon B., et al., eds., *Neonatology: Pathophysiology and Management of the Newborn*, 4th ed. Philadelphia: J.B. Lippincott Co., 1994, pp. 154–170.

46. Masaryk, Thomas J. Cystic lesions, vascular disorders, demyelinating disease and miscellaneous topics. In Modic, Michael T., et al., eds., *Magnetic Resonance Imaging of the Spine*, 2d ed. St. Louis: Mosby, 1994, pp. 388–433.

47. Mayo Clinic Cardiovascular Working Group on Stress Testing. Cardiovascular stress testing: A description of the various types of stress tests and indications for their use. *Mayo Clinic Proceedings* 71:43–52, January 1996.

48. Murphy, Mark D. Imaging aspects of new techniques in orthopedic surgery. *Radiologic Clinics of North America* 32:201–225, March 1994.

49. Pavlin, Charles J., et al. Ultrasound biomicroscopy in the assessment of anterior scleral disease. *American Journal of Ophthalmology* 116:628–635, November 1993.

50. Pearlman, Justin D., et al. Ultrafast magnetic resonance imaging: Segmented turboflash, echo-planar, and real-time nuclear magnetic resonance. *Radiologic Clinics of North America* 32:593–612, May 1994.

51. Peters, Mary Ellen. Mammography. In Juhl, John H., and Crummy, Andrew B., eds., *Paul and Juhl's Essentials of Radiologic Imaging*, 6th ed. Philadelphia: J.B. Lippincott Co., 1993, pp. 387–405.

52. Pettigrew, Roderic I. Magnetic resonance imaging of the heart and great vessels. In Schlant, Robert C., and Alexander, R. Wayne, eds., *The Heart*, 8th ed. New York: McGraw-Hill, Inc., 1994, pp. 2339–2359.

53. Puliafito, Carmen A., et al. Principles of operation and technology. In *Optical Coherence Tomography of Ocular Diseases*. Thorofare, NJ: SLACK Incorporated, 1996, pp. 3–15.

54. Ramsey, Ruth G. Embryology and normal cerebrovascular anatomy. In *Neuroradiology*, 3d ed. Philadelphia: W.B. Saunders Co., 1994, pp. 34–72.

55. ———. Supratentorial brain tumors. Ibid., pp. 250–330.

56. ———. Stroke and atherosclerosis. Ibid., pp. 431–494.

57. ———. Skull. Ibid., pp. 565–654.

58. ———. Spine and spinal cord. Ibid., pp. 786–943.

59. Reece, E. Albert, et al. Peripartum ultrasonography. In Sabbagha, Rudy E., ed., *Diagnostic Ultrasound Applied to Obstetrics and Gynecology*, 3d ed. Philadelphia: J.B. Lippincott Co., 1994, pp. 87–98.

60. Reed, Kathryn L. Doppler echocardiography. In Sabbagha, Rudy E., ed., *Diagnostic Ultrasound Applied to Obstetrics and Gynecology*, 3d ed. Philadelphia: J.B. Lippincott Co., 1994, pp. 483–490.

61. Reed, Kathryn L. Ultrasound during pregnancy. In Scott, James R., et al., eds., *Danforth's Obstetrics and Gynecology*, 7th ed. Philadelphia: J.B. Lippincott Co., 1994, pp. 245–267.

62. Reh, Thomas E., M.D. Personal communications.

63. Resnick, Donald, and Sartoris, David J. Imaging evaluation of patients with arthritis. In Stein, Jay H., ed.-in-ch., *Internal Medicine*, 4th ed. St. Louis: Mosby, 1994, pp. 2360–2371.

64. Reuter, Karen L., et al. The role of magnetic resonance imaging in problematic gynecologic diagnoses. *Magnetic Resonance Imaging* 12:569–576, 17 June 1994.

65. Rogers, Lee F. Normal anatomic variants and miscellaneous skeletal anomalies. In Juhl, John. H., and Crummy, Andrew B., eds., *Paul and Juhl's Essentials of Radiologic Imaging*, 6th ed. Philadelphia: J.B. Lippincott Co., 1993, pp. 291–316.

66. Rumberger, John A., et al. Electron beam computed tomography and coronary artery disease: Scanning for coronary artery calcification. *Mayo Clinic Proceedings* 71: 369–377, April 1996.

67. Runge, Val M., et al. Skull and its contents. In Runge, Val M., ed., *Magnetic Resonance Imaging of the Brain*. Philadelphia: J.B. Lippincott Co., 1994, pp. 85–531.

68. Schoenberg, Norman Y., and Beltran, Javier: Contrast enhancement in musculoskeletal imaging. *Radiologic Clinics of North America* 32:337–352, March 1994.

69. Sabbagha, Rudy E. Gestational age. In Sabbagha, Rudy E., ed., *Diagnostic Ultrasound Applied to Obstetrics and Gynecology*, 3d ed. Philadelphia: J.B. Lippincott Co., 1994, pp. 155–178.

70. ———. Cardiac scan. Ibid., pp. 449–482.

71. Sabbagha, Rudy E., and Minogue, John P. Altered fetal growth. In Sabbagha, Rudy E., ed., *Diagnostic Ultrasound Applied to Obstetrics and Gynecology*, 3d ed. Philadelphia: J.B. Lippincott Co., 1994, pp. 179–205.

72. Sabbagha, Rudy E., et al. Skeletal abnormalities. In Sabbagha, Rudy E., ed., *Diagnostic Ultrasound Applied to Obstetrics and Gynecology*, 3d ed. Philadelphia: J.B. Lippincott Co., 1994, pp. 539–556.

73. Sabbagha, Rudy E., et al. Early pregnancy evaluation. In Sabbagha, Rudy E., ed., *Diagnostic Ultrasound Applied to Obstetrics and Gynecology*, 3d ed. Philadelphia: J.B. Lippincott Co., 1994, pp. 581–602.

74. Sabbagha, Rudy E., et al. Sonography of the ovary. In Sabbagha, Rudy E., ed., *Diagnostic Ultrasound Applied to Obstetrics and Gynecology*, 3d ed. Philadelphia: J.B. Lippincott Co., 1994, pp. 655–681.

75. Shaw, Kathryn J. Placenta previa. In Mishell, Daniel R., and Brenner, Paul F., eds., *Management of Common Problems in Obstetrics and Gynecology*, 3d ed. Oxford: Blackwell Scientific Publications, 1994, pp. 201–205.

76. Socol, Michael L. Intrauterine transfusion. In Sabbagha, Rudy E., ed., *Diagnostic Ultrasound Applied to Obstetrics and Gynecology*, 3d ed. Philadelphia: J.B. Lippincott Co., 1994, pp. 145–152.

77. Sokol, Robert J., et al. Practical diagnosis and management of labor. In Scott, James R., et al., eds., *Danforth's Obstetrics and Gynecology*, 7th ed. Philadelphia: J.B. Lippincott Co., 1994, pp. 521–561.

78. Soldo, Stephen J., et al. MRI-derived ventricular volume curves for the assessment of left ventricular function. *Magnetic Resonance Imaging* 12:711–717.

79. Stevenson, Giles W. Normal anatomy and techniques of examination of the colon: barium, CT, and MRI. In Freeny, Patrick C., and Stevenson, Giles W., eds., *Margulis and Burhenne's Alimentary Tract Radiology*, 5th ed., vol. 1. St. Louis: Mosby, 1994, pp. 692–724.

80. Stewart, Edward T., and Dodds, Wylie J. Radiology of the esophagus. In Freeny, Patrick C., and Stevenson, Giles W., eds., *Margulis and Burhenne's Alimentary Tract Radiology*, 5th ed., vol. 1. St. Louis: Mosby, 1994, pp. 192–263.

81. Thompson, Bard H., and Stanford, William. Evaluation of cardiac function with ultrafast computed tomography. *Radiologic Clinics of North America* 32:537–551, May 1994.

82. Tio, T. L. Endosonography of the esophagus. In Freeny, Patrick C., and Stevenson, Giles W., eds., *Margulis and Burhenne's Alimentary Tract Radiology*, 5th ed., vol. 1. St. Louis: Mosby, 1994, pp. 264–271.

83. Touliopoulos, Paula, and Costello, Philip. Helical (spiral) CT of the thorax. *Radiologic Clinics of North America* 33:843–861, September 1995.

84. Verstraete, K. L., et al. First-pass images of musculoskeletal lesions: A new and useful diagnostic application of dynamic contrast-enhanced MRI. *Magnetic Resonance Imaging* 12:687–702, 25 July 1994.

85. Winter, Thomas C., and Laing, Faye. Hepatic ultrasound. In Freeny, Patrick C., and Stevenson, Giles W., eds., *Margulis and Burhenne's Alimentary Tract Radiology*, 5th ed., vol. 2. St. Louis: Mosby, 1994, pp. 1466–1485.

86. Wolf, Clifford R. Musculoskeletal system. In Runge, Val M., ed., *Magnetic Resonance Imaging: Clinical Principles*. Philadelphia: J.B. Lippincott Co., 1992, pp. 313–347.

87. Yasuda, Kenjiro, et al. Endosonography in the diagnosis and staging of pancreatic cancer. In Freeny, Patrick C., and Stevenson, Giles W., eds., *Margulis and Burhenne's Alimentary Tract Radiology*, 5th ed., vol. 2. St. Louis: Mosby, 1994, pp. 1127–1131.

88. Yochum, Terry R., and Barry, Michael S. Diagnostic imaging of the musculoskeletal system. In Yochum, Terry R., and Rowe, Lindsay J., eds., *Essentials of Skeletal Radiology*, 2d ed., vol. 1. Baltimore: Williams & Wilkins, 1996, pp. 373–545.

89. Zagzebski, James A. Physics and instrumentation. In Sabbagha, Rudy E., ed., *Diagnostic Ultrasound Applied to Obstetrics and Gynecology*, 3d ed. Philadelphia: J.B. Lippincott Co., 1994, pp. 3–43.

90. Zeman, Robert K. Anatomy and techniques of examination of biliary tract and gallbladder (oral cholecystography, computed tomography, cholescintigraphy, magnetic resonance imaging, and cholangiography). In Freeny, Patrick C., and Stevenson, Giles W., eds., *Margulis and Burhenne's Alimentary Tract Radiology*, 5th ed., vol. 2. St. Louis: Mosby, 1994, pp. 1223–1245.

91. Zeman, Robert K., et al. Helical (spiral) CT of the pancreas and biliary tract. *Radiologic Clinics of North America* 33:887–902, September 1995.

Chapter 19

1. Ahmad, Munir, M.D. Personal communications.

2. Arrighi, James A., and Dilsizian, Vasken. Radionuclide angiography in coronary and noncoronary heart disease. In Harbert, John C., et al., eds., *Nuclear Medicine: Diagnosis and Therapy*. New York: Thieme Medical Publishers, Inc., 1996, pp. 501–531.

3. Becks, Gregory P., and Burrow, Gerard N. Diagnosis and treatment of thyroid disease during pregnancy. In DeGroot, Leslie J., et al., eds., *Endocrinology*, 3d ed., vol. 1. Philadelphia: W.B. Saunders Co., 1995, pp. 799–820.

4. Beltran, Maria R. Testicular imaging. In Henkin, Robert E., et al., eds., *Nuclear Medicine*, vol. 2. St. Louis: Mosby, 1996, pp. 1110–1122.

5. Burt, Robert W. Cerebral perfusion imaging. In Henkin, Robert E., et al., eds., *Nuclear Medicine*, vol. 2. St. Louis: Mosby, 1996, pp. 1289–1312.

6. Cavalieri, Ralph R., and McDougall, I. Ross. In vivo isotopic tests and imaging. In Braverman, Lewis E., and Utiger, Robert D., eds., *Werner and Ingbar's The Thyroid*, 7th ed. Philadelphia: Lippincott-Raven, 1996, pp. 352–376.

7. Chen, Clara C. Parathyroid scintigraphy. In Harbert, John C., et al., eds., *Nuclear Medicine: Diagnosis and Therapy*. New York: Thieme Medical Publishers, Inc., 1996, pp. 429–438.

8. ———. The biliary system. Ibid., pp. 685–705.

9. Cush, John J., and Lipsky, Peter E. Approach to articular and musculoskeletal disorders. In Isselbacher, Kurt J., et al., eds., *Harrison's Principles of Internal Medicine*, 13th ed. New York: McGraw-Hill, Inc., 1994, pp. 1688–1692.

10. Daube-Witherspoon, Margaret E., and Herscovitch, Peter. Positron emission tomography. In Harbert, John C., et al., eds., *Nuclear Medicine: Diagnosis and Therapy*. New York: Thieme Medical Publishers, Inc., 1996, pp. 121–143.

11. Dillman, Wolfgang H. The thyroid. In Bennett, J. Claude, and Plum, Fred, eds., *Cecil's Textbook of Medicine*, 20th ed. Philadelphia: W.B. Saunders Co., 1996, pp. 1227–1245.

12. Dilsizian, Vasken. Nuclear imaging techniques for assessing myocardial ischemia and viability. In Harbert, John C., et al., eds., *Nuclear Medicine: Diagnosis and Therapy*. New York: Thieme Medical Publishers, Inc., 1996, pp. 461–500.

13. Early, Paul J. Radiation measurement and protection. Early, Paul J., and Sodee, D. Bruce, eds., *Principles and Practice of Nuclear Medicine*. St. Louis: Mosby, 1995, pp. 65–80.

14. Fink-Bennett, Darlene. Hepatobiliary imaging. In Henkin, Robert E., et al.,

eds., *Nuclear Medicine*, vol. 1. St. Louis: Mosby, 1996, pp. 997–1015.

15. Fisher, Delbert A. Thyroid physiology in the perinatal period and during childhood. In Braverman, Lewis E., and Utiger, Robert D., eds., *Werner and Ingbar's The Thyroid*, 7th ed. Philadelphia: Lippincott-Raven, 1996, pp. 974–983.

16. Fisher, Delbert A., and Polk, Daniel H. Thyroid disease in the fetus, neonate, and child. In DeGroot, Leslie J., et al., eds., *Endocrinology*, 3d ed., vol. 1. Philadelphia: W.B. Saunders Co., 1995, pp. 783–798.

17. Freitas, John E., and Freitas, Anne E. Parathyroid scintigraphy. In Henkin, Robert E., et al., eds., *Nuclear Medicine*, vol. 1. St. Louis: Mosby, 1996, pp. 877–885.

18. Fulham, Michael J. Neurological PET and SPECT. In Harbert, John C., et al., eds., *Nuclear Medicine: Diagnosis and Therapy*. New York: Thieme Medical Publishers, Inc., 1996, pp. 877–885.

19. Green, Michael V., and Seidel, Jürgen. Single photon imaging. In Harbert, John C., et al., eds., *Nuclear Medicine: Diagnosis and Therapy*. New York: Thieme Medical Publishers, Inc., 1996, pp. 87–120.

20. Harbert, John C. Radionuclide cisternography. In Harbert, John C., et al., eds., *Nuclear Medicine: Diagnosis and Therapy*. New York: Thieme Medical Publishers, Inc., 1996, pp. 387–400.

21. ———. The thyroid. Ibid., pp. 407–427.

22. ———. Vascular diseases. Ibid., pp. 533–551.

23. ———. The liver. Ibid., pp. 651–683.

24. ———. Adrenal glands and neural crest tumors. Ibid., pp. 745–785.

25. ———. The musculoskeletal system. Ibid., pp. 801–863.

26. Harbert, John C., et al. The genitourinary system. In Harbert, John C., et al., eds., *Nuclear Medicine: Diagnosis and Therapy*. New York: Thieme Medical Publishers, Inc., 1996, pp. 713–743.

27. Hay, Rick V., et al. Scintigraphic imaging of the adrenals and neuroecodermal tumors. In Henkin, Robert E., et al., eds., *Nuclear Medicine*, vol. 1. St. Louis: Mosby, 1996, pp. 855–876.

28. Higgins, Charles B. New cardiac imaging techniques. In Isselbacher, Kurt J., et al., eds., *Harrison's Principles of Internal Medicine*, 13th ed. New York: McGraw-Hill, Inc., 1994, pp. 972–979.

29. Johnson, Lynne L., and Pohost, Gerald M. Nuclear cardiology. In Schlant, Robert C., and Alexander, R. Wayne, eds., *The Heart*, 8th ed. New York:

McGraw-Hill, Inc., 1994, pp. 2281–2323.

30. Kim, Chun Ki, et al. Bone marrow scintigraphy. In Henkin, Robert E., et al., eds., *Nuclear Medicine*, vol. 2. St. Louis: Mosby, 1996, pp. 1223–1249.

31. Links, Jonathan. Radiation physics. In Braverman, Lewis E., and Utiger, Robert D., eds., *Werner and Ingbar's The Thyroid*, 7th ed. Philadelphia: Lippincott and Raven, 1996, pp. 330–341.

32. Moser, Kenneth M. Diagnostic procedures in respiratory diseases. In Isselbacher, Kurt J., et al., eds., *Harrison's Principles of Internal Medicine*, 13th ed. New York: McGraw-Hill, Inc., 1994, pp. 1163–1167.

33. ———. Pulmonary thromboembolism. Ibid., pp. 1214–1220.

34. Nalesnik, William, Ph.D. Personal communications.

35. National Council on Radiation Measurements. *Precautions in the Management of Patients Who Have Received Therapeutic Amounts of Radionuclides*. Report 36. Washington, DC: U.S. Gov't Printing Office.

36. Neumann, Ronald D., et al. Nuclear medicine tests for oncology patients. In Harbert, John C., et al., eds., *Nuclear Medicine: Diagnosis and Therapy*. New York: Thieme Medical Publishers, Inc., 1996, pp. 909–927.

37. Newhouse, Howard K., and Wexler, John P. Myocardial perfusion imaging for evaluating interventions in coronary artery disease. *Seminars in Nuclear Medicine* 25:15–27, January 1995.

38. Nickel, Richard A. Radiopharmaceuticals. In Early, Paul J., and Sodee, D. Bruce, eds., *Principles and Practice of Nuclear Medicine*. St. Louis: Mosby, 1995, pp. 94–117.

39. Park, Hee-Myung. The thyroid gland. In Henkin, Robert E., et al., eds., *Nuclear Medicine*, vol. 1. St. Louis: Mosby, 1996, pp. 830–854.

40. Podoloff, Donald A. Malignant bone disease. In Henkin, Robert E., et al., eds., *Nuclear Medicine*, vol. 2. St. Louis: Mosby, 1996, pp. 1208–1222.

41. Price, David C. The hematopoietic system. In Harbert, John C., et al., eds., *Nuclear Medicine: Diagnosis and Therapy*. New York: Thieme Medical Publishers, Inc., 1996, pp. 759–800.

42. Siegel, Michael E., and Stewart, Charles A. Peripheral vascular disease: Arterial and venous. In Henkin, Robert E., et al., eds., *Nuclear Medicine*, vol. 1. St. Louis: Mosby, 1996, pp. 798–827.

43. Silberstein, Edward B., et al. Skeletal scintigraphy in non-neoplastic osseous disorders. In Henkin, Robert E., et al., eds., *Nuclear Medicine*, vol. 2. St. Louis: Mosby, 1996, pp. 1141–1197.

44. Sisson, James C. Thyroid. In Early, Paul J., and Sodee, D. Bruce, eds., *Principles and Practice of Nuclear Medicine*. St. Louis: Mosby, 1995, pp. 617–640.

45. Sobel, Burton E. Acute myocardial infarction. In Bennett, J. Claude, and Plum, Fred, eds., *Cecil's Textbook of Medicine*, 20th ed. Philadelphia: W.B. Saunders Co., 1996, pp. 301–316.

46. Sostman, H. Dirk, Neumann, Ronald D. The respiratory system. In Harbert, John C., et al., eds., *Nuclear Medicine: Diagnosis and Therapy*. New York: Thieme Medical Publishers, Inc., 1996, pp. 553–584.

47. Thrall, James H., and Ziessman, Harvey A. Pulmonary system. In *Nuclear Medicine: The requisites*. St. Louis: Mosby, 1995, pp. 129–147.

48. ———. Hepatobiliary system. Ibid., pp. 191–225.

49. ———. Genitourinary system. Ibid., pp. 283–320.

50. Toskes, Phillip P. Malabsorption. In Bennett, J. Claude, and Plum, Fred, eds., *Cecil's Textbook of Medicine*, 20th ed. Philadelphia: W.B. Saunders Co., 1996, pp. 695–707.

51. Turgeon, Ronald, M.D. Personal communications.

52. Wackers, Frans J. Th. Myocardial perfusion imaging. In Harbert, John C., et al., eds., *Nuclear Medicine: Diagnosis and Therapy*. New York: Thieme Medical Publishers, Inc., 1996, pp. 445–459.

53. Wahl, Richard L. Radiolabeled monoclonal antibodies. In Early, Paul J., and Sodee, D. Bruce, eds., *Principles and Practice of Nuclear Medicine*. St. Louis: Mosby, 1995, pp. 678–701.

54. Walker, William J., and Jenkins, Lynn Evans. Radiation safety practices in the nuclear medicine laboratory. In Harbert, John C., et al., eds., *Nuclear Medicine: Diagnosis and Therapy*. New York: Thieme Medical Publishers, Inc., 1996, pp. 343–358.

55. Zaret, Barry L. Nuclear cardiology. In Bennett, J. Claude, and Plum, Fred, eds., *Cecil's Textbook of Medicine*, 20th ed. Philadelphia: W.B. Saunders Co., 1996, pp. 199–202.

56. Zeissman, Harvey A. The gastrointestinal tract. In Harbert, John C., et al., eds., *Nuclear Medicine: Diagnosis and Therapy*. New York: Thieme Medical Publishers, Inc., 1996, pp. 585–649.

Chapter 20

1. Aminoff, Michael J. Nervous system. In Tierney, Lawrence M., Jr., et al., eds., *Current Medical Diagnosis & Treatment*, 35th ed. Stamford, CT: Appleton & Lange, 1996, pp. 858–914.

2. Asbury, Arthur K. Numbness, tingling, and sensory loss. In Isselbacher, Kurt J., et al., eds., *Harrison's Principles of Internal Medicine*, 13th ed. New York: McGraw-Hill, Inc., 1994, pp. 133–136.

3. Atchison, James W., et al. Manipulation, traction, and massage. In Braddom, Randall L., ed., *Physical Medicine & Rehabilitation*. Philadelphia: W.B. Saunders Co., 1996, pp. 421–448.

4. Bach, John R. Pulmonary assessment and management of the aging and older patient. In Felsenthal, Gerald, et al., eds., *Rehabilitation of the Aging and Elderly Patient*. Baltimore: Williams & Wilkins, 1994, pp. 263–273.

5. Bradley, Nina S. Motor control: Developmental aspects of motor control in skill acquisition. In Campbell, Suzann K., et al., eds., *Physical Therapy for Children*. Philadelphia: W.B. Saunders Co., 1994, pp. 39–77.

6. Campbell, Suzann K. Understanding motor performance in children. In Campbell, Suzann K., et al., eds., *Physical Therapy for Children*. Philadelphia: W.B. Saunders Co., 1994, pp. 3–37.

7. Caplan, Louis R. Cerebrovascular disease (stroke). In Stein, Jay H., ed.-in-ch., *Internal Medicine*, 4th ed. St. Louis: Mosby, 1994, pp. 1074–1087.

8. Daroff, Robert B. Dizziness and vertigo. In Isselbacher, Kurt J., et al., eds., *Harrison's Principles of Internal Medicine*, 13th ed. New York: McGraw-Hill, Inc., 1994, pp. 96–99.

9. Day, Mary Jane. Diathermy. In Hecox, Bernadette, et al., eds., *Physical Agents*. Norwalk, CT: Appleton & Lange, 1994, pp. 143–162.

10. DiFabio, Richard P., and Badke, Mary Beth. Relationship of sensory organization to balance functions in patients with hemiplegia. *Physical Therapy* 70:542–548, September 1990.

11. Dombovy, Mary L. Rehabilitation concerns in degenerative movement disorders of the central nervous system. In Braddom, Randall L., ed., *Physical Medicine & Rehabilitation*. Philadelphia: W.B. Saunders Co., 1996, pp. 1088–1099.

12. Fond, Diana. Cryotherapy. In Hecox, Bernadette, et al., eds., *Physical Agents*. Norwalk, CT: Appleton & Lange, 1994, pp. 193–203.

13. Fond, Diana, and Hecox, Bernadette. Superficial heat modalities. In Hecox, Bernadette, et al., eds., *Physical Agents*. Norwalk, CT: Appleton & Lange, 1994, pp. 125–141.

14. Gajdosik, Carrie G., and Gajdosik, Richard L. Musculoskeletal development and adaptation. In Campbell, Suzann K., et al., eds., *Physical Therapy for Children*.

15. Garrison, Susan J. Geriatric stroke rehabilitation. In Felsenthal, Gerald, et al., eds., *Rehabilitation of the Aging and Elderly Patient*. Baltimore: Williams & Wilkins, 1994, pp. 175–186.

16. Geisel, Lynn, and Rhodes, Dina Fine. Electromyographic biofeedback for motor control. In Hecox, Bernadette, et al., eds., *Physical Agents*. Norwalk, CT: Appleton & Lange, 1994, pp. 367–375.

17. Gilman, Sid. Ataxia and disorders of balance and gait. In Isselbacher, Kurt J., et al., eds., *Harrison's Principles of Internal Medicine*, 13th ed. New York: McGraw-Hill, Inc., 1994, pp. 125–133.

18. Granger, Carl V., et al. Quality and outcome measures for medical rehabilitation. In Braddom, Randall L., ed., *Physical Medicine & Rehabilitation*. Philadelphia: W.B. Saunders Co., 1996, pp. 239–253.

19. Greenspan, John S. Oral manifestations of disease. In Isselbacher, Kurt J., et al., eds., *Harrison's Principles of Internal Medicine*, 13th ed. New York: McGraw-Hill, Inc., 1994, pp. 199–205.

20. Griggs, Robert C. Muscle spasms, cramps, and episodic weakness. In Isselbacher, Kurt J., et al., eds., *Harrison's Principles of Internal Medicine*, 13th ed. New York: McGraw-Hill, Inc., 1994, pp. 130–133.

21. Growdon, John H., and Fink, J. Stephen. Paralysis and movement disorders. In Isselbacher, Kurt J., et al., eds., *Harrison's Principles of Internal Medicine*, 13th ed. New York: McGraw-Hill, Inc., 1994, pp. 115–125.

22. Hecox, Bernadette. Thermal physics. In Hecox, Bernadette, et al., eds., *Physical Agents*. Norwalk, CT: Appleton & Lange, 1994, pp. 65–77.

23. ———. Hydrotherapy. Ibid., pp. 221–251.

24. Hier, Daniel B. Disorders of speech and language. In Stein, Jay H., ed.-in-ch., *Internal Medicine*, 4th ed. St. Louis: Mosby, 1994, pp. 1046–1051.

25. Iglarsh, Z. Annette. Education of patients. In Richardson, Jan K., and Iglarsh, Z. Annette, eds., *Clinical Orthopaedic Physical Therapy*. Philadelphia: W.B. Saunders Co., 1994, pp. 688–691.

26. Katz, Richard T. Management of spasticity. In Braddom, Randall L., ed., *Physical Medicine & Rehabilitation*. Philadelphia: W.B. Saunders Co., 1996, pp. 580–604.

27. Kistler, J. Philip, et al. Cerebrovascular diseases. In Isselbacher, Kurt J., et al., eds., *Harrison's Principles of Internal Medicine*, 13th ed. New York: McGraw-Hill, Inc., 1994, pp. 2233–2255.

28. Lewis, Carole B., and Bottomley, Jenifer M. Assessment Instruments. In *Geriatric Physical Therapy*. Norwalk, CT: Appleton & Lange, 1994, pp. 139–186.

29. ———. Neurological treatment considerations. Ibid., pp. 333–398.

30. McKinnis, David L. The posture-movement dynamic. In Richardson, Jan K., and Iglarsh, Z. Annette, eds., *Clinical Orthopaedic Physical Therapy*. Philadelphia: W.B. Saunders Co., 1994, pp. 563–601.

31. Mehreteab, Tsega Andemicael. Therapeutic electricity. In Hecox, Bernadette, et al., eds., *Physical Agents*. Norwalk, CT: Appleton & Lange, 1994, pp. 255–272.

32. ———. Effect of electrical stimulation on nerve and muscle tissue. Ibid., pp. 273–281.

33. ———. Clinical uses of electrical stimulation. Ibid., pp. 283–293.

34. ———. Iontophoresis. Ibid., pp. 295–298.

35. Michlovitz, Susan L. Cryotherapy: The use of cold as a therapeutic agent. In Michlovitz, Susan L., ed., *Thermal Agents in Rehabilitation*, 2d ed. Philadelphia: F.A. Davis, 1990, pp. 63–87.

36. ———. The use of heat and cold in the management of rheumatic disease. Ibid., pp. 258–274.

37. Mohr, J. P. Disorders of speech and language. In Isselbacher, Kurt J., et al., eds., *Harrison's Principles of Internal Medicine*, 13th ed. New York: McGraw-Hill, Inc., 1994, pp. 156–162.

38. Mysiw, W. Jerry, and Jackson, Rebecca D. Electrical stimulation. In Braddom, Randall L., ed., *Physical Medicine & Rehabilitation*. Philadelphia: W.B. Saunders Co., 1996, pp. 464–491.

39. Nelson, Arthur, Jr. Clinical electroneuromyography. In Hecox, Bernadette, et al., eds., *Physical Agents*. Norwalk, CT: Appleton & Lange, 1994, pp. 311–363.

40. Nicholson, Garvice G., and Clendaniel, Richard A. Manual techniques. In Scully, Rosemary M., and Barnes, Marylou R., eds., *Physical Therapy*. Philadelphia: J.B. Lippincott Co., 1989, pp. 926–985.

41. Reischer, Marcel A., and Spindler, Henry A. Rehabilitation management of pain in the elderly. In Felsenthal, Gerald, et al., eds., *Rehabilitation of the Aging and Elderly Patient*. Baltimore: Williams & Wilkins, 1994, pp. 303–318.

42. Rehabilitation Institute. Product line management at SSM Rehabilitation Institute leads to major patient benefits. *Insights* 1, 5, 7, and 9, Winter 1993.

43. Roth, Elliot J., and Harvey, Richard L. Rehabilitation of stroke syndromes. In Braddom, Randall L., ed., *Physical Medicine & Rehabilitation*. Philadelphia: W.B. Saunders Co., 1996, pp. 1053–1087.

44. Steinberg, Franz U. Medical evaluation, assessment of function and potential, and rehabilitation plan. In Felsenthal, Gerald, et al., eds., *Rehabilitation of the Aging and Elderly Patient*. Baltimore: Williams & Wilkins, 1994, pp. 81–96.

45. ———. Disorders of mobility, balance, and gait. Ibid., pp. 243–252.

46. Stout, Jean L. Gait: Development and analysis. In Campbell, Suzann K., et al., eds., *Physical Therapy for Children*. Philadelphia: W.B. Saunders Co., 1994, pp. 79–104.

47. Sweitzer, Ronald W. Ultrasound. In Hecox, Bernadette, et al., eds., *Physical Agents*. Norwalk, CT: Appleton & Lange, 1994, pp. 163–192.

48. Taylor, Lyn Paul. Massage. In *Taylor's Manual of Physical Evaluation and Treatment*. Thorofare, NJ: SLACK Incorporated, 1990, pp. 537–540.

49. ———. Massage muscle fatigue (and/or tension) relief. Ibid., pp. 541–543.

50. Timm, Kent E. Knee. In Richardson, Jan K., and Iglarsh, Z. Annette, eds., *Clinical Orthopaedic Physical Therapy*. Philadelphia: W.B. Saunders Co., 1994, pp. 399–482.

51. Walsh, Mart T. Hydrotherapy. The use of water as a therapeutic agent. In Michlovitz, Susan L., ed., *Thermal Agents in Rehabilitation*, 2d ed. Philadelphia: F.A. Davis, 1990, pp. 109–133.

52. Weber, David C. Physical agent modalities. In Braddom, Randall L., ed., *Physical Medicine & Rehabilitation*. Philadelphia: W.B. Saunders Co., 1996, pp. 449–463.

53. Weisberg, Joseph. Pain. In Hecox, Bernadette, et al., eds., *Physical Agents*. Norwalk, CT: Appleton & Lange, 1994, pp. 37–48.

54. ———. Electromagnetic spectrum. Ibid., pp. 49–53.

55. ———. Transcutaneous electrical nerve stimulation. Ibid., pp. 299–306.

56. ———. Point locator/Stimulator. Ibid., pp. 307–309.

57. ———. Ultraviolet irradiation. Ibid., pp. 377–389.

CREDITS

Chapter 2

Figure 2.1 From John W. Hole, Jr., *Human Anatomy and Physiology*, 3d ed. Copyright © 1984 The McGraw-Hill Companies, Inc. All Rights Reserved. Reprinted by permission. **TA 2.1** From John W. Hole, Jr., *Human Anatomy and Physiology*, 3d ed. Copyright © 1984 The McGraw-Hill Companies, Inc. All Rights Reserved. Reprinted by permission.

Chapter 4

Figure 4.1 From John W. Hole, Jr., *Human Anatomy and Physiology*, 5th ed. Copyright © 1990 The McGraw-Hill Companies, Inc. All Rights Reserved. Reprinted by permission. **Figure 4.2** From Kent M. Van De Graaff, *Human Anatomy*, 3d ed. Copyright © 1992 The McGraw-Hill Companies, Inc.The McGraw-Hill Companies, Inc. All Rights Reserved. Reprinted by permission. **Figure 4.3** From John W. Hole, Jr., *Human Anatomy and Physiology*, 6th ed. Copyright © 1990 The McGraw-Hill Companies, Inc. All Rights Reserved. Reprinted by permission. **Figure 4.4** From John W. Hole, Jr., *Human Anatomy and Physiology*, 3d ed. Copyright © 1984 The McGraw-Hill Companies, Inc. All Rights Reserved. Reprinted by permission. **Figure 4.8** From John W. Hole, Jr., *Human Anatomy and Physiology*, 6th ed. Copyright © 1990 The McGraw-Hill Companies, Inc. All Rights Reserved. Reprinted by permission. **TA 4.3** From John W. Hole, Jr., *Human Anatomy and Physiology*, 6th ed. Copyright © 1990 The McGraw-Hill Companies, Inc. All Rights Reserved. Reprinted by permission.

Chapter 5

Figure 5.3 From John W. Hole, Jr., *Human Anatomy and Physiology*, 3d ed. Copyright © 1984 The McGraw-Hill Companies, Inc. All Rights Reserved. Reprinted by permission. **Figure 5.8** From Kent M. Van De Graaff and Stuart Ira Fox, *Concepts of Human Anatomy and Physiology*, 3d ed. Copyright © 1992 The McGraw-Hill Companies, Inc. All Rights Reserved. Reprinted by permission. **Figure 5.9** From Kent M. Van De Graaff and Stuart Ira Fox, *Concepts of Human Anatomy and Physiology*, 3d ed. Copyright © 1992 The McGraw-Hill Companies, Inc. All Rights Reserved. Reprinted by permission. **TA 5.8** From Kent M. Van De Graaff and Stuart Ira Fox, *Concepts of Human Anatomy and Physiology*, 3d ed. Copyright © 1992 The McGraw-Hill Companies, Inc. All Rights Reserved. Reprinted by permission.

Chapter 6

Figure 6.8 From Karen Price, "St. Mary's First in St. Louis to Offer New DCA Procedure" in *St. Mary's Center News*. Copyright © St. Mary's Health Center, St. Louis, MO. Reprinted by permission.

Chapter 7

Figure 7.1 From John W. Hole, Jr., *Human Anatomy and Physiology*, 5th ed. Copyright © 1990 The McGraw-Hill Companies, Inc. All Rights Reserved. Reprinted by permission. **Figure 7.2** From John W. Hole, Jr., *Human Anatomy and Physiology*, 6th ed. Copyright © 1990 The McGraw-Hill Companies, Inc. All Rights Reserved. Reprinted by permission. **Figure 7.4** From John W. Hole, Jr., *Human Anatomy and Physiology*, 5th ed. Copyright © 1990 Wm. C. Brown Communications, Inc., Dubuque, Iowa. All Rights Reserved. Reprinted by permission. **Figure 7.5** From John W. Hole, Jr., *Human Anatomy and Physiology*, 5th ed. Copyright © 1990 Wm. C. Brown Communications, Inc., Dubuque, Iowa. All Rights Reserved. Reprinted by permission. **Figure 7.9** From John W. Hole, Jr., *Human Anatomy and Physiology*, 3d ed. Copyright © 1984 Wm. C. Brown Communications, Inc., Dubuque, Iowa. All Rights Reserved. Reprinted by permission.

Chapter 10

Figure 10.3 From Kent M. Van De Graaff, *Human Anatomy*, 4th ed. Copyright © 1995 The McGraw-Hill Companies, Inc. All Rights Reserved. Reprinted by permission.

Chapter 11

Figure 11.2 From Kent M. Van De Graaff, *Human Anatomy*, 4th ed. Copyright © 1995 The McGraw-Hill Companies, Inc. All Rights Reserved. Reprinted by permission. **Figure 11.5** From Kent M. Van De Graaff, *Human Anatomy*, 4th ed. Copyright © 1995 The McGraw-Hill Companies, Inc. All Rights Reserved. Reprinted by permission.

Chapter 12

Figure 12.1 From John W. Hole, Jr., *Human Anatomy and Physiology*, 5th ed. Copyright © 1990 The McGraw-Hill Companies, Inc. All Rights Reserved. Reprinted by permission. **Figure 12.2** From John W. Hole, Jr., *Human Anatomy and Physiology*, 5th ed. Copyright © 1990 The McGraw-Hill Companies, Inc. All Rights Reserved. Reprinted by permission. **Figure 12.3** From Stuart Ira Fox, *Human Physiology*, 3d ed. Copyright © 1990 The McGraw-Hill Companies, Inc. All Rights Reserved. Reprinted by permission. **Figure 12.7** From Kent M. Van De Graaff and Stuart Ira Fox, *Concepts of Human Anatomy and Physiology*, 3d ed. Copyright © 1992 The McGraw-Hill Companies, Inc. All Rights Reserved. Reprinted by permission. **Figure 12.10** From Kent M. Van De Graaff, *Human Anatomy*, 3d ed. Copyright © 1992 The McGraw-Hill Companies, Inc. All Rights Reserved. Reprinted by permission. **Figure 12.11** From Stuart Ira Fox, *Human Physiology*, 3d ed. Copyright © 1990 The McGraw-Hill Companies, Inc. All Rights Reserved. Reprinted by permission.

Chapter 13

Figure 13.1 From John W. Hole, Jr., *Human Anatomy and Physiology*, 5th ed. Copyright © 1990 The McGraw-Hill Companies, Inc. All Rights Reserved. Reprinted by permission. **Figure 13.2** From John W. Hole, Jr., *Human Anatomy and Physiology*, 3d ed. Copyright © 1984 The McGraw-Hill Companies, Inc. All Rights Reserved. Reprinted by permission. **Figure 13.3** From Kent M. Van De Graaff and Stuart Ira Fox, *Concepts of Human Anatomy and Physiology*, 3d ed. Copyright © 1992 The McGraw-Hill Companies, Inc. All Rights Reserved. Reprinted by permission. **Figure 13.4** From John W. Hole, Jr., *Human Anatomy and Physiology*, 6th ed. Copyright © 1990 The McGraw-Hill Companies, Inc. All Rights Reserved. Reprinted by permission.

Chapter 14

Figure 14.4 From John W. Hole, Jr., *Human Anatomy and Physiology*, 5th ed. Copyright © 1990 The McGraw-Hill Companies, Inc. All Rights Reserved. Reprinted by permission.

Chapter 15

Figure 15.3 From John W. Hole, Jr., *Human Anatomy and Physiology*, 5th ed. Copyright © 1990 The McGraw-Hill Companies, Inc. All Rights Reserved. Reprinted by permission.

Chapter 20

Figure 20.1 From John W. Hole, Jr., *Human Anatomy and Physiology*, 5th ed. Copyright © 1990 The McGraw-Hill Companies, Inc. All Rights Reserved. Reprinted by permission.